shakespearean criticism

"Thou art a Monument without a tomb,
And art alive still while thy Book doth
      live
And we have wits to read and praise to
give."

*Ben Jonson, from the preface
to the First Folio, 1623.*

Mr. WILLIAM SHAKESPEARES

COMEDIES, HISTORIES, & TRAGEDIES.

Published according to the True Originall Copies.

Martin Droeshout sculpsit London.

LONDON

Printed by Isaac Iaggard, and Ed. Blount. 1623.

Frontispiece to the First Folio (1623). By permission of the Folger Shakespeare Library.

ISSN 0883-9123

Volume 49

RSF
PR
286
.S44
v.49

shakespearean criticism

Excerpts from the Criticism of
William Shakespeare's Plays and Poetry,
from the First Published Appraisals
to Current Evaluations

Kathy D. Darrow
Editor

GALE GROUP

Detroit
San Francisco
London
Boston
Woodbridge, CT

STAFF

Kathy D. Darrow, *Editor*
Andrea Henry, *Assistant Editor*

Lynn Spampinato, *Managing Editor*

Maria Franklin, *Permissions Manager*
Kimberly F. Smilay, *Permissions Specialist*
Kelly A. Quin, *Permissions Associate*
Erin Bealmear, Sandy Gore, *Permissions Assistants*

Victoria B. Cariappa, *Research Manager*
Corrine Boland, Tamara C. Nott,
Tracie A. Richardson, *Research Associates*
Timothy Lehnerer, Patricia Love, *Research Assistants*

Dorothy Maki, *Manufacturing Manager*
Stacy Melson, *Buyer*

Gary Leach, *Graphic Artist*
Randy Bassett, *Image Database Supervisor*
Robert Duncan, Michael Logusz, *Imaging Specialists*
Pamela A Reed, *Imaging Coordinator*

Since this page cannot legibly accommodate all copyright notices, the acknowledgments constitute an extension of the copyright notice.

While every effort has been made to ensure the reliability of the information presented in this publication, The Gale Group neither guarantees the accuracy of the data contained herein nor assumes any responsibility for errors, omissions or discrepancies. Gale accepts no payment for listing; and inclusion in the publication of any organization, agency, institution, publication, service, or individual does not imply endorsement of the editors or publisher. Errors brought to the attention of the publisher and verified to the satisfaction of the publisher will be corrected in future editions.

This publication is a creative work fully protected by all applicable copyright laws, as well as by misappropriation, trade secret, unfair competition, and other applicable laws. The authors and editors of this work have added value to the underlying factual material herein through one or more of the following: unique and original selection, coordination, expression, arrangement, and classification of the information.

All rights to this publication will be vigorously defended.

Copyright © 2000 Gale Group, Inc.
27500 Drake Rd.
Farmington Hills, MI 48331-3535
Gale Group and Design is a trademark used herein under license.

This book is printed on acid-free paper that meets the minimum requirements of American National Standard for Information Sciences—Permanence Paper for Printed Library Materials, ANSI Z39.48-1984.

Library of Congress Catalog Card Number 86-645085
ISBN 0-7876-3144-2
ISSN 0883-9123

Printed in the United States of America
Published simultaneously in the United Kingdom
by The Gale Group International Limited
(An affiliated company of The Gale Group)
10 9 8 7 6 5 4 3 2 1

The Gale Group

Contents

60180

Preface

*S*hakespearean Criticism (SC) provides students, educators, theatergoers, and other interested readers with valuable insight into Shakespeare's drama and poetry. A multiplicity of viewpoints documenting the critical reaction of scholars and commentators from the seventeenth century to the present day derives from the hundreds of periodicals and books excerpted for the series. Students and teachers at all levels of study will benefit from *SC,* whether they seek information for class discussions and written assignments, new perspectives on traditional issues, or the most noteworthy analyses of Shakespeare's artistry.

Scope of the Series

Volumes 1 through 10 of the series present a unique historical overview of the critical response to each Shakespearean work, representing a broad range of interpretations. Volumes 11 through 26 recount the performance history of Shakespeare's plays on the stage and screen through eyewitness reviews and retrospective evaluations of individual productions, comparisons of major interpretations, and discussions of staging issues.

Beginning with Volume 27 in the series, *SC* focuses on criticism published after 1960, with a view to providing the reader with the most significant modern critical approaches. Each volume is ordered around a theme that is central to the study of Shakespeare, such as politics, religion, or sexuality. The topic entry that introduces the volume is comprised of general essays that discuss this theme with reference to all of Shakespeare's works. Following the topic entry are several entries devoted to individual works. Volume 49 is devoted to the topic of law and justice in Shakespeare's works, and provides commentary on that topic as well as on the plays *Henry IV, Parts 1* and *2, Henry V,* and *Measure for Measure.*

SC also compiles an annual volume of the most noteworthy essays published on Shakespeare during the previous year. The essays, reprinted in their entirety, have been recommended to Gale by an international panel of distinguished scholars. The most recent volume, *SC Yearbook 1998,* Volume 48 in the series, was published in October 1999.

Organization of the Book

Each entry consists of the following elements: an introduction, critical essays, and an annotated bibliography of further reading.

- The **Introduction** outlines modern interpretations of individual Shakespearean topics, plays, and poems.

- The **Criticism** for each entry consists of essays that are arranged both thematically and chronologically. This provides an overview of the major areas of concern in the analysis of Shakespeare's works, as well as a useful perspective on changes in critical evaluation over recent decades. Footnotes that appear with previously published pieces of criticism are reprinted at the end of each essay or excerpt. In the case of excerpted criticism, only those footnotes that pertain to the excerpted text are included.

- All of the individual essays are preceded by **Explanatory Notes** as an additional aid to students using *SC.* The explanatory notes summarize the criticism that follows.

- A complete **Bibliographical Citation** providing publication information precedes each piece of criticism.

- Each volume includes such **Illustrations** as reproductions of images from the Shakespearean period, paintings and sketches of eighteenth- and nineteenth-century performers, photographs of modern productions, and stills from film adaptations.

- The annotated bibliography of **Further Reading** appearing at the end of each entry suggests additional sources of study for the reader. Explanatory notes summarize each essay or book listed here.

- Each volume of *SC* provides the following indices:

  Cumulative Character Index: Identifies the principal characters of discussion in the criticism of each play and non-dramatic poem.
  Cumulative Critic Index: Identifies each critic that has appeared in *SC*.
  Cumulative Topic Index: Identifies the principal topics in the criticism and stage history of each work. The topics are arranged alphabetically, by topic.
  Cumulative Topic Index, by Play: Identifies the principal topics in the criticism and stage history of each work. The topics are arranged alphabetically, by play.

Citing *Shakespearean Criticism*

Students who quote directly from any volume in the Literature Criticism Series in written assignments may use the following general forms to footnote reprinted criticism. The first example pertains to material drawn from periodicals, the second to material reprinted from books.

[1]Gordon Ross Smith, "Shakespeare's *Henry V*: Another Part of the Critical Forest," in *Journal of the History of Ideas,* XXXVII, No. 1 (January-March 1976), 3-26; excerpted and reprinted in *Shakespearean Criticism,* Vol. 30, ed. Marie Lazzari (Detroit: Gale Research, 1996), pp. 262-73.

[2]Katherine Eisaman Maus, *Inwardness and Theater in the English Renaissance* (The University of Chicago Press, 1995); excerpted and reprinted in *Shakespearean Criticism,* Vol. 33, ed. Dana Ramel Barnes and Marie Lazzari, (Detroit: Gale Research, 1997), pp. 112-17.

Suggestions Are Welcome

The editors encourage comments and suggestions from readers on any aspect of the *SC* series. In response to various recommendations, several features have been added to *SC* since the series began, including the topic index and the sample bibliographic citations noted above. Readers are cordially invited to write, call, or fax the editors: *Shakespearean Criticism,* The Gale Group, 27500 Drake Rd., Farmington Hills, MI 48331-3535. Call toll-free at 1-800-347-GALE or fax to 1-248-699-8049.

Acknowledgments

The editors wish to thank the copyright holders of the excerpted criticism included in this volume and the permissions managers of many book and magazine publishing companies for assisting us in securing reproduction rights. We are also grateful to the staffs of the Detroit Public Library, the Library of Congress, the University of Detroit Mercy Library, Wayne State University Purdy/Kresge Library Complex, and the University of Michigan Libraries for making their resources available to us. Following is a list of the copyright holders who have granted us permission to reproduce material in this volume of SC. Every effort has been made to trace copyright, but if omissions have been made, please let us know.

COPYRIGHTED EXCERPTS IN SC, VOLUME 49, WERE REPRODUCED FROM THE FOLLOWING PERIODICALS:

Cardozo Studies in Law and Literature, v. V, Spring, 1993. Reproduced by permission.—*The Critical Quarterly,* v. 12, Spring, 1970. Reproduced by permission of Blackwell Publishers.—*ELH,* v. 49, Winter, 1982. Copyright © 1982 by The Johns Hopkins University Press. Reproduced by permission of The Johns Hopkins University Press.—*English Studies,* v. 74, February, 1993. Copyright © 1993, Swets & Zeitlinger. Reproduced by permission.—*Essay in Theatre,* v. 3, November, 1984 for "Hermione's Trial in 'The Winter's Tale' " by David M. Bergeron. Reproduced by permission of the author.—*Essays in Literature,* v. XVI, Spring, 1989; v. XXIII, Fall, 1995. Copyright © 1989, 1995, Western Illinois University. Both reproduced by permission.—*JGE: The Journal of General Education,* v. XXX, Fall, 1978. Copyright © 1978 by The Pennsylvania State University. Reproduced by permission of The Pennsylvania State University Press.—*Mosaic: A Journal for the Interdisciplinary Study of Literature,* v. 27, December, 1984. Copyright © Mosaic 1984. Acknowledgment of previous publication is herewith made.—*Philological Quarterly,* v. 58, Winter, 1979 for "That Within Which Passes Show: The Function of the Chorus in 'Henry V' " by Anthony S. Brennan. Reproduced by permission of the author.—*Shakespeare Quarterly,* v. 27, Summer, 1976; v. 32, Spring, 1981; v. 34, Spring, 1983; v. 39, Autumn, 1988; v. 45, Spring, 1994; v. 49, Winter, 1998. Copyright © The Folger Shakespeare Library, 1976, 1981, 1983, 1988, 1994, 1998. All reproduced by permission of Shakespeare Quarterly.—*Shakespeare Studies: An Annual Gathering of Research, Criticism, and Reviews,* v. IV, 1968 for "'Measure For Measure': Quid Pro Quo?" by A. D. Nuttall; v. XX, 1988 for "Richardian Law Reports and 'Richard II'" by W. F. Bolton. Copyright © 1968, 1988 The Council for Research in the Renaissance. Both reproduced by permission of the respective authors.—*Shakespeare Survey: An Annual Survey of Shakespearian Study and Production,* v. 30, 1977 for "The True Prince and the False Thief: Prince Hal and the Shift of Identity" by Norman Sanders; v. 37, 1984 for "'He Who the Sword of Heaven Will Bear': The Duke Versus Angelo in 'Measure For Measure' " by N. W. Bawcutt; v. 38, 1985 for "The Tragic Substructure of the 'Henry IV Plays' " by Catherine M. Shaw; v. 40, 1988 for " 'Henry V' as Working-House of Ideology" by Günter Walch; v. 49, 1996 for " 'Lawful Deed': Consummation, Custom, and Law in 'All's Well That Ends Well'" by Subha Mukherji. Copyright © Cambridge University Press 1977, 1984, 1985, 1988, 1996. All rights reserved. All reproduced by permission of Cambridge University Press and the respective authors.—*Texas Studies in Literature and Language,* v. 26, Spring, 1984. Copyright © 1984 by the University of Texas Press. Reproduced by permission of the publisher.—*University of Dayton Review,* v. 23, Spring, 1995. Reproduced by permission.—*Virginia Law Review,* v. 61, March, 1975. Copyright © 1975 by Virginia Law Review Association. Reproduced by permission.

COPYRIGHTED EXCERPTS IN SC, VOLUME 49, WERE REPRODUCED FROM THE FOLLOWING BOOKS:

Antony, Hammond. From " 'It Must Be Your Imagination Then': The Prologue and the Plural Text in 'Henry V' and Elsewhere" in *'Fanned and Winnowed Opinions': Shakespearean Essays Presented to Harold Jenkins.* Edited by John W. Mahon and Thomas A. Pendleton. Methuen, 1987. The collection as a whole, copyright © 1987 Methuen & Co. Ltd. The individual contributions, copyright © 1987 the contributors. All rights reserved. Reproduced the permission.—Bradshaw, Graham. From *Misrepresentations: Shakespeare and the Materialists.* Cornell University Press, 1993. Copyright © 1993 by Cornell University. All rights reserved. Used by permission of the publisher, Cornell University Press. All additional uses of this material—including, but not limited to, photocopying and reprinting—are prohibited without the prior written approval of Cornell University Press.

—Clary, F. Nick. From "Reformation and Its Counterfeit: The Recovery of Meaning in Henry IV, Part One" in ***Ambiguities in Literature and Film: Selected Papers from the Seventh Annual Florida State University Conference on Literature and Film.*** Edited by Hans P. Braendlin. Florida State University Press, 1988. Copyright © 1988 by the Board of Regents of the State of Florida. Reproduced by permission of the University Press of Florida.—Greenblatt, Stephen. From "Invisible Bullets: Renaissance Authority and Its Subversions" in ***Political Shakespeare: New Essays in Cultural Materialism.*** Edited by Jonathan Dollimore and Alan Sinfield. Manchester University Press, 1985. Copyright © Manchester University Press 1985. Reproduced by permission.—Hawkins, Harriett. From ***Likenesses of Truth in Elizabethan and Restoration Drama. Oxford, 1972.*** Copyright © Oxford University Press 1972. All rights reserved. Reproduced by permission of the executors of the Estate of Harriet Hawkins Buckley.—Hodgdon, Barbara. From ***The End Crowns All: Closure and Contradiction in Shakespeare's History.*** Princeton University Press, 1991. Copyright © 1991 by Princeton University Press. All rights reserved. Reproduced by permission.—Kastan, David Scott. From ***Shakespeare and the Shapes of Time.*** University Press of New England, 1982. Copyright © 1982 by David Scott Kastan. All rights reserved. Reproduced by permission of the author.—Kornstein, Daniel J. From ***Kill All the Lawyer?: Shakespeare's Legal Appeal.*** Princeton University Press, 1994. Copyright © 1994 by Princeton University Press. All rights reserved. Reproduced by permission.—Leggatt, Alexander. From ***Shakespeare's Political Drama: The History Plays and The Roman Plays.*** Routledge, 1988. Copyright © 1988 Alexander Leggatt. All rights reserved. Reproduced by permission of the publisher and the author.—McKenzie, Stanley D. From "The Prudence and Kinship of Prince Hal and John of Lancaster in 2 'Henry IV' " in ***Law and Philosophy: The Practice of Theory, Essays in Honor of George Anastaplo.*** Edited by John A. Murley, Robert L. Stone and William T. Braithwaite. Ohio University Press, 1992. Copyright © 1992 by Ohio University Press. All rights reserved. Reproduced by permission.—Seiden, Melvin. From ***Measure For Measure: Casuistry and Artistry.*** The Catholic University of America Press, 1990. Copyright © 1990 The Catholic University of America Press. All rights reserved. Reproduced by permission.—Trafton, Dain A. From "Shakespeare's 'Henry IV': A New Prince in a New Principality" in ***Shakespeare as Political Thinker.*** Edited by John Alvis and Thomas G. West. Carolina Academic Press, 1981. Copyright © 1981 John Alvis and Thomas G. West. All rights reserved. Reproduced by permission.—White, R. S. From ***Natural Law in English Renaissance Literature.*** Cambridge University Press, 1996. Copyright © Cambridge University Press 1996. Reproduced by permission of Cambridge University Press and the author.

PHOTOGRAPHS AND ILLUSTRATIONS APPEARING IN SC, VOLUME 49, WERE RECEIVED FROM THE FOLLOWING SOURCES:

Act III, scene iv, from William Shakespeare's *King Lear;* 'The Heath Scene,' photograph. The Department of Rare Books and Special Collections, The University of Michigan Library. Reproduced by permission.—Act IV, scene i, From William Shakespeare's *The Merchant of Venice;* Portia says to Shylock "nay, if the scale do turn, But in the estimation of a hair, Thou diest and all thy goods are confiscate." Cassell & Company, Limited, photograph. The Department of Rare Books and Special Collections, The University of Michigan Library. Reproduced by permission.—From a theatre production of William Shakespeare's *Henry IV, Part I.* Directed by Michael Langham and George McCowan, with Max Helpmann as King Henry IV, Stratford Festival, Stratford, Ontario, Canada, 1958, photograph. Courtesy of Stratford Festival Archives.—From a theatre production of William Shakespeare's *Henry IV, Part II.* Directed by Peter Moss, with Lewis Gordon as Sir John Falstaff, Stratford Festival, Stratford, Ontario, Canada, 1979, photograph by Robert C. Ragsdale. Courtesy of Stratford Festival Archives.—From a theatre production of William Shakespeare's *Henry IV, Part I.* Directed by Michael Langham and George McCowan, 'The Battle Scene,' Stratford Festival, Stratford, Ontario, Canada, 1958, photograph. Courtesy of Stratford Festival Archives.—From a theatre production of William Shakespeare's *Henry IV, Part I.* Directed by Stuart Burge, with (l-r) Eric Christmas as Bardolph, Douglas Rain as Prince Hal, Tony Van Bridge as Falstaff, Bruno Gerussi as Gadshill, and Heath Lamberts as Poins, Stratford Festival, Stratford, Ontario, Canada, June 14 to October 2, 1965, photograph. Courtesy of Stratford Festival Archives.—From a theatre production of William Shakespeare's *Henry V.* Directed by Michael Langham, with (center) Diana Leblanc as Katherine with ladies in waiting, Stratford Festival, Stratford, Ontario, Canada, 1966, photograph by Peter Smith & Co. Courtesy of Stratford Festival Archives.—From a theatre production of William Shakespeare's *Henry V.* Directed by Michael Langham, with (center) Christopher Plummer as Henry V, Stratford Festival, Stratford, Ontario, Canada, Festival Theatre, 1956, photograph. Courtesy of Stratford Festival Archives.—From a theatre production of William Shakespeare's *Henry V.* Directed by Michael Langham, with (center) Christopher Plummer as Henry V and Ginette Letondal as Katherine,

Stratford Festival, Stratford, Ontario, Canada, Festival Theatre, 1956, photograph. Courtesy of Stratford Festival Archives.—From a theatre production of William Shakespeare's *Henry V*. Directed by Peter Moss, with (l-r) Stephen Ouimette as The Boy, Amelia Hall as Mistress Quickly, Christopher Blake as Nym, Rod Beattie as Pistol, and John Cutts as Bardolph, Stratford Festival, Stratford, Ontario, Canada, Festival Theatre, 1980, photograph by Robert C. Ragsdale. Courtesy of Stratford Festival Archives.—From a theatre production of William Shakespeare's *Measure for Measure*. Directed by Amy Glazer, set design by Joe Regey, costume design by Elizabeth Poindexter and lighting design by Michael D. Ferguson at San José State University, November 14-21, 1997 Season; Gene Carvalho as Angelo and Frank Corrado as the Duke. Angelo is pleading his case in Act V, scene I, photograph by Dave Lepori. SAN JOSÉ STATE UNIVERSITY THEATRE. Reproduced by permission. —From a theatre production of William Shakespeare's *Measure for Measure*. Directed by Amy Glazer, set design by Joe Regey, costume design by Elizabeth Poindexter and lighting design by Michael D. Ferguson at San José State University, November 14-21, 1997 Season; Lucio (Paul Penza) exposes the Duke (Frank Corrado) in Act V, scene I, photograph by Dave Lepori. SAN JOSÉ STATE UNIVERSITY THEATRE. Reproduced by permission.—From a theatre production of William Shakespeare's *Measure for Measure*. Directed by Amy Glazer, set design by Joe Regey, costume design by Elizabeth Poindexter and lighting design by Michael D. Ferguson at San José State University, November 14-21, 1997 Season; Isabella (Kathleen Dobbs) and Claudio (Bryce Punty) in the prison, Act III, scene I, photograph by Dave Lepori. SAN JOSÉ STATE UNIVERSITY THEATRE. Reproduced by permission.—From a theatre production of William Shakespeare's *Measure for Measure*. Directed by Amy Glazer, set design by Joe Regey, costume design by Elizabeth Poindexter and lighting design by Michael D. Ferguson at San José State University, November 14-21, 1997 Season; Angelo (Gene Carvalho) and Isabella (Kathleen Dobbs) in Act II, scene iv, photograph by Dave Lepori. SAN JOSÉ STATE UNIVERSITY THEATRE. Reproduced by permission.

List of Plays and Poems Covered in *SC*

Volumes 1-10 present a critical overview of each play, including criticism from the seventeenth century to the present.
Beginning with Volume 11, the series focuses on the history of Shakespeare's plays on the stage and in important films.
The Yearbooks reprint the most important critical pieces of the year as suggested by an advisory board of Shakespearean scholars.
Beginning with Volume 27, each volume is organized around a theme and focuses on criticism published after 1960.

Volume 1
The Comedy of Errors
Hamlet
Henry IV, Parts 1 and 2
Timon of Athens
Twelfth Night

Volume 2
Henry VIII
King Lear
Love's Labour's Lost
Measure for Measure
Pericles

Volume 3
Henry VI, Parts 1, 2, and 3
Macbeth
A Midsummer Night's Dream
Troilus and Cressida

Volume 4
Cymbeline
The Merchant of Venice
Othello
Titus Andronicus

Volume 5
As You Like It
Henry V
The Merry Wives of Windsor
Romeo and Juliet

Volume 6
Antony and Cleopatra
Richard II
The Two Gentlemen of Verona

Volume 7
All's Well That Ends Well
Julius Caesar
The Winter's Tale

Volume 8
Much Ado about Nothing
Richard III
The Tempest

Volume 9
Coriolanus
King John
The Taming of the Shrew
The Two Noble Kinsmen

Volume 10
The Phoenix and Turtle
The Rape of Lucrece
Sonnets
Venus and Adonis

Volume 11
King Lear
Othello
Romeo and Juliet

Volume 12
The Merchant of Venice
A Midsummer Night's Dream
The Taming of the Shrew
The Two Gentlemen of Verona

Volume 13
1989 Yearbook

Volume 14
Henry IV, Parts 1 and 2
Henry V
Richard III

Volume 15
Cymbeline
Pericles
The Tempest
The Winter's Tale

Volume 16
1990 Yearbook

Volume 17
Antony and Cleopatra
Coriolanus
Julius Caesar
Titus Andronicus

Volume 18
The Merry Wives of Windsor
Much Ado about Nothing
Troilus and Cressida

Volume 19
1991 Yearbook

Volume 20
Macbeth
Timon of Athens

Volume 21
Hamlet

Volume 22
1992 Yearbook

Volume 23
As You Like It
Love's Labour's Lost
Measure for Measure

Volume 24
Henry VI, Parts 1, 2, and 3
Henry VIII
King John
Richard II

Volume 25
1993 Yearbook

Volume 26
All's Well That Ends Well
The Comedy of Errors
Twelfth Night

Volume 27
Shakespeare and Classical Civilization
Antony and Cleopatra
Timon of Athens
Titus Andronicus
Troilus and Cressida

Volume 28
1994 Yearbook

Law and Justice

INTRODUCTION

The intertwined concerns of human law and providential justice figure prominently in Shakespeare's dramas, regardless of genre, and have elicited considerable critical commentary in the late twentieth century. Legal conflict frequently appears in the comedies, romances, and problem plays, often leading to formal or mock trials of thematic significance. The use and abuse of law also abounds in the histories, and emerges in the tragedies, where the transcendental forces of justice dictate the outcome of human disputes. Overall, the sheer weight and diversity of legal terminology in Shakespeare's works has resulted in multiple lines of scholarly research on the topic. Commentators have considered allusions to the contractual obligations of marriage in the comedies; to the legalities of property, authority, and succession in the histories; and to the fallibility of worldly judgment in the problem plays and tragedies. This last subject, critics note, has tended to summarize Shakespeare's principal interest in human law as a flawed reflection of divine justice, which may only be redeemed when tempered with mercy.

Trials provide the centerpiece of any discussion of law in Shakespeare's dramas. This is no more apparent than in *The Merchant of Venice*, a work frequently cited by critics for its legal implications. Particular interest has tended to center on Antonio's trial, prompted as it is by Shylock's vengeful demand for a pound of flesh in exchange for the merchant's unpaid debt. In discussing the play, many critics have emphasized the legal acumen of (in the guise of the male law clerk, Balthasar) and the dynamics of courtroom persuasion featured in her often-quoted mercy and justice speech. Jay L. Halio (1993) represents such commentators, who laud Shakespeare's skillful dramaturgical use of the trial scene in *The Merchant of Venice* to demonstrate the theme of vengeance thwarted and justice achieved through mercy. Daniel Kornstein (1993) offers a complementary view of the play, seeing *The Merchant of Venice* as a legal parable that hinges on the subject of rigid versus flexible interpretations of law. Stephen A. Cohen (1994) considers the cultural contexts of this drama by focusing on the ideological threat that Shylock, as an outsider, presents to the aristocratic authority of Venice and by studying the use of law as a tool of social oppression.

Other formal and quasi-trials are represented elsewhere in the comedies, romances, and problem plays. *Measure for Measure*, among the problem plays, offers a legal framework and, according to John D. Eure (1975), expresses Shakespeare's statement on the limitations and competence of law. Employing an abstruse edict that invokes the death penalty for fornication, *Measure for Measure* dramatizes the folly of legal systems that seek to adjudicate human imperfections. The formal trial of Hermione in Act III of *The Winter's Tale* represents a similar treatment of the legal motif in Shakespearean drama. David M. Bergeron (1984) argues that the trial highlights the forces of irrationality, jealousy, and caprice that operate in any practical system of laws, and which may align to hinder justice.

While several of the darker implications of the law raised by the comedies and problem plays are resolved in some fashion within these dramas, Shakespeare's histories and tragedies offer a more critical vision of worldly justice. The question of legitimate authority and legal succession lie at the heart of most of the histories, which tend to display brutal miscarriages of justice and bold abuses of law. The plays of the *Henriad* contain numerous examples, as does *Richard III*, a drama that William C. (1992) claims encapsulates the relationship between law, succession, ritual, and hypocrisy. Carroll examines Richard's murderous violation of Natural Law in his attempt to win succession to the English throne. Obeying "the form of law" in word but not action, Richard demonstrates the susceptibility of legal authority to betrayal and treachery.

Critics have also noted that transgressions of Natural Law and their consequences are well-illustrated in the tragedies, principally *King Lear*. Janet M. Green (1995) views *King Lear* as both Shakespeare's recapitulation of the faults of the Jacobean legal system and his evocation of divine justice in the mode of Christian Last Judgment. Similarly, R. S. White (1996) provides a detailed study of the dramatic encounter between Natural Law and the corruption of worldly authority in *King Lear*. Among the other plays featuring similar themes, *Hamlet* and *Macbeth* generally draw the attention of critics interested in the interplay of justice, revenge, and the dynamics of violent political succession.

OVERVIEW

John D. Eure (essay date 1975)

SOURCE: "Shakespeare and the Legal Process: Four Essays," in *Virginia Law Review,* Vol. 61, No. 2, March, 1975, pp. 402-33.

[*In the following excerpt, Eure surveys themes of justice and law in Shakespeare's* The Merchant of Venice, Measure for Measure, *and* King Lear.]

The Merchant of Venice

The Merchant of Venice is the one Shakespearean play that, for better or worse, has come to the attention of nearly every lawyer, and especially every lawyer who writes about Shakespeare and the law.[22] In dealing with the familiar plot of this play, lawyers have understandably tended to emphasize that portion revolving around the trial of Antonio. This selective emphasis has caused most lawyer-critics, I think, to misinterpret the role of law in the play. It is perfectly valid to concentrate on the play's legal aspect, but in order to appraise it clearly, one must read the legal values expressed in terms of the larger scheme of the play.

Before examining the trial, it will be useful to look briefly at the contrasting characterizations of Shylock and Antonio. To a twentieth century audience, the insistence on Shylock's Jewishness is extremely unsettling, and may make the play unperformable in the terms in which Shakespeare wrote it. The Elizabethans, however, saw in Shylock a type of grotesque familiar from the medieval English stage; "Jew" was a moral metaphor embodying attributes contradictory to the Christian view of the universe. Shylock is frequently associated with the devil, a characterization derived directly from the medieval drama.[23] In his insistence on judgment according to the strict letter of the law, he represents the law of the Old Testament, the *lex talonis,* as opposed to the New Law of Christian mercy and forgiveness.[24] In terms of the human relationships established in the play, Shylock is deserted first by his servant, Launcelot Gobbo, and then by his daughter Jessica. Antonio, in contrast, is consistently depicted as one who lives to benefit others, and for whose welfare others are solicitous. The opening scene of the play reveals a crowd of friends trying to ease his melancholy. He gives friendship easily, and therefore receives it, as most clearly appears in his relation to Bassanio, for whose happiness he enters the bond with Shylock. Bassanio describes him as

> [t]he dearest friend to me, the kindest man,
> The best-conditioned and unwearied spirit
> In doing courtesies, and one in whom
> The ancient Roman honor more appears
> Than any that draws breath in Italy.
>
> (III.ii.292-96)

The contrast between Shylock and Antonio is emphasized by their actions within the explicitly commercial atmosphere of Venice. Shylock, a "breeder of barren metal," lends money for interest. Although the law allowed the charging of interest in Elizabethan England, and the government dealt, as all trading nations must, in international money markets,[25] popular sentiment retained the medieval Christian bias against making money by money; usury was evil. The usurious and miserly Shylock, the representative of that part of the commercial community that does not know how to use money for the improvement and enjoyment of life, reacts characteristically when Jessica elopes with a Christian, taking some of the family riches with her:

> Two thousand ducats in that, and other precious, precious jewels. I would my daughter were dead at my foot, and the jewels in her ear! Would she were hearsed at my foot, and the ducats in her coffin!
>
> (III.i.77-80)

Antonio, the merchant of the play's title, uses his wealth for human ends. He has lent much money to Bassanio already, and he gladly lends more: "My purse, my person, my extremest means / Lie all unlocked to your occasions." (I.i.138-39) His generosity in often saving debtors from Shylock's forfeitures (III.iii.22-23) exacerbates Shylock's hatred:

> I hate him for he is a Christian;
> But more, for that in low simplicity
> He lends out money gratis and brings down
> The rate of usance here with us in Venice.
>
> (I.iii.38-41)

Portia, too, we may note in passing, is characterized partly by her attitude toward money and its use. Her liberality with her great wealth in aid of Bassanio and his friends matches that of Antonio.[26] A further, otherworldly, dimension of Portia's character, however, contrasts explicitly with the frequent identification of Shylock with the devil and foreshadows Portia's role as the advocate of mercy. This dimension appears in a description given by Jessica in the scene immediately preceding the trial:

> (Bassanio) finds the joys of heaven here on
>   earth,
> And if on earth he do not merit it,
> In reason he should never come to heaven.
> Why, if two gods should play some heavenly
>   match
> And on the wager lay two earthly women,
> And Portia one, there must be something else
> Pawned with the other, for the poor rude
>   world
> Hath not her fellow.
>
> (III.v.69-76)

This too hurried summary has been designed to point out some of the resonances the principal participants in the trial carry with them into their encounter with the legal process. When Shylock repeatedly demands "the law," "justice" and the penalty set forth in his bond, his demand does not spring from that "impartial conduct of the soul," that "truth and upright inno-cency" that motivated the Lord Chief Justice [in *2 Henry IV*]. It is motivated instead by revenge and hatred. A basic similarity exists, however, between Shylock's claim and the Chief Justice's vision of jus-tice, which was both morally "good" and politically expedient. In *2 Henry IV* the "course of law" guards the "peace and safety" of the King and through him the entire social order. In *The Merchant of Venice* the enforcement of Shylock's claim, too, is insistently connected with the order and stability of the commer-cial state of Venice:

> He plies the Duke at morning and at night,
> And doth impeach the freedom of the state
> If they deny him justice.
>
> (III.ii.277-79)

Solanio is certain that the Duke will halt the pro-ceedings, but Antonio, the experienced businessman, replies:

> The Duke cannot deny the course of law;
> For the commodity that strangers have
> With us in Venice, if it be denied,
> Will much impeach the justice of the state,
> Since that the trade and profit of the city
> Consisteth of all nations.
>
> (III.iii.26-31)

Shylock in the trial repeats the connection:

> I have possessed your Grace of what I
>   purpose,
> And by our holy Sabbath have I sworn
> To have the due and forfeit of my bond.
> If you deny it, let the danger light
> Upon your charter and your city's freedom!
>
> (IV.i.35-39)

This "freedom" of contract, the "freedom" to bind oneself irrevocably to the performance of certain con-ditions, forms the foundation of a successful commer-cial state. Antonio recognizes that "no lawful means" (IV.i.9) can rescue him from Shylock's clutches. The Duke, presumably the chief judicial figure in the state, is unable to prevent execution, and even Portia, once Antonio confesses the bond, admits Shylock's unchal-lengeable right to execution of the penalty.

That in the end Shylock's plea to political expediency does not prevail, that his downfall does not "impeach the freedom of the state," summarizes the differing roles of law in *2 Henry IV* and *The Merchant of Venice*. The history is above all a political play, a prologue to Shakespeare's celebration of England's political golden age in *Henry V*. The paramount importance of estab-lishing a legitimate and lasting rule quite predictably finds partial expression in an idealized vision of hu-man justice. As I [have elsewhere] attempted to sug-gest, however, even in *2 Henry IV* Shakespeare could not participate fully in his intellectual ideal; the emo-tional core of the play rests in the more humane and down-to-earth world of Falstaff and Shallow. *The Mer-chant of Venice* is primarily concerned, not with the health of the state, but with the vitality of relation-ships between individuals that are at once more per-sonal and more universal than the "state." The basis of the social order celebrated at the end of the play is not political and economic stability, but rather human com-passion and love derived from divine love, and for which commerce and wealth, as I have suggested, are only metaphors. Unlike Henry's England, the state Shylock invokes is only a commercial city that com-mands no emotional allegiance. Similarly, Shylock's appeal to law as the mainstay of that state does not compel concern for the integrity of this commercial city; the continuing commercial viability of Venice is vindicated in the trial, but ultimately other issues com-mand the play's intellectual and dramatic energies.

Still, within the play's own terms, Shylock's political self-justification carries weight. Bassanio offers three times the sum named in the bond, or, in the alterna-tive, the forfeiture of his own life, in exchange for that of Antonio:

> If this will not suffice, it must appear
> That malice bears down truth. And I beseech
>   you,
> Wrest once the law to your authority.
> To do a great right, do a little wrong,
> And curb this cruel devil of his will.
> PORTIA: It must not be. There is no power in
>   Venice
> Can alter a decree established.
> 'Twill be recorded for a precedent,
> And many an error by the same example
> Will rush into the state. It cannot be.
>
> (IV.i.211-20)

The argument, although persuasive through its own internal logic and a familiar one to all lawyers, must fail to convince us, the audience, as it fails to con-vince all the trial participants except Shylock. Although Shylock's plea is perhaps "just" within its narrow perception of the economic welfare of the state, a wider sense of justice is terribly offended at his crabbed le-gality. This wider sense of justice takes into account all of those resonances that the trial participants bring with them into the courtroom.

The problem may be rephrased in another manner. To a certain extent the legal system in *The Merchant of Venice,* the backbone of the commercial life of the city, does exist in isolation from moral concerns. The bond between Antonio and Shylock, the two men of commerce, typifies the entire structure of that com-

Act IV. Scene i. Shylock and Portia. By J. D. Watson. The Department of Rare Books and Special Collections, The University of Michigan Library.

religious and moral themes that have permeated the play. Even this plea acknowledges that the law, as a system of rules by which the state defines itself, must enforce the bond unless mercy, a higher law, moves the plaintiff to relinquish his claim:

> The quality of mercy is not strained;
> It droppeth as the gentle rain from heaven
> Upon the place beneath. It is twice blest;
> It blesseth him that gives and him that takes.
> 'Tis mightiest in the mightiest; it becomes
> The throned monarch better than his crown.
> His sceptre shows the force of temporal
>   power,
> The attribute to awe and majesty,
> Wherein doth sit the dread and fear of kings;
> But mercy is above this scept'red sway;
> It is enthroned in the hearts of kings;
> It is an attribute to God himself,
> And earthly power doth then show likest
>   God's
> When mercy seasons justice. Therefore, Jew,
> Though Justice be thy plea, consider this:
> That in the course of justice none of us
> Should see salvation. We do pray for mercy,
> And that same prayer doth teach us all to
>   render
> The deeds of mercy. I have spoke thus much
> To mitigate the justice of thy plea,
> Which if thou follow, this strict court of
>   Venice
> Must needs give sentence 'gainst the
>   merchant there.
>
> (IV.i.182-203)

The law is here equated, as it was in the exchange between the Lord Chief Justice and Henry V, with earthly order and authority. Mercy belongs to an order apart from and above this merely temporal power. It ties human affairs into the New Law, the Christian ideal of grace by which mortals ultimately hope to be judged. But this is a concept that the human law of commercial Venice evidently cannot comprehend. Perhaps there are sufficient practical reasons embedded in the commercial well-being of the state to preserve this human law for administering mundane affairs. Certainly Antonio seems to feel that the Duke's inability to "deny the course of law" is acceptable for the maintenance of the "trade and profit of the city." But as valid as this law may be in the limited sphere of commercial regulation, it is totally inadequate for dealing with this situation. We cannot escape the conviction that this law ought to have built into it some mechanism for recognizing its own limitations.

Portia's solution, of course, is to go the strictly legalistic Shylock one better and apply the principle of strict construction to his bond. Although the law will allow him to exact his penalty, it will hold him to the

mercial world, and the law is, if you will, the cement that gives the structure form and certainty. The play repeatedly recognizes, in the passages quoted above, the validity of a certain type of appeal for the law's protection, and indeed a necessity that the law respond. But the law as interpreted and enforced by the Duke, and the commercial relationship protected by this law, is simply inadequate to deal with the issues presented in the case of Shylock v. Antonio. Even Portia, disguised as a doctor of laws and armed with the advice of the learned Doctor Bellario, cannot find a legal basis to challenge the enforceability of the bond. The Duke has earlier asked, "How shalt thou hope for mercy, rend'ring none?" (IV.i.88) and Shylock's response reveals a chasm between technical legality and morality: "What judgement shall I dread, doing no wrong?" (IV.i.89) In a narrow legal sense, he does no wrong. Measured by a higher law, however, his ruthlessness renders him liable to a judgment more terrible than any human judge can render. Portia's response to the unimpeachable legality of Shylock's claim is the famous plea for mercy, which focuses in the trial the express words—"a pound of flesh"—he used in formulating it. In a contest of cleverness, Shylock has been outdone. "For, as thou urgest justice, be assured / Thou shalt have justice more than thou desir'st." (IV.i.313-14) Since Shylock has already refused in open court payment of the principal in lieu of the penalty, he cannot now have even this. Moreover, Shylock's preparations to carve up Antonio have rendered him liable under a statute against the attempted slaying of a citizen.[27] This, and the strict construction of the bond, are admittedly pieces of legal sophistry, but they negate a threat to justice that should never have been possible in the first place.

The legal tricks by which Portia rescues Antonio and places Shylock under penalty of death are part of the legal system that has proven inadequate to its task so far. But to the extent that they are legal, they are hardly part of the ordinary working of that system. Neither the Duke nor Antonio saw any way the enforcement of the bond could be forestalled; only these bits of legal arcana rescued from oblivion by Bellario could accomplish this. They are delivered, we must remember, by an impostor whose qualifications are not legal, but nearly heavenly. Portia is the foremost of earthly women, who gives Bassanio the "joys of heaven here on earth." (III.v.69) She pronounces the judgment on Shylock that he richly deserves in terms of a higher moral law, and here the touted ideal of Christian mercy has a chance to display itself. Shylock, genuinely guilty, genuinely needs mercy, and it is given him. "That thou shalt see the difference of our spirit, / I pardon thee thy life before thou ask it." (IV.i.366-67) The Duke also remits the half of Shylock's goods that are forfeit to the state under the statute in exchange for a fine. Portia then asks, "What mercy can you render him, Antonio?" Antonio responds with a proposal that Shylock be given the use of all his money until his death, at which time it will all be conveyed by a deed of gift to Jessica and her husband.[28] Shylock is in addition forced to become a Christian, an action that may seem singularly unmerciful to modern audiences brought up in an age of comparative religious toleration. But in the terms of the play, and of Elizabethan morality, Antonio is having supreme mercy on Shylock's soul by giving him a chance for salvation denied him as a Jew, by giving him a chance to escape the devil with whom he has been identified. We may note that the legal system is used to institutionalize this dispensation of mercy. Shylock's future use of his property is to be within the framework of legal trusts, and a deed recorded in court is to insure his testamentary beneficence to his Christian daughter and son-in-law. Portia instructs her clerk to draw up the deed, and immediately following the courtroom scene we see the deed about to be delivered for Shylock's signature.

Shylock has attempted to use the law for evil purposes and has nearly succeeded. When an appeal to a higher,

divine law fails, human law is turned on its head through a bit of legal sleight-of-hand to dissipate the threat to Antonio. The higher law of mercy is then immediately applied to resolve the problem of how to punish Shylock, and to provide, through a judicious use of legal forms, for the well-being of Jessica and her husband. Human law alone has proven inadequate to the resolution of this particular disorder in the state. But perhaps the deepest insight that *The Merchant of Venice* offers from a legal standpoint is that human law is not an independent self-administering system that produces "justice" through some mechanical process. It is rather a tool, limited in scope, but powerful within those limits, which can be used by a variety of persons for a variety of ends. These applications of law have moral content measured by the moral character of those who apply it.

Once already in the play Bassanio has recognized this characteristic of the law—that it is a form capable of lending respectability and authority to virtually any substance:

> So may the outward shows be least
>   themselves;
> The world is still deceived with ornament.
> In law, what plea so tainted and corrupt
> But being seasoned with a gracious voice,
> Obscures the show of evil?
>
>   . . . . .
>
> There is no vice so simple but assumes
> Some mark of virtue on his outward parts.
>   (III.ii.73-77, 81-82)

Bassanio has to choose from three caskets—gold, silver, or lead—the one that contains Portia's likeness in order to win her for his wife, and this prompts his discourse on the frequent discrepancy between appearance and reality. This wider theme finds expression in the character of Shylock (cf. I.iii.93-98), in the whole series of scenes in which Portia's suitors choose caskets, and in the disguising of Portia and Nerissa, and the comic business that generates. In the context of the trial scene a variation on this theme yields the view of law we have been examining. Shylock's manipulation of the forms of strict legality nearly perpetrates gross injustice while the guardian and chief judicial authority of the state, the Duke, looks on helplessly. Antonio uses legal forms to confirm a beneficial distribution of wealth wrongfully gotten. And Portia, the representative of that higher order of justice to which human designs must always, in the end, conform, precipitates conformity in the dramatic present and prevents injustice from occurring in this particular comic environment through her use of a bit of legal sophistry. While the commercial laws of Venice have some outward "mark of virtue," the values that Portia represents transcend the commercial world and the law that supports it. They derive from a system of justice infinitely more comprehensive than human legality, but they must manifest themselves in human affairs through an essentially human response to human needs that is patterned after the divine mercy that has redeemed us though "in the course of justice none of us / Should see salvation." Although human law has a proper and necessary function in ordering human society, justice cannot be achieved merely through the mechanical application of the forms of that law; justice derives from the operation of a higher law motivating those who use human law.

Measure for Measure

Of all of Shakespeare's plays, *Measure for Measure* is the most thoroughly legal in its basic framework and in its concerns. The plot hinges on the sudden re-vivification, after a lapse of nineteen years, of a law imposing the death penalty on persons convicted of fornication. The sexual offense symbolizes all human imperfection and the particular law to be enforced exemplifies the legal system's all too frequent tendency to over-react in dealing with the constant fact of human imperfection. The play contains many perplexities, some of which may stem from textual imperfection, and it has occasioned much perceptive scholarly debate.[29]

As was the case with *The Merchant of Venice,* the legal issues are intricately woven into the entire fabric of the play, so that to separate them necessarily distorts the work. Several themes familiar from *The Merchant of Venice* reappear. We confront once more the problems of the need for consistency in the law, the role of mercy, and the possibility for humanizing influences in the application of the law. In a sense the play places characters whose concepts of the legal system are as crabbed and distorted as Shylock's in the judge's seat, and dramatizes the learning process that was imposed on Shylock by fiat at the end of the trial scene. While there are similarities between the two plays, *Measure for Measure* deals with two legal issues in more detail than did *The Merchant of Venice:* the nature and competence of the law as an institution and the nature of the judge-figure.

A statute imposing the death penalty for fornication may seem absurd to modern audiences,[30] but both historical data and intrinsic evidence support the possibility, if not the reasonableness, of the legal situation that obtains in Vienna at the beginning of the play. The control of sexual conduct by civil authority provided a subject for continuing debate in Elizabethan times, and from at least 1550 the Puritan faction of the Anglican church had been advocating the death penalty for fornication and adultery. In fact, in 1650, the Puritan government of the Commonwealth actu-

ally put such a law on the books. Before that, the only sexual crimes classified as capital offenses were rape, buggery, and carnal abuse of a female under ten years of age. Other sexual offenses were punished by the Ecclesiastical Courts, usually with fines or public penance.[31] When we find young Claudio sentenced to death for impregnating Juliet, we should be aware, as Shakespeare's audience was, that while Claudio's offense was not capital under Elizabethan law, amendment was certainly not unthinkable.

With this background in mind, we may more fruitfully examine the opening legal situation. The play opens as the Duke relinquishes for an indefinite period his control over Vienna to Angelo, an inexperienced young man of, apparently, scrupulously moral character. Old Lord Escalus, appointed second in command, vouches for Angelo's fitness for the office. (I.i.22-24) The power transferred by the Duke seems unlimited:

> For you must know, we have with special
> soul
> Elected him our absence to supply,
> Lent him our terror, dressed him with our
> love,
> And given his deputation all the organs
> Of our own power.
> (I.i.17-21)

> Hold therefore, Angelo:
> In our remove be thou at full ourself.
> Mortality and mercy in Vienna
> Live in thy tongue and heart.
> (I.i.42-45)

>   Your scope is as mine own,
> So to enforce or qualify the laws
> As to your soul seems good.
> (I.i.64-66)

Terror—love, mortality—mercy, enforce—qualify: these oppositions suggest a balancing process, a mediation between opposing forces, an avoidance of extremes. To them may be added tongue—heart, a distinction that proves crucial as the play progresses. Angelo is instructed to balance these contending forces "as to [his] soul seems good,"—not to his reason, or to his judgment, but to his soul, an explicit indication that there is a moral dimension in the conduct of government that necessarily derives from the essential nature of the governor. This is not a new concept for Shakespeare; we have met it already in the Lord Chief Justice's assertion that his judgment was guided by the "impartial conduct of [his] soul." (*2 Henry IV,* V.ii.36)

The Duke, as it turns out, has been concerned that the laws of Vienna have not been enforced:

> . . . so our decrees,
> Dead to infliction, to themselves are dead,
> And Liberty plucks Justice by the nose;
> The baby beats the nurse, and quite athwart
> Goes all decorum.
>
> (I.iii.27-31)

He has turned the government over to Angelo at least in part to reestablish the strict rule of law without himself seeming tyrannous or arbitrary. Angelo chooses to revive the long-dormant law against fornication, and to condemn Claudio to death as an example to all of the law's new strictness. But the statute cannot justly be applied to Claudio, if indeed it can be applied justly at all. He and Juliet have entered into a marriage contract that both the church and the state in Elizabethan England recognized as binding, and their marriage lacks only the transfer of the dowry and a final public confirmation to be fully effective. While Claudio is technically guilty of a violation, both Elizabethan custom and the position of one side in the church's continuing dispute about the status of a contracted marriage seem to have sanctioned his enjoyment of the physical pleasures of marriage.[32] In the source for *Measure for Measure,* Claudio's counterpart commits rape. Shakespeare has clearly chosen to mitigate the circumstances of his crime as much as possible while leaving it subject to the letter of the statute.

Regardless of the realistic Elizabethan status of Claudio's offenses, several characters in the play express an opinion about his offense, and the comments cover the spectrum. Claudio's sister, the saintly Isabella, who is preparing to enter an exceedingly strict convent, reacts with moralistic self-righteousness: "[it] is a vice that most I do abhor, / And most desire should meet the blow of justice." (II.ii.29-30) Lucio, the resident rake, flippantly calls it "a game of tick-tack" (I.ii.185), and it is "[g]roping for trouts in a peculiar river" (I.ii.86) to Pompey the bawd. Each of these views is a bit partisan, but the judgment of the Provost (jailor), who is consistently depicted as wholly admirable, humane, and clear-headed, seems to strike the proper balance: "a young man / More fit to do another such offense / Than die for this." (II.iii.13-15)[33]

The play is not, however, neutral on the issue of sexual incontinence. The Duke frequently expresses concern about the effects of sexual license. (See, for instance, II.iii; II.iv.26-34; III.i.17-41; and III.i.94.) The law, while unwisely applied in this particular case, and unreasonably harsh as a general matter, does represent a serious attempt to deal with a serious problem. Were this not the case, Claudio's initial acceptance of a certain justice in his condemnation (I.ii.118-19), Isabella's acceptance of his supposed execution in the final scene (V.i.444-45), and the vacillation of Escalus, who recognizes both the injustice of Claudio's conviction and a certain necessity for strict enforcement of the law (see II.i.4-16; II.i.64; III.ii.234-38), would be themselves absurd. Claudio's eventual deliverance would become no more than the most elementary and obvious justice, and Isabella's agony over whether to sacrifice her chastity in return for her brother's life would be empty puffing about a non-issue. Clearly chastity, or at least a reasonable control of the sexual drive, is valued highly, and the harsh law Angelo chooses to enforce is an extreme manifestation of a legitimate concern.

In a slightly different sense, however, Angelo's law is "absurd" in that in essence it punishes people for being human and for having fundamental human drives. The several overtly comic scenes involving Lucio, Pompey, and Mistress Overdone, the bawdy-house keeper, make it clear that thorough enforcement of such a law would depopulate the city in short order. This exchange between Pompey and Escalus puts the issue most succinctly:

> POMPEY: Truly, sir, I am a poor fellow that would live.
>
> ESCALUS: How would you live, Pompey? By being a bawd? What do you think of the trade, Pompey? Is it a lawful trade?
>
> POMPEY: If the law would allow it, sir.
>
> ESCALUS: But the law will not allow it, Pompey; nor it shall not be allowed in Vienna.
>
> POMPEY: Does your worship mean to geld and splay all the youth of the city?
>
> ESCALUS: No, Pompey.
>
> POMPEY: Truly, sir, in my poor opinion, they will to't then. If your worship will take order for the drabs and the knaves, you need not to fear the bawds.
>
> ESCALUS: There is pretty orders beginning, I can tell you; it is but heading and hanging.
>
> POMPEY: If you head and hang all that offend that way but for ten year together, you'll be glad to give out a commission for more heads. If this law hold in Vienna ten year, I'll rent the fairest house in it after three-pence a bay; if you live to see this come to pass, say Pompey told you so.
>
> (II.i.210-29)

Pompey is right, and at the core of the problems of government the play explores will be the dilemma of establishing a livable relation between elemental human nature and a society ordered by law. That the law takes upon itself to forbid something does not by any means settle the question. Severely repressive law, although usually "absurd" in this sense, and usually doomed to failure as is Angelo's law, is a familiar phenomenon, and there have been periods in our legal history characterized by a similarly strict theory of criminal law.[34] Shakespeare gives us, in essence, a plausible laboratory test of this type of law being administered at the farthest reach of its technical scope. This particular law deals with an element so basic to human character that all levels and types of characters can be vitally involved in the resolution of the issue. The testing is all the more interesting because of the nature of the judge who is also being tested.

As Angelo takes over the rule of Vienna, we know only that he seems virtuous and that his ability to govern is untested. (I.i.47-50) In I.ii Claudio's arrest is reported first in comic terms that deflate the solemnity of the passage of the reins of government in the preceding scene; the net effect so far has been to arrest a man for "groping for trouts," and to order all bawdy houses to be shut down, except for those in the city proper, which have been spared by the intervention of an influential businessman. (I.ii.82-100) So much for the initial wielding of "mortality and mercy in Vienna." The tone changes quickly, however, with the appearance of Claudio being led to prison as a public spectacle. (I.ii.112-15) However comic the situation may appear in the abstract, Claudio is in grave jeopardy of losing his life, and Angelo's experiment in law enforcement raises serious questions about his ability to govern:

> And the new deputy now for the Duke—
> Whether it be the fault and glimpse of
>   newness,
> Or whether that the body public be
> A horse whereon the governor doth ride,
> Who, newly in the seat, that it may know
> He can command, lets it straight feel the
>   spur;
> Whether the tyranny be in his place,
> Or in his eminence that fills it up,
> I stagger in—but this new governor
> Awakes me all the enrolled penalties
> Which have, like unscoured armor, hung by
>   th' wall
> So long that nineteen zodiacs have gone
>   round
> And none of them been worn; and for a name
> Now puts the drowsy and neglected act
> Freshly on me: 'tis surely for a name.
>
>   (I.ii.152-66)

"Tyranny" is strong language, but its application to Angelo's actions is ultimately justified.

The Duke, too, has doubts about Angelo's reaction to power that he expresses to the friar from whom he borrows a habit:

> Lord Angelo is precise,
> Stands at a guard with envy; scarce confesses
> That his blood flows, or that his appetite
> Is more to bread than stone. Hence shall we
>   see,
> If power change purpose, what our seemers
>   be.
>
>   (I.iii.50-54)

"Precise" means morally or religiously scrupulous. Angelo is a type of puritan who directs all his energy toward surpressing natural human instincts and toward enforcing an excessively rigorous morality for himself and, given political power, for those around him. Seen in this light, his decision to enforce a law against sexual license becomes easy to explain, and the resulting situation provides an especially appropriate test case for his whole approach to human nature.[35] The puritanical person either is ignorant of the complexity of human nature, or has repressed much of that nature in the interests of some abstract system of conduct. In his cold, mechanical, and restricted view of allowable human response, he shows that he does not understand his own humanity. Angelo is just such a repressed type: ". . . one who never feels / The wanton stings and motions of the sense, / But doth rebate and blunt his natural edge / With profits of the mind, study and fast." (I.iv.58-61)

Angelo's repression of part of himself represents one aspect of a wider concern in the play that may perhaps best be expressed in the phrase "know thyself." Angelo does not know himself, and during the course of the drama he will be forced to acknowledge and deal with facets of his nature that are common to all humanity. Isabella, too, eventually overcomes her almost pathological revulsion from the sexual part of her nature; there is something nearly hysterical in her reaction to Angelo's proposition, and in her rejection of her brother's very human pleas for life: "Then, Isabel, live chaste, and, brother, die: / More than our brother is our chastity." (II.iv.184-85) Her original solution had been withdrawal from the world into the convent of Saint Clare, whose votaries are severely restricted even in the most innocent contact with men. (I.iv.7-14) The necessity of pleading for her brother's life puts her ideas to as severe a practical test as Angelo's, and in the end she rejects her ascetic ideals in favor of life in the world as the Duke's wife. Escalus describes the Duke as "[o]ne that, above all other strifes, contended especially to know himself." (III.ii.218-19) In a curious exchange with the friar near the beginning of the play, the Duke appears to have been asked whether he has disguised himself in order to seek a wife or a lover. We do not hear the precise question, only the Duke's answer:

> No, holy father, throw away that thought;
> Believe not that the dribbling dart of love
> Can pierce a complete bosom;
>
>   (I.iii.1-3)

But when, at the play's end, the Duke proposes to Isabella, he has at least learned that he too is human to the extent that he can feel the "dribbling dart of love," and perhaps in a wider sense he has learned something about his role as the personification of the state. As he pardons all offenders in turn, he seems to have rejected that strict justice that he wanted Angelo to impose at the beginning. He has learned the lesson that Pompey tried to teach Escalus, that human nature is stronger than law, and that for law to stand any chance of being practically effective, it must, somehow, be made to reflect the diversity and imperfection of the human situation.

Escalus, pleading for Claudio, suggests that Angelo, too, must have felt impulses like those for which Claudio stands condemned. Angelo's idea of justice, which appears unobjectionable and even admirable at first glance, has no room for such a notion:

> We must not make a scarecrow of the law,
> Setting it up to fear the birds of prey,
> And let it keep one shape, till custom make it
> Their perch and not their terror.
>
> . . . . .
>
> 'Tis one thing to be tempted, Escalus,
> Another thing to fall. I not deny,
> The jury passing on the prisoner's life
> May in the sworn twelve have a thief or two
> Guiltier than him they try; what's open made
>   to justice,
> That justice seizes; what knows the law
> That thieves do pass on thieves? 'Tis very
>   pregnant
> The jewel that we find, we stoop and take't
> Because we see it; but what we do not see
> We tread upon, and never think of it.
> You may not so extenuate his offense
> For I have had such faults; but rather tell me,
> When I that censure him do so offend,
> Let mine own judgment pattern out my death
> And nothing come in partial. Sir, he must die.
>   (II.i.1-4,17-31)

Angelo visualizes an objective, self-righteous justice that adheres rigidly to the letter of the law, and that focuses single-mindedly on a result without scrutinizing the means—the characters of the judge and jury—used to render this "justice." Escalus can only respond with an appeal to a higher judge: "Well, heaven forgive him, and forgive us all." (II.i.37)

Immediately following this solemn description of the legal process we are introduced to Constable Elbow, one of that tribe of malaproping officers of the law who inhabit Shakespeare's comedies. Elbow's entrance, dragging to justice Pompey the bawd, "a precise villain

. . . void of all profanation in the world that good Christians ought to have," reasserts the comic context in which his fellow constables move, and which has been in danger of disappearing in *Measure for Measure:*

> ANGELO: How now, sir, what's your name? And what's the matter?
>
> ELBOW: If it please your honor, I am the poor Duke's constable, and my name is Elbow. I do lean upon justice, sir, and do bring in here before your good honor two notorious benefactors.
>
>   (II.i.44-49)

Angelo and Escalus attempt to interrogate the prisoners, and the "notorious benefactors" deny any wrongdoing.

> ESCALUS: He's in the right. Constable, what say you to it?
>
> ELBOW: First, an it like you, the house is a respected house; next, this is a respected fellow; and his mistress is a respected woman.
>
> POMPEY: By this hand, sir, his wife is a more respected person than any of us all.
>
> ELBOW: Varlet, thou liest; thou liest, wicked varlet. The time is yet to come that she was ever respected with man, woman, or child.
>
> POMPEY: Sir, she was respected with him before he married with her.
>
> ESCALUS: Which is the wiser here, Justice or Iniquity? Is this true?
>
> ELBOW: O thou caitiff, O thou varlet, O thou wicked Hannibal! I respected with her before I was married to her? If ever I was respected with her, or she with me, let not your worship think me the poor Duke's officer. Prove this, thou wicked Hannibal, or I'll have mine action of batt'ry on thee.
>
> ESCALUS: If he took you a box o' th' ear, you might have your action of slander, too.
>
> ELBOW: Marry, I thank your good worship for it; what is't your worship's pleasure I shall do with this wicked caitiff?
>
> ESCALUS: Truly, officer, because he hath some offenses in him that thou wouldst discover if thou couldst, let him continue in his courses till thou know'st what they are.
>
> ELBOW: Marry, I thank your worship for it. Thou seest, thou wicked varlet, now, what's come upon

thee; thou art to continue now, thou varlet, thou art
to continue.[36]

(II.i.152-81)

Angelo has proclaimed that the laws must be strictly
enforced and Elbow is attempting to do it, but his
effort becomes a parodic version of Angelo's lofty
theory. Elbow hardly understands the law he is enforcing, and, confused by his prisoner, he communi-
cates what little he does comprehend in a series of
malapropisms so outrageous that Escalus asks, "Which
is the wiser here, Justice or Iniquity?" The setting is
comic, but the question has serious implications for
Angelo as well as for Elbow. Both are personifica-
tions of justice ("my brother justice have I found so
severe that he hath forced me to tell him he is indeed
Justice," (III.ii.237-38) says Escalus at one point), and
as Elbow's inability to understand the law or speak
plain English dooms his attempt to enforce the law,
so Angelo's inability to understand human nature,
and to account for this nature in his application of
the law, also dooms his attempts at enforcement.
Something of the absurdity of a "law against lovers,"
as one popular eighteenth century version of *Measure for Measure* was called, is clearly shown in
Elbow's ridiculous efforts; iniquity is wiser than justice in recognizing the inevitability of human imperfection. But Angelo is not present to witness most of
this comic lesson in law enforcement, nor to hear
Escalus' pointed question. He has exited earlier in
the scene with the remark that he hopes Escalus will
"find good cause to whip them all." (II.i.130) Escalus
does not accept this advice because he has a much
wiser, more humane view of the law and his role as a
judge. Instead, the "notorious benefactors" are dismissed with a stern warning, the appropriate remedy.

Angelo's own articulation of his view of law and justice is proven defective during his interviews with
Isabella, who has come to plead for her brother's life.
During the first exchange (II.ii) Angelo remains obdu-
rate, although Isabella pleads for mercy in lines as
eloquent as Portia's appeal to Shylock:

> ISABELLA: Too late? Why, no: I that do speak
>   a word
> May call it back again. Well believe this,
> No ceremony that to great ones 'longs,
> Not the king's crown, nor the deputed sword,
> The marshal's truncheon, nor the judge's robe,
> Become them with one half so good a grace
> As mercy does;
> If he had been as you, and you as he,
> You would have slipped like him; but he, like
>   you,
> Would not have been so stern.
> ANGELO: Pray you, be gone.
> ISABELLA: I would to heaven I had your
>   potency,

> And you were Isabel; should it then be thus?
> No, I would tell what 'twere to be a judge,
> And what a prisoner.
> LUCIO [*aside to Isabella*]: Ay, touch him;
>   there's the vein.
> ANGELO: Your brother is a forfeit of the law,
> And you but waste your words.
> ISABELLA: Alas, alas;
> Why, all the souls that were were forfeit
>   once,
> And He that might the vantage best have
>   took,
> Found out the remedy. How would you be,
> If He, which is the top of judgement, should
> But judge you as you are? O think on that,
> And mercy then will breathe within your lips,
> Like man new made.
> ANGELO: Be you content, fair maid,
> It is the law, not I, condemn your brother;

(II.ii.57-80)

Isabella's plea is as ineffective as Portia's because
Angelo, like Shylock, is committed to a view of the
law as an abstract process, final and absolute in its
own right, a process independent of the character of
its administrator. Shylock himself recognized that he
pressed for the full penalty of the law out of hatred
and a desire for revenge, but Angelo's rigor stems
from no such personal enmity. He is, consequently,
capable of a further misunderstanding of the law with
which even Shylock cannot be charged: "Your brother
is a forfeit of the law. . . ."; "It is the law, not I,
condemn your brother; . . ." These statements do not
recognize the possibility of a judge sympathetic to
human imperfection, who interprets, modifies, and
humanizes the application of the abstract law; instead they visualize a neutral judge who merely enforces absolute legal standards. And in an even grosser
failure of self-knowledge, Angelo imagines his own
will to have become identical with the supposedly
external and abstract law: "Look what I will not, that
I cannot do." (II.ii.52)

Isabella continues to plead for pity (mercy), and Angelo
answers:

> I show it most of all when I show justice,
> For then I pity those I do not know,
> Which a dismissed offense would after gall,
> And do him right that, answering one foul
>   wrong,
> Lives not to act another. Be satisfied;

(II.ii.100-04)

This familiar defense of a uniform and harsh application of the laws may be heard in modern courtrooms.
Angelo's justifications—that the public needs protection from recidivism, and the offender benefits by being
prevented from committing a second offense—are ir-

relevant as applied to Claudio, who has offended only with his contracted wife-to-be, and seems to present no danger to the public at large. But Angelo's defense of his actions is flawed in a more general sense in that it assumes the perfect wisdom that would justify the absolute power he wields, and allows for no degrees of punishment since it recognizes no degrees of guilt. He has, in other words, an unrealistic conception of the relation of law to life. Isabella is quick to point out the necessary imperfection of human justice, and the folly of Angelo's position from the perspective of divine wisdom:

> So you must be the first that gives this
>   sentence,
> And he, that suffers. O, it is excellent
> To have a giant's strength, but it is tyrannous
> To use it like a giant.
>
> . . . . .
>
> Could great men thunder
> As Jove himself does, Jove would ne'er be
>   quiet,
> For every pelting, petty officer
> Would use his heaven for thunder,
> Nothing but thunder. Merciful heaven,
> Thou rather with thy sharp and sulphurous
>   bolt
> Splits the unwedgeable and gnarled oak
> Than the soft myrtle; but man, proud man,
> Dressed in a little brief authority,
> Most ignorant of what he's most assured—
> His glassy essence—like an angry ape
> Plays such fantastic tricks before high
>   heaven
> As makes the angels weep; who, with our
>   spleens,
> Would all themselves laugh mortal.
>
> . . . . .
>
> Because authority, though it err like others,
> Hath yet a kind of medicine in itself
> That skins the vice o' th' top; go to your
>   bosom,
> Knock there, and ask your heart what it doth
>   know
> That's like my brother's fault; if it confess
> A natural guiltiness such as is his,
> Let it not sound a thought upon your tongue
> Against my brother's life.
>   (II.ii.106-09, 110-23, 134-41)

Heavenly justice has the wisdom to discriminate between the "soft myrtle," Claudio, who merits only gentle correction, and the "unwedgeable and gnarled oak," the hardened offender, who needs harsher treatment. This human judge is ignorant of his own nature,

his "glassy essence," but his stupid confidence in his own self-knowledge results in perverse decisions— "fantastic tricks"—that would be terribly funny were they not so terribly wrong. The comparison of perspectives—heavenly and earthly—on human judgments is analogous to the dramatic contrast that precedes this scene: Angelo's solemn certainty about the nature of justice followed immediately by a comic vision of justice in action. Isabella reveals another flaw in Angelo's vision. There is a paradox in the very nature of human authority that its possession renders those who have it less fit to govern; authority blinds its possessors to their kinship in imperfection with those who are to be judged.

Isabella attacks Angelo's abstract view of his role with two arguments. First, mercy is the greatest attribute of earthly rulers because it is the most God-like. Second, and apart from any congruence between heavenly and earthly judgment, a human judge ought to recognize inevitable human imperfection, and this recognition ought to breed humility and caution in the judgment process. A man who recognizes both arguments is truly the "man new made," a phrase that echos the "brave new world" of *The Tempest*, and that resonates with the central truth of the Christian faith, that God's mercy in atoning for man's sinful nature has allowed us to be reborn into everlasting life. This religious overtone leads us directly to *Matthew* 7:1-2, the text from which the title of the play is taken. But even without invoking theology, Isabella's two arguments have a great deal to say about the purely earthly administration of justice, and Angelo is moved by them. "She speaks, and 'tis / Such sense that my sense breeds with it." (II.ii.141-42) He feels for the first time the sensual desire common to humanity, but ironically this newly awakened humanity impels him to attempt to use his authority to possess Isabella, rather than to practice Christian mercy by pardoning her brother for his transgression. In the first blush of his new passion Angelo does refute, however, his earlier argument about the nature of judges:

> . . . O, let her brother live:
> Thieves for their robbery have authority
> When judges steal themselves.
>   (II.ii.175-77)

At the beginning of the second interview with Isabella, Angelo confesses in soliloquy that his former confidence in his own virtue, and in his ability to judge rightly, has been profoundly shaken. He has tried to pray for guidance, but his imagination remains fixed on Isabella. The harmony between tongue and heart that the Duke enjoined in the opening scene (I.i.45), and that Isabella urged (II.ii.136-41), is no longer possible for Angelo. His "blood," a term meaning his passion, has overwhelmed his faculties of judgment and disabled them. He uses a revealing simile:

. . . and even so
The general, subject to a well-wished king,
Quit their own part, and in obsequious
    fondness
Crowd to his presence, where their untaught
    love
Must needs appear offense.

(II.iv.26-30)

The "precise" Angelo of the first act scarcely confessed that his blood flowed (I.iii.51-53; I.iv.57-61); now it is a flood tide that downs all other concerns. In choosing to compare his present state to a political body in which some of the citizens are unruly, Angelo has already learned something essential about the place of the "blood" in human nature. As the above-cited passages indicate, Angelo, at the play's beginning, considered "blood" an outcast in the miniature society of his own being, to be ignored or repressed; in this simile it has taken on the character of a citizen with, presumably, a proper although subordinate place in that society. He now sees his problem as one of the rightful ordering of legitimate parts of human nature, not as one of driving out an invader.

The tyranny of authority is an issue that surfaces several times in the play. Claudio has charged Angelo with it (I.ii.158-66), as has Isabella (II.ii.107-09). When Angelo's new-found passion for Isabella provokes him to all too human vices, but not to a generous human pardon of Claudio, Isabella recognizes a special danger in authority that is not tempered by the recognition of human failing, but is rather ruled by those failings themselves:

O perilous mouths,
That bear in them one and the selfsame
    tongue,
Either of condemnation or approof,
Bidding the law make curtsy to their will,
Hooking both right and wrong to th' appetite,
To follow as it draws.

(II.iv.172-77)

The Provost, one of those admirable peripheral characters in Shakespeare whose opinions are usually sure guides to proper audience reaction, calls Angelo a "bitter deputy" for his refusal to pardon Claudio. The disguised Duke replies ironically, since he already knows of Angelo's treachery:

Not so, not so; his life is paralleled
Even with the stroke and line of his great
    justice.
He doth with holy abstinence subdue
That in himself which he spurs on his
    power
To qualify in others. Were he mealed with
    that

Which he corrects, then were he tyrannous,
But this being so, he's just.

(IV.ii.74-80)

The burden of this discussion seems to be that authority, could it somehow be exercised by a perfectly wise and moral agent, would be "justified" in condemning humans according to the strict letter of the law. Not only is such a human judge impossible, however, but by the very nature of authority, power is wedded to the "will" and "appetite" of those individuals most subject to the corrupting influence of authority itself. Once again Pompey has hold of the truth of the matter:

'Twas never merry world since, of two usuries, the merriest was put down, and the worser allowed by order of law a furred gown to keep him warm; and furred with fox and lamb skins too, to signify that craft, being richer than innocency, stands for the facing.

(III.ii.5-9)

The merry usury is sexual license or prostitution, and the worser is authority, supported by the law. The same corrupt humans may practice both, a fact to which the more splendid trappings of authority should not blind us.

When Angelo, after recognizing his own humanity in his passion for Isabella, proves yet more basely human in his attempt to have Claudio killed despite his agreement with Isabella, the disguised Duke must take a more direct hand and apply "[c]raft against vice." (III.ii.260) The convolutions of plot that issue in the final judgment scene are too complex to rehearse here. Angelo stands condemned by the "very mercy of the law" for the supposed treacherous killing of Claudio. Isabella enters with a cry for "justice, justice, justice, justice!" (V.i.25), but she is met by a plea for mercy from Mariana, Angelo's secret betrothed whom he has cruelly repudiated. Only when Isabella, moved by Mariana's forgiveness of Angelo, learns to pity his human frailty, only when she can yield to Mariana's plea and herself beg mercy for Angelo, is he pardoned. Despite Isabella's legalistic argument (V.i.439-50), Angelo deserves punishment more clearly than any other offender in the play. But Isabella and the Duke have learned that to fix norms of behavior in a personal code of conduct or in the law will not guarantee conformity to those norms, and that imposing the maximum legal penalty is rarely the appropriate response to a violation. The law can define desired behavior, but as an instrument for compelling that behavior it is too indiscriminating a tool to be used without great care. And it is definitely a tool, not the abstract Justice that Angelo first perceives, that must be applied by distinctly human judges. At worst it becomes the shield for iniquity used by Angelo. At best it must be used with a clear awareness of ubiquitous human imperfection and a tolerance for failings in others that are latent in ourselves. This tolerance cannot, of course, become a license for unrestrained wrongdoing; there is a genuine need for the "[c]orrection and instruction" that are to be administered to the recidivist Pompey. (III.ii.30-31) Moreover, as has already been pointed out, unrestrained sexual license does violate values that need protection. But in the end, given the fallibility of human judges, it is better to err on the side of leniency, than to condemn too quickly and too harshly a first failing. The ultimate judgment of God will mete out any punishment the guilty deserve. This is, perhaps, the meaning of the puzzling pardon given to Barnardine, the incorrigible murderer who outrageously refuses to allow himself to be executed:

> There was a friar told me of this man.
> Sirrah, thou art said to have a stubborn
>   soul,
> That apprehends no further than this world,
> And squar'st thy life according. Thou'rt
>   condemned;
> But, for those earthly faults, I quit them all,
> And pray thee take this mercy to provide
> For better times to come. Friar, advise him:
> I leave him to your hand.
>   (V.i.475-82)

Barnardine is the extreme case. Angelo is more representative, and Mariana's plea for him expresses the wisdom the play teaches:

> They say best men are moulded out of faults,
> And, for the most, become much more the
>   better
> For being a little bad; so may my husband.
>   (V.i.435-37)

In the end the vices of humanity and the values that the law seeks to protect from those vices both remain. Although the Duke has not established the rule of law that he envisioned when he gave Angelo his commission, one critic has noticed that he has imposed another kind of order on society. The specific law against fornication cannot be too strictly applied without producing gross injustice, but the policy behind that law can be expressed and institutionalized in marriage, and thus we get four couples formed at the end—Claudio and his Julietta, Angelo and Mariana, Isabella and the Duke, and the unfortunate Lucio and Kate Keepdown.[37] This form of the rule of law is much more humane and accommodating than the harsh command and harsher punishment of the "law against lovers." It is a rule of law that accommodates itself to the facts of human nature instead of attempting to eradicate them.

A Note on King Lear

In *The Merchant of Venice* and *Measure for Measure* Shakespeare dissects and examines human justice and authority in light of both human fallibility and that heavenly "justice" that is mercy. In *The Merchant of Venice* the law and its procedures prove too rigid and narrow to cope with the plight of Antonio, but the "rule of law," in form at least, maintains a precarious existence with the aid of some obscure legal knowledge and a liberal portion of divinely-inspired mercy and forgiveness. In *Measure for Measure* both the institution of law as a method for dealing with human imperfection and the judge who administers it falter under the test of actual experience; order is restored with the aid of a new judge who has learned the lesson of mercy, and the social institution of marriage assumes the function of ordering and restraining human vice.

Justice in a broad sense and the misuse of authority are also central concerns of *King Lear*. C. J. Sisson, in an interesting short essay on justice in the play,[38] notes that in the opening scene Lear administers distributive justice in apportioning his kingdom among his three daughters according to their ostensible claims of merit. We may recall the eloquent defense in *2 Henry IV* of justice as the "sword" of the state, the guardian of the King's person and the stabilizer of the realm. Justice was a manifestation of order, and the alternative was the civil war that wracked England both before and after the reign of Henry V. With the perspective of *Measure for Measure* on authority's potential for abuse, we see in *King Lear* the terrible consequences of the misapplication of the royal dispensation of justice. When Cordelia fails to praise Lear sufficiently, retributive justice is visited both upon her and upon Kent, who insists upon telling Lear that he is acting foolishly. As in the histories, civil war is one result, but the chaos and destruction wrought on the state, and on the judge who failed in his duty, are more profound and more terrible than anything found in the histories. This is in part because the tragedy is tightly focused on the effect of events on an individual, whereas the impact of the histories is in part diffused by a concern with a more impersonal and ongoing stream of history. But a more profound difference in the world of *King Lear* sets it apart from all three plays that have been examined so far. The general sense of divine guidance that oversees *2 Henry IV* leads us to believe that God has willed Henry V's England. In both *The Merchant of Venice* and *Measure for Measure* the Christian world view, and specifically God's mercy on human sinfulness, present a pattern and an impetus for merciful dealings among the human characters. But *King Lear* takes place in a pagan setting, and the gods so often invoked lend no order and stability to the chaotic action of the play.

In the physical and psychological maelstrom into which Lear plunges, order is not to be found in human authority or human justice. Lear's exchange with Gloucester, who has, by this point, been blinded by Cornwall and Regan because of his loyalty to the old King, reveals the depths of Lear's disillusionment:

LEAR: . . . Your eyes are in a heavy case, your purse in a light; yet you see how this world goes.

GLOUCESTER: I see it feelingly.

LEAR: What, art mad? A man may see how this world goes with no eyes. Look with thine ears. See how yond justice rails upon yond simple thief. Hark in thine ear: change places and, handy-dandy, which is the justice, which is the thief? Thou hast seen a farmer's dog bark at a beggar?

GLOUCESTER: Ay, sir.

LEAR: And the creature run from the cur. There thou mightst behold the great image of authority— a dog's obeyed in office.

Thou rascal beadle, hold thy bloody hand!
Why dost thou lash that whore? Strip thy
    own back.
Thou hotly lusts to use her in that kind
For which thou whip'st her. The usurer hangs
    the cozener.
Through tattered clothes small vices do
    appear;
Robes and furred gowns hide all. Plate sin
    with gold,
And the strong lance of justice hurtless
    breaks;
Arm it in rags, a pygmy's straw does pierce
    it.
None does offend, none—I say none! I'll able
    'em.
Take that of me, my friend, who have the
    power
To seal th' accuser's lips. Get thee glass eyes
And, like a scurvy politician, seem
To see the things thou dost not.
                                    (IV.vi.144-69)

Marion Hope Parker has called these lines "the most passionate attack upon human justice ever made. . . ."[39] If they are, they derive from and recall Shakespeare's other, milder, criticisms of human law and authority. "Which is the justice, which is the thief"—the lines echo Angelo's initial self-righteous declaration that criminality in the judge is irrelevant to justice, and his later realization that "thieves for their robbery have authority / When judges steal themselves." As a reductive vision of the corrupt "great image of authority," the "dog obeyed in office" recalls Isabella's "angry ape." The beadle lashing the whore after whom he lusts blends Angelo's lust for Isabella with the comic spectacle of Constable Elbow pursuing Pompey and the frequenters of Mistress Overdone's bawdyhouse, but the image has been reduced to its crudest form, deprived of both eloquence and comedy. The usurer hanging the cozener may be Shylock become a judge, the great thief judging the petty. And for Lear, as for Pompey the bawd, "robes and furred gowns" hide the vices of the "worser usury" while it persecutes the "merrier," whose lesser sins show plainly through "tattered garments." The human justice Lear sees is a sham. At best, judge and judged are interchangeable and equally corrupt. At worst, the trappings of authority shield the great sins of the powerful, and the weak are punished for every petty offense. When he delivers this tirade late in the play, Lear has clearly lost his wits, yet he expresses in violent and concentrated form all the familiar challenges to human justice we have traced. As Edgar says of the speech, "O, matter and impertinency mixed; / Reason in madness." (IV.vi.171-72)

The action of *King Lear* may, as Sisson suggests, be seen in part as an exploration of the broad theme of justice. To trace this through the play is not my purpose here. I wish instead to focus on an unusual scene that occurs in the middle of the sequence on the heath, the trial of Goneril and Regan. The scene is short, and may be quoted almost in its entirety:

LEAR: It shall be done; I will arraign them
    straight.
[*To Edgar*]
Come, sit thou here, most learned justice.
[*To the Fool*]
Thou, sapient sir, sit here. Now, you she-
    foxes—
EDGAR: Look, where he stands and glares.
    Want'st thou eyes at trial, madam?
    Come o're the bourn, Bessy, to me.
FOOL: Her boat hath a leak,
And she must not speak
Why she dares not come over to thee.
EDGAR: The foul fiend haunts poor Tom in
    the voice of a nightingale. Hoppedance
    cries in Tom's belly for two white herring.
    Croak not, black angel; I have no food for
    thee.

KENT: How do you, sir? Stand you not so
    amazed.
Will you lie down and rest upon the
    cushions?
LEAR: I'll see their trial first. Bring in their
    evidence.
[*To Edgar*]
Thou, robbed man of justice, take thy place.
[*To the Fool*]
And thou, his yokefellow of equity,

Bench by his side. [*to Kent*] You are o'th'
  commission;

Sit you too.

EDGAR: Let us deal justly.

Sleepest or wakest thou, jolly shepherd?

Thy sheep be in the corn;

And for one blast of thy minikin mouth

Thy sheep shall take no harm.

Purr, the cat is gray.

LEAR: Arraign her first. 'Tis Goneril, I here
  take my oath before this honorable
  assembly, kicked the poor king her father.

FOOL: Come hither, mistress. Is your name
  Goneril?

LEAR: She cannot deny it.

FOOL: Cry you mercy, I took you for a joint-
  stool.

LEAR: And here's another, whose warped
  looks proclaim

What store her heart is made on. Stop her
  there!

Arms, arms, sword, fire! Corruption in the
  place!

False justicer, why hast thou let her 'scape?

EDGAR: Bless thy five wits!

KENT: O pity! Sir, where is the patience now
That you so oft have boasted to retain?

EDGAR: [*aside*]: My tears begin to take his
  part so much

They mar my counterfeiting.

. . . . .

LEAR: Then let them anatomize Regan. See
  what breeds about her heart. Is there any
  cause in nature that makes these hard
  hearts?

(III.vi.20-60, 74-76)

This scene takes place under some shelter near the
heath with the storm still raging outside. The cruelty
of Goneril and Regan, Lear's sorrow for his own treatment of Cordelia, and the storm have done their work.
"All the power of his wits have given way to his
impatience," says faithful Kent, and at the end of the
scene, when Gloucester asks for the King, Kent's
reply is, "Here, sir, but trouble him not; his wits are
gone." But mad Lear is curiously precise about his
legal forms. The daughters are arraigned, and evidence is ordered to be introduced. He uses a formality of language appropriate to a legal proceeding:
"Thou, robbed man of justice, take thy place, / And
thou, his yokefellow of equity, / Bench by his side."
A "commission," sometimes composed of judges from
both the law and equity courts, seems to have been
a proper and not unusual judicial unit for hearing
special cases. In dramatic terms, the scene can be a
most impressive stage presentation; Edgar, the Fool,
old Kent, and Lear all gravely mimic the formal pro-

ceedings of the courtroom. Two of the judges are a
madman and a fool, the prosecutor is mad, the defendants are two joint-stools, and much of the business
of the court is the babbling of "poor Tom."

This fantastical court, uniquely impressive and terribly poignant, dissolves in Lear's distraught mind as
quickly as it was constituted. It leaves the audience,
however, with ambiguous responses to this use of
formal legal process. On the one hand, this combination of formal procedural correctness and insane babbling creates an extraordinary image of the impotence
of human justice to deal with the crimes Goneril and
Regan have committed. When Lear in fact wielded the
power to dispense justice at the beginning of the play,
he misused his power. As Regan said at the time, "yet
he hath ever but slenderly known himself," and Goneril
replied, "The best and soundest of his time hath been
but rash. . . ." (I.i.292-95) *Measure for Measure* has
taught us that a judge's lack of self-knowledge will
fatally obstruct the process of human justice, and the
results of Lear's misjudgment have been disastrous.
We also know from that earlier play that authority
itself may incapacitate its holder from making clear
judgments. Lear, stripped of all the trappings and
powers of his kingship as a consequence of his misjudgment, has not only learned to judge his three
daughters rightly, but he has gained much self-knowledge. With this new self-knowledge so dearly bought
at the price of madness, he tries to use the royal prerogative of dispensing justice once more; all he can
accomplish is a mocking of the forms of normal human justice, comic in the ranting of Edgar, but desperately pathetic in the impotence of knowledge gained
too late to be translated into power.

In another sense, however, this mad trial, created by
an effort of Lear's will and imagination out of physical and psychological chaos, is an ordering into a familiar social form of the mind-and-heart rending experience Lear has undergone. Man has developed formal
legal process to deal with disorder in society, and these
forms, however imperfectly, do harness the threat of
chaos by constructing context within which we can
begin to control it. The trial ends the long, wild sequence on the heath, and after it Lear, for the first
time, is able to sleep. This process of justice is only
a delusion of Lear's tormented psyche, and judgment
cannot, of course, be executed by the officers of this
court; the eventual deaths of Goneril and Regan do
not result from any legal sanction. Indeed, the terrible
disorder and injustice expressed in the actual events
of the play contrast vividly with this attempt at reasoned order. But for Lear the familiar forms of justice
have allayed, at least temporarily, the demons that
torture his soul; Goneril and Regan have in a sense
been formally judged, and the process has been cathartic. We do not see Lear again for seven scenes,
and when he reappears his madness is as strong as

ever. We hear, among other things, the denunciation of justice that has already been examined. The calming effect has not been permanent, but this illusory trial has served a purpose uniquely appropriate to the legal process. In this short scene on the heath, in the midst of chaos, the use of legal process expresses the human need to attempt to deal with disorder in an ordered and "reasonable" way, even as it is also an image of the limits of that effort.

Before concluding, I think it may be appropriate to make a few general observations about the critical difficulties inherent in approaching a topic so diffuse as "Shakespeare and the law." These observations are in part implicit in the critical commonplace that the integrity of each artistic work must be respected, and in part derive from the special nature of this topic. "The law" is really a short-hand term for a complex group of related phenomena—rules, procedures, institutions, personalities—and Shakespeare's interest in "it" appears in correspondingly diverse circumstances—in plots, in characters, in imagery. Because his treatment of the law is scattered throughout a number of the plays, it will tend to be intractable to any critical discussion that seeks absolute conformity with some single Shakespearean ideal of the law. The plays span a working life of perhaps a quarter of a century, and it would be only natural to expect that, as the dramatist's experience with life and its representation on stage increased, and as he moved from one type of dramatic representation to another, his attitude toward the various aspects of the law that came his way would also change. Moreover, the law is rarely the central focus of attention, and its meaning in any given play is inextricably a function of all of the elements of that play. Fragments from a number of plays may well not form a coherent, consistent whole, and consistency may perhaps be had only at the expense of ignoring the integrity of the separate dramatic works from which the fragments come.

Finally, it seems to me that Shakespeare was not, and did not intend to be, a systematic legal philosopher.[40] His perspective is that of an exceptionally perceptive layman with a profoundly moral view of human experience who is interested in the law as a working system, not as a theoretical construct. He looks at the law in action, and he is interested not in technical precision, but in the people who enforce and who are affected by the law, and in the idea of human law as it encounters other values—political reality, political idealism, moral truth, psychological necessity. In addition, Shakespeare undoubtedly was attracted by the sheer dramatic potential of the law. His trial scenes are always meant to be taken seriously by his audience—they always focus important issues—but, whether or not Shakespeare was a trained lawyer, he was too good a dramatist to allow his dramatic momentum to become bogged down in the details of "correct" legal procedure.

The purpose of this article has been to explore some of the ways Shakespeare treats the law, and the selection of focal points has, admittedly, been somewhat arbitrary. I do think, however, that the [three] plays examined give a fairly accurate overview of Shakespeare's artistic and intellectual attitudes toward the law. As with most other subjects that interest him, Shakespeare has a variety of insights into the law and how it operates. It is sometimes a comic butt, as when Dogberry or Elbow tries to enforce it; sometimes a noble ideal, as when the Lord Chief Justice waxes eloquent about it; sometimes an all too human and imperfect construction that may actually impede the quest for justice, as in *The Merchant of Venice* or *Measure for Measure;* and sometimes a powerful metaphor for man's attempts to order and control his experience, as in the trial on the heath in *King Lear.* In all these settings, the law, a weak and distorted reflection though it is, derives a peculiar dignity from its analogous relation to the justice of God. The multiplicity of perspectives is entirely desirable; law is not, at least as most people experience it, an infallible system of pure reason, but rather an often distressingly, and sometimes joyously, human invention, with all the quirks and inconsistencies endemic in such human enterprises.

Notes

[22] The play has been used to provide arguments for those who claim expert legal knowledge for Shakespeare, and it has been cited as proof that he could not have been familiar with real courtroom procedure. German legal philosophers have been much interested in the jurisprudential content of the trial scene, usually from the standpoint of whether Shylock receives "justice." *See* G. Keeton, *supra* note 1, at 148-50, for a brief description of the discussion among the Germans. The participants and their relevant works are: R. von Jhering, *The Struggle for Law* (2d ed. J. Lalor transl., Chicago, 1915); A Pietscher, *Jurist und Dichter* (Dessau, 1881); and J. Kohler, *Shakespeare vor dem Forum der Jurisprudenz* (1st ed., Wurzburg, 1883; 2d ed., Berlin, 1919). One more recent treatise finds in the play an explicit recognition of the differing powers of courts of law and equity, and reads the trial scene as a plea for the supremacy of equity jurisdiction that was finally achieved in the famous case of *Glanville v. Courtney* in 1616. M. Andrews, *Law Versus Equity in The Merchant of Venice* (Boulder, Colo., 1965). W. Knight, *supra* note 10, at 178-90, advances similar ideas.

[23] Shylock as devil: I.iii.94 (by Antonio); II.ii.22-24 (by Launcelot Gobbo); II.iii.2 (by Jessica); III.i.18,69 (by Solanio); IV.i.215,285 (by Bassanio). *See generally* B. Spivack, *Shakespeare and the Allegory of Evil* (New York, 1958).

[24] Coghill, *The Governing Idea, 1 Shakespearian Quarterly* (Vienna, 1948), *quoted in part in* M. Parker, *The Slave of Life: A Study of Shakespeare and the Idea of Justice* 69-75 (London, 1955).

[25] C. Barber, *Shakespeare's Festive Comedy* 178, 190 (Princeton, 1959).

[26] The many implications of the concept of wealth in *The Merchant of Venice* have been treated thoroughly by several scholars of the play, and they have been no more than summarized most cursorily here. *See* C. Barber, *supra* note 25, at 163-91; J. Brown, *Shakespeare and His Comedies* 45-81 (2d ed., London, 1962); Cooper, *Shylock's Humanity,* 21 *Shakespeare Quarterly* 117 (1970).

[27] It would appear that it is the preparation to exact the penalty lawfully awarded, and not the mere prosecution of the action on the bond, that is culpable:

> BASSANIO: Why dost thou whet thy knife so
>   earnestly?
> SHYLOCK: To cut the forfeiture from that
>   bankrout there.
> GRATIANO: Not on thy sole, but on thy soul,
>   harsh Jew,
> Thou mak'st thy knife keen. . . .
>
> (IV.i.121-24)

[28] There is some question about the actual disposition of Shylock's property. G. Keeton, *supra* note 1, at 146-47, whom I have followed, reads the technical language in IV.i.378-88 as placing legal title to one half of Shylock's goods in Antonio, with a life estate in Shylock, and a vested remainder in Jessica and her husband. Antonio thus cannot be charged with benefiting monetarily from Shylock's downfall, a situation that would in any case flatly contradict the thematic structure of the scene. Andrews, wrongly I think, attributes the economic benefit from this property to Antonio for the duration of Shylock's life. *See* M. Andrews, *supra* note 22, at 74-75.

[29] Many literary critics have seen the play as something approaching an allegory, or at least a metaphoric representation, of divine mercy in human lives. The Duke, who abdicates for uncertain reasons at the beginning of the play, and who then oversees the ensuing action disguised as a friar before revealing himself and dispensing justice and mercy in a complex reconciliation scene, becomes a representative of the sometimes inscrutable ways of providence as viewed from an earthly perspective. Such a reading of the play does explain much of what is puzzling in the play's intellectual and moral structure. *See generally* G. Knight, *Measure for Measure and the Gospels* in *The Wheel of Fire* 80-106 (London, 1930); M. Lascelles, *Shakespeare's Measure for Measure* (London, 1953); E. Schanzer, *The Problem Plays of Shakespeare* 71-131 (London, 1963); Kirsch, *The Integrity of Measure for Measure,* 28 *Shakespeare Survey* (1975).

At least one literary critic has read the play as a primarily secular exploration of the problems of governing the state and the self. R. Hunter, *Shakespeare and the Comedy of Forgiveness* 204-26 (New York, 1965). This excellent essay confirmed and organized much of my own thinking about the play.

Curiously, most legal commentators, aside from the German legal philosophers (*see* note 22 *supra*), have shied away from extensive analysis of the play. *But see* G. Keeton, *supra* note 1, at 371-93.

The Duke presents one of the knottiest problems in Shakespearean criticism. His function and motivation, indeed his very nature, are the subject of lively debate. Since I did not think an extended treatment of him is necessary to my discussion, I have elected to say as little as possible about a very difficult subject. For commentary on the Duke, see H. Hawkins, *Likenesses of Truth in Elizabethan and Restoration Drama* 51-78 (Oxford, 1972); R.E.C. Houghton, ed., The New Clarendon Shakespeare edition of the play, 212-17 (Oxford, 1970); M. Lascelles, *supra,* at 118-19; G. Knight, *supra;* Leavis, *The Greatness of Measure for Measure,* 10 *Scrutiny* 234 (1942); Weil, *The Options of the Audience: Theory and Practice in Peter Brook's Measure for Measure,* 25 *Shakespeare Survey* 27 (1972); Wilson, *Action and Symbol in Measure for Measure and The Tempest,* 4 *Shakespeare Quarterly* 375 (1953); L. Owen, The Representation of Forgiveness in Shakespeare and The Medieval Mystery Play, (1975) (unpublished dissertation in Alderman Library at the University of Virginia).

[30] *See, e.g.,* Professor A.L. Goodhart's comment in *The Influence of Literature on the Common Law,* 21 Record of N.Y.C.B.A. 271, 279 (1966).

[31] The historical material is drawn from R. Hunter, *supra* note 29, at 209-12, 249-50.

[32] Schanzer, *The Marriage-Contracts in Measure for Measure,* 13 *Shakespeare Survey* 81 (1960).

[33] R. Hunter, *supra* note 29, at 208-09.

[34] *See* 1 L. Radzinowicz, *A History of English Criminal Law and Its Administration from 1750,* at 1-265; 611-734 (London, 1948); 4 *id.* at 303-53.

[35] *Cf.* Radbruch, *supra* note 2, at 131-32, on "The Psychology of the Man of the Law": Justice, as we have seen, is an empty category that may be filled with the most varied contents. So the madness of justice without purpose may dress the utmost monstrosity up as an ideal (Robespierre). Justice is a polar value, which

needs resistance if its essence is to prevail. Justice that is not again and again wrested from love becomes injustice, just as mercy would become unsteady weakness were it not in turn to be wrested again and again from justice. Justice without love hardens into self-righteousness, upon which the suppressed vital forces sooner or later terribly revenge themselves. In the figure of Angelo in *Measure for Measure,* Shakespeare has presented to us the image of the zealot of the law who slips into self-righteousness and injustice, the rebellion of suppressed desires running wild against the self-righteous norm.

[36] The end of this scene furnishes evidence of the realism of Shakespeare's portrait of the constable:

> Escalus: Come hither to me, Master Elbow; come hither, master constable. How long have you been in this place of constable?
>
> Elbow: Seven year and a half, sir.
>
> Escalus: I thought, by the readiness in the office, you had continued in it some time; you say, seven years together?
>
> Elbow: And a half, sir.
>
> Escalus: Alas, it hath been great pains to you; they do you wrong to put you so oft upon't. Are there not men in your ward sufficient to serve it?
>
> Elbow: Faith, sir, few of any wit in such matters. As they are chosen, they are glad to choose me for them; I do it for some piece of money, and go through with all.
>
> (II.i.243-55)

Although in theory every male citizen was expected to take a turn at the honorary office of constable, in practice persons like Elbow were often paid to perform the duties. *See* G. Keeton, *supra* note 1, at 103. Further evidence of the realism of Shakespeare's incompetent constables appears in contemporary statutes punishing constables severely for neglect of duty and references to the disreputable character of the holders of the office. *See* Frasure, *supra* note 11, at 384-86. In any event, the character was evidently popular with audiences, because a number of Shakespeare's contemporaries found places for similar figures in their plays. *Id.* at 389.

[37] *See* Sale, *The Comic Mode of Measure for Measure,* 19 *Shakespeare Quarterly* 55, 59 (1968).

[38] C. Sisson, *Shakespeare's Tragic Justice* 74-98 (London, 1963).

[39] M. Parker, *supra* note 24, at 138.

[40] As far as legal philosophies go, Shakespeare's vital interest in the concept of nature (see, for instance, the various uses of the term in *King Lear*) and his conviction that God's law is everywhere superior to mere human law, do place him in an intellectual tradition with the theorists of natural law. The Thomist tradition, with which Shakespeare has been identified by some critics, is a major contributor to the school of natural law. *See* M. Parker, *supra* note 24; Sister J. M. O'Malley, P.M., *Justice in Shakespeare—Three English Kings in the Light of Thomistic Thought* (New York, 1964). The possible relations are potentially complex, and would make an interesting subject for further study.

LAW IN COMEDY AND ROMANCE: TRIALS, MARRIAGE, AND MERCIFUL JUSTICE

David M. Bergeron (essay date 1984)

SOURCE: "Hermione's Trial in '*The Winter's Tale*'," in *Essays in Theatre,* Vol. 3, No. 1, November, 1984, pp. 3-12.

[*In the following essay, Bergeron argues that Hermione's trial in* The Winter's Tale *reflects a triumph of rationality over passion.*]

When Leontes and the others gather in the final scene of *The Winter's Tale* before the statue of Hermione, Paulina instructs them:

> It is requir'd
> You do awake your faith. Then all stand still:
> Or—those that think it is unlawful business
> I am about, let them depart.
>
> (V.iii.94-97)[1]

In a moment the music sounds and the statue moves. Puzzling, perhaps, is Paulina's word "unlawful". Robert Uphaus has argued that this word is appropriate because *The Winter's Tale* creates much "unlawful business;" it is "Shakespeare's most defiant romance."[2] The play continually violates our expectations. The most explicit example of defiance comes in Hermione's trial in Act III, a scene that in many ways is the obverse of the play's final restoration scene. The actual trial in Act III counters the trial of faith in the last scene, each producing its own special sense of wonder and the unexpected. My focus will be on Hermione's defense of herself in the trial, demonstrating how her rational approach contrasts with Leontes' passion and showing how her defense strengthens the presentation of her character. In several ways the trial foreshadows the restoration.

Generally, critics writing on *The Winter's Tale* have not paid much detailed attention to Hermione's trial. In an essay that explores the role of women in the play Peter Erickson in fact finds that Hermione's appearance in the trial confirms his view that she changes from a vibrant strength, seen early in the play, to weakness: ". . . she adopts a stance of patience and stoic passivity."[3] I will argue quite the opposite: the trial scene exhibits great strength in Hermione's character while it may also demonstrate patience. I see no evidence that she *adopts* the stance that Erickson suggests. What is indeed remarkable about Hermione here is how within social and legal confines she brilliantly defends herself in the trial, thereby helping us understand the great reservoir of moral courage that she possesses.

The natural outgrowth of Leontes' jealousy has been to send Hermione to prison in Act II on the, as yet unproved, assumption that she is guilty. His accusations against her in II.i.81-95 are clear but mistaken; and his precarious position is evident in his assertion: ". . . if I mistake / In those foundations which I build upon, / The centre is not big enough to bear / A school-boy's top" (II.i.100-3). The centre does not hold for Leontes; in part it does not hold because Leontes is himself the center, or so he thinks, building the foundations step by step on his jealousy. Fortunately for him and the state, a sufficient vestige of orderly procedure remains so that a formal trial of Hermione can be held. As Leontes says: ". . . as she hath / Been publicly accus'd, so shall she have / A just and open trial" (II.iii.202-4). Such is the primary business of the first part of Act III.

Shakespeare does not include many formal trials: the trial of Antonio in *The Merchant of Venice,* Katherine's in *Henry VIII,* and the one here in *The Winter's Tale.* Several other trials or legal proceedings are, of course, referred to but not given dramatic life. The semblance of a trial in *Measure for Measure* never acquires the formal characteristics of the ones above. Portia is the star in Antonio's trial as judge figure, not the defendant; throughout she truly has the upper hand. Katherine shares some similarities with Hermione, a point noted long ago by G. Wilson Knight in *The Crown of Life.* But her defense is primarily an attack on Wolsey, the formal charges against her never being articulated. Katherine has ostensible legal support from the learned reverend fathers. Hermione stands alone: defendant and sole legal counsel. As she notes, she has no other defense "But what comes from myself . . ." (III.ii.25). Solitary and vulnerable, she must make the best case for herself.

The orderly and formal structure of the trial belies the chaos, irrationality, and jealousy that bring it about, perhaps Shakespeare's way of indicating that Sicilian society may be capable of redemption. In other words,

to have such a trial implies that justice may yet be possible—certainly it is preferable to letting Hermione rot in jail. The odds against justice being achieved in the trial obtain so long as Leontes is the potential judge. The legalistic structure also counterpoints the mystical, transcendental oracle of Apollo that will finally determine the outcome of the trial, supplanting Leontes' judgement.

The assumption on which Hermione proceeds differs radically from that of Leontes. She observes in an "if" statement that contrasts nicely with Leontes' earlier one:

> . . . if powers divine
> Behold our human actions (as they do),
> I doubt not then but innocence shall make
> False accusation blush, and tyranny
> Tremble at patience.
>
> (III.ii.28-32)

For Hermione there is a center, and it holds. Shakespeare takes the seeds that he finds in Bellaria in Greene's *Pandosto* and gives them full development in Hermione. What I propose to examine in some detail is Hermione's legal defense: it is studied, calculated, logical, honest, and full of controlled passion. It is also at moments spontaneous as when she responds to Leontes' outbursts or questions; but basically, I think she has thought through the issues and has some kind of structure in mind for her argument. Her defense proceeds on the basis of the ancient modes of persuasion, enunciated by Aristotle: ethical, logical, and pathetic proofs (see Aristotle, *Rhetoric,* Book I, chapter 2). She engages not so much the subtleties of law as she practices the art of persuasion.

Leontes opens the proceedings by at least giving lip-service to the pursuit of justice:

> Let us be clear'd
> Of being tyrannous, since we so openly
> Proceed in justice, which shall have due course,
> Even to the guilt or the purgation.
>
> (III.ii.4-7)

He believes, of course, that he is right and will be vindicated by the trial. Leontes' word "purgation," though it means "acquittal," carries also the meaning of "catharsis"—what better description of what happens in the trial scene to both Hermione and Leontes? In one sense Leontes is also on trial even as he thinks Hermione is the only guilty party. As the prisoner Hermione is brought in, Leontes commands: "Read the indictment" (11). The Officer complies in what is, I believe, the only formal statement of charges in a trial in Shakespeare. The main burden of the indictment is thus:

Hermione, queen to the worthy Leontes, king of
Sicilia, thou art here accused and arraigned of high
treason, in committing adultery with Polixenes, king
of Bohemia, and conspiring with Camillo to take
away the life of our sovereign lord the king, the
royal husband . . .

(12-17)

In addition, she has presumably assisted in the escape
of Polixenes and Camillo. Adultery and conspiracy
are the fundamental charges. In contrast, Katherine in
Henry VIII is not accused of either of these crimes;
indeed, her main "fault" is that she has not produced
a male heir. Hermione's task is somehow to answer
the indictment. She cannot counter with tangible proof,
so she must try to move by persuasion. Her strength
grows from the knowledge that she is innocent and
that "powers divine" will exonerate her.

Hermione's first argument rests on establishing the
"ethos" of the speaker, that is, her moral, credible,
and upright nature (recall Brutus' speech given before
Antony's in *Julius Caesar*). She knows that it is insufficient merely to assert "not guilty," "mine integrity, /
Being counted falsehood . . ." (26-27). Instead, she appeals
to the common perception of her good character: ". .
. my past life / Hath been as continent, as chaste, as
true, / As I am now unhappy . . ." (33-35). One notes
that she does not rely on the considerable testimony
about her good character spoken by others earlier in the
play, like Paulina and Camillo, but seeks to make the
persuasive case herself. She argues by reciting simple
facts: that she is "A fellow of the royal bed," "a great
king's daughter," and "The mother to a hopeful prince"
(38, 39, 40). She also owns "A moiety of the throne,"
which makes her a political partner with Leontes. The
implication is clear: she is of such stature that she must
be listened to. She has, however, been left "To prate and
talk for life and honour . . ." (41). Illustrating Hermione's
control in logically defending herself is the skill with
which she grasps the words "life" and "honour" and
develops them in additional comments. Thus she contrasts sharply with the frenzy and irrationality of Leontes.
Her appeal to his "conscience" rests not on his good will
but rather on his recollection of how she was in his
merited grace before Polixenes came to Sicilia. If she
should be "one jot" beyond being totally honorable, then
"harden'd be the hearts / Of all that hear me, and my
near'st of kin / Cry fie upon my grave!" (52-54). The
note of finality that accompanies the statement suggests
that Hermione has come to the end of this particular
mode of arguing, as indeed she has.

Her case, however, does not rest on the ethos of her
character alone, for she moves next to logical proof,
that is, to answer explicitly the charges of the indictment. Point by point she responds to the formal accusation of adultery and conspiracy. About her relationship with Polixenes, Hermione responds:

. . . I do confess
I lov'd him as in honour he requir'd,
With such a kind of love as might become
A lady like me . . .

(62-65)

With irony Hermione notes that her expression of love
to Polixenes was none other than what Leontes had
himself commanded: "Which, not to have done, I think
had been in me / Both disobedience and ingratitude /
To you, and toward your friend . . ." (67-69). She signals her movement to the second point of the argument: "Now, for conspiracy . . ." (71); and she begins:
"I know not how it [conspiracy] tastes, though it be
dish'd / For me to try how" (72-73). All she knows is
that "Camillo was an honest man" (74); but why he
has left the court no one knows, not even the gods.
Her methodical approach to the details of the indictment underscores her attempt at logical proof and indicates a mind that has spent its time in prison sorting
out the issues and preparing her defense. As we sometimes comment that Leontes is his own Iago, perhaps
we can suggest that Hermione is her own Portia.

When Hermione finishes her logical proof, Leontes
counters with additional accusations, unmoved by what
she has said, and ironically adds: "Your actions are
my dreams. / You had a bastard by Polixenes, / And
I but dream'd it!" (82-84). On this illusion, of course,
rests all of Leontes' jealousy, the subsequent imprisonment of Hermione, and the trial. Leontes seems to
sense the conclusion of the legal proceeding, for he
renders judgement on Hermione: ". . . as / Thy brat
hath been cast out, . . . / . . . so thou / Shalt feel our
justice . . ." (86-87, 89-90). The justice he has in mind
is, in his own words, "no less than death" (91). But
Leontes is wrong, not reckoning on the strength of Hermione nor on her determination to follow through on her
final mode of argumentation: pathetic persuasion.

She begins bluntly enough: "Sir, spare your threats"
(91). No longer does she need to establish her good
character (ethos) or to answer the precise accusations
of the formal indictment (logic); the last movement of
her defense is clearly an appeal to the emotions (pathos). Even so—and this is one of the striking and
remarkable things about Hermione's defense—the pathetic proof also proceeds logically, step by step. Her
first point consists of enumerating the three things
("comforts" she calls them) that she has lost: "The
crown and comfort of my life" (94), namely Leontes'
favor; the "first fruits of my body," that is, Mamillius,
from whose presence she is barred "like one infectious" (97, 98); and the "third comfort," the baby who
has been taken from her breast and "Hal'd out to
murder . . ." (101). One notes the control of her rhetoric: the first "comfort" contrasts with the word "lost";
the "second joy" with "infectious"; and the "third
comfort" with "murder". Joining this profound sense

of loss is the recognition that she has herself been "proclaim'd a strumpet" (102) "on every post" and therefore denied her rights as a mother. She makes one final point in this part of the argument: she has been given inadequate time to recuperate from childbirth; instead, she has been rushed to the trial before she has "got strength of limit" (106).

Her peroration begins with her question: "Now my liege, / Tell me what blessings I have here alive / That I should fear to die?" (106-8). She no longer values her life—"I prize it not a straw" (110), but she does treasure her honor. Seemingly aware that she has pursued her several proofs, she warns Leontes that if she is condemned "Upon surmises, all proofs sleeping else / But what your jealousies awake, I tell you / 'Tis rigour and not law" (112-14). She knows that her defense is solid, and, of course, she knows that she is innocent. But the immediate warning grows from the full understanding of how the legal proceeding should function. Her condemnation would be "unlawful business," the ultimate expression of defiance. The irony works several ways: Hermione is herself quite defiant, but the trial is wrong; the trial has the semblance of pursuing justice, but it rests on fallacious notions of Leontes. The judgment that seems inevitable would in fact mock the cause of justice. She rests her case with an emotional appeal beyond the puny, mortal understanding of Leontes: "Apollo be my judge!" (115).

The trial verdict shifts from human judgment to divine intervention by the oracle of Apollo. Leontes has deluded himself in believing that he controls the trial; but, as he will soon learn to his peril, he is subject to higher law, the presiding spirit of Apollo in this play. Only the intransigence of Leontes fails to be moved by Hermione's persuasive legal defense; the Lords cry out for the messengers of the oracle to be summoned to court, and so they are. Cleomenes and Dion appear and are compelled to "swear upon this sword of justice" (124) that they have indeed been at Delphos and bring with them "This seal'd up Oracle, by the hand deliver'd / Of great Apollo's priest . . ." (127-28). They are the medium; Apollo is the message. Divine witness now clinches the case for Hermione and renders judgment. The Officer of the court reveals the Oracle:

> Hermione is chaste; Polixenes blameless; Camillo a true subject; Leontes a jealous tyrant; his innocent babe truly begotten; and the king shall live without an heir, if that which is lost be not found.

> (132-35)

Several things interest us about the Delphic oracle. First, it is both retrospective and prophetic; that is, it looks to the past and offers judgment on the characters, it imposes a stasis on the present, and it sees into the future with its riddle-like comment about Leontes' heir. In that sense it rather resembles the play itself at this moment: one large part of the action is coming to an end (past) while another strand of plot is developing (future). Further, the oracle parallels in some respects the indictment read at the beginning of Hermione's trial even to the point of naming the characters—Hermione, Polixenes, Camillo—in the same order as they appear in the indictment. It obviously responds directly to the accusations made in that indictment, the basis of which has been Hermione's presumed guilt; but the message of the oracle is clear and simple: "Hermione is chaste." With that all of Leontes' foundations of blame crumble. Though revealed by Apollo, the oracle sounds very much like the report of the jury at a trial's end; it systematically and concisely answers the charges made or implicit in Hermione's trial.

Little could Leontes know in Act II, scene i when he dispatched the messengers to Delphos that they would return with a judgment exonerating Hermione and condemning him, the logical conclusion of her trial.

Indeed, Leontes' reason for seeking word from Apollo is to satisfy others, as he says: "Though I am satisfied, and need no more / Than what I know, yet shall the Oracle / Give rest to th' minds of others . . ." (II.i.189-91). In *Pandosto* it is Bellaria who initiates the mission to Apollo, making the request on her knees before Pandosto. For Bellaria the Apollo appeal is one last effort to exonerate herself, but for Leontes it will merely confirm, so he thinks, what he already knows. The tone in *Pandosto* and in *The Winter's Tale* is strikingly different. Shakespeare has set the oracle matter in motion in order to bring the message in at the conclusion of Hermione's defense and not before. Leontes learns at the end of Act II that Cleomenes and Dion, the Delphic messengers, are back in the country (II.iii.192-96); but there is no necessary expectation that they will arrive and participate in the trial. Shakespeare delays their arrival so that it may coincide with the end of the trial; thus Apollo's message judges the trial itself as well as the character of the persons involved.

The "courtroom" response to the oracle's verdict reveals joy for some but continuing obstinance on the part of Leontes. At Leontes' order the Officer reads Apollo's verdict; but Leontes responds with an ambiguous question to the Officer: "Hast thou read truth?" (138). The Officer answers that he has read the document exactly "As it is here set down." But Leontes cries out: "There is no truth at all i' th' Oracle: / The sessions shall proceed: this is mere falsehood" (140-41). The reaction contrasts sharply with the comment of the Lords—"Now blessed be the great Apollo!" (136)—and with Hermione's simple but joyous "Praised!" (136). One might note in passing that this is Hermione's final word until her restoration in V.iii. Neither persuaded by Hermione's proofs nor moved by Apollo's oracle, Leontes lashes out in a desperate attempt to assert his will and control in the trial; he is now the defiant one. Obviously he has lost; and if he will not be sensitive to Hermione's defense nor to the will of the gods, then the dramatist offers one last convincing blow: the news that his son is dead. With lightning-fast conversion—resembling the speed with which Leontes initially expressed his jealousy—Leontes changes: "Apollo's angry, and the heavens themselves / Do strike at my injustice" (146-47).

Having lost in the trial and having lost his son and presumably Hermione as well, Leontes begins the painful process of finding himself, stripped of his pride and groundless jealousy. As Hermione's sins have been enumerated in the formal statement of the indictment, so Leontes' are rehearsed by Paulina at the end of the scene. (11. 175ff). She becomes his accuser and judge; thus, the trial continues, but of Leontes, not of Hermione. As Hermione has presumably died, Leontes withers into remorse, abetted by the knowledge of his guilt and the lashing tongue of Paulina. Defiance seems now to have had its day. Humbled and chastened, Leontes promises at the end of III.ii to visit the chapel where Mamillius and Hermione will lie, "and tears shed there / Shall be my recreation" (239-40). Time and again Leontes resembles figures from Greek tragedy—I think especially of Creon in Sophocles' *Antigone* whom the gods break across their superior power and will.

Antigone differs from Hermione, of course, because she knowingly and willfully breaks the law of Creon. But the defense of her action rests on the awareness that spiritual laws take precedence over man-made laws, and she buries her brother in accordance with the will of the gods. Hermione, too, is sensitive to those "powers divine" operating in her world; by such power she presents her impressive legal defense. She has for the moment seemingly won the battle but lost the war. The dramatist will, however, eventually show her triumphant in her restoration in the play's final scene.

Why the trial scene in *The Winter's Tale?* It establishes in compelling terms the strength of Hermione's character and by contrast the paltry insufficiency of Leontes'. It is the most extensive examination of Hermione in the play—nowhere else does she have such a scene. If what I have suggested is valid, namely that Hermione's legal defense is systematic and controlled, then we understand the rationality that dominates her character in contrast to Leontes'. Under the most extreme circumstances she thinks coolly, logically. Paradoxically, in Hermione's defiance is her rationality, and in her rationality is her defiance. Her control defies Leontes' passion; and by asserting herself in the trial, she strikes a blow for justice and logical proceeding. Leontes, on the other hand, defies the system of justice with his groundless accusations, and he defies the gods by insisting on his will—all prompted by passion, not logic. Leontes is left with unlawful business.

The trial scene is a concrete, explicit example of the several trials in the play as it is also the most developed. One thinks, for example, of the quasi-trial of Florizel by Polixenes in Act IV, scene iv, the sheep-shearing scene, where the father's judgment falls harshly on his insolent son. The confrontation between father and son begins with Polixenes' question: "Have you a father?" (IV.iv.393), to which an impertinent Florizel answers: "I have: but what of him?" Having tested his son, Polixenes, resembling the earlier irate Leontes, removes his disguise and renders a verdict of punishment: ". . . we'll bar thee from succession; / Not hold thee of our blood, no, not our kin . . ." (430-31). Somehow the play must also resolve the profound consequences of this "trial". On the metaphorical level we can see much of the play as the "trial" of Leontes. The legal form of the actual trial helps, I think, our perception of this metaphor.

The trial also assists the oracle's credibility by its coming as an explicit response to and judgment on the trial. Having witnessed the trial and heard Hermione's persuasive defense, we can readily see the necessity of the intervention of the gods in order to achieve justice. This intervention is not the spectacle of the vision of Diana in *Pericles* nor the magical descent of Jupiter in *Cymbeline;* rather it is a report from the god Apollo functioning like a jury—no less wondrous than the others but nicely tied to immediate human problems. The trial makes possible this orderly intervention of Apollo, and the oracle in turn ratifies the trial, confirming its procedure and rendering judgment. The trial needs Apollo, and the oracle needs the trial.

This legal proceeding also throws into high relief the social, political, legal, and emotional conflict between Leontes and Hermione. The orderly, objective form of the trial assists in the audience's judgment as well, underscoring our belief in Hermione and dismay at Leontes. What we are unprepared for is the consequence of the trial—Mamillius' actual and Hermione's apparent death. Defying or upsetting our expectations is at the heart of the dramatic strategy of III.iii in which Antigonus is destroyed and, of course, at the center of the play's final scene. The defiant, "unlawful" nature of the trial foreshadows the restoration scene. The intervention of Apollo produces wonder akin to if different from the wonder evoked in the final scene.

Not only may the trial foreshadow the last scene, but the restoration also fulfills the trial. Paulina, the singing master of the souls of Leontes and Hermione, has imprisoned them both, separately of course: Hermione, hidden away somewhere for sixteen years, and Leontes, incarcerated in a process of penance and renewal and a vow not to remarry without Paulina's approval. In a sense Paulina has usurped the position of Apollo, her own brand of defiance. The trial has imposed a sentence on both Leontes and Hermione; this sentence is revoked, fulfilled, overcome, commuted, and transmuted in the play's final scene. The reunions of husband and wife and of mother and daughter supplant the deaths in the trial. Defiance is now more artistic than personal. The statue of Hermione defies the laws of nature by its art (Leontes is puzzled why the statue should have such wrinkles) even as its nature defies art. Submission and forgiveness characterize the tone and action of the scene, demonstrating again how this scene is the obverse of the trial.

The gods judge Leontes in that last scene, accept his penance, and restore Hermione to him. Hermione's gracious acceptance of Leontes ratifies the judgment of the scene: Leontes has been on trial and it is now ended. The earlier trial scene mocked justice; the last scene mocks with art. When Hermione begins to move, Leontes cries out: "If this be magic, let it be an art/ Lawful as eating" (V.iii.110-11). The "unlawful business" of the trial and the "unlawful" nature of the restoration parallel and reflect on one another. In the trial scene and in the restoration—indeed throughout the play—we are forever meeting when we least expect "with things dying" and "with things new-born" (III.iii.112-13).[4]

Notes

[1] Quotations are from *The Winter's Tale,* ed. J. H. P. Pafford, the Arden edition (London, 1966).

[2] Robert W. Uphaus, *Beyond Tragedy: Structure & Experience in Shakespeare's Romances* (Lexington, 1981), p. 91.

[3] Peter B. Erickson, "Patriarchal Structures in *The Winter's Tale,*" *PMLA,* 97 (1982), 825. The essay is found on pp. 819-29. I take issue with a number of Erickson's points. Erickson argues, for example, for a diminution in the power of the women in the play, partly the result of their transformation from threatening to reassuring characters. I find no loss in their power, especially if one considers the enormous power that Hermione and Paulina wield in the last scene. Erickson suggests that "female roles, though significant, are narrow and fixed, arranged to be consistent with the emotional needs and institutional structures of men" (827). Even if that statement were entirely true, how then does *The Winter's Tale* differ in this regard from most of Shakespeare's other plays? Does not this presumed situation reflect both the practicalities of the theater and the realities of the political and social world in Jacobean England? Patriarchy, obviously, is a given in Shakespeare's world. The matter is partly one of perspective, but for me Shakespeare demonstrates in *The Winter's Tale* the extraordinary skill and power of women within their inherited social structure.

[4] I have examined the final scene in some detail in my "Hermione's Restoration in *The Winter's Tale,*" in *Shakespeare's Romances Reconsidered,* ed. Carol McGinnis Kay and Henry E. Jacobs (Lincoln, Nebraska, 1978), pp. 125-133. I further analyze the play at some length in terms of the family issue in my forthcoming book, *Shakespeare's Romances and the Royal Family* (University Press of Kansas, 1985).

Jay L. Halio (essay date 1993)

SOURCE: "Portia: Shakespeare's Matlock?," in *Cardozo Studies in Law and Literature,* Vol. V, No. 1, Spring, 1993, pp. 57-64.

[*In the following essay, Halio examines* The Merchant of Venice *as a play concerned with "mercy in the context of justice."*]

Much has been written about Shakespeare's legal prowess—or lack of it—in *The Merchant of Venice.* However intrinsically interesting these discourses are—and a good many of them are extremely interesting—I feel compelled to argue that almost all of it is irrelevant. Shakespeare was, first and foremost, a dramatist who made his fortune at the box office. His plays were intended to be "get pennies," sure to attract good audiences that would pay their penny at the gate and sometimes another penny for a seat in the gallery. His plays enjoyed popularity, if we can judge by the number that were published by 1600—with or without his authorization, and by such testimonials and other evidence that have come down to us. His plays were popular in the public theaters and at court, both with the Queen in the sixteenth century and with the King in the seventeenth. With good reason, James I became the patron of Shakespeare's company, thereafter known as the King's Men, soon after he ascended the English throne in 1603.

Scholars love to speculate about Shakespeare's activities during his so-called "lost years"—the decade between the time of his marriage to Anne Hathaway and the birth of his children, and the first mention of his presence in London as an actor and playwright in 1592. Some believe he was a schoolmaster; others, that he was a soldier, or a sailor. Or—now we come to it—a law clerk. Certainly his plays are studded with legal terminology as well as allusions to classical authors, seafaring terms, and soldier's lore. But the fact remains that we have no facts. We simply do not know what Shakespeare did during those "lost years." Not that I think it matters. Whatever he did, everything we know about him and his plays indicates that he had an uncommon ability to absorb ideas, stories, language, and events, and to transform them through the alembic of his imagination into the greatest poetic drama the world has known.

I say all this, which probably sounds like a recital of truisms, because I want to focus on the dramatic use of legal materials in *The Merchant* and avoid what could be a fruitless argument over the validity of Shylock's contract with Antonio, or the "trick" Portia uses later to entrap her victim, or other legal and quasi-legal issues. As other plays demonstrate, such as *Othello, The Winter's Tale,* and *Henry VIII,* Shakespeare became increasingly adept at using trial scenes—or what amounted to trials—for dramatic effect.[1]

Even before he wrote *The Merchant of Venice,* both in *Henry VI, Part II,* in the trial of the Duchess of Gloucester for witchcraft,[2] and in the deposition scene of *Richard II,*[3] the play written most proximately to *The Merchant,* Shakespeare learned how dramatically effective trial scenes could be on stage. He knew, as we do in our addiction to "Perry Mason," "Matlock," or "L.A. Law," how intrinsically dramatic the law can be, especially when cases are brought to trial. But his emphasis remained, I repeat, on the dramatic effect, not the legality. Law was the vehicle, however rickety at times, that carried the drama; but Shakespeare's point—like the dramatic effect—was of another order of magnitude.

The Merchant of Venice allows us to grasp this idea perhaps better than any other play. Act IV is a masterpiece of dramaturgy, and it scarcely matters whether or not it is really a trial or simply a hearing. True, the Duke appears prejudiced from the outset. In speaking with Antonio, he calls Shylock a "stony adversary" and "an inhuman wretch." (IV, i, 4) When Shylock enters, the Duke expects him to relent and tells him so flat out:

> Shylock, the world thinks, and I think so too,
> That thou but leadest this fashion of thy malice
> To the last hour of act, and then 'tis thought
> Thou'lt show thy mercy and remorse more
>   strange
> Than is thy strange apparent cruelty. . . .
>   (IV, i, 17-21)

Not only the Duke, but everyone else in the court is favourably disposed towards Antonio and against Shylock, including Portia, when she enters soon afterwards. Note that Shylock enters alone, unaccompanied by Tubal or any other *Landsmann;* I think it is an error (if I may digress for a moment) to have any other Jew present, as often the scene has been staged. Shylock is alone, and his isolation is meaningful. He is isolated from the Venetian Christian community, of course, but here also from the Jewish community. More to the point, dramatically he is a solitary figure, one against many. Hero or villain or clown, he is still solitary. He knows everyone is against him but he remains unfazed. He truly believes he has Antonio "on the hip," right where he has long wanted him, and he has the law on his side. Both Shylock (IV, i, 38-39 and 101-02) and Antonio (III, iii, 26-31) realize the dan-

gers to Venice (III, iii, 26-31) if the law is in any way compromised, let alone abrogated. Venice will lose status in the international community and, worse, trade (by which she thrives) will suffer. Armed thus with the law, as he and so far everyone else believes, and armed too with this political and commercial advantage, Shylock remains adamant in his suit.

He even believes he has morality on his side. He has pledged an oath, an "oath to heaven." (IV, i, 228) The slave-owning Christians, moreover, have given him a further moral advantage. In reply to the Duke's admonition for mercy, Shylock responds, "What judgement shall I dread, doing no wrong?" (89) He then draws a parallel between his ownership of a piece of Antonio and their ownership of whole human beings, whom "like your asses, and your dogs and mules, / You use in abject and in slavish parts, / Because you bought them." (91-3) So he concludes: "The pound of flesh which I demand of him / Is dearly bought as mine, and I will have it." (99-100)

Impasse—or so it seems. The Duke has sent to Dr. Bellario in Padua, the seat of juristic learning in Italy and throughout the Western world, for assistance in the case. But even before Portia enters as the good doctor's emissary, we get a clue as to the outcome of events when Bassanio tries to cheer Antonio up:

>   what, man, courage yet!
> The Jew shall have my flesh, blood, bones,
>   and all,
> Ere thou shalt lose for me one drop of blood.
>   (IV, i, 111-13)

Why have audiences, both on the stage and off, failed to see in these lines a solution to the dilemma? Why hasn't Shylock, astute as he is, foreseen his undoing? The answers are, of course, both legal and dramatic. Legally, one naturally assumes that Shylock is entitled to take his forfeiture along with everything else necessary (implied though not specified) to exact it. Dramatically, one is caught up—as we are meant to be—in the emotional tension that develops during the scene—until Portia springs Antonio loose by what many have called a legal "trick."[4] But Portia's device is much more than a trick, and it must be understood in its full dramatic context.

It is irrelevant, I believe, that Portia, like everyone else in the scene, is biased against Shylock. Never mind that she is wife to Bassanio, for whom Antonio entered into the bond in the first place. Never mind that it is with her money that Bassanio offers to repay Shylock for the loan. She comes in disguise—impenetrable disguise by Elizabethan stage convention—as Balthazar, a young law clerk wise beyond his years. Hence, she assumes and is credited with an air of proper impartiality; she fails even to distinguish between merchant and Jew, despite their different attire and accoutrements. (IV,i,176) Their identities made known, her strategy begins, and it is of the utmost importance to recognize and follow that strategy from start to finish.

She begins by establishing certain facts: first, that Venetian law cannot "impugn" Shylock or deny his suit; (177-79) secondly, that Antonio "confesses" the bond. Later, it will emerge that the state can—and certainly does—impugn Shylock as he proceeds against Antonio, but that is not the point here. The point now, as Portia puts it to Shylock, is that he must "be merciful." (182) I submit that this is the burden not only of her argument and the speech that follows, the famous "quality of mercy" speech, but of the whole scene and by extension much of the play, certainly of the last two acts. If *The Merchant of Venice* is about anything—and it is about many things—it is surely very much about mercy, *but mercy in the context of justice.* That is why Portia acts as she does. It is not that she wants to give Shylock enough rope to hang himself—literally, where Graziano is concerned—but that she wants to establish the right relation between justice and mercy: mercy in the context of justice. For without that context—without justice—mercy is empty, meaningless. It turns into sentimentality and becomes counterproductive, resulting in injustice. Fully to understand and value mercy, we need first of all to understand and grasp justice in all its rigor.

Shylock is impervious to Portia's exhortations. He "crave[s] the law," (206) and nothing but the law. I think it is a mistake, nevertheless, to see here an allegory of Old Testament law versus New Testament mercy, which some interpreters have claimed.[5] Mercy abounds in the Old Testament, as any reader of Genesis—even Shylock, who knows his Pentateuch—should realize. If, as Christians believe, the New Testament fulfills the Old, then one is not discarded in favor of the other; *both* are retained, one providing the context for the other. Thus justice and mercy go together. Or, in the words of the Hebrew Bible: "[W]hat doth the Lord require of you, but to do justly, and to love mercy, and to walk humbly with thy God?" (Micah 6:8).

This is not only the moral point behind Portia's speech on the quality of mercy, it is also the dramatic point of her subsequent behavior. She gives Shylock every opportunity to relent—and take treble the money for his pains. (234) She urges him at least to show a modicum of compassion and have a surgeon close at hand. (257) She does all this while at the same time agreeing to the legality of the bond and the apparent justice of Shylock's suit: mercy in the context of justice. But Shylock doesn't get it. He is relentless in his pursuit of plain "justice," as he conceives it, though we recognize it rather as the kind of "wild justice" Francis Bacon described in his essay, "On Revenge."

It is only now that Portia springs her trap. And it is here that lawyers become enmeshed in arguments that lie quite outside or apart from the dramatic context. If, at first, the law seems to allow the forfeit of a pound of flesh, and the court awards it, (300) "no jot of blood" can go with it. (306) Moreover, Shylock in cutting off the pound of flesh must do so precisely; he must cut no more or less than "a just pound." (327) These may seem like technicalities, but worse follows for Shylock. Moments later he stands accused and clearly guilty of the attempted murder of a Venetian citizen by an alien. For this crime the penalty is death and confiscation of all the criminal's worldly goods. (347-63) A second "Daniel come to judgment" (223) is Portia indeed, or so Graziano maintains. (333)

But Graziano is a little ahead of the action. As in the foregoing dialogue, where Portia was careful to establish the context of justice first, here she establishes a similar context. Justice first, then mercy. Portia's eloquent speech on the quality of mercy has not fallen entirely on deaf ears. Showing spontaneous charity, the Duke pardons Shylock's life before he begs it; further, he proposes that half of Shylock's estate owed the state become merely a fine, if Shylock shows appropriate humility. (376-77) But instead of "humbleness," (372) Shylock cries out in defiance borne of despair:

> Nay, take my life and all, pardon not that:
> You take my house when you do take the
>   prop
> That doth sustain my house; you take my life
> When you do take the means whereby I live.
> (374-77)

Now, it is Antonio's turn to show mercy, and he does—at least in Elizabethan terms. And this is where the scene becomes highly problematical for today's post-Holocaust audiences. One of the conditions that Antonio imposes for allowing Shylock to retain half his fortune—the half owing to the state—is that the Jew must convert to Christianity. (387) In this stipulation he is immediately backed up by the Duke, who threatens to revoke his pardon otherwise. (391-92) Harsh mercy though it must seem, it is mercy nonetheless, certainly as Elizabethans saw it. And it is framed in the context of a still harsher justice. Why else would Shakespeare have Shylock then agree to the terms, however grudgingly or reluctantly? In his reluctance, he is like Angelo in *Measure for Measure* or Bertram in *All's Well That Ends Well,* who are also the recipients—perhaps unmerited recipients—of mercy in the context of justice. Perhaps that is why a few critics, like W. H. Auden, have regarded *The Merchant of Venice* as another of Shakespeare's "problem comedies."

When he directed *The Merchant of Venice* in 1978 and 1981, first with Patrick Stewart and then with

David Suchet as Shylock, John Barton said that however different the productions turned out to be—and they were quite different—all three men agreed that Shakespeare portrayed Shylock as a bad Jew and a bad human being. They insisted, nevertheless, that the play was not anti-semitic.[6] We can probably argue the issue of anti-semitism endlessly, but there seems little question that Shylock is exactly as they say: a bad Jew and a bad human being. What professing Jew, such as Shylock pretends to be, would agree to such terms to save his life and fortune? The rabbis say that for the sake of life you may violate any of the more than 600 commandments in the Bible—except one, that prohibiting the desecration of God. By disavowing his religion, Shylock violates that commandment. (Exodus 20:3) By murderously lusting after vengeance, he shows himself, moreover, to be both a bad Jew and a bad human being, violating yet another commandment, "Thou shalt not kill." (Exodus 20:13)

Perhaps these lead us away from the play as Shakespeare and his audiences would have understood it. For them, this was a comedy and Shylock the villain, with roots not only in stage Jews from which Marlowe's Barabas also derived, but also in the *pantalone* of the *commedia dell'arte.* Elizabethans loved to see the biter bitten, the tables turned on the scheming machiavel. This happens quite ruthlessly in Marlowe's *Jew of Malta,* much less so in Shakespeare's *Merchant of Venice.* Although Act IV provides the major trial scene in Shakespeare's play, it is by no means the only one. Many trials occur, such as those in Acts II and III involving the caskets, and later on in Act V involving the rings Portia and Nerissa have given their husbands. Of the casket scenes, little need be said: the true character of the choosers emerges clearly enough through their choices, and I heartily agree with Lawrence Danson[7] and others who reject the view that Portia unfairly helps Bassanio choose correctly. Yes, the song sung while he deliberates has several lines that rhyme with "lead," (III,ii,62-65) and neither Morocco nor Arragon is so privileged. But Bassanio is after all somewhat dense; as we've seen, he misses an important clue he himself verbalizes in the trial scene, and in any case Portia disavows the opportunity to instruct her lover in the right choice and thus violate her oath. (III,ii,10-11) Perhaps the play undercuts these considerations in some ways—for the play is full of inconsistencies and contradictions, as Norman Rabkin has shown.[8] But in the theater, we are hardly mindful of them. Bassanio is the romantic hero and Portia the beautiful and clever heroine, who yet has one more lesson to teach before the play is over, one that neither her husband nor his friend Graziano is apt to forget.
In *Poethics,* Richard Weisberg has analyzed the significance of the ring business in Act V more than adequately, as several others have also done, pointing out that too often the play's endgame is overlooked.[9] In some nineteenth-century productions it was in fact

entirely omitted. I do not mean to slight it here at all, but I shall simply conclude by trying to place the action of Act V in a related context of justice and mercy.

Feminist critics must love what happens there. Maybe they are not overjoyed by the dialogue between Lorenzo and Jessica, who tends to become silent, if not stupefied, during or by her husband's long discourse on the music of the spheres. (V,i,60-88) But when the quarrel breaks out between Graziano and Nerissa over the missing ring and Portia joins in, those who champion women's rights begin to sit up and eventually cheer. For Portia soon has Bassanio "on the hip"—figuratively here, whatever happens later. She catches him out and has him dead to rights. He has foresworn his promise never to part with his wedding ring, and sure enough he has done so. Therefore, she will feel just as free to behave similarly and warns him that she will be as "liberal" as he has been. (V,i,226) It is simple justice, tit for tat. Once again, Antonio intervenes for the sake of mercy and pledges his soul this time as Bassanio's surety that her husband will never more break faith. (249-53) At this point, Portia and Nerissa return the rings to their husbands, permitting them momentarily to feel that they have been made cuckolds and to suffer consternation accordingly. Both Bassanio and Graziano thus pay a penalty, as justice exacts its due. Mercy follows, however, when Portia reveals the truth of events, with promises to answer all her husband's "inter'gatories." (296-9)

So the play ends, with Graziano punning bawdily on keeping Nerissa's ring. Is it a happy ending? It might seem so, but then there is Antonio, a kind of seventh wheel, quietly following the newlyweds—as the ending is sometimes staged—into Portia's house. And there is Jessica, who has not uttered a word since "I am never merry when I hear sweet music." (69) The play is assuredly a comedy, but what kind of comedy? Can its myriad conflicts successfully be resolved in performance? Should they be? Questions to be asked, perhaps, but we may never find definitive answers. Others abide our question, as Milton said, but Shakespeare remains "free." In the performance by the Peter Royston Players, taking a cue from Peter Alscher's notes, the play ended with some lines from the third scene of the play. Shylock's plea to Antonio, "I would be friends with you, and have your love," (I,iii,138) resonated here, reminding us of a theme that is often embedded in the play but scarcely developed—probably because it is short-circuited by Jessica's elopement with Lorenzo. That blow to Shylock and everything he holds dear really determines the viciousness of his vengeance, and the end of his "kindness." (I,iii,143) Like Jonathan Miller's 1970 production at London's National Theatre, which ended with an offstage cantor intoning the Mourner's *Kaddish,* we were therefore left feeling distinctly uncomfortable in what is, generically at least, supposed to be a happy ending. But Shakespeare seldom allows us to remain comfortable in what is, generically at least, supposed to be a happy ending. But Shakespeare seldom allows us to remain comfortable for long, even in the happiest of his comedies. *The Merchant of Venice* is no exception, and these endings, manipulated extra-textually or otherwise, stress the point.

Notes

* All cites to the play here are to Jay Halio, ed., *The Merchant of Venice* (Oxford: Oxford University Press, forthcoming 1993).

[1] *See, e.g.,* George W. Keeton, *Shakespeare's Legal and Political Background* (London: Pitman, 1967), pp. 151-76; O. Hood Phillips, *Shakespeare and the Lawyers* (London: Methuen, 1972), pp. 84-90.

[2] Keeton, *supra* note at 165-76.

[3] Phillips, *supra* note at 84-85.

[4] *See, e.g.* Lawrence Danson, *The Harmonies of "The Merchant of Venice"* (New Haven: Yale University Press, 1978), p. 118

[5] *See* Norman Rabkin, "Meaning and *The Merchant of Venice,*" *Shakespeare and the Problem of Meaning* (Chicago: University of Chicago Press, 1981), p. 9.

[6] John Barton, *Playing Shakespeare* (London: Methuen, 1984), p. 169.

[7] Danson, *supra* note 4 at 117-18.

[8] Rabkin, *supra* note 5 at 4-19, 27-30. Compare Danson, *supra* note 4 at 134-36.

[9] Richard Weisberg, *Poethics* (New York: Columbia University Press, 1993), pp. 100-4.

Daniel J. Kornstein (essay date 1993)

SOURCE: "Fie Upon Your Law!," in *Cardozo Studies in Law and Literature,* Vol. V, No. 1, Spring, 1993, pp. 35-56.

[*In the following essay, Kornstein evaluates* The Merchant of Venice *as a legal parable that weighs the conflict between rigid and equitable interpretations of law.*]

The Merchant of Venice is surely the Shakespearean play most closely linked in the popular mind with law. The crucial trial scene sears the legal and popular conscience like nothing else in Shakespeare. Over the centuries, *The Merchant of Venice* has spawned more commentary by lawyers than any other Shakespeare

play. Books and articles in large number have flowed from the busy pens of attorneys and others seeking to understand and explain the legal meaning of this play. And yet for all that has been previously written by lawyers about the play, there is still more to be said.

Commentary on the legal aspects of the trial in *The Merchant of Venice* is divided. One critic, not a lawyer, thinks the trial scene is so controversial that each reader must decide, like a Supreme Court justice, where to stand in the conflict.[1] The vast majority of scholarly commentary—an eight-to-one ratio—agrees with Portia's ruling.[2] For such scholars, the ruling of the court is a victory of the liberating spirit over the deadly letter of the law, of mercy over legalism, and of reasonable discretion over Shylock's demand for literal-minded justice. According to these majority commentators, Shylock gets just what he deserves—severe punishment for his miserly vengefulness. The consensus view is that the play dramatizes the struggle in Shakespeare's England for supremacy between the common law courts and the equitable Court of Chancery.

The minority view disagrees with Portia's judgment.[3] Those dissenters see Shylock as a victim of injustice, as the hero of the play, as shown no mercy by Portia, and as trapped by secret legalities. Rather than a fiend, Shylock strikes the minority as a tragic victim of religious and ethnic prejudice. Portia's judgment, to these contrarians, is a triumph of vengeance in the guise of justice. The more I think about *The Merchant of Venice,* the more I find myself in the minority camp.

As the sharp split of opinion might indicate, *The Merchant of Venice* has a persistent and uncanny grip on human imagination. Shakespeare's play strikes at the subconscious with a force extremely rare in literature, even in classics. When Dustin Hoffman played Shylock in London and on Broadway in 1989 and 1990, it was an international cultural event. And Laurence Olivier's film version of *Merchant* still captivates us. Part of what makes a classic is its capacity over time to yield new and different meanings. *The Merchant of Venice* has this ability to be meaningful to successive generations of viewers. Each playgoer brings personal experience and sensibility, a unique response and attitude to the play.

The sensibility and response of a lawyer may find new meaning in *The Merchant of Venice.* To someone trained in the law, the important and lasting message of *The Merchant of Venice* has an overwhelmingly legal cast. Although at its core *The Merchant of Venice* is about the complexity of the human spirit, the play is in many fundamental ways about law and about the need for law to reflect the folkways and mores of the community. The classic trial scene in Act IV is the climax of the play. But even apart from the trial scene, the entire play is from start to finish dominated by several legal themes. It is impossible to understand the play fully and in all its richness without grasping these legal themes.

The legal themes occur in the context of an attempt to enforce a contract. The main action in the play turns on a civil lawsuit, the material facts of which are simple, undisputed, and well known. Plaintiff Shylock is a Jewish moneylender; defendant Antonio is a Christian merchant in Venice who needs funds to help his friend Bassanio woo an heiress, Portia. The parties enter into a written agreement whereby Shylock departs from his usual practice of charging interest and lends money interest-free to Antonio. The loan agreement provides a grisly penalty—that if Antonio fails to repay the loan on time, then Shylock could cut out a pound of flesh nearest Antonio's heart.

Antonio's ships do not come in on time and the repayment date passes. Shylock, whose normally high level of resentment against Antonio's anti-Semitism is raised to irrational revenge on learning of his daughter's elopement with a gentile, now sues for deadly specific performance. Spurning repayment several times over, he wants his pound of flesh. At the trial, Judge Portia presides in the guise of Balthasar, a learned young Doctor of Laws recommended by Dr. Bellario, a noted jurist in Padua. Portia-Balthasar tells Shylock, "Of a strange nature is the suit you follow," (IV, i, 180) which is Shakespeare's way of saying it is what lawyers today would call a "case of first impression."

I. Liberty of Contract and Its Limits

One key to explaining the strange case of *Shylock v. Antonio* is the conflict between two legal doctrines: on one hand, liberty of contract and, on the other, limitations put on that liberty by public policy. The trick is to think of the contract in Shakespeare's play as void against public policy. Shylock wants the court to uphold freedom of contract, and asks to have his contract enforced according to the clear and unambiguous terms freely agreed to by the parties. From Shylock's point of view, the case is ripe for summary judgment.

Liberty of contract is of bedrock importance to Shylock. The ability to structure transactions as parties wish facilitates commerce and helped to overcome the economic inertia of feudalism. Equally important, that same ability shifts the focus away from one's inherited status by way of family or religion as a detriment to consensual agreements. This famous movement from status to contract creates social and economic mobility and allows far more personal freedom. A person has more rather than less freedom if he or she is allowed to make a legally binding contract, even though by making it some freedom is surrendered while the contract is in force.

Shylock seeks a literal reading of the contract. The contract says a pound of flesh of Shylock's choosing, and Shylock will settle for only that.

> So says the bond; doth it not, noble judge?
> Nearest his heart. Those are the very words.
> (IV, i, 261-262)

When Portia suggests that Shylock have a doctor at the ready to stop Antonio from bleeding to death, Shylock falls back upon a strict construction:

> Shylock: Is it so nominated in the bond?
>
> Portia: It is not so expressed, but what of that?
> 'Twere good you do so much for charity.
>
> Shylock: I cannot find it; 'tis not in the bond.
> (IV, i, 268-271)

Shylock here symbolizes literalness and technicality in the law, divorced from common sense, prudence, and practical wisdom.

By resting his case so heavily on legal technicality, Shylock draws the lines of battle on a treacherous field. Experienced trial lawyers know that getting one's adversary and the court to accept one's definition of the issues is half the battle, but here that tactic backfires. Shylock defines the issues in terms of literalness and technicality, and Portia reluctantly accepts his definition. But Shylock's reliance on technicality invites Portia to do the same, and Portia responds by giving a technical interpretation, though only after leading him on.

For a while, Portia appears to agree with Shylock's interpretation. She seems to accept the legality of the penalty clause, as she tells Shylock: "the Venetian law Cannot impugn you as you do proceed." (IV, i, 181-182) She adds that the law clearly allows the stipulated penalty:

> For the intent and purpose of the law
> Hath full relation to the penalty,
> Which here appeareth due upon the bond.
> (IV, i, 236-256)

And she looks as if she is ready to enforce it:

> Why, this bond is forfeit,
> And lawfully by this the Jew may claim
> A pound of flesh, to be by him cut off
> Nearest the merchant's heart.
> (IV, i, 236-239)

No wonder Shylock is emboldened to sharpen his knife. Portia's attitude up to this point has three consequences. First, it persuades Shylock to view her as someone who "know[s] the law" and whose legal judgment is "most sound" and authoritative. (IV, i, 243-244) He calls Portia, "A Daniel come to judgment! . . . O wise young judge," (IV, i, 228-229) "a worthy judge," (IV, i, 242) "most learned judge," (IV, i, 314) "most rightful judge," (IV, i, 311) "a well-deserving pillar" of the law. (IV, i, 245) The second consequence is to raise Shylock's expectation of legal victory so that he rebuffs munificent settlement offers of three times the principal of the loan. This inflexible and rigid settlement posture on Shylock's part means the matter will go to judgment; there will be no compromise. (A trial lawyer who had been around the block a few times would have advised Shylock that it is always risky and dangerous to reject a settlement recommended by the trial judge, no matter how airtight the case might seem.) Finally, Portia's early tilt toward Shylock beautifully sets the stage for the dramatic reversal that comes next. By lulling Shylock into a false sense of security on the very brink of his success, Portia—and Shakespeare— highlight the suddenness and the extremity of the change in circumstances that happens.

Portia abruptly pulls the judicial string on Shylock by resorting to an even more literal and hypertechnical interpretation than Shylock's. "Tarry a little," she says ominously to Shylock, "there is something else." (IV,i,315) Portia then points out that the contract says a pound of flesh but nowhere mentions blood. Therefore, she rules, Shylock must cut precisely one pound of flesh—no more, no less—and without shedding any of Antonio's blood—an obvious impossibility. Faced with such a hypertechnical reading, Shylock utters the incredulous cry of all disappointed litigants: "Is that the law?" (IV, i, 324)

It might or it might not be the law. It could be argued with some force—part of the extensive literature has in fact done so—that Portia's interpretation is not the law.[4] To hold, as Portia does, that Shylock may take a pound of flesh but no blood is transparently absurd. Although no one in the play makes this rebuttal argument, the bond must have implicitly authorized what was necessary for Shylock to get his pound of flesh, that is, the shedding of Antonio's blood. Portia's interpretation is like granting an easement on land without the right to leave footprints.

From this perspective, Portia's judgment seems to be a quibble, a ludicrously literalist reading of the contract; an empty, hypertechnical legalistic interpretation that is illogical, useless, impossible and absurd.[5] Portia shows herself as legalistic as Shylock. Portia and Shylock here demonstrate that law, literally construed, can be nonsense. They epitomize the empty and useless consequences of literalist and legalistic interpretation. Portia's legalistic and hypertechnical "flesh-but-no-blood" construction is probably also quite unnecessary. There are alternative rationales for denying Shylock's suit. Instead of resting her decision on in-terpreting the text of the bond, Portia could explicitly rely on public policy. Rather than ingeniously quibbling about the wording of the contract, Portia could have forthrightly addressed whether the bond was legal in the first place. It may be more accurate to understand Portia's ruling as in fact based on public policy, though explained by her in terms of construing contract language. We should perhaps focus on the result, not the rationale; we should watch what Portia does, not what she says.

Surely Portia's cram course with Dr. Bellario, the renowned legal expert in Padua who supposedly sent her to Venice in his place, taught her that liberty of contract has limits. She must have learned to ask the hardest question of all about freedom of contract: should every contract between consenting and adequately informed adults be enforced to the limit? Certain bargains, she has to have learned, are illegal, void, and unenforceable as against public policy. To find that public policy, Portia can look to legislation, common law, and the prevailing practices of the community of people and their notions as to what makes for the general welfare.

Rather than a strained, legalistic interpretation, Portia could have right away invoked the public policy against absurd contracts such as Shylock's. No court in any civilized society would even entertain the thought of enforcing a contract penalty calling for the death of one party. It would be obviously unconscionable, like a contract of self-enslavement. She could have immediately relied upon, as she ultimately does, the Venetian statute against attempted murder, not to punish Shylock but as a source of public policy. Portia would be on more solid legal ground here, especially when Shylock refuses to take three times the principal instead. Such a conclusion depends on no fine-spun parsing of contract terms but goes to the heart of the transaction—Antonio's heart.

Portia rules the contract unenforceable, both as to principal and penalty, but hardly stops there. She wheels on Shylock with legalistic fury, as she begins to deal with the second major phase of the case. According to the cited statute, Portia says Shylock must pay half his wealth to his intended victim, Antonio, and "the other half/comes to the privy coffer of the state." (IV,i,366-367) In the end, Shylock is even forced to convert to Christianity.

The legal underpinnings of Portia's ruling should be familiar to us. The doctrine that contracts against public policy are void is still very much alive. Under the law of New York and a number of other states, for example, a usurious contract is void and unenforceable, and the usurious lender must forfeit principal as well as interest. The case reports are full of lenders who, caught in the web of such usury laws, plead as ineffectively as Shylock did, "give me my principal and let me go."

(IV, i, 348) The newly emerging "lender liability doctrine," which makes lenders in certain situations liable for damage they cause to borrowers, may trace its roots to the seminal case of *Shylock v. Antonio.*

A classic example of a contract against public policy is an agreement in restraint of trade, and restraint of trade may lurk behind much of the action in *The Merchant of Venice.* Shylock and Antonio are competitors: Shylock lends money at interest, Antonio lends money without interest. Thus, on seeing Antonio in Act I, Shylock says in an aside:

> I hate him for he is a Christian;
> But more for that in low simplicity
> He lends out money gratis and brings down
> The rate of usance [i.e., interest] here with us
>   in Venice
>
> > (I, iii, 38-41)

To Shylock, Antonio is a hated below-cost competitor, and part of Shylock's motivation may flow from a desire on Shylock's part to rid himself of such off-price competition. In this sense, *Shylock v. Antonio* has antitrust aspects on which Judge Portia takes a pro-competitive stance.

Quite apart from public policy, other independent legal grounds exist for plausible rulings.[6] Portia could have refused the equitable remedy of specific performance on the ground that Shylock has an adequate remedy at law for damages, especially because he has been offered more than principal and interest. Indeed, mere tender of the principal plus interest could by itself suffice to rule against Shylock. Repayment is the only legitimate purpose of the contract.

Not everyone agrees with such legal objections to Shylock's suit. Several lawyers who have written on the play have concluded that Antonio's obligation is unconditional and automatic.[7] They argue that English common law and Roman civil law would prevent the cash tender in open court from rescuing Antonio if Shylock were to insist on the penalty.[8] Others contend that Roman law might have enforced Shylock's penalty against Antonio.[9] To me, these arguments have the smell of the lamp about them, out of touch with practical realities. Despite such legalistic arguments, the contract simply would not be enforced—under medieval Venetian law, under Roman civil law, under the English law of Shakespeare's time, under current American law—or under any other civilized system of law.

Portia might also have denied enforcement because of fraud. It can be argued that Shylock proposed the penalty clause to Antonio as a jest; Shylock himself told Antonio that the bond is "in a merry sport" (I, iii, 147) and not meant seriously (which may be the case until Shylock's daughter Jessica elopes with her Christian lover and takes Shylock's jewels with her). But the severity of the penalty, the seriousness with which Antonio understood it, and the solemnity of sealing the contract in writing all make fraud less likely.

Two other possibilities come to mind. It could be argued that the bond is an unenforceable gambling contract. Shylock's refusal to accept generous repayment is evidence that the bond is not an ordinary commercial guarantee at all, but truly a gamble on Antonio's life. A final legal ground could have been mutual mistake, as the play's last act reveals that three of Antonio's ships were not in fact lost (as all had thought) but returned to harbor safely and with great profit for Antonio, who can himself now pay the debt. At the least, the court might have let Shylock have his principal, without the burden of the additional punishments. Why should Shylock, who keeps his end of the bargain, be the only loser, and such a big one at that?

But, despite their availability, Portia uses none of these legal escape routes. Of course we must always remember that Portia is not a real judge, but merely a fictional character drawn temporarily into judicial service. Shakespeare wrote a play, not a judicial opinion. In such a context, the needs of drama trump the probabilities of the courtroom. Legalistic arguments based on technicalities provide good, efficient drama, more so perhaps than longwinded and hard-to-expound legal principles and public policy. Besides, only a legalistic argument teaches the lesson that technicalities and literalness beget technicalities and literalness. Portia's persnickety reading of the bond catches everyone, those in the play and in the audience, off guard, and allows the play to take a sharp, unexpected turn. Regardless of whether Portia's ruling is good law, it definitely is good theater, as it turns the tables on Shylock's lethal vengeance.

II. Law and Discretion

More broadly, Portia's ruling vividly illustrates a larger and ever present tension between rigid law and judicial discretion. Those who like Portia's decision (at least that part of it that avoids Antonio's death) say it shows how strict law can and should be mitigated by equity. One theory holds that Shakespeare may have been demonstrating the cruelty of English law and its necessary mitigation by the new courts of equity.[10] From this perspective, Portia's ruling is a metaphor of the struggle between rigidity and flexibility.

Shylock, a descendant of the People of the Law, aligns himself with the Rule of Law. "I stand here for law," he cries. (IV, i, 145) "I crave the law." (IV, i, 211) "If you deny me, fie upon your law!" (IV, i, 103) He seeks "law" and "justice" through a mechanical enforcement of the words of his contract. He relies on certainty and stability in the law merchant to bring him out all right. To the extent Shylock wants the judge to enforce contracts as written, he is an advocate of judicial restraint.

The need for certainty and stability in contracts generally is even more pronounced in the play's commercial setting. Then, as now, the ability to rely on contracts is of prime importance in commercial law. Even Antonio understands this requirement: "The Duke cannot deny the course of law," moans the bankrupt merchant,

> For the commodity that strangers have
> With us in Venice, if it be denied,
> Will much impeach the justice of the State,
> Since that the trade and profit of the city
> Consisteth of all nations.
>
> (III, iv, 29-34)

As Portia further explains:

> There is no power in Venice
> Can alter a decree established.
> 'Twill be recorded for a precedent,
> And many an error by the same example

In essence, Shylock is saying—and up to this point Antonio and Portia agree with him—that a ruling in Antonio's favor will upset the entire reliability of commercial contracts under Venetian law, and discourage merchants and moneylenders from doing business in Venice. As a policy consideration, Shylock's position, of course, has some merit.

Shylock's legal stance is far from the harsh caricature often portrayed. Shylock is an outsider in Venice, an unpopular minority member who is discriminated against, a hated alien who lacks the same rights as his adversaries. For such a victim of discrimination, it is entirely logical and reasonable—as Richard Posner insightfully points out in the most original, most important and most liberating contribution of his book *Law and Literature*—to trust in the apparent severity of a rigid but certain interpretation of law rather than in the discretion of a system that has already shown its bias.[11] Discretion can become arbitrariness, and worse than injustice is arbitrariness, the negation of law. Power is tolerated only if it is constrained. The majority does not need courts or law to protect its rights; a minority relies on law for protection precisely because it does not have the numbers to prevail in the political realm.

In this sense, Shylock stands for every minority member who ever sought protection in the safety of clear, precise, written law instead of the personal value judgments of a prejudiced local official. Shylock's concept of law—ridiculed for centuries, shunned by politically correct readers of Shakespeare—has some of the noble and attractive features that animated our own civil rights movement.

For such outsiders, the law of contracts is important. Law and order and the sanctity of contract are essential for them to compete in society. Their success depends on being scrupulous in obeying the law and abiding by contracts. Justifiable insecurity makes them that way.[12]

But Shylock begs the crucial question. When he claims to "stand here for law" and to "crave the law," he omits the key inquiry: what is law? He assumes his rigid approach is the only one possible. Of course he is wrong.

Portia defines law differently than Shylock. She understands that to be sensible, law requires judicial discretion. The rigor of the law, she thinks, must be softened with equity and mercy and tempered by individual circumstances. When Portia gives her moving "quality of mercy" speech, she puts into words an equitable concept of law that should inform all legal proceedings. To this extent, Portia is a judicial activist.

In finding a creative solution to a hard judicial problem, Portia, like King Solomon, shows signs of greatness. Greatness on the bench—as elsewhere—lies in creativity. But such creativity underscores a basic problem in the judicial process. We expect judges to enforce the law, while knowing they must exercise discretion in applying it to the intractable facts of life. How much law and how much discretion (or justice) are appropriate in the decision of a concrete case?

The Merchant of Venice thus sets up once again the ancient dilemma of rule versus discretion, of constraint versus leeway. Shylock symbolizes law as rigid rules; Portia personifies the spirit of equity. Perhaps because of Shakespeare's successful dramatic technique, our intellectual tradition tends to view Shylock's concept as bad and Portia's as good, but that is too simplistic. Both concepts are good, both are liable to abuse, and both are in frequent tension. This basic dilemma may be unavoidable; it may be embedded in the nature of a living legal system.

The implications of this dilemma are far-reaching. Although often discussed in terms of *Measure for Measure* and *The Merchant of Venice,* the tension between law and discretion can clearly be seen in the development of whole legal systems. The central legal dilemma so well illustrated in these two plays thus becomes a new way to measure and evaluate what a legal system is actually doing. Such a Shakespearean approach unexpectedly throws light, for example, on American legal history.

Like *The Merchant of Venice,* the history of American law shows two different approaches to discretion in government, both of which are designed in theory to enhance and protect liberty. One approach—Shylock's—is to limit such discretion; the other—Portia's—is to encourage it. They are part of the conflict within consensus in our attitudes toward interpreting our basic law, the Constitution. These differing approaches to the same professed goal of greater freedom have been from the beginning of American history continually in tension, as the yin and yang of American constitutional law.

III. Mercy Strained

Much has been written about the quality of mercy that Portia shows Shylock. We know she talks a good game: her moving "quality of mercy" speech during the trial has been read with pleasure, memorized by generations, and quoted to courts over and over again:

> The quality of mercy is not strained,
> It droppeth as the gentle rain from heaven
> Upon the place beneath. It is twice blest—
> It blesseth him that gives, and him that takes.
> 'Tis mightiest in the mightiest. It becomes
> The throned monarch better than his crown.
> His sceptre shows the force of temporal
>   power,
> The attribute to awe and majesty,
> Wherein doth sit the dread and fear of kings;
> But mercy is above this sceptred sway,
> It is enthroned in the hearts of kings,
> It is an attribute to God himself;
> And earthly power doth then show likest
>   God's
> When mercy seasons justice. Therefore, Jew,
> Though justice be thy plea, consider this,
> That, in the course of justice, none of us
> Should see salvation. We do pray for mercy,
> And that same prayer doth teach us all to
>   render
> The deeds of mercy.
>
>   (IV, i, 189-207)

One would think that the person who speaks those lines would feel and act on the sentiments behind them. One would hope that when such a person is in a position of power, she would season justice with mercy. One would expect merciful actions to match noble words.

One would be sorely disappointed. Portia's inconsistency between word and deed is vast. The gulf between her preaching about mercy dropping "as the gentle rain from heaven" and her vengeful punishment of Shylock is unbridgeably wide. On the one hand, she practically begs Shylock to be merciful, and, on the other, she acts with extraordinary cruelty to him only moments later. She could and should have stopped at merely denying Shylock's request for his pound of flesh. Is it absolutely necessary to appropriate all of Shylock's property? To put him under a death sentence? To make him convert to another religion? After all, Antonio did default on the loan. Is Portia's judgment fair? It certainly is not merciful.

Portia's huge inconsistency and terrible meanness leave haunting doubts about her character.

Those doubts only grow larger and larger. In addition to her hypocrisy and vindictiveness, we see her as a bigot, and not just a minor-league bigot, but a world-class, equal opportunity hate-monger. We know she is prejudiced against Jews by her enthusiastically reaching out to rely on the harsh, anti-semitic Alien Statute. And we also know she is a racist because of her comments about her African suitor's skin color: when the black Prince of Morocco makes the wrong choice in the lottery for Portia, she snaps with relief, "Let all of his complexion choose me so." (II,vii,80) To these character flaws, we add her jealousy of Antonio's suspect love for Bassanio. On top of all these defects is her corruption as a judge in a case in which she is closely interested.[13] Portia, for all her cleverness and verbal agility, is unattractive and infuriating, especially as a heroine.

For these reasons, I agree with William Hazlitt, who in the early nineteenth century wrote, "Portia is not a very great favorite with us."[14] To be sure, Portia has for the most part enjoyed good press over the centuries but it mystifies me that so sensitive an observer as Richard Weisberg can refer to Portia as an "exquisite heroine."[15] She strikes me more as the "eloquent mouthpiece"[16] than the lawyer's professional paradigm. She may be quick and legalistically nimble, but more judges like Portia would, in reality, cause a revolution by litigants and lawyers. By going beyond simply denying Shylock's suit and cruelly punishing him, Portia made herself no more of a hero than the infamous Judge Jeffries, notorious for his ruthless rulings during England's Glorious Revolution.

IV. The Casket Game

Even the casket game for picking Portia's husband can be read as a metaphor for law and justice. Portia's dead father's will insisted that her prospective suitors choose among three caskets—gold, silver, and lead—only one of which contains her picture. The suitor who picks the right casket can marry Portia. On the surface, this trial of the caskets seems unrelated to law, but, as the play and the casket trial teach, things are not always what they appear.

Consider the evidence. During the casket trial, the characters refer several times to Fortune and "blind Fortune," (II, i, 37) and Portia says once, "love is blind." (II, vi, 37) Justice, like Fortune and Love, is also supposed to be blind. Next, Portia says to one of her unsuccessful suitors, "To offend and judge are distinct offices," (II, ix, 63) which means, "You willingly chose the trial of the caskets; you should not presume to judge the verdict." A further linking of the caskets to law occurs when Portia's maid says: "Hanging [i.e., the results of law] and wiving [i.e., the results of the casket trial] go by destiny." (II, ix, 86) This in turn brings out the uncertainty of litigation generally, which is surely reinforced by both the play's express language and stunning outcome.

The whole casket game can be read as a metaphor about law and legal interpretation. Think of Portia's father's will as law. Just as "the will of a living daughter [is] curbed by the will of a dead father," (I, ii, 24-25) so too is our desire to govern ourselves constrained by the dead hand of the past. Like Portia's father's will, our law—constitution, statutes, common law—represents the past. In interpreting the Constitution, for example, in choosing how to apply it, we must—it is often said—defer to the intent of the Framers, who have long since departed the scene, rather than adapt to new circumstances. In this sense, we are in the same predicament as Portia, who complains, "the lott'ry of my destiny / Bars me the right to voluntary choosing." (II, i, 15-16) And yet Portia's song to Bassanio allows her, by interpretation, to bring about the outcome she wants.

The three caskets are themselves compelling evidence of a legal theme. The winning lead casket bears an inscription that continues the sub theme of chance: "Whoso chooseth me must give and hazard all he hath." (II, vii, 16) So it is with litigation. The silver casket, a loser, says, "Who chooseth me shall get as much as he deserves," (II, vii, 7) which is one definition of justice. Later, Portia adds to that definition: "In the course of justice, none of us / should see salvation. We do pray for mercy." (IV, i, 304-305) But it is the gold casket that is the most convincing.

The gold casket's legend is: "Who chooseth me shall gain what many men desire." (II, vii, 37) It symbolizes the gulf between appearance and reality; inside it says: "All that glisters is not gold." (II, vii, 66) When Bassanio considers which casket to pick, the first example to his mind of an "outward show" is legal:

> In law, what plea so tainted and corrupt
> But, being seasoned with a gracious voice
> Obscures the show of evil.
>
> (III, ii, 75-79)

After 20 years of practicing law, I can only say: 'tis true, 'tis true.[17]
The theme of the trial of the caskets—that things are not always what they seem—also runs through the trial of *Shylock v. Antonio.* Shylock's contract with Antonio appeared clear and unambiguous, but Portia shows that this is not the case. Even Portia herself is not what she seems. As the fianceé of Antonio's best friend for whom the loan was made, she is anything but a disinterested judge. Her bias removes the blindfold from justice. Indeed, Portia is neither a man nor a lawyer. In spite of her speech about mercy, she is unnecessar-

ily cruel to Shylock. Does all this mean Portia is a fraud? That justice is a fraud? Or merely uncertain?

V. Equal Protection

From a slightly different legal viewpoint, the play shows what happens when a society denies equal protection of the laws. Shylock's hate and revenge—what he calls the "ancient grudge" between Jews and Christians (I, iii, 44)—arise from the suffering, humiliation, injustice, and prejudice he and his co-religionists have borne. Shylock is not a cardboard figure of evil, but a complex and somewhat sympathetic man who has suffered much. We feel this with the intensity of his eloquent "Hath not a Jew eyes?" speech. (III, i, 52-65) As a non-Christian, Shylock could not even become a citizen of Venice. It is this discrimination that makes the crucial Venetian law—the vile Alien Statute—apply to him:

> It is enacted in the laws of Venice,
> If it be proved against an alien
> That by direct or indirect attempts
> He seek the life of any citizen. . . .
>
> (IV, i, 361-364)

This Alien Statute deserves strict scrutiny, as it is an outrage, at least to 20th century readers. Curiously, this odd and sinister law, so central to the play's outcome, has largely escaped careful legal analysis. In a new, pathbreaking paper, Peter Alscher, in this very number, brilliantly refocusses our attention on the vices of the statute. As Alscher points out, the law gives the state incredible power. If the statute is violated, the state has the legal authority to take all the property of a Jew or any other alien. Half goes to the Venetian citizen whose life has been threatened, and half to the government. The law also allows the state to execute the offender. These are severe punishments indeed.

The severity of the penalties under the Alien Statute is by no means matched by the severity of the crime for which they can be imposed. The law prohibits not only direct but also "indirect attempts" on the life of any citizen and includes merely "contriving against" such a life. The statute appears to apply even when the offender acts in self-defense or when no bodily harm is actually done. Ignoring the salutary distinction made by Isabella in *Measure for Measure,* the Alien Statute can be invoked not only for actions but also for intentions to act. The statute might be interpreted by Venetian citizens to prosecute "contriving against" a citizen's livelihood as well as his life, since property is the foundation of life. Conceivably, if an alien seeks repayment of a loan made to a citizen, such action itself could amount to "contriving against" the citizen's life.

These objections are nothing as compared to the fundamental flaw of the Alien Statute, which is its denial of equal protection of the laws. It discriminates against aliens, including Jews. There is no comparable Citizen Statute. A citizen who indirectly "contrived against" the life of an alien would not be subject to the same penalties. By virtue of this law, a Jew does not have the same rights as a citizen of Venice. This is the real vice of the Alien Statute: it constitutes unequal treatment by the state, it takes away the civil rights of Jews, and it deprives Jews of the right to private property. The statute would be clearly unconstitutional under American law.

A basic and obnoxious defect indelibly taints the Alien Statute. It embodies anti-semitism and encourages persecution against Jews. By making Jews' hold on life and property precarious, it foreshadows the infamous Nuremburg Laws of our own century, and reminds us of Jim Crow laws in this country and apartheid in South Africa. What strikes a modern reader is that no one in the play—not even Shylock—challenges or contests this awful law. Everyone seems to accept the awful premise of the Alien Statute. Have fundamental sensibilities changed that much?

Despite these deeply offensive qualities, the Alien Statute's application to Shylock has not drawn unanimous disapproval. On the contrary, the overwhelming majority of commentators do not object at all. But in the eyes of the minority, invoking the Alien Statute against Shylock is a horrible miscarriage of justice. After all, Shylock has no prior warning of this infuriating law. Rather, Portia previously told him that no other legal obstacle blocked his suit. For example, Portia asks Shylock to show mercy or else "this strict court of Venice / Must needs give sentence 'gainst the merchant there." (IV, i, 209-210) Portia brings up the Alien Statute for the first time only after Shylock has withdrawn his demand for a pound of flesh.

Taking all of the factors into consideration, Alscher proposes a radical resolution of the trial scene. In a dazzling set of new stage directions, Alscher makes the Alien Statute the true villain of the play. To challenge and eliminate this evil law, he introduces the statute itself as a paper scroll prop in the play. As Portia reads the scroll statute in Alscher's version, she has picked up Shylock's knife and uses it to point to the words. When finished, after saying that Shylock's life is at the mercy of the Duke, Portia gives Shylock's knife to Antonio, who starts and then stops in an effort to kill Shylock. The high point in Alscher's directions comes when Antonio raises high the knife and, for one potentially epiphnal moment, considers plunging the knife through the scroll.[18]

Shylock is not only a Jew, he is a symbol for any group that feels itself oppressed. Substitute African-Americans, women, or any other such group, and we understand the strength of their impatient feelings for

full equality. Shakespeare's play thus becomes a dramatic representation of the common-sense wisdom of the equal protection requirement of the Fourteenth Amendment. Rather than anti-Semitic, the play is prominority rights. It shows how inequality before the law breeds dangerous and divisive discontent, never a good thing in any society.

For at least one group—women—the play stands out as an example of triumph over inequality. Portia defies the codes of her milieu by assuming a commanding position of authority and respect as lawyer and judge in a man's world. She is skillful, witty, and learned. Despite occasional criticism from contrarian commentators like myself, Portia's name has become synonymous with eloquence and wisdom in a female attorney or judge. John Mortimer, the English lawyer and writer, has his fictional London barrister, Horace Rumpole of the Bailey, often refer admiringly to his female colleague Phillida Trant as "the Portia of our chambers." And at least one colleague on the Supreme Court has complimented Justice Sandra Day O'Connor—whom I once saw in June 1971 at the Folger Shakespeare Library—as "our Portia."[19]

Portia, moreover, rebels at the lack of choice in marriage. Intelligent and ambitious, Portia feels that society and her father's will fetter her choices. She is not resigned to her lot; she takes control.

But here, too, Portia's feminist triumph may not be all that it appears. Once the trial is over, Portia resumes her demure domestic role. Portia almost seems like two different persons, one the clever, forceful judge, the other a passive princess. Her rebellion over lack of marriage choice is more verbal than real: she complains but still submits to the marriage lottery. In sharp contrast, Shylock's daughter Jessica talks less but rebels more by running away from her father and marrying out of her faith. In this sense, Jessica may claim equal title as the feminist heroine of the play.

VI. Act V's Overlooked Legal Significance

The play's Fifth Act has often been neglected, but this would be a serious mistake, particularly from a legal point of view. Act V has the three sets of young lovers—Jessica and Lorenzo, Nerissa and Gratiano, and Portia and Bassanio—playfully bantering on the island of Belmont, where Portia lives. Coming as it does right after the tremendous tension of the trial scene in Act IV, the final act strikes many as anticlimactic and even superfluous. In fact, throughout much of the 19th century, English productions of *The Merchant of Venice* simply stopped the play after Shylock's humiliation at the end of the Fourth Act, dropping entirely the last act. Now, thanks to Richard Weisberg, we know just how much of an error it would be to overlook Act V.

Weisberg, in *Poethics,* sets forth an original and persuasive case for the crucial importance of Act V to the underlying legal themes of Shakespeare's play.[20] Unlike almost all other legal commentators on *The Merchant of Venice,* Weisberg goes beyond concentrating on the trial scene. According to Weisberg's trailblazing analysis, Act V is filled with legal imagery and talk of promises that represent a turnaround of the play's legal momentum. By the end of the play, Shylock may be vanquished, but his legalistic mindset has triumphed; everyone becomes as legalistic as Shylock.

The great change in Portia's attitude in Act V is hard to miss when we compare it to what happened in Act IV. At the trial, Shylock stands for sanctity of contract, the keeping of promises, and verbal expressions of commitment. The courtroom attack on Shylock is an attack on verbal obligation. Antonio, Bassanio, and their Venetian friends are casual oath-breakers and outright racists. Portia's ruling, however disguised in its own legalisms, encourages lighthearted breaches of contract and not taking seriously the making of a sacred oath. Equity won over law.

But all that changes in the often neglected Act V. There, Portia and Nerissa chide their lovers for giving away their wedding rings. Portia lectures Gratiano with words equally applicable to Bassanio:

> You were to blame—I must be plain with
>   you—
> To part so slightly with your wife's first gift,
> A thing stuck on with oaths upon your finger,
> And so riveted with faith upon your flesh.
>   (V, i, 167-170)

Now we have Portia, the symbol of equity, stressing the importance of oaths and their physical representation—rings. She asks Bassanio for "an oath of credit" that he will be faithful and never again give away her ring. (V, i ,564) Portia, having in Act IV allowed it as a judge, forbids oathbreaking in Act V. By play's end, law prevails over equity, oaths over breaches, and Shylock's ethical system over the Venetians' casualness toward obligations. Portia, in effect, adopts Shylock's values.

VII. Other Legal

If all this were not enough to demonstrate the legal themes in *The Merchant of Venice,* Shakespeare scatters throughout the text many other legal references. On first hearing Shylock's loan terms, for example, Antonio's companion says: "I like not fair terms and a villain's mind." (I, iii, 182) Every lawyer who ever drew a contract knows the importance of good faith: an honest person acting in good faith will abide by the sense of a contract however expressed; a villain will look for a way out of a contract no matter how tightly drawn. A lawyer can learn a lot about contracts, what to do and what not to do, and how to make them airtight and to protect against this or that contingency. But a handshake between honorable people is often the best contract. And sometimes letting people off the hook and letting them out of a commitment can be far more effective than holding them to the commitment.

Other legal comments abound. "The devil can cite Scripture for his purpose." (I. iii, 98) "Truth will come to light . . . in the end truth will out." (II,ii,72-74) A few lines from the end, Portia even gives us her view of pretrial discovery:

> And yet I am sure you are not satisfied
> Of these events at full. Let us go in,
> And charge us there upon inter'gatories,
> And we will answer all things faithfully.
>   (V, i, 318-321)

Courthouses usually have messages carved on them about law, and *The Merchant of Venice* could supply two more: "For, as thou urgest justice, be assured / Thou shalt have justice more than thou desir'st," (IV, i, 326-327) and "You must take your chance." (II, i, 40)

VIII. Revenge Through Law

Another theme, revenge through law, is important for the legal themes in Shakespeare. It indelibly marks *The Merchant of Venice,* a "revenge play" (common enough in Elizabethan times) in which crucial dramatic action turns upon a major character's drive to get even. With *Merchant,* Shakespeare puts a special twist on the standard revenge play by having Shylock seek revenge within the bounds of the law. Shylock does not take the law into his own hands and carry out private vengeance on Antonio through private violence. Rather, Shylock takes him to court, where the money lender attempts to enforce his legal rights to the limit, without pity, and even though Antonio's death might result. The legal system, in Shylock's hands, itself becomes the means for revenge.

The play is quite explicit about the theme of vengeance through law. After Jessica runs away with Shylock's jewels and money, and after Antonio is in trouble, Shylock is whipped up into a vengeful frenzy. "Let him look to his bond," (III, i, 41-44) Shylock says over and over again, believing he still has one way of getting back at Antonio. When Shylock's colleague Tubal asks what good will enforcing the bond do, Shylock answers: "[I]t will feed my revenge." (III, i, 47-48)

Then immediately follows Shylock's "Hath not a Jew eyes?" speech, during which he makes even more clear his use of legal process to work revenge:

And if you wrong us, shall we not revenge? If we are like you in the rest, we will resemble you in that. If a Jew wrong a Christian, what is his humility? Revenge. If a Christian wrong a Jew, what should his sufferance be by Christian example? Why, revenge. The villainy you teach me I will execute, and it shall go hard but I will better the instruction.

(III, i, 58-66)

Just in case we somehow miss the point, Shakespeare has Shylock repeat it before the start of the trial scene. "I'll have my bond! Speak not against my bond! / I have sworn an oath that I will have my bond." (III, iii, 5-7)

Shylock's use of litigation for revenge has a modern ring to it. It is a late development in the long evolution of law from violent private revenge to public enforcement by disinterested persons at a trial at law. In contrast with early use of revenge as a substitute for law, *Merchant* depicts the more recent phenomenon of vengeance through law. Venice is cosmopolitan and civilized; it has laws and a legal system for resolving disputes. Venetians go to law instead of doing bodily harm to those of their neighbors against whom they have claims.

Still, the thin veneer of civilization hardly wipes out so strong and deep-seated an emotion as revenge. Wise politicians and lawmakers know this psychological fact and, acting on it, create institutions and encourage habits to provide socially acceptable and orderly ways for venting vengeful feelings. "Law channels rather than eliminates revenge," as Judge Posner puts it, "replaces it as system but not as feeling."[21] Under the circumstances, nothing will mollify Shylock but revenge. Better it should be revenge through law than revenge as a substitute for law.

Despite its modern and salutary aspects, Shylock's use of law for revenge distresses us. It is as if Shylock is abusing modern law and even his own legal rights. He uses the means of the law for a bad end or purpose. In doing so, Shylock also does something nasty to himself, so misusing the law that he loses part of his mental and emotional balance and even some essential element of his humanity. Shylock is the embodiment of a character familiar to law offices today: the person obsessed with litigation. A victim of litigation psychosis, Shylock lives to inflict pain on his enemies through lawsuits. Any lawyer who has handled emotionally laden litigation—a bitter divorce case or a child custody battle or a *pro se* matter—knows the symptoms.

Shakespeare seems to take a dim view of Shylock's use of revenge through law. To be sure, one must always be careful when attempting to impute values or views to an author from something that author wrote in the realm of dramatic literature. Even so, and approaching the subject with diffidence, we can fairly conclude that Shakespeare rejects revenge in *The Merchant of Venice*. His portrayal of Shylock's ignoble quest through law, his handling of the trial scene, the very language and action all reflect a view of law in which the primitive impulse of revenge is disapproved. This theme, and the role of revenge in the evolution of law, will go on to figure prominently in later tragedies and histories, especially *Hamlet* and *Julius Caesar*.

IX. Classifications

Classifying *The Merchant of Venice* has always been difficult. Tradition lists it as a comedy, which would seem absurd unless comedy be defined as something apart from humor. Since convention requires of comedy only a sudden reversal of fate followed by a reconciliation of sorts, the play would be a comedy, though certainly a dark one. There is nothing funny about this play, and there is an apprehension of death that breaks all the rules. It is, truly speaking, neither a comedy nor a tragedy nor a history. It is a dramatic crystal of many legal issues, a rich text for a law school seminar. If a category is needed, let us invent one of legal parable.

As a legal parable, *The Merchant of Venice* may have influenced contemporary judges and changed the course of English legal history. King James I asked to see two performances of the play on two consecutive days. The leading modern champion of Shakespeare's impact on English jurisprudence—W. Nicholas Knight—insists that the 1616 case of *Glanville v. Courtney* shows the play's effect. In that case, which was a suit on a bond, Lord Coke, acting as Chief Justice of the common law courts, entered judgment for plaintiff. But the High Chancellor, Lord Ellesmore, issued an injunction to prevent enforcement of the bond. The result is considered to be a victory of equity over the common law, with the Crown siding with equity, just as the Duke did in *Shylock v. Antonio*.

Based on these facts, Knight speculates that the result in *Glanville v. Courtney* was due to *The Merchant of Venice*. If I understand Knight correctly, he is arguing that since *Glanville* was decided by judges who must have seen *Merchant,* then *Merchant* must have contributed to the legal result.[22] Such an argument is difficult to respond to. Yes, it is possible, but no proof exists for it. I appreciate Knight's wonderful and contagious enthusiasm for Shakespeare and the law but would be more restrained and hedged in my conclusions. The highly speculative nature of Knight's conclusions, provocative and fascinating though they may be, does not warrant the exaggerated style of certainty in which they are expressed.

Yet, others have sided with Knight on this point. A 19th century lawyer, on whose work Knight draws, also thought that the result in *Glanville* was due to Shakespeare's ideas. More recently, Harlan F. Stone, a justice of the Supreme Court for two decades in this century, once said that, "Often, in listening to *The Merchant of Venice,* it has occurred to me that Shakespeare knew the essentials of the contemporary conflict between law and equity."[23]

Whatever the true impact upon 17th century lawyers of *The Merchant of Venice,* we can surely appreciate its power over us. We can feel the power of the theatrical moment in our professional lives. The play, we know, is about human character, but it is also about law: liberty of contract and its limits, law and discretion, the meaning of mercy, the legal symbolism of the casket game, equal protection, and other legal themes.

As we leave a spiritually liberating performance of *The Merchant of Venice,* we hear over and over again in our minds what Portia says to Shylock, and what Shakespeare means the whole play to say to all of us: "The law hath yet another hold on you." (IV, i ,360)

Notes

[1] A. D. Moody, *Shakespeare: "The Merchant of Venice"* (London: Edward Arnold Ltd., 1964), p. 61.

[2] *See, e.g.,* Lawrence Danson, *The Harmonies of "The Merchant of Venice"* (New Haven: Yale University Press, 1977); Herbert Bronstein, "Shakespeare, The Jews and *The Merchant of Venice,*" 20 *Shakespeare Quarterly* 10 (1969); Anthony Hecht, *"The Merchant of Venice:* A Venture in Hermeneutics," *Obligati: Essays in Criticism* (New York: Atheneum, 1986), pp. 140-229; Edgar Elmer Stoll, *Shylock* (reprinted in the Signet Classic *Merchant of Venice,* 1965), pp. 157-172.

[3] *See, e.g.,* Moody, *supra* note 1; H. B. Charleton, *Shakespearean Comedy* (New York: McMillan, 1938), pp. 123-160; J. M. Murry, *Shakespeare's Method: "The Merchant of Venice"* (New York: ·Harcourt Brace, 1936), pp. 153-173; Judith Koffler, "Terror and Mutilation in the Golden Age," 5 *Human Rights Quarterly* 116 (1983).

[4] *See, e.g.,* Rudolf von Jhering, *Der Kampf um's Recht* (Vienna, 1886), translated in pertinent part in H. H. Furness, ed., *The Merchant of Venice: A New Variorum Edition of Shakespeare* (New York: Dover, 1964). Terry Eagleton, *William Shakespeare* (New York: Blackwell, 1986), pp. 36-37; Richard Weisberg, *Poethics, And other Strategies of Law and Literature* (New York: Columbia University Press, 1992), pp. 99-100.

[5] Hecht, *supra* note 2 at 186-187.

[6] *See, e.g.,* George W. Keeton, *Shakespeare's Legal and Political Background* (New York: Barnes & Noble, 1967), pp. 10-21.

[7] For a recapitulation of legal descriptions of the bond, *see* O. Hood Phillips, *Shakespeare and the Lawyers* (London: Methuen, 1972), pp. 102-116; on the automatic nature of the forfeiture, *see* Keeton, *supra* note 6 at 136.

[8] *See* Weisberg, *Poethics, supra* note 4 at 95.

[9] *Id.*

[10] M. E. Andrews, *Law Versus Equity in "The Merchant of Venice"* (Boulder: University of Colorado Press, 1965).

[11] Richard Posner, *Law and Literature: A Misunderstood Relation* (Cambridge: Harvard University Press, 1988), p. 97.

[12] Gertrude Himmelfarb, "Victorian Values/Jewish Values," 23 *Commentary* 28-29 (1990).

[13] *Accord* John Noonan, *Bribes* (Berkeley: University of California Press, 1984), pp. 323-25.

[14] J. William Hazlitt, *Characters of Shakespeare's Plays* (New York: Dutton, 1969), p. 322.

[15] Weisberg, *Poethics, supra* note 4 at 100.

[16] *Id.*

[17] *See* also the comment in Act Four of *Timon of Athens:* "Crack the lawyer's voice, that he may never more false title plead, Nor sound his quillets shrilly."

[18] Peter J. Alscher, *"The Merchant of Venice* and the Problem of Antonio: Staging a Radical Resolution of the Trial Scene," 5 *Cardozo Studies in Law and Literature* 1 (1993).

[19] John Paul Stevens, "The Shakespeare Canon of Statutory Construction," 140 *University of Pennsylvania Law Review* 1373, 1386 (1992).

[20] Weisberg, *Poethics, supra* note 4 at 93-104.

[21] Posner, *Law and Literature, supra* note 11 at 33.

[22] W. Nicholas Knight, *Shakespeare's Hidden Life: Shakespeare at the Law: 1585-1595* (New York: Mason & Lipscomb, 1973), pp. 178-190, 280-86.

[23] J. K. Emery, "Preface" to Andrews, *Law Versus Equity in "The Merchant of Venice," supra* note 10 at ix.

Stephen A. Cohen (essay date 1994)

SOURCE: " 'The Quality of Mercy': Law, Equity and Ideology in *The Merchant of Venice,*" in *Mosaic:*

A Journal for the Interdisciplinary Study of Literature, Vol. 27, No. 4, December, 1984, pp. 35-54.

[*In the following essay, Cohen probes the ideological threat to the dominant social order represented by Shylock's legal suit in* The Merchant of Venice.]

The interdisciplinary study of literature has received considerable impetus over the last two decades from the rise of New Historicism. Particularly in Renaissance studies, the work of Stephen Greenblatt, Louis Adrian Montrose and others has illuminated the relation of such diverse matters as exorcism, colonialism, architectural design and primogeniture to the cultural work performed by literary texts. One subject largely neglected by the New Historicists, however, is the law. This neglect may in part be attributable to the prominence of the law in older, positivist historical readings of Renaissance literature, and in turn to the New Historicists' desire both to distance themselves from this reflectionist model and to investigate unexplored areas of Renaissance culture. In any case, by conjoining the considerable work done by Renaissance legal scholars with New Historicism's characteristic questions—what are the sociopolitical functions of the cultural phenomenon in question, and how are those functions employed or adapted through the literary text—we may shed considerable light on both the law and the literature of the Renaissance.

Not surprisingly, given its explicitly economic central conflict and its intricately detailed legal climax, *The Merchant of Venice* has had considerable appeal for interdisciplinary critics. As O. Hood Phillips's investigations have shown, for over a century legal scholars and historians have studied the trial scene's relation to contemporary jurisprudence, debating its verisimilitude and its position in the period's jurisdictional and philosophical disputes, especially the conflict between the common law and equity (91-118). More recently, historical critics like Walter Cohen, Leonard Tennenhouse and Thomas Moisan have explored the play's relation to Renaissance social and economic history and ideology, and particularly its role in the period's transition from the cultural and financial structures of late feudalism to those of early capitalism. These two lines of inquiry have, however, remained almost entirely separate: legal readings of the trial scene tend to treat its legal significance in both cultural and textual isolation, failing to link it to the social and economic issues prominent in both text and cultural context; and socioeconomic readings of the play as a whole give little or no attention to the role of the trial's legal background in that framework.

A contemporary audience, however, would have made no such separation. The late 16th and early 17th centuries in England were notable both for unprecedented economic and social change and for a marked increase in legal activity; the connection between the two developments was sufficiently clear at the time that Francis Bacon could note almost as a commonplace that "times of peace, for the most part drawing with them abundance of wealth, and finenesse of cunning, doe draw also in further consequence multitudes of suits, and controversies . . . [which] do more instantly sollicite for the amendment of lawes, to restraine and represse them" ("Epistle Dedicatorie," n.p.).

Nor were such associations beyond the bounds of the theater. In the case of *The Merchant of Venice,* the susceptibility of the play's legal content to sociopolitical interpretation is attested to by no less a legal and political authority than Lord Chancellor Ellesmere, who in a 1615 judicial dispute over the power of King James to legislate economic policy without the concurrence of Parliament advised his fellow judges "to maintain the power and prerogative of the King; and in cases in which there is no authority and precedent, to leave it to the King to order it according to his wisdom and the good of his subjects, for otherwise the King would be no more than the Duke of Venice" (qtd. in Andrews 41). The significance of the reference—to the Duke's legal inability to act on his sympathy for Antonio—would not have been lost on James and his court, for whom *The Merchant of Venice* was performed twice in 1605 (Knight 108n8).

For its contemporary audience, then, the trial scene's legal conflict was firmly connected to the economic and political issues in which the period was increasingly embroiled. By bringing together the historical particularity of the play's legal critics and the ideological sensitivity of its newer historical readers, I hope to recapture the significance of this connection; and in shedding new light on the meaning of the trial scene's common law-versus-equity debate I will attempt to illuminate the role that *The Merchant of Venice* played in the culture of which it was a part.

The case that Shylock makes for the enforcement of his bond rests on three claims: 1) the self-evidence of the law's application to the case at hand; 2) the supremacy of that law over any other power, personal or governmental; and 3) the importance of that supremacy to the foundations of the state itself. "I [have] sworn / To have the due and forfeit of my bond," he tells the Duke as the trial opens; "If you deny it, let the danger light / Upon your charter and your city's freedom!" (4.1.36-39).[1] These three claims were the foundation of the case presented by the champions of the common law in their jurisdictional and philosophical conflict with the courts of equity. In supporting the inviolability of the common law's authority they argued that the order and security of the nation rested upon the adjudication of its increasingly complex web of rights and obligations by—as Sir Edward Coke phrased it—"the golden and straight mete-wand of the law, and not the incertain and crooked cord of discretion" (qtd. in Ives 125).

While acknowledging the technical legality of Shylock's suit—"Of a strange nature is the suit you follow, / Yet in such rule that the Venetian law / Cannot impugn you as you do proceed" (177-79)—Portia counters his claims by decrying the cruelty of the bond and the severity of the law that enforces it and insisting on the need for mercy "to mitigate the justice of thy plea" (203). The necessity of such mitigation was the basis of the argument presented by the advocates of equity's appellate superiority to the common law, in order, in the words of Lord Keeper John Williams, "to mix & temper mercie and equitie with the black and rigorous L[ette]re of the Law" (qtd. in Thomas 526). Consequently, Portia's victory has been read by legal critics like Mark Edwin Andrews, Maxine McKay and W. Nicholas Knight as Shakespeare's endorsement of the ethical importance of equity to mitigate the impartial but at times overly-strict justice of the common law.

As Lord Chancellor Ellesmere recognized, however, behind the ideological trappings of blind-but-strict law and corrective equity, the issue at stake in the trial plot is political power—specifically, the power of the Crown to further its social and economic agenda in the face of the legal challenge presented by the common law. As the complex, large-scale financial operations of early capitalism began to emerge in the middle years of the 16th century, its practitioners became acutely aware of the value of a comprehensive and predictable legal system that offered protection from arbitrary interference. As Max Weber notes:

> The modern capitalist concern . . . requires for its survival a system of justice and an administration whose workings can be *rationally calculated,* at least in principle, according to fixed general laws. . . . It is as little able to tolerate the dispensing of justice according to the judge's sense of fair play *in individual cases* or any other irrational means of principles of administering the law . . . as it is able to endure a patriarchal administration that obeys the dictates of its own caprice, or sense of mercy. . . . (qtd. in Whigham 107-08n14)

The common law, particularly after it began to recognize and incorporate the jurisprudence of the increasingly important international mercantile legal system (Hill 238), was clearly the law that best offered this protection, given its fundamental concern with *meum et tuum* property rights: "The person, goods and possessions of a man (as yow know) are the things which the Common lawes of England doe protect," wrote Edward Hake in the late years of Elizabeth's reign (69).

The Crown's difficulty with this conception of the common law was that the very same principles which facilitated the new economic activity could also be—

and increasingly were—employed to protect the profits of that activity from royal exploitation. The value to the nation of this new commerce and industry provided the Crown with a strong disincentive to violate or abrogate the common law; yet with the steadily growing financial pressure on the royal treasury in the late 16th century, the maintenance of state power came increasingly to require the diversion of the profits of English capitalism into the government's coffers. The means by which the Elizabethan state attempted this diversion—ad hoc financial and commercial regulation, extra-parliamentary taxation and forced loans that were never repaid—brought it into direct conflict with the necessary predictability and inviolability of the common law, and those profiting from the new economy were quick to invoke those principles in their own interest. Even Hake, who was by no means a wholehearted ally of the new capitalists (his revised *Epieikeia* was presented to King James), held that "concerning the subject's goods, neither subsidyes, taxes, contributions nor loans are by the lawe to take hold thereof or to be imposed upon any Englishe subject without his free consent"; thus "any seisures to be made of an Englishe subject's goods to the King's use withowt iust and lawfull tytle" were not to be considered (83-84).

Coupled with the ideological prestige of the common law's status as England's unique and indigenous legal heritage (insightfully described by J. G. A. Pocock), the Crown's reliance on the new economy made a royal attack on the common law in general both undesirable and impracticable. Instead, the Crown for the most part restricted its response to the particular instances in which the common law was used to oppose the Crown's will: thus while common-law tacticians cast their legal resistance to the state's unpopular financial devices as the defense of property rights against royal tyranny, the Crown countered by depicting that resistance as the economically self-interested *mis*use of the law contrary to the unity, order and security of the state. Equity, as the theoretical remedy for injustice produced by the misuse of the law, was consequently an essential component of the Crown's legal arsenal. While other legal weapons like the royally-dominated ecclesiastical courts, Star Chamber and the considerable direct prerogative power of the ruler himself would provide the Crown with greater practical power in the increasingly contentious years leading up to the Civil War, equity's established jurisprudential credentials allowed it to become one of the Crown's earliest and most powerful ideological tools in its efforts to stave off the political implications of capitalism's use of the common law.

Seen in this light, the broader social conflict behind the common-law/equity dispute is not the primarily economic battle between capitalism and feudalism, but the primarily political battle between two socioeconomic factions for the spoils of the nascent capitalist economy. These two factions were defined less by social status (aristocracy versus gentry or nascent bourgeoisie) than by a combination of economic interest and ideological affiliation. On one side were the merchants, financiers, landed gentry and even aristocrats who profited directly from the new economy and who perceived their interests—financial and otherwise—to be at least on occasion different from the Crown's (Stone, *Causes* 114-15). This group may be designated the "rising class," provided that we understand "rising" primarily in the economic rather than social sense and "class" as a taxonomy based on neither birth nor wealth but on economic activity.

Their opponents were the large landowners—Crown and older aristocracy—that for reasons both economic and social had been unable to adapt their financial practice to the new economy and who were consequently forced into an increasingly parasitical relationship to that economy—the Crown in the ways discussed above and the aristocracy as royal clients competing for monopolies and state offices (Tawney 9-13; Stone, *Crisis* 199-207). Despite the growing challenge posed by the rising class, this second group may still be referred to as the period's ruling class, for since Henry VII and Henry VIII subjugated the great noble families to the Crown, this royal-aristocratic bloc had wielded a nigh-hegemonic political and social power which in the late 16th century continued to hold most of the nation under its official or ideological sway.

Thus, while the immediate stakes in the conflict between the two groups were financial, the ultimate prize was much greater: the ability of the independent rising class to use the common law to thwart the sociopolitical will of the ruling class. Not simply a clash of legal principles or jurisdictions, the contest between common law and equity was one of the first and most important sites of the conflict between the rising and ruling classes that would climax (but not conclude) with the Civil War. As one of the earliest articulations—literary or otherwise—of this ideological struggle, the victory of Portia in the trial scene of *The Merchant of Venice* is not a simple reflection of a jurisprudential dispute or an all-but-complete economic shift but rather a highly partisan intervention in a growing cultural crisis.

As in the contemporary legal dispute, the trial's battle lines are drawn not between capitalism (Venice) and feudalism (Belmont), but between the socially and politically independent rising class (Shylock the Jew) and the ruling class and its ideological allies (the Christian aristocrats and Antonio). Even before the trial scene itself, the play makes clear that its target is neither capitalism nor common law *per se*. In response to Solanio's certainty that the Duke will void Shylock's bond, Antonio pointedly establishes not only the close connection between common law and nascent capitalism but also the importance of both to the economic survival of the state:

> The Duke cannot deny the course of law;
> For the commodity that strangers have
> With us in Venice, if it be denied,
> Will much impeach the justice of the state,
> Since that the trade and profit of the city
> Consisteth of all nations.
>
> (3.3.26-31)

During the trial, the legality of the contract itself, exemplar of both capitalist economics and common law, is never challenged: Antonio "confesses" the bond (181-82) and Portia declares, "Why, this bond is forfeit" (230)—that is, forfeited by Antonio upon his nonpayment. Instead, Shylock is vilified for the particular use to which he puts the law of contract: the enforcement of the bond's horrific stipulations at the expense of the Christian "royal merchant" Antonio.

The trial scene opens with a reassertion of its central sociopolitical division. Referring to Antonio by name, the Duke says: "I am sorry for thee" (3); the merchant responds by acknowledging the pains the Duke and the other "magnificoes" have already taken on his behalf (7-9; see also 3.2.279-83). Shylock, in contrast, is first referred to simply as "the Jew" (14), an epithet used throughout the trial to underline his social alienation. Despite (or more precisely because of) its prominence in the play's definition of his character, Shylock's religion is not to be taken at face value, but rather as an exemplary illustration of the play's mediation of Elizabethan sociopolitical reality for presentation on the stage. Without dismissing the importance of the considerable literature debating *The Merchant of Venice*'s anti-Semitism, I would argue that it is difficult to see Shylock primarily as a representative of Judaism. Shylock's Jewishness throughout the play is less theological than cultural: he is not identified by (and reviled for) his failure to accept Christ or the New Testament, but by his "Jewish gaberdine," his unwillingness to dine with his Christian business associates and especially his usury—in short, his social, economic and ideological alienation from Venice's dominant sociopolitical group.

Rather than a transparent religious designation, Judaism (certainly a flexible signifier in an England virtually devoid of professed Jews) functions in the play as a derogatory marker for a group extant but not fully delineated in the cultural consciousness of the late 16th century, a group characterized by its economic self-interest and its willingness to further that interest by opposing itself to the dominant social ideology: the rising class. If the play partakes in contemporary anti-Semitic stereotypes (greed, social separatism), it does so not in the service of their own furtherance, but in order to transfer those negative associations from the religious to the socio-economic sphere.

The Duke's first speech to Shylock (17-34) employs this transference in linking the trial's economic foundations to its larger social significance. Lacking the prerogative power to pardon Antonio—a power that belonged to the ruler only in criminal cases—the Duke resorts to the considerable extra-legal social power wielded by the ruling class. Antonio's financial straits, he says, should elicit pity and mercy not only from Christian hearts, but "from stubborn Turks, and Tartars never train'd / To offices of tender courtesy" (32-33). The Duke offers Shylock the following choice: either to remain more alien than even the Turks and Tartars in pursuing his suit, or to enter—as has Antonio—the hegemonic penumbra of the aristocracy by changing his pagan "malice" for Christian "courtesy" and economic cooperation. The full weight of the social pressure that the ruling class could bring to bear upon a recalcitrant individual is focused in the speech's final line (particularly in light of the recurring pun on gentle/gentile): "We all expect a gentle answer, Jew!"

In the not-too-distant Tudor past such a threat might well have proven the trump card that the Duke intends it to be. By the 1590s, however, the inviolability of the common law was providing the rising class with an increasingly effective shield with which to resist the Crown's efforts to assert its will over the law. Shylock's response to the Duke links the common law's economic domain, its class affiliation and its ideological status as foundation of the state:

> by our holy Sabaoth have I sworn
> To have the due and forfeit of my bond.
> If you deny it, let the danger light
> Upon your charter and your city's freedom!
>
> (36-39)

Throughout the trial scene, Shylock invokes the shield of the common law in the face of Christian attempts to coerce or cajole him by emphasizing his social exclusion or offering him inclusion at the price of his bond. "Till thou canst rail the seal from off my bond," he admonishes Gratiano, "Thou but offend'st thy lungs to speak so loud. / . . . I stand here for law" (139-42).

The lack of formal social submissiveness and regard for hierarchical distinctions implicit in both the substance and the tone of Shylock's response to his aristocratic opponents suggests the ultimate consequence of his common-law defense: the weakening of the sociopolitical hegemony that preserved royalist-aristocratic privilege. In keeping with the play's ideological agenda, this use of the law is presented as a threat to the safety and stability of a Venetian society whose social and juridical similarities to late 16th-century England would not be overlooked by a contemporary audience. This threat is clearest in Shylock's famous "Hath not a Jew eyes" speech (3.1.53-73).

Read in context—as a response to Salerio's suggestion that Shylock has nothing to gain by enforcing the bond—the speech is not the appeal to universal brotherhood it is often taken to be. Antonio's hostility towards Shylock is rooted in the latter's social alterity—"You call me misbeliever, cut-throat dog, / And spet upon my Jewish gaberdine" (1.3.111-12)—and it is this distinction between Jew and Christian that the speech rhetorically effaces. The result of this effacement, however, is not a pledge of mutual forbearance but a promise of retaliatory violence: "And if you wrong us, shall we not revenge? If we are like you in the rest, we will resemble you in that" (3.1.66-68). For Shylock, the bond's utility is not economic—"A pound of man's flesh," he tells Antonio and Bassanio, "Is not so estimable, profitable neither, / As flesh of muttons, beefs, or goats" (1.3.165-67)—but sociopolitical, through its power as an instrument of the common law to nullify the class privilege that protects Antonio from Shylock's vengeance. This association between the common law and violent social disruption is a crucial element of the play's ideological work.

The ruling class's response to Shylock's threat is presented by Portia. She begins by acknowledging both the validity of the bond (177-79) and the ideological power of the common law's promised consistency that underpins Shylock's confident intransigence. In reply to Bassanio's appeal to the Duke to "Wrest once the law to your authority" (215) she insists:

> It must not be, there is no power in Venice
> Can alter a decree established.
> 'Twill be recorded for a precedent,
> And many an error by the same example
> Will rush into the state. It cannot be.
>
> (218-22)

Consequently, her solution to Shylock's legal challenge—"Then must the Jew be merciful" (182)—at first seems identical to the Duke's. The mercy Portia seeks, however, is not the Duke's unconditional Christian mercy. While the Duke demands that Shylock forgive Antonio not only the interest owed but "a moi'ty of the principal" as well (26), Portia seeks not the abandonment of the bond but its payment, with justifiable interest, in place of the legal but abhorrent penalty Shylock demands. "Be merciful," she tells Shylock, "Take thrice thy money, bid me tear the bond" (233-34). It was precisely this type of mercy—that which does not mitigate justice for the sake of pity but mitigates (common) law for the sake of true justice—that the courts of equity claimed to dispense. Knight notes the distinction: "The 'mercy' of the High Court of Chancery's equitable decisions by the Lord Chancellor is not to be confused with . . . simple clemency or empathetic pity . . . for William West says: 'there is a difference between Equitie and Clemency: for Equitie is alwaies most firmly knit to the evil of the

Law which way soever it bends, whether to clemency, or to severity' " ("Equity" 95-96). Many in the play's contemporary audience would have recognized Portia's suggested compromise—the payment of appropriate interest rather than the contractually stipulated forfeiture—as a solution typical of the equity courts of the day (Keeton 137).

Like Shylock's use of common law, Portia's invocation of equity has social as well as legal significance. According to the theory of equity which emerged during Elizabeth's reign, while equitable mercy assured the justness of the law, equity's own justness was in turn guaranteed by its origin in the royal conscience (Thorne viii). The monarch's conscience itself was validated by his role as the earthly conduit for divine justice, which by virtue of its source was necessarily superior to, and thus the ultimate venue of appeal from, the merely human common law. William Lambarde, in his *Archeion,* writes:

> And considering that the Prince of this Realme is the immediate minister of Iustice under God, and is sworn at his Coronation, to deliver to his subjects *aequam & rectam Iustitiam;* I cannot see how it may otherwise be, but that besides his Court of meere Law, he must either reserve to himselfe, or referre to others a certaine soveraigne and preheminent Power, by which he may both supply the want, and correct the rigour of that Positive or written Law. . . . if only streight Law should bee administred, the helpe of GOD which speaketh in that Oracle of Equitie, should be denyed unto men that neede it.
>
> (42-44)

Accordingly, the court of Chancery was considered the "court of the King's conscience," its Chancellor deputized by the monarch to implement the justice of the royal will, correcting when necessary the injustices perpetrated by the common law by overruling the decisions of its courts. Contrary to the levelling effect of the common law that placed even the sovereign under the law, this construction of legal authority offered a hierarchical ideology which situated the monarch at the terrestrial pinnacle of the legal system.

Portia's response to Shylock's use of the common law is thus the jurisprudential reassertion of the fundamental value and necessity of social hierarchy, replacing his vision of inter-class violence with one of royally-regulated harmony. It is in this light that we must understand Portia's famous "quality of mercy" speech:

> The quality of mercy is not strain'd,
> It droppeth as the gentle rain from heaven
> Upon the place beneath. It is twice blest:
> It blesseth him that gives and him that takes.
> 'Tis mightiest in the mightiest, it becomes
> The throned monarch better than his crown.

> His sceptre shows the force of temporal
>   power,
> The attribute to awe and majesty,
> Wherein doth sit the dread and fear of kings;
> But mercy is above this sceptred way,
> It is enthroned in the hearts of kings,
> It is an attribute to God himself;
> And earthly power doth then show likest
>   God's
> When mercy seasons justice.
>
> (184-97)

Mercy, in short, descends from heaven into the heart of the monarch, allowing him to fulfill his role as the terrestrial conduit of God's justice, with which he "seasons" flawed human justice. In addition to justifying ideologically the supremacy of royal equity, however, Portia's speech also makes clear its practical implications. Her juxtaposition of the monarch's divine equitable authority with his "temporal power" sets up the speech's concluding union of Christian piety and *realpolitik* intimidation: "We do pray for mercy, / And that same prayer doth teach us all to render / The deeds of mercy" (200-02). The power that equity gives to the Crown by reinstating royal will as the ultimate legal authority assures that one can no more hope to prosper without the king's mercy than without God's, and that one who hopes for such mercy should be prepared to make concessions of his own. Some seven years after the play's composition, King James would make this same point less subtly in his July 1604 rebuke to a recalcitrant Parliament: "Justice I will give to all, and favour to such as deserve it . . . in cases of equity, if I should show favour, except there be obedience, I were no wise man" (qtd. in Kenyon 60).

While Portia replaces the social coercion of the Duke's Christian mercy with an equitable mercy which responds to Shylock's legal defense in kind, the ramifications of both threats are the same for him. To accept Portia's equitable resolution is to surrender his equal legal standing and accede to the existence of a higher legal and social authority. Not surprisingly, then, Shylock spurns Portia's veiled threat, preferring to rely on the power of his position under the common law to indemnify him from the need for royal mercy: "By my soul I swear / There is no power in the tongue of man / To alter me: I stay here on my bond" (240-42). What follows is one of the most dramatic—and ideologically potent—scenes in Shakespearean comedy, in which judgment is pronounced not once but twice, juxtaposing for the audience the results of the competing legal philosophies presented in the first half of the scene.

Portia's deliberations proceed first in accordance with the common law. When she declares the bond forfeit, Shylock esteems her for her knowledge of the law, suggesting the common law's justification of its judges' authority not by their own discretion but by their preeminent ability to administer consistently a time-tested body of law: "It doth appear you are a worthy judge; / You know the law, your exposition / Hath been most sound" (236-38). As the impartiality of the common law requires, Portia's ruling is pointedly faithful to the law of contract, despite her personal desire to offer mercy:

> Por: . . . lay bare your bosom.
> Shy: Ay, his breast,
> So says the bond, doth it not, noble judge?
> "Nearest his heart," those are the very words.
> Por: It is so. Are there balance here to weigh
>   The flesh?
> Shy: I have them ready.
> Por: Have by some surgeon, Shylock, on your
>   charge,
> To stop his wounds, lest he do bleed to
>   death.
> Shy: Is it so nominated in the bond?
> Por: It is not so express'd, but what of that?
> 'Twere good you do so much for charity.
> Shy: I cannot find it, 'tis not in the bond.
>   (252-62)

Alongside this emphasis on the strict legality of the procedure, however, is the no less insistent emphasis on the materiality of its outcome: the mutilation and almost certain death of Antonio. Present throughout the trial scene, this linking of common-law principle to its horrific results is unmistakable as the scene reaches its climax. As Shylock approaches Antonio with whetted knife, Portia again reminds us that what we see is the result of the court's obligation to proceed according to the law: "The law allows it, and the court awards it" (303). The result is a vivid and ideologically charged illustration of the irrelevance of the common law's human consequences to its inflexible requirements.

The clear injustice of this strictly legal proceeding is, of course, precisely what the flexible, case-specific judgments of the courts of equity claimed to remedy. Before Shylock can strike, Portia halts him—"Tarry a little, there is something else" (305)—and the trial shifts from the procedures of a common-law court to those of equity. Portia's famous "quibble"—Shylock may have his pound of flesh according to the bond, but on the condition that "if thou dost shed / One drop of Christian blood, thy lands and goods / Are by the laws of Venice confiscate / Unto the state of Venice" (309-12)—is a stratagem typical of the equity courts. While the common law traditionally held that if the law granted an individual a right (including the right to take possession of property) it also granted him the means to exercise that right (Andrews 77nA), the courts of equity would often thwart a common-law award by placing such stringent restrictions and protections on the property to be seized as frequently to make the path of least resistance that taken by Shylock, the

"voluntary" non-collection of the award (Andrews 66; Keeton 145). The relief and amazement, both on stage and off, at Portia's dramatic aversion of the travesty of justice almost perpetrated by the common law underscores the contrasting results of the two legal systems.

The audience's pleasure in Portia's victory is heightened by the irony of her use of Shylock's insistence on strict interpretation against him: "For as thou urgest justice, be assur'd / Thou shalt have justice more than thou desir'st" (315-16). In doing so, however, Portia has vexed legal scholars by belying the equitable principle most often associated with the trial scene, the mitigation of the strict letter of the law through recourse to its gentler spirit. The reason for this seeming contradiction lies in the political significance of Portia's legal device. While the mitigation of the letter of the law by its spirit or intent was indeed a central tenet of traditional equitable jurisprudence, in Shakespeare's time it was chiefly associated not with royally-controlled equity but with the judges of the common-law courts. Throughout the 16th century, as the limitations placed upon the common law by its codification into written rules became apparent, its judges began to revivify a procedure utilized by their predecessors in the 13th and 14th centuries: the interpretation of a law based on its intent rather than its precise wording (Thomas 515-16). Such an approach was entirely congruent with common-law ideology, basing the authority of the common-law judges to interpret rather than simply apply the law on their unmatched knowledge of its history and principles.

The practice of common-law equity was, of course, opposed by the equity courts, whose authority was based on the inadequacy of the common law to the requirements of justice and the necessity of an alternate source of justice—royal conscience—to remedy that inadequacy. To correct the letter of the law with its spirit was merely to affirm the ultimate wisdom of the common law. For this reason the principle of intent is emphatically not the basis of Portia's equitable decision. Portia herself discounts intent as a means of correcting the defects of the letter of the law when she pointedly acknowledges that the spirit as well as the letter of the law supports Shylock's claim: "the intent and purpose of the law / Hath full relation to the penalty, / Which here appeareth due upon the bond" (247-49). As the play takes pains to indicate, the intent of the law of contract is to protect the sanctity of contracts from external interference in order to ensure the rights of those who do business in Venice, regardless of the specific contents of those contracts.

The principle that Portia applies in reaching her verdict is not the mitigation of the letter of the law by its spirit, but the equally venerable equitable doctrine which holds that equity may mitigate the unjust results of the law's necessary generality by taking into account the aspects of a specific case of which the law takes no notice. This conception of equity is traceable to Aristotle's *Ethics,* in which he argues that "all law is universal but about some things it is not possible to make a universal statement which shall be correct. . . . this is the nature of the equitable, a correction of law where it is defective owing to its universality" (133; bk. 5, ch. 10). Elizabethan advocates of the courts of equity argued that the common law, in its quest for comprehensiveness and consistency, must operate on a general level and thus could never be made to take account of the "collaterall circumstances" of individual cases (Hake 123). As a result, equity was both necessary and necessarily superior to the common law, overruling the latter when the application of its general rules to a specific case produced evident injustice.

It was this theory of equity that was at the heart of the Crown's claims to legal authority: for even if superior knowledge of both the letter and the spirit of the common law must be conceded to the common-law judges, the individualized requirements of justice were the province of conscience: "the examination of the case by circumstances . . . doth necessarily appertayne to the high courte of Chauncery . . . by an Equity that is drawne from the only conscience of the Lord Chauncellor" (Hake 123). The stipulations in Portia's ruling concerning the spilling of blood and the removal of an exact weight of flesh underline the gruesome specifics excluded from the common law's generality even as they correct the injustice produced by that exclusion. Neither the letter nor the spirit of the law make allowances for contracts like Shylock's; it is left to Portia and equity to mitigate the effects of the law's generality by considering the circumstances of the case at hand, overruling the requirements of the law in order to satisfy those of justice.

The sociopolitical consequences of equity's victory over the common law are immediately and decisively registered in the treatment of Shylock by a legal system once again under the control of the ruling class. During the first half of the interpretational contest, Portia in her role as common-law judge sets aside the scene's emphasis on Shylock's cultural difference, addressing him not as "Jew" but by name. The shift to equity, however, returns social difference and discrimination to the law, indicated by Portia's invocation of the statute specifically criminalizing the shedding of "Christian blood." For the remainder of the trial Shylock goes unnamed, referred to only as "Jew" not merely by his avowed Christian enemies but also by Portia, the representative of justice. This connection between equity and social differentiation casts the freeing of Antonio as a reassertion of the distinctions between classes that Shylock's use of the law attempted to erase.

As Shylock tries to leave the court—"Why then the devil give him good of it! / I'll stay no longer ques-

tion"—he learns that "The law hath yet another hold on [him]" (345-47). Because Portia's equitable reading of the bond has disallowed the shedding of Christian blood as a contractually protected act, Shylock is guilty of attempted murder and thus subject under the criminal law to the forfeiture of life and property. The social basis of Shylock's predicament is suggested by the statute to which he falls prey, the law "against an alien, / That by direct or indirect attempts / [Seeks] the life of any citizen" (349-51).

Such a law is present in none of the sources of the pound-of-flesh plot; moreover, in late 16th-century England all felonies, including attempted murder, were punishable by death and loss of property no matter who the perpetrator (Auden 228; Keeton 146). There is thus no dramatic or historical justification for a law specifically targeting aliens except to emphasize the link between Shylock's social status and his fate forged by the power of the law to discriminate between—and against—social groups or classes: having resolutely maintained his status as cultural outsider, he now finds himself trapped by it. The pleasure we take in Shylock's resultant comeuppance reinforces the play's implicit rebuttal to the common law's central justification, the economic necessity of a law predictable and impartial even to the "strangers" whose "commodity" is so important to the nation. Punishing Shylock's abuse of the common law with a statue that explicitly discriminates against such "strangers" answers the economic arguments of the rising class by implying that despite its potentially deleterious effect on commerce a certain amount of regulation is necessary for the security and moral order of the state.

The reestablishment of the legal authority of the ruling class is complete when the statute places discretionary judicial power directly in the hands of the monarch: "the offender's life lies in the mercy / Of the Duke only" (355-56). Stripped of the common law's protection, Shylock is subject to Portia's earlier threat: his failure to grant mercy to Antonio puts him at the mercy of the Duke. That this mercy is not Portia's equitable mercy but instead the clemency which was the Crown's prerogative in criminal cases (as indicated by the Duke's use of the word "pardon" [369]) merely confirms the sociopolitical complicity of the two juristic principles.

Their legal power over him established, Shylock's antagonists immediately use it to nullify his socioeconomic threat: the loss of half of his wealth now to Antonio and the other half upon his death to Lorenzo places his economic power in the hands of the aristocracy and its allies, and his forced conversion symbolically completes his absorption by the dominant Christian-aristocratic culture. Notably, despite his earlier denunciation of Shylock's usury, Antonio makes no provision at this point to prevent its continuance; it would seem that the eventual appropriation of any profit made therein by the ruling class does much to mitigate usury's sinfulness. The Christians' true target is not Shylock's economic practice but the social and political ends to which it is employed.

Finally, the trial concludes with a further demonstration of the coercive power granted the Crown by the supremacy of equity that Portia intimates in the "quality of mercy" speech, as the Duke requires Shylock's acquiescence to Antonio's terms, "or else I do recant / The pardon that I late pronounced here" (391-92). Legally at the mercy of his enemies, Shylock can only accede to Portia's ironic query, "Art thou contented, Jew?" (393). Thoroughly humbled, he leaves the court not with the unregenerate curse of his attempted exit prior to the invocation of the law against aliens but with the entreaties of a broken man: "I pray you give me leave to go from hence, / I am not well" (395-96). The trial's last word, however, is given to Gratiano: "In christ'ning shalt thou have two godfathers: / Had I been judge, thou shouldst have had ten more, / To bring thee to the gallows, not to the font" (398-400). This taunting valediction, while reemphasizing the "mercy" granted Shylock in sparing his life, at the same time underlines the contingency of that mercy, suggesting how easily his fate could have been that which Gratiano prefers. That it was not is due less to the principles of equity than to the dramatic and ideological appropriateness of a punishment befitting Shylock's social and economic crime.

Seen from the dual perspective of legal and political history, the threat posed by Shylock to the Venetian social order is fundamentally the same threat that Lord Chancellor Ellesmere recognized nearly twenty years later in what was by then one in a growing number of legal challenges to the Crown's sociopolitical hegemony. Shylock's use of the common law represented to a contemporary audience a question not simply of jurisprudential principle, nor even of economic practice, but ultimately of "the power and prerogative of the King." And despite the efficacy of his defeat at Portia's hands in defining and resolving the conflict for the theater-going public in the interests of royal authority, the ideological battle fought in *Shylock v. Antonio* would prove to be but an early skirmish in the war between the rising and the ruling classes that was to dominate the next century of English politics.

Notes

[1] All quotations from *The Merchant of Venice* are from *The Riverside Shakespeare,* ed. G. Blakemore Evans. References to the trial scene (Act 4, scene 1) will be cited by line number only.

Works Cited

Andrews, Mark Edwin. *Law versus Equity in "The Merchant of Venice."* Boulder: U of Colorado P, 1965.

Aristotle. *The Nicomachean Ethics.* Trans. David Ross. London: Oxford UP, 1961.

Auden, W. H. "Brothers and Others." *The Dyer's Hand and Other Essays.* New York: Random, 1948. 218-37.

Bacon, Francis. *The Elements of the Common Lawes of England.* 1630. Amsterdam: Da Capo, 1969.

Cohen, Walter. "*The Merchant of Venice* and the Possibilities of Historical Criticism." *ELH* 49 (1982): 765-89.

Hake, Edward. *Epieikeia: A Dialogue on Equity in Three Parts.* Ed. D.E.C. Yale. New Haven: Yale UP, 1953.

Hill, Christopher. *Intellectual Origins of the English Revolution.* Oxford: Clarendon, 1965.

Ives, E. W. "Social Change and the Law." *The English Revolution 1600-1660.* Ed. E. W. Ives. London: Arnold, 1968. 115-30.

Keeton, George W. *Shakespeare's Legal and Political Background.* New York: Barnes, 1967.

Kenyon, J. P. *Stuart England.* Vol. 6 of *The Pelican History of England.* Harmondsworth: Penguin, 1978.

Knight, W. Nicholas. "Equity, *The Merchant of Venice,* and William Lambarde." *Shakespeare Survey* 27 (1974): 93-104.

———. "Shakespeare's Court Case." *Law and Critique* 2 (1991): 103-12.

Lambarde, William. *Archeion or, a Discourse upon the High Courts of Justice in England.* 1635 (written c. 1591). Ed. Charles H. McIlwain and Paul L. Ward. Cambridge: Harvard UP, 1957.

McKay, Maxine. "*The Merchant of Venice:* A Reflection of the Early Conflict between Courts of Law and Courts of Equity." *Shakespeare Quarterly* 15 (1964): 371-75.

Moisan, Thomas. " 'Which is the Merchant here? and which the Jew?': Subversion and Recuperation in *The Merchant of Venice.*" *Shakespeare Reproduced: The Text in History and Ideology.* Ed. Jean E. Howard and Marion F. O'Connor. New York: Methuen, 1987. 188-206.

Phillips, O. Hood. *Shakespeare and the Lawyers.* London: Methuen, 1972.

Pocock, J. G. A. *The Ancient Constitution and the Feudal Law: A Reissue with a Retrospect.* Cambridge: Cambridge UP, 1987.

Shakespeare, William. *The Merchant of Venice. The Riverside Shakespeare.* Ed. G. Blakemore Evans. Boston: Houghton, 1974. 254-85.

Stone, Lawrence. *The Causes of the English Revolution 1529-1642.* New York: Harper, 1972.

————. *The Crisis of the Aristocracy 1558-1641.* Abridged edition. London: Oxford UP, 1967.

Tawney, R. H. "The Rise of the Gentry, 1558-1640." *Economic History Review* 11 (1941). Rpt. in *Social Change and Revolution in England 1540-1640.* Ed. Lawrence Stone. London: Longman's, 1965. 6-18.

Tennenhouse, Leonard. *Power on Display: The Politics of Shakespeare's Genres.* New York: Methuen, 1986.

Thomas, G. W. "James I, Equity and Lord Keeper John Williams." *The English Historical Review* 91 (1976): 506-28.

Thorne, Samuel E. Preface to Hake. v-xii.

West, William. *Symboleography.* London, 1594.

Whigham, Frank. "Ideology and Class Conduct in *The Merchant of Venice.*" *Renaissance Drama* n.s. 10 (1979): 93-115.

Subha Mukherji (essay date 1996)

SOURCE: " 'Lawful Deed': Consummation, Custom, and Law in *All's Well That Ends Well*," in *Shakespeare Survey: An Annual Survey of Shakespearian Study and Production,* Vol. 49, 1996, pp. 181-200.

[*In the following essay, Mukherji studies the legal and contractual obligations of Renaissance marriage dramatized in Shakespeare's* All's Well That Ends Well.]

Having wed Helena at the king of Rossillion's behest, Bertram, the king's ward, refuses to bed her and flies to Italy with her dower, leaving a conditional letter for her: 'When thou canst get the ring upon my finger, which never shall come off, and show me a child begotten of thy body that I am father to, then call me husband; but in such a "then" I write a "never" ' (*All's Well That Ends Well,* 3.2.57-60).[1]

Bertram's marriage, overseen by king and priest, counts as a solemnized *de praesenti* union for all practical purposes. And as Henry Swinburne confirms in his *Treatise of Spousals,* 'Spousals *de praesenti,* though not consummate, be in truth and substance very Matrimony, and therefore perpetually indissoluble.' This treatise, written around 1600 but published in 1686, is the only systematic exposition of marriage laws and the first handbook of canon law to be written in England.[2] According to Swinburne, the use of long absence as a legal means for escape applied only to *de futuro* spousals.[3]

What, then, is Bertram resisting by refusing to sleep with Helena? What is the status of his apparently impossible condition? This moment in the action has been interpreted by critics as the transformation of a legal possibility into a 'fairy-tale' one, Bertram's stipulation being read as a purely fantastic setting of tasks in the romance mode.[4] But such readings fail to account for Helena's meeting of his terms as though they were an actual legal impediment, and her final securing of him in what is, effectively, a court of law. Bertram's instinctive belief that 'not bed[ding] her' somehow counteracts the effects of 'wed[ding] her' (3.2.21-2) does not stem simply from his own wrong-headedness, but from factors actually present in contemporary English society.

My point of entry into the play's engagement with law will be marital consummation as it figures in Bertram's conduct and Helena's response. I will interpret the concept of consummation in terms of its contrasting roles in Christian marriage and Christian divorce. But the act of sex in the social experience of marriage confounds these two functions, even as it conflates law and customary ritual. Its peculiar status in the play will be shown to hinge on its legal function as evidence. The problems of evidentiary procedure in English church courts provide an important focus for the play's treatment of marriage law. The two main forms of evidence that I will look at are the exchange of rings and pregnancy. My analysis of the ambiguities of evidence will refer to larger theoretical issues of motive and intention that are legally unresolvable but particularly conducive to exploration in drama.

In reconstructing the relevant legal history, I shall use Swinburne's treatise, which I will refer to as *Spousals.* This represents an attempt to codify as well as interpret the law, since Swinburne was dealing with an area of legislation that was not only supposed to discipline and punish but also to provide moral guidance for social and personal behaviour. *Spousals* seeks to mediate between legal theory and practice, the written word and the spoken, the spoken word and the sign, all of which constituted marriage as social practice. I shall also be drawing upon a draft fragment, preserved in Durham, which follows the completed *Treatise of Spousals* in what seems to be the authorial manuscript. Entitled 'Of the signification of divers woordes importing Matrimonye, etc.', this is, I take it, the beginning of the second part of what Swinburne originally intended to be a three-part treatise on spousals, marriage and divorces. I will refer to it henceforth as *Matrimony*.[5]

My other group of primary materials consists of surviving records of spousal litigation from contemporary church courts, mainly Durham, Chester, Norwich and Canterbury. Together, these two sets of texts provide a comprehensive picture of law as human action, and the contradictions in such action are dramatized in Shakespeare's *All's Well.*

The clue to our understanding of the nature of Bertram's conduct lies in the status of sexual consummation in popular custom, which derived elements from the theology, rituals and attitudes surrounding marriage, and its relationship with law. Among the many factors that constituted the overall sense of the accomplishment of a marriage, consummation had a role of special interest and curious standing. Theologically, a sacramental symbolism and sanctity attached to it, as reflected in *The Book of Common Prayer.* 'For this cause shall a man . . . be joined unto his wife, and they two shall be one flesh. This mystery is great.'[6]

In law, however, intercourse was not strictly a factor in the formation of marriage in sixteenth- or early seventeenth-century England. The church, which was in charge of matrimonial litigation, held, from the twelfth century onwards, that present consent, and not the sexual act, makes a valid and completed marriage.[7] This position was marked by Pope Alexander III's promulgation of consent as the basis of the institution, irrespective of either solemnization or consummation. In England, where the pre-Tridentine canon law of marriage survived the Reformation and did not change till 1753, informal or private contracts continued to have claim to legal recognition since consent was still the ultimate and sole criterion of validity. So, consummation was as irrelevant in 'law' as solemnization; hence the frequent clubbing together of the two by contemporary writers such as Swinburne as well as by legal historians in our own times.[8]

But given the inevitable confusions, uncertainties, and difficulties of proving consent, unsolemnized marriages were increasingly disapproved of by state and church. Certain 'legal effects'—property rights and benefits (*Spousals,* 15)—were made conditional upon solemnization, and Tudor and Early Stuart England floundered through the curious doubleness of a situation where validity and illicitness could coexist in the same union.[9] There was tightening pressure from both Protestant and Catholic reformers to regularize marriage, and one of its manifestations was an effort to impress on people that ecclesiastical solemnization alone made sexual union licit.[10] The denunciation of intercourse before or

without the public ceremony implied, firstly, that solemnization was seen by many as being connected with, indeed, guaranteeing and sanctioning consummation. Secondly, it suggests the association of intercourse with the social acceptance of a lawful union. Even among legal thinkers, there were those who, as Swinburne writes in *Matrimony* (120-1), made a distinction between 'matrimony initiate' or 'begunne' and matrimony 'consummate', between 'true' and 'perfect' marriage. 'This word *Nuptiae,* Marriages', he writes in *Spousals,* is not necessarily used to mean solely 'the Substance and indissoluble knot of Matrimony only, but doth often signifie the Rites and Ceremonies observed at the celebration of Matrimony' (*Spousals,* 8-9). It is in terms of a society where 'rites and ceremonies' were an essential constituent of the customary view and practice of marriage that Bertram's holding out against 'the great prerogative and rite of love' (2.4.41) has to be understood.

However, though it could not normally constitute a marriage in itself, there were a few specific circumstances in which sexual consummation could have a legal function. When a spousal was contracted between infants or between minors, it could be ratified and made into an indissoluble knot by willing cohabitation after attainment of the age of consent.[11] Sexual relations could give *de futuro* spousals between adults the effect of *de praesenti* marriage; they could also turn conditional spousals into matrimony.

If custom and ritual are major contributors to Bertram's perspective, these situations where intercourse has a proof-value form the other, more distinctly legal influence. Indeed, custom itself must have been conditioned by such legal associations. The witness depositions and the personal responses in contract suits of the period communicate a sense of how the specific legal functions of copulation led to a more general and undifferentiating notion of sex as being a factor that could make an otherwise uncertain match conclusive. In a Durham suit of 1570 for restitution of conjugal rights, cohabitation figures centrally in all the depositions. Isabel Walker's witness Richard Bell, keen to stress the validity of her marriage to William Walker and, thereby, *her* claims, says that they 'dwelte in house here in Durham togither, as man and wyfe by the space of one yere, or more'. On the other hand, William's witness emphasizes the finality of Isabel's marriage to her reportedly precontracted husband Robert Stathan; he deposes that 'he hath known . . . [them] . . . dwell to gyther in one house as man and wyfe, as this examinate and neighbours thereabouts dyd take ytt'.[12]

A different legal channel that influenced the way consummation was viewed proceeded from the laws regarding annulment, by which divorce could be obtained by proof of non-consummation in cases of precontract, duress, consanguinity, affinity or impotence.

The divorce of Lady Frances Howard from the Earl of Essex came through in 1613 when her allegation of his incompetence was confirmed by his admission that 'he could never know his said wife'.[13] The background to this law lies in the canonical tradition which associated indissolubility with the 'becoming one flesh' of married partners.[14] The question whether a man who, after his betrothal, feels a call to enter religious life was free to do so was met by Pope Alexander III with the answer that he could first marry and then leave off to become a monk if he did not follow up the marriage with carnal coupling. His premise was that the Christian prohibition against putting asunder those whom God had joined applied only to incorporated couples; his precedent, St John's turning to religion from a virginal marriage. But this contradicted the fundamental canonical assumption that consent, not coitus, is the substance—a position he himself upheld. His circumvention of this problem is described by J. T. Noonan as resembling 'a legal trick, of a lawyer's way of satisfying contradictory purposes by keeping form and sacrificing substance, of nominally honoring the oath to marry while permitting the actual subversion of the oath.'[15]

One way of reconciling the canonical contradiction is to make, as canon law obviously did, a distinction between the model of Christian divorce, provided by St John, and the example of Christian marriage, provided by Mary and Joseph.[16] The notion that mutual consent was the essence and physical union was the substance of marriage could thus be kept from a direct conflict and be channelled into two separate legal procedures. But this separation proved all too artificial in social practice. For consummation could function both as a constituent of marriage and as a sign of it. Originally, the constitutive function came into play mostly in clandestine or disputed marriages, while the signifying role was predominant in unions accomplished through the full formalities, being, as it were, an ultimate expression of the marriage. In a court of law, however, the two were easily conflated because in both capacities, the fact of consummation was required to establish certainties, to prove a status. Thus, in a Durham case of 1587, the doubts about the reality of the solemnized marriage of Sir Thomas Gray with Lady Catherine Neville arise because they have 'not cohabited continually'. That the marriage emerges as being viable and valid in court is due to the establishment of the fact that since a certain day they have 'nightly laid in one bed, as becometh man and wife'.[17] Anne Yate and George Johnson of Cheshire go through a very different event—a plebeian trothplight match, possibly *de futuro,* contracted through a witnessed handfast, but unsolemnized. But in the legal dispute over it in 1562, as in the previous case, the deponents confirm the marriage with reference to sexual union, and the causal relation suggested by their phrasing indicates the inseparability of consummation as sign of status

and as proof of contract. Oliver Foxe asserts that they were 'reputid and taken for man and wief amonge their neighboures' 'for they did lye in one house, and nothinge betwix them but a broken wall and a paintid clothe'. Cecilia Key confirms, 'the neighboures . . . did take them as man and wief, in somuche that they have laine together in bed, and so vsed them selves as man and wief'.[18] Does the importance of consummation here derive from its status as the criterion of indissolubility in the divorce paradigm? Or, from its assimilation into the formalities of making a marriage, and so its association with solemnization instead of consent? It is impossible to tell. What one can perhaps tell is that the deponents did not pause to work out such distinctions before giving testimony.

Thoughts about marriage and related legal actions covered and intertwined the issues of formation and validation of matrimony, as well as of the making and unmaking of marriage. The status of sexual union continued to be a focus of some of the dualities in marriage law, and Bertram's refusal is both a response to, and an expression of this doubleness. On the one hand, Bertram is holding out against the one formality that is left him to resist, having been rushed through the paraphernalia of 'contract' and 'ceremony'. From this point of view it is a token non-completion of the *ritual* stages of marriage in society. Marital non-co-habitation did draw considerable social attention in early modern England, was on occasions a ground for presentment in court,[19] and could even be disallowed by court decree.[20] A Yorkshire parochial presentment of 1568 states that 'They say all is well saving that John Pennye and his wif lyveth not to geither.[21]

But on the other hand, the resisted consummation is not, for Bertram, a mere external formality. Given that the legal validity of a marriage depended on mutual consent, he is exploiting the one remaining channel through which he can express his own consent or lack of it. Thus it comes to represent the substance of marriage, the indissolubility that it stands for in the canonical law of divorce. Here is a reconcilement of the apparently opposite standings of intercourse in the marriage and divorce paradigms that is less sophistical and more instinctive than the one offered by Alexander III. If the rationale behind granting importance to copulation is the idea that it expresses volition, the conflict is resolved. Especially in formally solemnized marriages like Bertram's, where the legally constituent elements are taken up in the self-generating momentum of ceremonies, the contract becomes more clearly an organized event than an expression of individual will; consequently, the post-legal stage of consummation becomes the clearer site of consent. 'I have wedded her, not bedded her, and sworn to make the "not" eternal', he writes to his mother, making a statement about the distinction, in his mind, between what has been achieved by legal form, and a voluntary and meaningful entry into the married state. The duality of the situation is further underlined by Bertram's language; the riddling and the cautious precision in his letters even while at one level he has committed himself—swearing 'to make the "not" eternal'—translates the sense of a lacuna written into the very language of the marriage ritual. The irony remains, of course, that Bertram's very defiance of law takes the form of an action prompted by legal instinct, neither custom nor social attitude being independent of law any more than law can function apart from these.

The transition of 'consummation' from its link with solemnization to its connection with intention is not peculiar to Bertram's psychology. Depositions from the period suggest that men and women did frequently associate the sexual act with 'consent'. The most telling example is that of Mawde Price alias Gregorie whose means of preventing her enforced and solemnized marriage to Henry Price from becoming real was to refuse to let him 'have . . . his pleasure apon her', and instead, having regular sexual relations, and two children, with her precontracted husband, Randall Gregorie. This becomes the single focus of each of the depositions in this Chester case of 1562, and is clearly regarded by the witnesses as being directly related to consent. Alice Dood's phrasing actually identifies copulation and matrimonial intention; she says that Henry and Mawde did not 'cohabete voluntarie together, nor did consent together as man and wiff'. Matilda Broke's testimony reinforces this equation; 'verelie they neuer consented together'. To Henry Price himself, Mawde's resistance to sex is a sign of the non-reality of the marriage, and moves him finally to seek judicial annulment. Randall, the precontracted husband, considers Mawde's refusal to have 'carnall dole' with Henry a sure indication of her 'not [accepting] hym as her husband'.[22]

Swinburne stresses the legal weight of 'voluntary Cohabitation' in converting child-marriages into 'true substantial Matrimony' and draws attention to the similarity of this criterion to the one that turns *de futuro* spousals into marriages. He goes on then to distinguish 'other more feeble Conjectures of kissings, . . . etc.' from those that 'are evident and urgent, and equivalent to the presumption of Carnal copulation' because it is required 'that this Consent, whereby Spousals are turned into Matrimony, do appear *evidenter, evidently*' (*Spousals*, 40-1). Talking of conditional contracts, he says that if the parties know each other carnally 'before the event of the condition', they are 'deemed to . . . yield their mutual Consents to Contract and Consummate pure and perfect Matrimony' (121). Swinburne, we must remember, was a legal practitioner, familiar with custom as well as legal theory. It is significant that his explicit association of consent with consummation is made problematic, if not contradicted, by his resorting to the law of pre-sumption elsewhere. Discussing complicated conditional spousals, he prescribes the 'favourable Presumption' that 'is to be preferred in all doubtful Cases' regarding the purpose of any sexual involvement that may have followed (219). If a man bound upon oath to marry one of three sisters lies with any one of them, 'he is presumed to have made choice of her as his Wife' (221). The difficulty of ensuring that this presumption is also the truth of intention arises most clearly in the marshalling of proof. The law of evidence, for all its safeguards against getting the intention wrong, can, more than any other legal endeavour, make 'consummation' an absolute tool, disjoined from its motive. So Swinburne says, 'Spousals do become Matrimony by carnal knowledge, albeit the Man were constrained, through *fear of death* to know the Woman' (226).[23] The process by which Bertram's condition is met in *All's Well* dramatizes the way in which the contradiction in Swinburne, which is also a contradiction in law, is produced by the peculiar demands of 'evidence'. This is paradoxical, given that the theoretical importance of sex in marriage law was based so largely on the belief that it could be, potentially, the surest proof of consent.

This is not the only way in which Bertram's instinctive 'use' of law rebounds on him. When, desperate not to let the marriage materialize, but powerless, as a ward, to prove duress, he resolves to 'End ere [he] [does] begin' (2.5.26), he is making a mental demarcation between public ritual and a private counterpart in consummation. Neither Helena nor anyone else has doubts about what law vouches to be hers (2.4.41-2; 2.5.79-82). What Bertram denies is the *relationship* that the contract is presumed to guarantee. He is reclaiming sexual union for the sphere of the personal from the sphere of legal validation. But he does not simply protest through inaction; he further makes consummation the condition for a fuller acknowledgement of the marriage. By himself positing sex as an evidence for Helena to establish the rights of love, he forfeits his rights to a personal scale of criteria. As Helena sets about to realize his condition, consummation becomes more public than ever, and more sharply distinguished from personal consent, by the very virtue of being used as proof, and hence being required 'to appear *evidenter*' in a legal space.

These reversions are the subject of the following section which will also make clear how Helena emerges as a defendant seeking to validate her marriage, while Bertram corresponds to the unenthusiastic party fumblingly attempting a sort of annulment. Seen within this structure, Bertram's preoccupation with non-consummation is entirely appropriate, and fulfils the legal expectation of a divorce suit. Helena's attainment and use of carnal union is equally appropriate to her own legal purpose. The meeting of the two 'causes' demonstrates schematically the coming together of sign and proof, of formation and validation, and with these, of the principles of union and those of annulment in the practised legality of marriage.

The process by which Helena earns the right to be acknowledged by Bertram as his wife is quasi-legal, but by the time it is completed, it looks like a proper legal validation. That is largely because this development is crossed with another, truly legal pattern of events consisting of the interaction between Bertram and Diana, leading to an actual trial where Bertram has to defend himself against Diana's claim of marriage and her allegation of marital disacknowledgement. These legal events, of course, are instrumental to the successful accomplishment of Helena's project, and stems from the plan to use Diana to set the stage for the bed-trick. A Shakespearian creation,[24] Diana stands at the intersection of the legal and the quasi-legal structures, and represents the inextricability of the one from the other. The Bertram-Diana part of the play illuminates the nature of Helena's use of evidence by exploring the ambiguities of proof in a more clear-cut legal framework.

The relationship between Bertram's condition and its fulfilment is also one between a promise and its performance, terms and their enactment, and so, between word and deed. In contract law, a bond, the common device to secure contractual settlements, was finalized by using a 'deed'—the term describing a document under seal. By the beginning of the seventeenth century, the notion of contract had already begun to extend from its original sense of 'a transaction . . . which transferred property or generated a debt' to include the modern sense of a consensual pact, an exchange of promise between individuals—a meaning formerly borne by the word 'covenant'.[25] Such agreements being transient events, the 'deed' is what made them concrete and gave them legal validity.

An examination of the principle underlying this importance of the 'deed', however, reveals its origins in evidentiary problems. In medieval town courts, a contract that had not been observed could be proved by the oath of the plaintiff. This inevitably began to be felt as inadequate: the very need of proof in this matter was prompted by an awareness of the elusive and indeterminate nature of words. This is what led to law's sharp distinction between mere words on the one hand and action or deeds on the other. By 1321 it was legally prescribed that 'the only acceptable evidence of a covenant in the royal courts was a deed'.[26] In its original sense of an exchange of property, a contract had to be executed in order to be effected—there was no notion of sueing an unperformed contract. When its sense expanded, the function of performance was taken on by the act of sealing the document of contract in front of witnesses—something done, and hence a deed. From this, its original meaning in law, the word 'deed' came to be applied by

transference to the product of the event—the document itself. Thus, a deed was both what made a contract in the legal sense, and what proved it. As well as being often signified by gestures such as a handclasp, it was itself a sign of the agreement.

The particular relevance of the word-deed hierarchy in marriage law is brought out through the liaison between Diana and Bertram. Persistent in his efforts at overcoming Diana's maidenly resistance, Bertram remonstrates, 'How have I sworn!' (4.2.21). Diana retaliates immediately that his oaths 'are words and poor conditions', and insists on a seal. This is not simply a metaphorical way of disputing Bertram's sincerity but a legal argument; an attempt to steer Bertram's private declarations into a contract that can be proved later in a legal event which, as she knows and he does not, has already been planned.

The explicit use of terms from contract law in connection with professed commitments of love dramatizes an actual link between spousal and contract litigation. Actions against breach of faith that came up as part of the church courts' bulk of marriage litigation were allied in principle to common law actions for breach of contract. Besides, there actually existed a common law action for breach of promise of marriage.[27] Likewise, contract suits formed a sizeable portion of the church courts' business in the sixteenth and seventeenth centuries, and the practice of settling for cash was comparable to the common law action.[28] The law of contract, after all, is essentially the 'law of obligations', as Baker puts it, one that 'governs those expectations of good faith which arise out of particular transactions between individual persons'.[29] This is exactly the issue in many spousal cases surviving from Tudor and Stuart times. Baker goes on to explain that this type of obligation could be dealt with either in terms of 'the right to performance of the contract or of the wrong of breaking the contract and thereby causing loss'. Helena's performance and validation of a conditional contract in the shape of Bertram's letter, and Diana's sueing Bertram for denying marital obligation dramatize these two complementary processes. The demarcation of the spheres of common law and canon law, thus, is among the several polarities that the play breaks down, in representing overlapping spheres of social experience.

When Diana expresses her misgivings about the 'unsealed' nature of a verbal promise, Bertram's reply supplies the possible nature of the deed that can seal it—

> Change it, change it.
> Be not so holy-cruel . . .
> Stand no more off,
> But give thyself unto my sick desires.
>   (4.2.32-6)

It is the act of sex, tacitly agreed upon thereafter, that Diana refers to when she talks of the need to 'token to the future our past deeds' (64). It is this, again, that Helena has in mind when she anticipates the 'lawful deed' planned for the night.

The marriage contract in Renaissance England can be seen as having consisted of a word component—the expression of present and mutual consent, and a deed component—the physical act of consummation. Like the written document in contract law, then, sexual intercourse is, potentially, what will clinch the private and unwitnessed agreement between Bertram and Diana as well as provide the evidence which Diana cynically suggests will be needed; it will draw his unsealed words into a legal 'deed' and ratify the verbal contract of espousal by performance.

The identification of the promissory and sexual components of a spousal pact with the verbal and the performative respectively, and of these, in turn, with the initial and legalizing aspects of a contract, was an element in the contemporary perception of the legality of marriage. This comes across in such court records as Matilde Price's personal response in the case of *Price v. Price* discussed earlier:[30] 'necque habuit carnalem copulam cum dicto Henrico, nec quia ex parte sua necque ratificauit hoc matrimonium re aut verbo . . .' [(she) neither had carnal copulation with the said Henry, nor on her part ratified this marriage by word or fact]. This is a case where the validation of an unsolemnized precontract and the invalidation of a solemnized marriage turn on the establishment of the fact of non-consummation in the latter; where *verba* becomes entirely secondary as the dispute in court diverts all attention to the superior ratifying power of *res,* which in this instance is 'carnal copulation'.[31] One of the meanings of the word 'ratify' in the sixteenth century was in fact 'to consummate' (*OED,* sense 3).

The 'deed' that is accomplished in *All's Well* through Diana's intervention, however, ratifies Bertram's earlier conditional contract with Helena, not his present one with Diana. It is the bed-trick in which all three senses of 'deed'—action, sealed contract and copulation—come together. The instrumentality of the subplot for the main plot, and their analogical relation highlight the fact that their distinctness is symptomatic of deeper divisions within the legal action in the main plot. One of the demonstrable instruments of the interlacing of plots is the pair of rings set in circulation by Diana. In serving this function, the rings as tokens of marriage and of intercourse alternate between two configurations in their relation to 'deed'.

While Bertram suggests sex as the seal called for by Diana, Diana demands his ring. This is the first ring to draw the audience's attention. Bertram's giving of it is analogous to a deed or to the signing of a 'deed',

either of which can be a seal on an agreement. This takes us right back to Swinburne's discussion of the role of the verbal formula. It is in asserting the assumed function of words in making a marriage that Swinburne is faced with their potential inadequacy, even treacherousness. He does ultimately hold up the validity of the *de praesenti* formula, but in the very process of confirmation, he has to concede that

> mortal man cannot otherwise judge of Mens meanings, than by their sayings for the Tongue is the Messenger of the heart; and although it sometimes deliver a false message, yet doth the Law accept it for true, when as the Contrary doth not lawfully appear.
>
> (*Spousals,* 87)

As court records show, the contracting parties were the least likely, especially at the moment of spousal, to be verbally precise, and not sure to be conversant with legal formulae; the witnesses were often uneducated and were mostly reliant on memory. Moreover, spousal disputes brought to court frequently involved secret contracts, with no witnesses to testify.

It is in recognition of such inadequacies or unavailability of the 'word' as evidence that Swinburne offers the exchange of rings as a possible solution (*Spousals,* 86). Moreover, he grants the ring a special position among the non-verbal signs that take on a demonstrative or validating function—deserving to be spoken of 'before all other signs' (207).[32] The giving and receiving of a ring was, indeed, one of the commonest gestures invested with special matrimonial significance in the period. The surviving depositions convey a vivid sense of why rings had such a hold on the popular imagination and how the imperatives of certain actual situations harnessed their symbolic importance to a legal one.[33]

Typically, rings assumed the greatest legal significance in settling disputes concerning unwitnessed and unsolemnized contracts, where material proofs were often the only available evidence.[34] In the case of *Thomas Allen v. Alice Howling of Norfolk* (1562), the determining factor is a 'Ring of gould'. In her personal response to Thomas's claim of matrimonial rights, Alice denies her alleged receipt of this ring 'in the waye of matrimony'. But her attempt at freeing herself is thwarted by John Smith and William Walker, who testify, in almost identical terms, that Thomas gave and Alice accepted the ring as an acknowledged token of present marriage.[35]

The popularly perceived value of ring-giving as a symbolic and integral ceremony in a matrimonial context derived, paradoxically, from its traditional association with solemnized weddings *in facie ecclesiae;* thus it almost lent a semblance of formality to clandestine marriages. The formalizing and mnemonic qualities of the ring come together in George Haydock's deposition about the runaway Sothworth couple of Chester (1565): 'what wordes what spoken betwene the parties, he certenlie cannot declare, biecause he did not marke them well'; what he does remember, though, is that 'gold and silver was put on the boke' and 'a ringe [was] put on her finger'.[36]

In Southern dioceses too, the Puritan challenge does not seem to have revolutionized custom.[37] In the Canterbury case of Wanderton v. Wild (1582), the ring clinches a contract—much in the manner prescribed by the pre-Reformation order of matrimony[38]—and gives a *de futuro* spousal the sanctity of present marriage, at least in the eyes of the deponents. After the parties uttered words of pledge to each other which, predictably, 'he remembreth not', Michael Haell, a witness to the contract, said to them, 'If you receaue any such thing as you pretend conclude the matter as it myght to be done els I will not medle in it.' 'Then the said Wanderton took the said Agnes by the handes', and they uttered what was, roughly, the formula of a *de futuro* contract. 'Then they losed ther handes, and Wanderton gaue her a Ring gelt saying to her take this as a token that you have confessed and I the like to you, you to be my wife and I to be your husband [. . .] and she receaued the same Ring thankfully' (176). Haell's claim is that they are well and truly married.[39] This bears out the popular currency, in some places at least, of the legal provision set out but qualified as being practically unsound by Swinburne— that in spousals *de futuro*, 'When as on[e] and above the words, there is an Accumulation of some Act joyned therewithal . . . For example: . . . the Man delivereth to the Woman a Ring, . . . hereby the Contract is presumed Matrimonial' (*Spousals*, 71). The delivery of a ring here has the status of an act or deed.

This is the function made to serve by Bertram's 'subarration' to Diana, which, in conjunction with his words, would technically count as a promise of marriage:

> Here, take my ring.
> My house, mine honour, yea my life be
>   thine,
> And I'll be bid by thee.
>
> (4.5.52-4)

We have, here, not only an evocation of the familiar situation of a private contract, and its characteristic method of establishing a formal context, but also the associated possibility of later dispute already present in the inception.

What Diana engineers, however, is an exchange of rings. This accords an altogether more complex set of values to the rings by the time they resurface together at the end, to constitute the comic and legal resolu-

tions. While the course of Bertram's ring gets deflected from its original path through the introduction of Diana, a new ring is imported by her dark promise to Bertram:

> And on your finger in the night I'll put
> Another ring that, what in time proceeds,
> May token to the future our past deeds.
>
> (4.2.62-4)

In its promised exchange with the first ring, it has already become associated with Diana's virginity— 'Mine honour's such a ring. / My chastity's the jewel of our house' (4.2.46-7). This is the jewel Diana pledges in return for Bertram's family jewel. In deed, though, it is Helena's chastity that is going to be its operative but invisible counterpart. The bawdy sense is reinforced by the verbal echo of Bertram's letter to Helena which posited, by linguistic juxtaposition, a cause-and-effect relationship between getting the 'ring upon [his] finger' and showing 'a child begotten of [her] body' (3.2.57-9).

Bertram's language is deliberately rendered ambiguous by Shakespeare to suggest an unmistakeable sexual meaning; 'the ring . . . which never shall come off' (3.2.57-8), with its multiple suggestion of a spousal ring with its eternal associations, Bertram's heirloom and the yet uncracked ring of Helena's virginity. It was, in Painter, far more clearly and singly the specific ornament belonging to Beltramo: 'I do purpose to dwell with her, when she shal have this ring (meaning a ring which he wore) vpon her finger, and a sonne in her armes begotten by mee.'[40] The change from 'her finger' to 'my finger' and from 'this ring' to 'the ring . . . which never shall come off' not only permits but invites a sexualized reading, and strengthens the syntactical link between the two conditions. It is this metaphorical connection that is taken up by Helena and literalized during the bed-trick.

The literal and bawdy meanings of 'ring' in Bertram's statement of his first condition are, however, taken apart and met separately, even as Helena's agency is divided between herself and Diana. Thus, the actual ring on Bertram's finger that Helena has to get in spite of his resolution that it 'never shall come off' (3.2.58) has already been obtained by Diana. But while its procurement was meant to be a proof of Helena's cohabitation with Bertram, it becomes an alleged token of his marriage to Diana in the scene of arbitration, and a confessed token of his supposed sexual deeds with her. Meanwhile, Helena's pregnancy takes on the role of signifying his actual 'deed' with Helena. This splitting of functions foregrounds the separation between the woman Bertram thinks he sleeps with, and the woman he actually penetrates. His ring gets reconnected with Helena's conception only at the very end, a connection that is explicitly underlined by Helena's words:

There is your ring.
And, look you, here's your letter. This it
   says:
'When from my finger you can get this ring,
And are by me with child', et cetera. This is
   done.

                              (5.3.312-15)

This is at once a realization and restatement of the implied connection between ring and sex in Bertram's letter, and a reuniting of divided agencies in the figure of Helena—a covering up of the many divisions through which her husband has had to be 'doubly won'.

Meanwhile, the second ring, the actual jewel that Helena has put on Bertram's finger 'in the night', spotted by Lafew as Helena's and by the king as his own gift to her, is defined ultimately as a proof that Bertram 'husbanded [Helena's] bed at Florence', since it is clear that 'this ring was . . . hers' (5.3.126-7). Part of the *raison-d'être* of this ring is its necessary role of providing additional support for Helena's claim of Bertram's paternity of her yet unborn child. Without this token of intercourse between Helena and Bertram, it would be less clear that Helena's conception followed from Bertram's night of pleasure in Florence.

Thus, if the first ring was initially analogous to the action or 'deed' that seals an oral contract, its later use as a sign of Bertram's supposed activities with Diana, and the use of the other ring as a seal and token of his actual congress with Helena, point to yet another relation between ring and deed in the play. 'Deeds', as what the rings, with their spousal and sexual associations, will help make evident, becomes clearly the act or acts of sex. Originally posited as a more reliable expression of intention than words, 'deeds' have now themselves become something to be proved; they, no less than words, are signs to be interpreted.

The special position given to rings by Swinburne and their centrality in the popular perception of marital obligations are borne out by their importance in the final episode. A scene of reconciliation and spousal negotiation quickly darkens into one of arraignment, as the 'amorous token for fair Maudlin' (5.3.69) is recognized by the king as the 'token' by which he would have relieved Helena, and as Bertram stakes all on it:

            If you shall prove
This ring was ever hers, you shall as easy
Prove that I husbanded her bed in Florence
                              (125-7)

The trial structure of this scene is officially established upon the delivery of Diana's letter. Stating with legal precision her claim of marriage, and clearly setting out the charge against Bertram, this letter takes the place of a libel which is defined by Henry Consett as 'a Writing which containeth the action' in his account of the practice of the church courts in Renaissance England.[41] Here, of course, the court is presided over by the king, instead of a doctor of law, but the royal presence itself is another factor which defines the legality of the space in the disclosure scene.[42] Diana's very phrasing—'and a poor maid is undone' (141-8)—evokes the ambience of the sex-related litigation of the church courts—recalling numerous pleas by women claiming to be used, deceived or abandoned. The legal situation gets wholly formalized with the king's declaration of his suspicion and the countess's call for 'justice' (152-6).

In this set-up, the rings become the *exhibita* or material objects produced in court to support allegations. Diana's presentation of the first ring—the one given her by Bertram—is clearly accorded a higher truth value than other forms of evidence such as witness testimony. When Bertram casts aspersions on Parolles's personal credibility, the king points out, 'She hath that ring of yours' (212).

The terms in which the characters respond to the rings suggest at least one of the reasons behind their evidentiary impact. The entire drama around the first ring starts when it catches the king's eye—'for mine eye, / While I was speaking, oft was fastened to 't' (82-3). Bertram's denial that it ever was Helena's is met with the Countess's assertion, 'Son, on my life / I have seen her wear it' and is corroborated by Lafew's 'I am sure I saw her wear it' (90-2). One remembers depositions like Christabell Andro's, who recounts the contract between William Headley and Agnes Smith, as well as registers its reality entirely in terms of images—'she . . . *sawe* the parties contract and gyve ther faith and trewth to gither . . . ; and the said William gave the said Agnes one pair of glowes and a bowed grote, and she gave unto . . . William one gold ring'.[43]

It is the impact of 'ocular proof' that Diana exploits when she presents this ring dramatically in court—' . . . O behold this ring' (5.3.194). The Countess immediately notes, 'he blushes and 'tis hit' (198). But Diana has hit the mark in more senses than one. Everyone else in the assembly reacts as much as Bertram does, and the Countess declares at this point, 'That ring's a thousand proofs.' (202) As Swinburne puts it, 'Not to be, and not to appear, is all one in Construction of Law' (*Spousals,* 181). The function of proof, therefore is to make the truth apparent or visible. *Enargáeia* was defined by Aristotle as an exercise which represents an object before the eyes of the viewers, and the Latin word for *enargaeia,* suggestively, is *evidentia.*[44]

Significantly, however, most of the deponents one encounters do not—and cannot—actually reproduce the incident or the facts they are seeking to ascertain. Rather, they attempt to narrate them vividly. Evidence, thus, involves an exercise in re-presentation and hence, inevitably, a metonymic relation between the truth sought to be proved, and the sign that is meant to evoke it. Even exhibits—be they letters, handkerchiefs, deeds or rings—are legal tokens. The way they make things evident is by symbolically or associatively evoking an entire situation before the eyes of the judge. The necessary translocation involved in evidentiary practice is dictated by the fact that the action or the intention to be proved cannot literally be shown in court, and yet has to be somehow made apparent. The inadequacies and ambiguities of this process gain a specially concise focus in the context of marriage law in which the crucial events and factors to be established were usually private acts and utterances, and very often the specific act of sex. *All's Well*'s dramatization of this area of law highlights a condition common to the theatre and the church courts. Both are faced with the task of often having to represent and legislate a realm removed from the public space of the stage or the court. Both, therefore, have to devise their own enargaeic modes to show what must necessarily be absent from this space but what is, at the same time, central to their motives of representation. The ring, here, inscribes this phenomenon, by virtue of its metaphoric valencies and its role as a 'monumental' token (4.3.18). Legally as well as theatrically it bodies forth what must lie outside the limits of representation.

This is part of the larger problem of an uneasy relation between intentionality and legal truths revealed by adventitious proofs. When the king confronts Bertram with the evident truth that Diana 'hath that ring of [his]', what Bertram denies in self-defence is not the fact that he gave it to her, nor indeed the implied fact of intercourse, but the matrimonial intention that is assumed and alleged to have informed both these acts (5.3.213-22). Exactly this argument is given by many defendants in debates over love tokens, especially rings, in disputed contract suits from the period. Alice Cotton of Canterbury says she received Thomas Baxter's gifts as 'mere gift' and not 'in . . . waie of marriage' (1574).[45] What comes closest to Bertram's disclaimer is perhaps John Smith's distinction between the use of tokens for a sexual contract and for a marital one in his personal response against Christian Grimsdiche's libel in a Chester trothplight case of 1562: 'beynge askid, for what intent' he gave her tokens, 'he sais, because he had, and wold have, to do with her, & knew her Carnally; & not for that he wold mary her'.[46] Such disputes highlight the difficulty of assessing the intention of the giver through the perception of the receiver and of others. From their position of privilege over the spectators or the judge at a law court, a theatre audience would have seen enough of Bertram and heard enough from him by the time he is brought to trial, to be clearly struck by the fallacy of a 'reasonable inference' of 'Wedlock' from the fact of Diana's possession of his ring.

The 'second' ring—the one that has travelled from the king to Bertram via Helena and Diana respectively, to surface in court as a proposed gift for Maudlin—turns out to be no less dubious a proof of intercourse and identity than the first ring is of spousal subarration. It is, of course, established that this ring was Helena's at one time, something that Bertram was confident could never be proved; but law's natural conclusion from this contingency, that Bertram 'husbanded her bed in Florence', completely eschews the question of intention in applying the formula for a valid marriage. Bertram thinks he sleeps with Diana, and if that act is to seal any marriage, it is his with her—as indeed it legally would—since the 'news' of Helena's death, arriving before the bed-trick, has met the stipulation of Bertram's *de futuro* spousal to Diana (4.2.72-3). The fact that he is 'quit' (5.3.301) is due to an arbitrary separation of fact and meant truth in the 'deed of darkness' in Florence.

The connection between this legal fiction and evidentiary law's reliance on what is visible is something Swinburne's *Spousals* is aware of: 'for proof is not of the Essence of Matrimony' (*Spousals*, 87).[47] But 'although . . . he which is the searcher of the heart doth well know their deceit and defect of mutual Consent', yet the 'judgement of Mortal man' must pronounce them married since 'the contrary doth not lawfully appear' (85). Hence such paradoxes as 'this deceit so lawful' 'Where both not sin, and yet a sinful fact' (*All's Well*, 3.7.38, 47). Hence, too, the irony that though 'not bedding but consent makes marriages' (*Matrimony*, 120), it is the bedding that, in this instance, proves it. The darkness and the silence that are the conditions for the bed-trick come to stand for the limits to the vision of the mortal judge, for what cannot be made evident either visually or by narration in a temporal court of law. Bertram's conditional pledge of love—'If she, my liege, can make me know this clearly'—touches precisely on the discomfort surrounding the knowledge law brings, but it is immediately forestalled by Helena's assertion—'If it *appear* not plain and *prove* untrue . . . ' (*All's Well*, 5.3.317-19). Helena's answer, in collapsing the gap between cognition and legal certification, articulates the rules that operate in the world of the play, as in law.

The Swinburnian unease around error and the inadequacy of law to accommodate its moral implications lies at the core of the bed-trick. In *Matrimony*, he states clearly and unproblematically that marriage contracted by those who 'doe not consent . . . for that they be . . . seduced by Error mistaking one person for another' 'is of no moment or effect in Lawe' since matrimony must be a 'coniunction of . . . myndes' (121-2). But where the issue is not mere definition but ascertainment of status in the case of a complex human situation, law and its agents have to face a dilemma. Thus, the bed-trick cannot be 'lawful meaning in a lawful act', since the act is joint, and involves two meanings.[48]

The bed-trick is a fictional situation that singles out a potential for fiction in law itself, by which the difference between the singleness of fact and the plurality of truth is collapsed, and a status is presumed. Its likeness to a legal fiction is highlighted by the mendacious means it adopts to achieve an ostensibly ethical end. It is no surprise that Helena, law's most self-aware user, should embody some of the dualities that the play's movement, largely through her energies, seeks to harmonize. To claim the honour that is hers, she has to 'steal' it surreptitiously (2.5.81) by becoming, as it were, a 'girl' of Italy, to make Bertram 'captive' to her service (2.1.21-2). The law trick that is the specific instrument of Helena's design turns on a logic familiar to a Renaissance English audience, but it acquires a specific status by being used in the context of subtle and strategic double-dealing by the heroine at her most 'Machiavellian' in the very land of plots and policies.[49]

But Helena's Italianate plotting does not ultimately create a simply negative sense of unsavoury cunning; nor is law reduced to a sceptic's quarry. Her character is in many senses Machiavellian in a positive way, and, paradoxically, her use of law and its particular literary location, even while they demystify law, result in a configuring of it as a peculiarly human and contingent measure. Her very first soliloquy (1.1.78-97) signals a transition in her attitude to fate, from passive resignation to a belief in the space it allows for individual enterprise—'The fated sky gives us free scope.' The only hindrance to exploiting such 'scope'—a concept akin to Machiavelli's *occasione*[50]—is our 'slow designs'. Her tough-minded confidence in possibilities and the expedient and inventive effort with which she sets about to achieve these brings her in line with the prudent protagonists—often heroines—of the *novellae,* whose *industria* is usually their main capital.[51]

The dual associations gathered by law in the course of the play lend the ending its distinctively mixed flavour. After the rapid escalation of legal dangers and implications in the final scene, Helena's spectacular entry must seem a relief in the immediate context, indeed some sort of a salvation. Back in Rossillion, Helena has shed her Italian character, and apparently displaces the world of sexual intrigue and precise legal wrangles as she steps into Diana's place to take over the limelight. She is not to be seen as one of those 'clamorous and impudent' women litigants that the likes of Lord Keeper Egerton and Chancery counsel Anthony Benn were, at the time, denouncing and attempting to keep out of the courts.[52] As in the bed-trick, so here, the status of an event is transformed by the replacement of one woman by the other: the lustful defiling of the

'pitchy night' and its legal and obligatory consequences are taken on by the Bertram-Diana sub-plot, while the central relationship of the play is strategically cleansed of its more degrading associations, and prepared for the 'renown' of the 'end'.

The moment that registers this change is when Helena and Bertram are brought to face each other for the first time in the scene, through Bertram's voluntary interposition. In response to the king's wonder at what seems to him an apparition—'Is't real that I see?'—Helena says,

> No, my good lord,
> 'Tis but the shadow of a wife you see,
> The name and not the thing.
>
> (5.3.308-10)

Even as the teasing, paradoxical mode of speech gets sublimated here into a medium that brings romance to the verge of anagnorisis, Bertram remonstrates, 'Both, both. O, pardon!' (310). If the bed-trick was the symbolic moment of the split between meaning and action, 'the name' and 'the thing', the present exchange between Bertram and Helena marks, no matter how fleetingly, the healing of these divisions in an act of forgiveness. An appropriate atmosphere is provided by Helena's self-presentation, aided by Diana, which creates an aura of miracle heightened by the regenerative associations of pregnancy. This sense of the wondrous is the main constituent of the romance mode which acts here as an equivalent of the social rituals that transform marriage from a contract into a mystery.

Yet the transition is not seamless. Even while status is attained, the contractual basis of marriage is not let out of sight. The particular instrument for sustaining this awareness is the continued and insistent mooring of the scene in the details of marriage law. Helena's achievement is to have foiled Bertram's attempt at seeking a divorce by establishing the fact of cohabitation: this is the specific significance of her staking 'deadly divorce' on the indisputability of the proofs of having met his terms (320). Thus, in the indistinct but comprehensive area covered between the two, both the marriage and the divorce paradigms behind their 'legal' actions get taken up and pursued till the end of the play where, finally, they are tied together.

Sex having been in *All's Well* the very site of a radical absence of volition, its centrality to the sacramental notion of indissoluble matrimony, which ostensibly contributes to the magic of the final reunion, extends the paradox of the earlier action. Swinburne's explanation of why 'Marriage is that great Mystery' is germane to what the pregnant wife's appearance relies on for its 'miraculous' impact: 'By Marriage the Man and the Woman are made one Flesh, so they are not by Spousals.' it is in the absence of such a union that he declares 'Spousals' to be 'utterly destitute of . . . mystical effect: And . . . Marriage is greater than Spousals . . .' (*Spousals,* 16). In *All's Well,* 'making one flesh' is in a sense what turns a spousal into matrimony, but the mystery around the incorporation of man and wife is at least partly replaced by consummation as an instrument of law and custom.

As the external symbol and visible outcome of this incorporation, Helena's pregnancy plays a crucial role in foregrounding the contractual basis of the revalidated union. While its procreational and promissory implications introduce a sense of romance quickenings, the function it serves in the resolution of the plot is legal. It is framed as an 'ocular proof' of the sexual consummation stipulated in Bertram's letter: 'one that's dead is quick— / And now behold the meaning!' (5.3.305-6).[53] This is in many senses a scene of remarriage—a familiar scenario, where the fact of intercourse acts as the single validating seal that at once proves and forms matrimony. Bridal pregnancy by itself was common enough in Elizabethan England;[54] and though prenuptial fornication was a punishable offence, in practice, judicial attitudes to it varied according to local custom, and were often quite tolerant where honourable intentions were clear or marriage had already followed.[55] But the remarriage in *All's Well* takes place not in church but in a virtual court. The visual resonances of a pregnant woman turning up in open court would evoke associations of incontinence and fornication—charges often spurred by illicit pregnancy. 'Pregnancies', Ralph Houlbrooke asserts, 'always figured prominently among the presentments made'; and, as he further puts it, 'rather more women than men were normally presented, because a pregnant woman was bound to be more conspicuous than her partner'.[56] As far as Bertram's conscious intention defines the deed that Helena's pregnancy proceeds from, the result is indeed symptomatic of the typical situation; only, it is transformed here by Helena's intention and her triumphant use of 'occasion'. What lends the legal connection of the scene its specific dubiousness is the combination of the marital and the evidentiary purposes behind Helena's action. As often in disputed suits of this kind, what is still at stake, implicitly, is Bertram's agency in the conception. In Shakespeare's time, determination of paternal identity was a troubling legal issue.[57] We have Swinburne's own pronouncement on the matter, in his discussion of why 'wedlock [is] called Matrimonye rather than Patrimonye': 'the mother is alwaies more certein than the father and truthe is stronger than opinion' (*Matrimony,* 118).

It is interesting to note one of Shakespeare's modifications of this source story. In Painter—as in Boccaccio—Giletta was 'brought a bedde of twoo sonnes, which were very like vnto their father . . .'. She enters Beltramo's banquet not pregnant but with these two, their resemblance to their father being pos-

ited and accepted as manifest evidence of paternity, strengthening the implication of her possession of his ring: 'for beholde, here in myne armes, not onely one sonne begotten by thee, but twayne, and likewise thy Ryng. . . . the Counte hearing this, was greatly astonned, and knewe the Ryng, and the children also, they were so like hym.'[58] If Shakespeare had left this episode unchanged, he would still have had the opportunity to evoke legal associations, for facial similarity has been known to have been a factor in establishing the father's identity in church courts.[59] But pregnancy as a presence in court was potentially more scandalous because there was an unavoidable uncertainty surrounding paternity and, by implication, a potential for the use of pregnancy for manipulation. It was not unknown for women to claim marital rights by offering their conception as proof of cohabitation. The motives could be various—as Martin Ingram puts it, women resorting to law to pressurize men into marriage could be 'naive, scheming, or . . . desperate'.[60] Among them, pregnant women not only had a stronger incentive but were 'in a better moral position to attempt coercion' than others.[61] They were also likely to receive local backing, not least owing to a concern about the threat of bastardy to the poor rates.[62] In the Salisbury case of Diar *v.* Rogers (1609), Henry Rogers is said to have promised that 'yf he did beget the said Alice with childe, that he would marry with her'. The witnesses for the manifestly pregnant plaintiff Alice Diar keep harping on the obligation that her conception has placed him under; as Alice Tante (?) puts it, it is 'in the respect of the said Henry Roger's faythfull promise [that] the said Alice offered her selffe to be begotten with child by . . . Henry'.[63] Even unconfirmed claims of pregnancy could create enormous pressure and a climate of opinion hard to cope with.[64] Not only can such a situation, irrespective of the truth or spirit of the alleged promise, be conducive to enforcement; the pressures incumbent on the defendant of such a suit are even known to have tempted women to have 'deliberately sought to become pregnant to induce the man to marry her'.[65] Such is the lingering sense of uncertainty that Bertram articulates, when he takes a faltering step back from his spontaneous 'Both, both. O pardon!' to qualify his acceptance of the situation:

> If she, my liege, can make me know this clearly
> I'll love her dearly, ever ever dearly.
>
> (5.3.317-18)

In a play where comic law operates through actual legal means, and recognition is arrived at through a trial, the incertitude surrounding the legal knowledge undercuts the absolute nature of the anagnoristic moment. This marriage, for all that the providential emplotment of Helena's 'course' suggests, is made not in heaven but in the bawdy court. Where the king is overwhelmed into a typical romance reaction (307—

9), the audience would be aware that the inevitable outcome of the discovery has as much to do with legal logic, by which the church court arbiter would probably order Bertram to take her back and live with her as married people should.[66]

As ever, though, it is in the figure of Helena, the employer of the legal tricks for the 'miraculous' ending, that the comic energy of the play as well as its use of law acquires a more complex status than mere stratagem can lay claim to. In her, policy and genuineness, simulation and sincerity, power and powerlessness have been inextricably compounded from the very beginning: 'I do affect a sorrow indeed, but I have it too' (1.1.51). It is this spirit that she infuses into the final scene. When she appears in court, big with child, her condition—betokening the triumph of her initiative—becomes a means for the strategic adoption of a traditional image of the obedient wife whose pleasure lies in being acted upon by her husband, a calculated evocation of domestic sanctities, so 'that man [can] be at woman's command, and yet no hurt done!'[67] Yet, as with the women 'who', in the words of *The lawes resolutions of women's rights* (1632), could 'shift it well enough' in the legal world of early modern England,[68] this is not simply a camouflaging of Helena's agency. It is also a pointer to her real vulnerability and, in an odd sense, passivity in the emotional transaction contained in the quasi-legal one. When she says, 'O, my good lord, when I was like this maid / I found you wondrous kind', her utterance is a gentle reminder to us that her active plotting has had to be executed through a virtual loss of identity in the act of sex; its humour lies in her acknowledged sexual enjoyment of even this imperfect emotional experience (5.3.311-12). As far as she is concerned, the seamier aspects of what has passed are not simplemindedly forgotten but deliberately put behind: 'This is done', she says, after curtailing her recitation of Bertram's conditional letter with a significant 'et cetera' (315). Peter Hall's 1992 production, appropriately, made Helena tear up the letter—which is also the contract—as she spoke these words.

Through her, then, law is finally felt to acquire a more positive value than merely being a sceptical alternative to either the *vera philosophia* or the perfect science that it was considered to be in some of the most prominent humanist traditions of jurisprudence. It emerges, rather, as an art of the probable, that involves prudence rather than wisdom—a perspective that was actually emerging in the Renaissance, questioning the more idealistic view of law.[69] Law is not in itself a transformative principle, but a pragmatic means of working through the essentially contingent human condition towards achievements that are necessarily provisional. It is for the individual to renounce and go beyond the legal devices to build on the possibilities made available to her by them. Over and above the obvious irony of the play's title, there is a sense in which it is felt to encapsulate the peculiar and hard-bought wisdom of the play. All one can begin with, in a sense, is this 'end'. This is not a romance, like *Pericles* or *The Winter's Tale,* where the children have been born and the regeneration has visibly begun. Helena's pregnancy, among its other expressive functions, suggests the play's projecting of fulfilments in the future. To take up the possibilities afforded by legal means is what the function of romance is posited as. Nor need the value of law necessarily lie in the discovery or assertion of certitudes; probability itself can be its gift to the human condition, and indeed a positive step towards knowledge. The king's words, as he accepts Helena's offer of her improbable 'medical' services, capture a perspective which the play ultimately invites the audience to accommodate:

Notes

[1] Though I use the Oxford Shakespeare, I retain the traditional name for the heroine. I should like to thank Ben Griffin for assistance with references.

[2] Henry Swinburne, *A Treatise of Spousals, or Matrimonial Contracts,* ed. Randolph Trumbach (London, 1985) (hereafter, *Spousals*).

[3] For influential examples of the critical opinion that Bertram's resistance is a legal escape route, see M. L. Ranald, 'The Betrothals of *All's Well That Ends Well*', *Huntington Library Quarterly,* 26 (1962-3), 179-92; p. 186, and Howard Cole, *The 'All's Well' Story From Boccaccio to Shakespeare* (Urbana, 1981) (hereafter, Cole), passim. Enforcement could be a ground for nullification, but only if it was raised by a party in court; Bertram's failure to do so at the relevant moment suggests the impracticality of this provision in a situation of authority and dependence. The one technically permissible objection a ward could raise—that against disparagement—is brought up by him but not sustained. On wardship, see Joel Hurstfield, *The Queen's Wards: Wardship and Marriage under Elizabeth I* (London, 1958).

[4] See Madeleine Doran, *Endeavors of Art: A Study of Form in Elizabethan Drama* (Madison, 1954), pp. 251-2, and W. W. Lawrence, *Shakespeare's Problem Comedies* (New York, 1960), pp. 32-77.

[5] Durham University Library, Palace Green, Mickleton and Spearman Manuscript 4, fol. 115-24. I am indebted to Sheila Doyle of the Durham University Law Library for drawing my attention to this manuscript volume.

[6] *The Book of Common Prayer 1559: The Elizabethan Prayer Book,* ed. by John E. Booty (Charlottesville, 1976), p. 297. Though, by this time, both the reformers and the bishops were clear that scripture did not

provide sanction for the sacramental status of marriage, its desacramentalization remained largely a matter of theological definition in England. To prevent it from being divested of dignity and solemnity in popular perception—an effect that was distinctly possible, and would threaten exactly the regularization sought by the reformers—the service was made to stress that marriage was a 'holy ordinance', and further, was coupled with the receiving of Holy Communion, at the same time as the sacramental language and claim were dropped. This was enough to preserve the sacramental sanctity of marriage for the common people, who did not pause to work out the technical distinctions of the reformers. See Eric Joseph Carlson, *Marriage and the English Reformation* (Oxford, 1994) (hereafter, Carlson), pp. 36-49.

[7] On church courts, see Ralph Houlbrooke, *Church Courts and the People during the English Reformation 1520-1570* (Oxford, 1979) (hereafter, Houlbrooke). For accounts focusing on marriage litigation, see Martin Ingram, *Church Courts, Sex and Marriage in England 1570-1640* (Cambridge, 1987) (hereafter, Ingram); R. H. Helmholz, *Marriage Litigation in Medieval England* (Cambridge, 1974) (hereafter Helmholz); and Carlson, pp. 142-180.

[8] See, for example, Helmholz, p. 27; Martin Ingram, 'Spousal Litigation in the English Ecclesiastical Courts, c. 1350-1640' in R. B. Outhwaite, ed., *Marriage and Society: Studies in the Social History of Marriage* (London, 1981) (hereafter, Ingram, 'Spousal'), pp. 35-57; pp. 37, 45; *Spousals,* p. 14.

[9] See G. E. Howard, *The History of Matrimonial Institutions chiefly in England and the United States* (Chicago, 1904), 3 vols., vol. 1, p. 339. The interplay of attitudes to Claudio and Juliet's sexual involvement in *Measure for Measure* turns exactly on this duality. For an incisive exposition of this point, see A. D. Nuttall's '*Measure for Measure:* The bed-trick' in Nuttall, *The Stoic in Love* (London, 1989), pp. 41-8.

[10] See James A. Brundage, *Law, Sex and Christian Society in Medieval Europe* (Chicago, 1987), pp. 551-74.

[11] See *Spousals,* pp. 21, 36-41; Sir Edward Coke, *The First Institute of the Lawes of England* (London, 1628), section 104.

[12] James Raine, *Depositions and other Ecclesiastical Proceedings from the Courts of Durham, extending from 1311 to the Reign of Elizabeth* (London, 1845) (hereafter, Raine), pp. 218-26.

[13] See J. O. Halliwell, ed., *The Autobiography and Correspondence of Sir Simonds D'Ewes* (London, 1845), vol. 1, pp. 87-9.

[14] See James A. Coriden, *The Indissolubility Added to Christian Marriage by Consummation: A Historical Study from the End of the Patristic Period to the Death of Pope Innocent III* (Rome, 1961), pp. 7-23.

[15] J. T. Noonan, *Power to Dissolve: Lawyers and Marriages in the Courts of the Roman Curia* (Cambridge, Massachusetts, 1972), p. 80.

[16] For Swinburne's reference to the marriage of Mary and Joseph as the authority behind the notion that 'carnall knowledge' is not essential for 'perfect matrimony', see *Matrimony,* p. 120.

[17] Raine, pp. 322-6.

[18] Furnivall, *Child-Marriages, Divorces, and Ratifications, &c. In the Diocese of Chester, A.D. 1561-6* (London, 1897) (hereafter, Furnivall), p. 58.

[19] See, for example, the 1623 case against John Cocke of Tillington and his wife, cited in P. Hair, ed., *Before the Bawdy Court: Selections from church courts and other records relating to the correction of moral offences in England, Scotland and New England, 1300-1800* (London, 1972) (hereafter, Hair), p. 107, or the Yorkshire presentment cited in n. 21 below.

[20] See E. D. Stone and B. Cozens-Hardy, eds., *Norwich Consistory Court Depositions 1499-1512 and 1518-1530,* Norfolk Record Society 10 (1938) (hereafter, Stone and Cozens-Hardy), no. 90.

[21] See T. M. Fallow, 'Some Elizabethan Visitations of the Churches belonging to the Peculiar of the Dean of York', *Yorkshire Archaeological Journal,* 18 (1905), 197-232.

[22] Furnivall, pp. 76-9.

[23] See also *Spousals,* p. 225.

[24] See Joseph Jacobs, ed., *The Palace of Pleasure: Elizabethan Versions of Italian and French Novels From Boccaccio, Bandello, Cinthio, Straparola, Queen Margaret of Navarre, And Others, Done into English by William Painter* (New York, 1966) (hereafter, Painter), 'The thirty-Eight Nouell'—Shakespeare's immediate source for the story of *All's Well.*

[25] Baker, p. 360. See also pp. 361 and 375.

[26] Ibid., p. 362.

[27] See S. F. C. Milsom, *Historical Foundations of the Common Law* (London, 1983), pp. 88-90 and 289.

[28] Ingram, 'Spousal', p. 52. On the reciprocal influence between common law, and canon law as prac-

tised in the church courts, see R. H. Helmholz, *Canon Law and English Common Law,* Selden Society Lecture, 1982 (London, 1983), esp. pp. 15-19.

[29] Baker, p. 360.

[30] See p. 186 above.

[31] Cp. Humphrey Winstanley *v.* Alice Worsley, a 1561 divorce suit from Chester, Furnivall, pp. 2-4.

[32] See also *Spousals,* pp. 71, 101, 206-12.

[33] On the various symbolisms of the ring, see *Spousals* pp. 207-9; A. H. Bullen, *An English Garner: Some Shorter Elizabethan Poems* (Westminster, 1903), p. 296, posy no. 15; J. E. Cirlot, *A Dictionary of Symbols and Imagery,* tr. J. Sage (London, 1971), p. 273; G. F. Kunz, *Rings for the Finger* (Philadelphia, 1917), pp. 193-248; Shirley Bury, *An Introduction to Rings* (London, 1948), pp. 15-17; Stith Thompson, *Motif-Index of Folk Literature* (Copenhagen, 1958), vol. 6, pp. 650-1.

[34] See Houlbrooke, 58, esp. n. 14; Peter Rushton, 'The Testaments of Gifts: Marriage Tokens and Disputed Contracts in North-East England, 1560-1630', *Folk Life* 24 (1985-6), 25-31. See also *Spousals,* Sections XII-XV.

[35] Norfolk and Norwich Record Office diocesan records (hereafter, NNRO), DN/DEP (deposition books of the consistory court) 9, bk. 8, 158v, 162-3v; DN/ACT (Act books) 9, bk 10.

[36] Furnivall, pp. 65-6.

[37] For attacks on the ring in Puritan writing, see Anthony Gilby, *A Pleasaunte dialogue, Betweene a Souldier of Barwicke, and an English Chaplaine* (Middleburg, 1581), M5r; Dudley Fenner, *Certain Learned and Godly Treatises* (Edinburgh, 1952), p. 96; Andrew Kingsmill, *A View of Mans Estate* (London, 1576), sig. K2r. Also, Donald McGinn, *The Admonition Controversy* (New Brunswick, 1949), pp. 218-19; Richard L. Greaves, *Society and Religion in Elizabethan England* (Minneapolis, 1981), pp. 184-5.

[38] *The Sarum Missal,* tr. A. H. Pearson (London, 1844), p. 552. See also 'The Form of Solemnization of Matrimony' as given in *The Book of Common Prayer,* pp. 290-3.

[39] Canterbury Cathedral Archives (hereafter, CCA), X.10.20, 173-6.

[40] Painter, p. 174.

[41] Henry Consett, *The Practice of the Spiritual or Ecclesiastical Courts* (London, 1685), p. 76.

[42] On the relation between the definition of a 'court' of law and the presence of the monarch, see J. H. Baker, *The Legal Profession and the Common Law* (London, 1986), pp. 153-69.

[43] Raine, pp. 238-40. See also Furnivall, pp. 187-96 (Edmund *v.* Bird) and pp. 65-7 (Sothworth *v.* Sothworth); Raine, p. 243 (Grynwill *v.* Groundye).

[44] *Rhetoric,* 3.11.1, 3.11.4, and 3.10.6, in *The Rhetoric and Poetics of Aristotle,* tr. W. Rhys Roberts and Ingram Bywater, ed. Friedrich Solmsen (New York, 1954). The potential of the image for being an instrument of proof is a well established concept in Aristotle and emerges from a collateral reading of the *De Anima* and *Nichomachean Ethics.* On the provenance of this notion in Renaissance England, see Kathy Eden, *Poetic and Legal Fictions in the Aristotelian Tradition* (Princeton, 1986), pp. 69-111.

[45] CCA, X.10.17, 152V. See also ibid., X.10.12, 182-V.

[46] Furnivall, p. 57.

[47] 'Legal fiction' may be roughly defined as a lie perpetrated with official or institutional authorization, in the interest of the commonweal. On 'legal fiction', see Ian Maclean, *Meaning and Interpretation in the Renaissance: The Case of Law* (Cambridge, 1992) (hereafter, Maclean), pp. 138-42.

[48] On Swinburne's upholding of legal presumption in 'such a favourable matter' as marriage, see *Spousals,* pp. 88, 98, 103 and 149.

[49] On the contemporary English stereotype of Italy, see Roger Ascham's interpolation at the end of the first part of his *Scholemaster* (c. 1570), quoted in Jacob's introduction to Painter, p. xix. See also Thomas Nashe, *The Unfortunate Traveller* in R. B. McKerrow, ed., *The Works of Thomas Nashe* (Oxford, 1958), vol. 11, pp. 301-2.

[50] See Quentin Skinner and Russell Price, ed., *Machiavelli: 'The Prince'* (Cambridge, 1988) (hereafter, *The Prince*), Chap. XXVII for the discussion of Caesar Borgia's prudence and ability (*prudentia* and *virtú*) manifested by his alertness to *occasione,* i.e. his recognition of the right opportunity and his acting upon it. See also Chap. XXI. Also relevant to this discussion is Machiavelli's stress on flexibility and adaptability to a particular circumstance or *fortuna* with all its limitations—see *The Prince.* Chap. XXV, pp. 85-7. This recipe for success is exactly what Helena's compromises are based on. Its link with prudence in Machiavelli, as stated in Chap. XV, is also an element in Helena's personality.

[51] See Cole, chap. II, esp. pp. 19-20, on the honour accorded to human effort, ability, and ingenuity in

Boccaccio. See also Lorna Hutson, 'Fortunate Travelers: Reading for the Plot in Sixteenth-Century England', *Representations,* 41 (1993), 83-103, on the 'transformative virtues' of prudence, enterprise and pursuit of occasion in Italian *novellae* and in Machiavelli, esp. pp. 88-90, 97, 99.

52 See W. Baildon, *Les Reportes del Cases in Camera Stellata 1593-1609* (1849), pp. 39 and 161; Bedfordshire Record Office, L28/46. See also W. R. Prest, 'Law and Women's Rights in Early Modern England', *The Seventeenth Century,* 6 (1991), 169-87; 182.

53 Cp. the function of Juliet's 'plenteous womb' in *Measure for Measure,* which 'expresseth [Claudio's] full tilt and husbandry' to the public gaze (1.4.42-3).

54 See Ingram, pp. 219-23, esp. p. 219.

55 Ibid., 223-6.

56 Houlbrooke, p. 76.

57 See L. A. Montrose, ' "Shaping Fantasies": Figurations of Gender and Power in Elizabethan Culture', *Representations* 1:2, Spring, 1983, 61-94 (72-3). For a historical study of the evolution of embryology, see J. Cole, *Early Theories of Sexual Generation* (Oxford, 1930).

58 Painter, vol. I, pp. 178-9.

59 See NNRO Dep. 4B, 30V; Dep. 5B, 173V; both cited in Houlbrooke, p. 77 (n. 74).

60 Ingram, 'Spousals', p. 47.

61 Ingram, p. 210.

62 Ibid., 210-11. See also G. R. Quaife, *Wanton Wenches and Wayward Wives: Peasants and Illicit Sex in Early Seventeenth-Century England* (London, 1979), pp. 218-20.

63 Salisbury Diocesan Records, deposition books preserved in the Wiltshire Record Office (hereafter, WRO), D1/26, 136V-137V; 140r-141v.

64 See, for instance, J. T. Fowler, ed., *Acts of Chapter of the Collegiate Church of St. Peter and Wilfred, Ripon, 1452-1506,* Surtees Society 64, 1875, p. 31ff.

65 Ingram, p. 225. See, for example, Office v. Rowden, WRO (1612), AS/ABO 11; and Office v. Greene (1621), WRO, AW/ABO 5.

66 See W. Hale Hale, *A series of precedents and proceedings in criminal causes extending from the year 1475 to 1640; extracted from act-books of ecclesias-* tical courts in the diocese of London (1847), p. 44; Stone and Cozens-Hardy, p. 90.

67 *All's Well,* 1.3.90-1.

68 T. E. *The lawes resolution of women's rights; or, the lawes provision for women* (London, 1632), p. 4.

69 On the jurisprudential debate on whether law was a science or an art, the conflicting visions of the status of law, and the argument for law emerging as an 'unphilosophical mixture of the necessary and the contingent in jurisprudence' that was 'in fact superior to that of philosophy', see Maclean, pp. 20-9. See also Donald Kelley, 'Vera Philosophia. The Philosophical Significance of Renaissance Jurisprudence', in *History, Law and the Human Sciences: Medieval and Renaissance Perspectives* (London, 1984), pp. 267-79. On the history of the idea of probability, see Ian Hacking, *The Emergence of Probability: a Philosophical Study of Early Ideas about Probability, Introduction and Statistical Inference* (Cambridge, 1975), and Douglas Lane Patey, *Probability and Literary Form: Philosophic theory and literary practice in the Augustan age* (Cambridge, 1984), esp. pp. 3-74.

> More should I question thee, and more I
>   must,
> Though more to know could not be more to
>   trust:
> From whence thou cam'st, how tended on—
>   but rest
> Unquestioned welcome, and undoubted
>   blessed.—
>
> > (2.1.205-8)

Like a promise, marriage, happy endings to stories and happiness itself, are all, in a sense, absolute and ignorant—like Pascal's wager with God, a leap of faith.

LAW IN THE HISTORIES: PROPERTY AND SUCCESSION

W. F. Bolton (essay date 1988)

SOURCE: "Ricardian Law Reports and *Richard II,*" in *Shakespeare Studies: An Annual Gathering of Research, Criticism, and Reviews,* Vol. XX, 1988, pp. 53-65.

[*In the following essay, Bolton considers the place of property law in* Richard II.]

The events in *Richard II* took place in 1398 and 1399. Just about two centuries later, Shakespeare wrote his play. Two hundred years after that, Shakespeare's editor Edmund Malone surmised that Shakespeare had undergone legal training, for even Malone—a practicing lawyer—needed to "brush up his black-letter law," as he put it, to understand some of Shakespeare's allusions.[1] Now, another two centuries along, we too can best understand some of the allusions in *Richard II* if we look at the old law books. They enable us to place the trial by combat in its correct context, to grasp some other legalisms scattered in the play, and to trace a central legal motif of plot and metaphor.

The black-letter law books included not only the legal documents of Shakespeare's own day, but also the sixteenth-century editions of medieval law reports, called Year Books.[2] The Year Books report proceedings before the King's Bench and the Court of Common Pleas. The manuscript reports were kept from about 1278 until 1535, and published from about 1483. Among those who took an active part in the publication were humanistic publishers like de Worde, Pynson, and Rastell, but none was so active as Totell, he of the *Songs and Sonnets,* who brought out over 225 separate editions between 1553 and 1591. Even so, publication was uneven; the Year Books for the reign of Richard II are still not all published, and in Shakespeare's time they had appeared in print only in Fitzherbert's *Abstracts* (1514) and in Bellewe's notes from them (1585). Yet these medieval law books were of much interest to Renaissance readers: In 1614 Bacon wrote that "As these Reports are more or less perfect, so the Law itself is more or less certain, and indeed better or worse," and even late in the seventeenth century Serjeant Maynard always carried one in his coach, preferring the old reports to any comedy.[3]

In the pleading that the Year Books report, both sides engaged in spontaneous debate at the Bar, trying first this plea and then that, allowed or disallowed by the Court. A plea once formally made by counsel and accepted by the Court, however, was binding on the party that made it, so the serjeants needed a report of what pleas had succeeded with which judges in similar cases. Of course they also needed a permanent record of the parties in the case and the outcome, so two sets of legal register came into being: the official Latin records (Plea Rolls) in unique exemplars, carefully preserving the details of judicial decisions, and the unofficial French reports (Year Books) in many copies, often containing verbatim accounts of courtroom exchanges.

In printed versions or in the widely circulated manuscript copies, the medieval Year Books were known and available in late sixteenth-century London. Yet F. F. Heard, explaining Pistol's *"obsque hoc"* in *2 Henry IV,* V.v.29, held that "in the absence of any explanation of this highly technical term of pleading in all reports and treatises extant in the time of Shake-

speare . . . , he must have obtained a knowledge of it from actual practice," which Phillips cites without comment.[4] A. R. Humphreys, in his Arden edition of the play (1966), says merely that the phrase may be a motto "or a legal tag." But the Year Books show that Heard's view is doubly mistaken, and Humphrey's guess is unnecessary. First, explanation of the plea *absque hoc* was indeed in "reports and treatises extant in the time of Shakespeare"; it appears throughout in the documents of 11-13 Richard II, as such in the records and as *sauns ceo* in the reports, where the meaning and use of the plea are often discussed between Bar and Bench (e.g., 11/55, 11/241) and where Shakespeare could easily have learned about it. Second, Pistol's phrase concludes *nihil est.* The reports show that the legalism does not include those words, so Pistol's phrase is probably not related to the "highly technical" plea after all, but—as Humphreys surmised—to a motto or proverb.[5]

Of the Latin records, the Plea Rolls, the editor of *11 Richard II* emphasizes the distinctive inviolability:

> In general, the records were made up with the utmost care. . . . Anything found to have been wrongly recorded was erased and rewritten, and omissions when discovered were supplied by interlineation. . . . [O]nce the record was enrolled, its contents could not be added to or amended. . . . Serjeant Hill asked for, and, as the record shows, obtained, the entry of a point on the strength of which he claimed judgment for his client. . . . And since the record once made was inviolable, it could be appealed to at a later stage of the proceedings and would be produced and read. In the famous fifteenth-century pictures of the law courts which hang in the Library of the Inner Temple, the clerks are shown holding membranes which . . . appear to be those of the rolls . . . ; possibly they were brought into court in case any demand should be made for oyer of the record.
>
> *(11/xxvi-xxvii)*

An "oyer" is the hearing of a document in court when one party refers to it and the other party "craves oyer" of it. Since the Year Books report the actual court pleadings, they include frequent references to oyer of the record (e.g., 11/78, 11/192), but I do not know of any record that refers to a report.

When Richard uses the legal verb "object" (*OED* s.v. 5[a]) to ask "Cousin of Herford, what dost though object / Against the Duke of Norfolk" (I.i.28-29), Bolingbroke in his reply calls on heaven to "be the record to my speech" (I.i.30), making a metaphor of the legal record; like Serjeant Hill, he wants his plea entered in an inviolable heavenly "Plea Roll" so that it can be read in a subsequent oyer, whether heavenly or not. In much the same way, Richard later asks Northumberland

If thy offences were upon record,
Would it not shame thee, in so fair a troop,
To read a lecture of them? If thou wouldst,
There shouldst thou find one heinous article,
Containing the deposing of a king,
And cracking the strong warrant of an oath,
Mark'd with a blot, damn'd in the book of
   heaven.

(IV.i.230-36)

Ure's note glosses "read a lecture" as "give a public 'reading'" and compares Bolingbroke's words to Mowbray's asseveration "if ever I were traitor, / My name be blotted from the book of life . . ." (I.iii.201-02). But "the book of life" is not "the book of heaven," and the relevant comparison is with Bolingbroke's appeal to heaven in Act I, not Mowbray's. For Richard too is making a metaphor of an oyer of the heavenly legal record.

Richard II abounds in such legal procedures, concepts, and vocabulary, from the question of succession to the throne down to Bolingbroke's image of his exile as an "apprenticehood" under the Statute of Labourers (I.iii.271-74); perhaps, next to *The Merchant of Venice,* it is Shakespeare's most "legal" play. But whereas the *Merchant* is concerned with contract law, a matter on which legislation did not begin to appear until the early fifteenth century, *Richard II* makes central use of property law as it stood in the late fourteenth century. In that way the play takes many of its dominant concerns and language from the past.

Diane Bornstein has argued to the contrary in these pages, holding that "the trial by combat scene in Act I of *Richard II* relates to a contemporary [i.e., Elizabethan] controversy on duels and honor . . ."[6] So, although she refers to one fourteenth-century work as a source for the controversy, the *Arbre des batailles* by Honoré Bonet or Bouvet, she takes most of her references from writings by Shakespeare's contemporaries, not Richard's. In this her interpretation resembles that of Jack Benoit Gohn, who regards the play as a legal brief on royal prerogative composed in response to the problem of succession that developed under Elizabeth I.[7] But it is one thing to say that the play takes history as its subject, as *Richard II* clearly does; it is another to say with Bornstein and Gohn that it uses history to comment on a contemporary issue. By connecting the legal episodes in the play with Elizabethan controversies, moreover, both Bornstein and Gohn overlook its legal metaphors such as Bolingbroke's and Richard's appeals to the celestial "record."

Implicitly criticizing interpretations like Bornstein's and Gohn's, the silk and Shakespearean Owen Hood Phillips has written (pp. 135-36) of

   a "conflict of laws in time and place" involved in the study of Shakespeare's law. If we want to

consider whether Shakespeare's use of legal expressions in the plays is "correct" . . . we must ask what legal system (if any) is appropriate. This will depend on the place and the period in which the action is supposed to be laid. Many legal writers have fallen down on this, by assuming that the law . . . ought to be what English law was in Shakespeare's time.

Clarkson and Warren had long before given an example: in the trial of *Falconbridge v. Falconbridge* before King John, the Bastard's retort "Of no more force to disposses me, sir, / Than was his will to get me" (I.i.132-33) is not in Shakespeare's source, but "correctly states the position of the law of England as it stood at the period portrayed, even though it was no longer the law at the time when he wrote his play," the pivotal legislation being the first Statute of Wills in 1540.[8] In accordance with Phillips's approach, the pre-1540 law, however Shakespeare came to know of it, is the only one that makes proper sense of the lines, because it was the 1540 law that made possible direct disposal of land, or disinheritance of an heir, by a written will.

If we use the late medieval law reports to apply Phillips's approach to the trial by combat in *Richard II,* we can correct some modern views of the trial scenes so prominent in the play. Peter Ure, for example, in his Arden edition, repeatedly turns to Dante's *De monarchia* for evidence about trial by combat, not a very relevant source for Shakespeare, and so he can assert that "trials by combat were . . . only proceeded with for want of other evidence to settle the case and not simply on the grounds given here . . . , the rejection of reconciliation by both appellant and defendant" (pp. 15-16, n. 199). One lengthy case in 1330 directly contradicts Ure's point, for it resulted precisely from the failure of appellant and defendant to reach reconciliation.[9] It even contradicts barrister-bardolator Phillips's own contention that "trial [by combat] was . . . almost obsolete by the end of the thirteenth century" (p. 165). And it hints at no connection between trial by combat and what Bornstein calls Richard's "presumptuous, unjust, unpatriotic, and un-English" attitude for allowing such a trial (p. 139).[10]

From a Ricardian standpoint, the trial by combat was a matter of fourteenth-century law, not of any sixteenth-century "cult of honor," so that—for example—Bornstein is mistaken to regard Bolingbroke's insistence that the quarreling lords wait "Till we assign you to your days of trial" (IV.i.106) as couched in "legalistic language [that] suggests that he is talking about trials in court rather than trials by combat" (p. 140). Such language also occurred in the 1330 trial by combat:

   Then Scrope [C. J.] inquired of the parties whether they knew any reason why the court ought not to award trial by battle. They said that they knew none.

Therefore Scrope told the parties to find pledges for the performance of the battle. . . . [Scrope]: You are adjourned to Monday, 5 March. . . . He then commanded the champions not to approach one another in the meantime, in any place.

(547-48)

As the presence of the Marshal and the Heralds indicates, the trial in *Richard II* is in the Court of Chivalry. The 1330 trial was in the Court of Common Pleas at a Northamptonshire Eyre, and at the combat Chief Justice Geoffrey le Scrope and his fellow justices performed most of the duties of the Marshal and the Heralds along with those of presiding judge.[11] Even so, the 1330 trial echoes the trial language in *Richard II* in phrases such as "deny it by the body"; the repetitions of legal formulas, "rehearsing the entire count without omitting a single word"; the presentation of the disputants' gloves to the presiding judge; the adjournment until the day appointed for battle; the charge to the champions to identify themselves and swear the justice of their cause; and the inspection and return of the champions' weapons.

In one detail, however, the report seems quite the opposite of the play, which has Richard preventing the combat even though the disputants could not be reconciled. In the 1330 case, by contrast, though the disputants did negotiate a settlement at the last moment, Scrope insisted

you have put the king's court to great labour. The court will therefore have its pleasure. The champions shall have at one another with shields and staves without the crooks and shall strike the blows for the king against one another and shall then fight.

(550)

But the detail from 1330 is not the contrast it seems with the trial of 1398, for it shows that as presiding judge Scrope, like Richard, had absolute power over the trial and the champions.

When in the accusation scene Bolingbroke tells Mowbray, "Pale trembling coward, there I throw my gage, / Disclaiming here the kindred of the king, / And lay aside my high blood's royalty" (I.i.69-71), he is accepting Mowbray's challenge (I.i.58-59), as Ure notes, by "waiving the fact of [his] kinship to the king (and the privileges attached to it)." But, the reports make clear, such a verbal disclaimer was not necessarily valid. In a case of 1389, a deed of feoffment was made to four men, three of whom took possession in the absence of the fourth: "the fourth came to them . . . and had view of the deed and said by parol that he did not want to have any of the said land nor to agree to the feoffment, but dissented from it . . ." (13/3). Later the court found that "it is beyond question that the issue in tail will not be disinherited by this verbal dissent"

(13/5), and in his introduction to the volume, the editor comments on this case and continues, "On the point of disclaimer in a court of record, we find nothing until 1591 when Coke . . . cited our case from Fitzhebert's version" (13/lix).[12] Bolingbroke's offer to disclaim his "high blood's royalty" would affect not only his title but more importantly his issue and most importantly his "oath and band" (I.i.2), that is his sworn obligation of loyalty to Richard. So, though the 1389 case was about a disclaimer of deed, not of title, it casts some doubt on the legal efficacy of Bolingbroke's offer, or his sincerity, or both.

The example of divestment by parol points to the place the law of property occupies in *Richard II*. In his complaint in Act II, Bolingbroke says,

I am denied to sue my livery here,
And yet my letters patents give me leave.
My father's goods are all distrain'd and sold,
And these, and all, are all amiss employ'd.

(II.iii.128-31)

This speech introduces a set of related legalisms that tie together literal and figurative terms elsewhere. Documents like the Ricardian law reports serve to illustrate just how the legalisms are related.

Even before Bolingbroke's complaint, York has asked Richard,

Seek you to seize and gripe into your hands
The royalties and rights of banish'd Herford?

. . . . .

If you do wrongfully seize Herford's rights,
Call in the letters patents that he hath
By his attorneys-general to sue
His livery, and deny his off'red homage,
You pluck a thousand dangers on your head. . . .

(II.i.189-205)

Clarkson and Warren quote Holdsworth *passim* to support their interpretation that

"On the death of the tenant in chief [such as John of Gaunt], he [the king] was always and under all circumstances entitled to first seisin". . . . The king took the fruits and profits of the land until the heir appeared, did homage and paid his relief, after which he might sue his livery, i.e. . . . "sue the tenements out of the king's hand . . . and get seisin."

(26)

The legal language sounds oppressive here, as it would be if every word had its "lay" meaning; but "seisin" is "possession," "to sue" means merely "to petition for," and "livery" is simply the act of delivering possession.[13] So Richard was well within the law to take the land, and even the "royalties and rights" from it, though the legalism "seize into his hands" does not make it sound that way. It was in refusing to accept Bolingbroke's homage and to permit him to sue his livery so as to regain seisin that Richard was lawless.

The law reports contain cases in point. One says:

> after the death of the tenant, the land and the manor were seised into the hand of the king, which manor the husband of full age and his wife within age sued out of the hands of the king, and had livery; . . . and . . . the husband . . . prayed livery out of the hand of the king of these tenements.
>
> *(12/21)*

Another passage shows that the process normally followed not only the death of the tenant but also his attainder: "if the husband commit felony for which he is attainted, all the land shall be seized into the King's hand, as well [held by the felon] in right of his wife as his own land . . . , and the wife shall sue to the King to have livery . . ." (11/271).

In Act IV of *Richard II,* Aumerle makes a figurative reference to "mine honour soil'd / With the attainder of his slanderous lips" (IV.i.23-24), where Ure's note explains that "attainder" means "accusation." It does not; it is instead the final legal *consequence* of accusation, as Mowbray implies in Act I when he swears "to defend my loyalty and truth / To God, my king, and my succeeding issue . . ." (I.iii.19-20). So the quarto reading has it, though the folio has "and his succeeding issue," which some editors have followed. But as Samuel Johnson observed of these lines, "Mowbray's issue was, by this accusation, in danger of an attainder, and therefore he might come among other reasons for their sake" (quoted by Ure 23, n. 20).

Legal attainder was the extinction of civil rights and capacities that followed the sentencing of a traitor or other felon. His estate was forfeited and he could pass nothing by inheritance. In the Ricardian law reports, attainder always follows outlawry, as it would not if attainder were merely "accusation."[14] Attainder also resulted in the felon's exclusion from suing livery for the seisin of his inherited tenements. Finally, as White notes, in a trial by combat, "if the accused was vanquished or killed . . . his blood was thereafter attainted, so that his heirs were cut off from inheriting from him, and all his posterity was made base and ignoble."[15] That is the literal fate that Mowbray as defendant seeks to avoid on behalf of his "succeeding issue," and it is the law on which Aumerle's figure of speech rests.

So far, these passages have associated "sue livery" with a further set of terms: "seisin," "tenements," and "attainder." While either death or attainder could re-

sult in the ordinary legal process called seisin, the extraordinary seizure of real or other property is called "distraint"—Bolingbroke says his father's lands are "distrained." The Ricardian law reports have

> J. and K. his wife granted, by a certain deed that is here, that if the said barley [rent] be in arrears, it should be lawful for him [from whom they held the land] to distrain on all other lands and tenements of which they were seised at the time of the making of this deed.
>
> *(11/15; cf. 11/21)*

Again the reports link our term, here "distrain," with "seise" and "tenement."

Early in the play, Richard makes his own complaint against Bolingbroke, using a legal figure of speech: Bolingbroke, he says, behaves "As were our England in reversion his, / And he our subjects' next degree in hope" (I.iv.35-36). It is a figure Richard's queen picks up in Act II: " 'Tis in reversion that I do possess . . ." (II.ii.38). As White points out (p. 234),

> The estate left after the termination of a life estate or an estate for years in a given tract of land, is reversion, and the estate arises by operation of law and not by deed or will. . . .
>
> The reversioner has the next right to the land, after the tenant of the term is through with the land. . . . [16]

Here an estate is not literally property but the relation that an owner or tenant bears toward the property. Figuratively, however, both "reversion" passages have connections that the Ricardian law reports best clarify. One serjeant argues, for example, "if a tenant for life lease to the reversioner he shall have a writ of waste against him" (13/53). It is this connection between the reversion of an estate and a tenant's waste on it that surfaces in *Richard II.*

In Act II, John of Gaunt complains to Richard that "The waste is no whit lesser than thy land" (II.i.103). "Waste," according to White, "is any damage or act which injures the inheritance of real estate done by a tenant for life or years, to the prejudice of the reversioner or heir" (pp. 234-35). So when Bolingbroke says that his father's goods "and all, are all amiss employ'd," or that Richard has "Dispark'd my parks and fell'd my forest woods" (III.i.23), he is bringing an accusation of literal, legal waste; his father, on the other hand, used the term figuratively.[17]

"Waste" by a tenant is not squandering property or letting it become ruinous, but more usually taking, selling, or alienating a landlord's commodities: "A writ of waste was brought against the tenant for a term of life . . . to wit one hundred oaks cut down and sold . . . two hundred beeches cut down and sold . . . and two villeins exiled by his wicked and tortious distress" (12/173). Because wood was especially valuable and vulnerable to waste by the tenant, it often appears in writs of waste, as it does in Bolingbroke's accusation that Richard has "fell'd my forest woods." One report has a particularly full account:

> A writ of waste was brought by an infant under age against T. FitzHugh as guardian . . . and the plaintiff affirmed the waste in a garden [and] in a wood in the felling and cutting down of certain ashtrees and oaks.

> *Markham,* for the guardian, said that a certain J. C., the plaintiff's ancestor, was seised of those same tenements wherein the waste is alleged, and of other tenements in his demesne as of fee. And he had issue of two daughters, to wit, the plaintiff who is under age and another who is of full age, and [he] died. . . . And after his death the two daughters entered, and the defendant took possession of [*seisist*] the wardship of the one under age on the ground that the tenements were held of him. . . . Afterwards the two daughters made purparty between them, so that the garden and wood . . . were allotted to the purparty of the one under age. . . . And because there were growing in the garden better and more valuable trees than in the purparty of her who is of full age, an agreement was made upon the purparty between them that she who is under age should cut down the same trees. . . .

> *(11/258-59; cf. 11/1, 12/30, 12/173)*

The trees involved might, that is, grow in a garden, not only in a wood or on open land.

John of Gaunt's accusation also holds that England under Richard has become "Like to a tenement or pelting farm" (II.i.60). Gohn thinks "tenement" in this passage is "rented rooms" (p. 957, n. 79), but Phillips's "time and place" doctrine rejects the meaning new in Shakespeare's time in favor of White's definition "A tenement in the law of real property, is anything of a permanent nature, which may be holden, as a house or a homestead" (p. 236), which is the meaning the Ricardian law reports quoted up to now reflect. Richard, though he is in reality lord paramount, has abused the country as though it were land "holden" and he were its wasteful tenant.

By relating tenancy to reversion and to waste, such remarks in the reports complete a picture in which the complaints of York and Bolingbroke, that Richard has prevented the latter from "suing his livery," prove to be the node of a set of references on which "distrain" (with "seize," as in "royalties and rights"), and by implication "waste," along with "attainder," "reversion," and "tenements," all converge. They are, the Ricardian reports bear witness, all members of a set of

legalisms drawn from the late fourteenth-century law of property, though the play distributes the members among the acts and characters of the play, using them both literally and figuratively. For although Shakespeare took some individual details of Ricardian legal history from Holinshed, the underlying legal system that enabled him to form this set of literal and figurative terms derives from other sources, such as the medieval law reports, as Shakespeare's imagination seized on them and molded them. Holinshed provided the literal basis for Bolingbroke and York's complaints, but not for the set of literary and figurative vocabulary based on them.

In the middle of the play, the gardener in York's oddly metaphorical garden observes that "Bolingbroke / Hath seiz'd the wasteful king" and further that if Richard had kept his "garden" properly, "himself had borne the crown, / Which waste of idle hours hath quite thrown down" (III.iv.54-55, 65-66). As a sequel to the figurative legalisms we have been viewing from the standpoint of the medieval reports, this reversal of action makes good sense: Richard is wasting his tenement, so Bolingbroke seizes him. A garden, the reports also show, is a pertinent venue for a commentary on waste. But the play is little more than half over, and the gardener's commentary, though it marks a turning point in the legal imagery, does not mark its climax. That comes near the end of Act V, when Richard says,

> . . . how sour sweet music is
> When time is broke and no proportion kept!
> So is it in the music of men's lives.
> And here have I the daintiness of ear
> To check time broke in a disordered string;
> But for the concord of my state and time,
> Had not an ear to hear my true time broke:
> I wasted time, and now doth time waste me. . . .
> *(V.v.42-49)*

The dominant image here, obviously, is music and musical time. But the chiastic wordplay of the last line. "I wasted time, and now doth time waste me," recalls also the figurative legalisms of the play, for Richard has committed waste as "a tenant for life or years, to the prejudice of the reversioner or heir," to quote again White's commentary.[18] A writ of waste, however, can lie only against a tenant, and Richard as lord paramount is the one person in the kingdom who cannot be a tenant, so no literal writ of waste can lie against him. But figuratively he has wasted time, of which he was indeed "a tenant for life or years," since life and years are time's tenements; and now time is "wasting," or suing for waste, its injurious tenant. And so in Richard's last long speech Shakespeare brings together the strands, explicit and implicit, of Ricardian property law in the play, though Richard can probably not see them. That we can see them now we may credit to those black-letter law books that help us, with Malone, to understand some of Shakespeare's allusions, and which, with old Serjeant Maynard, we may yet prefer to any comedy.

Notes

This paper was given in a shorter version at the section on "Shakespeare and the Middle Ages" of the Twenty-first International Congress on Medieval Studies, Kalamazoo, Michigan, May 1986.

[1] O. Hood Phillips, *Shakespeare and the Lawyers* (London: Methuen, 1972), pp. 176-77. Phillips offers excellent additional bibliography and a fascinating account of the study of Shakespeare by lawyers. See now also Edna Zwick Boris, *Shakespeare's English Kings, the People, and the Law* (Rutherford: Fairleigh Dickinson Univ. Press, 1978).

[2] My article addresses only those matters of law in *Richard II* related to the Year Books; it should be read in conjunction with Donna B. Hamilton, "The State of Law in *Richard II,*" *Shakespeare Quarterly,* 34 (1983), 5-17, who addresses other matters of law. For the Year Books, see William Craddock Bolland, *A Manual of Year Book Studies* (Cambridge: Cambridge Univ. Press, 1925), and *The Year Books* (Cambridge: Cambridge Univ. Press, 1921); Jacques Lambert, *Les Year Books de langue française* (Paris: Sirey, 1928); H. G. Richardson, "Year Books and Plea Rolls as Sources of Historical Information," *Transactions of the Royal Historical Society,* 4th ser., 5 (1922), 28-70; and Albert C. Baugh, "Chaucer's Serjeant of the Law and the Year Books," *Mélanges de langue et de littérature du moyen âge et de la renaissance offerts à Jean Frappier* (Geneva: Droz, 1979), 1. 65-76, which includes references to earlier studies of Year Books in general. Except for the 1330 case (for which see note 9 below), my Year Book quotations and translations are from *Year Books of Richard II: 11 Richard II, 1387-1388,* ed. Isobel B. Thornley (London: Spottiswoode, Ballantyne, 1937); . . . *12 Richard II, A.D. 1388-1389,* ed. George F. Deiser (Cambridge, Mass.: Harvard Univ. Press, 1914); and . . . *13 Richard II, 1389-1390,* ed. Theodore F. T. Plucknett (London: Spottiswoode, Ballantyne, 1929), cited as 11, 12, and 13, respectively (page numbers in these editions designate both the original French or Latin on the verso and the editor's translation on the facing recto). My quotations from *Richard II* follow the Arden edition by Peter Ure, 5th ed. (London: Methuen, 1961).

[3] Cited in Bolland, *Manual,* pp. 3, 4.

[4] F. F. Heard, *Shakespeare as a Lawyer* (Boston: Little, Brown, 1883), p. 48, cited in Phillips, pp. 181-82.

[5] Humphreys thinks that Pistol's following phrase, "'tis all in every part," is "apparently meant as a rough rendering of the quoted Latin tags." But *obsque hoc nihil est* is more probably either itself a translation of Falstaff's previous phrase "as if there were nothing else to be done," with its repetition of his "thinking of nothing else" (V.v.25-27), or—more probably still—Pistol's version of one of the 250 or so *absque hoc* proverbs, most of them containing a following negative, listed by Hans Walther, *Proverbia sententiaeque latinitatis medii ac recentioris aevi,* ed. Paul Gerhard Schmidt (Göttingen: Vandenhoeck & Ruprecht, 1982), 1. 32-47. The proverbs include for example no. 34372x3, *Absque Deo durabile nil est,* which may be similar to the model for Pistol's version.

[6] Diane Bornstein, "Trial by Combat and Official Irresponsibility in *Richard II,*" *Shakespeare Studies,* 8 (1976), 131.

[7] Jack Benoit Gohn, "*Richard II:* Shakespeare's Legal Brief on the Royal Prerogative and the Succession to the Throne," *Georgetown Law Journal,* 70 (1982), 943-73.

[8] Paul S. Clarkson and Clyde T. Warren, *The Law of Property in Shakespeare and the Elizabethan Drama* (Baltimore: Johns Hopkins Univ. Press, 1942), p. 215.

[9] Bolland, *Manual,* quotes this case from "an unprinted Year Book in Lincoln's Inn (p. 96), but it had in fact been printed by William Dugdale, *Origines Juridiciales,* 2nd ed. (1671), pp. 68-71. It has since been edited from several manuscripts by Donald W. Sutherland, *The Eyre of Northamptonshire 1329-1330* (Selden Society 98, 1983 for 1982), pp. 546-61.

[10] Mowbray's son certainly does not see the connection in *2H4,* IV.i.115-26.

[11] See G. Squibb, *The High Court of Chivalry* (Oxford: Clarendon, 1959), with excellent bibliography, to which add J. Derocquigny, "Note sur Shakespeare, Richard II, acte I, scène III," *Revue Anglo-Américaine,* 1 (1923-24) 430-31, which finds Shakespeare guilty of "solécismes" in several details of the trial by combat, including the performance by the Marshal of some roles properly those of the Constable, who does not appear in the play. But such telescoping of roles may not reflect Shakespeare's "nonchalance" and "ignorance," as Derocquigny would have it, so much as the influence of trials by combat like the one in 1330 and of roles like Scrope's in it. (Scrope was, by coincidence, the grandfather of the Sir Stephen Scroope who is a minor character in *R2,* III.ii and III.iii. See further Humphreys's note on *1H4,* IV.iv.3 [Arden ed., London: Methuen, 1960].)

[12] *Richard II* was written between 1595 and 1597, shortly after Coke made this citation. For Shakespeare's special interest in Coke, see George

W. Keeton, *Shakespeare's Legal and Political Background* (London: Pittman, 1968), pp. 43-66.

[13] For "tenements," see below. The legalism "livery" also occurs in *1H4,* IV.iii.62, referring to its use in *Richard II,* but elsewhere Shakespeare employs the word in the lay sense "garb." Ure's note on II.i.190 follows the *OED* and received opinion in defining "royalties" as "rights granted to a subject by the king," but Clarkson and Warren's "fruits and profits of the land" appears to give the word its present-day meaning, though it is one the *OED* does not know before the nineteenth century.

[14] E.g., 11/268-69, 11/279. The legalism is rare in Shakespeare, appearing elsewhere only in *LLL,* I.i.156, and *R3,* III.v.32. "Attaint," "attainded," and "attainture" are, however, more common.

[15] Edward J. White, *Commentaries on the Law in Shakespeare,* 2nd ed. (St. Louis: F. H. Thomas, 1913), p. 230.

[16] Another Shakespearean rarity, "reversion," occurs elsewhere only in 1H4, IV.i.53, and *Tro,* III.ii.92. Even as some legal scholars like White have explained the "reversion" passages in *Richard II* by reference to the law, others have explained the law by reference to the passages (Phillips 121).

[17] For reasons noted below, Bolingbroke could bring only an accusation, not a writ, of waste against Richard.

[18] It recalls too Gaunt's reference to. his own "time-bewasted night" (I.iii.220) and Richard's belief that "time hath set a blot on my pride" (III.ii.81).

KING LEAR: DIVINE JUDGMENT AND NATURAL LAW

Janet M. Green (essay date 1995)

SOURCE: "Earthly Doom and Heavenly Thunder: Judgement in *King Lear,*" in *University of Dayton Review,* Vol. 23, No. 2, Spring, 1995, pp. 63-71.

[In the following essay, Green discusses the workings of legal and divine judgment in King Lear.*]*

In *King Lear* (1605-1606) Shakespeare refers to the law and to judgment, both secular and divine, again and again, heightening the pressure and force of the tragic outcome. The repeated legal situations, rather than offering hope of a fair judicial decision or a merciful re-

prieve, intensify and mirror the characters' experiences of heavenly wrath, human cruelty, and hopeless pain.

It is illuminating to recapitulate as much as possible the ways in which Shakespeare's audience might have perceived these situations, concentrating on what Shakespeare might reasonably have expected the ordinary playgoer to know and understand. Almost certainly this ordinary playgoer had not read all the contemporary materials which modern critics have perused—nor, one suspects, had Shakespeare—yet we can posit a certain community of knowledge of some legal situations and terms that occur and re-occur in *Lear.* These can be grouped under two kinds of judgment: secular doom and divine thunder—Jacobean law courts and the Christian Last Judgment.[1]

Shakespeare's choice of legal situations demonstrates that the play's most powerful single dimension for spectators is "the nature and significance of human society" (Mack, *King Lear in Our Time*), for people's relations and responsibilities are set forth clearly in the law. Kiernan Ryan, while acknowledging that it is obvious Shakespeare's plays "have their historical basis in the social reality of his age," reminds us that more important is "ascertaining *how* that reality is perceived by the play, and *how we* are induced to perceive the play's representation of that reality" (26-27).

One of the realities is the highly litigious nature of Shakespeare's time. Going to law was common and frequent, as Shakespeare, and his father too, themselves demonstrated. An elaborate system of secular courts and legal entities with wide purposes and powers rendered judgments, not only to protect life and property, but to preserve the ranked structure of society and to encourage uniformity (Williams 217; Powell and Cook 41). Punishments were brutal, the range of felonies was wide, it was easy to bring prosecutions, and malicious litigation was widespread (Williams 248, 252).

Shakespeare's audience, like Lear himself, would condemn many things in such a legal system. Local justice was mostly in the hands of the much-criticized Justices of the Peace, who had both great responsibilities and great powers to enforce the law, which they did not always use with integrity. Sometimes, they might advocate clemency (as Lear does in the mock trial scene of 3.6 where he acts as a justice). Trial juries were known to be capricious, the attitude towards evidence often arbitrary, corruption and bribery prevalent, and haste could mar all procedure (Williams 231). A person could be—and often was—convicted one day and executed the next. Even the condemned ones making their farewells from the scaffold might be bidden by officials to make haste. The speed of resolutions in tragic drama resulting in the rapid heaping up of corpses which often seems artificial to us would not, perhaps, seem as contrived to Jacobeans.

Even more disliked than the secular courts, officials, and processes, were their ecclesiastical counterparts, which handled most matters of morality. Their autocratic approach and financial exactions "were resented and even hated by laymen" (Powell and Cook 86).

There was much to resent, fear and hate in both of these Jacobean legal systems, yet surely Shakespeare's audiences must have found the many highly dramatic renderings of judgment as fascinating as we do. The news-loving, lively Jacobeans were intensely interested in secular and religious trials, judgments and punishments, especially those with bizarre or gruesome details, or those involving the sad—perhaps satisfying—fall of great ones. John Foxe's *Book of Martyrs* still helped to feed the insatiable human appetite for gore, holy or otherwise. Accounts of trials were often printed for sale. Judgments (and their more interesting punishments) were enacted in the theatre. Public executions were common, often preceded by the condemned person's agreement with the judgment that had brought him (or her) to that dismal place. Secular judgment was a powerful reality to Shakespeare's audiences.

We see this consciousness in other works of Shakespeare, for example, *Measure for Measure, Much Ado About Nothing,* and *The Merchant of Venice.* It is most intensely mirrored and repeated in *King Lear.* In this tragedy, as in Jacobean life, legal terms and situations abound. In fact, they form an important framework for the action, from Lear's willful disposition of his kingdom in the first scene—that "trial of love"—until the end (Mack, *Everybody's Shakespeare* 162). When Lear summons his three daughters, it is to testify in a courtroom atmosphere.[2] In this scene, the royal judge metes out rewards and punishments like an overblown, arbitrary, powerful Jacobean magistrate, a character which would have been familiar to the audience. They would also have been aware of how contemporary laws of inheritance were violated by both Lear and Gloucester, and of how greed was threatening family ties (Kenneth Muir, *The Great Tragedies* 26). Many also would know the sensational story of Sir Brian Annesley. In 1603 when his eldest daughter and her husband sought to get him declared mad so they could gain his estate, Cordell, his youngest daughter, appealed to Sir Robert Cecil on his behalf.[3]

Other matters relating to law occur throughout *Lear,* almost too many to recount. For example, successful flight to avoid prosecution was then common (Williams 232) and, in 4.6 we see Lear running off to be pursued on the health by Cordelia's people. Some allusions to legal matters in the drama are almost glancing, like Goneril's arrogant pronouncement to her disgusted husband Albany that "the laws are mine, not thine" (5.3.158-59).

However, it is fitting that the most powerful, sustained, and effective images of judgment should center on the doomed king. The legal situations progress from the ceremonial disposition scene which opens the play, in which King Lear has all the power, and none of the understanding, to the mock trial scene (3.6) in which mad Lear has no real power but much better understanding. In this scene, he sets up his "courtroom" with Edgar (as poor Tom), the Fool, Kent and himself as justices. Cued by the Fool, Lear opens the proceedings:

> Fool: He's mad that trusts in the tameness
> of a wolf, a horse's health, a boy's love, or
> a whore's oath.
> Lear: It shall be done; I will arraign them
> straight
>
> (18-20).

So he does, arraigning Goneril, represented by a joint stool, on charges that she kicked him. "Let us deal justly," the Fool remarks (41).

This exhibition of the demented King presiding over a mad, surrealistic legal system must have pleased the original audiences, many of whom we can safely assume had had direct experiences with secular or ecclesiastical law and, very probably, not happy ones. Though the King in the play is insane, the arbitrariness and inconsistency of his legal pronouncements ring true. The apparent reversion to some kind of order in this scene—the structure of a law trial—is really a reversion to chaos and insanity, a point the audience could well appreciate. The mirror image effect not only increases the impression of Lear's weakening capacities, but reveals the marred nature and impaired truth of society itself. By all his incisive and telling words, Lear describes not only problems which the characters in the play face but problems in Jacobean life where legal judgment, like the fates of the drama's characters, could be arbitrary, inconsistent, brutally swift or hideously slow, crooked, unjust. The play's setting disguises the contemporary references somewhat, and the privilege of madness has allowed Lear, like Hamlet, to criticize the corrupt Jacobean social system without incurring punishment from the drama's other characters—or stimulating punishment of the playwright by authorities.

As the play goes on, the images of judgment become even more serious. As Lear goes increasingly mad, he becomes increasingly cogent as a social critic. Shakespeare skillfully enables us to recognize both states but trust the latter more. Lear, wandering about, continues to discourse in a seemingly disjointed manner but with penetrating acumen on injustice (4.6). Like George Eliot's famous pierglass image in *Middlemarch* (182), his egoism begins to organize random memories and experiences into a pattern of awareness, as a candle held close organizes the meaningless scratches on a metal pierglass into concentric circles. When Lear characterizes a barking dog who makes a beggar run away as the "great image of Authority: / A dog's obey'd in office" (4.6.160-61), we think of his own misused authority, as evidently he does also.

His scope widens to include other wrongs besides his own, but he characterizes the officer of the law (the punisher) as the real sinner, once again a reflection of his own crucial fault in disposing of his kingdom. The "rascal beadle," though he lusts for the whore, nevertheless lashes her back. The usurer, a magistrate guilty of lending money at usurious rates, hangs the cozener, only a petty cheater (Muir 180n; 4.6.162-65). Money protects the sinful from discovery and prosecution, and rich clothes disarm justice:

> Plate sin with gold,
> And the strong lance of justice hurtless
> 　breaks;
> Arm it in rags, a pigmy's straw does pierce it
> 　　　　　　　　　　　　　　　(167-69).

The audience must have realized, as Maynard Mack points out, "that it was listening to an indictment far more relevant to its own social experience than to any this king of ancient Britain could be imagined to have had." Lear, a king of the realm like their own King James, had "registered for all to hear the bankruptcy of the very body politic (and body moral) of which he was representative and head. . . . Even the most casual playgoer, who had looked about him reflectively in Jacobean England, must have experienced a shudder of self-recognition as Lear's 'sermon' proceeded" (107-08).

After indicting hypocrisy, Lear imitates an impossibly ideal magistrate, or perhaps the hoped-for merciful Christ at the Last Judgment, when he says, "None does offend, none, I say, none; I'll able 'em ("vouch for them"; 170). (He seems to revert to his old arrogance, however, when he adds the sinister reminder that he has "the power / To seal th' accuser's lips" (171-72)). But he has reversed the procedure usual in any court of judgment—in fact, destroyed its basis—by pardoning an offense before he knows what it is. Human mercy can do no more, nor can divine.[4]

Once Lear is reunited with Cordelia, the madman's judging ceases. The action quickens. The King, now restored to his wits but weak, and his adored Cordelia must suffer Edmund's unjust and extreme judgment upon them. Before this comes to pass, Lear, reunited with his darling, has one last happy moment. His eloquent address to her, "Come, let's away to prison," (5.3.8-19) may sound fanciful to us—and has had, like almost every passage in *Lear*, myriad interpretations—but the audience might have found it not a piece of deluded, senile, or symbolic imagination, but an anachronistic reflection of possibility. The legal system often granted surprising leniency to prisoners in Shakespeare's time, even to "traitors," if of high rank. Lear

does not live to enjoy the kind of imprisonment with Cordelia he describes, but it was not unreasonable for a king to expect it.

Shakespeare's use of such frequent allusions to secular judgment and to the legal systems must have deepened the playgoer's understanding of the tragedy and widened its meaning to include not only awareness of pagan Britain but of Jacobean England. And perhaps of life itself, for earthly judgments prefigured and mirrored in part God's final one.

Now we find in *Lear* more allusions to the judgment of the law than to Christianity's Last Judgment, even though religion was more pervasive in Jacobean daily life, but these Doomsday references reverberate powerfully, like the sounds of approaching thunder. They are fewer, of course, partly because *Lear* has a pagan setting, but also, it is likely, because overt references to religion could be dangerous. Prudent writers did not allude to religious matters except with great circumspection. The situation in Shakespeare's time resembled somewhat the circumstances surrounding the composition of most apocalyptic literature. Because it was often seditious and contemporary references dangerous, it was cryptic—as is Shakespeare's resolution of *Lear*. The consequences of offending the authorities could be severe. We cannot assume that Shakespeare stood aloof from the state religion of his time, for had he not conformed, S. Schoenbaum convincingly argues, he would have been noticed by authorities who were already hostile to the theatre on religious grounds (59-60).

The concept of the Last Judgment was one of the important ideas of Shakespeare's time (Weittrich 91). Queen Elizabeth had movingly referred to it in her Golden Speech in 1601.[5] King James, fascinated by theology, was obsessed with the Book of Revelation and his meditations on it were published in 1588 and 1603. Revelation pertained to the last age and would be fulfilled "in very short space," he wrote. Inspired by the King's concern, his subjects studied the subject enthusiastically (Weittrich 29-31). Besides the common verbal allusions to the Last Judgment were the common visual representations, like the paintings in churches (Lascelles 59-60). It seems reasonable to assume that the concept of the Last Judgment was as familiar to the ordinary playgoer as the creation of the world or the life of Jesus.

In church, sermons were preached on the Last Judgment, and in the liturgy Jacobeans heard and uttered references to it again and again. Church attendance was not optional, and the order of service, the creeds, and Scriptural readings were fixed. The use of and worship according to the *Book of Common Prayer* was enforced by statute, "and offenders were punishable by law," as described in "An Act for Uniformity of

Common Prayer" (BCP 6-13; 372). The vision of judgment in all its scarifying power was set before Shakespeare's contemporaries frequently in the Scriptural selections appointed to be read in particular Morning and Evening Prayer services and in the less frequent Holy Communion service (such as Matthew 13:47-50 and 25; and Luke 21).[6]

Judgment appears also in the Apostles' Creed used in Morning Prayer (and said in common by the whole congregation), and the Nicene Creed: "And He shall come again to judge both the quick and the dead." The Athanasian Creed which was said in common at the end of Evening Prayer on selected high feast days describes the Last Judgment in more detail: ". . . he shall come to judge the quick and the dead. / At whose coming all men shall rise again with their bodies: and they shall give account for their own works. / And they that have done good, shall go into life everlasting: and they that have done evil, into everlasting fire. / This is the catholic faith: which except a man believe faithfully, he cannot be saved" (64-67). The Apostles' Creed was used in Baptism (273) and several other services, and references to the Last Judgment appear in many places, even in the marriage ceremony: "I require and charge you (as you will answer at the dreadful day of judgment, when the secrets of all hearts shall be disclosed) . . ." (291). And of course the concept appears frequently in the Order for the Burial of the Dead, along with hope of mercy (309-13).

Many briefer, but still relentless, reminders of the same cataclysmic final day were contained in other portions of the church services. Two of the most important seasons of the church year, Advent and Lent, emphasized the individual's preparation for the fulfillment of God's ordinances.

There are not only reflections in *King Lear* of the general assumption that everyone knew about the Last Judgment, but there are echoes in it of the *Book of Common Prayer*. One service even reads like program notes for the villains in *Lear*. In the colorful and dramatic Office of Commination Against Sinners . . ."To Be Used Divers Times in the year," drawn chiefly from Deut. 27, the minister leads the congregation in denouncing various kinds of sinners (*BCP* 316-23). These kinds could describe characters in *Lear*:

> Cursed is he:
> "that curseth his father" (a description fitting Edmund);
> "that lieth with his neighbor's wife" (Edmund);
> "that smiteth his neighbor secretly" (Edmund, Goneril the poisoner);
> "that taketh reward to slay the soul of innocent blood"; (the Captain-hangman, Oswald)

> "that maketh the blind to go out of his way" (Cornwall, Regan).
> "Cursed are the unmerciful" fits Edmund, Goneril, Regan, Cornwall, Cornwall's servants, and Oswald. Gloucester and Lear, also, begin without the quality of mercy but advance towards it.

In this service of Commination, after the minister exhorts the congregation to return to God, "remembering the dreadful judgment hanging over our heads, and being always at hand," he reads a bloodcurdling description of that final day of wrath and vengeance, which it might have done even Edmund some good to hear.

It is well to remember in this discussion, though, that the Christian God is not possessed entirely by flaming judgmental wrath. It is also His property to have mercy. Mercy like the mercy Lear showed in the mock trial scene (3.6) when he forgave the sin before he knew the crime.[7] It was certain God accepted the repentance of the dying. So Shakespeare's audience might well have felt a sense of completion, of satisfaction, of justice, when even the villainous Edmund acknowledges a power greater than his own. Dying, he says, "I pant for life; some good I mean to do / Despite of mine own nature" (5.3.243-44).

The belief that God judges people on earth but also finally and dramatically—and not without mercy—in the life to come is so enshrined in the key protestations of Christian faith and Scripture that it must have affected the way in which Shakespeare's audience beheld their lives and his plays. What Joseph Weittrich terms "the apocalyptic myth" appears in other works, for example, *Anthony and Cleopatra* and *Macbeth* (6; Lascelles 56), and the comic murderers jest about Doomsday with perfect familiarity in *Richard III* (1.4.101ff). But it is in *Lear* that the concept is used most powerfully. The resemblances of *Lear*'s world to the world of Shakespeare's audiences were obvious. They would see more easily what modern critics so often quote, Keats's "fierce dispute betwixt damnation and impassioned clay" (380, lines 5-6). David Kranz writes that Shakespeare and his audience, "being Christian, would clearly see the pagan tragedy and the hidden Christian insights more easily than we do," though the insights are perhaps not so hidden as that statement implies (140). Even in a play with an undoubtedly pagan setting, says Bruce Young, "Shakespeare draws freely on the Christian idea of the Apocalypse, the era of tribulation and judgment that will accompany the end of this fallen world" (103).

Shakespeare knew the Geneva Bible, which with the *Book of Common Prayer* and the Homilies "profoundly nourished his imagination," concludes S. Schoenbaum (57). René Fortin goes further: "an ear attuned to Scripture would discern in Lear's ordeal resonances of the

Book of Revelation" (119). In *Lear* Shakespeare is particularly obsessed with the Doomsday idea (Weittrich 9-10). He seems to have before him, not the brief, flat statements of the Apostles' and Nicene Creeds, but the more terrifying vision of the Athanasian Creed (*BCP* 67):

> At whose coming all men shall rise again with their bodies: and shall give account for their own works.

> And they that have done good, shall go into life everlasting: and they that have done evil, into everlasting fire [the second death].

Apocalyptic events (as just described, and in Revelation and Daniel) take place, like the major events of *King Lear,* in a certain kind of time. Ordinary measured time ("chronos") is replaced by a period of massive change and danger, in which the sense of time is concentrated, quickened, and heightened because of the dramatic and important events that happen within it. This "chairos" (related to our term "crisis") brings change, good or bad, but always it brings anxiety and fear. In *Lear* we experience as the play progresses a growing sense of urgency, change, danger, and fear in which time is indeed heightened and rushes with unusual speed and force to the final destruction.

The effect is achieved not only by plot events but by the general atmosphere and by specific references. The quality of apocalyptic finality has occurred throughout the play—in trumpets, in thunders, in tempest. The hideous din of wind and rain on the heath seems to be at war "as if it were indeed Armageddon. . . . And everywhere "run tides of doomsday passion that seem to use up and wear away people, codes, expectations, all stable points of reference, till only a profound sense remains that an epoch, in fact a whole dispensation, has forever closed" (Mack, *King Lear* 85-86). In Keats's "vale of soul-making," the characters must make final choices, and in noise, chaos, madness, flight and battle their fates come upon them swiftly. "The wheel is come full circle," Edmund says. "I am here" (5.3.174).

Reference to another wheel has already brought to mind specific last things—Hell and punishment following Judgment. Lear seems to refer to a medieval torment in Purgatory (which the Protestants had abolished) when he wakes from his madness to behold above him the face of Cordelia:

> Thou art a soul in bliss; but I am bound
> Upon a wheel of fire, that mine own tears
> Do scald like molten lead
>
> (4.7.46-48)

Though the Established Church had rejected the doctrine of Purgatory, it could still linger in the minds of the audience and in the poetry of the playwright. Cordelia

has bent above her suffering father in one pietà; now at the end he bends above her in another (Barber 119).

The most obvious specific indication of the Last Judgment occurs at the end of the drama after Lear has expired over Cordelia's body. Commentators still dispute whether the ending is "Christian" or not, whether Lear is redeemed by his suffering or dies uselessly, and they variously interpret Lear's last words, "Look on her, look, her lips, / Look there, look there!" (5.3.310-11). Some say Lear actually thinks Cordelia revives, and his heart, like Gloucester's, bursts in joy, not anguish. Even if he dies in this happy belief, we know he is horribly mistaken and our pity is not diminished. Perhaps it is even increased. The reversal of the happier ending in the old Lear story could itself be authorized by the implications of Apocalypse (Weittrich 12). But whatever the interpretation, the deliberately evoked resonances of Doomsday, our sense of "chairos," magnify the sorrow of the scene. The audience's understanding of apocalyptic possibilities makes the deaths of Lear and his Cordelia more believable, more horrible.

The comments of the three remaining "good" characters seem to refer to a Christian Last Judgment:

> Kent: Is this the promised end?
> Edgar: Or image of that horror?
> Albany: Fall and cease
>
> (5.3.263-64).

Albany's enigmatic imperatives have been interpreted as "let heavens fall and all things cease" (Bevington 132n).

However, the above lines could also refer to the end of time ("eschaton"), which encompasses cataclysmic events like warning signs and disasters, the destruction of the world, the Last Judgment, and the final defeat of evil and death. Thus the possibility that Lear and Cordelia's tragic fate may be a sign that this end of time is near (is beginning?) makes Edgar ask, "Or image of that horror?"[8]

The final reference in the tragedy to a legal system returns to secular law. The meaning of Lear's suffering deepens into almost unbearable intensity when Kent uses the word "rack" as a figure for his sufferings. When Edgar tries to revive the dead King with "Look up, my Lord," Kent protests (as we do):

> Vex not his ghost: O! let him pass; he hates him
> That would upon the rack of this tough world
> Stretch him out longer
>
> (5.3.313-15).

The infamous rack connoted pain and suffering which must be endured, sometimes relieved only by death. It was known that the state used routine unwarranted, sometimes enthusiastic torture to get information, to ensure the veracity of the victim as a later witness whether yet brought to trial or not, to serve on occasion "to the example of others" (Williams 393). It was used to punish *and* to gain a confession—sometimes in that order.

Who would disagree with Kent's passionate plea, "O! let him pass"? The rack of Lear's sufferings has done too much to him. His mind has been dislocated as the rack might have maimed his body. In fact, in Caroline Spurgeon's famous words, through verbs and metaphors the drama's references to violence and bodily agony have finally created the image "of a human body in anguished movement, tugged, wrenched, beaten, pierced, stung, scourged, dislocated, flayed, gashed, scalded, tortured and finally broken on the rack" (339). Lear's pain has, it is true, yielded him greater compassion for his fellow beings and greater understanding of himself. He had long ago confessed his chief error—"I did her wrong," he had said flatly about Cordelia (1.5.24). But the price of gaining such knowledge has been too high. There can be no recompense. Kent says, "If Fortune brag of two she lov'd and hated, / One of them we behold" (5.3.280-81). Lear's increased sensitivity does show in his courteous dying request, "Pray you, undo this button: thank you, Sir" (5.3.309). Still it cannot redeem his suffering which had made him like a condemned soul to roam the earth in mad anguish. At the end, he is like a corpse tied to the gibbet for warning. True, Kent, Albany, and Edgar remain alive at the end of the play, but their virtue is pale and insufficient comfort for the sorrow and evil the audience has seen, the judgments—just and unjust—that have been implied and given.[9]

The unspoken connotative meanings of these judgments must have increased the powerful impression of the drama. As the audience left Shakespeare's theatre, their impression of the entire tragedy must have been undergirded by their knowledge, perhaps fear, of secular law, and as they dispersed, the thunder of the Last Judgment must have resonated in their minds.

Notes

[1] In this paper, acts, scenes, and line numbers refer to The Arden Shakespeare edited by Kenneth Muir, Methuen, 1963. The terms "Last Judgment," "Day of Judgment," and "Doomsday" (Old English "doom" meant "judgment") were in Shakespeare's time more or less synonymous and referred to a time when all people, the living and the dead, would be judged by God, after the world is destroyed and before a New Kingdom is created.

[2] René Girard in *A Theatre of Envy* says what Cordelia rejects in this scene is "mimetic rivalry" with her sis-

ters (182). This is an interesting point, since rivalry so often precedes violence. Rivalry is also the essence of litigation.

[3] Annesley died not long after Cordell's appeal, and the eldest daughter contested his will. Mack, *King Lear In Our Time* (45-47) and Muir in his edition of *King Lear* (xliii) summarize the details.

[4] A frequent New Testament idea is that sin and law reinforce each other, as in "for by the law is the knowledge of sin" (Rom. 3:20); "the strength of sin is the law" (1 Cor. 15:56); and "sin is not imputed when there is no law" (Rom. 5:13).

[5] To members of Parliament Elizabeth said: "I have ever used to set the Last-Judgment Day before mine eyes, and so to rule as I shall be judged to answer before a higher Judge, to whose judgment seat I do appeal, that never thought was cherished in my heart that tended not unto my people's good" (Neale 390).

[6] The 1559 edition of the *Book of Common Prayer* (hereafter *BCP*) was in constant use until 1604, when minor changes only were made. Further changes were not made until 1661-1662 (Booty, "History of the 1559 Book of Common Prayer" in *BCP* 329).

Some of the appointed Scriptural readings which included descriptions of the Last Judgment were: Acts 17:31; 2 Peter 3:9-13; 2 Cor. 5:10; 1 Cor. 4:4-5; 2 Thess. 1:7-10; and Jude 1:6—8 ("Proper Lessons To Be Read" and "An Almanac for Thirty Years." *BCP* 27-47).

[7] Cordelia, like Edgar, embodies Christian constancy; she gives especially eloquent voice to the doctrine of mercy when she hears how her deadly sisters had locked their doors against their father in the apocalyptic storm: "Mine enemy's dog, / Though he had bit me, should have stood that night / Against my fire" (4.7.36-38). The shining thread of mercy is interwoven in *Lear* with the harsh poetic justice described in these famous lines: "The Gods are just, and of our pleasant vices / Make instruments to plague us" (5.3.170-71).

[8] Yet another reading of these much discussed lines concludes that the three characters may refer to death itself. Kent laments the death of good people like Lear and Cordelia in such terrible circumstances ("Is this the promis'd end?"). Edgar adds that the horrible scene they behold is the first of many deaths ("Or image of that horror?"). Albany's remark reinforces that despair; once you die, there is nothing more ("Fall and cease"). For this interpretation I am indebted to Pastor Elizabeth Eaton and Father Conrad Selnick of Ashtabula. Ohio.

[9] Eaton and Selnick have conjectured that several apparently Christian references in the last scene may not be chance occurrences; Shakespeare may have deliber-

ately chosen them to soften the bleakness of the final events. (A pre-Christian setting did not require exact theology.) Edmund repents, providing the audience with a sense of resolution. Albany promises punishment and reward like the Christian God of the Last Judgment, thus providing a sense of justice and completion.

Some vocabulary has rich Christian connotations. Referring to the dead Goneril and Regan, Albany says, "*This judgment of the heavens, that makes us tremble, / Touches us not with pity*" (5.3.231-32). Lear says that if Cordelia lives, "It is a chance which does *redeem* all sorrows / That ever I have felt" (266-67). And Kent speaks of his imminent death as a journey he must undertake: "*My master calls me*" (322. Above italics mine).

Works Cited

Barber, C. L. "On Christianity and the Family: Tragedy of the Sacred." *Twentieth Century Interpretations of King Lear: A Collection of Critical Essays.* Ed. Janet Adelman. Englewood, NJ: Prentice-Hall, 1978. 117-19.

The Book of Common Prayer, 1559: The Elizabethan Prayer Book. Ed. John E. Booty. Folger Documents of Tudor and Stuart Civilization 22. Washington: Folger Shakespeare Library, 1976.

Eliot, George. *Middlemarch.* 1871-72. Ed. Bert G. Hornback. New York: Norton, 1977.

Fortin, René. "Hermeneutical Circularity and Christian Interpretations of 'King Lear,' " *Shakespeare Studies: An Annual Gathering of Research, Criticism and Reviews* 12 (1979): 113-25.

Girard, René. *A Theater of Envy: William Shakespeare.* New York: Oxford UP, 1991.

Keats, John. "On Sitting Down to Read *King Lear* Once Again" (sonnet). *Poetical Works.* Ed. H. W. Garrod. London: Oxford UP, 1969.

Krantz, David L. "Is This the Promis'd End?': Teaching the Play's Conclusion." Approaches to Teaching World Literature 12 (*King Lear*). Ed. Robert H. Ray. 1986. New York: MLA, 1992. 136-141.

Lascelles, Mary. "*King Lear* and Doomsday." *Aspects of King Lear: Articles Reprinted from Shakespeare Survey.* Eds. Kenneth Muir and Stanley Wells. Cambridge: Cambridge UP, 1982. 55-65.

Mack, Maynard. *Everybody's Shakespeare: Reflections Chiefly on the Tragedies.* Lincoln, NE: UP of Nebraska, 1993. Chapter 8 ("We Came Crying Hither: *King Lear*") uses material published earlier in his *King Lear in Our Time.*)

———. *King Lear In Our Time.* Berkeley: UP of California, 1965.

Muir, Kenneth. *The Great Tragedies.* 1961. London: Longmans Green, 1963. 25-32.

Neale, John E. *Elizabeth I and Her Parliaments: 1584-1601.* 1958. New York: Norton, 1966.

Powell, Ken and Chris Cook. *English Historical Facts: 1485-1603.* London: Macmillan, 1977.

Ryan, Kiernan. *Shakespeare.* Atlantic Highlands, NJ: Humanities P Intl., 1989.

Schoenbaum, S. *William Shakespeare: A Compact Documentary Life.* New York: Oxford UP, 1977.

Shakespeare, William. *King Lear.* Ed. David Bevington et al. 1980. New York: Bantam, 1988.

———. *King Lear.* Ed. Kenneth Muir. The Arden Shakespeare. London: Methuen, 1963.

Spurgeon, Caroline F. E. *Shakespeare's Imagery and What It Tells Us.* 1935. Cambridge: Cambridge UP, 1966.

Weittrich, Joseph. *"Image of that Horror": History, Prophecy, and Apocalypse in King Lear.* San Marino, CA: Huntington Library, 1984.

Williams, Penry. *The Tudor Regime.* 1979. Oxford: Clarendon P, 1983.

Young, Bruce W. "Shakespearean Tragedy in a Renaissance Context: *King Lear* and Hooker's *Of the Laws of Ecclesiastical Polity*." Approaches to Teaching World Literature 12 (*King Lear*). Ed. Robert H. Ray. 1986. New York: MLA, 1992. 98-104.

R. S. White (essay date 1996)

SOURCE: "Shakespeare's *The History of King Lear*," in *Natural Law in English Renaissance Literature,* Cambridge University Press, 1996, pp. 185-215.

[*In the following excerpt, White interprets* King Lear *as Shakespeare's most powerful demonstration of the struggle between Natural and worldly law.*]

In [many of] the plays by Shakespeare . . . a running debate is sustained between the rival claims of Natural Law and positive law in effecting 'poetic justice'.[1] So insistent is this debate that it is virtually a Shakespearian signature, and in *King Lear* we find no exception. In this play, moreover, Shakespeare sets in opposition particularly naked forms of the two legal systems, searches more profoundly the nature of their differences, and reveals in the ending an unsettling ambivalence which is a source of tragedy for the protagonists. The play is one of struggle and dialectic, dramatising, amongst other polarities, an archetypal clash between Natural Law and positive law, trust and mistrust in human beings, Aquinas' idealism about people and the scepticism of Calvin and Hobbes. That the struggle is inconclusive, as it is in *Love's Labour's Lost* and *Measure for Measure* does not diminish the play's power, and gives evidence of Shakespeare's preference for incomplete closure, leaving the audience scope for exercising judgment.

In one sense, as many critics have observed, *King Lear* gives us a very simple view of good and evil. In the terms of Natural Law, good is humanitarian, communitarian, and is driven by compassion, reason, and conscience. This rough generalisation applies not only to Kent, Cordelia, Albany, the King of France, and Edgar, but also to a host of 'little people', and it is a lesson eventually learned and acknowledged by the old men, Lear and Gloucester, through the recognition of their own violations of these principles. Evil is represented as an equation between power and positive law, without reference to conscience or any 'higher' morality, and it is fundamentally individualistic, corrupt, and self-seeking: a rerun of Angelo, and a forecast of Hobbes. Cornwall, Gonoril, Regan, and Edmund stand on this darker side of the division. Both Cordelia and Kent promise exemplary poetic justice along the lines of Natural Law, enabling us to admire and follow virtue, murmur at vice:

> CORDELIA Time shall unfold what pleated
> cunning hides.
> Who covers faults, at last shame them
> derides.

And so it does. But so it does not, at the same time, for although evil is unmasked, good cannot be said to triumph.

Where the play becomes problematical is in the failure of Natural Law to prevail in any *but* a moral sense. Cordelia, the agent most closely equated with Aquinas' maxim that one should follow reason and conscience, lies dead at the end. So, for that matter, do those who conspicuously and unrepentantly (unless we exempt Edmund's final 'good' deed done 'Despite of [his] own nature') violate Natural Law, but somehow the morally satisfying appropriateness of their demise pales into insignificance beside the failure of Natural Law to prevail. The deaths of Cornwall, Gonoril and Regan, and Edmund, have 'poetic justice', but the death of Cordelia makes victory to the virtuous less than Pyrrhic. Meanwhile, even the natural world is deeply ambivalent, at times presented as the pitiless storm which assaults the fragile human community, at others

aligned with the healing herbs that gently bring new life and nurture the human world. At the heart of *King Lear* lies a dialectic that underpins More's *Utopia*. Natural Law, based on the dictates of reason and conscience, is entirely vindicated and upheld in a moral sense, but its worldly failure raises disturbing questions about whether those who wield power in the state will ever allow it to be enacted in the world as it is.

The most significant, recent development in the study of *King Lear* is a reassessment of the relationship between the two printed versions. This appears at first sight to be of interest only to textual scholars, but the ramifications are very important for all branches of *Lear* criticism. The editors of The Oxford Shakespeare *Complete Works*, Stanley Wells and Gary Taylor,[2] succinctly state the basis of the 'revision theory', as a prelude to printing not one but two texts, *The History of King Lear* and *The Tragedy of King Lear:*

> *King Lear* first appeared in print in a quarto of 1608. A substantially different text appeared in the 1623 Folio. Until now, editors, assuming that each of these early texts imperfectly represented a single play, have conflated them. But research conducted mainly during the 1970s and 1980s confirms an earlier view that the 1608 quarto represents the play as Shakespeare originally wrote it, and the 1623 Folio as he substantially revised it.

Some of the evidence for this view, together with consideration of the implications for criticism and stage history, are collected in essays in *The Division of the Kingdoms: Shakespeare's Two Versions of 'King Lear',*[3] where the date of revision is proposed as 1608, contemporary with the writing of *Cymbeline,* whereas the Quarto was evidently written in 1605, and performed in 1606. Another, even more persuasive view put by Christopher Wortham, is that the Folio represents the play as Shakespeare originally wrote it (in line with the editors' stated principles), and the Quarto is as he substantially revised it for performance before the king, as the title-page announces.[4]

The differences between the texts for the purposes of the present book can be summarised in this way. Both Quarto and Folio texts constitute plays with significant Natural Law content, and this subject can be seen as an identifiable and central 'theme' of each. But there is an important difference in that where the Quarto presents *explicitly* issues of Natural Law, the Folio does so largely *implicitly,* so that in reading the latter we can either presuppose supportive knowledge acquired from the former, or presuppose a more hardworking reader or audience. Whichever tack we take, many of the episodes and characters who appear in the Quarto carrying the Natural Law refrain do not even appear in the Folio, and yet the action in the Folio still invites a Natural Law interpretation. This study is primarily based on the Quarto—what the Oxford editors call *The History of King Lear*—quoting many passages which simply do not appear in the Folio, and accordingly I supply references from the Quarto's Scenes (Acts are not used).

Trials and justice

There are many trials and quasi-trials in *King Lear,* and these reveal different forms in which justice and law are defined and executed in the play. In the tumultuous middle of the play, two scenes (in conflated texts, Act III, Scenes 6 and 7; Scenes 13 and 14 in the Oxford text of the *History*), are starkly juxtaposed on the issue of law itself. both scenes are set indoors, but in very different rooms—13 (III. 6) in the hovel standing against the wind and the rain on the open heath, 14 (III. 7) in Gloucester's castle. The one is a fantasy while the other is grimly 'real', but both in different senses parody the machinery of justice. In the former, Lear in his madness orchestrates an imagined, even hallucinatory trial of Gonoril and Regan. Fictional and fantastic as the situation is played out only in Lear's fevered consciousness, Lear follows strict legal procedure, anachronistically since he imports Elizabethan practice into Celtic England. He declares 'I will arraign them straight' (13. 16, III. 6. 20). Arraign means 'To call a prisoner to the bar of the court by name, to read to him the substance of the indictment, and to ask him whether he pleads guilty or not guilty'.[5] He nominates Edgar, impersonating Poor Tom, as the judge: 'Come, sit thou here, most learned justicer' (line 17). 'Thou robed man of justice, take thy place' (line 32). The Fool represents primarily the Elizabethan system of equity and secondarily the driving spirit of simple fairness behind law in general: 'And thou, his yoke-fellow of equity, Bench by his side.' That a fool should represent fairness is a comment on the explosive first scene which precipitated the action of the play. The presence of Lear, still thinking of himself as king, establishes that the court of equity, the king's court, is one presiding jurisdiction, while the 'robed man of justice' evokes a common-law setting. It was only under unusual circumstances that common law and equity sat down together in a 'commission', as, for example, in the trial of Mary Queen of Scots which continued to be controversial many years later, as we have seen in Spenser's case. Kent, disguised as servant to Lear, is also declared 'o'the commission' (line 39). Edgar intones 'Let us deal justly' before breaking off into apparent irrelevance. Addressing a joint-stool, Lear states the charge: 'Arraign her first. 'Tis Gonoril. I here take my oath before this honourable assembly she kicked the poor King her father' (lines 41-2). This is the formal indictment, basically a charge of cruelty and a metaphor for the ill-treatment Lear believes he has received from his daughters, which in his obsessive mind appears to be treasonous. There is no time to read the charge against the other defendant, pre-

sumably Regan, since she 'escapes' much to Lear's annoyance: 'False justicer, why hast thou let her scape?' (line 51). Both Kent and Edgar, for a moment moved by their feelings of pity for the mad king, step out of their 'counterfeitings', dismayed by Lear's state.

Lear now asks a very central question, and it is one that, in some form or another, the play keeps returning to: 'Then let them anatomize Regan, see what breeds about her heart. Is there any cause in nature that makes this hardness?' (lines 75-6). In the Folio the last phrase is 'these hard-hearts' which is perhaps more useful for our analysis of Natural Law content. Anatomy was a favoured study in the early seventeenth century[6] regarded as if it could reveal nature's secrets about human beings, and even generating its own literary form, the 'Anatomy'. Are the 'hard-hearts' in the play, Gonoril and Regan, Cornwall and Edmund, obeying some law of their own natures, or even nature in general, or are they violating their links with humanity in general? The unnervingly fundamental question radiates out into others. Are there any equally 'natural' impulses for good? Is a person's nature actively opposed to Natural Law (as an extreme Calvinist might argue), or can evil, indeed, be a product of nature at all? Are the hard-hearts after the Fall closed to reason and conscience, or are they wilfully denying the innate impulses 'natural' to people, and thus betraying their own place in nature? In the event, the 'trial' does not proceed, although, as a legal writer argues,[7] the scene achieves a double effect of providing 'a mocking of the forms of normal human justice' and also a cathartic process for Lear of dealing formal justice, after which he can sleep. But the question about human nature's capacity for knowing and obeying Natural Law remains, and it is one that the whole play interrogates.

Just as the play as a whole oscillates between hope and despair, good and evil, the scene in a quieter way unfolds another image of action which is of something equally basic, the exercise of compassion and fellow-feeling, for Edgar, Kent, and the Fool (by his continued presence, if not by his words) exhibit loyalty, sympathy, and the desire to protect Lear. It is one of many answers offered to the overriding question: in this case human beings *are* capable of knowing and implementing Natural Law, and 'hard' hearts are therefore not natural. It is a vision of community huddling in mutual protection against the elements. Gloucester adds one to the company when he enters and, having heard of an assassination plot, arranges for Lear, by now sleeping, to be conveyed to Dover to meet the French army with Cordelia. Edgar ends the scene by extolling the values of community and support to one who suffers. The mind, he says, can avoid much sufferance 'When grief hath mates, and bearing fellowship' (line 105), reflecting a favouring of community values over individualism. It appears that the machinery of poetic justice, the proof of Natural Law within the play's universe, is being wheeled onto the stage in preparation for the ending.

An immediate and brutal challenge to this expectation comes after the 'mad' cameo of justice. The following scene, III. 7 (line 14), may show a trial, and even some perverse version of fellowship among mates, but these are of a very different order, a dark parody of the hovel, where human nature itself is seen as 'hard'. Cornwall, Gonoril, and Regan have arrived at Gloucester's castle, full of fury that he has intervened to allow Lear to escape. Cornwall, who has now emerged as the decisive ruler and has taken prime authority upon himself, sends Edmund away, since the interrogation and punishment of Gloucester, he says, is not fit for the 'beholding' of a son's eyes, a somewhat uncharacteristic gesture towards the law of filial kind, in the light of these characters' treatment of Lear. He instructs Edmund to accompany Gonoril, so she also is absent from the rest of the scene. Cornwall and Regan, a married couple surpassing even the Macbeths in ruthlessness, now conduct an interrogation and 'arraignment' of Gloucester which is just as fanciful as Lear's, but far more nightmarish, in that these two as monarchs wield full, legal authority to carry out their sadistic and vindictive wishes. Cornwall is quite precise on this point, saying that although they must observe some due procedure of law, yet, even if the form is questioned, opponents will be silenced by their naked power:

> Though we may not pass upon his life
> Without the form of justice, yet our power
> Shall do a curtsy [courtesy?] to our wrath,
>   which men
> May blame but not control.
>
> (lines 23-6)

Here is one for whom Natural Law either does not exist, or cannot be known by mankind, or simply does not matter. 'The form of justice', positive laws made by worldly authorities, are the only ones that operate. This is legal positivism with a vengeance. Cornwall and Regan bind Gloucester, and, against his repeated appeals to the same conventions of hospitality that haunted Macbeth before the murder of Duncan ('You are my guests', 'I am your host'), proceed to charge him formally with treason and interrogate him about letters he has received from France and about why he has arranged to convey Lear to Dover. Gloucester is as stubborn as Cordelia and Kent had been formerly, in refusing to compromise conscience simply because authority demands—another competing sign of human comprehension of Natural Law—and Cornwall and Regan proceed to their 'punishment', the horrifying act of blinding Gloucester. The narrow legalism of the procedure may accord with Cornwall's 'form of justice', but its sickening inhumanity is thrown into sudden relief by the impetuous act of Cornwall's servant,

who relinquishes one duty of 'service' in favour of a duty of conscience:

> Hold your hand, my lord!
> I have served you ever since I was a child;
> But better service have I never done you
> Than now to bid you hold.
>
> (lines 70-4)

In his 'anger' (line 77), a further sign that moral virtue is based on instinctive knowledge and impulsive acts, he wounds Cornwall, mortally as it transpires, only to be stabbed in the back by Regan and later thrown upon the dunghill. His dying words beg Gloucester to witness the murder with his remaining eye, which provokes Cornwall to remove Gloucester's other eye. In extremity Gloucester calls upon his absent son to 'enkindle all the sparks of nature To quite [requite] this horrid act' (lines 84-5), but, as Regan gloatingly points out, his son Edmund in hatred had been the informant against his father. Immediately Gloucester in remorse realises 'Then Edgar was abused' (line 89), and prays for his own 'forgiveness' and his son's 'protection'. In this sense alone, the 'trial' has succeeded in repeating Lear's anguished question about 'nature', providing contrary and equally poised answers. The scene of legally sanctioned cruelty is ended with discussion between two more servants, like a jury passing a judgment which must by now be shared by the audience in either version of *King Lear,* even though the Folio does not have the words:

> SECOND SERVANT   I'll never care what
>   wickedness I do
> If this man [Cornwall] come to good.
> THIRD SERVANT   If she [Regan] live long.
> And in the end meet the old cause of death,
> Women will all turn monsters.
> THIRD SERVANT   Go thou. I'll fetch some flax
>   and whites of eggs
> To apply to his bleeding face. Now heaven
>   help him!
>
> (97-105 *passim*)

In these two scenes, the one painful for its pathos and the other for its cruelty, we see enacted several 'formal' trials and judgments: the first imaginary and inconclusive, ending with a question rather than a sentence, the second relentlessly moving through to sentence and punishment, a third the Servant's judgment on his master, a fourth the adjudication by Gloucester between his two sons, a fifth the commonsense judgment passed by the two Servants on Cornwall and Regan, and so on, reaching out to the audience's judgment about what has happened. Neither of the former sequences is any less 'mad' than the other in a play which questions the boundaries between imagined and real in, for example and in particular, the 'Dover Cliff' scene. The point is that *law and authority,* their officers alienated to roles, can themselves act with insane cruelty, but that *human beings* acting impulsively and from their own 'natures' can be kind and virtuous, ineffectual in the immediate situation but, if the Servant's case is taken into account, finally effective, since the Servant does kill Cornwall. To the question 'Is there any cause in nature that makes these hard-hearts?' we are directed, at least provisionally, to answer 'no' by witnessing the overwhelming evidence of other 'natural' and spontaneous responses to evil, such as anger, indignation, horror, self-sacrifice, fellowship, protection, and simple kindness. As in Aristotle's conception of justice, the audience's assessment may be based on the emotional grounds of pathos, but it carries weight.

One possible argument is that the 'cause' of evil lies not in nature or the human heart, but potentially in 'office' or institutional authority. Not nature, but vested power, creates these hard hearts. Like Angelo, once a person acquires power, he or she may change. Lear only fitfully realises that his own history, as one who ignored virtue and became hardened when in office, softened only when out of office, darkly exemplifies this conclusion. In allowing this judgment to surface, Shakespeare has placed the audience in the position of a jury, and has arranged the action along the lines of Thomas Wilson's advocate who, we recall, stirs the hearts of judges or a jury to pity the plight of the victims and arouse indignation against their oppressors, in order to find justice: 'In moving the affections, and stirring the judges to be grieved, the weight of the matter must be so set forth, as though they saw it plain before their eyes.' The Servants act as moral guides in our assessment of justice in the Quarto, but their absence from the Folio does not exclude the same conclusion, since the action itself *ipso facto,* stirs the 'affections' against those who blind Gloucester. However, the sardonic conclusion of the play, as of More's *Utopia,* is that on earth the positivists and the sceptics have one trump card, power itself, and this renders those who seek to live by Natural Law deeply vulnerable. The rest of this [essay] will trace the challenges they face, to the dismaying conclusion where poetic justice itself is swept aside in the sight of the limp, dead body of Cordelia in her father's arms. In the terms of this book, *King Lear* affirms the existence of Natural Law located in the human heart, and the hope that it can be implemented through poetic justice, but equally fundamentally questions the likelihood that it can survive more 'unnatural', institutionalised uses (or misuses) of positive law. Shakespeare, while agreeing with Hobbes about the jungle-like savagery of human struggles for power, opposes the Hobbesian assumption that only the state can deliver justice. Indeed, he tends to locate the true source of injustice in the state itself, and the only resistance to injustice lies within human reason and conscience.

The 'trials' in scenes 13 and 14 may be cruel parodies of justice, but they clearly tell us much about the rela-

tionship between positive law and Natural Law in the play. They are also perverse images for the most important trial of all, the one which opens the play when Lear tests his daughters' fitness to rule in his stead. The first scene presents a series of trials within trials. Each of them carries both senses of 'trial', as 'test' and also as quasi-judicial proceeding. First, King Lear puts his daughters on trial. If, in this absolute monarchy, his will is law, then he is making positive law in proposing to divide the kingdom into three parts, and to distribute them on 'merit'. His particular procedure is to promise disposal of the largest bounty 'Where nature doth with merit challenge' (I. i. 53), on the face of it an appropriate task for the machinery of justice. He puts to each of his three daughters in turn a question designed to test 'merit' by simultaneously testing 'nature' according to a version of the law of kind which is expected to operate in Renaissance family relations: 'Which of you shall we say doth love us most' (line 51). It is clear, however, that this is a 'show-trial' since his decision has already been made, and as each sister answers he will offer a predetermined moiety. His decision has been kept from his courtiers, Gloucester and Kent, since at the beginning they were discussing which of Albany (Gonoril's husband) and Cornwall (Regan's) is to gain the larger portion (emphasising in passing that although the women are tested the men are the ones who will financially benefit) but Lear has already made his decision and the public occasion is a ritual affirmation. He has reserved 'a third more opulent' than her sisters' for Cordelia. Gonoril and Regan, playing their part in the royal ceremony, treat Lear's question as a positive law and royal command. They trot out speeches that sound just as pre-scripted as Lear's, and they successfully meet the test. The asides heard by the audience from Cordelia generate the fundamental clash of legal and moral values which will throw the state into civil war and send Lear mad: 'What shall Cordelia speak? Love, and be silent' (line 62).

> Then poor Cordelia!
> And yet not so, since I am sure my love's
> More ponderous than my tongue.
>
> (76-8)

Appropriately enough for one whose name incorporates the word 'heart' (*cor*) she is speaking from the heart rather than from political expediency, from felt duty to conscience rather than hollow 'obedience' (line 278). None the less, when she speaks, her words have legal substance. To the question put by Lear she merely says 'nothing'—equivalent to a refusal to enter a plea of guilty or not guilty, and she redefines the nature of the trial. If, she says, Lear is proposing a contractual bargain (words in return for riches) then she cautions him in language of pure reason and law that such a contract is compromising other contracts:

> Good my lord,
> You have begot me, bred me, loved me.
> I return those duties back as are right fit,
> Obey you, love you, and most honour you.
> Why have my sisters husbands, if they say
> They love you all? Haply when I shall wed,
> That lord whose hand must take my plight
>   shall carry
> Half my love with him, half my care and
>   duty.
> Sure I shall never marry like my sisters,
> Love my father all.
> LEAR   But goes thy heart with this?
> CORDELIA   Ay, my good lord.
>
> (Scene 1, 87-98)

Cordelia is invoking the terms of Natural Law. Her 'heart' (conscience) informs an argument which is more soundly based on reason, conscience, and the law of kind than Lear's own command. She points out with legalistic precision that it is impossible for her sisters to claim to love a father 'all' when each is married and 'owes' love to her husband. Cordelia is not married, but she has been told by Lear that her future husband will be either the King of France or the Duke of Burgundy. At this stage, in a new sense, Lear himself is on trial, for his decree based on authority stands unexpectedly questioned in an impromptu court of Natural Law. Characteristically, he refuses to move his position, and equally true to character Cordelia remains consistent, so that there can be no meeting of minds. By disinheriting Cordelia, Lear is using his royal power in the fashion of Cornwall, to make another decree, directly opposing Natural Law with his authority to make positive law, and ironically displaying the 'hardness' of heart which he later recriminates. His own barely perceived recognition of the fragile basis of his judgment is, no doubt, one of the contributory causes, together with a sense of personal rejection, of his near-hysteria: reason and conscience may be working, but Lear suppresses them, and covers up any doubts he may hold.

The set of trials-within-trials is immediately followed by two others, where the same opposition between Natural Law and positive law is in issue. Kent accuses Lear of madness, folly, and bad judgment in giving his trust and power to the two eldest daughters over his youngest, and by doing so he aligns himself with Cordelia's Natural Law of reason and feelings, claiming to be Lear's 'physician' (line 153). Once again, Lear bases his judgment (if that is not too cool a word for his rage) on the felony of disobedience in trying to make a king break his vow (line 158), of attempting 'To come betwixt [his] sentence and [his] power' (line 160), and he banishes Kent. When he stands on his 'nature' and his 'place' (line 161) he is in reality simply asserting his power over a subject in the manner of positive law. The next trial is between France and

Burgundy, over who will choose Cordelia. Burgundy takes his lead from Lear, equating Cordelia with material wealth and since 'her price is fallen' (line 187) he does not feel contractually bound. France, preferring to follow the reasoning of Cordelia and Kent in declaring that 'Love's not love When it is mingled with regards that stands Aloof from the entire point' and that 'She is herself a dowry' (lines 233ff.), takes her in marriage. France takes her 'virtues' as the dowry and discovers that his love has kindled to 'inflamed respect' (line 255). We might add that after this succession of trials in the first scene, another immediately follows in the second, when Gloucester's claim to love equally his sons Edmund and Edgar is tested. Admittedly, this is precipitated by Edmund's trickery but Gloucester, who prefers astrology, superstition and the state's laws of 'legitimacy' to either reason or the feelings he claims to find within him, is an easy dupe. Effectively he is no better than Lear who arbitrarily disinherited his best loved daughter, since Gloucester first accepts society's prohibition against any rights for bastards, irrespective of his own 'natural' affections, and secondly he does not question allegations of Edgar's disloyalty. The results are just as calamitous for the Gloucester family as those stemming from Lear's mistake for his family, since both families are by the end of the play literally destroyed, except for the one survivor, Edgar.

Positive law, at least in this play, is simply the extension of the will of a sovereign ruler, while Natural Law has its source in the human mind and heart working independently of worldly authority. Lear has set up the situation where these systems are in direct conflict, and the titanic struggles which follow are as much in his own mind as in the state, and they are certainly his responsibility. His madness and his mental breakdown reflect the fundamentalist nature of the clash, and the play relentlessly follows the course of the dispute.

Positive law, authority, and evil

Cordelia, Kent, to some extent Edgar and the Fool, together with a procession of kindly servants, gentlemen (at least in the Quarto) and a doctor, all stand out against positive law on behalf of the Law of Nature in acts which the legal theorist John Rawls[8] would call conscientious resistance. Positive law, vested in worldly authority, however, is seen as immensely effective and destructive, even over Natural Law itself, and to understand its power we must examine its claims to legitimacy. Set against the essentially equitable and Natural Law appeal to feelings that lie behind conscience, charity and reason (in the sense of reasonableness rather than strict logic), lies Cornwall's appeal to authoritarian 'form of justice' as the basis for law. His argument is harder to parry in theory than in practice, for there is behind Cornwall's words a firm, if debatable, understanding of law itself. Law for him is positive law, without appeal beyond itself, and positive law is whatever a properly constituted authority deems it to be. Gonoril later makes the same point to Albany: 'the laws are mine, not thine, Who can arraign me for't?' (Scene 24, lines 154-5), and Lear, although now he lacks authority himself, knows that a king cannot be taken for coining since he is the king himself, owning or even 'being' both currency and law. In the general context of jurisprudence Roger Cotterell makes the point by quoting Emil Brunner:

> The Protestant theologian Emil Brunner wrote: 'The totalitarian state is simply and solely legal positivism in political practice . . . the inevitable result of the slow disintegration of the idea of justice'. And he adds: 'If there is no justice transcending the state, then the state can declare anything it likes to be law; there is no limit set to its arbitrariness save its actual power to give force to its will'.[9]

As many divine-right theorists argued, the monarch is the law, and is at the same time above the law, and one whom only God may judge. Whether or not Natural Law exists is virtually an unnecessary question in this formulation of authority, since not even the monarch needs to be credited with any understanding of it. The situation in the play's kingdom may be messy, with four rather than one in the position of monarchs, but the theory still remains. The only qualification is that authority must be backed up not by morality but by the brute power to enforce law, and it is clear that effectively power now lies with Cornwall, Gonoril, and Regan, Albany being marginalised. Within such an understanding, there is no room for appeals to Natural Law, nor are there *legal* checks against tyranny, arbitrariness, or corruption. Such sanctions as may exist are political (or military), the counter assertion of superior 'power'. The latter half of the twentieth century must be haunted by Hitler's apparent declaration after a massacre of his party members in 1934, ratified by *ex post facto* legislation: 'the supreme court of the German people consisted of myself'.[10] At every level in the system of authority which applies, justice is no more nor less than the will of the person wielding power, and such a will may be implicated in the very corruption which it seeks to judge:

> An the creature run from the cur, there thou might'st behold the great image of authority. A dog's obeyed in office.
>
> Thou rascal beadle, hold thy bloody hand. Why dost thou lash that whore? Strip thine own back.
>
> Thy blood as hotly lusts to use her in that kind
>
> For which thou whip'st her. The usurer hangs the cozener.

> Through tattered rags small vices do appear; Robes and furred gowns hides all.
>
> (Scene 20, lines 151-9)

Shakespeare is returning to the terrain of *Measure for Measure,* the corrupting potential of power, its hypocrisy, and its self-referential ability to enforce unreasonable laws. It is ironic that Lear should be the one who comments thus, since it was he who initiated the new, tyrannical regime by royal fiat, more or less as Sidney's Duke Basilius did in the *Arcadia* (a work which the play draws upon), or like Shakespeare's Duke Vincentio, who delegates rather than transfers authority but still effectively abdicates. Gonoril diagnoses Lear's own confusion: 'Idle old man, That still would manage those authorities That he hath given away' (Scene 3, lines 16-17), but it is perhaps a person who has once held, and then relinquished ultimate authority, who can best perceive the misuses and abuses of power exercised by others, and in recollection of himself in his former station, though he may not so readily admit the latter. Cornwall, Gonoril, and Regan think and act as if authority gives the holder free licence unconstrained by moral considerations or any notion beyond their own wills. The legal maxim, posed as a question, *Quis custodiet ipsos custodes?* is consistently and bleakly answered in this play by 'superior force'. Righteousness alone, however true it may be to reason and conscience, is impotent when rulers are not constrained by moral considerations. On the other hand, as we shall see in examining the virtuous side of the question, the final agents of what we might call rectificatory justice do not work directly, or even fully consciously, but they do oppose force: the Servant, Albany's conscience, even the apparently 'natural' tendency of evil characters to quarrel and destroy one another, are all ultimately effective in some way. Natural Law, like God, may act in mysterious and indirect ways, and apparent defeat can lead to ultimate victory. Milton was to place his trust in such a creed, and as we shall see in the next chapter, on issues such as the accountability of rulers and divorce, three hundred years passed before he was vindicated. For the virtuous forces in *King Lear,* to invoke a phrase in *Love's Labour's Lost,* 'That's too long for a play.'

In the context of a play, the positivist logic can be exposed as dangerous if not quite provably fallacious, but it is sobering to remember that the arguments of Hobbes and legal positivists alike, and the modern system of rule by law itself are, in essence, based on just such a logic. If this were not so, where would a properly elected government gain the authority to reverse law made by its predecessor, and why should common law generate new precedents that so qualify earlier ones that they appear to overturn them? Such checks as we have, lie respectively in the political process for passing statutes and in what the prevailing climate of opinion finds acceptable, not in the substance or procedures of law itself. *King Lear* may show positive law in the ascendancy and at its worst, but the train of events also presents at least 'pathetically' to the feelings of the judging audience in Wilson's sense, why some kind of Natural Law is necessary in a world where positive law rules. Authoritarian, positivist versions of law prevail, but audiences and readers are made aware of a coexisting, more benign and morally-based, form of judgment. That such legitimated injustice prevails over Natural Law in the political world of *King Lear* does not mean that the latter does not exist and operate in the play's moral scheme.

Edmund's law of nature

Before turning more fully to Natural Law in *King Lear*, we must address a different use of the word 'nature'. This second form of 'law of nature' (what in this book has been named natural philosophy as it links all the natural world) is the one under which Edmund at least claims to operate, and it is the driving force behind the other 'evil' characters as well. They obey what is popularly called by neo-Darwinians 'the law of the jungle' (incidentally slighting the peaceable kingdom of animals and plants, where in truth 'necessity' rather than competition is the basic driving force, and also misrepresenting Darwin). Without exception, all critics have interpreted Edmund's famous speech on 'Nature' at face value,[11] but it must be clear on close reading that he is *not* in fact invoking any recognisable version of 'nature'. Rather, he is perversely making himself the slave of the very social 'custom' that he reviles:

> Thou, nature, art my goddess. To thy law
> My services are bound. Wherefore should I
> Stand in the plague of custom and permit
> The curiosity of nations to deprive me,
> For that I am some twelve or fourteen
>   moonshines
> Lag of a brother? Why 'bastard'? Wherefore
>   'base',
> When my dimensions are as well-compact,
> My mind as generous, and my shape as true
> As honest madam's issue?
> Why brand they us with 'base'? with 'base,
>   base bastardy'?
> Who in the lusty stealth of nature take
> More composition and fierce quality
> Than doth within a stale, dull-eyed bed go
> To the creating a whole tribe of fops
> Got 'tween a sleep and wake? Well then,
> Legitimate Edgar, I must have your land.
> Our father's love is to the bastard Edmund
> As to the legitimate. Well, my legitimate, if
> This letter speed and my invention thrive,
> Edmund the base shall to th' legitimate.
> I grow, I prosper. Now gods, stand up for
>   bastards!
>
>   (Scene 2, lines 1-21)

The sense in which Edmund is appropriating 'nature' is semantic rather than substantive, deriving from the term 'natural child' for a bastard who is conceived, as he sees it, outside wedlock in animal passion, rather than within the dull habit of marriage. He also uses nature as antagonistic to society, in the same sense that during the storm scene several characters see the elements of nature as opposing mankind. Like Shylock, Edgar has a point, in so far as legitimate and illegitimate alike are 'natural' in the biological sense and there should be no basis for inequality. However, in his argument he is not appealing to anything beyond human institutions, and in so far as he is relying on a moral order it is merely as a challenge to positive law. He is showing up and railing against the contradictions in laws of inheritance. Renaissance law, for example, based rights to inheritance law on the issue of marriage, and Edmund's complaint is that 'legitimacy' is defined simply through this artificial construction, rather than parentage or even affection. A daughter born before a male heir, even 'legitimately', would have the same grievance. He is not appealing to a transcendent scheme of natural justice, but rather is condemning an existing, hypocritical system and asking for his proper inheritance rights as a 'natural' son, within society's own rules. In his spirit of acquisitiveness he wants not equality and morality as human values in themselves, nor even some form of fair, distributive justice, but rather property and money all to himself. He is no Raphael Hythlodaeus, challenging the basis of property from a 'Natural' point of view. Just as Gonoril and Regan feigned filial love to gain inheritance, so Edmund's plot to turn his father against the 'legitimate' Edgar is a stratagem to get land, not an action based on any kind of law observable in the world of nature. Like Cornwall's group, he basically wants power. Edmund's spurious reference to nature as a goddess is no more than a rationalisation of human greed. It carries no more weight than Lear's description of Cordelia as 'a wretch whom nature is ashamed Almost to acknowledge hers' (Scene 1, lines 202-3).

Obviously, later thinkers such as Hobbes and some followers of Darwin have elevated greed into a 'natural' law by calling it 'human nature', but such a conclusion is not necessitated by Shakespeare's words, nor is it for that matter necessitated by a reading of human history. We may be attracted to the energy and charisma of an actor who plays Edmund, but there are few signs in the text that such admiration should extend to his morality or his actions. They are certainly implacably opposed to the tenets of Aquinas and classical Natural Law.

For every power-hungry tyrant there have been thousands at least silently opposing him; for every greedy person there are many generous ones; for every militarist there have been many who prefer peace, and so on, and all these contrasting types are depicted in

Shakespeare's play. Edmund's 'nature' in *King Lear* is something of a red herring, and our reading of More's *Utopia* might invite us simply to replace his 'nature' with 'private property'. This is not to argue that Edmund does not have a just complaint against a society which allows his father to boast about the lust in which his son was conceived, while depriving that son of a share of the father's inheritance. Such a society is neither just nor fair in our terms. As a concession, Shakespeare mollifies the 'poetic justice' which kills Edmund at the end by giving him one last repentance, perhaps even a conscience, when in his dying moments he sends the order to reprieve Lear and Cordelia, an order that comes too late for Cordelia.

Where Edmund departs radically from classical Natural Law is in defining nature as a vindictive force and directly opposed to human society. He is merely employing the forms of social injustice and power-manipulations that he has learned from others, and the kind of positive law implementation that we have observed in Cornwall. The ruthless sexual acquisitiveness with which he throws Gonoril and Regan into competition against each other is evidence that even in intimate situations he follows these rules of power. Natural Law requires quite the reverse, centralising charity and the placing of social good above personal ends, co-operation above competition, drawing on the physical universe, if at all, only as a metaphor for 'laws' which are regular and consistent. Kent's 'The tyranny of the open night's too rough For nature to endure' (Scene 11, line 2) makes clear the reading of 'nature' as human and communitarian in essence, pitted metaphorically against the 'tyranny' of outward storms. The clearest contrast in the play lies between Edmund and Cordelia. Where his actions are motivated by the desire for individual power and status, and where his thoughts reveal little concern for conscience until his final gesture, Cordelia is willing to forfeit power and status when they are offered, before she will compromise on conscience. What we may be witnessing in the creation of Edmund is the birth of a modern myth of nature as red in tooth and claw, and an equally post-Hobbesian, Darwinian, assumption that human nature is the same.

Gonoril and Regan, and later Cornwall, also follow no 'natural' imperative. They simply want power, wealth and property, and given their chance the first two use unashamed flattery and unfelt sycophancy to achieve their ends. Once they have power, as we have seen, they equate law with their own wills, without reference even to the 'gods' that many others call upon, let alone to a system of morality or social justice. Gonoril and Regan, significantly, kill each other: dog may not eat dog in the world of nature (although it may eat, for example, rabbit for necessary food), but human may kill human when they enter the lists of power-play and competition, abandoning the Law of Nature written in

their hearts. Cornwall is killed by what can be interpreted as a rival moral system, more literally by a servant acting on behalf of an altruistic set of values, even if the Servant is himself slain. When we wish to answer 'no' to Lear's question 'is there any cause in nature that makes these hard-hearts?' we need not be sidetracked by Edmund's call to 'Nature' as his goddess.

Necessity, charity, and Natural Law

In our analysis of *King Lear* we may now move to a consideration of most of the major issues raised in this book. The play gives a representation of an absolutist political system where rulers seem rarely if ever constrained by moral considerations (the 'moral' man, Albany, loses power *because* he has qualms, and even when offered power at the end he refuses it) or by anything beyond military power itself. Might is considered, at least by the mighty, to be right, in a treatment by Shakespeare which could be read as a merciless satire on perversions of power. Despite many characters' calls upon gods, there are no *dei ex machina* and no evidence of manipulative gods.[12] The most virtuous character, Cordelia, ends up not only unrewarded but dead, and the two who might, as suffering indexes of good and evil, be said to have learned something, Lear and Gloucester, both also die. We should recall that Shakespeare has gone out of his way to create such an unrelieved and negative picture of the consequences of tyranny, since he has decisively altered most of his sources in giving us these deaths. If, as I have argued, Renaissance literature is, according to rhetorical theory, supposed to be morally educative, Rymer's question of *Othello* could be directed to *King Lear*: 'what learn you by that?', when all vestiges of poetic justice are violated, at least by Cordelia's death.

At the same time, this play above all others has been seen, especially in the twentieth century, as the most morally educative of all those by Shakespeare or any other writer. The contradiction—absence of an effective, implemented moral code within the play-world may paradoxically lead to the construction of a supremely moral experience for the audience—is resolved by the omnipresence of Natural Law in all its facets, and by the crucial 'participation' in Aquinas' sense, of readers and audiences in completing the circle. The resonant line 'Thou, Nature, art my goddess' could be appropriated from the reprehensible Edmund and redistributed in a different sense, certainly to Cordelia and also to each reader and each member of an audience. It is unseen Nature working its Laws of reason and conscience through virtuous characters, which dictates our capacity to make moral judgments on the action, and to distinguish between good and evil even where evil prevails in the worldly sense. The play is far from utopian, and indeed is despairing of social improvement until power itself is eradicated, but it does consistently endorse a code of values based on

Natural Law which leads virtuous characters to oppose authority's version of positive law. In turn, Cordelia, Kent, and others are driven by conscience and reason into positions of civil disobedience based on their beliefs in communitarianism, loyalty, and human sympathy. In a play which is backgrounded with the English adversities of common life, 'Poor pelting villages, sheep-cotes, and mills' (Scene 7, line 184), where the mere sight of beggars enforces 'charity' (line 186), a set of local communities with 'wakes and fairs and market towns' (Scene 13, lines 68-9), ranging in its *dramatis personae* from monarchs to a naked Bedlam beggar, it is significantly those who do *not* hold power who emerge as the most virtuous. They are driven by simple 'need', by 'necessity', and they are solicitous of others in need, only because they know what it is to suffer. In his unregenerate state, threatened with the disbanding of his personal followers, Lear had fulminated 'O, reason not the need! Our basest beggars Are in the poorest thing superfluous': 'Allow not nature more than nature needs, Man's life is cheap as beast's' (Scene 7, lines 423-6), but he speaks without the experience of true need. He is rationalising 'superfluities'. In the next scene but one, cold in the storm and seeking shelter, he recants, musing 'The art of our necessities is strange, that can make vile things precious' (Scene 9, lines 71-2). As the Fool reminds him, and as he altruistically realises, in a storm rain is wet, shelter is welcome. Lear finds that need does exist amongst humans, and furthermore that there is human responsiveness, and the impulse to help others. He has entered a new ethical arena, where 'need' *must* be 'reasoned', and where it is the imperative to charity, Luther's prime nutrient of Natural Law. The lesson is one that can be learned by Lear only in extreme adversity, divested of his pomp and ceremony. It is one of the play's starkest ironies that tenants, paupers, and beggars, all of whom have little means and many basic needs, are able to understand the basis of mutual aid in hardship, while kings, with all the resources at their disposal to eliminate poverty, cannot; that only need can recognise need, and, spurred by reason and conscience, try to meet it.

We have already noted the actions and words of servants who are more moral than their masters and mistresses, and to them we could add other characters who appear at least in the Quarto, such as Gloucester's tenant, the Old Man who offers to help him, the messenger who describes so eloquently Cordelia's grief (Scene 17, lines 17-24), the patient, understanding Doctor who helps Lear, and others. It seems no accident that the dramatic design puts Cordelia in the position of a disinherited child, Edgar into the disguise of a beggar, and Kent that of a Servant, and makes a Fool the trusted companion and political adviser to the fallen king, for it appears that virtuous action is the exclusive prerogative of the marginalised, the powerless, and the insignificant. While the great and lofty in power (including Lear as king) pursue self-interested motives, Machiavellian tactics for holding power, and a Hobbesian sense that human life is expendable, those at the other end of the social spectrum (including Lear himself when he is no longer king), demonstrate sympathetic charity. The 'intense imagining' of Edgar in his construction of the dizzying heights of Dover Cliff has not only a poetic and rhetorical but also a moral basis, and it is significant that his stage-managing of his father's 'fall' is, at least in Edgar's eyes, justified: 'Why I do trifle thus with his despair Is done to cure it' (Scene 20, lines 32-3). Cordelia's responses are consistently based on reason as the moral faculty and conscience as the stimulus to action. Her 'Nothing', simultaneously so disastrous in its results and so glorious in its courage, is based not on obstinacy, but a moral principle, in the face of a statement couched as a request but in reality a command:

> LEAR   But now, our joy,
> Although the last, no least to our dear love:
> What can you say to win a third more
>   opulent
> Than your sisters?
> CORDELIA   Nothing, my lord.
> LEAR   Nothing?
> CORDELIA   Nothing.
>   (Scene 1, lines 77-83)

Her earlier asides confirm her love for her father and her refusal to be drawn into a public declaration of it for personal gain. Love is silent in a context of power, her 'love's more richer than [her] tongue', to be proved by actions and not by words. Her reasoned response to Lear's demand is to assert some tenets of Natural Law: one loves according to some 'bond' of nature and inclination rather than to prescribed forms of words. Forced to 'heave' her heart into her mouth and use words when she would prefer to be silent, Cordelia must couch her response in terms that sound at first like positive law based on contractual obligations, but this implication is a coercion of Lear in setting up the situation. She is forced to answer authority with law. When we recall that axiomatically positive law is supposed to be in line with Natural Law, we can recognise that Cordelia is not standing upon a positive law—indeed, she is refuting Lear's positive 'law'—but instead explaining rationally the moral basis for the 'law of love' in the very terms introduced by Lear. 'Nothing', her answer to Lear's indecorous question supplemented by her explanations, carries the full weight of reason and conscience. When reluctantly talking, she cannot avoid altogether Lear's linguistic circuit, and, as he asserts an authoritarian version of law (rewards will be distributed according to royal whim), so she asserts a Natural Law (rewards and punishments are irrelevant beside the overwhelming compulsion of reason and conscience). Like most examples of conscientious resistance and refusal to obey authority's demands, Cordelia's gesture precipitates as much if not more anger and destruction than would outright opposition, for she is refusing to accept the basis for authority at all when it conflicts with conscience. The events of the play, dismaying as they are, unravel from this exchange. Responsibility, however, lies not with Cordelia but with Lear who, again like Basilius, attempts to assert positive law over Natural Law.

Kent's outburst, claiming the privilege of spontaneous and 'natural' anger at witnessing an injustice, is a different kind of political action. He implicitly accepts the absolute authority of Lear, but directly opposes his judgment and justice in the immediate case of appointing royal successors. Like Cordelia, Kent takes inspiration from the 'region' of his heart, but, in accusing Lear of madness, of folly, 'hideous rashness' and of bowing to flattery in misjudging his daughters, he is not questioning Lear's authority. He begs the king to reserve his state and apply 'best consideration' by reversing the decision, thus bringing positive law into line with manifest justice based on true deserts. He claims the position of a physician trying to cure a disease (lines 154-5), a metaphor which points to the 'naturalness' of his advice. Lear, speaking in Angelo's terms of alienated authority based on 'our sentence and our power' (an anticipation of Cornwall) asserts that neither his 'nature' nor his 'place' nor (more to the point) his 'potency' can accept such opposition, and he banishes Kent. Thereafter, Kent is completely and loyally consistent to his own self-defined 'bond', for, disguised as Caius, servant to Lear, he acts in willing servitude to his master. He refuses to accept the legitimacy of the new regime of rulers since, in his view, it is not based on a judgment consistent with reason and conscience. While Cordelia tacitly repudiates Lear's authority to act as he does, Kent accepts his authority but opposes his judgment (in both senses of the word, judicial and psychological), but they both agree that Natural Law is here opposed to positive law. Kent's touching farewell to Cordelia says as much:

> The gods to their protection take thee, maid,
> That rightly think'st, and hast most justly said.
>   (Scene 1, lines 172-3)

In the 'mini-trial' that follows, Burgundy refuses Cordelia in marriage, revealing that he sees her simply as property, as a dower, whereas France bases his decision to marry her on the basis of love and 'inflamed respect' ('She is herself a dowry'), and on 'reason without miracle' (Scene 1, line 213). Burgundy is establishing himself incidentally as a legal positivist in looking no further than immediate contractual circumstances of a dowry, France as a Natural Lawyer, looking beyond present authority to more ultimate values.

As the action unfolds, Cordelia becomes more and more equated with benevolent and healing natural forces. To her all natural things in distress are equally deserving of pity:

>   Mine injurer's mean'st dog,
> Though he had bit me, should have stood that
>   night
> Against my fire. And wast thou fain, poor
>   father,
> To hovel thee with swine and rogues forlorn,
> In short and musty straw? Alack, alack!
>   (Scene 21, lines 34-8)

Tears of sympathy and grief are her emblem, and virtually a whole scene (17) is devoted to them:

> GENTLEMAN . . .
> And now and then an ample tear trilled down
> Her delicate cheek . . .
> KENT   O, then it moved her?
> GENTLEMAN
> Not to a rage. Patience and sorrow strove
> Who should express her goodliest. You have
>   seen
> Sunshine and rain at once; her smiles and
>   tears
> Were like, a better way . . .
>   (Scene 17, lines 13-20 *passim*)

> 'What, i'th' storm? i'th' night?
> Let piety not be believed!' There she shook
> The holy water from her heavenly eyes,
> And clamour mastered, then away she started
> To deal with grief alone.
>   (Scene 17, lines 29-33)

Kent's comment in response that 'The stars above us govern our conditions' strikes us as glib in the manner of the superstitious Gloucester, when seen in the light of the constant equation drawn in the latter stage of the play between Cordelia and natural forces. It is she who brings the description of Lear,

> As mad as the racked sea, singing aloud,
> Crowned with rank fumitor and furrow-weeds,
> With burdocks, hemlock, nettles, cuckoo-
>   flowers,
> Darnel, and all the idle weeds that grow
> In our sustaining corn.
>   (Scene 18, lines 2-5)

She collaborates with the doctor who uses not drugs but nature and its 'simples operative', perhaps the 'idle weeds' some of which had curative functions, as Culpepper testifies, to induce sleep, and even, in the case of 'sweet marjoram' later mentioned by Lear, to allay madness:

> Our foster-nurse of nature is repose,
> The which he lacks. That to provoke in him

Are many simples operative, whose power
Will close the eye of anguish.
                        (Scene 18, lines 13-16)

Cordelia calls on nature itself to heal:

All blest secrets,
All you unpublished virtues of the earth,
Spring with my tears, be aidant and remediate
In the good man's distress!
                        (Scene 18, lines 16-19)

Cordelia's earlier, stubborn insistence on conscience is now linked with nature itself, as benevolent and as a moral force, to construct an emblem of Natural Law, brought into consistency with natural philosophy. Her nature is poles apart from Edmund's, which is closer to Hobbes's model of acquisitive 'human nature'. The victimisation and execution of her define more clearly than anything else could, that her enemies are also the enemies of both nature and Natural Law. The unutterable pathos (in Thomas Wilson's sense) of her death is generated from the echo of her natural imagery in Lear's anguished 'Why should a dog, a horse, a rat have life, And thou no breath at all?' (Scene 24, lines 301-4). Nature's companion has now become no more precious and unique than any of nature's beings. The image of her lifeless body makes a mockery of Albany's obtusely simple minded distribution of poetic justice:

All friends shall taste
The wages of their virtue, and all foes
The cup of their deservings.
                        (Scene 24, lines 297-9)

If this 'friend' is dead, then there is a sense in which virtue itself, far from being rewarded, has ceased to be.

If the audience and readers are in the position of a jury, then the ending of this play requires us to give our verdict by referring to our reasoning powers and activating our consciences, and in this case to feel outrage at the deeds of those who opposed Natural Law, while acknowledging the worldly destructiveness of evil. The educative function of the play, then, lies not in apportionment of rewards and punishments as Nahum Tate's eighteenth-century rewriting attempted to represent, but in making us 'feelingly', through witnessing victimisation, extend and implement the lessons of Natural Law, charity, and sympathy. An unfortunate inference is that outside Thomas More's state of Utopia, no such ideal world is available as a refuge, just as in *Utopia* itself the world of Europe remains incorrigible. Even Lear's comforting vision of prison as a place of observing gilded butterflies and acquiring the mystery of things is a whistle in the darkness.

The ambiguity discovered by critics in the line 'And my poor fool is hanged' (Scene 24, line 300), whether intended by the dramatist or not, points us towards another equation, that between Cordelia and the Fool.[13] The Fool also speaks from a basis in Natural Law, although he is more retributory and reproachful than Cordelia, losing no opportunity to bait Lear with the king's folly and injustice. He is the truly anti-authoritarian man, professionally licensed to challenge and undermine the power of those above him in the social hierarchy, and particularly the monarch at the top, and to disrupt even linguistic and conversational expectations. He taunts Lear, sometimes harshly, for dividing the kingdom so inequitably and for banishing his youngest daughter, but any cruelty in his attacks stems from loyalty towards Lear, love of Cordelia, and respect for a sense of collective good. He is more angrily subversive towards Gonoril when she holds power: 'I am a fool, thou art nothing' (I. iv. 192). In calculated puns, misdirections, underminings, he is directly threatening not only the authority of speakers, but that of language itself, at least in its assumed status as a stable signifier of 'meaning'. Unlike Kent and Cordelia, the Fool has no capacity to influence events. He even 'pines away' after Cordelia goes to France, and eventually out of the play altogether. His role is largely that of gnomic commentator on folly, injustice and breaches of Natural Law. His is the one lonely voice that refers, however·sceptically and strangely, to a utopia of justice, equality, and freedom from exploitation, and his mysterious 'prophecy' dwells on how natural these states are—as easy walking, in fact—and yet how unlikely they seem to be for mankind to achieve, at least in the 'confusion' prevalent in this play's Albion:

When every case in law is right;
No squire in debt, nor no poor knight;
When slanders do not live in tongues,
Nor cutpurses come not to throngs;
When usurers tell their gold i'th'field,
And bawds and whores do churches build,
Then comes the time, who lives to see't,
That going shall be us'd with feet.
                        (Folio only, *Tragedy* 3.2.87-94)

In other words, when the world is honest, then living will be as easily natural as walking. The weird comment that follows, sounding more the note of postmodern novels than a Jacobean play, 'This prophecy Merlin shall make; for I live before his time', throws the time of utopia outside the play and outside history itself, defining it as the kind of timeless state of Natural Law which is eternally present as a moral touchstone, but which the Fool, in his pessimism, sees as absent from the dealings of people in his world.

Lear himself is disingenuous in claiming to be 'more sinned against than sinning' (Scene 9, line 60) for it was he who precipitated all the disasters depicted as a consequence of the 'division of the kingdoms.'[14] The play can be rather reductively read as a punishment of

Lear and the kingdom as a whole for his violation of Natural Law at the beginning of the play, not only a breach of the 'law of kind' in rejecting his best loved daughter, but also an injustice in rewarding the unworthy daughters and punishing the virtuous one. The consequences of these 'sins' are to drive Lear into a direct confrontation with the very forces of nature which he has opposed. The storm scene can be read as allegorical in Spenser's sense, as the forces that Lear has gone against now humble and educate him. From this archetypal encounter Lear may learn some things, but too late for remedy. One thing he does learn about is 'the art of our necessities' (Scene 9, line 71), a concept legally and emotionally defined, which we have seen to be important in *Love's Labour's Lost*. 'Necessities' or needs are infinitely various, and depending on the situation 'can make vile things precious' (*ibid.*). But in this context they take us back to the notion of a minimal content of Natural Law. In order to survive in a violent storm when threatened with assassination, the text reveals, necessities are shelter and protection, literal and psychological, both of which require a form of human bonding which must be 'natural' in all senses, instinctive, and fulled by reason and conscience. Mutual aid and charity in its fullest sense take the place of self-defence in the struggle for survival, when the antagonist is the natural world of wind and rain rather than a human adversary.

The play gives an array of circumstances in which discrimination between what is a true need and what is not is raised as a problem. It is his daughters' dismissal of his 100 men that drives Lear to contemplate the issue. Gonoril and Regan clearly act politically rather than from their avowed distaste for the retinue's lack of house-training. To tolerate the existence of what amounts to a standing army loyal to the former king would, to these political pragmatists who believe that might is right, be courting the possibility of a reactionary coup. Regan questions Lear's 'need' of even one man in attendance, which unleashes his rather confused but enraged response:

O, reason not the need! Our basest beggars
Are in the poorest thing superfluous.
Allow not nature more than nature needs,
Man's life is cheap as beast's. Thou art a
  lady;
If only to go warm were gorgeous,
Why, nature needs not what thou, gorgeous,
  wearest,
Which scarcely keeps thee warm. But for true
  need—
You heavens, give me that patience, patience
  I need!

(Scene 7, lines 423-30)

Unregenerate as yet, Lear is simultaneously glimpsing and resisting the idea of 'need' as something that ap-

plies only in a world of deprivation, and not in that of a privileged 'lady' or a king. Even the poorest beggar wears what is superfluous to his needs, and once we 'reason' about whether something is needed, then we reduce man's life to the level of a beast's and strip it of all dignity. Ironically, a minute or so before, he had been speaking of 'Necessity's sharp pinch', and it is this he is about to encounter in the storm on the heath. Within a scene or two, Lear is to reassess his views, when he meets a 'philosopher' who wears virtually no clothes in a storm.

Lear is forced to test his analysis of 'need' by experiencing a situation offering little more than an animal's comfort in the wild (an analogy drawn by Cordelia), unprotected, 'bare-headed' (Scene 9, line 61) in the storm, 'minded like the weather, most unquietly' (Scene 8, line 2). Here, as he 'Strives in his little world of man to out-storm The to-and-fro conflicting wind and rain' (Scene 8, line 10) on a night when even the bear, lion, and wolf keep their fur dry, Lear learns a fundamental law that 'true need' provides a model for existing within nature and its laws. Increasingly, his perceptions embrace the lesson that previously, kept ignorant in the mantles of authority, he could not have understood. He sees the storm as a judicial scourge, finding out 'undivulged crimes Unwhipped of justice' (Scene 9, lines 52-3) crimes committed by the very people who claim to hold authority in the human world. Reduced to 'necessity' he sees that the true need for humanity is not a troop of men or gorgeous robes, but simple justice. Lear learns that in a storm his companion the Fool 'needs' shelter, the glimmerings of a moral sense which previously had been denied him. Extended to the social and political sphere, the logic leads towards *Utopia*'s:

Poor naked wretches, whereso'er you are,
That bide the pelting of this pitiless night,
How shall your houseless heads and unfed
  sides,
Your looped and windowed raggedness,
  defend you
From seasons such as these? O, I have ta'en
Too little care of this. Take physic, pomp,
Expose thyself to feel what wretches feel,
That thou mayst shake the superflux to them
And show the heavens more just.

(Scene 11, lines 25-33)

This marks a reversal of his outburst to Régan. Instead of saying even a beggar has more than he 'needs' to survive, and thus more than animals, he is saying that the beggar has *less* than is necessary, and he perceives that the injustice is directly caused by the superfluity appropriated by the rich and powerful. Gloucester, later reduced to similar need, discovers an equally communalistic, utopian-like basis of social justice, when in severe need himself he finds the compassion to give his purse to a presumed beggar:

> Heavens deal so still.
> Let the superfluous and lust-dieted man
> That stands your ordinance, that will not see
> Because he does not feel, feel your power
>   quickly,
> So distribution should undo excess,
> And each man have enough.
>
> (Scene 15, lines 64-9)

'Enough' for all is the maxim of Natural Law, 'distri-bution' is its basis for material justice, and the logic of 'feeling' is awakened by the Aristotelian advocate deploying the rhetoric of pathos. The sardonic point silently made by the play is that it seems impossible for anybody in authority to learn this lesson and im-prove things, simply because they are blinkered by the very fact of holding authority. They have too much to lose personally by instituting such a state of Natural Law.

Lear even finds his natural 'noble philosopher' (Scene 11, lines 141 and 159), his 'learned Theban' (line 144) of Natural Law, in Poor Tom who literally has 'noth-ing', and who is 'the thing itself! Unaccommodated man', a 'poor, bare, forked animal', and he removes his clothes in fellow-feeling (lines 98-9). Edgar's gib-berish in his role as Poor Tom associates him with unpleasant facets of nature, eating cowdung, old rats, and ditch-dogs, like the beggars described by Raphael Hythlodaeus who are 'whipped from tithing to tithing, and stock-punished, and imprisoned' (lines 122-3) sim-ply for existing.[15] He becomes for Lear the walking evidence of man's inhumanity to man, breaches of Natural Law, of injustice, and of the 'need' for con-science in making a human society. As well as being, with the Fool, the focus for Lear's new-found compas-sion, Edgar's condition also becomes in Lear's eyes the model of an ecologically non-exploitative exist-ence, owing nothing to the silkworm for silk, to cattle for leather, to sheep for wool, and to cats for perfume. In the role of Poor Tom, one of his many quick changes, Edgar is less a 'character' than a functional catalyst, an agency for change and moral awakening.

Lear's sentiments in this part of the play are as communitarian, anti-individualistic, and anti-authori-tarian as More's in his fictional version of Utopia. Once again, consistent with the Fool's despairing prophecy, neither Lear nor the play survives to see a state of justice according to Natural Law implemented in human society. Nor are there many signs that such a state will exist, without fundamental change in the world. It is for audiences and readers, as the judge and jury presiding over an 'as-if' scenario, to pass judg-ment and take the lessons into their own societies.

That, as in *Love's Labour's Lost,* is too long for a play and can occur only afterwards.

The parallel, interlocking plot of the Gloucester fam-ily, follows the course of Lear's. A father commits an injustice against his progeny, a sin against Natural Law, and not only does he suffer from his choice to follow vice and shun virtue, but so in different ways do the sons. In this case responsibility is shared (as it is be-tween Lear, Gonoril and Regan and Cornwall) because the plot is hatched and perpetrated by Edmund for his own, self-seeking reasons. At the same time, as I have suggested, it was Gloucester (like Lear or, again, like Basilius) who set in motion the train of events by his ambiguous attitude to Edmund, at once admiring him as a reflection of the father's amoral virility and yet disinheriting him according to society's laws on bas-tardy. In strictly narrative terms we might exonerate Gloucester by saying he is duped, but that would mean we could exonerate Lear also, on the grounds that he was deceived by Gonoril's and Regan's speeches in the first Act. Like Lear, Gloucester acts impetuously, without consulting the evidence of his own eyes and his experience about Edgar's filial affection. He su-perstitiously blames the 'stars' in the astrological sense instead of his own actions which were indifferent to human reason and conscience. As Lear begins sump-tuously dressed, surrounded by troops, and learns by being naked and alone, so Gloucester begins meta-phorically with sight which he neglects to use, and learns through blindness. When he is led to 'see' the scene of Dover Cliff through Edgar's poetic construc-tion, he is doing no more and no less than when he had 'seen' Edgar distorted through Edmund's eyes. He too has allowed positive law, the rules concerning 'legitimacy', to blind him to more important, human values. In this sense Edmund does have a grievance, and, although the play does not condone his actions, it does explain them, and in doing so places primary responsibility for the family fortunes squarely with Gloucester himself.

Power and injustice

Right through his writing career, from the debates on the use and misuse of power centring on Henry VI and Richard III to Gonzalo's vision of a political utopia in *The Tempest,* Shakespeare worried away at problems concerning the nature of justice and authority in po-litical worlds. He encompassed a dizzying kaleidoscope of models of justice, but the central distinction from which his plays derive much of their dramatic, moral, and intellectual energy is between man-made decrees, and something more 'natural' and eternal in its origin, beyond a world where people make mistakes of family justice and where humanity must perforce prey on it-self. This is precisely the distinction between positive law and Natural Law. And if the dialectic pervades all Shakespeare's plays, nowhere is it more central, more

Act III. Scene iv. Gloucester, Fool, Lear, Kent, and Edgar. By B. West (n.d.). The Department of Rare Books and Special Collections, The University of Michigan Library.

problematic, and more pressing than in *King Lear*. This is somewhat ironic, since it is a play, like *Love's Labour's Lost,* which itself flouts all conventions of the form of 'poetic justice' as classically defined. Virtue, far from being rewarded, lies dead. Expectations are unfulfilled at every turn. To suggest that Shakespeare is systematically requiring audiences and readers to act as jury in a case raising Natural Law issues of reason and conscience is, as the evidence of this book testifies, not anachronistic in the Renaissance, but fairly standard practice. Milton's *Areopagitica* is the greatest theoretical exposition of the obligation upon readers to form their own moral judgments, and his *Paradise Lost* is no less insistent a practice of this theory than is *King Lear*. We have constantly discovered through our exploration of Natural Law that, at least in its classical version, its main assumption is that people do not need to be *told* the difference between right and wrong, but that within each individual is the innate capacity to discriminate through the faculties of reason and conscience. Even one like Spenser

showing Calvinist influence can, in the medium of poetry, draw upon such a belief. Furthermore, according to the model, a person in tune with Natural Law by a kind of instinct inclines towards virtue and away from vice. In this sense *King Lear* becomes a clear example of a work in which the dramatist appeals to audiences to activate exactly these faculties. The plays of the period themselves bear witness to the fact that audiences were more imaginatively and morally active than those witnessing our post-Victorian stage practices. Brecht was one of the few who sought to tap the same active, judgment-forming faculties in his audiences, but it is arguable that entrenched, modern conventions were against him. Edward Bond follows in his footsteps, and it may be no accident that his most powerful plays are the adaptation called *Lear* and the play in which he represents Shakespeare writing *King Lear, Bingo*. Bond, like Shakespeare, gives no pat or easy solutions based on simple poetic justice, but rather he requires each member of his audience to search and construct a set of personal moral values out of the experience of the plays.

The most conspicuous point of both Shakespeare's versions of *King Lear* is the absence of a schematic 'poetic justice' which could easily have been applied by simply following sources, allowing Cordelia to live on, and take up the throne, or even to have allowed Lear to live on with his beloved daughter in autumnal reconciliation, as in Tate's version. Shakespeare has gone out of his way to reject his sources (whether legendary or historical), by killing off Cordelia and leaving a hiatus in the ruling of Britain. No self-respecting dramatist would expect his audience to accept this state of affairs as morally right, no matter what we think of the play's aesthetic qualities. The alternative 'happy ending' such as Tate's simply leaves the reader and audience in a state of cosy complacency, omitting the 'supplement' of manifest injustice chosen by Shakespeare.

An important but sadly overlooked book published in 1949 by Edmond N. Cahn, *The Sense of Injustice*,[16] posits that human beings may well be more 'naturally' able to recognise injustice than justice, as a prelude to the awakening of a desire for justice itself. Aristotle's emphasis on pathos in adjudicating a trial at law could be said to work on the same principle. The moral 'work' required of an audience by such a scheme clearly continues after the play is over, with an invitation to the reader and audience to transfer a largely tacit and emotionally pitched analysis and exemplification of good and evil into their own lives, as, in a very real sense, the capacity to judge came initially from their own experiences. It is in the nature of rhetoric, after all, to convince us 'feelingly' of injustice, without needing to spell out what justice itself compels. Once again, in lighter mode, *Love's Labour's Lost* emerges as the work, in terms of moral structure, oddly closest to *King Lear,* like a playful 'first run' for the immense tragic passion of the *Lear* plays. The crucial difference is that the courtiers in the earlier comedy 'deserve' the deferment and uncertainty of marriage they face at the close of the play, since they have overridden Natural Law by agreeing to obey a misguided edict, whereas Cordelia does not deserve death because she has, if anything, embodied Natural Law by instinctively following reason and conscience and by inclining to virtue. Here we might locate a more general 'law' of Shakespearian drama which has been overlooked in all the hundreds of accounts of 'the nature of comedy' and 'the nature of tragedy'. Shakespeare's comedies, at their heart, become a contemplation of the effecting of justice according to their own internal Natural Law of sexual attraction, while his tragedies become a contemplation of injustice, violations of Natural Law precepts. This is so even in plays with a more 'villainous' titular hero than Lear himself: nobody at the end of *Macbeth* can bring back Lady Macduff and her children, the innocent victims of tyranny, and at the end of *Coriolanus* there is no force that can resurrect all those civilians killed in war

by the military machine. The main offenders may be dead, and to this extent some version of poetic justice applies, but the profound injustices perpetrated by them cannot be rectified, and must instead remain as permanent witnesses to injustice. The lesson may be starker in *Lear* since the good and the evil alike are destroyed in a travesty of poetic justice, emphasising that injustice itself is intransigent when there are those around who do not follow innately the tenets of Natural Law.

Here lies an answer to the problems raised by the existence of 'two versions' of *Lear*. Whereas it is becoming common to describe the Quarto as compassionate and the Folio as harsh, we can equally argue that there is no fundamental moral difference between the two, and that if anything the Folio is more rigorously consistent to the underlying moral schema present in both. The Quarto gives more spoken guidance by offering choric voices and examples of human charity and Natural Law in operation which we may hang onto and identify with. The Folio, by shaving these away, leaves us more morally isolated, so that we must make up our own minds about good and evil without prompting, more or less like Milton's Adam and Eve at the end of *Paradise Lost.* It tests the reader and audience more starkly by requiring us to choose by reference to faculties which come from within us rather than being asserted by the play. This parallels exactly the morally active *practicum* of reading and interpreting advocated by Sidney, Milton in *Areopagitica,* and the Aristotelian theory of rhetoric described by Wilson. Cordelia, in this sense, has acted in lonely integrity, and the audience and reader are encouraged to do likewise.

The actual conclusions drawn by an audience from the Folio cannot be different in kind from those generated by the Quarto. For example, it would be considered frankly impossible for any audience not to be repulsed by the blinding of Gloucester, whether or not we have two Gentlemen moralising directly about it at the end of the scene. Their presence in the Quarto 'History' version may focus the humanist response by introducing voices of pity within the action, yet, although in the Folio 'Tragedy' the tone is different, there is no reason why the reader/audience does not feel directly the same pity and outrage, perhaps even more keenly because the stage spectators are ignoring callously some obvious moral assumptions. The Folio is, then, simply carrying a stage further. the Quarto's insistence that Natural Law is a 'need' from within which can be obscured by the existence of questionable positive laws enacted by worldly tyrants, but which can be retrieved by the exercise of human reason and conscience. While the Folio may give us the same number of violations of Natural Law as the Quarto, and fewer affirmations of it, this does not mean that Natural Law is excluded from its orbit. At the same time, Nahum Tate's *Lear* is different from Shakespeare's two versions. Tate eliminated all the doubts, uncertainties, ambivalences, and, in the currently voguish word, 'anxieties' of Shakespeare.

The little group of characters left huddling, exhausted, at the end of both versions of *King Lear* are like the audience in the position of Adam and Eve at the end of Milton's epic. They have witnessed something akin to the tragedy of the Fall of mankind in the evil perpetrated, and they have no refuge in the kind of platitudes and superstition which, for example, Gloucester had fallen back on. 'Speak what we feel, not what we ought to say', whoever says it (Albany in the Quarto, Edgar in the Folio), is a reproof to any glib or easy answer to the violations of Natural Law which we have witnessed: Lear's initial rejection of his loving daughter, Gloucester's failure to trust his son, the blinding of Gloucester, the hanging of Cordelia, and so on. Evil may be dead, but so is good. At the same time, like Adam and Eve, they know these sobered witnesses have the equipment for enlightened moral judgment, and realise also that they will be individually tested in their lonely attempts to follow virtue and shun vice. If they forget the lessons of Natural Law demonstrated by the actions they have witnessed and participated in, they may inadvertently fall themselves, or watch others fall into the blind and tyrannical ways of authority. They have reached a real but fragile point of moral awareness.

Readers and audiences occupy the same position, as, even more pertinently, do critics claiming any 'authority' over such a play. The logic of *King Lear,* with its decisive celebration of virtue over vice and its equally decisive extinction of virtue, folds back to catch in its snare those who would impose any kind of positive law, literary or legal, over Natural Law. As in *Utopia,* no matter how splendid is the prospect of a world based on reason and conscience, that world may not be achievable, because human greed and power-seeking are too deeply entrenched in the existing structures of authority and power: but the effort of trying should still go on. In answer to those who debate whether *King Lear* is an optimistic or a pessimistic play, we might conclude that it is optimistic in so far as Shakespeare believes in the existence, innate in the hearts of human beings, and the supreme importance of, Natural Law; pessimistic in so far as he does not give indications that we may foresee its imminent implementation in the political and legal processes of human society, because those who have power to change the political world for the better, are the 'hard-hearts' sealed against the promptings of Natural Law. If Shakespeare indeed has the transportability between cultures and times that have invited the term 'universality', the source lies not in his presentation of presumed verities, but his unsettling ambivalence about the possibility of ever arriving at such verities. His unerring focus on the central human activities of doing justice and injustice, and the problems each raises, is the central dynamic of all his plays and the reason

they are applicable in some way to such diverse cultures. In this focus, the dialectic between Natural Law and positive law is fundamental, and *King Lear* is its powerful exposition.

Notes

[1] This chapter draws freely from my previous publications, *Innocent Victims: Poetic Injustice in Shakespearean Tragedy* (second edition, Athlone Press, London, 1985), chapter 8, and 'King Lear and Philosophical Anarchism', *English,* 37 (1988), 181-200. I am not sure whether it is encouraging or dismaying that we go on discovering much later what we were trying to say on earlier occasions. In this case, research into Natural Law has clarified and simplified my thoughts on the play, and in no way reverses them. I also owe debts to John Danby, William Hazlitt, A. C. Bradley, G. Wilson Knight, and William Elton.

[2] William Shakespeare, *The Complete Works* (Oxford, 1986) p. 1025. Quotations taken from this edition.

[3] Edited by Gary Taylor and Michael Warren, Oxford Shakespeare Studies (Oxford, 1983).

[4] Christopher Wortham, 'Ghostly Presences: Dr Faustus meets King Lear', *Meridian,* 14 (1995), 65-74.

[5] *A Concise Law Dictionary,* ed. P. G. Osborn (London, 1964).

[6] John Donne's imagery is full of 'anatomy', and it was, after all, the age of William Harvey's discovery of the circulation of blood. See Devon L. Hodges' fascinating little book, *Renaissance Fictions of Anatomy* (Amherst, 1985).

[7] John D. Euce, 'Shakespeare and the Legal Process: four Essays', *Virginia Law Review,* 61 (1975), 390-433.

[8] John Rawls, *A Theory of Justice* (Oxford, 1971). Rawls' book, while not dealing directly with Natural Law, has been a continuing influence behind this book.

[9] Cotterell, *The Politics of Jurisprudence,* p. 143. I should point out, in defence of quoting at third hand, that Cotterell's book is an excellent 'Critical Introduction' which works largely through quotations, many of which are useful here.

[10] Cotterell, *The Politics of Jurisprudence,* p. 131, quoting Fuller.

[11] My analysis differs markedly from John Danby's in *Shakespeare's Doctrine of Nature. A Study of 'King Lear'* (London, 1949), although I readily admit my general indebtedness to this book. Although he does not ignore Natural Law, his main analysis deals with what I have called 'natural philosophy'.

[12] Among the many accounts of this contentious issue, see J. C. Maxwell, 'The Technique of Invocation in _King Lear_', _Modern Language Review_, 45 (1950), 142-7; Barbara Everett, 'The New King Lear' in _Critical Quarterly_, 2 (1960), 325-9; and compare William Elton, _King Lear and the Gods_ (San Marino, California, 1966).

[13] It has sometimes been argued that one actor doubled for Cordelia and the Fool. I find it very implausible that these two characters were played by the same actor, since both roles are identified with specialist actors, a professional comedian and a boy actor respectively.

[14] For the topicality of this issue in James I's reign, see Leah Marcus, _Puzzling Shakespeare_ (above, chapter 7, note 18).

[15] See Michael Goldman, _Shakespeare and the Energies of Drama_ (Princeton, New Jersey, 1972), pp. 94ff., for a graphic description of the kind of beggar's persona Edgar asumes.

[16] Edmond N. Cahn, _The Sense of Injustice: An Anthropocentric View of Law_ (New York and London, 1949).

FURTHER READING

Anderson, Linda. _A Kind of Wild Justice: Revenge in Shakespeare's Comedies_. Newark: University of Delaware Press, 1987, 195 p.

Explores the subject of justifiable revenge for "wrongs there is no law to remedy" in Shakespearean comedy.

Boris, Edna Zwick. _Shakespeare's English Kings, the People, and the Law: A Study in the Relationship between the Tudor Constitution and the English History Plays_. Cranbury, N. J.: Associated University Presses, 1978, 261 p.

Investigates late sixteenth-century English constitutional law as it applies to Shakespeare's two historical tetralogies and _King John_.

Buckley, G. T. "Was Edmund Guilty of Capital Treason?" _Shakespeare Quarterly_ 23, No. 1 (Winter 1972): 87-94.

Suggests that _King Lear_'s Edmund may not have been guilty of the charges of high treason brought by Albany, according to English common law.

Carroll, William C. " 'The Form of Law': Ritual and Succession in _Richard III_." In _True Rites and Maimed Rites: Titual and Anti-Ritual in Shakespeare and His Age_, edited by Linda Woodbridge and Edward Berry, pp. 203-19. University of Illinois Press, 1992.

Explores Richard III's transgression of the "form of law" in his pursuit of succession to the English throne in _Richard III_.

Cerasano, S. P. " 'Half a Dozen Dangerous Words.' " In _Gloriana's Face: Women, Public and Private, in the English Renaissance_, edited by S. P. Cerasano and Marion Wynne-Davies, pp. 167-83. Detroit, Mich.: Wayne State University Press, 1992.

Examines Hero's comic use of "honest slander" in her plot to encourage Benedick's and Beatrice's love in _Much Ado About Nothing_ in relation to the historical adjudication of Renaissance slander cases.

Echeruo, Michael J. C. "Tantistry, the 'Due of Birth' and Macbeth's Sin." _Shakespeare Quarterly_ 23, No. 4 (Fall 1972): 444-50.

Considers the argument that Macbeth's murder of Duncan was in some sense justified by Duncan's disregard of the law of tantistry—which states that a king's vacated throne, rather than being immediately succeeded to by his son, should be granted to the first ranking adult male of the royal family.

Graham, Kenneth J. E. " 'Without the form of justice': Plainness and the Performance of Love in _King Lear_." _Shakespeare Quarterly_ 42, No. 4 (Winter 1991): 438-61.

Discusses the importance of "plainspeakers" in _King Lear_ whose truthfulness contradicts the corruption of human judgment.

Hamill, Monica J. "Poetry, Law, and the Pursuit of Perfection: Portia's Role in _The Merchant of Venice_." _Studies in English Literature 1500-1900_ XVIII, No. 2 (Spring 1978): 229-43.

Focuses on the noble and complementary Renaissance pursuits of poetry and legislation as they are personified in the character of Portia.

Johnson, Lonnell E. "Shylock's Daniel: 'Justice More Than Thou Desir'st.' " _CLA Journal_ XXXV, No. 3 (March 1992): 353-66.

Probes allusions to the Biblical figure of Daniel as they relate to the resolution of the legal plot in _The Merchant of Venice_.

Jordan, Constance. "Contract and Conscience in _Cymbeline_." _Renaissance Drama_ XXV, New Series (1994): 33-58.

Analyzes contracts of family and state represented in _Cymbeline_.

Roth, Marty. " 'The Blood that Fury Breathed': The Shape of Justice in Aeschylus and Shakespeare." _Comparative Literature Studies_ 29, No. 2 (1992): 141-56.

Studies the legal dimensions of revenge, justice, and social exclusion in Aeschylus's drama _Eumenides_ and Shakespeare's _The Merchant of Venice_.

White, R. S. "*King Lear* and Philosophical Anarchism." *English* XXXVII, No. 159 (Autumn 1988): 181-200.

Examines the "anarchic" treatment of themes of authority and justice in *King Lear*.

Wilks, John S. "The Discourse of Reason: Justice and the Erroneous Conscience in *Hamlet*." *Shakespeare Studies* XVIII (1986): 117-44.

Comments on manifestations of providential justice and misaligned conscience in the figure of Hamlet.

Williams, George Walton. " 'With a little shuffling.' " In *"Fanned and Winnowed Opinions": Shakespearean Essays Presented to Harold Jenkins*, edited by John W. Mahon and Thomas A. Pendleton, pp. 151-59. London: Methuen, 1987.

Investigates the ambiguity of Claudius's succession in *Hamlet* as it hinges upon the metaphor of "shuffling"—an action that Walter argues only delays the inevitable retribution for Claudius's murder of his brother.

Henry IV, Parts 1 and 2

For further information on the critical and stage history of *1* and *2 Henry IV*, see *SC* Volumes 1, 14, and 39.

INTRODUCTION

Traditionally, critical discussion of *1* and *2 Henry IV* has centered primarily on Prince Henry, or Hal. In this vein, scholars have examined Hal's fitness as the future ruler of England and have compared him favorably or unfavorably to the serious-minded rebel, Hotspur. Closely connected to this focus is critical speculation over whether Hal's transformation from funloving ne'er-do-well to responsible heir is a sincere and natural result of his maturation or part of a calculated, cynical plan. Similarly, critics have debated the nature of the Prince's relationship with his father and with Falstaff. Many have argued that Falstaff acts as a surrogate father to Hal and that the Prince's subsequent rejection of the fat knight in *2 Henry IV* is cruelly Machiavellian; others have seen it as a necessary gesture of maturity. More recently, scholars have dispensed with efforts to pinpoint Hal's motives. Instead, critical discussion has concentrated on the tragic elements of the two history plays and how the characters and actions in *1* and *2 Henry IV* reflect Elizabethan mores as well as the shifting perspectives of both Elizabethan and modern society—particularly with regard to the issues of law and justice.

Of importance to several critics is the degree to which tragedy as a genre informs both *1* and *2 Henry IV*. Catherine M. Shaw (1985), for example, argues that for all their dependence on history, a tragic thread runs throughout both plays in the form of Henry IV's guilt-racked conscience for his part in the overthrow and assassination of his predecessor, Richard II. By contrast, Harry Levin (1981) asserts that the tragic focus is Falstaff, whose comic "vitality" and tragic "mortality" are in precarious balance—particularly in the more somber play, *2 Henry IV.*

These differing viewpoints regarding genre mirror what has been described as the two plays' ambiguous and, at times, contradictory perspectives: the raucous tavern scenes versus the politically charged Court scenes, Hal's unclear motives (Machiavellian or simply prudent), and Henry's role as usurper versus Hotspur's role as rebel. Increasingly, critics have been less apt to blame one character more than another for the moral ambiguity of the two plays and have instead looked to the audience, the playwright, and the times. For instance Marc Grossman (1995) suggests that Shakespeare created conflict between Falstaff's appealing roguery and Hal's royal responsibilities so that his audience would recognize and accept the gray areas that exist in Hal's predicament as well as in the audience's "everyday" life. F. Nick Clary (1988) also refers to Shakespeare's contemporary audiences in his discussion of Hal's dubious behavior toward Falstaff. He concludes that an interpretation of Hal's behavior depends on the social experiences of the viewer and that "during the Elizabethan Age, when the amorality of Machiavellian politics was practiced as much as it was criticized, a belief in Hal's moral recovery may, in fact, be a testimony to the possibility of regaining an ideal which had been lost." Stephen Greenblatt (1985) asserts that the source of the ambiguity in *1* and *2 Henry IV* resides not in the audience but more specifically in the politics of Elizabethan England and the fact that the theater of the time reflected a playwright's continual conflict between being faithful to his own ideas and submitting to royal censorship.

Ultimately, discussions of ambiguity of genre and perspective in *1* and *2 Henry IV* revolve around the issues of law and justice. Dain A. Trafton (1981) and E. A. Rauchut (1994) address the question of Henry's legitimacy as king. Trafton contends that since Henry fails to create "an entirely new order" consisting of his own rule of law and neglects to "obliterate even the memory" of Richard II's reign, he dooms himself to the continuing cycle of rebellion. Rauchut suggests that this rebellion is in part justified after Henry "ignor[es] the law of arms" and demands that Hotspur hand over his prisoners, thereby "committing a royal theft that causes civil war." Norman Sanders (1977), Stanley D. McKenzie (1992), and Daniel J. Kornstein (1994) link the themes of law and justice to Hal's ambiguous nature. All three see aspects of the Prince's behavior as part of his attempt to legitimatize his own eventual rule. Sanders, for example, argues that Hal shuns the "sick nation" he is due to inherit from his father and instead frequents the lawless world of the tavern so that he can one day "create single-handedly a totally new royal milieu" in which to rule legitimately. Similarly, McKenzie asserts that Hal's much debated rejection of Falstaff is in fact justified if the Prince hopes to be respected and obeyed by his future subjects. Indeed, McKenzie adds, while such behavior might seem brutal to a modern audience, an Elizabethan audience schooled in the tenets of Machiavelli would have considered Hal's actions wise. Finally,

Kornstein asserts that in *2 Henry IV* the "sober, solid, fair-minded lawyer figure" of the Lord Chief Justice is counterpoised against Henry IV as "a symbol of disorder." Thus Hal's coming of age occurs when he rejects his father's world which includes the lawlessness of Falstaff and turns to the legitimate rule personified by the Lord Chief Justice.

OVERVIEWS

Larry S. Champion (essay date 1978)

SOURCE: "History into Drama: The Perspective of *1 Henry IV*," in *JGE: The Journal of General Education,* Vol. XXX, No. 3, Fall, 1978, pp. 185-202.

[*In the following essay, Champion presents an overview of* 1 Henry IV, *examining its structure and characterization. The critic asserts that this play reveals Shakespeare's increasing expertise at combining impersonal history with personal, dramatic interest.*]

Following the composition of *Richard II* a conscious bifurcation seems to occur in Shakespeare's dramaturgy. The playwright in *Julius Caesar* continues to develop the focus of psychological analysis and the internalized protagonist which lead directly to his major tragic achievements. Brutus, like Richard II before him and Hamlet and Othello after him, confronts an ambiguous situation requiring decisions and commitments which cost him his life even at the point of his greatest sensitivity to the true nature of things. If Brutus' illumination is insignificant in comparison with that of Hamlet and Othello, he like them engages the spectators through soliloquies and asides in the intensely limited focus upon the spiritual agony of what Harley Granville-Barker terms the "war within himself."[1] In the *Henry IV* plays and *Henry V*, on the other hand, all probably written within two years of *Julius Caesar,* Shakespeare essentially returns to the fragmented perspective and the static characterization of *1, 2, 3 Henry VI*. In these plays he apparently was searching for a dramatic focus of sufficient scope to accommodate the movement of national forces through a significant portion of time. Even though an intense concentration upon a single individual would tend to blur the larger perspective by absorbing the spectators' interest and deflecting their attention from the broad social and political issues, he seemed progressively to realize that effective drama depends upon at least minimal emotional interaction between character and audience. And, especially in *3 Henry VI*, he moved toward a combination of the structural features which produce the detached view necessary for the historical theme and the devices of internalization which provoke a limited emotional response to the tragically inept title figure and the calculating and heartless political opponent

destined within a few years to be the most infamous of English kings. Such a perspective is basic also to *1 Henry IV*. Here, however, he combines multiple plot lines with an emphasis upon character ambivalence which yields far richer and more provocative interactions than anything in those earlier Lancastrian stage worlds. "Poised between tragedy and comedy,"[2] this work reflects the remarkable potential of the history play "as a separate form."[3]

The structural devices by which Shakespeare consciously shapes this broad perspective in *1 Henry IV* are readily demonstrated, For one thing, no single character dominates the action either physically or emotionally.[4] The principal figure in *Richard III*, by comparison, delivers well over thirty percent of the total lines (1127 of 3599); over five percent of the total lines (185 of 3599) involve him in soliloquies (eleven) or asides (five). Similarly Richard II speaks more than one-fourth of the total lines in his play (738 of 2755). While Richard's only genuine soliloquy occurs moments before his death at Pomfret Castle (66 11.), he gives the word-drunk impression throughout the play that he for the most part is talking to himself (or to the spectators) despite the presence of additional characters on stage. Moreover, in both plays the great majority of the other scenes focus sharply upon the protagonist through conversations about him—whether in *Richard III* from Margaret, Anne, Buckingham, and Richmond, or in *Richard II* from Bolingbroke, Carlisle, Gaunt, York, or the parasites. In *1 Henry IV,* to the contrary, the title character speaks only eleven percent of the lines (340 of 3049). Three characters, in fact, deliver a larger number, though none is as predominant as the central figures of the Richard plays (Hotspur—18.6%, 566 lines; Hal—18.7%, 569 lines; Falstaff—20.4%, 623 lines). In terms of developing a close emotional rapport between the character and the spectator, the devices of internalization are relatively insignificant in the play (5%—160 lines); the eight soliloquies are scattered among three characters, no one of whom speaks in private more than three percent of the total lines.

For another thing, Shakespeare simultaneously develops three individually significant plot strands—Henry IV's apprehensions concerning both his kingship and his relations with his son, the activities of the rebellious feudal lords which center on the impetuous Hotspur, and Hal's escapades at Eastcheap involving the world of Falstaff and his debauched associates. Totally unlike either the single dramatic focus on Richard III's Machiavellian ascent to the throne or the intersecting personal and political fortunes of Richard II and Bolingbroke—and equally unlike the thematically related experience of the two family units in *Hamlet* or *King Lear* which intensifies the dramatic focus—the plot strands of this play expand the spectators' vision. While extensive and important parallels do exist between the comic and the serious scenes, the more notable fact is that each strand depicts a vision of a different socio-political stratum, and consequently the dramatic perspective tends to become broad and diffuse rather than narrow and intensely personal. The emerging theme focuses not on the experiences of a single individual but on the evolving condition of a nation as reflected in the fortunes and misfortunes of several significant personalities.

Both the action and the setting of the play are committed to breadth. The scenes, for example, take place in such diverse points as Windsor, Rochester, Gad's Hill, Northumberland, Wales, Shrewsbury, Coventry, and London; even the London scenes move from the polarities of the palace to the tavern at Eastcheap.[5] And the disparate plot lines are carefully interwoven within the eighteen scenes as established in F1—the King's private concerns in three (I, i; III, ii; V, i—426 11.), the rebels' perspective in seven (I, iii; II, iii; III, i; IV, i; IV, iii; IV, iv; V, ii—1136 11.), the Falstaffian world in six (I, ii; II, i; II, ii; II, iv; III, iii; IV, ii—1279 11.). The lines coalesce, of course, in the final two scenes with principals from each strand in combat on Shrewsbury field. Prior to that point, however, the spectators view English society from several angles and from various geographical points, and the activities of both the Lancastrian lower classes and the aristocracy reflect the political and social instability which will culminate in open rebellion.

This theme of national instability Shakespeare accentuates by the juxtaposition of Henry and Hal as political foils in both *1* and *2 Henry IV*. Certain modifications which he imposed upon his sources, first described as such by A. R. Humphreys, underscore the dramatist's concern for such a conflict.[6] The historical events of the two plays are roughly in the chronological sequence found in the source, but the domestic events (Hal's relationship with his father) are essentially Shakespeare's own creation. Daniel makes no mention whatever of discord between father and son, while Holinshed notes only that the old King in the final year of his life had suspicions about the Prince; similarly, though there is much ado in *The Famous Victories* concerning the Prince's debauchery, it is again late in Henry's life that he laments the curse of a son who will destroy him.

While establishing this human element so vital to genuinely effective drama, Shakespeare also maintains a broad focus upon the larger design—specifically, the limited capacities of Henry IV as a ruler and the implications of those limitations for the body politic of England—by measuring Henry and Hal against the concepts of monarchy shared by those in his contemporary audience. These late sixteenth-century views, in very general terms, rest on two essential criteria—proper exercise of power and equitable dispensation

of justice. Concerning the former, the king, who should receive the scepter as a direct lineal descendant of the royal family, is God's vicar or lieutenant on earth; "The king, yes, though he be an infidel, representeth the image of God upon earth."[7] The duty, both religious and social, of the populace is obedience. As a homily published in 1571 states, "Such subjects as are disobedient or rebellious against their princes, disobey God and procure their own damnation."[8] In the body politic, obedience to the prince is essential; even a tyrant is preferable to anarchy, which would come with rebellion.[9] It is argued that monarchy in form arose from nature as an extended concept of the family unit.[10] The prince's duty is analogous to a father's duty; he exercises rule from the awareness of the need for order, for the welfare of the total community and nation. Hence, the king must be powerful, and he must be capable of using his authority to protect himself and his people.

Such, essentially, is Henry IV's concept of kingship, a concept, as Derek Traversi observes, predicated entirely on the ground of "political effectiveness."[11] Troubled by a realization that he has achieved the throne at the expense of the rightful King and by a sense of guilt for Richard's murder, he knows full well that his success as a ruler will be determined by his public virtue, specifically his ability to maintain civil order in the land. Regardless of whether Bolingbroke coldly and calculatingly planned to manipulate Northumberland as a stepping stone to political office, the fact is clear at the beginning of the play that Northumberland believes Henry to have broken his pledged word that he sought only the Dukedom of Lancaster. Moreover, established on the throne, the new King seems to shun the alliance from the north as readily as he had earlier embraced it. Dismissed from council, Worcester asserts, "Our house, my sovereign liege, little deserves / The scourge of greatness to be us'd on it, / And that same greatness which our own hands / Have holp to make so portly" (I, iii, 10-13).[12] The king with royal dispatch evaluates the rebels' strength and moves to confront them. There is no hesitation before Shrewsbury; the armies of the King are well directed and deployed to fight for protection of order in the land.

Certainly the spectators of the play would admire a king who, so unlike Richard II or Henry VI, exercises without hesitation his royal authority with a positive determination to uphold the law of the kingdom against the hydra-head of rebellion.[13] Yet the spectator would perceive with equal clarity that this same king attempts in practice—as Machiavelli did in theory—to separate public and private virtue. Certainly the clearest key to this emphasis on appearance occurs in *Part 2* in his deathbed speech to the king-elect:

> God knows, my son,
> By what by-paths and indirect crook'd ways

I met this crown, and I myself know well
How troublesome it sate upon my head.
To thee it shall descend with better quiet. . . .

. . . . .

And all [my] friends, which thou must make
    thy friends,
Have but their stings and teeth newly ta'en
    out;
By whose fell working I was first advanc'd,
And by whose power I well might lodge a
    fear
To be again displac'd; which to avoid,
I cut them off. . . .
                              (IV, v, 183-187, 204-209)

He is quick to counsel his son to "busy giddy minds / With foreign quarrels" (213-214) so that his own disjunction with his former allies might be put from the minds of the people. But in *Part 1,* as well, Henry explains the method by which he won the public opinion "that did help him to the crown" (III, ii, 42). By "being seldom seen" (46) and on such occasions dressing himself "in such humility" (51), Henry developed in reputation "like a robe pontifical" (52), which "Seldom but sumptuous, show'd like a feast" (58).

It is dramatically appropriate that this king, whose rule is vitally dependent upon decisive and powerful action in the face of danger and whose public reputation must appear inviolate even though his private actions smack so strongly of blatant practicality, should draw a specific analogy between Hotspur's valorous search for public glory and Hal's debauchery and apparent lack of concern for his public image. Indeed, Hotspur, "the theme of honor's tongue" (I, i, 81), "sweet Fortune's minion and her pride" (83), is a man of Henry's own heart; the King can understand, in a way in which he is never able to comprehend Hal, the political riser who is overtly conscious of public opinion. Kingly praise, it should be noted, comes even in the face of Henry's knowledge of Hotspur's rebellious action of denying prisoners to the throne. Furthermore, the King later praises Hotspur for his public display of virtue (III, ii, 115 ff.) in a scene immediately following Hotspur's compliance in a projected tripartite division of England. When the full effect of these scenes is considered, there can be little doubt that Shakespeare is utilizing Henry's praise of the "politic virtue" of Hotspur as yet another reflection of Bolingbroke's limited concept of rule. For certainly Henry praises, as one having "more worthy interest to the state / Than [Hal]" (98-99), a man who is specifically exposed as lacking qualities inherent in the ideal ruler.

In any event, Henry IV meets the sixteenth-century demands of a ruler who can and will exercise his power for the maintenance of unity in the kingdom. Beyond

that, however, the king, in whom public and private virtue must agree in the equitable dispensation of justice should rule for the welfare of the subject. Gascoigne in *The Steel Glass* (11. 114-134) strikes particularly at the ruler who would strive "to maintain pomp and high, triumphant sights" and "never care . . . to yield relief where needy lack appears." Castiglione[14] lists among the attributes of the ideal prince wisdom, justice, courtesy, and liberality in his treatment for and knowledge of his subjects. Similarly, Starkey[15] raises the specific issue that there is nothing more repugnant to nature than a whole nation governed by the will of a prince who neither understands the nature of his subjects nor knows their needs. Above all, it is Elyot who most clearly describes this concept of a king in his discussion of the training of a prince.[16] Like the "principal bee" the prince moves through society—not with "prick or sting" but with "more knowledge than is in the residue"; though, to understand his subjects, he might move temporarily among "herbs that be venomous and stinking," he gathers "nothing but that shall be sweet and profitable." Furthermore, though a prince study the classics diligently, his theoretical knowledge must be tempered by his experiences in society itself. And, as the prince moves in society, "What incredible delight is taken in beholding the diversities of people . . . to know the sundry manners and conditions of people, and the variety of their natures."

It would be difficult to escape the obvious contrast between Henry's constant concern to hold himself aloof from the people, and his son's ability to move with affable ease throughout the London populace. That the Prince is gaining useful knowledge of his future subjects through his associations is explicitly stated by Warwick in *Part 2:*

The Prince but studies his companions,
Like a strange tongue, wherein, to gain the
    language,
'Tis needful. . . .
The Prince will in the perfectness of time
Cast off his followers, and their memory
Shall as a pattern or a measure live,
By which his Grace must mete the lives of
    others,
Turning past evils to advantages.
                              (IV, iv, 68-79)

In *Part 1* the Prince suggests a similar advantage in a conversation with Poins: "They [the commoners of London] take it already upon their salvation, that though I be but Prince of Wales, yet I am the king of courtesy, and tell me . . . when I am the King of England I shall command all the good lads of Eastcheap" (II, iv, 9-15). In *Henry V* the new King notes to the French ambassador the use he made of his wilder days (I, ii, 268-269). Even Falstaff in his blustering manner implies that the Prince has tempered the cold-blooded valor which he inherited from his father by his association with and knowledge of his subjects (*Part 2,* IV, iii, 118-123).

In short, although Prince Hal inherits kingly valor and courage from his father—as is witnessed in his exploits at Shrewsbury and in his victories over the French armies at Harfleur and Agincourt—he possesses an attitude toward the monarchy which his father never achieves. Instead of a usurped throne, he inherits an established one; instead of striking internecine blows to protect an unsettled position of authority, he will use the power of a unified England for the positive advantage of expanding his realm; instead of concentration upon the power to punish, he exercises a justice tempered with mercy. Henry IV's cruel treatment of Richard II and his sentencing of Worcester and Vernon to immediate execution might have been politically expedient, but the comparison with Prince Hal's mercy is striking. Immediately after Worcester and Vernon are sentenced, the Prince requests and receives permission "to dispose" of Douglas. In signal contrast to Henry IV's death sentences, Hal delivers Douglas "Up to his pleasure, ransomless and free" (V, v, 28): "His valors shown upon our crests to-day / Have taught us how to cherish such high deeds / Even in the bosom of our adversaries" (29-31). This action is even more significant when one considers that the Prince is showing mercy to one who was at the very center of the rebellion. For Worcester had earlier utilized the capture of "Douglas' son" (I, iii, 261 ff.) as the sole motivation for Hotspur's rallying troops against the King in Scotland, and it was Douglas who very nearly carried the day for the rebels in his personal combat with the King. The Prince also tempers justice with mercy in the much-discussed rejection of Falstaff and his associates, for, although they are "banish'd till their conversations / Appear more wise and modest," the new King "hath intent his wonted followers / Shall all be very well provided for. . . ." (*Part 2,* V, v, 98-99, 97) In Hal's later action as King he is overtly merciful in his unwarranted freeing, just before the army's departure to France, of one "That rail'd against our person. We consider / It was excess of wine that set him on, / And on his more advice we pardon him" (*Henry V,* II, ii, 41-43). Even to Cambridge, Exeter, and Grey, the traitors who have accepted bribery from the French, Henry states that, concerning his person, he seeks no revenge, but that their execution is mandatory for the safety of the kingdom (II, ii, 174-175). Moreover, Shakespeare consciously emphasizes the king's mercy in his actions against the citizens of Harfleur, though historically no such mercy was shown.[17]

A further distinction in *1 Henry IV* between Henry and Hal emerges from the dialectical tension created by their perceptions of the other principal figures in the play. Henry's estimation of both Hotspur and

Falstaff, for example, is simplistic at best. The one he condones for his valor, merit, and ambition; the other he condemns for his morally reprehensible conduct and his parasitic attachment to the heir apparent. Hal's appraisals are sharply different; he sees both for what they are—individuals who, not devoid of charm, indeed possessing certain admirable qualities vital both to personal fulfillment and popular acclaim, are ultimately unbalanced, intemperate, and self-destructive. The dichotomy, more specifically, is established in the opening lines. Henry IV, as we have previously noted, admires Hotspur and would gladly believe the two Harrys to have been secretly exchanged at birth. Even facing a blatantly traitorous Hotspur at Shrewsbury in Act V, he for "considerations infinite" will not sanction a single combat between his son and the adversary of "great name and estimation" (i, 102, 98). Hal, to the contrary, while obviously recognizing Hotspur's courage and battlefield skills, also perceives the bravado and the unrestrained Herculean ambitions of the man. The one he parodies in conversation with Poins at the Eastcheap tavern:

> I am not yet of Percy's mind, the Hotspur of the north: he that kills me some six or seven dozen of Scots at a breakfast, washes his hands, and says to his wife, "Fie upon this quiet life! I want work." "O my sweet Harry," says she, "how many hast thou kill'd to-day?" "Give my roan horse a drench," says he, and answers, "Some fourteen," an hour after; "a trifle, a trifle."
>
> (II, iv, 101-108)

The other he addresses in soliloquy over Hotspur's body as an "Ill-weav'd ambition" which, by provoking and feeding the conviction that a kingdom itself is too small, has resulted only in "two paces of the vilest earth" (V, iv, 88, 91).[18]

Their views of Falstaff and the society of commoners are equally divergent. Henry IV characterizes his son's relationship with them as one of "riot and dishonor" (I, i, 85), of "barren pleasures, rude society" (III, ii, 14); like Richard II Hal "amble[s] up and down, / With shallow jesters" and grows "a companion to the common streets" (60-61, 68). Hal, to the contrary, is never even partially blind to Falstaff's dissolute qualities. From first to last, he addresses his fat companion bluntly and honestly, if good-naturedly. Falstaff is a time-waster, courting trouble with the law (I, ii, 5, 42-43, 66-68); he is a "fat-guts" (II, ii, 31), a liar ("gross as a mountain, open, palpable" [iv, 226]), a villainous thief (314), a devil in the shape of a fat man (447-448), an impudent rascal in whose bosom "there's no room for faith, truth, nor honesty" (III, iii, 153-154). Over his presumably dead body Hal declares that Falstaff would be sorely missed "If I were much in love with vanity!" (V, iv, 106). Illustrations could continue at considerable length, but surely we must assume that Hal from the opening scenes of the play

*Lewis Gordon as Sir John Falstaff and members of the Festival Company in a scene from
the 1979 Stratford Festival production of* Henry IV, Part II.

has no illusions whatsoever about his companion. Indeed, he specifically tells us as much in soliloquy. But he also sees beyond the present moment, suggesting that his present associations and actions will make him later shine more brightly when he throws off his "loose behavior" (I, ii, 208), just as the sun seems more brilliant when emerging from dark clouds. This tone of conscious analysis runs, in fact, like a thread through the entire play. Hal asserts that he is "of all humors" (II, iv, 92). He reports, in a statement which slices through the context of levity, that he eventually will banish "plump Jack" from his presence (479). And, on the battlefield he makes good his promise of his opening soliloquy; by openly referring to his truant youth and to an ostensibly instantaneous transformation, he dazzles those around him—even his enemy Vernon, who reports that he seems possessed of "such a grace / As if he mast'red there a double spirit / Of teaching and of learning instantly" (V, ii, 62-64).

Various structural features, then, such as multiple plot strands, the diversity of character and of setting, and the stylized juxtaposition of political concepts contribute to the broad historical perspective of *1 Henry IV.* Also fundamental to this perspective is the nature of the characterization. Since the central figures are static and do not command the close rapport and intensity of attention which would tend to blur the larger view of the scene, the spectators are held emotionally at arm's length from the principals; such a detached perspective encourages a breadth of vision not possible—and certainly not intended—in the major tragedies. The movement of the drama, like that of *Henry VI* plays in some respects, is created by the interplay of fixed types rather than by the developing nature of dynamic figures. Worlds removed, however, is the technique which lends to the characterization a degree of depth and dramatic vitality foreign to the stage worlds of the *Henry VI* plays. Henry, Hal, Hotspur, and Falstaff, for instance, do not develop in the course of the action, and hence they are essentially static figures. The spectators, however forced to view these principals in widely divergent situations, experience a mixed response; the angles from which the character is observed—whether of the public man, the private, the courageous, the cowardly, the melancholic, the philosophic, or the like—cumulatively produce an ambivalence that, for the spectators, moves far beyond the stylization of political theory.

Hal, more specifically, in no way grows or is educated in the process of the play. He announces his intentions when first on stage, and he fulfills them, at least in part, at the conclusion of *Part 1*. Along the way there is not the slightest doubt in the spectator's mind that he will do so. The difficulty Shakespeare has with the character, as Peter Alexander has written, is that "while he had to talk about the Prince's becoming a different man he also had to make it clear from the beginning that there is no change whatever."[19] To compare Hal's experience with that of the prodigal son, one must "so rewrite the parable that the prodigal may say as he departs for the far country, 'I'll so offend, to make offense a skill' " (p. 112). Similarly, to argue the morality tradition as the shaping force, one must accept an Everyman character who knows how to manipulate both sides to best advantage. If Hal is static, however, he is far from a simplistic figure of stylized ideality. Even placing the best interpretation on Hal's use of Falstaff's world is to become better acquainted with all elements of his future kingdom, one is hard pressed to sanction his occasional acts—his passive participation in a robbery involving physical violence and outright defiance of civil law, whatever the rationalization and the mitigating circumstances (II, ii); his refusal to consult with Sir John Bracy, an emissary from his father, at a time of political disruption, indeed permitting Falstaff to speak for him as the rogue sees fit (II, iv, 297 ff.); his arrant lie to the sheriff that Falstaff is not with him at the tavern, that instead he is employed on a special mission (513 ff.); his sudden determination, without explanation, to procure Falstaff an honorable position in the wars, this in the face of his full knowledge of Falstaff's character (545 ff.); and his willingness to grace the lie of Falstaff's slaying Hotspur in battle, an action which by implication at least condones Jack's earlier irresponsibility in substituting wine for his pistol[20] and his "discretionary" cowardice in feigning death—let alone his earlier gross abuse of funds for impressment of troops (V, v, 157 ff.). In a word, one can place little credence in the claim that Hal, the ideal king in waiting, is presented without flaw or that any early indiscretions can be excused by his progressive development in spiritual and physical fortitude. He is indeed guilty of occasional lapses in moral judgment—as much at the end of the play as at the beginning—and certainly from the outset he knows his companions for what they are and calculatingly weighs the political advantages of his actions. Either to whitewash his character or to view him as subject to a kind of repentance which obviates a canny sense of political pragmatism is to enforce a reductionism which the full text will not

support. Nor should he be viewed, with equal distortion, as a cunning schemer whose lust for power dictates his every move. If John Palmer begs the question with his assertion that Shakespeare "leaves us to decide for ourselves how far Henry really conducts himself according to plan, or how far he is merely creating an alibi for his misdemeanours,"[21] it is nonetheless true that the full context will support neither the view that Hal, morally beyond reproach, practices the golden mean of virtue[22] nor the view that he is a "self-complacent and self-centered" individual whose "incapacity for true feeling" leads him to discover a genuine Machiavellian energy.[23] Hal is, as it were, "his own foil."[24]

Neither saint nor sinner, then, Hal is an intriguingly human combination of virtues and vices with a taste for the wild life and the thrill of defiance, a tendency to rationalize and mitigate his actions, a remarkable capacity for good humor and a toleration for the boon companion who epitomizes it, a wiley perception of political strategy and of human psychology, a splendid courage and magnanimity on the battlefield, and a genuine dedication to the Lancastrian Throne. Certain characteristics may be dominant at times (suggesting perhaps a sense of development) but never to the exclusion of other features—hence, for example, the significance of the soliloquy declaring his self-knowledge in the midst of his antic moments with Falstaff and the law at the beginning of the play, and of his permitting Falstaff's lie in the context of his greatest military encounter at the end of the play. Hal, then, anticipates the throne and the responsibilities which it entails from his first moment on stage. He, as a static figure moving inexorably toward the throne which will bring fame and glory both to him and to England, does not—like Richard III and Richard II—emotionally engage the spectators in a restrictingly personal manner which would diminish the breadth of their perspective. At the same time he is a complex figure, far from the stylized qualities of heroism in Talbot, of virtue in Humphrey Duke of Gloucester, of villainy in Margaret of Anjou or Richard Duke of York.

The title figure the spectators know less intimately, perhaps in itself an indication of the playwright's concern for a broad focus—especially when one considers the significance of the title roles in the earlier *Richard III* and *Richard II*.[25] Henry IV, more specifically, speaks not one private line in *Part I,* and he appears in fewer scenes than any of the other principals. Again, too, there is no fundamental development in the character. Like Hal, however, he is a complex individual who commands the spectators' interest as they observe his personality from various angles. In I, i, for instance, we view the public Lancastrian face which seems carefully to calculate the political ramifications of every word. Henry is concerned for the kingdom so "shaken" with the "intestine shock . . . of civil butchery" (1, 12-13); were the sporadic insurrections to cease, he would as an act of national expiation lead an English force against the pagans in Jerusalem. Another aspect of the public face, admirably firm and decisive, is revealed in I, iii, in which Henry dismisses Worcester from the Council and sternly refuses Hotspur's conditions for delivering prisoners of war; in III, ii, he moves with confident dispatch to align the three components of his battle force; similarly, the play concludes with his staccato orders to pursue the rebels still at large. Yet another dimension, combining political acumen and magnanimity, is evidenced in the early moments of Act V. Prior to battle he extends "grace" and honorable reconciliation to the rebels (i, 106 ff.), an offer which even Worcester describes as "liberal and kind" (ii, 2). Distinctly different, however, is the remorseful father who senses that his son's profligacy is "the hot vengeance, and the rod of heaven" sent to "punish [his] mistreadings" (III, ii, 10, 11). Sensing in Hal's seeming disregard for the throne a repudiation of all he has achieved, Henry laments that his son is his "nearest and dearest enemy," likely to fight in Percy's pay from "Base inclination, and the start of spleen" (123, 125). The moment of reconciliation is charged with emotion, and a similar humanly vulnerable side is exposed later on the battlefield in words of gratitude to Hal for saving his life.

There may be no significant growth or alteration in personality, but Henry IV is not one dimensional; and the same is true for both Hotspur and Falstaff. Certainly, for instance, Hotspur in one sense fulfills Henry IV's simplistic description.[26] Vis-a-vis an effeminate lord from the court in I, iii, he is a veritable Mars on the battlefield, and he boldly asserts his position against the King himself. This same heroic stance the audience privately observes in Hotspur's disdain for those who shirk the battle from fear, yet claim political or domestic excuses: "he shows in this, he loves his own barn better than he loves our house. . . . What a frosty-spirited rogue is this!" (II, iii, 5-6, 20). And Hotspur bravely encounters Hal at Shrewsbury, lamenting in defeat that his sacrifice of "proud titles" is a far sharper pain than the loss of "brittle life" (V, iv, 78, 77). At the same time the spectators also see, far more plainly than Hal, the heir apparent's justification for mocking Hotspur's blustering and immoderate mien. Not only—following the King's order that all prisoners be delivered—does Hotspur develop such a passionate attack of logorrhea that his uncle declines further speech and his father brands him a "wasp-stung and impatient fool" (I, iii, 236); he also insists on alienating his ally, Glendower by bluntly calling him a liar (III, i, 58), and in a high dudgeon he insists that the river Trent be turned so that his division of the kingdom will be larger; in both cases only the cooler head of the Welsh leader preserves the fragile rebel alliance (an odious comparison indeed, since Glendower himself is given to such hyperbolic rant). Similarly he later disregards the defections from his ranks, vowing that since

"Doomsday is near" all will "die merrily" (IV, i, 134) and insisting—against the advice of all of his counsellors—that the charge take place that very night (iii, 1-29). But the spectator, unlike the royal father and son, perceives yet another side. When Lady Percy expresses concern for her husband's sleeplessness and loss of appetite and berates him for not sharing his innermost problems, not the heroism or the bravado but the humanity surfaces. Like Portia, Kate fears for her husband's safety; and, if Hotspur's response in II, iv, seems somewhat peremptory, his bantering tone hardly conceals his affection in III, i. Juxtaposed to the amorous pair, Mortimer and his wife, for whom language is a barrier, Hotspur bluntly proclaims Kate "perfect in lying down" (226). She wittily threatens to break his head unless he keeps silence, but he insists that she swear a "good mouth-filling oath" (254). The two are obviously well matched, and the impression conveyed by the scene is one of genuine intimacy. Whatever Henry's or Hal's single-dimensional perception of Hotspur, in other words, the spectators see him in a far more complex light. Not only must they balance the opposing views of the royal family (and the manner in which these views functionally develop the conflict of father and son); they must also accommodate the more personal vision of the man with wife, friends, and political allies.

The spectator's perception of Falstaff is no less complex. On the one hand, the character is indeed a fat parasite who, by inference at least, is a "grey Iniquity," a "villainous abominable misleader of youth" (II, iv, 453-454, 462-463).[27] On the other hand he is also a welcome participant in present mirth. Both views are readily illustrated. As a creature of malign influence, Falstaff is a "thief" (I, ii, 138; II, ii, 93) and a robber of the King's exchequer (55), a whoremonger and debtor to the hostess to the tavern (II, iii, 66), a traitor in his misuse of funds for assembling troops in a period of national emergency (IV, ii, 12), and an arrant coward on the field of battle (V, iii, 58-59; iv, 75 ff.). At the same time the Prince without question pays Falstaff's tavern debts (I, ii, 51) and time and again delights in his resourceful excuses and rationalizations—whether involving the counterrobbery at Gad's Hill (II, iv, 267-269), the pocket-picking at Eastcheap (III, iii, 164-166), or the parodic role-changing (II, iv, 376-481);[28] Hal will even tolerate dishonesty at Shrewsbury for the sake of such friendship:

Come bring your luggage nobly on your back.
For my part, if a lie may do thee grace,
I'll gild it with the happiest terms I have.
(V, iv, 156-158)

But there is yet another side to Falstaff which only the spectators perceive, and it is this quality which in large part accounts for the universal popularity of the character. Not only is this "huge hill of flesh" a voice of merry abandon; he also epitomizes that part of human nature which places a paramount value on life and survival and which disdains a commitment to violence and destruction for such pompous abstractions as national power and honor. Moments before the battle begins, for example, he privately shares with the spectators his catechism of honor—it may spur one to fight but it has never been able to set a leg or an arm or to mitigate the "grief of a wound" (V, i, 132). This concept of honor as a mere word for glorifying militaristic actions which result in death is a recurrent theme through several of his soliloquies in the final act.[29] Standing over the slain Sir Walter Blount, Falstaff sardonically observes the vanity of honor's prompting the nobleman to fight in the King's disguise (iii, 30-39); later, he is more grotesquely pointed: "I like not such grinning honor as Sir Walter hath. Give me life, which if I can save, so; if not, honor comes unlook'd for, and there's an end" (58-61). Similarly, when compelled to feign death to save life, he proclaims that he is "no counterfeit. To die is to be a counterfeit, for he is but the counterfeit of a man who hath not the life of a man; but to counterfeit dying, when a man thereby liveth, is to be no counterfeit, but the true and perfect image of life indeed. The better part of valor is discretion" (iv, 115-120).[30] He may at one moment be ashamed of the ragmuffins who follow him, but such embarrassment fails to dampen his enthusiasm for squandering the money he has appropriated (Iv, ii, 11 ff.). And he may at another moment vow to "purge and leave sack, and live cleanly," but he admits that he follows, "as they say, for reward" (V, iv, 164-165, 162). Falstaff, in a word, is worlds removed from the equally extreme battlefield heroics of Hotspur; but like Percy's son he is human in his habitude, and the interweaving of such powerfully ambivalent figures provides a rich and controlled perspective for dramatizing chronicle material.

In summary, Shakespeare's historical perspective reaches a new level of maturation in the two *Henry IV* plays and *Henry V,* a level which would seem flatly to refute the recent assertion by James Calderwood that the spectator "cannot simultaneously be involved in the immediate experience of the play and yet be detached from it."[31] On the one hand, no longer as in the *Henry VI* plays is character abstractly fitted to idea. For the most part flat and one-dimensional, the characters of those earlier stage worlds merely serve the purposes of the narrative. Consequently, the plot builds upon a series of scenes in which stylized character types are set in confrontation, and the perspective is broadly focused on the full range of action rather than on the complexity of a particular individual. On the other hand, Shakespeare—for the purposes of history at least—seems almost consciously to depart from the technique which, in his contemporary romantic comedies, directs attention to characters like Bassanio and Portia or Benedick and Beatrice who grow in the knowledge of love and, in his contemporary tragedies

like *Romeo and Juliet* and *Julius Caesar,* draws the spectators through soliloquies and asides to the private level of the protagonist. Whatever the nature of the external action in the tragic works, for example, and of the characters who move in opposition to the protagonist, the spectators' consuming interest is in the developing central figure whose critical moments they share. Perforce the perspective is both narrow and intense; the tragic impact arises from the spectators' personal identification with the protagonist and the quality of the insights gleaned from the suffering his error has provoked. The perspective of both *Richard III* and *Richard II,* although remarkably different in quality, shares this intensity of focus. Richard III celebrates his villainy with the spectators through a continuing run of soliloquies and asides forming a private level of perception. In *Richard II,* instead of the brittle relationship built on shared confidences about the gullibility of others, the perspective assumes a more emotionally empathetic quality as, in the final acts of the play, emphasis is focused more sharply upon the suffering of the man than the abuses of his royal office.

In *1 Henry IV* Shakespeare has developed a middle ground between these two polarities of dramatic technique. Several principal characters, each of whom reflects a significant aspect of the national culture, command relatively equal attention, thus projecting the focus beyond a single individual. These characters, by sharing private thoughts or critical moments with the spectators, exhibit an ambivalent human dimension which moves beyond the comprehension of the other characters on stage; the spectators alone realize the full dimensions of the several major figures and thus possess the perspective for responding to the human consequences of the historical events of the narrative. While ambivalent, however, these characters are essentially static and consequently serve the purpose of a broader design reflecting divergent philosophies of life and attitudes toward the kingship. Ultimately this design reveals an England emerging precariously from medieval feudalism, characterized in turn by guilt, decadence, fanatical heroism, and sagacious practicality. Neither an individual tragedy with historic setting nor a play which, for want of sufficient characterization, fails to engage the spectators dramatically, *1 Henry IV* presents a broad scene in which human interaction becomes history, unfolding the narrative of a nation struggling for unity at the expense of individual ambition in the lords and absolute integrity in the royal household.

Notes

[1] *Prefaces to Shakespeare* (Princeton: Princeton Univ. Press, 1946), I, 31.

[2] R. J. Dorius, ed., *Twentieth-Century Interpretations of Henry IV, Part One* (Englewood Cliffs: Prentice-Hall, 1970), p. 4.

[3] Harold E. Toliver, "Falstaff, the Prince, and the History Play," *SQ* 16 (1965): 65.

[4] William Empson describes "three worlds, each with its own hero" (*Some Versions of Pastoral* [London: Chatto and Windus, 1935], p. 43), while Alan C. Dessen speaks of "dual protagonists" ("The Intemperate Knight and the Politic Prince: Late Morality Structure in *1 Henry IV*," *Shakespeare Studies* 7 [1974]: 157). This absence of a single dominant role as a "star vehicle," according to Margaret Webster, has hurt the popularity of the play in the theater (*Shakespeare Without Tears* [New York: McGraw-Hill, 1942], p. 133).

[5] The prompt copy from the Smock Alley Theatre indicates the need for at least six different scene settings (Gunnar Sorelius, "The Smock Alley Prompt-Books of *1* and *2 Henry IV*," *SQ* 22 [1971]: 124).

[6] Ed., *The First Part of King Henry IV,* The Arden Shakespeare (London: Methuen, 1960), p. xxviii.

[7] Stephen Gardiner, *De Vera Obedientia, Oratio* (1535); see J. W. Allen, *A History of Political Thought in the Sixteenth Century* (London: Methuen, 1928), p. 126.

[8] Allen, p. 127.

[9] William Tyndale, "The Obedience of a Christian Man," in *Doctrinal Treatises and Introductions to Different Portions of the Holy Scriptures* (Cambridge, 1848), pp. 179-180.

[10] Sir Thomas Craig, *Concerning the Rights of Succession to the Kingdom of England* (London, 1703), p. 16. As Robert B. Pierce has recently observed, Shakespeare in *1, 2 Henry IV* "Displays the quest for political order as fundamentally like the quest for personal order within the family"—the Percies fail while the Lancastrians ultimately succeed (*Shakespeare's History Plays: The Family and the State* [Columbus: Ohio State Univ. Press, 1971], pp. 171, 213).

[11] *Shakespeare from Richard II to Henry V* (Stanford: Stanford Univ. Press, 1957), pp. 81-82.

[12] Line references to *1, 2 Henry IV* are to the edition of G. B. Evans, *The Riverside Shakespeare* (Boston: Houghton Mifflin, 1974).

[13] The topicality of the *Henry IV* plays has been investigated at length by Lily B. Campbell, *Shakespeare's Histories: Mirrors of Elizabethan Policy* (San Marino: Huntington Library, 1947), pp. 218 ff. The plays reflect the "delicate equilibrium of late sixteenth-century English society" (Charles Barber, "Prince Hal, Henry V, and the Tudor Monarchy," in *The Morality of Art,* ed. D. W. Jefferson [New York: Barnes and Noble, 1969]), p. 68; see also William B. Stone,

"Literature and Class Ideology: *Henry IV, Part One,*" *College English* 33 (1972): 894. Alfred Hart, in *Shakespeare and the Homilies* (Melbourne: Melbourne Univ. Press, 1934), asserts that *2 Henry IV* was heavily cut by the censor because of the possible parallel between Elizabeth and Henry IV, a king depicted as "refusing wise counsel" and "depressing his nobles" (p. 194).

[14] Sir Thomas Hoby, trans., *The Book of the Courtier* by Baldassare Castiglione (London: Dent, 1928), pp. 261 ff.

[15] *Dialogue Between Cardinal Pole and Thomas Lupset,* ed. Sidney J. Herrtage, The Early English Text Society (London, 1878), pp. 100-101.

[16] *The Boke of the Governor* (New York: Dutton, 1907), p. 9.

[17] J. H. Walter, ed., *King Henry V,* The Arden Shakespeare (London: Methuen, 1954), pp. xvii-xviii.

[18] James Hoyle describes the *tableaux vivant* as Hal standing "between the two extremes of self-indulgence" ("Some Emblems in Shakespeare's History Plays," *ELH* 38 [1971]: 525); see also Charles Mitchell, "The Education of a True Prince," *Tennessee Studies in Literature* 12 (1967): 19.

[19] *Introductions to Shakespeare* (London: Collins, 1966), p. 109.

[20] Rudolf B. Schmerl reminds us that such a scene would be far funnier to the comically detached spectator than to Hal ("Comedy and the Manipulation of Moral Distance: Falstaff and Shylock," *Bucknell Review* 10 [1961]: 132).

[21] *Political and Comic Characters of Shakespeare* (London: Macmillan, 1962), p. 186; see also Leonard Dean, "From *Richard II* to *Henry V*: A Closer View," in *Studies in Honor of DeWitt T. Starnes,* ed., Thomas P. Harrison and James H. Sledd (Austin: Univ. of Texas Press, 1967), rpt. in *Shakespeare: Modern Essays in Criticism,* ed. Leonard Dean, rev. ed. (Oxford: Oxford Univ. Press, 1967), p. 198. Such ambivalence is characteristic of the play as a whole (Cleanth Brooks and Robert B. Heilman, *Understanding Drama* [New York: Holt, Rinehart, Winston, 1948], p. 384; Anthony La Branche, " 'If Thou Wert Sensible of Courtesy': Private and Public Virtue in *Henry IV, Part One,*" *SQ* 16 [1966]: 381).

[22] William B. Hunter, "Falstaff," *South Atlantic Quarterly* 50 (1951): 89; Alan Gerald Gross, "The Justification of Prince Hal," *Texas Studies in Literature and Language* 10 (1968-1969): 28.

[23] S. C. Sen Gupta, *Shakespeare's Historical Plays* (Oxford: Oxford Univ. Press, 1964), p. 137; John

Masefield, *William Shakespeare* (New York: Holt, 1911), p. 112; Michael Manheim, *The Weak King Dilemma in the Shakespearean History Play* (Syracuse: Syracuse Univ. Press, 1973), p. 166.

24 Elmer M. Blistein, *Comedy in Action* (Durham: Duke Univ. Press, 1964), p. 10.

25 In this respect John C. Bromley aptly notes that Henry is a "wholly public figure" (*The Shakespearean Kings* [Boulder: Colorado Associated Univ. Press, 1971], p. 61), though to call his remorse "nothing but rhetorical posture" (p. 66) and to view him as a subtly drawn hypocrite (H. C. Goddard, *The Meaning of Shakespeare* [Chicago: Univ. of Chicago Press, 1951], I, 162) and a "cynically adept politician" (James Winney, *The Player King* [New York: Barnes and Noble, 1968], p. 87) is to oversimplify the character as it appears on stage.

26 Like Henry IV, writes David Riggs, Hotspur is engaged in "the ceaseless accumulation of 'proud titles' unrelieved by moments of social occasion or self-fulfillment" (*Shakespeare's Heroical Histories* [Cambridge: Harvard Univ. Press, 1971], p. 159). Of a bloody and vicious mind (W. Gordon Zeeveld, " 'Food for Powder'—'Food for Worms,' " *SQ* 3 [1952]: 310), Hotspur's instincts—"informed by the merely negative" (Raymond H. Reno, "Hotspur: The Integration of Character and Theme," *Renaissance Papers* [1962], p. 25)—are for "rebellion and anarchy rather than for order" (Northrop Frye, "Nature and Nothing," in *Essays on Shakespeare,* ed. Gerald W. Chapman [Princeton: Princeton Univ. Press, 1965], p. 43).

27 A sampling of the diversity of opinion will suggest the large body of criticism. Falstaff has been traced, for example, to various literary and folk antecedents—the allegorical figures of medieval drama (Bernard Spivack, "Falstaff and the Psychomachia," *SQ* 8 [1957]: 458), the mock king and Lord of Misrule (Northrop Frye, "The Argument of Comedy," *English Institute Essays* [1948], 71), the *miles gloriosus* of Plautus (J. Dover Wilson, *The Fortunes of Falstaff* [Cambridge: Cambridge Univ. Press, 1943], p. 83), the court fool and soothsayer (Roy Battenhouse, "Falstaff as Parodist and Perhaps Holy Fool," *PMLA* 90 [1975]: 32), the *picaro* of Renaissance fiction (Herbert B. Rothschild, Jr., "Falstaff and the Picaresque Tradition," *Modern Language Review* 68 [1973]: 14). Others find the origins in several characters of *The Famous Victories of Henry V* (D. B. Landt, "The Ancestry of Sir John Falstaff," *SQ* 17 [1966]: 70)—in particular in the influence of Richard Tarleton's striking impersonations in the role of Dericke (James Monaghan, "Falstaff and his Forebears," *Studies in Philology* 18 [1921]: 360)—in figures from the London streets of Shakespeare's day (Paul N. Siegel, "Falstaff and His Social Milieu," *Shakespeare Jahrbuch* 110 [1974]: 139), in the degen-

erate dependence upon the feudal order (T. A. Jackson, "Marx and Shakespeare," *International Literature* 2 [1963]: 87).

28 While John Shaw ("The Staging of Parody and Parallels in *1 Henry IV,*" *Shakespeare Survey* 20 [1967]: 64) and Paul A. Gottschalk ("Hal and the 'Play Extempore' in *1 Henry IV,*" *TSLL* 15 [1973-1974]: 609) perceive a broad parody and J. D. A. Ogilvy sees a comic attack upon both Euphuism and Arcadianism ("Arcadianism in *1 Henry IV,*" *ELN* 10 [1972-1973]: 185), Richard L. McGuire argues that the scene, far from being parodic, is the turning point for the relationship between Hal and Falstaff ("The Play-within-the-Play in *1 Henry IV,*" *SQ* 18 [1967]: 50); see also Fredson Bowers, "Shakespeare's Art: The Point of View," in *Literary Views,* ed. Carroll Camden (Chicago: Univ. of Chicago Press, 1964), pp. 54-55.

29 Shakespeare, according to Norman Council, makes the concept of honor—and the major characters' response to it—central to the play ("Prince Hal: Mirror of Success," *Shakespeare Studies* 7 [1974]: 144). This emphasis is "a mark of the secular atmosphere of *1 Henry IV.* . . . In the world of politics and civil war [honor] functions as a substitute for moral principle" (Moody E. Prior, *The Drama of Power* [Evanston: Northwestern Univ. Press, 1973], p. 202).

30 In an interesting article U. C. Knoepflmacher treats Falstaff's counterfeit rising as a parody of Hal's rising to glory at Shrewsbury ("The Humors as Symbolic Nucleus in *Henry IV, Part I,*" *CE* 24 [1963]: 501).

31 "*1 Henry IV:* Art's Gilded Lie," *English Literary Renaissance* 3 (1973): 138. Irving Ribner describes the plays as the "ultimate peak" in the development of Shakespeare's histories (*The English History Play in the Age of Shakespeare* [Princeton: Princeton Univ. Press, 1957], p. 193), and Edward I. Berry describes them as "subtler, more complex, more aesthetically coherent elaborations of dramatic techniques and political insights expressed in the first tetralogy" (*Patterns of Decay: Shakespeare's Early Histories* [Charlottesville: Univ. Press of Virginia, 1975], p. 104).

Barbara Hodgdon (essay date 1991)

SOURCE: " 'Let the End Try the Man': *1* and *2 Henry IV,*" in *The End Crowns All: Closure and Contradiction in Shakespeare's History,* Princeton University Press, 1991, pp. 151-84.

[*In the following excerpt, Hodgdon discusses various theatrical and cinematic interpretations of* 1 *and* 2 Henry IV, *focusing on the "multiple endings" of the two plays and how they are dealt with by different directors.*]

Taking Falstaff's part, A. C. Bradley begins "The Rejection of Falstaff" (1902) by asking, "Now why did Shakespeare end his drama with a scene which, though undoubtedly striking, leaves an impression so unpleasant?" Eventually, he concludes that *Henry IV*'s "chief hero" is the "wild" Prince Henry, who, in order to emerge "as a just, wise, stern, and glorious King," must, together with Bradley himself, banish Falstaffian plenitude.[1] Like Bradley, Orson Welles, a later Falstaffian conjuror, also begins with the end: discussing his 1966 film, *Chimes at Midnight,* an adaptation of *1* and *2 Henry IV* with traces of *Richard II, Henry V,* and *The Merry Wives of Windsor,* he comments, "I directed everything, and played everything, with a view to preparing for the last scene."[2] The close of his film, however, not only readdresses Bradley's question from a diametrically opposed position but, by staging Falstaff's body as its primary site of spectacle, turns *Henry IV*'s royal narrative, as in Hotspur's phrase, "topsy-turvy down" (*1 Henry IV,* 4.1.82).

In the cathedral space where Henry V is crowned, Welles's film articulates the rejection in a shot—reverse shot exchange consisting primarily of low- and high-angle close-ups and mid-close-ups in which two shots are especially striking. In the first, as Henry says "I know thee not, old man," he stands with his back to a Falstaff he clearly knows so well he does not even need to look at him; in the second, as the new King finally turns away from the "surfeit-swelled" old man to walk between massed banners toward the light, the film cuts to a mid-close-up of Falstaff, whose gaze registers pride in the splendid figure of his "sweet boy." When soldiers carrying lances bar his view of Hal, Falstaff moves slowly to stand alone next to a column, speaks with Shallow and, finally, moves out of the shot. As Shallow calls to him, a series of extreme long shots details his own procession as he walks away from the camera toward the darkened castle ramparts, his bulk growing smaller and smaller in the frame until, against deep, empty foreground space, his tiny silhouette disappears through a lit archway. As in Shakespeare's playtext, the Lords—here, the Bishop, Prince John, and the Lord Chief Justice—remark on the King's "fair proceeding"; but then Welles's textual rearrangements counterpose that judgment with its "fair" results: Doll is arrested, calling for Falstaff, who is ordered to the Fleet; his tiny Page, squirming through the crowd, tells Pistol that Falstaff is sick; and Bardolph comments, "The King is a good king, but it must be as it may." Before the castle battlements, Henry proclaims "Now, Lords, for France" and orders Falstaff released from prison—"We consider / It was excess of wine that set him on."

Now the camera pans right to follow Poins as he walks past the empty tavern "throne" where Falstaff and Hal had both played Henry IV and into the innyard, where he stops beside a huge coffin, resting on a rude cart:

"Falstaff?" "Falstaff is dead," says the page; and, after Mistress Quickly speaks his epitaph (*Henry V,* 2.3.9-24), she watches while the three men push the enormous coffin through the innyard gates across a snow-speckled landscape bounded by the distant castle walls. The camera slowly booms up to offer an omniscient perspective that traps this procession, in a high-angle extreme long shot, between tavern and court, and Ralph Richardson's authoritatively impersonal voice speaks a pastiche from Holinshed: "The new king, even at first appointing, determined to put on him the shape of a new man. This Henry was a captain of such prudence and such policy that he never enterprised anything before it forecast the main chances that it might happen. So humane withal, he left no offense unpunished nor friendship unrewarded. For conclusion, a majesty was he that both lived and died a pattern in princehood, a lodestar in honor, and famous to the world alway." Over a slow-motion film loop of a row of soldiers, nobles, and clerics, armed and ready for war, standing against the side wall of a church, pennon lances waving in the breeze, muffled drums beat out a rhythm that replaces his words.[3]

Rejected from the court by the King and from the tavern by Death, Falstaff's body inhabits a no-man's-land between the two spaces over which the voice of "history" presides, circumscribing and displacing Quickly's report of the fat knight's death with excerpts from Henry V's chronicle epitaph. Finally, the film reconstitutes the body, and the hierarchy, of the kingdom in an image that repeats itself endlessly, like the drums that simultaneously sound Falstaff's death knell and presage the coming war. If Welles's pseudo-Aristotelian complicity with tragedy generates a "finer end" (the Hostess's phrase), it also remaps the traditional territory[4] framed by "I know you all" and "I know thee not, old man" onto Falstaff's body to call Henry V's "carefully plotted official strategy" as well as the spectacle of rule into question. Strikingly, Welles's film is responsive not only to Bradley's praise, echoed by other readers, for Falstaff and his over-reaching creator, "caught up in the wind of his own genius"—"It is not a misfortune that happens to many authors, nor is it one we can regret, for it costs us but a trifling inconvenience in one scene"[5]—but also to more recent configurations of the *Henry IV* plays as an ideal testing ground for examining the relations between plebian and patrician discourses, the carnivalesque and the theater as sites of subversion that work, ultimately, to authorize the state.[6] Indeed Welles himself envisioned his film, not as a "lament for Falstaff, but for the death of Merrie England . . . a myth, which has been very real to the English-speaking world . . . the age of chivalry, of simplicity, of Maytime and all that."[7] When Steven Mullaney writes, of Falstaff's rejection, that "what surprises is not the event itself but the fact that the world being cast off has been so consummately rehearsed: so fully represented to us, and consequently, so fully foreclosed,"[8] he identifies quite precisely the rupture between "play" and "history" that shapes *2 Henry IV*'s close, a contradiction Welles's film reveals in the disjuncture between image and sound—the one recording what history excludes to hollow out the voice of official memory.

However split between a "prodigally lavish" Falstaffian economy and one of royal legitimation, between subversion and its containment, critical narratives of the *Henry IV* plays as well as late twentieth-century theatrical practice so consistently link its two parts into one that Falstaff's banishment becomes an end that indeed "crowns all." In fact, *Henry IV*'s "master narrative" not only subsumes *1 Henry IV*'s ending but absorbs the insistently coded closural gestures of *1* and *2 Henry IV*—what Samuel Crowl, writing on Welles's film, calls "The Long Goodbye"—into a pattern that arches over both plays to (always already) expel Falstaff. Reading *1* and *2 Henry IV*'s multiple endings from a "double vantage," I want not only to raise questions concerning their late sixteenth-century representation and reception but, by looking at several of their latter-day theatrical configurations, to examine how these reproduce or refashion, arrange or rearrange, social meaning as theatrical meaning. And I want to begin by describing *1 Henry IV*'s close in a version that, complete within itself, forecloses, so to speak, on the need for a second play.

Beerbohm Tree's 1895 *1 Henry IV*[9] constructs a highly idealized resolution of the play's contradictory, oppositional father-son relations. Omitting Hal's rescue of his father, Tree cuts from Falstaff's exit, taking a quick drink from the bottle Hal has just refused, to Hotspur's entrance, effecting a double exchange: rival son for rival father, true chivalry for its lack. As Hal and Hotspur recognize one another, the prompt copy indicates a trumpet flourish, followed by a pause and "picture" before an orchestral tremolo signals Falstaff's reentry to confront the Douglas. After the fights, Hal places a battle standard over Hotspur's body, turns briefly to address Falstaff, salutes Hotspur, and, with a sigh, exits. As the stage lights dim to an "evening effect," Falstaff glances over his shield; to the offstage clashing of swords, "very piano," he slowly rises and takes another drink from his bottle; but rather than taking up Hotspur's body, he falls to his knees and is about to lie down again when, seeing Hal and Prince John enter, he tries to creep away on his hands and knees. Helping Falstaff to his feet, Hal laughs, as Hotspur had done earlier in disbelief at his own death, and willingly gilds Falstaff's lie before proclaiming "the day is ours," at which a "15th and Final Flourish" sounds, backed by "hurrahs." Tree cuts Falstaff's promise to reform and moves directly to a mass entrance that fills the stage with soldiers, who frame a central tableau in which King Henry and Prince Hal embrace, surrounded by waving banners and triumphant

"Huzzahs." Not only does Hotspur's body remain on the stage to figure the rebels' defeat and Hal's victory but, since Tree himself played Falstaff and since the prompt copy indicates no exit for him,[10] this close gives Hal two fathers and celebrates his reconciliation with both amidst a splendid military spectacle.

Its pictorial realization reminiscent of eighteenth- and nineteenth-century commemorative paintings of famous battles, this sort of grand finale, its power greatly enhanced by the practice then common of playing the national anthem at the end of each performance, caps *1 Henry IV*s well into the 1950s.[11] While some performance texts, like Tree's, simply substitute military spectacle for the play's final scene, others, such as Bridges-Adams's for the Shakespeare Memorial Theatre in 1932,[12] by retaining King Henry's sentence of Worcester and Vernon, punish treason against the state and heal filial "treason" with the image of a Hal who kneels to his father at the final victory declaration. So transformed into moral myth, closure becomes a nostalgic fantasia in which rebellion has indeed lost its sway, mastered by heroism and military might embodied in a unitary spectacle that authenticates the relations between past and present cultures along a transhistorical continuum of idealized national and familial values.

In taking on such contours, these *1 Henry IV*s push to extremes the resolution of a story familiar to Elizabethans—the parable of the prodigal son, one well-known through two models, the biblical narrative and the equally mythologized tales, dramatized in the anonymous play, *The Famous Victories of Henry V*, of what Henry IV calls his son's "vile participation" (3.2.87).[13] In both versions, it is an exclusively male narrative directed toward working through father-son antagonisms and, in the case of the parable only, those between a dutiful elder son and his wastrel brother. Also in both, it is not the prodigal son's legitimacy that is in question but the need to establish his authenticity in relation to patriarchal law. Drawing on these paradigms as well as on chronicle materials, Shakespeare's play constructs a highly mythologized economy, structured through binary oppositions—court/tavern, honor/dishonor, time/timelessness, everyday/holiday, word/body, serious history/comic-popular discourse—in which the first term represents the desirable ideal, the second its inversion. As the only figure who can move flexibly between their boundaries, Hal encompasses their contradictions, for which Shrewsbury—represented on the one hand as history, and on the other as a purely theatrical invention—is the ideal testing ground.

Unlike Shakespeare's earlier histories, where conflict centers on genealogical descent in a struggle for the crown's rightful ownership, *1 Henry IV* positions the Percy-Northumberland rebellion against the state so that it serves Hal's mimetic rivalry with Hotspur as well as that between his authentic and counterfeit fathers, Henry IV and Falstaff.[14] In this extremely limited gender economy, structured by a desire for the male other that takes the form of aggression, women are positioned at history's margins: unnecessary to prove or deny Hal's or Hotspur's legitimacy (as, for instance, in *King John*), they simply delay historical time. Only the rebel leaders—Hotspur and Lord Mortimer—have wives, whose presence functions primarily to separate public from private domains and, by proving their husbands' heterosexuality, deflects the homoerotic into the homosocial; says Hotspur, "This is no world / To play with mammets or to tilt with lips" (2.3.87-88), nor has he time to listen to the Welsh lady sing (3.1.234). In their resistance to the male chivalric project, Kate Percy and Glendower's daughter are kin to Falstaff, a more substantial image of feminine "misrule," who lies within the tavern space, together with thieves, swaggerers, a Hostess-landlady, and "gentlewomen" who, it is said, "live honestly by the prick of their needles" (*Henry V*, 2.1.31-32). Although within the Oedipal narrative, Falstaff figures as Hal's surrogate father, he is coded in feminine, maternal terms:[15] his fat belly is the masculine counterpart of the pregnant woman; his Rabelaisian excesses of food and drink make him the Carnival antithesis to Henry IV's ascetic Lenten identity and his world of religious penance, bent as Henry IV is on expiating personal as well as national guilt with a crusade. It is Falstaff who accuses Hal of being the king's bastard son, and Hal, too, imagines him as female when, just before baiting Falstaff about his Gadshill cowardice and with Hotspur circulating in his mind and in his talk, he thinks himself into playing Percy and "that damned brawn" into "Dame Mortimer his wife" (2.4.104-5). That "play extempore" is then transformed into one where the roles of king and son become interchangeable, shared between Falstaff and Hal, and where women have no place: Falstaff's first "command" as "father-king" is "convey my tristful queen" (2.4.375).

But perhaps the most telling of Falstaff's multiform female guises of misrule is his association with Queen Elizabeth's virgin identity: "Let us be Diana's foresters, gentlemen of the shade, minions of the moon; and let men say we be men of good government, being governed as the sea is, by our noble and chaste mistress the moon" (1.2.23-27).[16] Desiring to undertake something like Essex's role in the annual Accession Day Tourneys that celebrated Elizabeth's powerfully mythic, theatricalized presence, his fantasy of social order would steal and invert Essex's chivalric image—echoed in Hotspur's "easy leap / To pluck bright honor from the pale-faced moon" (1.3.201-2)—in order to recode his own body. Chivalry's daytime, however, cannot admit an aging, corpulent "squire of the night's body," whose *2 Henry IV* counterpart, mentioned in passing, is Shallow's "bona roba," Jane Nightwork (3.2.188). Even Hal, "a truant to chivalry" and the "shadow" of his father's succession (5.1.94), must

transform himself to look the part of a May lord, "Ris[ing] from the ground like feathered Mercury . . . / As if an angel dropped down from the clouds," in order to confront Hotspur, a "Mars in swaddling clothes," the "king of honor" (4.1.106-8; 3.2.112; 4.1.10).[17] And although Sir John's body is also capable of metamorphosis, his transformations, and the codes he serves, work precisely to expose such glorious disguises.

Elizabethan spectators would have still other figures for Falstaff, and for his fluid gender identity, including his guise of eternal youth, that are distant from present-day readers and spectators. Spectators at *1 Henry IV*'s first performances, when Falstaff was called Oldcastle, would connect him not only with the character of the same name in *The Famous Victories* but also with a historical Sir John Oldcastle, a martyr celebrated in Foxe's *Actes and Monuments* and sentenced to death for treason by Henry V. Certainly some observers, the sixteenth-century Oldcastle descendants, Sir William Brooke and his son, the seventh and eighth Lord Cobhams, objected to such libel of the family name. And their objections had considerable weight, for Sir William was the Lord Chamberlain, with oversight responsibilities for the Master of Revels and the licensing of plays: given such sensitivity in high places, Shakespeare changed the name, and though traces of it remain in *1 Henry IV*, *2 Henry IV*'s Epilogue offers a public disclaimer that "Oldcastle died martyr, and this is not the man" (Ep., 27-28).[18] The subject of anecdotes, letters, and rival plays, the Oldcastle-Falstaff issue may well have been fueled by the character's impersonator, the famous clown, Will Kemp, whom Nashe described as "jest-monger and Vice-gerent general to the ghost of Dick Tarlton" and who "succeeded" Tarlton as a favorite of Queen Elizabeth as well as the general public.[19] David Wiles argues persuasively that the Oldcastle-Falstaff role was written with Kemp in mind and that Kemp's particular skills helped to shape it, especially his ability to produce the illusion, in speaking scripted words, of spur-of-the-moment improvisation. And the conventions that coded a clown's role—ambiguous social status and semi-androgynous identity, freedom to separate himself from the play's role and plot structure, metamorphosis and final exclusion[20]—rather precisely figure the attributes of Falstaff, who is both thief and knight, gentleman and marginal reveller, mother as well as father and giant "Power Baby,"[21] separate from but also central to the historical rebellion, protean liar, the excluded other. Throughout, but most especially at Shrewsbury, all of these images of his theatrical abundance come into play.

To "thrust in clowns by head and shoulders"[22] or, in this case, belly first, at Shrewsbury is, of course, Shakespeare's invention. The official chronicle sources record a battle in which the chief actors are Henry IV, Hotspur, and the Douglas, and position Hal simply as his father's helper, "a lusty young gentleman" who, though wounded, refuses to withdraw and continues to "fight where the battle was most hot."[23] And it is entirely possible to extract, from Shakespeare's own fictional account in *1 Henry IV*—in which his major additions to its royal plot are Hal's offer to oppose Hotspur "in single fight," his rescue of his father, his combat with Hotspur, his freeing of the Douglas, and the presence of Prince John—a "decent" version of Shrewsbury that avoids the "mingling [of] kings and clowns" that Sidney so deplores.[24] Indeed, these particular alterations are sufficient to reshape the chronicle record as a test of feudal and familial values, similar to those dramatized in the closing battles of the *Henry VI* plays. Selectively retold, such a decorously perfected narrative might begin as the King, with unexpected concern for his wounded son, begs him to retire; following Hal's refusal, both Henry IV and Hal praise John's valor in "hold[ing] Lord Percy at the point"—an event that gives Hal a second rival, his "true" brother. And when Hal's "fair rescue" of his father "redeem[s] his lost opinion, he dispels his "loose behavior" and supposed treachery—and with it the filial aggression dramatized in *The Famous Victories*[25]—as a rumor perpetrated by others: "they did me too much injury / That ever said I heark'ned for your death" (5.4.50-51). So prepared for, the Hal-Hotspur combat—what Graham Holderness calls "a vivid poem of feudal romance and chivalric adventure"[26]—is an exchange of "glorious deeds" for "indignities" that, with the death of the rival (rebel) son, ensures Hal's place as Henry IV's "authentic" heir. Finally, in the play's last scene, with the rebels vanquished and punished, Henry IV acknowledges that authenticity: Hal, granted leave by his father to dispose of the Douglas, not only redeems his prisoner, and so takes on the Hotspur-like qualities his father had so admired, but, in recognition of John's valor, transfers the "honorable bounty" to his brother just before his father, for the first time, and in the play's concluding speech, calls him "son Harry" (5.5.39).

In that Falstaff is kept apart from his kingly other, Shakespeare's fiction of Shrewsbury approaches this decorous ideal: during the battle, he appears only with Hal or alone on the stage and, in conformity with convention, is absent from its final "official" ending. Yet, curiously enough, Shakespeare's "double reading" of the chronicle takes license for Falstaff's appearance at Shrewsbury from details that, in keeping with his fictional status as a Lord of Misrule, are introduced as hearsay:

(as some write) the earl of Douglas struck [Henry IV] down, and at that instant slew sir Walter Blunt, and three other, apparelled in the kings suit and clothing, saying: I marvel to see so many kings thus suddenly arise one in the neck of an other. The king in deed was raised, & did that day many a noble feat of arms, for as it is written, he slew that day with his own hands six and thirty persons

of his enemies. The other on his part encouraged by his doings, fought valiantly, and slew the lord Percy, called sir Henry Hotspur.[27]

In *1 Henry IV*'s Shrewsbury, many also walk in the King's coats: indeed, Shrewsbury begins by killing the king, later recognized by Hotspur as Blunt, and so recirculates the question of the true king's identity, the central issue behind the Hotspur-Northumberland rebellion (5.3). Having others march in the King's armor represents the King's body both as powerfully doubled and redoubled in his subjects and as an empty lie; it also questions whether counterfeiting, dying as one's self or in another's guise, is honorable when put at the king's service, dishonorable when put into play by a Falstaffian subject.

For in *1 Henry IV,* it is Falstaff, not the King, who "rises," and the ambiguous "other on his part" becomes Hal who, as in Daniel's *Civil Wars,* saves his father's life.[28] While Holinshed represents the king-father's body as a multiform illusion, in *1 Henry IV,* it is Falstaff—whose "lying" nature the play codes in his body as well as his voice—who calls such illusion, and the omnipresence of fatherly law, into question. If, like the Douglas, the play's first, or first-time, spectators assume that, in killing Blunt, he has killed the king, they could also imagine that the Douglas does indeed kill Falstaff, especially since their attention is, so to speak, doubled, for the encounter occurs at the same time as Hal's mythic combat with Hotspur, Shrewsbury's most heroic event for which Falstaff is, at first, an observer:

> *They fight. Enter Falstaff*
> FALST. Well said, Hal, to it Hal. Nay you shall
> find no boys' play here I can tell you.
> *Enter Douglas, he fighteth with Falstaff, he
> falls down as if he were dead, the Prince
> killeth Percy.*
>
> (5.4.74-75)

When, later, Hal speaks double epitaphs—one for Hotspur's "stout" heart, one over Falstaff's stout body—the conventions alone dictate resolution, neatly rounded off in perfect, and perfectly accidental, closure that dispenses with both rival son and rival parent, throwing the rivals into relationship, joining antithetical perspectives on honor that the play has kept separate but parallel, restoring order in the play's most politically significant systems: father-son relations, the threatened division of the kingdom, and Hal's authenticity. Indeed, since the last six lines of Hal's eulogy on Falstaff even fall into rhyme, it is possible for spectators as well as readers to hear these "last words" as the end of the play. In present-day theatrical configurations of the scene, the pause that invariably follows Hal's exit certainly invites spectators to believe in both deaths: even when "Falstaff riseth up" to fals-ify the illusion, it is only his ability to speak, proclaiming himself "no counterfeit, but the true and perfect image of life indeed," that codes the moment as something other than a curtain call where, eventually, the two other bodies onstage—the players of Hotspur and Blunt, dressed in armor that counterfeits the King— would also rise to acknowledge spectators' applause.

Most present-day critical configurations of this moment claim that Falstaff's resurrection invites readers and spectators, first, to be complicit with him, welcoming his surprise return from death, and then reject him when he stabs Hotspur and leaves to claim Hal's glory as his own.[29] But in fact the playtext makes none of these moralistic judgments; rather, the only "moral work" is Falstaff's own, and it constitutes a riff on the infinite possibilities of theatrical dying (5.4.114-17). Here again, 1 Henry IV's Elizabethan spectators would have other options. For those who knew the character as Oldcastle, the fat knight's "rising" might take on specific topical resonances and be read as a lampoon on Oldcastle's alleged dying promise that he would "rise from death to life again, the third day."[30] And when his "killing" of Hotspur is read through the conventions associated with the clown, Falstaff's weapon takes on particular meaning. His sword first appears at Gadshill as a property that figures him as both Vice and adolescent, for the Vice's traditional weapon was a dagger of lath, similar to the wooden "waster" used by apprentices in the Sunday evening fights allowed them by their masters.[31] "Hacked like a handsaw" by Falstaff himself after the robbery, it is clearly a toy sword as well as a figure for his name—a "false staff" that, in figuring his lack of a potent phallus, is an emblematic weapon well chosen to represent his ineffectiveness in chivalry's, so to speak, metallic world. And it is this same child's toy with which he gives Hotspur a "new wound in [his] thigh" (5.4.127), an injury Shakespeare seems to transfer from the chronicler's Douglas—who "brake one of his cullions" in a fall and, having so lost his manliness, was pardoned by Henry IV[32]—to Hotspur. For all its insistent mythologizing of the heroic, Shrewsbury's battle is, finally, just what Falstaff claimed it was not: "boys' play."[33] And what gives it the lie and refutes its chivalric signs, making them serve his own interests, is the clown's interventionary presence. A creature who draws his own authenticity from the suspect realm of theatrical shadows, he, more than any other, is well aware that the counterfeit—the reproduced image of the authentic—has no value until it is put into circulation and exchanged.[34]

Curiously enough, it is the rupture within Hal's own chivalry—his failure to take favors from Hotspur and, instead, to give him his own—that enables Falstaff to recirculate Hotspur's body and claim for himself the father's honor. While it is usual to displace Hal's "fault" onto Falstaff and to read Falstaff as one who takes meaning from Hal, present-day theatrical configurations in which Hal demonstrates less than chivalric tactics in the fight show him sharing in Falstaff's brand of honor, a choice that can turn his gilding of Falstaff's lie into a kind of self-justification. Even more important, however, is Falstaff's ability to steal meaning from Henry IV. As he leaves the stage to "follow . . . for reward" (5.4.158), promising dietary reform, it looks as though Carnival will indeed yield to Lent and so, perhaps, create a new fiction of a Falstaff who can insert his transformed body into history. His words sound final—sound, that is, like the end of his role—and 1 Henry IV's final scene excludes him from its image of a reconstituted, rebellion-free royal hierarchy. Elizabethan spectators would recognize these moves as entirely "decorous," for the clown's final metamorphosis and his absence from the play's last scene were conventions of his role, and he would, in most cases, return to perform the traditional jig finale.[35] In the play's representational economy, convention works to dismantle narrative closure. By the last scene, Shakespeare seems to revert to reading the chronicle "straight": Henry IV never has knowledge of precisely which "other on his part"—whether Hal or Falstaff— has killed Hotspur. It is only Falstaff who, at least in some sense, has witnessed the event and turned it to imagined future advantage. And when, at the close, the King looks forward to "such another day," he reads into Shrewsbury's official account what 2 Henry IV will, at first, record as a lie destined for the ears of Hotspur's "crafty-sick" father and, then, as the means to reinstate a newly costumed, newly titled "valiant Jack Falstaff," and so to further transform 1 Henry IV's "mingle" of king and clown.

From the mid-1950s forward, theatrical configurations of 1 Henry IV's close for the most part avoid the seamless, unitary discourse of spectacle characteristic of late nineteenth- and earlier twentieth-century versions and so not only "play out the play" but extend its boundaries, though not, except in one case, in order to say more on Falstaff's behalf (2.4.460-61). In that it so clearly articulates patterns of substitution and replacement among rival sons and fathers, Terry Hands's 1975 Royal Shakespeare Company 1 Henry IV draws the closing scenes into what might be called a structuralist's dream.[36] In the Hal-Hotspur combat, Hotspur disarms Hal, who then seizes Hotspur's sword and aims two blows at his shield and a third at his stomach, which brings him to his knees; Hal then removes Hotspur's helmet and slashes his face with a dagger. On "I better brook the loss of brittle life," Hotspur grabs Hal and slowly stands, to die in his arms. To further cement their brotherhood, Hal lays Hotspur's body down and, kneeling beside it, enacts a series of ceremonial gestures: after wiping Hotspur's blood onto his own face, he places Hotspur's sword on his chest, crosses the dead hands over it, takes a red cloth from his own dagger to cover Hotspur's eyes, and finally stands and removes his own helmet while he praises his dead rival. In contrast, he pauses just long enough to see Falstaff and speak his epitaph but does not touch his body. When Falstaff returns to life, he not only performs a sequence of actions—speaking a few lines before rising to his knees and, finally, standing—that echo Hotspur's but repeats Hal's tactics by stabbing Hotspur with his own sword; linking him to both, his mimicry also calls the value of such gestures into question and, when he drags Hotspur's body offstage, subverts them completely. To further the transformed value of Hotspur's body, Hands repeats the image—not once but twice. As Falstaff exits, Hal reenters with John[37] and registers surprise at seeing neither Hotspur nor Falstaff; then Falstaff returns, dragging Hotspur's body behind him to hear a bemused Hal "gild" his lie. Left alone after Hal and John exit together, Falstaff again drags Hotspur's body out, undercutting his final promise to "live cleanly as a nobleman should do." Although this staging replaces Falstaff with John as Hal's companion, neither Hal's bond to Falstaff nor his to Hal is severed: indeed, this Hal seems to accept Falstaff's lie in order to accept his own counterfeiting self.

Hands's final stage images trace a further range of substitutions. Led in on ropes, Worcester and Vernon flank King Henry's central figure, while Westmoreland stands directly upstage of Henry, with Clarence and Humphrey at either side of him. Deliberately enforcing military justice, Henry drops, first, Worcester's rope and, after a pause, Vernon's. When Westmoreland and Humphrey exit with the prisoners, Henry moves downstage where, as Hal kneels at his right, asking for leave to dispose of the Douglas, and John moves to his father's left, both sons replace Worcester and Vernon, the traitors. On "ransomless and free," Hal stands, as Hotspur had earlier when Henry questioned him about his prisoners (1.3); and the echo of one son replacing another persists when Henry calls Hal "son Harry," puts an arm on his shoulder, and draws him toward a prominent downstage position before, pausing as though in doubt, he speaks his final line, "Let us not leave till all our own be won," which cues music filled with expectant drumbeats.[38] Hands's staging reconstitutes the initial image of Henry surrounded by roped prisoners as a Plantagenet family portrait: Clarence and John stand in Vernon and Worcester's positions, Humphrey directly upstage of King Henry, Westmoreland up left, and Hal, now the "authentic" heir, directly downstage of Henry. As in Hands's closing images for the *Henry VI* plays, this final tableau figures a hard-won stability and predicts the "true" successor. And if replacing traitors with sons and cousins also refigures rebellion as a family matter, freeze-framing the close not only suppresses such potential contradictions but makes them unreadable, masked by an image of exclusive familial hierarchy that perfectly expresses the self-regarding gaze of legitimated royal power.

While the formal satisfactions of Hands's close fix Shrewsbury's moment within time, the close of Trevor Nunn's 1982 *1 Henry IV,* again for the Royal Shakespeare Company,[39] goes beyond its limits to reread its victory through Henry IV's eyes. The final image rhymes with the opening spectacle, where a flickering candlelight procession of monks, all in white robes and cowls, moves slowly downstage, while the rest of the company fills the dimly lit boxlike rooms, walkways, and turrets of the set—watchers as well as participants assembled to sing a haunting *Te Deum.* There, the King, dressed in a gold-embroidered ceremonial white cope, emerges from the procession to stand at its head, encompassed by the symbolic weight of his costume; here, the close diminishes the full panoply of that opening tableau. Bare to the waist and wearing a large crucifix, King Henry kneels in a tunnel of light, a shadowy kingdom of men and women standing in darkness behind him to observe his solitary, agonized penance. Drawing on Henry's opening wish to undertake a pilgrimage, Nunn's ending positions Shrewsbury's victory as a tainted substitute for and displacement of Henry's desire to lead a crusade that will expiate his guilt. It is an image that can be doubly read. If read backwards through *Richard II'*s ending and forward through the King's speech on the crown (*2 Henry IV,* 4.5.178-219), the image sharply focuses Henry's private angst and, by showing him surrounded by onstage spectator-subjects, all eyes turned toward the King, enhances his vulnerability and, as in *Richard II'*s close, figures not royal power but its lack. But the image can also be read through the schematic opposition of rival fathers: although it is Falstaff who promises reform, here it is Henry IV who performs his Shrewsbury penance.

Only once in *1 Henry IV,* at the parley just before Shrewsbury's battle (5.1), do King Henry and Falstaff share the stage, within a context that flirts with equating carnival and rebellion. When the King asks Worcester how he came to rebel, Falstaff answers for him, "Rebellion lay in his way, and he found it," and Hal quickly silences him—"Peace, chewet, peace!" (5.1.27-28). Whether Henry IV either does not hear or simply chooses to ignore Falstaff's remark, he never addresses him; Falstaff himself does not speak again until, following Hal's offer to "Try fortune with [Hotspur] in a single fight" and the King's offer of amnesty for the rebels, he is alone with Hal and asks for "friendship": "Hal, if thou seest me down in the battle . . ." (5.1.121). But although the playtext denies the support of language to the moment, this does not rule out the possibility of a silent exchange between Falstaff and the King, and both Hands's and Nunn's performance texts took this opportunity to sketch in their rivalry. In Hands's staging, both the King and Falstaff start to leave, and when Falstaff turns back to plead with Hal, the King pauses to watch their encounter, as though to satisfy himself that Hal will indeed keep his promise to "redeem all this on Percy's head" rather than revert to playing holiday with Falstaff. And Nunn's Henry IV, caught between envy and contempt for Falstaff, turns away, his shoulders sagging in defeat as Hal jokes with Falstaff.[40] Emrys James, who played Henry IV in Hands's production, remarked in an interview with Michael Mullin that "one can conceive a marvellous scene being written about [Henry and Falstaff]—a meeting between them."[41] Two other performance texts—Welles's *Chimes at Midnight* and Michael Bogdanov's 1987 English Shakespeare Company *1 Henry IV*—provide such a meeting, though not, perhaps, the one James may have had in mind.

Welles's film extends Hands's and Nunn's exchange of speaking looks to read Shrewsbury's victory as a record of personal loss and, by including Falstaff in its final moves, changes the relations between history and carnival, between the official version of Shrewsbury and Falstaff's account. When Falstaff throws Hotspur's body to the ground, Hal kneels in the mud and turns the body over on its back; in a mid-long shot of Hal, seen across Hotspur's body, a figure enters the frame at left, only the bottom of his robe visible, and the camera, rising with Hal, moves left to reveal King Henry, facing his son, his back to the camera. In a tightly edited sequence of close-ups—Henry's anguished face; Hal's look, caught between his two fathers; Falstaff's glow of self-pleasure; Hal meeting his father's gaze—the film links the three figures in an ambiguous web of doubt, betrayal, and dishonor in which Falstaff's expectant "I look to be either earl or duke, I assure you" cancels what Hal wants to say but cannot: that he has killed Hotspur. In a long shot, father and son face each other across the dead body before the King walks past Hal, strides into the background, and, in the next several shots, mounts his horse, collapses over the saddle in anguish, and, recovering, raises his arm in salute as the camera pans right to follow rows of horsemen. The next sequence reveals Falstaff, surrounded by his entire crew of ragged soldiers, a huge wine keg in the background; as though the previous confrontation had not occurred, he speaks a truncated version of his dissertation on sherris-sack (*2 Henry IV*, 4.3.83-119) and offers a tankard to Hal, who takes it and drinks, his forced smile suddenly becoming serious as he turns away from Falstaff, not sharing in the general laughter. As Falstaff's own smile turns quizzical and disappears, Hal, seen in an extreme-long shot, walks away across the smoke-filled battlescape, dropping the tankard: the sound track registers only the wind's empty roar, and the shot fades out. Restating father-son oppositions, Welles's film deepens and sharply triangulates them to entrap a doubly orphaned Hal between his rival fathers—cut off by his father's gaze and rejecting Falstaff's sack-nurturing maternity himself—and, in eclipsing the image of Falstaff's bulk with that of Hal's receding figure, points forward to Sir John's ultimate rejection.

Deliberately quoting Welles's film, Michael Bogdanov's *1 Henry IV* not only reorders the play's final events but figures a more radical disjuncture between historical event and Falstaffian intervention than either *Chimes at Midnight* or Shakespeare's play.[42] In this eclectically dressed production, where costume ranges from Hal's blue jeans and open-necked shirt to nineteenth-century military uniform for Henry IV to commandolike garb for the rebels and camouflage gear for Falstaff, Hal and Hotspur wear tabards and chain mail for their mythic combat on a bare stage—bare, that is, except for the rounded hill of Falstaff's body. Toward the end of a long fight with heavy broadswords, Hal loses his and curls into a fetal position, as though overcome with infantile fear. With a grin, Hotspur slides the sword across to him; recovering immediately, Hal comes at him, slices across his gut in an ugly sweep, and then plunges the sword down from the shoulder, crosswise under the tabard, to his heart. Standing behind Hotspur and cradling his body, he stabs him once more, this time from the rear, on Hotspur's "And food for . . ."—an unnecessary overkill, this Hal's deliberate revenge on his father's obvious preference for Hotspur, as well as a coup de grace in tribute to Hotspur's bravery. As Hal returns his sword to the scabbard, he starts to exit, and then, seeing Falstaff, dismissively speaks his epitaph. When, after removing a NO ENTRY sign from his shirt, Falstaff rises, he uses a child's toy sword to saw at Hotspur's thigh before heaving him onto his back as he leaves the stage.

Now the King, Worcester, Westmoreland, Prince John, and Hal return for the play's final scene, but as Henry concludes his last speech, Falstaff enters with Hotspur's body and unceremoniously plunks it down center, in front of Hal (fig. 13). His "I look to be either earl or duke, I assure you" is spoken half to Henry IV, half to Hal; positioned between the two, his bulk separating father and son, he recounts his version of Shrewsbury. Henry IV crosses to the body, looks down at it and then up at Hal, silently accusing him, before turning away to exit upstage center; after a self-righteous smirk at his brother, John follows his father, and an angry Hal smashes his sword to the floor with both hands. Pulling a cart piled with dead bodies, a solider enters to circle the stage, weaving around Hal and Falstaff, stopping briefly at Hotspur's body before he exits. Now Hal bends over Hotspur's body, takes back the neckerchief he had worn in the earlier tavern scenes and had tied around the dead Hotspur's neck, and replaces it jerkily around his own—a mark of his kill through which he reaccepts the rivalry separating father and son. As though attempting to placate him, Falstaff delivers his promise to leave sack and live cleanly to a Hal who, without looking at him, orders him to "bring your luggage *nobly* on your back," an irony this Falstaff shrugs off as he exits, once again bearing Hotspur's body. Alone, Hal raises his sword with both hands straight over his head, turns upstage, and, his back rigid, exits toward his father into the gathering dark to the accompaniment of crashing brasses.

Like Welles's ending for Shrewsbury, Bogdanov's rewritten close sharply focuses Hal's entrapment. Although similar to Welles's strategy in catalyzing Hal's guilt through an exchange of gazes to turn him back into an unredeemed son, Bogdanov's close also more sharply calls the limits of counterfeiting into question. This *1 Henry IV* not only restores the father-son opposition but refuses to exclude a Falstaff who imagines his lie a Shrewsbury joke not unlike Henry IV's "shadows" marching in armor. By omitting Hal's gilding of Falstaff's lie, Bogdanov's rearranged ending permits Falstaff to take revenge for Hal's exposure of his Gadshill cowardice. And its final emphases rest not on Hal's rejection of Falstaff but on Hal's own exclusion, his need to prove himself once more and also, perhaps, to seek revenge against the father who, doubting his true son, believes the boastful lie of another, counterfeit, father. The close of Bogdanov's *2 Henry IV* will further transform, and interrogate, this finale to read Henry V's rejection of Falstaff as his final, bitter revenge on all such fatherly lies. . . .

Notes

[1] See A. C. Bradley, "The Rejection of Falstaff," 1902; reprinted in *Henry the Fourth, Parts I and II*, ed. David Bevington (New York, 1986), 81, 96.

[2] Quoted in Juan Cobos and Miguel Rubio, "Welles and Falstaff," 1966; reprinted in *Chimes at Midnight*, ed. Bridget Gellert Lyons (New Brunswick, N.J., 1988), 261.

[3] For discussions of Welles's film, see Jorgens, *Shakespeare on Film*, 106-21; Samuel Crowl, "The Long Goodbye: Welles and Falstaff," *Shakespeare Quarterly* 31 (1980): 369-80; and Dudley Andrew, *Film in the Aura of Art* (Princeton, 1984), 152-71.

[4] Sherman H. Hawkins reviews, judges, and extends the two-century-old debate over the plan, structure, and aesthetic unity of the plays, which ranges from Dr. Johnson and Malone to Harold Jenkins, in "Henry IV: The Structural Problem Revisited," *Shakespeare Quarterly* 33 (1982): 278-301. See also Calderwood, *Metadrama in Shakespeare's Henriad*, especially 111-16, and Berry, *Patterns of Decay*, 109. Giorgio Melchiori posits an "original" one-part play (based on *The Famous Victories*) comprising *1* and *2 Henry IV* and *Henry V*, rejected because of the Oldcastle controversy and later divided into three ("Reconstructing the Ur-Henry IV," in *Essays in Honour of Kristian Smidt*, ed. Peter Bilton, Lars Hartveit, Stig Johansson, and Arthur O. Sandved [Oslo, 1986], 59-77).

[5] Bradley, "Rejection of Falstaff," 97.

[6] See, for instance, Barber, *Shakespeare's Festive Comedy*, 214-16; Greenblatt, "Invisible Bullets," 265; Holderness, *Shakespeare's History*, 88-95; Bristol, *Carnival and Theater*, 180-83, 204-7; Barber and Wheeler, *Whole Journey*, 198-217; Tennenhouse, *Power on Display*, 83-84; and Steven Mullaney, "Strange Things, Gross Terms, Curious Customs: The Rehearsal of Cultures in the Late Renaissance," in Greenblatt, *Representing the English Renaissance*, 82-89.

[7] Quoted in Cobos and Rubio, "Welles and Falstaff," 262.

[8] Mullaney, "Strange Things," 87.

[9] Prompt copy in the Beerbohm Tree Collection, the University of Bristol Theatre Collection.

[10] Because Tree played Falstaff, he probably remained onstage, since common stage practice licensed actor-managers' presences at significant moments, especially at curtain, regardless of the playtext's stage directions. Whether or not his presence undercut the embrace between father and son is impossible to gauge. Although 5.5 was apparently returned at a later time (perhaps for the 1906 production), a second, less thoroughly marked, prompt copy for this production also highlights the Battle of Shrewsbury conceived as a spectacular tableau.

[11] For example, in Anthony Quayle's 1951 Shakespeare Memorial Theatre production; prompt copy at the Shakespeare Centre Library.

[12] Prompt copy at the Shakespeare Centre Library.

[13] Richard Helgerson, *The Elizabethan Prodigals* (Berkeley, 1977). See also Mullaney, "Strange Things," 83.

[14] In reading the substitutions and replacements in these character relations, I draw from V. I. Propp, *Morphology of the Folktale* (1928); reprint, trans. Laurence Scott (Austin, 1958); A. J. Greimas, "Elements of a Narrative Grammar" (1969), reprinted in *Diacritics* 7 (1977): 23-40; and Barthes, *S/Z*. See also my "Falstaff: History and His Story," *Iowa State Journal of Research* 53, no. 3 (1979): 185-90. For an analysis based on René Girard's concept of sacred mythic difference, see Laurie E. Osborne, "Crisis of Degree in Shakespeare's *Henriad*," *Studies in English Literature* 25 (1985): 337-59. On morality elements, see Dessen, *Shakespeare and the Late Moral Plays*, 55-90.

[15] On Falstaff's "curiously feminine sensual abundance," see Kahn, *Man's Estate*, 72. See also Valerie Traub, "Prince Hal's Falstaff: Positioning Psychoanalysis and the Female Body," *Shakespeare Quarterly* 40

(1989): 456-74. On the *Henriad* as an Oedipal narrative, see Ernst Kris, "Prince Hal's Conflict," *Psychoanalytic Quarterly* 17 (1948): 487-506. See also Richard Wheeler, *Shakespeare's Development and the Problem Comedies* (Berkeley, 1981), 158-67.

[16] Marcus also notes the connection (*Puzzling Shakespeare,* 94).

[17] See Tennenhouse, *Power on Display,* 83-84.

[18] On the Oldcastle connection, see Alice Lyle Scoufos, *Shakespeare's Typological Satire* (Athens, Oh., 1979). See also *Henry the Fourth, Part I,* ed. David Bevington (Oxford, 1987), 3-10. Gary Taylor argues for returning Oldcastle's name to the playtext ("The Fortunes of Falstaff," *Shakespeare Survey* 38 [1985]: 95-100). Holderness positions the Oldcastle controversy in relation to *The True and Honourable History of the Life of Sir John Oldcastle* and to Puritan risings (*Shakespeare's History,* 107-12).

[19] *Almond for a Parrat* (1590); *Apology for Actors* (1612); both quoted in David Wiles, *Shakespeare's Clown* (Cambridge, 1987), 11.

[20] See Wiles, *Shakespeare's Clown,* 116-20.

[21] I borrow Beverle Houston's apt phrase, "Power and Dis-Integration in the Films of Orson Welles," *Film Quarterly* 35 (Summer 1982): 2.

[22] Sidney, *A Defence of Poetry,* 77. On the clown's "disorder," see David Scott Kastan, " 'Clownes Should Speake Disorderlye': Mongrel Tragicomedy and the Unitary State," unpublished paper, Shakespeare Association of America, 1989.

[23] Holinshed, *Chronicles,* 521/1/74, reproduced in Bullough, *Narrative and Dramatic Sources,* 4: 191.

[24] Sidney, *A Defence of Poetry,* 77.

[25] See Holinshed's report of Hal coming to his father strangely attired (538/2/74, reproduced in Bullough, *Narrative and Dramatic Sources,* 4: 193).

[26] Holderness, *Shakespeare's History,* 122. See also Gerard H. Cox, " 'Like a Prince Indeed': Hal's Triumph of Honor in *1 Henry IV,*" in Bergeron, *Pageantry in the Shakespearean Theater,* 133, 135-47; and Derek Cohen, "The Rite of Violence in *1 Henry IV,*" *Shakespeare Survey* 38 (1985), especially 82.

[27] Holinshed, *Chronicles,* reproduced in Bullough, *Narrative and Dramatic Sources,* 4: 191.

[28] Daniel, *Civil Wars,* 4: 110-11, reproduced in Bullough, *Narrative and Dramatic Sources,* 4: 214.

[29] See, for instance, Edward Pechter, "Falsifying Men's Hopes: The Ending of *1 Henry IV,*" *Modern Language Quarterly* 41 (1980): 227-28. See also Barber, *Shakespeare's Festive Comedy,* 204-6; James Black, "*Henry IV:* A World of Figures Here," in McGuire and Samuelson, *Shakespeare,* 173-80; and Calderwood, *Metadrama in Shakespeare's Henriad,* 83-84, 119, 174. In Welles's film, Hal sees breath rising like steam from the kettle of Falstaff's armadillo-like armor, which turns his "Embowelled will I see thee by-and-by" (5.4.108) into a threatening joke.

[30] See Stow's account, taken from Walsingham; quoted in Scoufos, *Shakespeare's Typological Satire,* 109.

[31] See Wiles, *Shakespeare's Clown,* 120-22.

[32] See Holinshed, *Chronicles,* quoted in Bullough, *Narrative and Dramatic Sources,* 4: 191.

[33] Wiles also notes this (*Shakespeare's Clown,* 123).

[34] For a pertinent discussion of counterfeit images, see Sharon Willis, "Disputed Territories: Masculinity and Social Space," *Camera Obscura* 19 (1989): 5-23.

[35] See Wiles, *Shakespeare's Clown,* 110-15.

[36] Prompt copy at the Shakespeare Centre Library.

[37] Hands replaces 5.4.18-19 so that these lines cap Hal's praise of John—"Before I loved thee as a brother, John, / But now I do respect thee as my soul"—and gives Hal John's "But soft, what have we here?"

[38] In Michael Edwards's 1984 *1 Henry IV* at Santa Cruz, Hal "avoided the simple notion that Hal returns to the role his father offered him—deliberately refusing . . . to resolve the many-sided, partly contradictory aspects of the part 'into an overall theory about Hal.' " See Mary Judith Dunbar, "Shakespeare at Santa Cruz," *Shakespeare Quarterly* 35 (1984): 477.

[39] The prompt copy at the Shakespeare Centre Library provides practically no directions for the close. I rely on notes taken at an August 1982 performance. See also R. L. Smallwood, "*Henry IV, Parts 1 and 2* at the Barbican Theatre" (1983; reprinted in Bevington, *Henry the Fourth, Parts I and II,* 423-30). Tree's 1895 production also opened with a procession accompanied by a Gregorian chant (prompt copy in the Beerbohm Tree Collection, the University of Bristol Theatre Collection).

[40] See Smallwood, *"Henry IV, Parts 1 and 2,"* 425.

[41] Quoted in an interview with Michael Mullin, "On Playing Henry IV," *Theatre Quarterly* 7, no. 27 (1977): 31.

[42] My account combines details from a June 1987 performance in Toronto and a May 1988 performance in Chicago. In a September 1988 interview, Bogdanov indicated that his rearranged ending indeed drew from Welles's film, which he much admires.

LAW AND JUSTICE

Norman Sanders (essay date 1977)

SOURCE: "The True Prince and the False Thief: Prince Hal and the Shift of Identity," in *Shakespeare Survey: An Annual Survey of Shakespearian Study and Production,* Vol. 30, 1977, pp. 29-34.

[*In the following essay, Sanders contends that Prince Hal associates with outlaws such as Falstaff in order to dissociate himself from his own father's illegitimate rule and, ultimately, to "create" his own form of kingly "Justice."*]

Much of Shakespeare's drama is centrally concerned with men's need to make choices in life and the necessity for taking full responsibility for the actions which result from these choices. One of the dramatic techniques he often uses to explore this aspect of the human condition is an interchange of roles between characters who are in some way parallel, owing to a similarity in situation, personality, action, or attitude. Thus Edgar can 'represent' Cordelia during the storm scenes in *King Lear,* so that she becomes, in a sense, the philosopher on the heath from whom her father learns life's awful lessons. In a similar way, the lines of action open to Hamlet, but not followed by him, can be explored with their consequences in the persons of the other revenging sons, Laertes and Fortinbras. And the same device lies behind the handling of such different characters as Portia and Jessica, Viola and Sebastian, the twin Antipholi, Perdita and Hermione, and the pairs of lovers in *As You Like It.*

However, in no play does Shakespeare use this technique quite so deliberately in both verbal and dramatic forms as in the *Henry IV* plays. Further, the almost self-conscious consistency shown in its employment is clearly related to the conception of the character of Prince Hal; and consequently may throw light on the divergent attitudes that critics have taken to him.

Throughout the two plays, Shakespeare frequently lifts Hal out of his own person or transfers to another character some aspect of his identity. The most obvious verbal example of this is King Henry's desire, in the opening scene of Part 1, to have Hotspur for a son instead of Hal:

O that it could be prov'd
That some night-tripping fairy had exchang'd
In cradle-clothes our children where they lay,
And call'd mine Percy, his Plantagenet!
Then would I have his Harry, and he mine.
(*1 Hen. IV,* I, i, 85-9)[1]

The implications of these lines are clear. The king is seen as choosing for himself a more symbolically appropriate son than the one he has; for Hotspur, who is soon to be a rebel against the crown, is a proper heir to the man who sneaked home like a poor unminded outlaw and

In short time after he depos'd the King,
Soon after that depriv'd him of his life,
And in the neck of that task'd the whole
    state.
(*1 Hen. IV,* IV, iii, 90-2)

It is, of course, ironical that the act that provokes such a longing as this in the king is Hal's abandonment of court and family, which constitutes in practice exactly the severing of paternity that Henry so desires.

Another verbal transference of identity, rather more complex because it is a double one, takes place in the interview between father and son in III, ii of the first play. Here the king uses words which effectively detach Hal from his lineage:

Yet let me wonder, Harry,
At thy affections, which do hold a wing
Quite from the flight of all thy ancestors.
(*1 Hen. IV,* III, ii, 29-31)

He then reinforces this observation by vividly placing Hal in parallel with Richard II. First, he depicts himself as the model of retiring success:

Had I so lavish of my presence been,
So common-hackney'd in the eyes of men,
So stale and cheap to vulgar company,
Opinion, that did help me to the crown,
Had still kept loyal to possession,
And left me in reputeless banishment,
A fellow of no mark nor likelihood.
By being seldom seen, I could not stir
But like a comet I was wonder'd at,
That men would tell their children, 'This is
    he!'
Others would say, 'Where, which is
    Bolingbroke?'
And then I stole all courtesy from heaven,
And dress'd myself in such humility
That I did pluck allegiance from men's hearts,
Loud shouts and salutations from their
    mouths,
Even in the presence of the crownéd King.
(ll. 39-54)

This is the ideal that the father-usurper-king sets up for his erring son: one which, by his own testimony, is at odds with loyal possession of the crown. It is a picture of a man who 'stole courtesy from heaven', who 'plucks allegiance from men's hearts'. Against this tarnished figure is offered an equally vivid portrait of the legitimate monarch:

> The skipping King, he ambled up and down,
> With shallow jesters, and rash bavin wits,
> Soon kindled and soon burnt, carded his state,
> Mingled his royalty with cap'ring fools,
> Had his great name profanéd with their scorns,
> And gave his countenance against his name
> To laugh at gibing boys, and stand the push
> Of every beardless vain comparative.
>
> (ll. 60-7)

Both Henry and Shakespeare place Hal 'in that very line'—that is as heir to Richard; while the king is transformed into an earlier Hotspur:

> For all the world
> As thou art to this hour was Richard then
> When I from France set foot at Ravenspurgh,
> And even as I was then is Percy now.
>
> (ll. 93-6)

While Hal, the legal heir, is 'the shadow of succession', Hotspur 'hath more worthy interest to the state' that Henry stole. With such alternatives open to him, Hal can promise to fight Percy; but personally he can only vow

> I shall hereafter, my thrice gracious lord,
> Be more myself.
>
> (ll. 92-3)

It is in dramatic rather than poetic terms that an even more complex and significant transference takes place in the tavern's comic counterpart of the serious court interview. In answer to Falstaff's plea to Hal to rehearse his excuses to his father, two playlets are arranged. In the first of them, Falstaff (the King of Misrule with no moral right to reprimand personal disorder) will play King Henry (also a king of misrule, by virtue of his act of usurpation, who has no moral right to lament national disorder). Hal will play himself in his twin roles as legitimate son to his father and apparent spiritual son to his surrogate tavern father, Falstaff.

Falstaff's admonishment, as it winds its euphuistic way, actually makes in comic form some of the points repeated by the king to his son two scenes later. First, it questions the reality of the father-son relationship:

> That thou art my son I have partly thy mother's word, partly my own opinion, but chiefly a villainous trick of thine eye, and a foolish hanging of thy nether lip, that doth warrant me. If then thou be son to me, here lies the point . . . why, being son to me, art thou so pointed at?
>
> (1 Hen. IV, II, iv, 397-402)

Then Hal's truancy from court is questioned: 'Shall the blessed sun of heaven prove micher, and eat blackberries?' (ll. 402-4). Third, the question is raised as to whether Hal can associate with criminals without becoming criminal himself:

> There is a thing, Harry, which thou hast often heard of, and it is known to many in our land by the name of pitch. This pitch (as ancient writers do report) doth defile, so doth the company thou keepest.
>
> (ll. 406-10)

And finally, there is the extended praise of Falstaff himself.

It is at this point that Hal sets up the second playlet, in which the roles played are very different. The prince takes the part of his own father, and in that role castigates himself and his weaknesses in the person of Falstaff, who can aptly personate those associations to which Hal is committed by his conscious decision to separate himself from the illegality of his father's reign. As this second play proceeds, Hal 'deposes' his father, Falstaff; and then casts out his devil by turning away that element in his necessary truancy represented by the old Vice. Nowhere are Hal's position of aloneness and the isolation he feels in the England of the plays made more clear than when he utters his banishment of Jack Falstaff and 'all the world'.

Both in this scene and that with his father, it is plain that the prince conceives himself to be solely responsible for making his way to the crown in an environment that has nothing of the normal security and aids which an heir might expect to be available to prepare himself for future kingship. His society is sick; established authority is riddled with guilt; the opposition to this authority is doubly guilty; and the only condition which will effectively dissociate him from both parties entails engagement with the usual enemies of social order—idlers, rogues, and thieves. Hal can indeed only promise to be more himself, and accept the charges of coldness and machiavellian calculation that have been levelled at him.

As it has often been noted, the second part of the play, despite the brilliant realism of the scenes in Gloucestershire, moves very close at certain points to the manner of the old morality drama. And whatever one believes about the relationship between the two parts, it is demonstrable that some episodes in the second play do repeat, or make more explicit, or expand effects and events which the first part deals with more suggestively and (in my opinion) more subtly.

It is not surprising, therefore, that we find in two crucial episodes of Part 2 the same technique being used in the management of Hal's character. In the scene between the newly proclaimed Henry V and the Lord Chief Justice (v, ii), Hal once again juggles with his identities; only in this case he does so in a way that is complexly linked to the basic issues of kingship and its position in the social structure of the nation.

The Lord Chief Justice places Hal in the position of being his own father, even as Hal had himself in the tavern play scene:

> Question your royal thoughts, make the case
>   yours,
> Be now the father, and propose a son,
> Hear your own dignity so much profan'd,
> See your most dreadful laws so loosely
>   slighted,
> Behold yourself so by a son disdain'd:
> And then imagine me taking your part,
> And in your power soft silencing your son.
> After this cold considerance sentence me;
> And, as you are a king, speak in your state.
>   (*2 Hen. IV*, v, ii, 91-9)

Hal accepts the role and passes judgement on himself:

> You are right, Justice, and you weigh this well.
> Therefore still bear the balance and the
>   sword;
> And I do wish your honours may increase
> Till you do live to see a son of mine
> Offend you and obey you, as I did.
> So shall I live to speak my father's words:
> 'Happy am I, that have a man so bold
> That dares do justice on my proper son;
> And not less happy, having such a son
> That would deliver up his greatness so
> Into the hands of justice.'
>   (ll. 102-12)

But he goes further than ever his own father could; by abstracting the concept of Justice from its particular human representative, he places himself beneath the law in a classic formulation of the Tudor principle concerning the position of royal magistrates:

> I do commit into your hand
> Th'unstained sword that you have us'd to
>   bear,
> With this rememberance—that you use the
>   same
> With the like bold, just, and impartial spirit
> As you have done 'gainst me. There is my
>   hand.
> You shall be as a father to my youth,
> My voice shall sound as you do prompt mine
>   ear,

> And I will stoop and humble my intents
> To your well-practis'd wise directions.
>   (ll. 113-21)

Justice is thus dissociated from the reign of Henry IV and the wildness of Hal's youth and his father's illegal reign are firmly linked in the words used:

> believe me, I beseech you,
> My father is gone wild into his grave,
> For in his tomb lie my affections;
> And with his spirits sadly I survive
> To mock the expectation of the world,
> To frustrate prophecies, and to raze out
> Rotten opinion, who hath writ me down
> After my seeming.
>   (ll. 122-9)

In richly associative terms, Hal sees his blood, which had flowed in consciously adopted 'vanity' and was deflected from its true path of nobility by the decision forced upon him by his father's guilt, as reassuming its right channel:

> The tide of blood in me
> Hath proudly flow'd in vanity till now.
> Now doth it turn, and ebb back to the sea,
> Where it shall mingle with the state of
>   floods,
> And flow henceforth in formal majesty.
>   (ll. 129-33)

However one may react to the emotional and human impact of Henry V's final rejection of Falstaff in the last scene of Part 2, its terminology is perfectly consistent with the pattern of dissociation of identity I have tried to trace. Hal's experience has indeed been unreal and like a dream: one in which seeming has been taken for truth, where actual criminality has been necessary to achieve true legality, when the self has had to be split in two and one part of it turned away:

> I have long dreamt of such a kind of man, . . .
> But being awak'd I do despise my dream. . . .
> For God doth know, so shall the world
>   perceive,
> That I have turn'd away my former self; . . .
> When thou dost hear I am as I have been,
> Approach me, and thou shalt be as thou wast.
>   (*2 Hen. IV*, v, v, 49, 51, 57-8, 60-1)

If Shakespeare worked so deliberately and consistently to connect Hal with this pattern of dislocation from self and society, it follows that this means of dramatic portrayal must be connected with the way we are intended to view the prince and his unique difficulties in the situation in which he finds himself. And many other aspects of these plays seem to provide evidence that Shakespeare carefully constructed a world which forced upon Hal self-definition via apparent criminality as the only choice open to him.

First, both plays are loaded with reminders of the immediacy of Henry IV's ever-present guilt about what he did to get the crown, and with vivid recollections of the past by such characters as Hotspur, the Archbishop, and Worcester. These allusions are further reinforced by the cumulative effect of the imagery of sickness, weariness, and sleeplessness associated with Henry's reign, and also by the long shadow that Richard II's deposition and death throws over the plays. The rebels against this diseased rule are similarly devalued; for throughout both parts they are characterised by division, bickering, distrust, and weakness. In fact, despite the variety offered by such features as the violent and colourful animosity of Hotspur, the calculating illness of Northumberland, the pseudo-mysticism of Glendower, and the crafty manoeuvrings of Worcester, there is basically little to choose between the moral stances of the two sides. We find at various points in the plays definite interrelationships indicated between the moral deficiencies of both. In Part 2, the Archbishop accurately depicts the dilemma facing the usurper-king:

> the King is weary
> Of dainty and such picking grievances;
> For he hath found, to end one doubt by death
> Revives two greater in the heirs of life:
> And therefore will he wipe his tables clean,
> And keep no tell-tale to his memory
> That may repeat and history his loss
> To new remembrance. For full well he knows
> He cannot so precisely weed this land
> As his misdoubts present occasion.
> His foes are so enrooted with his friends
> That plucking to unfix an enemy
> He doth unfasten so and shake a friend.
> So that this land, like an offensive wife
> That hath enrag'd him on to offer strokes,
> As he is striking, holds his infant up,
> And hangs resolv'd correction in the arm
> That was uprear'd to execution.
> *(2 Hen. IV,* IV, i, 197-214)

The final image of family strife in the last five lines here is a telling one, for Hal's position between opposing forces is similar to that of the infant pictured between father and mother. In the first part of the play, Worcester describes the equally impossible situation in which the rebels find themselves:

> It is not possible, it cannot be,
> The King should keep his word in loving us;
> He will suspect us still, and find a time
> To punish this offence in other faults:
> Supposition all our lives shall be stuck full of
>   eyes,

> For treason is but trusted like the fox,
> Who, never so tame, so cherish'd and lock'd
>   up,
> Will have a wild trick of his ancestors.
> Look how we can, or sad or merrily,
> Interpretation will misquote our looks,
> And we shall feed like oxen at a stall,
> The better cherish'd still the nearer death.
> *(1 Hen. IV,* V, ii, 4-15)

It is this process of rebellion-repentance-recrimination-new rebellion-revenge set in train by Richard II's deposition and murder that Hal must put an end to. He must redeem that temporal pattern which decrees that

> heir from heir shall hold this quarrel up
> Whiles England shall have generation.
> *(2 Hen. IV,* IV, ii, 48-9)

Given these conditions, how else is Hal to create single-handedly a totally new royal milieu except by complete and apparently criminal dissociation from all the norms that a sick nation offers him? Shakespeare's dramatic solution is to make Hal's defection real to both the court and tavern worlds, while assuring the audience that the prince so offends to make offence a skill. His being, yet not being, a part of Falstaff's corrupt realm is typified by his role in the Gadshill robbery, in which the justice he creates is of his own rather than his society's making. He is for the same reason verbally detached from his father's lineage; even as he can strike his father's Justice, yet submit himself to the same Justice when it is the main prop of his own reign.

Because Hal's possession of the crown must be seen to be 'plain and right', Shakespeare devises a scene, which, although explicable in human terms, also shows Hal symbolically stealing the crown of England from his father rather than receiving it at his hands. In this scene *(2 Henry IV,* IV, V), Hal draws a careful distinction between the debt he owes his father as a loving son:

> Thy due from me
> Is tears and heavy sorrows of the blood,
> Which nature, love, and filial tenderness
> Shall, O dear father, pay thee plenteously, ·
> (ll. 36-9)

and the right he possesses by virtue of what he has made of himself:

> My due from thee is this imperial crown,
> Which, as immediate from thy place and
>   blood,
> Derives itself to me. [*Putting it on his head*]
> (ll. 40-2)

As Henry says, more truly than he knows, 'God put it in thy mind to take it thence. . . .   Thou wilt needs invest thee with my honours'; for no one else in his England can rightfully perform the ritual.

The Prince of Wales, in these two plays, faces alone the task of finding, while laden with an awesome duty, a *modus operandi* in an impossible world; just as the later Prince of Denmark was to undertake a not completely dissimilar task and meet it in a similar way. For Hamlet, the ultimate objective is the discovery of self and true being; whereas for Hal, it is the discovery of public role and right doing—which is to say that one is a tragic hero and the other a political one. As it is necessary for the greater prince to play the fool for wisdom's sake; so, for the lesser, a true prince may and does, for re-creation's sake, prove a false thief.

Notes

[1] Quotations are from the new Arden edition of the plays edited by A. R. Humphreys (1960, 1966).

Dain A. Trafton (essay date 1981)

SOURCE: "Shakespeare's Henry IV: A New Prince in a New Principality," in *Shakespeare as Political Thinker,* edited by John Alvis and Thomas G. West, Carolina Academic Press, 1981, pp. 83-94.

[*In the following essay, Trafton argues that Shakespeare intended to portray Henry IV as a calculating and impious usurper who, lacking "the creative qualities of a founder," fails to create a legitimate monarchy within his own lifetime.*]

Between the richly colored and dramatically imposing figures of Richard II and Henry V—at the very center, as it were, of Shakespeare's second tetralogy of plays about English history—stands the sober, curiously drab figure of Henry Bolingbroke. A mere outline of his career suggests a portrait that might have been composed almost entirely of highlights, both lurid and brilliant. Having seized the throne and murdered his cousin the king, Henry holds his prize against all comers, destroys his enemies at last, and bequeaths his conquests intact to his son. What this outline suggests, however, Shakespeare's art avoids. Throughout three plays notably filled with characters who dominate the stage, Shakespeare withholds from Henry the vividness that his story seems to warrant. Unlike other Shakespearean characters who commit outstanding crimes in the pursuit of thrones—Richard III, Macbeth, or Claudius—Henry has not been granted the moments of high dramatic intensity, the triumphs and the agonies, that make a hero. His is a study in grey. Moreover, as the tetralogy progresses from *Richard II* to the plays that bear his name, Henry literally recedes from view. A progressive diminishment of his presence on the stage occurs. In *Richard II* he is on stage

about half the time; in the first of the plays named for him, however, his role is reduced by half, and in the second a further reduction leaves him with only three scenes, which amount to less than one sixth of the work. One might conclude that Henry's character simply never engaged Shakespeare's full interest, but such a conclusion would miss the point. The sobriety of tone befits the special intention of Henry's portrait. That intention is neither tragic nor heroic, but essentially political. In the curiously muted presentation of Henry can be discovered one of Shakespeare's most searching political portraits—his most extended and also his profoundest political investigation of (to use the language of Machiavelli) a new prince in a new principality.[1] Other Shakespearean characters present the type in greater psychological and moral depth, and with greater dramatic power; none displays with such clarity and thoroughness the political implications of regicide and usurpation. Ultimately, moreover, the lusterless tones in which Henry is drawn point to Shakespeare's judgment upon the first Lancastrian king. As we shall see, the tetralogy's analysis of Henry's politics leads to a revelation of his essential deficiency.

According to Shakespeare, Henry's usurpation represents more than a simple change of dynasty. In defying, deposing, and eventually murdering Richard, Henry subverts not only the rule of a particular king, but also a fundamental principle of the realm. He violates, and thus undermines, the sanctity of monarchy itself, the belief that kings are God's deputies and that rebellion is a sin. Through the figures of Gaunt, Carlisle, York, and Richard himself, Shakespeare articulates this principle in all its religious dignity, and identifies it as an essential source of order in the traditional regime that exists at the beginning of the tetralogy. When the Duchess of Gloucester seeks revenge upon Richard for the murder of her husband, Gaunt sternly refuses to take action against "God's substitute, / His deputy anointed in His sight."[2] When Henry is on the point of taking the crown itself from "plume-pluck'd Richard," Carlisle steps forward to deplore "so heinous, black, obscene a· deed." If "the figure of God's majesty" is deposed, Carlisle warns,

> The blood of English shall manure the
> . ground,
> And future ages groan for this foul act.
>
> (IV.i.137-138)

Henry must be presumed as familiar with the weighty significance of these views as are his father and Carlisle; yet neither the memory of the former nor the eloquence of the latter turns him from an act of profound impiety against the regime. Noting the ambiguities and contradictions in his statements, and the fact that he is not depicted clearly as a villain, most critics have concluded that Shakespeare intended to present Henry as a rebel who drifts into his radical course without quite knowing, or quite admitting to himself, what he is doing.[3] At heart, these critics argue, Henry is more of an opportunist than a schemer; his maneuvers finally leave him no choice except to make himself king, but he is not the kind of man to have reflected much along the way. That Henry's statements are often ambiguous and that he is an opportunist cannot be denied. However, to conclude that he drifts into rebellion, that he has not reflected upon the implications of his deeds is to credit him too much or too little. In fact he is more thoroughly a rebel in thought than in action. He does not blink his own impiety; on the contrary, he guides his career consistently by a view of the world that is totally opposed to the one on which the traditional politics of the realm are grounded. Only when the extent of Henry's intellectual rebellion has come to light can the nature and cause of his deficiency as a new prince be perceived.

Interpretation of Henry's character is complicated by his evident prudence. Observation and his own admission inform us that he is an extremely politic man, constantly concerned with manipulating others and cultivating a public image:

> And then I stole all courtesy from heaven,
> And dress'd myself in such humility
> That I did pluck allegiance from men's
>   hearts.
>
> (*1 Henry IV*, III.ii.50-52)

Unlike Richard, who makes a parade of his thoughts and feelings, Henry is a man of masks. Yet masks, too, reveal—especially when they are recognized as masks; and we shall see that Shakespeare has designed Henry's so that they point to the reality they partly hide. In one scene, moreover, near the end of Henry's life, Shakespeare allows us to see him momentarily divested of his disguises, and speaking with shocking openness. Act III, scene i, of *Henry IV*, part 2, which contains Henry's only soliloquy, represents a spiritual crisis brought on by illness and the burden of a troubled reign. To his closest adviser, Warwick, Henry seems at times unbalanced during this scene, but his words provide an unusually clear insight into a mind that has discarded orthodox political ideals and has not flinched from deposing and murdering "the figure of God's majesty."

At the beginning of the scene Henry waits for Warwick and Surrey, whom he has just summoned to an impromptu midnight council, and soliloquizes on his insomnia. He wonders why he should suffer while the poor who lie in "smoky cribs" and the sailor on "the high and giddy mast" sleep soundly. "O sleep, O gentle sleep, / Nature's soft nurse, how have I frighted thee?" (5-6), Henry asks, but finds no cause in himself. Sleep is simply a "dull god" and "partial"; it is the general lot of kings to suffer. What is striking here is that Henry does not impute his troubles to his own deeds.

A more traditional mind might have invoked Carlisle's prophecy at this point, but Henry has turned away from that vision. For him there is no moral or religious significance in events: the god that governs sleep manifests no rational pattern of cause and effect. As the scene progresses, moreover, Henry's unorthodoxy becomes clearer. Warwick and Surrey arrive, but instead of attending immediately to the business at hand, Henry interrupts their advice with a long discourse upon the nature of things:

> Oh God, that one might read the book of
>   fate,
> And see the revolution of the times.
>
> (45-46)

He begins by calling on God, but the account of "the revolution of the times" that he goes on to give leaves God out entirely. Periodic cataclysms level mountains and dissolve coasts; the oceans themselves at times withdraw; and Henry sees in such events not the providential hand of God, but rather "how chance's mocks / And changes fill the cup of alteration" (51-52). To Henry, obviously, his father's and Carlisle's views of kingship are nothing more than pious myths. If the world is ruled by "chance's mocks," traditional religious restraints possess no more force than credulous minds are willing to give them.

In his present mood, however, Henry's view of the world seems more cause for despair than confidence. He has avoided one dread—the dread of sin—to discover another—the dread of meaninglessness as one drains "the cup of alteration." "O, if this were seen," he laments,

> The happiest youth, viewing his progress
>   through,
> What perils past, what crosses to ensue,
> Would shut the book and sit him down and
>   die.
>
> (53-56)

What motive to great actions can there be in a world subject to patternless change? As Henry rouses himself from depression one idea emerges as predominant in his mind—the idea of necessity. Turning from universal disorder to the infidelity of friends, he recalls Richard's accusation of Northumberland as the "ladder by the which / My cousin Bolingbroke ascends my throne," and interjects an apology—the 'only one he ever offers—for his usurpation: "necessity so bow'd the state / That I and greatness were compell'd to kiss" (70-74). And when Warwick seizes upon the idea, urging Henry to recognize the "necessary form" in his present difficulties, he responds with vigor:

> Are these things then necessities?
> Then let us meet them like necessities;

And that same word even now cries out on
  us.

(92-94)

For Henry, there is a necessity that compels in spite of "chance's mocks." To learn exactly what necessity means to him and how it operates in the world he envisions we must examine his earlier career.[4]

The earliest clear indication of the necessity that Henry recognizes occurs in the first act of *Richard II*, in Henry's response to his father's efforts to persuade him to accept his banishment patiently. On the surface, Gaunt argues simply that a wise man makes the best of everything. Beneath his stoicism, however, lies his belief in the sanctity of kingship. From Gaunt's point of view, a kind of necessity obliges Henry to submit to Richard's sentence; not to submit would be a sin:

Teach thy necessity to reason thus—
There is no virtue like necessity.

(I.iii.277-278)

Henry replies with a string of revealing rhetorical questions:

O, who can hold a fire in his hand
By thinking on the frosty Caucasus?
Or cloy the hungry edge of appetite
By bare imagination of a feast?
Or wallow naked in December snow
By thinking on fantastic summer's heat?
O no, the apprehension of the good
Gives but the greater feeling to the worse.

(I.iii.294-301)

No moral dimension complicates the three examples of simple physical pain that Henry employs; in each, the only conceivable "good" consists in alleviating the pain rather than in patiently bearing it. By implying that being banished is analogous to holding fire in one's hand or suffering from hunger or wallowing naked in snow, Henry makes it clear that the only good he apprehends is the end of banishment. He reduces what his father regards as a moral issue, involving a necessity imposed by divine law, to a matter of avoiding personal pain. Gaunt's advice violates nature as Henry understands it. Gaunt assumes a world informed by divine purpose, but Henry takes his bearings by the body. Just as physical necessity compels men to avoid fire, hunger, and cold, so the psychological pain of banishment will compel Henry to end it. A great deal has been written about the motive of Henry's actual return to England, but critics have failed to perceive the importance of this speech. To those who pay attention, Henry's words are a warning that he has already determined to come home as soon as he can. His later claim "I come but

for mine own" (III.iii.196) must be considered a politic lie; Northumberland's revelations immediately after the death of Gaunt (II.i.277-298) inform us that Henry has set out from Brittany even before the confiscation of his estate. Of course he wants his inheritance, but land is not what pricks him on. Not acquisitiveness but spirited self-assertion—an impulse that is strictly personal, and as compelling as the most powerful physical drive—impels Henry to violate the doctrine of kingship in which he does not believe, and to brave the mockery of chance in which he does. In a world bereft of the divine, the only necessity that obtains for a man derives either from his body's needs or from individual inclination; what but the sheer assertion of individuality leads one man to make himself king and another to "shut the book and sit him down and die"?

Obviously other possibilities exist—possibilities that lie somewhere between the violent course of usurpation and passive withdrawal from all effort—but they do not occur to Henry. Partly, of course, they do not occur to Henry because they do not occur for him. His condition precludes moderate courses. Given the necessity that brings him back illegally from banishment, he has no choice except to destroy Richard or be destroyed by him. Having defied the king, Henry can never be safe in England until he sits upon the throne himself, and until the old king lies dead. In a personal sense, at least, Henry's assertion that he and greatness "were compell'd to kiss" is true. At the same time, Shakespeare makes it clear that Henry considers the violent necessities of his own life to be not merely personal but also consistent with the design of nature as a whole. Indeed, Henry seems convinced that usurpation and regicide accord with "the revolution of the times." Logically, of course, there is no reason why "chance's mocks / And changes" should foster usurpation and murder any more than loyalty; under fortune, nature is promiscuous, but procreative as well as abortive, constructive as well as destructive. As we have seen, however, Henry's meditation on the nature of things focuses on destruction and disorder—on the vast calamities that alter the very face of the earth. In the minds of those who hold the world to be empty of God and governed by chance or fortune, the violent and destructive side of things tends to become ascendant. Lucretius reveals this subtly, Machiavelli emphatically. Henry conforms to the pattern.[5]

At Flint Castle, for example, Henry envisions his meeting with Richard in images of elemental struggle:

Methinks King Richard and myself should
  meet
With no less terror than the elements
Of fire and water, when the thund'ring shock
At meeting tears the cloudy cheeks of heaven.

(III.iii.54-57)

Max Helpmann as King Henry IV, with members of the Festival Company, in a scene from the 1958 Stratford Festival production of Henry IV, Part 1.

Here the violence upon which Henry bases his own career appears to reflect a universal disorder. Although he goes on to claim that in the coming confrontation he will be "the yielding water," the fact remains that Henry would not even have come to Flint Castle if he identified himself with the yielding elements. Earlier, indeed, he presented himself more frankly as a kind of natural force that might create a rain of blood:

> I'll use the advantage of my power
> And lay the summer's dust with showers of
> blood
> Rain'd from the wounds of slaughtered
> Englishmen.
>
> (III.iii.42-44)

And the image of a bloody rain recurs at the end of the play in a context that makes clear Henry's sense that one must live in accord with a violence that is essentially natural. Speaking of Richard's murder to the assembled court, Henry protests, "my soul is full

of woe / That blood should sprinkle me to make me grow" (V.vi.45-46). Whether Henry really feels sorrow or not, and if so how much, remains a matter of doubt; what cannot be doubted is that no scruple of conscience ever prevents him from pursuing the harsh course that his personal needs dictate. When he imagines himself a plant sprinkled with Richard's blood, Henry implies that Richard's murder must be seen as a necessary part of a natural process: just as a plant naturally requires rain, so Henry in the nature of things required the blood of the king whom he deposed.

In *Henry IV,* part 1, nothing illustrates Henry's view of life more clearly than his praise of Hotspur. Commenting on Hotspur's victory over the Scots at Holmedon, Henry describes him as "amongst a grove the very straightest plant" and "sweet Fortune's minion and her pride" (I.i.81-82). The best man, it seems, the man most likely to prosper in Fortune's·capricious eyes, is the best soldier. Like Henry himself, Hotspur lives by the needs of his own aggressive nature; and it is fully consistent with Henry's deepest convictions that his admiration increases when Hotspur's self-assertion aims at the throne. Having summoned Hal to the palace in order to rebuke him for his neglect of harsh necessity, Henry holds up the rebel Hotspur as an example of princely virtue:

> Now, by my sceptre, and my soul to boot,
> He hath more worthy interest to the state
> Than thou the shadow of succession;
> For of no right, nor colour like to right,
> He doth fill fields with harness in the realm.
>
> (III.ii.97-101)

According to Henry, who swears by his sceptre before his soul, the measure of Hotspur's worthiness for rule consists in his will and ability to take by force what he wants. In one contemptuous line, Henry dismisses the standards of legal and moral "right"; the only right he recognizes is the right established by might. "[E]ven as I was then is Percy now," he remarks, recalling his rebellion against Richard. No doubt Henry sees his own and Hotspur's careers as responsive to the same basic necessity—the need to assert oneself violently in a violent world, to use violence against others lest it be used against oneself.[6]

After Henry becomes king, of course, his admiration for men of similar virtue is necessarily restricted: his personal interests and the interests of the kingdom coincide. As exiled Henry Bolingbroke, he was fully prepared to "lay the summer's dust with showers of blood / Rain'd from the wounds of slaughtered Englishmen"; as King Henry IV, he abhors civil strife and seeks to bring order to the land. Nevertheless, the opening speech of *Henry IV*, part I, reveals that the same views that confirmed him in rebellion now inform his scheme for restoring order. Henry comes on stage "shaken" and "wan with care," but expressing optimism. Insurrection has plagued his reign from the outset, but he perceives at last an opportunity to transform domestic enmity into a foreign war. An expedition to the Holy Land will serve Henry's turn. Ostensibly the expedition is to be a crusade. Henry describes himself as a soldier of Christ and alludes to his original intention of journeying to the Holy Land in atonement for the murder of Richard. However, close attention to Henry's words reveals the wholly political motives that lie behind his religious professions:

> No more the thirsty entrance of this soil
> Shall daub her lips with her own children's
>   blood,
> No more shall trenching war channel her
>   fields,
> Nor bruise her flow'rets with the armed hoofs
> Of hostile paces; those opposed eyes,
> Which, like the meteors of a troubled heaven,
> All of one nature, of one substance bred,

> Did lately meet in the intestine shock
> And furious close of civil butchery,
> Shall now, in mutual well-beseeming ranks,
> March all one way, and be no more opposed
> Against acquaintance, kindred, and allies.
> The edge of war, like an ill-sheathed knife,
> No more shall cut his master.
>
> (I.i.5-18)

That Henry considers war abroad a proper preventive for war at home illustrates his conviction that violent courses conform to nature and are more likely to win the favors of Fortune. His imagery suggests that bloodshed is inevitable. The very earth thirsts for her children's blood, and if "this soil"—England—is to be denied what it longs for, the result will be an abundance for the soil of foreign lands. Men resemble meteors, conventional symbols of cosmic disorder; "all of one nature, of one substance bred," they nevertheless—or therefore—butcher each other. Civil war is an "ill-sheathed knife," but the obvious remedy of sheathing the knife correctly never arises; the only possible course, it seems, is to draw the knife completely and employ it on others. Later, Henry claims that his subjects "were moulded in their mothers' womb / To chase those pagans in those holy fields" (I.i.23-24). Men were born to fight; they carry from the womb an impulse to destroy. Just as Henry does not try to restrain that impulse in himself, his political program aims not at restraining his subjects but rather at channeling their violence outward towards foreigners. Peace is not his goal but rather a "well-beseeming" foreign war which will remove the destruction from England, and from Henry himself.

This political reading of the motives behind Henry's crusade is confirmed in *Henry IV*, part 2, during the king's final interview with Hal. There Henry analyzes his difficulties with the unruly noblemen of the realm who first helped him and now oppose him, and explains the policy by which he sought to check them:

> I cut them off, and had a purpose now
> To lead out many to the Holy Land,
> Lest rest and lying still might make them
>   look
> Too near unto my state.
>
> (IV.v.209-212)

According to Henry, Hal too must find a way "to busy giddy minds / With foreign quarrels." Of all Henry's references to a crusade, this one stands out as providing the most trustworthy account of his aims. Whereas earlier—in the presence of the court both at the end of *Richard II* and at the beginning of *Henry IV*, part 1—public consideration precluded frankness, nothing inhibits him here. He knows that he is on his deathbed, and he has no object beyond offering his political wisdom to his heir. The lesson that he conveys has nothing to do with religious atonement or any other sacred duty. He wants to teach Hal how to save his throne, not his soul. Although Henry mentions the "indirect crook'd ways" by which he obtained the crown (*2 Henry IV*, IV.v.183-185), and concludes with a nod toward the traditional doctrine of kingship—"How I came by the crown, O God forgive" (IV.v.218)—the rest of his long speech expresses no guilt. On the contrary, most of what Henry says amounts to a recommendation of his "indirect crook'd ways," and makes clear his opinion that success in politics depends upon them. One must grasp the potential for violence in things and wield it to one's own advantage. Even one's "friends" have "stings and teeth" (IV.v.204-205).

Occasionally, as in these last words of counsel to Hal, Henry's religious expressions seem merely perfunctory or ironic; characteristically, however, as in his proclamations of a crusade, he appeals to religion for obvious political reasons.[7] Having established his rule by force, Henry apparently hopes to render it more secure by arrogating to himself the religious awe of a traditional monarchy like Richard's. The crusade is the main device by which Henry attempts to throw a veil of piety over his deeds, but he is careful to identify his kingship with convention from the very moment of his accession. In order to maintain the illusion of an unbroken succession, he does his best to present Richard's deposition as an abdication; and when York arrives to announce that Richard has agreed to step down, Henry promptly announces, "In God's name, I'll ascend the regal throne" (*Richard II*, IV.i.113). Carlisle revolts at this brazenness and rebukes it; most of the court, however, seems prepared to accept, at least initially, Henry's assumption of divine favor along with the crown. York makes an extravagant show of loyalty in denouncing his own son's plot against Henry; and after Henry, yielding to the Duchess of York's pleas, pardons Aumerle, the Duchess thanks him with a phrase that seems to acknowledge his legitimacy in traditional terms: "A god on earth thou art" (V.iii.134).

Even before the end of *Richard II*, however, it becomes clear that Henry's efforts to make himself a sacred king in the old style cannot succeed. In spite of his follies and delusions, Richard's claim to be a kind of "god on earth" commands the loyalty of respectable men like Gaunt and Carlisle; Henry will never enjoy such dignity. The kingdom he has seized rises in arms against itself:

> the latest news we hear,
> Is that the rebels have consum'd with fire
> Our town of Ciceter in Gloucestershire.
>
> (V.vi.1-3)

His son and heir defies him. Contemptuous of his father's authority, Hal plays at robbery and beats the king's watch. Upon being informed of the royal "tri-

umphs" to be held at Oxford, he is said to have promised to appear wearing the "favour" of a prostitute. And these are but the portents of worse disorders. As many critics have pointed out, the *Henry IV* plays anatomize a kingdom split into factions, each seeking its particular ends and lacking the common bond of loyalty that shapes a regime: "this house is turned upside down since Robin Ostler died" (*1 Henry IV*, II.i.9-10), remarks the Second Carrier, unwittingly turning a wretched inn into a symbol for the realm. Falstaff's cynical comment on Justice Shallow—"If the young dace be a bait for the old pike, I see no reason in the law of nature but I may snap at him" (*2 Henry IV*, III.ii.325-326)—expresses the ethos that, through Henry's example, has contaminated the land. Under the circumstances, even the religious values that Henry tries to appropriate in his rhetoric turn against him. Appealing to "the blood / Of fair King Richard, scrap'd from Pomfret stones," deriving "from heaven his quarrel and his cause," the Archbishop of York "[t]urns insurrection to religion" (*2 Henry IV*, I.i.201-206). Rebellion engenders rebellion; the awe that protected Richard cannot portect his murderer.

Henry's effort to usurp the traditional sanctity of the throne along with the throne itself lays bare the fundamental defect of his policy. According to Machiavelli, a new prince in a new regime must make everything new; he must have the wisdom, skill, and courage to introduce an entirely new order that will obliterate even the memory of the old one. Left intact, or only impaired, the old order will return to haunt him. It furnishes a ready pretext and provocation to rebellion.[8] The truth of this teaching comes home to Henry with a vengeance. By attempting to resurrect in himself the principles of the old regime, by failing to exorcise Richard's ghost, Henry renders his usurpation abortive: he dooms himself to unceasing struggle, and afflicts both his dynasty and his kingdom. He and his direct heirs survive only by repeating his original violence over and over—first in England, then in France, then in England again. Both Henry and Hal spill blood continually and with considerable success; the reign of Henry VI, however, reveals the precariousness of their achievement. When the sword fails, the dynasty falls. As Shakespeare's contemporaries were aware, and as his earlier tetralogy of English history plays had already indicated, peace and stability return to the land only when the founder of a new dynasty—Henry VII, first of the Tudors—is able to revive the claims of traditional legitimacy, and present himself plausibly as God's deputy on earth.[9]

Ironically, it is the revolutionary boldness of Henry's thought that betrays him in the end. Having thrust him on to regicide, his radically new vision of the nature of things fails to provide him with the ground on which to create a new regime. He recognizes that stable political rule cannot be based on force and cunning alone, yet his view of life as essentially egotistical, violent, and governed by chance offers no principle of order that can replace the divine right that surrounded earlier English kings. A doctrine of individualism and violent necessity has no power to bind men together. As a result Henry is forced outside the characteristic range of his mind, and this necessity confounds him. He possesses one part of what is needful in a new prince in a new principality—an understanding of, and ability to use, violence—but he wants an even more important part—the creative qualities of a founder who is both armed and a prophet. The personal sense of necessity that drives him to make himself king finally traps him in the narrowness and harshness of his vision. Henry proves incapable of the extraordinary *virtù* attributed by Machiavelli to a Moses or a Theseus; we may consider him a type of Cain, but not of Romulus.[10]

England and Henry suffer for his sins, but they are not the sins of which Carlisle thought. Shakespeare's dramatization of Henry's career focuses not on the unfolding of God's judgment, but rather on the strictly political consequences of a usurpation only half achieved.[11] By the light of Shakespeare's analysis, we perceive that Henry misses the greatness that alone could redeem the heinous crimes of usurpation and regicide. He remains a usurper rather than a founder. It is to this deficiency, above all, that his drabness points.

Notes

1 Machiavelli defines the kinds of principalities in the first chapter of *The Prince:* "Principalities are either hereditary, in which case the family of the prince has been ruling for generations, or they are new. And the new ones are either completely new, as was Milan for Francesco Sforza, or they are like members joined to the hereditary state of the prince who acquires them, as is the kingdom of Naples for the King of Spain" (trans. Mark Musa [New York: St. Martin's Press, 1964], p. 5).

2 *Richard II,* I.ii.37-38. Act, scene, and line references are to the Arden editions of *Richard II,* ed. Peter Ure (Cambridge, Mass.: Harvard University Press, 1956), of *The First Part of King Henry IV,* ed. A. R. Humphreys (London: Methuen, 1961), and of *The Second Part of King Henry IV* (London: Methuen, 1966).

3 For expressions of the prevailing view that Henry is basically an opportunist, see John Palmer, *Political Characters of Shakespeare* (London: Macmillan, 1948), pp. 135-138; Brents Stirling, "Bolingbroke's 'Decision'," *Shakespeare Quarterly* 2 (1951), 27-34; Ure's Introduction to *Richard II,* pp. lxxiv-lxxv; A. L. French, "Who Deposed Richard II?" *Essays in Criticism* 17 (1967), 411-433; and Robert Ornstein, *A Kingdom for a Stage* (Cambridge: Harvard University Press, 1972), pp. 114-116.

4 The importance of Henry's idea of necessity has been recognized but never adequately studied: see, for example, Harold C. Goddard, *The Meaning of Shakespeare* (Chicago: University of Chicago Press, 1951), p. 162; Humphreys' note on III.i.72-74 in *The Second Part of King Henry IV;* and John C. Bromley, *The Shakespearean Kings* (Boulder: Colorado Associated University Press, 1971), p. 71. For more general remarks on the theme of necessity in the second tetralogy, see Humphreys' Introduction to *The Second Part of King Henry IV,* pp. xlv-xlvi and Derek Traversi, *Shakespeare: From Richard II to Henry V* (Stanford: Stanford University Press, 1957), pp. 135-136.

5 On Lucretius, see Leo Strauss, "Notes on Lucretius," in *Liberalism Ancient and Modern* (New York: Basic Books, 1968), pp. 76-139 (esp. pp. 76-85, 133-135). For other examples of Machiavelli's usefulness in analyzing Henry's career, see Irving Ribner, "Bolingbroke, A True Machiavellian," *Modern Language Quarterly* 9 (1948), 177-184; John F. Danby, *Shakespeare's Doctrine of Nature* (London: Faber and Faber, 1949), pp. 81-101; and Moody Prior, *The Drama of Power* (Evanston, Ill.: Northwestern University Press, 1973), pp. 219-248.

6 Near the end of *Henry IV,* part 1, it is true, Henry upbraids Worcester in terms that suggest a rather different view of man and nature:

> Will you again unknit
> This churlish knot of all-abhorred war?
> And move in that obedient orb again
> Where you did give a fair and natural
>   light,
> And be no more an exhal'd meteor,
> A prodigy of fear, and a portent
> Of broached mischief to the unborn times?
>   (V.i.15-21)

Contrary to Henry's praise of Hotspur, these lines imply that peace and obedience rather than war and rebellion are natural, but we must understand them in the light of the dramatic situation. Talking to Worcester, Henry has an obvious reason to stress the virtue of obedience, but there is no evidence that it is part of his private morality. Although he condemns Worcester for being a "meteor," earlier Henry compared himself complacently to a "comet" (III.ii.46-49).

7 Some critics have contended that Henry's expressions of guilt are sincere: see, for example, John Dover Wilson's note on I.i.1-28 in *The First Part of the History of Henry IV* (Cambridge: Cambridge University Press, 1946); Traversi, *Shakespeare: From Richard II to Henry V,* pp. 48, 51, 81; and M.M. Reese, *The Cease of Majesty* (New York: St. Martin's Press, 1961), p. 286. Such a view seems to me incompatible with everything else that Shakespeare shows us about

Henry. If Henry's religion is sincere, it never restrains his political actions in any way.

[8] See *The Prince,* chapter 6.

[9] See Shakespeare's presentation of Henry VII throughout the last act of *Richard III* (especially scenes ii, iii, and v).

[10] See *The Prince,* chapter 6. Henry's final speech in *Richard II* suggests the analogy between himself and Cain (V.vi.43-50). He condemns Exton as a kind of Cain, but recognizes his own guilt as well.

[11] Cf. Machiavelli's comment on "the present ruin of Italy": "And he [Savonarola] who said that our sins were the cause, said the truth; but they certainly were not the sins he thought, but rather the ones I have just recounted [military and political failures]; and since these were the sins of princes, they have come in turn to suffer the penalty for them" (Trans. Mark Musa, p. 101). That Shakespeare's second tetralogy departs from the moralized religious view of history favored by some of the Tudor chroniclers seems generally accepted by recent critics: see, for example, Alvin B. Kernan, "The Henriad: Shakespeare's Major History Plays," in *Modern Shakespearean Criticism,* ed. Alvin B. Kernan (New York: Harcourt, Brace, and World, 1970), pp. 245-275; and Moody Prior, *The Drama of Power,* pp. 14-33.

Stanley D. McKenzie (essay date 1992)

SOURCE: "The Prudence and Kinship of Prince Hal and John of Lancaster in *2 Henry IV,*" in *Law and Philosophy: The Practice of Theory, Essays in Honor of George Anastaplo,* edited by John A. Murley, Robert L. Stone and William T. Braithwaite, Ohio University Press, 1992, pp. 937-58.

[*In the following essay, McKenzie examines Prince Hal's rejection of Falstaff and Prince John's betrayal of the rebels at Gaultree, arguing that although their actions appear to be unjust, they are in fact attempting to protect the realm and provide legitimacy to their family's accession to the throne of England.*]

George Anastaplo continually explores the concept of prudence throughout his writings.[1] In his musings on literature, Anastaplo dismisses "dramatic necessities" in favor of inquiring "*why* a man of a certain character acted thus and so," and poses the ubiquitous Anastaplo question, "What is the right thing for a man to do in this situation."[2] He concludes that "in order to be able to choose correctly, one must be *prudent.* . . . Prudence tends to lead us to moderation, both personal and communal."[3] Hence for Anastaplo, Odysseus prevails because "he is a prudent man able to restrain himself."[4]

For a volume of essays in honor of George Anastaplo on the theme of "The Practice of Theory," it seems appropriate to apply his concept of prudence to the characters in one of Shakespeare's most complex history plays, *2 Henry IV.* Henry V's rejection of Falstaff remains the central critical subject of debate in this play. Is this rejection the proper fate of an unregenerate reprobate, or does it expose the new king as another Machiavellian Lancastrian placing policy above human feelings? A secondary but related problem concerns the manner in which Hal's younger brother, Prince John of Lancaster, defeats the rebels at Gaultree. Critical response has overwhelmingly condemned John, and the concern articulated by Samuel Johnson has not been adequately resolved to this day: "It cannot but raise some indignation to find this horrible violation of faith passed over thus slightly by the poet, without any note of censure or detestation."[5] Despite Dr. Johnson's protestation, there is considerable evidence that an Elizabethan audience in 1598 would view both Hal's rejection of Falstaff and John's "betrayal" of the rebels as prudent actions to be approved. Shakespeare enhances such a response through the structure and imagery of *2 Henry IV,* which associate Hal with John and create an ethic within which the actions of these Lancastrian brothers are prudent, commendable, and intrinsically akin.

Modern scholarship generally acknowledges the political necessity for the rejection of Falstaff, but there is no consensus as to how we should feel about Hal's method of effecting it. A. C. Bradley asserts that during the rejection speech the audience feels "a good deal of pain and some resentment,"[6] while, more recently, Catherine M. Shaw writes, "Intellectual moral justification for the expulsion of Falstaff can be accepted as can the historical actuality, but the disquietude which greets the end of *2 Henry IV* is not intellectual; it is emotional."[7] During the last decade, much attention has been given to Hal's role-playing throughout the *Henry IV* plays, but again with sharp disagreement: does this play-acting prove Hal to be a hypocrite with no underlying sincerity nor ethical base? Or is Hal admirably rehearsing for the day in which he will be forced to accept the burdens and responsibilities of "formal majesty" (5.2.133),[8] a role he does not desire, but which he is duty-bound to accept?[9]

Whereas Hal's rejection of Falstaff is increasingly being justified by critics, albeit often reluctantly and even apologetically, his brother's actions at Gaultree continue to be roundly denounced. Bradley is more damning than Dr. Johnson, referring to the Gaultree victory as a "detestable fraud," and describing John as "the brave, determined, loyal, cold-blooded, pitiless, unscrupulous son of a usurper."[10] E. M. W. Tillyard and Lily B. Campbell each provide some defense for John, but with the collapse of a single-minded Elizabethan world view has come nearly unanimous critical condemnation of John. These modern critics, however, have tended to ignore the fear of civil war ever-present throughout Elizabeth's reign. After the Northern Rebellion of 1569, a long "Homilie against Disobedience and Wylfull Rebellion" (1571) was read in every church throughout England, affirming that the sin of rebellion violates the Ten Commandments and entails all the seven deadly sins:

> For he that nameth rebellion nameth not a singular or one only sin, as is theft robbery murder and such like, but he nameth the whole puddle and sink of all sins against God and man.[11]

Elizabeth's propaganda machinery continually stressed that subjects had no right to judge their monarch (undoubtedly to discourage those inclined to do just that); to rebel against a bad king, with the notable exception of Richard III, was as sinful as to rebel against a good king. An Elizabethan could view Henry IV as an evil man (albeit penitent) inasmuch as he acquired the crown through rebellion,[12] but still as a good king in that he successfully crushed rebellions against him. God permitted the rebellions as punishment, but the rebels themselves were committing the mortal sin of disobedience to their king and deserved no mercy. That John's method of victory at Gaultree in *2 Henry IV* was consistent with Elizabethan policy of the 1590s can be seen in Lodowick Lloyd's *The Stratagems of Jerusalem* (1602), which recounts numerous examples of treachery being used to achieve peace and asserts that "all stratagems, victories, & good counsell cometh from the Lord."[13] Paul Jorgensen attributes the growing Elizabethan acceptance of deceit and treachery in dealing with rebels to the Irish wars. Faced with guerrillas who adeptly circumvented standard military efforts, the English for years had been resorting to treacherous policies, including the slaughter in 1580 of several hundred rebels who surrendered to Lord Grey at Smerwick.[14] Although theoretically despising Machiavelli, the Elizabethans were increasingly aware that many of his tactics could strengthen the security of the realm.[15]

Elizabethan perceptions of the historical John of Lancaster must also be taken into account when analyzing the events at Gaultree; Shakespeare has specifically altered his source materials in making John, rather than Westmoreland, the perpetrator of the deceit. Critics have argued that this historical change, along with the antipathy between John and Falstaff, serves to portray John as a cold-blooded, political Lancastrian in contrast to his warm and generous brother Hal.[16] This thesis is dubious, however, considering that John becomes the famous Duke of Bedford, whose reputation among the Elizabethans was nearly as great as his brother's. Shakespeare himself had previously portrayed Bedford in *1 Henry VI*, where at his death he is eulogized by Talbot and Burgundy as "valiant," "Courageous," "Undaunted spirit," and

> A braver soldier never couchèd lance,
> A gentler heart did never sway in court.
>
> (3.2.134-35)

On his deathbed, Henry V named Bedford protector of the realm for the infant Henry VI, and even after assuming the regency of France, Bedford remained instrumental in keeping peace at home between his brother Humphrey, Duke of Gloucester, and his uncle Henry Beaufort, Bishop of Winchester. Holinshed calls Bedford "a man both politike in peace, and hardie in warre, and yet no more hardie than mercifull when he had the victorie."[17] It seems likely that Shakespeare made John responsible for the events at Gaultree not to contrast him with Hal, but to use the future Duke of Bedford's reputation as a positive reflection on the method of victory; the brother's responsibility also serves to associate Hal more directly with these events that preserve the crown for him.

Henry V's rejection of Falstaff and John's betrayal of the rebels at Gaultree would be seen as essentially similar by a London audience in 1598 inasmuch as each manifests the triumph of order over disruptive forces threatening the security of the kingdom. For the brothers to have acted differently would have constituted a shocking and dangerous display of irresponsibility by those with whom God had entrusted the welfare of the realm. This political prudence may still be emotionally unattractive, however, especially for a modern audience, if it is viewed as calculatedly Machiavellian and personally unprincipled. The brilliance of Shakespeare's achievement within *2 Henry IV* is the manner by which he reinforces the cold lessons of political reality through the artistic devices available to the dramatist, especially imagery and thematic structuring. As the remainder of this paper will show, Shakespeare creates a functional ethos in the world of *2 Henry IV* where voracious appetite and greedy expectations surfeit, while moderation triumphs in the course of time.[18] Attuned to this ethos, Hal and John thrive and conform precisely to Anastaplo's definition of prudence as moderation and self-restraint which "may depend, ultimately, on a vital awareness of the *nature of things*."[19]

Turning first to Shakespeare's dramatic shaping of the play's literal plot, when the newly crowned Henry V stands between Falstaff and the Lord Chief Justice and is forced to make a final irrevocable choice, his commitment to justice and rejection of disorder contradicts the previously expressed expectations of every major character in the play.[20] Shakespeare nevertheless has carefully prepared for Hal's rejection of Falstaff throughout *2 Henry IV,* and those who empathize with Falstaff's expectations will find little encouragement within the text itself. The second scene of the play establishes the Lord Chief Justice and Falstaff as polar opposites; the Chief Justice does engage in battles of wit with Falstaff, but he also expresses his contempt with comments such as "the truth is, Sir John, you live in great infamy" (1.2.138-39) and "Thou art a great fool" (2.1.195-96). Prince Hal also treats Falstaff in this play with open contempt. He says, "I do allow this wen to be as familiar with me as my dog" (2.2.105-6), and claims that it is "profane" to spend time playing jokes on Falstaff (2.4.368-69). Except for one episode, Hal and Falstaff do not appear together until the final rejection scene, and the feeling that they are boon companions, established in *Part 1,* is lost in *Part 2.* At court, Warwick foreshadows Falstaff's rejection when he assures Henry IV that

> The prince but studies his companions
> Like a strange tongue, wherein, to gain the
>   language,
> 'Tis needful that the most immodest word
> Be looked upon and learned, which once
>   attained,
> Your highness knows, comes to no further
>   use
> But to be known and hated. So, like gross
>   terms,
> The prince will in the perfectness of time
> Cast off his followers. . . .
>
>   (4.4.68-75)

Such a rationale seems dubious in today's addiction-conscious society, but it was commonplace in sixteenth-century educational treatises. On the other hand, Henry IV's prediction of his son's reign (4.5.117-37) provides a horrifying description of England's fate if Henry V should not indeed cast out the "gross terms" he has learned.

Even the comic Gloucestershire scenes prepare for Falstaff's rejection. He traitorously misuses the king's press, receiving bribes from Moldy and Bullcalf, whom Shallow proclaims the best of the lot, to free them from impressment and taking in their place the decrepit Wart.[21] Furthermore, the relationship between Shallow and Falstaff parallels Falstaff's relationship with Hal; in each case one partner expects to use his fellow for his own advantage, while the other associates with the hanger-on solely for his own amusement. Falstaff thus unwittingly anticipates his own rejection when he says of Shallow, "Either wise bearing or ignorant carriage is caught, as men take diseases, one of another. Therefore let men take heed of their company" (5.1.78-80). Immediately after the final reconciliation between Hal and Henry IV, act 5 opens in Gloucestershire with Falstaff asking to be excused to leave; Shallow responds,

> I will not excuse you. You shall not be excused. Excuses shall not be admitted. There is no excuse shall serve. You shall not be excused.
>
>   (5.1.5-7)

Falstaff is soon not to be excused in a less comic sense as well. In the final Gloucestershire scene, Falstaff destroys any possible remaining sympathy for him when he learns that Hal is king and greedily cries out,

> Let us take any man's horses; the laws of England are at my commandment. Blessed are they that have been my friends, and woe to my Lord Chief Justice!
>
>   (5.3.140-43)

The new king, however, has already assured his brothers and the Chief Justice of his devotion to law and order. Henry V must still confirm his choice when confronted by both the Lord Chief Justice and Falstaff simultaneously, but Shakespeare has foreshadowed Hal's decision throughout the play.

Henry V nevertheless finds the rejection difficult to make, and he at first attempts to have the Chief Justice get rid of Falstaff for him: "My Lord Chief Justice, speak to that vain man" (5.5.44). Falstaff persists, however, and the new king must deal with him personally. The problem is that Falstaff's wit has seduced characters and audience alike; Hostess Quickly, whom Falstaff has constantly swindled, earlier choked up when he left for the wars, crying, "Well, fare thee well. I have known thee these twenty-nine years, come peascod-time, but an honester and truer-hearted man— well, fare thee well" (2.4.389-91). Falstaff's fascinating character makes plausible Hal's wasting time with him, but now judgment must be passed, and an objective look at Falstaff leaves no choice but for the prudent and moderate man to reject him.

Beginning with A. C. Bradley, the critics who claim that Shakespeare created such a genius of wit that he could not destroy him convincingly when the time came have themselves failed to distinguish between the genuinely witty Falstaff of *Part 1* and the Falstaff in *Part 2,* whose wit is so often based on other people's miseries.[22] Falstaff's entire environment has degenerated in *Part 2.* In *Part 1* Mistress Quickly apparently had an honest husband, well loved by the prince (*Part 1,* 3.3.98), and ran a respectable tavern, but in *Part II* she is a widow (2.1.82) and seems to be operating a brothel. Doll Tearsheet and Pistol, new additions to the Eastcheap populace in *Part 2,* are two of the grossest characters in any of Shakespeare's plays. Immediately before Falstaff's rejection, Hostess Quickly and Doll Tearsheet are hauled away to prison for having, along with Pistol, beaten a man to death (5.4.16-17). Although humorous, the voracious excesses of Falstaff and his companions have now become deadly.

When Henry V does reject Falstaff, Prince John comments, "I like this fair proceeding of the king's" (5.5.99) and then accurately predicts that Henry V will invade France. Shakespeare's giving John the final words in the play (except for the "Epilogue [Spoken by a DANCER.]") links John's moral approbation of Henry V with his own proceedings at Gaultree. Although dramatically John's betrayal of the rebels is of secondary importance to Henry V's rejection of Falstaff, the betrayal is likewise foreshadowed through advance warnings that the truce may not be all it seems. Mowbray, for one, is uneasy throughout the negotiations:

> There is a thing within my bosom tells me
> That no conditions of our peace can stand.
>
> (4.1.181-82)

Mowbray argues that the king must henceforth view everything they do with suspicion, and after both armies have presumably been dismissed, it is again Mowbray who suddenly feels ill while the others are drinking toasts. Prince John also provides a hint of what is to come when he reproaches the Archbishop for acting unlike a man of God in "Turning the word to sword and life to death" (4.2.10); it is likewise equally unnatural for John, a soldier and prince, to put up his sword and settle a rebellion with words.

The outward events of the play significantly take no notice of the moral issues involved in John's dissembling. Falstaff criticizes John's sobriety, but not his method of victory, and even the rebels go off to execution with minimal protest. Furthermore, no one in the royal family indicates that John's actions blemish Lancastrian honor. In *Part 1,* both King Henry IV and Hal had high praise for John's performance at Shrewsbury (5.4.15-22), and *Part 2* provides no evidence that Hal changes his mind about John, either before or after Gaultree; likewise, the dying king, who has consistently chastised Hal for perceived moral shortcomings, welcomes John back from Gaultree without qualification.

Although John's betrayal of the rebels is not foreshadowed as extensively as Hal's rejection of Falstaff, the literal plot level of *2 Henry IV* does prepare for both events and associates them with each other through John's approbation of his brother's action. Falstaff's defenders have argued that Shakespeare intends John's approval as a deprecation of Hal's character, in that only someone as treacherous as John could approve of the new king's cold-hearted treatment of his former companion; however, the symbolic or mythic elements and imagery patterns of the play also link Hal and John closely together and enhance the appropriateness of both brothers' actions.

Falstaff's bulk enables him to embody several symbolic and mythic aspects, all requiring his rejection by the new king. His roles as the Vice figure, the unregenerate "Old Man," the "Martlemas" beef, and the Lord of Misrule or scapegoat sacrificed to regenerate the wasteland have been so well established that when Justice Silence sings of "lusty lads" eating "flesh" at

"Shrovetide" (5.3.17-37) shortly before Falstaff's rejection, we may well recall that Shrovetide's feasting precedes the barren "winter" Lent leading to death and rebirth at Easter.[23] Thus the model Christian king's "sacrifice" of the symbolic scapegoat of riot and waste promises not only a new spirit of self-restrained frugality and strict order, but also future glories for England.

The psychoanalytical critics carry these symbolic aspects even further, claiming that Falstaff is a substitute father figure for Hal and must, like the ritually slain kings of Sir James Frazer's *Golden Bough,* be sacrificed before the land can regain its fertility under the rule of the young, virile son. Hal's real father-king, Henry IV, acquired his crown through the deposition and murder of Richard II, and "under the guilt-ridden, infirm, old king, England itself has become diseased."[24] Hal manifests parricidal tendencies toward his father throughout both parts of *Henry IV,* but according to these critics, these impulses are restricted to a displacement "killing" of the substitute father. Henry IV's natural death expiates the murder of Richard, but to renew England's strength, Henry V must bury his youthful vanities with the body of his father and sacrifice the spirit of excess and misrule by banishing his companions of those earlier, carefree days.

Falstaff's symbolic qualities encompass greedy appetite and disorder in general and are associated with the rebels in the play, even though these secondary political figures lack the abundance of specific mythic overtones that make Falstaff so rich a character. This association is made through imagery patterns that establish structural relationships among the major characters.[25] In the rejection scene, Hal calls Falstaff "surfeit-swelled" (5.5.50) and tells him that "the grave doth gape / For thee thrice wider than for other men" (5.5.53-54). The images echo the Archbishop's reference to "our surfeiting and wanton hours" (4.1.55) and Northumberland's claim that "my limbs . . . Are thrice themselves" (1.1.143-45). Lord Bardolph says the rebel messenger from Shrewsbury "had stol'n / The horse he rode on" (1.1.57-58), while Falstaff cries, "Let us take any man's horses" (5.3.140) upon learning that Hal is king, again linking him to the rebels. Both Falstaff and the rebels indulge in self-deception, entertaining hopes for which they have little basis and which ultimately fail. Falstaff continually deceives himself until the very end that Hal will still be his companion when king, while the rebels create false hopes in planning their campaign. Hastings acknowledges that "our supplies live largely in the hope / Of great Northumberland," (1.3.12-13) and cautious Lord Bardolph asserts that they need to be certain of Northumberland's questionable support, since "Conjecture, expectation, and surmise / Of aids incertain should not be admitted." (1.3.23-24). Yet after these self-acknowledged dangers, the rebels imprudently decide to proceed regardless of Northumberland's support and by the end of the scene are trusting their hopes entirely to circumstances.

Hal and John are likewise linked through the imagery of the play as they reverse the surfeits of their adversaries and return things to normal. The rebellion is a flooding (4.1.174) which John contains; when the "truce" is celebrated with drinks, the archbishop gets high, "Believe me, I am passing light in spirit" (4.2.85), while John's drinking is highly restrained, according to the play's preeminent drinker (4.3.89-90). Hal also stems a flood of excessive sanguinity when he becomes king:

> The tide of blood in me
> Hath proudly flowed in vanity till now.
> Now doth it turn and ebb back to the sea,
> Where it shall mingle with the state of
> floods
> And flow henceforth in formal majesty.
> (5.2.129-33)

Hal and John also meet their obligations, in contrast to the debt-ridden Falstaff (literally) and the rebels (morally). Thinking his father has died, Hal says,

> Thy due from me
> Is tears and heavy sorrows of the blood,
> Which nature, love, and filial tenderness
> Shall, O dear father, pay thee plenteously.
> (4.5.36-39)[26]

The Archbishop accuses John of breaking faith, but the prince claims,

> I pawned thee none.
> I promised you redress of these same
> grievances
> Whereof you did complain, which, by mine
> honor,
> I will perform with a most Christian care.
> (4.2.113-16)

John's punctiliousness contrasts with Northumberland's earlier argument that he must join the Archbishop's rebellion:

> Alas, sweet wife, my honor is at pawn,
> And, but my going, nothing can redeem it.
> (2.3.7-8)

Northumberland, however, once again fails to provide the support upon which the rebels are counting.

Several minor thematic images thus link Hal and John together, as well as Falstaff with the rebels. Disease, time, and unfulfilled expectations are the dominant and most frequently analyzed images of 2 Henry IV,[27] however, and these motifs create even larger structural relationships among the characters, in which the king is also grouped with Falstaff and the rebels in contrast to Hal and John. Beginning with disease, Henry IV, unlike the fighting king of Part 1, is ill throughout Part 2 and finally dies. Whereas the bad news of Shrewsbury cures the crafty-sick Northumberland (1.1.137-39), the good news of Gaultree hastens the king's death (4.4.102-11). Falstaff is preoccupied with everyone's diseases, and the analysis of his urine (1.2.3-5) reveals that he is thoroughly sick himself; he even boasts, "I will turn diseases to commodity" (1.2.251). Other characters in the play are likewise diseased. Falstaff insinuates that Doll Tearsheet and Hostess Quickly have syphilis, while of the prospective recruits at Gloucestershire, the two best are Moldy and Bullcalf, who claims he has been plagued with a "whoreson cold" through Henry IV's entire reign (3.2.183-87). The Archbishop, leader of the rebels, sums it all up:

> We are all diseased,
> And with our surfeiting and wanton hours
> Have brought ourselves into a burning fever,
> And we must bleed for it. Of which disease
> Our late king, Richard, being infected, died.
> (4.1.54-58)

This all-encompassing disease afflicts not only the people, but also the realm itself. The Archbishop speaks of a "bleeding land" (1.1.207), and even the king admits his land is diseased:

> Then you perceive the body of our kingdom
> How foul it is, what rank diseases grow,
> And with what danger, near the heart of it.
> (3.1.38-40)

All of England bears responsibility for the murder of Richard II through the popular support given Bolingbroke; now the sickness in the land is exasperated by new rebellions led by the same guilty men who helped Henry IV acquire his crown in the first place. Only Hal and John, too young to have participated in Richard's deposition, are healthy and free from the disease that afflicts England.

England's disease was caused by events that occurred in the past, but still affect the present times. Mowbray claims they all

> feel the bruises of the days before,
> And suffer the condition of these times,
> (4.1.98-99)

and the rebels constantly use time or the "times" as an excuse for their actions. The Archbishop tells Westmoreland,

> We see which way the stream of time doth
> run,

And are enforced from our most quiet there
By the rough torrent of occasion.

                                        (4.1.70-72)

But Westmoreland relies upon the identical rationale when he responds to the Archbishop's claim that the times make them rebel:

Construe the times to their necessities,
And you shall say indeed, it is the time,
And not the king, that doth you injuries.

                                        (4.1.102-4)

Warwick also claims the "necessary form" of "the hatch and brood of time" enabled Richard II to prophesy correctly that Northumberland would revolt against Henry IV (3.1.80-92), and even the king wishes he could

          read the book of fate,
And see the revolution of the times. . . .

                                        (3.1.45-46)

All these men, rebels and loyalists alike, are so caught up in capitalizing on the present moment to further their worldly ambitions and have such a highly developed consciousness of time's power over them that they become indeed "time's subjects," as Hastings claims (1.3.110).

Hal and John, however, do not subject their destinies to "the rough torrent of occasion" and never blame the times for their actions. Being young, they are scarcely concerned with time, and each makes only two direct references to it in *Part 2*. Hal, regretting his youthful imprudence, tells Poins, "Thus we play the fools with the time" (2.2.141), and when he learns that his father has been preparing for war while he has been playing tricks on Falstaff, he cries,

By heaven, Poins, I feel me much to blame,
So idly to profane the precious time.

                                        (2.4.368-69)

Attuned to the larger patterns of time that in due course will bring him to the crown, Hal views the present moment as a commodity for prudent use, but not a binding force. Similarly, John does not attempt to construe the necessities of the moment into a defense for his deeds and indeed claims that the rebels are

          much too shallow,
To sound the bottom of the after-times.

                                        (4.2.50-51)

John's only other use of the word comes when he tells Falstaff after Gaultree,

These tardy tricks of yours will, on my life,
One time or other break some gallows' back.

                                        (4.3.28-29)

Not the vagrancies of time, John says, but Falstaff's own actions will destroy him.

Falstaff is time's subject, however, in the sense that time brings old age and death. Throughout *Part 2* Falstaff tries to embody the eternal spirit of youth, but he cannot escape the fact that he has grown old and infirm, ever closer to paying the debt to God he managed to postpone at Shrewsbury. Like Henry IV and the rebels, Falstaff too is a diseased prisoner of his own past. The king and the rebels remember Richard II, but Falstaff and Shallow recall the even earlier era when John of Gaunt ruled England during the declining years of Edward III; Falstaff closes the scene by saying, "Let time shape, and there an end" (3.2.336-337).

The time imagery of *2 Henry IV* thus separates the major characters into two groups. Henry IV, the Archbishop, Northumberland, the other rebels, and Falstaff, the would-be exploiters of time, are instead all time's subjects, old "fathers" (the Archbishop is a "reverend father") whose voracious appetites and expectations have disrupted the established order.[28] Henry IV robbed Richard of his crown with the help of the rebels who now attempt to rob it from him, while Falstaff robs the king's "crowns," or money. These robberies create unpaid debts, and even though Henry IV claims he "purchased" the crown (4.5.199), he can pay for it only with his life. Purchasing is associated with death throughout the play, as when Shallow keeps asking the purchase price of animals while reminiscing about his youthful companions who have now grown old and died (3.2.39-54). Moldy and Bullcalf purchase their lives, but Feeble says, "We owe God a death" (3.2.240), punning on debt and echoing Hal's words to Falstaff before Shrewsbury in Part 1, "Why, thou owest God a death" (5.1.126). Despite Falstaff's incessant borrowing on even that debt, in *Part 2* the time for payment comes due, and all the old robbers are required to make a final reckoning. Hal and John, however, the healthy young sons from a new generation, are free from the guilty debts of the past that haunt the diseased old men of England. They do not blame the times but accept the state of affairs created by their elders; they attune themselves to the natural order of their world, assume their proper duties and responsibilities, and set out to shape a new future.

The final significant thematic motif connecting Henry IV, Falstaff, and the rebels is unfulfilled expectations. The king expects to expiate his murder of Richard II through a journey to Jerusalem, where it was prophesied to him he would die; instead he dies at home in a room called Jerusalem. He also expects his son to institute a reign of riot and says that Hal's premature taking of the crown "hast sealed up my expectation" (4.5.103), but Henry V becomes "the mirror of all Christian kings" (*Henry V,* 2 cho. 6). The rebels expect support from Northumberland, which they do not receive, and the Archbishop expects to have God's help, only to hear John credit his own victory to God. Mowbray does not think the peace can last, while his fellow rebels believe that the king will not chastise them after the truce; the peace does last, however, and John executes all the rebel leaders. Falstaff expects to be the boon companion of Henry V, but he is not to command the laws of England.

As with the disease imagery, unfulfilled expectations permeate *2 Henry IV* at every level, beginning with Rumor, who creates false expectations only to destroy them.[29] Hostess Quickly expects not only to get paid by Falstaff, but even to marry him; Justice Shallow thinks he will use Falstaff for his own gain; after Henry IV dies, the Chief Justice expects punishment from Henry V, Warwick now thinks Hal will be a riotous king, and even Clarence dreads having to speak well of Falstaff; but all three are wrong. Hal realizes that no one expects him to weep over his father, but he later does, and the crown that seems to be the "best of gold" turns out to be the "worst of gold" (4.5.160). The very language of the play creates unfulfilled expectations through the use of oxymora ("wrathful dove or most magnanimous mouse"); images such as Hal's simile that the crown is

> Like a rich armor worn in heat of day,
> That scald'st with safety;
>
> (4.5.29-30)

and even in set poetic passages such as the king's apostrophe to sleep which comes to the ship-boy in a deafening storm, but is denied to a king despite all his material comforts (3.1.4-31). This speech is parodied moments earlier by Falstaff as he tells Doll Tearsheet and Mistress Quickly "how men of merit are sought after. The undeserver may sleep when the man of action is called on" (2.4.382-84), providing yet another linkage between the king and fat knight.[30]

The theme of unfulfilled expectations is often developed through eating imagery, as in Henry IV's lament that fortune

> either gives a stomach and no food—
> Such are the poor, in health—or else a feast
> And takes away the stomach—such are the rich
> That have abundance and enjoy it not.
>
> (4.4.105-8)

Throughout the play, excessive "eating" leads not to contented satiation, but to surfeits and disease. The Epilogue promises more of Falstaff, "If you be not too much cloyed with fat meat" (Epi.26-27), and even the prostitutes' syphilis is associated with gluttony:

> FALSTAFF: You make fat rascals, Mistress
> Doll.

> DOLL: I make them? Gluttony and diseases make, I make them not.

> FALSTAFF: If the cook help to make the gluttony, you help to make the diseases, Doll. We catch of you, Doll, we catch of you.
>
> (2.4.41-46)

The images of voracious appetite, surfeits, disease, death, time, and unfulfilled expectations are all brought together in an early speech by the Archbishop that sets the tone for the entire play:

> The commonwealth is sick of their own
>   choice;
> Their overgreedy love hath surfeited.
> An habitation giddy and unsure
> Hath he that buildeth on the vulgar heart.
> O thou fond many, with what loud applause
> Didst thou beat heaven with blessing
>   Bolingbroke,
> Before he was what thou wouldst have him
>   be!
> And being now trimmed in thine own desires,
> Thou, beastly feeder, art so full of him
> That thou provok'st thyself to cast him up.
> So, so, thou common dog, didst thou disgorge
> Thy glutton bosom of the royal Richard;
> And now thou wouldst eat thy dead vomit up,
> And howl'st to find it. What trust is in these
>   times?
>
> (1.3.87-100)

In *2 Henry IV,* greedy expectations are not fulfilled as desired, but instead surfeit. Time is the ultimate betrayer, imprisoning men through past events and eventually defeating all desires through old age, disease, and death.

Surfeit is the result of gluttony, the opposite of prudent moderation and self-restraint.[31] Falstaff literally gorges himself with food and drink and tries to ingest everything else, including the very laws of England; Henry V calls the "surfeit-swelled" knight "The tutor and the feeder of my riots" (5.5.50,62). Henry IV hungered for Richard II's crown and dies repenting for the manner by which he became king. Northumberland and the other rebels who originally helped Henry now try to take the crown for themselves and are executed for their efforts. All these men create expectations based on lawlessly and gluttonously grabbing for things not belonging to them. Their expectations either remain unfulfilled or they surfeit on what they have imprudently ingested, become sick and die. England was jarred out of its naturally fertile state by Richard's misrule and his subsequent deposition and murder, but the men responsible continue trying to satiate their own opportunistic appetites and blame the times instead of their gluttony for the sickness they have caused.

Those characters who do not grab, but instead prudently accept what life brings to them, live on successfully at the end of the play. John, with typical restraint, foregoes a battlefield resolution and instead calmly lets the rebels fall into his clever trap, crediting God for the restoration of the peace. The Chief Justice also accepts his anticipated fate without making elaborate plans for his own safety. He does not expect Henry V to love him, but he is prepared "To welcome the condition of the time" (5.2.11); this passive acceptance of destiny without regard to personal benefit leads to an affirmative reversal of his expectations as he is retained in his position and honored by the new king. The most prudent non-grabber, of course, is Hal, whose only expectation is that he will be king. When he tries to fulfill this expectation himself, however, taking the crown before it belongs to him, he has to give it back. The last lesson Hal learns before becoming king is self-restraint and not to grab, but to wait prudently for things to descend to him in rightful order.

When Henry IV awakes to find that Hal has taken his crown, he cries out, "See, sons, what things you are!" (4.5.64), claiming that fathers who care for their sons are unnaturally "murdered for our pains" (4.5.77). When Hal again enters the room, the dying king continues:

> Dost thou so hunger for mine empty chair
> That thou wilt needs invest thee with my
>   honors
> Before thy hour be ripe? . . .
> Thy life did manifest thou lov'dst me not,
> And thou wilt have me die assured of it.
> Thou hid'st a thousand daggers in thy
>   thoughts,
> Which thou has whetted on thy stony
>   heart,
> To stab at half an hour of my life.
>
> (4.5.94-108)

Although the king is wrong in his assessment of Hal's parricidal motives, in this play the old "fathers"—secular, spiritual and sensual alike—give way to the young sons. Hal and John both defeat the expectations of the old generation as they impose new codes of strict moral justice on the forces of disorder. Henry IV, Falstaff, Northumberland, and the Archbishop are time's subjects, the products of their pasts, while Hal and John represent the future and are not bound by either the deeds or expectations of the fathers. Sons, however, must build the future on an inheritance from the past; they must not grab for the possessions of the fathers until they naturally descend in proper order. Henry IV's crown in due course comes to Hal, while the Chief Justice embodies the heritage of the deceased king. The Chief Justice is old, diseased, and time's subject; he does

not grab, however, and so lives on temporarily bridging the past and the new era of Henry V, who tells him, "You shall be as a father to my youth" (5.2.118).

The plot, characterizations, mythic and symbolic elements, themes, and imagery of *2 Henry IV* all work together to create a functional ethic of moderation and self-restraint in which gluttony surfeits, defeating the expectations of the glutton. Those who are attuned to this premise of personal and political prudence prosper, while those who defy it are destroyed.[32] The last step in the education of Prince Hal is learning not to be a glutton, but rather to be prudent and moderate; he voices this lesson when, as the newly crowned king, he speaks to Falstaff:

> I know thee not, old man. Fall to thy
>   prayers.
> How ill white hairs becomes a fool and
>   jester!
> I have long dreamt of such a kind of man,
> So surfeit-swelled, so old, and so profane,
> But, being awaked, I do despise my dream.
> Make less thy body hence, and more thy
>   grace.
> Leave gormandizing.
>
> (5.5.47-53)

Although Saturn devoured his own children, Falstaff is not permitted to ingest his "Jove."[33] To save the old glutton from temptation, Henry V provides him with a "competence of life" (5.5.66), and if Falstaff will be content with what he receives without grabbing for more, he will be given advancement.

Henry V's rejection of Falstaff is akin to John's betrayal of the rebels at Gaultree inasmuch as both curb voracious appetites by exercising moderation and self-restraint. The two Lancastrian brothers thematically are of similar character and possess Anastaplo's "vital awareness of the nature of things" in the world that Shakespeare has created for them. They recognize the death of the old order of things and accept the Machiavellian reality of the new order, but at the same time give legitimacy to this new order by immersing themselves in an ethos of natural succession. Indeed, Hal and John essentially affirm a comic vision of generational renewal as opposed to the tragic gluttonous vision of their forefathers. The functional ethic operating through the imagery and structure of *2 Henry IV* impels us to accept and to approve the prudence of both Hal's and John's actions and to recognize their inherent thematic kinship.

Notes

[1] See especially Anastaplo's "American Constitutionalism and the Virtue of Prudence: Philadelphia, Paris, Washington, Gettysburg," in *Abraham Lincoln, The*

Gettysburg Address and American Constitutionalism, ed. Leo Paul S. de Alvarez (Irving, Tex.: University of Dallas Press, 1976), pp. 77-170.

[2] Anastaplo, *The Artist as Thinker: From Shakespeare to Joyce* (Chicago: Swallow Press, 1983), p. 16; emphasis in original.

[3] Ibid.; emphasis in original.

[4] Ibid., p. 6.

[5] Samuel Johnson, *Johnson on Shakespeare,* ed. Walter Raleigh (London: Oxford University Press, 1959), p. 121.

[6] A. C. Bradley, "The Rejection of Falstaff," *Oxford Lectures on Poetry* (London: Macmillan, 1909), p. 251.

[7] Catherine M. Shaw, "The Tragic Substructure of the 'Henry IV' Plays," *Shakespeare Survey* 38 (1985): 65.

[8] All references to Shakespeare's plays are from *The Complete Signet Classic Shakespeare,* ed. Sylan Barnet et al. (New York: Harcourt Brace Jovanovich, 1972).

[9] See John W. Blanpied, *Time and the Artist in Shakespeare's English Histories* (Newark: University of Delaware Press, 1983); Derick R. C. Marsh, "Hal and Hamlet: the Loneliness of Integrity," in *Jonson and Shakespeare,* ed. Ian Donaldson (Atlantic Highlands, N.J.: Humanities Press, 1983), pp. 18-34; John Alvis, "A Little Touch of the Night in Harry: The Career of Henry Monmouth," in *Shakespeare as Political Thinker,* ed. John Alvis and Thomas G. West (Durham, N. C.: Carolina Academic Press, 1981), pp. 95-125; Harold Toliver, "Workable Fictions in the Henry IV Plays," *University of Toronto Quarterly* 53 (1983): 53-71.

[10] Bradley, "Rejection of Falstaff," p. 256.

[11] Cited by E. M. W. Tillyard, *Shakespeare's History Plays* (London: Chatto and Windus, 1964), p. 68. Both Tillyard and Lily B. Campbell, *Shakespeare's "Histories:" Mirrors of Elizabethan Policy* (San Marino, Cal.: Huntington Library, 1968), pp. 216-17, discuss this homily against rebellion. Campbell believes that Shakespeare's Henry IV plays specifically portray the 1569 Northern Rebellion, and she is one of the few critics to acknowledge that John's "peace-making . . . would, I think, have seemed quite orthodox to the Elizabethan audience" (p. 226). More recently, in an attempt to counter the current critical fad of Tillyard bashing, M. M. Reese, " 'Tis My Picture; Refuse It Not," *Shakespeare Quarterly* 36 (1985): 254-56, writes, "The contemporary [Elizabethan] conception of history expected it to be didactic and to teach immediate lessons. In the 1590s, under an aging and progressively erratic monarch, its duty was to emphasize the perils of disunity and secession" (pp. 255-56).

[12] In *2 Henry IV* the dying king confesses to his heir "By what bypaths and indirect crooked ways" (4.5.184) he acquired the crown.

[13] Sig. A 2^v; cited by Paul A. Jorgensen, "The 'Dastardly Treachery' of Prince John of Lancaster," *PMLA* 76 (1961): 490. Jorgensen cites several other sources from this period that affirm the same concept.

[14] The six hundred men slain at Smerwick were Spanish and Italian mercenaries sent by the Pope to aid the Irish rebels. Presumably Lord Grey never promised life as a condition of the surrender, and Queen Elizabeth was upset only at Grey's sparing some of the officers for ransom. This episode, however, was sensitive enough in 1598 that Edmund Spenser's spirited defense of Lord Grey in a *Veue of the Present State of Ireland* may have caused the difficulties encountered in getting the work published. Although registered with the Stationers on 14 April 1598, the work was not to be printed without further authority, and was not finally published until 1633 in Dublin. See Alexander C. Judson, "The Life of Edmund Spenser" in *The Works of Edmund Spenser: A Variorum Edition,* ed. Edwin Greenlaw and Charles Grosvenor Osgood et al., 11 vols. (Baltimore: Johns Hopkins University Press, 1966), 11: 89-92, 185-87. Judson states, "This horrible slaughter of the foreigners at Smerwick was unhappily quite in accord with the practice of the time" (p. 91).

[15] See *Coriolanus,* written ten years after *2 Henry IV,* where Volumnia urges her son to pretend to humble himself before the plebeians:

> I have heard you say,
> Honor and policy, like unsevered friends,
> I' th' war do grow together. . . .
>
> (3.2.41-43)

> If it be honor in your wars to seem
> The same you are not, which for your best ends
> You adopt your policy, how is it less or worse
> That it shall hold companionship in peace
> With honor as in war. . . .
>
> (3.2.46-50)

> Now, this no more dishonors you at all
> Than to take in a town with gentle words,
> Which else would put you to your fortune and
> The hazard of much blood.
> I would dissemble with my nature, where
> My fortunes and my friends at stake required
> I should do so in honor.
>
> (3.2.58-64)

See Stanley D. McKenzie, " 'Unshout the noise that banish'd Martius:' Structural Paradox and Dissembling in *Coriolanus*," *Shakespeare Studies* 18 (1986): 189-204.

[16] For example, George J. Becker, *Shakespeare's Histories* (New York: Frederick Ungar, 1977), states that "the cold-blooded calculation of Prince John by contrast adds to Hal's stature" (p. 53).

[17] Raphael Holinshed, *Chronicles of England, Scotland, and Ireland* (London, 1808), 3:184. Holinshed cites an impressive tribute to Bedford's valiancy by Louis XI, the son of the Dauphin (Charles VII) who had been Bedford's constant adversary. Tillyard claims that the Elizabethans believed that one source of the problems during Henry VI's reign was "the arrogance of the Duke of Bedford," which offended Burgundy, England's ally (*Shakespeare's History Plays,* p. 60). Bedford married Burgundy's sister, which cemented the alliance between the Lancastrain kings and the French duke until the lady's death in 1432. Holinshed recounts that the two dukes were then estranged by "flattering taletellers," and an attempted reconciliation failed when neither would travel to the other's lodging: "Thus by the proud disdaine and enuious discord of these two high stomached princes, Bedford not minding to haue anie peere, and Burgognie not willing to abide anie superior, shortlie after England much lost . . ." (Holinshed, 3:181). Unlike Tillyard, I do not believe this single episode stained Bedford's reputation among the Elizabethans.

[18] John Danby, *Shakespeare's Doctrine of Nature* (London: Faber and Faber, 1949), pp. 95ff., distinguishes between "Appetite" and "Authority" in *2 Henry IV.* Derek Traversi, *Shakespeare: From Richard II to Henry V* (Stanford, Cal.: Stanford University Press, 1957), pp. 108-65, sees the distinction being between those who act on passionate emotions and those who have the detached self-control of Hal and John, but which contains a certain moral loss and inhumanness. Norman N. Holland, Jr., Introduction to *2 Henry IV* in *The Complete Signet Classic Shakespeare,* pp. 678-85, sees craving appetite set in opposition to a stoical acceptance of destiny.

[19] Anastaplo, "Appendix B. Citizenship, Prudence, and the Classics," in *The Artist as Thinker*, p. 281.

[20] Sherman H. Hawkins, "Virtue and Kingship in Shakespeare's *Henry IV,*" *English Literary Renaissance* 5 (1975): 313-43, provides a detailed review of sixteenth-century treatises on the ideal education of a prince being in the cardinal virtues of justice, valor or fortitude, prudence, and temperance. Hawkins argues that Hal learns primarily temperance and valor in *Part 1* and justice and prudence in *Part 2.*

[21] J. Dover Wilson, *The Fortunes of Falstaff* (New York: Macmillan, 1944), pp. 84-85, points out that this episode echoes that in *Part 1* where Falstaff first recruited 150 men of means, who bought their release, then enlisted another 150 wretched "cankers" to fill the places. Furthermore, he sent his troops into the thick of the battle at Shrewsbury so that all but three were killed, and he could pocket the victims' belongings and pay.

[22] Traversi, *Richard II to Henry V,* pp. 118-33, effectively demonstrates the distinction between the Falstaff of *Part 1* and *Part 2.* See also Harry Levin, "Falstaff's Encore," *Shakespeare Quarterly* 32 (1981): 5-17 and J. McLaverty, "No Abuse: The Prince and Falstaff in the Tavern Scenes of 'Henry IV,' " *Shakespeare Survey* 34 (1981): 105-10.

[23] For studies of Falstaff as Vice, see Bernard Spivack, *Shakespeare and the Allegory of Evil* (New York: Columbia University Press, 1958), pp. 87-91, 203-5 and Walter Kaiser, *Praisers of Folly: Erasmus, Rabelais, Shakespeare* (Cambridge, Mass.: Harvard University Press, 1963), pp. 195-275; Kaiser provides a list of other critical analyses of Falstaff as a Vice (p. 197n). Falstaff as the "Old Man" in Paul's *Epistle to the Ephesians,* who must be cast off for renewal of spirit, is discussed by D. J. Palmer, "Casting Off the Old Man: History and St. Paul in 'Henry IV,' " *Critical Quarterly* 12 (1970): 265-83, and by Robin Headlam Wells and Alison Birkinshaw, "Falstaff, Prince Hal and the New Song," *Shakespeare Studies* 18 (1986): 103-15.

[24] Philip Williams, "The Birth and Death of Falstaff Reconsidered," *Shakespeare Quarterly* 8 (1957): 363; Williams provides one of the most convincing psychoanalytical analyses of this play.

[25] Many of the following points were explored in an undergraduate thesis I wrote at M.I.T. under the direction of Norman N. Holland, Jr. Professor Holland indicates an indebtedness to that original paper for several of the ideas he develops in his introduction to *2 Henry IV* in *The Complete Signet Classic Shakespeare,* and I take pleasure in acknowledging my indebtedness to him as teacher and scholar.

[26] In Hal's initial soliloquy in *Part 1,* he speaks of the day when he will "pay the debt I never promised. . . . Redeeming time when men think least I will" (1.2.206-14). Throughout *Part 1* Hal takes upon himself other people's obligations, including Falstaff's "debts," and makes them good when his mettle proves current, not counterfeit, at Shrewsbury.

[27] The images of time, disease, and unfulfilled expectations in *2 Henry IV* have been analyzed by Clifford Leech, "The Unity of *2 Henry IV,*" *Shakespeare Survey* 6 (1953): 16-24; Traversi, *Richard II to Henry V,* pp. 108-65; L. C. Knights, *Some Shakespearean Themes*

(London: Chatto and Windus, 1959), pp. 45-64; R. J. Dorius, "A Little More than a Little," *Shakespeare Quarterly* 11 (1960): 13-26; M. M. Reese, *The Cease of Majesty: A Study of Shakespeare's History Plays* (London: Edward Arnold, 1961), pp. 116-18, 286-92; Kaiser, *Praisers of Folly,* pp. 238-51; Holland, Introduction to *2 Henry IV,* pp. 678-84; Edgar T. Schell, "Prince Hal's Second 'Reformation,' " *Shakespeare Quarterly* 21 (1970): 11-16; Becker, *Shakespeare's Histories,* pp. 51-65; Levin, "Falstaff's Encore," pp. 5-7; and Blanpied, *Time and the Artist,* pp. 179-99.

[28] Dain A. Trafton, "Shakespeare's Henry IV: A New Prince in a New Principality," *Shakespeare as Political Thinker,* ed. John Alvis and Thomas G. West (Durham, N. C.: Carolina Academic Press, 1981), pp. 83-94, analyzes Henry IV's view of "necessity" from *Richard II* through *2 Henry IV* and argues that under Henry's reign the old men of England, including Falstaff, claim to be bound by the necessity of the times, but use this to justify their gluttonous desires and ambitions, hence contaminating the entire realm.

[29] Richard Abrams, "Rumor's Reign in *2 Henry IV:* The Scope of a Personification," *English Literary Renaissance* 16 (1986): 467-95, finds a close verbal relationship between Falstaff and the Archbishop: "As Falstaff's bellyful of tongues parodically subsumes the Archbishop's language gifts and the people's many-headed subversiveness, and as he re-establishes the spirit of Eastcheap riot in the peaceful Gloucestershire countryside, so all the dissident elements of 'unquiet' or rebellion are gathered under one head and jointly dispatched" (p. 492).

[30] Cited by Stephen Greenblatt, "Invisible Bullets: Renaissance Authority and its Subversion, *Henry IV* and *Henry V,*" in *Political Shakespeare: New Essays in Cultural Materialism,* ed. Jonathan Dollimore and Alan Sinfield (Manchester: Manchester University Press, 1985), pp. 40-41. Greenblatt· argues that the "structure of things [in *2 Henry IV* is called by] the twinned names of time and necessity" (p. 35).

[31] Dorius, "A Little More than a Little," argues that "what seems to set off the values of [Shakespeare's history] plays most markedly from those of the tragedies is the importance given by the histories to the virtues of prudence and economy"; Dorius defines the opposites of prudence and economy as "carelessness, excess, waste, and disease" (p. 13).

[32] Greenblatt argues that "Shakespeare does not shrink from any of the felt nastiness implicit in this sorting out of the right people and the wrong people; . . . the founding of the modern State, like the founding of the modern prince, is shown to be based upon acts of calculation, intimidation, and deceit. And the demonstration of these acts is rendered an entertainment for which an audience, subject to just this State, will pay money and applaud" ("Invisible Bullets," p. 39).

[33] Holland points out that "in the coronation scene, Falstaff calls out, 'My King! My Jove!' (thus identifying himself with Saturn, the Titan who devoured his own children)" (Introduction to *2 Henry IV,* p. 681). Earlier in the play, when Hal puts on a tavern drawer's leather apron to spy on Falstaff and Doll, whom he refers to as "Saturn and Venus" (2.4.269), the prince compares himself to Jove taking the form of a bull (2.2.170-73). Jove deposed his father-king Saturn as Hal now banishes his father substitute Falstaff.

Daniel J. Kornstein (essay date 1994)

SOURCE: "Old Father Antic the Law: *Henry IV, Parts 1 and 2,*" in *Kill All the Lawyers: Shakespeare's Legal Appeal,* Princeton University Press, 1994, pp. 135-42.

[*In the following essay, Kornstein emphasizes the themes of law and justice in 1 and 2 Henry IV, asserting that in these plays, Hal is meant to turn away from both Falstaff's thievery and the illegality of his father's rule, and embrace instead the "sober" lawfulness personified in the Lord Chief Justice.*]

With the two parts of *Henry IV,* Shakespeare spins a new and important legal theme. Like *A Midsummer Night's Dream,* the plays about Henry IV offer a theory of legal interpretation and perceptive comments on the role of law in society. But then the Bard does something unique and central to understanding his attitude toward law and lawyers. In the two *Henry IV* plays, Shakespeare gives us the most unqualifiedly, unmistakably complimentary portrait of a sober, solid, fair-minded lawyer figure in all the canon. Shakespeare's highly favorable and especially respectful description of the lord chief justice in the two parts of *Henry IV* is a powerful and effective antidote to those who think Dick the Butcher's line about killing all the lawyers should be taken at face value only.

To etch his most positive portrait of a lawyer that much more deeply, Shakespeare sets up a contrast. Early in Shakespeare's *Henry IV, Part 1,* Falstaff, the great comic creation of Shakespeare, gives his own candid view of the rule of law. Chatting merrily with Prince Hal, Falstaff asks, "Shall there be gallows standing in England when thou / art king?" (1.2.58-59). Why, asks Falstaff, should a thief's courage be cheated of its reward "with the / rusty curb of old father Antic [i.e., that old screwball] the law" (1.2.59-60)? The very phrasing, the offhand but colorful reference to the law gone awry, catches our attention and makes us anticipate something special about the role played by "old father Antic the law" in *Henry IV.* The two parts of *Henry IV* continue the story begun in *Richard II.* At the end of *Richard II*, Bolingbroke, having success-fully rebelled against Richard II, is crowned Henry IV. But both parts of *Henry IV* show that "uneasy lies the head that wears a crown" (*2 Henry IV*, 3.1.31).

King Henry is beset by troubles. He spends his time putting down new revolts by Hotspur and others who had originally helped the king achieve his power. Hal, the young prince of Wales, is a youth without any apparent sense of responsibility, who pains his father the king with the "bad element" he hangs around with. By the time *Part 2* closes, the new rebels are routed, Henry IV dies of natural causes, and ne'er-do-well Hal assumes the crown while foreswearing his past friends.

One of the underlying legal themes in *Henry IV* concerns the teaching function of government. Bolingbroke, the successful revolutionary, becomes, as Henry IV, a symbol of disorder. Under his reign, there is no lasting order. Lawlessness springs up all about him. One who acted as a street thug is king.

But *Henry IV* is not primarily about the educative role of government. According to a leading Shakespearean scholar, "the mainspring of the dramatic action" in *Henry IV* is legal.

In *The Fortunes of Falstaff*, published in 1944, John Dover Wilson, an English critic, argued that *Henry IV* hinges on "the choice . . . Hal is called upon to make between vanity and government."[1] Vanity is personified by Falstaff, and government by chivalry or prowess in the field (in *Part 1*) and justice (the theme of *Part 2*). In Wilson's analysis, Hotspur symbolizes chivalry and the lord chief justice stands for the rule of law or the new ideal of service to the state. *Henry IV* becomes a morality play, a struggle between vanity and government for possession of youth.

To choose vanity is, for Hal, to choose a disrespectful, even anarchic attitude toward law. He takes part in robberies. He even hits the chief justice, who sends Hal to jail. In this phase, Hal is always in trouble with the law.

Hal's antilegal attitude is the same as Falstaff's. He sees in Falstaff—and imitates—an entire absence of moral responsibility, a complete freedom. After Henry IV dies, and Falstaff thinks of his own influence over his friend Hal, Falstaff says, "Let us / take any man's horses—the laws of England are at my commandment . . . and woe to my Lord Chief Justice" (Part 2, 5.3.134-137). The law is "old father Antic the law."

Falstaff's interview with the chief justice nicely poses the basic choice facing Hal. When the chief justice asks for him, Falstaff tells a servant, "Tell him I am deaf" (*Part 2*, 1.2.67). In context, we can interpret this as "deaf to the law." And then a little later the chief justice upbraids Falstaff: "You hear not what I [i.e., the law] say to you" (*Part 2*, 1.2.121). In this interview, Falstaff comes off far wittier, which may help dramatize the choice for Hal.

In the same interview, Hal's friend speaks for Hal and youth in all times and in all places. Falstaff sums up generational conflict and youthful bridling at authority when he challenges the chief justice, in words that echo down to our own times: "You that are old / consider not the capacities of us that are young" (*Part 2*, 1.2.174-75). And soon after Hal inherits the throne, and adviser tells the chief justice, "Indeed I think the young King loves you [i.e., the law] not" (*Part 2*, 5.2.9).

But Hal's attitude changes. The lord chief justice of England, admirable symbol of the law, remains constant. Shakespeare portrays him throughout as sober, calm, incorruptible, fair, measured, and at all times fully in control of himself and the situation. The chief justice always speaks rationally and sensibly, without being overbearing or arch. He personifies justice in its eternal, ideal form.

The chief justice's symbolic role shows through, for example, in act 2 of *Part 2* when he restores order following Falstaff's arrest for nonpayment of a debt. Mistress Quickly sues Falstaff, and two officers come to a tavern to bring Falstaff into custody. A scuffle ensues until the lord chief justice and his men enter. "What is the matter?" asks the chief justice. "Keep the peace here, ho!" (*Part 2*, 2.1.63). The commotion subsides and the chief justice hears both sides, rendering judgment against Falstaff: "Pay her / the debt you owe her" (*Part 2*, 2.1.120-21).

But the real moment of truth—the theatrical moment of the play for the link between Shakespeare and the law—comes in the last act of *Part 2* when Hal has to make the choice of his life. Prince Hal has become King Henry V, and the chief justice recalls how he, the chief justice, has had, on occasion, to punish the wayward youth. The new king confronts the experienced, upright judge and sees the uncertainty in the judge's face.

The new king tells the judge, "You are, I think, assured I love you not" (*Part 2*, 5.2.64). The judge does not know if he will now be removed from office or, worse yet, punished by the new king for the judge's past strictness.

Bravely answers the chief justice, "I am assured, if I be measured rightly, / Your majesty hath no just cause to hate me" (*Part 2*, 5.2.65-66). "No?" responds the king with apparent sarcasm (though much depends on the actor's inflection).

> How might a prince of my great hopes forget
> So great indignities you laid upon me?

What—rate, rebuke, and roughly send to
   prison
Th'immediate heir of England? Was this
   easy?
May this be washed in Lethe and forgotten?
                      (Part 2, 5.2.67-71)

The chief justice's thoughtful comeback makes the play's legal symbolism explicit:

I then did use the person of your father.
The image of his power lay then in me;
And in th'administration of his law,
Whiles I was busy for the commonwealth,
Your highness pleased to forget my place,
The majesty and power of law and justice,
The image of the King whom I presented,
And struck me in my very seat of judgment.
                      (Part 2, 5.2.72-79)

Then the chief justice goes on to tell the new king that he should think how he would feel,

To have a son set your decrees at naught—
To pluck down justice from your awe-full
   bench,
To trip the course of law, and blunt the
   sword
That guards the peace and safety of your
   person,
See your most dreadful laws slighted . . .
                (Part 2, 5.2.84-87, 93)

The chief justice's cogent and dignified advocacy on his own behalf (and on behalf of law) moves the king. "You are right, Justice," answers Hal, and at last we know what his choice will be.

And you weigh this well.
Therefore still bear the balance and the
   sword;
And I do wish your honours may increase.
                  (Part 2, 5.2.101-3)

In an extraordinary passage, Shakespeare celebrates the notion that the law is supreme even over royalty. The playwright has Hal conjure up the possibility that one of his own sons would disobey the law, at which point Hal would say,

Happy am I that have a man so bold
That dares do justice on my proper son,
And not less happy having such a son
That would deliver up his greatness so
Into the hands of justice.
                 (Part 2, 5.2.107-11)

Hal returns the "unstained" sword of justice to the chief justice, reappoints him, and begs him to go on

administering the laws of England in this "bold, just, and impartial spirit" (*Part 2*, 5.2.115).

Then and there the new king chooses law over vanity as the touchstone for his reign. He puts off vanity and adopts justice as his father and guide. To the chief justice, Hal says:

You shall be as a father to my youth;
My voice shall sound as you do prompt mine
   ear,
And I will stoop and humble my intents
To your well-practised wise directions.
                  (Part 2, 5.2.117-20)

Shakespeare has created a portrait of a great judge and has paid an impressive tribute to the impartiality of courts.[2] So much for a superficial reading of Dick the Butcher's "Kill all the lawyers."

Here we have an allegory for all of us, lawyers or not. Each of us faces a choice similar to Hal's: youth standing between vanity and law or some other occupation. Somewhere around the time we finish college, consider what to do with our lives, decide whether to go on to graduate or professional school, and start to conduct our life's work, we first choose, as Hal chose, one over the other, profession over vanity. And then, as we live our lives in our work, we choose the way we will practice and conduct ourselves. Prince Hal is each one of us. This remembrance of choice quickens anyone's interest in the play.

There is proof of the large role of the law in Shakespeare's *Henry IV*. I find persuasive—and personally significant—the theory that the work is essentially a morality play about youth faced with a choice between law and vanity. But supplementing and even going beyond that theory is other evidence. Again and again Shakespeare makes us aware that the play is an allegory about law, sprinkled with casual but still stimulating legal references, some of which stay a while in the mind.

Consider the small but revealing matter of Mistress Quickly's lawsuit against Falstaff. In those days, lawsuits apparently began with more than a simple summons. Attachment of the person was the preferred method. In *Henry IV*, the two officers of the law who come to arrest Falstaff as a defendant in *Quickly v. Falstaff* are called Master Snare and Master Fang. Could Shakespeare have picked better allegorical names than Snare and Fang to reflect the dim, crabbed view debtors took of the law and its personnel?

Similarly, if the lord chief justice stands for the ideal element of the law, the mundane aspect of the law is represented by two local justices of the peace called Silence and Shallow. Justice Silence, true to his name, says almost nothing during the play. But Justice Shallow, hardly a deep fellow, is a fully developed character with many traits. The contrast between the lord chief justice and Justice Shallow could not be greater.

Shakespeare portrays Justice Shallow as a foolish old lawyer. Shallow makes several references to the time he spent as a young man at the Inns of Court (*Part 2,* 3.2.12-33, 275-83, 303-9). He reminisces about the wildness of his youth, his fighting, and his womanizing, for which he was then dubbed "lusty Shallow." At one point in the play a friend of Shallow even tries improperly to influence Shallow on behalf of a litigant. In the end, he comes off—especially in his dealings with Falstaff—as a stupid, gullible liar, ripe to be the victim of Falstaff's schemes.

Justice Shallow's allusions to the Inns of Court are significant. He refers to two by name—Clement's Inn and Gray's Inn; in only one other play, *Henry VI, Part 2,* does Shakespeare actually name another of the Inns (Middle Temple). We should recall that Clement's Inn is where Shakespeare's cousin John Greene had studied and Gray's Inn gave Shakespeare one of his first big breaks by inviting him to put on *Comedy of Errors* there. All of this shows the influence of the Inns of Court on Shakespeare.

It may also show that Shakespeare had some firsthand knowledge of the carousing that sometimes went on at the Inns of Court, and that "lusty Shallow" was not the only one who earned such a sobriquet. Some surviving evidence indicates that Shakespeare followed Shallow's habits after a performance of *Twelfth Night* at Middle Temple in March 1602. According to the unexpurgated diary of John Manningham, a barrister of the Middle Temple:

> Upon a time when Burbage played Richard the Third there was a citizen grew so far in liking with him, that before she went from the play she appointed him to come that night unto her by the name of Richard the Third. Shakespeare, overhearing their conclusion, went before, was entertained and at his game ere Burbage came. Then message being brought that Richard the Third was at the door, Shakespeare caused return to be made that William the Conqueror was before Richard the Third. Shakespeare's name was William.[3]

The Bard might then have been called "lusty Shakespeare."

Both parts of *Henry IV* stress the virtues of settlement and compromise, virtues that should not readily be lost on lawyers. In *Part 1,* just before the crucial battle at Shrewsbury where Hotspur is killed, King Henry offers to pardon the rebels if they will lay down their arms. Worcester, emissary of the rebels, decides for his own reasons not to relay the "liberal and kind offer of the King" (5.2.2), which Hotspur would have accepted. After the battle, with the rebels defeated, the king confronts Worcester about the generous settlement offer and on getting no satisfactory response orders Worcester killed.

In *Part 2* another settlement conference takes place. The king's representative offers the king's promise of mercy and attention to the rebels' grievances. Everyone knows it will be the last chance to settle before the battle:

> we may meet,
> And either end in peace—which God so frame—
> Or to the place of diff'rence call the swords
> Which must decide it.
>
> (4.1.177-80)

If litigation is a type of war, then attempts to settle are akin to peace negotiations. Viewed this way, the double mention of settlement in *Henry IV* takes on meaning. Once again, the lawyer knows Shakespeare is speaking about settling or calling down the swords. As almost every lawyer must have told a client at some time, the archbishop of York says:

> A peace is of the nature of a conquest,
> For then both parties nobly are subdued,
> And neither party loser.
>
> (*Part 2,* 4.1.315-17)

This is Shakespeare's version of the familiar lawyer's adage: "A fair settlement is better than a bad trial."

When the rebels have difficulty explaining their grievances, one of the king's men says, "A rotten case abides no handling" (*Part 2,* 4.1.159). Now there's a thought that must have gone through lawyers' minds more than once. How many rotten cases have attorneys handled? To what result? What is a rotten case?

Then there is a line full of special meaning about how a lawyer should best plead a case. The chief justice says to Falstaff:

> Sir John, Sir John, I am well acquainted
> with your manner of wrenching the true cause the
> false way. It is not a confident brow, nor the throng
> of words that come with such more than impudent
> sauciness from you, can thrust me from a level consideration.
>
> (*Part 2,* 2.1.111-16)

This passage compresses in a verse a whole primer on advocacy. The reader should linger on the lines a while, rolling them over delightedly in his or her mind, and meditate about their meaning.

Ability to wield the written or spoken word is a lawyer's primary weapon. Successful use of the basic technical skills of courtroom persuasion depend to a large extent on skillful use of language, on mobilizing language to the advocate's ends. We try to persuade by using words. Every great courtroom advocate grasps the vital importance of the written and oral word. "The power of clear statement," said Daniel Webster, "is the great power at the bar."

"The throng of words" has double application here. Both sentimental Richard II and pugnacious Hotspur—different personalities that they were—were similar in their wordiness. Shakespeare gives them good speeches, but in the end makes them both losers. They become victims of words, and one wonders if that too is a lesson for lawyers.

"Impudent sauciness"—a lawyer *should* be bold, even irrepressible, but there are limits. Overboldness runs the risk of sanctions; impudence is an unpleasant trait. We have all come across adversaries or colleagues who have said and done things with "more than impudent sauciness."

On the other hand, if deference became the hallmark of the legal profession, the law's creativity, its independence and willingness to challenge authority, its very excitement, may to some extent be lost.

Which brings us back full circle to the lord chief justice. Might it not be suggested that the chief justice uses some of the very qualities he taxes Falstaff for using? After all, does not the chief justice in his occasionally difficult dealings with young Prince Hal and new King Henry V display a "confident brow" and rely on a "throng of words," and even on what some might characterize as an "impudent sauciness"? Yet when the chief justice employs these traits, they are good, praiseworthy, and for positive ends. The lesson may be that skills are only skills in the service of deeper aspects of personality and character; skills depend on the purpose to which they are put, means have to be related to ends. These purposes and ends come under scrutiny in *Richard III*.

Notes

[1] John Dover Wilson, *The Fortunes of Falstaff* (Cambridge: Cambridge University Press, 1943), p. 17.

[2] G. W. Keeton, *Shakespeare's Legal and Political Background* (New York: Barnes & Noble, 1967), pp. 155-62.

[3] W. Nicholas Knight, *Shakespeare's Hidden Life: Shakespeare at the Law, 1585-1595* (New York: Mason & Lipscomb, 1973), p. 169.

E. A. Rauchut (essay date 1994)

SOURCE: "Hotspur's Prisoners and the Laws of War in *I Henry IV*," in *Shakespeare Quarterly,* Vol. 45, No. 1, Spring, 1994, pp. 96-7.

[*In the following essay, Rauchut discusses the laws governing prisoners of war in medieval England and concludes that Henry IV breaks these laws and aggravates his role as usurper when he commands Hotspur to hand over his prisoners to the crown.*]

Whether Hotspur is legally bound to turn over his prisoners and whether King Henry IV is justified in demanding them are questions that have long perplexed critics of Shakespeare's *1 Henry IV*.[1] Military and legal texts from the medieval and early modern periods suggest that although Henry asserts a royal right to all Hotspur's prisoners, his assertion flies in the face of both chivalric convention and the law of arms. A usurper's theft in the name of royal right thus becomes a cause for civil war as well as a dramatic *causa causans* of the play's robbery motifs.[2] I begin by considering some of the economic, legal, and political contexts of prisoners and ransom.

Prisoner ransom comprised war's greatest gain, a point that Camden illustrates in his history of Britain when he records that the Montgomerys' Pououny castle in Scotland was built with ransom paid for the "captive *Henry Percy*, sirnamed *Hotspur*."[3] Honore Bonet, in *The Tree of Battles*, suggests that a captor may demand "reasonable and knightly ransom, such as is possible for the prisoner to pay and according to the usage of arms and of his country, and not such as to disinherit his wife, children, relations and friends." James Turner, in *Pallas Armata*, notes, however, that because ransom demands are often extravagant, "an agreement is frequently made between the two parties who make the War, of a certain price to be paid by Officers, and Common Souldiers for their Ransomes according to their quality, and this seldom exceeds one Months pay, for any under the degree of Colonel." Francis Grose, in *Military Antiquities*, writes that the "usual price demanded for the ransom of a prisoner of war was . . . one year's rent of his estate," while a soldier without an estate might expect to pay a half-year's wages. In practice, however, captors often used the heat of battle and threats of death to extort top dollar from their prisoners, as Pistol does with the French Soldier in 4.4 of *Henry V*. As M. H. Keen explains, "the captor made a rough assessment of what his prisoner could at a pinch pay, threw in what his wealthier connections were likely to add to this, and asked for as much as he thought he could get."[4]

Laws governing prisoners and the distribution of ransom were similar to but more complicated than those governing other spoil. Prisoners became the property of their captors and, like other booty, were subject to laws of division. The soldier's share of ransom was the same whether he was paid wages or was armed by a prince. In England the king, captain, and captor each received a third of the ransom.[5]

The oath a prisoner swore to his captor was founded in the *ius gentium:* it was binding under the law of arms and formed a "close chivalrous bond" between captor and prisoner. This bond is dramatically underscored in *1 Henry IV,* where Hotspur's code of chivalric honor serves as a dramatic foil to Henry IV's *Realpolitik.*[6]

The transfer of prisoner rights involved a complicated formality entailing the prisoner's renunciation of faith to his original captor and a declaration of loyalty to his new master. In a provision of Meaux's 1422 treaty of surrender, for example, Henry V required the garrison to free its prisoners and each master formally to quit faith with each of his prisoners. Thomas Rymer, in *Foedera,* also records a formal transfer of loyalty in the Market of Mews, where "the Prisoners that thei have and with holden of the Subgetts and Obeysaunce and other of the Service of *the said Kings* . . . shall quitten pleinly all other Subgetts, Obeysauntes, and other of the said Services of the abovesaid Kynges, that have to hem made any Feith or Othe." Significantly, then, Henry IV's demand that Hotspur surrender his prisoners violates this formal oath, as well as the chivalric bond of honor between Hotspur and his captives.[7]

According to the law of arms, Henry IV can order Hotspur to turn over only those prisoners of noble blood, which in this case includes Mordake, Earl of Fife. The rest belong to Hotspur, who has the right to refuse even the king's demand for them. Henry, however, leaves no room for compromise: he claims all prisoners by royal right, making provision neither for a formal renunciation of faith nor for the traditional royal gratuity granted in exchange for prisoners.[8]

In demanding that Hotspur surrender all his prisoners, then, Henry asserts his royal right while ignoring the law of arms, traditional compensation, and the formal chivalric bond between Hotspur and his captives. In a real sense Henry attempts to steal the captives, and his court, as Stephen Greenblatt has observed, "comes to embody . . . glorified usurpation and theft."[9] The robber of the crown now robs the "hands" that "holp to make [him] so portly" (1.3.12-13), committing a royal theft that causes civil war.

Notes

[1] See, for example, Robert Hapgood, "Falstaff's Vocation," *Shakespeare Quarterly* 16 (1965): 91-98, esp.

95; Paul A. Jorgensen, *Shakespeare's Military World* (Berkeley, 1956), 246; and Edna Zwick Boris, *Shakespeare's English Kings, the People, and the Law: A Study in the Relationship between the Tudor Constitution and the English History Plays* (Rutherford, NJ, 1978), 174. Quotations of *1 Henry IV* follow the Oxford Shakespeare edition edited by David Bevington (Oxford, 1987).

Research for this note was conducted with the generous support of a Folger Short-Term Fellowship.

[2] Cf. Geoffrey Bullough, *Narrative and Dramatic Sources of Shakespeare,* 8 vols. (London, 1957-75), 4:162. For the idea of a kingdom without justice as a band of robbers, see St. Augustine's *City of God,* trans. Marcus Dods (New York, 1950), 112-13. For a discussion of this topos with reference to *1 Henry IV,* see W. R. Elton's "Shakespeare and the Thought of His Age" in *A New Companion to Shakespeare Studies,* Kenneth Muir and S. Schoenbaum, eds. (Cambridge, 1971), 180-98, esp. 197.

[3] William Camden, *Britain, or A chorographicall description of . . . England, Scotland, and Ireland . . .* (London, 1610). On the profitability of ransom, see also M. H. Keen, *The Laws of War in the Late Middle Ages* (London, 1965), 156; and Francis Grose, *Military Antiquities Respecting A History of the English Army, from the Conquest to the Present Time,* 2 vols. (London, 1812), 2:110.

[4] Bonet, *The Tree of Battles* (1387), ed. and trans. G. W. Coopland (Liverpool, UK, 1949), 153; Turner, *Pallas Armata: Military Essayes of the Ancient Grecian, Roman, and Modern Art of War* (London, 1683), 341-42; Grose, 2:111; and Keen, 158-59.

[5] For laws governing status and treatment of prisoners, see Giovanni da Legnano, *TRACTATUS: De Bello, De Represaliis et De Duello* (1360), ed. Thomas Erskine Holland, trans. James Leslie Brierly (Oxford, 1917), 270; Pierino Belli, *De Re Militari et Bello Tractatus* (1563), ed. James Brown Scott, trans. Herbert C. Nutting, 2 vols. (Oxford, 1936), 2:95; and Balthazar Ayala, *De Iure Belli Libri Tres* (1612), trans. John Pawley Bate, 2 vols. (Washington, DC, 1912), 2:38.

For distribution of ransom among captor, captain, and king, see Bonet, 152; Grose, 2:110-11; and also Keen, 146-47, 148, and 156.

[6] Keen, 164. On the potential for violence inherent in "the conflict between honor and obedience, the 'customary rites' of knighthood and the duty to 'right royal majesty,' " see Richard McCoy's *The Rites of Knighthood: The Literature and Politics of Elizabethan Chivalry* (Berkeley and Los Angeles, 1989), 2-3.

7 On the transfer of prisoner rights, see Keen, 166; and Rymer, *Foedera, Conventiones, Literae, et cujuscunque generis Acta Publica inter Reges Angliae,* 3d ed., 10 vols. (London, 1740), 4:65.

8 On the royal right, see Keen, 166. On exchange of prisoners of equal or greater rank and for examples of royal gratuity, see Turner, 341; Rymer, 3:2 and 3:13, where he records the award of two such gratuities in the year 1347, one granted for the prisoner David Bruce, King of Scotland, and another of 80,000 florins to Thomas Holland for his prisoner, the earl of Eu.

For more discussion of the legality of Henry's demand for Hotspur's prisoners in *1 Henry IV,* see commentaries by George Tollet in the Johnson-Steevens edition of 1773; George Steevens in the Malone Variorum (1821); Samuel B. Hemingway, editor of the Yale Shakespeare edition of 1917 (rpt. New Haven, 1943); and George Lyman Kittredge in his 1940 edition of the play.

9 "Invisible Bullets" in *Shakespearean Negotiations: The Circulation of Social Energy in Renaissance England* (Berkeley, 1988), 21-65, esp. 41.

AMBIGUOUS PERSPECTIVES

Stephen Greenblatt (essay date 1985)

SOURCE: "Invisible Bullets: Renaissance Authority and Its Subversion, *Henry IV* and *Henry V*" in *Political Shakespeare: New Essays in Cultural Materialism,* edited by Jonathan Dollimore and Alan Sinfield, Manchester University Press, 1985, pp. 18-47.

[*In the following essay, Greenblatt examines the subversive nature of 1 and 2* Henry IV, *arguing that it paradoxically serves to strengthen, rather than undermine, the legitimacy and power of the king.*]

In his notorious police report of 1593 on Christopher Marlowe, the Elizabethan spy Richard Baines informed his superiors that Marlowe had declared, among other monstrous opinions, that 'Moses was but a juggler, and that one Heriots, being Sir Walter Ralegh's man, can do more than he'.1 The 'Heriots' cast for a moment in this lurid light is Thomas Harriot, the most profound Elizabethan mathematician, an expert in cartography, optics, and navigational science, an adherent of atomism, the first Englishman to make a telescope and turn it on the heavens, the author of the first original book about the first English colony in America, and the possessor throughout his career of a dangerous reputation for atheism.2 In all of his extant writings, private correspondence as well as public dis-

course, Harriot professes the most reassuringly orthodox religious faith, but the suspicion persisted. When he died of cancer in 1621, one of his contemporaries, persuaded that Harriot had challenged the doctrinal account of creation *ex nihilo,* remarked gleefully that 'a *nihilum* killed him at last: for in the top of his nose came a little red speck (exceeding small), which grew bigger and bigger, and at last killed him'.3

Charges of atheism levelled at Harriot or anyone else in this period are extremely difficult to assess, for such accusations were smear tactics, used with reckless abandon against anyone whom the accuser happened to dislike. At a dinner party one summer evening in 1593, Sir Walter Ralegh teased an irascible country parson named Ralph Ironside and found himself the subject of a state investigation; at the other end of the social scale, in the same Dorsetshire parish, a drunken servant named Oliver complained that in the Sunday sermon the preacher had praised Moses excessively but had neglected to mention his fifty-two concubines, and Oliver too found himself under official scrutiny.4 Few if any of these investigations turned up what we would call atheists, even muddled or shallow ones; the stance that seems to come naturally to the greenest college freshman in late twentieth-century America seems to have been almost unthinkable to the most daring philosophical minds of late sixteenth-century England.

The historical evidence, of course, is unreliable; even in the absence of substantial social pressure, people lie quite readily about their most intimate beliefs. How much more must they have lied in an atmosphere of unembarrassed repression. Still, there is probably more than politic concealment involved here. After all, treason was punished as harshly as atheism, and yet, while the period abounds in documented instances of treason in word and deed, there are virtually no professed atheists. If ever there were a place to confirm the proposition that within a given social construction of reality certain interpretations of experience are sanctioned and others excluded, it is here, in the boundaries that contained sixteenth-century scepticism. Like Machiavelli and Montaigne, Thomas Harriot professed belief in God, and there is no justification, in any of these cases, for a simple dismissal of the profession of faith as mere hypocrisy.

I am not, of course, arguing that atheism was literally unthinkable in the late sixteenth century; rather that it was almost always thinkable only as the thought of another. This is, in fact, one of its attractions as a smear; atheism is one of the characteristic marks of otherness. Hence the ease with which Catholics can call Protestant martyrs atheists, and Protestants routinely make similar charges against the Pope.5 The pervasiveness and frequency of these charges then does not signal the probable existence of a secret society of freethinkers, a School of Night, but rather registers the operation of a religious authority that, whether Catholic or Protestant, characteristically confirms its power in this period by disclosing the threat of atheism. The authority is secular as well as religious; hence at Raleigh's 1603 treason trial, Justice Popham solemnly warned the accused not to let 'Harriot, nor any such Doctor, persuade you there is no eternity in Heaven, lest you find an eternity of hell-torments'.[6] Nothing in Harriot's writings suggests that he held the position attributed to him here, but of course the charge does not depend upon evidence: Harriot is invoked as the archetypal corrupter, Achitophel seducing his glittering Absolom. If he did not exist, he would have to be invented.

Yet atheism is not the only mode of subversive religious doubt, and we cannot entirely discount the persistent rumors of Harriot's heterodoxy by pointing to his perfectly conventional professions of faith and to the equal conventionality of the attacks upon him. Indeed I want to suggest that if we look closely at *A Brief and True Report of the New Found Land of Virginia,* the only work Harriot published in his lifetime and hence the work in which he was presumably the most cautious, we can find traces of exactly the kind of material that could lead to the remark attributed to Marlowe, that 'Moses was but a juggler, and that one Heriots, being Sir Walter Ralegh's man, can do more than he'. Further, Shakespeare's Henry plays, like Harriot in the New World, can be seen to confirm the Machievellian hypothesis of the origin of princely power in force and fraud even as they draw their audience irresistibly toward the celebration of that power.

The apparently feeble wisecrack attributed to Marlowe finds its way into a police file because it seems to bear out one of the Machiavellian arguments about religion that most excited the wrath of sixteenth-century authorities: Old Testament religion, the argument goes, and by extension the whole Judeo-Christian tradition, originated in a series of clever tricks, fraudulent illusions perpetrated by Moses, who had been trained in Egyptian magic, upon the 'rude and gross' (and hence credulous) Hebrews.[7] This argument is not actually to be found in Machiavelli, nor does it originate in the sixteenth century; it is already fully formulated in early pagan polemics against Christianity. But it seems to acquire a special force and currency in the Renaissance as an aspect of a heightened consciousness, fuelled by the period's prolonged crises of doctrine and church governance, of the social function of religious belief.

Here Machiavelli's writings are important, for *The Prince* observes in its bland way that if Moses's particular actions and methods are examined closely, they do not appear very different from those employed by the great pagan princes, while the *Discourses* treat religion as if its primary function were not salvation but the achievement of civic discipline and hence as if its primary justification were not truth but expediency. Thus Romulus's successor, Numa Pompilius, 'finding a very savage people, and wishing to reduce them to civil obedience by the arts of peace, had recourse to religion as the most necessary and assured support of any civil society'.[8] For although 'Romulus could organize the Senate and establish other civil and military institutions without the aid of divine authority, yet it was very necessary for Numa, who feigned that he held converse with a nymph, who dictated to him all that he wished to persuade the people to' (147). In truth, continues Machiavelli, 'there never was any remarkable lawgiver amongst any people who did not resort to divine authority, as otherwise his laws would not have been accepted by the people' (147).

From here it was only a short step, in the minds of Renaissance authorities, to the monstrous opinions attributed to the likes of Marlowe and Harriot. Kyd, under torture, testified that Marlowe had affirmed that 'things esteemed to be done by divine power might have as well been done by observation of men', and the Jesuit Robert Parsons claimed that in Ralegh's 'school of Atheism', 'both Moses and our Savior, the Old and the New Testament, are jested at'.[9] On the eve of Ralegh's treason trial, some 'hellish verses' were lifted from an anonymous tragedy written ten years earlier and circulated as Ralegh's own confession of atheism. (The movement here is instructive: the fictional text returns to circulation as the missing confessional language of real life.) At first the earth was held in common, the verses declare, but this golden age gave way to war, kingship, and property:

> Then some sage man, above the vulgar wise,
> Knowing that laws could not in quiet dwell,
> Unless they were observed, did first devise
> The names of Gods, religion, heaven, and
>   hell . . .
> Only bug-bears to keep the world in fear.[10]

Now Harriot does not give voice to any of these speculations, but if we look attentively at his account of the first Virginia colony, we find a mind that seems interested in the same set of problems, a mind indeed that seems to be virtually testing the Machiavellian hypotheses. Sent by Ralegh to keep a record of the colony and to compile a description of the resources and inhabitants of the area, Harriot took care to learn the North Carolina Algonkian dialect and to achieve what he calls a 'special familiarity with some of the priests'.[11] The Indians believe, he writes, in the immortality of the soul and in otherworldly punishments and rewards for behaviour in this world; 'What subtlety soever be in the *Wiroances* and Priests, this opinion worketh so much in many of the common and simple sort of people that it maketh them have great respect to their Governors, and also great care what they do, to avoid torment after death and to enjoy bliss' (374). The split between the priests and the people implied here is glimpsed as well in the description of the votive images: 'They think that all the gods are of human shape, and therefore they represent them by images in the forms of men, which they call Kewasowak. . . . The common sort think them to be also gods' (373).

We have then, as in Machiavelli, a sense of religion as a set of beliefs manipulated by the subtlety of the priests to help ensure social order and cohesion. To this we may add a still more telling observation not of the internal function of native religion but of the impact of European culture upon the Indians: 'Most things they saw with us', Harriot writes, 'as mathematical instruments, sea compasses, the virtue of the loadstone in drawing iron, a perspective glass whereby was showed many strange sights, burning glasses, wildfire works, guns, books, writing and reading, spring clocks that seem to go of themselves, and many other things that we had, were so strange unto them, and so far exceeded their capacities to comprehend the reason and means how they should be made and done, that they thought they were rather the works of gods then of men, or at the leastwise they had been given and taught us of the gods' (375-6). The effect of this delusion, born of what Harriot supposes to be the vast technological superiority of the European, is that the savages began to doubt that they possessed the truth of God and religion and to suspect that such truth 'was rather to be had from us, whom God so specially loved than from a people that were so simple, as they found themselves to be in comparison of us' (376).

What we have here, I suggest, is the very core of the Machiavellian anthropology that posited the origin of religion in a cunning imposition of socially coercive doctrines by an educated and sophisticated lawgiver upon a simple people. And in Harriot's list of the marvels—from wildfire to reading—with which he undermined the Indian's confidence in their native understanding of the universe, we have the core of the claim attributed to Marlowe: that Moses was but a juggler and that Ralegh's man Harriot could do more than he. It was, we may add, supremely appropriate that this hypothesis should be tested in the encounter of the Old world and the New, for though vulgar Machiavellianism implied that all religion was a sophisticated confidence trick, Machiavelli himself saw that trick as possible only at a radical point of origin: 'if any one wanted to establish a republic at the present time', he writes, 'he would find it much easier with the simple mountaineers, who are almost without any civilization, than with such as are accustomed to live in cities' (*Discourses*, p. 148).

In Harriot then we have one of the earliest instances of a highly significant phenomenon: the testing upon the bodies and minds of non-Europeans or, more generally, the non-civilised, of a hypothesis about the origin and nature of European culture and belief. Such testing could best occur in this privileged anthropological moment, for the comparable situations in Europe itself tended to be already contaminated by prior contact. Only in the forest, with a people ignorant of Christianity and startled by its bearers' technological potency, could one hope to reproduce accurately, with live subjects, the relation imagined between Numa and the primitive Romans, Moses and the Hebrews. And the testing that could then take place could only happen once, for it entails not detached observation but radical change, the change Harriot begins to observe in the priests who 'were not so sure grounded, nor gave such credit to their traditions and stories, but through conversing with us they were brought into great doubts of their own' (375). I should emphasise that I am speaking here of events as reported by Harriot. The history of subsequent English-Algonkian relations casts doubts upon the depth, extent, and irreversibility of the supposed Indian crisis of belief. In the *Brief and True Report,* however, the tribe's stories begin to *collapse* in the minds of their traditional guardians, and the coercive power of the European beliefs begins to show itself almost at once in the Indians' behaviour: 'On a time also when their corn began to wither by reason of a drought which happened extraordinarily, fearing that it had come to pass by reason that in some thing they had displeased us, many would come to us and desire us to pray to our God in England, that he would preserve their corn, promising that when it was ripe we also should be partakers of the fruit' (377). If we remember that, like virtually all sixteenth-century Europeans in the New World, the English resisted or were incapable of provisioning themselves and were in consequence dependent upon the Indians for food, we may grasp the central importance for the colonists of this dawning Indian fear of the Christian God.[12] As Machiavelli understood, physical compulsion is essential but never sufficient; the survival of the rulers depends upon a supplement of coercive belief.

The Indians must be persuaded that the Christian God is all-powerful and committed to the survival of his chosen people, that he will wither the corn and destroy the lives of savages who displease him by disobeying or plotting against the English. We have then a strange paradox: Harriot tests and seems to confirm the most radically subversive hypothesis in his culture about the origin and function of religion by imposing his religion—with all of its most intense claims to transcendence, unique truth, inescapable coercive force—upon others. Not only the official purpose but the survival of the English colony depends upon this imposition. This crucial circumstance is what has licensed the testing in the first place; it is only as an agent of the English colony, dependent upon its purposes and committed to its survival, that Harriot is in a position to disclose the power of human achievements—reading, writing, gunpowder and the like—to appear to the ignorant as divine and hence to promote belief and compel obedience.

Thus the subversiveness which is genuine and radical—sufficiently disturbing so that to be suspected of such beliefs could lead to imprisonment and torture—is at the same time contained by the power it would appear to threaten. Indeed the subversiveness is the very product of that power and furthers its ends. One may go still further and suggest that the power Harriot both serves and embodies not only produces its own subversion but is actively built upon it: in the Virginia colony, the radical undermining of Christian order is not the negative limit but the positive condition for the establishment of the order. And this paradox extends to the production of Harriot's text: *A Brief and True Report,* with its latent heterodoxy, is not a reflection upon the Virginia colony nor even a simple record of it—not, in other words, a privileged withdrawal into a critical zone set apart from power—but a continuation of the colonial enterprise.

By October 1586, there were rumours in England that there was little prospect of profit in Virginia, that the colony had been close to starvation, and that the Indians had turned hostile. Harriot accordingly begins with a descriptive catalogue in which the natural goods of the land are turned into social goods, that is, into 'merchantable commodities': 'Cedar, a very sweet wood and fine timber; whereof if nests of chests be there made, or timber thereof fitted for sweet and fine bedsteads, tables, desks, lutes, virginals, and many things else, . . . [it] will yield profit' (329-30).[13] The inventory of these commodities is followed by an inventory of edible plants and animals, to prove to readers that the colony need not starve, and then by the account of the Indians, to prove that the colony could impose its will upon them. The key to this imposition, as I have argued, is the coercive power of religious belief, and the source of this power is the impression made by advanced technology upon a 'backward' people.

Hence Harriot's text is committed to record what we have called his confirmation of the Machiavellian hypothesis, and hence too this confirmation is not only inaccessible as subversion to those on whom the religion is supposedly imposed but functionally inaccessible to most readers and quite possibly to Harriot himself. It may be that Harriot was demonically conscious of what he was doing—that he found himself situated exactly where he could test one of his culture's darkest fears about its own origins, that he used the Algonkians to do so, and that he wrote a report on his findings, a coded report, of course, since as he wrote to Kepler years later, 'our situation is such that I still may not philosophize freely'.[14] But we do not need such a biographical romance to account for the phenomenon: the

subversiveness, as I have argued, was produced by the colonial power in its own interest, and *A Brief and True Report* was, with perfect appropriateness, published by the great Elizabethan exponent of missionary colonialism, the Reverend Richard Hakluyt.

Yet it is misleading, I think, to conclude without qualification that the radical doubt implicit in Harriot's account is *entirely* contained. Harriot was, after all, hounded through his whole life by charges of atheism and, more tellingly, the remark attributed to Marlowe suggests that it was fully possible for a contemporary to draw the most dangerous conclusions from the Virginia report. Moreover, the 'Atlantic Republican Tradition', as Pocock has argued, does grow out of the 'Machiavellian moment' of the sixteenth century, and that tradition, with its transformation of subjects into citizens, its subordination of transcendent values to capital values, does ultimately undermine, in the interests of a new power, the religious and secular authorities that had licensed the American enterprise in the first place. What we have in Harriot's text is a relation between orthodoxy and subversion that seems, in the same interpretive moment, to be perfectly stable and dangerously volatile.

We can deepen our understanding of this apparent paradox if we consider a second mode of subversion and its containment in Harriot's account. Alongside the *testing* of a subversive interpretation of the dominant culture, we find the *recording* of alien voices or, more precisely, of alien interpretations. The occasion for this recording is another consequence of the English presence in the New World, not in this case the threatened extinction of the tribal religion but the threatened extinction of the tribe: 'There was no town where we had any subtle device practiced against us', Harriot writes, 'but that within a few days after our departure from every such town, the people began to die very fast, and many in short space; in some towns about twenty, in some forty, in some sixty and in one six score, which in truth was very many in respect of their numbers. The disease was so strange, that they neither knew what it was, nor how to cure it; the like by report of the oldest man in the country never happened before, time out of mind' (378).[15] Harriot is writing, of course, about the effects of measles, smallpox, or perhaps simply the common cold upon people with no resistence to them, but a conception of the biological basis of epidemic disease lies far, far in the future. For the English the deaths must be a moral phenomenon—the notion is for them as irresistible as the notion of germs for ourselves—and hence the 'facts' as they are observed are already moralised: the deaths only occurred 'where they used some practice against us', that is, where the Indians conspired secretly against the English. And, with the wonderful self-validating circularity that characterises virtually all powerful constructions of reality, the evidence for these secret conspiracies is precisely the deaths of the Indians.

Now it is not surprising that Harriot seems to endorse the idea that God is protecting his chosen people by killing off untrustworthy Indians; what is surprising is that Harriot is interested in the Indians's own anxious speculations about the unintended but lethal biological warfare that was destroying them. Drawing upon his special familiarity with the priests, he records a remarkable series of conjectures, almost all of which assume—correctly, as we now know—that their misfortune was linked to the presence of the strangers. 'Some people', observing that the English remained healthy while the Indians died, 'could not tell', Harriot writes, 'whether to think us gods or men'; others, seeing that the members of the first colony were all male, concluded that they were not born of women and therefore must be spirits of the dead returned to mortal form (an Algonkian 'Night of the Living Dead'). Some medicine men learned in astrology blamed the disease on a recent eclipse of the sun and on a comet—a theory Harriot considers seriously and rejects—while others shared the prevailing English interpretation and said 'that it was the special work of God' on behalf of the colonists. And some who seem in historical hindsight eerily prescient prophesied 'that there were more of [the English] generation yet to come, to kill theirs and take their places'. The supporters of this theory even worked out a conception of the disease that in some features uncannily resembles our own: 'Those that were immediately to come after us [the first English colonists], they imagined to be in the air, yet invisible and without bodies, and that they by our entreaty and for the love of us did make the people to die . . . by shooting invisible bullets into them' (380).

For a moment, as Harriot records these competing theories, it may seem to a reader as if there were no absolute assurance of God's national interest, as if the drive to displace and absorb the other had given way to conversation among equals, as if all meanings were provisional, as if the signification of events stood apart from power. This impression is intensified for us by our awareness that the theory that would ultimately triumph over the moral conception of epidemic disease was already at least metaphorically present in the conversation. In the very moment that the moral conception is busily authorising itself, it registers the possibility (indeed from our vantage point, the inevitability) of its own destruction.

But why, we must ask ourselves, should power record other voices, permit subversive inquiries, register at its very centre the transgressions that will ultimately violate it? The answer may be in part that power, even in a colonial situation, is not perfectly monolithic and hence may encounter and record in one of its func-

tions materials that can threaten another of its functions; in part that power thrives on vigilance, and human beings are vigilant if they sense a threat; in part that power defines itself in relation to such threats or simply to that which is not identical with it. Harriot's text suggests an intensification of these observations: English power in the first Virginia colony *depends* upon the registering and even the production of such materials. 'These their opinions I have set down the more at large', Harriot tells the 'Adventurers, Favorers, and Wellwishers' of the colony to whom his report is addressed, 'that it may appear unto you that there is good hope they may be brought through discrete dealing and government to the embracing of the truth, and consequently to honor, obey, fear, and love us' (318). The recording of alien voices, their preservation in Harriot's text, is part of the process whereby Indian culture is constituted as a culture and thus brought into the light for study, discipline, correction, transformation. The momentary sense of instability or plenitude—the existence of other voices—is produced by the monological power that ultimately denies the possibility of plenitude, just as the subversive hypothesis about European religion is tested and confirmed only by the imposition of that religion.

We may add that the power of which we are speaking is in effect an allocation method—a way of distributing resources to some and denying them to others, critical resources (here primarily corn and game) that prolong life or, in their absence, extinguish it. In a remarkable study of how societies make 'tragic choices' in the allocation of scarce resources (e.g. kidney machines) or in the determination of high risks (e.g. the military draft), Guido Calabresi and Philip Bobbitt observe that by complex mixtures of approaches, societies attempt to avert 'tragic results, that is, results which imply the rejection of values which are proclaimed to be fundamental'. These approaches may succeed for a time, but it will eventually become apparent that some sacrifice of fundamental values has taken place, whereupon 'fresh mixtures of methods will be tried, structured . . . by the shortcomings of the approaches they replace'. These too will in time give way to others in a 'strategy of successive moves' that comprises an 'intricate game', a game that reflects the simultaneous perception of an inherent flaw and the determination to 'forget' that perception in an illusory resolution.[16] Hence the simple operation of any systematic order, any allocation method, will inevitably run the risk of exposing its own limitations, even (or perhaps especially) as it asserts its underlying moral principle.

This exposure is at its most intense at moments in which a comfortably established ideology confronts unusual circumstances, moments when the moral value of a particular form of power is not merely assumed but explained. We may glimpse such a moment in

Harriot's account of a visit from the colonists' principal Indian ally, the chief Wingina. Wingina was persuaded that the disease decimating his people was indeed the work of the Christian God and had come to request the English to ask their God to direct his lethal magic against an enemy tribe. The colonists tried to explain that such a prayer would be 'ungodly', that their God was indeed responsible for the disease but that, in this as in all things, he would only act 'according to his good pleasure as he had ordained' (379). Indeed if men asked God to make an epidemic he probably would not do it; the English could expect such providential help only if they made sincere 'petition for the contrary,' that is, for harmony and good fellowship in the service of truth and righteousness.

The problem with these assertions is not that they are self-consciously wicked (in the manner of Richard III or Iago) but that they are highly moral and logically coherent; or rather, what is unsettling is one's experience of them; the nasty sense that they are at once irrefutable ethical propositions and pious humbug designed to conceal from the English themselves the rapacity and aggression that is implicit in their very presence. The explanatory moment manifests the self-validating, totalising character of Renaissance political theology—its ability to account for almost every occurrence, even (or above all) apparently perverse or contrary occurrences—and at the same time confirms for us the drastic disillusionment that extends from Machiavelli to its definitive expression in Hume and Voltaire. In his own way, Wingina himself clearly thought his lesson in Christian ethics was polite nonsense. When the disease had in fact spread to his enemies, as it did shortly thereafter, he returned to the English to thank them—I presume with the Algonkian equivalent of a sly wink—for their friendly help, for 'although we satisfied them not in promise, yet in deeds and effect we had fulfilled their desires' (379). For Harriot, this 'marvelous accident', as he calls it, is another sign of the colony's great expectations.

Once again a disturbing vista—a sceptical critique of the function of Christian morality in the New World—is glimpsed only to be immediately closed off. Indeed we may feel at this point that subversion scarcely exists and may legitimately ask ourselves how our perception of the subversive and orthodox is generated. The answer, I think, is that 'subversive' is for us a term used to designate those elements in Renaissance culture that contemporary authorities tried to contain or, when containment seemed impossible, to destroy and that now conform to our own sense of truth and reality. That is, we locate as 'subversive' in the past precisely those things that are *not* subversive to ourselves, that pose no threat to the order by which we live and allocate resources: in Harriot's *Brief and True Report,* the function of illusion in the establishment of religion, the displacement of a providential conception

of disease by one focused on 'invisible bullets', the exposure of the psychological and material interests served by a certain conception of divine power. Conversely, we identify as the principle of order and authority in Renaissance texts things that we would, if we took them seriously, find subversive for ourselves: religious and political absolutism, aristocracy of birth, demonology, humoral psychology, and the like. That we do not find such notions subversive, that we complacently identify them as principles of aesthetic or political order, is a version of the process of containment that licensed what we call the subversive elements in Renaissance texts: that is, our own values are sufficiently strong for us to contain almost effortlessly alien forces. What we find then in Harriot's *Brief and True Report* can best be described by adapting a remark about the possibility of hope that Kafka once made to Max Brod: There is subversion, no end of subversion, only not for us.

I want now to consider the relevance of what I've been saying to our understanding of more complex literary works. It is tempting to focus such remarks on Shakespeare's *Tempest* where Caliban, Prospero's 'salvage and deformed slave' enters cursing the expropriation of his island and exits declaring that he will 'be wise hereafter, / And seek for grace'.[17] What better instance, in the light of Harriot's Virginia, of the containment of a subversive force by the authority that has created that force in the first place: 'This thing of darkness', Prospero says of Caliban at the close, 'I acknowledge mine.'

But I do not want to give the impression that the process I have been describing is applicable only to works that address themselves directly or allusively to the New World. Shakespeare's plays are centrally and repeatedly concerned with the production and containment of subversion and disorder, and the three modes that we have identified in Harriot's text—testing, recording, and explaining—all have their recurrent theatrical equivalents. I am speaking not solely of plays like *Measure for Measure* and *Macbeth,* where authority is obviously subjected to open, sustained, and radical questioning before it is reaffirmed, with ironic reservations, at the close, but of a play like *1 Henry IV* in which authority seems far less problematical. 'Who does not all along see', wrote Upton in the mid eighteenth century, 'that when prince Henry comes to be king he will assume a character suitable to his dignity?' My point is not to dispute this interpretation of the prince as, in Maynard Mack's words, 'an ideal image of the potentialities of the English character',[18] but to observe that such an ideal image involves as its positive condition the constant production of its own radical subversion and the powerful containment of that subversion.

We are continually reminded that Hal is a 'juggler', a conniving hypocrite, and that the power he both serves and comes to embody is glorified usurpation and theft; yet at the same time, we are drawn to the celebration of both the prince and his power. Thus, for example, the scheme of Hal's moral redemption is carefully laid out in his soliloquy at the close of the first tavern scene, but as in the act of *explaining* that we have examined in Harriot, Hal's justification of himself threatens to fall away at every moment into its antithesis. 'By how much better than my word I am', Hal declares, 'By so much shall I falsify men's hopes' (I.ii.210-11). To falsify men's hopes is to exceed their expectations, and it is also to disappoint their expectations, to deceive men, to turn their hopes into fictions, to betray them. Not only are the competing claims of Bolingbroke and Falstaff at issue but our own hopes, the fantasies continually aroused by the play of absolute friendship and trust, limitless playfulness, innate grace, plenitude. But though all of this is in some sense at stake in Hal's soliloquy and though we can perceive at every point, through our own constantly shifting allegiances, the potential instability of the structure of power that has Henry IV at the pinnacle and Robin Ostler, who 'never joy'd since the price of oats rose' (II.i.12), near the bottom, Hal's 'redemption' is as inescapable and inevitable as the outcome of those practical jokes the madcap prince is so fond of playing. Indeed, the play insists, this redemption is not something toward which the action moves but something that is happening at every moment of the theatrical representation.

The same yoking of the unstable and the inevitable may be seen in the play's acts of *recording,* that is, the moments in which we hear voices that seem to dwell in realms apart from that ruled by the potentates of the land. These voices exist and have their apotheosis in Falstaff, but their existence proves to be utterly bound up with Hal, contained politically by his purposes as they are justified aesthetically by his involvement. The perfect emblem of this containment is Falstaff's company, marching off to Shrewsbury: 'discarded unjust servingmen, younger sons to younger brothers, revolted tapsters, and ostlers trade-fall'n, the cankers of a calm world and a long peace' (IV.ii.27-30). These are, as many a homily would tell us, the very types of Elizabethan subversion—masterless men, the natural enemies of social discipline—but they are here pressed into service as defenders of the established order, 'good enough to toss,' as Falstaff tells Hal, 'food for powder, food for powder' (IV.ii.65-6). For power as well as powder, and we may add that this food is produced as well as consumed by the great.

Shakespeare gives us a glimpse of this production in the odd little scene in which Hal, with the connivance of Poins, reduces the puny typster Francis to the mechanical repetition of the word 'Anon':

> *Prince.* Nay, but hark you, Francis: for the sugar thou gavest me, 'twas a pennyworth, was't not?

> *Francis.* O Lord, I would it had been two!
> *Prince.* I will give thee for it a thousand pound. Ask me when thou wilt, and thou shalt have it.

> *Poins.* [*Within*] Francis!
> *Francis.* Anon, anon.
> *Prince.* Anon, Francis? No Francis; but tomorrow, Francis; or, Francis, a' Thursday; or indeed, Francis, when thou wilt.

> (II.iv.58-67)

The Bergsonian comedy in such a moment resides in Hal's exposing a drastic reduction of human possibility: 'That ever this fellow should have fewer words than a parrot,' he says at the scene's end, 'and yet the son of a woman!' (II.iv.98). But the chief interest for us resides in the fact that Hal has himself produced the reduction he exposes. The fact of this production, its theatrical demonstration, implicates Hal not only in the linguistic poverty upon which he plays but in the poverty of the five years of apprenticeship Francis has yet to serve: 'Five year!' Hal exclaims, 'by'r lady, a long lease for the clinking of pewter' (II.iv.45-6). And as the Prince is implicated in the production of this oppressive order, so is he implicated in the impulse to abrogate it: 'But, Francis, darest thou be so valiant as to play the coward with thy indenture, and show it a fair pair of heels and run from it?' (II.iv.46-8). It is tempting to think of this peculiar moment—the Prince awakening the apprentice's discontent—as linked darkly with some supposed uneasiness in Hal about his own apprenticeship,[19] but if so the momentary glimpse of a revolt against authority is closed off at once with a few words of calculated obscurity designed to return Francis to his trade without enabling him to understand why he must do so:

> *Prince.* Why then your brown bastard is your only drink! for look you, Francis, your white canvas doublet will sully. In Barbary, sir, it cannot come to so much.

> *Francis.* What, sir?
> *Poins.* [*Within*] Francis!
> *Prince.* Away, you rogue, dost thou not hear them call?

> (II.iv.73-9)

If Francis takes the earlier suggestion, robs his master and runs away, he will find a place for himself, the play implies, as one of the 'revolted tapsters' in Falstaff's company, men as good as dead long before they march to their deaths as upholders of the crown. Better that he should follow the drift of Hal's deliberately mystifying words and continue to clink pewter. As for the prince, his interest in the brief exchange, beyond what we have already sketched, is suggested by his boast to Poins moments before Francis enters: 'I have sounded the very base-string of humility. Sirrah, I am sworn brother to a leash of drawers and can call them all by their christen names, as Tom, Dick, and Francis' (II.iv.5-8). The prince must sound the base-string of humility if he is to know how to play all of the chords and hence to be the master of the instrument, and his ability to conceal his motives and render opaque his language offers assurance that he himself will not be played on by another.

I have spoken of such scenes in *1 Henry IV* as resembling what in Harriot's text I have called *recording,* a mode that culminates for Harriot in a glossary, the beginnings of an Algonkian-English dictionary, designed to facilitate further acts of recording and hence to consolidate English power in Virginia. The resemblance may be seen most clearly perhaps in Hal's own glossary of tavern slang: 'They call drinking deep, dyeing scarlet: and when you breathe in your watering, they cry 'hem!' and bid you play it off. To conclude, I am so good proficient in one quarter of an hour that I can drink with any tinker in his own language during my life' (II.iv.15-20). The potential value of these lessons, the functional interest to power of recording the speech of an 'under-skinker' and his mates, may be glimpsed in the expressions of loyalty that Hal laughingly recalls: 'They take it already upon their salvation that . . . when I am King of England I shall command all the good lads in Eastcheap' (II.iv.9-15).

There is, it may be objected, something slightly absurd in likening such moments to aspects of Harriot's text; *1 Henry IV* is a play, not a tract for potential investors in a colonial scheme, and the only values we may be sure that Shakespeare had in mind, the argument would go, were theatrical values. But theatrical values do not exist in a realm of privileged literariness, of textual or even institutional self-referentiality. Shakespeare's theatre was not isolated by its wooden walls, nor was it merely the passive reflector of social and ideological forces that lay entirely outside of it: rather the Elizabethan and Jacobean theatre was itself a *social event.* Drama, and artistic expression in general, is never perfectly self-contained and abstract, nor can it be derived satisfactorily from the subjective consciousness of an isolated creator. Collective actions, ritual gestures, paradigms of relationship, and shared images of authority penetrate the work of art, while conversely the socially overdetermined work of art, along with a multitude of other institutions and utterances, contributes to the formation, realignment, and transmission of social practices.

Works of art are, to be sure, marked off in our culture from ordinary utterances, but this demarcation is itself a communal event and signals not the effacement of the social but rather its successful absorption into the work by implication or articulation. This absorption—the presence within the work of its social being—makes it possible, as Bakhtin has argued, for art to survive the disappearance of its enabling social conditions,

where ordinary utterance, more dependent upon the extraverbal pragmatic situation, drifts rapidly toward insignificance or incomprehensibility.[20] Hence art's genius for survival, its delighted reception by audiences for whom it was never intended, does not signal its freedom from all other domains of life, nor does its inward articulation of the social confer upon it a formal coherence independent of the world outside its boundaries. On the contrary, artistic form itself is the expression of social evaluations and practices.

One might add that *1 Henry IV* itself insists that it is quite impossible to keep the interests of the theatre hermetically sealed off from the interests of power. Hal's characteristic activity is playing or, more precisely, theatrical improvisation—his parts include his father, Hotspur, Hotspur's wife, a thief in buckram, himself as prodigal and himself as penitent—and he fully understands his own behaviour through most of the play as a role that he is performing. We might expect that this role-playing gives way at the end to his true identity—'I shall hereafter', Hal has promised his father, 'be more myself' (III.ii.92-3)—but with the killing of Hotspur, Hal clearly does not reject all theatrical masks but rather replaces one with another. 'The time will come', Hal declares midway through the play, 'That I shall make this northern youth exchange / His glorious deeds for my indignities' (III.ii.144-6); when that time *has* come, at the play's close, Hal hides with his 'favours' (that is, a scarf or other emblem, but the word also has in the sixteenth century the sense of 'face') the dead Hotspur's 'mangled face' (V.iv.96), as if to mark the completion of the exchange.

Theatricality then is not set over against power but is one of power's essential modes. In lines that anticipate Hal's promise, the angry Henry IV tells Worcester, 'I will from henceforth rather be myself, / Mighty and to be fear'd, than my condition' (I.iii.5-6). 'To be oneself' here means to perform one's part in the scheme of power as opposed to one's natural disposition, or what we would normally designate as the very core of the self. Indeed it is by no means clear that such a thing as a natural disposition exists in the play as anything more than a theatrical fiction; we recall that in Falstaff's hands 'instinct' itself becomes a piece of histrionic rhetoric, an improvised excuse when he is confronted with the shame of his flight from the masked prince: 'Beware instinct—the lion will not touch the true prince. Instinct is a great matter; I was now a coward on instinct. I shall think the better of myself, and thee, during my life; I for a valiant lion, and thou for a true prince' (II.iv.271-5). Both claims—Falstaff's to natural valour, Hal's to legitimate royalty—are, the lines darkly imply, of equal merit.

Again and again in *1 Henry IV* we are tantalised by the possibility of an escape from theatricality and hence from the constant pressure of improvisational power, but we are, after all, in the theatre, and our pleasure depends upon the fact that there is no escape, and our applause ratifies the triumph of our confinement. The play then operates in the manner of its central character, charming us with its visions of breadth and solidarity, 'redeeming' itself in the end by betraying our hopes, and earning with this betrayal our slightly anxious admiration. Hence the odd balance in this play of spaciousness—the constant multiplication of separate, vividly realised realms—and claustrophobia—the absorption of all of these realms by a power at once vital and impoverished. The balance is almost eerily perfect, as if Shakespeare had somehow reached through in *1 Henry IV* to the very centre of the system of opposed and interlocking forces that held Tudor society together.

When we turn, however, to the plays that continue the chronicle of Hal's career, *2 Henry IV* and *Henry V*, not only do we find that the forces balanced in the earlier play have pulled apart—the claustrophobia triumphant in *2 Henry IV*, the spaciousness triumphant in *Henry V*—but that from this new perspective the familiar view of *1 Henry IV* as a perfectly poised play must be revised. What appeared as 'balance' may on closer inspection seem like radical instability tricked out as moral or aesthetic order; what appeared as clarity may seem now like a conjurer's trick concealing confusion in order to buy time and stave off the collapse of an illusion. Not waving but drowning.

2 Henry IV makes the characteristic operations of power less equivocal than they had been in the preceding play: there is no longer even the lingering illusion of distinct realms, each with its own system of values, its soaring visions of plenitude, and its bad dreams. There is manifestly a single system now, one based on predation and betrayal. Hotspur's intoxicating dreams of honour are dead, replaced entirely by the cold rebellion of cunning but impotent schemers. The warm, roistering sounds overheard in the tavern—sounds that seemed to signal a subversive alternative to rebellion—turn out to be the noise of a whore and bully beating a customer to death. And Falstaff, whose earlier larcenies were gilded by fantasies of innate grace, now talks of turning diseases to commodity (I.ii.234-5).

Only Prince Hal seems, in comparison to the earlier play, less meanly calculating, subject now to fits of weariness and confusion, though this change serves less, I think, to humanise him (as Auerbach argued in a famous essay) than to make it clear that the betrayals are systematic. They happen to him and for him. He needn't any longer soliloquise his intention to 'Falsify men's hopes' by selling his wastrel friends: the sale will be brought about by the structure of things, a structure grasped in this play under the twinned names of time and necessity. So too there is no longer any need for heroic combat with a dangerous, glittering

enemy like Hotspur (the only reminder of whose voice in this play is Pistol's parody of Marlovian swaggering); the rebels are deftly if ingloriously dispatched by the false promises of Hal's younger brother, the primly virtuous John of Lancaster. To seal his lies, Lancaster swears fittingly 'by the honour of my blood'—the cold blood, as Falstaff observes of Hal, that he inherited from his father.

The 'recording' of alien voices—the voices of those who have no power to leave literate traces of their existence—continues in this play, but without even the theatrical illusion of princely complicity. The king is still convinced that his son is a prodigal and that the kingdom will fall to ruin after his death—there is a certain peculiar consolation in the thought—but it is no longer Hal alone who declares (against all appearances) his secret commitment to disciplinary authority. Warwick assures the king that the prince's interests in the good lads of Eastcheap are entirely what they should be:

> The Prince but studies his companions
> Like a strange tongue, wherein, to gain the
>   language,
> 'Tis needful that the most immodest word
> Be look'd upon and learnt, which once
>   attain'd,
> Your Highness knows, comes to no further
>   use
> But to be known and hated. So, like gross
>   terms,
> The Prince will in the perfectness of time
> Cast off his followers, and their memory
> Shall as a pattern or a measure live,
> By which his Grace must mete the lives of
>   other,
> Turning past evils to advantages.
>
> (IV.iv.68-78)

At first the language analogy likens the prince's low-life excursions to the search for proficiency: perfect linguistic competence, the 'mastery' of a language, requires the fullest possible vocabulary. But the darkness of Warwick's words—'to be known and hated'—immediately pushes the goal of Hal's linguistic researches beyond proficiency. When in *1 Henry IV* Hal boasts of his mastery of tavern slang, we are allowed for a moment at least to imagine that we are witnessing a social bond, the human fellowship of the extremest top and bottom of society in a homely ritual act of drinking together. The play may make it clear, as I have argued, that there are well-defined political interests involved, but these interests may be bracketed, if only briefly, for the pleasure of imagining what Victor Turner calls 'communitas'—a union based on the momentary breaking of the hierarchical order that normally governs a community.[21] And even when we pull back from this spacious sense of union, we are permitted for much of the play to take pleasure at the least in Hal's surprising skill, the proficiency he rightly celebrates in himself.

To learn another language is to acknowledge the existence of another people and to acquire the ability to function, however crudely, within its social world. Hal's remark about drinking with any tinker in his own language suggests, if only jocularly, that for him the lower classes are virtually another people, an alien tribe—immensely more populous than his own—within the kingdom. That this perception extended beyond the confines of Shakespeare's play is suggested by the evidence that middle- and upper-class English settlers in the New World regarded the American Indians less as another race than as a version of their own lower classes; one man's tinker is another man's Indian.[22]

If Hal's glossary initially seems to resemble Harriot's, Warwick's account of Hal's practice quickly drives it past the functionalism of the word-list in the *Brief and True Report,* with its Algonkian equivalents for fire, food, shelter, and toward a different kind of glossary, one more specifically linked to the attempt to understand and control the lower classes. I refer to the sinister glossaries appended to sixteenth-century accounts of criminals and vagabounds. 'Here I set before the good reader the lewd, lousy language of these loitering lusks and lazy lorels', announces Thomas Harman, as he introduces (with a comical flourish designed to display his own rhetorical gifts) what he claims is an authentic list, compiled at great personal cost.[23] His pamphlet, *A Caveat for Common Cursitors,* is the fruit, he declares, of personal research, difficult because his informants are 'marvellous subtle and crafty'. But 'with fair flattering words, money, and good cheer', he has learned much about their ways, 'not without faithful promise made unto them never to discover their names or anything they showed me' (82). Harman cheerfully goes on to publish what they showed him, and he ends his work not only with a glossary of 'peddlar's French' but with an alphabetical list of names, so that the laws made for 'the extreme punishment' of these wicked idlers may be enforced.

It is not at all clear that Harman's subjects—upright men, doxies, Abraham men, and the like—bear any relation to social reality, any more than it is clear in the case of Doll Tearsheet or Mistress Quickly. Much of the *Caveat,* like the other cony-catching pamphlets of the period, has the air of a jest book: time-honoured tales of tricksters and rogues, dished out cunningly as realistic observation. (It is not encouraging that the rogues' term for the stocks in which they were punished, according to Harman, is 'the harmans'.) But Harman is quite concerned to convey at least the impression of accurate observation and recording—clearly, this was among the book's selling points—and one of the principal rhetorical devices he uses to do so is the spice of betrayal: he repeatedly calls attention to his solemn promises never to reveal anything that he has been told, for his breaking of his word serves as an assurance of the accuracy and importance of what he reveals.

A middle-class Prince Hal, Harman claims that through dissembling he has gained access to a world normally hidden from his kind, and he will turn that access to the advantage of the kingdom by helping his readers to identify and eradicate the dissemblers in their midst. Harman's own personal interventions—the acts of detection and apprehension he proudly reports (or invents)—are not enough: only his book can fully expose the cunning sleights of the rogues and thereby induce the justices and shrieves to be more vigilant and punitive. Just as theatricality is thematised in the *Henry IV* plays as one of the crucial agents of royal power, so in the *Caveat for Common Cursitors* (and in much of the cony-catching literature of the period in England and France) printing is represented in the text itself as a force for social order and the detection of criminal fraud. The printed book can be widely disseminated and easily revised, so that the vagabonds' names and tricks may be known before they themselves arrive at an honest citizen's door; as if this mobility weren't quite tangible enough, Harman claims that when his pamphlet was only half-way printed, his printer helped him apprehend a particularly cunning 'counterfeit crank'—a pretended epileptic. In Harman's account the printer turns detective, first running down the street to apprehend the dissembler, then on a subsequent occasion luring him 'with fair allusions' (116) and a show of charity into the hands of the constable. With such lurid tales Harman literalises the power of the book to hunt down vagabonds and bring them to justice.

The danger of such accounts, of course, is that the ethical charge will reverse itself: the forces of order—the people, as it were, of the book—will be revealed as themselves dependent on dissembling and betrayal, and the vagabonds either as less fortunate and well-protected imitators of their betters or, alternatively, as primitive rebels against the hypocrisy of a cruel society. Exactly such a reversal seems to occur again and again in the rogue literature of the period, from the doxies and morts who answer Harman's rebukes with unfailing if spare dignity to the more articulate defenders of vice elsewhere who insist that their lives are at worst imitations of the lives of the great:

> Though your experience in the world be not so great as mine [says a cunning cheater at dice], yet am I sure ye see that no man is able to live an honest man unless he have some privy way to help himself withal, more than the world is witness of. Think you the noblemen could do as they do, if in this hard world they should maintain so great a port only upon their rent? Think you the lawyers could be such purchasers if their pleas were short, and all their judgements, justice and conscience?

Suppose ye that offices would be so dearly bought, and the buyers so soon enriched, if they counted not pillage an honest point of purchase? Could merchants, without lies, false making their wares, and selling them by a crooked light, to deceive the chapman in the thread or colour, grow so soon rich and to a baron's possessions, and make all their posterity gentlemen?[24]

Yet though these reversals are at the very heart of the rogue literature, it would be as much of a mistake to regard their final effect as subversion as it would be to regard in a similar light the comparable passages—most often articulated by Falstaff—in Shakespeare's histories. The subversive voices are produced by the affirmations of order, and they are powerfully registered, but they do not undermine that order. Indeed as the example of Harman—so much cruder than Shakespeare—suggests, the order is neither possible nor fully convincing without both the presence and perception of betrayal.

This dependence on betrayal does not prevent Harman from levelling charges of hypocrisy and deep dissembling at the rogues and from urging his readers to despise and prosecute them. On the contrary, Harman's moral indignation seems paradoxically heightened by his own implication in the deceitfulness that he condemns, as if the rhetorical violence of the condemnation cleansed him of any guilt. His broken promises are acts of civility, necessary strategies for securing social well-being. The 'rowsy, ragged rabblement of rakehells' has put itself outside the bounds of civil conversation; justice consists precisely in taking whatever measures are necessary to eradicate them. Harman's false oaths are the means of identifying and ridding the community of the purveyors of false oaths. The pestilent few will 'fret, fume, swear, and stare at this my book' in which their practices, disclosed after they had received fair promises of confidentiality, are laid open, but the majority will band together in righteous reproach: 'the honourable will abhor them, the worshipful will reject them, the yeomen will sharply taunt them, the husbandmen utterly defy them, the labouring men bluntly chide them, the women with clapping hands cry out at them' (84). To like reading about vagabonds is to hate them and to approve of their ruthless betrayal.

'The right people of the play', a gifted critic of 2 Henry IV observes, 'merge into a larger order; the wrong people resist or misuse that larger order'.[25] True enough, but like Harman's happy community of vagabond-haters, the 'larger order' of the Lancastrian State seems, in this play, to batten on the breaking of oaths. Shakespeare does not shrink from any of the felt nastiness implicit in this sorting out of the right people and the wrong people; he takes the discursive mode that he could have found in Harman and a hundred other texts and inten-

sifies it, so that the founding of the modern State, like the founding of the modern prince, is shown to be based upon acts of calculation, intimidation, and deceit. And the demonstration of these acts is rendered an entertainment for which an audience, subject to just this State, will pay money and applaud.

There is, throughout 2 Henry IV a sense of constriction that the obsessive enumeration of details—'Thou didst swear to me upon a parcel-gilt goblet, sitting in my Dolphin chamber, at the round table by a sea-coal fire, upon Wednesday in Wheeson week. . . .'—only intensifies. We may find, in Justice Shallow's garden, a few twilight moments of release from this oppressive circumstantial and strategic constriction, but Falstaff mercilessly deflates them—and the puncturing is so wonderfully adroit, so amusing, that we welcome it: 'I do remember him at Clement's Inn, like a man made after supper of a cheese-paring. When 'a was naked, he was for all the world like a forked radish, with a head fantastically carv'd upon it with a knife' (III.ii.308-12).

What is left is the law of nature: the strong eat the weak. Yet this is not quite what Shakespeare invites the audience to affirm through its applause. Like Harman, Shakespeare refuses to endorse so baldly cynical a conception of the social order; instead actions that should have the effect of radically undermining authority turn out to be the props of that authority. In this play, even more cruelly than in I Henry IV, moral values—justice, order, civility—are secured paradoxically through the apparent generation of their subversive contraries. Out of the squalid betrayals that preserve the State emerges the 'formal majesty' into which Hal at the close, through a final, definitive betrayal—the rejection of Falstaff—merges himself.

There are moments in Richard II in which the collapse of kingship seems to be confirmed in the discovery of the physical body of the ruler, the pathos of his creatural existence:

> . . . throw away respect,
> Tradition, form, and ceremonious duty,
> For you have but mistook me all this while.
> I live with bread like you, feel want,
> Taste grief, need friends: subjected thus,
> How can you say to me I am a king?
>
> (III.ii.172-7)

By the close of 2 Henry IV such physical limitations have been absorbed into the ideological structure, and hence justification, of kingship. It is precisely because Prince Hal lives with bread that we can understand the sacrifice that he and, for that matter, his father, have made. Unlike Richard II, Henry IV's articulation of this sacrifice is rendered by Shakespeare not as a piece of histrionic rhetoric but as a private meditation, the innermost thoughts of a troubled, weary man:

Why rather, sleep, liest thou in smoky cribs,
Upon uneasy pallets stretching thee,
And hush'd with buzzing night-flies to thy
   slumber,
Than in the perfum'd chambers of the great,
Under the canopies of costly state,
And lull'd with sound of sweetest melody?
                                        (III.i.9-14)

Who knows? perhaps it is even true; perhaps in a society in which the overwhelming majority of men and women had next to nothing, the few who were rich and powerful did lie awake at night. But we should understand that this sleeplessness was not a well-kept secret: the sufferings of the great are one of the familiar themes in the literature of the governing classes in the sixteenth century. Henry IV speaks in soliloquy, but as is so often the case in Shakespeare his isolation only intensifies the sense that he is addressing a large audience: the audience of the theatre. We are invited to take measure of his suffering, to understand—here and elsewhere in the play—the costs of power. And we are invited to understand these costs in order to ratify the power, to accept the grotesque and cruelly unequal distribution of possessions: everything to the few, nothing to the many. The rulers earn, or at least pay for, their exalted position through suffering, and this suffering ennobles, if it does not exactly cleanse, the lies and betrayals upon which this position depends.

As so often Falstaff parodies this ideology, or rather—and more significantly—presents it as humbug *before* it makes its appearance as official truth. Called away from the tavern to the court, Falstaff turns to Doll and Mistress Quickly and proclaims sententiously: 'You see, my good wenches, how men of merit are sought after. The undeserver may sleep when the man of action is called on' (II.iv.374-7). Seconds later this rhetoric—marked out as something with which to impress whores and innkeepers to whom one owes money one does not intend to pay—recurs in the speech, and by convention of the soliloquy, the innermost thoughts of the king.

At such moments *2 Henry IV* seems to be testing and confirming an extremely dark and disturbing hypothesis about the nature of monarchical power in England: that its moral authority rests upon a hypocrisy so deep that the hypocrites themselves believe it. 'Then (happy) low, lie down! / Uneasy lies the head that wears a crown' (III.i.30-1): so the old pike tells the young dace. But the old pike actually seems to believe in his own speeches, just as he may believe that he never really sought the crown, 'But that necessity so bow'd the state / That I and greatness were compell'd to kiss' (III.i.72-3). We who have privileged knowledge of the network of State betrayals and privileged access to Falstaff's cynical wisdom can make this opaque hypocrisy transparent. And yet even in *2 Henry IV*, where the lies and the self-serving sentiments are utterly in-

escapable, where the illegitimacy of legitimate authority is repeatedly demonstrated, where the whole State seems—to adapt More's phrase—a conspiracy of the great to enrich and protect their interests under the name of commonwealth, even here the audience does not leave the theatre in a rebellious mood. Once again, though in a still more iron-age spirit than at the close of *1 Henry IV*, the play appears to ratify the established order, with the new-crowned Henry V merging his body into 'the great body of our state', with Falstaff despised and rejected, and with Lancaster—the cold-hearted betrayer of the rebels—left to admire his still more cold-hearted brother: 'I like this fair proceeding of the King's' (V.v.97).

The mood at the close remains, to be sure, an unpleasant one—the rejection of Falstaff has been one of the nagging 'problems' of Shakespearean criticism—but the discomfort only serves to verify Hal's claim that he has turned away his former self. If there is frustration at the harshness of the play's end, the frustration is confirmation of a carefully plotted official strategy whereby subversive perceptions are at once produced and contained:

My father is gone wild into his grave;
For in his tomb lie my affections,
And with his spirits sadly I survive,
To mock the expectation of the world,
To frustrate prophecies, and to rase out
Rotten opinion. . . .
                                        (V.ii.123-8)

The first part of *Henry IV* enables us to feel at moments that we are like Harriot, surveying a complex new world, testing upon it dark thoughts without damaging the order that those thoughts would seem to threaten. The second part of *Henry IV* suggests that we are still more like the Indians, compelled to pay homage to a system of beliefs whose fraudulence somehow only confirms their power, authenticity, and truth. The concluding play in the series, *Henry V*, insists that we have all along been both coloniser and colonised, king and subject. The play deftly registers every nuance of royal hypocrisy, ruthlessness, and bad faith, but it does so in the context of a celebration, a collective panegyric to 'This star of England', the charismatic leader who purges the commonwealth of its incorrigibles and forges the martial national State.

By yoking together diverse peoples—represented in the play by the Welshman Fluellen, the Irishman Macmorris, and the Scotsman Jamy, who fight at Agincourt alongside the loyal Englishmen—Hal symbolically tames the last wild areas in the British Isles, areas that in the sixteenth century represented, far more powerfully than any New World people, the doomed outposts of a vanishing tribalism. He does so, obviously, by launching a war of conquest against the

French, but his military campaign is itself depicted as carefully founded upon acts of what I have called 'explaining'. The play opens with a notoriously elaborate account of the king's genealogical claim to the French throne, and, as we found in the comparable instances in Harriot, this ideological justification of English policy is an unsettling mixture of 'impeccable' reasoning[26] (once its initial premises are accepted) and gross self-interest. The longer the Archbishop of Canterbury continues to spin out the public justifications for an invasion he has privately said would relieve financial pressure on the Church, the more the audience is driven toward scepticism. None of the subsequent attempts at explanation and justification offers much relief: Hal continually warns his victims that they are bringing pillage and rape upon themselves by resisting him, but from the head of an invading army these arguments lack a certain moral force. Similarly, Hal's meditation on the sufferings of the great—'What infinite heart's ease / Must kings neglect that private men enjoy!'—suffers a bit from the fact that he is almost single-handedly responsible for a war that by his own account and that of the enemy is causing immense civilian misery. And after watching a scene in which anxious, frightened troops sleeplessly await the dawn, it is difficult to be fully persuaded by Hal's climactic vision of the 'slave' and 'peasant' sleeping comfortably, little knowing 'What watch the King keeps to maintain the peace' (IV.i.283).

This apparent subversion of the glorification of the monarch has led some recent critics to view the panegyric as bitterly ironic or to argue, more plausibly, that Shakespeare's depiction of Henry V is radically ambiguous.[27] But in the light of Harriot's *Brief and True Report,* we may suggest that the subversive doubts the play continually awakens serve paradoxically to intensify the power of the king and his war, even while they cast shadows upon this power. The shadows are real enough, but they are deferred—deferred until after Essex's campaign in Ireland, after Elizabeth's reign, after the monarchy itself as a significant political institution. Deferred indeed even today, for in the wake of full-scale ironic readings and at a time in which it no longer seems to matter very much, it is not at all clear that *Henry V* can be successfully performed as subversive. For the play's enhancement of royal power is not only a matter of the deferral of doubt: the very doubts that Shakespeare raises serve not to rob the king of his charisma but to heighten it, precisely as they heighten the theatrical interest of the play; the doubt-less celebrations of royal power with which the period abounds have no theatrical force and have long since fallen into oblivion.

The audience's tension then enhances its attention; prodded by constant reminders of a gap between real and ideal, facts and values, the spectators are induced to make up the difference, to invest in the illusion of

magnificence, to be dazzled by their own imaginary identification with the conqueror. The ideal king must be in large part the invention of the audience, the product of a will to conquer which is revealed to be identical to a need to submit. *Henry V* is remarkably self-conscious about this dependence upon the audience's powers of invention. The prologue's opening lines invoke a form of theatre radically unlike the one that is about to unfold: 'A kingdom for a stage, princes to act, / And monarchs to behold the swelling scene!' (3-4). In such a theatre-State there would be no social distinction between the king and the spectator, the performer and the audience; all would be royal, and the role of the performance would be to transform not an actor into a king but a king into a god: 'Then should the warlike Harry, like himself, / Assume the port of Mars' (5-6). This is in effect the fantasy acted out in royal masques, but Shakespeare is intensely aware that his theatre is not a courtly entertainment, that his actors are 'flat unraised spirits,' and that his spectators are hardly monarchs—'gentles all', he calls them, with fine flattery. 'Let us', the prologue begs the audience, 'On your imaginary forces work . . . For 'tis your thoughts that now must deck our kings' (18, 28). This 'must' is cast in the form of an appeal and an apology—the consequence of the miserable limitations of 'this unworthy scaffold'—but the necessity extends, I suggest, beyond the stage: all kings are 'decked' out by the imaginary forces of the spectators, and a sense of the limitations of king or theatre only excites a more compelling exercise of those forces.

To understand Shakespeare's whole conception of Hal, from rakehell to monarch, we need in effect a poetics of Elizabethan power, and this in turn will prove inseparable, in crucial respects, from a poetics of the theatre. Testing, recording, and explaining are elements in this poetics that is inseparably bound up with the figure of Queen Elizabeth, a ruler without a standing army, without a highly developed bureaucracy, without an extensive police force, a ruler whose power is constituted in theatrical celebrations of royal glory and theatrical violence visited upon the enemies of that glory. Power that relies upon a massive police apparatus, a strong, middle-class nuclear family, an elaborate school system, power that dreams of a panopticon in which the most intimate secrets are open to the view of an invisible authority, such power will have as its appropriate aesthetic form the realist novel;[28] Elizabethan power, by contrast, depends upon its privileged visibility. As in a theatre, the audience must be powerfully engaged by this visible presence while at the same time held at a certain respectful distance from it. 'We princes', Elizabeth told a deputation of Lords and Common in 1586, 'are set on stages in the sight and view of all the world.'[29]

Royal power is manifested to its subjects as in a theatre, and the subjects are at once absorbed by the instructive, delightful, or terrible spectacles, and forbidden intervention or deep intimacy. The play of authority depends upon spectators—'For 'tis your thoughts that now must deck our kings'—but the performance is made to seem entirely beyond the control of those whose 'imaginary forces' actually confer upon it its significance and force. These matters, Thomas More imagines the common people saying of one such spectacle, 'be king's games, as it were stage plays, and for the more part played upon scaffolds. In which poor men be but the lookers-on. And they that wise be will meddle no farther.'[30] Within this theatrical setting, there is a remarkable insistence upon the paradoxes, ambiguities, and tensions of authority, but this apparent production of subversion is, as we have already seen, the very condition of power. I should add that this condition is not a theoretical necessity of theatrical power in general but an historical phenomenon, the particular mode of this particular culture. 'In sixteenth century England', writes Clifford Geertz, comparing Elizabethan and Majapahit royal progresses, 'the political centre of society was the point at which the tension between the passions that power excited and the ideals it was supposed to serve was screwed to its highest pitch. . . . In fourteenth century Java, the centre was the point at which such tension disappeared in a blaze of cosmic symmetry.'[31]

It is precisely because of the English form of absolutist theatricality that Shakespeare's drama, written for a theatre subject to State censorship, can be so relentlessly subversive: the form itself, as a primary expression of Renaissance power, contains the radical doubts it continually provokes. There are moments in Shakespeare's career—*King Lear* is the greatest example—in which the process of containment is strained to the breaking point, but the histories consistently pull back from such extreme pressure. And we are free to locate and pay homage to the plays' doubts only because they no longer threaten us. There is subversion, no end of subversion, only not for us.

Notes

[1] John Bakeless, *The Tragicall History of Christopher Marlowe,* 2 vols. (Cambridge, Mass.: Harvard University Press, 1942), I, 111.

[2] On Harriot see especially *Thomas Harriot, Renaissance Scientist,* ed. John W. Shirley (Oxford University Press, 1974); also Muriel Rukeyser, *The Traces of Thomas Harriot* (New York: Random House, 1970), and Jean Jacquot, 'Thomas Harriot's Reputation for Impiety', *Notes and Records of the Royal Society,* 9 (1952), 164-87.

[3] John Aubrey, *Brief Lives,* ed. Andrew Clark, 2 vols. (Oxford University Press, 1898), I, 286.

[4] For the investigation of Ralegh, see *Willobie His Avisa* (1594), ed. G. B. Harrison (London: John Lane, 1926), appendix 3, pp. 255-71.

[5] See, for example, *The Historie of Travell into Virginia Britania* (1612), ed. Louis B. Wright and Virginia Freund (London: Hakluyt Society, 2nd. ser., no. 103, 1953), p. 101.

[6] Jacquot, 'Thomas Harriot's Reputation for Impiety', p. 167.

[7] See for instance Richard Baines's version of Marlowe's version of this argument: C. F. Tucker Brooke, *The Life of Marlowe* (London: Methuen, 1930), appendix 9, p. 98.

[8] Niccolò Machiavelli, *Discourses,* trans. Christian Detmold (New York: Random House, 1950), p. 146. See also *The Prince* in *Tutte le opere di Niccolò Machiavelli,* ed. Francesco Flora and Carlo Cordiè, 2 vols. (Rome: Arnoldo Mondadori, 1949), I, 18.

[9] Kyd is quoted in Brooke, *Life of Marlowe,* appendix 12, p. 107; Parsons in Ernest A. Strathmann, *Sir Walter Ralegh* (New York: Columbia University Press, 1951), p. 25.

[10] Quoted in Jean Jacquot, 'Ralegh's "Hellish Verses" and the "Tragicall Raigne of Selimus" ', *Modern Language Review,* 48 (1953), 1.

[11] Thomas Harriot, *A Briefe and True Report of the New Found Land of Virginia* (1588), in *The Roanoke Voyages, 1584-1590,* ed. David Beers Quinn, 2 vols. (London: Hakluyt Society, 2nd ser., no. 104, 1955), p. 375. (Quotations are modernised here.) On the Algonkians of southern New England see Bruce G. Trigger, ed., *Handbook of North American Indians:* vol. 15, *Northeast* (Washington, D.C.: Smithsonian, 1978).

[12] Cf. Richard Hakluyt, *The Principal Navigations, Voyages, Traffiques, & Discoveries of the English Nation,* 12 vols. (Glasgow: James Maclehose, 1903-5), X, 54, 56.

[13] On these catalogues, see Wayne Franklin, *Discoverers, Explorers, Settlers: the Diligent Writers of Early America* (University of Chicago Press, 1979), pp. 69-122.

[14] Quoted by Edward Rosen, 'Harriot's Science: the Intellectual Background', in *Thomas Harriot,* ed. Shirley, p. 4.

[15] Cf. Walter Bigges's account of Drake's visit to Florida in 1586, in *The Roanoke Voyages,* I, 306.

[16] Guido Calabresi and Philip Bobbitt, *Tragic Choices* (New York: Norton, 1978), p. 195. The term *tragic* is, I think, misleading.

[17] V.i.295-6. All citations of Shakespeare are to *The Riverside Shakespeare,* ed. G. Blakemore Evans (Boston: Houghton Mifflin, 1974).

[18] John Upton, *Critical Observations on Shakespeare* (1748), in *Shakespeare, the Critical Heritage,* ed. Brian Vickers, vol. 3: *1733-1752* (London: Routledge, 1975), p. 297; Maynard Mack, introduction to Signet Classic edition of *1 Henry IV* (New York: New American Library, 1965), p. xxxv.

[19] See S. P. Zitner, 'Anon, Anon: or, a Mirror for a Magistrate', *Shakespeare Quarterly,* 19 (1968), 63-70.

[20] See V. N. Volosinov, *Freudianism: a Marxist Critique,* trans. I. R. Titunik, ed. Neal H. Bruss (New York: Academic Press, 1976), pp. 93-116; the book was written by Bakhtin and published under Volosinov's name.

[21] See, for example, Victor Turner, *Drama, Fields, and Metaphors: Symbolic Action in Human Society* (Ithaca: Cornell University Press, 1974).

[22] See Karen Ordahl Kupperman, *Settling with the Indians: the Meeting of English and Indian Cultures in America, 1580-1640* (Totawa, N.J.: Rowman and Littlefield, 1980).

[23] Thomas Harman, *A Caveat of Warening, for Commen Cursetors Vulgarely Called Vagabones* (1566), in G mini Salg do, ed., *Cony-Catchers and Bawdy Baskets* (Harmondsworth: Penguin, 1972), p. 146.

[24] Gilbert Walker?, *A manifest detection of the moste vyle and detestable use of Diceplay* (c. 1552), in Salg do, *Cony-Catchers,* pp. 42-3.

[25] Norman N. Holland, in the Signet Classic edition of *2 Henry IV* (New York: New American Library, 1965). p.xxxvi.

[26] So says J. H. Walter in the New Arden edition of *Henry V* (London: Methuen, 1954), p. xxv.

[27] See the illuminating discussion in Norman Rabkin, *Shakespeare and the Problem of Meaning* (University of Chicago Press, 1981), pp. 33-62.

[28] For a brilliant exploration of this hypothesis, see D. A. Miller, 'The Novel and the Police', *Glyph,* 8 (1981), 127-47.

[29] Quoted in J. E. Neale, *Elizabeth I and her Parliaments, 1584 -1601,* 2 vols. (London: Cape, 1965), II, 119.

[30] *The History of King Richard III,* ed. R. S. Sylvester, in *The Complete Works of St Thomas More,* vol. 3 (New Haven: Yale University Press, 1963), p. 80.

[31] Clifford Geertz, 'Centers, Kings and Charisma: Reflections on the Symbolics of Power', in *Culture and its Creators: Essays in Honour of Edward Shils,* ed. Joseph Ben-David and Terry Nichols Clark (University of Chicago Press, 1977), p. 160.

Sections of 'this article originally appeared in *Glyph 8: Johns Hopkins Textual Studies* (Baltimore: Johns Hopkins University Press, 1981), pp. 40-61.

F. Nick Clary (essay date 1988)

SOURCE: "Reformation and Its Counterfeit: The Recovery of Meaning in *Henry IV, Part One,*" in *Ambiguities in Literature and Film: Selected Papers from the Seventh Annual Flordia State University Conference on Literature and Film,* edited by Hans P. Braendlin, Florida State University Press, 1988, pp. 76-94.

[*In the following essay, Clary suggests that an interpretation of Hal's character—that is, whether he indeed reforms or whether he is Machiavellian in his actions—depends upon an audience's perspective of human nature.*]

After a little tavern "play" designed to prepare Hal for a meeting with his father at court, Falstaff advises the Prince: "never call a true piece of gold a counterfeit." One editor prints, "thou art essentially mad, without seeming so," as Falstaff's next line. However, he glosses "essentially made" in his note for the line in question.[1] The Variorum editors list over three dozen entries which elaborate the controversy over this passage. Although the edition quoted above does not mention this controversy, the combination of the line and its gloss could provoke a similar confusion among readers unfamiliar with the available scholarship. The edition to which I have referred bears the label "An Authorized Text" on the title page; however, the paperback cover advertises "An Authoritative Text." I am not sure which label the editor would approve, and I hesitate to guess whether the author would consider this "revised" version of his play "a true piece of gold" or "a counterfeit."

From the earliest commentaries to the most recent critical studies, Shakespeare's Prince Hal has been the subject of persistent and varied controversy.[2] Literary scholars, however, have not so much created the controversy as revealed its inevitability; if the playwright has not written an intentionally ambiguous work, he has at least constructed a text that reveals the difficulties of interpretation. From the moment that Hal is first mentioned near the end of *Richard II* (V, iii), his words and actions are the objects of onstage commentary from every quarter.[3] The experience of Shakespeare's plays about Prince Hal approximates, in some respects, the reading of several source accounts concerning the exploits of Henry Monmouth.

Among the broad range of pre-Shakespearian sources, there is considerable variation. Whether the source is historical or nonhistorical in its methods, moral or political in its ideals, each interpretation is an effect of a particular appropriation of Prince Hal as a model and a testament to specific beliefs about the causes that shape events and the forces that govern the transformations in human character and behavior.[4] Conflicts of interpretation, which are the legacy of diversified source records, may have been a central concern of Shakespeare in his second historical tetralogy. Problems of interpretation will be my concern in this present reading of *Henry IV, Part One.*

In Shakespeare's earliest reference to Hal *(Richard II,* V, iii), the newly crowned King expresses concern about the political effect of his son's "madcap" behavior.[5] Although he has not seen the Prince for three months, Henry has heard rumors that Hal has been haunting the taverns of London. When he urges the nobles gathered at Windsor Castle to find out what they can about his son, his anxiety is clear: "If any plague hang over us, 'tis he." Hotspur is quick to report that he has seen Hal and told him of the jousting matches to be held at Oxford. Hal's answer, that he would go the "stews, / And from the common'st creature pluck a glove" to wear as a "favor" (V, iii, 16-19), would seem to confirm the King's suspicions. Yet Henry reads in this reply "some sparks of better hope, which elder years / May happily bring forth" (V, iii, 21-22).

Later, in the first scene of *Henry IV, Part One,* the King once again laments the "riot and dishonor" which "stain the brow" of his son. Between Henry's two references to Hal, no change has been reported in the Prince's behavior. The King's reading of his son, however, has grown less optimistic, for his hope now lies in the improbable fancy that fairies might have exchanged his Harry for Percy's when they were infants (I, i, 86-90). While offstage audiences may speculate about the meaning of Hal's behavior, Henry's reading of it as sometimes dangerously irresponsible and sometimes harmlessly immature indicates that the Prince's conduct can generate variant effects of meaning at different times and under different circumstances.[6]

When Shakespeare's Prince makes his first appearance in *Henry IV, Part One* (I, ii), his behavior in conversation is noteworthy in its strategy. Falstaff speaks first: "Now, Hal, what time of day is it, lad?" Hearing the question, Hal says that Falstaff cannot mean what his words signify. In light of what he believes about this speaker and of what he takes to be the situation, Hal claims, "thou hast forgotten to demand that truly which thou wouldst truly know." Initially Falstaff's inquiry about the time is taken to be an effect of forgetfulness induced by the speaker's idleness of life. Hal goes on to insist that the only way he can comprehend Falstaff is to assume that a system

of substitutions is in play which invests the question with its apparent identity:

> Unless hours were cups of sack and minutes capons and clocks the tongues of bawds and dials the signs of leaping-houses and the blessed sun himself a fair hot wench in flame-coloured taffeta, I see no reason why thou shouldst be so superfluous to demand the time of the day.
>
> (I, ii, 6-13).[7]

This first exchange is instructive, for Hal's reading of Falstaff illustrates how assumptions about a speaker and situation may be operative in the process of understanding. By extension, whether the interpreter is a father or a fat companion, an historian or a contributor to folklore, a literary scholar or an unsophisticated reader,[8] there will always be some interplay between perceptible data and the network of beliefs and habits that shape the interpretation of Hal's own words and actions.

As the scene in question continues, Hal baffles Falstaff at every turn and dismantles each of his attempted readings of the conversation in progress. Hal's evasions and indirections frustrate each of Falstaff's efforts to find familiar ground on which to stand. Failing to assure himself of the meaning of Hal's speech, the "old lad of the castle" finds himself in a verbal wilderness without a map, and he complains self-consciously about his condition (call it melancholy, vanity, or what he will). Falstaff, however, may not be the only one affected this way by Shakespeare's Prince. For example, those who might have expected that their direct experience of Hal would guarantee a clear and certain reading of his character and conduct might have found instead that the presence of the Prince has only served to dispel the hope that contact with him could be free of the subjectiveness that colors rumors and reports. In this scene Hal is exasperating, for he does not stand still long enough to be a stable object of attention. Whenever he seems to vanish behind clouds of verbal wit, offstage interpreters are left to consider their own operations in startlingly self-conscious ways. If they should ask themselves what they are doing, they might find that Falstaff is not the only one baffled by Hal.

Near the end of this scene, Poins enters to propose a robbery of pilgrims and traders outside London, and Falstaff is anxious to ask Hal to join in. The Prince replies, "Who, I rob? I a thief? not I, by my faith." When Falstaff accuses him of lacking "honesty" for refusing to be a robber, Hal adjusts his speech to the terms of the persuasion. If robbing is princely behavior in Falstaff's system, then Hal's refusal to be a thief must be accommodated. He responds, "Well then, once in my days I'll be a madcap." When Falstaff commends Hal, "Why, that's well said," the Prince clarifies his decision by insisting that, in light of the current exchange, madcap behavior can only mean staying at home and not participating in the robbery.

Before Hal is left alone on the stage, however, Poins urges him to join in a scheme to rob Falstaff and his confederates at Gadshill, insisting that the "virtue of this jest" will be in the "reproof" of Falstaff's lies afterwards. When Hal agrees, his "dissolute" conduct can be read as part of a program to reprove dishonesties. But whatever Hal's conversations with Falstaff and Poins might seem to illustrate, the meaning of his appearance so far in this scene cannot be understood as obvious or self-evident; it must be interpreted.

When Poins bids farewell and exits, Hal is left alone onstage. For the first time, Shakespeare's Prince speaks without the conditioning restraints of an onstage audience. In the conventional privacy of soliloquy, he claims to know precisely what he is doing. When Hal credits himself with success in creating his own reputation for "loose" behavior, he momentarily unsettles the available readings of his conduct. Whether the Prince's behavior has been consistently or variously read as dangerously irresponsible or harmlessly immature or indirectly reproving, it had never before been openly considered as part of a calculated political strategy. In this new light, his scheme looks like a Machiavellian gloss on the parable of the prodigal son. Although editorial notes may guide readers to interpret this speech in a particular way, and critical commentaries often encourage a specific assumption about the author's intention, when Hal anticipates the moment when he will throw off his "loose" behavior in a dazzle of "glitt'ring" reformation, he creates the possibility of conflicting interpretations at every turn.[9]

One important question that Hal's soliloquy raises is this: how can one recognize reformation when one sees it? In light of his speech, there are several ways to read the action that follows in the play. Insofar as a speaker's description of himself defines and determines the meaning of the actions he performs, it is possible to understand Hal as an essentially consistent character.[10] According to this reading, Hal may be said to remain committed to his plan of manipulating public opinion by engineering a moment when the illusion of "loose behavior" will give way to the impression of "glitt'ring" reform. No more virtuous than his father and no less calculating than Richard III, Hal's success would be a tribute to Machiavelli.[11] On the other hand, it is possible to understand Hal as a character who subsequently undergoes a remarkable transformation in a moment of actual conversion. This latter reading would find miracle, in place of manipulation, in Hal's story and dramatic irony, rather than political program, in his soliloquy. In this light, Prince Hal becomes the real convert that he had claimed he would only play.[12] Both of these readings depend on the fixing of refor-

mation in a single event. Whether played or actual, the casting off of dissolute behavior is "foreshadowed" as a moment of conversion which will be publicly recognized and generally welcomed. In order to be effective, Hal's reformation cannot be suspected of counterfeit; it must be indistinguishable from the real thing.[13]

The problem of distinguishing between reformation and its counterfeit, however, is not limited to one unrepeated occasion; it is a persistent condition of interpretation. In the tavern, at the palace, and on the battlefield, Hal enacts confessions of his misconduct and promises to reform. Onstage interpreters, whose experiences with the Prince are more restricted than those of offstage audiences, find themselves challenged to take the Prince at his word. For example, when the tavern play ends, in which Falstaff and Hal had alternately assumed the roles of King and Prince, Falstaff delivers a mock ultimatum: "banish plump Jack, and banish all the world." Hal makes a cryptic reply: "I do, I will." No one onstage seems to take the Prince at his word, for he is assumed to be merely playing.[14] Offstage interpreters, however, might recognize this scene as Hal's moment of mysterious conversion from a life of wayward prodigality. As such, it does not appear to be politically motivated, and it lacks the impact that his "reformation" was designed to have. Nonetheless, it is possible to read a firm purpose of amendment in his reply to Falstaff.[15] Although several critics and commentators have found this scene to be more purposeful than the comic diversion it is taken to be onstage, many consider Hal's closing remark to be either evidence of callousness in the speaker or irony in the playwright rather than reformation in the prince.[16] In most of the scenes after Hal's soliloquy, offstage audiences have discovered meanings in actions and words which go virtually unnoticed by those onstage.[17] Furthermore, offstage interpreters have regularly found themselves in considerable disagreement despite the advantage of seeing the events from a perspective which is not limited by onstage involvement in the action or biased by political allegiance.[18]

Later, under the pressure of his father's badgering speculations at the palace (III, ii), Hal has several opportunities to explain himself. Whatever designs the King might have in suggesting that his son's "vile participation" could be God's punishment for his own "mistreadings," he is surely not confessing his guilt.[19] When Hal is asked to explain his madcap conduct, he admits to "some things true," which he excuses as the "wanderings" of youth, and dismisses other charges as the "tales" of "pick-thanks and news-mongers."[20] Still, he asks pardon in the name of "true submission." Despite Henry's exclamation, "God pardon thee!," this king sees no place for morality within the political arena; when he presses on to lecture Hal on good conduct, he stresses effectiveness, rather than ethics. Describing his own political shrewdness and mocking

Richard's ineptitude, Henry details his success in sup-planting the annointed King. The time might seem opportune for Hal to reveal the politic method in his madness and to predict success for himself based on the simple logic of his soliloquy.[21] He promises in-stead, "I shall hereafter . . . be more myself." By now both speakers may be engaged in the kind of double-think that Worcester had earlier described: "The king will always think him in our debt, / And think we think ourselves unsatisfied" (I, iii, 283-284). Offstage audiences are left to infer the meanings taken by both of the onstage hearers which provide the contexts for interpreting the meanings of their replies. Not only is reference to some "subtext" required, but citations from "the text itself" are insufficient as evidence of meaning unless they are persuasively interpreted.[22] Onstage, however, Hal's apparent promise to reform leads directly to the King's denunciation of him as his "nearest and dearest enemy" who might fight against him "under Percy's pay."[23] To this, the Prince replies, "Do not think so; you shall not find it so,"[24] and he goes on to prophesy "some glorious day" when he will exchange his own indignities for Hotspur's "glorious deeds." When Hal promises to fight to the death for his father against the rebels and seals his pledge with a vow, the King exults.[25]

Whether the offstage audience is expected to forget Hal's soliloquy or Hal effectually forgets it himself, when his vow reintroduces God to the field of the con-versation, it could signal a diminishment of his belief in the efficacy of political strategy.[26] At any rate, as the generalities of his soliloquy are displaced by the par-ticulars of developing events, Hal's willingness to con-cede errors in his ways may be growing into a recog-nition of the essential error in his thinking. At this point in the play, offstage interpreters may notice in Hal's behavior a gradual recovery of the meaning of reforma-tion as a process, which depends for its achievement on the progressive unlearning of what he had seemed to know already. The idea that education is the proper process description for the Prince's reformation may have occurred to several offstage interpreters even be-fore Warwick's claim in *Henry IV, Part Two,* and the conclusion drawn by the Archbishop of Canterbury and the Bishop of Ely in *Henry V.*[27] The difference that I am suggesting here is that Hal's transformation is a counterprogressive process; it is not so much a gaining of knowledge through varied experiences as a losing of what he seemed to know in favor of more ancient wis-doms. The notion that Hal could have known already what he seems to be learning could be a way of gloss-ing Vernon's later description of him to Hotspur: it was "As if he mastered there a double spirit / Of teaching and of learning instantly" (V, ii, 63-64). In this light, Hal's transformation from a politically cynical strate-gist to an idealistic defender of the King is directly related to his repeated enactment of a promise to reform his life while confessing the looseness of his ways.

On the eve of the battle at Shrewsbury, Worcester and Vernon represent the rebels in a meeting at the King's camp (V, i). After Worcester and the King exchange accusations which trumpet their suspicions and distrust,[28] Hal steps forward to praise Hotspur for his celebrated "deeds" and to confess his own shame for having been a "truant to chivalry."[29] Fur-thermore, he offers to "try fortune" in a single fight with Hotspur, in order "to save the blood on either side" (V, i, 83-100). Whether offstage audiences read Hal in good faith (as gold) or with suspicion (as counterfeit), the King, for whatever reason, sets his son's proposal aside and offers his "grace" to the rebels if they will yield to him.[30]

When the meeting ends and the rebels leave, each negotiator for an alternative to open battle reveals his doubts and his suspicions of the others. Worces-ter, for example, expresses his fear of "suppositions" everywhere and his certainty that "interpretation" will always "misquote" his looks. In this, he reveals an-other problem which arises when one attempts to read others: the hazard of being read. The failure of peace-ful reconciliation here may be one of the inevitable consequences of private interpretation in an age of pervasive self-interest and profound disbelief.

In the final scenes of the play, while the rebel lead-ers are maddened by the King's men who march to their deaths "furnish'd like the king himself" (V, iii, 20), Hal relentlessly pursues Hotspur amid a flurry of reports that Percy has already been killed or captured.[31] Whatever doubts he might have about fulfilling his vow to "redeem" himself "on Percy's head" (III, ii, 132), when Hal rescues his father from Douglas, he declares that he "never promiseth but he means to pay" (V, iv, 42). As this echo from a line in his early soliloquy combines with Henry's announcement that his son has "redeemed" his "lost opinion" by driving Douglas off, Hal's politic plan and his filial pledge seem to coincide for an instant.

But the Prince does not declare his success on either count; rather he protests his father's continued suspi-cions and indirectly confesses his own failure to con-trol the readings given to his words and actions: "O God! they did me too much injury / That ever said I heark'ned for your death" (V, iv, 51-52).[32] Until the end of the play, as Hal's words repeatedly recall ear-lier scenes and other contexts, the challenge to de-cide who Hal is and what he is doing is unavoid-able.[33] While the characters onstage reveal the diffi-culties involved in reading others and in being read themselves, offstage audiences may feel pressured to hazard a belief which will provide a stable ground for reading Hal's story.

From the moment he encounters Hotspur until he gives Prince John the honor of setting Douglas free, Shake-

Members of the Festival Company in "The Battle Scene" from the 1958 Stratford Festival production of Henry IV, Part 1.

speare's Hal challenges his interpreters' beliefs. When he meets Hotspur in the field, Hal echoes his promise to the King, though presumption rather than prophecy sounds through his claim: "think not, Percy, / To share with me in glory any more. . . . all the budding honours on thy crest / I'll crop, to make a garland for my head" (V, iv, 62-73). When he mortally wounds Hotspur, completing his rival's final estimate of himself ("thou art dust, / And food for— / For worms, brave Percy" [V, iv, 85-86]), Hal might refresh the audience's memory of his soliloquy's cocky arrogance. But in the presumed privacy of his triumph, Hal goes on to eulogize the "great heart" fallen before him and to speak again of "ill-weaved ambition" and the ironies of human mortality, but this time with moral prudence.

This is no mere repetition; it illustrates how the effects of meaning can deepen and improve as they are reiterated.[34] When Hal bends to cover Hotspur's face with his own "favours," the image that he strikes refreshes a memory of noble chivalry and restores prophetic dignity to Hal's vision of the "glorious day" of

his redemption (III, ii, 132-137). However questionable his integrity and motives might be later when he promises to give Falstaff credit for killing Hotspur and when he grants Prince John the honor of disposing of Douglas, Hal's final words over the body of his fallen rival seem genuinely magnanimous:

> Adieu, and take thy praise with thee to
>   heaven!
> Thy ignominy sleep with thee in the grave,
> But not rememb'red in thy epitaph!
> (V, iv, 99-101)

As the play ends amid a swirl of promises and poses, offstage interpreters might experience momentary trials of belief involving Hal's conditions of mind, heart, and soul. In fact, the problems of distinguishing between counterfeit and the real thing, which persist to the last lines of this play, continue through the two plays which complete the story of Hal's succession to the throne.[35] There will be many more times when interpreters will find their subject involved in unexpected actions and uttering words which test their faith in the rightness of their "settled" readings.

Because it is possible for moral choice to coincide with political necessity, idealistic motives are sometimes inextricable from utilitarian ones.[36] In the shadow of pervasive ambiguity, the reading given to Hal at any point will be conditioned by the interpreter's assumptions about man's nature and the mysteries of human experience. In times of self-doubt, pretense, and suspicion, the belief that anyone can achieve nobility in his conduct might be a necessity. During the Elizabethan Age, when the amorality of Machiavellian politics was practiced as much as it was criticized, a belief in Hal's moral recovery may, in fact, be a testimony to the possibility of regaining an ideal which had been lost.[37] If counterfeit reformation was one of the effects of challenged authority and the failure of personal conscience, it might be said that Hal gives new currency to the "real" thing near the end of *Henry IV, Part One.* If so, then this play could be a clue to Shakespeare's sense of the value of historical thinking and an invitation to faith in the possibility of "redeeming time."

Notes

[1] Unless otherwise stated, I refer to the Sanderson edition in citations to *1 Henry IV,* ed. James L. Sanderson (New York: W.W. Norton and Company, 1969).

[2] In addition to the commentaries and studies cited in the glosses, the *Variorum Edition of Henry the Fourth, Part I* (Philadelphia: J. B. Lippincott and Company, 1936) and the *Supplement* (published in 1956 by the Shakespeare Association of America) include Appendices which sketch the major lines of the controversy. See especially *Variorum* 341-55 and 457-66; and *Supplement* 56-78 and 90-94. Recent articles and books indicate that the critical controversy is not likely to subside. I encourage my readers to attend to the documentation and consider its implications relative to the rules of evidence and persuasion.

[3] In addition to the characters in *1 Henry IV,* there are several others in *2 Henry IV* and in *Henry V* (including clerics, nobles, and the soldiery) who take various positions on the meaning of Hal's words and behavior. In these latter plays, characters are not the only commentators onstage: there is a Prologue (presented by Rumor) and an Epilogue (spoken by a Dancer, according to one recent edition) in *2 Henry IV;* in *Henry V* there are choral introductions to each act in addition to the Prologue and Epilogue.

[4] In their interpretations of the meaning of events, these writers reveal the anomalies that derive from attributing causes sometimes to the exercises of human will and sometimes to the workings of Divine Providence. Ornstein notes that ambivalences exist not only between but within various accounts: "In Hall's as in other sixteenth-century Chronicles, moralistic judgements stand side by side with shrewdly realistic observations of political life. Next to pious exclamations and simplistic moral portraits are clear-eyed statements of the Machiavellian facts of political struggle and intrigue." See Robert Ornstein, *A Kingdom for a Stage* (Cambridge, Mass.: Harvard University Press, 1972) 20-21.

[5] For a fertile introduction to the problems of sorting out facts from legend, see Croft's expanded footnote on Elyot's reference to the Lord Chief Justice incident (Henry Stephen Croft, *The Boke Named the Governour devised by Sir Thomas Elyot,* vol. 2 [London: K. Paul, Trench and Company, 1883] fn. 6, 61-71). Willey notes: "It may be that all thought is conditioned, and so 'unfree'; even so-called 'liberal' or 'objective' thinking is directed by presuppositions, however latent or unconscious they may be. We cannot help interpreting the world from where we stand, and with a view to some hoped for destination (Basil Willey, *The English Moralists* [New York: Doubleday Company, Inc., 1964, rpt. 1967] 82).

[6] The wording here has been intentionally groomed after Abrams's rendering of the deconstructive claims of Jacques Derrida (M. H. Abrams, *A Glossary of Literary Terms,* 4th ed. [New York: Holt, Rinehart and Winston, 1981]).

[7] See "Deconstruction" in Abrams for suggestions about the implications made available by the wording of this description of Hal's procedure in "reading" Falstaff.

[8] The distinction between "literary scholar" and "unsophisticated reader" is made in light of the First Folio's opening range of readers, from "the most able" to "him that can but spell" (A3). See discussions of "literary competence" in Jonathan Culler, *Structuralist Poetics* (Ithaca, N.Y.: Cornell University Press, 1975) 113-30, and of "informed" readership in Stanley Fish, *Is There A Text In This Class?* (Cambridge, Mass.: Harvard University Press, 1980) 303-71.

[9] As a dramatic device, the soliloquy is a versatile convention. Abrams notes: "the playwright uses this device as a convenient way to convey directly to the audience information about a character's motives, intentions, and state of mind, as well as for purposes of general exposition" (180). This versatility, however, introduces ambiguity: for instance, "intention" and "state of mind" may be proper labels for the remarkably different soliloquies spoken by Richard III (*Richard III,* I, i) and by Richard II (*Richard II,* V, v), respectively. In terms of Hal's speech, the difference between political rationale (an "intention") and psychological rationalization (a "state of mind") does not

appear to be a quibble. See also the commentary on "various modes of solo speech" in Daniel Seltzer, "Prince Hal and Tragic Style," *Shakespeare Survey* 30 (1977) 17-25, and notes on alternate ways that an actor might "play" this speech as well as the gloss on "variable effectiveness of the soliloquy . . . illustrated from accounts of performances" in *Shakespeare in Performance: An Introduction through Six Major Plays,* ed. John Russell Brown (New York: Harcourt Brace Jovanovich, Inc., 1976) 125-26. On the point of authorial intention, Empson notes: "Of course to decide on an author's purpose, conscious or unconscious, is very difficult. Good writing is not done unless it works for readers with opinions different from the author's." Yet Empson insists later in his book: "The crucial first soliloquy of Prince Henry was put in to save his reputation with the audience; it is a willful destruction of his claims to generosity, indeed to honesty, if only in Falstaff's sense: but this is not to say that it was a mere job with no feeling behind it . . . it cannot have been written without bitterness against the prince. . . . In having some sort of double attitude to the prince, Shakespeare was merely doing his work as a history writer" (William Empson, *Some Versions of Pastoral* [New York: New Directions Publishing Co., 1930, rpt. 1968] 3-5 and 102-05).

[10] The wording here has intentionally followed Rorty, who goes on to note that a speaker's description "may perfectly well be set aside" (Richard Rorty, *Philosophy and the Mirror of Nature* [Princeton: Princeton University Press, 1979] 349). In light of Worcester's complaints about the unalterability of the King's fixed reading of him (II, i, 282-85 and V, ii, 12-15), Hal's politic strategy might seem naive. The outcome of events in the play, however, could be introduced in support of both the optimism of Hal and the pessimism of Worcester, though they are mutually exclusive in their assumptions.

[11] Although Tudor historians indicate that Hal's contemporaries, including his father, suspected him of political plotting long befor the events of this play, Swinburne (who likened Hal to Louis XI and Caesar Borgia) was one of the earliest proponents of this reading, but it did not become popular until after Bradley, Yeats, and G. B. Shaw argued for it (see *Variorum* 461-63). By now it has become one of the recognized interpretations of Prince Hal/Henry V. See the commentary by Fredson Bowers, "Shakespeare's Art: The Point of View," in *Literary Views,* ed. Carroll Camden (Chicago: University of Chicago Press, 1964) 45-58, which is reprinted in Sanderson, esp. 313-16. Weiss has more recently turned the corner on this reading by commending rather than blaming Hal for his policy; he labels him "the ablest 'actor' " and a "royal counterfeit" who is well suited to a "topsy-turvy, bad time" (Theodore Weiss, *The Breath of Clowns and Kings* [New York: Atheneum, 1974] 277). On this latter note,

Mosse's assertion that "pious frauds" and "holy deceits" may imply "sincere attempts to meet the challenge of 'policy' and reason of state," rather than "mere hypocrisy," might shed more favorable light on Hal's reformation ploy (George L. Mosse, *The Holy Pretense* [New York: Howard Fertig, 1957, rpt. 1968] 5).

[12] In general, Tudor historians attempt to diminish the extent and/or intensity of Hal's dissoluteness by speaking of slanders and false rumors. Several, however, favor this reading, and there is considerable agreement among them about naming the time of Hal's "miraculous conversion" as the day of his coronation; see J. Dover Wilson's discussion of Fabyan's *Chronicle* of 1516 in *The Fortunes of Falstaff* (New York: Cambridge University Press, 1944) 15-35, which is reprinted in Sanderson, esp. 261-66. It might be well to mention that in *Henry V,* the Archbishop of Canterbury and the Bishop of Ely consider this interpretation but reject it, "for miracles are ceased" (I, i, 67). Brown glosses this passage: "protestants believed miracles ceased to occur after the revelation of Christ" *(William Shakespeare: The Life of Henry V,* ed. John Russell Brown [New York: The New American Library, 1965] 45). Modern historians tend to lament the lack of documentary evidence for Hal's dissolute conduct and to dismiss the possibility of miraculous conversion as a matter of superstition.

[13] Rabkin's discussion of the notion of "complementarity" might be valuable reading for those who recognize a problem here and see no convincing way to avoid what looks like an either/or choice at the crossroads of interpretation (Norman Rabkin, *Shakespeare and the Common Understanding* [New York: The Free Press, 1967] 1-29). In addition, I would like to recommend Stanley Fish, *Self-Consuming Artifacts* (Berkeley: University of California Press, 1972) 1-43 and Harold Bloom, "The Breaking of Form," *Deconstruction and Criticism* (New York: The Seabury Press, 1979) 1-22. After reading these, it might be possible to avoid lamenting the road(s) not taken.

[14] It might be argued that the Sheriff's knocking prevents any direct onstage response. It is curious, nonetheless, that while this knocking can effectively prevent interpretive responses onstage, it might be taken to be a specialized dramatic signal by interpreters offstage. See Goddard's discussion of "knocking" as a device used by Shakespeare "to betoken at a fateful moment the knocking of the inner mentor" (Harold Goddard, *The Meaning of Shakespeare,* vol. 2 [Chicago: University of Chicago Press, 1951] 207-09).

[15] Toliver, for example, calls it "a kind of official proclamation . . . a present impulse to reject comic ritual and to seek some other adjustment" (Harold O. Toliver, "Falstaff, the Prince, and the History Play," *Shakespeare Quarterly* 16 [Winter 1965]: 63-80, re-

printed in Sanderson, esp. 176-79). Furthermore, Dessen notes: "Shakespeare makes it clear that the prince's summary comment ('I do, I will') is based upon accurate knowledge of his companions (emphasized again through the papers from Falstaff's pockets), complete control of himself (in evidence since I, ii), and total awareness of the debt that remains to be paid, the role that must be assumed, and the world that must eventually be banished. Hal's four revealing words are in themselves enough to explain his ultimate victory over Hotspur if only in the vision that allows him to see the future in the present (as in his soliloquy) and steer his own independent course through uncharted political and moral waters" (Alan C. Dessen, "The Intemperate Knight and the Politic Prince: Late Morality Structure in *1 Henry IV*," *Shakespeare Studies* 7 [1974]: 159). See also Richard L. McGuire, "The Play-within-the-Play in *1 Henry IV*," *Shakespeare Quarterly* 18 (Winter 1967): 50.

[16] Traversi finds Hal's reply "true to the Prince's character and to the tragedy of his family": he will "banish everything that cannot be reduced to an instrument of policy in the quest for empty success" (D. A. Traversi, "*Henry IV, Part I:* History and the Artist's Vision," a revised reprint of his essay in *Scrutiny* [1947], in Sanderson, 322). On the other hand, Arthur C. Sprague sees "plenty of irony" in Hal's reply, though it was unavailable to audiences until the composition and presentation of *2 Henry IV,* and George L. Kittredge is careful to rule out an intention in the Prince to banish Falstaff, "for when this happens, he has 'turned from his former self'" (*Variorum Supplement,* 25-26). See also Seltzer's remarks on Hal's reply ("Prince Hal and Tragic Style" [26]).

[17] Sometimes onstage interpreters find themselves at a loss to understand Hal and must ask him for an explanation. For example, earlier in this same scene, Poins plays along with Hal in the baiting of Francis. Afterwards, however, Poins turns to Hal and says, "But hark ye; what cunning match have you made with this jest of the drawer? come, what's the issue" (II, iv, 100-02). Dessen finds no such difficulty offstage: "To the audience, Prince Hal is the obvious puppetmaster who can control Francis's reactions because of his knowledge of what makes the puppet work, whereas no one else understands the purpose of the test case" (158).

[18] With respect to the baiting of Francis (alluded to above), Ornstein describes the controversy it has spawned and notes one possible consequence of claims based on an assumption about Elizabethan conventions: "If Tillyard is correct the Francis episode is not a fascinating revelation of Hal's personality; it is an irrelevant and purposeless bit of low humor, which exposes Shakespeare's 'Elizabethan' snobbery and coarseness" (see Ornstein's discussion of this scene and of "Elizabethan 'thought,' " 8-11).

[19] Setting aside his own earlier readings of Hal (as dangerously irresponsible or harmlessly immature), the King now finds the reproving hand of God in Hal's dissoluteness. If Hal could be thought of as a conscious scourge of God, then his designs on the King might be inferred to be similar to the indirect reproval claimed as a possible explanation of his earlier agreement to rob Falstaff at Gadshill. Ornstein, however, considers Henry's first words "a scathing rebuke," though he notes an ambivalence in the King's lecturing of Hal: "Does Henry mistake his son? Or does he know precisely how to test Hal's mettle and how to expose the princely self behind the cloak of loose behavior?" (142-43).

[20] Hal does not enumerate or distinguish the "tales" from the "true things." The King and the offstage interpreters are left to assume that they know what he means.

[21] Though the phrase "method in his madness" may seem inexcusably trite, it is meant to recall the lines mentioned in the opening paragraph of this paper ("essentially mad/made"), and the commonplace that is popular in discussions of Hamlet's dealings with Claudius. See G. R. Hibbard, *"Henry IV and Hamlet,"* *Shakespeare Survey* 30 (1977): 1-12.

[22] Seltzer, on the issue of Hal's subtext in this play, notes: "The words of the text, in the mode of playwriting, themselves become referential; they demand for their full effectiveness an understanding of, or at least our assumption that the character possesses, an interior life which is developing its own energies, subtextually" (26). See also persuasions in Fish regarding ambiguity and indirect speech act (268-92) and to relativism and solipsism (317-21).

[23] Ornstein cites C. L. Kingsford's introduction to *The First Life of King Henry the Fifth* (Oxford: Clarendon Press, 1911) xxi, in support of his own suggestion: "We rejoice in the thought that the greatest monarch had misspent his youth, and much prefer this fictional prince to the real one, who apparently schemed with his allies to wrest the throne from his ailing father. We would rather believe that Hal boxed the ear of Authority than that he lusted for the crown" (140).

[24] Although these two statements may be taken as distinct declarations with respect to the King's claims (a denial of the charge that he is his father's enemy and an assurance that he will never take arms with the rebels against the King), it is possible to perceive conditional logic between them (If you do not believe that I am your enemy, then you will not find that I am your enemy).

[25] In light of Hal's vow (if he "break the smallest parcel," may he "die a hundred thousand deaths"), the King's triumphant reply, "A hundred thousand

rebels die in this," may be as richly ambiguous as Hal's "I do, I will."

26 Hal's invocation of God may be an unexpected effect of Henry's political hectoring or of his own repeated enactment of a resolution to change his ways. See C. S. Lewis, *Mere Christianity* (New York: Macmillan Co., 1943, rpt. 1960) 147; and Henri Bergson, *Matter and Memory* (New York: Macmillan Co., 1959) 102. Furthermore, his vow is not a denial of Henry's charge that his son is in Richard's line (III, ii, 85-87); rather it recalls a time when the God of Justice was believed to be the director of human events, a time like that invoked for a moment by Richard II when Mowbray and Bolingbroke were set on proving each other false (*Richard II,* I, i, and iii). In this connection, perhaps Mazzeo's analysis of Machiavelli's theory of reform might reveal a surprising irony: Machiavelli "blends two views of history—the cyclical and the regenerative. . . . Any hope of reform lies, analogically, in a retrograde movement to the more vigorous starting point. For example, any state that wishes to renew itself must return to its old ethos, a return which, Machiavelli says, can only be the work of one powerful man" (Joseph Mazzeo, *Renaissance and Revolution* [New York: Random House, 1965, rpt. 1967] 88. Ornstein, on the other hand, considers Hal's reply "a furious and boasting pledge" (142).

27 For a survey of some recent proposals concerning the implications of Hal's education, see especially Paul A. Jorgensen, " 'Redeeming Time' in Shakespeare's *Henry IV,*" *Tennessee Studies in Literature* 5 (1960): 101-09; Hugh Dickson, "The Reformation of Prince Hal," *Shakespeare Quarterly* 12 (1961): 33-46; Joan Webber, "The Renewal of the King's Symbolic Role: From *Richard II* to *Henry V,*" reprinted from *Texas Studies in Language and Literature* (1963) in James L. Calderwood and Harold E. Toliver, *Essays in Shakespeare* (Englewood Cliffs, New Jersey: Prentice Hall, Inc., 1970) 193-201; and Charles Mitchell, "The Education of the True Prince," *Tennessee Studies in Literature* 12 (1967): 13-21.

28 Worcester accuses the King of a "violation" of faith which drove the rebels "for safety sake to fly," while Henry charges that "insurrection" is always able to find "water colors to impaint his cause."

29 This Hal appears to be remarkably different from the gallant who had responded so cavalierly to Hotspur's announcement of the "triumphs at Oxford" (*Richard II,* V, iii, 16-19) and from the tavern cynic who had mocked Hotspur's braveries after his own "heroics" at Gadshill (*1 Henry IV,* II, iv, 92-101). In addition, offstage interpreters might have various expectations based on their "readings" of the scenes that have taken place in the meantime. For example, between the scene at the Palace and the eve of the battle

at Shrewsbury, Hal has returned to the tavern one more time. If there is a change in him, it is that he is less amused at Falstaff's shameless refusal to own up to his extravagant indulgences and debts. For his part, Hal admits to going through Falstaff's pockets and to paying back the robbery money after Gadshill, explaining, "I am good friends with my father and may do any thing" (III, iii, 161). Although Falstaff and Bardolph recognize this statement as a claim to be above the law and immediately propose another robbery, Hal abruptly changes the subject: "I have procured thee, Jack, a charge of foot." In a later scene, Vernon has announced to the rebel camp the approach of the King's army. His description of Hal mounting his horse (rising "like Mercury" from the ground and vaulting into his seat "As if an angel dropp'd down from the clouds" [IV, i, 106-08]) overturns Hotspur's more cynical request for news of "the nimble-footed madcap Prince of Wales," and evokes an image of "glitt'ring" reform. Hal's commitment to putting down the rebellion is complete, regardless of the motives or forces that direct him.

30 See John C. Robertson, "Hermeneutics of suspicion versus hermeneutics of goodwill" and Ben F. Meyer, "Response," in *Studies in Religion* 8, 4, (Fall 1979): 365-77 (Robertson) and 393-95 (Meyer).

31 In V, iii, Falstaff tells Hal that he has already "paid Percy" (45), though the Prince doubts him. And later, in V, iv, when the King claims to have seen Prince John holding "Lord Percy at the point," Hal replies, "O, this boy / Lends mettle to us all!" (20-23). See also Empson (43-44).

32 The King's suspicions are rekindled in *2 Henry IV* when he awakens to find Hal wearing the crown, though the soliloquy that Hal speaks reveals his anxiety about being King rather than his ambition. Furthermore, when the two exchange speeches it is clear that Henry has moved closer to contrition for his past than that expressed in his first meeting with Hal in *1 Henry IV.* Compare *1 Henry IV,* III, ii, and *2 Henry IV,* IV, iv.

33 I had originally written "where Hal is coming from" in the place now filled by "who Hal is and what he is doing" because the phrase seemed to aptly gather together suggestions about the process of reformation and the notion that Hal's recovery of meaning is a return to older and less amoral ideals. I have since thought better of it and chosen to avoid the slang idiom.

34 The effect of repetition here seems to be the reverse of what Falstaff had earlier called Hal's "damnable iteration" in alluding to a line which is recognizable from *Proverbs.* See I, ii, 76 and the editor's gloss.

35 In fact, the final scene of *Henry V,* which centers on Hal's/Henry's marriage proposal to Katherine of

France, may be as enigmatic as his first appearance with Falstaff and Poins in *1 Henry IV,* I, ii.

[36] In his study of Machiavellism, Meinecke notes: "If, after similar acts where idealistic and utilitarian motives might have been operating jointly, anyone were to put the question to himself sincerely as to how far his conduct had been determined by one or another motive, he would in the majority of cases be forced to admit that he was no longer able to distinguish clearly between the two types of motive and that they had intermingled imperceptibly. It is often the case that moral impulses do not make their appearance until after a dispassionate examination has revealed the usefulness and effectiveness of ethical action. . . . Between those sensations and motives which are moral in character and those which are amoral, there too often lie obscure regions of blending and transition; and it can even happen that these obscure regions come to occupy the entire space (Friedrich Meinecke, *Machiavellism,* trans. Douglas Scott [London: Routledge and Kegan Paul, 1924, rpt. 1957] 3-4).

[37] In this connection, see Meinecke's assertion: "The belief that there does exist an absolute, capable of being recovered, is both a theoretical and a practical need; for, without such beliefs, pure contemplation would dissolve into a mere amusement with events, and practical conduct would be irretrievably exposed to all the naturalistic forces of historical life. . . . There are only two points at which the absolute manifests itself unveiled to his gaze: in the pure moral law on the one hand, and in the supreme achievements of art on the other" (433).

Marc Grossman (essay date 1995)

SOURCE: "The Adolescent and the Strangest Fellow: Comic and Morally Serious Perspectives in *1 Henry IV*," in *Essays in Literature,* Vol. XXIII, No. 2, Fall, 1995, pp. 170-95.

[*In the following essay, Grossman argues that in* 1 Henry IV *the "comic" world of Falstaff and the "morally serious" world of the Court ultimately collide, rendering the audience's perspective of the play's actions and characters uncertain.*]

The figure of Prince Hal in *1* and *2 Henry IV* is notable for the divergent, and often vociferous, reactions it provokes. To Tillyard, for example, the prince is "a man of large powers, Olympian loftiness, and high sophistication, . . . Shakespeare's studied picture of the kingly type" (269). To Harold Bloom, on the other hand, he is a "cold opportunist . . . [and] a hypocritical and ambitious politician, caring only for glory and for power, his father's true son . . . [he] is best categorized by his own despicable couplet: 'I'll so offend, to

make offence a skill; / Redeeming time when men think least I will' " (3). As David Bevington remarks, and as Bloom's choice of quotation attests, in accounting for commentators' differing reactions to the prince "the interpretation of Hal's soliloquy (1.2 [of *1 Henry IV*]) is crucial." "Are we," Bevington asks, "to view it as evidence of bloodless calculation, or as reassurance for the audience of good intent, or perhaps as whistling in the dark?" (59) Other commentators, however, generally seem to view this speech as unproblematically performing an essentially explanatory function and more or less take for granted and follow one, or a combination, of the first two interpretations noted in Bevington's question.[1] These interpretations seem to me, however, to mistake the speech's dramatic function by treating it as an example of the kind of soliloquy, familiar both in Shakespeare and earlier Tudor drama, that serves principally as a mode of audience address and is fundamentally self-descriptive, or reportorial, or recitative in nature. This essay therefore proposes what I believe is a fresh reading of Hal's soliloquy, a reading that educes an understanding of Prince Hal that differs significantly both from the currently prevalent conception of him as a young "Machiavel" and from earlier views of him as a profligate prince who undergoes a morality play conversion into a responsible leader. As must any attempt at a satisfying account of the prince, the one offered here argues the significance of his companionship with, and subsequent banishment of, Falstaff. In joining that discussion I include an account of Falstaff that emphasizes the fantastic aspect of the character he embodies and that, in so doing, aspires to lay to its final rest the hoary debate over whether he is really a coward.

Focusing chiefly on *1 Henry IV,* I argue throughout that the most prominent and pervasive opposition established by that play is one between what I call "morally serious" and "comic" perspectives and that the play employs a variety of techniques for exposing the tension between the two—within a character, between characters, and, most inventively, within the audience itself. Most obviously, through the simple device of alternating historical and comic scenes throughout much of its first three acts, *1 Henry IV* confronts us with two contrasting worlds, whose opposition to each other is apt to emerge more powerfully in the theatre than in reading. The one inhabited by King Henry and his loyalists and by Hotspur and the other rebels is an essentially humorless and relentlessly judgmental world where qualities of moral character are regarded with the utmost seriousness. These historical characters assess themselves and others as being upright or deceitful, loyal or disloyal, courageous or cowardly, deliberate or rash, unassuming or arrogant, and so on, and although neither faction acts with unstained virtue or untainted motives, each is represented as having a measure of justice on its side, and as comprised of the kind of men who would not engage in such a contest without substantial conviction in the merit of their cause. Theirs, accordingly, is a world where conflict arises not only as a result of competing ambitions but as a result of opposing views as to the mandates of social justice, a world in which tragedy therefore looms as a continuous possibility. It is, in short, the world in which most of us live most of the time. I use such terms as "moral seriousness" and "a morally serious perspective" to denote, in a fully inclusive way, the perspective held by these characters and elicited in the audience by the play's historical scenes.

The other world dramatized in *1 Henry IV* is, of course, that of Falstaff and his fellow denizens of Eastcheap. Although its inhabitants are never portrayed as malicious or evil, in this world of pranks and high spirits moral seriousness is deflated with mockery and dissolved with laughter. It is a world that reflects its characters' tacit premise that life is short and the flesh is weak and their liberating lack of any sense of individual importance. Its reigning spirit is therefore one of mutual understanding and forgiveness, and it engenders in its audience the pleasure of a warm affection for all of its characters in all of their weakness and with all of their faults. It consequently is a world in which moral judgments are not the principal basis for the esteem in which a person is held. My use of such terms as "a comic perspective" and "seeing things comically" is intended to capture, once again in the broadest manner, the various facets of the *Weltanschauung* reflected, and elicited, by these East-cheap characters. Although, with a single salient exception, *1 Henry IV* maintains a quite sharp bifurcation between the morally serious perspective of the personages of the court and the non-morally serious, or comic, perspective of the habitués of the tavern, Shakespeare knows more ways of producing the effect of gray from black and white than simply by mixing the two together.

I

Many commentators unhesitatingly accept Hal's soliloquy as a straightforward audience-directed revelation that, in frequenting the tavern and becoming a companion to Falstaff, the prince is engaged in a calculated effort to cultivate a reputation for irresponsibility for the sake of achieving future political advantage, and their interpretation of motive in this one speech colors their entire experience of the play. To cite but one influential contemporary example, Stephen Greenblatt asserts:

> Hal is a "juggler," a conniving hypocrite, [whose] characteristic activity is playing [parts, including] himself as prodigal, and himself as penitent—and [who] fully understands his own behavior . . . as a role that he is performing, [thereby demonstrating that] theatricality . . . is one of power's essential

modes [and revealing that *1 Henry IV* presents an image of power that] involves as its positive condition the constant production of its own radical subversion and the powerful containment of that subversion.

(41, 46)[2]

In taking the soliloquy's account of Hal's motivation at face value, such readings disregard the extraordinary implausibility of the strategy the prince professes to be following. When stripped of its trite but powerful rhetoric, that strategy is so palpably unsound that the notion that anyone might seriously and steadily pursue it seems to me psychologically fantastic. It requires one to accept the premise that a young man, in anticipation of almost certainly one day holding a position of great social power and responsibility, might reasonably conclude that it would be shrewd to first convince his future subordinates of his utter incompetence and unsuitability for his destined role so that he can later surprise them by his diligence. The modern political expedient of intentionally lowering public expectations of one's performance is one thing; but deliberately to sow doubt, distrust and even contempt in those whom one would lead surely displays a most remarkable lapse in common sense. But does this blunt formulation of Hal's scheme distort or omit anything of importance from either his circumstances or his reasoning? Let's examine the prince's own words (1.2.168-90),[3] first the analogy to the sun and holidays.

It seems true enough that, just as the sun and holidays are "more wondered at" and more keenly "pleaseth" for their prior absence, responsible behavior may "show more goodly and attract more eyes" when performed by someone previously perceived as inadequate. But for Hal's scheme to have the least credibility, it must go beyond producing such transient effects as astonishment, appreciation, or relief to a reasonable expectation of some more substantial and lasting advantage, such as the enhancement of his ability to command the respect and loyalty he will require as king. But Hal's analogies to the sun and holidays do not even begin to support any such tenuous inference. For instance, Hal's personification of the sun as deliberately absenting itself so that we will the more admire its glory when it reappears does not take into account the skepticism as to its future reliability its willful withdrawal would inspire. And even if one supposes that Hal imagines the sun as able to dispel all such skepticism with a single timely burst of its radiance, what grounds can this idle, untried youth, possibly have for believing that he will have either the ability or the opportunity for deeds so glorious as to do likewise, much less for equating himself *now* to the very sun? It is more likely that his ascension to the throne would be attended instead, just as his father fears, with national contempt capable of undermining the integrity of the state.

In this last regard, it is instructive to compare Hal's soliloquy with his father's advice to him on the same subject (3.2.39-91). As is often noted, both speeches strongly rely on the notion that absence or deprivation of a good thing enhances appreciation for it, and both, by way of example, invoke the sun's reappearance after an absence. They also share not only a general pattern of imagery but specific words and phrases ("seldom," "rare," "clouds/cloudy," "wondered at," "eyes"). But the two speeches reach quite opposite pragmatic conclusions. For whereas the strategy Hal describes involves making himself common in the eyes of his countrymen and peers (the very same sort of behavior that Henry expressly cites as contributing to the downfall of Richard II), Henry advises his son to follow the example of his own ascension and achieve admiration, respect, and loyalty by maintaining an august distance from those he would lead, because, in a word, familiarity breeds contempt. The fact (as I take it) that Henry's cliché advice is both sounder and more often followed than the bizarre plan propounded by his son suggests that the repetition in the king's speech of concepts, images, and words used earlier by Hal may be intended to remind us of the soliloquy and to underscore the speciousness of its reasoning.

The weakness of its reasoning is not the only reason to distrust the notion that the soliloquy provides a factual explanation for Hal's biding his youth in the tavern with Falstaff. For in its opening lines Hal says:

> I know you all, and *will* awhile uphold
> The unyoked humor of your idleness.
> Yet herein *will* I imitate the sun. . . .
> (1.2.168-70; emphasis added)

That is, he does *not* say: "I know you all, and *do* awhile uphold (or *have* awhile up*held*) the unyoked humor of your idleness. Yet herein *do* I imitate the sun," which would be more natural and appropriate if Hal were here reciting to himself (for the audience's benefit) a rationale for his time in Eastcheap. Of course, the first "will" could be elliptical for "I will awhile *longer*." But while it could, there is no reason to suppose it must be. The second "will" might be thought to reflect the fact that Hal is beginning to contemplate his "reformation," which will of course occur in the future. However, he is not there referring to his reformation, but to his imitation of the sun and, specifically, the cloud-hidden sun. While that imitation will not be complete until Hal's reformation has occurred, if the act of imitating has itself been going on for some considerable time, why refer to it as something that he will do rather than as something he all along has been and is now doing? The soliloquy's closing lines are still more telling:

> I'll so offend to make offense a skill,
> Redeeming time when men think least I will.
> (1.2.189-90)

Here the future tense ("*I'll* so offend" rather than "I so offend") plainly suggests that Hal is contemplating some offense(s) he has *yet* to commit. Rather than being descriptive of past and current conduct, these words have the ring of affirmative resolution, and they impart that ring to the entire speech. But if Hal has long thought of himself as offending in this way, why should he need to resolve to do so now? As I will explain shortly, I take the tense of the three verbs I have cited to be indicative of what Hal is principally thinking about in his soliloquy and of the fact that he is not there *describing* something so much as *doing* something.

Finally, a further obstacle to accepting the soliloquy as an accurate statement of Hal's motivations is the stubborn impression, shared I believe by many readers and spectators of the play and actors and directors of the part, that the prince's enjoyment of and affection for both Falstaff and Eastcheap are neither feigned nor alloyed with any ulterior motive but are wholly genuine and fully sincere.

Even if one shares such discomforts as I have described, one could of course simply throw up one's hands and conclude that, in order to account for the incredible transformation of a truant prince into a glorious king to which he felt himself bound by the popular legend surrounding the youth of Henry V, Shakespeare "resorted to a most unpsychological explanation . . . but evidently he thought it sufficient" (Shaaber 16). Or one could follow the lead of those commentators who, in what strike me as little more than veiled versions of the same despair, appear to conclude that we are somehow meant to shut out of our minds the implausibility of the proposed explanation. Attempting to take Hal's words, as it were, out of his own mouth and heart, these commentators characterize the soliloquy as a kind of choric commentary (Tillyard 270-71) or prologue-like convention (Wilson 41) or assert that "[i]t is not a character speech at all . . . but a time-saving plot device, rather on the clumsy side, deliberately to remove from the audience any suspense that Hal was actually committed to his low-life surroundings" (Bowers 56). If, this being Shakespeare, one is reluctant to rest in such conclusions as these, then one is left with little choice than to search for an altogether different reading of Hal's speech.

Such a reading can be found in those commentators who, perceiving *1 Henry IV* as a richly developed and highly nuanced successor to the traditional morality play, construe the soliloquy as chiefly intended to assure the audience of the prince's awareness of the error of his ways and to announce his determination to reform, an announcement that serves to prepare us for a genuine reformation that is thereafter depicted.[4] The problem with this reading, however, is simple and bald: it completely ignores, and thus likewise fails to provide any satisfying explanation of, the improbable scheme set forth in the speech. Moreover, while Hal does indeed acknowledge his present behavior as "loose" and imagine himself in the future throwing it off and paying the debt he never promised, these accomplishments are neither the focus of his speech nor does he refer to them in language expressive of determination or resolution. He speaks of them, instead, as events whose eventual occurrence he takes for granted (or is resigned to): "So, *when* this loose behavior I throw off / And pay the debt I never promised. . . ." In contrast, he begins by saying "I . . . will awhile *uphold* / The unyoked humor of your idleness" and concludes with "I'll so *offend* to make offense a skill." Then, true to his word, his speech is followed by his participation in the Gad's Hill robbery. In short, while this speech may be construed as evidence of Hal's future good intent, it is at least equally evidence of his immediate intention to persist in "offending." And that is the intent that requires explanation. But if the morality-play reading of the soliloquy is at best incomplete and the politically oriented one is psychologically implausible, how else may that speech be understood? To answer this question we first need to recall the circumstances under which it is made.

Prince Hal, heir apparent to the throne of England, has just been asked by his closest companions to join in a highway robbery. He immediately declines: "Who, I rob? I a thief? Not I, by my faith" (1.2.120). Then, under the importuning of Falstaff, he momentarily relents: "Well then, once in my days I'll be a madcap" (1.2.124). Or perhaps he has not really relented but is only jovially pretending to have accepted Falstaff's typically sophistic argument that the prince's reluctance to join in his friends' endeavors is no mark of good character. In either event, he immediately once again declines: "Well, come what will, I'll tarry at home" (1.2.126). In the end, however, he is persuaded to involve himself by Poins's idea for turning the whole affair into a grand practical joke on Falstaff. His soliloquy immediately follows his agreeing to Poins's plan.

Hal has not lent himself to the Gad's Hill robbery for the purpose of enriching either himself or his companions, he is not himself to join in the actual theft, and one may even suppose that it has already occurred to him that he can later redeem the crime by making restitution, as he in fact will do. Hal might thus tell himself, with a measure of justice, that what he has really committed himself to is not a crime but a practical joke. On the other hand, it seems unlikely that he would now be wholly untroubled by the prospect of becoming complicitous in an act in which, just a moment before, he indignantly refused to participate. Taking my cue from that initial note of indignation— where he emphasizes not so much the illegality or impropriety of the robbery as its inconsistency with his upright character and royal status—I am proposing that it is reasonable, at the very least, to assume that

Hal's sense of his own integrity continues to be troubled by his acquiescence in a criminal enterprise out of his love of a practical joke. I am speculating, in short, that at the moment of his soliloquy Hal is contemplating his role in the Gad's Hill adventure not so much with anticipatory guilt as with anticipatory shame.

And if it is reasonable to imagine him troubled, then what could be more natural than for Hal to want somehow to explain away to himself the conduct in which he proposes to indulge? That, I submit, is what he is really doing in his soliloquy. As Hotspur does elsewhere (4.1.43-52 and 75-83), though in a less elaborate manner and unfortunately with total success, Hal is attempting to rationalize away misgivings, in part no doubt about the life he leads generally in Eastcheap but most especially a sense that the specific act he is about to perform crosses the boundary between defensible frivolity and the genuinely shameful. (Samuel Johnson, to my knowledge uniquely among commentators, likewise construes this speech as an act of rationalization, saying that it "exhibits a natural picture of a great mind offering excuses to itself, and palliating those follies which it can neither justify nor forsake" [170].[5]) Those who hear in Hal's soliloquy a calculating scheme are therefore not mistaken, but it is mistaken, I believe, to imagine that that scheme theretofore has been the actual ongoing premise of Hal's life and that what he is doing here is *reciting* that premise to himself and thereby informing the audience of it and explaining himself to them.

Instead, I suggest, the scheme is only just now, even as he speaks, taking shape in his mind. That is why he formulates it as something he *will* do rather than as something he has all along *been* doing. And, considered in the light of Hal's dubious circumstances, the speciousness of the reasoning behind that scheme flags its function as a rationalization. The political "strategy" described in his speech has therefore no more been a motive for Hal's companionship with Falstaff than it is a motive for his participation in the robbery; the real motive of both is just his love of the fun. I in no way mean to discount the probability of other, less conscious, motives, such as might be felt by any son of any father or by anyone who knows he must one day pay an enormous debt he never promised. But by interpreting himself to himself as playing the part of a prince secretly endeavoring to enhance his future authority as king, Hal fends off his shame by dressing up his conduct with a loftier purpose more befitting his youthful notion of how a prince ought to behave. Preposterous as the role in which he casts himself is, it projects a self-image he understandably might prefer to hold at this moment rather than feel obliged to forgo the Gad's Hill adventure or consider whether his attraction to it and his entire existence in Eastcheap are indicative of a genuinely dishonorable nature. To see all this more clearly, let us consider how Hal's lines might be read in light of my claim that they amount to an elaborate rationalization.

In that speech Hal is not speaking to us, the audience, for the purpose of (Shakespeare's) providing us with a highly implausible explanation for what might otherwise seem to us a highly implausible later transformation of his character. Nor is he pronouncing his judgment that his current companions and way of life are deserving of rejection and expressing his resolution to repudiate them and reform himself. He is a young prince who naturally fears that his complicity in a robbery will bring dishonor not only on himself but on the crown and who, speaking to himself, is engaged in an understandable attempt to persuade himself that it will not, ultimately, have any such consequence. When he begins by saying "I . . . will awhile uphold the unyoked humor of your idleness," he is thinking particularly (though probably not exclusively) about and reaffirming his commitment to the Gad's Hill escapade. From "Yet herein will I imitate the sun" through his speech's penultimate line he rationalizes that indulging himself now will make his inevitable later assumption of royal responsibilities seem more of an accomplishment and thereby redound to his own and his nation's greater good. By likening himself to the (hidden) sun, he is simultaneously striving to reassure himself of his fundamentally honorable nature and to persuade himself that the robbery and his "loose behavior" generally merely temporarily obscure his true merit, rather than constitute something by which it should be judged. And, beginning that strand of his rationalization that culminates in the soliloquy's final line, he is starting to comfort himself with the promise and fantasy that however he behaves now he will one day not only act worthily but will shine like the sun itself. His comparison of Falstaff, Poins, and the rest to "base contagious clouds" and "foul and ugly mists of vapors" may, in this context, be understood as more self-serving than sincere.

When he goes on to say *"when* [rather than "if"] this loose behavior I throw off / And pay the debt I never promised," he is neither prophesying to us his own destiny nor resolving to reform. He is simply *acknowledging* what he has always known will eventually be required of him and *assuming* (as the nature of his rationalization requires him to assume) that he will be equal to doing it. In characterizing his assumption of his future responsibilities as his "reformation," he is not conceding that he actually needs to reform but anticipating (correctly) how the outward change in his behavior will look to others. Although, as this speech shows, Hal's conviction as to the adequacy of his native character to his destined role currently requires shoring up, if he genuinely believed he needed to reform, he would hardly be likely to compare his current status to that of the (hidden) sun. (For reasons that will become evident, by the time of his audience with his

father [3.2], Hal's conviction will have become complete. For there, while accepting such censure as may be his due for "some things true wherein [his] youth / Hath faulty wandered and irregular" [3.2.26-27], he humbly but affirmatively *defends* himself against Henry's remonstrances by maintaining that his reputation exaggerates his faults, by asking to be judged not by what he is reputed to be but by what he really is, and by promising not that he will *amend* himself but that he will thereafter be *more himself.*) Finally, having for the moment become fully persuaded by his argument, Hal spurs himself on in his commitment to Poins's plan ("I'll so offend to make offense a skill") and concludes by augmenting his principal rationalization with one of the most common excuses of all: that he will make up tomorrow for the shameful thing he does today.

Construing Hal's soliloquy in this way immediately reveals several of its principal functions and features. First, the speech serves to disclose to the audience the acuteness with which Prince Hal, uniquely among the cast of *1 Henry IV,* internalizes, or mirrors, the tension between the two comic and morally serious perspectives, placed in opposition by the play. Second, the speech does not (unlike the previously described conventional readings) undercut in an oddly undramatic fashion whatever suspense the audience may be feeling as to the prince's true character. On the contrary, it is a device for creating suspense, or arousing false expectations. It either leaves the question of Hal's real nature open or suggests what will ultimately prove to be the wrong answer. For it leaves the audience to wonder: if this young man is capable of rationalizing his way into indulging himself now, may he not continue to do so later, even as king? Third, the soliloquy itself affords an instance of the prince's much noted proclivity for playing roles and illustrates what I shall maintain is generally true of Hal's "performances," at least throughout *Part 1:* that, contrary to the view of many commentators, they are primarily put on not for others but for himself. And finally, when heard as the temporization of a deeply divided youth, Hal's speech sheds its initial resemblance to those essentially self-descriptive soliloquies in which the speaker more or less directly expresses or reports his or her thoughts, emotions, ambitions, motives, or other interior life principally for the edification of the audience. (Consider, for example, Falstaff's soliloquy on honor [5.1.127-39].) Hal's speech emerges instead as an example of those dramaturgically more sophisticated soliloquies and other speeches that *exhibit* the speaker in the act of, say, trying to assimilate a particularly intense or painful experience (Troilus's "This is, and is not, Cressid"), or reaching for an understanding of how he or she has come to a particular pass (Macbeth's "Tomorrow, and tomorrow, and tomorrow"), or groping to explain himself to himself (Richard Gloucester's "Love foreswore me . . ."). The speech emerges, that is, as a specimen of the kind of playwriting that is capable of conjuring up what Janet Adelman aptly describes as "the voice of a fully developed subjectivity, the characteristically Shakespearean illusion that a stage person has interior being, including motives that he himself does not fully understand" (1).[6]

For those who may feel that Hal's initial refusal to join in the Gad's Hill robbery is the most slender of evidence from which to infer a seriously troubled state of mind, much less to use as a foundation for interpreting that important speech, I add the considerable evidence of 2.4, which is the first time we see Prince Hal after the Gad's Hill episode. That is the scene which takes place at the Boar's Head Tavern, where Hal and Poins are awaiting Falstaff's return from the robbery, and that opens with Hal soliciting Poins (in a reversal of their Gad's Hill roles) to play a practical joke on the drawer Francis. The playing of this extended joke involves Poins's stationing himself, as it were, off-stage and hidden in a private room, from which he periodically calls out for service while Hal engages Francis in a "conversation" largely incomprehensible to the hapless drawer. The beleaguered Francis is thereby torn between attending to his customer and rudely breaking away from the Prince of Wales. In the end the prince finally releases him to respond to Poins's calls, only immediately to summon him back, leaving Francis standing amazed and not knowing which way to turn. It is a bizarre and disquieting episode and when, after the joke has been played, Poins asks Hal, "But hark ye; what cunning match have you made with this jest of the drawer? Come, what's the issue?" (2.4.82-84), one may well feel that Poins is standing in for ourselves, who likewise may feel like asking the playwright, "So, where's the humor and what's the point of this long joke on poor Francis?" Hal answers Poins (and Shakespeare us):

> I am now of all humors that have showed themselves humors since the old days of goodman Adam to the pupil age of this present twelve o'clock at midnight.
>
> (2.4.85-88)

As I understand Hal's cryptic reply, the point of his "joke" lies precisely in its indefensibly gratuitous cruelty, or, more specifically, in its having enabled its perpetrator to have engaged in one of the most shameful forms of humor and hence to have plumbed one of the basest of temperaments. But why should Hal here seek so to debase himself? I can think of no better explanation than that, the actual crime having defeated his rationalization for participating in it, his shame is now wallowing in itself, brazening it out, as it were, by indulging in yet another shameful act. No other supposition seems to me to account so well not only for Hal's vile treatment of Francis but for the uncharacteristically haughty attitude he displays earlier at the very opening

of this scene. Let me, then, describe that opening upon the assumption that my supposition is correct.

Hal has come from Gad's Hill to the tavern burning with shame. He passes some time there "[w]ith three or four loggerheads amongst three or four-score hogsheads" (2.4.4-5) in an unsuccessful effort to drown his disgrace in drink. "To conclude," he thereafter reports to Poins, "I am so good a proficient in one quarter of an hour that I can drink with any tinker in his own language during my life" (2.4.15-17). Upon first rejoining Poins in the tavern, the prince is, accordingly, both bitterly ashamed of himself and reasonably drunk.[7] His bitterness, unleashed rather than checked by drink, then leads this normally unassuming youth and sometime companion of Bardolph and Peto suddenly to stand on his royal status and to recount to Poins, with haughty and therefore wholly uncharacteristic sarcasm, that he has just endured the convivial fellowship of three common drawers, who have been pleased to inform him that, notwithstanding his being Prince of Wales, he is after all just a good boy, a lad of mettle and certainly no proud Jack like Falstaff. In other words, reacting to the salt unknowingly rubbed in his wounded self-esteem by the drawers' innocent testimonials to his character, Hal self-defensively falls back on his hereditary class and station, taking offense at the drawers' temerity in presuming to pass judgment on him.

In this same spirit of uninhibited shame he goes on to reward poor Francis, who has pathetically bestowed on the heir apparent the favor of a pennyworth of sugar, by playing on him his cruel practical joke. But just as his expressions of scorn for the drawers have been born not from any genuine contempt for them but from his self-lacerating contempt for himself, so the true motive of his trick is not the mockery of Francis but that further humiliation of himself that he feels he so richly deserves. Ashamed for having participated in the robbery even as a practical joke, he now perversely seeks to repeat his shame for that defensible act by committing, in a second practical joke, what he this time knows full well to be the truly indefensible act of toying with a social subordinate for his sport. Excessive as his self-condemnation may be, it should not, in this light, be difficult to imagine how Hal might be moved to say that he has now acquainted himself with all humors known to mankind since its first experience of shame in the Garden of Eden.

After Hal's practical joke, Francis, having exited, momentarily reappears. Hal asks him the time and receives in reply only Francis's customary "anon, anon, sir" (2.4.89). The prince thereupon resumes his mocking of Francis's limited talents:

> That ever this fellow should have fewer words than a parrot, and yet the son of a woman! His industry is upstairs and downstairs, his eloquence the parcel

of a reckoning. I am not yet of Percy's mind, the Hotspur of the North, he that kills me some six or seven dozen of Scots at a breakfast, washes his hands, and says to his wife, "Fie upon this quiet life! I want work." "O my sweet Harry," says she, "how many hast thou killed to-day?" "Give my roan horse a drench," says he, and answers, "Some fourteen," an hour after; "a trifle, a trifle."

(2.4.90-99)

As is often remarked, Hal here performs a most stunning and puzzling conversational leap by proceeding from mocking Francis directly to mocking Hotspur. But the leap may seem less puzzling, even natural, when taken in conjunction with his earlier characterization of himself as Adam's pupil and when viewed as displaying the self-contempt he has been exhibiting from the start of this scene. That is to say, Hal's words here no more express his true opinion of Hotspur than his contemptuous references to Francis and the other drawers express his true feelings about them. Hal's real opinion of Hotspur is spoken at Shrewsbury over his corpse, and there, as in the prince's references to him during his interview with his father (3.2), his words express nearly unqualified admiration. I am suggesting that the figure of Hotspur suddenly springs to Hal's mind precisely because Hotspur represents to him someone approaching a paradigm of devotion to honorable conduct and that, by deriding Hotspur, Hal is adopting another defensive stratagem typical of shame—he is lashing out with derision both at the ideal he feels he himself has failed to live up to and at the person who for him most fully embodies that ideal.

In addition to supporting my interpretation of the soliloquy, this reading of the Francis episode provides an immediate dramatic motivation for certain additional features of Hal's interaction with Francis that have been brought out by others. For instance, in a fine essay on this remarkably rich and overdetermined little episode, J. D. Shuchter observes that, in probing the drawer's willingness to "show . . . a fair pair of heels and run from" his indenture (2.4.42-43), Hal is quite clearly probing the extent to which others experience conflicts similar to his, and thereby probing himself; that Hal. as tempter and Poins as customer "are playing roles . . . with respect to Francis [that] are functionally the same as those of Falstaff and King Henry with respect to Hal"; and that by causing Francis to feel irreconcilably pulled in two directions at once, Hal reproduces in him the stalemate in which he then finds himself (130-31). S. P. Zitner further points out that Francis's perpetual "anon, anon" serves something like the temporizing function of Hal's soliloquy (67). (That Francis functions in general as a surrogate for Harry of Monmouth is all but expressly announced in the prince's very first reference to him: "Sirrah," he tells Poins, "I am sworn brother to a leash of draw-

ers and can call them all by their christen names, as Tom, Dick, and . . . Francis" [2.4.6-8; ellipsis added].) By considering the foregoing observations in light of my own contention that, at the time of his by-play with Francis, Hal is experiencing the conflicts associated with his life in Eastcheap with an intensity sharpened by the Gad's Hill robbery, one can more readily understand *why* the prince is engaging in such semi-intoxicated soul-searching at just *this* juncture of the play.

If my readings of the soliloquy and the Francis episode are convincing, what can be learned from them? For one thing, they highlight the particular kind of writing that is contained in *1 Henry IV,* at least in the role of Prince Hal, and therefore the nature of the demand such writing makes on its audience or readers. It is writing in which, as I alluded earlier in connection with the soliloquy, a character's complex interior life is made known to the audience not by its being described or reported but by its being immediately manifested, or projected, moment by moment as it occurs, in the character's speech and behavior—projected in ways as fully complex and "indirect" as those one encounters outside the theatre. The soliloquy and the Francis episode thus exemplify a kind of writing in which a stage character's words and behavior "demand, for their full effectiveness, an understanding of, or at least our assumption that the character possesses, an interior life which is developing its own energies sub-textually," writing that consequently requires us to "consider the [character] as knowing and feeling neither more nor less at any given moment in time than *his* experience of the play, so to speak, allows him to have at that moment."

Considered as instructions or working hypotheses for reading such a play as *1 Henry IV,* these last two quotations seem to me as sound advice as any I know of. They are drawn from an essay by Daniel Seltzer, entitled "Prince Hal and Tragic Style" (26, 23), that is informed by a remarkable combination of scholarship and practical theatrical experience. Seltzer's object in that essay is to characterize and trace the evolution in Shakespeare's plays of a "technique" for the self-presentation of character which bears a strong resemblance to the kind of writing I have tried to elucidate. Suggesting that "it was in the histories that Shakespeare learned to focus upon the developing experience of a single character" (18), and finding the requisite technique for dramatizing that developing experience fully rendered in a sustained manner for the first time in the part of Prince Hal in *1* and *2 Henry IV,* Seltzer contends that Hal is "the stage character whose 'personality' is one of the most pivotal in the playwright's career, for in its composition he acquired the ability to make a character change internally" (14), an ability without which he "could never have carried Hamlet, Othello, Macbeth, or Lear to their ultimate moments of inner perception" (26).

While my particular readings of the soliloquy and the Francis episode are not those offered by Seltzer,[8] they point us toward an understanding of Prince Hal that is consonant with Seltzer's view of him as a figure who "is represented—in the writing—as constantly in touch with his own conflicted needs, whose acted expressiveness is in terms of those conflicts—as the life of the play develops" (22-23), a figure "the depths of [whose] character [therefore] correspond in interesting ways to depths which the center of tragic focus must achieve" (21). On such a view of the prince, his "playing of parts"—for instance in 2.4, first as Francis's tempter, then as Hotspur, and finally as both himself and his father in his mock interviews with Falstaff—constitutes, as Shuchter puts it, "a way of knowing, [a] dramatising [of] a situation [as] a way of clarifying the various positions within [a] conflict or of learning what the conflict really is" (133) and a device for "sifting, sorting and comparing" (135) with the object of discovering what he truly cares about, and how much. My readings point us, in other words, away from those interpretations of *1 Henry IV* in which Prince Hal is seen as an essentially "static," aloof, and manipulative character whose penchant for role-playing evidences that his conduct and demeanor are always studiedly adapted to his private purposes and consequently cannot be relied upon as expressive of his real inner nature (whether that is felt to be attractive and noble or meanly calculating). They direct us, instead, toward those readings which see the role of Prince Hal as a depiction of the development of a personality.

The common description of that development as the "reformation" of Prince Hal not only ignores the fact that the prince himself nowhere appears to regard his character as in need of reformation, but also does a great disservice by promoting a conception of him as a royal black sheep faced, at the outset of the drama, with the simple morality-play task of overcoming proclivities and renouncing companions that both he and we can readily recognize are wholly unworthy and deserving of outright rejection. The Hal of Eastcheap whom we observe in Acts 1-3 is not drawn to the disreputable life of the tavern because he is personally prone to the excesses of the flesh, or because he is altogether lacking in a sense of propriety, or because of corrupt desires or ambitions for himself or his companions. Like his involvement in the Gad's Hill escapade, which serves as its emblem, Hal's existence in Eastcheap and everything he does there have their source and reveal their meaning in his attraction to Falstaff. And Hal is attracted to Falstaff for the same reason we are.

To my knowledge, no one has articulated the source of Falstaff's appeal to us better than Bradley, who writes:

> The bliss of freedom gained in humour is the essence of Falstaff. . . . he is the enemy of everything that would interfere with his ease, and therefore of anything serious, and especially of everything respectable and moral. For these things impose limits and obligations, and make us the subjects of old father antic the law, and the categorical imperative, and our station and its duties, and conscience, and reputation, and other people's opinions, and all sorts of nuisances. I say he is therefore their enemy; but I do him wrong; to say that he is their enemy implies that he regards them as serious and recognizes their power, when in truth he refuses to recognize them at all. They are to him absurd; and to reduce a thing *ad absurdam* is to reduce it to nothing and to walk about free and rejoicing. This is what Falstaff does with all the would-be serious things of life. . . . These are the wonderful achievements which he performs, not with the sourness of a cynic, but with the gaiety of a boy. And, therefore, we praise him, we laud him, for he offends none but the virtuous and denies that life is real or life is earnest, and delivers us from the oppression of such nightmares, and lifts us into the atmosphere of perfect freedom.
>
> (262-63)

For each reference to Falstaff in this passage one could substitute the word "comedy," for Bradley's magnificent account of Falstaff is equally an account of comedy itself, and so of what it means to have a capacity for seeing things comically. (Falstaff likewise identifies himself with the capacity for a comic perspective when he says, in *Part 2*, "I am not only witty in myself, but the cause that wit is in other men" [1.2.9-10]). As Bradley's account registers, particularly in its concluding words, the hallmark of Falstaff/comedy is its ability to establish, or draw upon our natural capacity for achieving, that peculiar detachment from ourselves and our lives which, so long as it lasts, disengages the disapproval and intolerance with which we otherwise greet what we regard as morally unacceptable. (Which is perhaps why high comedy so often expressly directs our attention to the moon and the stars.) To say that Hal's life in Eastcheap has its source in his attraction to Falstaff is therefore to say that it expresses his enormous capacity for entertaining the very same perspective that we ourselves adopt when we are able to step back and contemplate with tolerant amusement matters we otherwise regard with the utmost gravity. Outside the theatre we continually slip in and out of this comic perspective, prizing it but also feeling that it must be kept in its place, though we are not always sure exactly what that place is. By alternating comic with historical scenes *1 Henry IV* elicits, inside the theatre, that shifting between comic and morally serious perspectives, together with the discomfort it can sometimes occasion, a feature I will later examine in greater detail.

Framed in these terms, the central question about Prince Hal with which the play opens is whether his appetite for seeing things comically has, through feeding on Falstaff, grown so boundless as to have wholly devoured his ability to respond and act in what he himself perceives to be a responsible and morally serious manner. That is the question the opening dialogue between Hal and Falstaff (1.2) seeks to raise in the mind of the audience, that Hal's soliloquy encourages, and that provides much of the suspense driving the drama. It also, of course, mirrors the question that so preoccupies Falstaff as he persistently tries to tease out of the heir apparent some explicit assurance that his hope for a future rule of license is well-founded. For the exact nature of Falstaff's uncertainty about the prince is revealed by the tactic by which he attempts to resolve it. His tactic throughout, from his opening dialogue with the prince through the play extempore, is never to appeal to Hal's baser instincts (since he knows he has none), but continuously to test and foster the prince's comic sensibility, as by portraying, say, thievery in an appealingly comic light: "Marry, then, sweet wag, when thou art king let not us that are squires of the night's body be called thieves of the day's beauty. Let us be Diana's foresters, gentlemen of the shade, minions of the moon . . ." (1.2.20-23). Hal is, of course, well aware that such a question is Falstaff's constant preoccupation, as he signals in his opening lines when he chides Falstaff, who has just asked him the time of day, for having "forgotten to demand that truly which thou wouldest truly know" (1.2.4-5). The fact that the prince then responds to Falstaff's subsequent probing only with evasive repartee shows, I believe, not merely that he enjoys the sport of keeping the fat rogue in doubt but that, at this point in the play, he himself is no more certain of the answer to that question than are Falstaff or we.

My reason for emphasizing that Hal's life in Eastcheap is an expression of his attraction to Falstaff/comedy is this. However much one may feel that attraction has led him astray, unless one believes that the capacity for a comic perspective is in itself objectionable and requires suppression, one will not conclude that the task facing Hal at the start of the play demands a morality-play renunciation of that part of himself given reign in Eastcheap. Hal's task in this drama, as I understand it, is not to stop seeing things comically and start taking them seriously but to stop seeing them so comically and start taking them more seriously. While I do not wish to split hairs, that difference seems to me to make all the difference. It means that what is required of the prince is not that he make a binary choice, thereby suppressing one part of himself in favor of another, but that he find the means for accomplishing a personally and socially acceptable accommodation of the two.

By depicting the prince in Acts 4 and 5 as rising without hesitation to the defense of his father's crown and as comporting himself in political conflict and martial combat with both nobility and valor, *1 Henry IV* ultimately leaves no room for doubt as to Hal's ability to put aside his comic perspective and assume a morally

serious one. But in making this shift, doesn't he in fact repudiate outright his own former self? This brings us, of course, to what is commonly referred to as the rejection of Falstaff, the event that occurs literally and publicly only in the coronation scene of *Part 2,* but which is prefigured at the conclusion of the play extempore in *Part 1.* By actually banishing Falstaff in *Part 2,* and by privately expressing his preparedness to do so in *Part 1,* isn't the prince obviously rejecting everything Falstaff represents and so renouncing his own former attraction to him? That seems to be the entrenched opinion, whatever the figure of Falstaff is taken to represent and whether Hal's banishment of him is seen as an unambiguously healthy step toward personal maturation and political regeneration or as a perhaps necessary but nonetheless regrettable act of self-mutilation. I am not at all sure that the question of the interior significance of the banishment to Prince Hal/Henry V can be definitively answered; but I do believe that the two plays invite reconsideration, and the response with which I am personally most comfortable requires that further discussion of Falstaff that is contained in the next part of this essay. With these provisos in mind, however, I will propose the following concerning the play extempore. The Gad's Hill escapade is not merely Shakespeare's way of fleshing out the popular legend of Henry V's wild youth. It is a critical event, a turning point, in the prince's development.

When, in the emotional aftermath of that event, and in reply to Falstaff's plea and warning, "Banish plump Jack, and banish all the world!" (2.4.427-28), Hal replies simply and flatly, first from within his role as King Henry, "I do," and then for himself, "I will" (2.4.429), he is for the first time answering the question about himself with which the play began, not only for the audience and for Falstaff (who of course proves unable or unwilling to hear the answer), but for himself as well. Despite his long-standing awareness that he must one day forsake Falstaff and Eastcheap, only now, in the act of uttering these words, while imagining himself to be his father and therefore his nation's king, with the news of open rebellion and the knowledge that he must shortly confront Henry at court fresh in his mind, and in the wake of his recent sense of his own self-disgrace, does he achieve the conviction that he possesses the inner resources actually to do it. In other words, despite arguments to the contrary (Gottschalk), I think there can be no serious doubt that this particular moment signifies a turn in the prince toward moral seriousness. As to whether that turn amounts to a full turnabout, let me for now merely say, first, that I can find no evidence, at least in *this* play, that the prince ever altogether loses that capacity for a comic perspective with which he begins and, second, that it does not diminish the dramatic significance of this moment to understand it as one of those small inward turnings which, while not a complete reversal of compass, is nonetheless definite and forever. In Hal's case it is a turning more fully toward a morally serious perspective by a youth in whom a comic perspective has until now predominated.

I want to conclude this portion of my discussion of Prince Hal by proposing a way in which many salient features of his situation and personality during the first three acts may collectively be comprehended. Hal's feeling torn between seeing things comically and taking them seriously; his finding himself chastised by his father and his falling into popular disrepute because his predilection for the former is mistaken for an incapacity for the latter, if not a native disposition to vice; his relish for idle raillery; his feeling burdened by the prospect of a heavy responsibility he never voluntarily assumed; his both wanting and fearing the responsibility for which he is destined; his being in any event socially precluded from assuming it, despite his physical and intellectual preparedness for doing so; his penchant for working through his conflicts and their attendant emotions by "acting out" or "trying on" a variety of possible solutions and selves; and his presentation as someone who, through continuous observation and assessment of both himself and others, is actively engaged in forming his values and thereby shaping his identity—all of these are, I think, characteristic of that stage of life we think of as distinctively adolescent. One will recall that at the time of the events chronicled in *1 Henry IV* the prince is only about 15 years old.

If this identification of Hal as an adolescent is a fair one, then his movement from immersion in the comic world of Eastcheap to prominence in the morally serious world of Henry and Hotspur may be understood as outward confirmation of the inward step he takes in the play extempore toward the resolution of his essentially adolescent "predicament" at the start of the play. Moreover, viewing the figure of Prince Hal in this light removes any inconsistency in character one might otherwise feel between the Hal of Eastcheap and the prince at Shrewsbury and with it the need for reconciliation of that inconsistency traditionally found in the prince's soliloquy. For seen in this way, the emergence of the staunch defender of his father's crown from the irreverent practical-joking companion of Falstaff constitutes neither the working out of the conscious design of a dissembling prince nor the reformation of a prodigal son. It marks a transition to adulthood by a young man who, so long as his circumstances permit, gives sway to his high spirited love of low fun, but who, when confronted with responsibilities commensurate with his status and abilities, displays that previously inchoate sensibility to duty and honor that has always equally been part of his native character.[9] (In the prince's reconciliation scene with the king [3.2] one may now begin to hear the commonplace voice of an anxious father expressing his fear that his adolescent son's persistence in irrespon-

sible frivolity signifies that he will never really grow up, and the son's equally commonplace reassurances that such worries are unwarranted.) I am proposing, in sum, that, as a foundation for whatever other levels of interpretation or criticism this play can bear, what might be considered the most simplistic view of *1 Henry IV*—that it shows us a young man "growing up"—may also be the best. I am proposing that Shakespeare has construed and presented the historical record of the youth of Henry V as providing heightened examples of both the elemental predicament of adolescence and of an otherwise ordinary passage from adolescence to adulthood.[10] Whether that passage is wholly successful, or whether in negotiating it Hal unhappily sacrifices something of value in himself, requires a fuller appreciation of who, or what, Falstaff is and of how the prince comes to understand him.

II

1 Henry IV poses the question of Falstaff's real nature as the question of whether he is a coward. The question is raised in the second scene by Poins's scheme for turning the Gad's Hill robbery into a prank on Falstaff, and thereafter the subject of cowardice is kept before us through the end of the play. Thus, at the scene of the crime, when Falstaff, learning that the thieves will be outnumbered by their intended victims, exclaims " 'Zounds! Will they not rob us?," Prince Hal retorts, "What, a coward, Sir John Paunch?" (2.3.57-58). To Falstaff's reply, "Indeed, I am not John of Gaunt, your grandfather, but yet no coward Hal," the prince responds, "Well, we leave that to the proof" (2.3.59-61). Then later, after the thieves have regrouped at the tavern and Hal's "plain tale" has exposed Falstaff's "incomprehensible lies," the prince continually rubs Falstaff's nose in the fact and manner of his flight at Gad's Hill, returning to the topic even after the interruption of the play extempore and with the sheriff at the door. And after Hal's own overt preoccupation with the matter has ended, we listen throughout the battle scenes to Falstaff's repeated expressions of fear and, finally, watch him sham death upon Douglas's engaging him in combat.

The most striking thing about the issue of Falstaff's cowardice is that it should command so much attention as it does (I mean *within* the play, though the degree of attention it has commanded among commentators is equally noteworthy[11]). The list of deficiencies in Falstaff's moral character seems so long, why should it matter much one way or the other whether cowardice may be added to it? I want to propose that the imputation of cowardice is raised by the play because of its peculiar suitability as a starting point for revealing exactly how extraordinary a character Falstaff is. I will further claim that the unproductive old scholarly debate over whether Falstaff is really a coward is, in fact, fully answered in *1 Henry IV*,

Eric Christmas as Bardolph, Douglas Rain as Prince Hal, Tony Van Bridge as Falstaff, Bruno Gerussi as Gadshill, and Heath Lambert as Poins in a scene from the 1965 Stratford Festival production of Henry IV, Part 1.

though not within the terms of the debate itself. I am going to argue that, like Prince Hal, Falstaff fully and outwardly reveals what he is only in passing from Eastcheap to Shrewsbury and that both the significance of the question of Falstaff's cowardice and its answer may be discovered by considering his behavior in the play's military scenes.

Falstaff's first appearance in those scenes (4.2) finds him recounting how he has abused his infantry commission for his profit. Subsequently, we learn that he has led his scraggly recruits to their death, discover that he has abandoned his pistol for a bottle of sack, and see him promptly feign death upon the onslaught of Douglas. Falstaff's persistence in flippant and wholly unprincipled behavior even after he has entered the morally serious dimension of the play suggests that, if Hotspur's problem is that he is unable (or unwilling) to put his regard for his own personal honor in perspective, that where he feels that a principle is at stake he will go to battle against all odds

and cavil on the ninth part of a hair, Falstaff's problem is that he is unwilling (or unable) to put his comic persona aside when his circumstances demand that he do so—that he does not know, so to speak, when (or how) to stop being Falstaff.

The reason he does not stop is disclosed, at least for me, when Falstaff, prompted solely by some vague dream of uncertain reward for himself, rises from his pretense of death to stab Hotspur's fresh corpse in the thigh. However much I may remind myself that Hotspur is, after all, already dead, Falstaff's gratuitous stabbing of the corpse of an honorable man, who never in any way offended him personally, seems a surpassingly vile and contemptible act. And it is hard to conceive a greater desecration of Hotspur and all that he represents than the sight of his corpse being carried off as a trophy of battle by someone who has proclaimed honor to be just a word. (That Falstaff stabs Hotspur in the thigh, rather than, say, the heart, keeps his act from seeming not merely contemptible but malicious or evil. And if, as I am told, stabbing someone in the thigh is a traditional act of the Vice figure, then the fact that it is a *corpse* that Falstaff so stabs tends to show just how far beyond a conventional Vice figure Shakespeare's Falstaff is.)

Coming as it does immediately after Prince Hal's stirring tribute to the soul he has just taken in battle (a tribute that Falstaff, lying "dead" on stage, has himself overheard), Falstaff's defilement of Hotspur inspires the thought that only someone wholly insusceptible to any feeling of shame could commit such an act. And if one shares such a thought one may come to realize both why the play poses the question of Falstaff's character as the question of his cowardice and what the answer to that question is. One may see that it is indeed inaccurate to think of Falstaff as a coward. For cowardice is not merely fleeing from danger, however slight; what such flight reveals is, at most, excessive timidity. To be a coward one must first value or believe in something—believe, that is, that some person, property or principle is worth risking one's own person, property or (even) principles to obtain or defend. And then one must shrink out of fear from trying to obtain or defend it. (I do not, of course, say that such shrinking is *always* cowardice.) But Falstaff *believes in nothing*. There is no other person and there are no principles or property for which Falstaff would risk his own person or property, and he would not risk his person to defend his person if he could instead flee. So, in effect, there is nothing for him to be either courageous or cowardly about. Falstaff does not certainly display cowardice at Gad's Hill, if only because he cannot with any assurance be called cowardly for declining to risk injury or his life in defense of his ill-gotten booty. As in most thefts, it is (as it were, morally) entirely up to the thief's own discretion to what extent he will risk himself to obtain or retain his prize. (Don't robbers in movies, for instance, often flee immediately upon the appearance of the police or any other significant threat to their success? Do we typically regard them as *cowards* for doing so?) But Falstaff's falling dead before Douglas likewise is not evidence of cowardice, because Falstaff simply has no belief in the justice (or injustice) of his side's cause in the conflict and no loyalty (or disloyalty) to his king or the prince. No more is at stake for Falstaff in his encounter with Douglas than would be at stake for you or me if we were suddenly to find ourselves in the path of a runaway horse. (In this sense Falstaff is indeed, as he says, a coward "on instinct" [2.4.246-47].)

Poins is therefore correct when he distinguishes Falstaff from Bardolph and Peto—not because Falstaff (as some would have it) is more courageous than they, but because to think of him as capable of displaying either cowardice or courage is to misunderstand what he is. Poins alleges that Bardolph and Peto are "as true-bred cowards as ever turned back" (1.2.158-59), whereas of Falstaff he says, "if he fight longer than he sees reason, I'll forswear arms" (1.2.159-60). The clear implication is that under no circumstance where he perceives any genuine risk will Falstaff see reason for long, for if that is not Poins's meaning, one would have to understand him as implying that one acquits oneself admirably only if one fights *longer* than one sees reason. And if Falstaff is likely to see reason for as long as anyone else might, how is Hal to take comfort from Poins's words, as he is obviously meant to, that in robbing the robbers he will have nothing to fear from Falstaff? In other words, when confronted with any real risk, Bardolph and Peto, Poins gives us to believe, will fly out of fear despite their feeling they ought to stand, and so will prove (and may feel themselves) ordinary cowards. Whereas Falstaff, Poins in effect tells us, will fly out of fear because he does not, or will not long, experience the object he happens to be pursuing, or any other consideration, as constituting a reason for which he ought to stand, and so will not be (and will not feel himself) a coward. Poins apparently intuits this fact about Falstaff, and that is why he himself never conceived his practical joke with a view to exposing Falstaff as a coward. "The virtue of this jest," he says, "will be the incomprehensible lies that this same fat rogue will tell us when we meet him at supper" (1.2.160-62).

Those "incomprehensible lies," I would add, are similarly revealing of Falstaff's real nature. For the transparency of his account of himself at Gad's Hill, like the lame incredibility of his fabrications generally, suggests that Falstaff tells his lies compulsively and with little or no regard for their plausibility, in an almost naive hope of catching from them whatever benefit he can. Indeed, the most notable thing about Falstaff's lies is their very pervasiveness. He seldom utters a plain statement of fact. Apart from asking questions concerning matters intimately affecting his personal self-interest, it is almost solely in the hope of gaining some benefit to himself that he speaks at all. For Falstaff, like ourselves, words are tools; only it is as if Falstaff is wholly oblivious of their having any use whatever other than in the service of his personal interests and wishes. It is, for example, as if Falstaff never so much as entertains the notion that when he utters a statement of fact what he says *ought* to be *true*.

Falstaff's "catechism" on honor (5.1.127-39) is therefore no shrewdly observant unmasking of an outdated chivalric code or hypocritical or callously elitist notion of honor. It is a speech about honor in the everyday sense in which it is used throughout this essay and in which one feels honorable for living up to, and shame at falling short of, whatever standards one accepts for one's conduct in one's various roles as citizen, soldier, parent, teacher, host, . . . and so on. And the speech's misguided evaluation of honorable behavior in terms of whether or not it serves one's self-interest confirms its speaker's utter incomprehension of what honor is about. Falstaff's soliloquy thus merely makes express what is implicit in his conduct throughout and made manifest in the military scenes—that (as in Bradley's previously quoted account of him[12]) Falstaff is just wholly insensible to any standards or ideals of conduct whatever. And being, consequently, literally and completely shameless, honor—to him—is indeed just a word.[13]

But if Falstaff is so wholly devoid of any internalized standards of personal conduct, then no matter how much we may enjoy him, what *are* we to make of him? Should we, can we, regard him as being fully human at all? The juvenile epithets continually hurled at Falstaff by others, and by Falstaff at himself, suggest that we may indeed be meant to regard him as something less than ordinarily human. He is, among other things: chops, ribs, tallow, clay-brained guts, bed-presser, horseback-breaker, sweet beef, huge hill of flesh, tun of man, trunk of humors, bolting hutch of beastliness, swollen parcel of dropsies, huge bombard of sack, stuffed cloakbag of guts and roasted Manningtree ox with the pudding in his belly. All of these terms are used by Hal, and most are taken from his speech when playing the part of the king to Falstaff's prince (2.4.397-409). All of them point, of course, to Falstaff's grotesque obesity. I do not mean to insist that our common association of great corpulence with an extraordinary largeness of spirit, particularly comic spirit, is wholly out of place in the case of Falstaff. But the crude terms applied to Falstaff focus our attention instead on the literal fact of his enormous dripping flesh, and many raise an image of him as being entirely "stuffed" with corporeal matter.[14]

The play's continual harping on Falstaff's monstrous bulk, and its persistent characterization of him in terms of sheer physical mass, are intended, I think, to lead us to regard Falstaff as being comprised, as Stanley Cavell has hinted (398), of nothing but flesh. They are meant to lead us to believe that Prince Hal, whether he himself then knows it or not, speaks the literal truth when he says to Falstaff: ". . .there's no room for faith, truth, nor honesty in this bosom of thine. It is all filled up with guts and midriff" (3.3.137-38). Or, to use the term whose recurrence marks a major preoccupation of *1 Henry IV*, they are intended to show us that Falstaff is a stage character whose lack of any capacity whatever for moral seriousness renders him a "counterfeit" of a man. ("Dost thou hear, Hal?" Falstaff pleads after he knows that his behavior at Gad's Hill has raised questions in the prince's mind about the nature of his companion, "Never call a true piece of gold a counterfeit" [2.4.439-40].) This notion of Falstaff as counterfeit suggests, in turn, a further reason why Falstaff with Hotspur's corpse slung across his back is so breathtakingly devastating a sight. For it

implies that Falstaff also speaks the literal truth when he assures the astonished Prince Hal that what he sees before him is "not a double man" (5.4.134). Falstaff with Hotspur's corpse on his back is, rather, a horrific parody of one single man, of that union of flesh and spirit of which each authentic human being is comprised. For there stands Falstaff, this creature who is all flesh, who is nothing but his flesh, monstrously coupled to the corpse of a man who, if he was not composed solely of spirit, was possessed of a spirit (however flawed) so large as to make it seem that even "a kingdom for it was too small a bound" (5.4.89).[15]

Can we, however, seriously and steadily imagine that any creature who, like Falstaff, walks (no matter how poorly) and talks (after all, so wittily) and otherwise so clearly resembles an ordinary person might actually be so lacking in any standards of personal conduct as to be utterly without any capacity for honor and shame? I believe that Falstaff is intended as an approximation to such a creature. (Bloom voices much the same view in venturing the judgment that "Shakespeare's Falstaff was a successful representation of what Freud thought impossible, a human being without a superego" [1].[16]) And it is as some such fantastic creature that Prince Hal himself ultimately comes to regard Falstaff. I say "ultimately" because I think that the prince, like ourselves, does not fully appreciate what Falstaff is until witnessing his conduct in the play's military scenes. Like us, he begins by responding to him as if he were an ordinary person, construing the Gad's Hill episode, for example, as raising the question of his cowardice. But at some point during those military scenes the prince does, I believe, achieve a kind of understanding of Falstaff. Perhaps he reaches it when he passes over in near silence the spectacle of Falstaff's pitiful recruits. Or perhaps it is later when, finding Falstaff's holster contains a bottle of sack, he refrains from much more than an expression of silent disgust. But if not on these earlier occasions, then certainly when he is subjected to Falstaff's outrageous claim to have vanquished Hotspur himself. For how better explain the mild magnanimity of the prince's response to Falstaff's desecration of the man Hal himself so fairly eulogized only moments before?

> Come, bring your luggage nobly on your
>   back.
> For my part, if a lie may do thee grace,
> I'll gild it with the happiest terms I have.
> (5.4.150-53)

And having ourselves no ready label to describe a Falstaff,[17] we should not be surprised that Prince Hal, even after having seen for himself what he is, is able to describe him no better than he does to his brother after they have listened to Falstaff's account of his conquest of Hotspur:

JOHN: This is the strangest tale ever I heard.
PRINCE: This is the strangest fellow, brother
John.

(5.4.149-50)

That may be as great an understatement as exists in all of literature.

We now have the foundation for considering the interior significance to Henry V of Falstaff's banishment. I proposed earlier that Bradley is correct in implicitly identifying Falstaff with (the capacity for) a comic perspective. To wish to banish plump Jack on account of what he affirmatively represents is indeed, therefore, to wish to banish, if not all the world (as Falstaff would like one to believe), nothing less than the claims of the flesh and a perspective enabling one to transcend, or at least temporarily step outside, a life otherwise relentlessly governed by the untempered demands of duty and honor. But as such an account of Falstaff/comedy implies, comedy is not just occasionally and incidentally, but is pervasively and inherently, morally subversive. And Falstaff, I have just argued, is an embodiment not merely of a comic perspective but of an *exclusively* comic perspective. May it not then be for that reason that he is banished by Henry V? May we not imagine that in banishing the particular stage character called Falstaff, Henry V is not so much rejecting what that character chiefly represents, and thereby rejecting that part of himself expressed in Eastcheap, as proclaiming the depth of his own commitment, as the new leader of his nation, to those qualities that character so completely lacks—proclaiming it as decisively as he can and for all the world to hear? I am conjecturing that in the coronation scene of *Part 2* we have yet another of Hal's famous performances, only now, and for the first time, one that is put on more for others than for himself.

III

By way of conclusion, I want to explain my opening observation that perhaps the most inventive of the techniques employed in *1 Henry IV* is one by which the play elicits in the audience itself a mirroring of the tension between comic and morally serious perspectives one finds within a single character (Prince Hal) and between characters (*e.g.,* Hal and Falstaff).

So long as Falstaff is confined to the world of Eastcheap we are able to enjoy his antics largely free of indignation at their impropriety. But as we listen to him boasting, on the road near Coventry amid the preparations for battle, how he has turned his commission to his financial advantage, leaving himself with a regiment comprised solely of the infirm and malnourished, a genuinely sour note may for the first time intrude upon our enjoyment of him. Our feeling of discomfort may continue when we later learn that,

though unscathed himself, he has led those pathetic troops to their slaughter and when we witness him fall down dead before Douglas, only to rise up to mutilate Hotspur's corpse. In view of our affection for Falstaff and the delight we previously have taken (and obviously been intended to take) in him, we may wonder if such feelings are appropriate and even try to suppress them. But I believe we do feel them. I am claiming, in other words, that, while it may come at a different point for some of us than for others, at *some* point during the play's military scenes our attitude toward Falstaff is likely to alter. We are likely to pass from experiencing him as an unambiguously and profoundly comic figure, whose frank and unmalicious disregard for everything respectable and morally serious would distress only a prig, to becoming sufficiently troubled by his behavior as to be made uncomfortable by our continued affection for him.

But what has changed? Clearly not Falstaff. Perhaps then it is the nature of what he does. But, surely, abusing one's military commission for profit or lack of enthusiasm for swordplay are not somehow *inherently* graver improprieties less susceptible to comic treatment than are, say, highway robbery or attempting to defraud one's hostess with false allegations of theft. How, then, explain our finding ourselves suddenly repelled by Falstaff, or at least no longer certain exactly how to respond to him, during those military scenes?

Acknowledging the possibility of such negative feelings toward Falstaff, but believing that Shakespeare means him always to have a purely comic effect, Bradley concludes that any opprobrium we may feel cannot be intended. Instead, he maintains, it must stem either from our misunderstanding of his conduct or from our inappropriately allowing our everyday moral seriousness to intrude, rather than attending, as Bradley thinks we are meant to throughout the play, solely to the comic aspects of Falstaff's "misdeeds." Our failure to maintain a purely comic perspective toward Falstaff "would," he says, "destroy the poet's whole conception" (265). Bradley's notion of Shakespeare's conception is, I submit, in this respect too narrow. He is wrong to dismiss our feelings of repulsion at Falstaff and to suppose that Shakespeare does not really intend them. The introduction of Falstaff into the historical dimension of *1 Henry IV* is the final step in a technique deliberately perpetrated by the playwright on his audience. By first shuttling us back and forth during the first three acts between scenes of comic low-life and scenes of solemn royal councils and sober conspiratorial deliberations on rebellion, the play successively elicits in us those scenes' opposed perspectives. By then wresting Falstaff—the very center and source of our comic focus—from his native Eastcheap and casting him into the morally serious world of Henry and Hotspur, the play produces in ourselves a collision between comic and morally serious perspectives that mirrors the one Prince Hal has himself been experiencing.

Accordingly, only by freely acknowledging *both* our affection *and* our repugnance for Falstaff are we likely to appreciate that part of Shakespeare's achievement in *1 Henry IV* is to cast the light of wonder on the everyday and familiar by forcing his audience to confront its two competing perspectives—without, however, requiring, or even inviting, it to reject one in favor of the other. Our repugnance at Falstaff's behavior in the play's military scenes is evidence of our inability wholly to detach ourselves from a morally serious perspective. Our persistent affection for Falstaff, despite that repugnance, is evidence of our unwillingness to forgo our capacity for a comic perspective as well. Our wish, like Bradley's, to find a way not to disapprove of Falstaff in order to continue to enjoy him—like our tendency to imagine that the emergence of the dutiful prince from the truant Hal must constitute a reformation of his character or be explained by the latter persona's having been a mask for the former—is evidence of the extent to which these two perspectives mutually eclipse one another. By propelling Falstaff onto the battlefield at Shrewsbury, Shakespeare leaves us, like poor Francis, amazed and uncertain which way to turn.

Notes

[1] Bevington provides no citation for, or other elucidation of, his cryptic suggestion that some commentators have construed the soliloquy as "whistling in the dark." See, however, the comments on the speech by Samuel Johnson and Daniel Seltzer (quoted, respectively, later in the text of this essay and in note 8) and by Edward Dowden (cited in note 9).

[2] The quotation is a composite of phrases from two portions of the text. For similar, and not always more charitable, assessments of the prince, each likewise grounded in a reading of his soliloquy, see Frye 76-78; Traversi 57-58; Goddard 171-75; Masefield 112-13; and Bradley 256-59.

[3] All citations of the text of *1 Henry IV* are to the second Norton edition.

[4] See, for example, Dickinson; Wilson 17-25; and Tillyard 265-69.

[5] For another commentator who comes close to such a reading, see note 8.

[6] The characterization of Richard Gloucester in the prior sentence is borrowed from Adelman.

[7] To whom other than himself is the Prince referring as "the drunkard" when learning of Falstaff's arrival at the end of this episode, he cries out. " 'Rivol' says the drunkard. Call in ribs, call in tallow" (2.4.100-01)? But perhaps the fact of the prince's intoxication is now so well accepted as not to require demonstration.

[8] I think our readings are, however, mutually consistent. Seltzer, for example, comes extremely close to reading the soliloquy as a rationalization when he describes its analogies as being "platitudes . . . which are to some extent alibis" (23) and characterizes the speech generally as "a shoring up of personal defenses" (24).

[9] For a similar view, see Dowden 210-12.

[10] The OED (2nd ed.) dates the words "adolescence" and "adolescent" to *circa* 1430 and to 1482, respectively. Lawrence Stone's brief discussion of adolescence (375-77) also tends to allay any qualms one may have about transporting the modern concept and experience of adolescence to Elizabethan England. Observing that "[t]he problem of adolescence . . . [was] familiar enought [sic] to Europeans since the fifteenth century . . . [that] the shepherd in Shakespeare's *A Winter's Tale* must have struck a familiar chord when he remarked, 'I would there were no age between sixteen and twenty-three, or that youth would sleep out the rest; for there is nothing in the between but getting wenches with child, wronging the ancientry, stealing, fighting,' " Stone asserts that a well-defined adolescent subculture existed throughout the period and concludes that "[t]he idea that adolescence, as a distinctive age-group with its distinctive problems, was a development of the nineteenth century is entirely without historical foundation." However, even if it were established that the modern experience of adolescence was not a sufficiently familiar fact of Elizabethan life to warrant my assumption that Shakespeare could have dramatized such an experience and expected his audience to recognize it as such, I would nevertheless be inclined to maintain that Hal is portrayed as undergoing, as a consequence of his own unique circumstances as heir apparent, an experience and a predicament that may appropriately be understood as precursors of those we now think of as distinctively adolescent.

[11] For a summary of the debate among commentators through the middle of this century over whether Falstaff is a coward, see Sprague.

[12] Bradley fails, however, to carry that account to its logical conclusion. Despite remarking at one point that Falstaff is "a character almost purely humorous, and therefore no subject for moral judgments" (260), he goes on to try to exonerate him from imputations that he is a liar and coward in a manner appropriate to an ordinary person, arguing that Falstaff seldom, if ever, intends his lies actually to deceive and never shows the craven fear Bradley takes as the mark of true cowardice (264-68).

[13] This paragraph was prompted by a conversation with John Zilliax. In continuing that conversation here, I want to emphasize that by discounting the cogency of any debunking of the concept of honor that comes from the mouth of Falstaff I do not mean to deny that other aspects of *1 Henry IV* raise provocative questions about appeals to individual or national honor as a motive or justification for destructive personal or social conflict.

[14] Much as I am indebted to Jonathan Grossman for calling my attention to the frequency with which Falstaff is specifically characterized as being "stuffed" with material substance, I am still more grateful for his patient advice and encouragement as I worked my way through drafts of this essay.

[15] Harold E. Toliver informs us that, in Elizabethan times, "a rider's control of his mount was a common figure for the soul's control of its body" (75). When this significance of a mounted rider is combined with the notion that Falstaff is comprised purely of flesh, it becomes clearer why both Hal and Hotspur are represented as accomplished horsemen, whereas Falstaff must have a charge afoot and go always uncolted.

[16] The most fully elaborated conception of Falstaff closest to that developed here is perhaps Franz Alexander's. Paralleling other themes developed in this essay, Alexander also notes that "[t]he double structure of [*1 Henry IV*] permanently forces us to look alternately at two different aspects of life which are in steady contradiction to each other," that Prince Hal "stands between" them and that the audience continually shifts during the play between identifying with each (596-97).

[17] Due to its conventional restriction to matters of conscience and duty, "amoral" is too narrow for the task, though it might be adequate in a culture with a shame-based Aristotelian concept of morality embracing not merely matters of right and wrong but the full range of standards by which one assesses oneself and others as acting well or ill, honorably or shamefully, in the multitude of one's daily roles. In addition to the psychoanalytic explications of Falstaff offered by Bloom and Alexander, one way to try to understand him might be by analogy to a very young, pre-socialized and incorrigible, child. Falstaff's childlike qualities are well brought out in Brooks and Heilman.

Works Cited

Adelman, Janet. *Suffocating Mothers*. New York: Routledge, 1992.

Alexander, Franz. "A Note on Falstaff." *Psychoanalytic Quarterly* 2 (1993): 592-606.

Bevington, David, ed. Introduction. *Henry IV, Part I*. By William Shakespeare. Oxford: Oxford UP, 1987. 1-110.

Bloom, Harold, ed. Introduction. *Falstaff*. New York: Chelsea House, 1992. 1-4.

Bowers, Fredson. "Shakespeare's Art: The Point of View." *Literary Views*. Ed. Carroll Camden. Chicago: U of Chicago P, 1964. 45-58. (Rpt. in part as "The Structural Climax in *Henry IV, Part I*" in Shakespeare, *Henry the Fourth, Part I* 309-16.)

Bradley, A. C. "The Rejection of Falstaff." *Oxford Lectures on Poetry*. 1909. London: Macmillan, 1963. 247-73.

Brooks, Cleanth, and Robert B. Heilman. "Notes on *Henry IV, Part I*." *Understanding Drama*. New York: Henry Holt, 1945. 376-87. (Rpt. as "Dramatic Balance in *Henry IV, Part I*" in Shakespeare, *Henry the Fourth, Part I* 215-29.)

Cavell, Stanley. *The Claim of Reason*. New York: Oxford UP, 1979.

Dickinson, Hugh. "The Reformation of Prince Hal." *Shakespeare Quarterly* 12 (1961): 33-46.

Dowden, Edward. *Shakespere: A Critical Study of His Mind and Art*. 3rd ed. 1875. New York: Barnes, 1967.

Frye, Northrop. *Northrop Frye on Shakespeare*. New Haven: Yale UP, 1986.

Goddard, Harold C. *The Meaning of Shakespeare*. Chicago: U of Chicago P, 1951.

Gottschalk, Paul A. "Hal and the 'Play Extempore' in *1 Henry IV*." *TSLL* 4.4 (1974): 605-14.

Greenblatt, Stephen. "Invisible Bullets." *Shakespearean Negotiations*. Berkeley: U of California P, 1988. 21-65.

Johnson, Samuel, *Selections from Johnson on Shakespeare*. Ed. Bertrand H. Bronson and Jean M. O'Meara. New Haven: Yale UP, 1986.

Masefield, John. *William Shakespeare*. New York: Henry Holt, 1911.

Seltzer, Daniel. "Prince Hal and Tragic Style." *Shakespeare Survey* 30. Ed. Kenneth Muir. London: Cambridge UP, 1977. 13-27.

Shaaber, M. A., ed. Introduction. *The First Part of King Henry the Fourth*. By William Shakespeare. Baltimore: Pelican-Penguin, 1957. 15-25.

Shakespeare, William. *Henry the Fourth, Part I*. Ed. James L. Sanderson. 2nd ed. New York: Norton, 1969.

————. *The Second Part of King Henry the Fourth.* Ed. Allan Chester. Baltimore: Pelican-Penguin, 1957.

Shuchter, J. D. "Prince Hal and Francis: The Imitation of an Action." *Shakespeare Studies* III (1967): 129-37.

Sprague, Arthur Colby. "Gadshill Revisited." *Shakespeare Quarterly* 4 (1953): 125-37. (Rpt. in Shakespeare, *Henry the Fourth, Part I* 278-95.)

Stone, Lawrence. *The Family, Sex and Marriage in England 1500-1800.* New York: Harper, 1977.

Tillyard, E. M. W. *Shakespeare's History Plays.* 1944. London: Chatto and Windus, 1980.

Toliver, Harold E. "Falstaff, the Prince, and the History Play." *Shakespeare Quarterly* 16 (1965): 63-80. (Rpt. with revisions in Shakespeare, *Henry the Fourth, Part I* 169-93.)

Traversi, Derek. *Shakespeare from* Richard II *to* Henry V. Stanford: Stanford UP, 1957.

Zitner, S. P. "Anon, Anon: or, A Mirror for a Magistrate." *Shakespeare Quarterly* 19 (1968): 63-70.

GENRE

Harry Levin (essay date 1981)

SOURCE: "Falstaff's Encore," in *Shakespeare Quarterly,* Vol. 32, No. 1, Spring, 1981, pp. 5-17.

[*In the following essay, originally presented in 1980, Levin examines the relationship between* 1 *and* 2 *Henry IV, and concludes that* 2 *Henry IV's function as a sequel is less important than its role in highlighting Shakespeare's shift from history plays and comedies to tragedies, noting that Falstaff's presence in the play signals this change of genre.*]

Any single work which entitles itself *The Second Part* starts from something of a disadvantage.[1] The compensating advantage is that it has been instigated by the widespread success of some forerunner, like *The Godfather.* But any sequel, necessarily presupposing a first part, is confronted by problems of autonomy. It is much easier for a novelist—a Dumas, a Proust, a Trollope, or a Fenimore Cooper—whose *roman-fleuve* can flow from book to book at the convenience of the reader. For a dramatist, well, the second part of *Faust,* one of the masterworks of the world's literature, rarely gets presented upon the stage. Cyclical presentation, as of Wagner's *Ring* at Bayreuth, has been rather the exception than the rule. Sophocles' three plays consti-

tuting the *Oedipus* trilogy were not composed in chronological sequence or produced at the same time. Dover Wilson believed that *The Second Part of Henry the Fourth* had been, and should be, performed within twenty-four hours of the first. A more recent playgoer and critic, Richard David, raises an objection to this continuity, insofar as it involves sitting through so much duplication and recapitulation. In general the critics seem to be equally divided, voicing strong opinions in both camps, on the composition of *Part Two,* its relationship with *Part One,* the inclusion of the pair in a trilogy with *Henry V,* and of all three into a tetralogy with *Richard II,* coexisting in synoptic unity. Samuel Johnson heads the roll of unitarians, who favor one grand overarching design. S. B. Hemingway, the *Varorium* editor of *The First Part,* speaks very forcefully on behalf of the pluralists, when he describes the two plays as "mutually exclusive."

Ambiguity is further clouded by the fact that *Part One* was not so designated until the First Folio, though it went through several more quartos than *Part Two.* The latter might today have been more aptly christened *Son of Henry IV.* The three parts of *Henry VI* were first numbered in the Folio, *Part One* making its maiden appearance there, whereas *Parts Two* and *Three* had previously been published in bad quartos under different titles. This and other Elizabethan examples do not really sustain the retrospective presumption that Shakespeare must have studiously planned and carefully executed a *Henriad* at long range. There are too many incidental disparities, readily traceable to the conditions of theatrical authorship. The second part of Christopher Marlowe's *Tamburlaine* had been prompted—so the prologue tells us—by "the general welcome" accorded to the first, and there would be an interval of twenty-six years between the first and second parts of Dekker's *Honest Whore.* We are promised and denied a reunion with the living Falstaff in *Henry V;* and we have instead the fortuitous caricature of him in *The Merry Wives of Windsor.* In the theatre it is not difficult to imagine a situation where an experimental playwright, like Marlowe, has been broaching a novel treatment of a broad subject, and relies upon the public reaction to encourage him toward continuance. In that respect, the *New Arden* editor, Arthur Humphreys, building on a study of Harold Jenkins, seems well warranted in characterizing the process as an "organic evolution." Shakespeare could have early contemplated the whole conception, but it remained to be worked out through his step-by-step artistic development.

He was working in a genre peculiar to the Elizabethans, which he made peculiarly his own, the history-play. This had its great run during the patriotic decade heralded by England's defeat of the Spanish armada in 1588. Covering the succession of British kings all the way back to the legendary Brut, drama served the forensic functions of propaganda and pedagogy. Formally it had to be episodic, depending upon the miscellaneous nature of annals and reigns and royal personalities. A weak but long-reigning monarch, Henry VI, could preside inertly in the background, while the foreground was animated by such episodes as the witchcraft of Joan La Pucelle, the rebellion of Jack Cade, and the usurpation of the Yorkists. The weakness of Richard II, under Shakespeare's lyrical touch, could become a theme for tragedy, following the venture of Marlowe in *Edward II.* The sinister force of Richard III could unify a play in the manner of Marlowe's more dynamic protagonists. However, Shakespeare found his most effective historical subject-matter in *Henry IV*—not so much in the uneasy crown of the self-made king as in the romance of Hotspur's losing cause, on the one hand, and the comedy of Falstaff's unpredictable presence, on the other. Just as he had taken comic conventions and moved them into the area of the tragic with *Romeo and Juliet,* so within the framework of history he created his greatest comic figure. Plot had been advanced by Aristotle as the first principle of poetics; yet it is character that predominates in Shakespeare; and for Hazlitt, as for many other readers and playgoers, Falstaff is "the most substantial character that ever was invented."

Hazlitt was playing upon the word *substantial,* to some extent; paranomasia is hard to resist in Falstaff's company. What surprises us is that Shakespeare, whose light-fingered way with source-materials has made heavy the hands of Shakespearean scholars, had so little to go by in this case. Henry V was perhaps the most popular ruler before the Tudors, having reconquered parts of France in the Hundred Years' War and then died prematurely. His popularity did not suffer from the rumors that he had led a prodigal youth and had reformed on acceding to the throne. Intangible gossip had crystallized into an anecdote, best known through Sir Thomas Elyot's *Book of the Governor.* One of his rowdy companions is sentenced for thievery; whereupon the Prince threatens to strike the judge, and in turn is sentenced for contempt; he gracefully accepts and duly serves the sentence. That is pure *exemplum,* demonstrating that no Englishman stands above the law, and that the Lord Chief Justice personifies regal power. It is interesting that Shakespeare ignores the episode in *Part One* and touches on it merely by offstage allusion in *Part Two.* The rumored wildness of Hal, from the pledge of reformation set forth in his first monologue, is consistently toned down. The dissolute playboy seems at heart to be a fun-loving boy-scout. In conquering Hotspur he seems to take over some of his rival's traits—even, occasionally in *Henry V,* the militant tone of voice. Harry's youthful fraternization with Tom, Dick, and Francis will have made him more humane as head of state than his aloof and crafty father has been. It completes his *Bildung,* his education, his kingly for-

mation, as Warwick advises Henry IV: "The Prince but studies his companions . . ." (*Part One,* IV.iv.68).

I

If you care to witness the princely box on the judicial ear, you should turn back to Shakespeare's crude old anonymous precursor, *The Famous Victories of Henry V.* There the chief comic *persona* was a clown named Dericke, played by the leading comedian, Richard Tarleton. Among the hangers-on of this unmistakably raffish prince is a silly old man addressed as Jockey. His given name is Sir John Oldcastle. Now it is common knowledge that Shakespeare originally used that appellation, was reminded that it had belonged to an actual person with ironically puritanical leanings, thereupon adopted "Sir John Falstaff" from a craven minor character in *1 Henry IV,* and offered an apologetic disclaimer in the Epilogue to *2 Henry IV.* The name's degree of resonance has been measured statistically by G. E. Bentley, in his monograph comparing the reputations of Shakespeare and Jonson during the seventeenth century. Professor Bentley finds that Falstaff was mentioned by other authors far more often than any other character (131 times, more than twice the number of the next figure on the list). If we have anyone in mind, it is he, when we talk of personages who walk out of books into our lives. (Indeed he led an independent existence in the clandestine theatre of the Commonwealth: one of Francis Kirkman's *Drolls* is simply patched together from Falstaff's scenes in *Part One.*) Critical formulation, in failing to pin him down, confesses with Dr. Johnson that he is "unimitated and inimitable." Numerous and various archetypes, from drama, literature, folklore, and anthropology, have been cited to throw light on his charisma. Frequently they do: he is a Braggart, a Parasite, a Trickster, a Scapegoat, a Fool, a Vice—all of these, and hence more than their sum.

He was the overwhelming surprise of *Part One;* he is the main attraction of *Part Two,* where he deliberately upstages everyone else and—at least until the put-down he seems to be asking for—all but runs away with the show. With a page as stooge, he shamelessly mugs; he appeals to the audience directly; he moves in and takes over situations, like *The Man Who Came to Dinner* on Broadway or his Hollywood counterpart, W.C. Fields. He behaves with atrocious rudeness and no respect for persons of high standing; the "sneap" (or snub) that he receives from the Lord Chief Justice is smartly returned "tap for tap," though it turns out to be a portent of the ultimate come-uppance (II.i.122, 193). Sociable and anti-social at once, he can be delightfully amusing and flagrantly immoral. We identify with him, in a kind of dionysiac empathy, because he invites us vicariously to shed our own inhibitions. The actor who plays the role faces the double task of commanding our sympathies while remaining a consummate rogue.

From the outset he is conscious that all eyes are fixed upon him: "The brain of this foolish-compounded clay, man, is not able to invent anything that intends to laughter more than I invent or is invented on me" (I.ii.7 ff.). In his pompous and peremptory letter to the Prince, he subscribes himself "Sir John with all Europe" (II.ii.134). He has become so famous that Coleville of the Dale surrenders to him without a fight, though Prince John's dry comment is scarcely a tribute to Falstaff's courage, and the entire engagement is anti-heroic. He has claimed the rewards for his "day's service at Shrewsbury," which—as the Justice acknowledges—has "a little gilded over your night's exploit on Gadshill" (I.ii.148-49).

Looking at the sources, A. L. Attwater suggested that *Part Two* was conceived as an encore to *Part One,* "hastily written" to exploit the fresh impact of Shakespeare's stunning characterization. We could admit the importance of that motive, without overlooking the arguments that support a more considered procedure. For one thing, *Part Two* runs about 250 lines longer than *Part One,* and Falstaff has the same proportion of lines (roughly twenty percent) in both parts. The roles of the King and the Prince have both been diminished under transition, the Prince's by just about half, while the Hostess has more than tripled her volubility and a variety of new comic characters has been recruited. The absence of Hotspur is emphasized by the false start, briskly linking the scene with the Battle of Shrewsbury through a misleading report, as well as by the choric lamentations of the Percies, bringing home the sense of an aftermath. Later on, instead of a heroic climax at Shrewsbury, we have the anticlimax at Gaultree Forest: a parley which leads not to battle but to betrayal. Thus history gets short shrift in *Part Two.* Three quarters of the Dering Manuscript, a conflation of both parts which is historically focused, derive from *Part One.* Though Holinshed's Chronicle included no lack of subsequent material, this was too discursive to be dramatized as Shrewsbury had so effectively been. *Part Two* is therefore centrifugal, where *Part One* had been centripetal; the cast of the second is twice as large as that of the first. *Part One* manages to balance the historic and comic elements, and to sound with Hotspur a tragic note. History, in *Part Two,* is outdistanced by comedy most of the way, yet ends by humbling comedy with a vengeance.

II

Honor, as a military virtue, sets the ethical standard of *Part One,* weighed in the equipoise between Hotspur's magniloquent apostrophe and Falstaff's reductive catechism. Justice is the civic virtue prevailing in *Part Two,* where misrule must capitulate to rule. Lacking a fit antagonist for outward historical rivalry, the Prince's conflict becomes a *psychomachia,* a morality-play in which the wavering hero must choose between the

guidance of two surrogate fathers: Falstaff, "that reverent Vice" (*Part One,* II.iv.453), and that newly authorized counselor, the Lord Chief Justice: "You shall be as a father to my youth" (V.ii.118). As a result, the moral paradigm is more expressly underlined, but it remains essentially the same—which has caused some commentators to remark that *Part Two* is rather an imitation than a continuation. After all, the Prince has made good his pledge and won his spurs on the battlefield. After that exploit of reformation, plus his reconciliation with the King, he can do little except repeat the performance at his father's death. No wonder he declares, on his belated entrance in Act II (for he is not onstage in Acts I and III), "Before God, I am exceeding weary" (II.ii.1). His half-hearted role-playing, his temporary backsliding among the riffraff, foreshadows the last line of the Epilogue: "My tongue is weary; when my legs are too, I will bid you good night." Erich Auerbach's *Mimesis* has a chapter whose starting-point is Hal's introductory dialogue, entitled "The Weary Prince." But it is not, like Auerbach's other chapters, an *explication de texte;* rather, it seizes the occasion to illustrate his theory deriving realism from the intermixture of grand and humble styles. "From a prince to a prentice? a low transformation!" (II.ii.174).

The interrelationship of the two plays is further complicated by the problematic interposition of *The Merry Wives of Windsor.* Evidence would seem to suggest that the writing of *2 Henry IV* was interrupted by the queenly command and courtly circumstance that evoked the Falstaffian comedy, although certain links with *Henry V* betoken a possible rewriting for public production. At any rate, *The Merry Wives of Windsor* sags with signs of having been written to order. Queen Elizabeth's wish to see Falstaff in love proved an unhappy inspiration, as it transpired, possibly because—as Dr. Johnson put it—"Falstaff could not love without ceasing to be Falstaff." He himself had explained the discrepancy by his exordium in *Part Two:* "I am not only witty in myself, but the cause that wit is in other men" (I.ii.9-10). In *The Merry Wives of Windsor* he is less of a wit than a butt, more laughed at than laughed with, repeatedly discomfited not by other men but by women, whose practical jokes fend off his clumsy advances. Insofar as he must momentarily dress as a woman, and two boys must compound the trickery by transvestism, the play may all too etymologically be considered a travesty. Falstaff suffers more of a comedown at Windsor than he does when the crowned Henry V rejects him. We are even tempted to surmise a connection between his unforeseeable reappearance in this play and his failure to reappear in *Henry V,* despite the Epilogue of *Part Two.* The happiest consequence of Elizabeth's idea, as W. H. Auden pointed out, would be the libretto for Verdi's last and most delightful opera. Yet we hesitate to chide Shakespeare with the stricture, which might well apply to Victor Hugo's melodramas, that foolish-sounding words may be redeemed by being set to music.

III

Let us then revert from the Garter at Windsor to the Boar's Head in Eastcheap, and consequently to the invidious and unavoidable comparison between the two parts of *Henry IV*. The second part is held by H. N. Hudson to represent a "falling off"; for R. G. White, at the opposite pole, it achieves "unsurpassed perfection." Critical judgment has ranged across that long-drawn-out spectrum, though much of it has come out somewhat closer to Hudson's view than to White's. Not only was Shakespeare daring enough to take us back again to the Boar's Head and vie with himself in the setting of a former triumph, but John Masefield has boldly asserted that this reprise is "the finest tavern scene ever written." It should serve accordingly as our touchstone, while we remember its longer and earlier model: the joke on the drawer Francis, the showdown between the Prince and Falstaff over the foray at Gadshill, the play-acting by way of celebration and rehearsal for serious business, the culminating apologia of Falstaff, and—after the interruption of the Sheriff—the reckoning in the form of the snoring Falstaff's unpaid bill. To this we should add our remembrance of a second scene taking place in that locale: Falstaff's hangover on a morning after, a change of tempo with the Prince's call to arms, and—after the others have marched off heroically—an ambivalent couplet, with Falstaff imaginably sitting down and pounding on the table:

> Rare words! brave world! Hostess, my
> breakfast, come!
> O, I could wish this tavern were my drum!
>
> (III.iii.205-6)

Honor will soon enough be reduced to a word; breakfast must come before everything else, and the tag-line leaves us wondering whether he wants to convert the tavern into a drum or a drum into the tavern, whether or not he would rather be taking his ease at his inn than be marching off to war.

As for the tavern, it has held a significance of its own in relation to the stage. It has been a continual hangout for playwrights, the alcoholic stimulus probably meaning less to them than the opportunities for confraternity and the chances to observe. We have heard a good deal more than we know about the Mermaid, much of it too easily sentimentalized. When Robert Herrick refers to the Sun, the Dog, and the Triple Tun, we gather that Ben Jonson and his disciples engaged in pub-crawls; yet Jonson's lively tavern scenes include—in *The Staple of News*—one at the Apollo room in the Devil, where he was particularly fond of holding forth. Another scene that stands out is in the collaborative *Eastward Ho*, where Captain Seagull spins a utopian fantasy about the Virginia colony. But the tradition has older and deeper roots.

From the standpoint of medieval homiletics, as expressed in *The Agenbite of Inwit:* "The tavern is the school of the Devil where his disciples study." As a licensed and licentious dispensary for the sensual pleasures of this world, it was regarded as an entry to the everlasting bonfire. It was the favorite haunt of those wayward clerks, the Goliards, whose major interests have been brazenly flaunted in the title of J. A. Symonds' translations, *Wine, Women, and Song*. In recoil from Christian asceticism, their Carmina Burana blasphemously set the tavern above the church: *"Magis quam ecclesiam / Diligo tabernam."* This matches, in cadence and sentiment, the well-known distich from another of their bibulous lyrics: *"Meum est propositum / In taberna mori."* Falstaff would be realizing that ambition to meet one's end in a pothouse.

In the morality plays, when the Vice did his damnedest to lead Everyman astray, the den of temptation was usually a tavern, which was often constructed as an *aedes* (or mansion) on the *platea* (or playing space). In the oldest vernacular miracle play, the thirteenth-century *Jeu de Saint Nicolas* of Jean Bodel, couriers rushing to and from the Crusades stop to refresh themselves at such a place, where there is dicing and brawling as well as drinking. While the thieves are roistering there, the saint makes his epiphany to reveal the stolen treasure. In the Digby *Mary Magdalene,* half-mystery and half-morality, the heroine is seduced on her harlot's progress by a gallant known as Curiosity in a tavern at Jerusalem. In the moralistic interlude, *Mundus et Infans,* Folly lures Mankind away from Conscience long enough to dine in Eastcheap and drink at the Pope's Head. To audiences, these machinations for lapsing into sins of the flesh may have been the most attractive stations on pilgrimages didactically conducted, just as the most dashing roles were those of Herod, the Devil, and the Vice. Just as the murder of children in *Richard III* and *Macbeth* can be put into perspective by recalling *The Slaughter of the Innocents,* so the tavern scenes of Shakespeare have behind them a rich backlog of dramatic convention. Not unlike his trial scenes, which reflect the institutional structure of English society and the legal nurture of English drama, tavern scenes were likewise displayed as set-pieces, testing the worldly wisdom of the dramatist. Moreover, they traditionally connoted the sobering assumption that rounds of festivity would be sooner or later offset by seasons of penitence.

IV

The tavern scene of *Part One* is more single-mindedly a carousal, to the point where Falstaff must sleep it off. Food suffuses the aura of imagery that surrounds his person, as when he is likened to a "roasted Manningtree ox with the pudding in his belly" (II.iv.452-53); but on his bill the "half-pennyworth of bread" is swamped by an "intolerable deal of sack" (l.540).

This emphasis on drink, like that on war, intimates that the field of action is perforce a man's world, as Hotspur pointedly reminds his wife. I am not suggesting that there is any drouth of liquor in *Part Two*. In lieu of his catechism on honor, Falstaff will recite his panegyric on sherry, which is praised as a sovereign instigator of wit. More specifically, he will credit it with making a better man of Prince Hal by warming up his cold Lancastrian blood. The contextual irony is that Prince John, through his deception of the rebels, has just shown a truly Falstaffian contempt for honor. There had been a few allusions to wenching in the first part, mainly with regard to Falstaff himself; but his accusation to the Hostess—"This house has turned bawdy-house" (III.iii.99-100)—was no more justified than Othello's frenzied denunciation of Emilia as a bawd. Shakespeare would not deal at first hand with the humors of the brothel until *Measure for Measure* and *Pericles*. Yet in *2 Henry IV* he introduced an unflinching component of illicit sex. No longer a baffled onlooker, the Hostess takes the initiative with a lawsuit; her complaints to the Chief Justice allege both unconscionable sponging and breach of promise. Falstaff charms her into not only pawning her goods to lend him more money, but procuring him another woman.

The tavern scene of *Part Two* is centered on that farewell assignation. It opens with an atmospheric quip, echoed in the talk of the drawers as they set the table. The Prince once teased Sir John, we hear, by placing a dish of six apple-johns (wrinkled winter apples) before him, then rising with a flourish to depart, and saying "I will now take my leave of these six, dry, round, old, withered knights" (II.iv.7-8). Verily, he will be taking his leave of this elderly lecher. Meanwhile the Hostess enters, clucking like a motherly hen, coddling and supporting the toughest of Shakespeare's heroines. The characterization of Mistress Quickly, we noted, has been much more fully developed. She already had a flair for mistaking the word, two centuries before Mrs. Malaprop, for abusing God's patience and the Queen's English, and for stumbling into many an off-color *double-entendre*. Malapropisms begin to charge the air as she comforts Doll Tearsheet, with whom we are making our first acquaintance. She had been signalized when the Page reported the rendezvous to the Prince, who suspected that she must be "some road," and Poins added, "as common as the way between Saint Albons and London" (II.ii.166-68). Coleridge, reading the Prince's epithet literally and chastely, proposed to emend Doll's surname to "Tearstreet." He must have skipped the passage where Falstaff threatens to toss Pistol in a blanket, and Doll encourages Falstaff by promising to canvass him "between a pair of sheets" (II.iv.225). But at the start she is in a contrary mood, tipsy, queasy, and truculent, having "drunk too much canaries" (l.26). When the Hostess inquires how she is

feeling, her ambiguous reply—"Better than I was. Hem!" (l.30)—thereby terminates with a hiccup.

Falstaff makes a loudly mock-heroic entrance, singing a snatch of an Arthurian ballad. But his own first words are "Empty the jordan" (l.34)—an injunction which Hugo would admire for its extroverted shamelessness. He had called for a cup of sack on entering the tavern in *Part One* and at every other opportunity, though he had ended in that play by vowing to "purge and leave sack" (V.iv.164). Now we find him calling for a chamber pot. It is rather uncomfortably consistent with the opening query he put to his diminutive page: "Sirrah, you giant, what says the doctor to my water?" (I.ii.1). Falstaff has been commonly numbered among the celebrants of Dionysus, in an intermingled cult of the vine and of the theatre. We think of him too as an oracle of Rabelais' Holy Bottle, imparting its monosyllabic message of good fellowship, the sound of clinking glasses, *trinc*. But, here in *Part Two*, his attention seems to be shifting from the ebullition of wine to its physiological end-product. His initial preoccupation with flagging health has continued into his dialogue with the Chief Justice, where his sanguine effort to stay young is countered by his interlocutor, listing the symptoms of old age: "a moist eye, a dry hand, a yellow cheek, a white beard, a decreasing leg, an increasing belly" (I.ii.180-82). Falstaff, after striving impudently and vainly to borrow a thousand pounds, has come away from the interview determined to "turn diseases to commodity" (l.248), to profit from malaise. Afflicted by the malady that goes with high living, the gout, he has cursed it and immediately realized that his curse itself is another affliction contracted by the habits of venery: "A pox of this gout! or a gout of this pox!" (ll.243-44).

When he encounters Doll in her qualm of indisposition, she greets him with a similar curse: "A pox damn you" (II.iv.39). He is not slow in reminding her that the pox is more likely to be one of her professional hazards. She, a seasoned veteran of the stews, absolves herself and blames his state on "gluttony and diseases" (l.42). The diagnosis of Falstaff as an individual has been macrocosmically projected when the rebel spokesman, the Archbishop of York, criticized the body politic:

> The commonwealth is sick of their own
>   choice,
> Their over-greedy love hath surfeited.
>   (II.i.87-88)

And, in apostrophizing the fickle multitude that had transferred its loyalties from Richard II to Henry IV, he pursued the metaphor from overeating through collective nausea to vomiting:

> Thou, beastly feeder, art so full of him,
> That thou provok'st thyself to cast him up.
>   (II.i.95-96)

As usual, the comic underplot runs parallel to the historic overplot, and thematic images connect Falstaff's revelry with the Archbishop's rebellion. "We are all diseased" (IV.i.54), the latter will repeat, in summing up his cause before the King's emissaries. The dying King himself, conferring with Warwick after his sleepless soliloquy, will compare his illness with that of his realm:

> Then you perceive the body of our kingdom
> How foul it is, what rank diseases grow,
> And with what danger, near the heart of it.
>
> (III.i.38-40)

Throughout, the concern for healthy appetite and sensuous fulfillment seems to be yielding to a clinical approach and a valetudinarian outlook. That the paragon of jesters should make his bow by inquiring about a urinalysis seems to bring Shakespeare uncharacteristically close to the medical vein of Molière.

V

Doll's and Falstaff's repartee is spiced with sexual innuendoes, which may help Mistress Quickly to reconcile these reproachful lovers, albeit with an unromantic and malapropistic reminder of their infirmities: "you cannot one bear with another's conformities" (II.iv.56-57). That, with ulterior wordplay on *bear,* has a melting effect upon Doll: "Come, I'll be friends with thee, Jack. Thou art going to the wars, and whether I shall see thee again or no, there is nobody cares" (ll. 65-68). Her subtext is a heartcry of loneliness from the stray lives of a prostitute and a soldier of fortune. At this juncture, the intrusion of a new character provokes an unruly incident. The mere announcement of Pistol's arrival is greeted by Doll's vituperative opposition: "Hang him, swaggering rascal . . . it is the foul-mouth'd'st rogue in England" (ll.71-72). The Hostess becomes suddenly concerned for the good repute of her house, having been warned by neighbors whom she quotes, with her habitual command of circumstantial detail and total recall. Falstaff resolves the dilemma by drawing a nice semantic distinction between swaggerers and cheaters; the newcomer is not a professional bully, he is just a confidence-man. Admitted on those credentials, aggressively drunk, Pistol attempts a toast—the byword is *discharge,* punning both on his own cognomen and on his more lascivious intentions. Doll will have nothing to do with him: "Away, you mouldy rogue, away! I am meat for your master" (ll.125-26). Mistress Quickly, who has abstained, tries to appease his pride by calling him captain, whereas he is no more than an ancient, Falstaff's ensign. "You a captain?" Doll goes on, "you slave, for what? for tearing a poor whore's ruff in a bawdy house?" (l.44).

Though she can be as foul-mouthed as he, she is a purist with him: "A captain! God's light, these villains will make the word as odious as the word 'occupy,'

which was an excellent good word before it was ill sorted" (ll.157-60). Yet *occupation* has its double meaning for her. Even the lowest characters exhibit a Shakespearean consciousness of language, and Bardolph will impress Justice Shallow by using the word "accommodated" (III.ii.66-67). As Pistol, venting his fury, speaks of being revenged on Doll, he dramatically changes his style. Damning her "to th' infernal deep," his rodomontade invokes the idiom of Thomas Kyd's tragedy of revenge and the theatrical school of night, "with Erebus and tortures vile also" (II.iv.157-58). When Mistress Quickly beseeches him to "aggravate" (l.162) his choler, of course, she means the reverse; but he takes her at her word and proceeds to garble the mightiest lines of Marlowe's *Tamburlaine:*

> Shall pack-horses
> And hollow pamper'd jades of Asia,
> Which cannot go but thirty mile a day,
> Compare with Caesars and with Cannibals
> And Troiant Greeks?
>
> (II.iv.163-67)

Pistol, it seems, is more than a roaring boy; he is an avid and impressionable playgoer; and, from this moment through *Henry V,* his idiolect will be a blank verse strung together with shreds and patches from the theatre. When the Hostess negatively answers his refrain from a lost play of George Peele—"have we not Hiren here?" (l.175)—he interacts by garbling a quotation from Peele's *Battle of Alcazar:* "Then feed and be fat, my fair Calipolis" (l.179). The histrionics wax louder and louder until, at Doll's insistence, Falstaff draws his sword and forces Pistol out and into a fall downstairs. He must content himself with his stoic maxim, spoken in a *lingua franca* of Italian and Spanish (or is it Esperanto?): *"Si fortune me tormente, sperato me contento"* (l.181).

Doll has rightly termed him a "fustian rascal" (l.189). Fustian, a coarse fabric, like bombast, which was padding, had come to be associated with playhouse ranting. When Falstaff impersonated the King in *Part One,* he had undertaken to rehearse "in King Cambyses' vein" (II.iv.387)—the rhetoric of an antiquated tragicomedy. But the speech he made from his joint-stool throne parodied the elegant Euphuistic prose of John Lyly. *Part Two* was enacted a decade after the Armada year, and its parodic echoes orchestrate the realization that Marlowe, Kyd, and Peele are dead and that their dramas of exotic conquest are outmoded. In less than another decade, with Francis Beaumont's *Knight of the Burning Pestle,* even Hotspur's speech on honor could be burlesqued into "a huffing part." Pistol, an anticlimactic replacement for Hotspur, is a more comfortable braggart captain than Falstaff. Unwittingly he marks the trend of fashion by exclaiming: "These be good humors indeed!" (l.163). The year 1598 saw the opening of the Globe Playhouse, though he must have preferred the old-fashioned productions at the Rose. That same year saw the rise of a literary movement exemplified by the sharply satirical comedy of Ben Jonson, *Every Man in His Humour.* Shakespeare would not be unaffected by it. Corporal Nym repeats Pistol's very words in *Henry V* (III.ii.26), and his personal watchword is "That's the humor of it" (passim). Though this third Henrician play was preordained to reach an epic conclusion, *Part Two* seems overshadowed beforehand by a Hogarthian strain which would be developed in dark comedies like *Measure for Measure,* and antic moods in the tragedies. The burlesque of theatricality in both parts of *Henry IV,* especially the second, heightens the reality of the *dramatis personae.*

VI

After Falstaff's victory over Pistol, the pace relaxes and the climate warms, moving from the bellicose to the amatory. Doll is ready to reward his valor, wherein she avows he has multitudinously outshone the Homeric heroes and the Nine Worthies. She sits on his lap, and they fondle and kiss, while Sneak's noise—an actually recognizable band of strolling musicians—suscitates their mutual caresses. "When wilt thou leave fighting a' days and foining a' nights," she asks him, "and begin to patch up thine old body for heaven?" (ll.231-33). He balks at this *memento mori* ("do not bid me remember mine end" [l.235]), but presently confesses "I am old, I am old," to which she consolingly responds: "I love thee better than I love e'er a scurvy young boy of them all" (ll.271-73). In the life of the senses, so keenly felt by the Renaissance, at such times the carnal aspect comes poignantly near to the charnel. The bodily appetites, eating, drinking, and sexuality, are sensitively edged by the prospect of death. So it is with this fat and bawdy old man, fighting and foining his way to the next world. In the meantime Bardolph has been making up to the hostess, while the Prince, with Poins, has sneaked in to listen and comment behind their billing and cooing. He is present during less than half of the scene, the only one where he and Falstaff are together, and the final one, except for their confrontation at the end. He and his fellow jokester go through a variation on their prank with the drawer in *Part One.* Both, who are dressed like Francis, appear and cry "Anon, anon, sir," when Falstaff calls for more sack. He has the laugh on them with his quick retort: "Ha? a bastard son of the King's? And art not thou Poins his brother?" (ll.282-84).

But they have overheard him freely and pungently disparaging them, and he must still extricate himself from this embarrassment, as he did from his prevarication about Gadshill. His excuse again is a piece of pharisaical casuistry: it is an act of friendship to dispraise one's friends before the wicked. Rising to a height of effrontery, he denounces the wickedness of Doll and Bardolph, and—himself the incarnation of

carnality and carnival—accuses the hostess of breaking lenten restrictions by serving meat. "All vict'lers do so." Her rejoinder, like Sir Toby's to Malvolio, is a plea for good living and for a sense of proportion. "What's a joint of mutton or two in a whole Lent?" (ll.346-47). Yet it leaves us with the feeling that we have survived a season of plenty and somehow lived on into leaner days. As in *Part One,* the ending is precipitated by knocking from outside, and tidings of the alert break off the tryst. The Prince, resuming the dignity of blank verse, regrets his idling in the shadow of duty, takes up his cloak and sword, and makes his exit. Falstaff, his self-importance reinforced by the news that a dozen captains await him, makes his farewells: "You see, my good wenches, how men of merit are sought after. The undeserver may sleep when the man of action is call'd on" (ll.375-77). Mistress Quickly, who in the morning was denouncing and suing him for his knaveries, breaks down: "I have known thee come peascod-time, but an honester and truer-hearted man—well, fare thee well' (ll. 382-84). Doll is in tears and can hardly speak. But there may yet be, as in *Part One,* a brief respite for dalliance. Falstaff sends Bardolph back for Doll, and the hostess despatches her to him: "O, run, Doll.... She comes blubber'd" (ll. 389-90).

Mrs. Inchbald thought that, whereas men liked Falstaff, women did not. But she was an eighteenth-century bluestocking, whose tastes obviously had little in common with those of Doll Tearsheet and Ursula Quickly. The continuing question—a question also raised, for example, about the reading of Rabelais—is what appeal he may hold for feminine sensibilities in a century which has tended to neutralize disparities between the sexes. Falstaff, at all events, must abandon his women for the manly sphere of martial action. There we watch him engaging not so much in soldierly exploits as in his old tricks of coney-catching. His round trip between London and Gaultree Forest is leisurely and rambling, since it stops off in Gloucestershire before and after the non-battle. His method of employing conscription to line his pockets was recounted by a monologue in *Part One.* It is just as well that we had no first-hand view of his ragged regiment, since later we are callously informed that all but two or three of them have been killed off. *Part Two* is resourcefully amplified by acting out the recruitment. One by one, five rustic types are called up and, as their names are pricked upon the roll, Falstaff makes an appropriate comment on each. During a short absence while drinking with his hosts, the recruits have a chance to buy their way off by bribing Bardolph. Those who can afford to, Bullcalf and Mouldy, do so; those who cannot, Shadow, Wart, and Feeble, must be courageous by default. As it happens, when Falstaff re-emerges, two stout fellows get excused, while three seedy weaklings are drafted into his battalion. Ensuing scenes will not bring us much nearer to genuine warfare than the inept preliminary drill that Bardolph puts them through.

VII

The theme of justice is mocked in the Gloucestershire episodes, where we are in the venue of the two doddering justices of the peace, opposites of Falstaff in all respects save age. Justice Shallow is as thin as Sir John is fat, as tame and timid as he is wild and brash. You might rate him the feeblest of Shakespearean characters, if Shakespeare had not outdone his feebleness in creating Justice Silence. Shallow's evocations of salad days, of youthful escapades with Sampson Stockfish and Jane Nightwork, contribute to the elegiac strain. But, as Falstaff soliloquizes, they are the fantasies of a dotard who was always a ninny. Bored by Shallow's prattle, he has listened politely for self-serving reasons. His response is succinct and noncommittal: "We have heard the chimes at midnight, Master Shallow" (III.ii.214-15). Like the Wife of Bath, Falstaff has had his world in his time; unlike Shallow, he has no need for nostalgia; he lives in the present, so long as he is alive. Ever with an eye for the main chance, he revisits Gloucestershire to borrow his thousand pounds from the foolish justice. Shallow's garden becomes an *al fresco* tavern for a last bout of conviviality, wherein Silence becomes surprisingly vocal. Davy, that "justice-like servingman," influencing Shallow's decisions to "bear out a knave against an honest man," is a comic role-model for what Falstaff soon expects to be: a friend at court who has the ear of the ascendant King (V.i.68, 48-49). This rural drinking scene is broken up by the arrival of Pistol, more welcome than at the Boar's Head for the information he now conveys: Henry IV is dead, long live Henry V! His bombastic diction affords the perfect medium for inflating the hollow expectations of Falstaff as he posts to the coronation.

We need not linger over the deflation. Many critics have been pained by the non-recognition scene, and have censured Henry for meeting his responsibilities, which could never have been fulfilled without the gesture of repudiation that he had explicitly anticipated all along. Given the groundwork, the ethos, the actualities involved, it could not conceivably have been otherwise. Henceforth he and Falstaff will go their separate ways, and each will be less engaging without the other. A. C. Bradley blamed not Henry but Shakespeare himself for overshooting the mark, for having permitted Falstaff to run away with our sympathies and hallowed him with that "touch of infinity" which Henry lacked. But infinity is by definition undefinable, and it seems more natural to envisage Falstaff as an innately corporeal creature. What would have occurred if the Chief Justice had been subjected to his tender mercies? "O God, that right should thus overcome might!" Mistress Quickly has exclaimed—a char-

acteristic reversal of what she intended, but true enough under the circumstances (V.iv.24-25). These are genuinely compromising, for they disclose aspects of a connection with the underworld that we have too long overlooked. Officers accompany the Hostess in her last scene as in her first; but she began, in seeking the arrest of Falstaff, with the law on her side. Here she is being arrested herself, along with Doll, and the charges are grave and grim. "Come, I charge you both go along with me," says the beadle, "for the man is dead that you and Pistol beat amongst you" (ll.15-17). Struggling and vituperating, pretending to be pregnant, Doll assails her officer: "Come, you thin thing, come, you rascal" (l.30). We are well aware of her preference for more corpulent men.

"Tavern on the Volcano" is the title of a suggestive essay on *Henry IV* by the Russian film-director, Grigori Kozintsev. From this vantage-point, the Boar's Head looks more like a Brechtian cabaret than a Shakespearean play-within-a-play. In *Henry V* we are given one receding glimpse of it, and the declination has been sealed by the marriage of Ursula to Pistol, who calls her Nell and is understandably ill at ease as mine host. Falstaff, now "in Arthur's bosom" (II.iii.9), is well out of the continental flurry and clangor. Instead of the "fat meat" (l.27) prefigured by the Epilogue to *Part Two*, we are given her famous account of his delirium and death. Inevitably, as the men confirm, "He cried out of sack . . . And of women" (ll.27, 29). It is best remembered that " 'a babbl'd of green fields" (ll.16-17). This was Lewis Theobald's emendation of a meaningless crux, a brilliant conjecture which leaves us with an untypical impression of pastoral pathos. But Mistress Pistol babbles on:

"How now, Sir John?" quoth I, "what, man? be a' good cheer." So 'a cried out, "God, God, God!" three or four times. Now I, to comfort him, bid him 'a should not think of God: I hop'd there was no need to trouble himself with any such thoughts yet. So 'a bade me lay more clothes on his feet. I put my hand into the bed and felt them, and they were as cold as any stone; then I felt to his knees, and so up'ard and up'ard, and all was as cold as any stone.

(ll.17-26)

Apart from the worldliness of the casual impiety, it has escaped much notice that she concludes with an outrageous pun. The coldness has settled into his most vital organs. Criticism, alienated from the Prince Hal who had become Henry V, and inspired by Maurice Morgann to rely upon "secret impressions" of character, has generally been more sentimental than Shakespeare in treating Falstaff. Not so Bradley's revisionist, L. C. Knights, who observes: "The second part of *Henry IV,* a tragicomedy of human frailty, is about the varied aspects of mutability, age, discontent, and decay." That is not the whole story; it is about some more spirited and vivacious matters withal; but its enormous vitality is posited upon its intimations of mortality, its attitude toward life as a unique performance which has no encores. Thus it points Shakespeare's direction from history and comedy toward tragedy. Its complex modality is that of the Duke—disguised as a friar—in *Measure for Measure,* when he advises Claudio to "Be absolute for death" (III.i.5) and admonishes each of us:

> Thou hast nor youth nor age,
> But as it were an after-dinner's sleep,
> Dreaming on both. . . .
>
> (ll.32-34)

Notes

[1] This paper was presented as the annual Shakespeare's Birthday Lecture on 23 April 1980 at the Folger Shakespeare Library.

Catherine M. Shaw (essay date 1985)

SOURCE: "The Tragic Substructure of the *Henry IV* Plays," in *Shakespeare Survey: An Annual Survey of Shakespearian Study and Production,* Vol. 38, 1985, pp. 61-7.

[*In the following essay, Shaw asserts that in* 1 *and* 2 Henry IV *Shakespeare makes use of the genre of tragedy to settle the scores and tie up the loose ends that remain at the end of his history play* Richard II *as the result of Henry's rebellion against the state.*]

In reporting Queen Elizabeth's conversation with William Lambarde, the Keeper of the Records in the Tower of London, about the staging of *Richard II* on Saturday, 6 February 1601, most scholars emphasize the Queen's words. 'I am Richard II, know ye not that?' Less often repeated but of much greater significance to the play which gave rise to the exchange and those that followed it, are the Queen's next words which, in referring to Essex, make significant comment on the dramatic role into which she cast the treacherous earl. 'He that will forget God,' she said, 'will also forget his benefactors . . .'[1] And Francis Bacon, who was one of the crown prosecutors at the trial which followed the unsuccessful insurrection, left no question as to the ultimate condemnation of any who would defy divine authority. In speaking of Sir Gilly Meyrick, one of Essex's supporters, Bacon said, 'So earnest hee was to satisfie his eyes with the sight of that tragedie which hee thought soone after his lord should bring from the stage to the state, but that God turned it upon their owne heads.'[2] Both of these speakers seem less concerned with Shakespeare's hero than they are with

the nature of Elizabeth's antagonist and with divine providence. 'That tragedie' which was to have been brought from 'the stage to the state' would seem to refer as much to the usurpation of Richard's throne as to his downfall and death, perhaps more. Their words, however, in addition to suggesting a tacit acceptance of Richard's fate, imply an impending dramatic aftermath ripe with potential for further tragic enactment—as if somehow, the play of *Richard II* is not yet over—and they are right. Shakespeare's *Richard II* ends in scenes which only partially fulfil the play's dramatic obligations; scenes which promise that the full tragic resolution will come only in the plays which follow—those titled with the name of the usurper king.

It is true that the tragedy of Richard II himself is, to all intents and purposes, over at the end of act 5, scene 5. Aumerle, Richard's last noble ally, has taken to his knees before the new king, and the playwright can now turn full dramatic attention to the death of Richard of Bordeaux. To use the metaphors of the play itself, Richard, having abused that divinely ordained time within which he should have been the caring gardener of the realm, must, in a kind of continuation of that strong morality theme dominant in the first tetralogy, pay for his errors against the state; for what Holinshed calls, 'wrongfull doings'.[3] And pay he does; one king falls and another takes his place.

As well as King Richard's private tragedy, these happenings also take care of the on-going narrative of the history plays; what A. P. Rossiter has referred to as the 'story-matter' gleaned from 'historical records to show that the course of events has been guided by a simple process of divine justice, dispensing rewards and punishments'.[4] We also know, however, from these records and the dramatization of them in the *Henry VI* plays and *Richard III,* that national tragedy has not yet run its course. And that is not all. Although divine ordination may have shortened Richard's days as king, *human* ordination shortened his physical life, and for this the wicked may not thrive. It is a deed, says Exton, 'chronicled in hell' (*Richard II,* 5.5.116).[5] Regardless, then, of what Shakespeare might owe to his audience in terms of a continuing historical narrative with all its political implications, he also must complete the artistic and moral obligations which tragedy demands. And Shakespeare pays these obligations in the *Henry IV* plays which, in many ways, are a return of the dramatic concerns of *Richard II*—only the actors who play the central parts are different. The roles played by protagonist and antagonist in *Richard II* are in the *Henry IV* plays reassigned to a larger cast of principals who, against a suitably expanded setting, continue the saga of misrule and insurrection. I am not referring here to the replaying of banishments and rebellion and the like; although scholars have long noted that Shakespeare emphasizes the parallel historical events in each reign. I mean that the potential for tragedy spills over from the last scenes of *Richard II* in which all four of the major figures of the next play are assembled, if not in person then in the conditioned mind of the audience, and operates subliminally in the *Henry IV* plays.

The 'unthrifty son' of the new King, however, the 'young wanton' Prince of Wales, already holds a special place in English hearts and indulgent smiles are the only reactions to references in act 5, scene 3 of *Richard II* to the undisciplined boy and his 'unrestrained loose companions' (5.3.7). Nothing disastrous can happen to England's favourite prodigal son who will one day wear the crown in victory at Agincourt. On the other hand, reason dictates that his lewd companions and, in particular, one fat knight, will be by then a youthful though sad memory. It is also fitting that young Harry Percy, the prince's rival in honour, be the person who responds to the King's question about his profligate son's reaction to summons to court. The prince's answer, repeated by the valiant Hotspur, was that

> he would unto the stews,
> And from the common'st creature pluck a
> 　glove,
> And wear it as a favour; and with that
> He would unhorse the lustiest challenger.
> 　　　　　　　　(*Richard II,* 5.3.16-19)

Although Hal's response is couched in appropriate gutter language (taking 'unhorse' as a pun on 'un whores') the words, heavy with irony, so prophesy Hal's strategy in *1 Henry IV* that one suspects the playwright went back and inserted them after the initial and overall planning of the second tetralogy had progressed well along into actuality. Be that as it may, it is Hal who redeems the nation from the moral bankruptcy which faces it at the end of *Richard II* and movement towards this redemption which has its climax under God's hand at Agincourt is the 'story matter' of the *Henry IV* plays. Besides that, if historical familiarity has not separated Hal from the others, then the dramatic Hal does it for himself in the soliloquy at the end of act 1, scene 2 of *1 Henry IV.* Unlike the others, Hal is made the conscious actor who creates a role which he will play until he 'please[s] again to be himself' (*1 Henry IV,* 1.2.195).[6]

Setting the future king aside then, as already having been given his role by history and by the playwright who was dramatizing it, we have at the end of *Richard II* his 'lustiest challenger', young Harry Percy, his 'unrestrained' companions later personified in Sir John Falstaff, and his father, the solemn guilt-ridden Henry IV; the three characters, I might add, who are in turn left behind when Hal moves on into his own play— prisoners of history within plays in which at the same time as they act and interact within the historical process, each pursues his own line of dramatic action. It

is these new players who act out the subliminal substructure for the *Henry IV* plays and which effect the necessary purgation, national and dramatic, before Henry V's reign of unexampled triumph can proceed.

Of these characters, Hotspur displays most clearly the potential for tragedy in the traditional sense of that word. Although introduced early in *Richard II* as 'tender, raw, and young', by the end of that play Harry Percy has already moved into a very firm position at Bolingbroke's side; almost, one might say, in the position of a son. Certainly Henry would wish that relationship, seeing in Hotspur valiant and princely traits in the opening scenes of *1 Henry IV* and later as a mirror image of himself when he arrived at Ravenspurgh. Hotspur is, however, more like the King than Henry might care to admit. Richard's words of Bolingbroke, that he is 'High stomach'd' and 'full of ire, / In rage, deaf as the sea, hasty as fire' (*Richard II,* 1.2.18-19), characterize that angry nobleman in the same way as do Northumberland's to his son, 'wasp-stung and impatient fool . . . / Tying thine ear to no tongue but thine own!' (*1 Henry IV,* 1.3.233-5). There is little doubt that both Henry and Hotspur say and do foolish things in anger. Once he is King, Henry does try very hard to control his temper and most times he succeeds, as when he defers judgement when prisoners are refused him after Holmedon. 'For more is to be said and to be done', he says at that point, 'Than out of anger can be uttered' (*1 Henry IV,* 1.1.105-6). When he does not, however, he makes provoking statements and commits rash actions just as Hotspur later does. Indeed, that very 'ire' coupled with conviction of personal injury and family dishonour is what leads Hotspur to rebellion and attempted usurpation just as surely as it had previously led Henry.

Henry, however, won and Hotspur does not. Why? For Henry it is because history wills it so; for Hotspur it is because Shakespeare wills it so. It is true, Holinshed records that 'the lord Percie' did die at Shrewsbury[7] but the Hotspur in *1 Henry IV* is almost totally of Shakespeare's creation and Shakespeare's Hotspur dies because his 'high stomach' and his 'ill-weaved ambition', characteristics which he holds in common with his king as surely as he holds bravery and valour and courage, lead him to rebel against that king and to his own disaster. And in this, Hotspur is acting out a tragedy in which the hero might just as well have been Henry Bolingbroke; their crimes are, after all, the same.

Hotspur's tragedy, however, is also personalized and his wilfulness is made the cause of peevish as well as dangerous actions. His uncle Worcester's exasperated words emphasize the flaws in the young man's nature:

> You must needs learn, lord, to amend this fault.
> Though sometimes it show greatness, courage,
> 　blood,
> —And that's the dearest grace it renders you—

Yet oftentimes it doth present harsh rage,
Defect of manners, want of government,
Pride, haughtiness, opinion, and disdain,
The least of which haunting a nobleman
Loseth men's hearts and leaves behind a
    stain
Upon the beauty of all parts besides,
Beguiling them of commendation.
                    (*1 Henry IV*, 3.1.174-83)

And after his death, it is not only Hal who acknowl-edges the tragic fall of a noble gentleman, but one of his own associates in the rebel cause, Lord Bardolph, confirms that for all his greatness, Hotspur

            with great imagination
Proper to madmen, led his powers to death,
And winking leap'd into destruction.
                    (*2 Henry IV*, 1.3.31-3)[8]

The fact remains, however, that the origins of rebel-lion, attempted usurpation, and national disorder lie in *Richard II*. As Herschel Baker has pointed out, in addition to *Richard II* recording 'the deposition of a king who showed himself unfit to rule', the play also dramatizes '*with indignation* the course and outcome of insurrection'.[9] Warning after warning has occurred in *Richard II* of what will be the inevitable outcome of 'gross rebellion and detested treason'. Someone must pay for these crimes as Richard paid for his errors and misgovernment and if history disallows Henry Boling-broke from the role then someone else must be his understudy: that understudy is Harry Hotspur. Thus, Hotspur is part of the tragic substructure of this play on two levels. At the same time as his personal trag-edy is independently significant, Hotspur's fall acts out within the historic scheme of things in *1 Henry IV* what could and perhaps *should* have happened to Bolingbroke had history not willed otherwise.

Sir John Falstaff is also a major actor in this tragic subtext of the *Henry IV* plays and his roles are without doubt the most complex of the play. In the opening scene of *1 Henry IV*, the new king may speak of the peace which, he says, has united 'acquaintance, kin-dred, and allies' (1.1.16), but the words are no sooner out of his mouth than the issues which are to become the dramatic conflicts of both *Henry IV* plays take the stage. These are not, however, new issues but a con-tinuation of old ones. The realm is, in fact, no better off for Richard's overthrow and murder. Rather, to that national disharmony for which Henry must now share the fault with Richard has been added dynastic disordering for which he is alone guilty. As Richard Plantagenet is dead, the responsibilities for national chaos and for the disorder of familial descent should fall on Henry Bolingbroke. History, however, let me repeat, has placed Henry as head of state and thus, within the drama, he may intone with great gravity

that royal 'we' which symbolizes the union of rightful king and nation. That dual role which personifies both national and dynastic disordering now passes to Sir John Falstaff. Both men, as James Winny has seen, have 'the semblance and manner of a king without the stamp of divine authority' and 'the farcical and disrespectful posture by Falstaff [in the play-within-a-play scene] gives visible form to the moral reality of Bolingbroke's kingship'.[10]

As Hotspur is the dramatic heir to that 'harsh rage', that 'want of government' in Henry's private nature that led him to challenge the King and embroil the nation in civil war, so Falstaff and Eastcheap are the visual representations of the public results of such actions. Falstaff's realm may be Eastcheap and his castle the Boar's Head Inn but the fat knight lords it both in misrule and in familial disruption. His very credo is lawlessness and he has at his side as devoutedly a wished-for heir in Hal as ever Hotspur is for Henry.

That such a realm has any permanence, however, is denied from the moment it is presented on stage. Like those of its king, the chief of 'Diana's foresters', its fortunes, although at the flood at the beginning of *1 Henry IV*, will also 'ebb' as Hal prophesies for the 'gentle-men of the shade', being 'governed as the sea is, by the moon' (1.2.26-33). The world of the stews represents in miniature the nation which Henry brought to further disorder by violating fealty and primogeniture. Law-lessness breeds lawlessness and history, at least Shake-speare's version of it, demands the reassertion of natural and familial unity. And, although Falstaff is a creation of the Shakespearian imagination, his fate in the role of king of Eastcheap is determined by the same historical factors as control the King for whom he provides a dramatic substructural counterpart.

Within this larger and historic scheme of things, Fal-staff's fall outlines as clearly as does any Shakespearian tragedy how the abuse of power and position can lead to personal and national disaster and that only by repu-diation of the perpetrator can the ordered state be re-established. As for the concerns of lineal disordering, Falstaff's pseudo-parental authority too must go. At the end of *2 Henry IV*, Hal chooses a new father in the Lord Chief Justice—Falstaff's *and Bolingbroke's* an-tithesis—the man who represents the time-honoured traditions of order and loyalty and justice. The new king expresses the dual transformation which has taken place both in himself and in the nation by picking up the earlier metaphor:

        The tide of blood in me
Hath proudly flow'd in vanity till now.
Now doth it turn, and ebb back to the sea,
Where it shall mingle with the state of floods,
And flow henceforth in formal majesty.
                    (*2 Henry IV*, 5.2.129-33)

As does Hotspur, however, Falstaff also acts out his own personal tragedy and his part within the subliminal tragic enactment of the *Henry IV* plays also has a multiple complexity. History may will that the nation must suffer and then be purged of treason, of chaos, and of dynastic discord, but Shakespeare wills that Falstaff's fall, like Hotspur's, be motivated by characteristics inherent within the very nature of his creation. And as Hotspur's weaknesses mirror those of Henry Bolingbroke, ironically, Falstaff's mirror those of Richard of Bordeaux who, like Falstaff, tries to perpetuate a mode of existence which is in direct conflict with the historical process of which he is a dramatic part. I say ironically because Richard's 'skipping' qualities (*1 Henry IV*, 3.2.60) which Henry lays to his son are in truth Falstaff's and not the Prince's. It is Falstaff's 'fattest soil' (*2 Henry IV*, 4.4.54) that, like Richard's, nurtures weeds. Both live *off* their realms, not *for* them. Both are egocentric. Both charm others and themselves with words. Both appear to move toward their dramatic expulsions refusing to see the danger signals so obviously there. Richard acknowledges the 'high pitch' to which Bolingbroke's 'resolution soars' (*Richard II*, 1.1.109) but proceeds not only to ignore it but also to add momentum to it. And who except Falstaff could ignore Hal's 'I do, I will' (*1 Henry IV*, 2.4.475) after the eloquent plea not to banish fat Jack from the Prince's world and then proceed to behave even more outrageously? And look to their endings. Richard has with him an unidentified groom to recall a regal past; not one of his noble subjects is left. Indeed, Richard's personal tragedy is, as many of Shakespeare's tragic heroes' are, one of progressive isolation. And so is Falstaff's. Isolated as he is already from his former world, Sir John has with him Shallow and Silence, lean-witted remnants of a past glory with whom he has been able to establish briefly another king-subject relationship. Pistol is there, and Bardolph who has escaped the purging of Eastcheap only because he hurried out of the city toward Gloucestershire. But they, like Aumerle, the last of Richard's royal associates, finally also become followers of a new king.

Both Richard and Falstaff also come to public humiliation and private self-recognition. These confrontations for Richard, however, come separately. Richard is first rendered defenceless against the new political world of Bolingbroke; then in the prison scene, stripped of previous misconceptions, he gains a majesty of self of magnificent proportion. For Falstaff, the exposures of public and private self come at the same time and the sudden abutting of the historical and the comic worlds is such that the personal tragic moment can be and indeed is most often overlooked.

The words which Falstaff calls out to Hal as he passes in the coronation procession are progressively more intimate: 'King Hal, my royal Hal!', 'my sweet boy!' and then 'my heart!' and they encourage the expecta-

tion of confrontation on a personal level. There is nothing intimate, however, in the King's response. Even the overture of an instinctive comic gesture is cut short by the King's abrupt 'Reply not to me with a foolborn jest' (*2 Henry IV*, 5.5.41-5). Intellectually, of course, ample preparation has been made for this moment. And visually, in the scene itself, the strewing of rushes in the street, the coronation procession which passes over the stage, all the grandeur of the royal regalia insist upon the public and ritualistic nature of the event. Historic reality not only breaks through the comic world as it has done on numerous occasions before in these plays, but this time it stays in full view. For the first time, says Robert M. Torrance in his study of the development of the type, 'a comic hero has met irrevocable defeat. . . . Death Falstaff could outwit, but from the righteous judgement of a Christian king there is no reprieve; he stands defenseless, as no pagan or heretic comic hero ever stood, against his anointed antagonist's monopoly of moral authority.'[11] All this is true, but surely there is more. Intellectual moral justification for the expulsion of Falstaff can be accepted as can the historical actuality, but the disquietude which greets the end of *2 Henry IV* is not intellectual; it is emotional.

As Falstaff stands staring after the departing King and his rag-tag band begin to shuffle their feet in the rushes, there is something quietly heart-rending in the way the fallen knight tries to gather about himself the shreds of his shattered dignity. To say that Falstaff really believes that Hal will call for him once out of the public eye is to misread every confrontation between the two in both plays. In a brief moment and in his own strange way, there is a splendid simplicity in Falstaff's attempt to assert a positive sense of self. The old man's words, 'I will be the man yet that shall make you great', have about them the same sense of desperate majesty as Lear's 'I will do such things;— / What they are, yet I know not' (*King Lear*, 2.4.283-4). Words, however, the weapons which served him so well in the past, are not enough to save him now any more than Richard's defence was able to ward off historic inevitability. Symbolically, Falstaff dies at this instant. No prison scene in Fleet allows further exploration of the tragic moment. All that is left is a sense of emptiness as the great girth moves from the stage. Torrance explains this emptiness and links it to a previous fallen knight. 'A kingdom', he says, 'that has lost first Hotspur, then Falstaff, along with all that they embodied, has been irreparably diminished, even though the excision be a condition for its survival.'[12]

King of Eastcheap—King of England: the parallels between these two are so obvious that it seems only fitting that on the national level Henry Bolingbroke should share with Falstaff the roles of Richard II. Each king faces similar political crises, as I suggested earlier, but there is more to being a king than merely acting out historical events. In his own plays, however, Henry is no longer the author of these events but their victim and, as such, he is forced into Richard's role. In addition, not only is the role of victim Henry's, so is the language. In act 4, scene I of *Richard II,* Richard hands over his crown to Henry; then in act 5, scene 1, he prophesies the cares and insecurities that will come with it. Once Henry's role changes from perpetrator to threatened victim and confidence in loyal allies 'converts to fear' (*Richard II,* 5.1.66), those very insecurities lead Bolingbroke to the same verbalizing of despair that Richard was prone to:

> Let all the tears that should bedew my hearse
> Be drops of balm to sanctify thy head,
> Only compound me with forgotten dust.
> Give that which gave thee life unto the
> worms;
> Pluck down my officers; break my decrees;
> For now a time has come to mock at form—
> . . . Up, vanity!
> Down, royal state!
>
> (*2 Henry IV,* 4.5.113-20)

The voice here is Henry's but the words might well be Richard's.

Shakespeare, however, denies to Henry Richard's heroic ending. The sense of loss at the death of Richard II is not felt when Henry dies. For one thing, unlike Richard's, and indeed unlike Hotspur's and Falstaff's, Henry's departure from the dramatic and historic world is underplayed. Warwick's news that the King has 'walk'd the way of nature' (*2 Henry IV,* 5.2.4) quickly turns to concern for the future of the Lord Chief Justice. M. M. Reese would add to this that 'long before the end the proud and confident Bolingbroke has shrunk into a sleepless neurotic'.[13] I'm not sure that this is true but if it is, the description refers to the private Henry; the Henry that has been for so long the source of sickness in the realm; the Henry that has hidden throughout his plays behind the role granted him by history while others act out what should have been his parts. At this Henry has been remarkably successful. Even at Shrewsbury he had 'many marching in his coats' (*1 Henry IV,* 5.3.25).

From the time he landed at Ravenspurgh, the public Henry is a winner. He achieves a crown and, although he gains little honour from either, his forces continue to be triumphant at Shrewsbury and Gaultree Forest. It is true that privately he is plagued by guilt but he is eventually able to dispel any fears he may have had of his son's capabilities to rule, to blame his sleeplessness on the heavy duties of wearing a crown, and to convince himself that he had committed treason because 'necessity so bow'd the state'. Warwick is also by to soothe him with platitudes when his mind runs to Richard's prophecy of a time when 'foul sin, gath-

ering head, / Shall break into corruption' (*2 Henry IV,* 3.1.73, 76-7). Finally, although he admits to the 'by-paths and indirect crook'd ways' that took him to the crown, he also assures Hal that 'the soil of the achievement' will go with him into the earth (4.5.184-90).

Dramatically, however, the soil of the achievement has passed to surrogates—Hotspur and Falstaff—and their demises, real or symbolic, are the prices paid for Henry's crimes against the state. But there remains 'one most heinous crime' for which Henry must pay his own piper—the murder of Richard Plantagenet. By Exton's use of direct quotation when he reiterates the king's words, 'Have I no friend will. rid me of this living fear?' (5.4.2), Shakespeare gives to Henry a scene in which he commits the grave error of allowing political expediency to hold sway over moral judgement. In other words, a quality which in all other regards has stood Henry in good stead and as a quality of kingship can be admired in him all the more because Richard so clearly lacks it, becomes in this instant a 'mole of nature'. I mean here that quality of knowing when to seize the moment, of knowing exactly when and how to motivate men and events to pursue his own ends. It is the dominant characteristic of Henry IV the political realist that emerges from the *Chronicles.* The Bolingbroke within the hollow crown in the *Henry IV* plays, however, is the playwright's artistic creation and Henry's decision not to abide Richard Plantagenet alive, whether made as the result of policy or in a fit of pique is, in Shakespeare's play, a tragic mistake in judgement.

The facts of history only deny Henry a Crusader's death but for this grave error Shakespeare's dramatic metaphor suggests another punishment. Although it is to the instrument of murder that Henry directs his biblical intonations at the end of *Richard II:*

> With Cain go wander thorough shades of
> night,
> And never show thy head by day nor light,
>
> (5.6.43-4)

Exton completely disappears from the dramatic progression. Shakespeare refuses to pass this crime on to a surrogate. Rather, Henry himself must bear the mark of Cain and live and ultimately die with the blood of Richard on his hands. Henry's plea, 'How came I by the crown, O god forgive' (*2 Henry IV,* 4.5.218), involves his treason and his violation of dynastic succession; Richard's death is parricide, linked by the Cain metaphor to the 'eldest primal sin,' and for this he is denied the true Jerusalem. This is the tragedy of Henry Bolingbroke.

Of Henry's former adversaries, Richard II had died weapon in hand, prophesying, 'Mount, mount, my soul! thy seat is up on high' (*Richard II,* 5.5.111);

Hal's words over the fallen Hotspur at Shrewsbury indicate that the Prince's praise will go 'to heaven' with the fallen warrior (*1 Henry IV*, 5.4.98); and Falstaff 'went away an it had been any christom child' (*Henry V*, 2.3.11-12). Even the loyal knight, banished Thomas Mowbray, after valiant years 'in glorious Christian field', gave up 'his pure soul unto his captain Christ, / Under whose colours he had fought so long' (*Richard II*, 4.1.93-100). But not so for Henry Bolingbroke. 'Then said the king,' reports Holinshed, 'Lauds be given to the father of heaven for now I know that I shall die heere in this chamber, according to the prophesie of me declared, that I should depart this life in Jerusalem.'[14] The words which Shakespeare gives to Henry carry no such tone of thanksgiving; no such surety of destiny. Rather, they are heavy with irony and the recognition of God's judgement and his own vanity:

> Laud be to God! Even there my life must
> end.
> It hath been prophesied to me, many years,
> I should not die but in Jerusalem,
> Which vainly I suppos'd the Holy Land.
> But bear me to that chamber; there I'll lie;
> In that Jerusalem shall Harry die.
>   (*2 Henry IV*, 4.5.235-40)

Thus, by the end of *2 Henry IV*, the crimes unpunished in the action of *Richard II* have all been accounted for in the tragic substructure of the *Henry IV* plays. It is true that in 'small time' civil war will again pitch Englishman against Englishman in the Wars of the Roses, but for the dramatic present, debts are paid and 'civil swords and native fire' (*2 Henry IV*, 5.5.106) may turn toward France and Agincourt.

Notes

[1] E. K. Chambers, *William Shakespeare*, 2 vols. (Oxford, 1930), vol. 2, pp. 326-7.

[2] Chambers, vol. 2, p. 326.

[3] Geoffrey Bullough, *Narrative and Dramatic Sources of Shakespeare*, 8 vols. (1957-75), vol. 3 (1960), p. 388.

[4] *Angel with Horns* (1961), pp. 1-2.

[5] William Shakespeare, *Richard II*, The Arden Shakespeare, ed. Peter Ure (1956). All references to *Richard II* are from this edition.

[6] William Shakespeare, *1 Henry IV*, The Arden Shakespeare, ed. A. R. Humphreys (1960). All references to *1 Henry IV* are from this edition.

[7] Bullough, vol. 4, p. 191.

[8] William Shakespeare, *2 Henry IV*, The Arden Shakespeare, ed. A. R. Humphreys (1966). All references to *2 Henry IV* are from this edition.

[9] Introduction to *Richard II, The Riverside Shakespeare*, ed. G. Blakemore Evans (Boston, 1974), p. 801.

[10] *The Player King* (1968), pp. 100, 107.

[11] *The Comic Hero* (Cambridge, Mass., 1978), p. 142.

[12] *Ibid.*

[13] *The Cease of Majesty* (New York, 1961), p. 312.

[14] Bullough, vol. 4, p. 278.

FURTHER READING

Berry, Edward I. "The Rejection Scene in *2 Henry IV*." *Studies in English Literature 1500-1900* XVII, No. 2 (Spring 1977): 201-18.

Examines the ways in which critics have misread Hal's rejection of Falstaff in *2 Henry IV* and suggests methods of interpreting the scene more fully.

Bevington, David. "Introduction." In *The Oxford Shakespeare: Henry IV, Part I*, edited by David Bevington, pp. 1-110. Oxford: Clarendon Press, 1987.

Provides an overview of *1 Henry IV*, including the play's sources, structure, and tensions between characters, as well as performances of the play and its place in history.

Candido, Joseph. "The Name of King: Hal's 'Titles' in the 'Henriad.'" *Texas Studies in Literature and Language* 26, No. 1 (Spring 1984): 61-73.

Looks at how Prince Hal's political savvy and respect for the past are linked in his efforts to solidify his right to the throne.

Cox, Gerard H. "'Like a Prince Indeed': Hal's Triumph of Honor in *1 Henry IV*." In *Pageantry in the Shakespearean Theater*, edited by David M. Bergeron, pp. 130-49. Athens: The University of Georgia Press, 1985.

Downplays the problematical aspects of Prince Hal's character, urging instead an evaluation of the Prince based on the conventions of chivalric pageantry.

Greenfield, Thelma N. "Falstaff: Shakespeare's Cosmic (Comic) Representation." In *Acting Funny: Comic Theory and Practice in Shakespeare's Plays*, edited by Frances Teague, pp. 142-52. Rutherford: Fairleigh Dickinson University Press, 1994.

Defines the classic comic figure and then demonstrates

the ways in which Falstaff is far more complex than this definition allows for.

Knowles, Ronald. "Honour, Debt, the Rejection and St. Paul." In *The Critics Debate: Henry IV Parts I & II*, pp. 73-86. London: The Macmillan Press Ltd, 1992.

    Provides an overview of the contrasting opinions of literary critics regarding Hal's rejection of Falstaff.

Leggatt, Alexander. "Henry IV." In *Shakespeare's Political Drama: The History Plays and the Roman Plays*, pp. 77-113. London: Routledge, 1988.

    Presents an overview of *1* and *2 Henry IV*, including their relationship to Shakespeare's other history plays and the interaction between the comedic world of Falstaff and the political world of the Court.

Paris, Bernard J. "Prince Hal." In *Character as a Subversive Force in Shakespeare: The History and Roman Plays*, pp. 71-90. Rutherford: Fairleigh Dickinson University Press, 1991.

    Traces the development and contradictions of Hal's character in *1 Henry IV*, through *2 Henry IV*, and up to the beginning of his rule in *Henry V*.

Prior, Moody E. "Comic Theory and the Rejection of Falstaff." *Shakespeare Studies* IX (1976): 159-71.

    Looks at the nature of comedy in relationship to the character Falstaff and describes Hal's rejection of Falstaff in *2 Henry IV* as "the triumph of the embodiment of power over the embodiment of the free spirit of comedy."

Rees, Joan. "Falstaff, St. Paul, and the Hangman." *The Review of English Studies* XXXVIII, No. 149 (February 1987): 14-22.

    Suggests ways in which Shakespeare makes full use in *1* and *2 Henry IV* of the textual ambiguity of biblical quotes.

Salingar, Leo. "Falstaff and the Life of Shadows." In *Shakespearean Comedy*, edited by Maurice Charney, pp. 185-205. New York: New York Literary Forum, 1980.

    Examines why audiences laugh at, or with, the character of Falstaff.

Somerset, J. A. B. "Falstaff, the Prince, and the Pattern of *2 Henry IV*." *Shakespeare Survey* 30 (1977): 35-45.

    Argues that *2 Henry IV* should receive more attention as a play in its own right rather than simply as a sequel to *1 Henry IV*.

Spiekerman, Tim. "The Education of Hal: *Henry IV, Parts One and Two*." In *Shakespeare's Political Pageant: Essays in Literature and Politics*, edited by Joseph Alulis and Vickie Sullivan, pp. 103-24. Lanham, MD: Rowman & Littlefield Publishers, Inc., 1996.

    Traces Hal's development into a legitimate king and how this development is affected by Hal's relationships with his father and with Falstaff.

Stewart, Douglas J. "Falstaff the Centaur." *Shakespeare Quarterly* 28, No. 1 (Winter 1977): 5-21.

    Compares the relationship of Hal and Falstaff to that of the heroes of Greek mythology and Chiron, the centaur/tutor.

Williams, Robert I. "Comic/Serious, Serious/Comic." In his *Comic Practice/Comic Response*, pp. 114-34. Newark: University of Delaware Press, 1993.

    Defines comedy of the absurd and applies this definition to *1 Henry IV*.

Henry V

For further information on the critical and stage history of *Henry V,* see *SC* Volumes 5, 14, and 30.

INTRODUCTION

Modern scholars writing about *Henry V* frequently remark on its distinctiveness. Unlike Shakespeare's other English histories, it focuses almost exclusively on the protagonist. Moreover, no other play in the Shakespeare canon uses a choric figure so extensively. *Henry V* is the last of Shakespeare's chronicle histories, and critics have characterized it as the most morally ambiguous as well. Up until about 1975, commentary on the play was sharply divided between those who embraced the heroic interpretation articulated by the Chorus and those who read *Henry V* as a caustic satire exposing the hypocrisy and cruelty of military adventurers. More recently, an increasing number of critics have moved away from an either/or position. Simplistic judgments cannot be substantiated, these commentators assert, because the play offers a number of competing viewpoints from which to evaluate such issues as patriotism, national unity, and the justice of foreign conquest.

Henry V is centrally concerned with the question of whether the invasion of France is justified, but it also deals with another important issue of law and justice: Henry's possession of the crown that his father usurped. Karl P. Wentersdorf (1976) maintains that the dynastic struggle between the houses of York and Lancaster is at the heart of the Southampton conspiracy, which Henry exposes in Act II, scene i. The critic points out that the principal conspirator, the earl of Cambridge, is married to the daughter of Edmund Mortimer—the brother of Richard II and Richard's appointed heir; thus Cambridge's infant son would be in the direct line of royal succession if Mortimer had become king instead of Henry IV. Wentersdorf asserts that placing Mortimer's grandson on the throne is the real reason for the conspiracy. David Scott Kastan (1982) declares that *Henry V* directly challenges the Tudor version of history and dynastic succession by exposing the fallacy of Henry's unquestioning assumption of the justice of the French war. Henry is so sure of the legitimacy of the invasion, Kastan remarks, that he brushes aside all suggestions of moral or legal ambiguities—raised, for example, by the aristocratic conspirators and by the commoners Williams and Bates; moreover, he ruthlessly condemns what he sees as the unlawful resistance of the citizens of Harfleur.

The most thoroughly uncritical view of the justice of the French campaign is provided by the Chorus in his prologues and epilogue. Indeed, the role of the Chorus in *Henry V,* and its implications for the play as a whole, have been the subject of a growing number of commentators, most all of whom reject the notion advanced by earlier scholars that these prologues were written by someone other than Shakespeare or that they were not originally part of the play. There is no similar unanimity, however, regarding the function of the Chorus's speeches. Anthony S. Brennan (1979) contends that the Chorus, who holds an unwavering belief in the nobility of war, represents an extreme position. Brennan points out that the Chorus's sentiments are regularly—and ironically—undercut by the scenes which immediately follow his prologues and which show what war looks like from the viewpoint of the common soldiers and the low-life characters from Eastcheap. Similarly, Lawrence Danson (1983) suggests that the Chorus exists to provide "a sense of perspective" and to demonstrate that an overly indulgent assessment of the king is mistaken. In contrast to Brennan, however, Danson argues that the dramatic action complicates the Chorus's preparation rather than contradicting it, and thus we become aware of Henry's human weakness as well as his greatness. Also recommending a balanced view of the king, Anthony Hammond (1987) maintains that the contradiction between the Chorus's descriptions of what will be shown on the stage and what we actually see is designed to underscore the duality that runs throughout the play. A dichotomy is built into Shakespeare's characterization of Henry, Hammond asserts, and while the play incorporates the Chorus's attitude toward the king and specific dramatic events, it also directly challenges that conception. Günter Walch (1988) relates the role of the Chorus to the play's representation of political doctrine, maintaining that the Chorus is profoundly involved in creating a national ideology. The unreliability of his information is central to the drama, Walch argues, for this exposes the illusory nature of national myths and legends, and demonstrates how they can be used as instruments of power.

Many late twentieth-century commentators have focused on the relation between power and ideology in *Henry V,* often from the perspectives of new historicism or cultural materialism. Jonathan Dollimore and Alan Sinfield (1985) contend that the play explores Henry's attempt to establish himself as the sole repository of political power. Henry's goal, they declare, is the complete suppression of all challenges to his authority, and he uses the ideological concept of national unity to achieve this. In their judgment, however, the play reveals, through numerous instances of dissension and threats of disobedience, the profound anxieties that accompany the imposition of ideological conformity on a nation comprised of diverse personal and political interests. Alexander Leggatt (1988) also examines the question of how *Henry V* portrays national unity, asserting that it shows the concept to be a "patriotic fantasy." He points out that Canterbury's refashioning of the traditional fable of the bees' commonwealth, in which all factions of an ideal state work together harmoniously, is juxtaposed to the depiction of disgruntled soldiers, scheming prelates, and France in ruins. Audiences and readers must work out these contradictions for themselves, Leggatt recommends, for the play offers both points of view and provides no simple resolution of this discrepancy. Similarly, Graham Bradshaw (1993) recently interprets *Henry V* as promoting uncertainty rather than a single, reassuring response to its representation of history. He contends that although the Chorus tries to control our reaction, and while Henry adroitly offers justification after the fact for the course he has already embarked on, the play's subversive connotations would not have been missed by those who first saw the play in performance. Like Leggatt and others, Bradshaw cautions that singleminded judgments of Henry, the justice of his war, and the integrity of the play's portrayal of history are unwise and reductive.

CHORUS

Anthony S. Brennan (essay date 1979)

SOURCE: "That Within Which Passes Show: The Function of the Chorus in *Henry V*," in *Philological Quarterly,* Vol. 58, No. 1, Winter, 1979, pp. 40-52.

[*In the essay below, Brennan views the Chorus as representing one side of a dialectical argument about the nature of war and national leadership. The critic believes that the Chorus's definition of war as a glorious undertaking and the grim perspective provided by the common soldiers are mediated by Henry's perception of the limitations and responsibilities of power.*]

The use of the Chorus in *Henry V* is really central to the whole question of what Shakespeare is doing when he reminds us so deliberately of the illusory nature of the play-world. Does the Chorus speak directly for Shakespeare in lamenting that the glorious history of England can receive no fully worthy representation on a tawdry stage? It has become a commonplace of criticism that any Shakespearian character who can be termed "choric" may often be taken to be presenting

the dramatist's own views on the action, inheriting the habit. Seneca gave the chorus of passing on didactic messages to the audience. How natural, therefore, to assume that we have Shakespeare's own scarcely disguised voice when he came to present a formal Chorus. We are told that Shakespeare "seems to have felt that his dramatic technique was inadequate to the subject"[1] and he "confessed ultimate failure to convert history into drama."[2] But surely if a writer is uncertain of success, and insecure about his technique, he does not strive to advertise his flaws and his fears throughout the play. Nor do any of the critics explain why Shakespeare felt no need of a narrator in, say, *King John,* which radically compresses historical time, sews several campaigns together, and bobs back and forth across the Channel like a tennis ball. Shakespeare's audience can never have expected the kind of panoply and "realism" for the absence of which the Chorus in *Henry V* apologizes. If they had accepted the tents of Richard III and Richmond a few feet apart on the same stage with ghosts flitting between, they were hardly likely to feel the lack of prancing steeds and of flotillas for crossing a channel that they had been imaginatively o'erleaping these many years by means of the poet's evocative language. We must find some explanation for the function of the Chorus other than as a vent for Shakespeare's frustration at working with productions governed by severe financial limitations. The only invention that would satisfy this literalist Chorus is the movie-camera. There is no evidence elsewhere of Shakespeare as an early D. W. Griffiths manqué. What there is evidence of everywhere is Shakespeare's overwhelming confidence that the simple, bare, thrust stage of his theatre could be used to present any kind of story in any kind of world whether real or imaginary.

The plays which Shakespeare presented on that bare stage were not naturalistic in the modern sense. Many critics, convinced that the acting style Shakespeare's company used was highly artificial and gestural, have ransacked books of rhetoric for evidence of a sort of formal sign language. Other scholars have argued that the actors eschewed the rhetorician's system and tended towards a more realistic portrayal. It is useful to remember that if characters were presented in an extremely formalistic manner many references within the plays become redundant and inexplicable. Shakespeare created a long string of characters who were frauds recognizable by their artificial and imperfect manners. Characters such as Osric, Sir Andrew Aguecheek, Lucio, or even Parolles can only be funny if there is some world of natural courtesy against which to measure their deviancy. Shakespeare was very much aware that the stage could present artificial fustian stuff and he puts parodies of such material into his own plays the better to set off a more natural world. The players' speeches in *Hamlet* parody the theatre in a way that tends to make us forget we are still in the theatre.

Falstaff in his Cambyses' vein, Pistol, or Don Armado, by their extravagant committment to thespian displays, tend to emphasize by contrast the natural behaviour of those around them. The mechanicals in *A Midsummer Night's Dream* amuse us because of their fears of success in the naturalistic style. They are hopelessly unaware that their limited acting skills will make it impossible for the audience, however willing, to suspend its disbelief. We can laugh at the failure of one level of illusion only in so far as we submit to the success of illusion at another level. When Shakespeare points our attention to the theatrical he does not weaken its hold over us, he strengthens it. This could only be true, of course, in a society which feels that, far from there being an enormous canyon separating the real world from theatre, there is in fact considerable overlap, a blurring of the line of demarcation which gives the dramatist considerable latitude in manipulating the audience.

The Chorus in *Henry V* apologizes for the tawdriness of the stage and implies that we can recreate history only by a vigorous exercise of our imaginations. We are immediately into the rich paradox that reality is a product of imagination, and that turns out to be the chief irony associated with the Chorus. The Chorus has a very selective imagination, it will deal only with glamour and bravery. This narrative voice is borrowed from the chronicles, but it is familiar in the older drama. Chorus figures and presenters are quite common in the plays of the 1570s and 1580s, but, as the skill of the dramatists improved, this device which belongs more to the narrative forms of prose than to drama began to disappear. Drama became a complete form when the various tatters of older forms—allegorical figures, prologues, inductions, choruses and so forth were digested by the play proper and the material was presented in terms of character in a self-contained world. It is odd, therefore, that Shakespeare who had already written many plays without resort to these old fashioned devices, should employ a formal chorus in the play which brings to a close his preoccupation with the history of England. Considering Shakespeare's complex skills by this stage of his career we have to assume some deliberate purpose in his employment of such an archaic device.

In *Henry V* Shakespeare broke the mold in which he had cast all his histories hitherto. That repetitive cycle of rise and fall, of factious barons roaming England and France to seek out their advantage, is finally thrust aside. The last remnant of that struggle, in the treachery of Cambridge, Grey and Scroop (II.ii) is an echo of the past. The King's decisive crushing of that conspiracy brings a whole era to an end. He advances on France with a united front, the factions having buried their enmity in a patriotic crusade. The concord among the nobles is remarkable and Shakespeare cleverly sets it off by relegating the conflict and factiousness to the commoners. He also contrasts the concord of the English high-command with the petty squabbles among the French barons.

The mixture of low-life comedy with the hallowed events of history was not Shakespeare's invention. In the source play, *The Famous Victories of Henry the Fifth,* from which he took many hints, we find a similar admixture. In the episodic nature of the source play there is little evidence of the unifying design, the total structure of ideas, that Shakespeare was to make of history. The source play does not relentlessly examine the traditionally received account of Henry's conquest, rather it follows tradition and enlivens it with comic interludes. The art of Shakespeare's drama is that of placing scenes, of setting up a contrast of attitudes which illuminates a structure of ideas regulating the play. For this purpose he elaborated much of Pistol's part, invented the whole of Fluellen's part and the group of common soldiers present at one of the critical moments of the play. One of the ways of balancing the views presented by this sub-plot world was to introduce the chorus.

The functions of this Chorus would at first sight seem to be straightforward. It provides narrative bridges and exhibits appropriately patriotic sentiments. But those critics who take the function of the Chorus for granted ought to realize that none of its speeches provide information absolutely necessary to our comprehension of the play, a fact noted by Johnson at the end of his 1765 edition of the play.[3] In comparison, say, with the spare and obviously functional employment of the chorus in *Doctor Faustus,* or with its essential narrative importance in Dekker's *Old Fortunatus,* Shakespeare's Chorus is supererogatory. If we excized the part, however, we would radically alter the structure of ideas and the mood and atmosphere of the play. In the Chorus it seems as though England had at last found its true voice; it is an abstract extension of the function that Shakespeare had first essayed in Faulconbridge. The cause of battle seems, in the glowing rhetoric of the Chorus, to have passed from individual personality to the whole nation.

I am not suggesting that Shakespeare specifically allegorizes the Chorus but he needed a voice that would represent one extreme of the spectrum of ideas on patriotism, as Pistol represents the other extreme. The King holds the balance. Henry cannot be the embodiment of patriotic zeal because he is faced with the human responses which separate men from their ideals. But if the King is to be properly heroic then no other man must overshadow him by an unquestioning acceptance of the virtues of patriotism. Shakespeare chose, therefore, a figure lacking both in personality and involvement in the action of the play. Being immune to the world it observes, the Chorus is static; its lyric exuberance persists throughout because there is no dynamic principle involved in its depiction which can induce development. The Chorus presents a play within a play, or rather a play within its own flow of grandiose rhetoric. The Chorus claims that the stage is not worthy to present reality but makes us aware that its own affinities are more with poetical transmutation, overblown hyperbole, than with reality.[4] It begs admittance to perform as our guide and appears regularly before the opening of each act to speed us on our way. We can come to an understanding of the significance of these choric prologues by weighing them against the content of each act.

The Chorus in the Prologue to Act I paints a rose-tinted spectacle of historical events. In attempting to inspire us to reach out for a glorious reality the speech of the Chorus begs us to forget the stage in language that forcibly reminds us of it. Because the Chorus embodies an unquestioning belief in the glory of war it presents a vision which does not adequately cover any man's actual experience of war. Shakespeare has many scenes to exhibit which are far from the pomp and glory of which the Chorus speaks, scenes which are tawdry indeed, ragged men who on this unworthy scaffold hardly aid the swelling scene. A play which capitalized on the tawdriness of the stage, on the ordinariness of human response, might seem more like real life, more real, indeed, than the tantalizingly impossible vision the Chorus presents.

In the first act we turn from the florid invocation to the political details of how the expedition came to be undertaken. The King establishes himself at once as a shepherd of his people intent on securing authoritative support for a just war. Whether we find the genealogical ramblings of Canterbury comic or not, it is clear that Shakespeare devotes a whole act to establishing the unity of the Church and the barons in England's cause. Shakespeare clearly indicates that we are in an entirely new world and to that extent fulfills the picture of a puissant nation which the Chorus had celebrated at the outset. The scenes constantly invoke that golden age of Edward III and the Black Prince so that our eyes are turned on this new king as a rising sun who will return England to its former glory (I.ii. 278-80).

The Prologue to Act II presents us with material designed for lyrical intensity, a patriotic hymn describing a nation girding its loins. The information concerning the conspiracy provides us with no material that we do not obtain by other means during the ensuing action. The information has a similar function to many of the Brechtian devices of anticipation. When we come upon the conspiracy, it does not disturb our faith in England's new found unity, because the Chorus has already informed us that we will ship for France. Thus we can concentrate on the masterly fashion in which the King deals with it.

It must also be observed that the speech which serves as Prologue to this Act makes no mention of the action which fills two-thirds of it. It can hardly be said that the scenes in Eastcheap contribute to the picture of an England transformed into an ideal state. Henry himself may be reformed but Shakespeare saw no point in abandoning his unrepentant associates when they could be used to elaborate richly on the major concerns of the play. The Chorus throughout the play exhibits no knowledge of this world resistant to the poetic vision of a mighty nation eager to fall upon its enemies. We do not expect the hyperbole of the Chorus to acknowledge their pedestrian concerns. But though the Chorus can ignore these characters, the King cannot, and the comic scenes add up in the audience's mind to illuminate the King's contemplation of: "the wretched slave / Who, with a body fill'd and vacant mind, / Gets him to rest, cramm'd with distressful bread" (IV.i.264-66).

In the Prologue to Act II we are prepared for the embarcation at Southampton: "The King is set from London, and the scene / Is now transported, gentles, to Southampton; / There is the playhouse now, there must you sit" (Prologue.II.34-36). The Chorus is interested only in the main line of the story, only in the King and his cause, not in any embellishments. There is even the implication that there is nothing further of interest in this narrative until the King appears: "But, till the King come forth, and not till then, / Unto Southampton do we shift our scene" (Prologue.II.41-42). The Chorus in elaborate manner rushes us forward to Southampton. It is with some surprise, then, that on entering Act II we find Shakespeare lagging behind in Eastcheap. Our sights have been set well above the Boar's Head Tavern:

> Now all the youth of England are on fire,
> And silken dalliance in the wardrobe lies;
> Now thrive the armourers, and honour's
>   thought
> Reigns solely in the breast of every man . . .
>   (Prologue.II.1-4)

Shakespeare tempers this public eulogy with the private humours of Pistol and Nym, which aim at a little less than the reign of honour. This inconsistency might, perhaps, be more easily explained by assuming a late shuffling and addition of scenes or incomplete revision, were it not in line with the entire development of the Chorus, whose poetic vision is played off against the reality of the everyday world. Those critics who have assumed that the Chorus was designed to link an episodic narrative together and prepare the audience for rapid transitions might note not only that it is almost entirely superfluous in that role, but also that its function might often be more fruitfully examined as a deliberate lack of bridging and preparation for what actually goes on.

It cannot be accidental that the first scene in the Boar's Head parodies the rhetoric of politics in the court world that we have just left. There is division over the title and possession of a piece of property, Nell Quickly; there is an exchange of insults; there is a determination to fight it out, and concord is established by linking us back to the major theme in the resolve to bury the quarrel in France. The "humorous" exchange between Pistol and Nym, with its absurdly overblown conceits and threats, is a comical reflection of the stern rebuttal of the Dauphin's insulting joke. The contrast here, of course, is in the excesses of the bragging, flyting match as opposed to the King's restrained and dignified retort to the French, and the lack of purposeful action that comes from the shouting match as opposed to the King's resolute expedition to conquer France. The overblown battle rhetoric of Pistol acts as admirable counterpoint to the genuinely ecstatic patriotism of the Chorus. Pistol's determination to profit by the war is a far cry from the honour which reigns in the breast of all the youths of England. It must be said, however, that the rogues, who give not a fig for honour, are gradually eliminated from the play. The Lord of Misrule, Falstaff, who had his being in more frivolous days, dies without being given opportunity to make an impact on the crusade, soon Bardolph is hanged, later Nym is reported to have been hanged, and Nell Quickly is said to be dead. Only Pistol, soundly battered, crawls back to England. None of them interacts with the King, save Pistol in his encounter with Harry "Leroy". The new England offers no secure place for the former revellers. This, however, does not prevent us from recognizing that the Chorus's version of events is a considerable gloss on reality.

The Prologue to Act III contains thirty-five lines, and of these only nine and a half at the most can be described as transmitting expository information. The rest is poetic embellishment. We have already learnt at the end of Act II that Henry is footed in France. The evocation of the channel-crossing in vivid pictorial imagery serves more as a transitional pause than for the contribution of information. The patriotic tone is reinforced with the description of a deserted England and the proud, invading army. Only at the close of the speech are we told rapidly about the siege of Harfleur as answer to the unsatisfactory French terms. The two succeeding scenes are set in dialectical contrast, reflecting on this invocation. The King continues the martial rhetoric in his Harfleur speech, living up to the ideal set by the Chorus. The laggards from Eastcheap fall away from that ideal, tempering valour with very heavy doses of prudence. Bardolph's entrance, opening Act III, Scene ii, inevitably puctures the vein of resounding rhetoric that Shakespeare has sustained unbroken for almost seventy lines. Anything less "Like greyhounds in the slips, / Straining upon the start" can scarcely be imagined. The rhetoric of the Chorus and Pistol is again juxtaposed; they both employ rhetoric of obviously literary origin. The Chorus aspires to the patriotic lyrical strains of a Spenser, magnifying honour to a point that ignores human weakness. Pistol borrows the fustian terms and epithets of the traditional stage braggart to hide his aversion to honour and to cover his human weakness. Hotson has described how the Chorus glorifies Henry while Pistol provides a comic parody of him:

> (Pistol's) gift is a daemon possessing him with the conviction that he is essentially a Locrine, a Cambyses, a Tamburlaine. Not, of course, the insane notion that he is a real tyrant king, but the wildly absurd one that he is a *player king*. Thus he can rehearse valour without requiring courage, carry tempest in his voice without running any measurable danger.[5]

By providing this parody of heroism Shakespeare induces us to believe the more in the genuine heroism of Henry. That Pistol will twice get his pretence of bravery accepted—Fluellen's eulogy of his work at the bridge and Le Fer's submission—indicates how careful one has to be in recognizing true valour. All the world's a stage to Pistol and he has his moments of glory even as he is also pelted with rotten vegetables when the audience, in this case Fluellen, sees through his performance.

The debate between Fluellen and MacMorris in Act III, Scene ii presents more evidence of the tawdry reality of war. The squabbling of the national representatives is a comic reduction of those factional struggles which had, in earlier plays, rent England asunder. The scene indicates the petty disputes, the touchy pride, the varying views on military strategy, which affect men in war. Shakespeare can thus represent the reality of war without allowing any factionalism to taint, in any serious way, the King's cause. In contrast to his days as Prince, Henry speaks to no one beneath captain's rank until the critical eve of Agincourt (IV.i.). It is well to keep this in mind when speaking of the King's much celebrated "common touch". There are many scenes which carry on a ribald commentary on the glorious action, but Shakespeare carefully disassociates the King from them all, despite his former proclivities, until late in the play. By that time, although we have not forgotten Prince Hal, we have had ample opportunity of recognizing the kind of king he has turned into.

In the Prologue to Act IV we look again in vain if we seek vital narrative informative. We have seen the English offer a challenge to battle, we have heard of the sickness of their troops, and we have observed already "The confident and over-lusty French" despising their English opponents. The Chorus merely reviews this material, but it also creates that midnight calm, that pause on the brink of the storm, in which Henry's tour among his soldiers can take place. The Chorus utters that magic word in English history and raises the spirit of the times—"The name of Agincourt". The function of the Chorus here is almost that of a priest presiding over and ushering in this sacred ritual of patriotism, this re-enactment of a miracle. The magnificent imagery of this speech could have been divided up among the characters but, isolated from the action, its cumulative impact swelling into a hymn of praise to the King helps to set up an atmosphere of reverence which causes the audience to pause and focus its attention. There is a sense here of ritual mimesis in which the priest-like Chorus announces the stages of the re-enactment, which are subsequently performed, thus bringing us to that sense of order and unity aimed at by religious rites. This hallowed atmosphere created by the Chorus is supported by echoes of Christian tradition in the action itself.

The King is something more than human in the speech of the Chorus. He is "like the sun" with miraculous restorative powers; as he moves in the darkness, "A little touch of Harry in the night", he has affinities with Christ as the light of the world. The King is the saviour of the English. As Christ came down to earth and took upon him the image of a humble carpenter's son, so the King walks among his men disguised, dividing his thoughts with them, attending to the humble almost as though they were his flock and he their shepherd. I am, of course, forcing to the surface those associations which must remain vaguely at the back of our minds as we watch these scenes. The imagery of communion, however, is obvious enough. Henry's famous battle speech to his soldiers, as unlikely a band of crusaders as the fishermen disciples themselves, emphasizes the significance of St. Crispian's day and the ritual sharing of blood:

> We few, we happy few, we band of brothers;
> For he today that sheds his blood with me
> Shall be my brother; be he ne'er so vile,
> This day shall gentle his condition;
>
> (IV.iii.60-63)

The speech draws its strength, too, from the tradition of the *comitatus,* but in its emphasis on the few, on the chosen, it reminds us of the disciples in a hostile land. Henry is depicted as God's chosen instrument to subdue the pride of the French who have little to say of God and are pictured almost as effete heathens hungering only for glory. The King's anguished soliloquy on the hard duties of being a chosen leader is also perhaps, uttered in the loneliness of the night on the eve of a great trail, a very distant reflection of Christ's agony in Gethsemane. Finally, and more fancifully, there is a very faint echo of the journey to Emmaus in Williams' exchange with Henry, for, having failed to recognize his master disguised in the night, the revelation comes as a shock later on with the King's bounty. These echoes work collectively to create a general atmosphere of religious dedication

which is ultimately rewarded with a miracle, the battle losses at Agincourt—"O God, thy arm was here!"

A great deal of this atmosphere of ritual stems, as I have suggested, from the speech of the Chorus. But we must also note that there are other elements in the Act which prevent it from becoming a totally formalized ritual and which place the battle firmly in the human sphere. We realize, if we think about it for a moment, that the Chorus' version of Henry's tour among his soldiers is deliberate misdirection, a lack of preparation for the scene as Shakespeare writes it. The King does not appear like a sun to thaw his soldier's fear, but moves disguised, unknown to his soldiers, not to impress and inspire them but to be depressed and dispirited by them. His experience among them begins with comic familiarity and insults from Pistol and ends almost in a brawl with Williams. In his debate with his soldiers the disguised King has to offer an elaborate theory of self-justification. He receives answers rooted in the immediate fears of men far removed from the theories by which the powerful seek to justify war. Instead of being inspired by a national ideal, or even a little touch of Harry in the night, they are suspicious, uncertain, anticipating the worst.[6] The rhetoric of battle may evoke greyhounds in the slips but the play also presents a king isolated in the understanding of his cause in Bates's: "Then I would he were here alone; so should he be sure to be ransomed, and a many poor men's lives saved" (IV.i.120-22).

In the King's soliloquy after the departure of his soldiers the dialectical arguments of the play are resolved. The King's talk of Ceremony and its pageantry deals with surface appearances, that triumphant exterior view which the Chorus has presented. In his talk with his soldiers the King has at last come in contact with its opposite, that care for the self, unmindful of greater causes. The King is incapable of living the carefree day to day existence of his soldiers or of being blinded by the ceremonial trappings of his office. He has to recognize, in full consciousness, the lonely burden of being of mortal clay with the superaddition of regal duty. At last in the history cycle a king appears who, by the nature of his strange education and his practical application of role playing, comes to an understanding of himself and of man's limitations while he is still at the top of Fortune's wheel. This understanding is affirmed by his unwearied ascription of his every success to God's favour.

The Prologue to Act V is the most functional of all in terms of transmitting narrative material, and it is the only one which concentrates on abridging the story. Since we return to the English camp in France immediately, it could be argued that there was no necessity for recounting the King's return home and from thence back to France. Shakespeare is so free in his treatment of history that there seems to be no reason why Henry

Christopher Plummer as King Henry V and members of the Festival Company in a scene
from the 1956 Stratford Festival production of Henry V.

could not have proceeded straight to the French court. But such telescoping of events was not to Shakespeare's advantage here. Even if historically Henry had not in fact returned home, it would have been necessary for Shakespeare to find some matter to form a transitional pause here. The atmosphere of war which has coloured this play must be brought to an end for the change in mood to the gay courtship which concludes the play. The description by the Chorus of Henry's reception in London not only crowns the patriotic fervor which has built up throughout the play but also neatly rounds off the preoccupation with war by a celebration of the return to peace. Even so we must note that the Chorus in providing the narrative link suppresses, in fact, more than it reveals. We are told of the triumphant return to England and a second visit to France for the composition of a treaty. No mention is made of Henry's second invasion of France, a four-year battle campaign the treaty for which was not concluded until five years after Agincourt. Shakespeare had chosen to reduce the battles of five years

to one swift and decisive campaign. This streamlining of events frees him to explore a sub-plot world and to elaborate a variety of moods and attitudes. The Chorus laments the inadequacy of the stage for transmitting history even as Shakespeare is using it to distort history in order to fit his own dramatic patterns.

Productions of this play in recent times have run to a variety of extreme interpretations. Olivier's film version, reflecting the miraculous heroism of the Battle of Britain, as the original play itself, many have claimed, celebrated the destruction of the Armada, appeared to operate on the assumption that Shakespeare's meaning was to be elicited from the attitude of the Chorus. A more recent London production played in tin hats and gas-masks among trenches, and Michael Langham's production at Stratford, Ontario in 1966 with its Brechtian emphasis, operated on the assumption that Shakespeare's sympathies lay with the informal "chorus" of soldiers. By a rather brutally managed irony the formal Chorus thus appeared to be jingoistic, ludicrously out of touch, in the painting of pretty verbal pictures, with the agonizing realities of war. To interpret *Henry V* in either of the above manners is to be unjust to the balance of evidence in the play. If we assume the Chorus to be Shakespeare's spokesman, we are hard put to it to give sufficient weight to the evidence of the soldiers. If we emphasize the soldiers' views exclusively, then we have to interpret large sections of the play in terms of a crude and heavily obvious irony that is not characteristic of Shakespeare. Henry is placed in a central position to mediate the dialectical contrast. Shakespeare has shaped Hal through two plays with a kind of education unique among the English kings of whom he wrote, so that at last the glories and horrors of martial struggles can meet in the perception of one man. The plainest thing about the complicated structure of this play is that Shakespeare was not writing heavily weighted propaganda for one side of the problem or the other.[7]

The Chorus, then, is throughout the play a strategically used device embodying the popular tradition which glowed, perhaps, in the memory of an Elizabethan audience. Tradition tends to rub away the encrustation of human detail, it glamourizes and has an infinite capacity to forget the human weaknesses among the human strengths. There is some truth still in tradition, but it is not the whole truth. Shakespeare did not wish to destroy the glory of Agincourt but he realized that by injecting episodic detail he could make it more convincing. The inclusion of Pistol and the disillusioned soldiers does not enhance the glory of the battle. There could be no greater travesty of chivalry than Pistol's dealings with Le Fer to contrast with Exeter's report of York's heroic death (IV.iv.7-32). The one must inevitably bring tears of laughter to our eyes even as the other brings tears of sorrow to Exeter's. But we accept Shakespeare's battle more readily than that of tradition because it is more firmly based in human experience.

In the final speech of the play the Chorus once again apologizes for the inadequacies of the stage, and yet we, who look back to all such scenes as Pistol grovelling before Fluellen's leek, are unlikely to concur in the judgement of the Chorus: "In little room confining mighty men, / Mangling by starts the full course of their glory" (Epilogue.V.3-4). The great art of Shakespeare's version of the story lies in the ample room that he has allowed himself and his mangling by starts, in such a varied way, the full course of the action.

Notes

[1] Geoffrey Bullough, *Narrative and Dramatic Sources of Shakespeare* (London: Routledge and Kegan Paul, 1962), III, p. 349.

[2] Virgil K. Whitaker, *Shakespeare's Use of Learning* (San Marino: The Huntington Library, 1964), p. 131.

[3] W. D. Smith finds the speeches of the Chorus so functionally unnecessary that he suggests that they were added by another hand for a performance at court in 1603. Without accepting this rather extreme conclusion, I would point to his discussion, which contains many useful examples of the redundancies, irrelevancies and often seemingly misleading passages in the choruses regarded from a functionally expository point of view. "The *Henry V* Choruses in the First Folio," *JEGP,* 53 (1954), 38-57.

[4] The contrast between the heroic view of war and the reality of its seamy side is made with devastating irony at the opening of *Troilus and Cressida.* The thunderously imposing hyperbole of the Prologue is immediately undercut by the sulkily adolescent, lovesick behaviour of Troilus. Shakespeare does not continue the Chorus in this play because it is enough to have the bludgeon satire of Thersites' choric commentary as a contrast to the overstuffed epithets of war emerging from the mouths of most of the other characters.

[5] Leslie Hotson, *Shakespeare's Sonnets Dated and Other Essays* (London: Rupert Hart-Davies, 1949), p. 61.

[6] Fluellen is used throughout the play to indicate the disparity between war as it should be fought according to hallowed tradition, and the kind of war that is actually fought with its murdering of defenseless boys, an act distressful to the Welshman because it deviates from the copy-book. Fluellen is a comic parody within the plot of the homage to tradition that the Chorus presents outside it.

[7] In Norman Rabkin, *Shakespeare and the Common Understanding* (New York: The Free Press, 1967), a similar balance of ideas is presented in exploring the concept of "complementarity" in Shakespeare's plays. Rabkin, however, believes that the polarized ideas of the play are held in an unresolved tension. He suggests (pp. 98-101) that since the audience cannot easily accept Henry's compromise with reality it must regard the play as a dream. It will be evident that I consider Shakespeare to have presented in the Chorus and Pistol views of the world that deliberately are not viable as alternatives to Henry's realism. Shakespeare's audience had waited patiently through many plays for a king who was neither sunk in the pleasure principle nor lost in the realms of impractical idealism.

Lawrence Danson (essay date 1983)

SOURCE: "*Henry V*: King, Chorus, and Critics," in *Shakespeare Quarterly,* Vol. 34, No. 1, Spring, 1983, pp. 27-43.

[*In the following essay, Danson calls attention to analogies between king and Chorus, suggesting that both the play and its principal character require an impartial, even sympathetic appraisal. Henry and the Chorus are both performers, the critic remarks, adept at creating images and self-images, myths and legends, and together depicting a king who is noble but flawed and who must make painful choices.*]

I would like to believe that *Henry V* was the first of Shakespeare's plays to be performed in his new Globe theatre, and in the absence of proof to the contrary I can at least dally with the surmise. Construction on the Globe began at the end of February 1599, and it must have been completed by late August or early September 1599. The date of *Henry V* is usually established by its reference to the Earl of Essex: the Chorus imagines in "loving likelihood" that "Were now the general of our gracious empress, / As in good time he may, from Ireland coming" (V. Chorus. 30-31), the people would welcome him as fervently as once they welcomed Henry V. Essex's campaign was in shambles by late summer; by the time the Globe was ready to open, his defeat looked certain. For this reason, editors have generally assumed that the play was written early in the year, before the debacle so clearly impended; and theatre historians have therefore generally assumed that the "wooden O" to which the Chorus repeatedly draws attention was *not* the Globe but the company's interim home, the Curtain. But the evidence is equivocal. *Henry V* is a play about a miraculous victory against impossible odds; an English victory in Ireland in late summer 1599 would have been such a victory, as clearly showing God's favoring hand as did, once upon a time, the victory at Agincourt. The Essex allusion does not rule out a date of composition in late August or early September. Such a pluckily defiant reference to temporary English setbacks could have been mighty cheering in that summer, a time enlivened anyway by the inauguration of the most splendid theatre ever built to celebrate the English in England.

I

Why, then, does the Chorus apologize for the theatre? The question of the Chorus' "apology" (the word, I will claim, does not adequately describe the tone) is as difficult to answer if we assume performance in the old Curtain as in the new Globe. No one, after all, forced Shakespeare to write this play in this particular way. If his flat unraised spirits couldn't bring forth so great an object on whichever unworthy scaffold, he could have chosen something else to write about. But of course it is no harder to bring forth an Agincourt than a Bosworth Field; and moonlight in the Athenian woods tests the theatrical muscle as much as do flickering campfires in France. The Chorus' apologies violate that elementary rule of English good breeding, "Never apologize, never explain"—not too much, at any rate, lest you keep the offense fresh in mind. The

Chorus calls attention to the ostensible fault in a way that makes us consider the fault rather than merely forget and forgive it. He makes us consider our theatrical environment. If that environment is the brand-new Globe, it might make sense for Shakespeare to call attention to it. The Chorus bids us travel in imagination to far off, wonderful scenes; but each such choric invitation, by making the process self-conscious, simultaneously keeps us in mind of our actual location in the theatre. To the extent that the imaginary jaunts to Southampton, Harfleur, Agincourt, or Troyes are successful, the theatre is successful. If the play works, the ostensible apologies only underscore the artistic triumph of Shakespeare's theatre of poor means: the fewer means, the greater share of honor.

No doubt there is an element of actual apology in what the Chorus says. The theatre does have certain limitations with regard to "real" life and to history; the best in this kind are but shadows, as needs no Chorus to tell us. But there is also an element of playing at apologizing. The Chorus enacts a sly version of the modesty topos, which (according to Ernst Curtius) was widely used by good orators "to put [the] hearers in a favorable, attentive, and tractable state of mind. How do this? First, through a modest presence. But one has to draw attention to this modesty oneself. Thus it becomes affected."[1] Affectation is a fault, and the use of such a hoary rhetorical ploy as the "modesty formula" could be dull. The Chorus solves those problems by mocking his own act with self-conscious exaggeration even as he earnestly enacts it. The profundity of the bow—"O pardon!"—lets us take his words in various ways. His tone tells us that he's sorry but proud, and proud of being sorry in such an ingenious way. Thus the Chorus woos the audience as King Harry does Kate: the one lacks a muse of fire, the other cannot look greenly nor gasp out his eloquence; the player lacks a kingdom for a stage, the King can only speak "plain soldier." But "nice customs curtsy to great kings" (V.ii.284), and the theatre's "imaginary puissance" (Prologue. 25) can work wonders.

Harry wins Kate, but notoriously he has not won the critics, from Dr. Johnson through Hazlitt to the recent editor who finds his wooing "ursine."[2] The critical reluctance to "cry, 'Praise and glory'" on Henry V's head is a curious case of theatrical *lèse majesté* because it is a vote of no-confidence, not just in Harry, but in that other noble speaker, Shakespeare's Chorus, as well. As the critical literature richly attests, and nowhere better than in Norman Rabkin's recent essay about the phenomenon, it is hard to know what to make of *Henry V,* because its various parts seem to tug us in such extremely different directions.[3] But hard as the play's problems are, they do not make it a gestaltist experiment, for the Chorus is there to give a sense of perspective, to establish the figure against the ground. The Chorus is simultaneously an actor in the play and a privileged voice outside it; we may not approve of privileged characters, but neither should we ignore them. So it is notable that critics hostile to Harry tend to neglect the evidence of the Chorus (other critics neglect other evidence); occasionally they fail to remark that their interpretations conflict with that of Shakespeare's own interpreter. The Chorus should pose a challenge to anyone who thinks we murder to ascribe a "meaning" to Shakespeare, while the distance between what he tells and some of what the intervening acts show challenges anyone who thinks that a privileged character ought to mean what he says.

II

In the matter of meaning, we need not take the extremes of all or none. The extremes do serve some purposes: those of the semiotician, for instance, to whom the play is like any other system of signs to be deconstructed into its many contradictory possibilities, or who searches along the text's small fissures in order to discover the social strains disguised by aesthetic sleights. For other purposes we may still value an interpretive *via media* where diversity is prized for the unity it can yield, and where coherent does not necessarily mean reductive. *E. pluribus unum* is a lively ideal in traditions as diverse as the Aristotelian and the Coleridgean and—most important for the immediate case—the theatrical. To the scholar alone in his famous study, *Henry V* may seem equally a rabbit and a duck, but I cannot imagine how you stage such duplicity. Audiences will buy complexity, but an optical illusion is what closes on Saturday night. Actors and directors cannot be relativists; they must make choices.

In *Henry V* there are many difficult choices to be made, and all the more difficult because Shakespeare lets us know what each choice excludes. Therefore he gives us the Chorus. The Chorus tells us how to respond as an audience, watching a play, watching a king. And he does this by linking the two circumstances, the theatrical and the historical, allowing us in both a coherent response. The Chorus reflects upon the nature of his own theatrical being at the same time that he holds up "the mirror of all Christian kings" (II. Chorus. 6). The images of *homo ludens* and *homo regens* are not identical; they exist in prismatic relation, the one image refracting interesting bands of light upon the other. The Chorus' presentation of Harry is as complex as its self-presentation. The Chorus can call attention to the play's inherent theatrical limitations at the same time that it invites us to revel in theatricality; and the play can show the human weakness of its hero at the same time that it celebrates his greatness. *Henry V,* partly through the prismatic relation of Chorus and King, allows us to see the weakness attendant on all human greatness yet to recognize that greatness when we see it.

As the audience is to the players, so Harry's men are to Harry. And, because the analogy points this way, as we are to the players so should we be to Harry—for the King too is only a man trying with limited resources to turn intractable reality into something resembling imaginative success. The King's actorliness has often been recognized by critics, though they have drawn various conclusions about it. Una Ellis-Fermor was dismayed that Henry V "is never off the platform," that man and role are so united in him that "there is no Henry, only a king." (The play existed for her as text rather than performance, and that may have something to do with her negative evaluation. "Generations of Shakespeare's readers have found little to love in this play," she wrote, just before a generation of moviegoers would start loving it in the Olivier version.)[4] James Calderwood also notices that "To play the king is to play the actor, for the king must have many roles in his repertoire." But Calderwood's evaluation of Harry's actorliness is more positive than Ellis-Fermor's, partly because he sees that acting one's self well, or acting well as if one were one's self, is not such a bad thing to do; and because he sees that the King's actorliness is related to what the play as a whole is doing: "Harry acts marvelously well, and the militant English road company for which he stars prospers apace."[5]

Less common than the recognition that the King is like an actor is the recognition that that special actor, Shakespeare's Chorus, is like the King. Michael Goldman makes the point in his fine reading, which is antipodal to Ellis-Fermor's in its precise attention to the play's performance qualities. "Once it is recognized that the Chorus sounds very much like the King, much of the play's method becomes clear," he writes; and "the figure of the Chorus rousing the audience to cooperation and excitement is rather like the figure of Henry addressing his men."[6] We can see this analogical relationship in other details too, for instance in Harry's ostensibly tongue-tied wooing and the Chorus' ostensible lack of theatrical means. The director Terry Hands points out that the line with which the King wraps up his Crispin Day speech—"All things are ready if our minds be so"—"is the same message uttered by the Chorus at the beginning of the play. It will serve for visual spectacle, or personal behaviour."[7] But most importantly we see this relationship overall in an attitude, and it is that attitude I want now to explore. The relationship of play-maker and audience is uneasy and dependent. If the Chorus can take pride in the theatre's limited resources (since the confession of those resources sets off, like a foil, the wonders the theatre can perform), he can do so only if he has a responsive auditory. The Chorus needs our sympathetic participation. We must "work" and "follow" and "eke out [the] performance" "in the quick forge and working-house of thought." We must be willing, for the success of the theatrical enterprise, not to overlook the theatre's limitations, but fairly to revel in the successful effort of overcoming them. "It's very hard," an interviewer commented to Alan Howard when he was playing the role of Henry V for the RSC, "to find a commentator from Dr. Johnson to Yeats who doesn't find the play shallow or jingoistic." "Why," the interviewer asked, "do you think that is?" "Well," said Alan Howard, "they haven't had to play it. . . . It is a *play*, after all, not a novel."[8] And a good audience to that play is neither hostile nor passive. It is mercifully critical, answering the Chorus' prayer "Gently to watch, kindly to judge, our play" (Prologue. 34).

III

The Chorus to Act IV is a good place to see the playfully self-conscious complexity of Shakespeare's attitude to his own theatrical accomplishment, and I will begin with it before going on to what it tells, by analogy, about Shakespeare's attitude to the King. The Chorus enacts the playwright's version of the inexpressibility topos, the most sublime form of the modesty formula. Once again, that is, just as thrice previously in the play, Shakespeare is showing to the capable imagination's eye what his words claim he cannot show. The burden is on the audience to "entertain conjecture of [the] time," because (as the Prologue had earlier told us) the unworthy scaffold and its cockpit cannot hold "the vasty fields of France" or "the very casques / That did affright the air at Agincourt" (Prologue. 10-14). This is the sort of technical problem that floored bully Bottom, but the Chorus in *Henry V,* even while it professes the canons of naive realism, shows how verbal art can overgo reality. The conjectured scene is so sensuously rich, its words at once so specific and suggestive, that (as the Olivier version shows) it becomes an embarrassment to the cinematographer's camera, which can only tag along and palely imitate what the instructed mind's eye can conceive. This Act IV Chorus is itself a protocinematic tour de force. It begins with a distant tracking-shot, which the imagination brings into more vivid focus than a passive camera could do. The tension with which we see and hear the uncreated scene is like the tension of the English and French "fix'd sentinels" who "*almost* receive / The secret whispers of each other's watch" (ll. 6-7). We strain to hear a murmur that is synesthetically "creeping" and to see a "dark" that is "poring" both because, by transference, it is "eye-straining" (Arden ed. note) and because, by punning, it is filling "the wide vessel of the universe" (ll. 2-3). The tenseness of the scene is embodied in a series of imagistic and syntactical oppositions, as "fire answers fire" and "steed threatens steed" (ll. 8, 10); and it is concluded in a way which simultaneously caps and releases the tension as "The country cocks do crow, the clocks do toll, / And the third hour of drowsy morning name" (ll. 15-16).

We cut quickly now to "The confident and over-lusty French" (l. 18), and for a moment the tension of our "conjecture" is relieved by the vigor of their dicing and chiding. But the image of "the cripple and tardy-gaited night / Who, like a foul and ugly witch doth limp / So tediously away" (ll. 20-22), brings back the dominant sense of action done with difficulty. That painful, slow limping is our cue to pan to another mid-shot and see "The poor condemned English." Their stillness, as they "Sit patiently, and inly ruminate / The morning's danger" (ll. 24-25), is in both moral and formal contrast to the French in the previous shot; and their insubstantiality ("lank-lean" and "war-worn," they are "So many horrid ghosts") sets off the vigor of the half-line, "O, now, who will behold" (l. 28).

"Behold": no mere conjecture, now, nor difficult straining to see and hear. The sudden appearance of "The royal captain of this ruin'd band" (l. 29) rewards and relieves our attentiveness. He is a gift to us as much as to his men. A refusal now to "cry, 'Praise and glory on his head!'" (l. 31) is a refusal of Shakespeare's poetry, a spurning of his virtuosity. And it is worth pausing for a moment (before concluding this little summary of the Act IV Chorus) to ask why we have so often refused the cry. Much of the answer will have to wait—all of it, in fact, having to do with the King's actions *in propria persona.* For the moment I am only interested in the part having to do with the Chorus' presentation.

Rarely in Shakespeare do we find poetry that has so palpable a design on us. Comparable things happen in epilogues, like Puck's or Prospero's; but an epilogue, because it "comes after all, imploring pardon," is safely set off from the preceding action. Its direct address is not felt as an interruption of the more usual modes of dramatic indirection. More nearly akin to the problem of the Chorus is the problem caused when a character steps out of dramatic context to serve, momentarily, a choric function. Such a moment occurs in *1 Henry IV,* just before the battle, in Vernon's description of Hal:

> I saw young Harry with his beaver on,
> His cushes on his thighs, gallantly armed,
> Rise from the ground like feathered Mercury,
> And vaulted with such ease into his seat
> As if an angel dropped down from the clouds
> To turn and wind a fiery Pegasus
> And witch the world with noble
>   horsemanship.
>
> (IV.i.103-9)

But here we are inclined to forgive the dramatic fault because of its transparency. Since there is absolutely no reason why Vernon should want to deject his troops (except to cheer up the audience), we can draw on our knowledge of non-naturalistic dramatic conventions and let it go at that. Elsewhere Shakespeare does this sort of thing better, so that there is no need to make allowances. Enobarbus dying of a broken heart while telling us how to respond to Antony's generosity is such a moment.

But the Chorus in *Henry V* is unique. The direct appeal is both intrusive and perfectly in character, and it is therefore possible to resent it. The Chorus is indulgent, not just of the King, but of himself: he indulges in oral/aural pleasures, with mouth- and ear-filling sensuousness. Emrys James, who played the Chorus to Alan Howard's Henry, confesses that "for years I used to do 'O for a Muse of fire' as my audition speech. And then maybe I would get the part and maybe I wouldn't, but that speech and the other Chorus speeches stayed with me in my head. I'd be walking down Oxford Street and there would be those extraordinary words, ticking over in my head, just there, for no reason at all, except that they'd been planted in my brain." Michael Goldman describes these speeches as "display arias for the commanding actor; they stimulate us to share his noticeable effort, to be aware of the glory and labor involved in making authoritative sounds."[9] But some of us resent authority and are suspicious of histrionic self-indulgence. People who are made uneasy by displays of virtuosity will find the Chorus more resistible than I do; and they may, by the same token, also resist the King's performance.

The end of the Act IV Chorus shows with what virtuosity both Chorus and King perform their parts. "Upon his royal face there is no note / How dread an army hath enrounded him," the Chorus assures us; "Nor doth he dedicate one jot of colour / Unto the weary and all-watched night" (ll. 35-38)—though fear and exhaustion, we will discover, are precisely what the King is feeling. But the Chorus' own description, in advance of the enacted revelation, makes the King's actions seem a calculated performance. Though beheld in close-up, in the concluding scene of this sequence, the King is still kept emotionally distant by the Chorus' imaginary lens. His feelings are suggested only by the negative assertion of what he does not reveal. His ostensibly easy movement "from watch to watch, from tent to tent" (l. 30) is the product of great effort, as he "freshly looks and overbears attaint" (l. 39). He exists for us as a source of emotion in others; so that while he is closely seen he is also held away, objectified, known chiefly by the effect he has, when

> every wretch, pining and pale before,
> Beholding him, plucks comfort from his
>   looks.
> A largess universal like the sun
> His liberal eye doth give to every one,
> Thawing cold fear, . . .
>
> (ll. 41-45)

This scene of the King begins with the direction "behold," and the final image returns to that word: "Behold, as may unworthiness define. . . . " These lines perfectly illustrate the playfulness of the Chorus' attitude. The phrase "as may unworthiness define," like the Chorus' other apologies, has the effect of turning our attention from the message to the medium. But what a moment to break the illusion, just as the Chorus is about to deliver himself of his finest line yet! It is like apologizing for the amazing Globe theatre. We hear the modest disclaimer, wait for the offense, and are rewarded with "A little touch of Harry in the night." The tenous delicacy of that "little touch" and the frightful portent of "the night" surround and set off the bold English name of "Harry"—the first time we have heard it in this speech, which has taken us from distant prospect to mid-range to close-up. The reward is all the more precious because there is no lingering on it:

> And so our scene must to the battle fly;
> Where, O for pity! we shall much disgrace
> With four or five most vile and ragged foils,
> Right ill-disposed in brawl ridiculous,
> The name of Agincourt. But sit and see;
> Minding true things by what their mock'ries
>   be.
>
> (ll. 48-53)

Again a name, "Agincourt," provides a satisfying climax instead of the anticipated disgrace. The apologetic "O for pity" functions like the previous "as may unworthiness define," acknowledging an obvious failure (not for us, today, "the very casques / That did affright the air" [Prologue. 13-14]), while granting us a different sort of aesthetic triumph.

IV

Thus with only his words and our charitably disposed imaginations the Chorus demonstrates the principle that less is more. In the political world of *Henry IV* this is a principle that Hal had known from the early days when he made his apparent moral poverty serve the ends of future greatness:

> So when this loose behavior I throw off
> And pay the debt I never promised,
> By how much better than my word I am,
> By so much shall I falsify men's hopes;
> And, like bright metal on a sullen ground,
> My reformation, glitt'ring o'er my fault,
> Shall show more goodly and attract more eyes
> Than that which hath no foil to set it off.
> I'll so offend to make offense a skill,
> Redeeming time when men think least I will.
>
> (*1 Henry IV,* I.ii.205-14)

At Agincourt, Prince Hal's shrewd accountancy is still recognizable in King Harry's making of "fewer men, the greater share of honour" (IV.iii.22). But if Harry's Crispin Day speech recalls Hal's politics it also, and more immediately, reflects the Chorus' imaginative investment. The Crispin Day speech is Chorus-like, not only because it makes more of less, but because it is specifically an aesthetic or imaginative sort of triumph that Harry aims for. It is his own legend, and his men's, that Harry is creating—writing, in effect, his own play. Like the Chorus, he involves his audience in a communal effort; and like the Chorus, he brilliantly manipulates the sounds of names:

> This day is call'd the feast of Crispian:
> He that outlives this day, and comes safe
>   home,
> Will stand a tip-toe when this day is nam'd,
> And rouse him at the name of Crispian.
> He that shall see this day, and live old age,
> Will yearly on the vigil feast his neighbours,
> And say, "To-morrow is Saint Crispian":
> Then will he strip his sleeve and show his
>   scars,
> And say, "These wounds I had on Crispin's
>   day". . . .
> . . . . Then shall our names,
> Familiar in his mouth as household words,
> Harry the king, Bedford and Exeter,
> Warwick and Talbot, Salisbury and
>   Gloucester,
> Be in their flowing cups freshly remember'd.
>   (IV.iii.40-48, 51-55)

Richard II had a similar talent for imaginative self-creation, but he could make it work for him only at the expense of life. His role was victim, his genre tragedy. Sitting upon the ground and telling sad stories of the death of kings, making dust his paper and with rainy eyes writing sorrow on the bosom of the earth, fretting for himself and Aumerle a pair of graves within the earth (complete with sad epitaphs), preparing for his queen the "lamentable tale of me" that would send her hearers weeping to their beds: repeatedly Richard was the author of his own self-sacrificial myth. Harry at Agincourt is in a similar way the author of himself; and like Richard's, his myth creates a mythic setting for his followers as well as for himself:

> This story shall the good man teach his son;
> And Crispin Crispian shall ne'er go by,
> From this day to the ending of the world,
> But we in it shall be remembered;
> We few, we happy few, we band of
>   brothers;
> For he to-day that sheds his blood with me
> Shall be my brother; be he ne'er so vile
> This day shall gentle his condition:
> And gentlemen in England now a-bed
> Shall think themselves accurs'd they were not
>   here,

> And hold their manhoods cheap whiles any
>   speak
> That fought with us upon Saint Crispin's day.
>   (IV.iii.56-67)

Unlike Richard's, Harry's tale ends in triumph.

Or so the story goes. The trouble is that texts (including plays and plays-within-plays) are notoriously unstable. Harry, committing himself (with the aid of Chorus) to the status of fiction, becomes by that token an object for interpretation.[10] Tellers can be unreliable; texts (some maintain) write their authors; language is symbolic, and any symbol can be read *in bono* or *in malo;* genre creates meaning, but irony subverts genre and can turn the heroic into the satiric. Whatever our school of criticism, the stories of such self-creative characters as Richard and Harry demand interpretation—a fact Shakespeare implicitly acknowledges and manipulates. In *Richard II,* while he leaves us ample room for interpretive shadings, he provides a series of characters whose function it is to ratify the broad outlines of Richard's account: the Bishop of Carlisle, the groom (and roan Barbary), the Queen, finally Bolingbroke himself with his vow to expiate Richard's death—each tells us that this is a tragedy rather than (say) a moral tale about a bad man who got what he deserved. We remain free to respond in a variety of ways to the tragedy, but the choric voice assures us that pity and fear will be among the appropriate responses and that certain other responses (indifference or contempt, for instance) may be less appropriate. And in *Henry V* Shakespeare gives us the Chorus, not to deprive us of the freedoms of interpretation but to give some direction to them. The Chorus in his own demeanor shows us and in his words tells us the spirit in which we are to understand Harry's plays—both the one he writes on Crispin's Day and the one Shakespeare and history wrote for him.

The sophisticated indirection of the Chorus' self-deprecation makes it likely that he will be indirect in his presentation of King Henry, too. Undoubtedly there are gaps (I will return to them) between some of the things he tells us and some of the things we actually see performed. Each such gap becomes an opportunity for interpretation, and the Chorus is clear in his directions "gently to watch, kindly to judge, our play." Our role is not to ignore or even to excuse Harry's shortcomings, any more than we are to ignore or excuse the theatre's. Sympathetic understanding, based on a sense of shared enterprise and shared humanity, will allow us to celebrate Harry's greatness—a greatness we recognize not despite but because he is flawed, because he is human. "In this theatre of man's life it is reserved only for God and the angels to be lookers on": some of the criticism of *Henry V* that stresses the play's putative dark ironies, turning it from heroic celebration to satiric denegation, proceeds as though it stood safely on the sidelines, exempt from the choric appeal for charitable identification.

V

I want now to take up just a few of the items of critical controversy with regard to the King, and to look at one specific scene with that choric appeal in mind. But I want to avoid, what the critical situation makes very hard to avoid, the air of an advocate answering a bill of indictment. I cannot, for gravest instance, justify the King's order to cut the throats of his French prisoners. I can try to understand the desperateness of the situation that gave rise to the order ("The French have reinforc'd their scatter'd men" [IV.vi.36]), but still I wish he hadn't done it. The case for the prosecution is well known: Harry is bloodthirsty, devious, a bad friend, a lousy lover, and he sounds too much like Tamburlaine. The case has been made thoroughly, vigorously, and I think that in recent years it has been made more frequently than the case for the defense.[11] My purpose is not to deny each item in the indictment, but to suggest how, in the spirit of the Chorus, some of them might be interpreted.

The first of the play's interpretable gaps falls right between the Prologue, with its heroic talk about "the swelling scene," and scenes i and ii, which are swollen mainly by the verbose efforts of Canterbury and Ely to forestall a bill to strip the Church of "the better half of our possessions" (l. 8). What seems most remarkable, in light of the choric preparation, is Shakespeare's decision to hew so closely to his historical sources, plunging us not into the world of brave physical combat but into the stickier world of political wheeling and dealing. If we expect our heroes pure, we will certainly be dismayed to find the King in the process of striking a deal: he will support the Church against the bill of sequestration, and in return the Church will lend its moral and financial support to the war in France. But the shock to our heroic expectation is exactly the point: this heroic King Henry does live— must, because he did live—in the real world he inherited and did not make.[12] Like the actors on the stage, this actor in history is a being strictly limited by his medium. Shakespeare allows us to watch Harry's (public) act of deciding the question of war, and thus he gives us once again the option the Chorus gives us. We can reject what Harry does because he does not do all we want him to do, or we can piece out his imperfections with our thoughts.

Shakespeare quickly reminds us of the circumstances Hal inherited when he became King: the churchmen speak of "the scrambling and unquiet time" that caused the bill to be deferred in "the last king's reign" (I.i.4, 2). Not much more needs to be said, directly, about the troublesome nature of Henry IV's reign. The danger of civil war is explicit at the beginning and the end of the play, and surely it must be intended to haunt the middle as well. The question of Harry's justification in his French war may take on a different shape if we recognize that the opposite of war abroad may not be peace but that greater horror, war at home. The King cannot know for sure, nor can we. (The creation of uncertainty is, I take it, Shakespeare's dramatic point in importing from his sources the Archbishop's interminable speech about Pharamond and Pepin and the Salic law. The attempt to establish legal certainty only creates dramatic uncertainty: the more of one, the more of the other, inevitably.) In the historical world where Harry must lead, no choice can be absolutely right. He could choose to despoil the Church for the good of the Crown. Or he could choose to invade France for the good of the Crown, making the Church his ally. My point is not that Harry makes the right choice; it is rather that we cannot know what the absolutely right choice is. Yet the theatrical circumstances force us to choose, as the historical circumstances force Harry to choose. If we reject the Chorus' positive estimation of Harry we indulge, I believe, an impossibly romantic notion of heroism. We expect omniscience and perfection in "the mirror of all Christian kings," when what we are shown is a human being trying to make the best of a bad thing.

That, according to the Chorus, is what actors do too. Perhaps it is not just the King's choice but the actorly manner of his choosing that makes us uncomfortable. It is your old stale argument against the players that they are always playing; their very virtuosity proves they are hollow men or uncanny puppets. In the second scene, with the churchmen and then the French ambassadors, the King plays his role so straight, never mugging or breaking frame, that it just might arouse one's antitheatrical prejudice. We can never know what Harry really thinks about the Salic law, only how he acts. The problem is more overt in Act II, scene ii, when Harry breaks the conspiracy of Scroop, Cambridge, and Grey. The Chorus has told us about the conspiracy in advance, and as the scene begins Bedford and Exeter remind us of it, remarking "How smooth and even [the traitors] do bear themselves" and assuring us that "The king hath note of all that they intend" (II.ii.3, 6). Thus our interest is less in the eventual outcome (of which we are assured) than in its technique, its self-conscious theatrical means. We regard Harry aesthetically, as a performer, and our ideas about theatricalism in everyday life are therefore engaged. Since the traitors are also playing roles (that is, pretending loyalty), we have here both play and counterplay, theatricalism becoming a form of craftiness in which the best actor is literally the winner. *Hamlet* displays one attitude toward that kind of situation, *Henry V* another.

My point is not simply the reverse of Miss Ellis-Fermor's. I do not claim that Harry is blameless because he is an actor. But I do claim that Shakespeare has chosen to place him in situations in which he must act (in all senses) and that he has, in part through the analogy with the Chorus/audience relationship, made sympathetic participation a more appropriate response to him than judgmental detachment. At times such sympathetic participation may evoke the joyful release of our applause; but it may also, at other times, evoke other feelings. We have seen how the Chorus prepares us for the "little touch of Harry" in the Act IV night. The Chorus there gives us our cues for response—sets a tone—but we must still encounter Harry himself, an encounter which complicates but does not contradict the choric preparation.

VI

The scene of Harry among his men, like the Chorus' description of it, is in icily objective close-up. Our focus is on a man under severe self-restraint. The range of his responses is strangely limited. During part of the scene he is at the periphery of the action, and even when he occupies its center—in the colloquy with Michael Bates—he remains an outsider from the larger group.[13] The effect of the close-up is therefore rather baffling than otherwise, for what it reveals is a kind of irreducible opacity in the character of Harry. Harry's encounters in this night, and the soliloquy that follows them, show the obverse of the choric lesson that less can be more. For the King, burdened with a superfluity of expressive means—his star billing, magnificent costume, elaborate script, cast of thousands (all the kingly appurtenances he calls "idol ceremony")—more is less, a weight hanging upon him and, even in this scene when he moves about under the cloak of old Sir Thomas Erpingham, keeping him a man apart. The Chorus leads us to expect that we will get from Harry the same little touch his men do and pluck, like them, confort from his universal largess. Instead we see precisely what his men do not see—the effort and the cost. The effect is anything but comforting, and one possible reaction (some of the play's critics show it) is a feeling of betrayal.

The scene begins with the King in his most thoroughly histrionic mode, cheering up his officers. Here is the smiling public man, full of platitudes and over-stretched *bonhommie,* that has so offended critics.[14]

> Gloucester, 'tis true that we are in great
>   danger;
> The greater therefore should our courage be.
> Good morrow, brother Bedford. God
>   Almighty!
> There is some soul of goodness in things evil,
> Would men observingly distil it out.
>   (IV.i.1-5)

At the very moment of his separating from this group, however, we find, in one delicate moment, the self-

consciousness (hence the effort) of the pose. Erpingham departs saying, "The Lord in heaven bless thee, noble Harry!"—itself the kind of line that might give offense if we did not accede to the choric appeal for imaginative participation. And Harry replies (probably out of Erpingham's hearing, as the old man exits), "God-a-mercy, old heart! thou speak'st cheerfully" (l. 34)—a line poised at gratitude and irony, admiration and desperation.

Immediately, from the imagined dark, comes Pistol, challenging the King in the language of the enemy, "Qui va la?"—to which the King replies, "A friend" (ll. 35-36). Their brief encounter is tensely comic, with the King's effort not to be recognized (hence the brevity of his responses) and with Pistol's swaggering impercipience (he takes "Harry le Roy" to be "a Cornish name"). Verbally, the encounter is dominated by Pistol. Pistol leaves and his place is taken by Gower and Fluellen engaged in a conversation the King overhears but in which he has no part; they remain unaware of his presence on stage. In a moment the King will be drawn into a conversation with Bates, Court, and Williams, and his attempt to shed kingly comforts on them will be less successful than the Chorus would have led us to believe. Indeed one of the most noticeable things about the scene, up to this point, is the readjustment of our dramatic expectations. Instead of the "cheerful semblance and sweet majesty" the Chorus had described (IV. Chorus. 40), we find in these successively isolating encounters a Harry unable to break out of the tight circle of his self-control, a commanding figure but by that same token an unapproachable one.

The interludes with Pistol, with Gower and Fluellen, and then with Bates, Court, and Williams, reveal another way in which the King's role is analogous to the Chorus'. He is Pistol's straight-man, and their encounter ends with a choric tag-line:

> *Pistol.* My name is Pistol called. [*Exit*].
>
> *K. Henry* It sorts well with your fierceness.
>   (ll. 62-63)

With Gower and Fluellen he is a silent presenter, and when their scene is over he offers, again, the choric summary: "Though it appear a little out of fashion, / There is much care and valour in this Welshman" (ll. 83-84). With the three soldiers, especially Williams, his choric role is put to the greatest strain. Harry tries to tell them, as the Chorus tries to tell us, how to respond to a man playing a king ("I think the king is but a man, as I am" [IV.i.101]). His direct appeal, like the Chorus' appeal for our sympathetic participation, is dramatically intrusive but perfectly in character; and, like the Chorus' appeal, Harry's does not win universal assent. For the most part, the analogy between

Chorus and King has worked to illuminate the King's role; here it also works in the other direction, to illuminate the Chorus'. The King, creator of the myth of Crispin Day, though in that mythopoeic moment he may imagine its future potency ("This story shall the good man teach his son" [IV.iii.56]), discovers by the campfire on Agincourt eve an audience's critical recalcitrance. Harry has only limited control over the reception of his own story. The Chorus incurs this difficulty too. The problem for both lies partly in the mode of direct address: if you argue and tell, someone may respond, and if you invoke authority (even narrative authority) someone is bound to counter it. The Chorus' awareness of his limitation is built into his role. The players can only be "ciphers to this great accompt," and the audience is asked to "piece out [their] imperfections," for it is as easy to overthrow a Chorus and his play as it is, in a kingdom, to create civil strife.

VII

That Michael Williams gets the better of Harry le Roy in their debate about the King's responsibilities is a truth that should not be universally acknowledged. Williams' case is a good one; it is, moreover, more attractively put than the King's rebuttal. The hypothetical scene Williams conjures is eerily evocative, passionate, with a dream-like specificity:

> But if the cause be not good, the king himself hath a heavy reckoning to make; when all those legs and arms and heads, chopped off in a battle, shall join together at the latter day, and cry all, "We died at such a place"; some swearing, some crying for a surgeon, some upon their wives left poor behind them, some upon the debts they owe, some upon their children rawly left. I am afeard there are few die well that die in a battle.

> (IV.i.135-44)

The King's response, by contrast, is imaginatively spare, his hypothetical cases the merest legal counters:

> So, if a son that is by his father sent about merchandise do sinfully miscarry upon the sea, the imputation of his wickedness, by your rule, should be imposed upon his father that sent him: or if a servant, under his master's command transporting a sum of money, be assailed by robbers and die in many irreconciled iniquities, you may call the business of the master the author of the servant's damnation. But this is not so; the king is not bound to answer the particular endings of his soldiers, the father of his son, nor the master of his servant; for they purpose not their death when they purpose their services.

> (IV.i.150-63)

The most charitably disposed audience could not muster much sympathy for that father or master or (for

that matter) king. But a couple of things should be said on the King's behalf, in the effort "gently to hear, kindly to judge." His argument rests on a distinction between his responsibility in the matter of a subject's death and his responsibility in the matter of a subject's damnation. A soldier dying may be damned, but not because he died for King Henry. "Every subject's soul is his own" (l. 183), and every subject must therefore bear responsibility for the state of his own soul. But a king's soul is *his* own, for which he bears the same responsibility as each subject bears. The King does not say, because it goes so absolutely without saying, that he accepts his proper responsibilities, which are heavy enough (God knows) without the addition Williams tries to make. Because "Every subject's duty is the king's," the subject does not sin in dying for him; but if the *King* dies and "the cause be not good, the king himself hath a heavy reckoning to make."

The argument between Williams and the King is a stand-off because they argue at cross-purposes. Williams himself gives the victory to the King's cause: "'Tis certain, every man that dies ill, the ill upon his own head; the king is not to answer it" (ll. 193-94). But for his muffled interlocuter the argument has gone in a different direction. For Williams, the question has been turned into that of the soldier's souls; for the King, it cannot ever be anything but the state of his own soul. The fact that Harry does not answer that latter question has seemed to some critics ironically to undermine him. It seems otherwise to me.

And this is the other simple thing that should be said on the King's behalf: that the cumulative effect of the scene on the night before Agincourt is to garner sympathy for this king whose mortal frailty is emphasized by his effort to unburden himself of the weight of his kingship and his mortality. We have seen, first, that he is unavoidably isolated from real fellowship with his men. We have seen, in the encounter with the three soldiers, that even a king (like a Chorus) cannot wholly control the text of his life. We have seen his vulnerability. And now, in the "idol ceremony" speech, his isolation and his weakness are again emphasized (both in what he says and in the understandable petulance of its saying), at the same time that they are accepted by him as his proper and unavoidable lot.

But the "idol ceremony" speech is not the scene's end. Erpingham enters with a simple line that expresses kingship's burdens as clearly as the King's own eloquent periods: "My lord, your nobles, jealous of your absence, / Seek through your camp to find you" (IV.i.291-92). It is Harry's cue for one last solitary moment and for his prayer to the "God of battles." Arguments about Harry's justification in the French war may miss the essential point that Harry himself cannot know whether he is right to undertake the war. Only its outcome can tell him that. And his prayer has all the panicky urgency of his lack of knowledge, even to the point of trying to bribe the deity. "Not to-day, O Lord! / O not to-day, think not upon the fault / My father made in compassing the crown!" (ll. 298-300). This is the single most poignant utterance in a play whose emotional range is purposefully narrow. It is a play rich in comedy and pageantry and in those communal emotions that can be entrusted nowadays to a Hollywood orchestra; but it is relatively poorer in the private and singular emotions. So the "God of battles" prayer, when Harry desperately bargains (he does not quite wrestle) with his God, is, for the audience, a precious moment.

And it is interesting that at the moment when this actor-king seems most the man and least the actor, at this moment of his intensest privacy, Harry should most clearly stand in analogous relation to the Chorus. Harry's audience is his God, and he addresses that audience directly, "imploring pardon" (IV.i.311)—the Chorus' word, too—while a most embarrassingly calling attention to the fault. Both King and Chorus worry about "the sense of reckoning" (l. 297)—here, as in the Chorus' prologue, a matter literally of numbers of men, of the poverty of means. But the "reckoning" is also a matter of judgments, and both King and Chorus know that they will be judged. Harry enumerates his penitential deeds with an urgency that counterpoints the Chorus' witty attempt, in his first appearance, to make "a crooked figure . . . attest in little place a million" (Prologue. 15-16). Harry's own fearful sense of reckoning edges toward panic:

> I Richard's body have interred new,
> And on it have bestow'd more contrite tears
> Than from it issued forced drops of blood.
> Five hundred poor I have in yearly pay,
> Who twice a day their wither'd hands hold up
> Toward heaven, to pardon blood; and I have
>   built
> Two chantries, where the sad and solemn priests
> Sing still for Richard's soul. More will I do. . . .
>
>   (IV.i.301-8)

Only God can know the sincerity of Harry's penitence, but almost anyone can know the fear in it. It is the fear of a man about to go into battle, or of a performer about to take the stage.

The King is called:

> My brother Gloucester's voice! Ay;
> I know thy errand, I will go with thee:
> The day, my friends, and all things stay for
>   me.

During the next scene, in the French camp, we know that the actor-king is in the wings or tiring-house preparing to go on. In the Olivier film the King instantly

materializes in response to Westmoreland's wish that they had "But one ten thousand of those men in England / That do no work to-day" (IV.iii.18-19). The camera meets him in his full rhetorical stride, already puffed up with the knowledge that he is doing his Crispin Day speech. But here is another instance of the theatre's less overgoing the movies' more. On stage, an entrance is a slower business; Harry cannot pop out on Westmoreland's cue. Rather, he has to be already on stage, listening to his men and being watched by us in his own (as we know it to be) fearfulness. The actor playing Harry playing king has a wonderful opportunity to enact his silent transformation from the uncertain, lonely man in the night to the inspiring leader of the day. Michael Goldman says of that leader, "We love him for his effectiveness" (p. 70). I would add that we can love him even more (though others have found it cause to love him less) because we have seen in the preceding scenes the all-too-human being out of whom the effective politician builds himself. We are moved partly by the spectacle of a man doing a difficult duty, submerging his clamorous self for the sake of a larger idea. Shakespeare allows us to doubt the validity of that idea, but his Chorus urges us to appreciate the nobility of Harry's attempt.

VIII

At the instant of Harry's transformation into the speaker of the Crispin Day speech, he reflects the Chorus' awareness that the theatre makes "imaginary puissance." As creator of the myth that unites his men, Harry is a cipher to the great accompt, working on his men's imaginary forces. We can, with some plausibility, wrench the Chorus' clear directive and find in it, for instance, "an underside of intimation that this warrior may be a crook, his followers moral zeros, and their power largely imaginary, indeed scaffold-bound."[15] The man in the play, like the play itself, is at our mercy.

And both are at the mercy of history. Though Shakespeare ends the action with a marriage, he adds a metadramatic epilogue that brings us back from comic fulfillment to the contingent world that both Chorus (representative of theatrical reality) and King (representative of historical reality) inhabit. I do not think that the Chorus' last lines are, as Norman Rabkin describes them, "harsh negation" (p. 51). Rueful, yes, but not without a touch of optimism about what can be achieved in a world that is, for better and for worse, so much like a stage. The Chorus' sonnet makes the experience of loss and failure another claim on our charitable indulgence: "and for their sake, / In your fair minds let this acceptance take" (Epilogue. 13-14). The pronoun "their" can refer both to the historical figures who lost France and made England bleed in the aftermath of Henry V's brief reign and to the actors who oft have shown it on our stage. For both the King and the actors, the play's action has been "Small time, but in that small most greatly liv'd" (Epilogue. 5). As we were promised, we have been shown "the accomplishment of many years [turned] into an hour-glass" (Prologue. 30-31). That compression was enforced by theatrical limitation, but it was simultaneously a source of theatrical intensity, as it was also the condition of Henry V's achievements. The Chorus' last "apology" is as sincere and as supererogatory as its apology for occupying "this wooden O" instead of "the vasty fields of France."

So I would like to believe that *Henry V* was performed in the great Globe itself, though I can imagine other possibilities.[16] It is Shakespeare's celebration of theatricality, on stage and off. But it is, of course, a tempered celebration. The Chorus plays at apologizing while doing superbly well the things he claims the theatre cannot do; still, the limitations he acknowledges are indeed limitations, if the performance is not eked out in the audience's mind. The playwright cannot control the reception of his play, and the King cannot control the course of history. The play's critical history shows how risky the venture is.

Notes

[1] *European Literature and the Latin Middle Ages,* trans. Willard R. Trask (New York: Bollingen Foundation, 1953; Harper & Row, 1963), p. 83.

[2] Herschel Baker, in *The Riverside Shakespeare* (Boston: Houghton Mifflin, 1974), p. 931. More indulgent to the character of the King is J. H. Walter, ed. New Arden *Henry V* (London: Methuen, 1954). I quote throughout from this edition.

[3] *Shakespeare and the Problem of Meaning* (Chicago: Univ. of Chicago Press, 1981). Rabkin's analogy is the optical illusion in which a pictured object is both a rabbit and a duck, depending on which is seen as figure and which as ground. *Henry V,* he claims, must be seen in two opposite, irreconcilable ways. A similar point was made by Anne Barton, for whom *Henry V* is "deliberately ambiguous . . . overtly a puzzle in which the audience is left to forge its own interpretation of action and characters with only minimal guidance from a dramatist apparently determined to stress the equivalence of mutually exclusive views of a particular complex of historical event." Nonetheless, Barton chooses one of the two equivalent views as the right one: Shakespeare "summon[ed] up the memory of a wistful, naive attitude toward history and the relationship of subject and king which this play rejects as attractive but untrue: a nostalgic but false romanticism." ("The King Disguised: Shakespeare's *Henry V* and the Comical History," in *The Triple Bond,* ed. Joseph G. Price [University Park: Pennsylvania State Univ. Press, 1975], pp. 102, 99.)

[4] *The Frontiers of Drama* (London: Methuen, 1945; 2nd ed. 1964), pp. 45, 47. On King Henry as role-player, see also Alvin B. Kernan, "The Henriad: Shakespeare's Major History Plays," in Kernan, ed., *Modern Shakespeare Criticism* (New York: Harcourt, Brace & World, 1970), especially pp. 260-78; and Thomas Van Laan, *Role-Playing in Shakespeare* (Toronto: Univ. of Toronto Press, 1978), pp. 32 ff.

[5] *Metadrama in Shakespeare's Henriad* (Berkeley: Univ. of California Press, 1979), pp. 170-71. Contrast the view of Roy W. Battenhouse, "The Relation of Henry V to Tamburlaine," *Shakespeare Survey,* 27 (1974): "The whole English community, as Shakespeare sees the situation, is being entranced imaginatively into role-playing, and without regard for the moral meaning of the assumed roles. And Henry, by treating himself as an actor caught up in his own play, is able to blind himself to the moral implications of his action" (p. 78).

[6] *Shakespeare and the Energies of Drama* (Princeton: Princeton Univ. Press, 1972), pp. 59, 61.

[7] "An Introduction to the Play," in Sally Beauman, ed., *The Royal Shakespeare Company's Production of "Henry V" for the Centenary Season at The Royal Shakespeare Theatre* (Oxford: Pergamon Press, 1976), p. 16.

[8] In Beauman, *Production,* p. 56.

[9] James, in Beauman, *Production,* p. 61; Goldman, *Energies,* p. 58.

[10] Thus, Mark Van Doren took this self-creative speech to be "the golden throatings of a hollow god" (*Shakespeare* [New York: Henry Holt and Co., 1939], p. 179).

[11] One of the most relentlessly pursued indictments is by Gordon Ross Smith, "Shakespeare's *Henry V:* Another Part of the Critical Forest," *Journal of the History of Ideas,* 37 (1976), 3-26. Smith is keener at scenting irony than at noticing humor or hearing poetry. He neglects the evidence of the Chorus while drawing promiscuously on historical documents that are only tangentially related to Shakespeare's play. Smith ironizes in the cause of a political ideology. For another comprehensive ironizing, in a different cause, see Battenhouse, "The Relation of Henry V to Tamburlaine," and his "*Henry V* as Heroic Comedy," in *Essays on Shakespeare and Elizabethan Drama,* ed. Richard Hosley (Columbia: Univ. of Missouri Press, 1962). David Quint argues against taking either Henry or history as exemplary in "'Alexander the Pig': Shakespeare on History and Poetry," forthcoming in *Boundary 2.* See also Andrew Gurr, "Henry V and the Bee's Commonwealth," *ShS* 30 (1977): 61-72.

[12] For a sensitive discussion of the gap between the Chorus' ideal vision and the rest of the play's "histori-

cal" sense, see Edward I. Berry, "'True Things and Mock'ries': Epic and History in *Henry V*," *Journal of English and Germanic Philology*, 78 (1979), 1-16. Also see Anthony S. Brennan, "That Within Which Passes Show: The Function of the Chorus in *Henry V*," *Philological Quarterly*, 58 (1979), 40-52. In "A Muse of Fire: *Henry V* in the Light of *Tamburlaine*," *Modern Language Quarterly*, 29 (1968), 15-28, Robert Egan treats "the dichotomy between conqueror and Christian" (p. 26) in King Henry's character. William Babula, "Whatever Happened to Prince Hal? An Essay on *Henry V*," *ShS*, 30 (1977), 47-59, sees a Henry who improves and matures over the course of the play.

[13] Gary Taylor interestingly analyzes this scene in light of the variants between Quarto and Folio. See Stanley Wells, *Modernizing Shakespeare's Spelling* with Gary Taylor, *Three Studies in the Text of "Henry V"* (Oxford: Clarendon, 1979), pp. 87-91. Taylor argues that Q is a memorial reconstruction of an abridged version of the play adapted for performance by a company of eleven actors. Thus the Chorus is absent from Q because he would require a twelfth actor.

[14] Cf. Van Doren's wonderfully fastidious description of him as "a mere good fellow, a hearty undergraduate with enormous initials on his chest" (*Shakespeare*, p. 176).

[15] Battenhouse, "Henry V and Tamburlaine," p. 77. A full account of the play would have to consider the comic or subplot characters and their relation to King, Chorus, and audience. Do they function "as a foil to contrast with, and so render still more admirable, the exploits of the 'mirror of all Christian kings'" (Richard Levin, *The Multiple Plot in English Renaissance Drama* [Chicago: Univ. of Chicago Press, 1971], p. 116)? Or are they "parodic commentary" showing that the king is a worse thief than Bardolph, and that Fluellen, in his "gullible loyalty," is one of "the willingly exploited" supporters "of a usurped title and of a diversionary war" (Smith, "Critical Forest," pp. 12, 24)? Obviously we can choose the latter point of view only by refuting the Chorus, or by ironizing his own choric "subplot" to a really dazzling degree.

[16] Another possibility is entertained by G. P. Jones, "*Henry V*: The Chorus and the Audience," *Shakespeare Survey*, 31 (1978), 93-104. Jones conjectures that the Chorus' "cockpit" was literally the Royal Cockpit and that the choric apologies pertain to a court performance, for which the Chorus was specially written. Jones's argument involves (as mine does) the question of the Chorus' tone; he assumes that it could only have been aimed at a "sophisticated and cultured audience," which "might have been more tolerant [than a popular audience] of appeals to understand and help compensate for the technical difficulties encountered by the dramatist" (p. 97). But there is no reason to think that a courtly audience would have been more

tolerant than Shakespeare's usual audience, and his own portrayals of well-heeled audiences suggest that Shakespeare had no illusions on that score: see Alvin B. Kernan, "Courtly Servants and Public Players: Shakespeare's Image of Theater in the Court at Elsinore and Whitehall," in *Poetic Traditions of the English Renaissance*, ed. Maynard Mack and George deForest Lord (New Haven: Yale Univ. Press, 1982), 103-22; also see Kernan's "Shakespeare's Stage Audience: The Playwright's Reflection and Control of Audience Response," in *Shakespeare's Craft: Eight Lectures*, ed. Philip H. Highfill, Jr. (Carbondale: So. Illinois Univ. Press, 1982), 138-56. Kristian Smidt, *Unconformities in Shakespeare's History Plays* (Atlantic Highlands, N.J.: Humanities Press, 1982), writes that "there is good reason to believe that the 'wooden O' referred to in the prologue is the new Globe theatre and not the Curtain" (p. 121)—assuming that the prologue is a late addition to a play written earlier and now revised. Anne Barton, "The King Disguised," asserts in passing that the play was given "in the new Globe theatre" (p. 93), but ours remains a minority opinion. (Both the New Cambridge and the New Arden editions assume first performance at the Curtain. Bernard Beckerman, *Shakespeare at the Globe, 1599-1609* [New York: Macmillan, 1962], pp. xi-xiv, also considers *Henry V* a pre-Globe play.) For a careful, recent overview of many of the play's problems, see H. R. Coursen, *The Leasing Out of England* (Washington, D.C.: University Press of America, 1982).

Anthony Hammond (essay date 1987)

SOURCE: "'It Must Be Your Imagination Then': The Prologue and the Plural Text in *Henry V* and Elsewhere," in *'Fanned and Winnowed Opinions': Shakespearean Essays Presented to Harold Jenkins*, edited by John W. Mahon and Thomas A. Pendleton, Methuen, 1987, pp. 133-50.

[*In the essay below, Hammond contends that the Chorus's description of the play and its protagonist is intended to contradict what we see in other parts of the drama. Duality is essential to* Henry V, *the critic asserts, and its disparate perspectives force us to consider both the complexities of heroism and the question of theatrical verisimilitude.*]

Among Shakespeare's plays only *Henry V* and *Pericles* employ the highly elaborated formal structure of prologue, choruses before each Act, and epilogue. Other plays employ some of these dramatic devices, but not even *Pericles* uses them as centrally and as structurally as does *Henry V*;[1] nor do the other plays which violate the unities as flagrantly as it. This fact has influenced interpretation of the play, often unconsciously. Everyone knows that *Henry V* is a play about war, and that Henry himself is a great warrior-hero.

How do we know? Because the Chorus (that is, the character who speaks these metatextual speeches) tells us so. Honest critics, examining the play closely, have been somewhat puzzled by this, because, in fact, there are no battles, really, in the play, and because although Henry plays numerous roles in the course of the action (he is politician, outraged feudal lord, orator, anxious general, bumbling lover, and so on), warrior is not one of them. This is all very perplexing. If it is not a patriotic play about a warrior-king, why does the Chorus say it is?

The absence of choruses from Q1 of *Henry V* has led some writers[2] to speculate that they were not by Shakespeare, but were the creations of that celebrated author, Another Hand. This supposition is self-evidently absurd, and no one who could seriously believe that 'O, for a Muse of fire' could have been written by anyone other than Shakespeare need be listened to on any issue whatever. Nonetheless, the assumption that if the choruses were not authorial they could safely be disregarded saved the begetter of this notion from the intellectual difficulty posed by them, and by their relationship to the body of the play. In the same way, those who read the play as a paean of patriotic enthusiasm are apt to say that it must have been written in a hurry, to account for its episodic structure and the apparent plethora of contradictory concepts it incorporates. These intellectual difficulties are the subject of the present paper: they deserve to be encountered firmly, and I hope in the process to shed some light on some of the interpretative problems in the play which continue to elude satisfactory definition. Certainly, I hope to present a solution of these difficulties more constructive than that of Q1, whose compilers, evidently judging that the provincial audience for whom (as Gary Taylor has shown[3]) that text was prepared was less sophisticated than that of the Globe, omitted not only the choruses, but most of the rest of the controversial matter in the play, thus making it 'exactly the sort of simple patriotic play critics have often taken *Henry V* to be'.[4]

If taken whole, *Henry V* is not an easy text, and most certainly not a simple patriotic play. Only by cutting and/or special pleading can it be made, as Laurence Olivier made it, patriotic propaganda about one of England's greatest warrior-kings, a triumphant celebration of the fact that England occasionally won wars handsomely rather than just muddling through them. Even some quite recent writers have maintained this view. John Dover Wilson's Cambridge edition, which appeared in 1947, dedicated to Field-Marshal Wavell, really belongs like the film to the Second World War. But J.H. Walter, in the introduction to his 1954 Arden edition, was at pains to demonstrate how Henry fulfilled Renaissance writers' conceptions of the ideal hero-king. It never seemed to occur to him that Shakespeare could have included all this ideology in his

play, only to leave us with a hero whose morality is persistently and pervasively equivocal: or, to put it another way, that Shakespeare just might have been able to see further than most, and in his play to reveal universal opinion to be mistaken or limited. Since Walter's edition appeared there has been Suez, the CND, the Cuban missile crisis, the Vietnam horror, the permanent catastrophe of the Middle East, Northern Ireland, Afghanistan and Cambodia, not to mention such lesser items of tragical-comical-historical-pastoral as the Falklands and Grenada: dear God knows how many other illustrations for our time that the military way is the worst possible way for the greatest number of people. One of the consequences of this newly-appalled perception of the horror and inefficiency of war is that *Henry V*'s condition has changed from that of honest history play to problem play. It is not, of course, the first time that this has happened; I believe that the first writer to express distrust of the military motive in the play was actually Hazlitt. 'And Hazlitt's convictions have become, for the most part, our own.'[5]

The essential clues to the contradictions built into the play are to be found in the choruses, and I would like to rehearse the issues in a little detail. The Chorus, in his prologue, adopts two tones of voice. First there is the heroic, which sustains some of Shakespeare's most thrilling rhetoric until line 8. In the middle of this line, the Chorus suddenly switches to an exculpatory mode:

> But pardon, gentles all,
> The flat unraised spirits that hath dar'd
> On this unworthy scaffold to bring forth
> So great an object. . . .

He continues in this vein for the rest of the prologue, apologizing for the fewness of the actors' numbers,[6] and for the absence of what in our time have come to be called 'special effects': especially the lack of horses. For the remedy of these deficiencies, the Chorus urges the audience again and again to use its imagination: 'let us . . . On your imaginary forces work'; 'Piece out our imperfections with your thoughts'; 'For 'tis your thoughts that now must deck our kings.' The Chorus to Act III is even more insistent: 'imagin'd', 'thought', 'Suppose', 'Play with your fancies . . . behold . . . Hear . . . behold', 'do but think', 'Grapple your minds', 'Work, work your thoughts, and therein see', 'Suppose', 'eke out our performance with your mind'. Well, goodness, we get the point. The audience is required to work for its living in *Henry V* along with the author and the actors.

One can scarcely refrain from recalling Theseus's defence of the mechanicals' play in *A Midsummer Night's Dream:* 'The best in this kind are but shadows, and the worst are no worse, if imagination amend them' (V.i.208-9). Theseus has been blamed for his seeming inability to distinguish between a play by Shakespeare and one by Peter Quince—but the plain fact is that people *are* moved, often to tears, by the most awful tripe: I cite, with due deference, the people that cry their eyes out at *Madama Butterfly* (or the children who bawl at *Bambi*), or the folks whose lives revolve around the polystyrene characters of soap operas. As Hippolyta acidly responds, 'It must be your imagination then, and not theirs', and she is undoubtedly right. To be greatly moved by art that is so inferior as scarcely to deserve the name at all requires a great imaginative faculty on the part of the spectator, reader, listener, or viewer. Theseus and his court decline, in fact, to exercise this faculty during the playing of *Pyramus and Thisbe*—'This is the silliest stuff that ever I heard'—and so does the audience at the pageant of the Nine Worthies in *Love's Labour's Lost*. The royal audience of 'The Mousetrap', however, finds his imagination suddenly working overtime, and experiences what used to be called character-identification.

All these plays-within-plays are silly stuff, but *Henry V* is clearly not: it may be perplexing, but it is certainly not stupid. Why, then, does the Chorus insist with such iteration on the importance of the audience's imagination and the inadequacies of the company? Obviously not because he seriously means nothing more than that the author and the company are unqualified for their subject.[7] On the whole recent critics have recognized the irony in the Chorus's apologies—Robert Ornstein remarks on 'the artfulness that wears so naive a guise' in them,[8] and Taylor recognizes that they are not 'reflections of a real sense of artistic dissatisfaction: rather the reverse' (1982 edn, 56). Indeed: there is something of a covert Jonsonian appeal to the understanding heads in the auditory in this process of apologizing for things that need no apology.

The Act II chorus follows the pattern of the prologue:

Now all the youth of England are on fire,
And silken dalliance in the wardrobe lies: . . .

Linger your patience on; and we'll digest
Th' abuse of distance . . .

There is the playhouse now, there must you
sit. . . .

The Chorus gets himself into a terrible tangle worrying about the unity of the place: 'the scene / Is now transported, gentles, to Southampton', he announces confidently, and goes on to promise safe passage across the Channel to France, only to recollect himself in the last two lines, when he remembers he has not got to Southampton yet. The lines are curious:

But, till the king come forth and not till then,
Unto Southampton do we shift our scene.

Walter complains that these lines 'hardly agree' with lines 35-6 (which asserted roundly that the playhouse is now in Southampton), and discusses the apparent inconsistency in his Introduction,[9] seizing upon a complex theory of revision to account for them. He seems unaware that the Chorus is saying something that on the literal level anyway is absurd and obviously untrue: the Globe is still firmly on the Bankside. Taylor in his edition provides a much more sophisticated explanation than Walter's, dismissing the idea that the concluding couplet is an afterthought, and remarking helpfully, 'Tonally, the last 12 lines of the speech lead very naturally into the comedy of 2.1.' He develops this insight further:

That the Chorus does nothing to prepare us for the scene which immediately follows is hardly surprising: the prologue does nothing to prepare us for 1.1. either. In both cases, Shakespeare arouses an expectation and then (temporarily) frustrates it, using the expectation not only as a contrast to the foreground scene, but as a means of sustaining our interest, assuring us of the main line of development, during an intermediate and subordinate action.

(Appendix B.I, 291)

This explanation actually describes Shakespeare's practice better in other plays than in *Henry V:* it suits very well the chorus and first scene of *Romeo and Juliet,* for instance. Here, the Chorus announces in a portentous sonnet the 'misadventur'd piteous overthrows' the 'star-cross'd lovers' will encounter; the speech's solemnity is thrown into extreme contrast by the coarse comedy of sex and violence of the opening dialogue. Shakespeare seems to have enjoyed *beginning* his plays with a peripeteia, and this is an easy way of achieving one. It does indeed establish a tonality for the entire play which survives the less-than-heroic first few scenes, and its language is instantly recognizable when Romeo and Juliet meet in a sonnet at the Capulets' ball. Of course, there are many ways of confounding audience expectation in the opening scenes: but the prologue is clearly one of them. Among its functions is to serve as a signal for peripeteia in the opening scene. The effect is not unlike that of, say, Mozart's Thirty-Ninth Symphony, whose grave introduction with its dissonant harmonies contrasts powerfully (yet satisfyingly) with the main subject of the allegro.

This description alone, however, will not do for the Chorus in *Henry V*, nor, for that matter, for the prologue to *Troilus and Cressida*. In this, the Prologue's stately language ('princes orgulous', 'strong immures', 'warlike fraughtage', 'massy staples /And co-responsive and fulfilling bolts') suddenly modulates, as the 'prologue arm'd, but not in confidence /Of author's pen or actor's voice' advises his audience that the play begins *in medias res*, 'starting thence away /To what may be digested in a play'. This mild concession to the limitations of the drama is not as apologetic as the Chorus's lines in *Henry V,* but is, as it were, cousin-german to them.

The chief objection to Taylor's explanation of the *Henry V* choruses is that the expectation aroused by them is not temporarily frustrated: it is *never* satisfied by action on the stage. Ornstein's comment that the Chorus's 'apology is as sly as it is gratuitous because Shakespeare makes no attempt in the play to represent an epic confrontation of armies',[10] makes the point clear. The audience must at some point become aware that as a prophet the Chorus is a great deal less than reliable, inspiring though he may be (a common enough condition amongst prophets, come to think of it). Taylor's argument will simply not suffice for a Chorus who contrives to get, really, *everything* wrong.

The prologue promises military wonders: Act I comprises two of the prosiest scenes in Shakespeare, as the churchmen wonder whether the new king will tax their revenues, and subsequently defend Henry's proposed invasion of France at mind-numbing length. (I have yet to see a performance of the play in which the Archbishop's 'So that, clear as is the summer's sun . . . ' did not get a laugh.) This leisurely politicking lasts some 318 lines (nearly a tenth of the play) before the French ambassador is called in (I.ii.222), and Henry given a handy opportunity to make the quarrel formal, and the fault of the French. All very necessary stuff, no doubt, but not the inspirational things the prologue talked of. In the same way, the chorus to Act II promises us that 'all the youth of England are on fire': that the war is universally popular; and that 'honour's thought /Reigns solely in the breast of every man'. But instead of seeing the youth of England on fire, we meet those tired old rogues, Nym, Bardolph, and Pistol, grumbling collectively; instead of finding honour in every breast, we are confronted with the treacherous conspiracy against Henry headed by the Earl of Cambridge.

This contrast is emphasized rather than contradicted by the chorus and first scene of Act III: the Chorus again lays stress on the bravery and gallantry of the expeditionary force, asking rhetorically

> For who is he, whose chin is but enrich'd
> With one appearing hair, that will not follow
> These cull'd and choice-drawn cavaliers to
>   France?

The chorus is followed by Henry's famous aria before the walls of Harfleur; but the dramatic point is that it *is* an aria, not an ensemble: while one presumes the stage to be as full of supers as the company's roster allows, the citizens are mum, say not a word. What actually *does* happen is that our friends Nym, Bardolph,

and Pistol come on again, and Nym, for one, is not sufficiently impressed by the oratory actually to do anything until Fluellen appears and beats him off to action (and all the action must be presumed to be taking place off-stage). There promptly follows what must be the great-grandfather of all the jokes that begin 'A Scotsman, an Irishman and a Welshman . . . ', the trio of Jamy, Macmorris, and Fluellen. There is no military action whatever.

Henry's oratory proves insufficient to rouse his troops to take the town; he needs another aria, this time directed at the citizens of Harfleur. In this, Henry's language modulates surprisingly from his former heroic-mindedness to threats that would not have sounded misplaced on Tamburlaine's lips;[11] in particular, as Jonathan Dollimore and Alan Sinfield remark,[12] his association of himself in imagery with the tyrant Herod is surely astonishing (explain it away as Walter tries) in a king from whom th' offending Adam had, so the Church declared, been whipped. Threats against women, children, and the aged are simply not attractive. Nor is it possible to evade the fact that Henry says he cannot control his army (III.iii.22-9), whose soldiers are characterized as 'rough and hard of heart', 'enrag'd', 'blind and bloody'—a far cry from the gentlemen-adventurers described by the Chorus. The scene has a desperate quality about it: the war has ground to a halt before Harfleur, and Henry must take the city if his campaign is to continue. The war he threatens is not pretty war; it is not heroic war, or idealized war such as the Chorus urges upon us: it rather foreshadows the total war of the twentieth century. Yet hard on Harfleur's surrender comes perhaps the most abrupt peripeteia Shakespeare ever wrote, as we find ourselves transported, gentles, to Princess's boudoir, for a scene of light comedy spiced with naughty double-entendres. The tonal lurch is almost impossible to exaggerate: it would be no more extreme to break into the middle of the last Act of *Tristan und Isolde* with a Gilbert and Sullivan patter song (an apt enough comparison, as even the play's language changes from English to French). Some productions choose to locate the interval between the two scenes, but such a division goes flatly against what seems to me a clearly purposeful juxtaposition of the two.

The chorus to Act IV follows the scene in which the French nobles await the Battle of Agincourt with careless impatience, and the Chorus prepares the audience's mind for the great event to come with some fine military metaphor suggesting the collective activity and anxiety that must pervade armies on the eve of battle. Shakespeare had done a good awaiting-for-battle scene before, in the fifth Act of *Richard III,* and it is instructive to compare the two, the most extended military sequences in the canon. That in *Richard III* occupies V.iii-V.v inclusive, or about 406 lines of dialogue; in *Henry V,* if we include the scene of the French anticipation and the chorus, Agincourt occupies III.vii-IV.viii, or no less than 1,175 lines, a third of the play and nearly three times as long as Bosworth (whose shadow, however, is cast over much of Act IV). Those of us who have seen (as who has not?) Olivier's famous film of the play will not be surprised by this figure, for he made of Agincourt one of the most memorable battle-scenes that the screen has ever achieved. But not very many of those 1,175 lines actually were spoken in the film. If we count again, and even if we exclude the scene of the French at the end of Act III, we find the extraordinary fact that 355 lines of the total are comedy, involving either Pistol and Le Fer or Fluellen and Williams. A third of the battle-scene is a joke, then, which makes us wonder again about the last lines of the chorus to Act IV: 'Yet sit and see; /Minding true things by what their mock'ries be'. Neither Walter nor Taylor glosses 'mock'ries', and indeed the principal meaning, of imitation in the dramatic sense,[13] is clear. But the other meaning, 'a subject or occasion of ridicule, a person, thing or action that deserves or occasions ridicule' (OED sb 1.b), was well-established. The same Chorus that makes puns about wooden Os and guilt/gilt is certainly not to be automatically exempt from suspicion of a pun here.

III.vii is itself at least partly comic, as the French nobles play languid word-games with each other. The ensuing chorus to Act IV first speaks of the armies' mutual preparation, then describes the alarming weakness and fatigue of the English troops. But Henry is reported to have the situation well in hand:

> For forth he goes and visits all his host,
> Bids them good-morrow with a modest smile,
> And calls them brothers, friends, and
>   countrymen.
> Upon his royal face there is no note
> How dread an army hath enrounded him. . . .

And the Chorus tells us that he cheers up everyone with the famous 'little touch of Harry in the night'. But once again the Chorus is mistaken: what Henry actually does is to borrow a disguise and go about the army in careful incognito. This entire episode is invented by Shakespeare: it does not occur in Hall or Holinshed.[14] But he was not without a model for it: I at least am reminded that, before Bosworth, Richard orders Ratcliffe,

> come, go with me:
> Under our tents I'll play the eavesdropper,
> To see if any mean do shrink from me.
> (V.iii.201-3)

Shakespeare does not have Henry play the eavesdropper, exactly; but he makes him retain his incognito even when, on any reasonable grounds, we might have expected him to drop it to encourage his sensible and yet anxious troops.

His own anxiety of mind is stressed by his soliloquy (IV.i.236f.)—his only serious soliloquy in the play.

We may therefore presume Shakespeare invented the scene as he wanted it, and that the apparent contradiction between the Chorus's account and what happens on stage subsequently is deliberate and purposeful. Even Taylor, who, as noted above, is more alert to the ambivalent functions of the Chorus than most editors, fudges this issue. His note on the 'little touch of Harry' concludes: 'in performance it is hard to exclude the extra-syntactical suggestion that we too will see a little touch of Harry; but this need not imply we will witness a dramatization of the *same* activity described here' (IV.o.45n.). One may justifiably respond that the case is on a par with the Chorus's general tendency to describe events that are not performed, which is not the usual function of a Chorus. On the contrary, it seems to me that the contradictions are absolutely essential to the function of the Chorus in this play, and this, the most blatant refusal on the dramatist's part to satisfy the expectations his Chorus has aroused,[15] is the key to understanding the nature of the entire play.

This understanding is confirmed by the final Act, whose chorus begins with further apologies and appeals to imagination, and contains eulogies similar to the earlier ones. Once again, it is followed by a scene of clownage: Fluellen's revenge upon Pistol; succeeded by a scene of political manoeuvring, followed by a scene of light comedy as Henry and Katharine come to an understanding. The Chorus concludes with an epilogue in sonnet form, which once more strikes the note of apology:

> Thus far, with rough and all-unable pen,
>   Our bending author hath pursu'd the story;
> In little room confining mighty men,
>   Mangling by starts the full course of their
>   glory.

It is difficult indeed to make a concord of this discord. The Chorus spends half of his time telling the audience of the glorious deeds that are the subject of the play, and the other half criticizing the company for their failure to achieve, in their art, the theatrical equivalent of those brave times. In the epilogue, quite clearly, he criticizes the author, in a vein that goes a good deal beyond the normally self-deprecating tone adopted for epilogues.[16] One thing he does not do is criticize the company for not performing what he said they were going to: I marvel that he left it out.

One way of dealing with the problem is to declare roundly that Shakespeare could not have written the choruses. We have dismissed that, but it affects a lot of critical thinking on the subliminal level: Consider, for instance, these remarks by John Wilders: 'The Chorus, who overlooks many of the subtleties in *Henry*

V', and 'the piety of Holinshed's portrait has found its way into the play (in the attitude of the Chorus, for example)'.[17] These observations really sound as if Wilders was bemused into thinking that the Chorus was a creatively independent entity from the 'Shakespeare' who composed the rest of the play. Perhaps it was just his way of putting it; but a text which encourages such apparently confused description from such an intelligent critic needs special care.

As I see it, there are two problems in *Henry V* which need to be treated separately, but which are ultimately part of a single issue. The first problem is that the Chorus seems to be describing a play he has heard about, but which is not the one that actually takes place. The second is the problem of the morality of Henry's behaviour. I have already said something about both problems, and propose now to try to summarize them. Let us take the second first. Many modern critics would like Henry to show some awareness of the ambivalent moral dimensions of the actions he undertakes. Partly, the absence of any such awareness arises from deliberate choice on the dramatist's part: Shakespeare gives Henry no opportunity to react to Falstaff's death. But his general coldness is often remarked upon: for instance, he shows no signs of feeling when Bardolph must be executed. Wilders, among others, rightly rejects Walter's learned defence of Henry on the basis of the rules of warfare: 'Shakespeare makes us think of the virgins and infants of Harfleur, not of the rules of warfare. These vivid details are, incidentally, Shakespeare's; they do not appear in Holinshed.'[18] He might have added that the 'rules of warfare' are made to look pretty silly anyway by Fluellen's absurd devotion to them. All these criticisms, and many more, must be conceded by those who admire Henry.

But those who find him dislikable must also concede that Shakespeare gives him two of the finest battle orations ever written, must concede his humility, his piety, and his refusal of the opportunity for self-promotion that Agincourt provides, and finally must concede that the play stoutly resists any attempt to play it in any sense hostile to Henry: if the production works at all, it will work by making the play more like the one the Chorus describes than most sceptical readers would be prepared to believe or, perhaps, prefer. Taylor confirms this with his observation that those who hold that Shakespeare himself disliked Henry, and tried to convey this to the audience, are faced with 'the fact that productions of the play apparently never succeed in communicating this message' (1982 edn, 1); indeed, most of us who have our reservations about Henry's morality will find these reservations at least temporarily silenced by the effect of a great, self-confident production.

The only intelligible conclusion is that the duality is built into the play: Henry is a great hero, and a cold, conniving bastard. Something similar can be said of Marlowe's *Doctor Faustus*, who is a great, poetic, imaginative spirit, and an absolute idiot as well. There are other examples, none perhaps as extreme as these two, in plays of the period which suggest that a *unified* character was not necessarily the dramatists' goal, and that contradictory feelings can not only be accommodated, but are even the *purpose* of some plays.[19] The ambivalences one feels towards other Shakespearian characters such as Shylock, Othello, Macbeth or, at a different level, Bertram or Claudio, are not the same thing: these are characters who reveal complex aspects of the single personality, some likable and admirable, some decidedly otherwise. But for Henry V we are holding two contradictory things in our minds: the Henry in the theatre who is a hero; the Henry whom we think about subsequently, or whom we read in the script, and whom we find objectionable. They cannot, as experience has shown, coexist on the stage, but they are both encoded into the text, and can be decoded on different occasions: their contradictions will jostle uncomfortably in our minds. That uncomfortable jostle is, perhaps, the true central experience of this particular play. The inconsistencies force us to *think,* not perhaps always comfortably, or comfortingly, about what it is that being a hero actually means. Ideology is challenged. And the Chorus forces us into awareness of the dichotomy by talking about only one of the Henries.

I find it useful here to draw upon Stanley Fish's concept of the disruptive text, that fails to fulfil the expectations it generates, thus challenging the reader to confront problems, difficulties, and questions which cannot readily be resolved into an easy and reassuring harmony. Fish calls this a 'dialectical' rather than a 'rhetorical' text, and comments further:

> A dialectical presentation . . . is disturbing, for it requires of its readers a searching and rigorous scrutiny of everything they believe and live by. It is didactic in a special sense; it does not preach the truth, but asks that its readers discover the truth for themselves, and this discovery is often made at the expense not only of a reader's opinions and values, but of his self-esteem.[20]

The 'rhetorical' text, by contrast, satisfies its readers or, to put it another way, endorses ideology. Another recent critical term can be helpful in understanding *Henry V:* Northrop Frye's elegant phrase, 'myth of concern'—the enunciation in imaginative writing of something that is held by the public to be believable.[21] In the 1590s there was a substantial ideology extant concerning Henry V, the last successful warrior-king in English annals. He was thought to have been one of the lads in his youth, but to have succeeded to the throne in gravity and then upon the field of battle to have become the 'star of England' the Chorus speaks of. This ideology became revitalized when the ageing Queen and the young Earl of Essex started playing out their dominance games.

Few would deny that the compliment to Essex that is woven into the chorus to Act V is an expression of this ideology, and that the play as a whole is a myth of concern, in which the ideology surrounding Henry is in part transferred to the current young hero, in a mixture of hope, optimism, and unspoken but apparent anxiety. That Henry did not need to invade France, and that Elizabeth could perfectly well have left the Irish alone, are irrelevant either to the ideology or the myth of concern: indeed the two come close together in this, as in most discussions of military activities.

The Chorus proposes a 'rhetorical' play, in Fish's terms: a myth of concern which will give expression to ideology: a drama which will reiterate Henry's greatness, and urge the military motive and its ideology as an ideal. What we are given, however, is a 'dialectical' play, which incorporates the Chorus's ideology and intentions, to be sure, but much more besides; it indeed is disturbing (as any challenge to ideology must be), and requires its spectators/readers to discover the truth for themselves, at the expense of their opinions and values, and possibly their self-esteem too. So *Henry V*, by insisting upon being taken plurally, by resisting any attempt to incorporate these contradictions which are so vital to its structure into a single reading, interprets and challenges ideology at once. It is, and is not, patriotic; it is, and is not, an attack on militarism.

Although it is seldom possible to transfer neatly critical concepts evolved for one literary form to another, a distinction drawn by Tzvetan Todorov may be useful to elucidate further the role of the Chorus in this process: 'The individual who says *I* in a novel is not the *I* of the discourse. . . . He is only a character. . . . But there exists another *I* . . . the "poetic personality" which we apprehend through the discourse.'[22] Critics of the drama will not be amazed at this revelation, since for them the problem of dissociating the 'implied author' (Wayne Booth's phrase) from the first-person statements of the dramatic characters has always been evident. Yet even such alert critics as John Wilders and Robert Ornstein have been misled by the *implied* special status of the Chorus into treating his pronouncements as if they were those of Todorov's 'poetic personality'.[23] In fact, they are the statements of a character in a play, a play which is a larger and more complex discourse than the play that the Chorus himself describes, or than *Henry V* without the Chorus would be. A three-dimensional sphere can look like a two-dimensional circle, but only if you restrict yourself to looking at it in two dimensions (as in a photograph). The range of discourses that exist in *Henry V* without the Chorus is indeed two-dimensional and, I suspect, inexplicable without further alteration of the text. With the Chorus, the 'poetic personality' in its plurality starts to make three-dimensional sense, a sense which is dependent on the seemingly contradictory meanings imposed upon it, as it were perpendicularly

to all its other dimensions, by the Chorus. Thereby, the play transcends both ideology and the myth of concern, by making their contradictions apparent, and thus producing new meanings.

We have still to relate the Chorus's persistent concern with the limitations and deficiencies of theatrical representation to the play itself. To do so I would like to return briefly to *A Midsummer Night's Dream*, the wonderful scene in which Peter Quince's company invent, independently of Brecht, the *Verfremdungseffekt*. Precisely for the purpose of alienation, Bottom proposes that Quince

> Write me a prologue, and let the prologue seem to say we will do no harm with our swords, and that Pyramus is not killed indeed; and for the more better assurance, tell them that I, Pyramus, am not Pyramus, but Bottom the weaver.

(III.i.15-20)

Epic theatre can seldom have been so concisely achieved. The terror of the lion is likewise deconstructed, and then the technical realistic difficulties of staging such perplexing features as the moonlight and a wall are pondered. In both cases the solution is the same: realistic, non-theatrical means are rejected: the idea of allowing the literal moonlight to shine into the chamber is canvassed, only to be dismissed in favour of a theatrical way of achieving the effect. Such effects as can be emblematized by the actors themselves are preferred.

The difficulties with the moon and the wall are very much those faced by the company in staging so great an object as Henry V's French wars. Even today, producers seem to puzzle themselves more about how to bring in the walls of Harfleur (as the fatally over-elaborate RSC production of 1984 demonstrated) than how to make the actors interpret their lines intelligently and intelligibly. In fact, it is very curious how companies flatly disregard the Chorus's apologies: as Taylor says, 'nineteenth-century theatres found the Chorus an embarrassment because they actually did their damnedest to cram within their wooden Os the exact number of casques that did affright the air at Agincourt' (1982 edn, 57). What the stage struggles to do, film achieves with ease,[24] and Olivier's *Henry V* was very much a play about the Battle of Agincourt, with enough horses for a thousand Westerns. Splendid and stirring though this was, and odd as it may seem to say so, it suggests that Sir Laurence had a lesser grasp of the essential nature of the theatre than did Bottom and Peter Quince.

Be that as it may, Bottom and Quince and the Chorus of *Henry V* are approaching the problem of theatrical verisimilitude with the same criteria in mind. Quince and Co. are afraid first that the effect of their play will be so lifelike that the audience will no longer be able to distinguish fiction from reality, and will fall into panic; and secondly that their resources do not admit of their staging their play adequately. On the first point, they are happily self-deluded, but this does not mean that they are mistaken in their belief that people *do* confound art and life, and the means Quince and his actors adopt to ensure that this does not happen are a delightful anticipation of Brecht's solution. More relevantly, their second concern leads them with equal sureness to purely theatrical solutions; in their innocence, they do not see the absurdity of their proposed devices. The Chorus to *Henry V*, however, is well aware of the limitations that restrict any theatrical action; far from fearing that the company's account of Henry's campaigns will generate panic in the audience, he is concerned that they will fail (in Coleridge's justly celebrated phrase) willingly to suspend their disbelief, and urges upon the audience the need for them to employ their own imaginations to help the enterprise out. But the Chorus's attitudes are not *ipso facto* the author's, the company's, or ours: in fact merely by introducing the question of the suspension of disbelief the Chorus ensures that an audience will be aware of the artifice of the theatre. He, too, of course, is a *Verfremdungseffekt*.

It does not always work: grumpy old Ben Jonson remained firmly unconvinced that an emblematic staging was worthwhile; and there are always those who rebel at anything other than realistic (that is, illusionistic) staging: Johnson wouldn't have liked Peter Brook's *Midsummer Night's Dream* either. The point is that both Quince and the Chorus are alert to the limitations of the theatre, and each, in their several ways, proposes to seek solutions within the theatrical frame, solutions which in the end are not so very different. The man who must say he is the man in the moon is not so very distant from the Chorus who asks us to 'Think, when we talk of horses, that you see them /Printing their proud hoofs i' th' receiving earth'; the difference is that it does not occur to Quince to think his solution problematic; the Chorus is only too aware that his is, and that all depends upon the willing imaginary powers of the audience. Not the willing suspension of disbelief, but the active employment of imagination.

Shakespeare seems to have been very actively interested in the theory of dramaturgy at this stage of his career: the early plays, with their showy demonstrations that he had mastered the techniques of rhetoric and the styles of earlier dramatists, give way to the more complex creations of the later 1590s, with their constant harping on what it is that drama does, and how it does it. Unlike John Dryden, Shakespeare never put into a non-imaginative, essay form his thoughts about artistic creation. Yet dull would he be of soul that would deny that these plays are centrally *about* the imagination and how it works. This is unmistak-

ably crucial to the comedies *As You Like It, A Midsummer Night's Dream* and *Twelfth Night* at the least. In such a context, the appeals of the Chorus of *Henry V* for imagination are more than conventional apologetics, and must be read or heard intertextually for their true force to be perceived.

Some have thought that because the Chorus apologizes for the limitations of the stage Shakespeare was really embarrassed by them. On the contrary, as we have seen, the Chorus's apologies are clearly ironical; what they are saying is not how the theatre has failed, but how it has triumphed:[25] and so it has, provided that the production has the nerve to *accept* the limitations of its nature and realize that what the Chorus 'apologizes' for are precisely the parameters of its imaginative options. In the same way, the appeals for imagination from the audience are the verso of a leaf whose recto is the glorious imagination of the poet and his company. 'Such tricks hath strong imagination': what Shakespeare has given his audience in *Henry V* is a play where imagination functions and demands at all sorts of levels. First we are asked to watch a history play, which accepts in ways that the younger Shakespeare would have found difficult that politics is a complex and often immoral business, whose choices play a bitter counterpoint to the brazen glory of military music. *Henry V* is an extended theatrical experience, which is not switched on at the rise of the curtain (as it were), and switched off at its fall, but something that continues to provoke and challenge its audience to grapple indefinitely with its plurality. The same, no doubt, can be said of all serious drama, but *Henry V* is somewhat different: its mimetic action attempts to end in closure, but the Chorus's epilogue denies the finality of that closure, and challenges the myth of concern by stressing the transitory nature of Henry's achievement. The only way this extended action will work is if we, the audience, indeed stretch our imaginations, not in the ways that the Chorus ironically fusses over, but to meet the challenges of the complexity of the moral action. It is, finally, not simply your imagination, or theirs, but both, which are the essence of the expression of this text.

Notes

[1] In any event, the question of the authorship of Gower's choruses in *Pericles* remains open. Throughout this paper I distinguish the Chorus, the character who speaks, from the chorus, the text spoken by that character.

[2] For instance W.D. Smith, 'The *Henry V* choruses in the First Folio', *Journal of English and Germanic Philology,* 53 (1954), 38-57.

[3] *Modernizing Shakespeare's Spelling* (by Stanley Wells) *with Three Studies in the Text of Henry V* (Oxford: Clarendon, 1979), pp. 72-123.

[4] ibid., p. 103n.

[5] Gary Taylor, ed., *Henry V* (Oxford: Clarendon, 1982), p. 3.

[6] Not as few as played the Quarto version, which, as Taylor has shown, was intended for a total cast of no more than nine or ten adults and two boy actors: thrift, thrift, good Horatio.

[7] I say 'obviously', yet heads as wise as those of Bullough and Whitaker have missed the point: see *Narrative and Dramatic Sources of Shakespeare,* vol. 3 (London: Routledge & Kegan Paul, 1962), p. 349, and *Shakespeare's Use of Learning* (San Marino: Huntington, 1964), p. 131.

[8] *A Kingdom for a Stage: The Achievement of Shakespeare's History Plays* (Cambridge, Mass.: Harvard University Press, 1972), p. 176.

[9] J. H. Walter, ed., *King Henry V* (London: Methuen, 1954), pp. xxxvi-xxxvii.

[10] Ornstein, p. 176.

[11] As John Dover Wilson noted, *King Henry V* (Cambridge: Cambridge University Press, 1947), p. xxvi.

[12] 'History and ideology: the instance of *Henry V*', in *Alternative Shakespeares,* ed. John Drakakis (London: Methuen, 1985), p. 226.

[13] *OED* sb 2: 'mimicry, imitation' (not then pejorative), citing this line.

[14] Kenneth Muir, *The Sources of Shakespeare's Plays* (London: Methuen, 1977), says the episode may have been suggested either by *The First English Life of Henry the Fifth* or by Tacitus's account of Germanicus (111).

[15] See Anthony Brennan, 'That within which passes show: the function of the Chorus in *Henry V*', *Philological Quarterly,* 58 (Winter 1979), 40-52: 'the Chorus' version of Henry's tour among his soldiers is deliberate misdirection, a lack of preparation for the scene as Shakespeare writes it' (48).

[16] There is, of course, no evidence whatever for Dover Wilson's romantic notion that Shakespeare himself played the Chorus.

[17] *The Lost Garden: A View of Shakespeare's English and Roman History Plays* (London: Macmillan, 1978), pp. 52, 58.

[18] ibid., p. 58.

[19] It is not within my brief to go into this in detail in this paper. But the characters of Webster's *The White Devil,* especially Vittoria, Flamineo, Brachiano, Monticelso, and to a lesser extent Francisco, seem to have been evolved with some such dramatic purpose.

[20] *Self-Consuming Artifacts: The Experience of Seventeenth-Century Literature* (Berkeley: University of California Press, 1972), pp. 1-2.

[21] *The Myth of Deliverance: Reflections on Shakespeare's Problem Comedies* (Toronto: University of Toronto Press, 1983), pp. 8-9.

[22] 'Language and literature', in *The Structuralist Controversy,* ed. R. Macksey and E. Donato (Baltimore, Md: Johns Hopkins University Press, 1970), p. 132.

[23] Ornstein says, 'in his Epilogue, Shakespeare meditates' (p. 202). Dover Wilson explicitly equates the two (xiii).

[24] Brennan remarks, aptly enough, 'The only invention that would satisfy [the] literalist Chorus is the movie-camera' (41).

[25] Brennan again remarks justly: 'When Shakespeare points our attention to the theatrical he does not weaken its hold over us, he strengthens it' (41).

Günter Walch (essay date 1988)

SOURCE: "*Henry V* as Working-House of Ideology," in *Shakespeare Survey: An Annual Survey of Shakespearian Study and Production,* Vol. 40, 1988, pp. 63-8.

[*In the following essay, Walch argues that the Chorus helps us distinguish the political ideology represented in the play from the protagonist and the play itself. Far from being an objective reporter of events, the critic contends, the Chorus is a propagandist who underscores the discrepancy between mythology and history, and highlights the use of ideology as a mechanism of power.*]

Among the features specific to the text of *Henry V* its apparent property of giving rise to particularly acrimonious division of opinion has often been noted. To say that there are two camps sharply opposing each other is indeed almost a commonplace of critical literature, the one camp fervently applauding what they see as a panegyric upon, indeed a rousing celebration of, 'the mirror of all Christian Kings'[1] and most successful English monarch of all the histories; and the followers of the other camp deriding with no less conviction the exaltation of a machiavellian conqueror in a rapacious and, after all, senseless war. Little wonder, then, that in 1939 Mark Van Doren should have thought even Shakespeare's genius baffled *vis-à-vis* such hopeless material;[2] that E. M. W. Tillyard should have considered *Henry V*, remarkably enough at the time of the Second World War, a dramatic failure on account of its puerile patriotism and lack of form;[3] or that Moody E. Prior should consider the play 'a theatrically handsome fulfillment of an obligation, performed with skill but without deep conviction'.[4] Puzzled by such an unprecedented attack of Tudor apologetics suffered by an author almost simultaneously engaged in composing *Julius Caesar* (1599) and *Hamlet* (1599-1601), scholars have since suggested readings of the text assuming either that 'the play is full of ironies, most of which challenge the legend, well-established at the time the play was written, of Henry the "mirror of all Christian Kings" '[5] or of disparate presentations co-existing in unbridgeable contradiction: Henry as ideal ruler *and* brutal conqueror for instance;[6] or as a politically strong monarch *and* weak human being;[7] or Harry as model ruler saddled with a nation sadly deficient in moral virtue,[8] to give just a few examples.

I am not quarrelling with interpretations of this kind which add inscriptions which can enhance our understanding of the text. But one of the things that seem to have happened in the process of an intensifying search for implicit ironies is that the dramatic character of the protagonist has dwindled in stature. He has been reduced even from Hazlitt's 'amiable monster' to a rather commonplace person, at times intensely unpleasant, occasionally a neurotic, compulsively circumnavigating the pressures of having to make decisions,[9] and so forth.

I'd better say at this point that this is not my view of the protagonist, not the image suggested to me by the text, and even less by its representations on the stage. For on the stage the young king appears to have a knack of capturing audiences by his youthful and intelligent vitality even against their will, as it were, in spite of all reservations, triumphing sometimes over directors whose sympathy he does not seem to enjoy. In fact, Harry on the stage seems to wrest sympathies from audiences understandably reluctant to embrace the ideological tenets, the Tudor orthodoxies, and above all the warmongering with which he must be associated. From that derives the point I wish to make. As Robert Egan has shown, negative as well as positive reactions to the text have, encouraged by the Chorus, usually been produced by identifying both the central character and the play as a whole with the ideological material represented in it.[10] But that is just what the text carefully sets out to avoid. That is why the general poststructuralist objection to all representation as establishing or reinforcing authority can be seen not to apply: Shakespeare does not reinforce authority by representing or re-writing or inscribing in the text an interpretation of an historical personage agreed upon in advance. As I shall argue, the dramatist does far more in the text than write a pageant, at best ambiguous—but ambiguity will not solve our problem—, about the audience's favourite ruler. He creates, through his text, the score for a theatricalization of that material, and in the process turns the text—if I may vary one of the Chorus's invigorating appeals to our imagination—into a 'quick forge and working-house' (5, Chorus, l. 23) of ideology.

The history of *Henry V* in the theatre and the other more recent mass media shows distinctly, more clearly perhaps than is the case with most Shakespearian plays, that the play's reputation has depended heavily on its political and ideological contexts. Since the Second World War theatres in many countries seem to have been somewhat wary of a text that in times of national crisis was put to superbly efficient use as a patriotic morale booster. Sir Laurence Olivier's war-time film, naturally always referred to in this connection, demonstrates this kind of significant use of the text, always keeping in mind some 1700 lines cut and others added by the filmmakers.

I am not quarrelling over violations of some presumed sanctity of the play's text, let alone of a text with a single fixed meaning. I share the interest in the text as an interest in the history of social uses of—in this case—dramatic material, uses without exception historically and socially specific. And I also believe that texts cannot be reduced to successive inscriptions during the course of history, but that accounts of the moment of the original production of a text, although rightly no longer privileged, are far from irrelevant.[11] *Henry V* is so pertinent to that kind of historical approach because it is not only, like all art, ideological in the sense of generally being part of the process of social consciousness. This text is rather special among Shakespeare's works in parading, or even flaunting, the ideology—in the narrower sense of the term—represented in it. This is the major function of 1.2, with the state's top dignitaries engaged in ideological preparation for the war against France. Thus the scene offers a rich choice of official thinking, culminating, first, in Canterbury's famous legalistic dispensation, and, second and even closer to the heart of authority, in the same speaker's no less renowned sermon on the commonwealth of the honey-bees, the lesson of which had been so well rehearsed by Shakespeare's audience in a lifetime of church attendance.

Although it would now be probably harder than it used to be to find romantic believers in Shakespeare's unqualified acceptance of the doctrine of Order and Degree and absolute ideological Obedience, the actual aesthetic significance of the dramatist's inclusion of such weighty contemporary ideological material is still widely underrated. Canterbury's disappearance from the play after that scene may tell us that he has done the job assigned to him within the plot, but certainly not that the rest of the play is unconcerned with ideology. On the contrary, concern with the consequences of, and the historical problems inherent in, the doctrine placed so obtrusively in the text, and all it stands for, is central to the play as a whole.

That this concern was felt to be disturbing or at least irritating may be inferred from 'the apparent modesty of its early success'[12] in striking contrast to much later exhilarating celebrations of the hero and hence of the play. A look at what the very first social uses of the text have to tell us can be quite revealing, even allowing for its somewhat hypothetical character. For if we do not confine ourselves to considering only the practical side of the genesis of the First Quarto of 1600 as 'a cut form of the play used by the company for a reduced cast on tour in the provinces',[13] but also, as the editor of the new Oxford edition suggests and as I think we should, the ideological quality of those cuts, we can indeed see that nearly all 'difficulty in the way of an unambiguous patriotic interpretation of Henry and his war'[14] have been removed: all references to the Church's mixed motives for, and its financial support of, the war; to Henry's personal responsibility for Falstaff's fate; to motives beyond bribery for the conspiracy against Henry; to Henry's 'savage ultimatum' and the devastation wreaked by him on France; Mac-Morris and some of the choruses.[15] In other words, it was not only that the touring company had to make shift with its casting. Profiting from the experience of the play's original performances, we may assume, they also saw to it that technically necessary textual reductions were employed to make the text less recalcitrant to meeting the conventional audience expectations of a dashing hero confirming their own superiority.

That recalcitrance is not restricted to isolated passages but deeply structures the text as a whole. To give at least an indication of this, I shall isolate the character of the Chorus as a means which, although behaving in a deceptively epic way as a character, can be shown, I believe, to have an essential dramatic function within the context of the work. This consists in playing with the audience's conventional expectations in a number of intricate ways. The Chorus titillates those expectations nurtured by the illustrious 'gentles all' (Prologue, ll. 8, 11) in the abjectly decried 'cockpit', but raised also by previous triumphs prepared by Shakespeare's 'rough and all-unable pen' (Epilogue, l. 1) for 'this unworthy scaffold' (Prologue, l. 10) which are then fulfilled grudgingly or not at all. The Chorus as Prologue promises battle scenes the grandeur of which the audience will have to use their 'imaginary forces' (Prologue, l. 18) to enjoy properly, while the gentles remember very well previous battles—Bosworth Field, Angiers, Shrewsbury—'Which oft our stage hath shown' (Epilogue, l. 13) so magnificently. The Chorus conjures up, or deplores the absence of, a super-cinemascopic verisimilitude the humble author and his platform stage never dreamt of supplying, or indeed had any need of.

The Chorus thus theatricalizes the whole problem of representation on the Elizabethan stage, only to use what is in effect a brilliant defence of Shakespeare's non-naturalistic aesthetic to lead the audience into assuming, from their previous experience and expectation, that they know very well what they can expect to see happening on the stage. In a puzzling way, they are both confirmed in this—as far as the manner of representation is concerned—and disappointed, concerning the matter of representation. Thus, for instance, while the 'Muse of fire', the 'casques' and the 'proud hoofs' of Agincourt are invoked by the Prologue, in contrast to previous history plays this one does not show us a single actual battle scene. The only scene set during the battle has the cowardly and greedy clown Pistol taking an equally scared Frenchman prisoner, a parody of heroic combat.

We are gradually made aware, by the way the Chorus operates, that he cannot be relied upon to be always talking of what is actually represented on the stage. On somewhat closer scrutiny, he does not seem to be operating innocently 'as a peculiar feature, connecting and explaining the action as it proceeds' at all, as he was thought to do by Charles Kean[16] and a majority, it seems, of scholars since. In fact, the Chorus seems quite far from 'describing and connecting the quick succession of events, the rapid changes of locality; and the elucidating passages which might otherwise appear confused or incongruous . . .'[17] We are made to stumble on such incongruity, created rather than elucidated by the Chorus, when the very first dialogue opens, and when after the Prologue's eulogy the very first line deals, not with patriotism, as we've been promised by the Prologue, but with ecclesiastic financial transactions, something nowhere hinted at in the Chorus. Equally, we certainly do not see the French 'Shake in their fear', even though evidently they should, and our expectations of seeing 'this grace of kings' (2, Chorus, ll. 14, 28) foil the heinous attempt on his life by the conspirators, whose sole motive he says is money (although 'crowns'—'crowns imperial, crowns and coronets' are given prominence as 'Promis'd' to Harry's 'English Mercuries' earlier on in the same Chorus; II, Chorus, ll. 7-11), our expectations are at least delayed because we are first introduced to the down-and-out Cheapside gang. About these, however, and the common soldiers so prominent in the play, the Chorus is conspicuously silent. They are mentioned only once, collectively, 'mean and gentle all', presumably flattered as joint recipients of 'A little touch of Harry in the night' (4, Chorus, ll. 45, 47), obviously for propaganda purposes. Again, contradicting 4, Chorus's announcement of a forth-going Harry 'Walking from watch to watch, from tent to tent' visiting and cheering up 'all his host' (ll. 30-33), Harry is actually shown as rather isolated throughout all the acts except the last. At least in the Folio text he does not approach the soldiers. They approach him, and what follows is the long, tortuous discussion, verbal fighting within his own camp taking the place of armed combat in that of the enemy. In the Quarto text, the dialogue has been changed drastically.[18] Here, Henry does approach the soldiers and speaks to them first, reversing the Folio situation and thus bringing it into line both with the Chorus and with audience expectations based on it and on Prince Hal's behaviour of yore. Just as 2, Chorus ('honour's thought / Reigns solely in the breast of every man', ll. 3-4), 3, Chorus, also announces the splendid readiness of the whole nation to achieve heroic deeds of war ('For who is he, whose chin is but enrich'd / With one appearing hair, that will not follow / These cull'd and choice-drawn cavaliers to France?' ll. 22-4). But we are made aware of a majority back home in England safely tucked up in bed.

The function of the Chorus cannot, then, possibly be confined to the epic one of providing information. The information provided by him is, in the first place, for the most part superfluous, for we learn nothing from it about the plot, about Harry and his world that we do not learn much better from the dialogues. Since 2, Chorus eagerly tells us how the traitor scene will end, obviously the structure and meaning of the events are meant to be more important than their mere course (the verdicts had been drawn up *before* the trial in any case).

This interpretative dimension of the Chorus has been appreciated both on the stage, for example by Mrs Kean's representation of the Chorus as Clio, the muse of history, but operating typically as 'the presiding charm'[19] of the play; and in Eamon Grennan's description a few years ago of the Chorus as a commissioned historiographer who shows his royal subject making history.[20] But if he is a historiographer, he is characteristically not merely recording events. He is bent on presenting his subject, the king, in the most glaringly idealized colours, and his war invariably in the rosiest of tones. He is much more than a functional epic device, neutral observer and reporter. He is a deeply involved maker of ideology. And while he is intent on convincing us that Harry is achieving the great victory virtually single-handed, and that with God's assistance he is thus making history as a Great Man of History, we are made to understand, through the different components of the complete play's text, that Henry, just as his historiographer and propagandist, is actually busy creating his, Harry's, legend.

The Chorus in *Henry V* is thus, in my understanding of the play, not a later addition, but indispensable to its functioning. The Chorus is an integral part of Shakespeare's strategy not in spite of his information being unreliable, but because it is unreliable, and because what he does not tell us is more important than what he does tell us. Shakespeare thus creates a unique dramatic structure in his last history play in order to do something completely different from what he had

been doing in his previous histories. The genetic context with *Julius Caesar* and *Hamlet,* which now appears anything but a *non sequitur* on the part of Shakespeare, can actually further our understanding of the play's relation to the other histories, in particular to *Richard II.* By this new structure, by emphasizing not the events but the functioning of ideology, the conspicuously ancient theatrical device is made to ask, through the means of its art, completely new and shocking questions concerning the function of the monarch himself ('O hard condition! / Twin-born with greatness'; 'thou idol ceremony', 4.1.239-40, 246). By showing the young king not shining in the world of the Chorus' creation but living in the world of history Henry becomes a complex character. Moreover, the play's questions are addressed to problems concerning the nature of history, its motivating forces and the ideological function of its representation. The Chorus can make the Elizabethan audience aware of the political significance of these questions by highlighting the discrepancies between the orthodox historical legend perpetuated by those in power and the ideology connected with it on the one hand, and the actual movement of history on the other, and thus shows the official ideology up for what it has become: an illusion effectively used as an instrument of power.

Notes

[1] 1, Chorus, l. 6. All references to *Henry V* (henceforth in the text) follow The Arden Shakespeare, edited by J. H. Walter (1954).

[2] Cf. Mark Van Doren, *Shakespeare* (New York, 1939), p. 179. For a brief summary of divergent criticism of *Henry V* see my 'Tudor-Legende und Geschichtsbewegung in *The Life of King Henry V:* Zur Rezeptionslenkung durch den Chorus', *Shakespeare-Jahrbuch* (East) 122 (1986), pp. 37f, notes 2-17.

[3] E. M. W. Tillyard, *Shakespeare's History Plays* (1944), pp. 304-314.

[4] Moody E. Prior, *The Drama of Power. Studies in Shakespeare's History Plays* (Evanston, 1973), p. 341.

[5] John Wilders, *The Lost Garden. A View of Shakespeare's English and Roman History Plays* (1978), p. 141.

[6] Valentina P. Komarova, '*Heinrich V* und das Problem des idealen Herrschers', *Shakespeare-Jahrbuch* (East) 115 (1979), pp. 98-116.

[7] W. L. Godshalk, 'Henry V's Politics of Non-Responsibility', *Cahiers Élisabéthains,* 17 (1980), 11.

[8] Prior, p. 272.

[9] Cf. Godshalk, *passim.*

[10] Robert Egan, 'A Muse of Fire: *Henry V* in the Light of *Tamburlaine*', in *Modern Language Quarterly,* 29 (1968), p. 15. Egan does not, however, follow up his own conclusions but reduces his analysis to another opposition of the kind mentioned before, that of conqueror and human being; cf. p. 19.

[11] Cf. Francis Barker and Peter Hulme, 'Nymphs and reapers heavily vanish: the discursive con-text of *The Tempest*', in *Alternative Shakespeares,* ed. John Drakakis (1985), p. 193.

[12] *Henry V,* ed. Gary Taylor, *The Oxford Shakespeare* (Oxford, 1982), p. 12.

[13] Walter, p. XXXV.

[14] Taylor, p. 12.

[15] For the details see Taylor, pp. 12, 20.

[16] Charles Kean (ed.), *Shakespeare's Play of 'King Henry the Fifth', Arranged for Representation at The Princess's Theatre, with Historical and Explanatory Notes.* As first performed on Monday, March 28, 1859 (n.d.), p. vi.

[17] John William Cole, *The Life and Theatrical Times of Charles Kean, F.S.A. Including a summary of The English Stage for the Last Fifty Years, and a Detailed Account of the Management of the Princess's Theatre from 1850 to 1859.* 2 vols (1859), vol. 2, p. 342.

[18] Cf. Taylor, p. 43.

[19] Cole, vol. 2, p. 342. Also quoted by Taylor, p. 57. Kean considered the idea of casting his wife as a female Chorus, which set a trend in productions of the play in England, very frankly and practically as 'an opportunity . . . to Mrs. Charles Kean, which the play does not otherwise supply, of participating in this, the concluding revival of her husband's management' of the Princess's Theatre. See Kean, p. vi.

[20] Eamon Grennan, ' "This Story Shall the Good Man Teach His Son": *Henry V* and the Art of History', *Papers on Language and Literature,* 15 (1979), 370-82.

LAW AND JUSTICE

Karl P. Wentersdorf (essay date 1976)

SOURCE: "The Conspiracy of Silence in *Henry V*," in *Shakespeare Quarterly,* Vol. 27, No. 3, Summer, 1976, pp. 264-87.

[*In the essay that follows, Wentersdorf explores the reasons why none of the principals on stage in Act II, scene i refers to the real motive behind the Southampton conspiracy: to make Cambridge or his son king of England. The critic points out that all the assembled nobles know that Cambridge's title to the English crown is as strong as Henry's—and at least as justifiable as Henry's right to the throne of France—but it's not in the self-interest of any of them to raise this issue.*]

I

In spite of the episodic nature of the materials out of which Shakespeare created *Henry V,* the drama, in the eyes of most critics, is notable for its unity of action and tone. There has been considerable disagreement, however, as to the precise nature of that tone. For some, the play presents the story of an ideal monarch and glorifies his achievements; for them, the tone approaches that of an epic lauding the military virtues. For others the protagonist is a Machiavellian militarist who professes Christianity but whose deeds reveal both hypocrisy and ruthlessness; for them, the tone is predominantly one of mordant satire.

The series of episodes giving rise to this controversy begins with the post-coronation episode at the end of *2 Henry IV.* Confronted by Falstaff outside of Westminster Abbey, the newly crowned Hal banishes his erstwhile tavern companion from the court and announces to "the world" that he will abandon altogether his former dishonorable way of life. Is this the praiseworthy action of a man righteously turning his back on a shameful past, or is it the act of a crafty politician, who has merely pretended to lead a riotous life in order to capitalize on the banishment of his "misleaders"? As is often the case with such controversies, the truth lies somewhere between the extremes. Hal's association with Falstaff is partly a matter of inclination—Falstaff's wit is entertaining—and partly a matter of political calculation: it suits the long-range plans of the prince. He never participates wholeheartedly in the "riots" and is never more than a patronizing acquaintance of the fat knight; Falstaff's belief that Hal is a personal friend is a blind spot in the old man's psychological makeup. Far, therefore, from feeling the shame of a prodigal son and an unfaithful friend, Hal experiences a sense of triumph when he moves, just as he had promised himself, from the obscurity of the tavern atmosphere into the brilliant spotlight that plays on the throne.

One need not overemphasize Falstaff's overweening folly in approaching the new king with "a fool-born jest" during a solemn ceremony, nor should one exaggerate Hal's heartlessness in silencing and banishing him with what has seemed to some critics like undue harshness. The speech and the action are precisely what would have been expected from a serious monarch by the "world" he pointedly refers to in the rejection speech; they are the necessary proof of the "reformation" he planned long ago and now demonstrates publicly. Even Falstaff comments that the king "must seem thus to the world" (V. v. 83),[1] failing to realize that the new royal stance is more than an official pose. It is ironic that Henry IV should have thought it necessary to lecture his son on the art of political one-upsmanship—telling how he, as Bolingbroke, had led a secluded life in King Richard's day and thereby impressed the people favorably on the rare occasions when he did appear in public. In matters of politics, there is little that Hal needs to learn from his father. His success in persuading the English world of his "reformation" is the first major political achievement of his reign. His image-building is no more hypocritical or ruthless than that of twentieth-century politicians, even if it is no more endearing.

A similar difference of opinion exists regarding Henry V's foreign policy. In the *Institutio principis* (1516), a much admired, cited, and imitated treatise on the nature of a Christian monarchy, Erasmus argued that the ideal king should be learned and well versed in theology, but also that he should allow himself to be counseled by wise men; and while he should always act to defend and preserve his country, he should also consider his responsibility—if he goes to war—for the deaths of many innocent people. How, then, is Henry to be judged in the light of his revival of Edward III's claim to the French throne and his invasion of France?

For some critics, the king is legally entitled to reopen the question and morally justified in using military force.[2] Does he not consult the spiritual leaders of the English Church, and is it not the primate himself who urges the new king to take the field in pursuit of his inheritance (*Henry V,* I. ii. 100-114)? In requesting and accepting advice from the Church, and in moving to attack England's ancient enemy and restore justice, Henry exemplifies his humility, his wisdom, and his concern for the state, as well as honor, courage, and an impeccable sense of rectitude. In every respect, according to this view of Henry, his public demeanor justifies the description of him put into the mouth of the Chorus: "the mirror of all Christian kings" (II. Chor. 6).[3]

To other critics, the king is a cold-blooded opportunist, acting on the advice given by his dying father: "Be it thy course to busy giddy minds / With foreign quarrels," so that these activities will wipe out memories of the Lancastrian usurpation (*2 Henry IV,* IV. v. 214-16). Instead of ostentatiously planning a crusade to the Holy Land, as his father had done, Henry embarks upon an imperialistic "foreign quarrel"—a war that is more promising of immediate and tangible dividends, not merely for himself and his nobles but also for common soldiers like Pistol (see *Henry V,* II. iii. 56-58), and one in which many innocent people on both sides are bound to be killed. From this critical standpoint, the description of Henry as "the mirror of all Christian kings" is a sobering piece of dramatic irony.[4]

At the opening of *Henry V,* the Archbishop of Canterbury is quite obviously motivated by more than legal and ethical considerations in offering to support the planned invasion of France with an unusually generous subsidy from the coffers of the Church (I. i. 1-81). The primate's public speech in defense of the English claim to the French throne (I. ii. 33-95), assuring Henry pontifically that he may proceed "with right and conscience" (I. ii. 96), is a masterpiece of ambiguous prolixity, and it astonishes as much by the information it omits as by the arguments it contains. Nowhere does it explain the basis for Edward III's original claim to be the rightful ruler of France through descent in the female line.[5] As for positive arguments in vindication of Henry V's similar claim, the Archbishop cites the cases of three French kings from long bygone times who had similarly claimed the crown through female descent; but he oddly undercuts the effect of his own arguments by characterizing two of those kings as usurpers and the third (the son of one of the usurpers) as a ruler troubled by an uneasy conscience.[6] And after a bellicose reminder of Edward III's victories in France (I. ii. 101-4), Canterbury concludes his advice by urging Henry to prosecute his rights "with blood and sword and fire" (I. ii. 130-31).

Is Henry, then, merely the victim of the sophistry of a cynical prelate? It has been argued that in developing the character of Henry V, Shakespeare jettisoned his earlier concept of Prince Hal—an independent person who goes his own way and thinks for himself—and introduced into the final Lancastrian play a pious young man given to action rather than thought, who seeks advice from others and acts upon it.[7] To accept this view is to fall into the dramatic fallacy. If Hal's thoughts and actions as Prince of Wales are any guide at all, there is no reason to believe that his public pronouncements and actions after his accession will be any less carefully calculated than those of his father. It is true that at the end of *2 Henry IV,* before the whole court, the new king adopts the Lord Chief Justice as a surrogate father and announces his intention to let himself be guided by the latter's wisdom (V. ii. 102-21). So also at the beginning of *Henry V,* he publicly asks Canterbury for advice in the realm of foreign policy, urging him to present the truth impartially and implying that he will accept the Archbishop's judgment (I. ii. 9-32). In both instances, the young king is obviously concerned, partly if not primarily, with building up his public image as a righteous monarch, earnestly devoted to justice and prudently willing to accept advice from his competent and more experienced elders.

As far as the invasion of France is concerned, there can be no doubt that war is being prepared for long before Henry arranges for the discussion of his claim to the French crown in the presence of the English court. Even as the coronation procession is moving away from Westminster Abbey, Prince John is wagering that the English will be fighting in France before the year is out (*2 Henry IV,* V. v. 111-14), and one of Henry V's first official acts is to submit to the French government a formal claim to "certain dukedoms" (*Henry V,* I. ii. 246-48). It is conceivable that Henry has not decided, prior to the open discussion in I. ii, whether to revive his great-grandfather's claim to the whole of France. Even so, however, it could not be seriously contended that Henry personally needs episcopal coaching regarding the historical background to his larger claim: what he does need, in addition to the public support of the great lords temporal, is the public blessing of the Church, whatever the precise goal of the invasion. In the persons of Canterbury and Ely, the Church gives its blessing to the larger claim; and in their turn, the nobles, represented by Exeter and Westmoreland, speak out in favor of fighting for the whole of France, a policy which Henry V thereupon pronounces to be a "well-hallowed cause" (I. ii. 293). But to argue that the king is indulging throughout this episode in diplomatic rhetoric is not to imply that he is simply a hypocritical villain. He might have been convinced of the justice of his claim to the French crown and still have desired public backing from what would seem to be a morally impeccable source—backing that would help to silence any opposition, existing or potential, to the planned war.

That there is some opposition, aided and abetted by the French themselves, becomes clear when the English preparations for war are described. To stop the invasion, the French have suborned three English leaders to assassinate Henry at the port of Southampton. The plot is mentioned in some detail in the prologue to Act II (Chor. 20-35), and it forms the subject matter of the second and longest scene of that act. When the scene opens, the king is already aware of the existence of the plot; he exposes the traitors publicly, denounces the enormity of their offense, and sends them off to execution without delay.

The Southampton conspiracy has called forth the same kind of widely differing responses as the earlier episodes regarding Shakespeare's attitude toward the materials he is using and his concept of the protagonist, but there has been much less discussion of this aspect of the controversy. Understandably enough, the critics who believe that Shakespeare thought of Henry V as a model Christian king see in this episode a further demonstration of Henry's virtues. The ideal monarch, Erasmus had argued, should establish justice in his kingdom, but he should show clemency to offenders and not decree punishment out of personal revenge. Does not Henry follow this policy when he denounces the evils of ingratitude and treachery, administers the law strictly but fairly, and energetically metes out the traditional capital punishment, not so much because his own life has been threatened as because the conspiracy has jeopardized the welfare of the whole country? At the other end of the critical scale, there are those who, without denying the guilt of the conspirators, regard Henry as being callous in playing a cat-and-mouse game with men he is about to send off to execution, brazen in accusing them of ingratitude (is it not his own ingratitude that brings on Falstaff's death of a broken heart?), self-righteous in claiming that he does not seek personal revenge, and hypocritical in holding forth about the enormity of a crime similar to the one of which his own father had been guilty—a crime of which he himself was still enjoying the fruits.[8]

Does Shakespeare's concept of the king's character and motivation in this episode lie once again somewhere between the critical extremes? More important, since the scene in which the plotters are exposed (unlike the discussion episode of I. ii) does not advance the main action, does it serve primarily as a mirror-scene reflecting ironically on the major problem of the play as a whole—the justice of the French war?[9] These questions call for a closer examination of the Southampton episode.

II

The Chorus at the beginning of Act II has already identified the "three corrupted men" by name, though with no indication of their role in affairs of state. Indeed, from the offhanded mention of their leader as "One, Richard Earl of Cambridge," it might be gathered that he was a relatively insignificant nobleman rather than a prince of the blood royal. The nature of the plot is spelled out briefly and with seeming clarity: the three noblemen have accepted "treacherous crowns" from the fearful French to kill "this grace of kings" and thus "divert the English purposes" (II. Chor. 12-35). The scene in which the plot is exposed can therefore begin *in medias res.*

From the opening remarks of the king's brother Bedford and his uncle Exeter—"His grace is bold, to trust these traitors" and "They shall be apprehended by and by" (II. ii. 1-2)—it is evident that the king is biding his time, for some reason best known to himself. When Henry V enters with the traitors, who accompany him expecting to receive documents confirming their recent appointment as royal commissioners, the reason slowly becomes apparent: Henry intends to create a situation in which, once exposed, the traitors will be seen in the most unfavorable light. He speaks to the conspirators with great affability ("my kind Lord . . . my gentle knight"), questioning them about the prospects of success in the coming campaign and about the attitude of the English people toward his French policy. Cambridge replies that none of Henry's subjects is unhappy under his rule, and Grey elaborates by asserting that even the enemies of Henry IV are now serving his son zealously, having steeped their galls in honey.[10]

Henry then announces his decision to pardon a man who has been jailed for railing against the king while in his cups; the nature of his dissatisfaction with the king or the royal policy is not mentioned. All three conspirators, anxious to prevent any suspicion that they might countenance disloyalty, swallow the bait and urge that the man be punished. The king reacts with heavy irony:

> Alas, your too much love and care of me
> Are heavy orisons 'gainst this poor wretch!
> If little faults, proceeding on distemper,
> Shall not be winked at, how shall we stretch
>   our eye
> When capital crimes, chewed, swallowed, and
>   digested,
> Appear before us? We'll yet enlarge that man,
> Though Cambridge, Scroop, and Grey, in
>   their dear care
> And tender preservation of our person,
> Would have him punished.
>
> (II. ii. 52-60)

Now that they have spoken out against showing mercy, even to a minor offender who has been under the influence of wine, the king hands them documents revealing that their plot has been discovered and asks them sarcastically why they blanch. The three immediately confess their guilt, asking for mercy, but the king replies that they have forfeited it by the advice given to him in the matter of the drunken railer (II.ii.71-80).

The king then sets forth his case against "these English monsters." First, he turns to the assembled princes and peers and denounces the Earl of Cambridge:

> You know how apt our love was to accord
> To furnish him with all appertinents
> Belonging to his honor. And this man
> Hath, for a few light crowns, lightly
>   conspired,
> And sworn unto the practices of France,
> To kill us here in Hampton.
>
> (II. ii. 86-91)

Next, Grey is dismissed in a couple of lines as one who is no less indebted to the king than Cambridge (II. ii. 92-93). Henry then turns to the third conspirator and addresses him directly in one of the most powerful speeches in the whole play:

> What shall I say to thee, Lord Scroop? Thou
>   cruel,
> Ingrateful, savage, and inhuman creature!
> Thou that didst bear the key of all my
>   counsels,
> That knew'st the very bottom of my soul,
> That almost mightst have coined me into gold
> Wouldst thou have practiced on me for thy
>   use,
> May it be possible that foreign hire
> Could out of thee extract one spark of evil
> That might annoy my finger?
>
> (II. ii. 94-102)

The king continues in this vein for a total of fifty lines: he insists on the devilish nature of Scroop's treason, comments at length on the traitor's hitherto virtuous way of life, and likens his revolt to "another fall of man" (II. ii. 140-42).

After the three have been formally charged with high treason, they again plead for mercy. Cambridge and Grey even profess to be glad that the assassination has been prevented. Henry then repeats his charge:

> You have conspired against our royal person,
> Joined with an enemy proclaimed, and from
>   his coffers
> Received the golden earnest of our death.
>
> (II. ii. 167-69)

He adds that the plot has threatened the whole kingdom with servitude and desolation. Denying that he is personally interested in revenge, he points out that as it is his duty to watch over the safety of his country, he has no choice but to have them executed.

There are various strange things about the episode. In the brief discussion of the affair by the top-level advisers of the king, immediately before he comes on, there is an allusion to the conspirator who had been the king's close friend—"the man that was his bedfellow, / Whom he hath dulled and cloyed with gracious favors" (II. ii. 8-9)—but no mention at this time of the man who was the leader and presumably the instigator of the plot, the Earl of Cambridge. Nowhere in the episode is there any reference to the fact that two of the plotters were men of authority as well as rank in the kingdom: Scroop was the Lord Treasurer, and Grey (a cousin of Hotspur) was a member of the Privy Council. Even more noteworthy is the almost complete failure of the conspirators to offer any justification for their treason. In both parts of *Henry IV* and in other histories, rebels are at great pains to present their activities in a favorable light. In *Henry V,* the plotters content themselves with swift confessions of guilt; they utter less-than-convincing protestations of joy at the detection of their plot; and with the exception of Cambridge, they accept without demur the repeated implication that they had acted on the basest of motives—the greed for money. Cambridge admits that he has received French gold but denies that the money was an end in itself: he accepted it, he says cryptically, in order "the sooner to effect what I intended" (II. ii. 155-57). Since he would hardly need French crowns to hire common assassins of the type who served Richard III, the intention of Cambridge (if his speech is to make sense) must have been more complex than the removal of Henry V for the benefit of England's foes. Finally, there is the strangeness of the king's own silence on this point. He has much to say, and what he says is interesting and rhetorically effective; but what he leaves unsaid is much more striking, as becomes apparent when the conspiracy is viewed in the wider context of the dynastic struggles in fifteenth-century England.

III

The Southampton conspiracy was but one of a long series of plots generated by disputes over the succession to the English throne. In October 1399, Henry Bolingbroke, heir to the Duke of Lancaster (fourth son of Edward III), was crowned king as Henry IV, after having deposed his cousin Richard II, heir to the Black Prince (first son of Edward III). The immediate opposition to the new Lancastrian line, the Oxford conspiracy of January 1400, provided Shakespeare with material for the concluding episodes of *Richard II*. A group of nobles and prelates plot to kill the newly enthroned Bolingbroke and restore Richard; their leader is Aumerle, elder son of the Duke of York (fifth son of Edward III). When the plan accidentally becomes known to York, Aumerle anticipates his father's denunciation of the plot to Bolingbroke, confesses his guilt to the new king, and obtains his promise of mercy. Ex-king Richard's other supporters are captured and executed by friends of Henry IV.

The next revolt against the Lancastrian government provides the basic material for *1 Henry IV*. The men most instrumental in helping Bolingbroke to the crown, the Earls of Northumberland and Worcester, realize that Henry is mistrustful and fear that he will turn against them. With the aid of the Scots and the Welsh, therefore, the Northern Earls conspire to replace Henry IV by Edmund Mortimer, fifth Earl of March, who—through his grandmother Philippa—is the great-grandson of the Duke of Clarence (third son of Edward III). Since the second son of Edward III had died without heirs, Richard II, before leaving England on his Irish expedition, had proclaimed Mortimer heir-presumptive to the throne.[11] But although Mortimer, under the law of primogeniture, has a stronger right to the crown than Henry IV,[12] there is little popular support for his cause. Furthermore, neither the Welsh nor Northumberland himself appear at the climactic confrontation near Shrewsbury in July 1403. In Shakespeare's play,

the rebels charge the king with perjury, regicide, and failure to ransom the true heir to the throne from captivity. To these charges, Henry IV has no better rejoinder than that such arguments appeal only to "fickle changelings and poor discontents." With Prince Hal's unexpected offer to save bloodshed by fighting Northumberland's son Hotspur in single combat, attention is distracted from the moral and legal points at issue. In the ensuing battle, the rebels are decisively beaten; Hotspur is killed, Worcester captured and executed.

In *2 Henry IV*, Northumberland seeks revenge by conspiring with Archbishop Scroop of York, an uncle of the Lord Scroop who will participate in the Southampton plot. Scroop and his confederates are captured and executed; Northumberland is defeated in battle. There is no mention of Mortimer in this play.

These setbacks to the enemies of the Lancastrians did not remove all danger to the throne. After the death of Henry IV in 1413, it was rumored that Richard II was still alive in Scotland, and this rumor was probably a major consideration in Henry V's decision to reinter the murdered king. Nevertheless, domestic dissension plays a relatively minor role in *Henry V*. The real significance of the abortive Southampton conspiracy of January 1415 is overshadowed by the spectacular invasion of France, which effectively diverts attention from political problems at home and focuses it on an international dynastic dispute. The overwhelming victory of the English at Agincourt is followed by a treaty in which the defeated French ruler disinherits his son and heir-apparent, the Dauphin Charles, agrees to the marriage of his daughter to Henry V, and solemnly recognizes Henry V as the true heir to the French crown.

The hollowness of Henry V's military and diplomatic victories becomes apparent when he dies in 1422, before his son Henry is one year old, and the rule of his territories passes into the hands of a council of ambitious and quarrelsome nobles. The quarreling takes place within the boy-king's immediate family as well as between the Lancastrian and Yorkist branches of the Plantagenet dynasty. The dissension undermines the English rule of France and threatens the domestic peace of England. The heir of Henry V turns out to have none of his father's abilities as a leader: in France, his right to rule is successfully challenged by the disinherited Dauphin, and at home his authority is questioned and finally rejected by the Yorkists.

The head of the house of York in *1 Henry VI* is Richard Plantagenet, son of the executed Earl of Cambridge. Confronted with the weakness of Henry VI, he is as ambitious as Bolingbroke had been in the time of Richard II. His immediate aim is to regain his family's honors and possessions; and since he is also the heir to Edmund Mortimer, he intends, when the time is ripe, to revive in his own person Mortimer's claim to the throne itself. He achieves the first step toward his main goal when young Henry VI, displaying a greater sense of justice than hard-headed political wisdom, restores him to his father's earldom and at the same time equitably invests him with his deceased uncle's dukedom of York.

The first move by the new Duke of York in his campaign to obtain the crown is made in *2 Henry VI* with the private announcement of his ambitions to some powerful friends. Later in the play, he accepts the command of the English forces in Ireland; but before departing, he persuades a Kentish soldier named John Cade to impersonate Mortimer and raise a revolt against Henry VI—a rebellion which reveals considerable opposition to the Lancastrian rule before it is suppressed by the king's forces. Seizing the opportunity created by the disorders, York returns to England with an army, allegedly to suppress Cade but in reality to "pluck the crown from feeble Henry's head." He soon finds a pretext for denouncing the king's impotence and publicly proclaims his own right to the crown. With this challenge, the Wars of the Roses get under way.

At the beginning of *3 Henry VI,* York appears in parliament and calls on Henry to abdicate: the king weakly agrees to make York his heir, provided that he will swear to keep the peace and let Henry remain on the throne for life. Though York takes the oath, the supporters of both leaders are dissatisfied with the agreement, and war breaks out again. When York is captured and killed, his rights devolve upon his eldest son, Edward, Earl of March. After further fighting, the direct Lancastrian line is wiped out; and Edward, grandson of the Earl of Cambridge, establishes the Yorkist dynasty on the English throne.

IV

This brief review of Shakespeare's treatment of fifteenth-century rebellions against the Lancastrian kings makes it clear that the Southampton conspiracy in *Henry V* is part of a much larger dynastic struggle, which begins with the Oxford plot to kill the usurper Henry IV and restore Richard II. The ranking conspirator in that plot, Aumerle, is forgiven by Henry IV (partly, at least, because he does not represent a dynastic threat to the new king) and permitted to inherit the dukedom of York when his father dies; he himself falls, leading the English vanguard, at Agincourt (*Henry V,* IV. viii. 108). When Henry V succeeds to the throne and history repeats itself with the Southampton plot of 1415, the ranking leader this time is Aumerle-York's younger brother, the Earl of Cambridge. Now Cambridge is not only a cousin of the king,[13] as well as heir-presumptive to his brother York (the latter being married but childless); he is also the husband of Anne Mortimer, sister and heir-presumptive to the Edmund Mortimer who had been desig-

nated heir to the throne by Richard II. Furthermore, by Anne Mortimer, Cambridge is the father of Richard Plantagenet (born 1411), who later, after having been created Duke of York by Henry VI, would revive the Yorkist opposition to the Lancastrian usurpers.

The most striking aspect of Shakespeare's treatment of the Southampton plot is the conspiracy of silence among the characters regarding the family ties and political motives of the Earl of Cambridge. In the other history plays, there is ample explanation of the genealogical connections behind the various dynastic claims being made and the actions taken. But nowhere in *Henry V* is there any reference to the obvious interpretation to be placed on the motives of the plotters in accepting help from France. According to Holinshed, Cambridge wanted to replace King Henry by Edmund Mortimer: "Diverse write that Richard earle of Cambridge did not conspire with the lord Scroope & Thomas Graie for the murthering of king Henrie to please the French king withall, but onelie to the intent to exalt to the crowne his brother in law Edmund earle of March. . . ."[14] There was, of course, more than mere altruism behind this intention: Mortimer was not only without children but "for diverse secret impediments, not able to have issue." The role played by Cambridge must therefore be interpreted as a move toward his own acquisition of supreme power, either as king in the right of his wife Anne or as regent on behalf of his young son by her. As Shakespeare's source put it, "the earle of Cambridge was sure that the crowne should come to him by his wife, and to his children, of hir begotten."[15]

In view of the silence in the play regarding this crucial aspect of the historical conspiracy, would the dynastic circumstances be apparent at all to an audience? Goddard argues that "the long shadow that the incarcerated Mortimer casts across this play is not visible from a seat in the theater."[16] This observation is undeniably true of today's audiences as well as of today's readers who know only *Henry V.* Even modern playgoers who have seen the other plays in the Lancastrian-Yorkist cycle are unlikely to have a clear grasp of the genealogical details and are therefore apt to fail to realize the significance of the status and actions of the Earl of Cambridge. It would be wrong, however, to make any such assumptions about Shakespeare's audiences, at least about the historically-minded persons in those audiences. The Wars of the Roses and their origins were of special interest to the Elizabethans— witness the popularity of chronicles like those of Halle and Holinshed, not to mention epics like Samuel Daniel's monumental poem, *The Civil Wars* (1595, revised 1609), which ran through several editions.[17] And Shakespeare's eight plays on the subject, written between ca. 1589 and 1599, were among the most successful of his dramas, both with theatre audiences and with the reading public.[18]

In the course of this Shakespearean history cycle, the basic facts regarding Mortimer and Cambridge are introduced several times. Early in *1 Henry IV*, Hotspur clashes with the king over the question of ransoming his brother-in-law Mortimer, who has been taken prisoner while leading English forces against the Welsh under Owen Glendower. Henry IV vehemently denounces Mortimer as a traitor who betrayed his own troops and then compounded the treachery by marrying Glendower's daughter; for these reasons, the king refuses to ransom him. Later, when Hotspur comments—presumably with exaggeration—on the king's fearful reaction at the mention of Mortimer, Worcester says that he cannot blame the king: "Was not [Mortimer] proclaimed / By Richard that dead is the next of blood?" When Northumberland confirms the truth of this, Hotspur's response seems, at first, to be out of character: "Did King Richard then / Proclaim my brother Edmund Mortimer / Heir to the crown?"[19] It is impossible to imagine that he would have been ignorant of Mortimer's royal descent; but since Shakespeare's Hotspur is a very young man, he might well have been unaware of Richard's proclamation some years earlier. I would argue that Shakespeare makes Hotspur ignorant of it in order to obtain the necessary dramatic emphasis on this point. Finally, Worcester suggests that the Northern earls join forces with Mortimer, Glendower, and the Scots, for the purpose of overthrowing their mutual enemy. In this powerful episode of three hundred lines (I. iii), the position of Mortimer on the national scene is the major topic. Subsequently in the play, Lady Percy guesses that her husband is taking the field because her "brother Mortimer doth stir / About his title" (II. iii. 84-85), and Mortimer does in fact participate with the other rebels in planning the tripartite division of the kingdom (III. i). Shortly before the battle of Shrewsbury, Hotspur informs the royal envoy of the rebels' charges against Henry IV; not only was he responsible for the deposition and death of Richard II, but

To make that worse, suffered his kinsman
  [Mortimer, Earl of] March,
Who is, if every owner were well placed,
Indeed his king, to be engaged in Wales,
There without ransom to lie forfeited.

(IV. iii. 90-96)

As it happens, Mortimer and Glendower are both absent from Shrewsbury when Hotspur and Worcester are defeated by the king.

Mortimer reappears as a character in *1 Henry VI*. In this play, he is presented as a prisoner in the Tower of London, dying of old age and sorrow after having been held in "loathsome sequestration" ever since Henry V came to the throne (II. v. 23-25). Modern historians note that the Tower episode is fictitious; Mortimer was imprisoned by Henry IV but not by his succes-

sors. Holinshed implies, however, that he died after a long confinement: "Edmund Mortimer, the last Erle of Marche of that name (whiche long tyme had been restrained from his liberty, and finally waxed lame) diseased without issue, whose inheritaunce discended to lorde Richarde Plantagenet. . . ."[20] Shakespeare goes even further: his Mortimer says that he had been imprisoned "all [his] flowering youth / Within a loathsome dungeon" (II. v. 55-57).

Just before introducing Mortimer, Shakespeare brings on his nephew Richard Plantagenet and other nobles in a scene at the Temple Garden (II. iv. 80-120). During an argument over an unspecified point of law, Somerset calls Plantagenet a yeoman. Warwick rejects the insult, drawing attention to Plantagenet's royal descent: "Spring crestless yeomen from so deep a root?" Somerset justifies the affront by pointing out that since the late Earl of Cambridge was executed for treason, his son has been *ipso facto* "attainted,. . . . and exempt from ancient gentry," and that until the family titles are restored to him, he will remain a yeoman. Plantagenet intervenes with a legal quibble: "My father was attached, not attained." And after his enemies have left the scene, he is encouraged by Warwick's hope that the blot on his family will be wiped out during the next parliament.

Plantagenet thereupon visits Mortimer in the Tower and (in the most poorly motivated introduction of genealogical information in all of the histories) asks the dying man to tell him why Cambridge was put to death, "for I am ignorant and cannot guess." Mortimer explains in detail how his own claim to the throne was stronger than that of the usurper Henry IV. He then tells how the Northern Earls had wanted to advance him to the throne, and how in their "haughty great attempt . . . to plant the rightful heir" he lost his liberty and they their lives (II. v. 51-81). He concludes his story with an account of the Southampton conspiracy itself:

. . . When Henry the Fifth,
Succeeding his father Bolingbroke, did reign,
Thy father, Earl of Cambridge, then derived
From famous Edmund Langley, Duke of
  York,
Marrying my sister, that thy mother was,
Again in pity of my hard distress
Levied an army, weening to redeem
And have installed me in the diadem:
But, as the rest, so fell that noble Earl
And was beheaded.

(II. v. 82-91)

As Mortimer has no issue, he names Plantagenet his heir. When the latter angrily denounces the execution of Cambridge as "nothing less than bloody tyranny," Mortimer cautions him to be silent and politic, feeling that it would be futile to attempt to unseat the "strong-fixed" house of Lancaster (II. v. 92-103). Wishing his nephew prosperity, Mortimer dies; and Plantagenet hastens away to the parliament at which he is in fact "restored to his blood" and also created Duke of York (III. i. 149-77).

In *2 Henry VI*, when York appeals to Salisbury and Warwick as potential supporters of his future bid for the throne, the genealogical situation is once again set forth in pedestrian fashion. The sons of Edward III are named, Bolingbroke's usurpation is denounced, and the point is made that there is no surviving issue of the first and second sons. York then presents his case. Through his father he is descended from York, the fifth son; but he is also heir to Clarence, the third son, through his mother Anne Mortimer: "By her I claim the kingdom." He then repeats the details of Anne Mortimer's descent from Clarence and concludes: "If the issue of the elder son / Succeed before the younger, I am king." Warwick agrees that York's claim is better than that of Henry VI (descended from the fourth son of Edward III), whereupon he and Salisbury acknowledge York to be England's true monarch (II. ii. 1-82).

The final allusion to the Southampton plot occurs in the opening episode of *3 Henry VI*. York seats himself on the royal throne and is challenged by Exeter: "For shame, come down. He made thee Duke of York." And when York replies, "'Twas my inheritance, as the earldom was," Exeter reminds him: "Thy father was a traitor to the crown" (I. i. 77-79). In this exchange, York is referring to his uncle's earldom of March, and Exeter is adverting to the conspiracy. Shakespeare evidently felt that at this point the basic facts were sufficiently well known to make another detailed discussion of the genealogical issue unnecessary.

The interest taken by the public in Shakespeare's histories is reflected in the production by the rival Admiral's Men of *Sir John Oldcastle*, late in 1599.[21] Written as a counterblast to the slur on the memory of the Lollard leader in *Henry IV* (the character Falstaff was originally named Oldcastle) and staged only a few months after *Henry V* was first acted,[22] the play of *Oldcastle* offers a more elaborate version of the Southampton plot and makes the dynastic aspect quite explicit. First, Cambridge explains his interest in the throne to Scroop, Gray, and Chartres, a French envoy. After presenting genealogical data comparable to those in Shakespeare's *Henry VI*, he argues that his wife Anne "ought proceede, / And take possession of the Diademe / Before this Harry. . . . " His listeners agree that the cause is just: the murder of Richard II must be avenged, and Harry must resign or die (III. i. 1-65). The conspirators then approach Lord Cobham, formerly Sir John Oldcastle, counting on his assistance. But Cobham is loyal to the king, in spite of

persecution on account of his religion; he therefore pretends to support the plotters and persuades them to give him a signed statement of their aims (III. i. 66-201). Later, he hands over the incriminating document to King Harry (IV. ii. 121-37). Finally, the conspirators are overheard by the king while discussing the best way to murder him. Scroop opts for poison and volunteers his services ("I am his bedfellow"), Cambridge favors a public assassination, and Gray offers to kill him in the council chamber. At this point, the king reveals himself, comments sardonically on the practicability of their proposals, and orders them dragged to their deaths (V. i. 1-52).

V

There is, in short, abundant contemporary evidence for the familiarity of Elizabethan theatregoers with the story of the Mortimers under the Lancastrians. But why does Shakespeare refrain from any mention of that story in *Henry V*? Dover Wilson acknowledges that the real motivation of the Southampton plot was dynastic and comments: "it seems odd that Shakespeare did not make it more explicit, until we remember that he must avoid anything that casts doubts on the legitimacy of Henry V."[23] But is it Shakespeare who must avoid this, or Henry himself? Matthew agrees with Wilson, believing that "no patriotic Elizabethan, lost in admiration for the usurper's son, would care to hear" a word in defense of the rebels.[24] In my view, this argument is specious. There were undoubtedly many visitors to the Globe who thrilled uncritically to the near-epic treatment of the national hero's deeds; but there were also others, politically more sophisticated, who were interested in the problem of legitimate succession (a problem still of grave concern in the year 1599) and who would soon have become aware of the ironic contrast between the rhetoric of the characters and the realities of the action. For such playgoers, whether they sympathized with the Lancastrians or the Yorkists, the silence on the dynastic issue might well have been a more intriguing tour de force than a historically unfounded public dispute.

Since the background of the Southampton conspiracy was generally known, some at least in Shakespeare's audience would have noted the weak points in the rhetoric of Henry's oversimplified explanation of the would-be assassins' motives. But how would they have interpreted the curious absence of any reference whatsoever to the background? Is the conspiracy of silence adequately motivated in terms of the overall action? Why is it that the accused noblemen remain unresponsive when the king alleges that their treachery has sprung from the most sordid of motives—the desire for gold? Why is it that the Earl of Cambridge does not offer a rebuttal, dignified or outraged, that would explain the dynastic basis for his role in the plot—a rebuttal comparable, perhaps, to Hotspur's defense of the Northern Earls' rebellion and of Edmund Mortimer's right to be king? And why does Cambridge fail to point out that if Mortimer and his heirs are to be denied their rights to the crown on the ground that Mortimer is descended from Edward III in the female line, Henry V can scarcely proceed in conscience with his war to obtain the French crown on the basis of a claim likewise through descent in the female line?

The answer to these questions lies partly in the circumstance that the three conspirators, unlike Hotspur at the time of his defense, are already in the hands of the king; but the overwhelming reason for the conspirators' silence is the nature of the punishment meted out to those found guilty of treason. Traitors lost not merely their lives: their titles and possessions were also forfeited to the crown. This meant that the widow and children of an executed traitor were left destitute and stripped of all the rights and privileges to which the dead man's rank in society had entitled him and his family. In such a situation, it would be folly of the worst sort for the plotters to antagonize the king still further by reminding the "world" that he is the son of a usurper, and that Cambridge's young son has a clearer legal claim to the throne than the incumbent. The conspirators remain silent on this point because they do not want to jeopardize the survival of their families: they hope that the king will acknowledge their restraint by mitigating the almost inevitable suffering of their innocent wives and children.

Justification for this interpretation of their failure to come to their own defense is explicit in Shakespeare's prime source for the play and implicit in the Temple Garden episode of *1 Henry VI*. "These prisoners," Holinshed reports, "upon their examination, confessed, that for a great summe of monie which they had received of the French king, they intended verelie either to have delivered the king alive into the hands of his enimies, or else to have murthered him before he should arrive in the duchie of Normandie."[25] After recounting this public confession, however, Holinshed gives a detailed account of the main reason for the conspiracy— a reason evidently not touched upon at the public examination of the three men: their object, with French aid, was to place Edmund Mortimer on the English throne,[26] the throne that would ultimately pass, since Mortimer was "not able to have issue," to the son and heir of Anne Mortimer and the Earl of Cambridge. The chronicler then comments on the motive behind the public confession made by Cambridge: "And therefore (as was thought) he rather confessed himselfe for need of monie to be corrupted by the French king, than he would declare his inward mind, and open his verie intent and secret purpose, which if it were espied, he saw plainlie that the earle of March should have tasted of the same cuppe that he had drunken, and what should have come to his owne children he much doubted. Therefore destitute of comfort & in despaire of life to save his children, he feined that tale, desiring rather to save his succession than himselfe. . . . "[27]

When the traitors beg Henry V to pardon them, then, what they have in mind is not an act of mercy that would save them from death: Cambridge implies, while Scroop and Gray state explicitly, that they are ready to pay for their fault with their lives (II. ii. 151-65). The pardon which they request is for their families. The fears of Cambridge are not unjustified: the family was to remain stripped of its titles and rights for many years. Even in adulthood, the earl's heir, Richard Plantagenet, is taunted publicly with being a mere yeoman; and this incident, invented by the dramatist to highlight the dynastic situation, takes place shortly before the pious son of Henry V restores Plantagenet to his family's titles and possessions.

As for the silence of Henry V himself regarding the real motives of the conspirators, how could he mention the plotters' intention to make Mortimer king without drawing attention gratuitously to the weak legality of his own claim to the crown?[28] His problem is to distract attention from the potentially explosive political situation, and he approaches the problem with a rhetorical skill that is little short of masterly. First he displays great affability in order to prepare the onlooking nobles and courtiers for subsequent reminders of his past favors to the three men, and to bolster the anticipated revulsion at the thought of their ingratitude. For the main thrust of his attack, he chooses to concentrate on the charge that they were motivated by French bribes, knowing that the conspirators will have the good sense not to challenge it. Then, in place of a detailed denunciation of the ringleader, the king launches into a long tirade against Lord Scroop of Masham—the Lord Treasurer, a trusted counselor, and for many years a close personal friend of the king. After expressing surprise that "foreign hire" could tempt a man of Scroop's sterling character to participate in such a "savage and inhuman" deed, Henry goes on to offer an explanation for such incredible behavior:

> . . . whatsoever cunning fiend it was
> That wrought upon thee so preposterously
> Hath got the voice in Hell for excellence.
> All other devils that suggest by treasons
> Do botch and bungle up damnation
> With patches, colors, and with forms being
>   fetched
> From glistering semblances of piety.
> But he that tempered thee bade thee stand up,
> Gave thee no instance why thou shouldst do
>   treason. . . .

In short, the "demon . . . with his lion gait" that influenced Scroop must have been the Devil himself (II. ii. 102-25). In the light of Scroop's upbringing and temperament, Henry asks in effect, what other explanation is conceivable?

> . . . . Show men dutiful?
> Why, so didst thou. Seem they grave and
>   learned?
> Why, so didst thou. Come they of noble
>   family?
> Why, so didst thou. Seem they religious?
> Why, so didst thou. Or are they spare in diet,
> Free from gross passion or of mirth or anger,
> Constant in spirit, not swerving with the
>   blood,
> Garnished and decked in modest complement,
> Not working with the eye without the ear,
> And but in purged judgment trusting neither?
> Such and so finely bolted didst thou seem.

Not even the best endowed are safe from suspicion any longer, for Scroop's revolt is like "another fall of man" (II. ii. 127-42). If the rebellious Scroop is Adam, then Henry V is God; and this is no mere hyperbole. Henry is subtly reminding all present that whatever the background of the current dynastic situation, he is their anointed monarch and thus (as the Bishop of Carlisle said of Richard II) "the figure of God's majesty."[29]

This striking tour de force is no unpremeditated outburst. The king's words and tone are partly a genuine expression of strong feelings, partly a clever piece of histrionics, foreshadowed by his play-acting in the discussion of the drunken railer, and calculated to quash doubts regarding a political challenge by stimulating horror at a personal betrayal. Like his earlier pronouncements as monarch, the "fall of man" philippic is a public speech artfully developed for the maximum rhetorical effect. The conclusion which Henry reaches is often taken at its face value. For instance, in a recent discussion of the episode, Scroop's participation in the plot is said to have resulted from "a disposition to rebel without any apparent reason" and to be "explainable only figuratively by reference to demonic influence"; he "is possessed by the spirit of Cain as is no other character in the tetralogy."[30] From the standpoint of Henry V's supporters, there would have been validity in the comparison of Scroop's crime with the fall of Adam; and it may be that the theatre audience was intended to think of Henry as carried away by his own arguments. To deduce,..however, that Shakespeare himself conceived of Scroop's offence in the same terms as some of his *dramatis personae* would be to fall once again into the dramatic fallacy.

It seems more likely that when Henry proclaims his inability to understand the motivation for such a crime, he is speaking in character, as an astute politician, keeping the discussion away from the embarrassing heart of the matter. It is very convenient for him to advance the simple explanation that Scroop must have been deceived by the Devil, and it is also politic for everyone else to accept this uncomplicated solution to the puzzle. But most if not all of those present at the exposure of the plot are aware of the inescapable fact that Cambridge and Scroop are challenging Henry V's right to the English throne on grounds at least as convincing as those justifying Henry's challenge to the French king. To them, the king's assertion that Scroop had no impelling motive—"no instance why thou shouldst do treason"—must sound, whatever their sympathies, somewhat hollow.

The problems raised by the Southampton conspiracy are more complex than those surrounding the revolts in other plays—as regards both the circumstances and the personalities. Henry V is not a widely detested tyrant, like Richard II and Richard III; nor, technically speaking, is he a usurper, like Richard III. Though he is the son and beneficiary of a man guilty directly of usurpation and indirectly of regicide, he himself, as his father assures him, is personally untained (*2 Henry IV*, IV. v. 184-202). Nevertheless he remains uneasy in his conscience because he enjoys the proceeds of his father's crimes (*Henry V*, IV. i. 309-22). There is no knowing how many of his subjects are likewise uneasy; but it is a fact that some of them are willing to risk death by supporting the claim of Mortimer and his Yorkist heirs, not only in 1415 but on several other occasions in the decades to come. And though many of the Yorkist sympathizers are probably actuated by the hope of rewards in the form of wealth or power, some may be idealists with a desire to see justice done, akin in spirit to the self-sacrificing Bishop of Carlisle.

If Henry V is no Richard II, Scroop is no Earl of Worcester (whose defection while one of Richard II's ministers is recalled in *1 Henry IV*, V. i. 34-38). Lord Scroop—and the point is emphasized by Holinshed—had always been a man of impeccable character. In cataloging the fallen man's virtues, the king may at first sight seem to be exaggerating a little, but he would be creating a credibility gap if the portrait he gives were not known to his nobles to be substantially true. Moreover, Scroop has indeed been, as Henry states, a close and trusted friend on whom he has relied for advice in important matters. What explanations can there be for the defection of such a man? The possibility that he has been corrupted by French gold, a charge directed against the conspirators as a group, is quite unconvincing. The theory that his deed is an ultimately inexplicable example of devilish malignity is conceivable only if the background of the conspiracy is left out of consideration. The one explanation that makes sense in the case of Scroop is that Shakespeare conceived of him as a political idealist, and this is an explanation that Henry V quite understandably ignores.

Unless Henry V is an extraordinarily bad judge of character, Scroop is a virtuous man to whom the very thought of betraying a friend and murdering a king must have been abhorrent. Only considerations of the utmost gravity could have led him to participate in treason. Whether or not he has any scruples concerning the invasion of France is impossible to tell. In any case, he has been worked upon by the adherents of Mortimer and persuaded that justice should be done to the claimant to the throne who, as is made clear in the earlier plays, is not merely denied his royal rights but is being held prisoner by Henry V in a loathsome dungeon. To judge from his long association with Henry, Scroop can hardly be as certain of the rights and wrongs of the situation as Carlisle is when he denounces Bolingbroke's usurpation; it can only have been with great reluctance that Scroop switched his allegiance to Mortimer.

In support of this interpretation, it is pertinent to note that the subject to which Shakespeare probably turned after writing *Henry V* was the assassination of Julius Caesar, and the major theme of the new play was misguided political idealism. The description of Henry, returning victorious from Agincourt, as a "conquering Caesar" (V. Chor. 28) may indicate that Shakespeare was already thinking about his next play before the final act of *Henry V* had been completed. The new work was to be the tragedy not of Caesar himself but of Marcus Brutus, a politically naive but patriotic nobleman who agrees to join the conspiracy against Caesar only after he has been persuaded that the assassination is a necessity for the ultimate good of the state. The portrait of Brutus could thus be regarded as a full-length study in naive political idealism, influenced or possibly even prompted by the briefly sketched role of Scroop—an attempt to deal in depth with the psychological problem which Henry V professes to find unfathomable.

The similarities between Scroop and Brutus are noteworthy. Each is publicly respected as a man of great probity and self-control. Each deservedly enjoys a high reputation for patriotism and piety. Each is held in great affection by the man he agrees to kill, and both rulers react to the treachery with incredulity. *Henry V* has no counterpart to the episode in *Julius Caesar* in which the altruism of Brutus is finally acknowledged even by his enemies (V. v. 68-79); but then Scroop is not himself a dynastically significant figure. Furthermore, Brutus is eulogized only after he and his co-conspirators have been totally destroyed, whereas the deaths of Scroop and Cambridge do not eliminate the danger to the house of Lancaster from the heirs of Mortimer—the danger which ultimately overwhelms the Lancastrians.

Scroop was a man, says Holinshed, who "represented so great gravitie in his countenance, such modestie in behaviour, and so vertuous zeale to all godlinesse in his talke, that whatsoever he said was thought for the most part necessarie to be doone and followed."[31] It is not inconceivable, then, that Antony's sentiments regarding Brutus come close to epitomizing the truth about Scroop:

> All the conspirators, save only he,
> Did that they did in envy . . .
> He only, in a general honest thought
> And common good to all, made one of them.
> (V. v. 69-72)

At the very least, it must be recognized that Scroop's motives in turning against his friend are as ambiguous as those of Henry V in invading France. Even if Scroop is not the mirror of all Christian patriots, neither is he a diabolically possessed opportunist. He is a perplexed man who has been convinced that he had compromised his honor by allowing the claims of personal friendship to outweigh the demands of political justice, and who has joined Cambridge in a belated attempt to right an earlier wrong.[32] The biblical elements in Henry's rhetoric are obviously intended to suggest that the exposure of the conspiracy is proof of God's adverse verdict on the justice of Scroop's decision to support the Mortimer family. The irony is inescapable: Shakespeare's audience knows that the verdict will be reversed when Mortimer's heirs overthrow the Lancastrian dynasty and establish the Yorkist line on the throne.[33]

VI

The role of the Earl of Cambridge and his supporters in attempting to overthrow the established monarch is analogous to that of Henry V and his noblemen in challenging the French. The difference in method—an underhanded assassination as opposed to a courageously fought hand-to-hand combat—should not be permitted to obscure the similarities in motivation and goal, especially in the complexity of the legal and moral aspects of the two bids for justice. Henry V asserts that the conspirators have no compelling reason for their conspiracy; might not precisely the same be said regarding his invasion of France? He denounces them for hiding behind "semblances of piety"; is not this what he himself is doing, in asking for the approval of ecclesiastics whose motives are mercenary and political? He claims that the plotters would have sold Englishmen to "oppression and contempt, / And . . . desolation" (II. ii. 172-73); what else is he bringing to the people of France, as he himself admits, but "waste and desolation . . . heady murder, spoil, and villainy" (III. iii. 17-32)? Henry is by no means the monster he has seemed to some critics, witness his appeal to the French king to spare his subjects the horrors of war (II. iv. 102-9); given the exigencies of the military situation, the threats made to the Governor of Harfleur are not the expression of a blood-thirsty delight in death and destruction for their own sake, but rather an effective piece of psychological warfare. On the other hand, however, Henry is not the saintly leader of a crusade. He is a soldier-adventurer engaged in war for shrewd political motives that have as much to do with potential troubles at home as with territorial gains abroad.

It is not by chance, therefore, that the successful invasion of France is capped by a series of striking dramatic ironies. During the wooing of the French Princess Katherine, Henry roguishly boasts that he and his wife-to-be will together breed a warrior son "that shall go to Constantinople and take the Turk by the beard." Can this have sounded anything but laughable to those who recalled that the son born to them would one day sit on a hilltop sighing for a hermitage, while his doughty wife leads his army in battle? When the French king is compelled to disinherit his son the Dauphin and adopt Henry V as his heir, what historically-minded playgoer would not have reacted with the sobering thought that the weakling Henry VI will also have to face a warlike challenger and will likewise be compelled to disinherit *his* son? Above all, there is the French king's pious hope that the peace treaty between England and France will plant "Christianlike accord / In their sweet bosoms": is this a genuinely felt expression of hope, or is it nothing but a platitude, the face-saving rhetoric of a king trying to justify his inglorious surrender? In any case, it is belied only minutes later by the gloomy predictions of the *Epilogue.*[34]

In the course of writing his great history cycle, Shakespeare had become increasingly aware of the difficulty of arriving at an objective view of major historical events, and of the ease with which the truth can be misrepresented. The play of *Henry V* completes his exploration of the true role played by the house of Lancaster in precipitating the Wars of the Roses. Nowhere are the problems in the way of understanding that role more strikingly illustrated than in the controversial nature of the French war, and in the episode which mirrors the ambiguities of that war—the Southampton conspiracy.

Notes

[1] The text cited in this paper is that of G. B. Harrison, *Shakespeare: The Complete Works* (New York, 1952).

[2] In his edition of *King Henry V* (New Arden Shakespeare; London: Methuen, 1954), J. H. Walter argues, p. xxiii, that if Shakespeare believed Henry's claim to be justified, he was in agreement with Alberico Gentili, "the greatest jurist of the sixteenth century," who in his *De iure belli* (1588, 1598) expressed the view that the claim was legal; Walter does not point out, however, that Gentili was writing while a refugee in England and is not necessarily an impartial witness.

[3] For some modern views of Henry V as an ideal monarch, see John Dover Wilson, *The Fortunes of Falstaff* (Cambridge: Cambridge Univ. Press, 1943), pp. 60-81, 114-28; J. H. Walter (1954), pp. xiv-xxiv; M. M. Reese, *The Cease of Majesty* (London: Edward Arnold, 1961), pp. 319-23; R. Berman, "Shakespeare's Alexander: Henry V," *CE,* 23 (1962), 532-39; G. W.

Keeton, *Shakespeare's Legal and Political Background* (New York: Humanities Press, 1968), p. 282; F. P. Wilson, *Shakespearian and Other Studies* (Oxford: Oxford Univ. Press, 1969), pp. 41-42.

[4] Notable among critics who believe that Shakespeare presents Henry V and his foreign policy in an unfavorable light are Mark Van Doren, *Shakespeare* (New York: H. Holt, 1939), pp. 170-79; J. Palmer, *Political Characters of Shakespeare* (London: Macmillan, 1945), pp. 221-44; H. C. Goddard, *The Meaning of Shakespeare* (Chicago: Univ. of Chicago Press, 1951), pp. 218-26; H. Matthews, *Character and Symbol in Shakespeare's Plays* (Cambridge: Cambridge Univ. Press, 1962), pp. 51-65; R. Battenhouse, "*Henry V* as Heroic Comedy" in *Essays on Shakespeare . . . in Honor of Hardin Craig,* ed. R. Hosley (Columbia, Univ. of Missouri Press, 1962), pp. 169-80; H. M. Richmond, *Shakespeare's Political Plays* (New York, 1967), pp. 184-96. That the problem is an acute one is evident from the commentary of E. K. Chambers—*Shakespeare, A Survey* (London, 1925)—who asserted that Henry is "the ideal king, the divinely chosen representative and embodiment of the spirit of England" (pp. 137-38) and yet recognized in him "the prototype of the blatant modern imperialist" (p. 143); the discrepancy is noted by Robert Ornstein, *A Kingdom for a Stage* (Cambridge, Mass.: Harvard Univ. Press, 1972), p. 177.

[5] After King Philip IV of France had been succeeded by his three sons, each of whom in turn died without issue, the French then chose as their ruler the son of Philip IV's younger brother. The new king was challenged by Edward III, the son of Philip's only daughter Isabella, on the ground that the law of primogeniture gave him a prior claim to the French throne. For an Elizabethan dramatic treatment of this claim and the ensuing war, see *Edward III,* repr. in *The Shakespeare Apocrypha* (Oxford: Oxford Univ. Press, 1908), pp. 67-101; the pertinent genealogical details are presented in I. i. 1-50, pp. 69-70. It is interesting to note that *The Famous Victories of Henry V,* a play well known to Shakespeare, likewise makes it clear that Henry V's claim to France came to him through Edward III's mother, Isabella.

[6] The illogic of citing the example of the French usurpers is noted by Goddard (p. 221) and Battenhouse (pp. 173-74).

[7] Thus, E. M. W. Tillyard, *Shakespeare's History Plays* (London, 1944), pp. 309-11.

[8] For views that Henry's handling of the situation demonstrates his kingly qualities, see Walter, pp. xvi-xxv; Reese, p. 327; Keeton, pp. 282-83. Unfavorable views of Henry's treatment of the conspirators are expressed by Goddard, pp. 228-31; Matthew, p. 55; Richmond, pp. 181-82.

[9] A brief example of the mirror technique is provided by the scene in which Bardolph, Pistol, and Nym—thieves in England and looters in France—are dawdling near the walls of the besieged city of Harfleur. Their intention in France, in Pistol's words, is to act "like horse-leeches, my boys, / To suck, to suck, the very blood to suck" (II. iii. 58-59). The scene begins with Bardolph's ineffectual exhortation to his companions, "On, on, on, on, on! To the breach, to the breach" (III. ii. 1-2); it ends with their boy's comments on the utter dishonesty of the three men (III. ii. 29-57). Coming as this does right after the blood-tingling speech which Henry V makes to his troops at the same siege, "Once more into the breach, dear friends, once more" (III. i), the mirror-scene can hardly fail to reinforce doubts as to the propriety of Henry V's presence in France.

[10] The image has ironic implications, since honey soon cloys. It is precisely this that Henry IV has in mind when he reproves Hal and likens him to Richard II as a self-indulgent man who, "being daily swallowed by men's eyes, / They surfeited with honey and began / To loathe the taste of sweetness" (*I Henry IV*, III. ii. 70-72).

[11] Shakespeare's source, Holinshed's *Chronicles* (2nd ed., 1587), mistakenly says that Edmund Mortimer was proclaimed "heire apparant"; see *Narrative and Dramatic Sources of Shakespeare*, ed. G. Bullough (New York: Harcourt, Brace, 1962), IV, 184. In point of fact, the man proclaimed heir-*presumptive* was Roger Mortimer, fourth Earl of March. The error is unimportant: when Roger died before King Richard, his rights as heir-presumptive passed to his son Edmund.

[12] For recent discussions of the Elizabethan view that orderly succession to the crown went by primogeniture, see Sigurd Burkhardt, *Shakespearean Meanings* (Princeton: Princeton Univ. Press, 1968), pp. 167-68; Keeton, pp. 251-57.

[13] It is strange that modern editors of the play, in listing the *dramatis personae,* identify York (who speaks a mere two lines) as "cousin to the king," but list Cambridge separately and without a similar description. Strictly speaking, York and Cambridge were first cousins to Bolingbroke and thus second cousins to Henry V.

[14] Bullough, IV, 386. The real motive is noted briefly by various editors, including J. D. Wilson and J. H. Walter.

[15] Bullough, IV, 386.

[16] Goddard, p. 229.

[17] According to Tillyard, p. 238, Daniel "was in high repute just before Shakespeare began his second his-torical tetralogy. . . . " Daniel sets forth Cambridge's motivation—the replacement of Henry V by the childless Earl of March, thereby assuring that the crown would descend to his own heirs—in Book IV, st. 26-38 (or Bk. V, st. 24-36 in the edition of 1609). See *The Civil Wars of Samuel Daniel,* ed. Laurence Michel (New Haven: Yale Univ. Press, 1958), pp. 183-87.

[18] Abundant evidence of this popularity is provided by the numerous quarto editions of the histories, both pirated and legitimate, as well as contemporary allusions: for the latter, see E. K. Chambers, *William Shakespeare* (Oxford: Oxford Univ. Press, 1930), II, 188, 205, 233, 326-27.

[19] The captive Edmund Mortimer (married to Glendower's daughter and brother-in-law to Hotspur) was actually an uncle of the Edmund Mortimer who was Earl of March and heir to the rights of the Duke of Clarence. Holinshed confuses the two, and Shakespeare follows suit; but again, the error is dramatically unimportant.

[20] Bullough, III (1960), 47.

[21] See E. K. Chambers, *The Elizabethan Stage* (Oxford: Oxford Univ. Press, 1923), III, 306-7. The play was revived in 1602; quarto editions appeared in 1600 and 1619. The text is reprinted in *The Shakespeare Apocrypha,* pp. 127-64.

[22] That the authors of *Oldcastle* were writing with *Henry V* (as well as *Henry IV*) in mind is indicated by some unmistakable echoes in their counterblast: for example, the passage in which Harpoole makes the Sumner eat the Bishop's warrant (*Oldc.,* II. i. 56-86) imitates that in which Fluellen makes Pistol eat the leek (V. i); the pre-battle gambling scene where King Harry, in disguise, argues with Sir John of Wrotham (*Oldc.,* IV. i. 51-152) parallels the pre-battle scene where Shakespeare's disguised king disputes with Williams (IV. i); and the denunciation of Cobham as a traitor by the Bishop and King Harry (*Oldc.,* IV. ii. 54-84) recalls the denunciation of Scroop by Shakespeare's king (II. ii).

[23] *King Henry V,* ed. J. Dover Wilson (New Cambridge Shakespeare; Cambridge: Cambridge Univ. Press, 1947). p. 140.

[24] Matthew, p. 35.

[25] Bullough, IV, 384-85.

[26] Ibid., 386. That the Yorkist Earl of Cambridge accepted aid from the French in his abortive bid to unseat the king is hardly surprising: so did the Lancastrian Earl of Richmond, in his successful attempt to overthrow the last Yorkist monarch (*Richard III,* IV. iv. 523, V. iii. 315-36). Furthermore, like Cambridge (on

behalf of the Yorkists), Richmond claimed the throne in virtue of descent from Edward III in the female line.

[27] Bullough, IV, 386.

[28] Battenhouse believes, pp. 174-75, that Henry is "blindly" unaware of the weakness in his position—unaware that in claiming to inherit through the female line in France, he is undermining his position in denying Mortimer's right to inherit through the female line in England; but to assume that Henry is really blind, rather than diplomatically so, is to deny his obviously high degree of intelligence.

[29] Bolingbroke's deposition of Richard II is likewise characterized, by the Queen, as "a second fall of cursed man" (*R2*, III. iv. 73-77), and Richard identifies himself with Christ when he talks of being delivered to his sour cross (IV. i. 239-42).

[30] Robert L. Kelly, "Shakespeare's Scroops and the 'Spirit of Cain'," *SQ*, 20 (1969), 79. Earlier in the essay, p. 73, Kelly argues that Scroop and his uncle, the Archbishop of York in *1* and *2 Henry IV*, "stand for Satanic evil under an appearance of piety. . . . The evil symbolized by these men, having no apparent source in motives of greed, ambition, or vengeance, is ultimately inexplicable[!], and all the more difficult to detect and root out."

[31] Bullough, IV, 384.

[32] The sinfulness of supporting the Lancastrian usurper is emphasized not only in Richard II's public and admittedly partisan denunciation of the heinous offense committed by North umberland and other adherents of the new regime (*Richard II*, IV. i. 232-42) but also in Hotspur's private admission that the supporters of Bolingbroke share in his crime of "murderous subornation" (*1 Henry IV*, I. iii. 160-79).

[33] For a brief discussion of the evidence that Shakespeare himself believed in the justice of the Mortimer-Yorkist claim, see Keeton, p. 257.

[34] Erasmus (cited by Walter, p. xvii) notes that it is good for a Christian monarch to marry, but points out that marriage for the sake of an alliance is liable to create further strife.

David Scott Kastan (essay date 1982)

SOURCE: "'The King is a Good King, but it must be as it may': History, Heroism, and *Henry V*," in *Shakespeare and the Shapes of Time*, University Press of New England, 1982, pp. 56-76.

[*In the essay below, Kastan argues that Henry's moral certitude prevents him from questioning the justice of*

his cause or permitting anyone else to challenge it. The critic maintains that the king is convinced that God is on his side and that the war against France is legally as well as divinely sanctioned, and so he ignores or suppresses any suggestion of moral ambiguity or complexity.]

As Spenser and Milton understood so well, the reformation forced a significant revaluation of the traditional ideas and images of heroism. Human strength must be a problematic virtue in a world shaped by and charged with the will of God, but even more so when faith rather than deeds is understood as the source of justification. The Pelagian thrust of heroic action was countered by St Paul's insistence that

> by grace are ye saued through faith, and that not of your selues: it is the gifte of God, Not of workes, lest any man shulde boaste him self.
>
> (*Ephesians* 2:8-9)

In Book I of *The Faerie Queene*, Spenser sounds the Pauline theme, warning against the 'boasts of fleshly might', since

> If any strength we haue, it is to ill,
> But all the good is Gods, both power and eke will.
>
> (I.10.1)

Similarly, Milton's Gabriel reminds Satan of the true nature of creatural power:

> I know thy strength, and thou know'st mine,
> Neither our own, but giv'n; what folly then
> To boast what Arms can do.
>
> (*Paradise Lost*, IV.1006-8)

Both poets, however, see that Protestantism demands not a repudiation of heroic ideals but a redefinition, and each succeeds in re-establishing the claims of heroic achievement. Spenser's poem records and rehearses the heroism of fallen man struggling to be re-educated 'in the virtues which he lost with the Fall',[1] while Milton's celebrates 'the better fortitude / Of Patience and Heroic Martyrdom' (IX.30-1). The heroic image is validated and revitalized by locating it firmly within a matrix of Christian history. The 'adventurous act' may occasion wonder and admiration, but it has significant meaning only in a world where God's love of man—the grace that can authenticate and guarantee heroic value—and man's love of God—the faith that can animate and direct heroic energy—are each axiomatic.

In the world of Shakespeare's history plays, however, grace and faith are not axiomatic. Their open-ended structures, as I have argued, stand as dramatic challenge to the providential assumptions of most Tudor historiography. Here history demands to be understood as secular history—history denied any participation in the economy of salvation. In such a world, heroic energy and moral purpose necessarily lack authority and direction. The achievements of 'the righteous Artegall', in book five of *The Faerie Queene,* are limited, vulnerable to irony and time; yet, for Spenser, even in an age of iron, the sanctions upon which action rests are simple and unambiguous: 'All creatures must obey the voice of the most high' (V.ii.40). The histories, however, mute 'the voice of the most high', and therefore the ground of human action is uncertain and insecure. The Bastard in *King John* provides the perfect emblem of man in Shakespeare's history plays:

> I am amazed, methinks, and lose my way
> Among the thorns and dangers of this world.
> (IV.iii.140-1)

In *Henry V,* Shakespeare examines the claims of heroic achievement as they appear 'among the thorns and dangers of this world'. He satisfies our desire and need for the heroic image at the same time he allows us to see its costs and limitations. Henry is indeed a hero, but he is so only because of his willingness to deny the character of the time that mocks heroic achievement. (However, the appeal of the heroic image need not be diminished by this fact. If the destructive action of time frustrates heroic attainment, it also insures the value of the heroic image. Against the flux of time, the heroic image functions as an at least psychologically necessary assertion of human dignity and worth.) Henry proceeds always as if he acts on a stage filled with sacred time and purpose— that is, as if he has succeeded in 'redeeming time' (*1 Henry IV,* I.ii.205)—but the open ends of the play themselves declare his presence in a more secular theatre. Time charged with the will of God is benign and restorative, but the open-ended history play frames the time only of 'this breathing world' (*Richard III,* I.i.217)—a time that continues relentlessly, denying men 'surety', 'hope', and 'stay'.[2] Though England under Henry reaches its greatest medieval glory, his reign, as Shakespeare so clearly realizes, brings no lasting changes. Interestingly, this is the judgment of most modern historians. A. R. Myers writes that 'he won unity for his realm and glory for himself at the price of immediate misery for France and eventual confusion for England'.[3] And Harold Hutchison, who allows that Henry provided 'a heroic myth for generations to come', condemns 'the barrenness of his glory and the futility of his achievement'.[4]

Unlike their modern counterparts, historians in the sixteenth century were willing to isolate the victorious acts of Henry V from the temporal context in which they occur. From such a vantage point, they saw only the peerless warrior-king, and it is their uncritically heroic conception of Henry that informs the voice of the Chorus. Echoing the language of Hall and Holin-

shed, the Chorus sees Henry as 'the mirror of all Christian kings' (II.cho.6) and the 'star of England' (epi.6). Even scholars who are sharply critical of Henry recognize the Chorus' celebration of 'this grace of kings' (II.cho.28). Indeed, the irony that they find in Shakespeare's treatment is located precisely in the disparity between the heroic promise of the Chorus and the action delivered by the play. 'Through the Choruses', writes Harold Goddard, 'the playwright gives us the popular idea of his hero. In the play, the poet tells the truth about him.'[5]

Yet the dynamics of Shakespeare's multiple focus are more complex than Goddard suggests. Shakespeare does not so simply play off the myth and the man, for the 'truth' about Henry includes though certainly is not identical with the heroic conception of popular account. Shakespeare acknowledges this partial truth in the lines of the historical plot, giving the history of the reign virtually mythic shape and significance essentially by virtue of three omissions from the chronicles' narrative.[6] First, the anti-Lancastrian rebellions and the Lollard activity that dominated the first eighteen months of Henry's reign are ignored in Shakespeare's play, replacing the reality of a divided and distrustful country with the illusion of a unified England unquestioningly committed to the will of its king.[7] Second, the events of the French war are selected and compressed in such a manner that the great victory at Agincourt leads directly to the peace at Troyes, omitting the intervening four years of intensive campaigning that brought about a peace in 1420. Finally, the peace settlement in Shakespeare's play concludes the fighting and looks toward a time of 'Christian-like accord' (V.ii.337). Holinshed, on the contrary, writes of the Dauphin Charles'[8] refusal to accept the peace terms, forcing Henry to return to France. This subsequent invasion was not as successful as the first, and in 1422 Henry died, having failed to subdue the stubborn Dauphin.[9]

Thus, the broad outline of Shakespeare's dramatic version of the military history shows England's Harry leading a small band of loyal and brave soldiers against a much larger force of arrogant and decadent Frenchmen. The astounding victory at Agincourt ends the threat from France and confirms England's military and moral pre-eminence. The formulation is undeniably a cliché of propagandistic plotting, but it serves perfectly to reveal the play's transformation of history into patriotic myth.

Shakespeare, however, forces an audience to recognize the instability of the shape of this restructured history. Certainly we are allowed (in fact, made) to see and glory in the great military and political successes of Henry's rule—and no reading of the play will suffice that does not respond to these as significant and substantial achievements—but the mythic outlines dissolve in the more complex temporal (and moral) context that the play provides. We are made to feel the scope and appeal of Henry's famous victories, but we see simultaneously what D. A. Traversi calls 'certain contradictions, human and moral, inherent in the notion of a successful king'.[10] We see Henry as a hero, but we see more clearly than ever Henry does exactly what this means.

After the Chorus disingenuously laments the inadequacy of artistry and stage that prevents more perfect realization of 'this great accompt' (I.cho.17), the scene reveals not the anticipated heroic posture of the English king but the political manoeuverings of a worldly church. The Bishops of Ely and Canterbury, concerned lest they 'lose the better half of [their] possession' (I.i.8), search for ways to 'resist' the enactment of a bill that would give to the king 'all the temporal lands which men devout / By testament have given to the church' (I.i.9-10). An audience not familiar with the chronicles must wonder what this has to do with the promised confrontation of 'two mighty monarchies' (I.cho.20). Holinshed, for his part, makes it clear that the impetus for the French war emerges from the desire of the churchmen to prevent the Leicester parliament from enacting the confiscatory law:

> they thought best to trie if they might moue with some sharpe inuention, that he [Henry] should not regard the importunate petitions of the commons wherevpon on a daie in the parlement, Henrie Chichelie, Archbishop of Canturburie, made a pithie oration, wherein he declared, how not onelie the duchies of Anjou and Maine, and the countrie of Gascoigne, were by undoubted title apperteining to the king, as to the lawfull and onelie heire of the same; but also the whole realme of France, as heire to his great grandfather king Edward the third.[11]

Apologists for Henry have argued that Shakespeare does not follow the pattern indicated by Holinshed. 'It is clear from his text', writes Dover Wilson, 'that before the Archbishop takes any hand in the affair at all, not only has the whole question of Henry's title in France been broached' but the king has 'long since decided for an invasion. . . . It is not the Archbishop who sets the king awork, but the king the Archbishop'.[12]

Yet if this account is accurate one may well wonder why the scene exists at all. At best it is irrelevant, and at worst it leads to a serious misvaluing of the action that follows. Wilson, however, has in fact overstated the differences between Shakespeare's account and that of Holinshed, for we can find in the first scene of *Henry V* indication that, as in Holinshed, the French war is strategically urged by the churchmen to prevent passage of the expropriation bill.[13] Ely's question about the king's inclination towards the bill elicits Canterbury's revealing reply:

> He seems indifferent,
> Or rather swaying more upon our part
> Than cherishing th' exhibiters against us;
> *For I have made an offer to his majesty,*
> Upon our spiritual Convocation
> And *in regard of causes now in hand*
> *Which I have opened to his grace at large*
> *As touching France,* to give a greater sum
> Than ever at one time the clergy yet
> Did to his predecessors part withal.
> 　　　　　　(1.i.72-81, emphasis mine)

The king, at least in the archbishop's account, sways to the churchmen's part because of ('For'—the conjunction that Jonson calls the 'cause renderer')[14] the 'offer' to finance an operation which the Archbishop himself has 'opened to his grace at large / As touching France'. Though this discussion between the king and the Archbishop of Canterbury has taken place in the undramatized time before the events which open the play, we cannot say with Dover Wilson that the question of Henry's title has been raised 'before the Archbishop takes any hand in the affair at all'. Certainly, Canterbury's refutation of the Salic law merely sanctions a course of action that Henry already favours, but an audience has been made aware that earlier negotiations have taken place. What remains unresolved (and unresolvable) is the issue of whether Henry's 'thoughts concerning us and France' (1.ii.6) occasion or are occasioned by the bishops' offer to finance the war. In either case, the scene seems designed to prevent an audience from feeling unreserved patriotic emotions. Shakespeare deliberately complicates our response by evoking this undramatized past. Our search for the ground of action is frustrated. The play makes us aware of the difficulty of recovering motives from 'the dark backward and abysm of time' (*The Tempest*, 1.ii.50).

The objection may be raised that too much importance is being placed on verbal subtleties not evident in performance, yet the reply must be that dramatically no other interpretation seems possible. In *The Famous Victories,* well before the archbishop ever speaks, an audience hears of the king's 'embassage' to tell France that 'Harry of England hath sent for the Crowne, and Harry of England will have it' (ll. 723-5). Similarly, the temporal ordering of Holinshed gave Shakespeare the opportunity to follow the heroic promise of the opening Chorus with Henry's passionate defiance of the Dauphin, for in the Chronicles the insult precedes the convocation of the Leicester parliament of 1414.[15] Shakespeare chooses instead to ignore the precedents and to place the scene with the calculating bishops between the Chorus and Henry's decision to go to war. The logical fallacy, *post hoc ergo propter hoc,* is often a dramatic truth, and the interposed scene can only serve to raise doubts about 'the well hallowed cause' that motivates the war.

The lustre of the celebrated war will certainly be tarnished if it is understood not 'on the high moral grounds of righting lost wrongs and regaining lost rights'[16] but as the self-serving device of a Church desperate to retain its wealth. The contrary has, of course, been argued by those who hold that the archbishop's sanction itself establishes that the war has been righteously undertaken;[17] but the archbishop's confirmation of Henry's right should not provide much comfort to Henry's uncritical supporters. If an audience loses the thread of the labyrinthine speech, the archbishop's assurance that the complex proof is 'as clear as is the summer's sun' (I.ii.86) must seem a laughable effort to rescue the argument from the appearance of sophistry which it almost inevitably assumes. If, on the other hand, an audience closely follows Canterbury's argument, Henry fares little better. Once the principle of 'claiming from the female' (I.ii.92) is affirmed, Henry's right not only to the throne of France but also to that of England itself can be challenged, for Mortimer's descent from Philippa (daughter of Lionel, Duke of Clarence) has undeniable primacy in the line of Edward III from which both claims originate.

In either case, Canterbury is of demonstrably insufficient moral stature to fulfil the role that many would thrust upon him. He is an all-too-worldly prelate whose opposition to the bill of confiscation reveals his repudiation of such traditional church responsibilities as the 'relief of lazars' and the establishment of 'almshouses right well supplied' (I.i.15,17). Henry may 'hear, note, and believe in heart / that what you [i.e. the archbishop] speak is in your conscience washed/ As pure as sin with baptism' (I.ii.30-2), but an audience, having witnessed the first scene, will of necessity be more critical.

One might argue that Henry is in no way tainted by these considerations. Indeed Charles Barber claims that 'the churchmen may have politic reasons for encouraging the war, but for the king all ulterior motives are excluded'.[18] Yet if this is true then Henry is no more than an unwitting pawn of the bishops' policy, scarcely an appropriate role for one who Barber maintains is intended to 'represent the aspirations of the Tudor monarchy'.[19] And if Henry is not used by the bishops but in fact is using them, certainly we are no closer to the 'ideal monarch' that Barber seeks in the play.

J. H. Walter, like Barber uncritical in his praise of Henry, would rescue the king from this skeptical line of argument by asserting that 'to portray Henry as the dupe of two scheming prelates, or as a crafty politician skillfully concealing his aims with the aid of an unscrupulous archbishop is not consistent with claiming at the same time that he is an ideal king'.[20] Surely he is right; one cannot reconcile a view of Henry as pawn or politician with a view of him as an ideal king. Nevertheless, what must be reconsidered is not the first part of his formulation, as Walter would have it, but the second. Shakespeare's Henry is not an ideal king at all, merely a successful one.

This is a distinction that perhaps is foreign to the conqueror drama of the 1580s, where soldier-kings commonly glory, as Othello once did, in 'the big wars / That make ambition virtue' (III.iii.349-50). In these plays the ethic of heroic achievement blurs the differences between the ideal and the successful. For Shakespeare, on the other hand, the differences are always clear and crucial. Though shadowy creatures such as the gracious Edward in *Macbeth* or the virtuous Richmond in *Richard III* appear to suggest ideal patterns of kingship, they do not so much exist *in* as exist *in spite of* the historical world Shakespeare depicts. The histories consistently reveal his awareness of the matrix of human fallibility in which all political action is grounded. Indeed, in *Henry V,* it is by allowing an audience to see the uncertain genesis of the famous victories that Shakespeare begins his exploration of the necessarily imperfect man that lies beneath Ceremony's 'intertissued robe of gold and pearl' (IV.i.248).

The opening scenes of the play insist upon the exercise of a moral pressure that the Elizabethan conqueror drama suppresses. We are made to ask, with a rigor greater than Henry's own, whether he may 'with right and conscience make this claim' (I.ii.96); and though the play's self-conscious evocation of anterior time prevents us from answering with any real assurance, it at least forces us to recognize the inadequacy of Henry's answer in his characteristic idiom of moral certainty. He may be confident of 'his cause being just and his quarrel honorable', but we must agree with the soldier Williams that 'That's more than we know' (IV.i.120-2). Almost never do wars begin where the 'wrongs' of one party alone give 'edge unto the swords / That makes such waste in brief mortality' (I.ii.27-8); and surely the French war, justified by a genealogical claim that has but questionable applicability to Henry and which Edward III had himself relinquished in the terms of the treaty of Bretigny (1360),[21] is not the rare exception.

Henry, however, does not wish to be confronted with ethical considerations that might give pause to his heroic energy. He wants to be assured that the war is but the extension of his 'rightful arm in a well-hallowed cause' (I.ii.294), yet the moral probity that he apparently seeks is perhaps less an indication that he is Shakespeare's ideal king than that he is Shakespeare's idealistic king. His vision of the world is marked by an insistent moral idealism in which the truth of almost every issue 'stands off as gross / As black and white' (II.ii.103-4).

Recognition of this tendency suggests a possible solution to a long-standing puzzle. Critics have often wondered about Henry's silence at Cambridge's confession that

> the gold of France did not seduce,
> Although I did admit it as a motive
> The sooner to effect what I intended.
>
> (II.ii.155-7)

They gloss the traitor's actual intent easily enough by reference to the historical events that Shakespeare recalls in *1 Henry VI* (II.v.63-92). There he writes that Cambridge 'Levied an army, weening to redeem/ And have installed [Mortimer] in the diadem'. For his rebellion Cambridge 'was beheaded. Thus the Mortimers/ In whom the title rested, were suppressed'. Yet though Cambridge's allusion is easily enough annotated, the reason why Henry should fail to respond to this hint of the dynastic controversy or even why the hint is given at all has been more elusive. Surely it is inadequate to argue that Henry's silence shows Shakespeare's unwillingness to raise the issue of the Lancastrian usurpation.[22] If this were so, there could be no reason (and much reason not) to have Cambridge admit to any motive other than 'the gold of France'. However, as it stands the episode accurately reveals the existence and limitations of Henry's idealism. The absolutism of his moral vision is achieved and maintained only by radical simplification of experience. If he does not react to Cambridge's allusion, it is because to do so would be to allow complexity and contradiction to intrude into his universe.

Cambridge's treachery, which might serve to remind Henry of the weak foundation on which the Lancastrian succession rests, never troubles the English king. The abortive 'revolt' seems unequivocal in its implications—indeed to Henry it seems 'Another fall of man' (II.ii.142). Henry ignores the disquieting reminder in Cambridge's confession, for in it rests a challenge to the heroic posture he adopts. Having worked to assure himself of the unambiguous moral character of his undertaking, Henry will not even hear the words that must qualify the moral authority he claims. Heroic action demands unconditional moral supports, and Henry allows nothing to affect his assertive spirit.

Whatever surprise and disappointment the treachery occasions quickly fades before Henry's certainty of the 'glorious' future before him:[23]

> We doubt not now
> But every rub is smoothed on our way.
>
> (II.ii.187-8)

For Henry, the plot against his crown is merely an obstacle inconveniently 'lurking in our way/To hinder our beginnings' (II.ii.186-7). Now that it has been exposed, more than ever is he confident of the justice of his cause and the success of his 'enterprise':

> We doubt not of a fair and lucky war,
> Since God so graciously has brought to light
> This dangerous treason.
>
> (II.ii.184-6)

Rather than disturbing his conscience, as well it might, the incident as Henry understands it confirms his moral certitude: God has seen fit to reveal the treachery, therefore God must approve of the war.

The simplistic moral assurance that Henry takes from this episode is precisely that which gives rise to the discomforting excess of his speech at Harfleur. Convinced of the sanctity of his undertaking, Henry can only see the resistance of the city as blasphemous opposition to his legitimate presence. Harfleur is 'guilty in defense' (III.iii.43) and thus deserves to suffer all that he threatens.

> What is it then to me if impious war,
> Arrayed in flames to the prince of fiends,
> Do with his smirched complexion all fell
>   feats
> Enlinked to waste and desolation?
> What is't to me, when you yourselves are
>   cause . . .
>
> (III.iii.15-19)

The destruction of the city is of course avoided as Harfleur yields, and Shakespeare, ignoring Holinshed, has Henry order Exeter to 'use mercy to them all' (III.iii.54).[24] Yet even without its fulfilment, the imaginative force of the threat is profoundly disturbing. Modern editors have attempted to justify the speech by reference to contemporary military practice and the authority of *Deuteronomy* 20,[25] but such extra-literary explanations ignore the moral index provided by the poetry. The Deuteronomic law-giver maintains that a city 'if it wil make no peace' may be besieged and sacked after its deliverance:

> thou shalt smite all the males thereof with the edge of the sworde.
>
> Onely the women, and the children, and the cattel, and all that is in the citie, *euen* all the spoile thereof shalt thou take vnto thy self, and shalt eat the spoile of thine enemies, which the Lord thy God hathe giuen thee.
>
> (*Deuteronomy* 20:13-14, Geneva translation)

This, however, is far from the apocalyptic fury of Henry's threat. 'Look to see', Henry warns the citizens of Harfleur,

> The blind and bloody soldier with foul hand
> Defile the locks of your shrill-shrieking
>   daughters;
> Your fathers taken by the silver beards,

And their most reverend heads dashed to the
  walls;
Your naked infants spitted upon pikes,
Whiles the mad mothers with their howls
  confused
Do break the clouds, as did the wives of
  Jewry
At Herod's bloody-hunting slaughtermen.

(III.iii.34-41)

The ferocity of the minatory outburst unquestionably
disturbs the received idea of Henry's heroic stature.
He threatens literally to out-Herod Herod, and the
speech manifests the same blustering sadism and self-
righteousness of the Herod of the Corpus Christi play.

Shakespeare's procedure here is, to say the least, unusual. He suppresses Holinshed's mention of the
plunder of Harfleur, replacing it in the play with
Henry's order for leniency. Yet equally unmindful
of his source, Shakespeare places the savage threats
in Henry's mouth instead of following Holinshed's
account of the chivalrous conduct of the English
before the city.[26] The effects of these manipulations
of the source seemingly cut in two opposing directions. On the one hand, Henry's order to 'use mercy'
works to confirm his own account that he is 'no
tyrant, but a Christian king' (I.ii.242), but the speech
at the city's gates suggests precisely the reverse.
Both the brutal speech and the merciful treatment of
Harfleur must be viewed together, however, and both
may be seen as behaviour consistent with a man supremely confident of his moral authority. The terrible
threats are not evidence that Henry 'does not see the
horrors of war feelingly',[27] but evidence that he does
not see the moral complexity of this war at all. Convinced of his legitimacy and thus of the unlawfulness
of the city's resistance, Henry can do no other than
enter the city or reduce it to 'ashes' (III.iii.9). 'France
being ours', says Henry earlier, 'we'll bend it to our
awe/Or break it all to pieces' (I.ii.225-6). When
Harfleur's governor yields to Henry's 'soft mercy'
(III.iii.48), the vision of the English king is confirmed.
'It is pointless even to wonder', as Michael Manheim
writes, 'whether Henry would carry out his threats at
Harfleur. It never crosses his mind or anyone else's
that the citizens would resist his challenge.'[28]

Henry's confidence, complete however reductive, in his
moral authority also dominates the scenes at Agincourt.
He is unshaken by the observation of the soldier
Michael Williams that 'if the cause be not good, the
king himself hath a heavy reckoning to make' (IV.i.127-
8), for he has been assured that his cause is indeed
'good'. Yet oddly he fails to provide the answer that
Williams seeks. He might have asserted, as Richmond
does at Bosworth, that 'God and our good cause fight
upon our side' (*Richard III*, v.iii.241), but instead he
evades the direction of the soldier's probing:

So, if a son that is by his father sent about
merchandise do sinfully miscarry upon the sea,
the imputation of his wickedness, by your rule,
should be imposed upon his father that sent him;
or if a servant, under his master's command
transporting a sum of money, be assailed by
robbers and die in many irreconciled iniquities,
you may call the business of the master the author
of the servant's damnation.

(IV.i.139-46)

The analogies fail to convince, for what Henry takes
for granted, 'the business of the master', is precisely
that which Williams questions.

Williams will readily agree with Henry that 'every
man that dies ill, the ill upon his own head—the king
is not to answer it' (IV.i.176-7), but this is not the
thrust of the soldier's questioning. Williams has asked
not about the king's responsibility for 'the particular
endings' of his fighting men but about the king's
responsibility for the justice of the cause for which
they fight. But to this Henry has no answer.[29] Uncritically committed to the absolute probity of his
undertaking, Henry will not permit a thorough hearing of this issue. Just as he did with the traitor Cambridge, Henry responds selectively, and what might
frustrate his heroic energy remains unaddressed. Here
he speaks not to the question of the king's terrible
responsibility but to those concerns which are to his
mind more immediate to a fighting man about to enter
battle: 'Every subject's duty is the king's, but every
subject's soul is his own. Therefore should every soldier in the wars do as every sick man in his bed—
wash every mote out of his conscience' (IV.i.166-70).

The 'little touch of Harry in the night' (IV.cho.47)
primarily serves to reveal Henry's unwillingness to
confront the moral challenge his soldiers offer, and
the soliloquy that follows indicates how deeply internalized that evasion is. The speech 'Upon the king'
gives no more evidence than the interview with Williams and Bates of serious moral struggle.[30] It is a
rather conventional account of the 'polished perturba-
tion' and 'Golden care' (*2 Henry IV,* IV.v.22) which,
as prince, Henry recognized in the crown, exceptional
perhaps only in the splendour with which Henry invests the very 'Ceremony' he derides.[31] Henry laments
that the burdens of kingship deny him the easy rest of
even the most 'wretched slave' (IV.i.254), but no moral
dilemma contributes to these burdens. Even in this
rare moment when we see and hear the private man
that exists behind 'thrice-gorgeous ceremony' (IV.i.252),
Henry reveals the same radically simplified moral
perspective that marks his public behaviour. 'The terrible responsibilities of his office' for Henry do not
stem from any recognition of the moral demands it
makes. His uneasy sleep results only from the constant
'watch the king keeps to maintain the peace' (IV.i.269).

He is able to deny the office the tragic moral complexity that Shakespeare so clearly sees. If he knows that 'his ceremonies laid by, in his nakedness he appears but a man' (IV.i.101-2), he finds neither contradiction nor ambiguity arising from the dislocation between the private man and the public mask he wears. For Henry, although kingship imposes awesome obligations, its moral claims are remarkably uncomplicated. He must 'maintain the peace', and, almost incredibly yet entirely characteristically, he sees no tension between this charge and his presence in France at the moment he speaks the words.[32]

Were it not for the soliloquy, our twentieth-century political sensibilities might lead us to praise Henry as a realistic and pragmatic ruler who, if not an example of kingship such 'as it should be', is at least an example of kingship 'as it might best be' given the nature of fallible humanity and the political world in which he must function.[33] Indeed several recent critics have seen Henry as 'a Machiavel conceived of in the happiest terms Shakespeare knows',[34] successful because of his ability to create images of authority that obscure his human weaknesses. Yet, were Henry intended to be this Machiavellian monarch, the soliloquy should reveal a mind conscious of the trade-off of moral excellence for effective political leadership. In fact this moment of self-revelation suggests something quite different. Though some have argued that Henry's 'moral sense is the servant of his policy',[35] the soliloquy discloses the exact reverse: Henry's policy is always the servant of his unconditional moral sense. He is not the pragmatist willing to accept the moral loss that must accompany political success but the idealist who, in conceiving of his responsibility as no more and no less than the maintenance of peace, tries to deny that any such loss takes place at all.

Nowhere is this more clear than in Henry's prayer before Agincourt, for his petition to the 'God of battles' (IV.i.275) indicates no awareness of the moral vulnerability of his position. He has not been led by Williams' skeptical argument to re-examine his 'right and conscience'. Certain that both are untainted, he asks only that God 'think not upon the fault/[his] father made in compassing the crown' (IV.i.279-80). The justice of the war in France remains unquestioned, as Henry piously catalogues his acts of expiation for his father's sinful disruption of the Angevin line fifteen years earlier.

Yet if Henry's prayer reveals his unchanged confidence in the moral propriety of his presence in France, his speech to Westmoreland reveals significantly less confidence in the military consequences of that presence. He perceives the desperate situation of his outnumbered forces, although, perhaps surprisingly, he is unwilling to take comfort, as Richard II does, in any thought that 'God omnipotent/Is mustering in his clouds

on our behalf/Armies of pestilence' (*Richard II*, III.iii.85-7). To make such a claim is to risk the very examination of the justice of his cause that Henry has worked so hard to prevent anyone—even himself—from undertaking. Perhaps to preclude any such inquiry or merely because he knows that 'The Goddes do help the doers',[36] he appeals to the pride not the piety of his small band of Englishmen:

> gentlemen in England now abed
> Shall think themselves accursed they were not here,
> And hold their manhoods cheap whiles any speaks
> That fought with us upon Saint Crispin's day.
> (IV.iii.64-7)

Led by their inspiring leader, the English soldiers, of course, win a decisive victory. When, asks Henry, 'was ever known so great and little loss/On one part and on th' other?' (IV.viii.105-6). Indeed, Shakespeare presents the English achievement at Agincourt as little short of miraculous. Chronicles and play agree that this was the great military achievement of medieval England, but the chronicles, unlike the play, emphasize that success was in part gained by 'a politike inuention'.

> He [Henry] caused stakes bound with iron sharpe at both ends of the length of fiue or six foot to be pitched before the archers, and of ech side the footmen like an hedge, to the intent that if the barded horsses ran rashlie vpon them, they might shortlye be gored and destroied.[37]

In *The Famous Victories of Henry V*, the same fact is given prominence. Henry is shown ordering the stakes deployed, and this strategy is the *only* aspect of the battle that elicits comment from John Cobler and Robin Pewterer:

> John: But, Robin, didst thou see what a pollicie the king had? To see how the french-men were kild with the stakes of the trees!
>
> Robin: I, Iohn, there was a braue pollicie.[38]

Shakespeare, on the contrary, omits all reference to this 'braue pollicie'. His Henry pointedly claims that victory came

> without stratagem
> But in plain shock and even play of battle.
> (IV.viii.103-4)

The defeat of the French against the 'fearful odds' (IV.iii.5) that the English face would perhaps be explicable if mention were made of the superior military tactics of the 'happy few', but Shakespeare seems deliberately to emphasize the improbable nature of the victory.

The casualty report reinforces the miraculous aspect of Agincourt. The French, as in the chronicles, are said to have lost ten thousand men, while the English lose only

> Edward the Duke of York, the Earl of
>   Suffolk,
> Sir Richard Ketly, Davy Gam, esquire;
> None else of name; and of all other men
> But five-and-twenty.
>
> (IV.viii.98-101)

This is almost an exact transcription from Holinshed, but it omits the rest of the sentence where Holinshed writes that this is only 'as some do report'.[39] Hall, even more incredulous, adds to a similar account, 'if you will geue credite to suche as write miracles'.[40] Both historians are well aware that 'other writers of greater credit affirme, that there were slaine aboue fiue or six hundred persons'.[41]

Even at the larger figure the victory is of enormous proportion, and Shakespeare's adoption of the report of least credit (along with the omission of the fact that the English made use of the sharpened stakes) suggests that probability is here being deliberately eschewed. The credible is rejected in favour of the miraculous; the historical logic of probable cause, in favour of the poetic logic of giant-killing.

Henry, of course, claims no personal credit and is quick to acknowledge God's agency. Five times in eighteen lines he rings changes on the theme,

> O God, thy arm was here!
> And not to us, but to thy arm alone,
> Ascribe we all!
>
> (IV.viii.101-3)

This is the exact attitude of the historian Hall, who writes that God

> sent to [Henry] this glorious victory, whiche victory is almost incredible if we had not redde in thee booke of kynges that God likewise had defended and aided them that onely put their trust in hym and committed themselues to his gouernaunce.[42]

Henry has put his trust in God, or, more accurately, he at least assumes that God has put His trust in Henry.

Clearly his professions of piety are not the conventional shows of modesty that Renaissance manuals of military conduct advise,[43] yet neither are they compelling evidence of a profound and mature Christianity. Henry is unquestionably sincere, but his piety after the battle reflects his characteristic moral stance. Before Agincourt Henry does not invoke God's authority, but now he can praise God comfortably without fear of raising troublesome moral issues, for the outcome, to Henry's mind, is powerful testimony to the justice of his cause. To attribute the victory to God is to confirm the sanctity of his enterprise, and the psalms which Henry orders sung appropriately serve the moral absolutism of his vision. The sheer reiteration of Henry's claim 'that God fought for us' (IV.viii.115) may itself suggest that Shakespeare holds up Henry's piety for critical examination, but if not, certainly Fluellen's scarcely convincing, or convinced, agreement with Henry must:

> Yes, by my conscience, he did us great good.
>
> (IV.viii.116)

Henry has begun the campaign by taking assurance from the archbishop that he may 'with right and conscience make this claim', and he ends by taking assurance from God Himself that this is so. All that might contradict or even complicate such confidence Henry relentlessly suppresses. 'Knowledge', in Nietzsche's apothegm, 'kills action', and Henry carefully forestalls the death. The ironies of the archbishop's speech, the hint of dynastic controversy in Cambridge's confession, the skeptical thrust of Williams' questioning are all ignored as Henry marches swiftly and triumphantly through France. If he is Shakespeare's most successful king, he is so precisely because his uncritical moral intelligence forges the unambiguous moral environment that heroic action demands.

In *King John*, the Bastard's political and military success results from his complete awareness of the problematic moral character of time; Henry's success in this play results from his refusal to acknowledge that character. 'The scambling and unquiet time' (I.i.4) of *Henry V* has moral contours no less indistinct than those of *King John*, but Henry wilfully denies them. His heroic posture is animated and maintained by a restricted moral vision that creates images of simple and certain moral oppositions.

For this very reason, Moody Prior argues that '*Henry V* fails us because whereas the preceding [history] plays are permeated with the ambiguities and harsh dissonances of the political world, the king in this one is separated from them and is presented as politically uncontaminated'.[44] But *Henry V* does not fail us, because it is not the play that separates the king from 'the ambiguities and harsh dissonances of the political world' but the king himself. Henry V, not *Henry V*, seeks to deny the heavy moral price that political success exacts. His unconditional moral vision does not admit the tragic implications of kingship that Shakespeare explores in all the histories. Shakespeare knows well that the fallible humanity of even this 'mirror of all Christian kings' makes large the gap between the ideal and the real. 'The king is a good king', as Pistol says, 'but it must be as it may' (II.i.121).

Diana LeBlanc as Katherine and ladies-in-waiting in a scene from the 1966 Stratford Festival production of Henry V.

The final scene, however, tempts us to assent to Henry's own vision. The peace with France and the marriage with Katherine provide potent images of comic resolution. Eugene Waith observes that 'The pattern of romance asserts itself powerfully here in preparations for a marriage to reward the efforts of a hero and to symbolize the attainment of harmony'.[45] Yet clearly this is less Shakespeare's vision than Henry's own. The greatest English king sees his reign as a romance, but the greatest English playwright makes us see it as a history.

Henry knows that 'nice customs curtsy to great kings' (v.ii.260), and in the final scene he would have the nice custom of royal marriage sanctify and guarantee his conquest. Marriage indeed might serve as a powerful image of healing and harmony, as in Hall's account of 'the union of Matrimony celebrate and consummate betwene the high and myghty Prynce kyng Henry the seuenth and the Lady Elyzabeth his mooste worthy Quene'. In that marriage, Hall claims that 'al men'

may apparantly perceiue, that as by discorde great thynges decaie and fall to ruyne, so the same by concorde be reuiued and erected. In likewise also all regions whiche by deuision and discension be vexed, molested and troubled, bee by union and agrement releued, pacified, and enriched.[46]

Only Henry is 'enriched' by this marriage, however, and his territorial drive is too naked for the promised wedding to authenticate the harmony it would effect. Not God's will but Henry's dictates the marriage. 'I am content', he says imperiously to Katherine's father, 'so the maiden cities you talk of may wait on her. So the maid that stood in the way for my wish shall show me the way to my will' (v.ii.312-14). The absence of all but enforced 'concorde' prevents this union from serving as a symbol of restoration and a promise of renewal. As prince, Henry could 'drink with any tinker in his own language' (*1 Henry IV*, II.iv.18), but as king he cannot even speak with his intended wife in hers.

If we are troubled, however, Henry is not. He insists upon the romance ending that Shakespeare would disrupt. Always to Henry time appears unthreatening and providential,[47] and he has no reason to doubt that it shall bring fulfilment of the French Queen's prayer:

> God, the best maker of all marriages,
> Combine your hearts in one, your realms in
>   one!
> As man and wife, being two, are one in
>   love,
> So be there 'twixt your kingdoms such a
>   · spousal
> That never may ill office, or fell jealousy,
> Which troubles oft the bed of blessed
>   marriage,
> Thrust in between the paction of these
>   kingdoms
> To make divorce of their incorporate
>   league;
> That English may as French, French
>   Englishmen,
> Receive each other! God speak this Amen!
>   (v.ii.343-52)

But God does not 'speak this Amen' (unlike the 'Amen' He does speak to Richmond's prayer at the end of *Richard III*). If, as Exeter says, Henry 'weighs time /Even to the utmost grain' (II.iv.137-8), the sand he measures is of a character different than he thinks. Time reveals not the restorative action of romance but the destructive action of history. Henry himself, the epilogue tells us, is granted but 'small time' (epi.5), and his son, who Henry prophesied should 'go to Constantinople and take the Turk by the beard' (v.ii.203), becomes that unfortunate monarch,

> Whose state so many had the managing
> That they lost France and made his England
>   bleed.
>   (epi.11-12)

Time in the histories is inescapable and relentless. When Henry is concerned that Katherine should not love him, he is assured by Burgundy that 'maids well summered and warm kept are like flies at Bartholomew-tide . . . then they will endure handling which before would not abide looking on' (v.ii.296-300). Henry replies to this with a wisdom greater than he knows:

> This moral ties me over to time and a hot
>   summer.
>   (v.ii.300-1)

He is indeed tied to time. The open ends of the play powerfully declare this bond and declare the failure—even as they establish the appeal—of his heroic effort to deny the moral and chronological loss that existence in time demands.

Notes

[1] Maurice Evans, *Spenser's Anatomy of Heroism* (Cambridge: Cambridge University Press, 1970) p. 29. See also Paul J. Alpers, *The Poetry of* The Faerie Queene (Princeton: Princeton University Press, 1967) pp. 334 - 69.

[2] *King John,* V.vii.67-9.

[3] *England in the Late Middle Ages* (8th ed.; Baltimore: Penguin, 1972) p. 122.

[4] *Henry V* (New York: John Day, 1967) p. 225.

[5] *The Meaning of Shakespeare* (Chicago: University of Chicago Press, 1951) p. 218.

[6] The anonymous play, *The Famous Victories of Henry V,* makes these same omissions in dealing with the reign.

[7] The treason of Grey, Scroop, and Cambridge is here the exception that proves the rule. Cambridge's enigmatic hint of a 'motive' other than the 'gilt of France' is left undeveloped, the dynastic controversy is ignored, and the treason is viewed as a military device of the French designed solely 'To hinder our beginnings' (II.ii. 187).

[8] Historically, three sons of Charles VI, Lewis, John, and Charles, successively became Dauphin during the period covered by the play. Shakespeare compresses all three into a single, nameless 'Dauphin'.

[9] *Chronicles,* 3. Sig. 318ᵛ-3K2ᵛ.

[10] *Shakespeare: From* Richard II *to* Henry V (Stanford: Stanford University Press, 1957) p. 177. We must also notice that these contradictions are (as the edited text for Olivier's film version of 1944 makes clear) present in the play itself and not merely the result of considering *Henry V* in the light of the *Henry IV* plays. Cf. Moody Prior, *The Drama of Power* (Evanston: Northwestern University Press, 1973) pp. 314-17.

[11] *Chronicles,* 3 Sig. 3G1ʳ.

[12] *Henry V,* ed. Dover Wilson (Cambridge: Cambridge University Press, 1947) pp. xx-xxi.

[13] This reading of the first scene was advanced over sixty years ago by Gerald Gould, 'A New Reading of *Henry V*', *The English Review,* 29 (1919) 42-55.

[14] *Ben Jonson,* i. 550. C. H. Hobday notes that 'that word *for* is decisive' in his 'Imagery and Irony in *Henry V*', *Shakespeare Survey,* 21 (1968) 110.

[15] *Chronicles,* 3, Sig. 3G1ʳ. In Hall, as in Shakespeare, the Dauphin's insult occurs at the opening of the Leicester parliament.

[16] Campbell, *Shakespeare's Histories*, pp. 263-4.

[17] In addition to Campbell, pp. 270-1, see also Irving Ribner, *The English History Play in the Age of Shakespeare*, p. 187; M. M. Reese, *The Cease of Majesty*, p. 324; Dover Wilson's New Cambridge *Henry V*, p. xxiii; and J. H. Walter's New Arden *Henry V* (London: Methuen, 1954) pp. xxii-xxiii.

[18] 'Prince Hal, Henry V, and the Tudor Monarchy', *The Morality of Art*, ed. D. W. Jefferson (London: Routledge, 1969) p. 73.

[19] 'Prince Hal, Henry V, and the Tudor Monarchy', p. 72.

[20] New Arden *Henry V*, p. xxii. Ralph Berry's chapter on *Henry V* in *The Shakespearean Metaphor* (London: Macmillan, 1978) pp. 48-60, effectively challenges this view.

[21] Holinshed, *Chronicles*, 3, Sig. 2D3ᵛ.

[22] See, for example, the comment of Dover Wilson in the New Cambridge *Henry V:* 'it seems odd that Shakespeare did not make it more explicit, until we remember that he meant to avoid anything that casts doubt on the legitimacy of Henry V' (p. 140n). See also Karl P. Wentersdorf's 'The Conspiracy of Silence in *Henry V*', *SQ* 27 (1976) 264-87, which looks closely at the political issues raised by the scene.

[23] For an alternative reading of this scene, see James Winny, *The Player King*, pp. 184-6. Winny argues that the rapid 'transformation of outlook' from Henry's 'shocked depression' to his 'happy assurance' of success indicates a fundamental contradiction at the heart of the play. Norman Rabkin sees these contradictions everywhere, sees them indeed as the very pattern in the carpet. In 'Rabbits, Ducks, and *Henry V*', *SQ* 28 (1977) 279-96, he argues that the play serves as an example of 'complementarity' in which the contradictions reveal that the 'inscrutability of *Henry V* is the inscrutability of history'.

[24] Holinshed reports that 'The souldiors were ransomed, and the towne sacked, to the great gaine of the Englishmen' (3, Sig. 3G3ᵛ).

[25] See Dover Wilson's New Cambridge *Henry V*, p. 150n; and J. W. Walter's New Arden edition of the play, p. 66n.

[26] Holinshed writes that Henry sent word to Harfleur 'that except they would surrender the towne to him the morrow next insuing, without anie condition, they should spend no more time in talke about the matter. But yet at length through the earnest sute of the French lords, the king was contented to grant them truce until nine of the clocke the next sundae, being the two and twentith of September; with condition, that if in the means time no rescue came, they should yeeld the towne at that houre, with their bodies and goods to stand at the kings pleasure'. *Chronicles*, 3, Sig. 3G3ᵛ.

[27] See Robert Ornstein, *A Kingdom for a Stage*, p. 189.

[28] *The Weak King Dilemma in the Shakespearean History Play*, p. 175. Manheim, however, views the speech not as evidence of Henry's moral absolutism but as evidence of his profound Machiavellianism. It is a bit of 'play-acting' designed to create an 'image for himself which if he keeps in fact will assure his success' (pp. 175-6). For a criticism of this view, see pp. 69-70.

[29] Henry Kelly, in contrast to the position I take, argues that perhaps we are not meant to be disturbed by Henry's evasion. Williams, he writes, 'speaks as if Henry has completely answered his argument, and we are perhaps to assume that the objection which Henry answered was implicit in Williams' mind at the close of his speech' (*Divine Providence in the England of Shakespeare's Histories*, p. 239n). The assumption that Henry is a mind-reader seems, however, far less convincing than the assumption that he deliberately chooses to answer a different argument than Williams presents.

[30] The contrary, of course, has usually been argued. See for example M. M. Reese, *The Cease of Majesty*, p. 330; 'The soldiers' blunt questioning moves Henry to a further examination of his conscience, and when he is alone he contemplates the terrible responsibilities of his office'.

[31] See Robert Ornstein's *A Kingdom for a Stage*, p. 196.

[32] Shakespeare obviously needed no source for Henry's factitious use of 'peace' in the speech, but he could have found in *The Annales* of Tacitus, which did serve as a source for *Henry V*, the complaint against the Romans under Agricola: 'To take away by maine force, to kill and to spoile, falsely they terme Empire and gouernment: When all is waste as a wildernesse, that they call peace' (trans. Richard Greneway, London, 1598, Sig. R5ᵛ).

[33] The quoted phrases are used by Spenser in his letter 'To the Right noble, and Valorous, Sir Walter Raleigh knight', *The Poetical Works of Edmund Spenser*, ed. J. C. Smith (1909; Oxford: Clarendon Press, 1964) 486.

[34] Manheim, *The Weak King Dilemma in the Shakespearean History Play*, p. 169. In addition to Manheim's chapter (pp. 167-82), see also Robert B. Parker, 'The Prince and the King: Shakespeare's Machiavellian Cycle', *Revue des Langues Vivantes*, 38 (1972) 241-53; and Michael Goldman (though he does not explicitly invoke Machiavelli), *Shakespeare and the Energies of Drama* (Princeton: Princeton University Press, 1972) pp. 58-73.

[35] S. C. Sen Gupta, *Shakespeare's Historical Plays* (London: Oxford University Press, 1964) p. 146. Herbert R. Coursen, Jr. also claims that 'morality subserves policy', in 'Henry V and the Nature of Kingship', *Discourse* 13 (1970) 288.

[36] Erasmus, *Proverbs or Adagies,* trans. Richard Taverner (London, 1569) Sig. G6[r].

[37] Chronicles, 3, Sig. 3G5[r].

[38] ll. 1168-73. *Chief Pre-Shakespearean Drama*, ed. J. Q. Adams (Cambridge, Mass.: Houghton Mifflin, 1924) p. 616.

[39] *Chronicles,* 3, Sig. 3G6[r].

[40] *The Union of the Two Noble . . . Families,* Sig. d2[r].

[41] Holinshed, *Chronicles,* 3, Sig. 3G6[r]. See also Hall, Sig. d2[r].

[42] *The Union of the Two Noble . . . Families of Lancaster and York,* Sig. d2[r-v].

[43] See Paul Jorgensen, *Shakespeare's Military World* (Berkeley: University of California Press, 1956) pp. 89-90.

[44] *The Drama of Power* (Evanston: Northwestern University Press, 1973) pp. 340-1. See also Joanne Alteri, 'Romance in *Henry V*', SEL 21 (1981) 223-40.

[45] *Ideas of Greatness* (New York: Barnes and Noble, 1971) p. 103. More skeptical responses to the final scene may be found in Marilyn Williamson's 'The Courtship of Katherine and the Second Tetralogy', *Criticism* 17 (1975) 326-34; and Ornstein's *A Kingdom for a Stage*, pp. 198-9.

[46] *The Union of the Two Noble . . . Families,* Sig. A1[r-v].

[47] Even when Henry is aware of time's passage he finds no significant loss. The body may fail, he tells Kate, but 'a good heart . . . shines bright and never changes, but keeps his course truly' (v.ii.157-63). And in his claim of being unhandsome, he concludes that 'the elder I wax the better I shall appear', since 'old . . . age can do no more spoil upon my face' (v.ii.222-4).

POLITICS AND IDEOLOGY

Alexander Leggatt (essay date 1988)

SOURCE: "*Henry V*," in *Shakespeare's Political Drama: The History Plays and The Roman Plays,* Routledge, 1988, pp. 114-38.

[*Below, Leggatt considers possible readings of the play, its depiction of war, and its portrait of political authority. He invokes the need for audiences to be engaged as well as skeptical, particularly with respect to appraising Henry, whom the critic sees as a man motivated by obedience—the same virtue that Canterbury cites as the means of keeping all parts of an ideal nation working in harmony for a common purpose.*]

Henry V presents the anatomy of a war. We see the causes and the aftermath, the leaders and the common soldiers, the heroism that lives in legend and the grumbling, sickness, and petty crime that generally do not. Only strategy and tactics are underplayed. Shakespeare is more interested in the feelings and imaginations of his characters than in the way they move on a map—just as in *Richard II* he was more interested in the mentality that led the King to abuse his office than he was in the abuses themselves. The play's function as anatomy is connected with its episodic quality. We are not so much following an action as looking all round a subject, often in a discontinuous way. This includes not only characters and events but attitudes towards them, even ways of dramatizing them. *Henry V* provides evidence that can be used in a wide variety of readings, from romantic celebration to ironic satire. In that way it anatomizes not only its subject but the possible responses of its audience. In criticism and performance it becomes, perhaps more obviously than any other play of Shakespeare's, a way of revealing the biases of its interpreters.

As a patriotic pageant it gives a view of the past very different from the view in previous history plays. When York attacked Richard II for betraying the standards of his grandfather, Edward the Black Prince, the moment was typical in its contrast of a heroic past and a diminished present (*Richard II*, II. i. 171-85). Early in *Henry V*, on the other hand, Canterbury exhorts Henry:

Look back into your mighty ancestors:
Go, my dread lord, to your great-grandsire's tomb,
From whom you claim; invoke his war-like spirit,
And your great-uncle's, Edward the Black Prince.

(I. ii. 102-5)

Edward can be revived; he is no longer a lost hero but an inspiration to achievement in the present. In the process, the dynastic problem created by Bolingbroke's usurpation is forgotten. Ely, supporting Canterbury's exhortation, does not examine the lines of Henry's family tree in any detail. The blood is the same; that is enough:

> You are their heir, you sit upon their throne,
> The blood and courage that renowned them
> Runs in your veins.
>
> (I. ii. 117-19)

The continuity that matters lies in the office and the tradition of valour Henry has inherited. We are close to Henry VI's description of Richmond as framed by nature to be England's king.

Even the knockabout comedy of the scene where Fluellen forces Pistol to eat a leek ends with an assertion of the importance of the heroic past. Gower draws the moral as a lesson to Pistol to respect 'an ancient tradition, begun upon an honourable respect, and worn as a memorable trophy of predeceased valour' (V.i. 73-5). Henry represents that 'predeceased valour' come to life again. Recalling the terrible achievements of the Black Prince at Crécy, the French King warns his nobles, 'he is bred out of that bloody strain / That haunted us in our familiar paths' (II. iv. 51-2).[1] England itself becomes a magic kingdom. Scotland, Ireland, and Wales send representatives to support it;[2] even traitors profess delight at being caught (II. ii. 161-4). The divisions we have seen in previous plays are replaced, as at the end of *2 Henry IV,* by a common purpose: 'So may a thousand actions, once afoot, / End in one purpose' (I. ii. 211-12); 'Therefore let every man now task his thought, / That this fair action may on foot be brought' (I.ii.309-10). It is, we note, *action* that brings England together. England is unified not by what it is but by what it is doing: 'They sell the pasture now to buy the horse' (II. Chorus, 5). The land itself, a garden in *Richard II* and a suffering body in *2 Henry IV,* has become simply a resource to feed the action. The national imagination has been fired to the point of ecstasy: even before the war begins, the hearts of Henry's followers 'have left their bodies here in England / And lie pavilion'd in the fields of France (I. ii. 128-9). The French make their contribution to this patriotic fantasy. In *Henry VI* and *King John* the French, like all sensible people, speak English. In *Henry V,* especially when alarmed or excited, they break into French; and it seems to be Princess Katharine's native language. This sense of the Frenchness of the French has an initially comic effect, especially in Pistol's scene with Monsieur le Fer, but it also gives them a quality of otherness. Bickering and leaderless on the eve of Agincourt, they greet their first setback with 'The devil take order now!' (IV. v. 22), and the next we hear they have attacked the boys

and the luggage. The contrast with the unity and control of the English under a strong leader is obvious. Against Henry's promise—

> he to-day that sheds his blood with me
> Shall be my brother; be he ne'er so vile
> This day shall gentle his condition.
>
> (IV. iii. 61-3)

—we set the concern of the French Herald Montjoy to separate the corpses into classes: 'For many of our princes—woe the while—/ Lie drown'd and soak'd in mercenary blood' (IV. vii. 77-8). At certain points the French seem to be comic-book villains who make satisfyingly foreign noises when defeated. At others they display dignity and intelligence (this is true especially of the King and the Constable), but these qualities are clearest at moments when they show their respect for Henry and his followers.

Part of the excitement of Agincourt is the contrast between the small, tattered English army, 'warriors for the working-day' (IV. iii. 109), and the vastly greater numbers of the French, gorgeously overdressed and arrogant: 'let us but blow on them, / The vapour of our valour will o'erturn them' (IV. ii. 23-4). This is the eternal satisfaction of watching Jack kill the Giant. War is also the Great Game. Henry responds to the Dauphin's present of tennis-balls by challenging him to a set that 'Shall strike his father's crown into the hazard' (I. ii. 263), and tells his men at Harfleur, 'I see you stand like greyhounds in the slips, / Straining upon the start. The game's afoot' (III. i. 31-2). Excitement is not the only feeling to be played on. The deaths of York and Suffolk are frankly sentimental: 'The pretty and sweet manner of it forc'd / Those waters from me which I would have stopp'd' (IV. vi. 28-9). The French are allowed epic dignity when their King goes through a roll-call of the nobility, and the names themselves produce a sudden charge of excitement (III. v. 40-7).[3] The dignity turns sombre when Henry reads the names of the dead at Agincourt (IV. viii. 82-114). The disproportion in the casualties—10,000 French to 29 English—produces a feeling of shock even in the victors. Henry's immediate reaction is to ascribe the victory to God, and there seems (on the evidence of the play) no other explanation. In *Richard II* God seemed deaf to all invocations, and York concluded bitterly, 'Comfort's in heaven, and we are on the earth' (II. ii. 78). Here, at a time of violent action, God seems to have drawn suddenly close to human affairs, and Henry, whose earlier invocations may have sounded perfunctory, is not just gratified but stunned:

> be it death proclaimed through our host
> To boast of this or take that praise from God
> Which is his only.
>
> (IV. viii. 116-18)

The campaign ends with a formal celebration of God's action: 'Do we all holy rites: / Let there be sung "Non nobis" and "Te Deum" ' (IV. viii. 124-5).

Fairy-tale excitement, epic dignity, religious awe: the play gives us all of these, drawn together in the myth of the hero-king. But we also see the grubby reality. The unglamorous side of the war is evoked in the stage direction 'Enter KING HENRY . . . and his poor soldiers' (III. vi. 89SD). Sickness spreads through the army (the historical Henry would die of camp fever), and Grandpré's gloating over the English includes a memorable description of their sick horses (IV. ii. 46-52). Faced with the prospect of carnage, Henry cleverly turns it into a threat that the smell of English corpses 'shall breed a plague in France' (IV. iii. 103), but in doing so he evokes a real horror, the stench of a battlefield when the game is over. France has its revenge in a small way when Doll dies 'i' the spital / Of malady of France' (V. i. 85-6); the nationality of the pox is an old joke, but in this case it connects the spread of disease with the war. Army surgeons do not just deal with wounds. The play also reminds us that between the crises of a war there are long, dreadful periods of waiting: the night before Agincourt seems to stretch for ever, and the French and English are equally on edge. The French while away the time with a convincing barrack-room conversation whose principal themes are sex and horses. The rhetoric of war in the largest sense includes not only patriotic speeches like Henry's great battle orations but a good deal of swearing and grumbling.[4] For every utterance on the level of 'Once more unto the breach' there must be thousands on the level of 'By Cheshu, I think a' will plow up all if there is not better directions' and 'By Chrish, la! tish ill done: the work ish give over' (III. ii. 67-8, 91-2). On this level of war, official history is generally silent; Henry V is not.

But at least Fluellen and Macmorris, authors of the complaints just quoted, are committed to the war. Pistol and his companions are in it for their own reasons, delicately suggested in Pistol's 'I shall sutler be / Unto the camp, and profits will accrue' (II. i. 111-12). But though Pistol exhorts his friends, 'Let us to France; like horse-leeches, my boys, / To suck, to suck, the very blood to suck' (II. iii. 56-7), they seldom rise above the level of stealing lute-cases and fire-shovels (III. ii. 44-9). The Boy has an even better idea: 'I would give all my fame for a pot of ale, and safety' (III. ii. 12-13). In Henry IV the low life of Eastcheap went its own way till the final disaster. In Henry V the Eastcheap characters are more directly touched by history, enlisted in the great national enterprise. But they keep their own interests and voices. They died off one by one, as though history is determined this time to crush them slowly and thoroughly; but Pistol remains. Like Parolles in All's Well That Ends Well and Pompey in Measure for Measure, he is a survivor:

Well, bawd I'll turn,
And something lean to cut-purse of quick
   hand.
To England will I steal, and there I'll steal:
And patches will I get unto these cudgell'd
   scars,
And swear I got them in the Gallia wars.
                          (V. i. 89-93)

The grubby life of the underworld not only survives but retains its power to mock respectability. Pistol settles into a parody of the boasting old veteran of the St Crispin's Day speech.

As he did in Richard II and will do again in Coriolanus, Shakespeare gives us early in the play a set piece describing the ideal state. In each case the vision of perfection is at odds with the intractable human reality shown by the play as a whole. Appropriately for a play that presents an anatomy, the state is seen by Exeter as a body: 'While that the armed hand doth fight abroad / Th'advised head defends itself at home' (I.ii. 178-9). Exeter's concern with the state in action, each part in harmony with the others, leads into Canterbury's extended description of the bees' commonwealth:

> Therefore doth heaven divide
> The state of men in divers functions,
> Setting endeavour in continual motion;
> To which is fixed, as an aim or butt,
> Obedience: for so work the honey-bees,
> Creatures that by a rule in nature teach
> The act of order to a peopled kingdom.
> They have a king and officers of sorts;
> Where some, like magistrates, correct at
>   home,
> Others, like merchants, venture trade abroad,
> Others, like soldiers, armed in their stings,
> Make boot upon the summer's velvet buds;
> Which pillage they with merry march bring
>   home
> To the tent-royal of their emperor:
> Who, busied in his majesty, surveys
> The singing masons building roofs of gold,
> The civil citizens kneading up the honey,
> The poor mechanic porters crowding in
> Their heavy burdens at his narrow gate,
> The sad-ey'd justice, with his surly hum,
> Delivering o'er to executors pale
> The lazy yawning drone.
>   (I. ii. 183-204)

The emphasis on action is characteristic of the play; everyone is doing something, and the penalty for doing nothing is death. The key word, isolated at the beginning of a line, is 'Obedience', for this is what such order depends on. The issue of obedience will return, however, in Henry's debate with his soldiers on the eve of Agincourt, and we shall see that it is not so simple a virtue for men as it seems to be for honey-bees. As the speech progresses, its tone becomes increasingly light and jocular, crossing the border from a serious political lesson to a comic fantasy like Mercutio's Queen Mab speech. The comedy does not, as in Menenius' fable of the belly, sharpen the lesson; it seems more a decoration, even a distraction. The fantasy is not the serious fantasy of Gaunt, taking us to a higher level of imagination. Like Drayton's *Nimphidia* it has about it a disconcerting touch of Walt Disney. In theory this speech presents a working model of the ordered, effectively functioning state that is the play's ideal for England; but when ranked with equivalent speeches in other plays—Gaunt's England, Cranmer's prophecy of Elizabeth—this is the hardest to take seriously.

Looking at the speech with twentieth-century eyes, we note that the bees are (as we would say) exploiting their environment. But pillaging the countryside is part of a system that includes creativity in town, 'The singing masons building roofs of gold'. There is no disturbance here. The play's second set piece about a kingdom, Burgundy's lament for France, gives us only ruin:

> Her vine, the merry cheerer of the heart,
> Unpruned dies; her hedges even-pleach'd,
> Like prisoners wildly overgrown with hair,
> Put forth disorder'd twigs; her fallow leas
> The darnel, hemlock and rank fumitory
> Doth root upon, while that the coulter rusts
> That should deracinate such savagery.
>
> (V. ii. 41-7)

The suggestion of human breakdown is developed in what follows:

> Even so our houses and ourselves and children
> Have lost, or do not learn for want of time,
> The sciences that should become our country,
> But grow like savages, as soldiers will
> That nothing do but meditate on blood,
> To swearing and stern looks, diffus'd attire,
> And every thing that seems unnatural.
>
> (V. ii. 56-62)

The picture of the disordered garden we saw in *Richard II* has become a larger picture of destruction embracing the land and the people. Henry has done what the Gardener wanted: he has ordered the garden of England—including, in the arrests at Southampton, some necessary pruning. But the result is that he has ruined the garden of France. In each case the effect of the set piece is not to summarize but to disturb, one by implication, the other directly. Canterbury's formula is too neat to account for our responses to the likes of Pistol and Bardolph, not to mention the late Sir John Falstaff, who would surely be executed as drones in this commonwealth—as some of them are in Henry's. Burgundy's speech disrupts our enjoyment of the English victory by reminding us that the French are people with a land and culture of their own, which the war has ruined.

The celebration of order is jocular and leaves us detached; the vision of ruin, taken by itself, is sombre and persuasive. Yet Burgundy has to compete with the charm and glamour of the victorious Henry. His speech, no less than Canterbury's, is challenged by its context. This throws the problem out to the audience: what is our final judgement of the war? Is Burgundy's speech a minority report, to be listened to respectfully and then shelved, or does it overturn the play's apparent satisfaction at Henry's achievement? The problem of interpreting the play, of judging between the heroic and the realistic visions, comes down to the question of how we put things together. It appears at the end—how do we relate Henry to Burgundy?—and it appears, most strikingly, at the very beginning, as we examine the cause of the war. After the stirring invocations of the Prologue, the play opens unexpectedly with a bit of backroom politicking by two very worldly sounding bishops. They are threatened with a bill that will strip the church of a large part of its possessions, applying the proceeds to such unchurchly ends as the King's honour and the relief of the poor, aged, and sick. They see their best hope in the favour of the King, who is not only 'a true lover of the holy Church' (I. i. 23) but has received an offer of massive clergy support for his war with France (I. i. 79-83). Through the bland ecclesiastical manner we glimpse the eternal cynicism of the backroom politician: they assume the King can be bought. Yet in the following scene, when Canterbury expounds the Salic law to assure Henry he has a valid claim to France, there is no mention of the bill against the clergy. Holinshed makes the connection, telling us that in the excitement of war preparations the bill was set aside;[5] Shakespeare leaves the issue hanging. How, then, are we to judge Canterbury's encouragement of the King? Is it simply a piece of political jobbery? Or do we accept the legal argument as valid, dismissing his motives for putting it forward as secondary to the main question? This is bound up with the problem of the Salic law speech itself. It presents two perfectly clear arguments: that the Salic land is not France, and that French kings have in the past taken inheritance through the female line as valid. Put as baldly as this, the case is simple; but the speech is so overlaid with incidental detail that it *sounds* confusing, and the line 'So that, as clear as is the summer's sun' (I. ii. 86) seems to invite the laugh it usually gets. Which quality should be uppermost, clarity or muddle?[6] Finally, what do we make of the fact, never mentioned in the play, that if inheritance can pass through the female line then Henry has no right to the throne of England?

The play's episodic quality leaves us to make connections for ourselves, and leaves us wondering which

Stephen Ouimette as The Boy, Amelia Hall as Mistress Quickly, Christopher Blake as Nym, Rod Beattie as Pistol, and John Cutts as Bardolph in a scene from the 1980 Stratford Festival production of Henry V.

connections to make. In theatrical tradition the Boy is killed onstage; but in the text he tells us at the end of IV.iv that he is going to guard the luggage, and Gower announces in IV. vii, ' 'Tis certain there's not a boy left alive' (IV. vii. 5). We have to make the connection ourselves. This case is relatively easy. But does Henry's order to kill the French prisoners mean that Pistol (who in the Quarto greets the order with a cry of 'Couple gorge!' but is not even on stage in the Folio) kills Monsieur le Fer? Assuming he does, Gary Taylor takes it as a surprising insight into his character, for in killing his prisoner Pistol is losing ransom money that would have set him up nicely; having exercised the play's key virtue of obedience, he returns to England destitute.[7] What do we make of the fact that Henry's attack on Scroop is framed by the two scenes of the death of Falstaff? What Robert Ornstein makes of it is that Quickly's affection for the man who mocked and cheated her shows up very well against Henry's unforgiving tirade.[8] Do we connect Henry's promise, in the St Crispin's Day speech, that

the survivors will have something to boast of with his later order that boasting will be punishable by death (IV. viii. 116-18), and so accuse him of hypocrisy? Or do we conclude that Henry was not expecting a victory that was so obviously the hand of God, and that circumstances alter cases?

As the last two examples show, the more we put things together, the more critical and satiric the play becomes. The patriotic reading means being swept along by the flow of the play, taking each moment as it comes; the critical reading means stopping and speculating, ferreting in the cracks between scenes, noting silences and omissions—like the conspicuous absence of the Dauphin in the last scene, when his inheritance is being given away. (Or is it conspicuous? Do we even think of him?) The whole play can be made decisively ironic by making a connection back to *2 Henry IV,* seeing Henry as taking his father's advice to busy giddy minds with foreign quarrels. On this reading, the fact that this motive is never mentioned only makes the cynicism deeper. There is also the question of how the comic characters function. There is a mischievous juxtaposition between the departure of Pistol and his comrdes for the war and the opening of the next scene with the French King's announcement, 'Thus comes the English with full power upon us' (II. iv. 1). But if there is satire here it is not clear whether the English or the French are its targets. When Bardolph opens III.ii with 'On, on, on, on, on! to the breach, to the breach!' (1-2), we may take this as a parody of Henry's speech in the previous scene, or as a sign of that speech's power to inspire even the basest of Henry's troops. Other parallels between high and low life are equally uncertain in their effect. As Henry unifies England, Bardolph reconciles Pistol and Nym so that they can go to France as 'three sworn brothers' (II. i. 12). As at Harfleur, we wonder whether Henry's achievement is being parodied or confirmed by its low-life shadow. Fluellen admires Pistol's eloquence (III. vi. 64-5), as Canterbury and the audience admire the King's. But he is quickly disillusioned. Should we take this as simply a sign that Pistol's rhetoric and the King's are not to be compared, or should we take the parallel to its logical conclusion?

The play not only persists in raising such questions but at one point actually dramatizes the problem—possibly for our guidance. Fluellen's comparison of Henry with Alexander the Great may be a parody, as T.J. B. Spencer suggests, of the historical method of parallel lives Shakespeare found in Plutarch.[9] But it also plays on the whole critical activity of parallel-hunting, and the initial effect is ludicrous: 'There is a river in Macedon, and there is also moreover a river at Monmouth . . . and there is salmons in both' (IV. vii. 27-32). Just as we are relaxing—and, if we have been doing this kind of thing throughout the play, starting to laugh at ourselves—Fluellen compares Alexander's killing of Cleitus with Henry's turning away of the old fat knight whose name Fluellen cannot remember. But we remember instantly. And, while our memories are working, Gower's apparently sensible objection, 'Our king . . . never killed any of his friends (IV. vii. 42-3), is answered by the voice of Mistress Quickly, earlier in the play: 'The king has killed his heart' (II.i.88). Minutes before this, Henry has ordered the killing of the French prisoners, a desperate and controversial act that Shakespeare could easily have omitted if he had wanted our view of the King to be simple. The human cost of Agincourt is related to the human cost of the self-fashioning that has made Henry what he is. If this scene is a clue for the audience—and I think it is—what it tells us is that while the critical activity of making connections between unlike things may occasionally look silly it is always worth risking. We must discriminate, and be on the lookout for forced and arbitrary parallels; but our memories were given us for a purpose, and in watching this play we are meant to use them. Quite simply, the lapse in Fluellen's

memory—'I have forgot his name'.(IV.vii.52)—makes us aware of the functioning and the value of ours.

The Chorus also makes the audience self-aware, as we find ourselves comparing our readings with his. If we really are concerned with making connections, as I think we should be, we find him at times surprisingly unreliable. His claim that the French 'Shake in their fear, and with pale policy / Seek to divert the English purposes' (II. Chorus, 14-15) is too simple an account of the French response, which includes intelligent military preparation and over-confident boasting. The Chorus's announcements of what is coming are often baffled by events: he leaves us unprepared for the first bishops' scene, the first East-cheap scene, and the leek-eating scene, all of which come immediately after he has told us (incorrectly) where the play is going next. The Chorus to Act II is particularly odd, with the announcement, 'the scene / Is now transported, gentles, to Southampton' (34-5), followed by clumsy second thoughts: 'But, till the king come forth, and not till then, / Unto Southampton do we shift our scene' (41-2). We find ourselves in Eastcheap. Granted that Shakespeare himself may have changed his mind in the course of writing, the effect of a crude patch-up could have been avoided so easily that we wonder if it is deliberate.

More overtly, the Chorus makes us compare what we are told to imagine with what we actually see, and thus alerts us to the inadequacies of the theatre:

> can this cockpit hold
> The vasty fields of France? or may we cram
> Within this wooden O the very casques
> That did affright the air at Agincourt?
> (Prologue, 11-14)

Agincourt itself, he complains, will be fought with 'four or five most vile and ragged foils' (IV. Chorus, 50). As in *Richard II,* theatre degrades. It also omits. The Chorus talks of things we cannot see—a fleet in the Channel, Henry's return to England, the opening of peace negotiations. Some of this we have no particular desire to see, and the Chorus to Act V especially makes us feel we are examining the chippings on the floor of a sculptor's studio. Some of it we see anyway, through the Chorus's words, and here his more positive function comes into play. The passages that work best—the descriptions of the fleet and of the two camps the night before Agincourt—do so because they fire our imaginations in response. The Chorus's function is not just to complain of the inadequacies of the theatre but to enlist us in the effort to overcome them: 'Piece out our imperfections with your thoughts . . . For 'tis your thoughts that now must deck our kings' (Prologue, 23, 28). He works on us as Henry works on his men.[10]

In the Chorus to Act III we are asked not only to imagine the English expedition but to join it:

> Follow, follow!
> Grapple your minds to sternage of this navy,
> And leave your England.
>   (17-19)

The Chorus goes on to appeal like a recruiting sergeant to the audience's pride and manhood (20-4). Then, by a stage trick, the charm seems to work, and imagination begets reality:

> the nimble gunner
> With linstock now the devilish cannon
>   touches,
> [*Alarum, and chambers go off.*
> And down goes all before them. Still be kind,
> And eke out our performance with your mind.
>   (32-5)

As Hippolyta puts it, it must be our imaginations and not theirs. But their stage effects, simple though they are, co-operate to make us believe that our imaginations are working, our minds and the performance are becoming one.

This is very different from the critical detachment, the standing back to put two and two together, that is, I have argued, an important part of our experience of the play. The Chorus's role as patriotic spokesman is connected with his technical function of sweeping us along, filling in the gaps between acts, precisely those gaps where our questions occur. A full reception of the play demands both engagement and questioning; and the common factor is that we are aware, as in *Richard III,* of our activity as audience. The play in a sense is about us—our judgements, our imaginations. The first tetralogy ended with the emergence of a great mythic figure. So does the second, but the differences are crucial, and they are not just the differences between villain and hero. Both are figures of considerable scale, and both are great manipulators. But while Richard III was stylized and simplified, and subject to a clear judgement from within the play, which included our own withdrawal from him, Henry is varied and elusive, and while the judgement of the play seems to go all one way— 'Praise and glory on his head!' (IV. Chorus, 31)— the judgement in the audience's mind is allowed to be more open and questioning. In *Henry IV* we found both Hal and his father hard to read, hard to judge. Here our difficulties are compounded, for the play is so thoroughly Henry's story that the problem of interpretation affects every area of it. To a degree unusual even for him, Shakespeare is setting the material before us, leaving its contradictions intact, and inviting us to make of it what we can. This effort must be centred on Henry himself.

The Chorus tells us that, if Shakespeare had a kingdom for a stage and princes to act,

> Then should the warlike Harry, like himself,
> Assume the port of Mars; and at his heels,
> Leash'd in like hounds, should famine, sword,
>   and fire
> Crouch for employment.
>   (Prologue, 5-8)

This is the superhuman figure we hear of at the opening of *1 Henry VI:* 'His brandish'd sword did blind men with his beams: / His arms spread wider than a dragon's wings' (I.i. 10-11). But this is precisely the figure the stage cannot and will not show. On 'this unworthy scaffold' (Prologue, 10) there has to be an ordinary, life-sized actor. Shakespeare accepts—more gladly, I think, than the Chorus does—that to put Henry in the theatre is to make him human. The limits of time are also important. Henry commits himself to a single action, all or nothing:

> or there we'll sit,
> Ruling in large and ample empery
> O'er France and all her almost kingly
>   dukedoms,
> Or lay these bones in an unworthy urn,
> Tombless, with no remembrance over them.
>   (I. ii. 225-9)

The myth Henry hopes to create concerns not his office but himself. Richard II was concerned with being a king; Henry is concerned with winning or losing a war. He will be, according to the outcome of his own efforts, a hero or a forgotten man.

Richard's range of performances was limited: the Lord's anointed and the suffering victim. He showed an actor's versatility only in his prison soliloquy, for him a nightmare of indecision. Henry is naturally, endlessly versatile. Canterbury describes him as a man for all occasions:

> Hear him but reason in divinity,
> And, all-admiring, with an inward wish
> You would desire the king were made a
>   prelate:
> Hear him debate of commonwealth affairs,
> You would say it hath been all in all his
>   study:
> List his discourse of war, and you shall hear
> A fearful battle render'd you in music:
> Turn him to any cause of policy,
> The Gordian knot of it he will unloose,
> Familiar as his garter; that, when he speaks,
> The air, a charter'd libertine, is still,
> And the mute wonder lurketh in men's ears,
> To steal his sweet and honey'd sentences.
>   (I. i. 38-50)

What Canterbury emphasizes is the King's eloquence; he always has the right words. Like Tamburlaine, he conquers not just with his sword but with his language. But, while Tamburlaine was obsessed and single-minded, Henry is flexible. Tamburlaine swept across the map as an irresistible force; Henry works on different people in different ways. We have evidence of his ability to make just the right impression when Canterbury describes his reaction to the bill against the clergy:

> He seems indifferent,
> Or rather swaying more upon our part
> Than cherishing th'exhibiters against us.
>
> (I. i. 72-4)

The appearance of sympathy, but no real commitment—Henry is canny. And Fluellen might note that while Alexander cut the Gordian knot Henry unties it.

Arresting the conspirators at Southampton, he contrives a little morality play (recalling the scene with the Lord Chief Justice), which uses theatrical trickery and surprise to highlight his mercy and justice and their unworthiness. He insists there is nothing personal in it; he is doing what law and the kingdom's safety require (II. ii. 174-7). His most bloodthirsty utterances are controlled by the demands of the occasion. His response to the Dauphin's insulting gift of tennis-balls may sound like a tantrum, but it is shaped by the wit of the tennis analogy and ends with an acknowledgement of the rights of ambassadors: 'So get you hence in peace' (I. ii. 294). His notorious threat to Harfleur, in which the fine fighting animals of 'Once more unto the breach' become murderous thugs who will run wild if the town does not surrender, is followed, once the surrender has been achieved, by Henry's command to Exeter, 'Use mercy to them all' (III. iii. 54), and his weary recognition of his real position: 'The winter coming on and sickness growing / Upon our soldiers, we will retire to Calais' (III. iii. 55-6). The terrible cruelty of the speech is introduced by Henry's statement of his role, 'as I am a soldier, / A name that in my thoughts becomes me best' (III. iii. 5-6), and switched off as soon as it has served its purpose. With Montjoy Henry plays, attractively, the gallant underdog, not glossing over his difficulties but putting the best face on them. His tribute to the herald, 'Thou dost thy office fairly' (III. vi. 145), is the greeting of one professional to another.[11]

Responsible statesman, bloody conqueror, good fellow—Henry plays them all. His most surprising and controversial performance is his last. Wooing Katharine, he presents himself, eloquently and at length, as a plain blunt man with no command of language. The last feat of eloquence, of course, is to make itself disappear. But this time we are more aware than usual of the pressure of a contrary reality behind the performance. With self-effacing charm Henry begs Katharine to accept him; but he has the whip-hand, and they both know it. The man who declared in the first act, 'France being ours, we'll bend it to our awe / Or break it all to pieces' (I. ii. 224-5), is now in a position to make that boast good. We see the true relations between Henry and the French when the French King, trying to preserve a shred of dignity, holds out on a small but significant piece of protocol, the addressing of letters. He will yield, he says, if Henry asks him to; the unspoken message is that it would be gracious of Henry not to ask. Henry's reply is soft but firm: 'I pray you then, in love and dear alliance, / Let that one article rank with the rest' (V. ii. 363-4). The disparity between the true relations of victor and vanquished and Henry's pose as wooer is made clear from the outset:

> *K. Hen.* Yet leave our cousin Katharine here
>   with us:
> She is our capital demand, compris'd
> Within the fore-rank of our articles.
> *Q. Isa.* She hath good leave.
> [*Exeunt all but King Henry, Katharine, and
>   Alice.*
> *K. Hen.*   Fair Katharine, and most fair,
> Will you vouchsafe to teach a soldier terms
> Such as will enter at a lady's ear
> And plead his love-suit to her gentle heart?
>
> (V. ii. 95-101)

This time we cannot miss the connection. The words 'capital demand' start an undercurrent that runs through the scene. In reply to Katharine's question, 'Is it possible dat I sould love de enemy of France?', Henry is cheerfully frank: 'in loving me, you should love the friend of France, for I love France so well that I will not part with a village of it; I will have it all mine' (V. ii. 174-80). Katharine's replies are for the most part guarded—'I cannot tell wat is dat'; 'I cannot tell'; 'I do not know dat' (V. ii. 183, 203, 221)—and when she pays Henry a compliment it is somewhat backhanded: 'Your majesté 'ave fause French enough to deceive de most sage damoiselle dat is en France' (V. ii. 229-30). Actresses can play the Princess as charmed, attracted, even flirtatious; the words will allow that. But all the bare text conveys at her moment of surrender is a recognition of political reality combined with Canterbury's virtue of obedience:

> *K. Hen.* . . . wilt thou have me?
> *Kath.* Dat is as it shall please de roi mon
>   père.
> *K. Hen.* Nay, it will please him well, Kate; it
>   shall please him, Kate.
> *Kath.* Den it sall also content me.
>
> (V. ii. 260-4)

Her surrender is sealed with a significant gesture. Henry refuses to respect the French custom that unmarried ladies do not kiss; with the words 'therefore, patiently and yielding' (V. ii. 291) he kisses her on the mouth, and she is silent for the rest of the play.

Why did Shakespeare choose to end Henry's career in this way? The scene can look flat on the page, and critics frequently see it as a sad and puzzling let-down. But in the theatre, played by a witty and attractive actor, it is often the climax of the evening. It is not just the last in a string of Henry's performances; in a number of important respects it is special. Nowhere else in the play does the actor have so many chances to get laughs; this draws the audience to the character more directly than before, as we feel his control working on us.[12] At the same time we see more fully than ever that it *is* a performance: the disparities between role and reality are, I have suggested, unusually clear. On both counts it is an effective way of summing up the public Henry: a performance, but a powerful one. It is also an effective way of summing up the war with France. The Chorus has complained that the theatre cannot do battles properly; and in fact we never quite see Agincourt. At the centre of the great battle sequence in the Olivier film is a single combat between Henry and the Constable, in which Henry's victory stands for the English victory as a whole. Shakespeare could not give us anything like Olivier's cavalry charges and flights of arrows; but he could give us, as he did in *Richard III,* something like that scene. Instead, Henry sets out to battle, there are alarums and excursions, then Pistol captures Monsieur le Fer, then we see the French in panic and disarray—and we realize with a shock that Pistol and le Fer stand for the great English victory.[13] Our imaginations, we feel, may have to work overtime on this one. There are more alarums, and there is a certain amount of confusion. In one of the play's most realistic touches, Henry does not realize he has won until Montjoy tells him so (IV. vii. 85-8). He has barely started to savour his victory when he has to be polite to Fluellen, who is rattling on about the good service the Welsh did at Crécy (IV. vii. 94-119).[14] We see the tension before the battle, and the aftermath of victory; we never quite see the victory itself.

Where we see Henry win France is in V. ii, at the moment when he plants a kiss on the lips of the French Princess. The connection is suggested when Henry's victory at Harfleur is followed by a scene in which the Princess decides she had better learn English—'il faut que j'apprenne à parler' (III. iv. 4-5)[15]—surveying the parts of the body and ending with bawdy puns on 'le foot et le count' (III. iv. 57). Henry has listed the rape of virgins among the atrocities he will unleash at Harfleur; after the town falls, the French complain that their women are threatening to 'give / Their bodies to the lust of English youth' (III. v. 29-30). Bourbon tries to rally his fellows after the first disaster at Agincourt:

And he that will not follow Bourbon now,
Let him go hence, and with his cap in hand,
Like a base pandar, hold the chamber-door
Whilst by a slave, no gentler than my dog,
His fairest daughter is contaminated.
                                        (IV. v. 12-16)

Conquest and disgrace in battle have their sexual conterparts; and in V. ii. itself the word-play on 'maiden cities' that 'war hath never entered' (V. ii. 344, 340-1) encourages us to see the connection. Having conquered France, Henry conquers Katharine; the second event stands for the first, and is easier to show in the theatre. The peace is cemented by treaty, and Henry will marry Katharine, not rape her; yet we have seen an element of enforcement in both cases, and while there is much talk at the end of a marriage of kingdoms (V. ii. 366-86) the bride and groom, like Mortimer and his wife, do not speak the same language. The fact that the wooing is conducted mostly in English suggests the usual fate of a conquered people.

Henry impresses us, then, through a series of performances; and his climatic performance, like the opening performance of Richard of Gloucester, is a wooing scene, an act of persuasion. This also suggests something about the nature, and the means, of his victory. We hear little of the technicalities of war. Henry's principal strategy is summed up in the words 'All things are ready, if our minds be so' (IV. iii. 71). His petition to God is 'steel my soldiers' hearts' (IV. i. 295). His address to them at Harfleur reads like instructions to an actor, including a strong sense of decorum, of what is proper to the occasion:

In peace there's nothing so becomes a man
As modest stillness and humility:
But when the blast of war blows in our
    ears,
Then imitate the action of the tiger;
Stiffen the sinews, conjure up the blood,
Disguise fair nature with hard-favour'd
    rage.
                                        (III. i. 3-8)

The ferocity of the fighting man is a disguise, something laid on top of his ordinary nature. He expects of his men something of his own capacity to behave as the situation requires; and he knows that, if ferocity were to be man's normal state, life would sink to the level of horror described in Burgundy's speech. Agincourt presents a different problem, and requires Henry to inspire his men in a different way. Here the overwhelming odds and the fear of certain death pose a threat to morale. While Hotspur at Shrewsbury roused his fellows with the cheerful cry, 'Doomsday is near; die all, die merrily' (*1 Henry IV,* IV. i. 134), Henry asks his men to imagine themselves back in England, enjoying the 'pot of ale, and safety' the Boy longed for at Harfleur:

He that shall see this day, and live old age,
Will yearly on the vigil feast his neighbours,
And say, 'Tomorrow is Saint Crispian':
Then will he strip his sleeve and show his
    scars,
And say, 'These wounds I had on Crispin's
    day'.
Old men forget; yet all shall be forgot,
But he'll remember with advantages
What feats he did that day.

                                        (IV.iii.44-51)

Henry's phrasing implies a realistic admission that not everyone will survive; without that the speech would not be so persuasive. But its main effort is to make the idea of survival concrete. The scene is domestic and familiar, a far cry from the heroics of Harfleur, and the old veteran is made more convincing by Henry's joking suggestion that he will exaggerate a little. But like the scene at Harfleur it shows Henry's awareness that his principal task is not the arrangement of his soldiers on the field but the preparation of their minds.

Henry asks his men to imagine themselves as something different: tigers, greyhounds, old men. He asks of them, in other words, the versatility he shows himself. That versatility prompts the question: is there an essential Henry? Is there a man behind the public performances? One of his conversations with Fluellen raises the problem with special urgency:

> *Flu.* . . . the duke hath lost never a man but
> one that is like to be executed for robbing
> a church: one Bardolph, if your majesty
> know the man: his face is all bubukles, and
> whelks, and knobs, and flames o'fire; and
> his lips blows at his nose, and it is like a
> coal of fire, sometimes plue and sometimes
> red; but his nose is executed, and his fire's
> out.
>
> *K. Hen.* We would have all such offenders so
> cut off: and we give express charge that in
> our marches through the country there be
> nothing compelled from the villages,
> nothing taken but paid for, none of the
> French upbraided or abused in disdainful
> language; for when lenity and cruelty play
> for a kingdom, the gentler gamester is the
> soonest winner.

                                        (III. vi. 103-18)

As in his scene with the Lord Chief Justice, Henry stands for the principle of law, and he adds to it a principle of the conduct of war. But we feel like shouting at him, 'Dammit, it's *Bardolph!*' Of that fact, Henry shows not a flicker of recognition. Though Fluellen himself does not know it, his words 'if your majesty know the man' are a direct challenge. We know the importance of our memories; how good is Henry's?

As Hal, he joined in the jokes about Bardolph's face that we are now hearing for the last time. Actors may fill in the moment with recognition of one kind or another;[16] what Shakespeare gives us is a deliberate silence, a refusal to acknowledge private life. Henry's own account of his self-control suggests it is enforced: 'our passion is as subject / As is our wretches fetter'd in our prisons' (I. ii. 242-3). But the control is so complete that no effort actually shows. There seems to be a formal surrender of private life in Henry's attack on Scroop. Scroop appeared to be the ideal friend—dutiful, grave, learned, noble, and, like Horatio, no slave to passion (II. ii. 127-37). Scroop was also, Henry declares, a man who knew him intimately: 'Thou that didst bear the key of all my counsels, / That knew'st the very bottom of my soul' (II. ii. 96-7). The breaking of this ideal friendship is for Henry 'like / Another fall of man' (II. ii. 141-2). Throughout the play as a whole, Henry has no relationships; all his encounters with other characters are exemplary, designed to illustrate a point. Is Henry's relation with Scroop any different? The answer, I think, is no. Its sheer formality makes it hard to feel there was ever a real friendship to be betrayed; Scroop is not so much a man as an example. The scene is framed by the death of Falstaff, as though to remind us of a much fuller relationship, one whose course and end could not be seen so reductively.

We need to look for the private Henry, assuming there is one, on the eve of Agincourt. On the edge of action—'Brother John Bates, is not that the morning which breaks yonder?' (IV. i. 85-6)—Henry tries to snatch a few minutes' solitude, and we realize that we have never seen him alone: 'I and my bosom must debate awhile, / And then I would no other company' (IV. i. 31-2). But solitude does not come easily; he keeps running into other people. Nor can he really shed his identity, despite his borrowed cloak. His encounter with Pistol may suggest a reversion to his Eastcheap past, but not if we remember that Hal and Pistol never met. When Henry introduces himself as 'Harry le Roy' we realize (assuming our French is better than Pistol's) that his present identity and public role are very much in place. Even his attempt to assert the King's common humanity is equivocal: 'I think the king is but a man, as I am: the violet smells to him as it doth to me; the element shows to him as it doth to me; all his senses have but human conditions: his ceremonies laid by, in his nakedness he appears but a man' (IV. i. 101-6). Only in that last touch, when he comes down to Lear's bare forked animal, does he see the King as simply 'a man'. But that is to go from one abstraction to another, from the role to the species. If somewhere in this process there is an individual, we have missed him. This apparently private scene only confirms that Henry is the King, and that his life consists in dealings with others. Those dealings involve a necessary distance, as we see when Williams speculates that the King will allow himself to be ransomed:

K. Hen. If I live to see it, I will never trust his word after.

Will. You pay him, then! That's a perilous shot out of an elder-gun, that a poor and a private displeasure can do against a monarch.

(IV. i. 202-5)

Henry imagines that a common subject can pass judgement on a monarch, and the common subject finds the notion ridiculous.[17] The later development of the two men's relations confirms this distance: the glove trick is a practical joke conducted by remote control, and ends with Henry giving Williams a substantial tip.[18] The soldier's refusal of Fluellen's much smaller tip (IV. viii. 70) is in all likelihood the defiance he would like to utter to the King but knows he cannot.

The true relations of king and subject are authority and obedience. For Bates this is a comfort: 'If his cause be wrong, our obedience to the king wipes the crime of it out of us' (IV. i. 133-4). We see here that obedience is an equivocal virtue, freeing underlings from moral responsiblity. Williams takes the argument a stage further, insisting that all responsibility for the carnage of war finally falls on the king: 'if the cause be not good, the king himself hath a heavy reckoning to make' (IV. i. 135-6). The subject may be free, but the king is trapped. At last Henry is touched on a nerve, and a number of other moments fall into place around this one. Throughout the play Henry is touchy on the question of responsibility, always trying to shift the burden—to Canterbury, for inciting him to war; to the Dauphin, for sending him the tennis-balls; to the French King, for resisting his claim; to the citizens of Harfleur, for presuming to defend their town (I. ii. 18-28; I. ii. 282-4; II. iv. 105-9; III. iii. 1-43).

His occasional deference to God (I.ii.289-90) may be another way of easing the burden. Henry has taken so much on himself that the thought of an authority above him may console him as it does Bates. Yet the burden of responsibility cannot finally be shifted; it can only be limited. Henry cannot, and does not, refute Williams's insistence that he is responsible for the war; he only jibs at the further implication that he is responsible for the souls of men who do not die in a state of grace: 'Every subject's duty is the king's; but every subject's soul is his own' (IV. i. 182-4). In the great doom picture that opens his speech, Williams imagines the soldiers as suffering victims with bereaved families, guilty only of the violence that war has made them commit (IV. i. 135-46). Henry imagines them, or some of them, as escaped criminals whom God will punish, using war as an opportunity to make good the lax judgements of men (IV. i. 163-74). Each man's view has its own narrowness; there is, as we see elsewhere, a distance between them. Williams's view is from the streets, Henry's from the bench. And their debate is

conducted in general terms that make it seem, like Henry's other encounters, an illustration of a principle. But the fact that Williams has touched on something personal is hinted by the illustration Henry uses to begin his argument: 'So, if a son that is by his father sent about merchandise do sinfully miscarry upon the sea . . . ' (IV. i. 150-1). The mercantile image is part of the Bolingbroke style we remember from *Henry IV;* but why son and father, not just master and servant? Is it because Henry himself has been sent on a dangerous errand by his father, who instructed him to busy giddy minds with foreign quarrels? Or is the mission his father gave him kingship itself? The recognition of Henry as not just king but son flickers only for a moment, and very lightly; it will return at the end of the scene.

Finally alone, Henry complains bitterly of Williams's attempt to put everything on him:

> Upon the king! let us our lives, our souls,
> Our debts, our careful wives,
> Our children, and our sins lay on the king!
> We must bear all. O hard condition!
> Twin-born with greatness, subject to the breath
> Of every fool, whose sense no more can feel
> But his own wringing.

(IV. i. 236-42)

The echoes of Williams's speech (IV. i. 135-49) are direct, and his reference to Williams as a self-centred fool is bitter and unfair; Henry is giving way for once to an anger that makes him unreasonable. But he does not say this time that Williams is wrong. He goes on to complain that the only compensation for his burden is ceremony. Richard II saw the symbols of his office as essential signs of its divine sanction. Henry sees them as external trappings: 'The intertissued robe of gold and pearl, / The farced title running 'fore the king' (IV. i. 268-9).[19] He complains of ceremony, as Falstaff did of honour, that it hath no skill in surgery: 'Canst thou, when thou command'st the beggar's knee, / Command the health of it?' (IV. i. 262-3).[20] Like his father, he protests that the common people can sleep better than he does. All this is fairly generalized; but what follows is startlingly particular:

> Not to-day, O Lord!
> O not to-day, think not upon the fault
> My father made in compassing the crown!
> I Richard's body have interred new,
> And on it have bestow'd more contrite tears
> Than from it issued forced drops of blood.
> Five hundred poor I have in yearly pay,
> Who twice a day their wither'd hands hold up
> Toward heaven, to pardon blood; and I have
>   built
> Two chantries, where the sad and solemn
>   priests

Still sing for Richard's soul. More will I do;
Though all [that] I can do is nothing worth,
Since that my penitence comes after all,
Imploring pardon.

(IV. i. 298-311)

This man who keeps shifting responsibility to others is himself haunted by the guilt of a crime he did not commit. The lineal succession he boasted of at the end of *2 Henry IV* included more than the crown. On the eve of his great victory his mind goes back to the past, and he reveals that the problem created in *Richard II* has not been solved and may be insoluble. It seems to bother no one else in the play; but it bothers him. Why does Henry connect his inherited guilt and his war with France? He does not say explicitly, but we may make the connection ourselves. Kingship can never again be the sacred office it was for Richard; the best it can be is a vehicle for worldly achievement, and on those limited but real terms Henry is determined to restore it, to undo the damage his father did—if only the guilt incurred when the office was desanctified does not hold him back.

The look back to *Richard II* is the furthest reach of the play's historical vision. The furthest reach of its personal vision is the discovery of Henry's spiritual isolation. He is convinced that the ceremonies of prayer, like the ceremonies of kingship, are in his case worthless. To the official loneliness of a king is added the more terrible spiritual loneliness of a man convinced that his prayers are not being heard. Whatever he achieves in the world must be set against this. Surrounded by the praises of men, Henry is finally aware of the silence of God. Yet the routines of prayer go on, and Henry promises, 'More will I do'. At the end of the scene we have our final insight into him, when his brother Gloucester calls him: 'I know thy errand, I will go with thee: / The day, my friends, and all things stay for me' (IV. i. 313-14). He finally accepts, as calmly as his father accepted the role of scapegoat, that the whole burden of his kingship falls on him. There is none of the plaintiveness of Hamlet's 'The time is out of joint. O cursed spite, / That ever I was born to set it right' (I. v. 196-7). He has faced his pain, complained of it, found it incurable, and accepted it. This is what lies behind the panache and high spirits of his public performances: a man who has seen through his life to a point at which another man might despair, and is determined to carry on. He carries on alone; his own brother is merely a voice calling him to duty. Like Hotspur's last speech, his prayer ends with an incomplete line, but this time there is no one to finish it for him. The scene as a whole has insisted that Henry's kingship is inescapable; even the private man is defined by it. While Henry envies the life of the peasant, his own imagination—throwing up images like 'vacant mind' and 'distressful bread' (IV. i, 275-6)—tells him he

could never live it. His father's references to 'smoky cribs' and 'loathsome beds' (*2 Henry IV*, III. i. 9, 16) show a similar realism; neither man sentimentalizes the life of the poor as Henry VI does. But of course the question goes deeper than class. Richard II's kingship was unremovable because of its sanctity; Henry's is unremovable because it is a lifelong duty. Like his subjects, he is a man under obedience.

As a hero who brings English history to a moment of triumph, he is like Richmond, but of course we never see into Richmond in this way. Nor does Richmond seem subject as Henry is to the workings of time. Shakespeare carries over from *Henry IV* the sense of time as ultimately ruinous, making any achievement provisional and temporary. Even at Agincourt the first flush of victory simply means new effort: 'Well have we done, thrice-valiant countrymen: / But all's not done; yet keep the French the field' (IV. vi. 1-2). We go to the deaths of York and Suffolk, the order to kill the prisoners, and the attack on the luggage. The follow-up to the first excited realization that the English are doing well is by turns painful, brutal, and squalid. When Henry himself jokingly claims a Falstaffian immunity to decay, the effect is to remind us of his mortality: 'But, in faith, Kate, the elder I wax the better I shall appear: my comfort is, that old age, that ill layer-up of beauty, can do no more spoil upon my face' (V. ii. 240-3). It didn't. Not long after his marriage to Katharine, he was dead. His achievements died with him. His astonishing victory at Agincourt may or may not be a sign that God has answered his prayer and released him from his father's guilt; it is one of those connections we are not sure whether to make. What is clear is that there was to be no release for England. Cambridge's hint of a deeper reason for his treachery than the gold of France (II. ii. 155-7) is a cryptic reference to the unsolved dynastic problem that will surface again in the Wars of the Roses. Later in the play, faint but deliberate memories of *Henry VI* are stirred. Henry's list of the heroes of Agincourt, 'Bedford and Exeter, / Warwick and Talbot, Salisbury and Gloucester' (IV. iii. 53-4), is also a list of names familiar from the earlier plays. Henry's dream of reviving the crusade, another inheritance from his father, produces the sharpest irony of all: 'Shall not thou and I, between Saint Denis and Saint George, compound a boy, half French, half English, that shall go to Constantinople and take the Turk by the beard?' (V. ii. 215-18). Henry, we notice, does not offer to go on a crusade himself; perhaps he senses that he has done all he can, and it is not for him to make John of Gaunt's dream a reality. But the boy they compounded was Henry VI. The marriage, technically a comic ending, produces a child who will preside over disaster.

One thing Henry envies in the peasant life is the simplicity of its relations to time:

next day after dawn,
Doth rise and help Hyperion to his horse,
And follows so the ever-running year
With profitable labour to his grave.

(IV. i. 280-3)

Like a Book of Hours, this sees country labour as a matter of regular cycles. For Henry time is more urgent. Exeter describes him as weighing it 'to the utmost grain' (II. iv. 138), as though he knows how little he has; the French King complains that he forces the pace (II. iv. 145-6). *Carpe diem* is one solution; another is to include posterity in the audience Henry is playing for: 'our history shall with full mouth / Speak freely of our acts' (I. ii. 230-1). He combines this with the idea of cyclical time in his prediction that

Crispin Crispian shall ne'er go by,
From this day to the ending of the world,
But we in it shall be remembered.

(IV. iii. 57-9)

The secular achievement will go into the calendar as a saint's day, just as the day of the Queen's accession became an annual festival in Elizabethan England. In a way, Henry gets what he asks for. The play itself, less regular then a religious feast but still recurring, is a guarantee of his survival. That is why we are constantly aware, in *Henry V* as in none of the other histories, of the play as play. The Chorus began by complaining of the narrowness of the medium in which the great subject had to be confined. But when he declares, 'Small time, but in that small most greatly liv'd / This star of England' (Epilogue, 5-6), 'small time', in the movement of the speech, seems at first to refer to the brevity of the play rather than that of Henry's life. Finally, of course, it means both. The Chorus accepts that as a short life was enough for Henry, who weighed time to the utmost grain, two hours or so were enough for Shakespeare. As Henry has accepted his role, so the Chorus has finally accepted his medium, now that the play has demonstrated what it can do. The Epilogue is in the form of a sonnet, the form Shakespeare used elsewhere to insist on the permanent achievements of art.[21]

The Chorus also claims, as the Sonnets do, that only art survives:

Henry the Sixth, in infant bands crown'd
    King Of France and England, did this king
    succeed;
Whose state so many had the managing,
    That they lost France and made his England
    bleed:
Which oft our stage hath shown.

(Epilogue, 9-13)

If our memories stretch back—as they are now invited to—to the earlier plays, we may conclude that this is

where we came in: a disunited group of nobles squabbling over the body of a hero who was 'too famous to live long' (*1 Henry VI*, I.i.6). History, which we normally think of as a straight line moving through time, turns back on itself and forms a circle, an image not of perfection but of futility. We keep coming back to the same point: loss and ruin. That is what Shakespeare's art shows us of our life in history. But the Chorus adds, 'and, for their sake, / In your fair minds let this acceptance take' (Epilogue, 13-14). Who are 'they'? The clearest reference seems to be to the cast of *Henry VI;* but perhaps they stand for all time's subjects as the history plays have shown them. And what is 'this' we are to accept? *Henry V,* and (I think) the whole historical vision that lies behind it. We are to accept the play, as Henry accepted his unrewarding role and the Chorus his imperfect medium. That is the last of our many responsibilities as audience. Our acceptance is our way of recognizing that the fusion of the hero with the art that creates him—however we may judge the imperfections of either—offers a chance to protect human achievement from the erosion of time. Taken together, Henry's prediction about Saint Crispin's Day and the Chorus's prediction about England's future imply that as history darkened again men would still remember this light from the past. As *Henry VI* shows, they did. The business of *Henry V* is to keep that memory alive through art, in a future even Shakespeare could not have imagined.

Notes

[1] In Laurence Olivier's film version, Harcourt Williams delivers this speech with a shudder of superstitious dread.

[2] Jamy's loyalty in particular is a striking contrast to the traditional enmity of 'the weasel Scot' (I. ii. 170) which concerns Henry in the first council scene.

[3] The power of the speech was shown in Michael Langham's 1956 production at Stratford, Ontario: Gratien Gelinas, who played the French King as a bewildered invalid confined to a chair, rose to his feet during the speech and began unsteadily to walk, electrifying his court and the audience.

[4] In the preface to his Great War book *In Parenthesis* David Jones complains, 'I have been hampered by the convention of not using impious and impolite words, because the whole shape of our discourse was conditioned by the use of such words' (New York: Viking Press, 1963), p. xii.

[5] See Geoffrey Bullough (ed.), *Narrative and Dramatic Sources of Shakespeare,* vol. 4 (London: Routsledge & Kegan Paul, 1962), p. 380.

[6] Anyone who has seen Tony Church's brilliant reading of the speech in the LWT series *Playing Shake-*

speare knows it is possible—if only just—for a skilled actor to capture both qualities.

[7] Introduction to the Oxford edition of *Henry V* (Oxford: Oxford University Press, 1982), p. 65.

[8] Robert Ornstein, *A Kingdom for a Stage* (Cambridge, Mass.: Harvard University Press, 1972), p. 188.

[9] T.J.B. Spencer, *Shakespeare: The Roman Plays* (London: Longmans, Green, 1963), p. 16.

[10] See Michael Goldman, *Shakespeare and the Energies of Drama* (Princeton, NJ: Princeton University Press, 1972), p. 59.

[11] One of the most attractive touches in the Oliver film is the mutual liking of the two men, which creates a separation between their private feelings and the business they have to do.

[12] Herbert Whittaker, reviewing the 1956 Stratford, Ontario, production, wrote, 'In this last scene, [Christopher] Plummer held his audience . . . in the hollow of his hand, capping an evening of slowly-mounting triumph': 'French, English-speaking actors are united', *Globe and Mail,* 18 June 1956.

[13] See William Babula, 'Whatever happened to Prince Hal? An essay on *Henry V',* *Shakespeare Survey,* 30 (1977), 55-6.

[14] In this scene in the 1964 Royal Shakespeare Company production, jointly directed by John Barton, Peter Hall, and Clifford Williams, Henry (Ian Holm) was kneeling and trying to pray; Fluellen (Clive Swift) was at his elbow, distracting him.

[15] In the Royal Shakespeare Company's 1975 production, directed by Terry Hands, the wall that represented Harfleur sank down to reveal Katharine standing on the stage. See Gary Taylor, *Moment by Moment by Shakespeare* (London: Macmillan, 1985), p. 118.

[16] Ian Holm allowed a flicker of pain to show on his face and turned aside to cross himself, seen only by the audience. Douglas Rain (in Michael Langham's 1966 production at Stratford, Ontario) pointedly showed no recognition, though the body of Bardolph was dumped at his feet. In Adrian Noble's 1984 Royal Shakespeare Company production, Henry (Kenneth Branagh) was forced to watch in growing discomfort as Bardolph was slowly garrotted before his eyes; the extravagance of the effect made one appreciate the economy of Shakespeare's version. Alan Howard, who played Henry in the 1975 Royal Shakespeare Company production, said of the execution of Bardolph, 'That he doesn't do that coldly, and without a struggle, can be seen in the ramblings, the indecision, the contradictions of his

speech to Montjoy immediately after Bardolph's death': quoted in Sally Beauman (ed.), *The Royal Shakespeare Company's Production of Henry V for the Centenary Season at the Royal Shakespeare Theatre* (Oxford: Pergamon Press, 1976), p. 57. The use of Bardolph's death to show Henry's commitment to justice may go back to the fact that it was in a dispute over Bardolph that Hal struck the Lord Chief Justice.

[17] See Marilyn L. Williamson, 'The episode with Williams in *Henry V',* *Studies in English Literature,* 9 (1969), 277.

[18] See Anne Barton, 'The king disguised: Shakespeare's *Henry V* and the comical history', in Joseph G. Price (ed.), *The Triple Bond* (University Park and London: Pennsylvania State University Press, 1975), p. 101.

[19] See Philip Edwards, 'Person and office in Shakespeare's plays', *Proceedings of the British Academy,* 56 (1972 for 1970), 104.

[20] See Norman Rabkin, 'Rabbits, ducks, and *Henry V',* *Shakespeare Quarterly,* 28 (1977), 287.

[21] See Ornstein, op. cit., p. 202.

Graham Bradshaw (essay date 1993)

SOURCE: "The Historical Challenge," in *Misrepresentations: Shakespeare and the Materialists,* Cornell University Press, 1993, pp. 46-63.

[*In the following excerpt from a chapter in which he challenges historicist and materialist readings of* Henry V, *Bradshaw argues that members of an Elizabethan audience would have responded in a variety of ways to the play's presentation of history. Depending on their principles, their personal interests, and their political sympathies, the critic contends, some would have embraced the Chorus's version of events and Henry's justifications of the war, but others would have noticed the play's skeptical questioning of the "official" account.*]

Critics have argued at length about Henry's motives for going to war with France, and whether he is right or wrong to do so. Such arguments usually polarize into pro-Henry and anti-Henry readings, in which the critical assumption that we need to establish what view the play "really" takes produces incompatible readings; old and new historicist interventions often depend on assumptions about what view (not views) the Elizabethan audience would have taken. But then history never tells us what Henry's motives were, because it can't; in this simple but important sense a history play that pretended to make Henry's motives clear would be historically irresponsible.

Holinshed does indeed tell us, in a very interesting passage with no parallel in Hall, that when Henry was dying he was especially anxious to have it understood that his motives were of the best:

And herewith he protested unto them, that neither the ambitious desire to inlarge his dominions, neither to purchase vain renowne and worldlie fame, nor anie other consideration had moved him to take the warres in hand; but onlie that in prosecuting his just title, he might in the end atteine to a perfect peace, and come to enjoy those peeces of his inheritance, which to him of right belonged: and that before the beginning of the same warres, he was fullie persuaded by men both wise and of great holinesse of life, that upon such intent he might and ought both begin the same warres, and follow them, till he had brought them to an end iustlie and rightlie, and that without all danger of Gods displeasure or perill of soul.[21]

But of course what this *also* tells us is that other, less favorable accounts of Henry's motives were circulating, so that he found it necessary to "protest." It evidently told Shakespeare as much, since his play is historically responsible, both in its ultimate reticences and in its habitual way of exposing the Chorus's hagiographic account of "the Mirror of all Christian Kings" to other, competing interpretative possibilities. Whether Henry was right or wrong to go to war with France is a question that depends not only on whether the "title" was "iust" but on whether one is taking what Edward Powell's book on Henry V calls a "king's-eye view" or, say, the view of the French king, or of a dead conscript's widow, or of Shakespeare's Michael Williams, or of Archbishop Chicheley. In other words, the historiographical challenge involves what Shakespeare's King of France calls seeing "perspectively," and the challenge corresponds with the poetic-dramatic framing of opposed or discrepant perspectives.

Any argument that the play presses us toward one single, inclusive judgment deflects the historiographical challenge and (what is really the same thing) smothers the play's interrogative, skeptical, and exploratory energies. To suppose that the play "addresses its audience as a collectivity" short-circuits its dramatic thinking, in which the challenge is that of seeing "perspectively." The Chorus does indeed keep calling for some such collective or communal response in accord with his own "king's-eye view," which in turn steadily and sturdily assumes that the interests of a nation continually and happily coincide with those of its ruler or ruling class. Even in the first Prologue, which is often taken as an engagingly modest and indirect authorial appeal, the Chorus is richly characterized and anxious in interesting ways. To address the mixed audience as "Gentles all" is strategic precisely because they are not all "Gentles." It flatters, and appeals to, the audience in the very same way that Henry will appeal to his straggling army:

let us sweare,
That you are worth your breeding: which I
  doubt not:
For there is none of you so meane and base,
That hath not Noble luster in your eyes.
            (2.1.27-30)

The Chorus is *right* to fear that neither the play nor the audience can be relied upon to become "Cyphers" to the "great Accompt" (line 18). "Into a thousand parts divide one Man," he appeals, even as he seeks to bond the audience and make them as one. He withdraws, asking us "Gently to heare, kindly to judge," but without in any way preparing us for the play's first jolting, ungentle probing of competing interests—when we find ourselves eavesdropping on a necessarily private conversation between the Archbishop of Canterbury and the Bishop of Ely. This descent is moral as well as stylistic; doubt and division thrive.

As the bishops consider the danger posed by the Crown's claim on the Church's "temporall lands"— that is, those properties not used for strictly religious purposes, which make up "the better halfe of our Possession" (1.1.8)—they are not concerned to consider whether anything might justify or give credence to the Crown's claim. In Canterbury's indignant summary, almshouses and the needs of the lepers and indigent take their place alongside Henry's wish to provide for fifteen earls, fifteen hundred knights, over six thousand esquires, and the King's own "Coffers":

Cant. And to reliefe of Lazars, and weake
  age
Of indigent faint Soules, past corporall toyle,
A hundred Almes-houses, right well supply'd:
And to the coffers of the King beside
A thousand pounds by th' yeere. Thus runs
  the bill.
Ely. This would drink deepe.
Cant.   'Twould drink the cup and all.
Ely. But what prevention?
Cant. The King is full of grace and fair
  regard.
Ely. And a true lover of the holy Church.
            (1.1.15-23)

That break in the meter, when Ely puts his practical question, orchestrates a small but significant adjustment[22]: now Canterbury reminds Ely that to resolve the practical problem, which is already in hand, will require a very different style of public performance. The guileless bluntness of Ely's question is no more spiritually becoming than Canterbury's near-blasphemous joke about drinking the cup; the worldlywise must know when and how to seem unworldly. Ely responds at once, like a *commedia dell'arte* player recognizing his cue to improvise; to lean on the phrase a little, these men are not bishops for nothing. So we have that sudden, *seemingly* inconsequential duet on the King's miraculous virtues: the man who wants to "strip" the Church to fill his "Coffers" is now praised as "a true lover of the holy Church." The subtext to this hymn of praise is that the miraculous reformation is unbelievable: "Miracles are ceast," after all—"And therefore we must needes admit the meanes, / How things are perfected" (lines 67-69). We have entered a world where role-playing is crucial, and a world of which the Chorus knows nothing. He *believes* that Henry is "the Mirror of all Christian Kings," whereas these bishops know when to *say* such things—so that the printer's abbreviation of "Canterbury" to Cant seems, in its fortuitous way, singularly happy. In his unholy worldliness, Canterbury resembles Pandulph in *King John:* he is not the man to represent "right and conscience," so that when Henry deferentially speaks as though he is, it is hard to know who is using whom, or whether the two are functioning as accomplices in a more or less cynical public routine. Since Canterbury also reveals that he has had a private meeting with Henry which was interrupted by the ambassador's arrival, it is worth asking why Shakespeare chose not to stage it so. The most plausible answer, I suggest, is that this first scene is busily working to promote—not resolve—uncertainty about Henry's motives for going to war with France.

To hear Canterbury argue why Henry should go to war is still more unsettling and divisive. Here it's worth emphasizing that there is no reason to doubt that individual members of an Elizabethan audience would have responded in very different ways. Some would have seen how the argument is contrived, both as a tactical diversion to ensure that the bishops retain "our possession" and in its substantive claims: as the New Arden editor observes, Pharamond was the "legendary king of the Salian Franks," and the "Salic Law was actually a collection of folk laws and customs and had nothing to do with the right of succession" (15). Some would have seen how the biblical text that Canterbury cites to establish the right of succession on the female side ("When the man dyes, let the Inheritance / Descend unto the Daughter") is certainly to the point but produces a potentially catastrophic difficulty: accepting this argument would destroy Henry's claim to the *English* throne, so that he, like King John, would be no more than a de facto king.[23] For others, who are only thinking about the claim to the French throne, Canterbury's argument might seem good enough on its own quasi-legal terms. But then these terms are also being exposed to scrutiny, and here the argument's remoteness figures as an important part of its dramatic effect. Even as the speech ponderously tracks back through centuries to revive and give weight to the seventy-year-old dynastic claim entered by Henry's great-grandfather Edward III, it summons a sense of France's historical, geographical, and cultural *separateness*. This is also why it matters in this play that the French frequently speak French, and make their

own appeals to "God"; as Alexander Leggatt remarks, in "*Henry VI* and *King John* the French, like all sensible people, speak English," but in *Henry V* they have a curious habit of breaking into French, "especially when alarmed or excited."[24] And when Canterbury goes on to recall the thrilling "Tragedie" played out "on the French ground" when Edward III "Stood smiling, to behold his Lyons Whelpe / Forrage in blood of French Nobilitie," his jubilantly bloody-minded celebration of what our boys once did and might still do to "the full pride of France" emphasizes the traditional enmity between these countries and cultures. (Here Canterbury's lines on the Black Prince are so close to those of the King of France (2.4.53-62) as to suggest what could be, and perhaps was, gained by giving both' parts to the same actor, who would then deliver the two passages with a wholly different emotional emphasis.) It is clear enough that the historically remote and self-aggrandizing dynastic claim makes war not love, as Henry's brutal joke in the final scene also reminds us: "I love France so well, that I will not part with a Village of it: I will have it all mine." This war is obviously not being undertaken for France's good—but then whom, among the English, could it benefit? The dynastic ambitions and interests of a particular royal family are utterly remote from the concerns and interests of the Williamses of this world. "Unckle Exeter," "brother Lancaster," "brother Clarence," and the others who eagerly join with Canterbury in urging the King to press his claim can at least hope, like the King, to fill their Lancastrian "coffers." To say that the burden of deciding whether to go to war falls on the king is only another, more "mystifying" way of saying that *he* can choose not to—whereas in Henry's reign, as in Elizabeth's, a conscripted common soldier had no choice, little prospect of profit and none of ransom, and would be lucky to survive. So, Henry very solemnly reminds Canterbury that he must, "in the Name of God, take heed," since

> never two such Kingdomes did contend
> Without much fall of blood, whose guiltlesse drops
> Are every one, a Woe, a sore Complaint,
> 'Gainst him, whose wrongs gives edge unto the swords
> That makes such waste in brief mortalitie.–
> (1.2.24-28)

Here Henry himself is exposing that moral can of worms which Williams's speech will open. The crucial difference is that Henry always takes for granted the coincidence between his family and caste interests and those of the common weal, whereas Williams needs more convincing.

So will members of the audience who notice what the dramatic sequence tells us about Henry's way of pressing his claim. *Henry IV* had finished with Prince John's prediction of war:

SHAKESPEAREAN CRITICISM, Vol. 49

HENRY V

Christopher Plummer as King Henry V, Ginette Letondal as Katherine, and members of the Festival Company in "The Royal Wedding" scene from the 1956 Stratford Festival production of Henry V.

I will lay oddes, that ere this yeere expire,
We beare our Civill Swords, and Native fire
As farre as France. I heare a Bird so sing,
Whose Musicke, to my thinking, pleas'd the
    King.

In *Henry V* we then hear Canterbury regretting that, since his preliminary private meeting with the King was interrupted,

        there was not time enough to heare,
    As I perceiv'd his Grace would faine have
        done,
    The severalls and unhidden passages
    Of his true Titles to some certaine
        Dukedomes,
    And generally, to the Crowne and Seat of
        France.

                                    (1.1.83-88)

However, there evidently was time (first things first) to float the financial deal:

    As touching France, to give a greater Summe,
    Then ever at one time the Clergie yet
    Did to his Predecessors part withall.

                                    (1.1.79-81)

The more alert will wonder how this could have found "good acceptance of his Majestie" *before* any discussion of the justice of the claim. The next scene picks up and develops that quietly suggestive irony. As soon as we see the King, we hear him piously emphasizing his need to "be resolv'd" (1.2.4) before he sees the French ambassadors. Apparently, no decision will be taken before the Archbishop's judgment of what "Or should or should not barre us in our Clayme":

    And God forbid, my deare and faithfull Lord,
    That you should fashion, wrest, or bow your
        reading . . .
    For God doth know, how many now in
        health,
    Shall drop their blood, in approbation
    Of what your reverence shall incite us to.

263

Therefore take heed how you impawne our
  Person,
How you awake our sleeping Sword of
  Warre.

(1.2.13-14, 18-22)

Only after being "well resolv'd" that he can indeed "with right and conscience make this claim" will Henry call in the French ambassadors—or so it seems. But then we learn from the ambassador's speech that Henry has already claimed "some certaine Dukedomes" (the phrase is repeated) as one of his first actions on becoming king:

Your Highnesse lately sending into France,
Did claime some certaine Dukedomes, in the
  right
Of your great Predecessor, King *Edward* the
  third.
In answer of which claime, the Prince our
  Master
Sayes, that you savour too much of your
  youth.

(lines 246-50)

This dramatic revelation becomes the pivot for the whole stunningly structured scene, and for that very reason it's worth emphasizing how there is nothing like this in the chronicles. True, Holinshed's report of the Archbishop's oration is preceded—characteristically, without comment—by an account of the clergy's anxiety about the threat to its properties. But then his narrative becomes very diffuse, spanning large distances and periods of time. We learn that "during" the same parliament, "there came to the king ambassadors, as well as from the French king that was then in the hands of the Orlientiall faction, as also from the duke of Burgognie, for aid against that faction," and that Henry then sent Exeter, Grey, and others to the French king who "receiued them verie honorablie, and bancketted them right sumtuouslie" (*Chronicles,* 67). In time, Henry's ambassadors tell the French king that if he will "without warre and effusion of christian bloud, render to the king their maister his verie right and lawfull inheritance, that he would be content to take in marriage the ladie Katharine, daughter to the French king, and to indow hir with all the duchies and countries before rehearsed"; the French ask for time to consider, promising to "send ambassadors into England," whereupon Henry—evidently dissatisfied with that stalling—determines to make war and set forth. The Chorus in Shakespeare's play would be happy with a versified dramatic version of this and, if he noticed how the account raises questions, would certainly not want to see them pressed.

Shakespeare presses them and shows how the whole court scene is being staged by Henry himself. If we understand the significance of the ambassador's rev-

elation, it affects our sense of everything that happens in this richly equivocal, and richly dramatic, scene. We now see that the claim was entered before Canterbury's ponderously prepared speech "inciting" the King to war and taking "The sinne upon my head"; but now Canterbury can see that too, and a good production might let us see him seeing that—as any doubt about which man was using the other is resolved. We now see that Henry had already made his claim when he declared his need to be "resolv'd" and spoke so solemnly of the horrors of war; but the court can now see that too, and it is neither critical of the King nor any less determined to go to war. Once we know that this claim is what provoked the Dauphin's insult, the moment—a few lines earlier—when Henry declared himself "well prepar'd to know the pleasure / Of our faire Cosin Dolphin" seems wonderfully or appallingly insouciant; having heard him add, with regal casualness, "we heare, / Your greeting is from him, not from the King," we might reflect that nobody seems concerned to wait for the King of France's reply. We can also now see why the discreet ambassador offered to deliver the Dauphin's message to the King "sparingly," and why it was politically shrewd of the King to prefer to be insulted before his court. First he can affirm, stirringly, "We are no Tyrant, but a Christian King." Then, once the insult has been received, it—rather than the Archbishop's superfluous *nihil obstat*—can be treated as the incitement to war:

tell the pleasant Prince, this Mocke of his
Hath turn'd his balles to Gun-stones, and his
  soule
Shall stand sore charged, for the wastefull
  vengeance
That shall flye with them: for many a
  thousand widows
Shall this his Mocke, mocke out of their deer
  husbands;
Mocke mothers from their sonnes, mock
  Castles down:
And some are yet ungotten and unborne.
That shal have cause to curse the *Dolphins*
  scorne.
But this lyes all within the will of God,
To whom I do appeale, and in whose name
Tel you the *Dolphin,* I am comming on,
To venge me as I may, and to put forth
My rightfull hand in a wel-hallow'd cause.
So get you hence in peace: And tell the
  Dolphin,
His Jest will savour but of shallow wit,
When thousands weepe more then did laugh
  at it.

(lines 281-96)

Henry's adroitness in providing himself with retrospective justifications for what he has already determined to do is characteristic; we will see it again when

Henry makes the slaughter of the boys a justification for the order he has already given, to cut the French prisoners' throats. The speech to the ambassadors is another powerful imaginative summons to consider how the horrors of war will devastate the lives of so many, including those who "are yet ungotten and unborne"; but as soon as the ambassadors leave with that "merry Message," the merry Harry England can urge his loyal lords to "omit no happy howre" in preparing for "this faire Action."

Henry and his army will already be at Harfleur when we learn, in the Chorus's prologue to Act 3, that

> th'Embassador from the French comes back,
> Tells *Harry,* That the King doth offer him,
> *Katherine* his Daughter, and with her to
> Dowrie,
> Some petty and unprofitable Dukedomes.
> The offer likes not: and the nimble Gunner
> With Lynstock now the divellish Cannon
> touches,
> *Alarum, and Chambers goe off.*
> And down goes all before them. Still be kind.
> (lines 29-34)

And here, once again, the dramatic sequence exposes troubling questions that the Chorus's official hagiography doesn't acknowledge, let alone consider. Those critics (like Leonard Tennenhouse) who suppose that the marriage to Katherine is the crucial "article" in the English attempt to dominate France all too often fail to notice how Henry could have achieved that merely by accepting the King of France's offer—without risking his soldiers' lives and the nation's safety, and without making "such waste in briefe mortalitie." Characteristically, the play includes the evidence for this damaging line of argument, but without ever suggesting that Henry himself ever considers that rushing to war might have been imprudent or wrong; Shakespeare's Henry seems no less convinced than Holinshed's that he is "prosecuting his iust title," "without all danger of Gods displeasure or perill of soul." No less characteristically, the dramatic sequence is exposing the Chorus's loyally royal version of history to scrutiny: just as we see how the Chorus's rousing "down goes all before them" is followed by a scene showing the English army in retreat, we see what is unthinking in the Chorus's simple, too automatic assumption that this mirror of Christian kings is right to dismiss the French king's attempt to prevent war.

Of course, to say "we see" begs a question: not everybody does see, or would have seen, what is there to be seen. Yet we can be perfectly sure that the play's (various) subversive implications were not lost on some members of the original audience—precisely because the Elizabethan audience wasn't a monolithic entity, as old historicists liked to suppose.[25] The representa-

tional complexities in this first act suggest a sure knowledge of how mixed that audience's responses would be: the play plays to—sifts, and explores—such differences, and it is a measure of the power of that extraordinary second scene that the responses of individual spectators are also likely to be mixed or divided. To take one instance: once we are at last in a position to see how the King has been several steps ahead of Canterbury, do we approve or disapprove? Given the detonating force of the ambassador's revelation on our sense of all that we have seen so far, it is perfectly possible that we will be more engaged by other issues. It is also possible that we will be both relieved that the king—or, shifting the emphasis, the theatrical protagonist—is too clever to be used, and uneasy that Henry as prince and king is so adept at using others and exploiting any occasion. Much depends on whether the actor playing Canterbury is more or less formidable; on whatever we are bringing to the show, in our own attitude to the (Catholic) church and ecclesiastical politicians, or to the horrors of war, or to the French; and on our intellectual adequacy to issues raised by Canterbury's speech on the Salic law. The challenge to think is directly related to the play's refusal to tell us what to think.

As for the original audiences, we can be sure that they included some who agreed with Michael Williams, along with others who did not; those whose approval or disapproval of Henry's French expeditions reflected their attitude to the contemporary French, Spanish, and Irish expeditions; those who admired the way in which Henry forbids looting, and those who glumly observed the workings of a double code that allows only the well-born their pickings; those who knew from their reading of the chronicles what really happened after the surrender of Harfleur,[26] and others who hadn't read the chronicles or couldn't read; those severe "morallers" who thought the king right to make no exception for Bardolph and Nym, and those who were disgusted by such glacial firmness; those who were as patriotic as the Chorus, and those who were terrified of being conscripted and forcefully wrenched from their families and livelihoods; those who were profiting from the contemporary wars—from monopolies, patents, and other court perks—and those who were being crushed by the ever-increasing burden of taxation during the last years of Elizabeth's reign (when, to take one example, the Irish establishment cost nearly two million pounds); those groundlings who felt a bit lost and fidgety while Canterbury is insisting that "the Art and Practique part of Life, / Must be the Mistresse to this Theorique," elders who nodded sagely, and clever irreverent young men from the Inns of Court who reflected that, far from showing how praxis is the mistress to theory, Canterbury's own actions, words and motives show how theoretical principle is a willing whore to practical self-interest.

Here it is worth noticing that the Chorus's dramatic function is sometimes to remind the audience of pressing perplexities and provokingly contemporary issues that the Chorus would prefer to deny or ignore. So, although the play might seem to be prudently silent on the dangerously topical matter of conscription, the loyally flagrant lie in the second Chorus is also a dramatically devious reminder that both Henrician and Elizabethan actualities were very, very different:

> Now all the Youth of England are on fire,
> And silken Dalliance in the Wardrobe lyes:
> Now thrive the Armorers, and Honors thought
> Reignes solely in the breast of every man.
>
> (Prol. 2, lines 1-4)

As a stirring fantasy this is superb; the Chorus similarly asks, in Prologue 3 who "will not follow / These cull'd and choyse-drawne Cavaliers to France." Yet Edward Powell's study of criminal justice in Henry's reign gives a somewhat different picture, for instance when Powell remarks that "the muster-roll of the earl of Arundel's retinue at the siege of Harfleur . . . reads like a catalogue of those indicted in king's bench."[27] The historical Henry V followed Edward I's practice of giving criminals, including rapists and murderers, pardons (and military training) in return for military service. Of course Shakespeare's Henry leads a very different kind of army—if we are to judge from "Once more unto the breach" or the Crispin's Day speech; but then Henry's speech before Harfleur summons a much more familiar and terrifying vision of the "blind and bloody Souldier" whose "licentious Wickednesse" can only with difficulty be restrained from "Murther, Spoyle, and Villany." As for culled and choice-drawn cavaliers, Elizabethans were likely to know what the studies by C. G. Cruikshank and Lindsay Boynton amply confirm: although an Elizabethan army would usually include a few "gentlemen volunteers" (not all of them on fire with honor's thought) and a few ordinary volunteers who joined up as privates, by far the largest part of the army consisted of conscripts of two kinds—honest men taken away from steady employment (which was not often waiting for them when and if they returned), and "the unemployed, rogues, and vagabonds."[28] Cruikshank's study concluded with this somber account of those years in which the second tetralogy was written and staged:

> The nation became more and more war-weary. . . . The evasion of military service by one device or another became more frequent. Burghley sadly exclaimed that the country was weary of the ceaseless expenditure of money and life in foreign service. The Privy Council became apprehensive at the hostile attitude of the people. By the end of the century it was well-nigh impossible to raise money for troops.
>
> (283)

Peter Clark's magnificently detailed study of English provincial society presents an even more somber picture of social and economic crisis.[29] After the returns on land had been driven down in the early 1590s by unusually bountiful harvests, a run of ever more disastrous harvests produced a crisis in the food supply; increases in recruitment, taxation, and indirect levies like patents and purveyance all contributed to the severe economic recession. There was a great increase in crime, vagrancy, poverty, and disease, and severe outbreaks of bubonic plague drove the mortality levels still higher. The government could neither resolve nor delegate all the problems posed by the destitute families of dead soldiers and by the returning soldiers who were maimed, diseased, and unable or unwilling to find employment. Clark's account of town suburbs that were infested with emaciated soldiers raiding houses and terrifying the inhabitants reminds us that, whatever his medieval credentials, Pistol was a thoroughly contemporary figure and not so bad as some. Yet in all this misery a voice was heard: "Now all the Youth of England are on fire, / And silken Dalliance in the Wardrobe lyes."

This is to say that the Chorus has his work cut out, in relation to both audience and play—and, up to a point, knows it. His conviction that everybody *should* respond as he does to the inspiring "Story" about "the Mirror of all Christian Kings" if only the play can do justice to the "great Accompt" is, on a sympathetic view, naive but decent. On a less sympathetic view it resembles the conviction of so many politicians that opposition to their policies cannot be opposition to their policies but must be attributable to some reparable breakdown in public relations or "presentation." Having real horses is not the answer, although those who admire [Kenneth] Branagh's jejune travesty are unlikely to see that joke. But then the Chorus also betrays intuitive anxieties that, as often happens, are more obviously justified than his passionate convictions: he is quite right to fear that the dramatic representation won't be adequate to his view of history, and right to fear that the mixed audience's "imaginary forces" may not function in a docile, unremittingly obedient fashion as mere "Cyphers to this great Accompt." When the Chorus worries that the play's make-believe won't be adequate to the glorious history, the play's eruptive, complicating energies break in and expose the element of make-believe (or make-them-believe) in the Chorus's own attempts to collectivize and control the audience's responses, as well as the inadequacy of the Chorus's approach to the problems of "doing" history. What the Chorus would unite the play divides: so, after each eloquent choric attempt to bond the audience in a single, stirringly eloquent vision, the play uncovers those divisions and conflicts of principle, interest, or sympathy which the Chorus would prefer to edit or suppress and which speak to and explore the differences and divisions within the audience itself. So far as the audience is concerned, the Chorus thinks like Greenblatt while the play behaves like Brecht.

In Prologue 2 the Chorus's troubles begin even before he has finished. His dream of England ("O England!") as a "little Body with a mightie Heart," in which "Honors thought / Reignes solely in the breast of every man" collides with the facts (some values are more fact-laden), while the hasty explanation that the "Traitors" were seduced by "the gilt of France" is later contradicted by Cambridge's own dark claim that "for me, the Gold of France did not seduce" but was merely another "motive, / The sooner to effect what I intended"—that is, the Yorkist attempt to make Edmund Mortimer king (2.2.155-57). Before that, we see Pistol and Nym resolving to go to France not from thoughts of "honour" but from the hope that "profits will accrue" (2.1.107)—just as the Chorus's wistfully rhetorical question in Prologue 3, "who is he, whose Chin is but enrich / With one appearing Hayre, that will not follow / These cull'd and choyse-drawn Cavaliers?", is no less wistfully answered by the Boy's feelings about the war in which he will soon be slaughtered: "Would I were in an Ale-house in London, I would give all my fame for a Pot of Ale, and safety" (3.2.10). Such effects douse the Chorus's noble dream with cold splashes of reality.

But then, although the relation between whatever the Chorus says and what the play shows or suggests is so challengingly interrogative, this doesn't mean that the Chorus's thoroughly pro-Henry views only make an anti-Henry view more compelling. The "Henriad" nowhere suggests that any of the rebel leaders and factions are less inclined than the monarchs to identify their own interests with those of the common weal.[30] This might prompt bleak thoughts about power and history, or a more positively pragmatic sense of Henry's relative merits, but it doesn't make an anti-Henry view more compelling; if anything, it suggests why indulging a narrowly characterological judgment is simplistic and reductive, a form of social unrealism that (like Joyce's Mrs. Mooney in *Dubliners*) deals "with moral problems as a cleaver deals with meat."

The final act brings another, more perplexing but climactic collision between the Chorus and the play. The Chorus is historically correct when he reminds "those that have not read the Story" that Henry and his army returned to London after Agincourt, and that five years passed between the battle of Agincourt and the Treaty of Troyes, which is represented in the play's final scene. To the extent that this protest against "abridgement" seems in place, in a straightforwardly historical sense, it might appear to be an unequivocal example of the way in which—as Herbert Lindenberger assumes—"Shakespeare awkwardly excuses himself" through the Chorus, recognizing that "the modest

theatrical piece he has created can at best supply a few hints about the glory it purports to depict."[31] For A. P. Rossiter, who wrote so superbly about "ambivalence" in the history plays, *Henry V* is an exception, a "propaganda-play on National Unity"—the sort of play the Chorus would certainly prefer; Sigurd Burckhardt similarly supposes that in this play Shakespeare "knowingly chooses a partial and partisan clarity" so that we hear his "epic," rather than his "dramatic," voice—which, once again, is just what the Chorus would wish, although he certainly wouldn't agree with Burckhardt that this amounts to taking "a rest."[32] Yet when the Chorus asks "such as have read" the "Story" to

> admit th'excuse
> Of time, of numbers, and due course of
>   things,
> Which cannot in their huge and proper life,
> Be here presented.
>
> (Prol. 5, lines 3-6)

something more complicated, and deviously intricate, is happening, which should—if we ourselves are not taking a rest—render far more suspect the idea of a self-deprecatory Shakespeare apologizing through the Chorus.

First, we might notice how the Chorus's use of the word "Story" unleashes ironies he certainly does not intend. As a late Elizabethan who prides himself on his knowledge of history, he takes for granted that his own "king's-eye" version of the "Story" is the truth. This precludes any concern with the way in which a historical narrative is constructed and shaped, like any fictional story, by the narrator's sense of how best to make sense of events and lives. Just as the Chorus is entirely untroubled by historiographical doubts, he is entirely innocent of any *positive* conception of dramatic and narrative form, and complains about what the play cannot do without ever registering what it does do. Pistol would have no place in his "great Accompt," but then, far from considering what the "low" characters and episodes are doing in the play's version of the "Story," the Chorus never even acknowledges their existence: he always speaks about the play he so nervously inhabits as though they weren't there, and as though he himself weren't a part of it either. Here, as ever, he places himself between the play and its audience and apart from both, while worrying whether either will measure up to his "Story." Clearly he is apart from the dramatic action, which spans the period from April 30, 1414 to May 20, 1420; Fluellen is the amateur historian within the play's action, and still another fervently loyal, take-me-to-your-leader historian. So, as Anthony Brennan nicely observes, Fluellen provides "a comic parody within the plot of the homage to tradition that the Chorus presents outside it."[33] But to reflect on the relation between the Chorus and Fluellen as amateur historians is to respond to the play's very different way of presenting the "Story" and to see how, although the Chorus is apart from the play's action, he is very much a part of its dramatic thinking. Seeing himself as a judiciously detached and wholly authoritative commentator who can appraise, correct, and (in his own account of the king's triumphal return) supplement the play, he cannot see how he is assimilated into it, or how the play's irony enfolds his own nonironic use of the word "Story." When he apologizes for the play's inability to present things in their "huge and proper life" the play eats him, smiles expansively, and suggests why his own ideal version of the "Story" is so *small* and proper.

His version is more like Branagh's, not just in having real horses and more than four or five vile and ragged foils, but in altogether suppressing scenes like 5.1—which, as Branagh himself explains, isn't even very funny.[34] The Chorus wants a linear, annalistic account of what the high and mighty did from one year to the next, which keeps closer to the chronicles while carefully excluding anything like Holinshed's "some say" or "others allege," since such things let on that the "Story" hasn't been universally received as the Truth. Although seemingly unstructured, this ideal version would be forcefully structured or "abridged" by its automatic omissions and "proper" suppressions, and by the Chorus's unwavering assumption that the truth about how it really was—Ranke's *wie es eigentlich gewesen*—can and must be "presented" in a unified and uniformly "high" or "epic" fashion. In the Chorus's terms 5.1 is doubly offensive: the already displeasing, historically inaccurate "abridgement" makes room for another "low" and irrelevant comic scene or side-show thrown in for those groundlings who are incapable of responding to the "Story" like true "Gentles." But in that case what *is* 5.1 doing in Shakespeare's play?

Far from being apologetic, Shakespeare builds in another teasing, wittily defiant provocation. For as soon as the Chorus leaves the stage, 5.1 gives the contrary impression that the army has never left France, that barely any time has passed between 4.8 and 5.1, and that the victorious Henry proceeds directly from the battlefield to the French court. True, the King's final words in Act 4 referred to the return to Calais, then England; but that token gesture toward getting the "Story" right, in the Chorus's sense, has little dramatic weight if set against the impression of continuity. Act 5 abruptly opens in *"France. The English camp,"* and in the course of a further conversation between Fluellen and Gower, which we pick up as the latter remarks, "Nay, that's right: but why weare you youre Leeke to day? / S. *Davies* day is past." Fluellen replies, "There is occasions and causes why and wherefore in all things," and explains that he is looking for "that rascally, scauld, beggerly, lowsie, pragging Knave *Pistoll,* which you and your selfe, and all the World, know to be no petter then a fellow, looke you now, of no merits" (5.1-5.8). It is at once clear that this is

unfinished business. In 4.1 Pistol had assured the disguised king that he would "knock" Fluellen's "Leeke about his Pate upon S. *Davies* day," and now the angry Fluellen reports the insult he received "yesterday," when Pistol "prings me pread and sault yesterday, looke you, and bids me eate my Leeke: it was in a place where I could not breed no contention with him; but I will be so bold as to weare it in my Cap till I see him once againe, and then I will tell him a little piece of my desires" (lines 9-13). We have just heard the Chorus telling us of the *years* that passed between 4.8 and 5.1, but, as we readjust to the play's quite different way of telling the "Story," who counts the number of times St. Davy's day must have passed?

Here, instead of supposing that Shakespeare is "awkwardly excusing himself" by ventriloquizing through the Chorus, we should notice how he is engineering this exuberant collision between the Chorus and the play's different ways of "doing" history. So far as the "abridgement" of time is concerned the Chorus is right, and 5.1 is wholly irrelevant to the kind of play or dramatic "chronicle" this play makes its Chorus want and expect. Why conclude the play and the second tetralogy in such a fashion? Dr. Johnson was famously dismissive, commenting that "the poet's matter failed him in the fifth act, and he was glad to fill it up with whatever he could get."[35] Yet an alternative possibility, to which that climactic, finely engineered collision points, is to consider the fifth act as a highly organized design or poetic-dramatic conceit, in which the two final scenes make up an ironic diptych of "low" and "high" conclusions framed by the Chorus's protesting prologue and still more discontented epilogue. Act 5.1 may not be very funny in Branagh's sense, but it is a remarkably witty and disconcerting example of Shakespeare's dramatic rhyming. . . .

Notes

[21] Raphael Holinshed, *Chronicles of England, Scotland and Ireland,* 6 vols. (London, 1808), 3:132-33. As Phyllis Rackin usefully emphasizes in her important study *Stages of History: Shakespeare's English Chronicles* (London and New York: Routledge, 1990), the chronicles are the product of collaborative effort in which we hear a "plurality of voices": they "included the work of many writers—predecessors whose work was incorporated, successors who augmented the narratives after their authors' deaths, and collaborators at the time of their production" (23). See F. J. Levy's pioneering work, *Tudor Historical Thought* (San Marino, Calif.: Huntington Library, 1967).

[22] See George T. Wright's comments on "squinting lines," which "produce an effect that no manner of printing so far devised can make clear to the reader"; Wright, *Shakespeare's Metrical Art* (Berkeley: University of California Press, 1988), 103.

[23] For an excellent discussion of these issues, see Karl T. Wentersdorf, "The Conspiracies of Silence in *Henry V*," *Shakespeare Quarterly* 27 (1976): 264-87, especially 265-68, 280, 283. As Wentersdorf observes: "If Mortimer and his heirs are to be denied their rights to the crown on the ground that Mortimer is descended from Edward III in the female line, Henry V can scarcely proceed in conscience with his war to obtain the French crown on the basis of a claim likewise through descent in the female line," while "Cambridge and Scroop are challenging Henry V's right to the English throne on grounds at least as convincing as those justifying Henry's challenge to the French king."

The *King John* analogy is particularly interesting, in relation to Sigurd Burckhardt's arresting claim in *Shakespearean Meanings* (Princeton: Princeton University Press, 1968) that "what *King John* presents us with is a world in which authority is wholly untrustworthy" (138), and in which "he that holds his kingdom holds the law" (132). Several essays in Deborah T. Curren-Aquino, ed., *King John: New Perspectives* (London: Associated University Presses; Newark: University of Delaware Press, 1989) take up that challenge, as does David Womersley, "The Politics of King John," *Review of English Studies* 40 (November 1989): 497-515. But Burckhardt himself suggested that the latter history plays became "a kind of holding operation, with the work of discovery going on beneath the surface" (143); as far as *Henry V* is concerned, the important question is whether (as Marsha Robinson's essay in *King John: New Perspectives* assumes) the later play disregards the earlier play's challenging "discovery," and in this sense goes backward. This is what Annabel Patterson seems to think happened even between the Folio and Quarto versions of *Henry V*, since the Quarto eliminates so much of what I have called the historiographical challenge in the Folio; see Patterson, "Back by Popular Demand: The Two Versions of *Henry V*," in *Shakespeare and the Popular Voice* (Oxford and New York: Blackwell, 1989), 71-92, and the earlier version of this chapter in the 1989 volume of *Renaissance Drama*. However, since we do not know why these cuts were made, Patterson's argument reinforces the authority of the Folio text as the Shakespearean *Henry V*.

[24] Alexander Leggatt, *Shakespeare's Political Drama* (London and New York: Routledge, 1988), 115.

[25] "Thou art a blessed fellow to think as every man thinks," Hal wryly observes to Poins. "Never a man's thought in the world keeps the roadway better than thine" (*2H4*, 2.2.56-59). I do not want to deny that there were roadways; yet we should not assume that Shakespeare and every member of his audiences kept to them, or that establishing what they were and where they ran is a straightforward matter of consulting of-

ficial maps—that is, discovering what those in authority said people should believe.

Would Elizabethans, for instance, have been repelled by the "incestuous" marriage of Claudius and Gertrude? Although nobody in *Hamlet* apart from the Ghost and Hamlet seem troubled enough to mention it, Harold Jenkins admits no doubt in his edition of Hamlet (London: Methuen, 1982): the relationship was incestuous, and repellent, because the Leviticus-based Elizabethan law condemned such unions. He doesn't explain why the *other* relevant biblical text considers the question when an unmarried brother *should* marry a deceased brother's widow; chap. 7 of John Scarisbrick, *Henry VIII* (London: Eyre and Spottiswoode, 1968) provides a magisterial account of the significance of these conflicting texts (Lev. 18.16, 20.21; Deut. 25.5) in relation to Henry's busy marital itinerary. As it happens, the corresponding Scottish law was, until very recently, still based on Leviticus: like the Elizabethan law, it made no distinction between sleeping with one's sister and with one's sister-in-law. The law was finally changed, since many Scots thought there was a difference, and thought it important; but Jenkins's argument about "the" Elizabethan audience would also oblige him to deny that contemporary Scots could think any such thing—until that moment when the law was changed, and suddenly they all thought and felt differently!

[26] See Christopher Hibbert, *Agincourt* (London: Batsford, 1975), 33, and the telling discussion in Graham Holderness, Nick Potter, and John Turner, *Shakespeare: The Play of History* (London: Macmillan Press; Iowa City: University of Iowa Press, 1988), 63-67. Holinshed records that "soldiers were ransomed, and the towne sacked, to the great gain of the Englishmen," and warily mentions that others have made "mention of the distresses whereto the people, then expelled out of their habitations, were driven" (73-74); two thousand of the town's poor and infirm were expelled, and each was allowed to take no more than a small bundle and five sous.

Shakespeare's departure from his historical source material at this point is admittedly problematic. Some see it as evidence of a hagiographical determination to idealize power. In that case it's hard to understand why Shakespeare made Henry's speech so ruthless—and followed it with the governor's dignified and deflating speech, where the reason given for the surrender is the failure of reinforcements to arrive at the expected time. My own view is that the change is being assimilated to a long-range exploration of ends and means. The "Henriad" exposes short memories: many who would defend the Harfleur speech by arguing that Henry wanted to save lives would balk at defending Prince John's treacherous treatment of the rebels at Galtree, which also saves the lives of loyal soldiers. Moreover, in having Henry forbid looting, Shakespeare suggests the disquietingly ironic view that (as Hibbert's study confirms) the spoils of war were being reserved for the rulers and officers. Someone like Williams gets nothing at all, unless he accepts what the King and Fluellen give him; Pistol has to accept Fluellen's groat, but his obedience in butchering Le Fer means destitution. As ever, Shakespeare allows a view from the ranks—and a very topical one, since the frequently appalling situation of returning soldiers was something Cecil himself frequently bewailed, without being able to remedy it.

[27] Edward Powell, *Kingship, Law, and Society: Criminal Justice in the Reign of Henry V* (Oxford: Clarendon Press, 1989), 233-34.

[28] C. G. Cruikshank, *Elizabeth's Army,* 2d ed. (Oxford: Oxford University Press, 1968), chap. 2; Lindsay Boynton, *The Elizabethan Militia* (London: Routledge and Kegan Paul, 1967), chap. 6.

[29] Peter Clark, *English Provincial Society from the Reformation to the Revolution* (Brighton: Harvester Press, 1977).

[30] A similar pragmatic point might be made about *The Tempest* if, instead of basing our response on whatever general position we take in response to "post-colonial" critiques, we consider the particular characters who would dominate this particular island: Prospero, who will leave the island with no trace of regret once it has served his purpose, yet who is not simply an imperialist villain; Trinculo and Stephano, who have no sponsors; and Caliban, who cannot be considered merely as a dispossessed and much wronged "native" when he wants to rape Miranda and paunch Prospero with a stake.

[31] Herbert Lindenberger, *Historical Drama: The Relation of Literature and Reality* (Chicago: University of Chicago Press, 1975), 78. The assumption that Shakespeare is speaking through the Chorus persists, for example in Dollimore and Sinfield's essay on this play (Jonathan Dollimore and Alan Sinfield, "History and Ideology: the Instance of *Henry V*," in John Drakakis, ed., *Alternative Shakespeares* [London and New York: Methuen, 1985], 206-27), but it has also been challenged in several good discussions of the Chorus's role. See Anthony Brennan, "That Within Which Passeth Show," *Philological Quarterly* 59 (1980): 40-51, and Brennan's more recent chapter on *Henry V* in *Onstage and Offstage Worlds in Shakespeare's Plays* (London and New York: Routledge, 1989), 173-208. See also Eamon Grennan, "This Story Shall the Good Man Teach his Son," *Papers on Language and Literature* 15 (1979): 370-82; Gunter Walch, "Henry V as Working-House of Ideology," *Shakespeare Survey* 40 (1988): 63-68. As Walch observes, "The Chorus is an integral part of Shakespeare's strategy not in spite of his information being unreliable, but because it is unreliable, and because what he does not tell us is more important than what he does tell us" (67).

[32] A. P. Rossiter, *Angel with Horns,* (London: Longman, 1961), 57; Burckhardt, *Shakespearian Meanings,* 193; Lindenberger quotes these critics in *Historical Drama.*

[33] Brennan, *Onstage and Offstage Worlds,* 189.

[34] Kenneth Branagh, *Shakespeare: Henry 5* (London: Chatto & Windus, 1990), 11. Branagh declares the scene "resoundingly unfunny," without considering what the resonances might be if Shakespeare's complex design were regarded as anything more than a vehicle for the ego of actors with a crippling Olivier complex.

[35] Quoted in Lindenberger, *Historical Drama,* 78.

FURTHER READING

Ayers, P. K. " 'Fellows of Infinite Tongue': Henry V and the King's English." *Studies in English Literature 1500-1900* 34, No. 2 (Spring 1994): 253-77.

Relates Henry V's mastery of diverse modes of speech to the complex pattern of historical and theological issues raised by the play. Ayers believes that the king's verbal strategy has several different purposes: to reshape his public and private personas, erase the objective past, and obscure his own sins.

Babula, William. "Whatever Happened to Prince Hal?: An Essay on *Henry V*." *Shakespeare Survey* 30 (1977): 47-59.

Asserts that *Henry V* is concerned with the same theme as the two parts of *Henry IV:* the education of a ruler. Babula contends that Henry slowly but gradually progresses from a rash youth who avoids responsibility and whose speech is highly artificial to a mature, plain-spoken monarch who fully appreciates the values of peace and moderation.

Barton, Anne. "The King Disguised: Shakespeare's *Henry V* and the Comical History." In *The Triple Bond: Plays, Mainly Shakespearean, in Performance,* edited by Joseph G. Price, pp. 92-117. University Park: Pennsylvania State University Press, 1975.

Argues that in *Henry V* Shakespeare employed the popular motif of a disguised monarch's encounter with his subjects—a recurring feature of medieval ballads and late sixteenth-century history plays—to show that a sovereign is, by virtue of his office, no ordinary mortal but rather an emotionally isolated man.

Battenhouse, Roy. "*Henry V* in the Light of Erasmus." *Shakespeare Studies* XVII (1985): 77-88.

Views Henry as a pseudo-pious monarch who violates many of the norms set forth in Erasmus's *Praise of Folly* and *The Christian Prince*. Battenhouse holds that just as Erasmus satirizes rulers and their associates who adhere to pagan rather than Christian notions of kingship, Shakespeare's perspective on Henry's notions of justice and public welfare—and on Canterbury's as well—is deeply ironic.

Black, James. "Shakespeare's *Henry V* and the Dreams of History." *English Studies in Canada* 1, No. 1 (Spring 1975): 13-30.

Considers how Henry tries to meet the expectations of those who hold chivalric dreams of the past while at the same time shaping a new image of heroism for himself. Black distinguishes enthusiasm for epic wars and illustrious conquests—expressed by the Chorus and many others—from what he sees as Henry's workmanlike approach to war, which emphasizes shared fame and fellowship rather than personal glory.

Dean, Paul. "Chronicle and Romance Modes in *Henry V*." *Shakespeare Quarterly* 32, No. 1 (Spring 1981): 18-27.

Proposes that the Nym-Bardolph-Pistol subplot has a double function, serving as both a dramatic foil to the main plot and a subversive critique of Henry. Dean also comments on elements in the play derived from conventional "romance histories, particularly the episodes in which Henry appears in disguise and when he plays the role of lover."

Dollimore, Jonathan, and Alan Sinfield. "History and Ideology: the Instance of *Henry V*." In *Alternative Shakespeares*, edited by John Drakakis, pp. 206-27. New York: Routledge, 1985.

Provides a materialist analysis of ideology and power in *Henry V*, focusing on the play's treatment of national unity and internal conflict.

Gurr, Andrew. "'Henry V' and the Bees' Commonwealth." *Shakespeare Survey* 30 (1977): 61-72.

Examines the various motivations for war as well as Henry's conduct as a Christian monarch. In Gurr's judgment, *Henry V* demonstrates that a commonwealth is typically made up of a variety of self-interested persons who must be brought together to achieve a common goal—in this case the conquest of France. The critic also believes that Henry is principally driven by his need to achieve personal distinction and secure an untarnished title to the English throne.

Herman, Peter C. "'O, 'tis a gallant king': Shakespeare's *Henry V* and the Crisis of the 1590s." In *Tudor Political Culture*, edited by Dale Hoak, pp. 204-25. Cambridge: Cambridge University Press, 1995.

Contends that in *Henry V* Shakespeare challenges the validity of the Tudor view of history by articulating late sixteenth-century skepticism of established authority. Herman asserts that Bates and Williams's mistrust of royalty, Pistol's critical demeanor toward authority, and the consistent undermining of the Chorus's "official" view of Henry all contribute to a subversive questioning of Tudor propaganda and the myth of Henry as a paragon of virtue.

Hodgdon, Barbara. "'A Full and Natural Close, Like Music': *Henry V*." In *The End Crowns All*, pp. 185-211. Princeton, N.J.: Princeton University Press, 1991.

Assesses possible readings of the quarrel between Fluellen and Pistol, the prologue and epilogue to Act V, and the wooing scene. Hodgdon also describes the contradictory ways these passages were represented in three late twentieth-century stage productions and in Olivier's 1944 film adaption, and she considers the question of whether the play ends with a harmonious resolution of its discordant perspectives on history.

Holderness, Graham. "*Henry V*." In *Shakespeare: The Play of History*, edited by Graham Holderness, Nick Potter, and John Turner, pp. 62-82. Iowa City: University of Iowa Press, 1987.

Argues that the discrepancy between historical reality and theatrical representation in *Henry V* calls into question the ideology of national unity. Holderness maintains that despite the play's protestations regarding equality and a united kingdom, Henry suppresses the issue of civil dissent with his victory at Agincourt, and the values of chivalry and feudal aristocracy remain in place at the close.

Mossman, Judith. "*Henry V* and Plutarch's *Alexander*." *Shakespeare Quarterly* 45, No. 1 (Spring 1994): 57-73.

Suggests that Shakespeare made significant use of Plutarch's *Life of Alexander* in developing the structure and characterization of *Henry V*. Although Mossman sees Henry as "a more virtuous version of Alexander," she concludes that they are both complex figures—epic heroes who must contend with the duties, challenges, and tribulations of kingship.

Paris, Bernard J. "*Henry V*." In his *Character as a Subversive Force in Shakespeare*, pp. 91-109. Rutherford, N. J.: Fairleigh Dickinson University Press, 1991.

A psychoanalytic appraisal of the disparity between the play's idealistic rhetoric and its realistic portrayal of Henry. Noting that the rhetoric celebrates Henry as an exemplary king and superlative military hero, Paris argues that the protagonist is actually a contradictory character: convinced of the justice of his cause but also violently aggressive, self-effacing yet compulsively ambitious, and a perfectionist who frequently doubts his worthiness.

Ross, A. Elizabeth. "Hand-me-Down-Heroics: Shakespeare's Retrospective of Popular Elizabethan Heroical Drama in *Henry V*." In *Shakespeare's English Histories: A Quest for Form and Genre,* edited by John W. Velz, pp. 171-203. Binghamton, N.Y.: Medieval & Renaissance Texts & Studies, 1996.

Contends that in *Henry V* Shakespeare challenges Elizabethan literary ideals of the epic and the heroic. Ross is principally concerned with the many parallels and contrasts between this play and Marlowe's *Tamburlaine*—especially the choric figures, the function of rhetoric, and the use of irony and ambiguity—but she also evaluates Act IV, scene i in terms of the conventions of heroic ballad plays.

Taylor, Mark. "Imitation and Perspective in *Henry V.*" *Clio* 16, No. 1 (Fall 1986): 35-47.

Focuses on the way two episodes—the exposure of the English nobles' conspiracy and Henry's justification of his cause to Williams, Bates, and Court—highlight the king's attempts to manipulate others. On the first occasion, Taylor maintains, Henry successfully projects his point of view onto the conspirators so that they applaud their own death warrants; on the second occasion, however, the common soldiers maintain their own perspectives and thwart Henry's efforts to substitute his personal version of reality for theirs.

Tucker, E. F. J. "Legal Fiction and Human Reality: Hal's Role in *Henry V.*" *Educational Theatre Journal* 26, No. 3 (October 1974): 308-14.

Evaluates the question of Henry's moral transformation in terms of the Elizabethan concept of the King's Two Bodies. In Tucker's judgment, the scenes leading up to Agincourt show Henry struggling with—and ultimately accepting—the need to sacrifice his personal schemes so that he can fulfill his public responsibilities.

Vickers, Brian. "'Suppose you see': The Chorus in *Henry V* and *The Mirror for Magistrates.*" In *Shakespearean Continuities: Essays in Honour of E. A. J. Honigmann,* edited by John Batchelor, Tom Cain, and Claire Lamont, pp. 74-90. London: Macmillan, 1997.

Proposes that the Chorus's appeals to the audience's imagination represent Shakespeare's witty reminder of the collaborative nature of theater—in which author, actors, and spectators share responsibility for the success of a performance. Vickers also suggests that the prose prefaces in *The Mirror for Magistrates* may be a model for the Chorus in *Henry V.*

Wilcox, Lance. "Katherine of France as Victim and Bride." *Shakespeare Studies* XVII (1985): 61-76.

Regards Katherine as serving two dramatic functions: to represent the victims of military and sexual aggression, and to temper our view of Henry as a ruthless conqueror. Wilcox argues that although the wooing scene is designed to redeem Henry's image by showing him as a gracious lover, this episode fails to soften the grim portrayal of the king as a brutal invader.

Measure for Measure

For further information on the critical and stage history of *Measure for Measure,* see *SC,* Volumes 2, 23, and 33.

INTRODUCTION

Often identified as one of Shakespeare's "problem plays," *Measure for Measure* begins on a serious note, drawing audiences in with its focus on the moral dilemmas of its major characters. By the second half of the play, however, the tone shifts to a comic one, which distances audiences from the characters and their plights. This discordance is one of the issues that makes the play "problematic." Another such issue is the play's stance on law, justice, and mercy. In analyses of these themes, critics are unable to agree on what message Shakespeare intended to convey. Often, such discussions focus on the characters of the Duke and Angelo, who, as governmental leaders, are in a position to interpret the law and dispense justice and mercy. Other topics of modern critical debate include the role of sexuality in the play, as well as Shakespeare's use of substitutions in the play.

In examining the inconsistencies in *Measure for Measure*, A. D. Nutall (1968) states that the "Grand Inconsistency" of the play is that "between the ethic of government and the ethic of refraining from judgement." Nutall examines Angelo and the Duke as rulers and heroes and maintains that it is possible to view Angelo as a good Machiavellian ruler, who retains a certain integrity throughout the play. The Duke, Nutall argues, is frivolous and cannot be taken seriously as a satisfactory hero. In exploring the attitudes of the Duke and Angelo regarding the law and its application, N. W. Bawcutt (1984) claims that *Measure for Measure* presents a dual image of the law, in which the law is ignored without consequence but may suddenly mete out harsh punishment with a certain arbitrariness. Mercy, Bawcutt demonstrates, is similarly presented in a variety of ways, whereas justice and the law are relatively indistinguishable from one another.

Other critics focus on how specific aspects of the law are treated in *Measure for Measure*. Margaret Scott (1982) reviews the play's vague law against fornication and cautions against approaching the play through the examination of Elizabethan marriage contracts. Jonathan (1985) studies the regulation of sexuality in the play, suggesting that, as in Elizabethan and Jacobean England, such regulation was a reaction of the State against the fear of anarchy.

In examining the apparent structural inconsistencies between the two halves of the play, Herbert Weil, Jr. (1970) argues that if the falling action of the play is viewed as light comedy, even farce, then the action does in fact "fit into a comprehensive design." Weil maintains that through the comic subplot involving Lucio, Pompey, and Mistress Overdone, Shakespeare prepares the audience for the comic reversals of the second half of the play. Furthermore, Weil suggests that Shakespeare deliberately altered his sources in order to engineer the audience's disappointment resulting from the failure of the action to resolve the characters' moral dilemmas. The purpose of this alteration, Weil asserts, was to highlight, through Shakespeare's parodying of the melodrama of his sources, the limitations of comic form and devices. At the same time, Shakespeare "stretches [comic conventions and implausible devices] into new possibilities." Like Weil, T. A. Stroud (1993) emphasizes the importance of the play's comic substructure, arguing that the comic plot initiated by Lucio was intended to balance, (and nearly does so, according to Stroud), the "quasi-tragic plot initiated by Angelo." Stroud stresses that an analysis of this doubling or balancing could resolve "some of the widespread critical dissatisfaction with this play." In her analysis of *Measure for Measure* as tragicomedy, Harriett Hawkins (1972) outlines some of the major discrepancies between the first and second half of the play and describes it as "a magnificent failure." Hawkins states that the most pervasive problem of the play is "that the memory of the characters, their speeches, and their conflicts between mutually exclusive moral alternatives simply cannot be revoked by the theatrical intriguing of a Duke. . . ."

The sexual relations between men and women play a major role in *Measure for Measure*. Kathleen McCluskie (1985) contends that the dilemmas in the play and the sexuality of its female characters are conceived of in entirely male terms: Mistress Overdone is a bawd, Juliet is obviously pregnant, and Isabella, in her nun's habit, denies sexuality. Only Mariana's position is ambiguous, since she is not a maid, widow, or wife. The organization of the second half of the play is designed to rectify this problematic status, McCluskie argues, and to reinstate Mariana within the male prescribed sex roles. Susan Carlson

(1989) on the other hand, maintains that the play offers a "fragile" and "unusual" alternative to male dominated sexuality. This alternative, according to Carlson, is simply "the acknowledgement of qualities, options, and relations for both men and women not sanctioned by the standard sexual politics." In the end, Carlson notes, the possibility for the existence of this alternative, which challenges the play's male order, is eliminated.

In *Measure for Measure*, characters are repeatedly substituted for one another. Alexander Leggatt (1988) reviews some of these substitutions: Mariana for Isabella in the bed-trick, Angelo for the Duke, Barnardine for Claudio, and Ragozine for Barnardine. The critic maintains that the substitutions in the play either fail to achieve their intended purpose or are in some other way unsatisfying, concluding that the substitutions are both "revealing" and "fascinating" but incomplete. Additionally, Leggatt states that Shakespeare did not deliberately write an imperfect play in order to highlight the imperfections of his art. Hutson Diehl (1998) directly challenges Leggatt's view, insisting that this is indeed what Shakespeare has done. Diehl argues that Shakespeare explores, through the use of substitutions, the power and limitation of theatrical representation, and that in doing so, he creates a dissatisfaction·in the audience's response to *Measure for Measure*. By creating this dissatisfaction, Diehl explains, Shakespeare uses the theater for "the project of reforming human behavior even as he acknowledges the limits of that project and distances his theater from the extremist views of radical Puritanism." Through *Measure for Measure*, Diehl concludes, Shakespeare inspires in his audiences a sense "of the infinite space that separates them from the divine."

LAW AND JUSTICE

A. D. Nutall (essay date 1968)

SOURCE: "Measure For Measure: Quid Pro Quo?," in *Shakespeare Studies: An Annual Gathering of Research, Criticism, and Reviews,* Vol. IV, 1968, pp. 231-51.

[*In the following essay, Nutall examines the inconsistencies and "ethical collisions" in* Measure for Measure. *In particular, the critic scrutinizes the ethics of government and judgment and contrasts Angelo's moral character with that of the Duke.*]

Some people seem to have little difficulty in understanding *Measure for Measure;* for example, Professor Wilson Knight. His summary of the play's theme is at once lucid and deeply attractive: "'justice' is a

mockery: man, himself a sinner, cannot presume to judge. That is the lesson driven home in *Measure for Measure*."[1] It is difficult not to respond gratefully to this thesis, which exalts the loving prostitute above the censorious prig, charity of heart above Olympian pride of intellect. If mankind is frail, then we, as part of mankind, are frail, and the proper response to our situation is not judgement, but love. Further, Professor Knight's thesis is not only *inherently* attractive; it also accords well with the main movement of the plot, which is from judicial retaliation to forgiveness and harmony. Again, it attaches itself closely to certain passages in the play—passages which derive their beauty from their enormous moral power:

> How would you be
> If He, which is the top of judgement, should
> But judge you as you are? O, think on that,
> And mercy then will breathe within your lips,
> Like man new made.
> *(II.ii.75-79)*

> But man, proud man,
> Dress'd in a little brief authority,
> Most ignorant of what he's most assur'd—
> His glassy essence—like an angry ape
> Plays such fantastic tricks before high heaven
> As makes the angles weep. . . . [2]
> *(II.ii.118-123)*

Within the world of *Measure for Measure* Professor Knight's thesis exalts, say, the forgiving Duke high above the frigid Angelo, which would seem to be very good sense, since the Duke is obviously the hero and Angelo the villain.

Unobviously, however, the situation is quite otherwise. If we allow ourselves to look at all hard at the play, a shadowy structure of a disturbingly alien shape becomes visible under the comedy surface. One thing we can learn quite quickly is, for example, the fact that Angelo is, on a modest computation (as Swift would say) worth about six Dukes. One begins to suspect that the whole trouble with Professor Knight's account is its very smoothness. It is occasionally salutary to ask oneself "If I had never read or seen *Measure for Measure,* but knew it only from Professor Knight's essay, what sort of idea of the work would I have? What surprises would I get when I turned to the play itself? In what ways would the real experience of *Measure for Measure* differ from the experience Professor Knight had led me to expect?" I think it is fair to say (and this goes not just for Professor Knight's account but also for the varying interpretations of Roy Battenhouse, Nevill Coghill and even F. R. Leavis)[4] that Shakespeare would give such a reader a much *rougher ride* than he had looked for. The first thing he would learn from a virgin text is that *Measure for Measure* is a jagged play.

It is also a highly dialectical play, perhaps the most audaciously metaphysical of all Shakespeare's dramas. In *Measure for Measure* Shakespeare (who had after all trained himself on such stories asthat of *The Comedy of Errors*) wove a plot of astonishing ingenuity. As long as this play is treated as a work of abstract art, it will be found as smooth as your mistress's glass. So considered, its primary characteristics are intricacy and celerity. The principal idea (of vicarious action) is worked out in a very pretty sequence of variations meeting in a final resolution. For example, one may hear the theme in brilliant *accelerando* if one traces that strand of the plot which brings Lucio into contact with the Duke. In III.ii. Lucio slanders the Duke to the Friar, not knowing that the Duke and the Friar are one and the same person (though he seems to know that the Duke has disguised himself). Then, at V.i.130f., he slanders the Friar to the Duke, not knowing—again—that they are the same person. Thus Lucio's fertility in slander is frustrated by the Duke's fertility in subterfuge. The variety of the Duke's appearances cancels out the variety of Lucio's mendacity, leaving a single net offence—the slander of a prince.

So one pole of the play is, we may say, *technical* neatness. The other is, of course, *metaphysical* disorder. Thus the effect of the play may be expressed by describing it as having the tempo and intervals of a minuet worked out in a sequence of violent discords. For example: it is likely that the substitution of Mariana for Isabel in Angelo's bed is one of the elements in the plot which we owe to Shakespeare alone. The episode illustrates very clearly the double character of ingenuity and discordancy which I impute to the play as a whole. On the one hand it is expert comedy-plotting, a dramatic structure in itself intricate and mirroring other elements in the play, as for example the Friar-Duke-Lucio relationship I have just described. Isabel is a lady who has dedicated her virginity to God. She expresses herself as willing to give anything to save her brother's life. Angelo then turns the tables on her by asking for the one thing she feels she cannot give. In effect, the Duke's delegate strives to usurp the place of God in Isabel's life (for she is betrothed to God). But Angelo is (or was) betrothed to Mariana. Thus Isabel is able, by breaking faith with Angelo, to keep her faith with God. The venial sin of Mariana in sleeping with her betrothed formally echoes the venial sin of Claudio who slept with *his* and so began the whole chain of events. The stratagem of Isabel and the Duke mathematically cancels out the stratagem of Angelo, who is brought to commit the very crime for which he had sentenced Claudio. Angelo's attempt at usurpation is countered by another usurpation (Mariana's); and the double falsehood issues in a strange propriety. Thus we have a *peripeteia* within a *peripeteia*. What could be more elegant?

And yet, as we watch it happen, what could be more appalling? How can Isabel who so imperiously denounced her brother's action—"There is a vice that most I do abhor, / And most desire should meet the blow of justice . . ." (II.ii.29-30)—assent with such sprightly readiness to the suggestion that Mariana perform the self-same action—"The image of it gives me content already . . ." (III.i.260). Note that Shakespeare could, had he wished, have made this much more comfortable for us. He could easily have caused Isabel to argue from the first that Claudio in effect committed no sin with Juliet.[5] This would have had the further consequence of making Isabel's duet with Lucio (in which they together try to divert the harsh purpose of Angelo) altogether more harmonious. But Shakespeare preferred to show us an Isabel forced by vicissitude into strange company, into what is almost an unholy alliance. Theoretically, she is really (as Mary Lascelles saw[6]) much closer to Angelo than to Lucio. Both are ethical precisionists. Both abhor the confusion of charity with indulgence, of licence with true mercy. Yet Isabel must plead against an insinuating counterpoint from Lucio which almost amounts to a parody of her argument. Certainly, the episode comes off more smoothly in Whetstone. But who prefers Whetstone's scene to Shakespeare's?[7]

That the play is full of ethical collisions, not to say inconsistencies, needs little labour to show. Isabel not only turns, in the words of Sir Arthur Quiller Couch,[8] from a saint into a bare procuress; she also lets down the Christian historicist critic. Thus in her early clash with Angelo we are told that anyone who thinks Isabel *ought* to submit to Angelo is the victim of a modern prejudice; that it could never have occurred to an Elizabethan that there could be anything vicious in fidelity to a vow of chastity. What's supernatural is supernatural. What's natural is only natural. And then, when all our learning has been lavished in defence of her supernatural dedication, she marries the Duke. Of course, such a defence of the automatically over-riding status of Isabel's vows was always bad history of ideas. Raymond Southall has shown[9] how the distinction between social and spiritual grace formed the material of open controversy in the sixteenth century—that is, if I have correctly understood the opening sections of his essay. J. W. Lever has[10] an interesting quotation from Tyndale on the pride of Lucrece, "which pryde god more abhorreth than the whordome of any whor." More could be added from Erasmus.[11] Indeed Lever has observed[12] that the affirmation of specifically "natural" values is a commonplace of humanism. To bring the argument nearer home we might observe that in the source-stories both of Cinthio and Whetstone the Isabel-figure actually does the inconceivable thing; she yields, and yet remains the heroine. If a Shakespearean voice is wanted to show that people *could* think unfavourably of chastity, there is Parolles—"virginity is peevish, proud, idle, made of self-love . . ." (*AWW*, I.i.149). Or, if Parolles disgraces the witness box, it must be granted that the Duke, in the present play, distinguishes plainly enough between an introverted preoccupation with one's own virtue and an outward-turned beneficence in his words to Angelo at I.i.29:

> Thyself and thy belongings
> Are not thine own so proper as to waste
> Thyself upon thy virtues, they on thee.[13]

These are dangerous sentiments to leave lying about in the neighbourhood of Isabel.

Of course I am aware that answers can be made to all these points; and, in particular, that Isabel can readily be cleared of the charge of simple egoism. I can even agree with E. M. Pope that the dominant feeling of the time would endorse Isabel's refusal to yield to Angelo.[14] I only submit that for a play as dense in texture as *Measure for Measure* to register a "dominant feeling" is not enough. We must be receptive to the presence of varying undermeanings. To assimilate the present scene to the basic tenets of the Elizabethan World Picture (which I begin to think was as real an entity as the Twentieth Century World Picture—imagine a critic three hundred years hence operating on, say, Muriel Spark, with *that*) is to empty the scene of stress. As it stands, the collision of values is immense. A crack runs rapidly across the scorched earth; the direct love of God is split from the love of neighbour. The two basic commands of the Gospels of which George Herbert wrote: "O dark instructions; ev'n as dark as day!"[15] prove, after all, not wholly perspicuous. There once appeared an ecclesiastical cartoon which showed a little monk praying fervently while his superior angrily shouted "Are you going over my head?" *Fabula docet.* As soon as we learn how to enter into a direct relationship with God, our relationship with the world can be viewed as a distraction. As long as one's love of God is naturally discharged by love of one's neighbour, Isabel's dilemma is impossible. Only with the birth of the monastic ideal and of the notion that I can love God best if I withdraw from my neighbour's society, does it become possible. Only then can God and my neighbour become rivals. In *Measure for Measure* God has two rivals for the love of Isabel, one loved and one detested but who working together are almost dangerous—namely Claudio and Angelo. Certainly Isabel's situation is ill described as egoism under attack. She cannot forget her own honour for the sake of Claudio since she has pledged that honour to God. If the reader feels something preposterous in this high piled metaphysical structure—something reminiscent of, say, Graham Greene, I am inclined to agree with him. I fancy Shakespeare felt it too; after all, he created the ironic witness Lucio and even Isabel cannot keep it up. But the metaphysical terror, though wafer-thin, is real.

Isabel's marriage, then, is as inconsistent as her attitude to sexual intercourse between engaged persons. But this is of small importance compared with the Grand Inconsistency of the whole play—namely the inconsistency between the ethic of government and the ethic of refraining from judgement. But having named this conflict I propose to postpone its discussion. It may profitably be left to germinate for a while in the reader's consciousness.

I have suggested a discrepancy between the "technical" smartness of this play and its ideological discordancy. The application of this distinction to, say, the character of Angelo is straightforward. Its effect is greatly to weaken the force of the plain man's argument against him, already cited: "Angelo is the technical villain; therefore it makes good sense to hold that he is contemptible." Isabel is the technical heroine, but she is not permitted to survive unmarked. Perhaps a correlative dispensation is extended to Angelo.

To begin from what is generally accepted: we all know better than Hazlitt now. Angelo is not a common hypocrite.[16] Isabel is at her very best when she says of him

> I partly think
> A due sincerity govern'd his deeds
> Till he did look on me.
>
> (*V.i.443-445*)

The tone of this is subtle. It represents an effort of objectivity. It also expresses a kind of bewilderment. Isabel is finding that she has not really understood what happened, does not really understand Angelo. And indeed it is a question whether he is intelligible at all. His loneliness is so nearly complete.

His first words in the play—

> Always obedient to your Grace's will,
> I come to know your pleasure
>
> (*I.i.25-26*)

—are perhaps faintly ridiculous. But the speech should be so delivered as to defeat an incipient risibility in the audience by its sheerly factual character. It is a part which should be played with a complete insensitivity to social overtones, and a complete attention to radical meaning. As the figure of Angelo moves before us we find a certain note struck again and again. It is the fundamental idea of the play—vicariousness—but in Angelo it finds its most intricate and powerful expression.

Angelo is, in the inherited story of the play, a deputy, the Duke's Vicar. But Shakespeare has extended this notion to color the very essence of Angelo. He is in himself a sort of surrogate human being. The Duke, gazing at Angelo on his first appearance, observes that the virtue of so excellent a man requires and merits public exercise. The sentiment is ordinary enough. But also present in the speech is the merest hint of a much more radical—indeed, a philosophical—idea, namely that virtue is essentially a matter of behaviour, that the man whose virtue is invisible cannot meaningfully be said to be virtuous at all. It is a speech I have already touched on:

> Thyself and thy belongings
> Are not thine own so proper as to waste
> Thyself upon thy virtues, they on thee.
> Heaven doth with us as we with torches do,
> Not light them for themselves; for if our
>   virtues
> Did not go forth of us, 'twere all alike
> As if we had them not.
>
> (I.i.29-35)

The Arden editor notes that this passage echoes language used elsewhere by Shakespeare of procreation. It also recalls Ulysses' philosophical exhortation of Achilles (though the similarity is in thought and style rather than in vocabulary):

> . . . no man is the lord of anything . . .
> Till he communicate his parts to others;
> Nor doth he of himself know them for ought
> Till he behold them form'd in the applause
> Where they're extended; who, like an arch
>   reverberates
> The voice again, or like a gate of steel
> Fronting the sun, receives and renders back
> His figure and his heat.
>
> (Troilus and Cressida, III.iii.115-123)

Angelo is the man suggested by the philosophizing of Ulysses; in himself nothing, pure function (at ll.ii.39 he actually uses the word "function" of himself). The Duke forthwith appropriates his identity: "be thou at full ourself" (I.i.43). The purely instrumental status of Angelo is repeatedly brought to our notice:

> Whether the tyranny be in his place,
> Or in his eminence that fills it up,
> I stagger in.
>
> (I.ii.152-154)

> I have on Angelo impos'd the office.
>
> (I.iii.40)

> How will you do to content this substitute . . . ?
>
> (III.i.186-187)

> Lord Angelo dukes it well in his absence.
>
> (III.ii.91)

Through all the proliferating substitutions of the play, Angelo remains (so to speak) the supreme vicar. Yet he has his own kind of solidity (and it is a moral kind).

Professor Coghill makes much[17] of his refusal personally to sift the evidence in the case of Froth and Bum—

> This will last out a night in Russia
> When nights are longest there. I'll take my
>   leave,
> And leave you to the hearing of the cause;
> Hoping you'll find good cause to whip them
>   all.
>
> (II.i.133-136)

It is, however, doubtful whether there is anything discreditable in the delegation of this tedious business to Escalus. Physical chastisement has acquired in modern times an added character of traumatic outrage and thus Angelo's parting words may shock a present-day audience where they would earn a sympathetic laugh in a Jacobean theatre. Nevertheless, the line retains a distinctly unpleasant force, which is principally located in the word "hoping." A certain relish of anticipation is implied. Perhaps we might say that this is the first faint sign in Angelo of the lust which will destroy him. But the real tenor of the speech is missed if we stop here. There is a further phrase in the line which, coming from the lips of Angelo, has the power to check and channel the suggestion of "hoping": I mean the phrase "good cause." At the very moment when Angelo's blood quickens, his grip tightens on the law. Although the tension of this speech is so gently hinted and so soon over, it is really present and foreshadows the later development of Angelo. Our dominant impression is still that of a hollow man, a sort of lay-figure. But as the play progresses we see that there persists in Angelo, even through the usurpation of his own soul by lust fully revealed and irresistible, a kind of integrity.

Which is more than can be said for the Duke. The Duke is a ruler who has let things slide. In order to restore good order in Vienna he appoints a substitute who will bear on his shoulders all the odium of renewed severity. This is the Grand Substitution of the play at the purely political level.

For this play is profoundly political. Roy Battenhouse described it (but without any consciousness of paradox) as "a Mirror for Magistrates founded on Christian love."[18] We can now look a little more closely at the conflict I have already alluded to—the conflict between the ethic of government and the ethic of refraining from judgement.

Anyone who has read through Cinthio's tale and Whetstone's two-part play can watch for himself the growth of a serious and rebarbative preoccupation with legal utility in the transplantation of this story from Italy to England. Mary Lascelles has noted[19] how the law in Cinthio has the status of a purblind dotard guarding an orchard from children among whom it is a point of honour to rob the trees; whereas in Whetstone we find a Tudor reverence for law itself with criticism reserved for defects in its administration. It seems doubtful whether Whetstone realized what a formidably un-Christian ethical force he had released by honouring human law in such a context. Indeed, to men who were seriously concerned with the ordering of institutions, the revolutionary morality of *Matthew,* vii, *Mark,* iv, and *Luke,* vi (the Scriptural sources for the title of this play) presented grave difficulties. Elizabeth Marie Pope has brilliantly shown what sort of effect these passages had on the magisterial mind. For example she quotes[20] Calvin and William Perkins to the effect that such Biblical texts should not lead a man to condone open and serious wrong. Attempts were made to resolve the difficulty by distinguishing between the actions of a private individual and the actions of the state. Private citizens may—indeed, should—be as Christian as possible, but judicial clemency is "limited in practice to considerations of ordinary common sense."[21]

But what then of the Prince, who, in his own person, *is* the State? Presumably he should *not* indulge a promiscuous clemency. Of course the Prince who condemns does so not in his own name but as the minister and vicar of God.[22] This in a way reproduces the dual morality of those Scriptural passages which lie behind the title "Measure for Measure." For example, in the verses from *Matthew,* vii we are told to refrain from judgement, not because judgement must be transcended by love, but "that ye be not judged." In *Mark,* iv[23] the over-riding context of divine retribution is even clearer. So the Prince *qua* man has no duty save to love and forgive his fellow creatures, but as God's substitute he must hunt out and punish the malefactor.

If we press hard on the argument, the ruler might appear to be metaphysically in a cleft stick. As the bloodless instrument of God's will he must perform actions which in a human creature count as sins; his office is eschatologically a millstone round his neck, for the obligation it confers is an obligation to sin.

There is, of course, a short way to resolve this difficulty. The only disquieting thing about it is that if we adopt it we come near to absolving Angelo of guilt in his treatment of Claudio. Thus we may point out that to say X does such and such a thing in the name of Y means that Y, not X, bears the responsibility for the action. Thus God, not the Prince, bears the responsibility for official executions. Now Angelo certainly condemns Claudio in the Duke's name. So whose is the responsibility now? It may be replied that this is sheer sophistry since the Duke never authorised Angelo to do *that.* But is it? The Duke was fully aware of Angelo's character. Hence, indeed, his appointment as substitute. The Duke wants Angelo for the job just because he will condemn people like Claudio. And to condemn the Claudios of Vienna is not just politically

imprudent; it is too dirty a job for the Duke's squeamish conscience. Would not this reformation of justice seem more dreadful in yourself than in a deputy? Asks Friar Thomas:

> I do fear, too dreadful.
> Sith 'twas my fault to give the people scope,
> 'Twould be my tyranny to strike and gall
>   them
> For what I bid them do: for we bid this be
>   done,
> When evil deeds have their permissive pass,
> And not the punishment. Therefore indeed,
>   my father,
> I have on Angelo impos'd the office;
> Who may in th'ambush of my name strike
>   home,
> And yet my nature never in the fight
> To do in slander
>   (I.iii.34-43)

There are two arguments here: the first is straight Machiavelli: delegate unpopular actions. We need not look far in *The Prince* for an analogue to the Duke of Vienna:

> the province was a prey to robbery, assaults, and every kind of disorder. He [Cesare Borgia], therefore, judged it necessary to give them a good government in order to make them peaceful and obedient to his rule. For this purpose he appointed Messer Remirro de Orco, a cruel and able man, to whom he gave the fullest authority. This man, in a short time, was highly successful in rendering the country orderly and united, whereupon the duke, not deeming such excessive authority expedient, lest it should become hateful, appointed a civil court of justice in the centre of the province under an excellent president, to which each city appointed its own advocate. And as he knew that the harshness of the past had engendered some amount of hatred, in order to purge the minds of the people and to win them over completely, he resolved to show that if any cruelty had taken place it was not by his orders, but though the harsh disposition of his minister. And having found the opportunity he had him cut in half and placed one morning in the public square at Cesena with a piece of wood and bloodstained knife at his side. The ferocity of this spectacle caused the people both satisfaction and amazement.[24]

But to be sure, the Duke of Vienna pardoned Angelo.

Of course, to show that a character is Machiavellian is not *ipso facto* to prove him a villain. The idea that a ruler should delegate odious offices is Aristotelian[25] and was referred to with approval by Erasmus[26] before it was adopted by Machiavelli. Mario Praz has shown[27] how Machiavellian principles were implicitly approved by Thomas More, Montaigne and Spenser. Mary Lascelles notes[28] that the ideal governor in Elyot's *The*

Image of Governaunce (1541) is allowed to use sub-terfuge to ensure a just outcome. There is a whole essay to be written round what might be called the "White Machiavel" in Shakespeare. Such an essay might begin from Sonnet 94 ("They that have power to hurt") and end in a discussion of the supreme White Machiavel, Prince Hal. W. H. Auden has already pointed out[29] that one style is common to the solilo-quies of Iago and Hal. Plainly, any writer with as strong an interest as Shakespeare's in government could not long escape seeing the bitter duties of a prince whose care for his people was more than sentimental. But have we a White Machiavel in *Measure for Measure?* I think perhaps we have, but the Duke is not he.

The good Machiavellian ruler, if we allow him to be saveable at all, is saved by his resolute dedication to a good end. No such powerful direction is discernible in the tergiversations of the Duke. Certainly, he pre-serves the luxury of a technically uncorrupted con-science; certainly he ensures that the laws are rein-forced, even if he proceeds by his orgy of clemency at the close to undo all the good achieved. Note that we can approve his behaviour at the end of the play only at the cost of condemning his behaviour at its outset. A man can play football or cricket; but he cannot score goals with a cricket bat. At whichever end of the ethi-cal spectrum you begin, you will never make a satis-factory hero of the Duke. I suspect that the essential frivolity of his nature really shows itself in the speech with which he ends I.iii—

> Lord Angelo is precise;
> Stands at a guard with Envy; scarce confesses
> That his blood flows; or that his appetite
> Is more to bread than stone. Hence shall we
>   see
> If power change purpose, what our seemers
>   be.

Is it too curious to detect in this speech a certain relish of anticipation? Is there not a slight shifting of ground from the opening scene in which the Duke professes his trust in, and grave respect for, the ascetic probity of Angelo? Is there not the merest shadow of a Lucio-like sneer at the chastity of Angelo? It is Lucio who echoes the Duke's language at I.iv.57-58—"a man whose blood / Is very snowbroth." Again it is a mat-ter of exclusive alternatives. If we welcome the mock-ing tone of these lines, then we must surely reject as priggish the grave eulogy at I.i.26-40. As Clifford Leech has observed,[30] the Duke cannot *both* be test-ing a suspected nature and tightening up the admin-istration of Vienna by the most reliable means to hand. But perhaps this is too dubious an instance to hang an entire interpretation on. A surer index is the Duke's unblushing readiness to hear confessions (and talk about them afterwards). The priestly disguise holds no embarrassment for him: "I have confess'd

her, and I know her virtue" (V.i.524). The Duke in *Measure for Measure* is, at the political level, at best an off-white Machiavel, incongruously elevated to the position of Presiding Genius. At the metaphysical level he is, perhaps, mere Machiavel.

The bare mention of Machiavelli, however, raises the ethical question of ends and means. Ought we to per-form an action in itself wicked in order that a greater good may come of it? This question is fundamental in *Measure for Measure,* and I fancy that in raising it I have reached the point at which I can no longer even hope for unanimity in the responses of readers. Christian opinion is itself divided on the point. On the one hand there is the tender-minded view, as expressed by the Thomist Jacques Maritain (writing on Machiavelli); moral conscience, he says "is never allowed to do evil for any good whatsoever."[31] On the other hand Hilaire Belloc took up the tough-minded position when he defined sentimentality as the inability to see that the end justifies the means. I suppose most modern Englishmen implicitly assent to the proposition that the end justifies the means. Any clergyman, for example, who allows the pos-sible existence of a just war thereby ranges himself with Belloc and against Maritain.[32] The Elizabethans, with their fear of anarchy, were, I think, a little quicker to see this than we. Having assembled my apparatus I must set it to work. According to the terms elaborated we may find in *Measure for Mea-sure* two fundamental ethical views, tender and tough, of which the first must be subdivided into two fur-ther sections. Let us label them *Ia, Ib* and *II.*

Ia may be expressed as follows: No man who is not himself perfect has the right to judge a fellow crea-ture. Man can only forgive and exercise charity. For example:

> *Isabel*
>   Go to your bosom,
>   Knock there, and ask your heart what it doth
>   know
>   That's like my brother's fault. If it confess
>   A natural guiltiness, such as is his,
>   Let it not sound a thought upon your tongue
>   Against my brother's life.
>
>   *(II.ii.137-142)*

Compare also II.ii.75f., IV.ii.81-83. Persons who hold to this opinion tend in practice to believe that the end cannot justify the means. The connection between these two notions is not immediately obvious. My own guess is that both stem from a powerful awareness of the supernatural authority of God and a correspondingly low estimate of man. To such a mind ethics tends to consist of a series of God-given imperatives. These imperatives cannot be appraised or placed in order of value by merely human intelligence. Ours not to reason why. This granted, man's right to ethical judgement is no greater than the child's right to judge the proficiency of his schoolfellow in, say, French prose composition. And to form projects involving the considered subjection of means to ends involves a similar assumption of Olympian authority. View *Ia* almost certainly lies behind the repulsion Escalus feels at Angelo's account of the law as a scarecrow, which if left unchanged will become the object of contempt (II.i.1f). Note that if we side with Escalus here we place ourselves in opposition to the Duke whose loving state-craft is very fairly represented by Angelo's words. But we are growing accustomed to these uncomfortable choices. Such then is ethic *Ia;* the high Christian variant of the tender view.

Ib is on the contrary, low and non-Christian, though still, of course, tender. It goes something like this: anybody without a bit of generous vice in him isn't properly human. The sexual appetite is in itself good; it is of the heart, and heart is more than head. This has a very twentieth-century flavour but is certainly present in *Measure for Measure*—most obviously in the "low" dialogue of the play, though the implied collision of values is never so clearly expressed as by Escalus in his rueful comment on Angelo's austere judicial conduct:

> Well, heaven forgive him; and forgive us all.
> Some rise by sin, and some by virtue fall.
>
> *(II.i.37-38)*

The same ethical collision is asserted "from below," as the Arden editor noticed, in the comic misplacings of Elbow:

> But precise villains they are, that I am sure
>   of, and void of all profanation in the
>   world, that good Christians ought to have.
>
> *(II.i.54-56)*

To hammer the point home Escalus is here given a "Here's a wise fool" response. Isabel, after she has been battered down from her high Christian position, has recourse to the low-tender view: "'Tis set down so in heav'n, but not in earth" (II.iv.50).

Ethic *II,* the tough-minded one, has much less power (it will be noticed at once) to give us warm feelings. To begin with, it is white Machiavellianism. Ends (in this fallen world) justify means; to resist this is to lapse into sentimentalism; *of course* none of us is perfect but *of course* we must judge; the man who is willing to abolish the police force in order to luxuriate in a private orgy of conscience is less merciful than the magistrate who administers the law in the interests of the community. This ethic is impersonalist, pragmatic and anti-sentimental. Above all it is the ethic of Angelo. Ethic *II* yields no passages of moving poetry,

as e.g. *Ib* does, in Lucio's "blossoming time" speech at I.iv.40f. That, I suspect, may be part of the point. Its ugliness and inaccessibility are correlative with the ugliness and inaccessibility of Angelo himself. It is supported "from below" by the dramatist, but in a manner appropriate to its nature. All the scenes in which the corruption of Vienna is conveyed work on its behalf. For, observe, human sexuality in *Measure for Measure* has two faces, one fair and one (from which Professor Wilson Knight appears to have averted his eyes) very foul indeed. Anyone who thinks of this play as a simple celebration of the procreative processes should read through, say, III.ii.

Now concerning these rival ethics I should like to put what might well be thought an indecorous question. Which of them, *as argument,* cuts deepest? Wood cuts butter; so Isabel cuts through the simple monster of ferocity she takes Angelo to be. Steel resists wood, so the real Angelo meets and parries every ethical thrust Isabel can produce from all the warmth of her heart and her understanding. In order to obtain a fair hearing for Angelo I must ask the reader to consider the moral questions before him not as if they were in a romance (where we should all applaud indiscriminate clemency without a moment's compunction) but as if they were a part of real life. *Measure for Measure* deserves no less. Now, do we really think that because none of us is perfect so no one should judge—that is, in hard terms, there should be no law-courts, no penal system, no juries, no police? Certainly judges are imperfect, but equally certainly it is a job that someone has to do. Men of tender conscience may preserve their charity intact, but only so long as others are willing to tarnish theirs a little.

Angelo grants at once that those who judge are not themselves free from sin. This may mean that they lack, at the metaphysical level, a "right" to judge, but it certainly does not mean that they cannot, at the practical level, do it:

>   I not deny
> The Jury passing on the prisoner's life
> May in the sworn twelve have a thief, or two,
> Guiltier than him they try. . . .
>
> *(II.i.18-21)*

The naked intelligence of this transfixes the naive casuistry of the Duke's evasion of guilt at I.iii.36-40.

Of course Angelo is only half a man. He is, until invaded by terrible desire, pure intellect. But it may be salutary to remember how much less human beings can be, even than that. Angelo's lust is moved, strangely, and terrifyingly, by Isabel's virtue (II.ii.162, 168-70, 174-75, 180-84). It is as if he discovered that he was a pervert who could be stimulated only by manifest goodness in another person (note, once more, the conceptual audacity of *Measure for Measure:* those lines dispose finely of that slovenly abstractness of mind which defines love as a passion directed at the soul and lust as a passion directed at the body).

So Angelo falls. But notice how, as a dialectician, he is still in a manner secure. Nothing has happened to over-throw his original position. He had always been enough of a realist to know that among the jurors there might be one guiltier than the defendant. The conclusion is clear, and Angelo never shirks it. He is now himself properly the victim of the superhuman law.

For Angelo's view of the law is naturally impersonalist:

> It is the law, not I, condemn your brother;
> Were he my kinsman, brother, or my son,
> It should be thus with him.
>
> *(II.ii.80-83)*

This must always have been coldly shocking but per-haps a Jacobean audience would be quicker than we to think of Junius Brutus who condemned his own sons—to connect Christian sin with Roman virtue. Certainly the notion of an heroic suppression of hu-manity would be alien even then, but not perhaps entirely inaccessible.

The most invidious action of Angelo's is perhaps his going back on the promise to release Claudio. At this point in the play Angelo has descended into hell and it would plainly be absurd to defend its morality, yet a sort of consistency may persist even here. Consider it for a moment from the point of view of a white Machiavel. Remember that you are committed to the thesis that a strict administration of the law is in the best interests of the people, and that these interests have an overriding claim upon the conscience of the administrator. Suppose, then, the administrator finds himself drawn by a purely personal entanglement to remit the normal course of law—what ought he to do? Clearly, on such principles, he should disregard his personal commitment in deference to the general. He should pull himself together and exercise strict au-thority according to the law.

In fact however, the reason Angelo gives in his solilo-quy is much less creditable than this. He says that he is afraid that Claudio, if allowed to live, may take vengeance on the ravisher of his sister. That at least is the most natural way (and, let us confess, the *right* way) to take this speech. Yet there is an awkwardness in the expression which seems to betray the presence of a contrary idea, struggling for admission. The line are these:

> He should have liv'd;
> Save that his riotous youth, with dangerous sense,

> Might in the times to come have ta'en revenge
> By so receiving a dishonoured life
> With ransom of such shame.
>
> *(IV.iv.26-30)*

The crucial word is "By." Read without any aware-ness of context, that "By" would most naturally be taken as following closely on "have ta'en revenge." The meaning of the whole sentence would then be: "He should have been allowed to live, except that, if he had, his youthfully riotous nature might subsequently have taken a kind of revenge on him, by accepting a life of dishonourable vice, since that life had been bought in so shameful a way." The sentiment would then be parallel to that of Angelo's earlier speech at II.ii. 101-105. It might be objected that such a reading places an odd interpretation on "receiving," but the objection could not be sustained for long. Compare for example, *Twelfth Night,* III.iv. 199-200, "I know his youth will most aptly receive it,—into a most hid-eous opinion" or *Henry VIII,* II.iv. 168, "My conscience first receiv'd a tenderness." No, the real difficulty is that there is a much more probable interpretation—the one I have already stated—available. The only prob-lem facing the orthodox interpreter is the word "By." *This* difficulty is not dispelled by citing instrumental uses of *by* such as "By this Lord Angelo perceives he's safe" (V.i.492). What is rather needed is a *caus-ative* use of *by.* This, though very rare, appears to be possible Shakespearean English: for example:

> . . . the remembrance of my former love
> Is by a newer object quite forgotten.
> *(Two Gentlemen of Verona, II.iv.196-197)*

To show that a causative use of *by* is possible is, I think, to clinch the orthodox case. But to prove that an expression is possible is not to prove it normal. One can still legitimately feel that the sentence is oddly put together, that the thought is subject to a certain strain. It may be significant that by a trifling change of per-spective a different, yet in one respect a *consistent* picture of Angelo's motivation emerges.

Whichever view is uppermost in Angelo's mind, his grip on it is uncertain. His next words betray unhap-piness and bewilderment:

> Would yet he had liv'd.
> Alack, when once our grace we have forgot,
> Nothing goes right; we would and we would not.
>
> *(IV.iv.30-33)*

Where, then, does this leave us? The judgement of the law must be imposed (all agree to that, except perhaps Lucio and his associates). To the question: Who shall impose the law since none of us is perfect? Angelo and the Duke return different answers. Angelo's answer is that men must sink their individuality in the law; that men must judge according to the law, and, when they err, submit to the same law; if it seems grotesque that a man should sit in judgement on other men, one should remember that the judge also is subject to the same rules. The Duke's answer is: Get someone else to do it.

This brings us back to the Duke's speech of explanation at I.iii.34f. I said that there were two arguments in this speech, the first being the Machiavellian thesis that unpopular actions should be delegated, according to the example of Cesare Borgia. The second argument I have yet to discuss. At first sight it looks more respectable.

> Sith 'twas my fault to give the people scope.
> 'Twould be my tyranny to strike and gall
>   them
> For what I bid them do.

That is to say, it is not only imprudent for me to enforce the law personally, it would also be immoral; I should be a tyrant in so switching from indulgence to rigour. That this argument is slightly more poisonous than the other appears on a very little reflection. For the Duke *is* switching from indulgence to rigour. Such a process is hard on the more sentimental sort of conscience, and the Duke is struggling to keep his untroubled by wrapping it in a tissue of evasions. Angelo would say at once that if rigour is really what is required then no tyranny but rather benevolence is involved in its exercise (as he argues to Isabel at II.ii.101-105 that there is a more genuine mercy in the enforcement of the law than in its neglect). But the Duke's intelligence, unlike Angelo's, is cunning rather than comprehensive. Morals to him are not contextual. Every action is intrinsically good or bad. To release a prisoner is to be charitable. Actually to prosecute a prisoner is uncharitable. Such an atomistic view of morals rapidly breeds what might be called meta-ethical situations. Thus, it is uncharitable suddenly to change course and enforce the law (that is basic ethics) but somehow it seems as if that is what *ought* to be done (meta-ethics!). The contextual view of an Angelo, whereby ends justify means, instantly resolves this dilemma, of course. But which view does *God* incline to, the atomistic or the contextual? The thunderingly simple commands in the Gospels, urged with such power by Isabel, suggest that God is more than half an atomist, and, by implication, that the eschatological structure of the universe will reflect an atomistic ethic. In plain terms they suggest that a man who does not perform charitable actions (like releasing criminals)—for whatever reason—is a sinner, and may go to Hell.

It is, of course, a primitive ethic, but it is deeply embedded in the ritual comedy-story of the play. To perceive its presence is to learn that the Duke is not merely a political Machiavel; he is also (so to speak) a metaphysical one. The device which saves his reputation also preserves his soul. Certain kinds of practical virtue (being technical sins) are beneath the saintly charity of the Duke, so someone else must be found as a surrogate. This situation is exactly paralleled by Isabel's adoption of Mariana as her substitute.

The idea of substitution is paramount. One might map it with reference to two poles, Machiavelli in the south and Christ in the north. For, as Roy Battenhouse saw, the Grand Deception of the Atonement moves just as certainly beneath the surface of the drama as does the bloody subterfuge of Cesare Borgia. It is explicitly conveyed in some of the most moving words of the play:

> Why, all the souls that were, were forfeit once,
> And he that might the vantage best have took
> Found out the remedy.
>
> *(II.ii.73-75)*

If we contemplate the structure of the Atonement for a while, we may be willing to draw the last, and most terrifying, lesson from this play. Mankind lay groaning under a burden of sin, of which the wages are death. The Son of God took these sins away from us, bore them on his own shoulders, and by his death on the Cross, discharged our debt. Thus Christ, by taking our sins, was the supreme substitute.

Battenhouse, with some difficulty, sought to identify the God of the Atonement with the Duke. This can be done as long as we restrict our attention to God the Father—as long, that is, as we ignore the cardinal fact of substitution, which above all else connects *Measure for Measure* with the Atonement. Suppose we ask, who, in this play, most obviously corresponds to the figure of Christ? It is not surprising that this question has been avoided. The answer is both unthinkable and only too plain.

There is a story[33] by Jorge Luis Borges about a certain theologian of the city of Lund who began by suggesting that Judas played the noblest part in the drama of the Crucifixion in that it was he who shouldered the necessary burden of sin—and ended by arguing that Judas was the real Christ. Readers who find this story just silly will probably be unwilling to follow me further. For I wish to suggest that the Doctrine of Atonement which underlies *Measure for Measure* is closer to that of Nils Runeberg of Lund than it is to that of Irenaeus or Anselm; that it is, in short, a critical version. After all, Shakespeare borrowed nothing which he did not change.

One element in the traditional doctrine which is obstinately unclear is the phrase "took upon his shoulders our sins." How could this be, since Christ was without sin? Of course one can deal with the phrase by saying that it simply means that Christ took upon his shoulders the *consequences* of our sins. But as soon as one substitutes this account one gets the feeling that something has been lost—that the central mystery of Christ's incarnation has been removed. If God really became man, if the crucifixion really involved the voluntary self-humiliation of God, then—we feel—"took upon his shoulders our sins" must bear a slightly stronger sense. But then we are confronted once more by the first difficulty. The good Christian cannot say that Christ *became a sinner* just like the rest of us. It is too much to require of God that he should deny his nature.[34]

Yet that is what is required of Angelo. In the atonement of *Measure for Measure* the ·implications of vicarious guilt are followed out to the very end. Angelo takes on his shoulders the necessary sins of human judgement. But in the morality of this comedy there is no such area of uncertainty as we found in the Christian doctrine of the Atonement. Angelo, unlike Christ, really sins. His hands do not remain clean.

Under the pressure of Shakespeare's genius the figure of the atoning sufferer begins to take on the lineaments of his anthropological ancestor, the scapegoat. Thus, while I must plead guilty to introducing the *bete noire* of present day criticism, the Christ-figure, yet Angelo is certainly a Christ-figure with a difference. For he is also a Devil-figure. We are now in a position to account for the strange resonance of Isabel's cry in the last scene—"You bid me seek redemption of the devil" (V.i.30). Angelo is at once a Redeemer and the polluted. Earlier in this essay I was forced to acknowledge (for what it was worth) that Angelo at the close of the play is forgiven by the Duke. At the civil level this must be seen as a mitigation of the Duke's Machiavellianism. But the Duke is also, as we have seen, a metaphysical Machiavel. And I am not sure that, at this level, his forgiveness of Angelo is not his finest stratagem. It had always been a necessary consequence of Angelo's view of law that that administrator should desire for himself, if found guilty, the same punishment he would impose on others:

When I that censure him do so offend,
Let mine own judgement pattern out ·my
    death,
And nothing come in partial.

(II.i.29-31)

Angelo (how different, here, from Hazlitt's arch-hypocrite!) is absolutely consistent on this point when the crisis comes:

No longer session hold upon my shame
But let my trial be mine own confession.

Immediate sentence, then, and sequent death
Is all the grace I beg.

(V.i.369-372)

Angelo's plea to cut short his own inquisition is no sort of evasion, for he knows that he is unmasked. In such circumstances he can scarcely hope that the knowledge of his crimes will be kept from the populace. His proposal is not a trial in *camera* but a full confession from the guilty party. Further, the paradoxical description of punishment as "grace" is not just a verbal flourish. It expresses a paradox *in rebus*.

I crave death more willingly than mercy;
'Tis my deserving, and I do entreat it.

(V.i.474-475)

Again, the word "deserving" is not mere rhetoric. Angelo is pleading for justice. The ending of *Measure for Measure* is really not very like the ending of *The Winter's Tale* or *Cymbeline*. For Angelo the Duke's indulgent benevolence does not confer felicity; rather, it perpetuates his anguish. Any producer who has Angelo leave the stage at the close of the play in a state of happy tranquillity simply does not know his business. The fact that Angelo's eye quicknes when Claudio is produced alive will bear another construction than that which the Duke places on it ("By this Lord Angelo perceives he's safe," line 492). If Angelo were preoccupied with his own safety he would have responded differently to Isabel's pleas on his behalf (441-75). The play leaves him in a state of torture, mitigated only by the fact that Claudio is not, after all, dead. The lines I quoted are the last Angelo is given. He longs to discharge his debt, to rest his burden. The Duke makes sure that he carries it to the end.

What, then, of the Duke? Just as Angelo is both Christ and Devil, so the Duke is both the Heavenly Father and supremely contemptible. Critics have joyously pounced on the lines which deify him:

. . . your Grace, like power divine,
Hath looked upon my passes.

(V.i.367-368)

and have forthwith become enmeshed in the difficulties which ensue. It is no part of my case that Angelo does nothing vile. On the contrary it is essential to it that he does. But I do want to say that the play gives him immense moral stature. Similarly with the Duke; I will not trouble to argue that he is not the hero, the presiding genius, the Prospero of the play. According to the Atonement structure I discern in it, he occupies the position of the Father. But I do want to say that he is utterly wanting in moral stature. Why else does Shakespeare repeatedly subject him to a kind of minor humiliation at the hands of the low persons of the play (see II.ii.89-92 and V.i.520-21)? Why else is he so utterly transcended (it is the only word) by *Barnardine?* Johnson's religious instinct was sure when he recoiled[35] from that awful Ciceronian consolation which the Friar-Duke churns out over the head of the suffering Claudio. According to the Runebergian heresy God the Father *is* a very odd character.

The whole of this argument concerning Angelo has, of course, a limited scope. I have tried, in a manner, to "account for" the mysterious resonance of Angelo's character by showing that the evil he does has its place in a necessary scheme of redemption. But not all the evil Angelo does can be accounted for in this way. The theory is readily applicable to Angelo's sin of harsh and presumptuous judgement (in Professor Knight's view the cardinal sin of the play). It does not apply at all to Angelo's sin against Isabel. It was no necessary part of his duties as redeeming scapegoat to fall victim to lust (though certain psychologists might see it as one of the hazards of the job). That is why I have been unable to claim for my scheme any higher status than that of a "substructure." If I am asked what is the relation between substructure and superstructure in this play, my reply must be "ragged and uncertain."

I certainly do not wish to suggest that Angelo and I are of one mind on questions of morals. He is (forsooth!) too illiberal for me. Yet I prefer his belief in the essential benevolence of the law to such liberalism as the Duke purveys.

At the beginning of this essay I expressed dissatisfaction with those critics who make *Measure for Measure* sound like a naive morality play. I now find myself concerned lest, in my reaction, I have fallen into the far grosser error of making it sound like something by Bernard Shaw.[36] Curiously, the charge of making it sound like Graham Greene frightens me far less. The ingenious structure of Machiavellian redemption, of substitution and atonement which I discern in this play is only an element in a larger whole. There is an exploratory reverence, a diffidence before the indefinitely recessive humanity of the persons of the play, which excludes all Shavian facility. Yet if the play has a fault it is perhaps a Shavian one. The vertiginous paradoxes with which the dramatist assaults his audience are achieved at some cost to reality. For example, we are led to suppose that the duties of government place man in a simple dilemma; either he must punish all, or he must forgive all. Some glimmerings of a third, less dramatic course appear in the person of Escalus but that is all. A great part of the tension of the play consists in the clash of theoretic absolutes.

Yet no play of Shakespeare is so moving in its assertion of concrete fact. The imminent death of Claudio and his fear entirely transcend the theoretic extravagance of Isabel. I am aware that in saying this I may offend some historicist critics who will tell me that to the Jacobean mind death was unreal compared with becoming a nun. I can only ask such readers to listen to the verse. The poetry given to Isabel works as hard for Claudio as it does for her:

> The sense of death is most in apprehension;
> And the poor beetle that we tread upon
> In corporal sufferance finds a pang as great
> As when a giant dies.
>
> *(III.i.77-80)*

Let the historicist have his say: "Taken in their context, the lines clearly mean that even a giant feels at death no more pain than a beetle does." Of course. But is it pure accident that the common reader has always taken it to mean just the opposite?

Notes

[1] "*Measure for Measure* and the Gospels," in his *The Wheel of Fire,* the 1964 reprint of the 4th edition of 1949, p. 76.

[2] All references to *Measure for Measure* are to the Arden Edition of J. W. Lever, 1965. All other Shakespearean references are to W. J. Craig's three volume Oxford Edition of 1911-12.

[3] W. M. T. Dodds noticed this twenty years ago in an admirable, if one-sided, article, "The Character of Angelo in *Measure for Measure*," *MLR,* XLI (1946), 246-255.

[4] Roy W. Battenhouse, "*Measure for Measure* and Christian Doctrine of the Atonement," *PMLA,* LXI (1946), 1029-1059; Nevill Coghill, "Comic Form in *Measure for Measure*," *Shakespeare Survey,* VIII (1955), 14-27; F. R. Leavis, "*Measure for Measure,*" in his *The Common Pursuit* (London, 1962), pp. 160-172.

[5] So plead the Isabel-figures Epitia and Cassandra in the sources. See Geoffrey Bullough, *Narrative and Dramatic Sources of Shakespeare* (London, 1958), II, 422, 452-453.

[6] See her *Shakespeare's Measure for Measure,* 1953, p. 65.

[7] One is tempted to answer here, "Professor Coghill does." At least, the part of Lucio was pruned away from II.ii. when he helped to produce the play for the BBC in 1955. See J. W. Lever's Arden Edition of *Measure for Measure* (London, 1965), p. lvii.

[8] The New Cambridge Shakespeare *Measure for Measure* (London, 1961), p.xxx.

[9] "*Measure for Measure* and the Protestant Ethic," *Essays in Criticism,* XI (1961), 10-33.

[10] In his Arden Edition, pp. lxxx-lxxxi; J.C. Maxwell has argued that this quotation is irrelevant because Lucretia's situation is quite unlike Isabel's; see his "*Measure for Measure,* 'Vain Pity' and 'Compelled Sins,'" *Essays in Criticism,* XVI (1966), 253-255. Nevertheless, Tyndale's observation remains perfectly good evidence for the modest claim that chastity could, at this period, be regarded as springing from pride.

[11] See for example "Courtship," "The Girl with no Interest in Marriage" and "The Repentant Girl" in *The Colloquies of Erasmus,* trans. C.R. Thompson (Chicago, 1965), pp. 86-98, 99-111, 111-14.

[12] Arden Edition, p. lxxiii.

[13] Again, noted by Lever, *ibid.,* p. lxxiii.

[14] See her "The Renaissance Background of *Measure for Measure,*" *Shakespeare Survey,* II (1949), 66-82.

[15] From "Divinitie," in *The Works of George Herbert,* ed. F. E. Hutchinson (Oxford, 1941), pp. 134-135.

[16] See Hazlitt's *Characters of Shakespeare's Plays,* first published in 1817, in *The Complete Works of William Hazlitt,* ed. P. P. Howe after the edition of A. R. Waller and Arnold Glover (London, 1930), VI, 346.

[17] *Op. cit.,* p. 19.

[18] Battenhouse, *op. cit.,* p. 1059.

[19] Lascelles, *op. cit.,* p. 59.

[20] Pope, *op. cit.,* pp. 68, 69.

[21] *Ibid.,* p. 75.

[22] *Ibid.,* p. 69.

[23] The strong context of unmasking villainy together with the presence of the injunction not to hide one's light under a bushel (possibly echoed in the Duke's speech to Angelo at I.i. 26f.) suggest that of the four Scriptural *loci* it may be *Mark* that was dominant in Shakespeare's mind at the time of writing *Measure for Measure.*

[24] Machiavelli, *The Prince,* the translation by Luigi Ricci revised by E. R. P. Vincent (London, 1935), pp. 31-32.

[25] Aristotle, *Politics,* v.11 (1315a).

[26] Erasmus, *The Education of a Christian Prince* (first published 1516), trans. L.K. Born (New York, 1936), p. 210.

[27] Mario Praz, "Machiavelli and the Elizabethans," Annual Italian Lecture of the British Academy, 1928, p. 10. The essay is reprinted in *Proc. Brit. Acad.,* vol. XIII.

[28] Lascelles, *op cit.,* p. 100.

[29] W. H. Auden, *The Dyer's Hand* (London, 1963), pp. 205-206.

[30] "The Meaning of *Measure for Measure,*" *Shakespeare Survey,* III (1950), 66-73.

[31] Jacques Maritain, *"The End of Machiavellianism"* [first published in *The Review of Politics, IV* (1942)] in *Machiavelli: Cynic Patriot or Political Scientist?,* ed. De Lamar Jensen (Boston, 1960), p. 93.

[32] It may be objected that my account reduces Maritain's position to absurdity; that fighting Hitler would not count as doing evil for the sake of good since fighting Hitler is itself good. Of course it is perfectly possible to give an ethical description of an action with reference to its purposive context, but to do so is to reject any open consideration of the question of ends and means. As soon as we re-admit the distinction we shall see that such an objector (just *because* his ethical assessment of actions is conditioned by their ends) belongs with the tough-minded faction. And, naturally, to the tough-minded, Maritain's position *is* absurd.

[33] "Three Versions of Judas," in his *Ficciones* (Buenos Aires, 1962), pp. 151-157. My attention was drawn to this story by my colleague Gabriel Josipovici.

[34] The relevant passages in the New Testament do not make the matter any simpler: "Himself took our infirmities, and bare our sicknesses," *Matthew,* viii.17; "Who his own self bare our sins in his own body on the tree . . . ," *1 Peter,* ii.24; "For he hath made him to be sin for us, who knew no sin," *2 Corinthians,* v.21. Augustine (*Enchiridion,* chap. XLI, in Migne's *Patrologia Latina,* vol. XL) raises the question whether there is adequate textual authority for the view that Christ sinned, and rejects it. Writing against the Manichaeans who shrank from the notion that Christ really died on the cross, Augustine stresses the element of curse, says that a curse is the fruit of sin but nowhere concedes that Christ actually sinned (*Contra Faustum Manichaeum,* XIV.4, in Migne, vol. XLIII). It was left to the more extravagant theologians of the Reformation to draw the most disturbing conclusions from this language; Luther, in his 1535 Lectures on Galatians, strenuously affirmed that Christ on the cross was the accursed of God, and guilty of all sins (III.13; in *Luther's Works,* ed. J. Pelikan and W. A. Hauser [Saint Louis, Mo., 1963], XXVI, 287-290; in *D. Martin Luthers Werke,* [Weimar, 1883-1921], XL, 448-452). Calvin, likewise, is not content to say that Christ ac-

cepted our punishment, but wishes to add that, in a manner, he accepted our guilt: "This is our absolution, that the guilt, which made us obnoxious to punishment, is transferred to the person of the son of God," *Institutes of the Christian Religion,* II.xvi, in John Allen's translation (Philadelphia, 1935), I, 460. See also J. S. Whale, *The Protestant Tradition* (Cambridge, 1955), pp. 76-80. John Donne speaks as a good Anglican when he describes the Redemption as Christ's humiliation (*The Sermons of John Donne,* ed. E. M. Simpson and G. R. Potter [Berkeley, Cal., 1953], VI, 341.)

[35] See Johnson's note on the lines; in the Augustan Reprint Society's *Johnson's Notes to Shakespeare,* ed. A. Sherbo, (Berkeley, Cal., 1956), p. 35.

[36] Shaw's comments on the Atonement are, in fact, not wholly irrelevant. He held that Christ may have bewitched Judas into betraying him. See the Preface to *Androcles and the Lion,* in *Prefaces by Bernard Shaw* (London, 1934), p. 545.

Margaret Scott (essay date 1982)

SOURCE: "'Our City's Institutions': Some Further Reflections on the Marriage Contract in *Measure for Measure,*" in *ELH,* Vol. 49, No. 4, Winter, 1982, pp. 790-804.

[*In the essay below, Scott discusses how the law against fornication is viewed and applied in* Measure for Measure, *demonstrating that throughout the play the audience is shown that the situation of Angelo and Mariana is greatly similar to that of Julietta and Claudio. However, Scott maintains, both the Duke and Isabella fail to recognize these similarities.*]

> 'Tis very pregnant
> The jewel that we find, we stoop and take 't
> Because we see it; but what we do not see
> We tread upon, and never think of it.
>   (II. i. 23-26)

It might seem that these lines, taken from their context, have done much to shape some recent critical approaches to *Measure for Measure.* There has been a widespread, if wistful, conviction that a jewel exists to be found, that a single shining solution to the long-canvassed problems of the play's interpretation lies ready for the taking. There has also been a marked anxiety that this jewel might be missed, trodden beneath layers of forgotten knowledge and decayed assumptions, and never thought of. No other of Shakespeare's plays has provoked more anxious fossicking among extrinsic and sometimes extraneous materials.

Predictably, the most common source of solutions, or, at least, of that which might be said to furnish "the problem of a problem play"[1] has been the Bible.[2] "To Shakespeare," Arthur C. Kirsch reminds us, "the Bible was not simply an eschatological document but a revelation of human as well as divine truths, and it is precisely the relationship between the two that *Measure for Measure* is about."[3] Some commentators have passed beyond Matthew's rendering of the Sermon on the Mount or St. Paul's epistle to the Romans to a survey of contemporary religious doctrine.[4] Features of Puritan thought, such as the Ramist "disjunctive syllogism"[5] or the Calvinist championing of individual conscience against authority[6] or, contrariwise, "Shakespeare's sympathy with Roman Catholic institutions"[7] have all been presented as important keys to meaning.

The most recent full length study of the play, Darryl Gless's Measure for Measure, *the Law, and the Convent,* contains an exploration of an impressive array of materials belonging to "the play's immediate intellectual background." These range from the familiar biblical passages to the doctrinal writings of "leaders of each of the major divisions of Reformation Christianity" and the antimonastic satire of Chaucer and Jean de Meun. Together, it is claimed, such materials "provide solutions" to virtually all the "vexing questions" that have bedevilled the *explication de texte.*[8] Many of the biblical and doctrinal sources which Gless examines are concerned with law, albeit in the broad sense of divine or natural law, and it is law which Gless sees as "the play's central subject."[9] Accordingly, he extends his search for solutions into the area of commentary that treats of law in its earthly as well as its divine manifestations. And here, too, though he may range further afield than some of his predecessors, Gless begins his exploration by traversing some well-trodden ground. David L. Stevenson and Peter Alexander are among those who, like Gless, have sought illumination in James I's *Basilican Doron,*[10] while a number of critics have preceded Gless in his use of the work of the seventeenth-century jurist, Henry Swinburne, consistory judge in the ecclesiastical courts at York and author of the *Treatise of Spousals* (London, 1686).[11]

The frequency with which authorities such as Swinburne have been invoked is understandable. For one thing, it is tempting to discover an autobiographical connection between the two marriage contracts in the play and Shakespeare's own experience. Neither Claudio and Julietta nor Angelo and Mariana are married in the presence of a priest before Act V, yet Claudio in Act I speaks of Julietta as his wife, and the Duke assures Mariana that Angelo is her husband "on a pre-contract" (IV.i.72). The ambiguous ties uniting the two couples appear similar to that kind of hand-fast marriage which was widely accepted in Elizabethan England and which may have united Shakespeare and Anne Hathaway before they were married in church. In addition, Alfred H. Schouten points out the pertinency of the case history of Shakespeare's friend, William Russell, who contracted an informal marriage in 1603, shortly before *Measure for Measure* was written.[12] Equally pertinent is the case of Shakespeare's aunt, Agnes Arden, who was recognised as the wife of Thomas Stringer for three months before her church wedding.[13]

But recourse to Swinburne and other authorities on Elizabethan matrimonial law is also prompted, I suspect, by the beguiling prospect of exactitude. In the midst of its ambiguities *Measure for Measure* raises what look like specific questions: Would an Elizabethan audience accept Claudio's assertion that Julietta is "fast my wife" (I.ii.150)? What would such an audience make of the Duke's claim that Angelo is Mariana's husband, or of his reference to "a pre-contract" (IV.i.72)? It seems that questions such as these can be readily decided by reference to a contemporary authority, or to a reputable legal history, or even to the *Encyclopaedia Britannica.* It seems, too, that once such questions have been answered it is but a short step to deciding how "just" or "severe" Angelo's verdict on Claudio is meant to appear, and to seeing the Duke, who proposes the bed-trick, and Isabella, who accepts it, in their true colors. What D. P. Harding has called "the central problem"[14] of the play—that is, the apparent inconsistency between Isabella's detestation of Claudio's "fornication" and her cheerful acceptance of Mariana's copulation with Angelo—seems within an ace of solution, and, in consequence, at least some of the doubts concerning the total coherence of *Measure for Measure* as a dramatic structure look very much as though they are to be laid to rest at last.

Unhappily, this apparently ready and easy way to the heart of the play's mysteries has proved to be full of pitfalls, and nothing of great value has emerged from the studies that have followed upon Harding's thoughtful appraisal of the way in which Isabella's attitudes to espoused couples might reflect the inconsistencies of Elizabethan England at large. Yet the nature of the perils involved in approaching *Measure for Measure* through an examination of Elizabethan marriage contracts is itself of some interest. This paper represents an attempt to identify the more obvious dangers of the method, and to indicate the importance of several features of the play and its background, which, in the widespread enthusiasm for English canon law, have been largely neglected.

The first and most obvious pitfall consists in forgetting that the law of the play is "story-book law."[15] Angelo's "drowsy and neglected act" (I.ii.173) against fornication is kept deliberately vague in a way that, say, the Salic Law in *Henry V* is not. It is fictional law, the like of which has never been enacted in England, nor, so far as I know, in Vienna. It seems reasonable to assume, then, that other subsidiary legislation in the play, including that relating to marriage contracts, is also part of the texture of a world which is in some sense self-enclosed. If it is inapposite to break in upon the world of Shakespearean tragedy with questions about Lady Macbeth's children, then it is perhaps equally futile to inquire the precise form of words used by the betrothed couples before *Measure for Measure* begins. And Vincentio's Vienna is not even endowed with the limited realism of Macbeth's Scotland, but lies at a greater distance from actuality in the province of romance.

Even in his histories and in those tragedies based upon sources which his age regarded as historically sound, Shakespeare was not primarily concerned to construct a replica of actual events. As everyone knows, he tampered with his Holinshed when he made Prince Hal and Hotspur similar in age, and he never entertained the Jonsonian conviction that the superior status of tragedy depends on its rendering of the kind of truth that emerges from a scrupulous use of Plutarch and Livy.

Whatever the genre of *Measure for Measure*—"problem play," "dark comedy," "tragi-comedy" or "romance"—it is certainly neither a history nor a full-blown tragedy. It is based on Cinthio and Whetstone, rather than on Holinshed or Plutarch. It may deal seriously with the realities of human depravity and idealism, justice and mercy, or law and conscience, but these realities are not apprehended by a precise and detailed matching up of the characters' experience with either our own or that of the Elizabethan audience. Even where we respond with that intense personal involvement evoked by painfully recognizable feelings and probable or necessary events, the imagination is stimulated much more by expressions of fear or guilt or pride, which convince us that the characters' circumstances are real, than by any specific parallelism with a set of historically verifiable conditions. And, notoriously, of course, the responses which *Measure for Measure* evokes are variable ones. If part of the play demands the kind of sympathetic participation that characterizes reactions to tragedy, other parts seem to enforce an almost Brechtian detachment of the sort elicited by Prospero's dispensations on his magical island.

This is not the point at which to consider whether or not these different responses are effectively played off against each other or ultimately synthesized. My concern is simply to point out that, since *Measure for Measure* is not a history play, even of the rather unhistorical Shakespearean kind, it is unlikely to contain much detail which accords specifically with a given historical situation; that apprehension of its realities, tragic or otherwise, is unlikely to depend upon recognition of the kind of authenticity to which a Henry Swinburne can attest; and that, finally, since at least some part of the play is cast in the romantic mode, it is ill-advised to predicate any exact correspondence between Vincentio's world and our own.

Considerations such as these might have done something to temper the dogmatism with which it has been
claimed that the characters of *Measure for Measure*
react differently to the two marriage contracts because
one is a *de praesenti* contract and the other *de futuro*.[16] These terms are not, of course, used in the
dialogue, but they are easily imported from the English ecclesiastical courts by any commentator who is
prepared to assume "a one to one correspondence
between the dramatic and social conflicts as if the
former were mere wooden replicas of the other."[17]
Ernest Schanzer has been effectively criticized by J.
Birje-Patel for making just such an assumption, but no
one, apparently, has challenged Schanzer's conclusions
by indicating a further set of considerations which, in
their turn, might have lent a more tentative note to
"The Marriage Contracts in *Measure for Measure*."

The law of *Measure for Measure* is not only story-
book law, it is also, on the face of it, foreign, Roman
Catholic law. Anyone dealing in "one to one corre-
spondences between the dramatic and social conflicts"
might be expected to recognize that Shakespeare goes
to some trouble to make it clear that Vienna, if not
much like the city of that name, is certainly not London. There is talk of "the Duke, with the other dukes"
coming to "composition with the King of Hungary"
(I.ii.1-2), and, much more important, a wealth of detail
to remind us that this Vienna is a state still faithful to
Rome. There is Isabella, about to enter the cloister; the
sister of St. Clair with her exposition of votarists' vows;
the friars Thomas and Peter; and the masquerade of the
Duke, who not only assumes a friar's habit but also
models his conduct so closely on that of a "true friar"
that he hears Julietta's confession. One might imagine
that the significance of this emphasis on allegiance to
Rome would be clear to anyone engaged in a search
for historical parallels with the play's law, but, rather
oddly, not much account has been taken of the manner
in which the Tridentine decree of 1563 had wrought
major changes in the marriage law of Catholic nations
and so had introduced important differences between
this law and that of Protestant states.[18]

A number of those who have elected to examine the
nature of the marriage contracts in *Measure for Measure* have pointed out that the canon law which was
collected and codified in the thirteenth and fourteenth
centuries recognized the central principle that marriage requires nothing more than the free consent of
the parties, expressed in any way sufficient to show
their purpose. No banns, no public ceremony, no priest,
no witnesses, and no specific form of words (provided
they constituted present consent) were necessary to
make the marriage valid and indissoluble. The church,
of course, frowned upon such irregular unions. The
parties rendered themselves liable to the spiritual penalties of penance, and might either be punished for
failing to solemnize their union, or at least ordered to

do so under threat of ecclesiastical censure. Yet, throughout Christendom, both church and state recognized "the
consent of two parties expressed in words of present
mutual acceptance" as "actual and legal marriage"[19]
until the sweeping change effected by the Council of
Trent. The Council passed a "Tamesti" decree (Sessio
XXIV, cap. i, *De Reformatione Matrimonii*) which
stated that whereas clandestine marriages had previously been held valid, though blameworthy, in future
all would be deemed invalid unless they were celebrated before a priest and at least two witnesses. The
Council, which was, of course, intended to secure the
union of Christendom under the See of Rome, destroyed by its decree the uniformly accepted marriage
law of Western Europe. The new restrictions were
accepted in Roman Catholic states, but were not, of
course, received by Protestant nations. In England
recognition of the simple marriage of consent continued until Lord Hardwicke's Marriage Act of 1753.

In a Catholic city after 1563, neither Claudio's union
with Julietta nor Angelo's pre-contract with Mariana
would have been accepted as valid marriage. If, by
indicating the allegiance of his Vienna to Rome, Shakespeare intended to remind his audience of this, then
all the debate about whether one couple or both had
expressed present consent to marry or whether they
had merely agreed to marry in the future becomes not
simply injudicious but irrelevant. So, too, of course,
do the more complicated arguments surrounding the
effects of the consummation of the unions. In England
it was held that sexual relations subsequent to a contract by *verba de futuro* automatically converted the
contract into a present, indissoluble one. An English
ecclesiastical court in 1604 would have accepted
Claudio's claim that Julietta was his wife, though it
would have condemned the marriage as blameworthy
and irregular. The question of whether the pair had
expressed present or future consent before getting into
bed would have been set aside, provided that the court
was satisfied that there had been some kind of definite
agreement to marry. The case of Angelo and Mariana
would probably have been viewed in the same way,
since the pre-contract by which, according to the Duke,
Angelo is Mariana's husband is followed by the night
meeting in the garden-house. In the eyes of an English
court Angelo's copulation, like Claudio's, would have
made the precise nature of his pre-contract irrelevant.
An error as to person might have provided Angelo
with grounds for subsequent divorce, but would not,
presumably, have changed his marital status, once he
had known Mariana in the sexual sense.

The inadvisability of this kind of movement out of the
play and into the courts would need no further demonstration if it were accepted that Shakespeare set the
action of *Measure for Measure* in a Catholic Vienna
in order to remind us that in states still loyal to Rome
the hand-fast marriage was no longer valid. Of course,

to assume at once that Shakespeare must have known about the Tridentine decree, or that he must have presupposed a knowledge of it in his audience—above all that he must have intended us to see his Vienna as akin to an actual Catholic state in law as well as religion—is to commit exactly the kind of error which has vitiated much of the discussion of the play's marriage contracts, and to fall headlong into the first pitfall that I have described as lying open for all those who insist on treating romantic fiction as historical fact. Yet it remains clear enough that the emphasis laid on Roman Catholicism in the play deserves at least some consideration before the inception of any attempt to solve the legal riddles by appeal to English law and Protestant practice. Moreover, while very little attention has been given to the suggestion that the transfigured marriage law of Catholic Europe is an element in the play's background, the idea has a certain force and merits exploration. If it does not solve all the problems with which *Measure for Measure* confronts us, it certainly seems to lead us to a point at which we can see what the real problems are.

Arguments concerning Shakespeare's knowledge of affairs and, still more, assertions about what his audience might have been expected to know are, as often as not, mere guesswork. Yet it does not seem especially rash to suggest that many people in Shakespeare's London might have known that the Catholic Church had, for many years, differed from the Church of England in its view of hand-fast marriage. A number of Shakespeare's fellow dramatists had travelled in Europe and there were plenty of Europeans (and Catholics) in London. And it is probable that Shakespeare's audience would be more likely to have grasped one plain fact than to have acquainted themselves with the tangled subleties of the law relating to *de praesenti* and *de futuro* marriage contracts. The audience would know, I imagine, that one could be married in England without going to church and that the ecclesiastical authorities frowned on such unions, but it seems doubtful that anyone short of Lord Bacon would make sense of Isabella's inconsistency by rehearsing in his mind the kind of arguments that have been advanced by Ernest Schanzer.

When Shakespeare wanted his audience to understand some confusing complexity, he normally explained, as he does in the case of the dynastic claims in *Henry VI Part One* (II.v) or the English title to the French crown in *Henry V* (I.ii.35-95); but where there is one clear fact concerning a foreign practice (that Denmark was an elective monarchy, say, or that the Scottish king designated his own successor) we are usually left to attend to the nature of the action and the assumptions of the characters. The English experience is allowed to flow in as a kind of ground swell that directs our attitude to the foreign custom. In the early scenes of *Hamlet,* for instance, we recognize rather vaguely that

in Denmark a king's son has no automatic title to his father's throne, while at the same time feeling that Claudius is already tainted in some sense by the usurpation of which, in England, he would have been guilty. The situation in *Measure for Measure* seems similar. Here is a Catholic state in which hand-fast marriage is no longer accepted as valid, but an awareness that Claudio could not in England have been punished for fornication flows in under our recognition of foreign difference to deepen our disapprobation of Angelo's severity.

If one watches the play with the effects of the Tridentine decree in mind, then behind Angelo's sudden revival of a law which makes the winked-at transgression a capital offence there lies another layer of events in which the valid, if blameworthy, union has become in the twinkling of an eye the sin of fornication. That atmosphere of moral ambiguity which is the native element of the play grows still more palpable, and the European background becomes the figure of Angelo's new stringency writ large. This background also stands as the emblem of that theme of changed appearance and shifting judgment which underpins the play's demonstration of the fallibility of human justice. "That in the captain's but a choleric word / Which in the soldier is flat blasphemy" (II.ii.131-132) gains added resonance in a world in which Isabella's church has seen a man as a husband one day and as a fornicator the next.[20]

It has been suggested that Claudio's "odd and inappropriate"[21] feelings on his arrest, his mingled shame and self-justification, are to be seen as a reflection of that blend of misapprobation and acceptance with which the hand-fast marriage was regarded in England.[22] But Claudio's attitude becomes rather more comprehensible if we see him as a citizen of a Catholic state in which the Tridentine decree had been received, backed by some draconian local legislation, and then largely ignored. We can then see his conscience as stirred by the knowledge that his church has damned his act as sinful, and his appeal to custom as sustained by his recollection of an older dispensation which the Council's decree and the state's laws have not yet extirpated from the minds of the people.

Whatever their attitude to Claudio's imminent execution, all the characters in the play are sure that he is guilty as charged. Schanzer suggests that Isabella makes no reference to her brother's contract with Julietta because she knows nothing about it.[23] But if we are to assume that English law is operative in this Vienna, then it might have occurred to Isabella to enquire whether such a contract, which would make all the difference to her brother's fate, had ever existed. And even if Isabella is to be seen as too "enskied and sainted" (I.iv.34) to give thought to the customary English defence against a charge of fornication, one might expect Escalus, who is as pregnant as any in "our city's institutions and the terms / For common justice" (I.i.10-11) to give some thought to the matter. Above all, it might be expected that Lucio, who has been told all about the marriage agreement (I.ii.148-156), would mention Claudio's "true contract" when he is egging on Isabella to importune Angelo in Act II. At this stage in the play it is difficult to escape the conclusion that Shakespeare has invoked his Vienna's allegiance to Rome in order to remind us that English Protestant law, while inevitably shaping our responses, cuts no ice at all in Vincentio's state.

Up until Act III, recollection of the Council of Trent's decree does much to make the action of *Measure for Measure* more explicable and its meanings more resonant. The difficulties arise, of course, with the proposal of the bed-trick. For at this point, as has so often been demonstrated, the Duke and Isabella suddenly change their attitude towards unsolemnized union and accept that, while Julietta is a fornicatress, Mariana will be committing "no sin" (IV.i.73) in copulating with the man she once agreed to marry. Yet in the eyes of the Catholic church both women would, after 1563, have been guilty of fornication. And if the Tridentine view of what constituted valid marriage is accepted in Shakespeare's Vienna, as it seems to be in Claudio's case, then Angelo is just as much a fornicator as the man he has condemned, and the substitution of his affianced bride for the object of his lust cannot in law make the slightest jot of difference.

Recollections of the Council of Trent's decree, then, seem in the end only to make the notorious impasse of Act III more formidable than ever. There is no longer any hope of proving that the Duke and Isabella see the two pre-contracts differently because there is a real difference between them. Claudio and Julietta's "true contract" may have been *de praesenti* and Angelo and Mariana's "pre-contract" may have been *de futuro,* as Schanzer has argued, or the reverse may be true, as Nagarajan has suggested. But if the definition of fornication operative in Vienna derives from Trent, such claims do nothing to solve the riddle of the characters' *volte face.* We are left confronting a situation in which Angelo's position is ironically similar to Claudio's, and neither the Duke nor Isabella is prepared to recognize the similarity.

But if this is where we are left, it is, perhaps, where we should stand, for there are many elements in the play which operate in the same way as a recollection of the Tridentine decree in prompting us to face the same conclusions. Shakespeare clearly went to some trouble to point up the similarity rather than the difference between the two marriage contracts in the play. Angelo is guilty of more sins than Claudio, but his contract, like that of the man he condemns, forms part of a network of action and language that links sex with money throughout the play. In each case we are told of solemnities delayed because of difficulties in getting hold of the dowry. Both Julietta and Mariana are apparently without parents (and their isolation is made more striking by their appearance in sequestered places, the prison and the moated grange[24]); Mariana's dowry has been lost at sea, along with her brother Frederick, while Julietta's remains "in the coffers of her friends" (I.ii.154), who are, it seems, unwilling to disburse until they have formed a favorable opinion of their charge's bridegroom.

Similarities such as these place the two marriage contracts at the heart of an intricate pattern of parallel and exchange. Parallels between individual scenes which bear upon the Claudio-Julietta and Angelo-Mariana relationships are frequent. There are, for example, the Duke's interviews with Isabella and Mariana in IV.i, in which he cooperates with one in urging the other to give herself to Angelo in order to save Claudio's life. This scene in the moated grange recalls and in some sense reverses both the prison scene in which the Duke urges Julietta to repent of her fornication, and the scene at the nunnery in which Lucio, the Duke's anarchic parody and opposite, persuades Isabella to emerge from her cloister and "assay the power" she has to soften Angelo (I.iv.70-77). In these scenes, as elsewhere, the contracts and sexual union at large are constantly associated not only with money but also with death. Claudio's getting of "his friend with child" (I.iv.29) leads to the death sentence; Angelo proposes to Isabella that she yield up her maidenhead to save her brother's head; death caused Angelo to deny his bond with Mariana, the existence of which makes possible the substitution of one maidenhead for another on the very night that, in the prison, the head of the dead pirate Ragozine is substituted for that of Claudio.[25] In Act V Angelo and Claudio both excape the block to marry their brides, while Lucio stands poised between a whore and a halter. This association of sex with death penetrates the comedy in which Pompey turns from bawd to executioner, and it permeates the language of the play at every level— from Claudio's likening of men in their sexual passion to "rats that ravin down their proper bane" (I.i.132) and Isabella's vow that she would "strip myself to death, as to a bed / That longing have been sick for, ere I'ld yield / My body up to shame" (II.iv.101-103), through to Pompey's punning on the "mysteries" of painting and hanging (IV.ii.37-41).

The linking of sex with a death which is, in the event, held at bay for all but the pirate, Ragozine, is in turn part of a complex structure of language and action in which almost any character or any act can change its complexion according to the bias or the acuity of the perceiver, and in which any quality may become the associate or even the propagator of its contrary. Death may be "the best of rest" (III.i.17) "That makes these odds all even" (III.i.41), or it may be "To lie in cold obstruction and to rot" (III.i.119); it may be the arbitrary penalty exacted "for a name" (I.ii.172) or the just punishment that deters those left alive from "future evils" (II.ii.92-99). The act of copulation may be "most mutual entertainment" (I.ii.157), "full tilth and husbandry" (I.iv.44), "sweet uncleanness" (II.iv.53), "abhorr'd pollution" (II.iv.182), "a merriment" or "a vice" (II.iv.115). The thief may stand in the dock or sit on the jury, the fornicator lie condemned in his prison or sit in judgment in his palace, the jewel may be taken up or trodden underfoot. The Duke may be Vincentio or a friar; the first may be abused as "a very superficial, ignorant, unweighing fellow" (III.ii.140) or defended as "a scholar, a statesman, and a soldier" (III.ii.147), while the second may be an "unreverend and unhallow'd Friar" (V.i.306), a "bald-pated, lying rascal" (V.i.354), or "a man divine and holy" (V.i.144).

Similarly, the same sun that makes the carrion putrid makes the violet fragrant (II.ii.165-168), and the devil "to catch a saint" uses a saint to bait his hook (II.ii.180-181). The showing of Claudio to the world (I.ii.119) for the crime of "loving" Julietta (II.iv.141) leads on to the secret lust of Angelo, while at the night meeting in the garden-house, deceit, disguise, and substitution become the "crimes," which, "making practice in the times," draw forth the "ponderous," "substantial" (III.ii.274-277), and open dispensation of justice in the final scene.

The two marriage contracts must, I think, be seen as typical elements in these ambivalent structural patterns. They supply both the supreme parallel in the play and twin links in that sequence of exchange and substitution in which the altered aspect of reality rests always in the eye of the beholder. If, then, we insist on turning Shakespeare's Vienna into the ecclesiastical courts at York, and seek to prove an essential difference between Angelo's "pre-contract" and Claudio's "true" one, we are tearing a whole web of meaning from the support upon which it is built.

Anxiety to save Isabella's face and the Duke's by suggesting that, because Angelo's contract is different from Claudio's, his copulation is somehow less culpable, has led to still more perverse violations of meaning. Angelo is urged over and over again to recognize a Claudio in himself. Escalus enquires whether, "Had time cohered with place or place with wishing" (II.i.11), the deputy might not have "Err'd in this point which now you censure him" (II.i.15). Isabella harps on the same string:

> Go to your bosom,
> Knock there, and ask your heart what it doth
> know
> That's like my brother's fault.
>
> (II.i.137-139)

The phrase "weigh thy brother by thy self" (II.ii.127 and V.i.111) rings through the play until in Act V the Duke in sentencing Angelo to death—an Angelo for a Claudio—declares: "Like doth quitlike, and Measure still for Measure" (V.i.413). Certainly, as Isabella points out, Angelo does not succeed in forcing an unwilling virgin to his will (V.i.453). Neither he nor Claudio is guilty of rape. But if the two are not both guilty of fornication, if Angelo is not, in the end, revealed as having engaged in the same sequence of consent and copulation as the man whom he condemns, then much of the play's irony is blunted and its coherence impaired.

If we do accept that the two marriage contracts are of the same kind,[26] then the Duke, who views them differently, becomes rather less than "power divine" (V.i.371) and Isabella, who accepts the Duke's guidance, becomes capable of self-deceit or at least of a willingness to be misled.[27] Yet this is not to consign the play once more to the realm of cynicism and dark comedy from which it has been gradually recovered. The Duke, as everybody knows, tells a great number of lies and, from the start, seems to go darkly to work in the belief that the most devious of means are justified by their ends. I suggest that he is also the play's prime example of that inconsistency in perception and judgment which, in Measure for Measure, is everywhere apparent, and which, in Vincentio himself, is ironically counterpointed by his resentment of Lucio's new and scurrilous portrait of "the old fantastical Duke of dark corners" (IV.iii.157).

Against the background of a Catholic, post-Tridentine Vienna, the Duke's adjustment of his view of the unsolemnized union stands out sharply, yet his inconsistency is, of course, no foreign vice and remains a pertinent comment on the confused and shifting attitudes to hand-fast marriage—and much else—in Elizabethan England. But, in the end, the Duke is more remarkable for his virtues than for his faults. The mercy with which he eventually judges in Act V reminds us that fallible man has no warrant for the kind of dogmatic legalism exemplified by an Angelo and discernible, albeit in less significant form, in much of the discussion that has surrounded the marriage contracts in Measure for Measure.

Notes

1 Ronald Berman, "Shakespeare and the Law," Shakespeare Quarterly, 18 (1967), 142. All citations of Shakespeare are from The Riverside Shakespeare, ed. G. Blakemore Evans (Boston, 1974).

2 See especially R. W. Battenhouse, "Measure for Measure and the Christian Doctrine of Atonement," PMLA, 61 (1946), 1029-59, and G. W. Knight, "Measure for Measure and the Gospels," in his The Wheel of Fire (London, 1930), 73-96.

[3] Arthur C. Kirsch, "The Integrity of *Measure for Measure*," *Shakespeare Survey*, 28 (1975), 91.

[4] Notably, Elizabeth M. Pope, "The Renaissance Background of *Measure for Measure*," *Shakespeare Survey*, 2 (1949), 66-82.

[5] Harold Fisch, "Shakespeare and the Puritan Dynamic," *Shakespeare Survey*, 27 (1974), 81-92.

[6] William John Roscelli, "Isabella, Sin and Civil Law," *The University of Kansas City Review*, 28 (1962), 215-227.

[7] D. J. McGinn, "The Precise Angelo," *Joseph Quincy Adams Memorial Studies* (Washington, 1948), pp. 129-140.

[8] Gless, (Princeton, 1979), pp. ix-xi.

[9] Gless, p. 35.

[10] David L. Stevenson, *The Achievement of Shakespeare's* Measure for Measure (Ithaca, 1966); Peter Alexander, "*Measure for Measure*: A Case for the Scottish Solomon," *Modern Language Quarterly*, 28 (1967), 478-488.

[11] These include A. D. Nuttall, "*Measure for Measure*: The Bed-Trick," *Shakespeare Survey*, 28 (1975), 51-56; Ernest Schanzer, "The Marriage Contracts in *Measure for Measure*," *Shakespeare Survey*, 13 (1960), 81-89; J. Birje-Patel, "Marriage Contracts in *Measure for Measure*," *Shakespeare Studies*, 5 (1969), 106-111.

[12] Alfred H. Schouten, "An Historical Approach to *Measure for Measure*," *Philological Quarterly*, 54 (1975), 68-84. For further information concerning Russell's marriage see William Empson, *The Structure of Complex Words* (London, 1951), p. 286, and Leslie Hotson, *I, William Shakespeare* (London, 1937), pp. 137-40, 203-10.

[13] For further details of Agnes Arden's marriage see J. S. Smart, *Shakespeare: Truth and Tradition* (London, 1928), pp. 60-61.

[14] D. P. Harding, "Elizabethan Betrothals and *Measure for Measure*," *JEGP*, 49 (1950), 156.

[15] The phrase is A. D. Nuttall's. In his illuminating article on the bed-trick, he shows that he is well aware of this particular pitfall.

[16] Schanzer argues that the contract between Claudio and Julietta is *de praesenti* and that between Angelo and Mariana *de futuro*. S. Nagarajan takes the opposite view in "*Measure for Measure* and Elizabethan Betrothals," *Shakespeare Quarterly*, 14 (1963), 115-119.

[17] Birje-Patel, 106.

[18] Peter Alexander makes reference to the Tridentine decree and admits that in a Vienna inhabited by monks and nuns, "one might have expected to find marriage practiced in accordance with the regulations laid down by the Council of Trent." But he concludes that the Duke nonetheless "conducts matters as if he were in the Scotland of James' day" (486). The decree is also noted by Karl P. Wentersdorf in "The Marriage Contracts in *Measure for Measure*: A Reconsideration," *Shakespeare Survey*, 32 (1979), 129-144. But Wentersdorf goes on to claim: "Except for the severity of its statute making fornication a capital offence, the fictional Vienna of *Measure for Measure* undoubtedly reflects the laws, customs, and thinking of Shakespeare's England" (143).

[19] Sir William Scott's judgment in the famous case of *Dalrymple* v. *Dalrymple* (2 Hagg. Con. Rep.54), quoted in Howard W. Elphinstone, "Notes on the English Law of Marriage," *The Law Quarterly Review*, 5 (1889), 48. Other useful modern commentaries on the canon law relating to espousals, and to the effects of the Tridentine decree on European legislation, are: James Bryce, "Marriage and Divorce Under Roman and English Law," in *Select Essays in Anglo-American Legal History* (London, 1968), III, 782-833, and especially 809-812; R. H. Hemholz, *Marriage Litigation in Medieval England* (Cambridge, 1974), pp. 25-74; Joseph Jackson, *The Formation and Annulment of Marriage* (1951; 2nd ed., London, 1969), pp. 10-19. Pollock and Maitland, *The History of English Law* (1895; 2nd ed., Cambridge, 1968), II, 368-385, provides an authorative discussion of the canonical doctrine of marriage, but does not deal with the Tridentine decree or its effects.

[20] Karl P. Wentersdorf has pointed out that the decree did not invalidate hand-fast marriages contracted before 1563 (133). But this means only that a man who had had sexual relations with his hand-fast wife before the promulgation of the decree was still regarded as a husband, whereas if he did exactly the same thing for the first time a day later he was regarded as a fornicator.

[21] L. C. Knights describes Claudio's attitude in this way in "The Ambiguity of *Measure for Measure*," *Scrutiny*, 10 (1942), 225.

[22] Schanzer, 82.

[23] Schanzer, 86.

[24] I am indebted to E., A. M. Colman for pointing out that certain of Shakespeare's other young heroines are without parents (Olivia, Beatrice, the Helena in *All's Well*) and that almost all, apart from Juliet, are without mothers. While, as Professor Colman suggests, this

may have been brought about by a need to restrict cast size, in *Measure for Measure* and elsewhere, Shakespeare can turn the exigencies of theatrical life to dramatic profit.

[25] Jan Kott makes some useful comments on the substitutions in the play in "Head for Maidenhead, Maidenhead for Head: The Structure of Exchange in *Measure for Measure*," *Theatre Quarterly*, 8 (1978-79), 18-24. Yet Kott's conclusions on the "corrupted law and corrupted sex" of Shakespeare's Vienna are unnecessarily pessimistic.

[26] Several of those who have concerned themselves with the *de praesenti* v. *de futuro* issue have come eventually to the same conclusion. See, for example, Roscelli, who decides that both contracts are of the *de praesenti* variety. Others, who have avoided embroilment in English canon law, have also pointed to the similarity of the two agreements and their sequels. William Empson makes the point with his usual trenchancy: "What the Duke urges Mariana to do ('He is your husband on a pre-contract; To bring you thus together is no sin') can only be distinguished, if at all, by a technicality from what Claudio is to be killed for doing ('she is fast my wife . . . ')." See *The Structure of Complex Words,* p. 282.

[27] Peter Alexander defends Isabella by reminding us that the Duke is disguised as a religious figure and that Isabella is eager to submit to the discipline of a religious order. He claims, moreover, that the Duke has "a natural air of authority" which would have its effect on the young novice. See "*Measure for Measure:* A Case for the Scottish Solomon," 483. This may all be true, but it does not alter Isabella's readiness to deal in double standards; she, like everyone else in the play, needs to recognize the force of her own appeal to Angelo. Since man can never see with the clarity of heavenly vision, mercy becomes him better than severity.

N. W. Bawcutt (essay date 1984)

SOURCE: "'He Who the Sword of Heaven Will Bear': The Duke Versus Angelo in *Measure For Measure*," in *Shakespeare Survey: An Annual Survey of Shakespearian Study and Production,* Vol. 37, 1984, pp. 89-97.

[*In the essay that follows, Bawcutt explores the distinctly different attitudes of the Duke and Angelo toward the law and how it is applied in Vienna, arguing that it is oversimplifying the matter to state, as critics often do, that Angelo personifies the Law while the Duke stands for Mercy.*]

'Law', 'Mercy', and 'Justice' are three of the main concepts repeatedly used in *Measure for Measure*.

There are no simple deductions to be made from this fact: the meaning of the play cannot be summed up as a kind of mathematical equation, Law plus Mercy equals Justice. The words themselves are not presented unambiguously. 'Law' is usually qualified by adjectives implying that Viennese law is harsh by its very nature—'strict statutes and most biting laws' (1.3.19), 'the hideous law' (1.4.63), 'the angry law' (3.1.201)—but there is also a series of striking, sometimes faintly ludicrous, images suggesting that the law is despised and ineffective. Law is like 'an o'er-grown lion in a cave / That goes not out to prey' (1.3.22-3) or the 'threatening twigs of birch' (1.3.24) used to whip children; if not applied effectively it will be like the motionless scarecrow that the birds of prey regard as 'Their perch, and not their terror' (2.1.4), or will 'Stand like the forfeits in a barber's shop, / As much in mock as mark' (5.1.319-20). The result is a paradoxical double image: the law can frequently be ignored with impunity, but may suddenly and unpredictably inflict savage punishment, with a kind of arbitrariness that is half accepted and half resented, as in the opening speeches of Claudio.

'Mercy' also is qualified in a variety of ways: 'lawful mercy' (2.4.112) is quite different from the 'devilish mercy' (3.1.64) offered by Angelo to Isabella. For Escalus, too much mercy does more harm than good:

> Mercy is not itself, that oft looks so;
> Pardon is still the nurse of second woe.
>
> (2.1.280-1)

In its personified form mercy sometimes behaves very unlike the gentle creature we might expect it to be:

> Mercy to thee would prove itself a bawd.
>
> (3.1.149)

> This would make mercy swear and play the tyrant.
>
> (3.2.188-9)

> The very mercy of the law cries out
> Most audible, even from his proper tongue:
> 'An Angelo for Claudio; death for death.'
>
> (5.1.405-7)

The term 'justice' is not sharply distinguished from 'law', especially in the first half of the play, and when, in the concluding trial scene, Isabella calls for 'justice! Justice! Justice! Justice!' (5.1.26) against Angelo, 'a murderer . . . an adulterous thief, / An hypocrite, a virgin-violator' (5.1.41-3), it is clear enough that at this point in the scene, whatever may happen afterwards, she wants him to be severely punished.[1] (And we should perhaps bear in mind that many readers have regarded the final mercy shown to Angelo as very far from doing justice to his particular case.)

If the terms themselves are probed and examined in the course of the play, and sometimes overlap and sometimes oppose each other, this is all the more reason for not treating the play allegorically and assigning one abstraction exclusively to a single character. Three of the most important characters—Claudio, Isabella, and Angelo—are tormented by divided loyalties and impulses, a turmoil so vividly presented that it is surely impossible to see any of them as a static personifcation. It is natural enough that we should compare the Duke to Angelo—both are judges and administrators faced with complex legal problems—but it seems a little too easy to say, as so many critics do, that Angelo stands for the Law, rigidly applied, while the Duke represents Mercy. It is not false, but it is an over-simplification. The differing attitudes of the two men towards the law and its application need a more thorough examination than has been made so far, and this will involve a consideration of certain words used in the play which tend to be overlooked, such as 'severe' and 'severity', and the group consisting of 'tyrant', 'tyranny', and 'tyrannous'.

Rather than work through the play consecutively, I want to begin in the middle and work outwards. The Duke learns of Angelo's attempt to blackmail Isabella in act 3, and when left to himself at the end of that act he meditates, in the light of Angelo's behaviour, on the duties of a ruler. This passage in couplets has almost always been treated unsympathetically. As recently as 1922 Dover Wilson was willing to endorse the common view that the lines were a spurious interpolation,[2] and even those who accepted them as genuine were often puzzled by their presence and felt obliged to devise some ingenious theory to account for their existence. A good example is provided by Mary Lascelles: 'One conjecture remains permissible; at some performance, Shakespeare's play was given in two parts, a pause intervening, and on this occasion it was judged prudent to remind the audience, on renewal of the performance, of the theme and situation.'[3] But there is not a scrap of evidence to support this, and even if we regard *Measure for Measure* as a kind of two-part play the section in couplets is surely as much an epilogue to Part I as a prologue to Part II.

There is no need to swing to the other extreme and regard the passage as the very core and centre of the play, the neglected key which will unlock the secret meaning of *Measure for Measure*. It is not great verse, and none of its lines embed themselves in the mind like 'man, proud man, / Dress'd in a little brief authority' (2.2.118-19) or 'Ay, but to die, and go we know not where' (3.1.117). It is written in a condensed and elliptical style which sometimes leads to obscurity, and parts of it may betextually corrupt, though most of the editorial tinkering inflicted on it has surely been quite unnecessary. Even so, we do not have to agree with Rosalind Miles that 'the Duke is only making appro-

priate sententious noises to close a climactic movement of the play.'[4] I prefer to assume that Shakespeare himself wrote the passage, intended it to occur at this particular point, and expected his audience to treat it as a necessary part of the play, demanding full and sympathetic attention.

J. W. Lever's analysis of the structure of the passage seems basically right to me.[5] It is plausible that a couplet has dropped out between lines 267 and 268; if so, the passage originally consisted of twenty-four lines which can be divided into four sections, each of six lines or three couplets. The first section is a generalized statement on the qualities required in a good ruler, while the second is a rebuke to Angelo for failing to show those qualities. The third section is a puzzle, especially if a couplet is missing. Lever feels that the Duke is 'asking how Angelo's abuses are to be rectified' and asserts that the 'idle spiders' strings' in line 268 are an allusion to 'the Renaissance commonplace . . . that the laws were like spiders' webs which caught the small flies but let the big insects break through'. To my mind the image is rather that of a heavy load or weight pulled along by threads which are as flimsy as a spider's web. The four sections of the Duke's meditation seem to alternate between the general and the particular: the first and third sections are generalizations applicable to all men, the second and fourth are specifically about Angelo. The third section could perhaps be interpreted, with allowance for textual deficiencies, as the Duke's recognition in general terms that a guilty hypocrite can make important consequences follow from totally spurious appearances. In the final section the Duke decides to turn Angelo's own weapons against him: deception will be used to counter deception.

The Duke's meditation opens with a couplet that editors rarely discuss in any detail:

> He who the sword of heaven will bear
> Should be as holy as severe.
>
> (3.2.254-5)

The sword is a symbolic instrument of punishment—even, presumably, of capital punishment. It is 'of heaven' and therefore has a divine origin or sanction.[6] This suggests that religion endorses punishment quite as much as it endorses mercy. The implications of the second line are slightly elusive. I take the primary meaning to be that anyone who wishes to wield the sword of justice should be holy in equal proportion to the degree of his severity. There is no condemnation of severity: it follows logically that he may be as severe as he wishes provided that he is correspondingly holy. The couplet is a gnomic utterance that can stand on its own, but it is also a condensation of an exchange between Escalus and the Duke a few lines earlier, where Escalus tells the Duke that he has pleaded in vain for clemency towards Claudio:

I have laboured for the poor gentleman to the extremest shore of my modesty, but my brother-justice have I found so severe that he hath forced me to tell him he is indeed Justice.

Duke. If his own life answer the straitness of his proceeding, it shall become him well: wherein if he chance to fail, he hath sentenced himself.

(3.2.244-51)

The logic here is quite explicit: if the strictness of Angelo's private life corresponds to his strictness as a judge, his severity will be admirable. If it does not correspond, he ought to receive the same sentence himself.

There is plenty of evidence in the scene leading up to the Duke's meditation to indicate that he has no indulgence whatever to sexual licence. When Pompey is brought in charged with being a bawd, an accusation he makes no attempt to deny, the Duke attacks him furiously for living off the 'abominable and beastly touches' of prostitutes and their clients (3.2.23), and the Duke's description of prostitution as a 'filthy vice' (line 22) is a curiously close echo of a phrase used earlier by Angelo to Isabella, 'Fie, these filthy vices!' (2.4.42). When Lucio complains that Angelo 'puts transgression to't' (3.2.91-2), the Duke defends Angelo ('He does well in't', line 93), and answers Lucio's suggestion that Angelo might show 'A little more lenity to lechery' (line 94) by asserting the need for harshness: 'It is too general a vice, and severity must cure it' (line 96). This seems to echo or parallel the earlier comments of Escalus and the anonymous Justice at the end of act 2, scene I:

Justice.
Lord Angelo is severe.
Escalus.   It is but needful.

(2.1.279)

In these exchanges the Duke and Escalus both appear as upholders of severity. The theme becomes overtly comic in the Duke's horror and embarrassment when he himself is casually described by Lucio as a habitual libertine, who 'would mouth with a beggar though she smelt brown bread and garlic' (3.2.177-8). Pompey and Lucio are both disreputable characters whom the Duke would be unlikely to find congenial, but even in his discussion with the nobly penitent Juliet in an earlier scene he refers to her 'most offenceful act' three times as a 'sin' (2.3.19-31). If Angelo is to be called a puritan, so too is the Duke.

At first sight the Duke's conversation with Friar Thomas in act 1, scene 3, would seem to prove irrefutably that the Duke approves of severity in certain circumstances. Angelo, we are told, has been put in charge of Vienna in the expectation that he will strictly enforce the neglected laws of the city, so the Duke can

hardly blame him if he does precisely that. Here, however, we encounter a difficulty. Friar Thomas is merely a rather clumsy stage device used by Shakespeare to enable the Duke to share his thoughts with the audience without resorting to a soliloquy which would have been over fifty lines long. No other character in the play has any clear idea of the Duke's purposes; both his departure and his return are shrouded in mystery and confusion. As M. D. H. Parker notices, 'Angelo is not told to be rigorous';[7] indeed, the formality of the play's opening scene rather conceals the fact that neither Escalus nor Angelo is given a precise indication of how the Duke expects him to behave. Escalus is told that he already knows so much about law and administration that further advice would be superfluous. Angelo is admonished in biblical language not to hide his light under a bushel or bury his talents; he is given exactly the same powers as the Duke, but it is twice made clear that he is totally free to use them as he wishes:

In our remove, be thou at full ourself.
Mortality and mercy in Vienna
Live in thy tongue, and heart

(I.I.43-5)

    Your scope is as mine own,
So to enforce or qualify the laws
As to your soul seems good.

(ll. 64-6)

It is hardly surprising that the two men should want to meet in order to clarify their position:

Escalus.
 A power I have, but of what strength and
     nature
 I am not yet instructed.
Angelo.
 'Tis so with me.

(ll. 79-81)

Possibly the written commissions are detailed and specific, but they are not read out to the audience.[8] The only way I can put all this together is to assume that the Duke hopes and expects that Angelo will restore strict discipline to Vienna. But he has reservations about Angelo's integrity (see 1.3.50-4), and in order to make a genuine trial of Angelo the Duke must leave him completely free to expose his true nature.

The next four lines of the Duke's meditation help to bring out the implications of the opening couplet:

Pattern in himself to know,
Grace to stand, and virtue, go:
More nor less to others paying
Than by self-offences weighing.

(3.2.256-9)

Lever's paraphrase of the first line, 'to know that the precedent for his judgements lies in his own conduct', is curiously muted, as though Lever is reluctant to acknowledge the full force of the line. 'Pattern' here is surely used in *OED*'s sense 1, 'an example or model deserving imitation': if the ruler wants a model of the right sort of human behaviour, he should be able to find it by looking into himself. The next line is a little more specific, if we expand it in the way most modern editors do: 'he must have grace in order to stand, and virtue in order to go'.[9] The ruler needs divine grace to keep him morally upright, but by itself this might seem merely passive, so he also needs virtue as an active principle. This helps to lead us forward to the second couplet, which deals with the ruler's attitude when he functions as a judge: he pays out, or inflicts, neither more nor less punishment to others than is determined by weighing up the amount of evil in himself. (It is not, of course, specifically said that the 'paying' refers to punishment, but the reference to 'self-offences' in the next line makes this the most plausible interpretation.)

In this context 'weighing' clearly has a moral significance, and the concept of assessing or judging other people in terms of ourselves is central to the play. When Isabella tells Angelo, 'We cannot weigh our brother with ourself' (2.2.127) her remark appears to mean simply that we cannot judge everybody by a single standard, since those in authority can successfully commit offences which would be punished in ordinary people. It is little more than a piece of worldly wisdom, and Lucio is surprised to find her so shrewd ('Art avis'd o' that?', line 133). But when she urges Angelo:

> Go to your bosom,
> Knock there, and ask your heart what it
>   doth know
> That's like my brother's fault. If it confess
> A natural guiltiness, such as is his,
> Let it not sound a thought upon your
>   tongue
> Against my brother's life
>
> (ll. 137-42)

her speech is a turning-point in the play, though its effect is ironically not what she intends. Angelo does look into his bosom, and finds that like Claudio he can feel urgent sexual desire, but the discovery does not prompt him towards sympathy or mercy. In the last scene of the play Isabella's earlier phraseology is picked up by the Duke in his pretended refusal to believe that Angelo could have behaved in this manner:

> it imports no reason
> That with such vehemency he should pursue
> Faults proper to himself. If he had so
>   offended,

> He would have weigh'd thy brother by
>   himself,
> And not have cut him off.
>
> (5.1.111-15)

This provides, I think, a useful gloss or expansion of lines 259-60 in the couplet speech at the end of act 3.

It is characteristic of the play, and indeed of Shakespeare's normal dramatic technique, that there should also be comic treatment of the theme. Abhorson the executioner is shocked that he should be expected to use Pompey the bawd as his assistant ('he will discredit our mystery', 4.2.26-7), but the Provost can see nothing to choose between them: 'Go to, sir, you weigh equally: a feather will turn the scale' (ll. 28-9).[10]

Lucio too has his own debased and simplified version of judging others in terms of oneself: as Lucio sees it, Angelo is severe simply because he is quite incapable of having sexual feelings. Lucio wants the Duke to return because the Duke is an old lecher whose experience of begetting bastards would make him more tolerant: 'He had some feeling of the sport; he knew the service; and that instructed him to mercy' (3.2.115-17). A related theme is that of putting oneself in another person's position, of seeing things from the opposite point of view; Isabella, for example, vividly imagines how first her brother and then she herself would have behaved if they had exchanged places with Angelo:

> If he had been as you, and you as he,
> You would have slipp'd like him, but he like
>   you
> Would not have been so stern.
> *Angelo.*   Pray you be gone.
>
> *Isabella.*
> I would to heaven I had your potency,
> And you were Isabel! Should it then be thus?
> No; I would tell what 'twere to be a judge,
> And what a prisoner.
>
> (2.2.64-70)

This can easily be pushed a little further by Shakespeare and treated literally as a plot device of physical substitution, Angelo for the Duke, Mariana for Isabella, and so on.

In the light of all this evidence it surely becomes increasingly clear that the Duke, in terms of his own statements, does not differ from Angelo by advocating mercy, a word he rarely uses and completely omits from his meditation on the duties of a ruler. The difference is rather that the Duke, in contrast to Angelo, believes in a personal or reflexive view of the law: when faced with a prisoner the judge must look into himself, and is disqualified from judgment if he is guilty of the same offence. If, however, the judge has been able to restrain his own tendency to a particular sin, he is perfectly entitled to punish that sin in other people. This attitude clearly emerges in a passage not mentioned so far, when the Duke and Provost are together in the prison at midnight, waiting in the hope that Claudio will be pardoned. The Provost criticizes Angelo ('It is a bitter deputy') but is rebuked by the Duke:

> Not so, not so; his life is parallel'd
> Even with the stroke and line of his great
>   justice.
> He doth with holy abstinence subdue
> That in himself which he spurs on his power
> To qualify in others: were he meal'd with
>   that
> Which he corrects, then were he tyrannous;
> But this being so, he's just.
>
> (4.2.77-83)

For Isabella, in an earlier scene, tyranny occurs when a ruler exercises his full powers of punishment to their uttermost:

> O, it is excellent
> To have a giant's strength, but it is tyrannous
> To use it like a giant.
>
> (2.2.108-10)

For the Duke, tyranny is not merely the infliction of harsh punishment; it is the infliction of harsh punishment by someone who is not in a moral position to do so. The same attitude underlies the Duke's explanation to Friar Thomas of why he has chosen Angelo to reform Vienna instead of himself:

> Sith 'twas my fault to give the people scope,
> 'Twould be my tyranny to strike and gall
>   them
> For what I bid them do: for we bid this be
>   done,
> When evil deeds have their permissive pass,
> And not the punishment.
>
> (1.3.35-9)

By being excessively lax in the past, the Duke has disqualified himself from exercising severity in the present.

Angelo explicitly rejects the personal view of law at the opening of act 2. His first speech, affirming that the law must be genuinely terrifying and not merely a scarecrow, seems to answer an off-stage plea from Escalus for mercy towards Claudio. Escalus then tries various approaches, one of which is to suggest, in a rather awkward and tentative fashion, that Angelo himself might have committed the same offence if circumstances had been particularly favourable. In other words, he invites Angelo to put himself in Claudio's

position. Angelo is unperturbed: for one thing, he knows perfectly well that he has never committed precisely the same offence as Claudio. In addition, even though some administrators of justice may be corrupt:

> I not deny
> The jury passing on the prisoner's life
> May in the sworn twelve have a thief, or two,
> Guiltier than him they try
>
> (2.1.18-21)

the fact has no great importance: 'What knows the laws / That thieves do pass on thieves?' (ll. 22-3). The tone appears to be contemptuous: 'why should you expect the law to be at all concerned about the fact that one thief is passing sentence on another?' For Angelo the whole process of the law is impersonal; crimes come to light, are punished by the appropriate law, and that is that. He is merely an agent, 'the voice of the recorded law' (2.4.61), and he feels no personal involvement in the sentence he has passed on Claudio: 'It is the law, not I, condemn your brother' (2.2.80). It is not until Angelo feels desire for Isabella that he makes any move towards the personal view of law: 'Thieves for their robbery have authority, / When judges steal themselves' (2.2.176-7); but the change is not powerful enough to alter his behaviour.

Angelo's conduct is so clearly shown to be wrong by the whole course of the play that it would seem perverse to argue in his defence, but it has to be said that most normal systems of law operate on principles closer to Angelo's than the Duke's. A sentence made by due process of law on adequate evidence could hardly be appealed against on the grounds that the judge himself had subsequently been discovered to be guilty of the offence for which he had sentenced the prisoner. The response would surely be that the judge himself must now stand trial, but his verdict need not be overturned. The Duke's insistence that a judge should be aware of his own human fallibility is admirable, but if pushed to extremes can lead to gross injustices. If you are convicted of a particular offence, the sentence you receive will not depend exclusively on the gravity of your offence, but also on the extent to which the judge has weaknesses of the kind for which you have been convicted. It is as though on each occasion the judge must put himself on trial as well as the prisoner, and in such circumstances there can be no uniformity of sentencing.

What is the Duke's response to Angelo's behaviour? The most explicit statement comes in the second section of his meditation at the end of act 3:

> Shame to him whose cruel striking
> Kills for faults of his own liking!
> Twice treble shame on Angelo,

To weed my vice, and let his grow!
O, what may man within him hide,
Though angel on the outward side!

                                        (3.2.260-5)

The only point here that provokes much editorial discussion is 'my vice' in line 263; opinion is divided between a personal interpretation (the vice created by the Duke's negligence) and an impersonal (the vice of other people in contrast to Angelo's). The personal reading surely fits the context better and is much more powerful. The Duke is angry because the man he chose as his substitute, while busily weeding out the vice for which the Duke feels personally responsible, is simultaneously creating a fresh crop of his own. This brings out the main emphasis of the Duke's complaint: what he objects to is not Angelo's severity but his hypocrisy. It could be argued that 'cruel striking' and 'Kills' to some extent imply that the Duke regards the sentence on Claudio as inherently severe. This may be so, but the way the argument develops suggests that Angelo is cruel not just because he is rigorous but because he is punishing others for his own offences.

The problem of interpreting these lines prompts a question which has important implications, though at first sight it might seem a triviality of the 'How many children had Lady Macbeth?' type. When precisely does the Duke decide to intervene on Claudio's behalf, and why does he do so? It is assumed sometimes that the Duke makes up his mind to rescue Claudio as soon as he hears of Angelo's harsh sentence. For Bertrand Evans the turning-point is the Duke's examination of Juliet (act 2, scene 3): 'This is a crucial interview: if there is a precise point at which the Duke commits himself to the cause, it is here, when he finds Juliet's penitence honest, and, being so, to merit forgiveness.'[11] Evans may be right, but there is nothing in the scene to compel us to think so. The decisive and unmistakable intervention comes in act 3, at the point where Isabella is about to storm out in horror at her brother's willingness to prostitute her body to save his own. The Duke comes forward with a plan for coping with the problem, which must have been thought out beforehand, but he could quite easily have devised it only a few minutes in advance, while listening to the increasingly emotional debate between Claudio and Isabella. Indeed, the device he suggests, the 'bed-trick' substitution of Mariana for Isabella, would have been quite pointless at an earlier stage when Angelo was not lusting after Isabella. The conclusion seems to be that the Duke intervenes only at the point where he discovers that Angelo is a hypocrite who is in no position to condemn others. It might even be true that if Angelo had continued to behave with rectitude, the Duke would have allowed Claudio to go to his death. Of course it is foolish to speculate on what fictitious characters in a work of art might have done

in different circumstances: I put it in this way only to bring out the full implications of the issue.

The exact way in which the Duke intervenes has a bearing on the way we respond to his character. The Duke is sometimes seen by those who dislike him as a cold-hearted manipulator, handling human beings rather as an experimental psychologist might treat the rats in his laboratory, subjecting them to unsuspected shocks in an arbitrary way that needs to be justified. It is true that in acts 4 and 5 he frequently allows the other characters to remain ignorant of the truth in a way that might cause undeserved suffering, as when Isabella is told, quite untruthfully, that her brother has been executed. The trial scene in act 5 proceeds for much of its length on assumptions that the Duke knows to be totally false, and he even persuades Isabella, somewhat to her embarrassment (4.6.1-4), to pretend that she has been deflowered by Angelo. Now if we assume that the Duke decides to rescue Claudio and Juliet as soon as he learns of their predicament, it follows that his use of this kind of deception begins virtually as soon as he puts on the robes of a friar, and in particular, that his great speech attempting to reconcile Claudio to death is a kind of sham because he knows perfectly well that Claudio is not going to die. If, however, the Duke does not decide to intervene until Angelo's hypocrisy has been revealed, the interview with Juliet and the speech on death to Claudio can be taken at their face value. Until he overhears the agonized discussion between Claudio and Isabella in prison, the Duke knows no more than anyone else: Angelo might of course change his mind at the last minute, but all the signs suggest that Claudio is going to die, and the Duke bases his conduct on this assumption.

My argument also applies to an earlier scene in the play, the Duke's account to Friar Thomas in act 1, scene 3, of his motives for putting Angelo in charge of Vienna. It has become increasingly fashionable for sophisticated critics to invoke chapter 7 of Machiavelli's *The Prince* in this connection. When Cesare Borgia had gained control of the Romagna in Italy, he found it 'rife with brigandage, factions, and every sort of abuse' through the weak and avaricious behaviour of its previous rulers.

> So he placed there messer Remirro de Orco, a cruel, efficient man, to whom he entrusted the fullest powers. In a short time this Remirro pacified and unified the Romagna, winning great credit for himself.

> There were, however, dangers in allowing this efficient cruelty to persist too long; the servant's brutalities were making the master unpopular.

> Cesare waited for his opportunity; then, one morning, Remirro's body was found cut in two

pieces on the piazza at Cesena, with a block of wood and a bloody knife beside it. The brutality of this spectacle kept the people of the Romagna for a time appeased and stupefied.[12]

We are invited to compare this to *Measure for Measure* and to see the Duke as a kind of white, or perhaps we should say grey, Machiavellian who tries to avoid unpopularity by getting a subordinate to do his dirty work for him. But there is no evidence that Shakespeare had read a word of Machiavelli or had the slightest admiration for him, and I cannot believe for a moment that Shakespeare would have expected or welcomed the comparison. If there are some similarities between the Duke's behaviour and Cesare Borgia's, there are also striking differences. The Duke's account of his motives for delegating power may not strike us as fully convincing, but it harmonizesso well with his deepest convictions about the way a ruler should behave that there is no need to regard his action as a repulsive duplicity.

I have already emphasized that the ideas discussed so far are not intended to provide a complete interpretation of the play. All the same, it would be natural, and legitimate, to ask whether the way we interpret the Duke's couplet speech at the end of act 3 has any bearing on our response to the second half of the play and in particular to the concluding trial scene which occupies the whole of act 5. When the Duke temporarily hands over his power at the beginning of the play, he has two motives for doing so: one is to test Angelo, the other is to bring about a stricter enforcement of the laws of Vienna. At the end it would seem that the first aim has been accomplished, with a negative result, while the second has been discreetly put aside and is not supposed to be present in the audience's mind. If, however, we take seriously the Duke's idea about personal justice, then his second aim is dependent on his first: the law cannot be enforced with severity if the man brought in to enforce the law proves to be corrupt. The danger of this sort of argument is that it can sound glib, and it must be admitted that the Duke never says anything of the kind explicitly. At the same time, there is nothing in act 5 to support those critics who argue that the play shows us an educative process in which the Duke, or Angelo, or possibly both together, learn that justice needs to be tempered with mercy, that the ideal is some kind of blend or balance. The alternatives at the end of the play are not light punishment and heavy punishment, but rather punishment in general as against mercy and forgiveness. In the opening scene the Duke had said to Angelo: 'Mortality and mercy in Vienna / Live in thy tongue, and heart' (1.1.44-5), and the play seems to offer us little between these two extremes, death on the one hand, and forgiveness on the other.

The disparity between the first half of *Measure for Measure,* up to the Duke's intervention, and the sec-

ond half is a major critical problem of the play. The first half has an almost tragic intensity as the characters clash with each other in a way that painfully reveals their innermost character. Everything is spontaneous and unpredictable. In the second half, there is a strong sense of intrigue and manipulation: Shakespeare possibly wanted the trial scene in act 5 to have the same dramatic tension as the earlier scenes involving Claudio, Isabella, and Angelo, but in the trial scene there is an air of contrivance, with the Duke as both actor and director in a play-within-the-play. There are of course reasons for this shift of emphasis, even if they do not provide full artistic justification. In all other versions of the story the woman corresponding to Isabella goes to bed with the Angelo-figure, and it is she who complains to the judge's overlord when she realizes she has been duped. Shakespeare did not want his heroine to lose her virginity, so he provides a substitute, but he could hardly make Isabella herself suggest this device or provide her own substitute. Inevitably the Duke takes over as the organizer of the action.

The consequences of Shakespeare's decision may seem unfortunate, but the decision was consciously made. The last section of the Duke's meditation at the end of act 3 helps to prepare us for the intrigue of the last two acts:

> Craft against vice I must apply.
> With Angelo tonight shall lie
> His old betrothed, but despised:
> So disguise shall by th' disguised
> Pay with falsehood false exacting,
> And perform an old contracting.
>
> (3.2.270-5)

Clearly Angelo will be outwitted—the play will not end tragically—but the 'craft' used to counter his 'vice' will entail disguise and falsehood, so we need not be unduly surprised if the virtuous characters tell lies. The Duke could simply have revealed himself, but this would have brought the play to an abrupt conclusion, and more importantly, Angelo would not have been forced to experience intimately the deception and false appearances he has inflicted on other people. Angelo is thus receiving measure for measure, particularly if we gloss the word 'measure' according to sense 15 of *OED*, 'treatment meted out to a person, especially by way of retribution or punishment'. Those who dislike the second half of *Measure for Measure* will not be made to change their minds by any analysis, however subtle, of the Duke's meditation at the end of act 3. But if the evidence suggests, to a degree unusual in Shakespeare, that he deliberately and consciously altered the mode of his play, we ought to be cautious before passing judgement on it. Whatever artistic flaws there may be in *Measure for Measure,* they are not the result of carelessness or inadvertence on Shakespeare's part.

Notes

[1] Isabella, it is true, knows perfectly well that Angelo has not in fact blackmailed her into sexual submission, but she genuinely believes that he has treacherously executed her brother.

[2] *Measure for Measure,* ed. A. Quiller-Couch and J. Dover Wilson, New Cambridge Shakespeare (Cambridge, 1922), pp. 139, 141.

[3] Mary Lascelles, *Shakespeare's Measure for Measure* (1953), p. 104.

[4] Rosalind Miles, *The Problem of Measure for Measure* (1976), p. 180.

[5] *Measure for Measure,* ed. J. W. Lever, the Arden Shakespeare (1965), pp. 93-4. All my references are to this edition.

[6] The sword is of course a common attribute of justice, but in this context there may be a biblical allusion to the Epistle to the Romans, chapter 13, in which Christians are ordered to obey 'the powers that be'. Part of verse 4 reads as follows in the 1560 Geneva version: 'if thou do euil, feare: for he beareth not the sworde for noght: for he is the minister of God to take vengeance on him that doeth euil.'

[7] M. D. H. Parker, *The Slave of Life* (1955), p. 112.

[8] Escalus is ordered not to 'warp' (diverge) from his commission (line 14), so presumably it gives him detailed instructions.

[9] H. C. Hart, in the first Arden edition (1905), suggested that 'and virtue go' could mean 'if his virtue should fail him'. But the combination of 'stand' and 'go', in the senses of 'keep upright' and 'walk', seems to be a stock Elizabethan usage; compare a story in Thomas Lupton's *Siuqila: Too Good to be True* (Part II, 1581) in which a girl spends all night tied to a tree, sig. V2, 'I was neither able to goe nor stande', and V4, 'I vnbound hir, who was so frozen with the cold, that then she could neither go nor stand'. This book contains a version of the *Measure for Measure* story which may have been known to Shakespeare.

[10] This conjunction of 'weigh' and 'scale' suggests that Lever is right to gloss 'scaled' as 'weighed as in scales (his moral worth truly estimated)' at 3.1.256, where the Duke claims that Angelo, 'the corrupt deputy', will be 'scaled' if Isabella goes ahead with the bed-trick.

[11] Bertrand Evans, *Shakespeare's Comedies* (Oxford, 1960), p. 193.

[12] Machiavelli, *The Prince,* translated by George Bull (Harmondsworth, 1961), pp. 57-8.

Melvin Seiden (essay date 1990)

SOURCE: "A Trial: Make-Believe Confounds Reality," in *Measure For Measure: Casuistry and Artistry,* The Catholic University of America Press, 1990, pp. 116-43.

[*In the following essay, Seiden analyzes the trial scene in* Measure for Measure, *arguing that the theatricality, trickery, and game playing of the play's final scene "creates an exhilarating and satisfying climax that the whole play has been designed to achieve." Furthermore, Seiden states that the Duke's role-playing in the mock trial "makes a mockery of justice."*]

> All the world's a stage,
> And all the men and women merely players.
> They have their exits and their entrances,
> And one man in his time plays many parts.
> (*As You Like It,* II.vii.139ff.)

In *The Merchant of Venice,* written about ten years before *Measure for Measure,* Shakespeare had discovered the exciting dramatic device of the courtroom trial in which the law, mated, it would seem, to injustice, is ultimately, almost miraculously, brought back into the service of justice. The trial scene in *The Merchant of Venice* (IV.i) is both melodramatic and sophisticated, raw and crude, psychologically and poetically refined. The tables are going to be turned on Shylock—in E. E. Stoll's memorable phrase, the formula is "the Biter bit"—and it is this powerful formula that controls the development of the action.

Shylock is confident that the Venetian court must grant him the pound of flesh owed him by Antonio's default; Antonio is resigned to his fate, seeing himself as "a tainted wether of the flock, / Meetest for death" (IV.i.114-15); Portia, disguised as an attorney, Balthasar, intervenes in the proceedings to support the strict and unyielding law, thus puffing up the confidence of Shylock, who gloats in the self-congratulatory and self-deceived refrain, "A Daniel come to judgment!" (l. 223), but at the point at which all the Christian friends of Antonio, including the duke of Venice, despair of saving the good merchant's life— "You must prepare your bosom for his [Shylock's] knife" (l. 245), says Portia-Balthasar to Antonio, and the surgeon stands by—the action wheels around and the tables are turned on the Jew: "This bond doth give thee here no jot of blood" (l. 306). Portia has used her wit to find a loophole, the legal quibble that will free Antonio and, with structural and moral symmetry, put Shylock's life in jeopardy. To the accompaniment of the second refrain, "O upright judge!

Mark, Jew. O learned judge!" (l. 313), Shylock submits to the humiliating punishments meted out by the court. What seemed at first, a fraudulent trial, a mockery of justice, has been transformed by Portia's ingenious intervention into a victory for compassion and Christian casuistry.

For the first three hundred lines of the scene, the audience, like Antonio's friends, has been terrorized. Shylock's knife presides over these long, tense minutes in which a judicial murder threatens. (The vengeful knife, unlike Hedda Gabler's pistols, must not be used, must be rendered impotent, just as Shylock is stripped naked, defanged, and spiritually emasculated.) In the approximately three-quarters of the scene that passes before Portia executes her stunning reversal, enormous suspense is generated. Anticipatory fear fuels the fire of suspense. In tragedy, such fear turns out to have been all too justified: there is no escape from the consequences of the blunders and misconceptions. In *The Merchant,* the fear is dissipated in one breathtaking peripety, a U-turn so swiftly and satisfyingly maneuvered that it compensates us generously for the pain of the anger we have felt as Shylock's "merry sport" played itself out.

In the resolutions of *Measure for Measure* Shakespeare will deploy, but with greater complexity and sophistication, the formal punitive development he had first used in *The Merchant of Venice.* Preparing Mariana for the trial scene that is to ensue in act 5, scene 1 (IV.vi, a fifteen-line scene), Isabella warns,

> If peradventure
> He [the Duke] speak against me on the
>   adverse side
> I should not think it strange, for 'tis physic
> That's bitter to sweet end.
>
> (ll. 5ff.)

We too are being reassured that no matter how bitter the medicine administered, not only to Angelo but to Isabella and Mariana, the "sweet end" will more than compensate for the pain. Shall we call this an example of crude telegraphing? We can, certainly, but what is remarkable is how brilliantly the scene works despite what might seem the redundant reassurances. In any case, the duke, who makes his entrance at the beginning of act five no longer disguised as a friar, now wears a moral disguise: he plays the role of the gullible and corrupt judge: gullible because he is corrupt, corrupted anew because he is so contemptibly gullible.

The duke begins the scene by bolstering Angelo's confidence with a suave ambiguity:

> We hear
> Such goodness of your justice that our soul

> Cannot but yield you forth to public thanks,
> Forerunning more requital.
>
> (V.i. 5ff.)

If we or anyone in the play were in a position to ask Vincentio the question, Did Angelo do wrong in sentencing Claudio to death? he would be hard put, surely, to offer a simple answer. Because "justice" here includes what Angelo has done or tried to do to Isabella and Mariana, the duke utters an ironical equivocation: the irony promises "public thanks" and "requital" that will be the very opposite of what they lead Angelo to expect.

Continuing in the same fashion, the duke "praises" Angelo in florid verse:

> Oh, your desert speaks loud, and I should
>   wrong it
> To lock it in the wards of covert bosom
> When it deserves, with characters of brass,
> A forted residence 'gainst the tooth of time
> And razure of oblivion.
>
> (ll. 9ff.)[1]

Irony, surely: the knife lancing the flesh so deftly that the patient, drugged with praise, does not realize that the physician has begun the bloodletting. But something else is happening here, something that complicates and enriches the fork-tongued irony. Caught up in the charade in which Vincentio is convincingly a shameless, colluding crony and a captive judge, we, in a certain way, take him at his word, just as Angelo does, and are goaded into a perplexed sort of resentment. Simultaneously, one might almost say *magically,* the drama allows us to see that Vincentio is pulling the wool over Angelo's eyes and yet, somehow, is having the wool pulled over his!

There is a superb example of Shakespearean dramaturgical magic that may serve as a model for the duality of audience response we have been describing here. It can be found in the interplay between Gloucester and Edgar when the father, wishing to commit suicide, is lovingly manipulated by his devoted son (*King Lear,* IV. vi). The "perpendicularly" steep cliffs of Dover are evoked in flashing cinematic images: "crows and choughs that wing the midway air," "fishermen that . . . [a]ppear like mice," a ship's small boat "[d]iminished too . . . a buoy / Almost too small for sight" (ll. 12-20). It is not, however, the Dover cliffs but only a little knoll from which the blind, distraught Gloucester tries to leap to his death. It is a hoax. Edgar knows and we know that it is not true that "hadst thou been aught but gossamer, feathers, air, / So many fathoms down precipitating, / Thou'dst shivered like an egg." Edgar, like Vincentio, a good physician and a noble-hearted liar, plays with his father's raw emotions (and our sensory confusions) in order to teach him and us wisdom, to make Gloucester and every member of the audience recognize that "Thy life's a miracle" (l. 55). What is extraordinary is how we are caught up in the illusion that tricks Gloucester: the vertiginous height, the sickening fall, the miraculous reprieve from death. At the same time that we are fully aware that it is a trick, this blind man's leap, and that Edgar's pictures of the "dread summit" are intended to deceive Gloucester, not us, we cannot shake free of the acrophobic dread that Edgar's images evoke and then purge in us. Shakespeare can make use of the irony that inheres in our being in on Edgar's therapeutic ruse yet audaciously play with our fears. The pyrotechnics of special effects in the movies are only more technically but not more artistically accomplished than the verbal trompe l'oeil of Gloucester's suicide leap.

When the duke plays the part of the gull while covertly retaining control as impresario, director, and deft actor in his own miniplay ("The Loyal Duke and His Slandered Deputy"), Shakespeare is using a "special effect" in a way that is almost as daring as the Gloucester-Edgar scene in *Lear.* [In *Measure for Measure* the tense duality of audience response is sustained throughout a long and emotionally turbulent one-scene act. In *Lear,* Shakespeare's inspired filmflam, like Edgar's, is subordinate to the thematic purpose of effecting a spiritual rebirth in Gloucester. Trickery is a means to a higher end. I shall argue that the tricky game playing in act 5 of *Measure for Measure*—"theatricality" in the pejorative term of disapproving criticism—creates the exhilarating and satisfying climax that the whole play has been designed to achieve.

Preparing Isabella for the trial, the duke had said, "Accuse him [Angelo] home and home" (IV.iii.148), and so she does, but when she cries out, "justice, justice, justice, justice!" the duke immediately turns her over to the tender mercies of Angelo: "Here is Lord Angelo shall give you justice. Reveal yourself to him" (ll. 27-28). Isabella denounces Angelo, and if the passion is more controlled, the eloquence more shapely and stylized than the outbursts aimed at her brother (in III.i), that may in part be because this is a staged trial, a prearranged indictment, the enactment of the duke's contrivance:

> That Angelo's foresworn, is it not strange?
> That Angelo's a murderer, is't not strange?
> That Angelo is an adulterous thief,
> A hypocrite, a virgin-violator,
> Is it not strange and strange?
>
> (ll. 38ff.)

Undoubtedly, the formal, patterned rhetorical structure distances us somewhat from the "content" of the emotion: that altogether genuine and unfeigned indignation that assures Isabella that Angelo is a "virgin-

violator," no matter that she is not the violated virgin. The lie would be a moral truth even if Angelo had not possessed Mariana. Though we remind ourselves that this is a mock trial, a simulated perversion of justice, we are caught up in the authentic passion that validates the charge. Five times Isabella repeats the word (or variants of) *true* in her reply to the duke's "Nay, it is ten times strange":

> It is not truer he is Angelo
> Than this is all as true as it is strange.
> Nay, it is ten times as true, for truth is truth
> To the end of reckoning.
>
> (ll. 43ff.)

The duke plays his role, that of the credulous judge, with great skill; the judge who relies on appearances is bound to think that such outlandish accusations as these bespeak "the infirmity of sense," a woman "touched with madness." But we, after all, know that Vincentio is playacting the part of a judge both credulous and corrupt. Why then does this knowledge not work to give us a comfortable and comforting reassurance that justice will not be perverted? Why, again, do we respond to this travesty of a travesty of justice as if it were the real thing?[2]

A clue to the paradox may be found in Isabella's spontaneous and unfeigned denunciation of Angelo earlier in the play. In her first interview with Angelo (in II.ii), Isabella had inveighed against the abuse of power, authority, the office that confers a Jove-like invulnerability upon the officeholder who lords it over those less fortunately franchised:

> But man, proud man,
> Dressed in a little brief authority,
> Most ignorant of what he's most assured,
> His glassy essence, like an angry ape
> Plays such fantastic tricks before high Heaven
> As make the angels weep. . . .
>
> (ll. 118ff.)

Isabella might have used the words of Lear: "See how yond Justice rails upon yond simple thief. . . . Change places and, handy-dandy, which is the Justice, which is the thief?" (*King Lear,* IV.vi.154ff.).

There is a perpetually unfair contest between the "simple" soul, the powerless individual who runs afoul of the law, and constituted authority with its overbearing power. Up against socially sanctioned justice, the solitary defendant, innocent or criminal though he or she may be, is always at a disadvantage. This, at any rate, is what might be called the civil libertarian view of legal justice, and it is the view that fires Isabella's eloquent denunciation of "authority [which], though it err like other, / Hath yet a kind of medicine in itself / That skins the vice o' the top" (II.ii. 133ff.).

When, therefore, the duke pretends to discredit Isabella, our residual memory of Angelo's misuse of authority is attached to this corrupt judge, the duke. The presence of Angelo, the genuine corrupter of justice and authority, suggests that the duke's feigning of that role reenacts what has already and truly taken place. The duke plays his part wonderfully well, plays, that is, with nice verisimilitude at being an Angelo. Angelo played badly, played, that is, dishonestly at being a duke. Handy-dandy, which is the ruler, which is judge? Early in the scene, we understand that handy-dandy is indeed the game when the duke says, "Here is Lord Angelo shall give you justice. / Reveal yourself to him" (ll. 28ff.).

Isabella tells her story to a disbelieving judge while Angelo stands off to the side in silence. She must tell the indispensable lie that has lodged within it the redemptive truth: how "To [Angelo's] concupiscible intemperate lust . . . [she] did yield to him [her virginity]." There are multiple ironies in the duke's reply; he begins and ends his speech (ll. 106ff.) with the premise that she has been "suborned"; the charge she makes against Angelo is so incredible that it must be that "Someone hath set you on. / Confess the truth, and say by whose advice / Thou camest here to complain" (ll. 112ff.).

There are a surface irony and a more subtle irony that depend on and intensify the more obvious one. What is most obviously perceived by us is the black humor of the duke's speculating that Isabella must be the tool of "Someone [who] hath set you on." That someone is Vincentio himself; the duke, Isabella, and we know this; only Angelo does not. The director who wants cheap and easy effects (or who does not trust the intelligence of the audience) will encourage his Vincentio to grimace portentously as he speaks these lines—a mistake. It is a mistake not only because it is crude; nudging the audience will obscure the secondary irony. *That* irony points to what I have called the civil libertarian view of justice. From this point of view, it is the duke and Angelo who collude to subvert justice. Insofar as the duke is convincing, he acts like the kind of judge who has been bribed to bedeaf to the pleas of the weak, the innocent, especially women in a world in which men make, enforce, judge, and corrupt the laws. If the first and admittedly more dramatic irony is comic, the more subtle irony is intellectual and serious. It is an irony that takes Lear's handy-dandy "impertinency" and enacts it in a bitter farce in which the judge (who is guilty of colluding with a powerful malefactor) charges the victim of injustice (Isabella) with precisely his own crime: that is, of having been "suborned" by a nameless co-conspirator.

In dismissing Isabella's charge against Angelo, the duke speculates, "If he [Angelo] had so offended, / He would have weighed thy brother by himself, / And not

have cut him off" (V.i.110-11). It's a foursquare, commonsensical argument, and, of course, flatly wrong. It was self-hatred that led Angelo to hasten the execution of Claudio, in order, we might say, to eliminate his doppelgänger. So much for speculative psychology. There is another important point concealed in the duke's hypothesis. If proof were needed at this late stage that Isabella was right to refuse Angelo's offer of a reprieve for Claudio in exchange for her chastity, it is here. Having as he believes had the use of Isabella's body, Angelo orders the immediate execution of Claudio. True, the question posed by Isabella's dilemma is a moral one: Angelo's behavior demonstrates that, had she accepted his proposal, she would nevertheless have failed to rescue Claudio. Capitulation would not have saved his life. An admirably principled moral stubbornness is corroborated by a practical consequence, but we in the audience do not need to make this overt inference when we hear the duke speculate about Angelo's behavior; the duke's plausible but erroneous reasoning will carry us back to those anguished moments when Isabella faced Angelo and then her distraught brother—and made the right choice, we now see.

In her answer to the duke's blockheaded credulity Isabella's language again echoes that of *Lear:*

> Then, O you blessed ministers above
> Keep me in patience, and with ripened time
> Unfold the evil which is here wrapped up
> In countenance!
>
> (ll. 115ff.)

As we have seen, Isabella's denunciation of prostituted "authority" (in II.ii) echoed Lear's shattering insight that "Justice," alas, is more often determined by social and institutional privilege than by disinterested principles of equity, and here in the final moments of the play injustice compounds itself with each new development. The duke is about to have Isabella rushed off to prison: "Shall we thus permit / A blasting and scandalous breath to fall / On him so near us?" (ll. 121ff.). What is being staged in this charade is not merely a powerful political figure protecting a crony. The duke is shielding himself. It's a question of fallout in which the corruption of the underling threatens the more important figure who is the source of the lesser man's power. In our time, cases of self-protecting collusion between big and little fish—in government, medicine, business, the armed services, and indeed academic institutions—can be found in the daily newspaper. A cynic might say that what is shown in *Measure for Measure* to be an extreme perversion of law and justice is in contemporary life commonplace, a ubiquitous "fact of life."

Now aping the duke's servility with Angelo, Friar Peter colludes with the duke as the mockery of justice continues. Isabella, he claims (l. 140), has "Most wrongfully accused your substitute." (The word *substitute* reinforces the idea that Angelo is not only the duke's agent; here in this trial the duke and Angelo are twinned: the duke as corrupt judge does Angelo's dirty work for him, just as earlier the duke had delegated Angelo to do his for him. Friar Peter's *substitute* is another handy-dandy.) The situation resembles the phenomenon in which ordinary folk support the powerful oppressor and not the powerless victim, not, that is, the person with whom the weak and defenseless ought to feel a natural kinship. Friar Peter is not just "a little man." Symbolically, the church is tainted when Friar Peter jumps on the bandwagon to support the duke and his agent.

Friar Peter is a real friar, and his complicity in injustice is feigned: he has been enlisted into Vincentio's secret plan in act 4, scene 5. But his feigning represents the way in which the church all too often allies itself with the rich, the powerful, and the corrupt. Friar Peter is another "authority" figure; only Isabella and Mariana, mere women, victims, and sex objects, lack any sort of socially sanctioned authority; they can rely only on their own honesty and truth, slingshots to hurl against the heavy artillery of government, judiciary, and now, church, in league against them.

Friar Peter, like the duke, is both gullible dupe and ironist, and when he claims that Isabella has "wrongfully accused" Angelo "who is free from touch or soil with her," he is speaking factual truth, making the assertion, however, in the service of a moral lie, the lie being the implication that it is Angelo, not Isabella, who is the victim of slander. And again, we know perfectly well that Friar Peter is in on the duke's game and is not the corrupt clergyman he impersonates. Even so, this new injustice works on us as if it were genuine and unfeigned; it generates an anger that will have a swift and satisfying catharsis in the developments that follow.

As the next stage of the miniplay unfolds, "Isabella is carried off [to prison] guarded," and Vincentio, still playing the role of credulous judge, says to his confederate, "Do you not smile at this, Lord Angelo?" (l. 163).[3] "Mariana comes forward," presses her claim that Angelo is her husband, and insists that not only is he guiltless of fornication but "I had him in mine arms / With all the effect of love" (ll. 197-98) at the time when, supposedly, he was making love to Isabella. After Angelo has explained how and why he jilted Mariana and she again insists, "He knew me as a wife" (l. 230), Angelo begins the speech with which he intends to demolish the plot against him with the remark "I did not smile till now" (l. 233). So this crucial stage in the action is marked by a smile enjoyed at its beginning and a smile repressed at its most intense moment, both signaling a deep and

complex irony. To appreciate it fully we must place ourselves in Angelo's position.

When Isabella presses her case against Angelo, he, we can be sure, is in a panic of guilt and fear. It is his word against hers, but he has had the good luck to find support in his claim of innocence from both the duke and Friar Peter. The reputation for rectitude that won him the position of substitute duke serves to discredit the "blasting and scandalous breath" of Isabella's charge. Angelo believes that Isabella speaks the truth; what he does not and cannot know is that Isabella's truth, as far as he is concerned, is a lie. He has just had, therefore, the narrowest of escapes and his pulse races when Mariana comes forward to claim him as wife and lover. Having just miraculously escaped the crime for which (as he believes) he deserves hanging, Angelo now has a stroke of good fortune so stunning it may seem too good to be true; in fact, that is exactly what it is *not*: Mariana speaks the truth, but he is sure it is a lie.

The corrupt and complaisant gods, he thinks, have delivered to Angelo the best gift a criminal might hope for: a new charge that happens to be false! The expression that blossoms in his face when he begins his demolition of Mariana's (to him) absurd claims is the look of innocence, the smile of a man who has gambled and won, the smile of renewed confidence, the smirk of a born-again sinner, reborn not to faith and humility but to arrogant and scornful righteousness.

> I did but smile till now.
> Now, good my lord, give me the scope of justice.
> My patience here is touched. I do perceive
> These poor informal women are no more
> But instruments of some more mightier member
> That sets them on.
>
> (ll. 233ff.)

Angelo concludes, "Let me have my way, my lord / To find this practice out"; the duke assents: "And punish them to your height of pleasure" (l. 240).

Anthony Brennan does not denigrate Shakespeare's art in the fifth act; to the contrary, he asserts, "Shakespeare was not, however, afflicted by sudden amnesia about how to sew varied elements into a coherent design."[4] Because he admires the dramatic structure of the fifth act, Brennan subjects it to careful and detailed analysis. And though he makes many illuminating points, he fails to recognize the tensions and cross currents at work in Angelo. Commenting on the crucial speech "I did smile till now" (l. 232ff.), Brennan observes, "It is Angelo above all who refuses to learn the lesson ['judge not lest ye be judged'] and his response to Mariana's claim is to ask more assertively

Lucio (Paul Penza) exposes the Duke (Frank Corrado) in Act V, scene i, of the
San José State University 1997 production of Measure for Measure.

for the power of judge, 'the scope of justice.'" Brennan's interpretation is correct but insensitive to the deputy's most urgent concerns. His analysis is more didactic than dramatic. At the point at which Angelo says, "Let me have my way, my lord, / To find this practice out," he believes that Mariana's false claim—and that is what her charge of sexual intimacy indubitably is, he is sure—will turn the tide in his favor. Nothing in the fifth act is more important than the fact that Angelo, at this point, believes that he has the upper hand, is counting his chickens, while we, our confidence sorely tried, ask ourselves when, if ever, the all too convincingly stupid duke will make his move, will "like an o'ergrown lion in a cave . . . [go] out to prey" (I.iii.22-23).

"I'm home free," Angelo tells himself; we understand that, though Shakespeare's supposedly faulty art is too refined to allow Angelo to say any such thing.

The duke, concealed and indecipherable (to Angelo) behind his mark of stupid credulity, has the pleasure of watching his victim puff up like a blowfish. Whose pleasure is more keen: that of the man who thinks he has been blessed with a double portion of good luck and is now untouchable or that of the man who knows that his prey has ensnared himself in an invisible web? (If we recall Iago's pithy "With as little a web as this will I ensnare as great a fly as Cassio" [*Othello,* II.i.169], it will also occur to us that Angelo is both spider and fly, or rather an erstwhile spider, soon to discover that he is the fly that has been lured into the trap woven by, shall we say, a superspider?) Angelo, at any rate, will do the smiling, and Vincentio will preserve a grave and sober mien. That way he can savor his pleasure more deliberately, contemplatively.

What about us, we who ache to see Angelo exposed and to have that sickening smile erased from his pinched and unforgiving face? Temporarily, we are left to a dry, pleasureless indignation. When Angelo says that Mariana and Isabella "are no more / But instruments of some more mightier member," (l. 238) the irony is insufficient compensation for our disappointment; again Angelo has emerged without a scratch; and everything in the speech and demeanor of the duke camouflages his true position, his covert pleasure, and his old pledge to Isabella, and therefore to us, that he is part of the "remedy," not one who aids and abets the disease. (To reassure Isabella, Vincentio as friar said, "To the love I have in doing good a remedy presents itself" [III.i.203]).

Experiencing the play in the theater, we respond to what the overt duke overtly does and not to the maneuverings of the covert Vincentio. A long time ago (as dramatic time goes) Vincentio, about to go underground in the guise of a friar, had made the promise to "see, / If power change purpose, what our seemers be" (I.iii.54). In the fifth act Vincentio is in every way the equal of Angelo as "seemer," but whereas we are never taken in by Angelo's seeming, having been privy to the terrible split between his public persona and his private agonies as shown in act 2, scenes 2 and 4, Vincentio's seeming tricks us into a kind of hypnotized gullibility. Somewhere in the back of our mind we know perfectly well that he is not stupid, not corrupt, not malleable clay in the greasy hands of Angelo, and not any of the demeaning roles he plays in this mock trial that makes a mockery of justice. Even so, we take his shamming for the reality; we respond, as we must, to his words, not to the subtext.[5] Only in the study are we fully responsive to the duke's camouflaged pleasure as Angelo smiles infuriatingly.

And only in the study are we likely to recall how Vincentio modestly declared, "I love the people, / But do not like *to stage me* to their eyes" when he took leave of Angelo in act 1, scene 3 (emphasis added). If we want to make Vincentio out to be a supersubtle con man, we might suppose that he professes to be no good at playacting on the political stage all the better to practice the roleplaying so brilliantly enacted here in the fifth act. There is a better way of reconciling Vincentio's earlier demurral with his later and brilliant demonstration of precisely the skill he professes to lack. On the political stage, undisguised and transparently himself, he is shy and diffident. In the fifth act, which is virtually a play within the play, he is disguised, first in the by now familiar and comfortable disguise of the friar, then as precisely the person he is not: a foolish, credulous, and corrupt judge; a political crony; not a sovereign who is solicitous of the well-being of his subjects.

Vincentio's stage metaphor, casual when it is first used, turns out to be a revelation: the too modest and too inward Vincentio has the potentiality to be a fine actor; however, like many another actor, he needs to conceal his own face to do the job. In all likelihood, Vincentio spoke the truth when he described himself as someone who was no good at playing the game of political stagecraft.

In *Measure for Measure,* as in a Portuguese corrida, there is no need for a literal kill; the creature to be

dispatched is sacrificed symbolically. Angelo's smile marks the point at which he commits his last and most grievous offense against *us*.[6] For we are the court of last appeal, and it is our sense of justice, in collaboration with Isabella's and Mariana's, that cries out, and this before Vincentio states the bloodthirsty principle, "An Angelo for a Claudio, death for death!" Angelo does not know that the "boss" who has allowed himself to become Angelo's "stooge" has outperformed him in the cunning business of seeming. Angelo does not know that he has lost everything, but we cannot quite make ourselves believe—never mind all those whispered confidences and promises made byVincentio—that Angelo is going to have the tables turned on him.

The airplane races toward the landing strip. Green swirls and white cubes become trees and houses; the insects are automobiles. You reassure yourself with statistics, prop up your confidence with probabilities. Not until the motors roar into reverse do you believe that you are not going to—indeed that you did not—crash. In the play we have to wait many painful minutes—more than one hundred lines are spoken after Vincentio allows Angelo to "have [his] way" as judge and jury in his own case—before we can truly believe that Vincentio is going to put a stop to the cant, deception, and injustice. Our respite does not come until Lucio "Pulls off the friar's hood and discovers the Duke."

But now Shakespeare introduces a new variation on the theme of justice denied. Vincentio, having allowed Angelo the license "Do with your injuries as seems you best" (l. 257), leaves and returns "in his friar's habit." It is now Vincentio as friar who is to be the victim of blind, prejudiced "justice," but this time there is no feigning by the accuser; he is none other than good, kindly, tolerant Escalus, who, with the best of intentions, denounces this friar, who has had the temerity to criticize Escalus' beloved duke. There is, of course, the comedy of Escalus' not knowing that the friar he attacks (in loyalty to the duke) is the duke. There is the irony that inheres in Escalus' being both wrong and genuine: he does not know that he has been dragged into a labyrinthine struggle between Angelo and Vincentio; he does not pretend (as Vincentio and Friar Peter pretended) to support injustice; Escalus, in his passionate attachment to justice, is guilty of unintended injustice:

> Why, thou unreverend and unhallowed friar,
> Is't not enough thou has suborned these women
> To accuse this worthy man, but . . . then to glance from him
> To the Duke himself, to tax him with injustice?
> Take him hence, to the rack with him!
>
> (ll. 307ff.)

Finally, then, there is the third level of irony: though the friar whom Vincentio has impersonated has indeed been reverend and hallowed, Escalus speaks truer than he knows when he charges that the friar "has suborned these women"; Escalus cannot know that the anonymous friar has suborned them to do good, not to broadcast slander.

Vincentio, still hiding behind the friar's mask, indicts degenerate Vienna: "I have seen corruption boil and bubble / Till it o'errun the stew" (ll. 320-21), thus angering again Escalus, who accuses him of uttering "slander to the state." Now a most incongruous trio forms to stand against the truth-speaking friar: both Lucio and Angelo join Escalus in attacking him. An unholy alliance: the man of goodwill, old, somewhat feeble, and a bit too willing to take the establishment's side in the argument; the fantastic, decayed gentleman whose native element is the brothel; the Puritan sinner, a man who only recently has undergone his first encounter with sexual passion and experienced it with all the intensity of an epileptic seizure—three men who have nothing in common except their alliance in the cause of silencing a truth sayer.

Escalus, raging over the insults spoken by Vincentio as friar against Vincentio as duke, says:

> Take him hence, to the rack with him! We'll touse you
> Joint by joint, but we will know his purpose.
> What, "unjust"!
>
> (ll. 312ff.)

There's something of the sputtering, impotent *senex* in these lines, and they serve as a transition to the overt comedy that follows.

In the next development, Lucio, with shameless sang-froid, makes the friar—Vincentio—the author of those libelous words against Vincentio: "And was the Duke a fleshmonger, a fool, and a coward, as you then reported him to be?" (ll. 336-37). Now it is Lucio's turn to march to the shambles. Just as Angelo smiled and smiled at the very moment when he had overreached, so Lucio goes on the offensive at the very moment when he is about to be cut down. "Why, you bald-pated, lying rascal, you must be hooded, must you? Show your knave's visage. . . . Show your sheepbiting face, and be hanged an hour!" (ll. 356 ff.). How satisfying to witness Lucio's discomfiture. He "[p]ulls off the friar's hood, and discovers the Duke" and, as he is immediately to learn, uncovers his true fantastic self. But before the duke gets around to sentencing Lucio, he must deal with Angelo; the comedy of the jocose liar is prologue to the grave business of dealing with a shamefaced and self-lacerating liar: Angelo. It may seem like having the sweet before the main course. Perhaps, though, there is a

dramatic imperative in Shakespeare's serving up Lucio before Angelo: that way, the edge is taken off our punitive appetite. Having enjoyed the settling of Lucio's hash, we can accept considerably less than an ultimate punishment for Angelo.

Vincentio confronts Angelo as soon as his disguise has dropped: "Hast thou or word, or wit, or impudence, / That yet can do thee office?" (ll. 368-69). Angelo lacks Lucio's impudence, that guiltless comic audacity that is never at a loss to improvise reasons, concoct excuses, explain away embarrassments. Angelo will do none of these things. To the contrary, he hastens to judge himself as mercilessly as he has judged Claudio:

> O my dread Lord,
> I should be guiltier than my guiltiness
> To think I can be undiscernible
> When I perceive your Grace, like power divine,
> Hath looked upon my passes. . . .
> Immediate sentence then, and sequent death,
> Is all the grace I beg.
>
> (ll. 372 ff.)

What is said of the thane of Cawdor might be said of Angelo: "Nothing in his life / Became him like the leaving it." The difference between the two men, of course, is that "execution" is done on the disloyal Cawdor, whereas Angelo is to be spared. Angelo has his most impressive moment when, with stolid dignity, he faces his disgrace, does not plead for understanding or pity, and is willing to die. If we can remember that far back—and in the theater it is unlikely that we can—we will recall that Angelo made a promise that here he fulfills. To Escalus he had boasted, "When I that censure him [Claudio] do so offend, / Let mine own judgment pattern out my death. . . . " (II.i.28ff.). If at the time this seemed to us an empty boast, a shrewd debating point, we now know better.

It is hard not to be awed by Angelo's pitiless self-condemnation. Bravery, even if suicidal, is always impressive, and here Angelo shows that he has the courage to accept the justice of his own death. Were he an antique Roman like the disgraced Antony, he Angelo succumbed to the one vice from which he thought himself immune, anesthetized; sexual lust taught him the intolerable truth that he and Claudio were brothers in weakness. But Angelo's weakness, his vulnerable humanity, will never bring him to his knees as Claudio's unmanned him, making him beg, "Let me live." For Angelo life at any cost is contemptible. A disgrace as humiliating as his, therefore, must be paid for by death.

Angelo is not the sort of man for easygoing compromises, shifting opinions, muddling through, and stammering regrets. He was willing to be loathed for his exalted standards of conduct, and he is willing to die for having betrayed those standards. The speedy "sequent death" he asks for may be more bearable than the prolonged recitation of crimes that he may fear he has yet to endure. Do we recall the words of Claudio, "If I must die, / I will encounter darkness as a bride, / And hug it in mine arms" (III.i.83ff.)? Claudio cannot abide by his resolution and falters; Angelo, though perhaps he is not tested as severely as Claudio, never falters. For whatever reasons, Angelo was unable to accept the role of bridegroom, but he has no difficulty imagining himself mated to death.

A dissenting view would insist that it is not strength but weakness that prompts Angelo to embrace death, weakness and sadism. The guilt-ridden, self-despising, sex-denying sickness that makes Angelo a sadist (the psychoanalytic argument might claim) still rages in him, and it is this sadism, turning against itself, that seeks oblivion. We can accept this insight but must not use it to denigrate him, because it is evident that the exceptionally mild punishment meted out to Angelo constitutes a kind of reward for virtues. Many nonpejorative terms suggest themselves to describe these virtues: pride, a sense of honor, absolute and uncompromising principles, a queer but genuine integrity. If we do not recognize what is admirable in Angelo we forfeit the right to be censorious about what is so appalling in his character. If then we grant that Angelo deserves these terms of praise, we can also accept the idea of "sadism" as well. Is criticism that embraces these antinomies guilty of slovenly eclecticism? It is *Measure for Measure,* not baffled and improvisatory criticism, that embraces contradictions, discontinuities, and incompatible extremes of behavior and belief. In Angelo Shakespeare paints a portrait of a deformed goodness that is repugnant, to be sure. Who could possibly love "this Angelo [who, it is said] was not made by man and woman after this downright way of creation" (III.ii.111ff.)? But who could fail to admire and to respect a man who, like a god, refuses to hear his own voice cry out, "Let me live" and condemns himself to death. Angelo is frightening because he imagines himself standing above the muck and the mire of humanity; Angelo is Isabella's "pelting petty officer"; but he is also a failed "Jove" (II.ii.111-12), someone, it is fair to say, who still possesses remnants of his original angelic beauty. In aspiring to perfection he took the greatest risk of all.

In any case, to some contemporary readers it is Duke Vincentio who seems the sadist as he persists in manipulating his puppets in the mock trial that he directs and plays a part in. He continues to conceal from Isabella the crucial fact that her brother lives; he plays cat and mouse not only with Angelo but with the two women as well. Is Vincentio then a cruel god who relishes toying with and tormenting these puny, all-

too-human creatures? And had not Angelo imputed a godlike status to the duke when he addressed him in these words?

> O my dread lord,
> I should be guiltier than my guiltiness
> To think I can be undiscernible
> When I perceive your Grace, like power
>   divine,
> Hath looked upon my passes.
>
> (ll. 372 ff.)

Whether as a fatherly pedagogue or as a sadist, Vincentio seems to be working on Isabella: students and critics often feel that he is working her over. When he turns to her and says, "The very mercy of the law cries out . . . 'An Angelo for Claudio, death for death!'" (ll. 412ff.), he is putting her to the test. To sharpen the point that Isabella is now on trial, Mariana, told that the imminent execution of Angelo threatens to make her a widow, begs Isabella to add her voice to that of the new bride in beseeching the duke to spare his life. The woman who was willing to sacrifice her brother's life to the cult of personal chastity now has a second chance to discover her own humanity. Once hard, inflexible, and uncharitable, a changed Isabella somehow finds it in her to judge Angelo's case with the tolerance and sympathy she had denied Claudio.

This point of view is intellectually attractive, and it is surely not wrong. Nevertheless, I shall argue that it is a way of looking at the final moments of the play that obscures the essential dramatic thrust; it is an emphasis that substitutes a doctrinal principle, that Isabella must be tested so that a more mature and womanly woman can emerge, for an exciting and powerful dramatic situation in which Isabella is only one of the parties involved. If we focus on Isabella and the moral problem—will she rise to the occasion and become a compassionate woman?—we point the critical spotlight, in fact, on the wrong person.

Who then is the right person? It must be Angelo: Angelo who, it is true, remains absolutely silent while the two women speak all the lines and command our attention; it is Angelo who is the crucial character even while it is Isabella, ostensibly, who is on trial. In the debate that ensues, we cannot forget that what is at issue between the duke, Isabella, and Mariana is Angelo's life. If Isabella fails as an advocate, he dies. Just as Antonio's life depended on Portia's forensic ingenuity, so Angelo's fate rests not in Isabella's hands but on her tongue, with her words, her rhetorical skill. In both plays, however, while the arguments and counterarguments are made, the man whose very being hangs in the balance stands before us as a reminder that neither in Venice nor in Vienna is this a moot court: an apparently doomed man stands off to the side; he can do nothing to help his own cause; he is probably resigned to death; indeed, there is reason to believe that (like Antonio) he is half in love with easeful death; yet he must also struggle to repress an all too human and Claudio-like fear of death. Antonio and Angelo, potential victims, believe that they face genuine threats of death, and even the proud and steely Angelo must feel his pulse's quickening as the reality of his situation presses upon him.

The essential purpose of what from one angle of vision may be seen as the testing of Isabella is, dramatically, the turning of the screw on the duke's instrument' of torment for Angelo. Throughout this long scene he has been suffocating with fear of humiliation through exposure; now, as Isabellatries to say whatever can be said to mitigate his guilt, the sweat again streams down his back. Antonio had said to his guilt-stricken friend, Bassanio, "I am a tainted wether of the flock, / Meetest for death" (*Merchant of Venice*, IV.i.114). Angelo knows, even if some critics forget, that he too is "meetest for death" and that is what the contest is about: whether he should live or die.

Angelo as judge condemns himself to death; Angelo as merely man may hope for life; if the duke hands down a harsh, Angelo-like verdict, the death sentence should be satisfying to the Angelo of old: the absolutist who refuses to make deals, even with himself. If, however, the duke spares his life—well, Angelo must accept, though grudgingly perhaps, this windfall that he would be the first, no doubt, to admit is undeserved. The gift of life, after all, comes from his master, the duke, and cannot be spurned. In any case, even a would-be but failed saint might find it beyond his moral strength to reject what must seem to him a second life. As he silently listens to charge and rebuttal in the Vincentio-Isabella contest, Angelo finds himself in a tight squeeze: either decision will cause him spiritual pain. But it is equally correct to say that whatever fate is measured out to him by the duke, one side of his personality will approve of what is being done to him. Indeed, it turns out that everyone, Lucio excepted and Angelo included, essentially gains his or her heart's desire, and that is what the tragi-comic form amounts to.[7] Angelo, like Claudio, is granted the most urgent desire of all—life.

The accomplished actor will show us a man who is riven by equivocal hopes, contradictory fears, and every kind of confusion; these perplexities will play themselves out on Angelo's tense body and imperfectly masked face. Perhaps he does not know what he wants for himself; and witnessing his silent perplexity, we find it all the harder to decide what we want for him, what we want done to him. Thus it is that when finally Angelo's life is spared we do not reject the duke's reprieve as charity misguided, misapplied, and shamelessly unprincipled. These are the charges brought against the duke, and Shakespeare, by critics who are

members of what might be called the Angelovean school, because, like Angelo, they are stern and unforgiving moralists who would like Angelo's time on the rack to be longer and harder than the duke and Shakespeare decree. Critics who remain unappeased by the kind and duration of Angelo's punishment remind one of the Hamlet who might but does not "do it pat" when he finds Claudius at prayer; Hamlet seeks a revenge "that has no relish of salvation in it"; the Angeloveans would prefer a punishment for Angelo that would "trip him, that his heels may kick at Heaven / And that his soul may be as damned and black / As Hell whereto it goes" (*Hamlet*, III.iii.73ff.). But the spirit of tragi-comedy is tolerant and forgiving. The Angeloveans ask for a strict and quantified measuring of justice, whereas the tragi-comic point of the play, surely, is that no such moral precision can be achieved, certainly not by casuistry and possibly not by God, even though He surely sees the prejudices and blind spots of all human judges. The duke himself speaks like an Angelovean when he calls out, "An Angelo for Claudio, death for death!"; but the tragi-comic irony is that the duke, still feigning, still taking bad or bigoted positions, still the corrupt judge who mocks Angelo's corruption by parodying it, discredits the very principle he propounds. Moral comparability is illusory at best, blind and vicious at worst.

What about Isabella: does not she invoke moral comparability in the crucial speech "Look, if it please you, on this man condemned / As if my brother lived" (ll. 449 ff.)? The duke gives short shrift to her arguments; he dismisses them with, "Your suit's unprofitable." He is saying in effect, "My savage measuring is the only acceptable one; yours, I reject out of hand." His argument seems simpler thanit is: because Claudio died for the crime of fornication, Angelo too must die for the same crime. The duke's equation must imply that Angelo's thwarted fornication with Isabella—and the workings of the bed trick have already been exposed—is tantamount to an act of commission. It is the wicked intention lodged in Angelo's evil soul that Vincentio wishes to scourge in this climactic moment of moral assessment and counterassessment. But it is not only punishments that are being measured to fit crimes; it is also one kind of comparability, the duke's, measured against another, Isabella's. But comparability simply does not work; it cannot solve the moral problems.

What are we to make of Isabella's arguments?[8] There is a genuine humility and generosity in her claim "A due sincerity governed his [Angelo's] deeds, / Till he did look on me" (ll. 452-53). It is, however, a testimony to her innocence that she supposes herself to be making a cogent argument when she mentions this point. Sincerity? As we know, Angelo's sincerity—if that is the right word for it—is in some ways worse, at least in its devastating consequences for himself (to say nothing of Claudio, had he not been under the protective wing of Vincentio), then Lucio's blithe insincerity. A jurist might say that this argument is very weak; a literary critic would counter with this rejoinder: in preparing us to accept the duke's generous treatment of Angelo, soon to follow, Shakespeare takes us back to Angelo's vain attempt to pray himself back into wholeness and to the abject "sincerity" of his confession "Heaven hath my empty words, / Whilst my invention, hearing not my tongue, / Anchors on Isabel" (II.iv.2ff.).

This is Isabella's main argument:

> My brother had but justice,
> In that he did the thing for which he died.
> For Angelo,
> His act did not o'ertake his bad intent,
> And must be buried but as an intent
> That perished by the way. Thoughts are no
>   subjects,
> Intents but merely thoughts.
>
> (ll. 453ff.)

We are the jury, and though we may think Isabella's argument a simplistic solution to a fiercely complex moral problem, we must vote not guilty. How can we refute the point that Angelo did not in fact fornicate with Isabella?[9]

As a prologue to his eye-for-eye principle, Vincentio indicts Angelo for multiple crimes:

> But as he adjudged your brother—
> Being criminal, in double violation
> Of sacred chastity, and of promise breach
> Thereon dependent, for your brother's life—
> The very mercy of the law cries out . . .
> "An Angelo for Claudio, death for death!"
>
> (ll. 408ff.)

There are three, possibly four, crimes mentioned here: (1) the attempted rape of Isabella, which converted into (2) the encounter with Mariana ("double violation"), (3) the broken promises to marry Mariana, and (4) the sparing of Claudio's life in return for Isabella's sexual favors. It is not easy to say which of these is the more grave offense or whether any one crime warrants the death penalty.

Isabella, shrewdly, homes in on the one crime that Angelo indisputably did not commit! She ignores her new friend Mariana's "sacred chastity" (we might wonder whether the propounder of the bed trick is in any position to use that pious phrase), and because the second crime has been brushed aside there is no point in considering the third (the broken promise to marry Mariana). The fourth would support Vincentio's vindictive position and, had Isabella been foolish enough to examine it, would have been extremely damaging

to her plea for clemency. (Vincentio might have argued, "Not only did the scoundrel try to rape you, he reneged on his promise to let Claudio live as the payoff for the use—abuse!—of your body!") So Isabella is clever to hammer at Angelo's noncrime, the crime that only a deception prevented him from committing, the one crime that Claudio, alas, did commit.

In the theater we cannot and probably need not rely on long memories, but in the study, memory allows us to make revealing connections; in this case, we can go back to the origins of Isabella's argument that "Thoughts are no subjects" to the law's strictures. It was none other than Angelo who had first enunciated Isabella's principle. "'Tis one thing to be tempted, Escalus," Angelo had insisted, "Another thing to fall" (II.i.18-19). When Angelo dismisses Escalus' tenderminded request that he imagine himself in Claudio's position, the deputy's icy distinction between deeds and intentions strikes us as a hollow legal formalism; we agree with Escalus, and because what we want most is an understanding and charitable disposition of Claudio's case, Angelo's distinction, we are certain, is a heartless and un-Christian one. Christian morality, after all, is above all concerned with crimes of the heart and is not, like secular and legal morality, narrowly confined to overt deeds. Thus it is that in *The Brothers Karamazov,* as we have seen, the central moral point is that Dmitri Karamazov, who did not murder his father but did harbor murderous thoughts against him, is from a Christian point of view guilty. Justice was done. Secular injustice represents God's justice.

Isabella uses what had once seemed the bad argument of Angelo to try to save Angelo from threatened death at the hands of the duke. This argument, however, is not "Angelovean" in the way that we have been using this term; to the contrary, it is the very opposite, because its purpose is indeed the Christian one of forgiving Angelo's "bad intent." If then we are tempted to view Isabella's argument as a legalistic evasion of the important moral questions, we might recall that her forensic sister, Portia, also used a legal loophole for a charitable end: to save an innocent life. In the case of Portia and Shylock, Christian morality is explicitly evoked in "The quality of mercy" speech; if, risking the trap of false comparability, we compare Portia's legalism with Isabella's, we see that the former is a quibble, sleight-of-hand, semantic dexterity ("The words expressly are 'a pound of flesh'"), whereas Isabella's defense of Angelo is based on a commonsense distinction universally believed and wished for: that we be tried for deeds done, not evil thoughts contemplated.

Recognizing that Isabella's crucial argument has its genesis in Angelo's once unacceptable distinction between temptation and falling, we must therefore reject those readings of *Measure for Measure* that tell us that the Isabella who pleads for Angelo's life is a newly enlightened, humane, and maturewoman; she has, we are told, changed, learned, developed; she is not the same person who condemned Claudio to death. The prude of the third act has metamorphosed into a sensitive woman, a womanly woman. How or why Isabella makes the transition from cruelty to compassion it is not easy to say. Does she harbor a secret guilt? But the supposedly "new" Isabella who claims, "My brother had but justice, / In that he did the thing for which he died" manifests no guilt whatsoever.

Isabella's principle is precisely secular, legal, and non-Christian. Suspect means (such as the bed trick) are often used to achieve good ends in this play; so far as Isabella's character is concerned, the dubious claim that she has achieved some sort of "Christian" compassion is based on an argument that, Christian though it may be in intention is nevertheless unabashedly secular and legalistic in content. But because in the theater we do not hear the voice of Angelo the serpent speaking when Isabella the dove begs the duke to let Angelo go free, we may entertain the illusion that her character has undergone some sort of progressive development. More accurately, one might say that she regresses in espousing Angelo's old (and once repudiated) idea that in order for the law to function with equity and coherence, it must confine its purview to deeds done and not to those dark and dank chambers of the heart in which wicked thoughts fester. Cogent or merely ingenious, Isabella's argument, however, is rejected by the duke, and the rejection does not seem to disappoint Angelo.

Notes

[1] Though it is unlikely that Vincentio's phrase "razure of oblivion" will in a staged performance recall to the spectator Angelo's soliloquy at the conclusion of act 2, scene 2, the critic may remember the anguished sentence "Having waste ground enough, / Shall we desire to raze the sanctuary, / And pitch our evils there?" (ll. 170ff.). For Angelo "to raze the sanctuary" is an act of despoilment of the same awful magnitude as the rape he contemplates. For Vincentio the "razure of oblivion," is, as the Arden editor points out (note 14, p. 126), like the idea of injurious time in Sonnet 122. Thematically, Angelo's *raze* and Vincentio's *razure* have this in common: the one is used in the context of false, perjured, and diseased love; Duke Vincentio's fulsome praise of Angelo, if it were sincere (as we know it is not), would be as corrupt as Angelo's "love" of Isabella; it is, in fact, however, false and perjured, but for therapeutic and ultimately benevolent purposes.

[2] An uncompromising rejection of the fifth act can be found in Marco Mincoff's essay, "*Measure for Mea-*

sure: A Question of Approach," *Shakespeare Studies,* (1966), 141-52: "And then comes the wearisome business of the unmasking, from which all the salt has gone, and we are asked to follow the peripeteias as though we did not know that it was all an elaborately staged ritual" (p. 146). Wrong though Mincoff is in the claim that "all the salt is gone" out of the maneuverings of the fifth act, he is right when he remarks that Shakespeare makes use of "his frequent method of having things both ways by pointing our emotions in one direction when the logic of the whole context would pull them the other" (p. 146). Mincoff believes that "Shakespeare overstepped the limits of illusion," whereas my analysis attempts to show that even with the knowledge that Vincentio "stages" a parody trial in which he is a caricature judge, we, nevertheless, feel the injustice done to the suppliant women, feel genuine outrage as Angelo seems successfully to escape punishment. Shakespeare is having it both ways, but audiences are capable of complex reactions in which knowledge does not dissipate fear or credulity.

[3] Mary Lascelles understands that the fifth act is a "play within the play," and her analysis recognizes Vincentio's design "not to confound Angelo at the outset, but to put him off his guard and so make sure that he will settle into the trap" (*Shakespeare's Measure for Measure* [Athlone Press, London, 1953]), p. 124. And though she sees what many critics miss—the theatrical brilliance of the trap ("All this is *very good theater*") she offers an epistemological rather than a dramatic analysis of the duke's role in the final moments of the play: "He knows now what is behind the fair shows of society . . . he knows, but he cannot make his knowledge effectual. . . . He can, that is, see and speak, but he cannot act—until, with the disclosure of his identity, knowledge and power are at last effectually joined" (p. 127). Vincentio can act any time he chooses to do so; he does not act against Angelo, not because of impotence but by design: he is allowing Angelo to enjoy his delusory triumph over the women who accuse him. In this play within the play Vincentio is playing the part of the venal judge; he feigns stupidity and corruption so that our indignation may be fired to a white heat and so that our satisfaction, when it finally comes, may be all the greater: that is the best part of this "very good theater." In the chapter concerned with the fifth act, "The Verdict," casuistry, it might be said, weighs more heavily than artistry for Lascelles; a good case can be made for reversing the emphasis.

[4] Anthony Brennan, *Shakespeare's Dramatic Structures* (Routledge & Kegan Paul, London, 1986), p. 71ff.

[5] Anthony Caputi seems to recognize that the duke's behavior causes us pain ("Scenic Design in *Measure for Measure," Journal of English and German Philo-*

logy, 60 [1961], 423-24, reprinted in *"Measure for Measure": A Collection of Critical Essays,* ed. George L. Geckle [Prentice-Hall, Englewood Cliffs, N.J., 1970]). "Clearly the primary function of Act V is to cause our sense of distress to yield to a sense of reassurance, to supplement our perception of the precariousness of civilized foundations with the perception that with understanding man can regulate, if not remedy, his difficult situation . . ." (p. 95). However, Caputi's bland duke is described as a man who "simply sits back in Act V to let the intrigue work itself out"; in fact, the duke is very busy behaving like a caricature of a blind and bigoted ruler and judge.

[6] R. L. P. Jackson's analysis of the fifth act takes a benevolent view of Angelo ("Necessary Ambiguity: The Last Act of *Measure for Measure," Critical Review,* 26 [1984], 114-29). "If, as I take it we do, we squirm a little uncomfortably in our seats, then the squirming is partly on Angelo's behalf" (p. 116). In his emphasis on ambiguity, the critic assures us, "Shakespeare awakens our sympathies to what it would be like to be an Angelo . . ." (p. 117). In Jackson's view, "we're all on trial in this last act" (p. 123), and apparently are not better than Angelo and probably have "been too easy on our own (as we think them) benignly humanitarian impulses" (p. 120). Such tolerance of Angelo leads to a blurring of moral distinctions. The only revenge that Jackson discusses is that of the duke against Lucio. He does not recognize that our "squirming" expresses the desire to have Angelo stopped, exposed, and punished. It may reflect badly on us, but we cannot identify with Angelo. To the contrary, his success in brazening out the charges leveled against him, until finally the tables are turned, angers us. Traditional moral notions are not on trial, and if we who are guided by these are on trial, it is not in the sense in which Jackson means to humble us. The trial requires us to endure a great deal of sustained frustration in the hope that punitive justice, demanded by Angelo's crimes, will be forthcoming: in the hope that our moral discomfort will be assuaged.

[7] The critic A. D. Nuttall asserts, "The play leaves [Angelo] in a state of torture, mitigated only by the fact that Claudio is not, after all, dead" ("*Measure for Measure:* Quid Pro Quo?" *Shakespeare Studies,* 4 [1968], p. 247). If it is true that "any producer who has Angelo leave the stage at the close of the play in a state of happy tranquillity simply does not know his business," what is the final effect of what Nuttall calls Vincentio's "orgy of clemency"? Do we leave the theater with punitive desires unassuaged and in a state of irritation?

Nuttall's paradox whereby the Judas-like Angelo takes "upon his shoulders our sins" allows him to explain, at least partially, the "mysterious resonance" that, unarguably, attaches to the duke's deputy. Exploring the paradox (found in Borges' "Three Versions of

Judas" in *Ficciones*) Nuttall displays his gifts as a casuist. Angelo in Nuttall's essay seems to suffer exclusively from a moral anguish. But it is in the ferocious miscegenation of principled morality and uncontrollable sexual feelings that Angelo's character is created—or should we say *destroyed?* Nuttall might have made an even better case for Angelo's bifurcated status as devil and saint if he had confronted the explicitly sexual nature of the deputy's torment.

[8] A. P. Rossiter (*Angel with Horns* [Theatre Arts Books, New York, 1961]) is dissatisfied with Isabella's "plea for Angelo"; it "comes too suddenly, too like a Beaumont and Fletcher switchover—without *thought* . . . Shakespeare does not let her open her mind to us. This is worse than her silence for over eighty lines at the end of the play, before she declines coyly into the ex-Friar's bosom" (p. 162). As has been pointed out (Chapter 6, n. 2), nowhere in the play does Shakespeare "let [Isabella] open her mind to us" through the kind of introspective soliloquy that twice affords a window to Angelo's thoughts and feelings. The eighty lines of silence come after Vincentio has declared, "Your suit's unprofitable" (l. 460). Isabella's plea, on behalf of Angelo and, more important, Mariana, who is her true client, has failed, at least momentarily, and to the extent that Angelo values his own life—a problematic point—Angelo will suffer in much the same way Claudio suffered when Isabella had to spurn him as he begged for life. And so the subtle but potent tension, not recognized by Rossiter, keeps Angelo on tenterhooks—he has "crav[ed] death more willingly than mercy"—while Vincentio attends to other matters. If Angelo wants to die, he will soon be punished with life and marriage; if he wants to live, he is being tormented with the threat of death. Rossiter does not focus on the primary character in these final moments of the play: Angelo, who is in the dock, not attorney Isabella.

[9] Northrop Frye tells us that when Isabella "pleads for Angelo's life on the ground that he is less villainous than self-deluded . . . we understand that this is really what the whole second half of the play is about" (*The Myth of Deliverance* [University of Toronto Press, Toronto, 1983] p. 29). Her speech, "Look, if it please you, on this man condemned / As if my brother lived" (V.i.449-50), Frye claims, "expresses the genuine kind of love, the charity which is the supreme virtue, that Isabella had dimly in mind when she first wanted to be a nun."

We must be pleased to find Northrop Frye willing, charitably, to speak of Isabella's charity. He believes in "the genuine sanctity of Isabella," and so do we. Frye goes on to say that, with the reprieve of Angelo, "the law has been, not annulled or contradicted, but transcended; not broken but fulfilled by being internalized" (p. 30). Frye then makes what is surely an unsupportable statement. "*Measure for Measure* is among other things a subtle and searching comedy of humors in which Angelo andIsabella are released from the humors of different kinds of legalism, or what Blake would call moral virtue" (p. 38). This, however, ignores the obvious fact that it is a legalism, a quibble, that makes it possible for Isabella to argue for Angelo's freedom. Earlier, Frye had glanced at *The Merchant of Venice.* Strange then that he does not recognize that Isabella, like Portia, uses the law to achieve the deliverance that is the subject of Frye's study. However exalted the aims of these two amateur attorneys, their means are those of the tricky lawyer. As we say nowadays, Portia "gets her client off on a technicality," and so does Isabella. Frye need not have evaded the fact that Isabella uses legalistic means to achieve noble ends. After all, the play as a whole is characterized by the use of expedience to achieve pleasing results.

SUBSTITUTIONS

Alexander Leggatt (essay date 1988)

SOURCE: "Substitution in *Measure for Measure,*" in *Shakespeare Quarterly,* Vol. 39, No. 3, Autumn, 1988, pp. 342-59.

[*In the essay below, Leggatt stresses that not only is the use of substitutions pervasive in* Measure for Measure, *but that the substitutions are all problematic in that they fail to achieve the intended ends, or they are in some way unsatisfying. Leggatt concludes that the substitutions, although revealing, are incomplete.*]

In the sources that Shakespeare used for *Measure For Measure,* the heroine gives her own body to the judge in order to save her brother. Shakespeare spares Isabella that fate by putting Mariana in her place. This substitution is part of a pattern of substitution, virtually a chain reaction, that runs through the play. A. D. Nuttall has called "vicarious action" the "principal idea" of the play,[1] and James Black has shown how pervasive the idea is: not only does Mariana substitute for Isabella, but Angelo substitutes for the Duke; then Isabella asks Angelo to put himself in Claudio's place, and he does. When the bed-trick fails, "Maidenhead-for-maidenhead" becomes "head-for-head";[2] Barnardine for Claudio; Ragozine for Barnardine. In fact, Ragozine has the distinction of being a substitute substitute. Not long ago I took part in a production of this play;[3] at the first rehearsal when we were allegedly off book, the Provost approached Angelo and asked, "Is it your will Angelo shall die tomorrow?"—leaving Angelo somewhat at a loss for an answer that fitted the script. Throughout rehearsals—and performances—the transpositions continued. Quite late in the run Escalus was

heard to exclaim, "But yet, poor Angelo!" The names chime together: Angelo and Claudio, Barnardine and Ragozine; but this was only a symptom of something deeper. Some gremlin of substitution was in the air, like the evil spirits that haunt performances of *Macbeth.* This gremlin can be seen at work in the text. Why does Friar Peter take over from Friar Thomas? One could be clever and say that as part of the play's comic movement we go from the doubting apostle to the rock on which the Church is founded; but I suspect it's simply the gremlin at work. Part of the manufactured confusion of the last scene stems from the fact that characters do not speak for themselves. Friar Peter identifies himself as Friar Lodowick's mouth-piece, "To speak, as from his mouth, what he doth know / Is true and false" (V.i.157-58).[4] He does this rather oddly, seeming to defend Angelo and attack the women, while the "real" Friar Lodowick does just the opposite. Angelo says of Isabella and Mariana:

> I do perceive
> These poor informal women are no more
> But instruments of some more mightier member
> That sets them on.
>
> (V.i.234-37)

Lucio casts the Friar in his own role as slanderer of the Duke:

> Had he been lay, my lord,
> For certain words he spake against your Grace
> In your retirement, I had swing'd him soundly.
>
> (V.i.131-33)

Later the Duke, as Friar, declares, "You must, sir, change persons with me, ere you make that my report" (V.i.334-35). Part of the business of the dénouement is quite simply getting people to appear as themselves and speak as themselves, clearing away substitutions and reversing transposed identities.

The idea of substitution appears not just in the comic machinery of the play, where its presence could be seen as conventional, but in the language of the more serious scenes. When Angelo hints that Claudio could be saved by sin, Isabella takes it that he sees mercy as a sin, and she offers to assume the guilt herself:

> . . . you granting of my suit,
> If that be sin, I'll make it my morn prayer
> To have it added to the faults of mine,
> And nothing of your answer.
>
> (II.iv.70-73)

She offers, in effect, to take his place. When Claudio at first agrees with her refusal to give up her chastity, she declares, "There my father's grave / Did utter forth a voice" (III.i.85-86); Claudio is speaking as her father, saying what he would say. His declaration, "I will encounter darkness as a bride / And hug it in mine arms" (III.i.83-84) suggests another bed-trick, with death taking the place of Juliet. The idea has other ramifications. Not just in the Duke's peculiar decision to leave Angelo in charge of the city, but in the normal workings of society as a whole, substitution is pervasive. Elbow owes his job to it; he says of his neighbors, "As they are chosen, they are glad to choose me for them." Escalus's order, "Look you bring me in the names of some six or seven, the most sufficient of your parish" (II.i.265-70), makes it clear that he is going to find a substitute for Elbow.

In Isabella's plea for mercy, we touch on the greatest substitution of all:

> Why, all the souls that were, were forfeit once,
> And He that might the vantage best have took
> Found out the remedy.
>
> (II.ii.73-75)

This is the doctrine of the Atonement. Since this is arguably the central and defining doctrine of Christianity, it is tempting to do what some critics have done and see it as central to the play,[5] but that is to ignore the theatrical effect of its placement in the scene. It is part of Isabella's argument but not the climax of it; it has no effect on Angelo, and the scene sweeps on past it. Angelo puts himself not in the place of Christ but in the place of Claudio; Isabella herself, as James Black has noted, will not take the way of substitution: she will not sacrifice herself to save Claudio.[6] Another kind of divine substitution is suggested when Angelo laments his fallen spiritual state. His line, "Heaven in my mouth" should almost certainly read "God in my mouth";[7] it has been damaged by the general expunging of oaths in the Folio. The passage then reads:

> God in my mouth,
> As if I did but only chew his name,
> And in my heart the strong and swelling evil
> Of my conception.
>
> (II.iv.4-7)

The bread of the communion substitutes for the body of Christ; and Angelo's image suggests that in chewing the name only, with his heart full of evil thoughts, he is incurring the condemnation of which St. Paul writes: "he that eateth and drinketh unworthily, eateth and drinketh damnation to himself, not discerning the Lord's body" (I Corinthians, 11:29). Angelo's image is central to Christian liturgy, as Isabella's is central to Christian theology; but once again, this time more directly, the context makes it ironic. One route of salvation is ignored, the other is perverted.

God acts on man through a series of substitutions: the Incarnation, the Eucharist, and the priesthood—represented here by a Duke who dresses up as a Friar and goes around hearing confessions in a manner that would produce a major scandal in an actual Catholic community. In every case the substitution, as it appears in *Measure for Measure,* is in some way clouded by irony. The substitutions that are central to the plot are all, in various ways, unsatisfying. Angelo and Elbow have this in common: they fail to perform adequately in the roles assigned to them. The bed-trick fails to appease Angelo; the substitution of Barnardine for Claudio is called off when Barnardine refuses to die. We need, then, to do more than note the pervasiveness of substitution in the play; we need also to note its problematic quality, for this may help us to understand why Shakespeare was so interested in it and took the trouble to explore it from such a great variety of angles.

Let us begin with the first of the play's substitutions, Angelo for the Duke. The Duke has two deputies, but in the first scene he speaks to them in very different terms. He tells Escalus,

> . . . I am put to know that your own science
> Exceeds, in that, the lists of all advice
> My strength can give you. Then no more remains
> But that, to your sufficiency, as your worth is able,
> And let them work.
>
> (I.i.5-9)

The passage is obscure in detail but its drift is clear: the Duke trusts to Escalus's own ability. He is worthy in himself; nothing needs to be given to him. In sharp contrast, the Duke bestows his own role on Angelo, as though Angelo himself is nothing and must be given the Duke's office and capacities before he can function:

> What figure of us, think you, he will bear?
> For you must know, we have with special soul
> Elected him our absence to supply;
> Lent him our terror, drest him with our love,
> And given his deputation all the organs
> Of our own power. What think you of it?
>
> (I.i.16-21)

His persistent questioning suggests an edginess about the decision, as does his repeated insistence on Angelo's substitute role later in the scene: "In our remove, be thou at full ourself" (l. 43); "Your scope is as mine own" (l. 64). Angelo is also nervous about his assignment:

> Now, good my lord,
> Let there be some more test made of my metal,

Before so noble and so great a figure
Be stamp'd upon it.

(I.i.47-50)

He imagines that the Duke will give him his identity as the stamp turns a piece of metal into a coin; but he wonders if the metal itself is worthy of the impression.

Why does the Duke make Angelo his substitute? We will consider the Duke more fully later; but we may note here that the motives he expresses overtly come close to cancelling each other out: Angelo will make up for the Duke's failure to clean up the city, and in the process his own nature will be tested. The first motive suggests trust in Angelo, the second distrust. We may also note that certain similarities link the two men: both profess a dislike of crowds, though the Duke's is qualified—"I love the people, / But do not like to stage me to their eyes" (I.i.67-68)—while Angelo is more simply critical of the "foolish throngs" (II.iv.24). There may be more to this than an expression of sympathy for James I's similar feelings. The Duke's love of "the life remov'd" (I.iii.8) is something that links him both with Angelo, who takes on public office with reluctance, and with Isabella, who has to be practically dragged out of the convent to plead for her brother's life. Making Angelo act for him solves a problem for the Duke's reputation: Angelo

may in th' ambush of my name strike home,
And yet my nature never in the fight
To do in slander.

(I.iii.41-43)

He is made to undergo not only the responsibility but the public exposure the Duke shuns. The Duke picks for this role not someone who enjoys the limelight but someone who in this respect is like himself; and Angelo is made to undergo worse than this. The Duke's "Believe not that the dribbling dart of love / Can pierce a complete bosom" (I.iii.2-3) is the equivalent of Angelo's "Eve[r] till now / When men were fond, I smil'd, and wonder'd how" (II.ii.186-87). The Duke throws Angelo, on his behalf, not only into the arena of power but into the arena of sexual experience.[8] Angelo suffers the disgrace and torment; the Duke comes along when it is all over and proposes marriage.

To put it that way may seem to credit the Duke with a foreknowledge of the plot that is hardly believable. But his curiosity about how Angelo will behave is centered on the question of whether he can control his appetites:

Lord Angelo is precise;
Stands at a guard with Envy; scarce confesses
That his blood flows; or that his appetite
Is more to bread than stone. Hence shall we
    see

If power change purpose, what our seemers
be.

(I.iii.50-54)

To take on power is to undergo temptation, and Angelo is to do both on the Duke's behalf. The Duke professes abstinence; so does Angelo. In seeing how Angelo behaves, the Duke may be revealing a curiosity, even anxiety, about himself. "Our seemers," interestingly, is plural. We see how nettled the Duke is by Lucio's slanders; and most of these concern his sexual behavior. A similar defensiveness is suggested by the Duke's jest with the Provost, when he asks to be left alone with Isabella: "My mind promises with my habit no loss shall touch her by my company" (III.i.176-77). This is odd and pointless—even, in view of what Isabella has just been through, a bit tasteless. Like his reactions to Lucio, it may reflect the Duke's touchiness about his own sexuality.

In more than one sphere, then, the Duke gets Angelo to do his dirty work. Rosalind Miles observes that "the Duke's realisation of the mistake of trying to enforce the law too strictly seems to have been learned entirely through Angelo, and at his expense."[9] Whether the Duke *does* realize the mistake is a moot point, but it is certainly true that Angelo, on the difficult matter of law enforcement, takes both the risk and the blame. He is clearly the most unpopular man in Vienna. If the tough action needed to clean up the city involves some risk to the soul, or at least to the moral nature, of the authority who tries it (it is not business for a saint), then Angelo must bear that too.[10] In being the Duke's substitute, Angelo is also his victim. Moreover, there is only one respect in which the substitution is clearly successful. The defiance of Pompey and the final distribution of pardons make law enforcement look futile; there is no certainty that the city will ever be cleaned up. Though Angelo may be taking the risk of erotic involvement on the Duke's behalf, the connection is not so clearly established as it might be, and in any case Isabella's silence in the face of the Duke's proposal leaves the theme unresolved. What has been achieved, without question, is the testing, exposure, and humiliation of Angelo. Whatever his last thoughts are after the dénouement, his last words express a longing for death. As achievements go, this one is negative.

In the last scene, the Duke's initial action of withdrawing from Vienna and leaving deputies to rule for him is not just reversed but parodied. Putting Angelo and Escalus in charge of the inquiry into Isabella's accusations, the Duke leaves the stage again. He then returns as the Friar and asks for himself. Escalus's reply, "The Duke's in us" (V.i.293) is sharply ironic. The Duke is not in Angelo or Escalus; he is on stage in the person of the Friar. And when Escalus in the Duke's name goes on to badger and threaten the Friar, the effect is increasingly comic. We would expect

Isabella (Kathleen Dobbs) and Claudio (Bryce Punty) in the prison, Act III, scene i, of the

San José State University 1997 production of Measure for Measure.

Shakespeare, as part of the dénouement, to have the Duke finally speak and act for himself, but he goes beyond this, subjecting the whole idea of political substitution to ironic comedy, making it look futile.

The play's other major substitution, the bed-trick, has its own futility. Quite simply, Angelo takes his price and orders Claudio's execution anyway. And just as the Duke's motives in putting Angelo in his place seem mixed and shadowy, so there are aspects of the bed-trick that remain curiously unexplored. Experts may debate whether Mariana loses her virginity under the same legal conditions as Juliet did; what the play is at pains to emphasize is that the personal relationship is utterly different. Claudio and Juliet are simply in love: the key word for their sexual relationship is Juliet's "Mutually" (II.iii.27). Mariana, on the other hand, is obsessed with a man who wants nothing to do with her, and who beds her thinking she is someone else. This raises questions about the nature and quality of their sexual encounter, questions that I think are more than just vulgar curiosity. In the production I was involved in, Angelo and Mariana spoke to each other in

the last moments of the play, in dialogue that, since it was not intended to be heard by the audience, gave the performers a certain latitude for mischief. One night Angelo asked Mariana, "How was I?" to which she replied, "Well, I still want to marry you."

In the text there is nothing of the kind. We do not know how Angelo feels about the experience he was so desperate to have; his decision to have Claudio executed might indicate disappointment, but I think it more likely reflects the peculiar legal turn of his mind. The self-disgust he shows in his final soliloquy is nothing new; he has felt it all along. Certainly he feels no better, and he has evidently made no attempt to meet Isabella again; once was enough. About Mariana's feelings we know nothing. Should we expect to know anything? We have the precedent of Helena's words following the bed-trick in *All's Well That Ends Well:* "O my good lord, when I was like this maid, / I found you wondrous kind" (V.iii.307-8). The sad, touching irony of this line reverberates through the whole relationship of Bertram and Helena. He was a good lover for her because he thought she was someone else. He also seems to have been a better lover than his cynical indifference to Diana once the encounter is over would indicate; he is not just a lecherous young brute. Or is Helena's "wondrous kind" a charitable exaggeration? Or, to take a darker reading, is she simply grateful for anything? However one takes it, the line encourages speculation about the quality of the encounter, speculation that illuminates the characters in a variety of ways. No such illumination is provided in *Measure for Measure*. We have no indication that the encounter humanizes Angelo or satisfies Mariana; neither character seems different. There is something blank and anonymous about it. James Trombetta has suggested that "Sexuality is deeply threatening to Angelo because it presents itself as the solvent of character, a fall into anonymity";[11] whether this is true of Angelo's own thinking, it certainly seems true of the bed-trick. All cats are grey in the dark. It does not represent a stage in the relationship of the participants, as it does for Bertram and Helena. One simple sign of this is that we know Helena is pregnant at the end of the play, while about Mariana's condition we know nothing.

But at least Mariana, like Angelo, has taken the risk of acting for another person, and she has done so more willingly than he. As James Black points out, "Here is the first act of wholehearted substitution."[12] We might add that for Mariana all cats are not grey in the light. Angelo has added to his other offenses the intention (and, so far as he knows, the act) of infidelity. The Duke points out,"It is your husband mock'd you with a husband" (V.i.416). He was consummating their relationship only in the most literal, physical way; in his mind he was having sex with Isabella. In that sense he was not the real thing but a substitute, a mock-husband. Yet when the Duke offers to give Mariana Angelo's estate "To buy you a better husband" she replies, "O my dear lord, / I crave no other, nor no better man" (V.i.423-24). For her there is a point at which the game of sunstitution has to stop; for whatever reason, Angelo's value to her is unique, and no other man will do. If there is indeed something impersonal and anonymous about sex, this is Mariana's answer to it.

We may think that the bed-trick frees Isabella from all risk and all responsibility. Mariana will simply do the job for her. But Isabella is not let off: in the last scene their relationship is reversed, as she substitutes for Mariana. She has to undergo the embarrassment and— it must seem for a while—the very considerable danger of accusing Angelo in public, claiming he has done to her what he actually did to Mariana. She undergoes this trial with characteristic reluctance:

> To speak so indirectly I am loth;
> I would say the truth, but to accuse him so
> That is your part; yet I am advis'd to do it,
> He says, to veil full purpose.
>
> (IV.vi.1-4)

Mariana has nothing worse to confess than the fact that she has slept with her husband; Isabella must confess, falsely and publicly, to the fornication she actually refused to commit. This is not the same as doing the deed, of course, but theatrically she is forced to imitate the fallen woman she would not be in reality; in its own way this is a kind of surrogate action.

She goes further in her plea for Angelo's life. Once again she acts on Mariana's behalf, answering the other woman's request, "Sweet Isabel, take my part" (V.i.428), speaking not for what she wants but for what Mariana wants. But she can do more than just substitute for Mariana. In one sense her plea is very different, cold and reserved as Mariana's is not:

> I partly think
> A due sincerity govern'd his deeds
> Till he did look on me.
>
> (V.i.443-45)

This is not Mariana's style. In another way, however, Isabella's plea has far greater force. Mariana can do little more than express her own desire and her hope that Angelo will reform. Isabella, as the party most deeply wronged, can address with real authority the central question of Angelo's offense. Since there is no self-interest behind it, a plea from her has greater weight than a plea from Mariana. As Mariana, not Isabella, was the sexual partner Angelo should have had, so Isabella, not Mariana, is the advocate he really needs.

This substitution, like the others, fails in its apparent purpose. The Duke's reply, "Your suit's unprofitable" (V.i.453), makes it seem futile, and his ultimate intention of mercy means that it was never necessary in the first place. Or, at least, it was never necessary as a way of saving Angelo. It was necessary, instead, as a test of Isabella. In every case we have examined so far, the substitution fails in its overt intent but tests the character of the substitute. Angelo does not clean up Vienna but reveals his own nature. Mariana's giving of her body does not save Claudio but tells us something of her own capacity for commitment; Isabella's plea does not save Angelo, but the fact that she can make it at all shows a measure of charity that her harsh words to Claudio made us doubt. In testing and revealing the character of the substitute, each episode also reveals that the substitution cannot be exact; one person simply does not equal another. Angelo is not the Duke, Mariana is not Isabella, nor is Isabella Mariana. Made to act on another's behalf, they reveal their own individuality. In Brecht's *Mann ist Mann*, individuality is meaningless, and the porter Galy Gay can become for all practical purposes the missing soldier Jeraiah Jip. The play ends with him fixed in his new identity. Shakespeare's human material is less tractable and more significant.

The political and sexual substitutions in the play have of course been much discussed; critics have been less interested in the attempted substitution of Barnardine for Claudio, but I think it was very important for Shakespeare. He took unusual pains to bring the characters together theatrically. Between his great scene with Isabella and his wordless appearance in the finale Claudio appears only once, when the Provost asks that he and Barnardine be fetched out together. Only Claudio appears, explaining that Barnardine is "As fast lock'd up in sleep as guiltless labour / When it lies starkly in the traveller's bones" (IV.ii.64-65). Wakeful and obedient, Claudio initially contrasts with Barnardine—but parallels accumulate. The Duke takes Barnardine as a challenge, determining to "Persuade this rude wretch willingly to die" (IV.iii.80). He has tried the same with Claudio, not altogether successfully; it is safe to predict that with Barnardine he will fail. (There is, incidentally, another substitution in the last scene as Friar Peter is given Friar Lodowick's old job of spiritual advisor to Barnardine—arguably a harder fate than Lucio's.) Later the Duke orders the Provost, "put them in secret holds, / Both Barnardine and Claudio" (IV.iii.86-87), as though they were similar material to be stored in adjacent bins. In the last scene they enter together, suggesting again some equation between them. Shakespeare is hinting, I think, that there is more to Barnardine's relationship with Claudio than the fact that he has a head to sever.

Mary Lascelles notes an echo of the Duke's speech to Claudio on the emptiness of life in the Provost's description of Barnardine as "A man that apprehends death no more dreadfully but as a drunken sleep" (IV.ii.140-41). She calls this echo "unintended and unlucky,"[13] but I am not so sure. Both men cling to a life the Duke describes as "an after-dinner's sleep" (III.i.33); his question, "What's yet in this / That bears the name of life?" (III.i.38-39), is directed at Claudio but applies with equal or greater force to Barnardine. The Provost says of the latter, "He hath evermore had the liberty of the prison: give him leave to escape hence, he would not" (IV.ii.145-47). One reading of this is that wherever Barnardine may be physically, he is always spiritually in the prison of himself; he carries his own cell with him. Physical escape would be pointless and meaningless. This, according to Isabella, is the life Claudio would have if he let himself be rescued at the cost of his sister's shame:

> . . . perpetual durance; a restraint,
> Though all the world's vastidity you had,
> To a determin'd scope.
>
> (III.i.67-69)

Claudio too would carry his prison with him.

But the substitution of Barnardine for Claudio does not, like the bed-trick, fail; it does not even take place.

Not only does Barnardine refuse, but in literal terms he was never a good duplicate in the first place. The Provost objects, "Angelo hath seen them both, and will discover the favour"; the Duke replies, "O, death's a great disguiser; and you may add to it. Shave the head, and tie the beard" (IV.ii.172-75). Though the Duke shows his usual confidence, it is clear that this will need more technical work than the bed-trick seems to do. In the end it is Ragozine who takes Claudio's place (and Barnardine's). He is "more like to Claudio," "A man of Claudio's years; his beard and head / Just of his colour" (IV.iii.75, 71-72). His severed head makes a brief appearance, but he is otherwise unseen. He never establishes, like Barnardine, an onstage identity that makes him an individual. All we know of him is that he is "a most notorious pirate" who has just died of "a cruel fever" (IV.iii.69-70). He might be linked with the sanctimonious pirate of I.ii, who went to sea with the Ten Commandments minus one; but that too is an offstage character, and while we may say of Claudio and Angelo that they respect all the commandments but one, the connection is, I think, too general to be very significant. Ragozine's "fever" might have suggested the fires of lust if such imagery had been as pervasive in this play as it is in *Troilus and Cressida;* but it is not. There are suggestions, perhaps, that Ragozine bears the sins of the other characters and purges them by his death; but these suggestions do not go very far, and the main impression, certainly the theatrical impression, is that Ragozine will do as a Claudio-substitute because he is not really an individual. Barnardine is; so, of course, is Claudio. When the Provost unmuffles him at the end of the play, he calls him "As like almost to Claudio as himself" (V.i.487). The phrasing really conveys that there is no one like Claudio. He is, like all human beings, unique and irreplaceable. So is Barnardine. When Barnardine is simply described, he sounds expendable. When we actually see him, we recognize in his brute stubbornness and pride—"If you have anything to say to me, come to my ward" (IV.iii.61-62)—something we would hate to lose. Shakespeare acknowledges this by bringing Barnardine on stage for public forgiveness. In strict plot terms Barnardine is a red herring. We could cut him and go straight to Ragozine, and the story would be unaffected. But he is there as an acid test of the principle that no human being is replaceable or expendable. If we can say that of Barnardine, we can say it of anybody.

The question of whether Barnardine can really be equated with Claudio has other implications for the play's treatment of substitution, to which I would now like to turn. Angelo is like the Duke and unlike him; Barnardine is like Claudio and unlike him—and so on through the play. Characters, ideas, and actions are explored for their similarities and differences, and the result is a series of mirroring effects, of likenesses that are striking but not quite exact (just as a literal mirror image is not quite exact, since it flattens and reverses what it reflects). Claudio's crime is fornication, Barnardine's is murder, and different characters pick away at the possibility of an equation between these crimes. Lucio asks Claudio if his crime is murder or lechery (I.ii.129). For Angelo there is no real difference:

> It were as good
> To pardon him that hath from nature stolen
> A man already made, as to remit
> Their saucy sweetness that do coin heaven's
>   image
> In stamps that are forbid. 'Tis all as easy
> Falsely to take away a life true made,
> As to put mettle in restrained means
> To make a false one.
>
> (II.iv.42-49)

He then goes on to give Isabella the choice of sex with him or death for her brother. Her decision, "I had rather my brother die by the law, than my son should be unlawfully born" (III.i.188-90), continues the experiment of weighing sex and killing in the same set of balances. From this point of view Claudio has violated life no less than Barnardine has. It is an interesting notion. But we should listen to the straightforward common sense of the Provost, comparing the two men: "Th' one has my pity; not a jot the other, / Being a murderer, though he were my brother" (IV.ii.59-60).

The equation of Claudio and Barnardine is unexpected, interesting, and worth pursuing for a while, but it finally breaks down.[14] The same could be said of other character equations. For example, the two great scenes that pit Angelo and Isabella against each other bring out ironic resemblances between them. Both have been led out, reluctantly, into a world of practical action that is dangerous to them. The Duke's words to Angelo—

> Heaven doth with us as we with torches do,
> Not light them for themselves; for if our
>   virtues
> Did not go forth of us, 'twere all alike
> As if we had them not.
>
> (I.i.32-35)

—form a rough parallel to Lucio's insistence that Isabella come out of the convent to save her brother. Describing the frailty of women, Isabella uses the image Angelo had used for his own frailty: " . . . we are soft as our complexions are, / And credulous to false prints" (II.iv.128-29). More important, their two scenes together are mirror images of each other. In the first, Isabella argues against absolute standards—"That in the captain's but a choleric word, / Which in the soldier is flat blasphemy" (II.ii.131-32)—while Angelo insists on them. In the second, it is Angelo who argues against the absolute, reacting to Isabella's "'Tis set down so in

heaven, but not in earth" with "Say you so? Then I shall pose you quickly" (II.iv.50-51), and driving her into the strict legalism that had been his. There is some point in his challenge, "Were you not then as cruel as the sentence / That you have slandered so?" (II.iv.109-10). In the first scene, Angelo is backed into a corner, and he ends the scene with a soliloquy expressing his dilemma; in the second, this move is repeated by Isabella.[15] She admits, up to a point, that she has used dubious arguments that he can now turn against her:

> *Ang.* You seem'd of late to make the law a
>   tyrant,
> And rather prov'd the sliding of your brother
> A merriment than a vice.
> *Isab.* O pardon me, my lord; it oft falls out
> To have what we would have, we speak not
>   what we mean.
> I something do excuse the thing I hate
> For his advantage that I dearly love.
>
> (II.iv.114-20)

Yet she never succumbs to Angelo's attempt to equate her legalistic cruelty with his:

> Ignomy in ransom and free pardon
> Are of two houses: lawful mercy
> Is nothing kin to foul redemption.
>
> (II.iv.111-13)

Like the Provost, she insists on a clear, final distinction based on common sense.

Angelo's offense, up to a point, resembles Claudio's. Isabella asks him to imagine an exchange: "If he had been as you, and you as he, / You would have slipp'd like him" (II.ii.64-65), and later, more directly,

> Go to your bosom,
> Knock there, and ask your heart what it doth
>   know
> That's like my brother's fault.
>
> (II.ii.137-39)

These are the words that trigger his first guilty aside: "She speaks, and tis such sense / That my sense breeds with it" (II.ii.142-43). Escalus has already raised the question of Angelo's committing Claudio's sin, and Angelo has given the answer:

> You may not so extenuate his offence
> For I have had such faults; but rather tell me,
> When I that censure him do so offend,
> Let mine own judgement pattern out my death,
> And nothing come in partial.
>
> (II.i.27-31)

It appears at the end that this is exactly what will happen:

'An Angelo for Claudio; death for death.
Haste still pays haste, and leisure answers
    leisure;
Like doth quit like, and Measure still for
    Measure.'
Then, Angelo, thy fault's thus manifested,
Which, though thou would'st deny, denies
    thee vantage.
We do condemn thee to the very block
Where Claudio stoop'd to death, and with
    like haste.

                                        (V.i.407-13)

Far from denying the justice of the sentence, Angelo insists on it: "'Tis my deserving, and I do entreat it" (V.i.475). Yet it is central to Isabella's plea that the cases are not alike:

    My brother had but justice,
    In that he did the thing for which he died:
    For Angelo,
    His act did not o'ertake his bad intent,
    And must be buried but as an intent
    That perish'd by the way.

                                        (V.i.446-51)

She means that Angelo did not sleep with her, but with Mariana; and her words have a greater resonance than she knows, for he did not kill Claudio either. (The Duke's words have a similar resonance: so long as Angelo is condemned to the block where Claudio died, he is perfectly safe.) Isabella makes a legal distinction between the sexual offenses, making Angelo's seem lighter. We have already made a personal distinction that makes it heavier: we cannot react to the meeting of lovers, mutually agreed, as we do to Angelo's brutal commands, "Fit thy consent to my sharp appetite" and "Redeem thy brother / By yielding up thy body to my will" (II.iv.160, 162-63). The equation of Angelo's offense with Claudio's is an irony that is significant up to a point; but beyond that point it fails.

The same could be said of equations that surround it, that are touched on more lightly: Lucio's image for Claudio and Juliet, "her plenteous womb / Expresseth his full tilth and husbandry" (I.iv.43-44), is echoed by the Duke's hope for the bed-trick: "Our corn's to reap, for yet our tithe's to sow" (IV.i.76). Yet the differences, as we have seen, are crucial. Isabella and Juliet are adopted cousins (I.iv.45-48); Angelo sees himself as taking their relationship a stage farther: "Give up your body to such sweet uncleanness / As she that he hath stain'd" (II.iv.54-55). But the parallel is false, for there is no sweetness in what he offers. This denial of apparent resemblance is repeated in incidental touches throughout the play. The First Gentleman's "Well, there went but a pair of shears between us" is countered by Lucio's "I grant: as there may between the lists and the velvet" (I.ii.27-29). More important, when Escalus

feels called upon to defend Claudio's sentence, he adopts one of Angelo's arguments: "Mercy is not itself, that oft looks so; / Pardon is still the nurse of second woe" (II.i.280-81). Minutes later Angelo will declare that he shows pity

        most of all when I show justice;
    For then I pity those I do not know,
    Which a dismiss'd offence would after gall,
    And do him right that, answering one foul
        wrong,
    Lives not to act another.

                                        (II.ii.101-5)

The difference is that Escalus adds, in his next breath, "But yet, poor Claudio!" (II.i.282), and we see at once that the two men cannot finally be equated.

In setting up parallels only to question them, the play is in effect examining its own processes, for the drawing of parallels through action, images, and ideas is a device that lends both unity and resonance to the work as a whole. The play produces several variations on Lear's "change places, and handy-dandy, which is the justice, which is the thief?" (IV.vi. 153-54), a question that might well be asked of Angelo and Claudio. Elbow's "mistaking words" is a conventional stage-constable joke, but in transposing varlets and honorable men, and making "respected" a term of abuse, he casts an ironic light on the respected varlet Angelo. When Abhorson objects to having Pompey as his assistant, the Provost retorts, "you weigh equally; a feather will turn the scale" (IV.ii.28-29). Pompey's jests about cutting off men's heads and women's heads (IV.ii.1-4), given that fornication is a capital offense in Vienna, make the crime and the punishment alike. Given the bawdy implication of "serve your turn" (cf. Love's Labor's Lost, I.i.289-90), Pompey's punning on the word "turn" is more than just gallows humor (IV.ii.54-57). As Josephine Waters Bennett points out, in calling out Abhorson's customers he is acting as pimp to the headsman.[16] Coming from brothel to prison, Pompey does not notice much difference: "I am as well acquainted here as I was in our house of profession: one would think it were Mistress Overdone's own house, for here be many of her old customers" (IV.iii.1-4). His catalogue of prisoners is like the catalogue of brothel customers that forms one of the stock devices of Jacobean comedy.[17] Also conventional in Jacobean comedy is the linking of the whore and the usurer, both illicit breeders.[18] This lends some point to Pompey's complaint, "'Twas never merry world since, of two usuries, the merriest was put down" (III.ii.6-7). Wedding and hanging, proverbially equated, come together in the punishments that threaten Angelo and Lucio. The latter complains, "Marrying a punk, my lord, is pressing to death, / Whipping, and hanging" (V.i.520-21). The sex-death equation returns here, as it does in Pompey's change of jobs. If bedding and killing are imaginatively so close, there would seem to be something finally interchangeable about life and death. As Claudio declares, "To sue to live, I find I seek to die, / And seeking death, find life" (III.i.42-43).

Yet however we may play with the idea, death and life are not finally the same. The Duke's insistence on wedding but not killing, and on keeping everyone, even Barnardine, alive at the end of the play, shows Claudio's resolve as heroic but out of tune with the comic world. The ironic equation of brothel and prison is perhaps more convincing, but Pompey finally admits that the new life of the inmates is not really the same as the old one: they were "all great doers in our trade, and are now 'for the Lord's sake'" (IV.iii.18-20). And for all his breezy self-confidence, Pompey the assistant executioner is a smaller figure than Pompey the bawd. We see him taking orders from Abhorson, as he never does from Mistress Overdone (in their relationship he seems, if anything, to have the initiative). The Provost's "Come, sir, leave me your snatches, and yield me a direct answer" (IV.ii.5-6) suggests that his other role as clown will be restrained from now on; while the Fourth Act may create the impression that he will survive and prosper, he lapses into uncharacteristic silence partway through his last scene, and in the Fifth Act he has simply disappeared.

The play of likeness and difference also affects Isabella's plea to Angelo. Not to Isabella but to Claudio and Lucio—and eventually to Angelo himself—it is like a sexual seduction. Claudio imagines that her appeal will be physical, not just intellectual:

> . . . in her youth
> There is a prone and speechless dialect
> Such as move men. . . .
>
> (I.ii.172-74)

Egging her on from the sidelines and refusing to let her leave till she has won her man, Lucio behaves in the first Angelo-Isabella scene very much as Pandarus does in the first encounter between Troilus and Cressida.[19] Angelo's pun, "She speaks, and 'tis such sense / That my sense breeds with it" (II.ii.142-43), acknowledges the link. His odd instruction to his servant when Isabella comes for the second meeting, "Teach her the way" (II.iv.19), suggests that Isabella is about to enter a labyrinth, and this idea is echoed in the elaborate instructions for finding the place of their sexual encounter: "he did show me / The way twice o'er" (IV.i.40-41).[20] In both scenes she comes for a debate on a legal, moral, and spiritual question of great importance to her only to find that what is on the line is not her mind but her body. But of course the equation of her plea with a sexual seduction breaks down as soon as we see her own reaction when the trap is sprung. We may note another parallel, smaller but suggestive: the scene in which the Duke brings the

two women together is followed immediately by the scene in which the Provost brings Pompey and Abhorson together. A small spark leaps from the Duke's line, "Welcome; how agreed?" (IV.i.65), to the Provost's "Are you agreed?" (IV.ii.46). But the comic piquancy of the resemblance, like the irony of Isabella's plea-cum-seduction, depends as much on difference as on likeness.

Can characters stand for each other? Can actions stand for each other? *Measure for Measure* gives the usual Shakespearean answer: yes and no. Much of its imaginative and intellectual life depends on this play of likeness and difference, which is also a play on one of the essential conditions of poetry itself, which both examines the likeness of things and asserts their uniqueness: lovers are a pair of compasses, my mistress' eyes are nothing like the sun, a rose is a rose is a rose. The play also provokes the question, can characters stand for concepts larger than themselves? It is remarkable how often in criticism of the play the characters have been assigned allegorical roles. Some critics have whole lists of these assignments. Here is G. Wilson Knight's: "Isabella stands for sainted purity, Angelo for Pharisaical righteousness, the Duke for a psychologically sound and enlightened ethic. Lucio represents indecent wit, Pompey and Mistress Overdone professional immorality. Barnardine is hard-headed, criminal, insensitiveness."[21] Here is M. C. Bradbrook's: "Angelo stands for Authority and for Law, usurping the place of the Duke, who is not only the representative of Heavenly Justice but of Humility, whilst Isabel represents both Truth and Mercy." Bradbrook later refines Angelo's role, making him stand for "the letter of the Law, for a false Authority" and for "Seeming or False Semblant."[22] The marriage of Isabella and the Duke has been seen, variously, as "the marriage of understanding with purity; of tolerance with moral fervour"[23] and as the wedding of erring but forgiven humanity with Christ the Bridegroom.[24] Other critics have cautioned against such allegorical readings, pointing to the complexity and inconsistency of the characters.[25] The good sense of this warning seems obvious; yet, just as there is some gremlin in the text that makes actors transpose names, there is another that makes critics think they are reading a morality play.

Angelo pursues Claudio "To make him an example" (I.iv.68), as his insistence on parading him through the streets suggests. He is to stand for the fornicators of Vienna, as Lucio realizes when he undertakes to save him "for the encouragement of the like, which else would stand under grievous imposition" (I.ii.177-79). Isabella's "Who is it that hath died for this offence? / There's many have committed it" provokes Lucio's comic aside, "Ay, well said" (II.ii.89-90). Vienna, we are told, is seething with corruption, and it is a rare production that does not fill out the lowlife scenes with additional silent characters miming various kinds of debauchery. The text itself, however, is surprisingly economical. We hear something of Lucio's conduct, but in theatrical terms Claudio and Juliet stand for it all; they are the only couple the play picks out. In I.ii we hear of an unnamed "younder man" carried to prison (ll. 56-85), but the text is ambiguous at this point, and the man could be Claudio himself. The Provost, speaking from within the play, is struck as Isabella is by the unfairness of the legal procedure: "All sects, all ages smack of this vice, and he / To die for't!"(II.ii.5-6). We as audience may be struck by the unfairness of the dramatic procedure. Claudio's case is too special, the extenuating circumstances too great to let him stand for the sexual corruption of Vienna.[26] The problem comes to a head in Isabella's bitter accusation, "Thy sin's not accidental, but a trade" (III.i.148), against which we instinctively protest: Claudio is not Pompey.

Pompey, Lucio, Froth, and Mistress Overdone stand for the trade itself and for its clients. As Jonathan Dollimore points out, the actual prostitutes "have no voice, no presence."[27] There are no brothel scenes as such; we hear a little about the life of the stews, but theatrically we stay on the fringes of it. Escalus's inability to get a clear account of what happened to Mistress Overdone is the comic equivalent of our inability to see past the individual characters to the brothel life they represent. In the same way, the unseen Flavius, Valencius, Rowland, and Crassus, with the visible but silent Varrius—if they are not simply ghost characters—stand for a network of power the Duke uses but the play never allows us to see (IV.v.6-13). In all these cases the characters are given roles that seem to be representative, but what they represent remains shadowy. And when the characters themselves are cast, by themselves or others, into the sort of allegorical roles critics have wished on them, these identifications are shot through with irony. We may bridle at Isabella's "You do blaspheme the good, in mocking me" (I.iv.38), but she gets her comeuppance when Angelo casts her in the allegorical role of "woman" and demands that she play it (II.iv.133-37). In the same scene, he identifies himself as "the voice of the recorded law" (l. 61), and Escalus later remarks, somewhat grimly, "he hath forced me to tell him he is indeed Justice" (III.ii.247-48). His phrasing suggests that this is not a compliment. In a cooler moment Angelo tries to distance himself from such identification: "It is the law, not I, condemn your brother" (II.ii.80). In fact one of the many resemblances between Angelo and Isabella is that both, as characters, try to stand for large principles: Law, Justice, Goodness, Chastity. But it is the character, not the playwright, who makes the identification. What the playwright shows is that Angelo's allegorical role is sabotaged by his own nature, and Isabella's by a cruel dilemma in which the virtues of charity and chastity are set in conflict.

Looking for some ultimate order we turn, finally, to the Duke. It is he who arranges so many of the play's substitutions, and who seems better placed than any other character to embody its final vision of order, authority, and wisdom. Yet in several respects he is a substitute himself, and the ironies that affect others in this role also affect him. His role as Friar Lodowick is a disguise, and to call it a substitution may be cracking the wind of the poor phrase. But he is taking on, like Angelo, power that is not his own. He gives spiritual counsel, though his advice to Claudio is more Stoic than Christian; more remarkably, he hears confessions. He says of Mariana, "I have confess'd her, and I know her virtue" (V.i.524). This is after the masks have fallen, and we have no reason to disbelieve him as we disbelieve his earlier claim to be Angelo's confessor (III.i.165-66). For anyone who takes this sacrament seriously, the implications of the Duke's conduct do not bear thinking about.[28] There is no such thing as a substitute priest, and the Duke's assumption of priestly power means, among other things, that he is giving false absolutions to people on the point of death. By the narrowest interpretation, if Claudio were to die in this condition, his state would be like that of the elder Hamlet, and he has some reason to be fearful. Yet the Duke seems blandly unconcerned with this problem and so, as far as we can tell, is the play—unless, of course, the Duke's blandness and the lack of criticism he encounters on this point are meant to horrify us with an image of power abused and the abuse accepted.

There are other substitutions of whose effect we can be more certain. The notorious shadowiness of the Duke as a character—for one critic he speaks in many voices, for another he has no distinctive style[29]—may be related to the fact that he stands for various figures who are essentially outside the play. One of these is God. Angelo's "your Grace, like power divine, / Hath looked upon my passes" (V.i.367-68) makes the identification explicit, though we need to notice that it is a simile: the Duke is *like* God in his omniscience. He is also, at times, like Him in his power over the characters and the action, re-creating Angelo in his own image[30] and producing a providential solution for Isabella's dilemma. His solution does not work, however, and providence itself has to bail him out by providing Ragozine. Nor is the Duke so omniscient as Angelo thinks; Angelo himself can catch him by surprise. Darryl J. Gless gives a sensible statement of how far this particular identification can go: "Of course, he is not providence, but an earthly and therefore imperfect and intermittent simulacrum of it."[31] He can also be seen as a representative on stage of God's substitute in Westminster, King James I. His thinking about government, his love of withdrawal and dislike of crowds, his delight in his own "craft," his acute sensitivity to criticism—on all these points he is like the King.[32] King James evidently admired his grandfather James V, who practiced the Duke's trick of going disguised among his people.[33] Yet Josephine Waters Bennett, who gives a very full account of the reasons for seeing the Duke as a compliment to James, also points out that direct impersonation would have given offense; indeed, the King's Men had already got into trouble for a play about the Gowry conspiracy.[34] If the identification were too direct, the Duke's occasional failures would compound the offense. Where a court masque turns to the King himself, present in the audience, for its image of kingship, the play (which we know was performed at court) gives instead an image of an imperfect ruler, leaving the presence of the King in the audience to act, for the loyal imagination, as a standard by which the Duke may be judged and found wanting.[35]

Finally, and most important for our purpose, the Duke is a surrogate for the playwright himself. This is in line with the play's own interest—characteristic of such earlier comedies as *Love's Labor's Lost* and *A Midsummer Night's Dream*—in examining its own procedures, an interest that I have already touched on. The last act has all the characteristics of a play-within-the-play, contrived by the Duke.[36] In an odd touch in his scene with Friar Thomas, the Duke seems to be trying to write the Friar's part of the dialogue: "You will demand of me, why I do this" (I.iii.17). Bennett, finally withdrawing from an identification of the Duke with King James, imagines Shakespeare himself playing the role, with some piquant ironies when we see the Duke at a loss, needing Providence's help, unable to control Lucio.[37] I would argue, in fact, that the identification of Duke with playwright, whether reinforced by casting or not, is mostly ironic in its effect, for the Duke is not a very good playwright. Giving himself motives for leaving the city, he seems to be doodling; the motives, as we have seen, do not add up, and the effect of the scene with Frair Thomas is of a rough draft that needs more work to bring it to consistency. At other times he is arbitrary. His deception of Isabella, when he tells her Claudio is dead, is notorious:

> . . . I will keep her ignorant of her good,
> To make her heavenly comforts of despair
> When it is least expected.
>
> (IV.iii.108-10)

We may wish other motives on him—making Isabella realize how much her brother's deathmeans to her, sharpening the test on her when she is asked to plead for Angelo—but the motive the Duke professes is a playwright's motive: he will heighten the effect of Isabella's final joy by putting her through a period of suffering first. But good playwrights do not impose suffering on their characters arbitrarily. Everything they undergo is accounted for by their own actions, or by some logical turn in the plot. The Duke simply lies. The flurry of contradictory

letters he sends to Angelo and Escalus suggests an attempt to create that period of confusion that precedes the resolution of a comedy. Again it is arbitrary, confusion for confusion's sake. Equally arbitrary are the twists and turns that make the final scene so complicated. We may contrast this with what Shakespeare does in plays like *The Comedy of Errors* or *A Midsummer Night's Dream,* where every stage in the confusion is honestly earned.

The Duke as playwright, then, works no better than any of the other substitutions—indeed, it is less successful than some. But we may also wonder how much of the play's irony at the Duke's expense is cast back at the figures he is representing: if he stands for God, for James I, and for Shakespeare, how much of his imperfection can be seen as a reflection of theirs? The author of *King Lear* was not afraid to question and even to protest the ways of Providence; anyone who would criticize Providence might also (in a tactfully implicit way) criticize James I; and for a writer to poke fun at himself is one of the oldest tricks of the trade. Is there, in fact, one last substitution to discuss—that of *Measure for Measure* for the play Shakespeare would have liked to write? Rosalind Miles observes that "any discussion of *Measure for Measure* eventually comes down to a discussion of the play as it seems to have been intended, rather than as it is."[38] Its inconsistencies are central and notorious: Isabella's moral dilemma is solved by an unprepared technical trick; the scrupulous Angelo of the first two acts is replaced by a cynic who rejects Mariana for material reasons; at the end, key relationships—Angelo and Mariana, Isabella and Claudio, Isabella and the Duke—are left hanging in silence. The central figure, on whom so much depends, seems not so much a bewildering character as a bewildering piece of characterization. It seems appropriate that the comedy should end with a marriage proposal to which no answer is given. I am not saying that Shakespeare, in order to make a point about the imperfection of his art, deliberately wrote an imperfect play. I would prefer to believe that every play of his is as good as he could make it, and I am tempted to add that none of them is perfect. He seems, however, to have found *Measure for Measure* a harder struggle than most, and as he faced the gap between conception and embodiment, his imagination generated image after image of representations that are vivid but not quite adequate, and substitutions that are revealing and fascinating but incomplete.

Notes

[1] "*Measure for Measure:* Quid Pro Quo?" *Shakespeare Studies,* 4 (1968) 231-51, esp. p. 232.

[2] "The Unfolding of 'Measure for Measure'," *Shakespeare Survey,* 26 (1973), 119-28, esp. pp. 124, 125.

[3] The production, directed by Ronald Bryden, played at the Robert Gill Theatre, University of Toronto, in March 1987.

[4] All references to *Measure for Measure* are to the Arden edition, ed. J. W. Lever (London: Methuen,1965). References to other Shakespeare plays are to *The Complete Works of Shakespeare,* ed. David Bevington (Glenview, Ill.: Scott, Foresman and Co., 1980).

[5] See especially Roy W. Battenhouse, "*Measure for Measure* and Christian Doctrine of the Atonement," *PMLA,* 61 (1946), 1029-59.

[6] Black, p. 124.

[7] Lever admits this in his note on the passage, but retains the Folio reading, as do most editors except J. M. Nosworthy in the New Penguin edition (Harmondsworth: Penguin Books, 1969).

[8] This was pointed out to me by Kate Helwig in an extremely interesting undergraduate essay on *Measure for Measure* and *The Tempest.*

[9] *The Problem of* Measure for Measure (London: Vision Press, 1976), p. 214.

[10] See Nuttall, "Quid Pro Quo?" p. 245.

[11] "Versions of Dying in *Measure for Measure,*" *English Literary Renaissance,* 6 (1976), 60-76, esp. p. 67.

[12] Black, p. 124.

[13] *Shakespeare's* Measure for Measure (Univ. of London: Athlone Press, 1953), p. 110. Lascelles goes on to point out that Claudio has a vivid apprehension of death, Barnardine none at all.

[14] According to Darryl J. Gless, Angelo's equation of murder with fornication was against contemporary Protestant doctrine, which insisted that some sins were heavier than others. See Measure for Measure, *the Law, and the Convent* (Princeton: Princeton Univ. Press, 1979), pp. 122-24.

[15] This was reflected in the blocking of Ronald Bryden's production, in which first Angelo, then Isabella, was cornered behind a desk; the two soliloquies were delivered from the same position on stage.

[16] Measure for Measure *as Royal Entertainment* (New York and London: Columbia Univ. Press, 1966), p. 41.

[17] See, for example, Marston's *The Dutch Courtesan* (II.ii) and Sharpham's *The Fleer* (III).

[18] See, for example, the alliance of Syndefy and Security in Chapman, Jonson, and Marston's *Eastward Ho;* and the marriages of Hoard and the Courtesan in Middleton's *A Trick to Catch the Old One,* and of Throat and Frances in Barry's *Ram Alley.*

[19] On the erotic overtones in Lucio's encouragement, see Richard Fly, *Shakespeare's Mediated World* (Amherst: Univ. of Massachusetts Press, 1976), p. 68.

[20] Black also notes that Angelo's locked garden is like Claudio's prison, p. 125.

[21] *The Wheel of Fire,* (1930; rpt. London: Methuen, 1949), p. 74.

[22] "Authority, Truth and Justice in *Measure for Measure,*" *Review of English Studies,* 17 (1941), 385-89, esp. pp. 385-86, 387.

[23] Knight, p. 95.

[24] Gless, p. 255.

[25] See, for example, Lever, Arden Introduction, p. lix.

[26] See Lever, p. lxxv.

[27] "Transgression and Surveillance in *Measure for Measure,*" in *Political Shakespeare,* eds. Jonathan Dollimore and Alan Sinfield (Ithaca and London: Cornell Univ. Press, 1985), pp. 72-87, esp. p. 86.

[28] See Clifford Leech, "The 'Meaning' of *Measure for Measure,*" *SS,* 3 (1950), 66-73, esp. p. 70.

[29] See, respectively, Bennett, p. 107, and Miles, pp. 180-81.

[30] See Gless, p. 24.

[31] See Gless, p. 248.

[32] For a full discussion of the resemblances, see Bennett, pp. 78-104.

[33] See Bennett, p. 97.

[34] See Bennett, pp. 105, 107.

[35] If William Blissett is correct, there is a bolder effect in *Bartholomew Fair,* where Overdo is a joking version of the King in the audience. See "Your Majesty is Welcome to a Fair," in *The Elizabethan Theatre,* 4, ed. G. R. Hibbard (Toronto: Macmillan, 1974), pp. 80-105.

[36] See Trombetta, p. 72.

[37] See Bennett, pp. 135-37.

[38] Miles, p. 285.

Huston Diehl (essay date 1998)

SOURCE: "'Infinite Space': Representation and Reformation in *Measure for Measure*," in *Shakespeare Quarterly*, Vol. 49, No. 4, Winter, 1998, pp. 393-410.

[*In the essay that follows, Diehl maintains that Shakespeare's use of "representational strategies," such as substitutions, in* Measure for Measure *reflect his experimentation "with a Protestant aesthetic of the stage."*]

Measure For Measure is a deeply dissatisfying comedy, so problematic that, as Jean Howard argues, it "puts critics under stress."[1] They typically respond by judging, finding fault with the play's structure, the Duke's elaborate manipulations, Isabella's ethical choices, Shakespeare's use of the bed-trick, and, especially, the final trial scene, with its exaggerated theatricality, its failure to effect any real reformation, and its unsettling subversion of the conventional comic ending.[2] Identifying a pattern of failed, inadequate, and problematic substitutions in *Measure for Measure*, Alexander Leggatt, like many other critics, concludes that the play is flawed:

> I am not saying that Shakespeare, in order to make a point about the imperfection of his art, deliberately wrote an imperfect play. . . . He seems, however, to have found *Measure for Measure* a harder struggle than most, and as he faced the gap between conception and embodiment, his imagination generated image after image of representations that are vivid but not quite adequate, and substitutions that are revealing and fascinating but incomplete.[3]

Taking Leggatt's disclaimer as my starting point, I want to examine Shakespeare's representational strategies in *Measure for Measure*, and the dissatisfaction they arouse, in order to make precisely the opposite claim. I will argue that Shakespeare deliberately calls attention to the imperfection of his art, and I will show how the inadequacy of the multiple substitutions is a crucial factor in Shakespeare's conception of his drama, producing—not undermining—the play's meaning as well as its peculiar power. What Leggatt attributes to a breakdown in the creative process—resulting in the proliferation of incomplete and inadequate substitutions and the contrived nature of the final revelations—are, I think, better understood as products of the playwright's experimentation with a Protestant aesthetic of the stage.

Shakespearean criticism has long been alert to the play's religious themes, biblical allusions, and theological subtexts. The references to the Sermon on the Mount and to St. Paul; the dramatization of the conflict between law and mercy; the association of the Duke with divine providence; the parodies of the Annunciation and the Last Judgment; the language of grace, ransom, and remedy; the appropriation of such religious genres as hagiography, parable, and *contemplatio mortis:* scholars have discussed these and many other theological aspects of *Measure for Measure,* though without arriving at any consensus about how Shakespeare employs this theological material or to what end.[4] But to a surprising degree, scholars who focus on the play's religious dimension ignore the contested nature of religion in early modern England, preferring to speak of a universal Christianity in ways that obscure the controversies fracturing the Christian church during the Reformation.[5] And critics who take issue with these attempts to read *Measure for Measure* in terms of Christian themes are much more likely to insist on the play's having a secular or even antireligious nature than to evaluate the historical assumptions about religion that inform such studies.[6] Even those new historicists who use *Measure for Measure* as a key text in their studies of early modern English culture tend to treat religion as a conservative and stable orthodoxy in the service of the state and monarchy.[7]

But, of course, in post-Reformation England Christianity was in crisis, religious ideology unstable, and theological doctrines vigorously disputed. Even among English Protestants religious beliefs and practices were so much the subject of contentious debate that one of James's first acts as the king of England was to convene in January 1604 a conference of bishops and puritans at Hampton Court to try to resolve some of their long-standing differences and perhaps "to begin a further reformation of the Church."[8] Yet to illustrate my point, that historical event goes unmentioned in virtually all treatments of *Measure for Measure* as a play written for or about James even though Shakespeare's 1604 comedy, in staging a conflict between a rigid reformer and a woman intent on entering a strict Roman Catholic religious order, rehearses the extremist views—radical puritan and Catholic—that James sought to suppress at the Hampton Court conference.[9] According to Kenneth Fincham and Peter Lake, James used the conference, on the one hand, "to construct and support a common Protestant front against Rome" and, on the other, to contain radical puritanism by "driving a wedge between the moderate and radical wings of Puritan opinion."[10]

I mention King James's ecclesiastical policy not to argue that Shakespeare advocates or allegorizes it but rather to suggest how fully *Measure for Measure* engages many of the religious controversies of Jacobean England, exploring theological issues—about monasticism, celibacy, idolatry, auricular confession, merit, righteousness, hypocrisy, reformist zeal, and moral discipline—that trouble and divide James's subjects in the early years of the seventeenth century. Set in the Roman Catholic city of Vienna and featuring a number of characters who are, desire to be, or pretend to be members of the Roman Catholic clergy, the play questions the possibility of achieving either celibacy or a disciplined withdrawal from the world. By using the clerical habit of the friar as a disguise that the Duke puts on and off and eventually discards, the play also demystifies monasticism, perhaps even reinforcing Protestant associations of friars with a fraudulent theatricality, their "humblest habits" with "a false disguise."[11] At the same time, the play depicts the very pressing urban problems that preoccupied the Protestant authorities of Jacobean London and critiques the draconian measures proposed by radical puritans to reform human behavior, revealing these measures to be both inhumane and ineffective. It also exposes the moral depravity and hypocrisy of a character associated with these extreme reformist policies—the precise and legalistic Angelo. Thus marking Vienna for its early modern London audiences as a setting simultaneously alien and familiar, papist and puritan, *Measure for Measure* identifies Isabella's monastic vocation and Angelo's reformist zeal with a false—or counterfeit—righteousness. Angelo's hypocritical and tyrannical behavior, to be sure, is depicted as far more abhorrent than Isabella's idealistic, if excessive, commitment to the rigid rules observed by "the votarists of Saint Clare" (1.4.5). But efforts to read the play as either pro-Catholic or nostalgic for a Catholic past fail to address the ways in which Shakespeare appropriates the representational strategies of English Calvinism, distancing his theater from a fraudulent theatricality widely associated in Protestant England with the Roman Catholic Church while also challenging the vehement antitheatricality of radical Protestants.[12]

There was, most historians agree, a Calvinist consensus within the national church under King James, who sought at the beginning of his reign to win over moderate puritans "through the incorporationof evangelical Calvinism into the Jacobean establishment."[13] Indeed, Patrick Collinson asserts that "Calvinism can be regarded as the theological cement of the Jacobean church . . . 'a common and ameliorating bond' uniting conformists and moderate puritans."[14] But although Calvinism is the cement that binds together different factions of the Jacobean church, various segments of the population appropriated and adapted it to their own needs and interests—"consumed" it in Michel de Certeau's sense of this word.[15] Calvinism was employed in the service of competing authorities and rival political factions and invoked to achieve a range of multiple and even conflicting goals, not all of them religious in nature.

A case in point is the battle over the legitimacy of the stage. As literary scholars have frequently noted, antitheatricalists often draw upon Calvinist distrust of theatricality in their attacks on the stage, tapping into their Protestant readers' deepest anti-Catholic sentiments by aligning the London theaters with the "false" ceremonies, "idolatrous" spectacles, and "cunning" theatricality of the Roman Church.[16] But apologists for the stage also appropriate basic tenets of Calvinist theology to wield against their opponents, a phenomenon that has for the most part been ignored in the critical literature. In his refutation of Stephen Gosson's *Schoole of Abuse,* Thomas Lodge, for example, counters Gosson's point that Plato banished the poets from his republic by accusing Plato of idolatry, thus attempting to undermine Plato's authority by associating him with the "idolatrous" Roman church; he also insists that poetry is a gift from God, an argument that Calvin and his followers repeatedly use to justify certain kinds of art.[17] Lodge is just one of many writers who appropriate Calvinist arguments and tropes to defend the stage. They charge the antitheatricalists with employing Roman Catholic modes of interpretation, argue that the stage exposes rather than produces the fraudulent kind of theatricality Calvinism distrusts, and apply Calvinist notions of the conscience to their theories of dramatic art.[18]

Shakespeare, I suggest, participates in these efforts to legitimate the theater by aligning it with the moderate Calvinism of the established English church. At the same time, he raises provocative questions about the challenge of knowing, judging, and reforming in a Calvinist universe. In a sustained exploration of the power and limits of representation, including his own theatrical representations, Shakespeare formulates an aesthetic of the stage that marks and preserves the gap between the sign and the thing signified, arouses and frustrates the desire to know directly and fully, and compels his audiences to confront both the inadequacy of all human knowledge and their own imperfect judgment. By eliciting an enabling kind of dissatisfaction in *Measure for Measure,* he claims for the theater the project of reforming human behavior even as he acknowledges the limits of that project and distances his theater from the extremist views of radical puritanism.

Knowing

Rather than assume that Shakespeare's play is flawed because the substitutions staged in the course of *Measure for Measure* are inadequate or incomplete, I propose to examine its pattern of substitutions in terms of Calvin's insistence that the physical world is itself a *representation*. English Calvinists encourage the faithful to discern in the visible world signs of another truer and more real world, to find in the transient present images of a permanent future, and thus to see how the world they inhabit mirrors (however imperfectly) the divine. Calling the created world "painted tables, by which al mankinde is provoked and allured to the knowledg" of God, Calvin argues that "God dothin the mirror of his workes shew by representation both himself and his immortall kingdome," and he urges his readers to discern "certaine markes" and "ensignes" of God's glory that God has "graven" and "displaid" in the "whole workmanship of the world."[19] Indeed, Calvin imagines the world as a magnificent theater and its inhabitants as spectators capable of knowing God indirectly by beholding the beauty of his creation. "For what else is the world," he asks in a sermon on Ephesians, "but an open stage wheron God will haue his majestie seene?"[20] Man, he asserts in the *Institutes,* "is set as it were in this gorgeous stage to be a beholder" of God's works.[21]

To take an example that might shed light on Shakespeare's duke and deputy, in such a construction of the world a magistrate is in a sense always a representation of the divine judge—God's substitute, if you will—and always to be viewed in terms of both his likeness to the divine (his authority, power, and capacity to judge and punish) and the limitations of that comparison. Calvin defines civil magistrates as "deputies of God" who "altogether beare the person of god, whose stede they do after a certaine maner supply." Ideally, they "are true examplars and paternes of hys bountifulnesse" in whom "the lord himself hath emprinted and engraved an inuiolable maiesty."[22] The practice of hanging paintings of the Last Judgment directly above the magistrate's seat in the law courts of Northern Europe visually reinforced the notion that the magistrate was an earthly proxy for the divine judge.[23] But to see the magistrate as an image of the all-judging God was to understand not only how he derives his authority from God but also how inadequate he is in relation to God. Even as he urges magistrates to "represent in themselues unto men a certaine image of the providence, preservation, goodnesse, good wil, & righteousnesse of God," Calvin addresses the problem of tyrannical, severe, deceitful, vengeful, and violent rulers, noting how far they have strayed from the God they should figure.[24] The comparison between the earthly magistrate and the divine Judge thus inevitably produces dissatisfactioń, a longing for that which is represented but absent, the God who cannot be seen in this world face to face.

The peculiar way in which the characters of *Measure for Measure* seem to point beyond themselves to divine things, even as their flaws firmly locate them in the human world of Vienna, may well reflect Shakespeare's attempt to represent the physical world as it was understood in the age of Reformation, to write not an allegory but a play about living in an allegorized world. For if, as Calvin teaches, the world that humans inhabit is understood to be a theater in which God manifests himself indirectly through images and signs, then Shakespeare's theatrical practice—in the Globe, no less-is a representation of a representation, one that engages its spectators in the challenge of knowing indirectly, partially, by means of signs. In *Measure for Measure* characters repeatedly define the human condition in representational terms, describing themselves as figures, mirrors, coins, stamps, prints, and forms that image something else. Even Angelo's name, which calls to mind both the spiritual creature and the English coin stamped with the image of the archangel Gabriel, reminds Shakespeare's audiences that a deputy bears the image of the divine and gains his value from that image. The spectators in the Globe of 1604, I am suggesting, were encouraged to engage in acts of interpretation that replicated the way the established English Church—in sermons and catechisms—had taught them to interpret the world. "Because he [God] hath made hym self knowen unto us by his woorkes," the child in an English catechism is taught to respond, "it is necessarie for vs to seeke hym out in them. For our capacitie is not able to comprehende his Diuine substaunce, therefore he hath made the worlde as a Glasse, wherein wee maie beholde hym in such sorte, as it is expedient for us to knowe hym."[25] Central to this mode of experience is a profound sense of the gap between the fallenworld and the celestial one it can only shadow.

For early Protestants the challenge of living in a world where human knowledge is partial, indirect, and limited centered on the need to curb the all-too-human tendency to mistake the sign for the thing it signifies. According to Calvin and his English followers, people are always prone to confusing the substitute with the original because they long for direct knowledge and they overvalue the things of this world. "Even the children of God," a 1581 English catechism warns, "feele themselves so intangled in the delight of earthly thinges which of themselves are good" that they commit idolatry, attributing "that to the creature which ys due to the creator."[26] The Protestant reformers identify this as one of the chief errors of papistry, evidenced in the doctrine of transubstantiation, the cult of the saints, and the worship of images. In their attack on "idolatrous" theater, the antitheatricalists accuse playwrights of perpetuating this error, claiming that stage plays tempt spectators "to giue that which is proper to God, unto them [the players and their theatrical illusions] that are no gods."[27]

In *Measure for Measure* Shakespeare seems intent on guarding against this danger, both by thematizing it and by marking his own representations as representations. From the opening scene when the Duke deputizes Angelo, to the bed-trick when Mariana is substituted for Isabella, to the complicated substitution of Ragozine's head for the unrepentant Barnardine's so that it in turn can be substituted for Claudio's head, to Elbow's comic malapropisms (substitutions that force the audiences to listen for the gap between the literal word and the intended meaning), to the dizzying proliferation of substitutions in the last act: Shakespeare not only explores the capacity of the substitute to stand in for the original but also nurtures a highly self-reflexive awareness of the nature of representation and the problem of indirect knowledge. To illustrate, let me briefly discuss three key episodes: Angelo's sudden and inexplicable lust for Isabella, which I interpret as a classic example of idolatry; the bed-trick and the subsequent playing with the notion of carnal knowledge, which I read as an inquiry into the nature of embodiment; and the often-overlooked but highly significant substitution of the Duke's seal for the deputy's death warrant, which I see as a test of faith.

In the fascinating and disturbing scene in which Isabella, goaded by Lucio, pleads with Angelo for her brother's life, the righteous deputy who has never before experienced sexual passion finds himself overwhelmed by desire for a woman who wishes to enter a convent. Many scholars interpret this sudden and unexpected eruption of sexual desire in Angelo in psychoanalytical terms. Focusing on the relation between repression and desire, they argue that for Angelo "prohibition is aphrodisiac"; but the widely held assumption that "Angelo desires a woman because she is forbidden" obscures, I think, the way this scene locates the origin of Angelo's sexual desire for Isabella in his sense of his own righteousness, identifying his lust for the virtuous woman with his love of virtue.[28] "Dost thou desire her foully," Angelo asks himself incredulously after Isabella departs, "for those things / That make her good?" (2.2.178-79).[29] Imagining that the devil uses a saint to ensnare him in his own saintliness, he concludes:

> O cunning enemy, that, to catch a saint,
> With saints dost bait thy hook! Most dangerous
> Is that temptation that doth goad us on
> To sin in loving virtue. Never could the strumpet,
> With all her double vigour—art and nature—
> Once stir my temper; but this virtuous maid
> Subdues me quite.
>
> (ll. 184-90)

How can loving virtue be the source of sin?

Shakespeare, I submit, depicts Angelo's lust for Isabella as idolatry, for when the deputy is aroused by the novice's saintliness—that is, for the way she images the divine—he immediately seeks to know that saintliness directly and carnally. In other words, he substitutes the woman who reflects divinity for God himself, a substitution that simultaneously "foul[s]" Isabella and alienates him from God. Once he is aroused by Isabella's virtue, he can think of her only with a lust he himself identifies with misplaced devotion:

> When I would pray and think, I think and pray
> To several subjects: heaven hath my empty words,
> Whilst my invention, hearing not my tongue,
> Anchors on Isabella. . . .
>
> (2.4.1-4)

Enacting the error of idolatry as it was understood by early Protestants, Angelo is, in effect, "so snared with . . . affection" for one of the "creatures that God hath made for our use" that "the Lord is . . . altogether . . . thrust out of place."[30] His imagination "[a]nchors on Isabella" and not the God who created her. Angelo's attempt to "know" Isabella's virtue by "knowing" her body, however farfetched it may sound to us today, conforms to a pervasive early Protestant belief that idolatry—perceived as misplaced devotion, a substitution of the creature for the Creator—leads directly to physical lust and "abominable concupiscences" because it privileges the carnal over the spiritual.[31] To interpret Angelo's lust as a misplaced desire to know God directly and carnally—that is, to understand it in theological rather than psychoanalytic terms—is not therefore to deny the utter perversity of it; rather, it is to recognize how dangerous, how fundamentally depraved, the idolater in the Calvinist schema was believed to be. English reformers equate idolatry with "spirituall fornication," and they warn that the idolater—alienated from God, paradoxically, by trying to physically possess the divine—inevitably falls into "carnall fornication, and all uncleannesse," indulging in "Sodomie," "the stewes," "whoredoms and fornications."[32] The idolater, in other words, was understood to be someone who, like Angelo, gives his "sensual race the rein" (2.4.160).

If we understand Angelo's fundamental error as epistemological—a confusion of the sign for what it signifies, a misidentification of the substitute as the original—we can see how provocatively Shakespeare explores the problem of knowing in the bed-trick, where he literalizes Angelo's error in order to expose its absurdity. When the Duke substitutes Mariana for Isabella, tricking Angelo into sleeping with the woman he has wronged and rejected, he exploits Angelo's tendency to apprehend—as the Duke says of Barnardine—"no further than this world" (5.1.475) and forces a recognition of the danger of equating the image with the truth. The bed-trick thus does not simply trap Angelo in his own perverse lust, hypocrisy, and betrayal; it also reveals his central epistemological error, an error that he is in danger of repeating endlessly: mistaking his limited power for absolute power and confusing his asceticism with perfection, as well as desiring Isabella in placeof God.

Before she reveals her identity in the trial scene, the veiled Mariana speaks enigmatically, first declaring "I

*Angelo (Gene Carvalho) and Isabella (Kathleen Dobbs) in
Act II, scene iv, of the San José State University
1997 production of* Measure for Measure

have known my husband, yet my husband / Knows not
that ever he knew me" and then claiming to the startled
onlookers that Angelo is her husband and the man
"Who thinks he knows that he ne'er knew my body, /
But knows he thinks that he knows Isabel's" (ll. 184-
85, 198-99). Her riddles, like Lucio's comic assertion
"I know what I know" (3.1.390) earlier in the play,
call to mind an enigmatic passage from First Corinthians in which Paul, preaching against idolatrous
practices, questions the validity of all human knowledge and insists that "loue" rather than knowledge
"edifieth": "If any man thinke that he knoweth any
thing," Paul declares, "he knoweth nothing yet as he
oght to knowe."[33] In appropriating this Pauline text,
which identifies any belief in one's own capacity to
know with vanity, pride, and idolatry, Mariana unsettles Angelo, for she not only denies his version of
the truth but also challenges the very ground upon which
he has passed judgment on others. She plays, too, of
course, with the double meaning of the word *know,* a
joke that underscores Angelo's epistemological error,
highlighting his presumption that what he knows carnally is valid and emphasizing that the very nature of

embodiment impedes direct and full apprehension.
Through the bed-trick Angelo thus quite literally experiences the partiality and inadequacy of corporeal
knowledge, in the "shadow and silence" (3.1.239) mistaking the substitute for the woman he illicitly desires.

The play, I suggest, produces a similar experience for
theater audiences, who are simultaneously invited to
believe that what they see embodied on the stage is
true and reminded that the theater, after all, is nothing
but a "fantastical trick" (l. 340) involving masks and
disguises, lies and indirections, shadows and substitutions. But while the artifice of the bed-trick calls attention to the gap between representation and reality,
eliciting dissatisfaction in audience members who prefer drama to achieve greater verisimilitude, Shakespeare
never entirely demystifies his representations but rather
promotes a faith in signs as well as a skepticism about
theatrical illusions. Indeed, in one particularly significant scene, he casts as heroic the character who acts
solely on the basis of faith in a sign.

I refer to the scene in which the Provost receives
Claudio's death warrant from Angelo. Having arranged
the bed-trick in order to save Claudio, the disguised
Duke is unprepared for this turn of events. Rather than
reveal his true identity, he asks the Provost to disobey
his superior and delay the execution, thereby risking his
own death. Refusing, at first, to violate his oath, the
Provost changes his mind when, told that the Duke
approves the delay, he is shown "the hand and seal
of the Duke" and encouraged to recognize "the character . . . and the signet" (4.2.177-78). Replying simply, "I know them both" (l. 179), the Provost chooses
to honor the signet of the absent Duke and to ignore
the deputy's death warrant. Except for the Duke's seal
and handwriting, the "amazed" Provost has only the
assurance of an obscure friar that the Duke's approval
of this dangerous course of action is "a certainty" (l.
173). Although the friar promises that the truth will
eventually be revealed and the Provost's actions vindicated, he speaks in cryptic and mysterious riddles, offering only more signs to interpret. "Look," he tells the
Provost, "th'unfolding star calls up the shepherd" (ll.
185-86). In this scene Shakespeare explores the challenge of exercising faith in the absence of direct proof.
This was a central concern of early Protestantism and
one that English reformers, articulating the tenets of a
Calvinist covenant theology, frequently addressed by
using the analogy of the king's seal or signet.[34] Shakespeare champions the character who has the capacity to
recognize, interpret, and trust the sign of an absent authority, and he constructs as heroic the ability to act
on the basis of faith in such a sign even though one's
own knowledge is indirect and incomplete. In the
end Claudio's life is spared not (as in Shakespeare's
source) because the lustful deputy was provided with
a sexual partner but because a seal and signet were
honored by the faithful and courageous Provost.

The last act promises to resolve the problem of indirect, partial, and imperfect knowing through the anticipated comic resolution, but, significantly, that promise is not fully realized.[35] Shakespeare stages a fictional moment in which the gap between sign and thing signified is eradicated and substitution gives way to identity: the hooded friar *is* the Duke; the veiled Mariana, the woman who slept with Angelo; the muffled man, Claudio. But the desire for direct knowledge that the play has aroused in the audiences is thwarted, the promise deferred, by Shakespeare's stagecraft. Although the multiple unveilings invoke the Pauline promise of direct knowledge and clear vision, the scene insists on its own dark and fantastical artifice. The Duke's plan resembles a comic script too complex and contrived to be credible; the return of the Duke requires the disappearance of the friar he has been playing, highlighting the theatrical convention of doubling and its attendant problems; the Duke and Friar Peter rehearse the ending with Mariana and Isabella, coaching them on how to relate their story, perform their roles, and "veil full purpose" (4.6.4); and Lucio serves as a skeptical audience member, stripping away the theatrical disguise of the friar, refusing the fiction. Even the stunning revelation that Claudio lives is made ambiguous by the Duke's odd insistence that the muffled man resembles and stands in as a substitute for Claudio rather than actually being Claudio. Presenting the mysterious prisoner "As like almost to Claudio as himself," the Duke withholds any assurance of certainty, telling Isabella that "If he be like your brother, for his sake / Is he pardoned" (5.1.483, 484-86), thereby reintroducing a gap between the substitute and the longed-for original.

By calling attention to the artifice, the staginess, of his comic resolution, Shakespeare denies his audiences the pleasure of believing, even for a moment, that the image and the thing imaged are one. The promised revelations are, after all, only theatrical illusions, reminding the audiences that the players cannot escape their own bodies or the play its own representations. But the resulting dissatisfaction, I suggest, is energizing and productive. The trial scene arouses the audience members' deepest desire for completion and revelation, direct knowledge and certainty. By eliciting a longing for certainty that is promised but perpetually deferred, the play does not merely frustrate; it encourages its audiences to view both the world they inhabit and the fictional world of the play as representations, which are inadequate, to be sure, but also potentially significant, even powerful.

Judging

Scholars interested in Shakespeare's treatment of the law in *Measure for Measure* have examined English ecclesiastical and civil laws pertaining to marriage, adultery, and fornication in some depth, but they generally ignore Reformation theories of the law and, in particular, Calvin's emphasis on the epistemological function of the law. And yet Shakespeare seems far less interested in details of the English legal system— one critic calls the law of Vienna "story-book law"[36]— than in exploring the relation between law, broadly defined, and the problem of knowing and judging. Central to his play's inquiry into the law, I suggest, is a Calvinist insistence that self-knowledge can be achieved only by recognizing one's utter inability to fulfill the law, a recognition that necessarily precludes passing judgment on others.

Emphasizing the immeasurable gulf between any individual and perfection, Calvin teaches that no one is capable of obeying the law. His discussions of the law focus not on ethical behavior, discipline, and punishment but on knowledge. "By the law," he writes, "is the knowledge of sinne."[37] For him, the law does not correct or control sin but rather represents it, showing people the multiple ways they have transgressed. The law, he writes, is a "loking glasse" that "representeth unto us the spottes of our face," a mirror that reveals to people how utterly they have defaced the divine image in which they were made.[38] English Protestant catechisms of this period invariably advance Calvin's interpretation of the law, rehearsing the notion that the law is a "glasse" that teaches "that we be imperfect in all our workes," thereby making us aware of "our naughtiness sinne and defectes."[39] That awareness, moreover, is productive, for it creates the conditions for repentance and redemption. "And so by our own euells we are stirred to consider the good things of God," Calvin writes, "and we can not earnestly aspire towarde him, untill we begin to mislike our selues."[40] For Calvin, the law thus serves a vital function: by revealing our inherent sinfulness, it produces dissatisfaction with the self, a dissatisfaction that, because it initiates the process of repentance, is essential for salvation.[41]

When Calvin defines the law as a mirror that works to "admonish, certifie, proue gilty, yea and condemne euery man of his owne unrighteousenesse," he declares any belief in one's own righteousness a fantasy; insisting that none "shall come to the mark of true perfection, unlesse he be loosed from the burden of his body," he warns that to presume that one has "any woorthinesse" or "any meane or abilitie to doo good (of himself:)" is "too step intoo Gods place," that is, to confuse one's own powers with God's, usurping the place of the Creator.[42] The law thus serves as a continual reminder that "there is none righteous, no not one" (Romans 3:10) by enabling people to see their transgressions, imperfections, and failings. Calvin insists that the person who believes himself to be righteous is deluded by self-love,

> so long as he measureth it [his strength] by the proportion of his own will. But so sone as he is

compelled to trie his life by the balance of the law, then leaving the presumption of that counterfait righteousnesse, he seeth himself to be an infinite space distant from holinesse: againe, that he floweth full of infinite vices, wherof before he semed cleane. For the evels of lust are hidde in so depe and croked privuie corners, that they easily deceiue the sight of man.[43]

Setting aside the tantalizing linguistic echoes of this passage in *Measure for Measure,* I want to suggest how Calvin's theory of law informs Shakespeare's play and, in particular, its theatrical insistence on the gap, the "infinite space," between "counterfait righteousnesse" and "holinesse."

Measure for Measure dramatizes a conflict between two characters who trust in their own capacity to obey the law and to lead virtuous lives: a reformist magistrate smugly confident of his own righteousness and a Roman Catholic novice earnestly preparing to join a strict religious order. Through their confrontation both discover the "infinite space" between their behavior and perfection. Angelo commits a crime far more repugnant than the one for which he has condemned Claudio, and in the trial scene he is forced to acknowledge the distance between the laws he administers and his own rapacious and unruly appetites. Isabella experiences a range of conflicting emotions when she is confronted with Angelo's terrible proposition that requires her to choose between her chastity and her brother's life. Passionately pleading for her brother's life, actively participating in the duplicitous bed-trick, and deliberately giving false testimony against Angelo in order to take her revenge on him, she, too, fails to live up to her ideals of purity and holiness.

The play's insistence that neither the rigorous discipline of the religious novice nor the severe laws of the precise puritan can produce a state of righteousness surely must have resonated in a powerful way with the audiences of post-Reformation England, where questions of human merit, good works, and righteousness were vigorously debated. Protestant reformers vehemently denounce the clerics and saints of the Roman Church because they "most shamelessly call" their lives "Angelike, doing herein verily so great injurie to the Angells of God" when in reality they are nothing more than "whoremongers, adulterers, and somwhat ells muche worse and filthier."[44] And satiric attacks on radical Protestantism skewer puritans for assuming they could attain a state of righteousness, exposing that belief to be a grand delusion and exposing them as contemptible hypocrites.[45] Many recent critical readings of the play, however, ignore these contemporary religious controversies and especially the intense anti-Catholic and anticlerical sentiments they generated in Jacobean London. Feminist criticism in particular tends to valorize Isabella's commitment to a monastic life of celibacy and saintliness, viewing the cloistered life of a nun as an admirable assertion of "female autonomy" that is inherently subversive of patriarchal society. From this perspective, Isabella's public humiliation in the final act is an inexcusable violation of both Isabella's independence and her religious vocation, a shameless "shaming of a nun."[46]

For these critics the play's ending, which turns on Isabella's capacity to forgive the man who tried to coerce her into having sex with him, is profoundly disturbing, for that forgiveness represents to them not an admirable willingness to relinquish a "counterfait righteousnesse" but a regrettable surrender to patriarchal authority; and the Duke's subsequent pardon of Angelo constitutes a nullification of the grievous wrongs committed against Isabella. Declaring the final trial scene "aesthetically and intellectually unsatisfying . . . [and] personally infuriating," Harriett Hawkins, for one, complains that "the Duke's decision to grant mercy to everybody revokes the rule of law, and to revoke the rule of human law is to revoke the idea of consequence, of necessity."[47] Such an intense resistance to the play's resolution provides insights into late-twentieth-century democratic notions of law and justice, criminals and victims, power and submission. But it may also illustrate the way *Measure for Measure* challenges traditional notions of merit that were being contested in Shakespeare's own day. The play arouses but thwarts a deeply felt desire for "justice, justice, justice, justice!" (5.1.25), eliciting a profound dissatisfaction, a dissatisfaction inherent in Calvin's premise that the law exists not to control the dangerous behavior of a few but to reveal everyone's imperfections.

In deliberately violating the conventions of poetic justice, Shakespeare not only challenges traditional belief in human merit but also interrogates his own theatrical practices. Many critics have noted that the final trial scene resembles a play that the Duke carefully scripts, rehearses, and stages. The insistent metadrama of this final scene, I suggest, underscores how theatrical representation can thwart self-righteous judgment and compel self-knowledge.

In compliance with the Duke's script, the chaste (and chastened) Isabella plays the role of the defiled woman in the trial scene and publicly proclaims that she has slept with Angelo. Although Shakespeare depicts her as self-conscious about the role she reluctantly agrees to play, heightening his audience's awareness of the pretense, he insists on the value of her role-playing. Isabella experiences her theatrical performance as profoundly humiliating, but her public humiliation enables her to identify and empathize with Mariana. Required to step into Mariana's place, Isabella, "with grief and shame" (l. 96), declares herself a "fallen" woman and is treated as an object of scorn and approbation. Imaginatively reversing the earlier physical substitution of

Mariana for Isabella, a substitution that put Mariana at risk in order to save both Isabella's brother and her chastity, the Duke's casting thus forces Isabella to recognize that she, like the woman she plays, is vulnerable, conflicted, passionate, imperfect, and at risk. It is this recognition, the product of a theatrical fiction, that enables Isabella to join Mariana in pleading for Angelo's life.

The Duke's theatrics force Angelo, too, to acknowledge his imperfection. When Isabella and Mariana accuse Angelo of terrible crimes and demand justice, the Duke, in a shocking move, turns the legal proceedings over to the accused, placing him in the seat of judgment and telling him, "be you judge / Of your own cause" (ll. 165-66). Rather than reasserting his authority, the Duke delegates his power of judgement to his deputy, the very man whom he knows to have flagrantly abused that power and who is the subject of judicial inquiry. The Duke then stages an elaborate theatrical performance, one in which Angelo is positioned as both dramatic protagonist and judging spectator. Shaken and exposed by this performance, Angelo confesses his crimes and repents. If Shakespeare calls attention to the contrived and scripted nature of Angelo's trial, he nevertheless attributes its efficacy—its capacity to make Angelo's transgressions visible to himself and others and to elicit self-examination and confession—largely to the Duke's representational strategies: his use of indirection; his substitution of Isabella for Mariana; his deployment of a paradoxical riddle; his teasing theatrical presentation of a mysterious, veiled woman; his own complicated doubling as friar and Duke; and the way he forces Angelo to pay attention to the discrepancies between what Angelo thinks he knows and what is. By foregrounding the confusing gaps between language and meaning, knowledge and truth, the substitute and the person she stands in for, the disguise and the person in disguise, the Duke's theater disrupts and confounds its spectators, ultimately revealing to them what has been hidden, denied, or misunderstood.

In *Measure for Measure,* as in *Hamlet,* Shakespeare insists on the capacity of theater to activate the conscience, arouse guilt, and elicit confessions of wrongdoing. In both plays he draws on Calvinist theories of the conscience to explain the powerful affect of theater, and in both he nurtures as well as thematizes the interiorized, reflexive, and self-disciplinary gaze that those theories seek to inculcate. According to the many English Protestant tracts on the conscience which proliferated in the wake of the Reformation, the conscience enables a person to see his or her actions from God's perspective and therefore to render "'a man's judgment of himself, according to the judgment of God of him.'"[48] Angelo confesses his crimes and declares his heart "penitent" as soon as he realizes that the Duke, "like power divine," has been privy to his most secret

acts and private transgressions—that is, as soon as he imagines his actions from the viewpoint of a judging authority:

> O my dread lord,
> I should be guiltier than my guiltiness
> To think I can be undiscernible,
> When I perceive your grace, like power
> divine,
> Hath looked upon my passes.
>
> (5.1.358-62)

It is, significantly, the Duke's theater that provides Angelo with this perspective by positioning him as a spectator and judge at his own trial. In this scene, as in the performance of "The Murder of Gonzago," Shakespeare claims for the stage the power to activate the conscience—that internalized and self-regulating spectator, "God's spy," "man's . . . overseer," and a keeper "ioyned to man, to marke and watch all hys secretes"—that Protestant reformers taught has the power "to prescribe, prohibit, absolute and condemne *de iure.*"[49] In a play that questions the capacity of any individual to achieve righteousness, he imagines a theater that nurtures reflexivity, produces guilt, and thwarts the impulse to judge others.

Reforming

Inasmuch as the Duke's theater seeks to initiate an internal reformation in its spectators by arousing dissatisfaction with the self, it conforms to the kind of art approved by Protestant theologians. Although they condemn as idolatrous images and plays that seduce, dazzle, and trick the beholder, the English reformers routinely defend art that "provoke[s]" us "to consider ourselves . . . and to condemn and abhor our sin," that serves as "stirrers of men's minds," and that enables its viewers "to remember themselves, and to lament their sins"; and they approve of art that awakens the conscience and nurtures moral self-examination.[50] In his defense of the stage, written a few years after Shakespeare's comedy, Thomas Heywood fully articulates a theory of dramatic representation based on these Protestant defenses, arguing that theater has the capacity to "new mold the harts of the spectators" by enabling them to "see and shame at their faults."[51] Louis Adrian Montrose asserts that the arguments advanced by Heywood and other apologists for the stage "remain constrained within the terms of the dominant antitheatrical discourse" and thus "do not fully comprehend the cultural practice" they seek to defend.[52] He looks instead to the antitheatrical tracts, and especially their pervasive fear of the seductive pleasures of the stage, for a more accurate sense of theater's power over its spectators. But I would like to suggest that, by the beginning of the seventeenth century, Shakespeare and his fellow playwrights were actively appropriating Calvinist theories of representation and creatively exploring the disciplinary potential of their medium in an effort to legitimate the stage in the face of virulent antitheatrical attacks.

Steven Mullaney also takes Heywood's claims seriously, using them to illustrate how the early modern stage was understood to be "a potent forum for the reformation as well as the recreation of its audiences." However, he associates the dramatic practice of inducing apprehension and shame with the suppressed Roman Catholic practice of auricular confession, arguing that early modern playwrights appropriate the "internal drama" of the forbidden sacrament, which was "performed before a judgmental authority, at times harrowingly silent, at times sharply inquisitorial."[53] Certainly auricular confession is, as he suggests, a "specter" that haunts *Measure for Measure,*[54] but Shakespeare's play questions its efficacy and, in the final scene, stages another kind of confession, a public and communal rehearsal of mutual guilt that conforms much more closely to Calvinist than to Roman Catholic rituals of confession.

In eliminating the sacrament of auricular confession and instituting a reformed confession, the English Protestant Church substituted one form of apprehension for another. In fact, what the Calvinist reformers most strenuously objected to in the Roman Catholic sacrament of auricular confession was not so much that it aroused apprehension and shame, as Mullaney argues, as that it relieved it in a particularly offensive way. Calvin complains that

> men hauing made confession to a Priest, think that they may wype their mouth and say, I did it not. And not onely they are made all the yeare longe the bolder to sinne: but al the rest of the yeare bearing themselves bolde upon confession, they neuer sighe vnto God, they neuer return to themselues, but heape sinnes vpon sinnes, til they vomit vp all at once as they thinke. And when they haue once vomited them vp, they thynke themselues discharged of their burden, and that they haue taken away from God the iudgemente that they haue geven to the Priest, and that they haue brought God in forgetfulnesse, when they haue made the Priest priuie.[55]

For him the Catholic sacrament is "pestilente" because it confers on the priest the power to absolve sin, a power he insists resides only in God.[56] He seeks instead to devise religious practices that provoke men to "sighe unto God" and "return to themselves," to feel their guilt continuously and reflect on divine judgment.

Calvin privileges the individual's private and internal confession of sins before God, but he also imagines that such a confession will naturally be followed by a voluntary and public confession before men "not only to whisper the secret of his heart to one man, and once and in hys eare: but oft and openly, and in the bearing

of al the world simplye to rehearse . . . his own shame."[57] Indeed, he imagines an ideal Protestant community as one in which all members share publicly the knowledge of their own failings, rehearsing their shame. "We shoulde lay our weaknesse one in an others bosome," he writes, "to receiue mutuall counsel, mutual compassion & mutual comfort one of an other: then that we be naturally priuie to the weaknesses of our brethren; shoulde praye for them to the Lorde."[58] Far from being eliminated from Protestant confessions, then, shame is understood to be shared, and its rehearsal in public is believed to be salutary, arousing the desire for an absolution that no human can confer, nurturing a continual process of self-reflection and repentance, and fostering a sense of community.

In the final scene of *Measure for Measure,* Shakespeare stages just such a public rehearsal of shame, one in which the comic ending is governed by mutual confessions of weaknesses and transgressions and repeated requests for forgiveness rather than the conventional triumph of love and mirth. Even Escalus and the Provost, who appear relatively blameless, and Isabella, who was clearly wronged, confess their faults and ask—publicly—to be pardoned for their behavior; and Angelo, the most obviously guilty character, not only requests forgiveness but is also asked to forgive the Provost for sending him the head of Ragozine instead of Claudio. Indeed, the Duke himself, having discarded his clerical disguise along with all pretense that he has the power to absolve sins, asks to be pardoned, confessing to Isabella that he is responsible for the supposed death of her brother and even declaring his kinship with the condemned man (5.1.487). All of these confessions are offered spontaneously and openly to the entire community after Lucio inadvertently reveals that the friar is, in truth, the Duke. To the extent that these confessions nurture a sense of community based on shared guilt—that is, a Calvinist community of sinners—they may be understood to liberate Isabella, Angelo, and the other characters from the isolation of their counterfeit righteousness.[59]

But that community, forged out of the painful awareness of a common guilt, is necessarily imperfect. As many critics have pointed out, the Duke does not achieve the complete reformation he desires. Isabella struggles to forgive Angelo, making a reluctant and qualified plea for his life; Angelo marries Mariana under duress, never speaking a word of affection to her; Lucio resists the Duke's order to marry Kate Keepdown, his wit still directed toward the bawdy and subversive; Barnardine stubbornly refuses all efforts to reform him; and Isabella does not answer the Duke's marriage proposal, her silence unsettling the comic ending. Although he asserts the power of theatrical representation to arouse guilt and produce the conditions for repentance, Shakespeare questions the capacity of the stage to reform its spectators.[60] When, in the final act, he makes his own activity as dramatist visible through a Duke who constructs fictional narratives, traffics in substitutions, manipulates desire, cleverly scripts comic endings, and seeks to reform his audiences, he depicts his central character as an imperfect, even a bungling playwright.[61]

Why might Shakespeare create a figure of a playwright who cannot be trusted, who devises tricks that raise troubling ethical questions, who employs an improbable and highly contrived script, and who cannot even produce the conventional comic ending, unable as he is to reform the transgressors or persuade his romantic heroine to assent to the traditional marriage proposal? One answer may be that, by calling attention to the imperfection of his own art, Shakespeare deliberately cedes the reforming powers of the artist to a higher, divine authority and sacrifices the satisfactions of a comic ending in order to create a felt need for grace. It is surely significant that grace in Shakespeare's play is on everyone's tongue (in the repeated utterance of the words *grace* and *gracious*) yet is so noticeably absent.[62] The persistent references to grace, like the pattern of inadequate substitutions, function to arouse desire for what the play cannot, on its own, achieve; for in *Measure for Measure* authority remains stubbornly outside both the world of the play and the realm of the author. Like the law as Calvin conceives it, the play can only reveal, not correct, imperfection, and it thus arouses a longing for what it acknowledges it cannot deliver: divine forgiveness. But even as he exposes the inadequacies of his representational theater, Shakespeare brilliantly exploits them. By portraying an imperfect playwright-Duke, by marring his own comic ending, and by depicting a series of inadequate but evocative substitutions, Shakespeare cultivates a knowledge of lack that is not only dissatisfying but also productive. He creates in his audiences a profound sense of the infinite space that separates them from the divine.

Notes

[1] Jean E. Howard, "*Measure for Measure* and the Restraints of Convention," *Essays in Literature* 10 (1983): 149-58, esp. 149.

[2] See, for example, Rosalind Miles, who argues that "there remains an unshakeable sense that it [the trial scene] fails to conclude the play in a way that leaves us entirely content; it does not fully resolve the issues and release the dramatic tensions which the course of the play has created" (*The Problem of* Measure for Measure: *A Historical Investigation* [New York: Barnes and Noble, 1976], 250); Anthony Dawson, who argues that "the elaborate restitution at the end of *Measure for Measure* is more hoax than reaffirmation" ("*Measure for Measure,* New Historicism, and Theatrical Power," *Shakespeare Quarterly* 39 [1988]: 328-

41, esp. 341); Robert N. Watson, who sees the final revelation as "an illusion manipulated by a fake holy man for his own aggrandizement" and argues that "all the strategies of secular immortality, all the fantasies (religious, artistic, familial) of resurrection . . . lie mortally wounded amid the formulaic resurrections of the final scene" ("False Immortality in*Measure for Measure:* Comic Means, Tragic Ends," *SQ* 41 [1990]: 411-32, esp. 423); and Richard Wheeler, who comments on "Shakespeare's inability to find an ending that responds fully to the whole action" (*Shakespeare's Development and the Problem Comedies: Turn and Counter-Turn* [Berkeley: U of California P, 1981], 12).

[3] Alexander Leggatt, "Substitution in *Measure for Measure,*" *SQ* 39 (1988): 342-59, esp. 359.

[4] See, for example, Katharine Eisaman Maus, *Inwardness and Theater in the English Renaissance* (Chicago: U of Chicago P, 1995), 172-77; Louise Schleiner, "Providential Improvisation in *Measure for Measure,*" *PMLA* 97 (1982): 227-36, esp. 227; Julia Reinhard Lupton, *Afterlives of the Saints: Hagiography, Typology, and Renaissance Literature* (Stanford, CA: Stanford UP, 1996), 110-40; and Michael Flachmann, "Fitted for Death: *Measure for Measure* and the *Contemplatio Mortis,*" *English Literary Renaissance* 22 (1992): 222-41. For earlier treatments of the play's religious content, see also Roy W. Battenhouse, "*Measure for Measure* and Christian Doctrine of the Atonement," *PMLA* 61 (1946): 1029-59; Darryl J. Gless, Measure for Measure, *The Law, and the Convenant* (Princeton, NJ: Princeton UP, 1979); and George Wilson Knight, *The Wheel of Fire: Interpretations of Shakespearian Tragedy, with three new essays* (London: Methuen, 1949).

[5] Elizabeth Pope, for example, explicitly argues that in *Measure for Measure* Shakespeare "touches . . . only on such elements of traditional theology as were shared by Anglican, Puritan, and Roman Catholic alike" ("The Renaissance Background of *Measure for Measure*" in *Aspects of Shakespeare's 'Problem Plays',* Kenneth Muir and Stanley Wells, eds. [Cambridge: Cambridge UP, 1982], 57-73, esp. 71). Making no distinctions between Roman Catholic and Protestant views of chastity, Jonathan Dollimore assumes that "the Church" approves of Isabella's renunciation of her sexuality; see "Transgression and surveillance in *Measure for Measure*" in *Political Shakespeare: Essays in Cultural Materialism,* Jonathan Dollimore and Alan Sinfield, eds. (Ithaca, NY: Cornell UP, 1985), 72-87, esp. 82. Leggatt remarks that were a duke to disguise himself as a friar and go "around hearing confessions," he would create "a major scandal in an actual Catholic community" (344), but he never considers how a dramatic representation of such an action might play to a Protestant audience in early modern England. Carolyn Brown does not address the radically different views

of Roman Catholics and Protestants on religious flagellation, asserting instead that the practice of flagellation "did not die in the Middle Ages but, to the contrary, survived and flourished through the sixteenth century in most of Europe" ("Erotic Religious Flagellation and Shakespeare's *Measure for Measure*," *ELR* 16 [1986]: 139-65, esp. 141).

[6] Watson, for example, ignores Protestant condemnation of vows of chastity when he argues that because the play makes "a mockery of the pious notion that virginity is a plausible or even permissible way to pursue immortality," it is subversive of all religion, and he suggests that the play is "potentially heretical, even blasphemous" (426 and 415). Harriett Hawkins suggests that the play reveals how "organized religion itself . . . provide[s] solutions that are false, ways out that are too easy" ("'The Devil's Party': Virtues and Vices in 'Measure for Measure'" in Muir and Wells, eds., 87-95, esp. 95).

[7] See, for example, Dollimore, 72-87; Jonathan Goldberg, *James I and the Politics of Literature* (Baltimore: Johns Hopkins UP, 1983); Stephen Greenblatt, *Shakespearean Negotiations: The Circulation of Social Energy in Renaissance England* (Berkeley: U of California P, 1988); andLeonard Tennenhouse, "Representing Power: *Measure for Measure* in Its Time," *Genre* 15 (1982): 139-56.

[8] I quote from Frederick Shriver, "Hampton Court ReVisited: James I and the Puritans," *Journal of Ecclesiastical History* 33 (1982): 48-71, esp. 48; see also, William Barlow, *The Summe and Substance of the Conference . . . at Hampton Court* (London, 1604).

[9] "James's ecclesiastical policy was often conceived and presented as a via media between these two extremes" of puritanism and papistry, write Kenneth Fincham and Peter Lake, who note that "the king himself never tired of pointing out the equivalence of these two menaces" ("The Ecclesiastical Policy of King James I," *Journal of British Studies* 24 [1985]: 169-207, esp. 170). They argue that "James I not merely identified and opposed the threats of popery and Puritanism but also endeavored to emasculate the political dangers that both contained" (171).

[10] Fincham and Lake, 175 and 172.

[11] See, for example, in Henry Peacham's *Minerva Britanna* (London, 1612), the emblem of a hypocrite, who wears a friar's habit and carries a rosary and staff (198); Peacham identifies the friar's "humblest habits" with "a false disguise" that cloaks his "hidden villainies."

[12] In her fascinating analysis of what she calls "the relics of hagiography in Shakespearean drama," Julia Reinhard Lupton finds in this play "a residually *Catholic* discourse not fully subject to its Reformation into secular literature" (140). She argues provocatively that *Measure for Measure* stages "the founding of secular literature on the supersedure of Christian forms" (135), but in identifying the Protestant Reformation with the "classicizing . . . humanist, rationalist, and empiricist initiatives of the Renaissance" (xxxii), she is, I think, too quick to equate early English Protestantism with the secularizing impulses of modernity.

[13] Fincham and Lake, 207.

[14] Patrick Collinson, *The Religion of Protestants: The Church in English Society 1559-1625* (Oxford: Clarendon Press, 1982), 82.

[15] Michel de Certeau, *The Practice of Everyday Life*, trans. Steven Rendall (Berkeley: U of California P. 1988).

[16] See, for example, Louis Adrian Montrose, "The Purpose of Playing: Reflections on a Shakespearean Anthropology," *Helios* 7 (1980): 51-74; and Michael O'Connell, "The Idolatrous Eye: Iconoclasm, Anti-Theatricalism, and the Image of the Elizabethan Theater," *ELH* 52 (1985): 279-310. Both argue that the early modern London theater develops in reaction against Protestantism, a religion they assume is hostile to all theater. Montrose has recently distanced his position from O'Connell's; see Louis Adrian Montrose, *The Purpose of Playing: Shakespeare and the Cultural Politics of the Elizabethan Theatre* (Chicago: U of Chicago P, 1996), 32n.

[17] Thomas Lodge, "A Reply to Stephen Gosson's *Schoole of Abuse:* In Defence of Poetry Musick and Stage Plays" (1580?) in *The Complete Works of Thomas Lodge,* 4 vols. (Glasgow: Robert Anderson for the Hunterian Club, 1883), 1:A4^r, A7^r, and B2^r. I would even suggest that it is Lodge, in his reply to Gosson, who first formulates a position on the stage that draws on Calvinist theology. It is only when Gosson answers Lodge's critique of his first tract that he fully develops the relation between antitheatricality and Protestant theology.

[18] For a detailed discussion of these Calvinist defenses, see my book, *Staging Reform, Reforming the Stage: Protestantism and Popular Theater in Early Modern England* (Ithaca, NY: Cornell UP, 1997), 71-72 and 205-7.

[19] John Calvin, *The Institution of Christian Religion, written in Latine,* trans. Thomas Norton (London, 1562), Bi^v and Avi^r. Subsequent references to the *Institutes* follow this sixteenth-century edition.

[20] John Calvin, *The Sermons of M. Iohn Caluin, upon the Epistle of S. Paule too the Ephesians,* trans. Arthur Golding (London, 1577), fol. 87.

[21] Calvin, *Institutes,* Biiiiᵛ, Giʳ⁻ᵛ, and Niiiᵛ-Niiiiʳ. Calvin elsewhere laments that most men are blind to these signs, preferring to "rest in beholding the workes without hauing regard of the workeman" (Biᵛ).

[22] Calvin, *Institutes,* QQQviiʳ, RRRvᵛ, RRRviiᵛ, and SSSiʳ.

[23] For a discussion of these pictures, see Craig Harbison, *The Last Judgment in Sixteenth-Century Northern Europe* (New York: Garland Press, 1976), 52-61.

[24] Calvin, *Institutes,* RRRiʳ. In an extended discussion of civil government, Calvin raises many of the central issues that Shakespeare explores in *Measure for Measure,* including the problems caused by too severe and too lenient administration of the law.

[25] John Calvin, *The Catechisme, or maner to teache Children the Christian Religion* (London, 1580), A4ᵛ.

[26] William Wood, *A Fourme of Catechising in true religion* (London, 1581), C1ʳ. For Calvin, G. R. Evans writes, "The signs are present in this world, seen by our eyes and touched by our hands. Calvin's fear is that if this spatial separation of sign and thing signified is not emphasized there will be idolatry" ("Calvin on signs: an Augustinian dilemma," *Renaissance Studies* 3 [1989]: 35-45, esp. 40). Early Protestants repeatedly define idolatry in terms of substitution: see, for instance, Calvin, *Institutes,* Biiiʳ; "An Homilie Against perill of Idolatrie, and superfluous decking of Churches" in *Certaine Sermons or Homilies Appointed to be Read in Churches in the Time of Queen Elizabeth I . . . A Facsimile Reproduction of the Edition of 1623,* ed. Mary Ellen Rickey and Thomas B. Stroup (Gainesville, FL: Scholars' Facsimiles and Reprints, 1968), 11-76, esp. 49; and William Perkins, *A Treatise of Mans Imaginations* (Cambridge, 1607), B12ᵛ-C1ʳ.

[27] Stephen Gosson, *Playes Confuted in fiue Actions* (London, 1582), D7ᵛ.

[28] Maus, 164 and 163. See also Janet Adelman's discussion of "the battle within [Angelo] between fierce repression of sexual desire and equally fierce outbursts of degrading and degraded desire"; Adelman concludes that for Angelo "desire is necessarily the ravishing of a saint" ("Bed Tricks: On Marriage as the End of Comedy in *All's Well that Ends Well* and *Measure for Measure*" in *Shakespeare's Personality,* Norman N. Holland, Sidney Homan, and Bernard J. Paris, eds. [Berkeley: U of California P, 1989], 151-74, esp. 164).

[29] Quotations of *Measure for Measure* follow *The Norton Shakespeare, Based on the Oxford edition,* ed. Stephen Greenblatt et al. (New York: W. W. Norton, 1997).

[30] Wood, B8ᵛ-C1ʳ.

[31] "An Homilie Against perill of Idolatrie," 49.

[32] "An Homilie Against perill of Idolatrie," 49; and William Perkins, *A Warning against the Idolatrie of the last times. And an Instruction touching Religious, or Diuine worship* (Cambridge, 1601), F6ʳ.

[33] 1 Corinthians 8:1-2. Biblical quotations in this essay follow the 1560 *Geneva Bible* and will hereafter be cited parenthetically in the text.

[34] See, for instance, Calvin, *Sermons upon Ephesians,* fol. 85.

[35] Although he does not discuss this play in terms of Calvinist theology or the Reformation, R.L.P. Jackson makes a similar observation in "Necessary Ambiguity: The Last Act of *Measure for Measure,*" *The Critical Review* 26 (1984): 114-29, esp. 117.

[36] Margaret Scott, "'Our City's Institutions': Some Further Reflections on the Marriage Contract in *Measure for Measure,*" *ELH* 49 (1982): 790-804, esp. 794. For interesting discussions of civil and ecclesiastical law and *Measure for Measure,* see Victoria Hayne, "Performing Social Practice: The Example of *Measure for Measure,*" *SQ* 44 (1993): 1-29; and Maus, 157-81.

[37] Calvin, *Institutes,* Diiiᵛ.

[38] Calvin, *Institutes,* Diiiᵛ. According to John T. McNeill, "the term 'law' for Calvin may mean (1) the whole religion of Moses . . . ; (2) the special revelation of the moral law to the chosen people . . . ; or (3) various bodies of civil, judicial, and ceremonial statutes." He notes that "Of these, the moral law, the 'true and eternal rule of righteousness' . . . is most important" (John T. McNeill, ed., *Institutes of the Christian Religion,* trans. Ford Lewis Battles, 2 vols. [Philadelphia: The Westminster Press, 1960], 1:348n).

[39] Edmond Allen, *A shorte Catechisme: A briefe and godly bringinge up of youth in the knowledge and commandements of God.* ([Zurich] 1550), C5ᵛ and D3ᵛ. See also *A Short Catechisme, or Playne Instruction* (London, 1553), B5ᵛ; John Dod and Richard Cleaver, *A Plaine and familiar Exposition of Ten Commaundments, with a methodicall short Catechisme* (London, 1605), Ff4ᵛ; and Stephen Egerton, *A Briefe Method of Catechizing* (London, 1631), A5ʳ-A7ʳ and C6ʳ.

[40] Calvin, *Institutes,* Aiʳ.

[41] Alexander Nowell writes that the law "striketh their heart with a wholesome sorrow, and driveth them to . . . repentance" (*A Cathechisme written in Latin* [1570],

trans. Thomas Norton, ed. G. E. Corrie [Cambridge: Parker Society, 1854], 141).

[42] Calvin, *Institutes,* Diii[r] and Dii[v]; Calvin, *Sermons upon Ephesians,* fols. 77[v]-78[r].

[43] Calvin, *Institutes,* Diii[v].

[44] Calvin, *Institutes,* GGGiiii[r].

[45] See, for instance, Ben Jonson's portrayal of the Anabaptists in *The Alchemist* (1610) and of the puritan Zeal-of-the-Land Busy in *Bartholomew Fair* (1614).

[46] Mario DiGangi, "Pleasure and Danger: Measuring Female Sexuality in *Measure for Measure,*" *ELH* 60 (1993): 589-609, esp. 596; Laura Lunger Knoppers, "(En)gendering Shame: *Measure for Measure* and the Spectacles of Power," *ELR* 23 (1993): 450-71, esp. 462. Knoppers believes that Isabella's desire to enter a convent is "threatening" to patriarchal society (464). See also Brown, who laments that the Duke's shaming of Isabella "prevents her from ever returning to the protection of the convent" (216).

[47] Harriett Hawkins, *Likenesses of Truth in Elizabethan and Restoration Drama* (Oxford: Oxford UP, 1972), 70 and 68. See also Richard Ide, who writes: "For Barnardine to be forgiven along with Claudio also seems an abuse of justice on the part of the lenient Duke" ("Shakespeare's Revisionism: Homiletic Tragicomedy and the Ending of *Measure for Measure,*" *Shakespeare Studies* 20 [1987]: 105-27, esp. 119).

[48] William Ames, *Conscience with the Power and Cases Thereof* (London, 1639), B1[r]. For a discussion of early Protestant notions of the conscience, see John S. Wilks, *The Idea of Conscience in Renaissance Tragedy* (New York: Routledge, 1990).

[49] Jeremiah Dyke, *Good Conscience or A Treatise Shewing the Nature, Meanes, Marks, Benefit, and Necesity thereof* (London, 1624), B7[r]; Calvin, *Institutes,* DDDi[v]; Richard Carpenter, *The Conscionable Christian* (London, 1620), Hi[r].

[50] Thomas Cranmer, *The Bishop's Book* (1537), quoted here from John Phillips, *The Reformation of Images: Destruction of Art in England, 1535-1660* (Berkeley: U of California P, 1973), 57; "The Contents of a Book of Articles devised by the King," quoted here from *The Actes and Monuments of John Foxe* (1570), ed. Stephen Reed Cattley, 8 vols. (London: R. B. Seeley and W. Burnside, 1937-41), 5:163.

[51] Thomas Heywood, *An Apology For Actors* (London, 1612), B4[r] and F4[r]; see also G1[v]-G2[r]. For a detailed discussion of Heywood's defense of the stage and

Protestant theories of conscience, see my book, *Staging Reform.*

[52] Montrose, *The Purpose of Playing,* 44-45.

[53] Steven Mullaney, *The Place of the Stage: License, Play, and Power in Renaissance England* (Chicago: U of Chicago P, 1988), 95, 98, 101, and 100.

[54] Mullaney, 99.

[55] Calvin, *Institutes,* CCvii[v]-CCviii[r].

[56] Calvin, *Institutes,* CCvii[v].

[57] Calvin, *Institutes,* CCiiii[r].

[58] Calvin, *Institutes,* CCii[v].

[59] In "The Politics of Theatrical Mirth: *A Midsummer Night's Dream, A Mad World, My Masters,* and *Measure for Measure*" (*SQ* 43 [1992]: 51-66) Paul Yachnin argues that *Measure for Measure* represents "theater as the place of private conversial work rather than as the gathering-place of politically reconciliatory mirth," and he contends that Jacobean comedy, in sharp contrast to Elizabethan comedy, seeks "to exert itself with respect to the individual *as individual* rather than as a member of the community" (62). But he ignores the way the final scene's public rehearsal of mutual guilt creates a community of sinners. Victoria Hayne, in "Performing Social Practice," argues that "the audience is repeatedly invoked as witness, compurgator, congregation, jury" (21); and it might be possible to argue along these lines that the final act positions Shakespeare's audience as a congregation, witnessing these public confessions. But while she examines puritan emphasis on the congregation's judgmental role, I focus on Calvin's emphasis on the importance of the congregation's identification and compassion.

[60] Noting that Viennese "society seems singularly unaffected" by the Duke's efforts to inflict "anxiety for ideological purposes," Stephen Greenblatt argues that "salutary anxiety is emptied out in the service of theatrical pleasure," thereby calling into question the Duke's goals (141 and 138). Greenblatt argues that the pleasure the audience experiences is "bound up with the marking out of theatrical anxiety as represented anxiety—not wholly real, either in the characters onstage or in the audience" (135). But I want to suggest that salutary anxiety, rather than simply being emptied out, has both an aesthetic and a disciplinary function.

[61] Anne Righter Barton makes a similar observation in *Shakespeare and the Idea of the Play* (London: Chatto and Windus, 1962) when she notes that "the Duke's managerial rôle flatters neither himself nor the theater" (178).

[62] The word *grace* or *graces* occurs twenty-five times in *Measure for Measure,* the words *gracious* and *graciously* eight times; see T. H. Howard-Hill, ed., *Oxford Shakespeare Concordance:* Measure for Measure (Oxford: Clarendon Press, 1969).

SEXUALITY AND GENDER RELATIONS

Susan Carlson (essay date 1989)

SOURCE: "'Fond Fathers' and Sweet Sisters: Alternative Sexualities in *Measure for Measure*," in *Essays in Literature,* Vol. XVI, No. 1, Spring, 1989, pp. 13-31.

[*In the essay below, Carlson contends that* Measure for Measure *presents a "fragile and unusual"alternative sexuality in which relationships for both men and women that are not endorsed "by the standard sexual politics" are acknowledged. However, Carlson explains, the effort to create such a sexuality challenges the male order of the play and is terminated in the play's final scene.*]

Measure for Measure insists on defining its women in terms of their sexual relations to men. Such definition is clearest in the play's final scene when the Duke concludes Mariana must be "nothing" if she is not maid, widow, or wife (V.i.177-78).[1] The definition is corroborated by Lucio with his addition of a more tawdry fourth alternative, "punk," to the unchallenged list of female types. Many critics responding to the play in recent years have explored this seeming equation of a woman's worth with her sexuality to conclude that the play's sexual attitudes result from a persistent male fear of women.[2] Their feminist connection between gynophobia and the play's restrictive sexual definitions has helped explain many of the ambiguities in the play's highly sexualized fabric. But although they call into question privileged, male-powered sexuality, none of them studies alternative sexualities in *Measure for Measure*. Other critics have begun to characterize the play's diversified sexualities, however, by combining a feminist perspective with their exploration of multiple cultural and social paradigms. While in general terms both Stephen Greenblatt and Jonathan Dollimore have urged that a dominant power structure persists because it allows for, even demands subversion, Jacqueline Rose, Kathleen McLuskie, and Dollimore himself have ventured specific readings of *Measure for Measure* which assume that the play's sexuality is a plurality of behaviors conditioned by cultural, social, and literary norms.[3]

The finding of literary scholars that sexuality is pluralistic and mutable is corroborated by the recent work of anthropologists, sociologists, and historians. Elizabeth Janeway, Carole Vance, Gayle Rubin, Jeffrey Weeks, Lawrence Stone and others deny essentialist assumptions that sexuality is a monolithic force existing prior to social life and offer, instead, their finding that sexuality is a social construct constantly "renegotiated" in the intersections of cultural, social, and political relations.[4] Guided by such critical reappraisals, I want to identify and explore *Measure for Measure*'s principal alternative sexuality. Whereas the dominant sexuality in the play includes both the traditional definitions of women advanced by the Duke and Lucio and other predictable patterns of relations between men and women, the most viable alternative sexuality in the play is articulated by its women. The sexual realm controlled by the women affirms life as it is not affirmed elsewhere in the play by supporting reorganized relations between men and women and by broadening the sexual options for women. While the whisper of this second sexuality is rarely heard above the commanding din of the dominant order, its resilient presence disturbs the play's characters and influences their actions in significant ways. McLuskie tells us that nothing in the play dislodges the men's established power, and Dollimore cautions that the play's termination offers more exploitation than resistance.[5] Although I join them in cautioning that the presence of the women's alternative sexuality does not lead to feminist reformation, I find both unusual and notable the play's fragile openness to sexual redefinition.

Others have convincingly established that the play's dominant sexuality is masculine and authoritarian, operating under the twin assumptions that women are enticements to sexual sin and that women threaten a life of dangerous fecundity. Out of the fear attached to these assumptions grows an elaborate system of double standards designed as a protection against female concupiscence as well as an intricate grammar which linguistically positions women as passive objects— direct objects, indirect objects, prepositional objects.[6] An even more subtle controlling standard is the corollary assumption that the sexuality of women as well as men is known and defined in a single way. Yet ironically, in spite of the powerlessness into which women are cast by such logic, they remain a potent enough threat to merit extensive guardianship. In fact, the insistence with which the play's women are defined in these limited ways is suspiciously myopic. For the assumption that there is only one sexuality is belied by the energy expended to protect the dominant order, an energy which suggests as much the possibility of an alternative as it does the exclusivity of the status quo. Before I turn to a study of the second sexuality that does exist in the play, I need to review two factors that complicate the play's alternative image of women and their sexuality: Isabella's anomalous position in the power structures of the play and *Measure for Measure*'s adaptation of comic patterns.

Because the second sexuality is, practically, a way of redressing the power imbalance of traditional sexual roles, it is most closely attached to the women who have been powerless. This alternative can not simply be equated with the play's most visible woman, Isabella, however. Like the rest of the play's women, Isabella somewhat surreptitiously expresses her sexual nature, but unlike them, does so mostly in accordance with the assumptions of the dominant sexuality. Richard P. Wheeler finds that the judicial decisions of the play's powerful men—the Duke and Angelo—are tied to their repression of sexual desire. For Wheeler, Angelo's failure to integrate his own sexual desires into the power structure he administers accounts for his overriding of what would normally be compelling moral, familial, and political strictures. The Duke, he adds, avoids his sexuality by channeling his fear of it into a generalized death wish expressed with false aphoristic certainty.[7] While Isabella is the only woman to join the play's men in the repression of sexuality and while her response is—like theirs—evasive, she has fewer options than they do for rechanneling her sexuality since she lacks their authority in social and political arenas. So while the men wield power in response to sexual urges, Isabella can only avoid that power and the world and roles it has created. Although her actions are an extension of the men's, Isabella's necessarily more defensive response to the play's power structures is aligned—in result if not in intention—with subversive strategies all the play's women adopt to survive in a sphere where they are denied power.

Jane Lapotaire, analyzing Isabella from an actress's point of view, concludes that her retreat to the convent is an escape from a world where she has suffered some sexual trauma related to male power. Dollimore, similarly, sees in Isabella's renunciation her seeking "to be preserved specifically from men" and assumes, like Lapotaire, that Isabella knows enough about male power to want to avoid it.[8] Indeed, as soon as Isabella is faced with the inhuman logic of Angelo's law, she displays a passionate rhetoric seemingly rooted in personal knowledge of the abuses of power. She belittles the authoritarian as "man, proud man, / Dressed in a little brief authority, / Most ignorant of what he's most assured" (II.ii.117-19). And in II.iv, when Isabella has both Angelo's licentiousness *and* his abuse of authority to respond to, she chooses to berate *only* his power (II.iv.172-77). Both Isabella's desire to escape authority and her berating of its abuses are replicated in the actions of the play's other women. But Isabella's sexual repression, her compliance, and her lack of self-knowledge prevent her from standing at the middle of the play's second order of power and sexuality, even though she is the most fervid in her outbursts against the men's power. Along with the other women, she contributes to an alternative, but not one of the women is strong enough, finally, to resist the men's power and paradigm.

The limited sphere of the play's second sexuality observable in Isabella's paradoxical role is countered, in part, by the play's comic inversion. Even though this play does not reproduce the joyousness of earlier Shakespearean comedies, it does share in the comedies' rich reversals. While I agree with Jean Howard and Marcia Riefer that the play's comic form does not lead to the creation of a power-wielding heroine,[9] I find, nevertheless, that comic inversion is at work in creating a world disordered enough that its women can test an alternative sexual order. The Duke himself invokes customary comic license when he describes his Vienna as a world out of its order:

> And Liberty plucks Justice by the nose;
> The baby beats the nurse, and quite athwart
> Goes all decorum.
>
> (I.iii.29-31)

While for several of the play's critics the Duke's conception of Vienna's inverted power structure is negative, the inversion and the prominence it accords women signal the welcomed hope of a second order. Meredith Skura labels the inversion a critique of the phallocentric order; Howard finds that the reversal allows for both convention and its critique; and Carol Thomas Neely argues that the expansion and alteration of comedy in *Measure for Measure* (as well as *All's Well That Ends Well*) act in part to protect women's sexuality in the rough world of these problem plays.[10] The events of the play do suggest that the central power structure is enticingly changeable. Yet any alternative order in the play is not as powerful, ascendant, or inspiring as these critics would like to believe. Dollimore makes it soberingly clear that the play's Bakhtinian inversion is largely illusory, and worse, that the power released by such inversion is nearly always contained.[11] An alternative sexuality generated through women is strengthened by the play's comic inversions, however. The alternative has a limited life, but it interrupts the control which the dominant sexuality wields over the language and actions in the play.

Five scenes mark the existence of the play's tenuous counter sexuality. The most important of these is I.iv, for it makes the fullest statement about what constitutes the sexual alternative in the play. In the exchange between Isabella and Francisca that opens the convent scene, critics usually note how Isabella's overzealous desire for restrictions signals her extreme repression of the life she is about to abandon outside of the convent walls. Just as important, however, is the protest against conventional sexual definitions initiated here. As Marilyn French points out, we know the convent only by its gender-based rules, which are premised on the assumption that piety necessitates the women's avoidance of men.[12] Holiness ranks above sex and men in the priorities of this world. The women's abstention from sex is not a denial of sexuality, however, but a component in their redefinition of it. Virginity and chastity are as much ways of embracing sexuality as are acts of making love, for chastity is not the emblem of a sexless soul, but the acknowledgment of a sexual desire that will not be acted on. The nuns' choice of a self-willed unavailability indicates a control over their lives that Isabella, however, never achieves. Her chaste sexuality is suspiciously aggressive. While the community of abstemious nuns she is about to join seem contented in their vows of chastity, Isabella substitutes for their acknowledgment of desire a repression of it. Those famous first five lines of the scene notify us that Isabella is not completely harmonized with her community. It is worth stressing that Isabella is only a novitiate, on the eve of taking her religious vows. This too, in a sense, marks her difference from the community of nuns. And this difference will be crucial to Shakespeare, whose Duke eventually offers Isabella the option of a marriage vow to replace a religious one.[13]

As I noted above, Isabella is a paradoxical presence in the play, even among its women; she remains, however, a crucial part of a female community which offers alternatives here. In fact, Isabella's idiosyncratic presence in I.iv is one sign of several complex cultural echoes in the nuns' protected sexuality. Maurice Charney reminds us that because of their chastity, nuns have always been enticing figures for pornography. And Lisa Jardine, in detailing the sexuality Isabella, in particular, inherits from the saints, clarifies the power in such chastity. Such power, she suggests, grows out of the legacy of silence and wrongful accusation contained in the saints' lives, and contributes to the dignity and heroism of Isabella and Francisca's sexual restraint and sequestration.[14] In short, the combination of self-reliance and sexuality implied in the nuns' chastity is a threat to men. In I.iv, the pious life-choices of the women imply the marginality of men in the convent world and register an unvoiced though diversified protest against the male world outside of the nunnery.

Verbal representations of women in I.iv also suggest a reordering of priorities. In this scene, as in others, most of the references to women put them in classes— like those the Duke and Lucio list in V.i—that do not threaten the prevailing order. References to nuns— "the sisterhood, the votarists of Saint Clare" (5) and "sister" (19)—to "maids" and "Maidens" (32, 80), and to "virgins" (33) identify groups of women who are comfortably defined in their relationship to men. All but one of these references comes from Lucio. Isabella opens up the possibilities of meaning that lie beyond such standard definitions of women, however, when she recalls the "apt affection" (48) she and Juliet shared, an affection so intense they have expressed their closeness by adopting the familial term "cousin" for one another. The relationship, significantly, does

not recall any category proposed by the Duke and Lucio because the women are defining themselves outside of their relationship to men. When Isabella calls up the image of herself and Juliet as "schoolmaids" (47) she introduces a second new category of female behavior, one which marks women's intellectual capacities. The double meaning of "sister," first introduced in this scene, also contributes to the broadening of social and sexual roles for women. While Lucio jokes about Isabella's double role as sister—"a novice of this place, and the fair sister / To her unhappy brother, Claudio" (19-20)—for Isabella the double role later becomes a source of power. In II.ii, Angelo is mildly surprised to learn of Isabella's double sisterhood (19-22) and perhaps is disarmed by this conflation of roles. Later in the scene, Isabella instinctively depends on the doubled role, bolstering her pleas as a sibling with the support of her sisterly convent community (II.ii.153-55). Shaken by the fervor of Angelo's sexual desire in II.iv, Isabella is less able to draw on her multivalent power; yet even in her refusal she fuses the meaning of her two sisterly roles to gain some ground:

> And 'twere the cheaper way:
> Better it were a brother died at once
> Than that a sister, by redeeming him,
> Should die forever.
>   (II.iv.105-108)

Although in III.i Isabella separates the two sisterly roles in arguing with Claudio, by V.i—in her plea for justice—she has returned to the power she can call up through the doubleness: "I am the sister of one Claudio . . . I, in probation of a sisterhood" (69, 72).[15] In I.iv women are presented as several things at once: friends, students, novices, siblings, and rhetoricians. They cannot be one-dimensionally stereotyped.

It is not just the women in the scene who benefit from the transformative power of a new set of assumptions. In fact, when Lucio intrudes into the female world of the convent, we get our clearest picture of the alternative sexuality the scene offers. Even though Lucio brings into this world the harsh news of Angelo's laws, both he and his tale are altered by his telling it in this female environment. Lucio, by several accounts the bawdiest character in the play, can here deliver the play's only description of the sexual relationship between Claudio and Juliet which is alluring, lyric, and positive:

> Your brother and his lover have embraced;
> As those that feed grow full, as blossoming time
> That from the seedness the bare fallow brings
> To teeming foison, even so her plenteous womb
> Expresseth his full tilt and husbandry.
>   (I.iv.40-44)

It is dangerous, of course, to take Lucio's words at face value, for he seems to be gauging his usual raucous language for Isabella's unworldly ears. Indeed, his rhetorical proficiency has already been proven in the scene. He has opened with a somewhat stiff and rusty graciousness: "Hail, virgin, if you be, as those cheek-rose / Proclaim you are no less" (16-17). And he has moved through direct jest—"For that which, if myself might be his judge, / He should receive his punishment in thanks" (27-28). Yet as Lucio builds to his description of Claudio and Juliet's relationship, he discards jest and formality, and the resulting directness—"Do not believe it. Fewness and truth, 'tis thus" (39)—flowers into the simple, convincing simile of lines 40 to 44. In spite of the urgency of his mission, in a place the women have made us feel is different, Lucio seems to relax and expresses his message in a language that defers to the values of this female environment. It is hard to know how sincere Lucio is, but at the least the women's world of I.iv has liberated a generous and optimistic sentiment that Lucio does not (or cannot) express elsewhere. Outside of the convent and the influence of its women, Lucio's gracious acceptance of others' sexuality will sour to a petty self-protection. In II.ii, still in the company of Isabella but back in a male world, he reverts to a directness that is harsh, jests that are clever but cutting, and even disrespect—as is clear in his reference to Isabella as a "wench" (124). But in the female space of I.iv, he renounces his "familiar sin" to "jest" with "virgins" (31-33) and is selfless in depicting sex as beautiful and life-producing.

Lucio's role in this scene is emblematic of his connection with the alternative sexuality throughout *Measure for Measure*. Like the women, he is outside of the conventional hierarchies of men's power and must of necessity learn the best ways to make his less-than-welcome voice heard. Lucio has the slight advantage, of course, of retaining the male privilege to make direct his criticisms of authority, as the women rarely can. Lucio shares his welcome in this second society with only one other male, Pompey. Perhaps because of the outcast status Lucio and Pompey share with the women, they alone are able to form relationships with the women on a non-sexual, non-familial basis. In I.iv, Lucio and Isabella initiate a comradely fight to rescue Claudio. And even though Lucio recognizes the sexual overtones of Isabella's pleas to Angelo during II.ii, his responses focus not on them but on her rhetorical skill. Mistress Overdone and Pompey are also able to share an unconventional relationship; because they deal *together* in sex as a business, they too can relate to one another without being confined by a limited model of male-female relationships. But predictably, both men pay a price for their collusion with women. While the play's subversive women are placed under the protection of men, the play's subversive men are imprisoned.

While I.iv does offer two of the women in *Measure for Measure* a rare opportunity to be together, it is even more significant for the way it broadens definitions of women and their sexuality. Here sex is affirmatively attached to life, and the attachment stimulates new attitudes toward men and women. Even though Isabella cannot completely embrace the possibilities of the environment, both she and Lucio appear at their best here. The openness and directness of I.iv are evident again in II.iii, the brief scene in which Juliet and the Duke review her sexual sin. Charney has noted that this scene occupies a significant position separating the tense confrontations of Isabella and Angelo in II.ii and II.iv.[16] Not surprisingly, then, one of this interlude's main functions is to underscore the sexual dimension of the struggle between Angelo and Isabella. Through Juliet's defiance in II.iii, Shakespeare highlights the rejection of conventional power that undergirds Isabella's more obtuse pleas. And when Juliet refuses to align her actions and thoughts with the sexuality the Duke seeks to impose on her, her unexpected assertiveness transforms the scene into a second forum for the play's alternative sexuality.

Two references to Juliet before she enters predict that the standard view of sexuality will not prevail here. The Provost claims her as "a gentlewoman of mine" (10) and describes her compassionately as one "Who, falling in the flaws of her own youth, / Hath blistered her report. She is with child" (11-12). He lacks Lucio's convent-inspired grace and vision, but not his goodwill, a quality rare in the men's responses to women. When Juliet enters, the Duke's catechism on sin and repentance begins, yet his control is compromised almost immediately and for the first time in the play. While Juliet's responses are mainly compliant and her manner decorous, she rejects the equation of female sexuality with sin by following each proper response with a qualification which subverts her original answer *and* the dominant sexuality. When the Duke asks her if she repents the sin she carries, she first replies "I do," but then adds, "and bear the shame most patiently" (20). When the Duke asks her whether she loves Claudio, her "yes" is followed with "as I love the woman that wronged him" (25). Juliet's unmistakable statement of self-love is rare in a play where self-hatred is the rule. Juliet repeats both her subversive independence and her personal contentedness in her final comment to the Duke, when once again her proper answer—"I do repent me as it is an evil"—is followed by her gentle defiance, "and take the shame with joy" (35-36). With this final line, Juliet not only interrupts the Duke, but leaves him only enough room for an uncharacteristically brief and neutral response, "There rest." Juliet accomplishes what few others do in the play: by refusing to accept the Duke's definitions of her sexual act, Juliet takes from the Duke his power to preach, rule, and pontificate.

Juliet refuses to privilege the shame the church attaches to her sexual act and instead proudly affirms her sexuality, her self, and the new life she is carrying.[17] Her decorous defiance also includes a redefinition of male-female relations. She acknowledges the shared responsibility in her sex with Claudio, so that when the Duke reminds her of a double standard which determines "Then was your sin of heavier kind than his," she can accept and absorb his scorn: "I do confess it, and repent it, father." Her repentence, it seems, can come without the shame the Duke seeks to invoke. Both Juliet's independence and her sexual redefinitions influence our responses to Isabella in the two scenes which sandwich II.iii. As we have seen, unlike Juliet's, Isabella's sexuality is largely conditioned by her submission to the dominant order: she represses her sexual urges, denounces sexual desires in others, and finds women responsible for sexual sins. Yet, when Isabella refuses to accept the sexual bargain Angelo offers, her disgust at his power engenders a defiance much like Juliet's. Jardine suggests that Isabella's refusal of the sex Angelo would force on her constitutes the breaking of a stereotype, since Isabella would have been expected to submit to disgrace and then to kill herself.[18] The positioning of Juliet's defiance in II.iii, then, together with Isabella's own protests, suggests that Isabella's integrity—like Juliet's—is threatened by conventional alignments of power and sexuality. Isabella is simply less cognizant of her compromised position than Juliet. Since she has little to lose, Juliet reacts by refusing standard definitions of love and sex; because she has accepted significant portions of these standard definitions, Isabella's recantation of the primary sexuality is less clear.

Juliet makes two other appearances in the play, both silent. In I.iii she appears briefly and pregnant to serve as a visual reminder of her and Claudio's sexual acts. And in V.i, she joins the ranks of the soon-to-be-married. Her words and her subversive compliance in II.iii are, consequently, uncharacteristic and avoidable. Why then does Shakespeare choose to include the prison interlude? At this strategic point, before Isabella is burdened in II.iv with knowledge of Angelo's corruption, we are encouraged to remember that alternatives, especially alternative sexualities, exist in this world. This scene, however, is the last clear expression of such options. After the major tonal shift in III.i, when the Duke resumes his directing role, the play is mainly given over to his drive to fortify the play's dominant sexuality.

There are, however, two more scenes, before Act V, in which the play's alternative sexuality is evident. Neither makes the strong statements of I.iv and II.iii, but both indicate that the women in the play remain the conduits of heterodox sexual attitudes. In IV.i, at Mariana's "moated grange," we return to an environment where women have a respite from male control.[19] And as in II.iii, the Duke enters as an outsider into a

world where women can speak openly and honestly. When we learn from Mariana that she has "sat here all day" (19-20), we register a more leisurely world than the turbulent, discordant Vienna which is the dominant setting in the play. In this new environment, love is the main topic. We begin, in the song, with an acknowledgment that sexual contact can go by the name of love; lovers who up to now in the play have been bodiless acquire "lips" and "eyes." The verse also centers on a metaphor of light and dawn, a rare occurrence in a play that is pervasively dark in both imagery and tone. Even though the song's new day is one of fresh betrayal and self-abusive desire, the darkened love is informed by the play's second sexuality. Mariana's grange, however, mournful, is a home for reveries on the possibilities of love, fulfillment, corporality, and sensuality.

Like Juliet, however, Mariana knows that her relaxed behavior is not sanctioned. Because of this, like Juliet, Mariana has two modes of behavior—one for the Duke and one for a world without the Duke. The boy and his lyrics are dismissed hastily as soon as the Duke appears, and Mariana launches into an excuse for her leisure. The linguistic convolutions of her explanation signal the illogic of her divided life:

> I cry you mercy, sir, and well could wish
> You had not found me here so musical.
> Let me excuse me, and believe me so,
> My mirth it much displeased, but pleased my
>   woe.
>
> (10-13)

As the Duke censures her behavior and her music (almost at her invitation), he assumes control of the scene and the environment; and in the process the alternative world of the grange dissipates. No longer do the women act together as any sort of community, much less suggest an alternative order. While Mariana and Isabella meet for the first time in this scene, they directly exchange only four lines of dialogue (58, 67-69) in seventy-five. Isabella, by this time, has relinquished her passionate protests and her references to alternative options. Early in III.i, her chastity has hardened into a death wish for both herself and her brother, and she gives over any remaining volition to the Duke later in the same scene. Isabella has not, like Juliet or Mariana, displayed a wide range of behaviors dependent on her environment, but by the time of this first scene with Mariana, even her behavior has narrowed and the protests of I.iv, II.ii, and II.iv are gone (except, of course, for moments when the Duke calls them up for his own purposes in the final scene). But while the alternative sexuality of the scene remains more suggestion than actuality, the unusual environment still encourages unconventional actions in the Duke. Although elsewhere he is seen separating people and admonishing sins of collusion, here he brings the two women together, telling Mariana "Take then this your companion by the hand" (54). He also acknowledges the necessity of sex as he manipulates events to allow Mariana and Angelo to consummate their wedding contract. In fact, the location of IV.i may help explain why the Duke sanctions sexual behavior here that he seems to abhor elsewhere. In this world where feelings and flexibility are encouraged, the belated fulfilling of Mariana and Angelo's *de futuro* contract makes every sense and can be encouraged. The Duke's agricultural image is a final sign of his subtle transformation; echoing the natural growth and increase Lucio celebrated in I.iv, the Duke explicitly acknowledges life processes: "Our corn's to reap, for yet our tithe's to sow" (75).

In IV.vi, the last scene before the Duke's triumphant re-entry in V.i, we have our final exposure to the play's other mode. Unlike the other scenes in which an alternative sexuality operates, IV.vi does not take place in a protected environment like the nunnery, the prison, or Mariana's grange. In the transitional space of this scene—a Viennese street—the brief exchange of Isabella and Mariana becomes emblematic of both the alternative order the women have offered and their difficulty in holding onto that alternative once they are reestablished in the official world of Vienna. In the nine lines the women exchange before Friar Peter ushers them off, they discuss the indirect behavior the disguised Duke has directed them to adopt. They comment not only on their upcoming deception, however, but also on the clandestine, subversive nature of their actions throughout the play. Priding herself on her directness, Isabella opens the scene by complaining: "To speak so indirectly I am loath; / I would say the truth" (1-2). Yet by the end of the same four-line speech, she has adopted a passive role—"Yet I am advised to do it" (3). Her passivity, together with the acceptance Mariana urges in her command—"Be ruled by him"—reestablishes here the inclination of the play's women to submit, at least in public, to the desires of others. Thus, in one of the rare moments we see the play's women alone together, we note little of the tentative reorganization suggested in I.iv and II.iii. Instead, we see only the women's consciousness of the indirection they engage in, their reluctance to accept it, and their helplessness in doing anything about it. Our response to their aversion is qualified, however, by our knowledge that both women have, since we saw them last, acted the leading roles in the bed trick. Yet their mendacity is not the compromised behavior it first seems. In the women's sexual paradigm, directness, vitality, and naturalness determine actions; but when the women must operate in the standard sexual paradigm, they adopt the subversive tactics they have needed to survive in the men's world where women are assumed to be concupiscent and threatening bearers of life. Just as Lucio and the Duke modulate their actions and words when in the women's sphere, the

women, in the men's world, pragmatically adopt behaviors that will ensure their survival.

Before I move to the play's final scene, I want to consider Mistress Overdone and her connection to the play's woman-based alternative sexuality. In my scenic analysis above, she has been notably absent. Because of her differences from the play's other women (differences of class and profession) she does not appear in their relatively protected spots; yet her fleeting presence is a telling comment on the sexual redefinition the other women more visibly undertake.

Mistress Overdone appears only twice, under constraints each time. In I.ii, her entry into the bawdy exchange of Lucio and his friends is compromised not only by their ridicule of her but also by her own contradictory behavior. After informing Lucio and the others of Claudio's arrest, she becomes the seemingly uninformed audience for Pompey's lewd jokes about the same news.[20] Perhaps she is deferring to Pompey's authority even though she knows full well what he is about to tell her, and thus is falling in line with the general tendency of the play's women to defer to men. What is more constraining about her appearance in I.ii, however, is that she is mocked from the start. Because she is laughingly equated with sexual disease and sexual excess (she has had nine husbands), the power of her sexuality is trivialized and defused. When Mistress Overdone appears briefly again in III.ii, she is physically constrained, on her way to prison. She is also the solitary woman in an atmosphere increasingly commanded by traditional attitudes toward women. Against condemnation and disgust from Escalus and the Provost, she constructs a meagre self-defense by accusing her accuser Lucio of illegal fornication and by offering the heretical thought of herself as a foster mother to his child. While defiance is implied on the occasion of both scenes, Mistress Overdone finds her voice only briefly, once, in I.ii, when she is left alone on stage (after the exit of Lucio and the gentlemen and before the entrance of Pompey) to bemoan her increasingly difficult situation: "Thus, what with the war, what with the sweat, what with the gallows, and what with poverty, I am custom-shrunk" (I.ii.78-80). This lament connects Mistress Overdone to the play's subversive sexuality, as it offers a compact view of Mistress Overdone as a woman much affected by the sexual laws Angelo imposes. But more importantly, her soliloquy reminds us that Mistress Overdone represents a community of whores who can be found only in the margins of the play. It is the absence of this community which is the most telling aspect of her "presence" in the play. Both Dollimore and Alexander Leggatt have noticed this remarkable void in a play about sexuality.[21] Not only are the women physically absent, but references to Mistress Overdone's business further erase the women by recalling a male community, not a female one (most notable is Pompey's

IV.iii comparison of the prison community to the community at Mistress Overdone's). The ephemeral appearance of Mistress Overdone and the absence of her community of prostitutes both suggest, once more, how women and their sexuality are marginalized in the play. Mistress Overdone does not contribute much to the alternative order the play's other women hint at; but her isolation is in harmony with the dim nature of those other women's attempts to define their lives.

The play's final scene has necessarily become the linchpin for most interpretations of *Measure for Measure*. It has always been a key to characterizations of the Duke and to studies of the play's genre. It must be a part of any analysis of this play's power structures or its portraits of rule. The scene's movements toward closure are also crucial for my reading of the alternative sexuality, for the efforts to establish a sexuality which runs contrary to the play's male order are effectively terminated here. The structure of the scene draws perversely on comedy, but the reestablishment of order that comes with even a forced comic conclusion truncates any liberty or space the women in the play have found (see pp. 15-16 above). Yes, the scene abounds in ironies and may be, as Anthony Dawson contends, "self-subverting,"[22] but in it we watch the firm reassertion of the play's traditional sexuality. Repeated references to women call up stereotypes based on women's concupiscence and sexual culpability. In this scene, as noted earlier we have the Duke and Lucio categorizing women according to types—wife, widow, maid, and punk. There is also the persistent equation of women with sexual desire and sin, when Escalus calls Isabella and Mariana "giglets" (344), and also when the Duke publicly attaches Mariana to sin and conspiracy—"and thou pernicious woman, / Compact with her that's gone" (239-40). Throughout the scene, in fact, one of the principal logical weapons that the Duke wields is his certainty that his audience will want to assume women are weak, concupiscent, and subversive. The indirection that has been foregrounded by Mariana and Isabella in IV.vi is repeatedly attributed to women here by the Duke, Escalus, Angelo, and Lucio, who variously find the women "informal" (234), "pernicious" (239), and "light" (278). Even men who have elsewhere seemed compassionate and sensitive reflexively display such simplistic responses. Escalus allows Lucio to joke about Isabella's night with the Duke (269-80), and Friar Peter (as part of his role in the Duke's scheme) accuses Isabella of lying and sinning (158-62). These charges of overweening desire and subversion all go unanswered by the women who have agreed to lie about certain things and who have learned to be silent about others.

The linguistic stereotyping of the women is reinforced by the choreography of their appearances during the scene. Most important, Isabella and Mariana are separated for most of the 534 lines. Isabella must make her charges against Angelo on her own in the first part of the scene, and later Mariana must confess her entrapment of Angelo without Isabella's presence. And while Isabella may exit after her line at 125, she can, as most editors suggest, remain on stage until 162, in which case her exit immediately precedes Mariana's entrance. The crossing actions accentuate the separation of the two women. When they later plead together for Angelo's life, it is at the Duke's suggestion, not the women's inclination, that they finally coordinate their efforts.

The play's final response to the alternative sexuality the women sporadically intimate lies in the marriages proposed in this scene. In Shakespearean comedy, marriage can be a blessing on love, a sign of order reestablished, a reward for perseverance, or a natural outlet for sexual desire. Yet marriage can also be, as feminist critics like Carol Thomas Neely, Peter Erickson, Shirley Nelson Garner, and Clara Claiborne Park have pointed out, an end to female characters' language and freedom.[23] I suggested earlier that the play's comic plotting encourages an alternative sexuality, even though that alternative is fleeting. In adopting comedy's tumble toward marriage, *Measure for Measure* further highlights the dissonance in its comedy, for the pairing off of Angelo and Mariana, Isabella and the Duke, Claudio and Juliet, and Lucio and Kate Keepdown calls to mind marriage's threat of pain more than its promise of happiness.[24] Throughout the play, marriage has represented everything *but* a dream or a goal. When Claudio adopts marriage as the metaphor for death, for example, he turns marriage's togetherness into doom:

> If I must die,
> I will encounter darkness as a bride,
> And hug it in mine arms.
>
> (III.i.83-85)

For Elbow, as II.i makes clear, marriage is a constant trial of unrewarded watchfulness. And for Angelo and Lucio, marriage is predominantly punishment. Angelo's only verbal response to his forced marriage to Mariana is indirect, but his craving "death more willingly than mercy" (V.i.472) strongly suggests his choice of death over marriage. Lucio has been much more vocal in denouncing marriage. In IV.iii he jokes to the disguised Duke that he has narrowly escaped marriage to the "rotten medlar" he has gotten pregnant (169), and his fear is realized in this final scene when he responds, in horror, to the Duke's actualizing of this very punishment of marriage: "Marrying a punk, my lord, is pressing to death, whipping, and hanging" (V.i.517-18). Along with Claudio and Juliet, who we may assume give silent approval to the marriage ordered for them, only Mariana looks joyously on the prospect of marriage. The others display various shades of reticence. We have seen that horror colors Lucio's response. Angelo asks for death instead of marriage and then resigns himself to silence for the rest of the play when his request is denied. The Duke, who has earlier denied his own need for sex—dismissing it as "the dribbling dart of love" (I.iii.2)—twice offers marriage to Isabella, though only in moments when her emotions are safely engaged elsewhere. And Isabella can only join Angelo in silence as a response to the prospect of marriage. We know his silence is in protest; we can only assume hers *could* be. Such silences and disinclinations, although they carry many other meanings, are the scene's only echo of the play's alternative sexuality: the joylessness of these final marriages suggests that other sexual options *have* disturbed the traditional order.[25] As the final signal of a reestablished order, marriage is a vault in which is buried the play's alternative sexuality.

I can clarify both the tenuousness of this alternative sexuality and its rarity in the canon by examining similar situations in other plays, particularly *All's Well That Ends Well. Measure for Measure*'s comic inversion is a structural reminder, of course, that it shares its general narrative movement with less troubled comedies like *As You Like It, The Merchant of Venice, Much Ado About Nothing,* and *Twelfth Night.* The way Rosalind and Celia clear a space for themselves in the forest of Arden recalls the female enclaves of the nuns or of Mariana, although in *As You Like It,* the heroines must rely on male disguise to gain their leisure and liberty. Rosalind is fully cognizant of sexual double standards and their effect on women, but she can silently join in the comic reversion to the status quo because this play's dominant view of women and their sexuality is characterized more by generosity and love than by fear and misogyny. *The Merchant of Venice* offers an even more enduring alternative order than does *As You Like It.* Belmont is, essentially, a female territory where Portia and Nerissa (later Jessica) promote their definition of male-female relations and sexuality. They are constrained, of course, by the mechanism of the caskets and must, like all of Shakespeare's women, take subversive measures to retain their independence. Yet in spite of such handicaps, Portia alone keeps her world (and that of Venice) sane, and manages to maintain an unruliness to the end of the play.[26] But as in *As You Like It,* the women-powered spaces in *The Merchant of Venice* are less a retreat from misogyny than women's interpretations of their union with men. The comedies are far from being feminist paradises, but they do allow for, even encourage, a dialogue between the sexes that is not entirely on the men's terms.

In marked contrast, *All's Well That Ends Well* reproduces many of the concerns that give rise to *Measure for Measure*'s alternative sexuality. In both plays, sexuality is a troubling preoccupation, chastity is the standard measurement of a woman's worth, an assumed culpability for sin undergirds talk of women, and the

ending is both forced and unfixed. Yet in *All's Well* an alternative sexuality is not the clear result of these conditions. Two major factors account for these differences in *All's Well:* first, since marriage is more central to the narrative development, alternatives to it are not explored; and second, since Helena is, on her own, such a threat to the male order, an alternative sexuality is both less necessary and less viable. This play is a comment on, not a copy of *Measure for Measure*'s multiple sexualities.[27] The best way to register these differences between the plays is to note how in neither of *All's Well*'s women-influenced locations—the home of the Count of Rossillion and the Widow's house in Florence—do women actively pursue non-traditional sexual options for themselves.

While the two spiritual leaders of the Rossillion household, Helena and the Countess, are women, nothing like the alternative sexuality of *Measure for Measure* springs up under their guidance. The women's constant interaction and concern with men and marriage replaces the protest and withdrawal of *Measure for Measure*'s women. For example, I cannot argue, although it is tempting, that in the female environment of the opening scene Helena and Parolles' bantering about virginity establishes an alternative view of women's sexuality. The assumptions about men's and women's sexuality that the exchange is based on are, in fact, little different than those the men later use in similar contests of wits. Virginity, which *Measure for Measure*'s nuns prize as a mature commitment and which Isabella would die for, is here merely an object of banter. For Helena, who would gladly lose her virginity to Bertram, the banter marks a pragmatic step towards marrying him, not a definition of other relational options. In addition, Helena's expression of sexual desire is only seemingly uninhibited. Her delivery of revelatory soliloquies both before and after this exchange suggests that when she is with Parolles neither the time nor the place has allowed for her honest expression.

Neither does the second scene at Rossillion give rise to a woman-influenced counter order. As I.iii opens with the Countess and Lavatch discussing his sexual desires, the Countess' playful responses appear to sanction a non-judgmental view of Lavatch's situation. Yet her acknowledgment of his lust, unabashed as it is, is but a familiar acceptance of the unlasting nature of sexual desire. Her openness, though more unusual in her sex, cannot be attributed to her sex. Of more significance is the fact that while Lavatch talks freely of his sexual desires, his talk is only passively welcomed by the Countess. She does not join in except to prod him to further performance. In I.i it was Parolles; here it is Lavatch who talks of sexual matters. The women are encouraging listeners unwilling or unable to articulate their own opinions. In the meeting of the two women at the end of the scene there is also little evidence for their attachment to an alternative sexuality. Even here Helena relaxes only enough to confess, not confide, her love for Bertram; and although the women conspire to further Helena's dreams, they display little consciousness of being handicapped by the traditional order of things. It is Helena's will to have Bertram, not the women's common sex or their shared affection that moves them from confession to plan of action. When Helena and the Countess next meet at the palace in III.ii, Helena is so distracted by her disgrace at the hands of Bertram that her return has little to do with a reunion of the women (who are never alone together). And once more, Helena can express her true feelings only in soliloquy. Both I.iii and III.ii are models of how the play accommodates its women differently than does *Measure for Measure*. In none of the palace scenes do the women seek release from their bonds with men, and so they have little need to isolate themselves from men or to rail against them.

Neely argues that all the women in the play identify with each other "feeling sympathy and offering help where hostility and rivalry might have been expected."[28] While it is hard to connect such mutual aid between Helena and the Countess with the creation of an environment the women can call their own, in the scenes at the widow's home in Florence, connections among women do mark a spot of relief from men and their assumptions. Yet these scenes also make clearest that Helena's assertiveness has, in large part, replaced the community-based power of *Measure for Measure*'s alternative scenes. Before Helena enters a third of the way through III.v, the Florentine widow, her daughter Diana, and their neighbor Mariana anticipate the appearance of the Florentine army by discussing a maid's peril at the hands of Parolles and Bertram. Although obviously enchanted by Bertram's attentions, Diana acknowledges the truth in Mariana's warnings about endangered maidenhoods. And as Diana pledges "You shall not fear me" (27) she places her ties with women above her infatuation with men. Since women in *Measure for Measure* were not primarily engaged in searching for men, such direct talk about the dangers of sexual entanglements did not transpire there. But the sense of women's shared burden in traditional male-female relationships implicit in *Measure for Measure* is explicit here at the Widow's. The combination of community and protest early in the scene is as close as we come, in *All's Well,* to an alternative women's space. Later in the scene the Widow suggests the bed trick to Helena. Although Helena's new women friends then plan with her an alternative action, their move is guided as much by Helena's desire for Bertram as by the women's belief in the possibility of a different kind of life.

When Helena and the Widow meet two scenes later to transact the business of the bed trick, it is even more evident that Helena's strong character has replaced the kind of alternative that was suggested by enclaves of women in *Measure for Measure*. Helena's appraisal of Bertram's sexual desire for Diana—"Now his important blood will naught deny / That she'll demand" (III.vii.21-22; see also 26-28)—marks her frankest assessment of human sexuality. Yet this moment of Helena's clear-headed assessment is not a sign of a new forthrightness, since its context is her purchase of the Widow and Diana's aid. When compared to Isabella and Mariana's comparatively passive participation in *Measure for Measure*'s bed trick, Helena's single-minded determination seems excessive, tawdry, and selfish. As Jardine points out, it is Helena's education which extends what is already a potent sexual threat in the play.[29] Such intellectual status also separates her from the others; so while Helena's subversive behavior bring her a husband, any benefits (besides monetary) of the alternative action are confined to her.

The tenor of Diana's conference with Bertram in IV.ii underlines, finally, the singular presence of Helena in the play's development. More than any other in *All's Well,* this scene recalls Juliet's defiance of the Duke. At least until Diana begins the ring bartering in line 39, her responses to Bertram neutralize his suggestive comments and suggest alternatives. Though his jargon is love and the Duke's was religion, the pattern of response between man and woman is the same. To Bertram's first plea for physical contact with her, Diana replies by transforming his lust into her honesty and duty (3-13). In her two longer speeches to follow (17-20, 21-31), she continues to speak of truth and of oaths in garden metaphors and with heavenly references that characterize this defiance as hers, not Helena's. And even as she must seem to acquiesce to Bertram later in the scene, her loyalty to a women's sphere echoes Juliet's. Her protest concludes when, after he leaves, she declares herself always chaste— "I live and die a maid" (74). But while Juliet's defiance highlights Isabella's, Diana's is sacrificed to the relentless pursuit of Helena's plan. In the final scene, when Diana's still protestingspirit withstands the aspersions of Bertram, LaFew, and the King, she deftly makes possible Helena's triumph. But she can be repaid by both Helena and the King only with a dowry for a husband she has renounced in IV.ii. In *Measure for Measure* we could blame the Duke for the final, public abuse of Isabella and Mariana. Here we must blame Helena.

Since its suggestions of a second sexuality are sporadic and dim, *All's Well* does not close, like *Measure for Measure,* with a final scene in which forced couplings bury women's unconventional options. Generally marriage—the plot preoccupation throughout—is a tonic, not a punishment. Helena considers it her reward. And even Bertram, who has done his best to escape marriage to Helena, shows us, in his eagerness to wed Maudlin, that it is Helena, not marriage, that he objects to. Although the happiness at the end of the play is forced, at least for Bertram and Diana, protest against it is not a disruption, as in *Measure for Measure*. Both marriage and men are acceptable to women in *All's Well*. And conversely, women are acceptable to men.[30]

In *All's Well* a less forceful dominant sexuality compels a less forceful counter sexuality. And the female protest that exists in the play is channeled into Helena's individual battle, which appears independent from a series of women's spaces. Instead of *Measure for Measure*'s multiple options of chastity, of women's community, of mutually enjoyed sex, *All's Well* offers an assertive woman. *All's Well*'s constricted portrait of sexual relations is, finally, helpful in identifying how Isabella's singular presence contributes to *Measure for Measure*'s alternative sexuality. While the clear misogyny of *Measure for Measure* undoubtedly provokes the feminine counterforce of the women's second sexuality, the strength of its collective locations is a reflection of Isabella's reticence as well as of a tyrannical world.

As this comparison should emphasize, the alternative sexuality of *Measure for Measure* is both unusual and fragile. It is the rare and instructive result of a particular collection of dramatic components. But although it is more suggested than actualized, it cannot be discounted as a spectral re-channeling of sexual desires. This alternative is the acknowledgment of qualities, options, and relations for both men and women not sanctioned by the standard sexual politics. It is the testing of new constellations of power in relationships between men and women. It is the abandonment of restrictive stereotypes. It is the affirmation of bodies and of life. And as *All's Well* makes so clear, this sexuality is nourished only in locales outside the purview of the official paradigm. The play's fond fathers have reconfirmed their power by the final scene of *Measure for Measure*, but the intermittently visible sweet sisters never completely relinquish theirs. The presence of a second sexuality helps explain the tensions of *Measure for Measure* and why, for so long, we have felt inclined to scour the play for indications of joy and affirmation that counterpoint its oppressive sexual morality.

Notes

[1] Quotations from *Measure for Measure* and *All's Well That Ends Well* are taken from *The Pelican Shakespeare*, ed. Alfred Harbage (New York: Viking, 1969).

[2] See Richard P. Wheeler, *Shakespeare's Development and the Problem Comedies: Turn and Counter-Turn* (Berkeley: U of California P, 1981); Meredith Skura,

"New Interpretations forInterpretation in *Measure for Measure*," *Boundary* 27 (Winter 1979): 39-59; Marianne Novy, *Love's Argument: Gender Relations in Shakespeare* [Chapel Hill: U of North Carolina P, 1984); and David Sundelson, *Shakespeare's Restorations of the Father* (New Brunswick: Rutgers UP, 1983). Marilyn Williamson makes a slightly different point in coupling fear of women with fear of a growing population; see her *The Patriarchy of Shakespeare's Comedies* (Detroit: Wayne State UP, 1986).

[3] Stephen Greenblatt, "Invisible Bullets: Renaissance Authority and its Subversion," *Glyph* 8 (1981): 40-61; Jonathan Dollimore, "Introduction: Shakespeare, Cultural Materialism and the New Historicism," in *Political Shakespeare: New Essays in Cultural Materialism,* ed. Dollimore and Alan Sinfield (Ithaca: Cornell UP, 1985) 2-17; Jacqueline Rose, "Sexuality in the Reading of Shakespeare: *Hamlet* and *Measure for Measure*," in *Alternative Shakespeares,* ed. John Drakakis (London: Methuen, 1985) 95-118; Kathleen McLuskie, "The Patriarchal Bard: Feminist Criticism and Shakespeare: *King Lear* and *Measure for Measure*," in *Political Shakespeare* 88-108; Dollimore, "Transgression and Surveillance in *Measure for Measure*," in *Political Shakespeare* 72-87. Anthony Dawson is not writing as directly about women and sexuality, but his reading of *Measure for Measure* in the context of new historicist criticism similarly points to the complexity of making conclusions about the play's sexual politics. See his "*Measure for Measure,* New Historicism, and Theatrical Power," *Shakespeare Quarterly* 39 (1988): 328-41.

[4] See Elizabeth Janeway, "Who is Sylvia? On the Loss of Sexual Paradigms," *Signs* 5 (1980): 573-89; Carole S. Vance, "Gender Systems, Ideology, and Sex Research," in *Powers of Desire: The Politics of Sexuality,* ed. Ann Snitow, Christine Stansell, and Sharon Thompson (New York: Monthly Review Press, 1983) 371-84; Gayle Rubin, "Thinking Sex: Notes For a Radical Theory of the Politics of Sexuality," in *Pleasure and Danger: Exploring Female Sexuality,* ed. Carole S. Vance (Boston: Routledge and Kegan Paul, 1984) 267-319; Jeffrey Weeks, *Sexuality and Its Discontents: Meaning, Myths, and Modern Sexualities* (London: Routledge and Kegan Paul, 1985); and Lawrence Stone, *The Family, Sex, and Marriage in England 1500-1800* (New York: Harper and Row, 1977). There is also much work which relates this notion of mutable sexualities to the psychology of identity formation. See, for example, Julian Henriques, Wendy Hollway, Cathy Irwin, Couze Venn, and Valerie Walkerdine, *Changing the Subject: Psychology, Social Regulations and Subjectivity* (London: Methuen, 1984).

[5] See McLuskie 97-98; and Dollimore, "Transgression and Surveillance" 86.

[6] While the Duke most clearly creates a climate in which women are grammatically objectified—both in

his language and in his directing of the women after III.i—the assumption that women will play passive roles invades the language of nearly every character, from Claudio to Elbow, from Angelo and Escalus to Isabella. Angelo's comment that "these poor informal women are no more / But instruments of some mightier member / That sets them on" (V.i.233-36) puts in sharpest relief the way women are circumscribed by a male-determined grammar of objectification which refuses them volition.

[7] See Wheeler 98, 100, 121-37. Rose notes that such repression is replicated on the critical level, especially in interpretations of Isabella which replace sexual ambiguity with clear censure (103-105).

[8] Lapotaire's comments are related in Judith Cook, *Women in Shakespeare* (London: Harrap, 1980) 43. See also Dollimore, "Transgression and Surveillance" 82. Darryl F. Gless finds, like Lapotaire, that Isabella has fled the world based on her knowledge of it; see his *Measure for Measure, The Law, and the Convent* (Princeton: Princeton UP, 1979) 97-8.

[9] See Marcia Riefer, "'Instruments of Some More Mightier Member': The Constriction of Female Power in *Measure for Measure*," *Shakespeare Quarterly* 35 (1984): 157-69; and Jean E. Howard, "*Measure for Measure* and the Restraints of Convention," *Essays in Literature,* 10 (1983): 149-58.

[10] Skura, 53; Howard, 149-58; Carol Thomas Neely, *Broken Nuptials in Shakespeare's Plays* (New Haven: Yale UP, 1985) 60-2. Covering slightly different territory, Catherine Belsey notes that we can usually gain pleasure from the sexual plurality opened up in Shakespearean comedy. Although she does not refer to *Measure,* she is discussing a liberty similar to that Skura and Howard identify. See her "Disrupting Sexual Difference: Meaning and Gender in the Comedies," in *Alternative Shakespeares* 185.

[11] Dollimore, "Transgression and Surveillance", 73.

[12] Marilyn French, *Shakespeare's Division of Experience* (New York: Summit Books, 1982) 189.

[13] M. C. Bradbrook offers a careful reading of the possibilities for Isabella's religious status. While she suggests that references to Isabella as "a sister" in II.iv.18 and III.i.150 technically should indicate that Isabella *has* taken her vows (perhaps between the first and second interviews with the Duke), she concludes, more reasonably, that Isabella has probably deferred her vows. See "Authority, Truth, and Justice in *Measure for Measure*," in *William Shakespeare's Measure for Measure,* ed. Harold Bloom (New York: Chelsea House, 1987) 13; rpt. from *Review of English Studies* 17.68 (1941).

[14] Maurice Charney, "'To Catch a Saint': Sexual Reciprocities in *Measure for Measure,*" *Shakespeare Bulletin* 21 (1983): 13-16; Lisa Jardine, *Still Harping on Daughters: Women and Drama in the Age of Shakespeare* (Sussex: Harvester Press, 1983) 186-91.

[15] A. P. Rossiter more generally speaks of a doubleness in Isabella's character, although he does not read this as a sign of strength. See his work on *Measure for Measure* from *Angel With Horns,* ed. Graham Storey (Longman, Green, & Co., Ltd. Theatre Art Books, 1961); rpt. in *William Shakespeare's Measure for Measure:* 51-4.

[16] Charney 15.

[17] Juliet's obvious pregnancy and its affirmation of life are repeated in the pregnancies of Mistress Elbow and Kate Keepdown. Elizabeth Sacks also argues that Mariana is pregnant by the end of the play, and that Isabella soon will be. See her *Shakespeare's Images of Pregnancy* (London: Macmillan, 1980) 55. Such possibilities only reinforce my argument that the women of *Measure for Measure* represent a vitality feared by most of the play's men.

[18] Jardine, *Still Harping* 190-2.

[19] Gless interprets the isolation of Mariana's grange negatively, suggesting that the confinement here, like that in the play's prison, "generates an atmosphere of claustrophobic repression" (95-96). My disagreement with this reading rests on the autonomy that women have a chance at only in such unsanctioned locales.

[20] Mistress Overdone's strange behavior may be the result of authorial error. Nevertheless, it functions curiously well as an example of women's public deference to the play's men.

[21] See Dollimore, "Transgression and Surveillance" 86; and Alexander Leggatt, "Substitution in *Measure for Measure,*" *Shakespeare Quarterly* 39 (1988): 356.

[22] Dawson 338.

[23] See Neely, *Broken Nuptials in Shakespeare's Plays;* Peter Erickson, "Sexual Politics and Social Structure in *As You Like It,*" *Massachusetts Review* 23 (1982): 65-83; Shirley Nelson Garner, "*A Midsummer Night's Dream:* 'Jack Shall have Jill: / Nought shall go ill,'" *Women's Studies* 9 (1981): 47-63; Clara Claiborne Park, "As We Like It: How a Girl can be Smart and Still Popular," in *The Women's Part: Feminist Criticism of Shakespeare* (Urbana: U of Illinois P, 1980) 110-16.

[24] Williamson discusses the dissociation between marriage and desire in the play (101-5).

[25] See Philip C. McGuire for a thorough analysis of the silences which surround this play's conclusion in marriage: *Speechless Dialect: Shakespeare's Open Silences* (Berkeley: U of California P, 1985) 63-93.

[26] Both Lisa Jardine and Karen Newman refer specifically to Portia's continued "unruliness." See Jardine's "Cultural Confusion and Shakespeare's Learned Heroines: 'These are old paradoxes,'" *Shakespeare Quarterly* 38 (1987): 16-18; and Newman's "Portia's Ring: Unruly Women and Structures of Exchange in *The Merchant of Venice, Shakespeare Quarterly* 38 (1987): 19-33.

[27] Neely studies thoroughly the image of marriage in *All's Well;* see *Broken Nuptials* 64-92. Jardine amplifies the potent threat Helena so singly represents by suggesting that her threats of sexuality are bolstered by her rare intellectual accomplishments. See her "Cultural Confusion and Shakespeare's Learned Heroines." My work on *All's Well* has also been influenced by Barbara Hodgdon's "The Making of Virgins and Mothers: Sexual Signs, Substitute Scenes and Doubled Presences in *All's Well That Ends Well,*" *Philological Quarterly* (1987): 47-71. Hodgdon finds the play's sexuality is expressed clandestinely, in a series of doubles and substitutes.

[28] Neely 74.

[29] Jardine, "Cultural Confusion and Shakespeare's Learned Heroines" 5-12.

[30] My reading of the position of women at the end of the play differs from both Williamson's and Neely's. Williamson argues that Shakespeare's splitting of his central female figure into Helena and Diana diffuses women's power (69-72). In her discussion of the women in the play, Williamson rarelywrites of the women together, suggesting how easy it is, even in a feminist analysis of the play, to deal with the play's women only in relation to men. Neely *does* directly write about the community of women in the play, finding ultimately that the women's bonds—especially those of Helena, Diana, and the Widow—are so strong that they intrude on the traditional heterosexual coupling of the play's conclusion (72-78).

STRUCTURE, IMAGERY, AND INCONSISTENCIES

Herbert Weil, Jr. (essay date 1970)

SOURCE: "Form and Contexts in *Measure for Measure*," in *Critical Quarterly,* Vol. 12, No. 1, Spring, 1970, pp. 55-72.

[*In the essay that follows, Weil studies the apparent discrepancies between the form of the first and second halves of* Measure for Measure, *arguing that Shakespeare's design can be viewed as comprehensive only if the play's falling action "is played in a light comic, often farcical, vein." Weil maintains that Shakespeare parodies the melodrama of his sources and highlights the limitations of comic conventions, but at the same time "stretches them into new possibilities."*]

I

Among the most challenging problems presented by *Measure for Measure* is why Shakespeare so thoroughly terminates before mid-play the dramatic intensity of his early acts. Although readers and critics have recognized this slackening of tension and suspense, few have been willing to grant that the dramatist may have carefully planned this change of mode. None, so far as I can discover, has shown convincingly why he turns his action to such frustrating anti-climax. Nor has any critic presented a theory of the play's unity that indicates why Shakespeare chose most of the details we find in his last acts. I feel that only if much of the descending action is played in a light comic, often farcical, vein, can all of its speeches fit into a comprehensive design.[1] I use the phrases 'light comic' and 'broad comedy' to represent passages which aim to arouse our laughter as our *immediate* response. This need not limit the seriousness of the subject matter, the after-effects, or the implications. Comedy then does not indicate any lack of serious thematic relevance or resonance—unlike the limited seriousness of threats in the fable.

Unless we recognize this increasingly comic mode we cannot understand the unusual formal coherence that Shakespeare creates through his juxtaposition of such discordant elements as potential tragedy and farce. Until the decisive change in Act III, our responses alternate between moderate suspense for the main plot and laughter at the sub-plot—perhaps mingled with some confusion. After the eavesdropping Duke Vincentio, disguised as a friar, steps in to interrupt Isabella's angry denunciation of her brother Claudio, powerful moral and intellectual concerns seem to be ignored. The resulting frustration felt by most readers and critics has been a major cause for two prevalent, but misleading, attitudes toward the final and longer part of the play. One interpretation recognizes that mode and spirit do change drastically in Act III, scene 1, but maintains that thereafter the play is carelessly conceived and carelessly executed.[2] The most common and influential examples of this approach tend to view the play as if it were tragicomic melodrama; they continue to emphasize the threats posed by the villain Angelo. The other approach argues for the play's unity by focussing upon the character of the Duke.[3] But its proponents find this unity only at the expense of neglecting significant speeches which suggest a paradoxical conflict between the Duke's role and his moral attributes. Prompt-books for every production of *Measure for Measure* since 1945 at Startford-on-Avon show significant cuts in passages that tug against playing the Duke as heroic or as reliable.

Critics seeking excitement and deepening involvement with Isabella or Angelo naturally find the final acts lacking in proper seriousness. Critics who see the play as successfully unified about the Duke, in effect, ask us to believe that the play becomes more serious in its second half—that the seriousness of characters and story are sacrificed for some higher seriousness. In so arguing, they falsify the relaxed confident mood of the final acts. Both of these approaches impose on the play's descending action demands that Shakespeare makes no attempt to satisfy. Consequently they prevent any valid judgment of the unity and accomplishment of the play as a whole. I shall attempt to show how deliberately Shakespeare alters both the mode and structure of his sources and of his own opening acts. With the discordant form that results, he attempts to create an unusual direction for our disappointment at the failure of his action to resolve in convincing depth the moral dilemmas and physical dangers his characters face.

Especially significant is the way in which Shakespeare carefully calls our attention to the extreme shift in subject matter, style, and tone at that moment—Act III, scene 1, line 152—when the Duke interrupts Isabella's outburst against her brother.[4] For the remainder of the play, the Duke and the comic characters—Lucio, Pompey. Barnardine—become increasingly prominent. Whenever Lucio or Pompey is on-stage, he tends to transform the spirit of the play with irreverent jests. This comic mode, foreshadowed at intervals during the earlier acts, now affects every aspect of the situation of the monstrous proposal—including the Duke who takes it in hand. Those critics who admire him with few reservations lean too heavily on the power of the Duke to avert any catastrophe. They do not explain why he speaks in such an awkward and pompous way nor why he repeatedly makes a fool of himself in response to Lucio and Barnardine.

Because the fifth act of *Measure for Measure* mirrors the structure of the whole play, it supports our discovery of Shakespeare's carefully planned design. As in the complete action, reversal, discordance, and anticlimax are vital. Major moral problems are first convincingly posed and then resolved very superficially or evaded altogether. By treating this final act as a mirror as well as a conclusion, we return to the difficulties created by the use of the spectator's frustrated involvement. Is *Measure for Measure* a better play because Shakespeare engages our minds with significant moral questions—the relation of justice to mercy, of chastity to sexual license—even though the play's action does not work them out in any depth? What finally holds the play together when the author so strikingly changes its spirit and the responses of his audience?

II

Most emphatic among the objections to the descending action of *Measure for Measure* is the preface to the new Cambridge edition by Sir Arthur Quiller-Couch. He accurately observes that, after the Duke intervenes, subject matter and style generally lose the intense vigorous quality of earlier passages. This has been generally accepted, but Quiller-Couch goes on to claim:

> The two halves of this scene cannot be made of a piece by anyone possessing even a rudimentary acquaintance with English prose and poetry . . . We say confidently that the two parts could not have been written by the same man, at one spell, on one inspiration, or with anything like an identical or even continuous poetic purpose.[5]

Although many of us may have shared his disappointment during our first reading, we should not argue from our initial response that there is a major flaw in Shakespeare's design. Shakespeare prepares for this reversal and takes pains to make it so conspicuous. He uses it to signal his audience that they should not feel disturbed suspense over the dangers to the heretofore prominent Claudio and Isabella. The scenes to follow are not melodramatic; they should be played as broad comedy of farcical insults, non-sequiturs, and fantasy.

If the spectator is to feel a radical shift of emphasis after the impassioned debates, the comic elements in the early scenes must not stand out too strongly. But if the shift in tone and emphasis is to surprise the spectator rather than shock or amaze him, the early acts must contain the seeds that make the later change credible. This Shakespeare accomplishes through his use of the comic sub-plot. In an atmosphere of coarse (and, at times, perhaps intentionally humourless) jesting, we first learn about the central situation of the main plot, the sentencing of Claudio to death. Through Lucio, Pompey, and Mistress Overdone, the spectator further learns about the widespread corruption in the city, about Angelo's proclamations that close the houses of prostitution and reinstate the long dormant death penalty against fornication, and about Isabella at the convent of St. Clare. After feeling offended by Lucio's initial greeting, the heroine quickly recovers and becomes closely linked with him. He accompanies the girl to her first debate with Angelo, and she later defends him against the angry Duke.

In addition to these expository functions, Shakespeare's comic characters help establish an important, unobtrusive rhythm. Repeatedly, an idealistic statement is succeeded by clowning and broad jests. In the first scene of the play, the Duke delegates his power to Angelo, claiming that he has no time to explain his motives, but taking time to expound upon the ruler's duties and the need for mercy. Instead of developing or applying directly any of these principles, Shakespeare shifts to a scene of broad comic gossip and jesting about venereal disease. When we first see Isabella in scene iv, she is requesting 'a more strict restraint' upon the sisters of the convent. Lucio then bursts in to interrupt with his mood-shattering. 'Hail virgin, if you be'. The next scene opens with an argument between Escalus and Angelo, who insists that penalizing fornication with death is proper and that his own virtue will support his extreme decree. But any expectation we might have that Angelo's lines will lead to a straight-forward investigation of the nature of justice or to a development of tragic potentialities for the judge or his prisoner is promptly eliminated. The constable Elbow and the tapster Pompey enter, and in the broadest farce of the ascending action use Angelo and Escalus as straight men, constantly interrupting their judges and each other. Angelo reveals mainly his inability to deal with concrete problems of corruption, but he does so in a joyous context that leads to Elbow's defence of his wife:

> If ever I was respected with her, or she with me,
> let not your worship think me the poor Duke's
> officer. Prove this, thou wicked Hannibal, or I'll
> have mine action of battery on thee.
>
> (II. 1. 814-8)

From this use of comic characters for exposition, atmosphere, and rhythm, we, of course, receive no certain proof that the story will end happily. But such frequent comic interruptions, combined with the audience's knowledge that the Duke is watching over Angelo, should help prevent our feeling that there has been no adequate preparation for the relaxed optimistic mood of the final acts.

Rather than try to hide the disparities between the two halves of his play by involving our emotions, Shakespeare calls our attention to his changes by unmistakable contradictions and discords. As the ascending action of *Measure for Measure* ends in the midst of Act III, scene i, the highest ethical position of each character in the plot of the monstrous proposal has been shattered. Angelo has learned that his self-controlled purity has been an illusion; Claudio has learned that his resolution to die nobly is weak; and Isabella has shown the audience that her love of mercy is not reflected in her action toward her brother. She cannot sympathize with Claudio's cowardice and his desire to live; her last words to him are:

> Mercy to thee would prove itself a bawd.
> 'Tis best thou diest quickly.

Because these three characters can neither resolve their dilemmas not face them nobly, it becomes necessary for an outsider to assume control over these problems.

But no sooner does Vincentio step from his hiding place than the play's mode shifts completely into another key. The Duke opens the descending action with praise for Isabella at her most brutal moment with deceptive lies to Claudio that would deprive him of all hope to live, and with his proposal of the bed-trick. Even the Duke's clumsy prose, full of awkward repetitions, formulas, and clichés, contrasts sharply with Isabella's preceding lines of blank verse ranting. It is surely significant that this transition comes in mid-scene when we are most likely to notice it.

Such a transition clearly suggests that there will no longer be any real dangers on the story level; it should also prepare us for a dénouement that does not depend on careful moral deliberation. There is little visible need for the Duke's deception of Claudio in such statements as 'Angelo had never the purpose to corrupt her [Isabella]' or 'tomorrow you must die;' these lies can hardly be accorded the intensity or verisimilitude which the debates have established. Only a few lines later, the Friar introduces his device of the bed-trick which, if it is successful, will contradict his statements to the condemned Claudio. Even if attentive spectators who notice these discrepancies have no ready explanations for them, they would realize that they were no longer to take the dilemmas and dangers of Claudio and Isabella with the seriousness that they deserved in the ascending action. Isabella now need only acquiesce in the devices arranged by the Friar. Claudio does not even receive an honest account of his temporal situation. Until the end of the play, he is rarely on stage and apparently should only prepare himself for death.

The language of the Duke suggests how the mode changes from danger, debate, and moral responsibility to mere justification of non-moral plot devices. He offers a rather long-winded defence of the bed-trick, concluding, 'the doubleness of the benefit defends the deceit from reproof.' Interestingly enough, Vincentio here, to justify a trick, uses ethical arguments strikingly similar to those Isabella rejected when they were used by Claudio and which her prototype accepted and acted upon in *Promos and Cassandra*.[6] Although she refused to sacrifice her virginity when Claudio, attempting to save his life, begged, 'Nature dispenses with the deed so far that it becomes a virtue,' she agrees happily to the Duke's scheme for Mariana, The image of it gives me content already; and I trust it will grow to a most prosperous perfection.'

That Shakespeare in *All's Well That Ends Well* and twice in *Measure for Measure* provides extended expository apology for the bed-trick, seems to indicate that he could not, or felt that he could not, rely on the facile acceptance by his audience of this familiar convention.[7] His procedure indicates that he does not want any such unquestioning acceptance; he uses the general mood of his scene and the Duke's clumsy reiterative explanations to Isabella in order to suggest to his audiences that they are no longer watching the same morally serious world as that of the ascending action. This focal scene shows us that he intends us to change our perspective as he changes his tone.

Shakespeare's treatment of the turning point in his action distinguishes him from the writer of melodrama. This term, however anachronistic, describes clearly the dominant mode in the sources and analogues for *Measure*. In effective melodrama, the writer cannot invite a detached and critical response to his plot mechanics, much less burlesque them. The spectator at a melodrama usually suspends any belief he might have that a dire and seemingly inevitable catastrophe will be averted. Because he must not feel any relaxed confidence in a happy ending, he must not be shown how that ending will be reached. In *Measure for Measure,* however, before mid-play we share the knowledge of the controlling character and feel sure that the dangers will not come to pass.[8]

Through the remainder of the episodic third and fourth acts, the stage is dominated by the Duke and by comic characters who establish the mood and who insist on commenting about the main action. Shakespeare changes his dramatic focus by repeatedly inventing new, incidental and often comic characters—Mariana, Kate Keepdown, Barnardine, Ragozine, Abhorson— as foils for figures in both main and sub-plot. These new characters draw our attention from, and tend to decrease our involvement with, Angelo's potential victims, Claudio and Isabella. In addition, Shakespeare reduces the activity of these formerly prominent characters, while he increases that of the Duke. During the descending action either Duke Vincentio or some comic character is present for all but seventy lines. The sequence of substitutions through which Vincentio saves Claudio becomes progressively more farfetched. Although the Duke has successfully preserved Isabella's chastity by substituting Mariana for her in Angelo's bed, his first trick has failed to save Claudio's life. Because Angelo breaks his agreement, Claudio's situation—to outward appearance—remains what it was before either Isabella or the Duke interfered. Conveniently, the Duke discovers a substitute for Claudio, one Barnardine. This prisoner, we learn, is 'Drunk many times a day,' is 'fearless of what's past, present, or to come,' and 'hath evermore the liberty of the prison; give him leave to escape hence, he would not.' Why he is offered the opportunity to run away we never discover, for Barnardine is represented with the minimal credibility he needs to be a foil for Claudio and a test for the Friar. The tone of this episode is set by the first lines spoken to him—Pompey's 'Master

Barnardine, you must rise and be hanged, Master Barnardine.' The condemned criminal refuses the clown, 'Away you rogue. I am sleepy.' He will treat the disguised Duke in the same way. When the Duke begins his instruction, 'Sir, induced by my charity and hearing how hastily you are to depart, I am come to advise you, comfort you and pray with you,' the impatient prisoner refuses to listen:

> Friar, not I: I have been drinking hard all night
> . . . I will not consent to die this day, that's
> certain . . . I swear I will not die today for any
> man's persuasion.
>
> (IV. iii. 56-63)

And he does not. After interrupting the Friar-Duke, he storms off the stage, reappearing only in the final act to receive an unconditional pardon.

It is hard to imagine playing this scene as anything other than broad comedy. And it is even more difficult to take seriously the device which finally succeeds in saving the life of Claudio. Only seven lines after Barnardine leaves, the Duke and the audience suddenly learn, 'There died this morning of a cruel fever/One Ragozine, a most notorious pirate/A man of Claudio's years.' The Duke exclaims, 'O, 'tis an accident that heaven provides!' and dispatches his head to Angelo.

Such a fast-paced farcical treatment of Claudio's impending execution eliminates any possible fear or tension the most literal-minded spectator might feel. Even if he has somehow taken quite earnestly the Duke's plans for the substitution of Mariana, the second and third ready-made substitutions would strain his belief. They clearly push too far an initially shaky plot device. Barnardine's unwillingness to serve as a substitute parodies Mariana's docility and transforms a grotesque situation into broad comedy. By such exaggeration, Shakespeare signals that he does not wish the spectator to remain emotionally involved with his story.

Barnardine's refusal to cooperate with the Duke climaxes a series of meetings between the disguised ruler and the comic characters. These scenes help to set the tone of the descending action. More important, but less obviously, they reflect essential personal traits in the controlling character himself. For all his power and good intentions, Vincentio, when confronted by a member of the sub-plot, usually tends to become a comic character himself. The comic aspects of the Duke apparently need stressing because most recent critics who praise the unity of *Measure for Measure* focus on his character or role but tend to omit any thorough discussion of his shortcomings. G. Wilson Knight, F. R. Leavis, Francis Fergusson, and David L. Stevenson treat the Duke either as a symbol for Divine Providence, as a tribute to the newly crowned James I, as the ideal ruler, or as a figure for the author-director, 'whose attitude, nothing could be plainer, is meant to be ours.'[9] It is often argued that the Duke as director of the action provides its unity by working out some central theme, usually the relation of justice to mercy or of chastity to natural sexual desires. But a unifying theory based upon the virtues of the Duke leaves unexplained such major questions about the final acts as: Why does Lucio so constantly harass the disguised Duke with 'compliments' to his lenient rule and his alleged sexual prowess? Why does the Duke-Friar use such clumsy devices to manipulate the action? Why does he tell Isabella in Act V that her petition for Angelo's pardon is in vain? And why does he repeatedly praise himself with such awkward prose? Studies that discover a neat, allegorical resolution to *Measure for Measure* do not recognize how fully the split in mid-play has affected its mode.

Perhaps our best evidence that the reiterated and verbose self-praise by the Duke is not merely awkward or careless writing comes from his direct confrontations with the comic characters. After his interview with Claudio and Isabella, in quick succession Vincention meets Elbow, Pompey, Lucio and Mistress Overdone. These meetings help create contexts for the Duke's behaviour quite unlikethose in the earlier acts when he never confronted any of the comic characters. Now the Duke's reactions to them, usually exaggerated beyond either the requirements of the plot or the demands of verisimilitude, betray his own character. For example, the Duke, just after leaving Isabella, shows his lack of competence and compassion when he sees Elbow and Pompey. Elbow appears only twice in *Measure for Measure*. Each time he is leading Pompey to jail. The parallel responses that the constable and his prisoner elicit, first from Angelo and then from the disguised Duke, provide an important implicit connection between the ruler and his deputy. Vincentio first exclaims, 'O heavens! what stuff is here?', and then goes on to berate Pompey:

> A bawd, a wicked bawd!
> The evil that thou causest to be done,
> That is thy means to live. Do thou but think
> What 'tis to cram a maw or clothe a back
> From such a filthy vice . . .
> Canst thou believe thy living is a life,
> So stinkingly depending?
>
> (III. ii. 20)[9]

Pompey stumbles, admits that his life does 'stink in some sort, sir, but yet, sir, I would prove . . . ' The Friar does not permit Pompey to finish. As if forgetting his disguise, Vincentio instructs his constable. 'Take him to prison, officer . . . This rude beast will profit.' Like Isabella's outburst against Claudio at the climax of the previous scene, the Friar-Duke's attack on Pompey is meant to show us angry vituperation far

in excess of any immediate justification. His lines remind us of Angelo's disgust at Elbow and Pompey and his desire that both be punished.

Two choral comments tend to reinforce this exposure of flaws that Vincentio does not recognize in himself. His next speech about 'the rude beast' Pompey is a cryptic aside:

> That we were all, as some would seem to be,
> [Free] from our faults, as faults from seeming
>   free.
>
> (III. ii. 40-1)[10]

With the protracted wordplay and the enforced emphasis of the eighteen monosyllables in this couplet, the Duke shifts the tone of the dialogue and interrupts the action. Vincentio suggests how Pompey (the final 'faults') is superior to the idealistic, hypocritical Angelo The Duke acknowledges—for this one moment—virtues in the comic characters that the spectator has probably long felt. Pompey's essential quality has been captured during his first arrest when he answers Escalus, 'I am a poor fellow that would live.' When we last see him he gaily presents the most concrete, visual example Shakespeare will provide of reform in corrupt Vienna: 'I have been an unlawful bawd time out of hand, but yet I will be content to be a lawful hangman.' In this delight, vitality, and flexibility, not in any disgust or morbid cynicism, lies the spirit of the comic sub-plot.[11] Unlike Angelo, unlike most men, and unlike the Duke himself, Pompey and the comic characters avoid all 'seeming' or pretence to a virtue they do not possess.

Lucio, like Barnardine and Pompey, reminds us that Vincentio is not as noble as he thinks himself.Their arguments are central in the descending action, much as Isabella's debate with Angelo had been in the earlier acts. The audience knows that Lucio cannot win, that the Friar is really the Duke. But even with all his advantages, the Duke appears foolish. Often we laugh at the Duke's imperceptive egoism as he turns Lucio's intended compliments into insults. It is clear that Lucio incriminates himself with 'pretty tales of the Duke' and of his own wenching. But if we notice only this obvious, facile self-revelation, we miss completely the richness and suggestiveness of their doubled-edged witcombats. Lucio first greets the disguised Duke with varied rumours concerning his absence, concluding, 'It was a mad fantastical trick of him to steal from the state and usurp the beggary he was never born to.' He then leads Vincentio into defending the harsh measures of Angelo. With his most hyperbolic comic metaphors, Lucio declares that, 'Angelo was not made by man and woman after this downright way of creation . . . Some report a sea-maid spawned him; some that he was begot between two stock-fishes. But it is certain that when he makes water his urine is congealed ice, that I know to be true.' In burlesquing Angelo's view that denies the natural in procreation, Lucio shifts his idiom easily, from fantastic rumour to fantastic certainty. Equally fantastic are the rumours he repeats and his claims to certain knowledge.

Lucio means to compliment the Duke both as ruler and as man by contrasts with the unnaturally cruel Angelo:

> Why, what a ruthless thing is this in him, for the rebellion of a cod-piece to take away the life of a man! Would the Duke that is absent have done this? Ere he would have hanged a man for getting a hundred bastards, he would have paid for the nursing a thousand. He had some feeling of the Sport, he knew the service, and that instructed him to mercy.
>
>   (III. ii. 121-8)

Angered by the sexual allusion, Vincentio praises himself, thereby denying Lucio's statements and leading his comic gadfly on to exaggerate, in turn, his alleged knowledge of the 'absent' Duke. When the Duke commends himself, 'Wise? Why no question but what he was,' Lucio now takes the opposite stance, 'A very uperficial, ignorant, unweighing fellow.' Losing all self-control, the angered Duke explodes:

> Either this is envy in you, folly, or mistaking. The very stream of his life and business he hath helmed must, upon a warranted need, give him a better proclamation. Let him be but testimonied in his own bringingsforth, and he shall appear to the envious, a scholar, a statesman, and a soldier.
>
>   (III. ii. 149-55)

I find it difficult to believe that the audience was expected to treat such self-praise as reliable characterization. To interpret the Duke as a tribute to James I, as the ideal Renaissance ruler, or as an allegorical figure for Providence requires that we ignore his angry and wonderfully funny reactions to Lucio.

As Duke Vincentio repeatedly defends Angelo and stresses his own puritanical abhorrence of sex, his resemblance to the deputy becomes much more clear. Although Lucio's allegations may be unfair to the Duke as a private person, they are credible deductions from his negligent practice as a ruler. Ironic self-incrimination is suggested in Lucio's 'Friar, thou knowest not the Duke so well as I do.He's a better woodman than thou tak'st him for.' Lucio speaks to the character who earlier declared, 'Believe not the dribbling dart of love can pierce a complete bosom (I. iii. 1).' We might well expect such lines from Angelo. The misogyny and pride so emphatically expressed are carefully placed at the opening of scene iii when the Duke 'returns' to Vienna and discloses to the audience the

deception he practised in the opening scene. The Duke who moves from this description of himself to propose marriage with the Isabella who wants to be a nun may well be a better 'woodman' than he recognizes. Vincentio offers in the lighter contexts of the final half of the play a clear parallel to Angelo's false confidence in his ability to rule efficiently and to resist love or temptation. And Lucio repeatedly scores these failures in the man who 'above all other strifes contended especially to know himself.'

III

This presentation of the Duke as a well-meaning powerful figure who delights in his own manoeuvring but who fails to understand his own weaknesses will help explain many otherwise perplexing details of Act V. Much of this act must seem trite or irrelevant if one attempts to understand the play either as a romantic melodrama designed to arouse suspense over the fate of threatened characters or as a didactic morality which demonstrates the fair and proper meting out of justice and mercy by the ruler. For example, most commentators have felt that after the Duke reveals that he has saved Claudio, Shakespeare simply forgot to give speeches to the boy and to his sister, for each remains silent. Shakespeare seems, however, to attend carefully in his closing lines to such minor details as the Provost's failure to carry out Angelo's order and the freeing of Barnardine. In fact, Shakespeare in his final lines spends more time on the pardoning of Barnardine and on the punishing of Lucio than on any of the major characters from the monstrous proposal plot.

But Shakespeare's conclusion becomes readily intelligible when we view this last act as a mirror of his structure and strategy throughout the play. In the first part of the scene, we watch the devices of the Duke (about which the audience has been specifically forewarned in the closing moments of Act IV) and his comic badgering by Lucio. The Duke's praise for Angelo recalls the play's opening scene; Angelo tries his accusers, Isabella and Mariana, as he judged Pompey. The emotional and ethical climax comes in Isabella's plea that Angelo be spared. Her speech works out a moral pattern that has been implicit since her petition for Claudio. It therefore should not surprise the reader but rather impress him as morally and formally right. Like her suit to Angelo for Claudio, it is refused—to be succeeded, again, by the intentional anticlimax of the Duke's manipulating—his hasty pardons, marriage proposal, and extended dialogue with Lucio.

The need to resolve the main plot, which has hinged on Angelo's 'monstrous proposal' and Isabella's response, can explain why the heroine and Mariana accuse the deputy. But only the demands of the broadly comic perspective established by the descending action can account for Vincentio's surprising departure in the midst of the trial when he leaves instructing Angelo as deputy to punish his accusers 'to the height of your pleasure.'

Why, when Angelo has been truly accused, should he be left to judge his own case? Isabella and Mariana—mingling truth with falsehood—have claimed that Angelo has lain with them. Isabella's false charge has seemed true to Angelo; Mariana's true accusation has made public information about Angelo's behaviour that only the Duke, the two women, and the audience knew. The continueddeception is not necessary as a means to trap Angelo. He promptly and simply confesses 100 lines later when Lucio pulls the Friar's hood from the Duke. The multiple lies and Vincentio's unjust delegation of power—which he himself shortly will attack while wearing the Friar's habit—are necessary only so that an aspect of the story, seemingly secondary to the monstrous proposal plot, can be included in the resolution. Shakespeare has constructed his act carefully so that his dramatic emphasis falls upon the disguises and manipulation of the Duke.

When he returns to the stage, again disguised as Friar Lodovick, the Duke, who has always refused to listen to comparable criticism by Lucio or Pompey, strongly objects to his own policy and rule. Now as he addresses Isabella and Mariana, he claims:

> The Duke's unjust . . . to put your trial in the villain's mouth . . . I have seen corruption boil and bubble till it o'er-run the stew; laws for all faults stand like the forfeits in a barber's shop as much in mock as mark.

These lines have the surface function of leading Lucio on so the Duke can spring his carefully laid trap. But they also bind the Duke's role as ruler more closely to his personal character. Because Vincentio has consistently shown himself to be inefficient and sometimes unmerciful, we cannot consider his initial departure from Vienna and his disguise as mere plot devices.

Only the Duke's desire to emphasize his own tricks and their effectiveness in preserving Claudio explains why the ruler handles Isabella's petition as he does—first carefully shaping the context in which she pleads and then denying her request for mercy. There should be little doubt of the rightness of Isabella's petition. On formal grounds, she makes the only satisfying choice. Isabella earlier told Angelo she would grant mercy if she were in his position; Angelo has repented and confessed; we know his crimes have been only of intent, except for his lying with Mariana, and we certainly expect the final resolution to pardon Claudio for a similar 'crime'. Perhaps most important, mercy fulfills the highest moral ideal of the play's action. Here in her final speech Isabella shows extremely effective humility and simplicity. Earlier she has shown an ide-

alized devotion to mercy, but no ability to practise it. In her scene with Claudio, we ignore Shakespeare's dynamic moral action if we emphasize the rightness of Isabella's decision to preserve her chastity, rather than the cruelty with which she answers the brother she believes soon to be executed. Because her choice of mercy is not inevitable, her truly merciful behaviour to Angelo is the moral climax of the play. This climax achieves its success largely because it grows from and momentarily transcends the confused and untested values which Isabella upheld. It satisfies us because Shakespeare creates a situation that would permit a cynical or grotesque conclusion—and then rejects the conclusion. He thereby gives us the feeling that, even in this world of Vienna, the morally and logically right decision can be made.

The context in which Isabella pleads is vital. Lucio has just unfrocked the Friar and revealed the Duke; Angelo has been forced to wed Mariana; the audience and the Duke know that Claudio lives. As the newly-wed couple re-enter, the Duke, who has just assured Isabella that Claudio is happier because he is dead, now tells her that she must pardon Angelo because he did not achieve his evil intent. But in the same sentence, the Duke continues:

> But, as he adjudg'd your brother
> Being criminal, in double violation
> Of sacred chastity and of promise-breach
> Thereon dependent, for your brother's life—
> The very mercy of the law cries out
> Most audible even from his proper tongue,
> 'An Angelo for Claudio, death for death!'
> Haste still pays haste, and leisure answers
>   leisure
> Like doth quit like, and Measure still for
>   Measure.
>   (V. i. 408-16)

Particularly important here is Vincentio's ironic use of the idea of equal substitution and especially of the play's title. Only now, when both the audience and the speaker know that there has been no harm done—that the specific reference to Claudio's death is false—does Shakespeare introduce the title of his play. We cannot accept either the threat of Angelo's execution or the moral appropriateness of the words 'Measure still for Measure' in this context because both are contingent upon 'An Angelo for Claudio, death for death.' The Duke has deprived Isabella's petition of any credible influence on events. Here, as in the pivotal scene where the eavesdropping Friar takes control, moral conflict tends to separate from dramatic action.

That Isabella does not speak again suggests that the dramatist does not want her to detract from the impression she has just created. In his closing lines, Shakespeare deliberately underplays the plot of the monstrous proposal in order to end the action on a comic and anti-climactic note. In one sentence of confused syntax, the Duke, who thoroughly dominates the stage, reveals Claudio, pardons him, and proposes to Isabella:

> If he be like your brother, for his sake
> Is he pardon'd; and for your lovely sake—
> Give me your hand and say you will be
>   mine—
> He is my brother too.
>
>   (V. i. 495-8)

The wedding of the misogynist Duke-Friar to the chaste novice Isabella, who 'most abhors' the sexual vice of her brother, achieves a comic rightness, for Shakespeare combines the formal, conventional resolution with a variation that surprises precisely because neither character has shown the least desire to marry.

The next lines between the Duke and Lucio seem to burlesque not only the hastily presented resolutions in marriage but also the continuing motif of the Duke's fair meting out of justice. Vincentio turns to Lucio with, 'And yet here's one place I cannot pardon'. As usual, Lucio causes the Duke to betray—in a comic manner—his own weakness as a ruler. The one character who has insulted the manipulating Duke remains his anathema. The Duke demands that Lucio marry the woman he has 'wrong'd. The nuptial finished, let him be whipp'd and hang'd.' Although Lucio pleads that to marry him to a whore will make him a cuckold, the Duke insists upon the dubious justice of this marriage—which parodies the three other more happy weddings:

> Upon my honour, you shalt marry her.
> Thy *slanders* I forgive; and therewithal
> Remit thy other forfeits.

Lucio's last line, 'Marrying a punk, my lord, is pressing to death, whipping, and hanging,' may gain him nothing, but once again he reveals Vincentio's ineptitude. The Duke is provoked to contradict explicitly his 'forgiveness' of five lines earlier when he replies to Lucio '*Slandering* a prince deserves it.'

This concluding scene builds to a dramatic climax which coincides with its moral peak—only to lead to intentionally anti-climactic, non-moral manipulation. We move from the plot of the monstrous proposal to the bawds with whom the Duke proves so futile. In this comic world, Vincentio has the last word, but he must answer Lucio who has the next-to last word.

IV

Any criticism of *Measure for Measure* as a unified play must account for rather than evade the implica-tions of its inconsistent details, its fluctuating focus upon different characters, and especially the levels of intensity that distinguish its two halves. For a full understanding of the play, it is necessary to consider the action from two contrasting, overlapping formal perspectives. On one hand, Shakespeare involves us in the situations of his major characters and the dilemmas they face. But he never works these out in convincing depth. This perspective we may call the 'problematic' if we use this term as it refers to a work (or major aspect of a work) in which the author poses significant and disturbing moral problems, for which he *intentionally* offers only superficial resolutions. One can readily see that the critic can discuss this perspective only with very limited precision.

On the other hand, when we consider the story in *Measure* and our attitudes toward the threats Angelo poses, we see that Shakespeare offers an increasingly comic approach. The ascending action builds up our concern for Claudio's life and our antipathy toward Angelo because the death penalty seems harsh and excessive. But Shakespeare carefully concentrates his intensity in the first part. The three debates when Isabella faces first Angelo and then Claudio comprise less than 800 lines and all come within the second quarter of the play. Even here, Shakespeare uses Lucio to accompany Isabella when she first meets Angelo and he carefully shows the audience the disguised Duke hiding, but learning all that takes place, when Isabella tells her brother of the deputy's monstrous proposal. The Duke's presence implies the existence of some eternal force that will prevent a direct working out of the dilemmas posed. Once the Duke interrupts Isabella's tirade against her brother, never for more than a moment need we feel concern over the effectiveness of the devices by which Claudio is saved as we would if we were watching an effective melodrama.

In the descending action, the problems of justice, mercy, and sexual promiscuity, posed so forcefully by Isabella and Angelo, remain important, but their relevance often is adapted to the world of Barnardine and Kate Keepdown. The transformation of mood and control proves so complete after the Duke reduces Isabella's dilemmas to such devices as substituting heads or virgins that we must recognize that ethical choices are no longer vital to work out the story. The action of *Measure for Measure* does not lead us to any new discoveries that can resolve bitter conflicts between mercy and justice. In the final scene, as the Duke has contrived the climactic choice, *both* mercy and justice require that Angelo be pardoned. And the final weddings surely are not meant as an earnest solution to the excesses of promiscuity and of chastity—for the last comment on the subject is Lucio's objection that forcing him to marry a punk will make him a cuckold.

Once the critic of *Measure* recognizes its over-all comic structure and its increasingly comic perspective, his approach often tends to flatten out or ignore vital distinctions between the early debates and the later farce.[12] Yet the play has become increasingly popular with modern audiences and readers largely because of the early atypical scenes—and their emotional and intellectual engagement which other comedies so rarely can create. While Shakespeare remoulds his overt action, and the moral problems in so far as they are embodied in that action, he expects the alert responsive spectator to feel disturbed. Anti-climactic rhythms and structure call the disparities between problem and solution to the attention of the spectator. Through Lucio and Pompey, the dramatist repeatedly draws our attention to the inadequacy of solutions that the perfectionists in the play—Angelo, Isabella, and the Duke—profess to find adequate. They all share a lack of the self-knowledge which each claims. This false conception leads each to impose demands for extreme purity on those subject to his power, and then to abuse them cruelly when they prove flawed.

Shakespeare, then, creates an action to which we respond in distinct ways. We know that on the level of the fable, no harm will be done. Yet we feel certain that the explanations given by well-meaning, apparently reliable characters do not provide the meaning of the experiences represented. That the Duke saves Isabella and Angelo from the consequences of their self-deception should satisfy us, especially because it comes through their testing and increased awareness. The comic characters, in turn, remind us of the Duke's own pretences and thereby help construct the underlying integrity of the play. The Duke's flaws become laughable because of the contexts in which they are presented and because he does save Claudio and Isabella—as we have long felt confident he would. In this respect, they are similar to the weaknesses of heroes in Shakespeare's romantic comedies. But in keeping with the increased seriousness of tone and subject matter in *Measure for Measure,* they are more consistent and significant. From the perspective of the spectator's immediate response, such flaws suggest a playful comic author. In respect to the thematic issues—the private character of the ruler, the need for mercy and justice, the discrepancies between major flaws and mild effects—all raised in emphatic contexts, we remain aware of unresolved problems as Shakespeare's use of the problematic structure generates a play of mind which is *not* completely reabsorbed by the action itself. It would be a mistake therefore to suggest that *Measure* is completely unified or that any interpretation of it could explain away all disappointment and discomfort. Shakespeare's technique is a daring and experimental one, for this play of mind, held under minimal control, may well become subjective and tangential to the matters actually represented. (The failure of many critics to limit their own play of mind has been one major cause of the general failure to distinguish the internal comic action of the play from its suggestions about the 'everyday world' external to the formal action.)

My argument here indicates some ways in which we can discriminate more precisely the mingling of the serious, the comic, and the problematic. Shakespeare again and again calls our attention to the disparity between the emotional involvement with his action and the facile formal resolution that seems inherent in comedy. It is clear that *Measure for Measure* is no attempt at tragedy or melodrama. The excitement of the early acts creates an energy that is not absorbed in the latter partof the play. This energy leaves us appropriately disturbed over the pretences of the characters—pretences perhaps best exemplified by the Duke's misleading praise for Isabella when he interrupts her tirade. But for the spectator, this energy like the suspense, is, for the most part, transformed into a joyous, playful, mocking comedy. Shakespeare parodies the melodramatic structure he took over from his sources. He reveals a hero pompous and apparently successful, yet failing to recognize his own weaknesses. He finally makes us aware of the limitations of the very comic conventions and implausible devices he uses as he stretches them into new possibilities.

Because it combines intellectual vigour and delight with its challenging problematic side, *Measure for Measure* may well be Shakespeare's finest achievement in comedy.

Notes

[1] Performances of *Measure for Measure* at Stanford University in May 1962 demonstrated clearly that an audience can readily recognize and respond to the interpretation proposed in this essay. Such opportunities unfortunately have been uncommon. Even the production of the play which Tyrone Guthrie directed for the Bristol Old Vic company in 1967 developed the humour only for the characters of the sub-plot. Many of the Duke's clumsier lines were cut thus losing the dual-edged critical humour. Guthrie's production of the play for the Festival Theatre in 1929 may have been the first in this century to make much of its broad humour.

[2] See for example the introduction to the new Cambridge edition of the play (1922) by Arthur Quiller-Couch; E. M. W. Tillyard, *Shakespeare's Problem Plays,* (London, 1949); and Virgil K. Whitaker, *Shakespeare's Use of Learning,* (San Marino, 1953), 215-22.

[3] See for example, F. R. Leavis, 'The Greatness of *Measure for Measure*' Scrutiny, (1942). This essay has probably been more influential than any other in proposing the view most prominent in recent criticism

357

of the play. Further development will be found below in Footnote 9.

[4] Line references, with the single exception cited, are taken from *Shakespeare Complete Works,* ed., William Allan Neilson and Charles Jarvis Hill (Boston, 1942).

[5] Quiller-Couch, op. cit., XXXIX.

[6] Close comparison with George Whelstone's *Promos and Cassandra* indicates that Shakespeare probably used its text while writing *Measure for Measure,* but that he invariably reacted strongly against the moral evaluations and the tone of this source. Whetstone's play, perhaps never produced, is most conveniently available in Geoffrey Bullough, ed; *Narrative and Dramatic Sources of Shakespeare,* Vol. II., (New York, 1958).

[7] For an influential opposing view, see W. W. Lawrence, *Shakespeare's Problem Comedies,* (New York, 1931).

[8] Perhaps the most extreme statement of the often-held view that Shakespeare strives for melodramatic suspense may be found in Bertrand Evans, *Shakespeare's Comedies* (Oxford, 1960),203: 'With infinite shrewdness the dramatist made Isabella describe the details of the route to the garden house so vividly that now the mind's eye can trace the course while the outer eye observes the substitute action.'

[9] This phrase comes from F. R. Leavis, 'The Greatness of *Measure for Measure*' reprinted in the *Best of Scrutiny* (New York, 1948), 154. It is quoted with enthusiasm by David L. Stevenson, 'The Role of James I in Shakespeare's *Measure for Measure,*' ELH, XXVI (1959), 188-206. The other references are to G. Wilson Knight, *The Wheel of Fire* (London, 1930), Ch. IV, and Francis Fergusson, 'Philosophy and Theatre in *Measure for Measure,*' Kenyon Review, XIV (1952), 102-23.

[10] This cryptic couplet has received many various emendations. I have used the form in the Folio, adding only 'Free' the initial word of the second line. Unlike most emendations, this adds only a word that must be assumed whether or not it is expressed.

[11] For strong expressions that the play is careless and disgusting, see Coleridge's *Writings on Shakespeare,* ed. Terence Hawkes, (New York, 1957), 249-50. Among numerous more recent examples of such distaste for the play are Una Ellis-Fermor, *The Jacobean Shakespeare* (London, 1936), 260; Mark Van Doren, *Shakespeare* (New York, 1943), 186; and Caroline F. E. Spurgeon, *Shakespeare's Imagery and What it Tells Us* (Boston, 1958), 289. One might suggest here the need for special attention to contexts in studies of

imagery in comedies. Even A. P. Rossiter, in *Angel with Horns* (New York, 1961), 108-28, 152-70, the most perceptive study of the play's darker side and character relationships, concludes his essays with emphasis on 'the tottering values and the distorted will, 166' and 'the lack of inner conviction, 169' that he considers are the mark of the play.

[12] See for example Josephine Waters Bennett, *Measure for Measure as Royal Entertainment,* (New York, 1966), 158: 'The play is, from beginning to end, pure comedy, based on absurdity, like *The Mikado*'.

Harriett Hawkins (essay date 1972)

SOURCE: " 'They That Have Power to Hurt and Will Do None': Tragic Facts and Comic Fictions in *Measure for Measure,*" in *Likenesses of Truth in Elizabethan and Restoration Drama,* Oxford University Press, 1972, pp. 51-78.

[*Below, Hawkins discusses the discrepancies between the two halves of* Measure for Measure, *and maintains that as tragicomedy, the play "is a magnificent failure" in that the contradictions in the play—between "equally valid claims to human devotion" and between the comic and tragic forms—may be irreconcilable.*]

> We ourselves esteem not of that obedience, or love, or gift, which is of force.
>
>   Milton

It is an old paradox of literary history that certain works which confront their critics with conspicuous flaws (like *Measure for Measure*) nevertheless remain greater than similar works whichpose no serious difficulties (like Marston's *The Malcontent*). Indeed, the simple fact that a play which creates insoluble critical problems can still demand the adjective 'great' (nobody calls *Measure for Measure* 'good') serves as an important reminder of the essentially mysterious nature of literary greatness. The most brilliant critic living cannot tell a gifted young poet how to write a masterpiece any more than our categories of genre can explain why masterpieces so often transcend generic categorization. And *Measure for Measure* still stubbornly defies the whole modern range of critical methods and historical information to solve its problems. There are at least three books on Shakespeare's tragicomedy and there have been discussions galore.[1] But nobody has come up with any over-all interpretation of the play which cannot be refuted or countered by some opposing interpretation with equal, if separate, validity. The play itself splits into parts so essentially different that they compete with each other,[2] and so do our conflicting, mutually contradictory, responses to them. The detached point of view predominant in the second half of the play does not extend back to encompass the first half, and the intense personal involvement aroused by the first half is not sustained or even permitted in the second half. In short, the first half of the play has the power to hurt; the second half will do none. The play refuses to do the thing it most did show. The first half moves others (us) to desire tragedy and then the second half asks them (us) to be unmoved, cold, and to temptation slow. Each half thus represents a dramatic country on which the other half has declared war. And there are other problems as well. Maybe a quick account of the way *Measure for Measure* differs from *The Malcontent*—a comparable and very successful tragicomedy—followed by a discussion of key difficulties with *Measure for Measure* can help explain why it remains a great play which haunts the memory and the imagination, and also remains a frustrating, annoying companion, constantly nagging about probblems which nobody can solve for it, since they are problems that have no social, theological, or dramatic solution.

It is obvious at a glance that the general tragicomic outlines of *Measure for Measure* and *The Malcontent* are similar, and their similarities can be swiftly, if dully, described. Within the corrupt societies of both plays a disguised duke manipulates characters and intrigues so that the outcome of a play which might otherwise have developed in the pattern of revenge tragedy results in mercy and harmony. Here the similarity ends and some illuminating differences emerge. Where the ending of *Measure for Measure* creates disturbing problems for its audience, the conclusion of *The Malcontent* satisfies its audience, or at least a common reader has no objection to that conclusion. Where Marston's play is all of a piece throughout, the language and action of Shakespeare's play split into two distinct parts. But the most noticeable difference between the two tragicomedies lies in their initially differeing modes of characterization.

Marston's characterization poses no problems for his audience. His characters are, every one of them, familiar types on the Elizabethan stage. The disguised Duke Altofronto, speaking as Malevole, sounds enough like Jonson's Macilente and other characters of the same type to be readily accepted as the play's satiric spokesman from the moment he first opens his mouth. Marston's villain, Mendoza, is a nicely portrayed Machiavel with a Marlovian flair for overstatement. The other characters need no more detailed introduction to any audience or reader even superficially familiar with their dramatic predecessors and contemporaries. We have Celso, the loyal friend and confidant; Bilioso, the doddering old man; various licentious courtiers; a fool; a virtuous duchess; a bawd. However bitter Marston's presentation of his upsidedown world may be, its inhabitants are our old dramatic friends whose ancestors, siblings, and progeny people many of the

most popular plays on the Elizabethanstage. Familiarity, in this instance, breeds relaxed acceptance and enjoyment. We know exactly what to expect from Marston's characters, and they gratify us by living up to our expectations (in the manner of Jonson's 'humour' types). All Marston has to do, given his skilful depiction of these well-known types, is to set them in action in a series of interesting intrigues. And his characters are such conventionally theatrical figures that even when the action moves in an ominous direction, nobody in the audience really worries. The highly theatrical posturing, running about, double murder assignments, and masque are lively, vivid, and fun to watch. Marston's world is certainly out of joint, but from the beginning it is so obviously a theatrically disordered world that there is no surprise when the playwright—via his spokesman and agent, Malevole-Altofronto—manages, theatrically, to set it right. For any problems created by the dramatic intrigues of one set of characters may be effectively solved by the dramatic intrigues of another group of characters, and dramatic 'humours' can be expelled dramatically. Also, the satire is consistently, if savagely, funny. The perfume sprayed on the stage in the opening scene, Malevole's gleeful exposures of everyone, Mendoza's exaggerated, contradictory, speeches about the nature of women, all move the play's satirical thrust in the direction of comedy. Marston further makes it impossible to worry seriously about the fate of his characters because he continually reminds us that Malevole-Altofronto will take over just as soon as time and place adhere. Their predicaments are serious, and the corrupt court of *The Malcontent* evokes righteous indignation from its inhabitants; but Marston rightly calls his play a comedy since, however dark and devious his dramatic world may be, his primary emphasis falls on the dramatic intrigues, and not on the suffering which it causes.[3]

The situations presented in the first half of *Measure for Measure* cause some extreme suffering, and Shakespeare's major characters evoke no laughter. If, in the first half of his play, Shakespeare exaggerates the traits of Angelo and Isabella, he does so in ways significantly different from Marston's stylized exaggeration. Where Marston gives us old dramatic acquaintances, Shakespeare gives us characters different from any of the dramatis personae in his own works or in those of his contemporaries. Where Marston anchors his characters and action in the dramatic tradition, Shakespeare looses our dramatic moorings at the same time that he disturbs familiar ethical and moral assumptions. There are lots of villains like the machiavellian Mendoza—there is none like Angelo. Isabella's concern for her chastity goes far beyond the conventional purity of Marston's Maria (or Whetstone's Cassandra) and becomes the fiery asceticism of a medieval saint. Until Act III, Scene i, line 153 of this play, Angelo, Isabella, and Claudio (when he faces death) have the classical intensity of figures in the *Antigone*. The three are all absolutists. Angelo is absolute for the letter of the law, then for Isabella. Isabella is absolute for chastity. Claudio soon becomes absolute for life. In their great confrontation scenes Shakespeare moves this triumvirate in what seems to be an inexorably tragic direction. Surely an audience which has watched these confrontations is left not with a vague impression but with the absolute conviction that, given their situation, each of these characters would choose to bring tragic suffering upon another. Indeed, Angelo, Isabella, and Claudio themselves (in turn) convince us that Angelo would, without doubt, take Isabella and dishonour her in spite of his own horrified conscience; that Isabella would never yield to Angelo, even to save her brother's life; that Claudio could not willingly choose death, even to save his sister's honour. In the first half of the play Shakespeare makes these tragic decisions seem both probable and necessary. Thus, just before he alters the course of action in the direction of comedy, he passes a dramatic point of no return. For he creates in his audience a very simple and passionate appetite to watch these characters enact their tragic choices.

Furthermore, whether we approve or violently disapprove of them, and however they may shock or infuriate us by their personal assumptions and behaviour, Angelo, Claudio, and Isabella force us to experience their dilemmas with them. On a personal and intimate level, which the words of Marco Mincoff both illustrate and describe, the first half of this play gives us 'a man who believes he is more than his fellows, who stumbles and falls, and struggles blindly to understand how he has become the thing he despises'. The true meaning of Angelo, for Mr. Mincoff, may lie in 'the fact that we have experienced his fall with him . . . have felt his very repressions bursting out with double force, and his bewilderment when the staff he has always relied on, his freedom from temptation, collapses under him' and 'that we have felt, even in him, something of the potential splendour of humanity'. It gives us a girl, 'with an ideal of virtue beyond this world', who is faced 'with the necessity of consigning her own brother to death, and turning from him in horror when he sinks to the level of her tempter'. It gives us her brother, 'brought up to regard death as preferable to dishonour and steeling himself to meet it steadfastly, yet breaking down when a hope of life offers itself. And it shows them to us in a complex set of interactions that form a moving and exciting story. It does not ask us either to accept or to reject the assumptions on which these people believe they must act, it only asks that we should feel with them, and realize how hard it may be to live up to such assumptions. It presents these figures to us in a language so pregnant and splendid that it lends to them an added significance and an added depth, so that they seem both larger and truer than life.'[4] If only half of a play can evoke this kind of response from a perceptive and intelligent critic (and from many others like him),

it is surely part of a very great play. But the deeply involved, highly personal nature of this response suggests that this half of *Measure for Measure* is more readily comparable to *Hamlet* than to *The Malcontent* or *The Tempest.*

Throughout *The Malcontent,* the point of view of Malevole-Altofronto, the satirist who exposes and castigates the vices and follies of the other characters, is the predominant one, the one which we in the audience are encouraged to share. Marston's comedy is an imitation of follies and vices which the playwright (in the words of Sidney's *Apology*) 'representeth in the most ridiculous and scornfull sort that may be, so as it is impossible that any beholder can be content to be such a one'. And Marston's stylization of his characters allows us to heap our scorn and ridicule on them from a safe dramatic distance. In *The Tempest* Prospero's perspective (the perspective which dominates the play and which we are encouraged to share) allows us to view the characters and action from a great height, like a god contemplating the theatre of the world without tears or fear. Too frequently, I think, modern criticism takes it for granted that we watch *all* plays and their characters either with the diagnostic, highly critical, moralistic superiority of the satirist, or with the cosmic, philosophical detachment of a Prospero who can control his own emotions as perfectly as he controls the action. Mr. Mincoff's vision of the characters and action of *Measure for Measure* fits neither of these categories. It is very personal, as well as aesthetic; very emotional, as well as rational. He speaks as a human being engaged by the play as well as a critic detached from it. He has been *moved* by Shakespeare's 'hart-ravishing' presentation of 'virtues, vices, and passions so in their natural states, laide to the view' that the spectator, along with the characters and their language, 'may be tuned to the highest key of passion' (Sidney's phrases about poetry's power to move its audience). Where *The Malcontent* and *The Tempest,* for their individual and proper dramatic reasons, subordinate their emotional impact for the sake of and by means of other kinds of effects, the first half of *Measure for Measure* makes a direct assault on the emotions. For this reason, Mincoff's response seems to me to be much truer to this part of the play than a critical approach which assumes that we are detached, distant, anduninvolved, unmoved and unchanged by the dramatic experience, and which assumes that our perceptions of the play can only be distorted by our emotions.

D. L. Stevenson, for instance, has argued that the audience, throughout this play, is encouraged to examine the moral decisions and conflicts of the characters with 'a sardonic detachment equal to that of the Duke', and that the characters here are 'deliberately simplified and made less interesting in themselves than is Hamlet, for instance, or Falstaff'.[5] Much of what Mr. Stevenson has to say is perfectly true—of *The Malcontent*. And do we really want to see *Measure for Measure* turned into a duplicate of Marston's play? On the contrary, the history of criticism of *Measure for Measure* reflects just about every possible attitude towards the moral decisions and conflicts of the characters except sardonic detachment. For while it is true that a detached perspective on the characters and action is encouraged by the second half of the play, initially there is no dramatic insulation between our personal responses and characters who arouse in us simultaneous pity and terror and, in the process of doing so, sear themselves into our imaginations. The Duke (who will be discussed later) reveals no firm standpoint remotely comparable to the consistent attitudes provided for us by Malevole and Prospero. There is no traditionally satiric, comic, or romantic stylization of the central characters or their language that effectively lends aesthetic distance. Again, the first half of *Measure for Measure* has the dramatic impact of a play comparable to *Hamlet*.

Certain great plays may be compared to the remarkable characters they so frequently contain, or to the stars who act in them, since they are all capable of demanding an indelible and passionate response from their observers. This capacity is ultimately mysterious, like the appeal of a supremely vivid human personality, whether it be expressed in the play, *Hamlet;* embodied in its central character; projected by its star player; or inherent in its author. Play, character, actor, and playwright all may share the power to evoke not only an aesthetic, impersonal fascination, but also to compel a deep, instinctual, highly emotional, and private response from their observers and in doing so to take on an independent existence in the observer's imagination. For instance, characters like Hamlet and Falstaff have had, throughout the years, personal after-lives in the imaginations of their admirers that exist quite independently of their original dramatic contexts. They have somehow transformed themselves from component human parts in given dramatic spectacles into spectacular human beings interesting for their own sakes. Earlier criticism, such as *The Fortunes of Falstaff,* Coleridge on Hamlet, Bradley's *Shakespearean Tragedy,* bears witness to this phenomenon. Modern criticism, which frequently argues that such characters have no right to any existence apart from their immediate dramatic context, tends to imply that this phenomenon does not or should not exist. But whether or not it should, it does. The passionate adoration which individual critics accord to their own, private, saintly, or lovable Isabellas, and the equally passionate revulsion which other critics express towards their own smug, vixenish, intolerant, selfish Isabellas, testify to Isabella's after-life in the heavens or hells assigned to her by individual imaginations.[6] This phenomenon, as it recurs over time, demonstrates that, like Falstaff, the plays, characters, artists, and individuals who have the

mysterious power to move—to delight, to hurt—are the cause of wit in others. They somehow make people see better, know things, feel them intensely, and it does not especially matter (in art) whether the insight communicated is beautiful or terrible, good or evil, disturbing, pleasant, or amusing. It is doubtful if the secret of this power can be rationally explained. There is something irrational and compulsive about any rapt reader or audience. Tolstoy thought that the vogue for Shakespeare was a kind of contrived mass mania, and perhaps this is exactly what certain great plays and characters create—a mass mania, contrived by their creators and admirers, that survives the tests of time and truth posed by the imagination of individual readers. As Dr. Johnson said, a substantial period of time is necessary to establish the enduring validity of a classic writer or work, and in the experience of the individual reader or playgoer the same principle applies. Our personal classics—plays, characters, or writers—are remembered for a lifetime and sought out again and again in different periods of that lifetime. They make it impossible for us to forget them. They will not let us go.

The first half of *Measure for Measure* has these indelible qualities. The characters, their lines, their cruel dilemmas are quite impossible to forget; for Shakespeare forces us along with Angelo, Isabella, and Claudio on their way to 'temptation where prayers cross'. He exhibits before us, with ruthless and disturbing power, the irreconcilable contradictions which very frequently arise, in life itself, between equally valid claims to human devotion. He shows us the contradiction between Isabella's ideal of her own chastity-integrity and the claims of her devotion to her brother; the contradiction between Claudio's will to live and his devotion to his sister; the intrinsic contradictions between the claims of the rule of law, the claims of ideal justice, and the claims of Christian mercy. Here, surely, the truths of literal reality and the artist's imaginative presentation of them are fused, for the sheer power of Shakespeare's dramatic exhibition of these conflicts drives home the harsh but undeniable fact that certain contradictions between equally valid claims to human devotion may be totally irreconcilable. And the major problem in this 'problem play' is precisely that the memory of the characters, their speeches, and their conflicts between mutually exclusive moral alternatives simply cannot be revoked by the theatrical intriguing of a Duke who argues that measures can always be taken, that solutions can always be found, that 'all difficulties are but easy when they are known'.

It is true that all things are possible in the drama. Shakespeare has a perfect right to change his mode of characterization and the direction of his action in the middle of the play if he wants to. The problem here is that he cannot alter the memory of his own audience. For by the time Shakespeare shifts his dramatic emphasis in the direction of intrigue and comedy, his earlier movement towards tragedy has become part of the spectator's memory, part of his personal experience, part of his own private past. And, in the words of Milton,

> Past who can recall, or done undo?
> Not God Omnipotent, nor Fate!

Not even Shakespeare. For while we can easily be taught something new, we cannot be commanded to forget information which is implanted in our minds by the command itself: 'Try to count to ten without thinking of a rabbit.' The dramatic shock of watching an Angelo previously unmoved and invulnerable to temptation become obsessed by a young novice makes its awesome dramatic impact before Mariana's name is ever mentioned. The subsequent references to his marriage contract and the action based on this contract are therefore, except for the obvious contrivances of the plot, more annoying than effective. They remind us of the earlier Angelo who has claimed our imagination and who will not let us go. The same thing is true of Isabella. The memory of the original Isabella causes acute resentment of the Duke's proposal of marriage. Whether we approve of extreme asceticism or not, the passion for chastity which Isabella expressed with such uncompromising conviction in the opening scenes of the play makes it impossible to believe that the same woman would ever willingly marry anyone. 'Get her to a nunnery,' one student snarled. Mary Lascelles points out that it is the very idleness of criticism to ask how this play's new-married couples will settle down together,[7] and it is certainly true that Shakespeare frequently ends his comedies with matches which no marriage counsellor would sanction. And yet none of the parties to his other matches are creatures endowed with personalities so fundamentally hostile to a stock romantic future as Isabella and Angelo. It is their earlier, unforgettable selves who, haunting the memory of their audience, ask how they could settle down with Mariana and the Duke. In fact, their own ultimate silences in this connection are eloquent enough to raise the question. I realize there may be textual omissions in the final scene, but Angelo's last lines in the play as it stands plead for justice, for consequences, for death:

> I crave death more willingly than mercy;
> 'Tis my deserving, and I do entreat it.
> (V. i. 474-5)

Angelo never once, in the text we have, expresses the slightest desire 'to marry a good woman and be happy'. Isabella's last lines are about Angelo's desire for her. She says not a single word about the Duke's proposal.[8] Given Shakespeare's powerful initial presentation of these characters and their own stubborn refusal to ac-

cept officially the futures assigned to them, it seems fair enough for an audience to wish that Shakespeare had allowed them to face the truths and the consequences of dilemmas and desires which once seemed their own dramatic business—not the Duke's.

The real trouble with *Measure for Measure* begins when, in the course of some acutely human events, Shakespeare suddenly endows the Duke of Vienna with the superhuman, omniscient, manipulative powers of a Prospero—powers far beyond those of Marston's manipulator-spokesman, Malevole. An audience will readily accept superhuman intervention from benevolent manipulators like Oberon or Prospero, who initially demonstrate their power and announce that all will be well for the human mortals who enter their domains. But the same audience may justifiably question such intervention when a previously undistinguished character in a realistic dramatic context suddenly begins, half-way through the action, to exercise prerogatives that are traditionally associated with a dramatic divinity. There is just not enough evidence provided early in the play that Shakespeare's Duke (even to the degree of Marston's Duke Altofronto) can, wants to, or will be able to control the situation in festering urban (and suburban) Vienna. Indeed, the first motive the Duke gives for leaving the city is that the legal and social situation there has got out of his control and he wants somebody else to clean up the mess which his own permissiveness has created (I. iii. 19-43). This motive hardly entitles him (morally or dramatically) to put an objecting Angelo (I. i. 48-51) to a test, or to cause unnecessary suffering for a number of his subjects merely in order to find out what might lie behind Angelo's stony exterior (I. iii. 50-4). And if the Duke knew all along that Angelo had jilted Mariana, as he says later on (III. i. 206-17), he would hardly have needed to test Angelo for flaws in the façade. F. R. Leavis argues that we should not analyse the Duke as if he were 'a mere character, an actor among the others', but there is no evidence early in the play that he is anything more. In the long run we cannot analyse him as such because he will not stand up under the kind of analysis which we can give with no effort at all to, say, Lucio or Barnardine. So one alternative is to interpret the Duke allegorically, to see in him the workings of a mysterious Providence. But are a few allusions to Power Divine, a disguise as a priest, a speech informing us that the Duke has ever sought to know himself (III. ii. 218-19), really enough to exalt him, late in the action, to the status of a 'more-than-Prospero' as Leavis calls him?[9] I think not. He is much less than the real Prospero, who makes his powers and the limits of his powers clear, who analyses himself and controls himself along with the situation and the other characters. But I wonder, in fact, if any form of *deus ex machina* introduced in the third act of *Measure for Measure* could be successful, any more than some super-Polonius, disguised, providentially, as a priest, could, half-way through the play, convincingly manipulate Hamlet and Claudius into reconciliation and shift the action from revenge tragedy to comedic mercy. The personal conflicts and the intellectual dilemmas presented in the first acts of *Measure for Measure* are, like those in *Hamlet*, too deeply rooted for any happy resolution.

Indeed, the fundamental clash between the claims of the rule of law, the claims of abstract justice, and the claims of mercy which Shakespeare introduced in the opening scenes of *Measure for Measure* may not admit of any final solution at all apart from the tragic non-solution which the same conflicts produce in Melville's *Billy Budd* and which similar conflicts produce in the *Antigone*. In an imperfect world (and Vienna is notably imperfect) the realm of law is necessarily a realm of judgement and choice which dialectically conflicts with the realm of Christian idealism where all judgements are regarded ultimately as simple: Forgive your enemies; judge not that ye be not judged.[10] And Isabella's contrast between a god's or even an individual's renunciation of vengeance and a governor's enforcement of the law is an unfair one. Shakespeare knew this perfectly well. Henry V makes clear distinctions between divine mercy, an individual's renunciation of vengeance, and legal punishment:

> God quit you in his mercy! Hear your
>   sentence.
>
> Touching our person seek we no revenge;
> But we our kingdom's safety must so tender,
> Whose ruin you have sought, that to her laws
> We do deliver you.
>
>   (*Henry V,* II. ii. 166-77)

Much of our annoyance with Duke Vincentio stems from his consistent refusal (and this refusal seems to be the most consistent thing about the Duke) to face up to the dilemmas and responsibilities of a governor who, whether he likes it or not, is bound to enforce the law. In other plays where the justice-mercy conflict arises, Shakespeare emphatically distinguishes between a ruler's personal pity and forgiveness and his duty to the law, even when the law is cruel or silly. 'We may pity, though not pardon thee' (*Comedy of Errors,* I. i. 98) is the typical statement of the Shakespearian governor. In *A Midsummer Night's Dream* Shakespeare explicitly contrasts the magical domain of Oberon, who is free from human law and necessity, with the realm of Theseus, who rules by the statutes of Athens:

> For you, fair Hermia, look you arm yourself
> To fit your fancies to your father's will,
> Or else the law of Athens yields you up—
> Which by no means we may extenuate—
> To death, or to a vow of single life.
>
>   (I. i. 117-21)

In *The Merchant of Venice* the Duke is very sorry for Antonio, and does his best to qualify Shylock's rigorous course, but Antonio himself realizes that 'The Duke cannot deny the course of law', and Portia agrees:

> . . . there is no power in Venice
> Can alter a decree established;
> 'Twill be recorded for a precedent,
> And many an error, by the same example,
> Will rush into the state.
>
>   (IV. i. 213-17)

And Escalus, the closest thing to a *raisonneur* in *Measure for Measure,* reminds us of the characteristic dilemma of a virtuous Shakespearian governor:

> *Escalus.* It grieves me for the death of
>   Claudio;
>   But there's no remedy.
> *Justice.* Lord Angelo is severe.
> *Escalus.* It is but needful:
>   Mercy is not itself that oft looks so;
>   Pardon is still the nurse of second woe.
>   But yet, poor Claudio! There is no remedy.
>
>   (II. i. 266-71)

This essential and dramatic clash between the law, justice, and mercy appears in *Measure for Measure* well before Angelo becomes obsessed with Isabella. Vienna is in a state of misrule because of the Duke's refusal to enforce the laws:

> We have strict statutes and most biting laws,
> The needful bits and curbs to headstrong
>   steeds,
> Which for these fourteen years we have let
>   slip;
> Even like an o'ergrown lion in a cave,
> That goes not out to prey. Now, as fond
>   fathers,
> Having bound up the threat'ning twigs of
>   birch,
> Only to stick it in their children's sight
> For terror, not to use, in time the rod
> Becomes more mock'd than fear'd; so our
>   decrees,
> Dead to infliction, to themselves are dead;
> And liberty plucks justice by the nose;
> The baby beats the nurse, and quite athwart
> Goes all decorum.
>
>   (I. iii. 19-31)

So the Duke brings in Angelo, who rigidly enforces the letter of the laws on the books and arrests Claudio under an exceptionally severe old statute against fornication. Still, under the law, Claudio is guilty as charged, and though his pre-contract and intent to marry Julietta make the deathpenalty completely unjust, it is nevertheless perfectly legal. In her arguments with

Angelo, Isabella never denies the legality of Claudio's sentence or even questions the validity of such a cruel statute ('O just but severe law!' II. ii. 41)—she appeals to Christian mercy. And Claudio himself blames 'too much liberty' for his current predicament. Given the situation in Vienna, Angelo's decision to enforce the letter of the law seems no less (though no more) acceptable than the Duke's repeated decisions to ignore law and pardon everybody on his criminal docket. In one case, severity plucks justice by the nose, in the other case, liberty does.[11] And, unlike the Duke, Angelo intellectually confronts the issues inherent in a judge's responsibility, and he makes some valid points in his arguments with Isabella:

> It is the law, not I condemn your brother.
> Were he my kinsman, brother, or my son,
> It should be thus with him.
>
> (II. ii. 80-2)

A cluster of Shakespearian associate justices—the Duke in *Othello* (I. iii. 67-70), Henry V and the Lord Chief Justice of England (*2 Henry IV*, v. ii. 70-117)—would assent to the impartiality of Angelo's enforcement of the law. And Angelo's statement about precedent,

> Those many had not dar'd to do that evil
> If the first that did th'edict infringe
> Had answer'd for his deed
>
> (II. ii. 91-3)

has strong support from the Duke's own original account of the legal and social mess in Vienna.

An exceptionally good gloss on the cruel legal dilemma surrounding Claudio appears in Melville's *Billy Budd*. Captain Vere is faced by the paradox that though the vicious Claggart was rightly struck down by Billy, 'the angel of God', the Mutiny Act requires that 'the angel must hang'. At the Last Assizes, Vere says, ultimate justice will acquit Billy. 'But how here?' he asks. In a navy threatened by spreading mutiny, Vere decides that he must proceed under the law of the Mutiny Act:

> For suppose condemnation to follow these present proceedings. Would it be so much we ourselves that would condemn as it would be martial law operating through us? For that law and the rigor of it, we are not responsible. . . . But the exceptional in the matter moves the hearts within you. Even so too is mine moved. But let not warm hearts betray heads that should be cool. Ashore in a criminal case will an upright judge allow himself off the bench to be waylaid by some tender kinswoman of the accused seeking to touch him with her tearful plea?[12]

Now the problems and the conflicts introduced in both *Measure for Measure* and *Billy Budd* are not essentially literary problems and conflicts. They are universally relevant social, human, and legal dilemmas which have, in this fallen world, no perfect social, human, or judicial solution. Laws can be cruel, they can go out to prey, they can bite, they can hurt. But without them liberty may become licence, the baby may beat the nurse, and headstrong steeds (or weeds) may run wild. Indeed Shakespeare's initial appeal to the facts of human experience represents a threat to certain theological ideals, for it reveals that the law set down in heaven, 'judge not that ye be not judged', offers no solution to the earthly problem. It is a spiritual law set down for mortals to obey when they renounce personal vindictiveness or choose tolerance. It has never been set down on earth as an explicit guide for the conduct of magistrates, for it would then be a commandment to command them from their function—it is their business to judge. Furthermore, in the first half of *Measure for Measure*, Shakespeare gives the Duke's permissiveness and Angelo's severity (for which the Duke's earlier permissiveness and retreat is responsible) equal blame for the grievous personal and social suffering displayed. Thus, when the Duke gives pardon to everybody in the end, there are all sorts of ghostly stage whispers chorusing 'Remember me' from the cellarage. They come from the reverberating echoes of earlier statements by the Duke, Angelo, and Escalus concerning precedent and the rule of law. And any argument that the Duke has somehow developed an intellectual and moral conviction that his earlier permissiveness was socially and legally justified all along is just as shaky[13] as an argument that the personalities and passions of an Angelo or an Isabella can be as readily and satisfactorily altered as stock comic humours—neither argument is supported by the text on the desk. Furthermore, if this Duke is Providence, his own continuing improvidence turns him, in the play as it stands, into a contradiction in terms.

For, both socially and dramatically, the Duke's decision to grant mercy to everybody revokes the rule of law, and to revoke the rule of human law is to revoke the idea of consequence, of necessity (the law may be a kind of dramatic metaphor for blind necessity in this play). It does not impose order (providential or otherwise) on the action, it imposes the disorder of incredibility. Of course it attempts to transform what is a fundamentally human and tragic situation into some sort of comedy, but whether this transformation is successful is a debatable point. Whether it is desirable is another one. As it is made in *Measure for Measure* the transformation deprives the characters (including the Duke) of human and dramatic dignity by denying them the full measure of responsibility that comes from facing the consequences of their own decisions and desires. And it deprives the audience of watching them make the terrible choices between equal claims to their devotion. In effecting his final shift from a tragic to a comic mode, Shakespeare, by breaching it, calls to our attention an essential decorum described in a tale by Isak Dinesen:

Gene Carvalho as Angelo and Frank Corrado as the Duke. Angelo is pleading his case in Act V, scene i of the San José State University 1997 production of Measure for Measure.

[Tragedy is] a noble phenomenon, the noblest on earth. But of the earth only, and never divine. Tragedy is the privilege of man, his highest privilege. The God of the Christian Church Himself, when He wished to experience tragedy, had to assume human form. And even at that . . . the tragedy was not wholly valid, as it would have become had the hero of it been, in very truth, a man. The divinity of Christ conveyed to it a divine note, the moment of comedy. The real tragic part, by the nature of things, fell to the executors, not to the victim . . . Tragedy should remain the right of human beings, subject, in their conditions or in their own nature, to the dire law of necessity. To them it is salvation and beatification. But the gods, whom we must believe to be unacquainted with and incomprehensive of necessity, can have no knowledge of the tragic. When they are brought face to face with it they will, according to my experience, have the good taste and decorum to keep still, and not interfere. . . . [And] we, who stand in lieu of the gods and have emancipated ourselves from the tyranny of necessity, should leave to our vassals their monopoly of tragedy, and for ourselves accept the comic with grace. Only a

boorish and cruel master—a parvenu, in fact—will make a jest of his servants' necessity, or force the comic upon them.[14]

In *Measure for Measure,* those lords of the theatre, Shakespeare and his Duke, make a jest of their servants' necessity by interfering with the tragic, by forcing the comic upon the characters and the audience; and thus, as we shall see later, they call the validity of this particular kind of tragicomedy into question. Certainly when mercy is granted to Angelo it denies his (and our) pressing requests for necessity, for consequences:

> Immediate sentence then, and sequent death,
> Is all the grace I beg.
>
> (v.i. 371-2)

And by so frustrating the desire for consequences, for tragedy, which he himself earlier created, Shakespeare may very well increase it, since, over the years, whether they are common or uncommon, Christian or agnostic, readers have found the ending of *Measure for Measure* not only aesthetically and intellectually unsatisfying, but personally infuriating. In this instance, critics as temperamentally different as Coleridge and Dr. Johnson use the same word—'indignation'. For Coleridge, the ending 'baffles the strong indignant claim of justice', and Dr. Johnson believed that 'every reader feels some indignation when he finds [Angelo] spared'.[15]

Prospero, as we all know, granted universal mercy too. But Prospero set everybody free to pursue their private destinies, for good or ill. In legal jargon, Prospero dismissed the jury and let the defendants go. Similarly, Marston's Duke Altofronto simply kicks out Mendoza and allows the other characters to pair off as they choose. But Duke Vincentio limits the freedom of his subjects to the incongruous futures that he chooses for them. Barnardine is placed in the custody of a friar (v.i. 483-4). The severe Angelo and the rakish Lucio are alike ordered into shot-gun weddings. And then the Duke proposes marriage (of all things) to Isabella. All this sounds closer to the comic sentences of *Volpone* than to the comic release of *The Tempest.* But watching the action of *Volpone,* we watch the characters create their own dramatic designs and destinies, and they are permitted their own morality or immorality. In *Measure for Measure* the Duke forces his own arbitrary morality and his own dramatic designs upon the action. F. R. Leavis argues that the Duke's total attitude 'is the total attitude of the play'.[16] But where does the Duke articulate a 'total attitude'? We watch the Duke appear severely righteous with Julietta (II. iii), condemning her 'most offenceful act'—without irony or sympathy—as 'a sin'. Then later we hear him tell Mariana that, since Angelo is her husband on pre-contract, ''tis no sin' for her to do virtually the same thing that Julietta did (IV. i. 70-1); and because no clear legal or moral distinctions between *de praesenti* and *de futuro* betrothals are given us, what appears to be simply a double standard on the part of the Duke is naturally confusing to any common sense of either justice or morality. Elsewhere we watch the Duke deliberately put Angelo to a test (I. iii. 50-4), then condemn him for failing it, and finally take the credit for forgiving Angelo while conveniently forgetting that he himself was directly responsible for Angelo's original predicament and therefore for all the suffering in the play. Prospero's situation was very different. Prospero's 'rarer action' represented his personal forgiveness of people who injured him personally: Prospero himself has suffered, and we watch him struggle to forgive. But so far as the text of *Measure for Measure* is concerned, the worst thing that the Duke of Vienna faces in his entire dramatic life is a series of rather amusing insults from Lucio. And the Duke finds these personal insults harder to forgive than any other offences in the play—major or minor, attempted or committed. But in his final judicial role, the person to compare the Duke with is not Prospero but Henry V, andthe Duke does not come off very well. Henry readily takes into account extenuating circumstances and grants pardon to a drunk who slandered him personally; then he personally forgives the traitors, but he finally turns them over to the law. It is in *Henry V* and not in *Measure for Measure* that we find an upright judge who does his best to achieve a viable legal and human solution to the legal and human dilemmas inherent in his role as governor.

In order to justify the Duke as Providence Divine, or the Image of an Ideal Ruler, or a Compliment to James, it becomes necessary to transform Shakespeare from the greatest of poets into the kind of philosopher that Sidney set beneath the poet: 'I say the *Philosopher* teacheth but he teacheth obscurely so as the learned onely can understand him, that is to say, he teacheth them that are alreadie taught.' The poet, in contrast, 'beginneth not with obscure definitions which must blurre the margent with interpretations, and loade the memorie with doubtfulnesse'. Now on a literal (as opposed to any symbolic) level, Shakespeare's Duke has much less in common with either Providence Divine or an Ideal Ruler than he has in common with Ben Jonson's tyrant Tiberius. Jonson's enigmatic Emperor and Shakespeare's Duke of dark corners both deliberately retire from view and in doing so they get 'seconds' (Angelo and Sejanus) to do their political dirty work for them. Later on they both write contradictory letters, and finally they manifest their full power and overthrow their deputies. But Jonson's tyrant obviously represents neither Providence Divine nor an Ideal Ruler. In the words of *Sejanus,* a tyrant 'is a fortune' sent to test the virtue of Roman citizens. Gradually, in the course of the action, Jonson equates the inconsistent, arbitrary behaviour of Tiberius with the inconsistent, arbitrary behaviour of the Roman deity Fortune. In parallel scenes, Fortune and Tiberius turn

away from Sejanus, and we learn in the end that Tiberius, not Sejanus, has turned fortune's wheel in Rome from the very beginning. But Tiberius does not himself change his mode of behaviour. We are simply given progressively fuller information about him that changes our attitudes towards him and incorporates his modes of behaviour into the over-all meaning of the play. Shakespeare's Duke changes his attitudes and actions as the plot requires, moving from incompetence to omniscience, from advocating severity to advocating leniency, with no modulation in between.

No matter how hard we try to incorporate the Duke's behaviour into some over-all interpretation of the play, all the incorporation and all the interpreting appears to be ours—not Shakespeare's. If, uncertain how to justify the intrusion of his *deus ex machina* and unable to resolve the essential dilemmas of the first acts without doing so, Shakespeare made his text hard to follow because of *non sequiturs,* contradictory moral attitudes, impressive-sounding references to Power Divine, and elaborate in-jokes to compliment James, then we shall have great difficulty in finding out exactly what Shakespeare intends us to understand. We shall have to reason it out much as we reason out a notice in some language we do not fully understand. Thus some pretty strenuous reasoning may be interposed between the author's conceptions and our interpretation of them, and it is strangely easy to forget that in this specific instance the reasoning was not Shakespeare's, but all our own.[17] The strenuous reasoning behind most of the critical justifications of the Duke, behind all the allegorical and historical interpretations of *Measure for Measure,* appears to me to have been done by individual critics rather than by Shakespeare, who, in the text as it stands, seems to treat the Duke with something like poetic contempt. For while he lavishes great poetry on the early Angelo, Isabella, and Claudio, and while he treats them, even in their moments of extreme cruelty or cowardice, with great dramatic sympathy, he never gives the Duke a speech which is not self-contradictory or contradicted by the action itself. In fact, the reader in search of the tritest lines in the play, or even the tritest lines in the complete works of Shakespeare, need look no further than the Duke's summing-up of *Measure for Measure*. The same final lines issue a command just as silly and as unenforceable as the legal commandment against fornication. The Duke says 'Love her, Angelo'. Now if human biology cannot be subjected to magisterial command, neither can human emotion. Love your enemies and forgive them if you can. But do not command them to love you, or to love each other. Not even Prospero, Shakespeare's most powerful dramatic manipulator, commanded or expected that. King Lear learned the folly of such commandments too. But Duke Vincentio learns nothing. He admits no limits to his power and he never once analyses the total situation. And so, in defiance of all our critical efforts, Duke

Vincentio, in the second half of *Measure for Measure,* remains outside any meaning, an external plot-manipulator, a dramatic engineer of a comic ending, who never sees beyond his single theatrical goal.

Thus, precisely because of the Duke, throughout the final scene of *Measure for Measure* I feel great sympathy for Angelo, who was placed in a position to be tempted, given a dramatic appetite, then cheated of the satisfaction of gratifying it and piously condemned because he tried to do so. The play is comparable to a lady who first deliberately excites desire, then refuses to satisfy it. The ending implies that we ourselves should overcome any temptation to demand consequences and retributive justice, just after it has provocatively tantalized us with precisely this temptation. If Shakespeare wished to lead us, in the course of this play, from an appetite for tragedy (for *Hamlet*) to an appetite for comedy (for *The Tempest*) this is not the way to do it, and this specific experiment in tragicomedy is a magnificent failure. The rarer action may be in virtue than in vengeance, but we like to choose virtue for ourselves; we do not like having virtue thrust upon us any more than we like to see it thrust upon characters who are not born virtuous and do not achieve virtue for themselves in the course of the action. Indeed we may rebel against virtue imposed more than against punishments imposed. For if the facts of life have always rebelled against conventional poetic justice because it simply is not true that virtue is inevitably rewarded and vice always punished, it is even less true that divine or ducal intervention will finally make everybody be good. And do we, in fact, truly want everybody to be good at the dramatic price exacted from us by the Duke?

One school of modern criticism, on its knees before the Duke, overlooks the obvious fact that the Duke's protection ultimately forces personal and dramatic diminution on those he protects. It forces the awesome Angelo to lie down in the second-best bed of the faceless Mariana, and it blithely passes this off as the best of all dramatic destinies. At the very same time that it shelters the characters from the ultimate consequences of their own decisions and desires, it denies them the dramatic magnificence which comes only from facing such consequences. And it deprives the audience itself of an ultimate dramatic confrontation with the terrible facts of life, with the crushing dilemmas, the human vice, the human pathology which all lurk in the wings at the end of *Measure for Measure* but which the Duke, by ignoring them, tries to keep out of our sight. Indeed the Duke would seem to have precisely the same essentially patronizing designs upon us that he has upon Isabella: his palpable didactic design attempts to make us feel merciful, and his mechanical comic design attempts to make us forget the reality and the suffering of the first half of the play. For these reasons, it is good and proper that Isabella and Angelo

remain silent at the end. In the 1970 production of the play at Stratford, Isabella, with stunning effect, remained alone on the stage at the end. It would be equally interesting to see Angelo coolly manifest resentment and contempt as he stands before the Duke, for this would dramatically deprive the Duke of his all too easy victory, leave Angelo with his original individuality, and lend the impact of truth to the conclusion:

> Forgive me not, Vincentio,
> My will remains my own;
> You know it not, but I well know
> I still remain Lord Angelo,
> By choice myself alone.[18]

Still, in the long run, the violence of all these aesthetic, intellectual, and emotional objections to *Measure for Measure* testify to the play's continuing power. It is impossible to forget either its power to hurt or the things it most did show. But here any analogy with Sonnet 94 breaks down, since even some of the bravest dramatic weeds cannot outbrave the dignity of Shakespeare's festered lily. Who would prefer to have written *The Malcontent* if he could have written the great first half of *Measure for Measure?* Nevertheless, the fact remains that *The Malcontent* works as a whole, while *Measure for Measure,* taken as a whole, leaves us all knotted up in a snarl of contradictions. The play appears to show us that extremism in the pursuit of anything (chastity, sex, mercy, law) causes such damage that it becomes a vice. But at precisely the same time, the play emphatically demonstrates that while extremism in the pursuit of chastity, sex, or law may produce very great drama, extremism in the pursuit of a happy ending most definitely will not. Similarly, in defiance of the Duke's decisions (which suggest that they will suffice) the over-all action of the play demonstrates that the laws set down in heaven will not work down here on earth. And likewise, in defiance of its artificial reconciliations, the play haunts us with the cruel fact that there may be totally irreconcilable contradictions between equally valid claims to human devotion. *Measure for Measure* also clearly reveals that there are certain equally irreconcilable contradictions between comic and tragic form. For this particular tragicomedy amounts, in structure, to a dramatic self-contradiction.

In *The Malcontent* Marston took a satiric *via media* between comic and tragic form, and the result is a consistent dramatic intrigue which is governed by a consistent satirical perspective. Likewise, the dramatic realm of *The Tempest*—ruled by magic and governed with benign, philosophical detachment—transmutes comic and tragic elements alike into a rich and strange substance of its own. But the first half of *Measure for Measure,* so far as its major characters are concerned, is exclusively tragic, while the second half is a network of comic intrigues. And these two dramatic modes of presentation admit no more reconciliation than the original conflict between Isabella's desire to maintain her own chastity and her desire to save her brother's life. A decision between them is necessary; and where its major characters decide for tragedy, the play decides for comedy. But if comedy gets the last word, tragedy gets the first word, and the first word prevails because it is more powerfully expressed poetically and dramatically, and also because the word rings true. The first half of the play shows us what is in fact the case; the second half is escapist fiction. Indeed it may be a fact of dramatic life that without magic, and certainly without a clear, consistent, imaginative modulation or assimilation of them, the literal facts of human necessity, human evil, and human passion will inevitably threaten any moral or dramatic idealism that guarantees that All will be Well, and assumes that all things are but easy when they are known. For if, as Leavis argues, in the second half of the play the Duke affords us a 'criticism of life', the facts of life in the first half of the play afford us with a devastating criticism of the ducal contrivances of the second half. For Vincentio's realm was vividly introduced as a threatening world of striving and failing, of choices and judgements, a world of necessity, where people are condemned by laws they never made—in short, as the world we know. The second half of the play is thus doomed to fail the test of truth when it attempts to replace, reject, or ignore the nature of its own original dramatic dispensation. And so, and still, the phoney dramatic solution imposed upon this play's problems only calls our attention to its own ineffectuality, and thus unofficially makes us notice what we are apparently not officially supposed to notice. For by so abruptly moving into the conventionally theatrical realm of *The Malcontent*—the realm of intrigues and the expulsion of humours—only after powerfully exhibiting a series of insoluble human dilemmas, the play creates its own insoluble artistic dilemmas. And this is its major problem. And this is where we came in.

One kind of aesthetic experience creates the appetite for a different kind, and after a confrontation with *Measure for Measure*—a play which involves us personally, emotionally, intellectually, and morally, and poses problems on all these levels—it is a refreshing change to turn to a Restoration comedy which holds us morally at arm's length and sets out, without any apologies, to entertain us with some enduringly fashionable and fascinating human vices and follies. There are times when a play like Etherege's *The Man of Mode* can satisfy a very genuine dramatic need, otherwise

> In Briton why shou'd it be heard,
> That Etheredge to Shakespeare is preferr'd?
> Whilst Dorimant to crowded audience wenches,
> Our Angelo repents to empty benches: . . .
> The perjur'd Dorimant the beaux admire;

> Gay perjur'd Dorimant the belles desire:
> With fellow-feeling, and well conscious gust,
> Each sex applauds inexorable lust.[19]

Steele's Epilogue to *Measure for Measure* goes on to cry 'For shame!' and to ask his readers to 'scorn the base captivity of sin'. I shall make no such request of mine. In fact the whole gist of my discussion of *The Man of Mode* may be introduced by echoing some conventional wisdom: when faced by attractive and amusing immorality (in art, of course) it is best to relax and enjoy it.

Notes

[1] For a good survey (and bibliography) of criticism of this play see Jonathan R. Price, '*Measure for Measure* and the Critics: Towards a New Approach', *Shakespeare Quarterly*, xx (1969), 179-204.

[2] A full account of the stylistic differences between the two halves of the play appears in E. M. W. Tillyard's *Shakespeare's Problem Plays* (London, 1951), pp. 123-38.

[3] See Marston's Prologue to *The Malcontent*, which reminds the reader of the lively action which his comedy had on the stage. Of course a satiric point of view similar to Marston's governs the action of contemporary tragedies as well as contemporary comedies. The same point of view and a markedly similar cast of characters, appropriately darkened for tragic purposes, appears, for instance, in Tourneur's *Revenger's Tragedy*. In both *The Malcontent* and *The Revenger's Tragedy* the stylized characters and the satirical perspective on them lend aesthetic distance to the action.

[4] See the full discussion by Marco Mincoff, '*Measure for Measure*: A Question of Approach', *Shakespeare Studies*, ii (1966), 141-52.

[5] D. L. Stevenson, *The Achievement of Shakespeare's 'Measure for Measure'* (Ithaca, N.Y., 1966), pp. 12, 14. Mr. Stevenson himself later changes his mind and acknowledges that 'what is held brightly in focus is an excited and intensified sense of the immediate knowableness of a created and complex being: a Hamlet, an Isabella' (p. 120).

[6] For examples of saintly or lovable Isabellas see Roy Battenhouse, '*Measure for Measure* and Christian Doctrine of the Atonement', *PMLA*, lxi (1946), 1029-59; R. W. Chambers, 'Measure for Measure', in *Man's Unconquerable Mind* (London, 1952), pp. 277-310; Eileen Mackay, 'Measure for Measure', *Shakespeare Quarterly*, xiv (1963), 109-13, and others cited by D. L. Stevenson (n. 5, above), p. 89. For smug, selfish Isabellas see Arthur Quiller-Couch's Introduction to his edition of the play (Cambridge,

1922), pp. xxix-xxxiii, and U. M. Ellis-Fermor, *The Jacobean Drama* (London, 1958), p. 262.

[7] Mary Lascelles, *Shakespeare's 'Measure for Measure'* (London, 1953), p. 137. I am indebted to studies of the play by Miss Lascelles and by A. P. Rossiter throughout this chapter.

[8] F. R. Leavis (*The Common Pursuit* (London, 1952), p. 172) argues that we should willingly 'let Angelo marry a good woman and be happy', and we might—if Angelo himself ever expressed a desire to do so. The effect of Lucio's dramatic punishment might likewise be altered if Lucio verbally decided to accept and make the best of his fate, like the character tricked into marrying the witty whore in *A Chaste Maid in Cheapside*. But the characters in *Measure for Measure* express no resignation, much less enthusiasm, concerning their dramatic destinies. In *Shakespeare's Problem Comedies* (New York, 1931), pp. 106-7, W. W. Lawrence notes that Isabella does not formally assent to the Duke's proposal in the closing lines of the play, but he does not think that 'there is any doubt that Isabella turns to him with a heavenly and yielding smile'. I myself would prefer to see her turn away from him with a frowning sneer, and I do not see why my preference is any more (or less) subject to doubt than Lawrence's, since the text itself gives not one shred of evidence concerning Isabella's response.

[9] *The Common Pursuit*, p. 169. For interpretations of the Duke as Power Divine, and the play as a kind of Christian allegory, see G. Wilson Knight, '*Measure for Measure* and the Gospels', *The Wheel of Fire* (London, 1930), pp. 80-106, and the essays by Roy Battenhouse and R. W. Chambers (p. 58, n. 6, above).

[10] For a full account of the essential conflicts between the rule of law and theological mercy see Reinhold Niebuhr, *Love and Justice* (New York, 1967).

[11] See Elizabeth M. Pope, 'The Renaissance Background of *Measure for Measure*', *Shakespeare Survey*, ii (1949), 74, who quotes a contemporary distinction between two kinds of equally bad judges. The first are men such as the Duke, 'such men, as by a certain foolish kind of pity are so carried away, that would have nothing but *mercy, mercy,* and would . . . have the extremity of the law executed on no man. This is the high way to abolish laws, and consequently to pull down authority, and so in the end to open a door to all confusion, disorder, and to all licentiousness of life.' The second kind are men such as Angelo: 'such men as have nothing in their mouths, but the *law*, the *law; and Justice, Justice;* in the meantime forgetting that Justice always shakes hands with her sister mercy, and that all laws allow a mitigation. . . . These men, therefore, strike so precisely on their points, and the

very tricks and trifles of the law, as (so the law be kept, and that in the very extremity of it) they care not, though equity were trodden under foot.' There is a middle ground—equity—but its spokesman in *Measure for Measure* is Escalus, not the Duke (see Ernest Schanzer, *The Problem Plays of Shakespeare* (London, 1965), p. 116).

[12] Ultimately, in this story, 'the condemned man suffered less than he who mainly had effected the condemnation'. Such is the potentially tragic dilemma of judges. For a contrasting view of what might be expected from an upright judge see W. W. Lawrence (*Shakespeare's Problem Comedies,* p. 114): 'an audience would hardly see virtue in a man who insisted on sending a youth to death for a venial offence, in the face of moving appeals for mercy uttered by a beautiful heroine.'

[13] See Clifford Leech, 'The "Meaning" of *Measure for Measure*', *Shakespeare Survey,* iii (1950), 69.

[14] See Isak Dinesen, 'Sorrow-acre', in *Winter's Tales* (New York, 1961), pp. 52-3. See also A. H. Maslow, *Toward a Psychology of Being* (Princeton, N.J., 1962), p. 198, who clearly distinguishes between living in a realm of the imagination which is free from the laws of necessity, in the 'inner psychic world' of love, poetry, art, and fantasy, and 'living in and adapting to the non-psychic reality which runs by laws [the individual] never made and which are not essential to his nature even though he has to live by them'. By contrast with 'the more effortful, fatiguing, externally responsible world of "reality", of striving and coping, of right and wrong, of truth and falsehood', the world of the imagination may be called 'Heaven'.

[15] Coleridge and Johnson are quoted by George L. Geckle in 'Coleridge on *Measure for Measure*', *Shakespeare Quarterly,* xviii (1967), 71-2.

[16] *The Common Pursuit*, p. 163.

[17] I have applied to *Measure for Measure* the same treatment that P. B. Medawar gives to obscure modern philosophical writing in 'Science and Literature', *Encounter* (January 1969), p. 19. Medawar concludes that 'in all territories of thought which science or philosophy can lay claim to, including those upon which literature has also a proper claim, no one who has something original or important to say will willingly run the risk of its being misunderstood'.

[18] My apologies to Mr. Auden.

[19] Steele, 'Epilogue to *Measure for Measure*', quoted by Joseph Wood Krutch in *Comedy and Conscience After the Restoration* (New York, 1924), p. 245.

Phoebe S. Spinrad (essay date 1984)

SOURCE: "*Measure for Measure* and the Art of Not Dying," in *Texas Studies in Literature and Language*, Vol. 26, No. 1, Spring, 1984, pp. 74-93.

[*In the following essay, Spinrad examines the correlation between the prison imagery in* Measure for Measure *and the concept of death as an escape from the prison of life.*]

In many ways, Shakespeare's *Measure for Measure* may be considered a culmination of the Morality tradition that extends from *Pride of Life* to *Doctor Faustus:* a tradition that poses the moment of death as an understanding of life, offers the soul a last chance on earth to choose salvation or damnation, and dispatches the soul accordingly. But in *Measure for Measure,* the soul is not dispatched. And in this respect, Shakespeare's "problem" play mirrors the "problem" of life itself: that even though death offers the perfection of salvation to an imperfect world, we are often afraid to accept the terms of the offer; and that when we have overcome our fear and are ready to embrace death as a release, the kindly offer may be withdrawn.[1]

This is not to suggest that *Measure for Measure* is a grim forerunner of the twentieth-century existentialist school, or that we are meant to leave the theater shaking our heads in pity over the bad fortune that has inflicted life upon the characters of the play. Claudio, Isabella, and Angelo, we feel—yes, and even Lucio and Pompey—will be as moderately happy with their lots as any human creatures can hope to be. But there *are* some grim sets of images that dominate the action of the play, of which the primary and most pervasive is that of the prison, both the literal prison of Vienna and the figurative prison of life.

The pivot of the action in *Measure for Measure* is, of course, Claudio's death sentence, and throughout all but the first and last scenes of the play, Claudio remains in prison. To this prison come the duke, Isabella, Lucio, and Pompey; in this prison reside the provost and Abhorson, the executioner; and ordering the affairs of this prison are Angelo and Escalus. Outside the prison walls are more walls: Isabella's convent, Mariana's moated grange, and Angelo's double-locked garden and chamber. By the end of the play, although some of the characters will elect to remain in their enclosures, or will exchange one enclosure for another, most of the original doors will be opened, and the inmates will be allowed to leave. What is interesting, however, is that each character will first come to realize that there are more ways out of prison than the one that he or she has planned, and that one of the doors is Death.

In several of the possible sources of Shakespeare's play, this alternate exit is indeed made the subject of

a grim joke. Juriste, the Angelo-counterpart of Cinthio's *Epitia* (1582), also promises to free Epitia's brother from prison if she will go to bed with him; but after she has done so, Juriste sends her the dead body of her brother with a messenger who explains: "This . . . is your brother whom my lord Governor sends you freed from prison."[2] In the play that Cinthio himself made from this story in the *Hecatommithi,* the joke becomes more elaborate; the messenger is made to deliver the message twice (once to the maid and once to Epitia), and Juriste's sister, Angela, explains the irony to the audience, who may have missed the point:

> *Angela:* My brother I have cursed. . . .
> He answered, that he promised Epitia
> To give her Vico freed from prison, true,
> But never promised to release him living;
> So that she has exactly what he promised.
>   (III.ii; Bullough, p. 436)

In George Whetstone's *Promos and Cassandra* (1578), another promiser fulfills his pledge ironically. With the head sent to Cassandra, Promos sends a message that: "To Cassandra, as Promos promised thee, / From prison, lo, he sends thy brother free" (IV.ii; Bullough, p. 469). And in Thomas Lupton's *Too Good to Be True* (1581), although no such ghastly message is carried to the gentle-woman with her husband's body, the judge speaks in what appear to be deliberately equivocal terms: "and whereas your husband should have been executed tomorrow in the morning, I will dispatch him and send him home tomorrow unto you before noon at the furthest, if it be not before" (Bullough, p. 520). The gentlewoman's husband is, of course, "dispatched" by the hangman.

Shakespeare omits this sadistic joke from his play—probably to make Angelo less evil and more forgivable.[3] But the underlying irony of the joke is one that is inherent in a more serious tradition: the *de contemptu mundi* view of life itself as a prison and death as a release. A motif running through both Roman Catholic and Protestant Arts of Dying, it was first and most forcefully stated by Pope Innocent III in *De Miseria Condicionis Humane:*

> "Infelix homo, quis me liberabit de corpore mortis huius?" Certe non vult exire de carcere qui non vult exire de corpore, nam carcer anime corpus est.

> ["Unhappy man that I am, who will release me from the body of this death?" Surely, no man wishes to escape from prison who does not wish to escape from the body, for the body is a prison to the soul.][4]

And again, of the just man, Innocent says: "Sustinet seculum tanquam exilium, clausus in corpore tanquam in carcere" (II.18; "He endures the world as though he were in exile, locked up in his body as in a prison").

The 1576 translator of Innocent's treatise, H. Kirton, indeed editorializes further on the theme: "Beholde the lamentation of the silly soule, which would fayne be discharged out of prison. Whereof the Psalmist sayth thus. O lorde bring my soule out of captiuitie. There is no rest nor quietnesse in anye place heere in this world."[5] And the translator of Petrus Luccensis's *Dialogue of Dying Wel* (trans. 1603) carries the analogy still further to Claudio's case:

> When an imprisoned malefactor hath receaued sentence of death and knoweth he cannot escape, oh how many waylings, and how many lamentings maketh the wretche in that time, seeing that assuredly he must foorthwith be put to death. In this case are all men liuing found to bee, against whome as soone as euer they be borne, in this miserable and transitorie lyfe, the seuere sentence of death is pronounced.[6]

That such a motif had become almost a commonplace by the time of *Measure for Measure* is evident not only from its appearance in treatises, poems, and broadsides but also from the sardonic remark made by Sir Charles Mountford on his release from prison in Thomas Heywood's *A Woman Killed with Kindness* (ca. 1603), a play whose subplot also requires that a sister sacrifice her honor for her brother's well-being:

> *Keeper:* Knight, be of comfort, for I bring
>   thee freedom
> From all thy troubles.
> *Sir Charles:*   Then am I doom'd to die;
>   Death is th' end of all calamity.[7]

And in this sense of death as a release from prison, the famous Act III prison scene of *Measure for Measure* may be considered a series of attempts by the duke and Isabella to offer Claudio every possible escape route out of his prison, while Claudio obdurately refuses them all.

Shakespeare's audience would certainly have understood the duke's, "Be absolute for death" speech (III.i.5-41)[8] as a compendium of many traditional Christian exhortations on the vanities of life—and if, as some critics have maintained, the speech contains allusions to such pagan philosophers as Lucretius,[9] it is Lucretius filtered through Christian homiletics. Pope Innocent himself had used many of the figures and analogies that the duke uses: the baseness of the flesh, the revolt of the organs of the body, and the afflictions that torment all living creatures regardless of age, class, or virtue. Treatise after treatise had echoed Innocent in these figures and had echoed as well his comparison of death to a welcome sleep, just as does the duke:

> *Duke:*   Thy best of rest is sleep;
>   And that thou oft provok'st, yet grossly
>   fear'st
> Thy death, which is no more.
>
>   (III.i.17-19)

But in order to welcome sleep, one must first be weary, and Claudio is by no means weary of his life. Consequently, the duke, like the preachers before him, must first evoke in Claudio a sense of the frustrations of life:

> *Duke:*   Reason thus with life:
> If I do lose thee, I do lose a thing
> That none but fools would keep. A breath
>   thou art,
> Servile to all the skyey influences
> That dost this habitation where thou keep'st
> Hourly afflict.
>
>   (III.i.6-11)

This idea of the insubstantiality of human existence is certainly not contrary to Christian belief, as J. W. Lever has claimed;[10] it does not deny the divine origin of the soul, but rather contrasts the soul's heavenly importance with the laughably frail, earthly shell in which the soul resides. E. Hutchins, in his popular and rather lovely religious handbook, *David's Sling against Goliath* (1598), had made many such comparisons about human life on earth:

> Now therefore reason with me. Shal we feare death for the losse of a shadow: shall wee by sighs and sobs storme againste the Lorde for the loss of a vapour? . . . So y[t] our life is like a ruinous house, alwayes readie to fall: like a thin thred, alwaies readie to rotte: like a running cloude, whereof we are vncertaine, where and when it falleth.[11]

Considering the downfall of Claudio's expectations, he should certainly be receptive to such preaching.

But unfortunately, weak, mortal creatures seldom respond as they should and, when subjected to uncertainties in life, usually assume that they can find compensating certainties in that same life. Such was Everyman's assumption; such is Claudio's. At first, it is true, he seems to have resigned himself to death and to be giving the theologically proper response: "To sue to live, I find I seek to die, / And seeking death, find life. Let it come on" (III.i.42-43). Christopher Sutton's *Disce Mori* (ca. 1600) had said much the same thing: "That which we call life, is a kinde of death, because it makes us to die: but that which we count death, is in the sequele a very life: for that in deede it makes us to liue."[12] Or, in Kirton's translation of *De Miseria*: "We then are dying whiles we liue, and then doe we cease from dying, when we cease to liue. Therefore it is better to dye, always to liue, than to liue to dye euer. For the mortall lyfe of man is but a liuing death."[13] For Claudio, so far, so good. But he and the audience know something that the duke does not know: Isabella has been to see Angelo about

Claudio's pardon and is even now on her way to the prison—to open, as Claudio thinks, an exit for him other than dying. As long as he retains this hope for another exit, he cannot be "absolute for death."

There is, furthermore, another element missing from Claudio's apparent preparation for death: repentance. The *de contemptu mundi* sermon which the duke has given him was traditionally only the first step toward readying the dying man; it forms the first of three parts in Innocent's *De Miseria,* the other two of which deal with the deadly sins and the pains of hell; and it serves primarily as an introduction to the serious business of death in all the Arts of Dying. But the duke does not have a chance to proceed to the second step of his deathbed counseling; he is interrupted by the arrival of Isabella.[14] And from the moment Isabella enters, we know that Claudio has not really accepted the fact of death.

Claudio's first question—"Now, sister, what's the comfort?" (III.i.53)—is much like Everyman's questioning, in that it is posed in temporal rather than eternal terms; his "comfort," at this point, should be the ghostly comfort that the duke has given, but Claudio speaks only in terms of life on earth. Isabella apparently senses his weakness and his excessive attachment to life at any cost. Although she has earlier assured herself that her brother would gladly die "On twenty bloody blocks" to save his soul and hers (II.iv.176-82), his plea for "comfort" seems to frighten her into a circumlocution. Instead of blurting out Angelo's perfidy and the choice which Claudio must make, she spins an elaborate conceit on Claudio's coming journey to heaven, where he will be an "everlasting leiger," an ambassador in the court of God (III.i.56-60). It is noteworthy that she has omitted any mention of the words "die" and "death" and has inverted the traditional figure of "Death, the mighty messenger" to make Claudio the messenger instead.

But Claudio is still looking for a way out and, by a series of more and more insistent questions, forces his sister into telling him what he does not want to know:

Claudio: Is there no remedy?
Isabella: None, but such remedy as, to save a head,
  To cleave a heart in twain.
Claudio: But is there any?
(III.i.60-62)

The audience, here, might remember parts of the first debate between Angelo and Isabella, in which earthly and heavenly "remedies" were compared:

Isabella: Must he needs die?
Angelo: Maiden, no remedy.

. . . . .

Angelo: Your brother is a forfeit of the law,
  And you but waste your words.
Isabella: Alas, alas!
  Why, all the souls that were, were forfeit once,
  And He that might the vantage best have took
  Found out the remedy.
(II.iii.48, 71-75)

Why does Isabella not point out this heavenly "remedy" to Claudio? Perhaps because his mode of questioning has already indicated to her, as it has to us, that he is not open to heavenly comfort yet, that he is still too concerned with earthly comforts.

Isabella, then, becomes a shrewder comforter than the duke has been, although she, too, will fail temporarily. Taking her cue from Claudio's questions, she turns not to the *de contemptu mundi* (which her brother will not believe) but to the Christian humanist's approach to death: the appeal to heroism and the integrity of the human spirit. She begins in the negative vein, evincing doubt about Claudio's courage—perhaps as a natural expression of her new fear, but also as a plea for Claudio to prove her wrong:

Isabella: O, I do fear thee, Claudio, and I quake
  Lest thou a feverous life shouldst entertain,
  And six or seven winters more respect
  Than a perpetual honour. Dar'st thou die?
  The sense of death is most in apprehension,
  And the poor beetle that we tread upon
  In corporal sufferance finds a pang as great
  As when a giant dies.
(III.i.73-80)

This is much like two of the arguments used by the Christian humanist Thomas Lupset in *A Compendious Treatise Teachynge the Waie of Dieyng Well* (1530): first, that it is just as foolish to haggle over a few years of life as it would be for a condemned felon to demand to approach the scaffold last in line; and second, that the pain of dying is of necessity a short one, feared more by beasts than by men.[15] "Let vs then take a lusty courage of this desperation," Lupset had said, "seeinge there is no remedy: lette vs manfully go to it" (p. 280). And this ploy, for the moment, seems to work on Claudio. Flushed with resentment, he demands hotly, "Why give you me this shame?" And just as he has echoed the religious tone of the *de contemptu mundi* in reply to the duke, so he echoes the heroic tone of Lupset's "good pagan" in reply to Isabella:

Claudio: If I must die,
I will encounter darkness as a bride,
And hug it in mine arms.

(III.i.82-84)

Alas, alas, as Isabella would say. The sexual imagery and conditional "if" clause bode no good. But since Claudio has apparently responded to the humanist's call to honor, Isabella reinforces her appeal in the positive vein, congratulating him on his nobility and adding a confirmatory appeal to family as well as individual honor: "There spake my brother: there my father's grave / Did utter forth a voice" (III.i.85-86). Claudio, after all, as the eldest male in the family, *should* be willing to lay down his life for his sister's honor. But can there be some subliminal warning bell that causes her, even in the midst of her approving speech, to answer Claudio's "if" with such a positive "yes"? "Yes," she says, "thou must die" (III.i.86).

Claudio is still bargaining. To be sure, he can expect more than the "six or seven winters" which Isabella has predicted for him, and for a man still too firmly attached to this world to see things in terms of the next, even six or seven years seem better than six or seven hours. Perhaps he may even find a way, in those years, to redeem his honor—and his soul. But he is in the position, now, of Lupset's convict, merely dropping back a place in line each time the line moves toward the hangman; and every time he drops back, he makes death harder for himself.

Both the duke and Isabella may indeed have misjudged the nature of Claudio's fear, or at least the nature of his worldly attachment. He is not merely clinging to the outward trappings of fashion, as the duke has imagined; nor is he merely flying from the fear of corporal pain, as Isabella has imagined. Claudio is more pagan than either of his comforters has realized; he fears and half believes in the total annihilation of self. The first words of his last desperate appeal for life are a cry of horror at self-disintegration—a cry couched solely in terms of the body, the only self he knows:

Claudio: Aye, but to die, and go we know
not where;
To lie in cold obstruction, and to rot;
This sensible warm motion to become
A kneaded clod . . .

(III.i.117-20)

The very words of the *de contemptu mundi* have become, for Claudio, not a reason to prepare for death but a reason to dread it.

When Claudio turns his mind to the possibility of an afterlife, he is perhaps not quite pagan, but not quite an ideal Christian either. He gives no thought to heaven, but pictures in turn the fires of the preachers' hell and the torments of Dante's Inferno: the "thick-ribb'd ice" of the traitors and the windblown eternal motion of the uncommitted and the lustful. All his thoughts are of dissolution, agony, and damnation; he has succumbed at once to the traditional deathbed temptations of infidelity, impatience, and despair.

In such a state of mind, Claudio may well cry out, with Hamlet, that the suffering of life may be preferable to the sleep of death, that "the dread of something after death" (in Claudio's case, perhaps, the dread of Nothing after death) "makes us rather bear the ills we have / Than fly to others that we know not of" (*Hamlet,* III.i.78-82):

Claudio: The weariest and most loathed
worldly life
That age, ache, penury, and imprisonment
Can lay on nature, is a paradise
To what we fear of death.

(III.i.128-31)

He cannot now believe the preachers who have tried to tell him the opposite: "Yea, this case of the soule is such a cage of filth, as a man of God hath said, that no Bocardo, no dungeon, no sinke, no puddle, no pitte is in any respect so evil a prison for this bodie, as the bodie is of the soule."[16]

This is not to suggest that Claudio is wrong to fear death; no preacher or poet would have claimed that such fear is unnatural. But all would have remarked upon Claudio's failure to overcome his fear, whether by faith or by reason, and would especially have pointed out that to bargain for life at the expense of one's soul is a mortal sin: "Saynt Austyn sayth: More greate is the dommage of one soule the which is loste and deed by dampnacyon than it is of ye dethe of a thousande bodyes deed of the dethe corporall and by putryfaccyon."[17] How much worse, then, to bargain for life at the expense of someone else—a deed that will encompass the "dampnacyon" of not one, but two immortal souls.

Claudio, however, is beyond the reach of traditional appeals. He is a Worldly Man in a sense undreamed of by the sixteenth-century Moralists: the man who sees Nothing beyond the limits of his own consciousness, the quasi-solipsist who in his own demise sees the disappearance of the universe. Both the medieval and the Renaissance Christian formulas are therefore meaningless to him, since both posit a universe independent of his own being; for him to accept death, he must be convinced of the existence of things outside himself, of a continuity of Being once he is gone. And Isabella, whose impulsiveness so often bursts out in wild and whirling words, in her own desperation hits upon the right cure for her brother:

Isabella: O you beast!
O faithless coward! O dishonest wretch!
Wilt thou be made a man out of my vice?
Take my defiance,
Die, perish! Might but my bending down
Reprieve thee from thy fate, it should
  proceed.
I'll pray a thousand prayers for thy death;
No word to save thee.

                    (III.i.135-37, 142-46)

It is an angry speech, a furious speech, a violent rush
of words from a young woman at the end of her rope.
And almost from the earliest performances of *Measure for Measure,* critics have either denounced the
speech or made tortuous excuses for it.[18] But ironically, the one thing that both Isabella's detractors and
her champions have glossed over too quickly in their
analyses of her words is the most important thing about
them: they work where all else has failed.

Up to now, Claudio has managed to control his universe, despite the sentence of death, and has thus
managed to maintain his sense of being the universe.
He has sent for his sister, and his sister has arrived.
He has tossed off the correct response to the duke's
sermon, and the duke has been satisfied. He has juggled
with the seven deadly sins to make Angelo's proposition seem sinless, and he has convinced himself and
fully expects to convince his sister. Even the apparent
coincidence that the "precise" Angelo should suddenly
act out of character in a way that may save Claudio's
life is proof that Claudio's will makes and remakes
the universe. How, then, should he die?

The only answer is Isabella's. Her defiance, her thrusting of death in his face when he has it least in mind,
her very refusal to listen to his repeated cries of "Oh,
hear me, Isabella!" are all concrete evidence of a world
outside Claudio's control. And Claudio, who has declared himself unafraid of "age, ache, penury, and
imprisonment," is shocked back to reality by something far worse than any of them: a sister's contempt.

To be sure, his immediate response to Isabella's outburst is no more promising than was his response to
the duke's sermon, or to Isabella's first appeal: "I am so
out of love with life that I will sue to be rid of it"
(III.i.170-71). We have heard those words before, and
then have heard Claudio retract them. But his preface
to them, this time, *is* promising: "Let me ask my sister
pardon." Theologically, he has taken the first step toward repentance, and psychologically, he has taken the
first step toward acceptance: he has admitted that there
is Being outside himself, and at least a human being, if
not a divine one, more important than himself.

The results of Isabella's shock treatment become most
evident later in the play, when Claudio and Barnardine

are served their death warrants. Claudio now evinces
a calm acceptance of his mortality, and when asked
about Barnardine, uses a simile which links his own
past with Barnardine's present: "As fast locked up in
sleep as guiltless labor / When it lies starkly in the
traveller's bones" (IV.ii.64-65). Despite the implicit
irony of the word "guiltless" (Claudio is not above
sarcasm himself), this is not the traditional metaphor
of sleep as a type of corporal death, but rather a
metaphor which the duke has introduced earlier: sleep
as a type of spiritual death—an insensibility to the
meanings of life and death alike: "Thou hast nor youth,
nor age, / But as it were an after-dinner's sleep /
Dreaming on both" (III.i.32-34). The provost himself
sees Barnardine in these terms: "A man that apprehends death no more dreadfully but as a drunken sleep"
(IV.ii.140-41). And when Barnardine receives his summons to death, he flatly refuses to die.

In the old Morality Plays, and even in the new secular
tragedies, Barnardine would have had no choice. Humanum Genus and Everyman at first refused to die;
Tamburlaine and Macbeth refused to die; and all of
them died. Why Barnardine is allowed his refusal we
shall see later; but the refusal itself, at this point,
serves as an almost allegorized extension of Claudio's
previous denial and bargaining, and thus throws his
present acceptance into sharper relief. Indeed, the
connection between the two men is reinforced by the
nature of Barnardine's imprisonment, a form of transitional half-life similar to his "drunken sleep." He is
the prisoner who cannot and will not be released to
life or death; he has gained stay after stay of execution, and, the provost says, if he were offered a chance
to escape, he would not go. Like Claudio, he prefers
the circumscribed prison of his own ordering, where,
by denying the power of forces outside himself, he
can maintain the semblance of control. Does he not
have "the liberty of the prison" (IV.ii.145-46)? But it
is a prison after all.

The duke's evaluation of Barnardine's insensibility—
"Unfit to live or die. O gravel heart!" (IV.iii.63)—is,
then, a commentary on Claudio's earlier behavior as
well. But as always in this play where people say
much more than they think they mean, the duke is
speaking not just of Barnardine and Claudio but of
all the major figures who move around him in prisons of their own making—including himself.

Like Claudio in his physical and mental prison, Angelo,
Isabella, and the duke begin by thinking that they can
order the universe to their own requirements. Angelo
in particular is the Puritan mind carried to its coldest
extremes, a man who has mentally segregated humankind into the all-good and the all-bad, with no room in
his world for the mixed creature who can sin, repent,
and sin and repent again. But although—or perhaps
because—he so easily sends the reprobate to a literal

prison, he does not see that he is creating a separate but equal figurative prison for the elect.

Raymond Southall has postulated Angelo as an extreme post-Reformation Catholic type who relies too much on outward signs of grace, and Isabella as an extreme Protestant who relies too much on inward, individual signs; both, says Southall, must recombine into "Medieval Christianity."[19] But such an interpretation seems curiously perverse—or at least makes Shakespeare seem curiously perverse in his methods. Why, after all, clothe a symbol of radical Protestantism in a nun's habit, unless to confuse the audience needlessly? And why refer to a Roman Catholic as "precise" (I.iii.50), a term used almost exclusively of Puritans in Shakespeare's day? Indeed, Shakespeare's audience might have recognized Angelo as a Puritan even without references to his "precision" and would certainly have recognized the dangerous nature of his Puritanism: the frighteningly sincere distinction between good and evil that allows for no compromise and will make no exceptions, even for oneself.

To speak of Angelo's sincerity might sound as self-contradictory as to speak of Iago's honesty. But Isabella is only partly correct, during the judgment scene, when she says, "I partly think / A due sincerity govern'd his deeds / Till he did look on me" (V.i.443-45). A due, if warped, sincerity has governed Angelo's deeds even *after* he has looked on Isabella; he is as sincere in his sin as he was in his virtue. It is especially interesting to watch him chart his moral regression throughout the play and to match the chart against the Calvinist preacher William Perkins's outline of the progress of sin:

> Actuall sinne in the first degree of *tentation,* is, when the mind upon some sudden motion, is drawne away to thinke evill, and withall is tickled with some delight thereof. For a bad motion castinto the mind, by the flesh and the devill, is like unto the baite cast into the water, that allureth and delighteth the fish, and causeth it to bite. Sinne in *conception,* is when with the delight of the mind, there goes consent of the will to do the evill thought on. Sinne in *birth,* is when it comes forth into an action of execution. Sinne in *perfection,* is when men are growne to a custome and habite in sinne, upon long practice. . . . And sinne thus made perfect, brings foorth death.[20]

In Angelo's first stage, temptation, he does indeed use the image of the bait and fish: "O cunning enemy, that, to catch a saint, / With saints dost bait thy hook!" (II.ii.180-81). And when he has failed to master his temptation, he speaks of his "conception":

> *Angelo:*   Heaven in my mouth,
> As if I did but only chew his name,
> And in my heart the strong and swelling evil
> Of my conception.
>
>   (II.iv.4-7)

Even his shocking double entendre to Isabella, "Plainly conceive, I love you" (II.iv.140), may carry more than double meaning in this sense; he is inviting Isabella to give consent of her will to sin. And by the time he tells her, in no uncertain terms, "Fit thy consent to my sharp appetite" (II.iv.160), he has looked ahead to the next stages of his sin: "I have begun, / And now I give my sensual race the rein" (II.iv.158-59). He is predicting, here, not merely the birth, or action, of the sin of fornication, but perfection in sin, the next sin that he will "perform in the necke of" the first (Perkins, p. 98)—lying to cover his tracks: "Say what you can, my false o'erweighs your true" (II.iv.169).

Having charted his course so accurately, he must now expect that his "sinne thus made perfect, brings foorth death." And indeed, when we next see him alone, he explains in soliloquy that his reason for ordering Claudio's execution, in violation of his promise, was not gratuitous villainy, but an attempt to stave off retribution for a while:[21]

> *Angelo:*   He should have liv'd;
> Save that his riotous youth, with dangerous sense,
> Might in the times to come have ta'en revenge
> By so receiving a dishonor'd life
> With ransom of such shame. Would yet he had lived.
>
>   (IV.iv.26-30)

That last phrase is a telling one. Angelo, knowing that he deserves death, half craves the punishment—but fears the consequences. For him, in his state of sin, death means hell.

From the beginning of the play, Angelo has served as his own prosecutor, judge, and jury. He sincerely believes what he has told Escalus:

> *Angelo:* When I that censure him do so offend,
> Let mine own judgement pattern out my death,
> And nothing come in partial.
>
>   (II.i.29-31)

When he does "so offend," then, he convicts himself utterly, leaving no room for a repentance that he, as a reprobate, cannot expect to be granted. Consequently, although he dreads the damnation that he knows will follow death, when his sins are exposed during the judgment scene, he twice demands his right to die—almost, we feel, with a touch of relief that the flight from death is over:

> *Angelo:* Immediate sentence then, and sequent death

Is all the grace I beg.

. . . . .

I am sorry that such sorrow I procure,
And so deep sticks it in my penitent heart
That I crave death more willingly than
   mercy;
'Tis my deserving, and I do entreat it.
                        (V.i.371-72, 472-75)

Before we applaud Angelo's self-judgment, however, we must remember that a "penitent heart" does not refuse grace, mercy, or a chance to amend. This is not acceptance of death, but something uglier: despair. Isabella may forgive him; Mariana may forgive him; the duke and all the laws of man and God may forgive him; but unless something drastic happens, Angelo will never forgive himself. Like Barnardine refusing to escape from jail, Angelo is locked into the prison of his rigid, ultra-Puritan belief: once a sinner, forever damned.[22]

Isabella herself, who stands in opposition to Angelo throughout the play, opposes him only in the sense that a mirror image opposes the thing it reflects. She, too, wants to order the universe. Her idea of order, however, leans more to an ideal of neatness than to a system of rectitude; she is far more willing than Angelo to make moral exceptions for other people and is not above special pleading for a cause which she does not wholeheartedly espouse. It is especially noteworthy that when she learns that her brother has impregnated Juliet, her immediate response is not moral horror but commonsense practicality: "O, let him marry her" (I.iv.49). But although she grants human society the right to go to hell happily on the road of its own choosing, she herself wants a divorce from that society and would choose for herself a martyr's crown—and a martyr's isolation.

There is no need to condemn the whole system of monasticism, or to assume, as Darryl F. Gless has recently done, that Shakespeare is condemning it,[23] in order to see the self-imprisoning nature of Isabella's choices. She is not content with the already severe restrictions placed on the Poor Clares, whom she seeks to join, but would have the whole order translated into an ideal society of martyrs, one which probably cannot exist among fallible human creatures:

Isabella: And have you nuns no farther
   privileges?
Nun: Are not these large enough?
Isabella: Yes, truly; I speak not as desiring
   more,
But rather wishing a more strict restraint
Upon the [sisterhood], the votarists of Saint
   Clare.[24]

                                      (I.iv.1-5)

Whether Lucio is indeed "mocking" her when he calls her "a thing enskied and sainted" (I.iv.34) is a moot point; the important point is that Isabella would like to see her chosen world in these terms and that she finds it difficult to accept the existence of her own noble thoughts in the mind—or on the lips—of an ignoble creature from the outside world.

There is no reason, then, to doubt Isabella's word when she twice offers to lay down her life for her brother. It is the heroic thing to do, and Isabella yearns to be a saintly hero. The very words that she uses about her voluntary martyrdom show that she has adopted her ideas about sacrifice from the luridly detailed martyrologies of the time, as well as from the combined sensual and spiritual imagery of Loyolan meditation and the new poetry:

Isabella: [W]ere I under the terms of death,
   Th' impression of keen whips I'd wear as
      rubies,
   And strip myself to death as to a bed
   That longing have been sick for, ere I'd
      yield
   My body up to shame.
                              (II.iv.100-05)

But Isabella is not now in the ideal world of the martyrologies, and her imagery only whets Angelo's sensual appetite. Furthermore, not even the audience is allowed to retain Isabella's romantic view; we are made too vividly aware that those "keen whips" are in the hands of the rough-hewn Abhorson and the bumbling Pompey, an ex-pimp.

Nothing goes the way Isabella expects. Angelo turns her brilliant logic-chopping against her; the noble Law makes illicit propositions; her glorious martyrdom must be traded for a sordid tumble; and her valiant brother, who should rush to her protection, turns out to be a sniveling coward. It is small wonder that when the duke greets her after her disastrous interview with Claudio, she can hardly wait to get back to her nice, safe convent. "I have no superfluous leisure," she says. "My stay must be stolen out of other affairs; but I will attend you awhile" (III.i.156-58). This is no mere social excuse; Isabella has found the world too disappointing—yes, even too messy—and wants only to return as soon as possible to her ideal world where there are (she thinks) no loose ends and no human frailties.

It is exactly at this point that the duke steps in and begins arranging the "happy" denouement. As Rosalind Miles, who perhaps unconsciously uses the prison metaphor in her analysis, points out:

With this structure of character and plot involving Isabella, Angelo, and Claudio, the audience comes to realize that there is no help for these three from each other. Shakespeare has closed the trap of the plot upon them, and it is a trap which can only be opened from the outside. They must have external help, and that help must be the Duke's.[25]

It is true; we do feel that there is, at this point, no way out but a guilty life or death for the three. But the "trap" of which Miles speaks is Shakespeare's only at second remove, and each of thecharacters has come to the trap through the mental trap each has built for himself or herself. Furthermore, the duke's "external help" is itself a product of his own mental prison.

Miles's observation that the duke's "outside intervention is bound to be artificial and unreal" (p. 260) is a good one, but again it focuses too much on Shakespeare's plot making at the expense of the duke's. The duke, after all, could just as easily have revealed himself at this point and saved the three in a more straightforward manner. But he, too, is circumscribed by a need to order the universe—a need that combines the active meddling impulse of Angelo with the passive withdrawal impulse of Isabella. From such a mixture can come only disaster.

From the beginning of the play, it is obvious that the duke has been an anti-Machiavel, a ruler who wants to be loved more than feared by his subjects, and who has consequently been both too removed from and too permissive toward the people of Vienna. He has "ever lov'd the life removed," he tells Friar Thomas (I.iii.8), but his failure to become more involved with the punitive aspects of his ducal responsibility has caused sin to run riot in Vienna. Friar Thomas's commonsense reply to this—"It rested in your Grace / To unloose this tied-up justice when you pleas'd" (I.iii.31-32)—is not, however, to the duke's liking. He pleads that it will seem "tyranny" in him to enforce the laws that he has previously ignored and, in a revealing bit of rationalization, explains why he has given that chore to Angelo:

> *Duke:* I have on Angelo impos'd the office,
>   Who may in th' ambush of my name strike
>   home,
>   And yet my nature never in the fight
>   To do in slander.
>
> (I.iii.40-43)

We may recognize here the sentiments of every official, major or minor, down to the present day: the desire to be loved as a beneficent figure and a source of recourse against one's own rigorous enforcement agencies.

But things do not go according to plan for the duke, any more than they do for Angelo, Isabella, or Claudio. Like the eavesdropping kings and queens of Shakespeare's history plays before him,[26] the duke discovers

that his people do not universally applaud him, and he must listen to some unpleasant truths about himself even from the most slanderous tongues.

And what of the famous bed trick? It is indeed "artificial and unreal," as Miles has said, and so flimsy that we can hardly imagine Isabella agreeing to it if it had not been endorsed by a friar. Furthermore, at the introduction of the bed trick, the play begins to change with an audible creaking of machinery. But there is one thing about the bed trick that has been consistently overlooked by critics who condemn it: the bed trick does not work.

In the tales and plays that used the trick before *Measure for Measure,* the ploy does what it is supposed to do: it brings about recognition, reconciliation, or revenge. Even in Shakespeare's own *All's Well That Ends Well,* Helena gets the man she wants through a bed trick—regardless of what we think about the scoundrel that she gets. But in *Measure for Measure,* the trick makes everythingworse: it hastens the order for Claudio's execution, temporarily blackens the reputations of both Isabella and Mariana, and throws Angelo into a dangerous state of despair. The duke himself is placed in a quandary by Angelo's response to the trick; he must suddenly change all his plans, must find a new way to save Claudio's life and Barnardine's soul, must very nearly reveal himself to the provost ahead of schedule, and must later subject himself and the two women to public scorn. What has gone wrong?

The men and women of *Measure for Measure,* when they assemble at the judgment scene, have wrought havoc with their own lives, with the lives of others, and with the storybook ending that we expect of a comedy. There have been too many playwrights at work within the play, each working from a script that the others have not seen. Even after the final revelations and pardons, many of them seem only to have left one prison for another. Mariana has come out of her moated grange to be tied for life to the Puritanical Angelo. Angelo himself is in a state of despair that leads only to hell. Isabella, after what she has undergone, is as firmly locked out of her convent as she was once locked in. The duke must abandon his own quasi-monastic dreams to undertake marriage and the resumed rule of Vienna. Pompey has moved from the whorehouse to the executioner's shed. Barnardine, in or out of prison, remains in his "drunken sleep." And Lucio is married to a prostitute. Nothing, it seems, has changed, except possibly for the worse. Or has it?

The falloff which so many audiences have seen in the second part of Shakespeare's play is a reflection of the falloff which his characters have seen in their ideal worlds, as they learn to accept both death and life— their own and others'. And as in *Everyman* and the Arts of Dying, the central event of Claudio's death sentence has taught the lesson. Death, far from being the glorious martyrdom of Isabella's dreams, the comfortable sleep of the duke's dreams, the nuisance of Barnardine's, the punishment of Angelo's, or the horror of Claudio's, is in fact simply a part of life, to be accepted on its own terms and neither fled from nor sought after. The readiness, as Hamlet would say, is all; and the readiness itself casts a steadier light on life, revealing that it cannot be perfect but must not therefore be scorned. If life, in fact, is second best to heaven or whatever perfection each person imagines as his or her own ideal, second best to perfection is not a lowly status after all.[27]

This, then, is why Angelo and Barnardine must not be allowed to die. Theologically, they have not achieved repentance, and psychologically, they have not yet learned to live. In the end, what Mariana has said of Angelo is the lesson that all the great but fallible human creatures of *Measure for Measure* are in the process of learning about existence as they leave us:

> *Mariana:* They say best men are molded out
> of faults,
> And, for the most, become much more the
> better
> For being a little bad. So may my husband.
> (V.i.444-46)

Death, as Sir Charles Mountford has said, is the end of all calamity—but in the words of the old Jewish proverb, "You don't die so easy; you live with all your aches and pains."[28] The universe itself is a compromise of warring elements, and it is only through a truce with death that we may begin to negotiate with life.

Notes

[1] My discussion deals primarily with the individual's response to impending death and with his or her concept of death itself. I do not address the reactions to Claudio's supposed execution because this convention of illusory death (used in such plays as *Romeo and Juliet, Antony and Cleopatra, All's Well,* and *A Winter's Tale*) has more to do with the survivor than with the potential victim.

[2] Cinthio, *Hecatommithi,* 8.5., ed. Geoffrey Bullough, in *Narrative and Dramatic Sources of Shakespeare* (London: Routledge & Kegan Paul, 1963), II, 425. All references to Bullough are to this volume. Where Bullough gives the old spelling, I have modernized it for uniformity.

[3] The only remnant of the figure is the duke's, "He hath releas'd him, Isabel,—from the world. / His head is off, and sent to Angelo" (IV.iii.114-15). But the duke offers comfort immediately afterward, and knows, besides, that Claudio is alive.

[4] Innocent III, *De Miseria Condicionis Humane,* ed. Robert E. Lewis (Athens: Georgia University Press, 1978), I.19. Translations from this text are mine.

[5] Idem, *The Mirror of Mans Lyfe,* trans. H. Kirton, STC 14093, D3[v].

[6] Petrus Luccensis, *A Dialogue of Dying Wel,* trans. R. Verstepan, STC 19815, A8[r-v].

[7] Thomas Heywood, *A Woman Killed with Kindness,* in *Revels Plays,* ed. R. W. Van Fossen (London: Methuen, 1961), x.18-20.

[8] All quotations from *Measure for Measure* are from the Arden edition, ed. J. W. Lever (London: Methuen, 1965).

[9] See especially Arthur H. Scouten, "An Historical Approach to *Measure for Measure,*" *Philological Quarterly,* 54 (1975), 75; and Lever's introduction to the Arden edition, p. lxxxvi.

[10] Lever, ed., p. lxxxvii.

[11] E. Hutchins, *David's Sling against Goliath,* STC 1403, pp. 186-87, 188-89.

[12] Christopher Sutton, *Disce Mori. Learne to Die,* STC 23474, p. 114.

[13] *Mirror of Mans Lyfe,* D5[r].

[14] Whether the duke knows, at this point, that he will save Claudio's life along with his soul is a fruitless speculation. However, that he does plan to continue his sermon is evident from his parting words: "Dear sir, ere long I'll visit you again" (III.i.46).

[15] In *The Life and Works of Thomas Lupset,* ed. John Archer Gee (New Haven: Yale UniversityPress, 1928), pp. 281, 280.

[16] Hutchins, p. 174.

[17] *The Arte or Crafte to Lyue Well or to Deye Well* (Anon., ca. 1506), STC 793, F. lii.

[18] See Rosalind Miles, *The Problem of* Measure for Measure (New York: Barnes & Noble, 1976), for an excellent account of the centuries-long argument over Isabella's denunciation of her brother.

[19] Raymond Southall, "*Measure for Measure* and the Protestant Ethic," *Essays in Criticism,* 11 (1961), 10-33.

[20] William Perkins, *The Whole Treatise of Cases of Conscience,* ed. Thomas F. Merrill (Nieuwkoop: B. De Graaf, 1966), p. 98.

[21] Critics who defend Claudio's willingness to lay down Isabella's honor for his life may well take note that even Angelo expects better of him and understands what Claudio's society would demand of him in such a crisis.

[22] Although both Luther and Calvin had posited a state of quasi-despair as the prerequisite for conversion, Calvin's doctrine of perseverance in grace allowed for no fall and second conversion; any recurrence of despair was a sign that the soul was reprobate (see Calvin's *Institutes,* esp. III.iii.32 and III.v.3): Angelo, having once thought himself of the elect, stands self-convicted of reprobacy and hence of an inability to repent.

[23] Darryl F. Gless, Measure for Measure, *the Law, and the Convent* (Princeton: Princeton University Press, 1979), esp. chaps. 1-3.

[24] I do not agree with Lever's substitution of "sisters stood" for"sisterhood" in this line. It seems just as likely that "sisterstood" in F was a typo, since it was corrected to "sisterhood" in F2 and subsequent editions.

[25] Miles, p. 260. Although Miles obviously disagrees with critics who see the duke as a Christ figure who returns to mete out justice and mercy, she gives a good account of the duke's eschatological—and folkloric—associations (see esp. her pt. 2, chap. 1-2).

[26] See, e.g., *3 Henry VI,* II.v; *Richard II,* III.iv; *2 Henry IV,* II.iv; and *Henry V,* IV.i.

[27] As for Lucio's cry that "Marrying a punk . . . is pressing to death, / Whipping, and hanging" (V.i.520-21), can we really see Lucio choosing death before dishonor? Like the other characters in the play, he has tried to order his own destiny—in this scene, by requesting whipping instead of hanging. After the duke first offers him both and then remits both, all Lucio can bargain for is a remission of the marriage as well. But he, too, must learn to live with someone else's idea of justice and mercy.

[28] Like all proverbs in other languages, this is a difficult one to translate accurately. "Meh shtarbt nisht azoi gring; meh lebt un mitchet zich" is really a response both to "These troubles will kill me" and to "I wish I were dead." The use of the reflexive verb, "mitchen zich," also implies that the troubles or griefs are the function of oneself—not necessarily in the sense of assigning blame, but in the sense that the human condition is inherently a condition of trouble, that we breathe in pain as we breathe in air. But we continue to breathe.

T. A. Stroud (essay date 1993)

SOURCE: "Lucio and the Balanced Structure of *Measure for Measure,*" in *English Studies,* Vol. 74, No. 1, February, 1993, pp. 84-95.

[*In the essay that follows, Stroud argues that the comic plot initiated by Lucio is intended to balance the more serious, "quasi-tragic" plot initiated by Angelo.*]

The title of Shakespeare's problem play is an open invitation for readers to speculate about its polarities, especially about which of the symmetrical oppositions are crucial to its interpretation. Long ago Lever adequately summarized its 'contrasts and antimonies juxtaposed and resolved',[1] of which a memorable example is Stevenson's analysis of Angelo and Isabella as 'paired and balanced representatives of human nature'.[2]

No matter how obtrusive Lucio may have seemed to Lever, however, and to others who search for 'a unified ideological message' in the play,[3] they generally dismiss him as a 'comic scapegoat figure'[4] unworthy of further speculation except by those who depend on his remarks to denigrate the Duke's character, either as Satan's emissary or as 'a pious bawd'.[5] In a recent article Swann 'refutes' the traditional view of Lucio (a favorite goal of post-modernists) most ingeniously as a 'benefactor' who for whatever reason seeks to punish the authorities for corrupting him . . . if by Jacobean standards he was corrupt at all.[6] I hope that my conception of his role as intended to balance Angelo's will constitute an indirect refutation.

As a Formalist, I initially assume that *Measure for Measure* is one of many imaginative narratives, dramatic or novelistic, whose plots constitute aesthetically delightful configurations which cannot be explained by, enhanced by, or subsumed to one message, or even to two unreconciled ones.[7] I agree rather with Professor Levin that critics who assume that some moral or social generalization provides an art work with its *raison d'être* seldom feel any need to explain its pattern or enhance its value. The message they discern in most fictions is as banal as it is socially acceptable, and is rendered ineffective by the fact that other critics often opt for quite different meanings.

Early in this century Sir Arthur Quiller-Couch found it to be 'one of the puzzles of the play that the jackanape Lucio should take so much of the limelight as he does in the finale . . . '[8] But few have taken the puzzle seriously. M. C. Bradbrook did comment briefly on his 'symbiotic' relationship with the Duke: ' . . . Lucio, who at the beginning of the play organizes what action there is, becomes as it were another deputy for the Duke; first giving his own character to the absent ruler, then fathering his own aspersions upon the Duke himself, in his role of Friar'.[9] Similarly, H. W. Bennett observedthat Lucio is 'the thread on which the action of the play is strung',[10] but never explained his contribution to what A. D. Nuttall cryptically described as the 'elegant intricacy of [its] plot',[11] an elegance which I propose to credit in large measure to the interplay of plot symmetries.

Shakespeare varies his primary source (*Promos and Cassandra*) in a number of ways, but the significant variations generally involve a reprise of a plot motif or a doubling of its characters. Professor Nevo's impressive list of such doublings begins with the Duke's choice of not one but two polarized deputies[12] and the Duke's decision to balance both of them by remaining in Vienna. Such features of Shakespeare's plays are not really surprising, however, when one realizes how frequently symmetries, polarities and doublings appear whenever he introduces novel characters or plot units into his versions of other plays, notably the 'Chinese box' sequence of overheard lovers in *Love's Labor's Lost,* the parallel hoaxing of Benedick and Beatrice, the 'interweaving of the stories of two generations' in *The Winter's Tale,* and the Caliban-Ariel opposition in his last comedy.[13] Perhaps the most obvious example is *The Comedy of Errors,* in which adding a second set of twins greatly increases the number of 'successive episodes of mistaken identity [which] follow an almost mathematical pattern of permutations and combinations';[14] but as Kermode points out, in such plays as *Hamlet* and *Lear* the playwright's 'doubling' may be less obvious but hardly less basic.[15] Is it too much to suppose that human beings have an insatiable craving for symmetries and that no writer ever excelled Shakespeare in satisfying that need?

Admitting the possibility that the text of *Measure for Measure* suffered significant damage before being preserved in the First Folio, I still maintain that some of the widespread critical dissatisfaction with this play is attributable to an incompleted but intentional balancing or doubling thus far overlooked—namely, the plots initiated by Lucio and Angelo. In formulating these plot strands, I find myself agreeing at times with Professor Miles's observation that 'any discussion of *Measure for Measure* eventually comes down to a discussion of the play as it seems to have been intended, rather than as it is'.[16] In this instance, I believe that the playwright either scaled down his original conception of the Lucio-Angelo opposition as he fleshed out the scenes or conceived it too late for it to function smoothly in the total configuration. In either case, critics have failed to perceive how nearly the play comes to balancing a quasi-tragic plot initiated by Angelo against a satirically comic one initiated by Lucio. Without being adjusted to that Angelo-Lucio polarity, any thematic interpretations based solely on other polarities are likely to be inadequate or misleading. Thus, for example, Professor Altieri denies that the play can be unified because the low comic group is used to 'travesty' rather than modify the main action.[17]

Both plot strands originate in the Duke's attempt to reconcile the highest degree of morality (in his subjects) with the most mercy (toward the offenders), a condition supposedly existing in Vienna fourteen years earlier (II, i, 19-21), and soon becomes a frantic effort to straighten out the resulting mess. Each strand has its own protagonist, however, and unfolds concurrently without either assimilating the other. (Isabella does at times dominate the play, but always as an antagonist reacting to the others.) Lucio, Angelo and Claudio all try to manipulate her, but none succeeds; later the Duke employs her to solve his crisis and chooses her to help him co-exist with a recalcitrant society.

As to whether Shakespeare intended by the Duke's activities to flatter King James or to censure him, today's historical critics cannot agree, and may be even more confused now that the traditional view of the the Duke as a surrogate for God[18] has been challenged by critics who accept Lucio's view of him as sensually reprehensible.[19] Such vital disagreements bring into question most thematic interpretations, and are enough to justify focusing on the aesthetic consequences of positing dual plot strands in *Measure for Measure.*

Since there is no disguised ruler in Shakespeare's sources, having a Lucio figure slander him is of course original with this play, and so are any doublings of characters and repetitions of plot motifs that depend on Lucio's presence. The subplot in which Promos's henchman easily obtains the favor of a courtesan while Promos struggles to overcome Cassandra's resistance may be the germ of the balanced structures, but the earthy scenes inserted almost at random in *Promos and Cassandra* do little to account for Shakespeare's variations.[20]

Few would question that Angelo is the protagonist in a serious plot strand. But why cannot Lucio, as he attempts to save Claudio from Angelo's judgment, then in frustration seeks to defame the Duke, and finally appeals in vain to escape a punishment befitting his crime, provide a non-serious plot strand intentionally (though imperfectly) balancing the other? If Shakespeare's goal was merely to undermine the seriousness of the Angelo plot, it would have been easy to have Angelo slander the Duke without knowing his identity, thus making the comic plot superfluous. By inventing Lucio to serve this purpose, however unequal at times the bulk of his contribution, and setting his comic slandering against Angelo's unsuccessful seduction-revenge, the playwright achieves the play's present configuration.

The first hint of a balance between Angelo and Lucio involves the names Shakespeare gave them: like Lucifer, Lucio's name is derived from 'lux', but 'light' here is a metaphor for 'loose' rather than 'moral'; Angelo's is cognate with angelic, but really serves to contrast his sinful potential with his reputation. Lucio's renown among the Viennese for sneering at virtue, for 'blaspheming the good', balances Angelo's monopoly of rectitude. Lucio is a comic talent (that is, a person adept at making others look ridiculous) prone to attribute his own vices to everyone else; Angelo is a moralist ready to punish others for the vices which he denies sharing. Neither is a hypocrite, but Lucio wants credit for more sins than he has committed, while Angelo is inordinately proud of his moral superiority. In the play, neither is guilty of more than idle words and vicious intentions: Lucio because his slanders are vented primarily on his victim, the Duke; Angelo because his victim gets help from the only man capable of preventing the crime, the Duke.

The first two scenes initiate the structural opposition. The first opens with a pillar of rectitude being summoned to the palace, to be ceremoniously but enigmatically assigned the task of reforming his society; the second with an idle gentleman exchanging cheap and pointless insults with two others whose only function in the play is to lose a 'dismal punning match',[21] in the process of which they implicitly agree that rulers in general are neither desirous of moral improvement nor capable of improving others. While Angelo is being formally empowered to constrain the immorality of the subjects, Lucio appears as a powerless onlooker; yet he focuses the general assumption of the Viennese underworld that Vincentio's drastic move to reform the society is as Machiavellian[22] as it is futile.

In the first scene the Duke is curiously hesitant, even ambiguous about which laws he wants enforced, uncertain about the virtues which 'must go forth from us' (II, i, 30): Thus he begins confusingly:

> Of government the properties to unfold,
> Would seem to me t'affect speech and
>   discourse . . .
>
> (I, i, 22-23)

and continues to be so confused that Angelo is given no guidance or limits for his campaign to restore moral order to Vienna. The opening scenes introduce two counterposed plot strands: in one strand the conspicuously moral Angelo eventually commits himself to actions so heinous that he must conceal them from the world, particularly the Duke, in the other a 'merciful' Lucio would convince the world that the Duke has committed equally heinous crimes without letting him learn the identity of the slanderer. Thus, the audience soon becomes ironically aware that this particular deputy is no more likely to reconcile 'morality and mercy in Vienna' (I, i, 45) than Lucio would be.

If audiences wonder at all about this juxtaposition, they are soon drawn into three acts of events so intense that the evidence for such a balance is overlooked. The readers who agree with Tillyard that 'the play is not of a piece but changes its nature half way through',[23] must be ignoring the opening juxtaposition of a a prudish Angelo pharisaically aching to reform the society with a bored and licentious Lucio craving even more licence. Once they comprehend Lucio's role,

however, the notion that the tragedy 'goes to pieces' when Marianna is introduced becomes less plausible.[24]

In the first scene Angelo accepts (though with modest hesitation) an opportunity to display his moral superiority; in the second, Lucio's being asked to intercede for Claudio affords a welcome outlet for his sexual obsessions and a self-serving cause to pursue. As the instrument which the Duke chooses to redeem Vienna, Angelo lacks the touch or taint of humanity which Lucio (and the Viennese in general) have in excess. When Claudio appeals to Lucio for help, he first assumes that Angelo will relent (I, ii, 124), then that the Duke will countermand an obviously excessive punishment, and even after learning of the Duke's absence, continues to suppose that Claudio's sentence can easily be rescinded. Claudio's telling Lucio that the punishment had some justification (I, ii. 121-26) is ironical, for no one is less likely to take him seriously than Lucio, to whom Claudio appeals for aid, perhaps because he does not feel he deserves a better defender against the authorities. And Lucio is too tainted with cynical irresponsibility to do much, at least not until the cause becomes personal.

Lucio's nature is exemplified by his ambiguously cynical greeting to Isabella: 'Hail, virgin, if you be . . .' (I, iv, 16). When Lucio's every speech reflects his captious cynicism, why should audiences suppose that Lucio is sincere in complimenting Isabella (I, iv, 34-7), especially as flattery here is serving the purpose of a natural hypocrite? When he calls her a saint, Isabella herself doubts his sincerity: 'Sir, make me not your story' (I, iv, 29). There is little to indicate that Lucio is ever tinged with idealism[25] and less that he ever wants to 'curb his own lechery' (IV, iii, 152).

In the source(s) of this play, the female intercessor needs no one to urge her on, whereas urging the sexually repressed Isabella requires a modest degree of rhetorical skill, especially by a roué like Lucio, to have her ask mercy for her brother. At this point Lucio still believes that an appeal to the Duke (of whose absence he has just learned) will be an adequate last resort. In directing Isabella's plea as though he were a master of one-upmanship coaching an apprentice, Lucio foreshadows his role in Act V.[26] Lucio urges Isabella to violate her fundamental beliefs both to save her brother's life and (as far as he is concerned) 'for the encouragement of the like, which else would stand under grievous imposition' (I, ii, 182-83). When she indulges in rhetorically inappropriate insults such as 'it is tyrannous to use it as a giant', they strike him as 'well said' (II, ii, 107-09), and when she naively stumbles into hinting bribery (II, ii, 146), he disapproves only when it has an adverse effect on Angelo. By the time of the second confrontation, of course, Lucio's absence is essential to Angelo's blackmail; and after all, Lucio has no reason to suppose his presence is needed.

In this interplay of the two plot strands, Lucio contributes to Angelo's temptation by insisting that Isabella not merely persist in her pleading but also be sexually provocative.[27] What Lucio craves above all is a passionate (i.e., sexually oriented) delivery: 'Hang upon his gown' (II, ii, 45) and 'You are too cold' (II, ii, 56). However excusable, even enviable, Lucio considers Claudio's affair with his betrothed, he never asks the prudish Isabella to pursue loopholes in the law itself. Lucio's comments, though they are as pithy as Angelo's are verbose, partly account for the faulty rhetoric and equivocal language in her plea,[28] and balance Angelo's speeches primarily by their incongruity and audacity. The laughs Lucio gets (from the audience?), in spite of the intensity of the scene, help him to feel smug about the outcome, and it is only after learning of Angelo's verdict that he seeks to punish those responsible for his failure. Later, since his slanders are spoken directly to a victim rendered defenceless by the demands of his own role, Lucio has all the skill he needs to drive them home. Vincentio's later soliloquy: 'Millions of false eyes are stuck upon three. Volumes of reports . . . rack thee in their fancies.' (IV, i, 60-1) indicates that he thinks Lucio's slanders are endlessly proliferating.

The situation also explains why Lucio does not choose to slander Angelo, a man whose 'urine is congealed ice' (III, ii, 118), 'one who was not born of woman' (III, ii, 97). Instead Lucio chooses a more vulnerable target, a conveniently absent ruler who is—after all—ultimately, responsible for the miscarriage of justice. There is good reason to suppose that the Duke's disguise was a mystery to Lucio, for otherwise he would not later have risked stripping off the ruler's cowl; yet Lucio's paranoid speculations about the Duke do give the play a further 'air of design', another 'turn of the screw'. Reacting to Lucio's slanders 'with rare intensity', Vincentio continues to brood about them in private,[29] feeling as desperate to defend himself against Lucio's slanders as he is to forestall Angelo's machinations. Those who credit Lucio's charges despite the absence of any other internal evidence seem suspiciously anxious to 'refute' traditional views.

The abnormal situation created by the Duke's mysterious disappearance frees Lucio to besmirch Angelo's sponsor, yet only after having his impulse to save Claudio frustrated does he begin to slander the Duke. No matter how many sexual allusions are identifiable in Lucio's initial conversation, the snide remarks about the Duke and his fellow rulers imply nothing personal about his sexual habits. Similarly, Angelo's obsession with having Isabella emerges only after she appears before him in the habit of a novice and convinces him of her chastity: 'O cunning enemy that, to catch a saint, / With saints dost bait thy hook.' (II, ii, 180-81). Thus, Claudio's predicament stirs what may be the only components in Lucio's personality capable of diverting him from an aimless and foppish existence, while Claudio's novice sister may well stir the only iniquitous impulse which Angelo is incapable of suppressing (a situation reminiscent of the minister's reaction to a repentant prostitute in Maugham's short story, 'Rain'). And as the Duke becomes more and more engaged in thwarting the consequences of Angelo's lechery, he becomes increasingly vulnerable to Lucio's slanders.

Since the Angelo-Lucio counterpointing tends to blur in the middle episodes, however, audiences of every age have overlooked or dismissed this structural balancing and settled for labeling Lucio an obtrusive hanger-on. I propose instead that the playwright has sent in a substitute—a move hardly unexpected if Professor Leggatt is correct in finding this a play rife with substitutions.[30] Viewing Pompey as a low-class counterpart of Lucio not only seems plausible but allows the structural balancing with Angelo to be extended into the middle scenes. As Professor Carlson points out, the two share their outcast state alone, enthusiastically agree that women are defined in terms of their sexual relations to men, and prefer the same vulgar language.[31] In his very first appearance Pompey out does Lucio in selfish cynicism as he discredits Lucio's motivation for acting on behalf of Claudio. Also Pompey's 'groping for trouts in a peculiar river' neatly echoes Lucio's pun-loving reactions to the situation: 'filling a bottle with a tun-dish' (III, ii, 182) or more poetically: ' . . . her plenteous womb / Expresseth his full tilt and husbandry' (I, iv, 43-44).

I suggest that Lucio and Pompey are as deliberately correlated in this play as are Mercutio and the Nurse in an earlier tragedy, in which they function as equally bawdy and garrulous 'nurses' of Romeo and Juliet respectively.[32] As the aristocratic Mercutio tries unsuccessfully to promote Romeo's welfare, so gentleman Lucio tries in vain to save Claudio by having Isabella charm Angelo, both proponents being driven by a macho cynicism inconsistent with their goals. Similarly, Juliet's Nurse and Pompey both tease and circumvent the Establishment, until in a sense they join it. Only the supernaturally-tinged powers of the Duke prevent *Measure for Measure* from ending as disastrously as *Romeo and Juliet*.

Pompey's next appearance (II, i), according to Professor Miles, is an 'amusing stroke of dramatic parallelism'.[33] But it should be noted that, like Lucio's badinage with the Gentlemen, Pompey's defense of Froth primarily aims at the denigration of authority. Given the circumstances, Lucio had come as close to defending Claudio as Pompey does for Froth, and in the same spirit. By causing Elbow, that weakest limb of the law, to look even stupider than usual, and by frustrating Escalus with his digressions and incoherencies, Pompey also foreshadows Lucio's climactic assault on the Duke, that torso of the law who symbolically but temporarily combines the church and the state. Pompey impudently exploits Elbow's malapropisms to show Angelo as unequal to routine administrative duties as he is to justice.

Another possible link is the juxtaposition of the Duke's attack on Pompey's 'filthy vice' (III, ii, 22) and Lucio's complaint to the disguised Duke that Angelo might have 'A little more lenity to lechery' (III, ii, 94). Admittedly, Pompey does not participate in Lucio's verbal abuse of the Duke, who after all is in disguise when he insists that Pompey receive 'correction and instruction' as a bawd (III, iii, 32) but his success in ridiculing the Duke's surrogates neatly equates him with Lucio. Pompey's talent for distracting authorities temporarily postpones his whipping and incarceration; and even after the sentence is pronounced, he gets unexpected relief in the form of an ironically appropriate job as hangman's assistant, for whose duties he becomes even more enthusiastic than the professional Abhorson. In the fifth act Lucio similarly threatens the judicial proceedings with chaos as he first pleases onlookers with his witty slanders of the Friar-Duke, only to have his sentence temporarily postponed by having successfully duped Escalus, and even after being condemned to whipping and death, he suffers only the indignity of retroactive cuckoldry (not that his macho code would ever let him admit his relief).

The hint that Lucio had informed on Pompey and on Mistress Overdone (III, ii, 60) suggests Lucio's callousness and meanness, but hardly more than Pompey's encouragement to Barnardine: 'Awake till you are executed and sleep afterwards' (IV, iii, 33). When the prison-bound Pompey appeals to Lucio for help, in a reprise of Claudio's earlier entreaty, Lucio dismisses the plea with the same derision Pompey would have accorded his acquaintances: 'Farewell, good Pompey. Commend me to the prison, Pompey; you will turn good husband now, Pompey . . . ' (III, ii, 67-68), a sneer perhaps hinting at Lucio's imminent 'shotgun marriage'!

Critics haunted by the feeling that the deadly seriousness of the major characters in Angelo's strand aesthetically demands a tragic outcome,[34] tend to hold that the play breaks 'into disparate halves' in order to permit a comic ending. But the break is minimized if we credit Lucio-Pompey with a major role, one which includes inciting laughter during Isabella's pleas for her brother's life, and insolently taunting the authorities.

With Pompey's help, Lucio becomes the center of a society so earthy that the idea of a male being condemned to death for fornication is too fantastic to support a tragic tone. As the Lucio-surrogate Pompey speculates 'If you head and hang all that offend that

way but for ten years together' (II, i, 238-39), there won't be any left to behead. In moving from the intensely emotional confrontations between Isabella and Angelo to the satirical interplay between the Duke's frantic schemes and Lucio's foolhardy malignity, the play admittedly demands somewhat different reactions from the audience; yet in the early scenes Lucio's role, properly understood, should already bring into question the notion that the last two acts are appended as a wish-fulfillment dream sequence[35]. The Duke's musing on greatness in IV, i., may seem 'irrelevant and insufficient',[36] but it strengthens the likelihood that Lucio's activities constitute a contrapuntally opposed plot strand.

One particularly intriguing opposition is that referred to as the 'bed trick' and the 'head trick'.[37] The first is a comic element as out of place in the serious plot as the second is in the comic plot. In the serious plot, introducing a woman who craves to lose her maidenhead to Angelo allows Isabella to defy Angelo successfully despite Claudio's refusal to die quietly. In the comic plot, Barnardine's obstinate refusal to supply the needed head (which parodies Claudio's refusal) requires an even more far-fetched comic 'deus ex machina' to furnish a substitute, while the irrepressible Pompey, along with several representatives of the criminal class, unwittingly help Lucio torment the Duke.

Although one may question whether Pompey, even with the incidental support of the other riff-raff, supplements Lucio enough to balance the Angelo plot in the middle sequences, the strands are clearly balanced in the final scenes. It is no surprise that a critic perhaps unaware of the balance remarks that Lucio does 'noticeable damage to the ostensible solemnity of the play's climax'.[38] Once more Lucio has fewer lines than the so-called 'major' characters, but the difference this time is relatively small.

In the presence of the disguised Duke, Lucio desperately redoubles his slanders, while Angelo reinforces his lies as a cushion against exposure (IV, iv). Now we have the ironical switch from a Duke who must endure Lucio's slanders to preserve his disguise to a ruler who cannot prevent further slanders without spoiling the trap triggered by his disguise. Lucio, whose primary motive now is to avoid punishment, joins Isabella in longing for the Duke to appear; Angelo fears her accusations and dreads the Duke's appearance. Then both characters feel unduly safe for a brief period: Lucio because he thinks to have nullified any charges of the pseudo-friar by slandering him in advance, Angelo because the Duke apparently defends him against Isabella's charges.

Hoping to expose the conspiracy, the Duke now calls on Escalus, but finds him so thoroughly entangled in

Lucio's lies that his slanders seem to have triumphed. Likewise, Angelo, thinking he has an opportunity to bury the evidence of his misdeeds, feels he has escaped exposure. The Duke tricks Angelo into admitting his guilt only after panic has caused him to augment his lies; and in switching roles to achieve that goal, the Duke inadvertently emboldens Lucio to strip off the Duke's cowl, thereby simultaneously exposing Lucio's comic viciousness and nullifying Angelo's power to sneer at human weakness, much less to punish sins according to his lights.

Both characters are condemned to death; then the sentence is reduced to forced marriages with their victims, by which action Angelo is redeemed, Lucio undone. And by being given husbands, Kate Keepdown and Mariana are both made 'honest' women, Kate despite her bastard, Mariana despite her lost virginity. Angelo, as abject as Lucio is unrepentant, emerges as a quasi-tragic figure undergoing the equivalent of shock treatment:

> I am sorry that such sorrow I procure,
> And so deep sticks it in my penitent heart
> That I crave death more willingly than
>   mercy;
> 'Tis my deserving, and I do entreat it.
>
> (V, i, 472-75)

After Angelo realizes the depths of his turpitude, we may assume that he will prove worthy of Mariana's long-suffering love (though the assumption is not shared by those who indulge in the recent fad of 'attacking the terminality of the ending').[39]

If it is the Duke's nature to test the morality of others, it is ironical that Lucio and Angelo serve to test him in complementary ways: Lucio his passive tolerance, Angelo his active ingenuity. Of all the persons whose traits the Duke sought to elevate, only Lucio remains untouched. Even as he suffers a paralyzing reversal, he never ceases struggling to regain his status as a 'comic talent': 'I beseech your Highness do not marry me to a whore. Your Highness said even now, I made you a Duke; good my lord, do not recompense me in making me a cuckold' (V, i, 510-12). To suppose that he 'pays dearly for all his jests',[40] as some critics do, is to ignore all this balancing of the plots. The fact that Lucio's sentence is withheld until the last moment, that his punishment so neatly fits the crime in subverting his talent for ridiculing or maligning others, and that in the original production he may well have been the last to leave the stage, should lend weight to the balancing of strands. Since Lucio's protests save him from execution, then from beating, why would not he (like Brer Rabbit threatened by the Briar Patch) vehemently protest the cruelty of being forced to marry the 'punk' who bore his son (V, i, 522-23). Lucio is no court jester insulting a ruler for the social good,

nor is he in any way redeemed by his experience. Instead he becomes a climactic test of the Duke's capacity for clemency, which now preserves Lucio from the execution appropriate to such a crime in Shakespeare's world.[41] Furthermore, the audience finds the Duke's decision aesthetically acceptable because it so appropriately destroys Lucio's power to ridicule or slander.

The play ends, moreover, with four of the most varied and equivocal engagements imaginable. In his 'festive' comedies, Shakespeare ends with three or more engagements or marriages, most of which are romantic in tone; the four he offers here could hardly be less romantic or more diverse.[42] Lucio's plot strand mates a whoremaster and his whore; Angelo's a woman without pride and a man without honor; Claudio is already married except for a technicality, and the Duke has simply found a worthy consort. Lucio has a child already, Claudio's is near, Angelo's wife may have just conceived; but the Duke gives no sign of sex being relevant to his plans, nor is there any reason to suppose that Isabella has changed her mind about sexual activity. Her failure to respond verbally to the Duke's offer has even been interpreted by recent 'refuters' as a refusal;[43] but it seems much more likely to reflect the silence of the 'the Votarists of Saint Clare'. Why should audiences be surprised that no word of love has crossed their lips? The compassion she displays for her would-be ravisher and (as far as she knows) the killer of her brother (though perhaps tainted by self-regard), is consistent with her seeing herself as a nun choosing another, perhaps even 'more strict restraint'.

At the close, therefore, the plot strands clearly renew their contrapuntal balance. Viewed in this perspective, the Duke's verdicts are highly appropriate; any arguments that the punishment of Angelo is indulgent and that of Lucio disturbingly harsh[44] ignore the symmetry. That Angelo has undergone a permanent reformation is implied in the Duke's plea: 'Forgive him Angelo, that brought you home / The head of Ragozine for Claudio's (V, i, 526-27). Just the opposite can be inferred from Lucio's responses; in fact, only if Lucio is right about the Duke, as 'refuters' would have us believe, are we justified in charging the Duke with cruelty. Since most of the evils attributed to the Viennese seem to involve fornication, marrying off the various participants ironically suggests that the citizens can be reformed simply by legalizing their sins. Undoubtedly Vincentio learns from the experience, but what he learns leaves him—and the audience—no closer to reconciling morality and mercy than he was before. Given the 'pretty tales' about the Duke's sexual habits (so inexplicable to him!) and his acquisition of a wife capable of paradigmatic mercy, he is no more likely to reform the state than he was when he delegated the task to a 'hatchet man'—an outcome delightful for those who prize the ironies of comedy, but hardly one appropriate to religious allegory or conducive to moral improvement.

However driven at this period of his life Shakespeare may have been by a desire to reconcile morality and sexuality,[45] themes which undeniably function as opposites in this play, this view of the plot questions the reconciliation with which it has been credited. Admittedly, the play acknowledges many aspects of the moral dilemma, the need for mercy, love, and justice, but implies no remedies. Rather (to return to the initial comment by Nuttall), Shakespeare 'unites elegant intricacy of plot with the greatest possible inconsistency of ethical principle'. To those—like me—who treasure complexity integrated into an aesthetic whole, it confirms Shakespeare's persistent fascination with the aesthetic potential of symmetry.

Notes

1 J. W. Lever, ed., *Measure for Measure,* Arden edition (London, 1965), pp. xliii, lvi, ciii, etc. (All quotations are taken from this text.)

2 D. L. Stevenson, 'Design and Structure in *Measure for Measure*', *ELH* 23 (1956), 266.

3 C. Swann, 'Lucio: benefactor or malefactor', *Crit. Q.* 29 (1987), 56. An earlier exception is Lucio's thematic function in Terry Eagleton, *William Shakespeare* (New York and Oxford, 1986), p. 53.

4 Robert Rogers, *A Psychoanalytic Study of the Double in Literature* (Detroit, 1970), p. 75.

5 Nevill Coghill, 'Comic Form in *Measure for Measure*', *SS,* 8 (1955), 23-24, finds him a minor Satan. Geoffrey Bullough, ed., *Narrative and Dramatic Sources of Shakespeare* (London, 1958) II, 410, calls Lucio an 'advocatus diaboli'; as do Francis Fergusson, *The Human Image in Dramatic Literature* (New York, 1957), p. 135; and Louise Schleiner, 'Providential Improvisation in *Measure for Measure*', *PMLA,* 97 (1982), 227-36.

6 Swann, p. 56.

7 Richard Levin, 'Some Second Thoughts on Central Themes', *MLR,* 66 (1974), pp. 3-4.

8 *Measure for Measure:* A. Q-C and J. Dover Wilson (eds.), New Cambridge Edition (Cambridge, 1922) p. xl.

9 *The Artist and Society in Shakespeare's England* (Brighton, Sussex, 1982), pp. 152-53.

10 *Measure for Measure as Royal Entertainment* (New York, 1966), p. 90.

11 '*Measure for Measure:* The Bed Trick', *SS,* 8 (1975), 51.

12 Ruth Nevo, '*Measure for Measure:* Mirror for Mirror', *SS* 40 (1988), 107-22.

13 Marion B. Smith, *Dualities in Shakespeare* (Toronto, 1966), p. 23; *Shakespeare Design* (Cambridge, Mass., 1972), pp. 27-67.

14 Robert Grudin, *Mighty Opposites: Shakespeare and Renaissance Contrariety* (Berkeley, Cal., 1979), p. 8.

15 Frank Kermode, *Forms of Attention* (Chicago, 1985), pp. 38-44.

16 Rosalind Miles, *The Problem of Measure for Measure* (New York, 1976), p. 285.

17 Joanne Altieri, 'Style and Social Disorder in *Measure for Measure*', *SQ,* 25 (1974) 16.

18 Roy W. Battenhouse, '*Measure for Measure* and the Christian Atonement', *PMLA,* 61 (1946) 1029-59; G. Wilson Knight, *The Wheel of Fire,* rev. ed. (New York, 1957), pp. 74 ff.

19 W. J. Martz, *The Place of 'Measure for Measure' in Shakespeare's Universe of Comedy* (Lawrence, Kansas, 1982), p. 92, suggests that Angelo's reactions hint that the Duke is homosexual.

20 Bullough, II, 444-45; Kenneth Muir, *Shakespeare's Sources I: Comedies and Tragedies* (London,1957), pp. 101-9; Anthony Brennan, *Shakespeare's Dramatic Structures* (London, 1986), pp. 80-82, finds Shakespeare's changes in Cinthio's story to be even more fundamental.

21 Louise Schleiner, 'Providential Improvisation in *Measure for Measure*', *PMLA* 97 (1982), 227-36.

22 Harold Skulsky, *Spirits Finely Touched: The Testing of Value and Integrity in Four Shakespearean Plays* (Athens, Ga., 1976), pp. 100-104. Richard Fly, *Shakespeare's Mediated World* (Amherst, Mass., 1976), p. 71. Lever, p. xx. suggests that this episode was inserted to reinforce Lucio's 'prominence'. But unless he has more function than is usually supposed, one wonders why. Moreover, if the references in I, ii to laws, prayers and the 'peace of heaven' do foreshadow the monastic features of the plot [D. L. Gless, *Measure for Measure: The Law and the Covenant* (Princeton, N. J., 1979), pp. 20-21.], they also give context for the neglected law whose drastic enforcement by Angelo strikes at the heart of Lucio's world.

23 E. W. M. Tillyard, *Shakespeare's Problem Plays* (London, 1950), p. 78.

[24] Michael O'Donovan (Frank O'Connor), *Shakespeare's Progress* (Cleveland, Ohio, 1960), pp. 152-58.

[25] Harriet Hawkins, *Likenesses of Truth in Elizabethan and Restoration Drama* (Oxford, 1972), p. 51.

[26] Deconstructors who hold that many of her words are equivocal, such as 'potency', 'prone', and 'skins', ignore the fact that Angelo must believe that she is unconscious of their sexual connotations; otherwise her saintliness would not have baited the hook. The Elizabethans had attached sexual meanings to so many common words that it would have been difficult, I submit, to phrase an emotional plea without employing equivocal words.

[27] Patrick Swindon, *An Introduction to Shakespeare's Comedies* (London, 1973), p. 152.

[28] Rogers, p. 171.

[29] Nevo, p. 117.

[30] Alexander Leggatt, 'Substitution in *Measure for Measure*', *SQ* 39 (1988). pp. 342 ff.

[31] Susan Carlson, ' "Fond Fathers" and Sweet Sisters: Alternative Sexualities in *Measure for Measure*', *Essays in Literature* 16-17 (1989-90), pp. 13-8.

[32] Brian Gibbons, ed., *Romeo and Juliet,* New Arden ed., (London, 1980), p. 40.

[33] Miles, p. 256. Viewing the plots as balanced helps explain why Wylie Sypher, 'Shakespeare as Casuist in *Measure for Measure*', *Sewanee Rev.,* 58 (1950). 268-70, is puzzled by the Duke's exemplifying both 'comic irresponsibility and ethical responsibility'.

[34] Lever, p. 99ff.

[35] Contrary to Wheeler's position, it is only in Angelo's world that 'phallic sexuality typically leads to self-alienation and emasculation' (p. 111). In Lucio's world the danger is purely external.

[36] Lawrence, p. 450; Lever, p. 99ff.

[37] James Black, 'The Unfolding of *Measure for Measure*', *SS,* 26 (1973), 122. That the 'bed trick' was 'unpleasant to modern feelings' a generation ago (Tillyard, p. 270) must be hard for the young to credit.

[38] Brennan, p. 79-101.

[39] 'Refuting Shakespeare's Endings. Part 2', *MP,* 75 (1977), 132-58; Arthur C. Kirsch, *Shakespeare and the Experience of Love* (Cambridge, 1981), p. 146.

[40] William W. Lawrence, '*Measure for Measure* and Lucio', *SQ,* (1958), p. 451.

[41] Arthur A. Scouton, 'A Historical Approach to *Measure for Measure*', *PQ,* 54 (1975) 71.

[42] 'Refuting Shakespeare's Endings', *MP,* 71 (1975), 337-49; Part 2, p. 171.

[43] *Ibid,* p. 77-81; D. A. Stauffer, *Shakespeare's World of Images* (Bloomington, Ind., 1964), p. 144.

[44] Wheeler, pp. 124-27, notes that the other couples say little or nothing.

[45] Even if David Aers and Gunther Kress are correct in holding that 'the themes of justice, law, authority, and order illustrate the differing effects the concepts have on the individual' in this play ['The Politics of Style: Discourses of Law and Authority in *Measure for Measure*', *Style,* 16 (1982), 36], they still offer no clue whatever to the configuration of the play, which avoids even considering the 'rewards and punishments after death' (Wheeler, p. 117).

FURTHER READING

Baines, Barbara J. "Assaying the Power of Chastity in *Measure for Measure*." *Studies in English Literature 1500-1900* 30, No. 2 (Spring 1990) 283-301.

  Argues that the in the play, chastity is clearly aligned with power and that Isabella's situation and "choice" represent cultural, societal values--not simply Isabella's own religious values.

Black, James. "The Unfolding of 'Measure for Measure'." *Shakespeare Survey* 26 (1973): 119-28.

  Analyzes Shakespeare's use of the bed-trick and maintains that the playwright intended "to convey the sense that Mariana in sleeping with Angelo has done something right, and that the playturns upon the positive virtue of her action."

Bradbrook, M. C. "The Balance and the Sword in *Measure for Measure*." In *The Artist and Society in Shakespeare's England: The Collected Papers of Muriel Bradbrook*, Vol. I, pp. 144-54. Sussex: The Harvester Press, 1982.

  Examines the treatment of justice in the play, pointing out the play's confusion between ecclesiastical and civil law as they pertain to marriage and sexual offenses.

Brennan, Anthony. "'What's yet behind, that's meet you all should know': The Structure of the Final Scene of *Measure for Measure*." In *Shakespeare's Dramatic Structures*, pp. 70-101. London: Routledge & Kegan Paul, 1986.

  Maintains that the play's structure is not broken in

half, as many critics have argued, but that it logically builds throughout the first four acts to a point where the characters "are ripe for a complete transformation."

Brown, Carolyn E. "The Wooing of Duke Vincentio and Isabella of *Measure for Measure*: 'The Image of It Gives [Them] Content.'" *Shakespeare Studies* XXII (1994): 189-219.

Suggests that the Duke's marriage proposal to Isabella may not be completely unmotivated and is perhaps more than a weak attempt by Shakespeare to resolve plot complications.

Dollimore, Jonathan. "Transgression and Surveillance in *Measure for Measure*." In *Political Shakespeare: New Essays in Cultural Materialism,* edited by Jonathan Dollimore and Alan Sinfield, pp. 72-87. Manchester: Manchester University Press, 1985.

Argues that the State's anxiety regarding the socially disordering effects of both fornication and drunkenness in Elizabethan and Jacobean England is reflected in the play through the efforts of those in power to regulate sexuality.

Gibbons, Brian. Introduction to *Measure for Measure*, by William Shakespeare, edited by Brian Gibbons, pp. 1-72. Cambridge: Cambridge University Press, 1991.

Provides a detailed overview of the play, discussing the composition date, contemporary political and religious influences, the sources used, the play's themes and characters, and the play in production.

Jaffa, Harry V. "Chastity as a Political Principle: An Interpretation of Shakespeare's *Measure for Measure*." In *Shakespeare as a Political Thinker*, edited by John Alvis and Thomas G. West, pp. 181-218. Durham, N.C.: Carolina Academic Press, 1981.

Explores the themes of the law, justice, and sexual politics in *Measure for Measure*.

Kirsch, Arthur C. "The Integrity of 'Measure for Measure'." *Shakespeare Survey* 28 (1975): 89-105.

Argues that the play's "intellectual and formal structures" have been misunderstood by its critics, who have failed to accurately read the play as it would have been received by Shakespeare's original audiences.

McCluskie, Kathleen. "The Patriarchal Bard: Feminist Criticism and Shakespeare: *King Lear* and *Measure for Measure*." In *Political Shakespeare: New Essays in Cultural Materialism,* edited by Jonathan Dollimore and Alan Sinfield, pp. 88-108. Manchester: Manchester University Press, 1985.

Argues that the female characters in the play represent a variety of sexual relationships and asserts that feminist criticism has no "point of entry" into the play because the issues related to sexuality "are constructed in completely male terms."

Nevo, Ruth. "'Measure for Measure': Mirror for Mirror." *Shakespeare Survey* 40 (1988): 107-22.

Contends that the play repeats its situations and doubles its personae "because that is the way the play works through, and divulges, the fantasies which energize it. It is a masterly study of repression, and of the repressed. . . ."

Palmer, Christopher. "Selfishness in *Measure for Measure*." *Essays in Criticism* XXVIII, No. 3 (July 1978): 187-207.

Asserts that the greatness of the play stems from the manner in which it allows the characters to stress their singularity, or selfishness, in an uncompromising way. Yet in their assertion of the self, Palmer states, the characters "resist complete submission to the moral."

Guide to *Shakespearean Criticism* Series

VOLUMES 1-10	Provides an historical overview of the critical response to each Shakespearean work. Includes criticism from the seventeenth century to the present.
VOLUMES 11, 12, 14, 15, 17, 18, 20, 21, 23, 24, 26	Examines the performance history of Shakespeare's plays on the stage and screen through eyewitness reviews and retrospective evaluations of individual productions. Also provides comparisons of major interpretations and discusses staging issues.
VOLUMES 27, 29-31, 33-36, 38-41, 43-47, 49	Focuses on criticism published after 1960. Each volume is ordered around a theme, such as politics, religion, or sexuality, with a topic entry that introduces the volume and several entries devoted to individual works.
Yearbooks: **VOLUMES 13, 16, 19, 22, 25, 28, 32, 37, 42, 48**	Compiled annually beginning in 1989. Includes the most noteworthy essays of the year published on Shakespeare as recommended by an international advisory board of distinguished Shakespearean scholars.

Cumulative Character Index

The Cumulative Character Index identifies the principal characters of discussion in the criticism of each play and non-dramatic poem. The characters are arranged alphabetically. Page references indicate the beginning page number of each essay containing substantial commentary on that character.

Calphurnia
Julius Caesar
Calphurnia's dream **45:** 10

Cambridge
Henry V See **traitors**

Canterbury and the churchmen
Henry V **5:** 193, 203, 205, 213, 219, 225, 252, 260; **22:** 137; **30:** 215, 262

Cardinal Wolsey
Henry VIII See **Wolsey**

Cassio
Othello **25:** 189

Cassius
Julius Caesar **7:** 156, 159, 160, 161, 169, 179, 189, 221, 233, 303, 310, 320, 333, 343; **17:** 272, 282, 284, 344, 345, 358; **25:** 272, 280; **30:** 351; **37:** 203

Celia
As You Like It **46:** 94

Chorus
Henry V
role of **5:** 186, 192, 226, 228, 230, 252, 264, 269, 281, 293; **14:** 301, 319, 336; **19:** 133; **25:** 116, 131; **30:** 163, 202, 220

the churchmen
Henry V See **Canterbury and the churchmen**

Cinna
Julius Caesar
as poet **48:** 240

Claudio
Much Ado about Nothing
boorish behavior **8:** 9, 24, 33, 36, 39, 44, 48, 63, 79, 82, 95, 100, 111, 115; **31:** 209
credulity **8:** 9, 17, 19, 24, 29, 36, 41, 47, 58, 63, 75, 77, 82, 95, 100, 104, 111, 115, 121; **31:** 241; **47:** 25
mercenary traits **8:** 24, 44, 58, 82, 91, 95
noble qualities **8:** 17, 19, 29, 41, 44, 58, 75
reconciliation with Hero **8:** 33, 36, 39, 44, 47, 82, 95, 100, 111, 115, 121
repentance **8:** 33, 63, 82, 95, 100, 111, 115, 121; **31:** 245
sexual insecurities **8:** 75, 100, 111, 115, 121

Claudius
Hamlet **13:** 502; **16:** 246; **21:** 259, 347, 361, 371; **28:** 232, 290; **35:** 104, 182; **44:** 119, 241

Cleopatra
Antony and Cleopatra
Antony, relationship with **6:** 25, 27, 37, 39, 48, 52, 53, 62, 67, 71, 76, 85, 100, 125, 131, 133, 136, 142, 151, 161, 163, 165, 180, 192; **25:** 257; **27:** 82; **47:** 107, 124, 165, 174
characterization **47:** 77, 96, 113, 124
contradictory or inconsistent nature **6:** 23, 24, 27, 67, 76, 100, 104, 115, 136, 151, 159, 202; **17:** 94, 113; **27:** 135

costume **17:** 94
creativity **6:** 197; **47:** 96, 113
death **6:** 23, 25, 27, 41, 43, 52, 60, 64, 76, 94, 100, 103, 120, 131, 133, 136, 140, 146, 161, 165, 180, 181, 192, 197, 208; **13:** 383; **17:** 48, 94; **25:** 245; **27:** 135; **47:** 71
personal attraction of **6:** 24, 38, 40, 43, 48, 53, 76, 104, 115, 155; **17:** 113
self-knowledge **47:** 77, 96
staging issues **17:** 94, 113
as subverter of social order **6:** 146, 165; **47:** 113
as superhuman figure **6:** 37, 51, 71, 92, 94, 178, 192; **27:** 110; **47:** 71, 174, 192,
as tragic heroine **6:** 53, 120, 151, 192, 208; **27:** 144
as voluptuary or courtesan **6:** 21, 22, 25, 41, 43, 52, 53, 62, 64, 67, 76, 146, 161; **47:** 107, 174

Cloten
Cymbeline **4:** 20, 116, 127, 155; **22:** 302, 365; **25:** 245; **36:** 99, 125, 142, 155; **47:** 228

Collatine
The Rape of Lucrece **10:** 98, 131; **43:** 102; **48:** 291

Cominius
Coriolanus **25:** 245

Conrade
Much Ado about Nothing See **Borachio and Conrade**

Constance
King John **9:** 208, 210, 211, 215, 219, 220, 224, 229, 240, 251, 254; **16:** 161; **24:** 177, 184, 196

Cordelia
King Lear
attack on Britain **25:** 202
characterization **2:** 110, 116, 125, 170; **16:** 311; **25:** 218; **28:** 223, 325; **31:** 117, 149, 155, 162; **46:** 218, 225, 231, 242
as Christ figure **2:** 116, 170, 179, 188, 222, 286
gender identity **48:** 222
rebelliousness **13:** 352; **25:** 202
on stage **11:** 158
transcendent power **2:** 137, 207, 218, 265, 269, 273
women, the Christian ideal of **48:** 222

Corin
As You Like It See **pastoral characters**

Coriolanus
Coriolanus
anger or passion **9:** 19, 26, 45, 80, 92, 157, 164, 177, 189; **30:** 79, 96
as complementary figure to Aufidius **19:** 287
death scene (Act V, scene vi) **9:** 12, 80, 100, 117, 125, 144, 164, 198; **25:** 245, 263
as epic hero **9:** 130, 164, 177; **25:** 245
immaturity **9:** 62, 80, 84, 110, 117, 142; **30:** 140

inhuman attributes **9:** 65, 73, 139, 157, 164, 169, 189, 198; **25:** 263
internal struggle **9:** 31, 43, 45, 53, 72, 117, 121, 130; **44:** 93
introspection or self-knowledge, lack of **9:** 53, 80, 84, 112, 117, 130; **25:** 296; **30:** 133
isolation or autonomy **9:** 53, 65, 142, 144, 153, 157, 164, 180, 183, 189, 198; **30:** 58, 89, 111
manipulation by others **9:** 33, 45, 62, 80; **25:** 296
as military leader **48:** 230
modesty **9:** 8, 12, 19, 26, 53, 78, 92, 117, 121, 144, 183; **25:** 296; **30:** 79, 96, 129, 133, 149
narcissism **30:** 111
noble or aristocratic attributes **9:** 15, 18, 19, 26, 31, 33, 52, 53, 62, 65, 84, 92, 100, 121, 148, 157, 169; **25:** 263; **30:** 67, 74, 96
pride or arrogance **9:** 8, 11, 12, 19, 26, 31, 33, 43, 45, 65, 78, 92, 121, 148, 153, 177; **30:** 58, 67, 74, 89, 96, 129
punishment of **48:** 230
reconciliation with society **9:** 33, 43, 45, 65, 139, 169; **25:** 296
as socially destructive force **9:** 62, 65, 73, 78, 110, 142, 144, 153; **25:** 296
soliloquy (Act IV, scene iv) **9:** 84, 112, 117, 130
as tragic figure **9:** 8, 12, 13, 18, 25, 45, 52, 53, 72, 80, 92, 106, 112, 117, 130, 148, 164, 169, 177; **25:** 296; **30:** 67, 74, 79, 96, 111, 129; **37:** 283
traitorous actions **9:** 9, 12, 19, 45, 84, 92, 148; **25:** 296; **30:** 133
as unsympathetic character **9:** 12, 13, 62, 78, 80, 84, 112, 130, 157

the courser and the jennet
Venus and Adonis **10:** 418, 439, 466; **33:** 309, 339, 347, 352

Cranmer
Henry VIII
prophesy of **2:** 25, 31, 46, 56, 64, 68, 72; **24:** 146; **32:** 148; **41:** 120, 190

Cressida
Troilus and Cressida
as ambiguous figure **43:** 305
inconsistency **3:** 538; **13:** 53; **16:** 70; **22:** 339; **27:** 362
individual will vs. social values **3:** 549, 561, 571, 590, 604, 617, 626; **13:** 53; **27:** 396
infidelity **3:** 536, 537, 544, 554, 555; **18:** 277, 284, 286; **22:** 58, 339; **27:** 400; **43:** 298
lack of punishment **3:** 536, 537
as mother figure **22:** 339
objectification of **43:** 329
as sympathetic figure **3:** 557, 560, 604, 609; **18:** 284, 423; **22:** 58; **27:** 396, 400; **43:** 305

Dark Lady
Sonnets **10:** 161, 167, 176, 216, 217, 218, 226, 240, 302, 342, 377, 394; **25:** 374; **37:** 374; **40:** 273; **48:** 346

the poets
Julius Caesar **7:** 179, 320, 350

Polixenes
The Winter's Tale
Leontes, relationship with **48:** 309

Polonius
Hamlet **21:** 259, 334, 347, 386, 416; **35:** 182

Porter
Henry VIII **24:** 155
Macbeth **3:** 173, 175, 184, 190, 196, 203, 205, 225, 260, 271, 297, 300; **20:** 283

Portia
The Merchant of Venice **4:** 194, 195, 196, 215, 254, 263, 336, 356; **12:** 104, 107, 114; **13:** 37; **22:** 3, 69; **25:** 22; **32:** 294; **37:** 86; **40:** 142, 156, 197, 208

Posthumus
Cymbeline **4:** 24, 30, 53, 78, 116, 127, 141, 155, 159, 167; **15:** 89; **19:** 411; **25:** 245, 319; **36:** 142; **44:** 28; **45:** 67, 75; **47:** 25, 205, 228

Prince Henry
King John See **Henry (Prince Henry)**

Prospero
The Tempest
characterization **8:** 312, 348, 370, 458; **16:** 442; **22:** 302; **45:** 188, 272
as God or Providence **8:** 311, 328, 364, 380, 429, 435
magic, nature of **8:** 301, 340, 356, 396, 414, 423, 458; **25:** 382; **28:** 391; **29:** 278, 292, 368, 377, 396; **32:** 338, 343
psychoanalytic interpretation **45:** 259
redemptive powers **8:** 302, 320, 353, 370, 390, 429, 439, 447; **29:** 297
as ruler **8:** 304, 308, 309, 420, 423; **13:** 424; **22:** 302; **29:** 278, 362, 377, 396
self-control **8:** 312, 414, 420; **22:** 302; **44:** 11
self-knowledge **16:** 442; **22:** 302; **29:** 278, 292, 362, 377, 396
as Shakespeare or creative artist **8:** 299, 302, 308, 312, 320, 324, 353, 364, 435, 447
as tragic hero **8:** 359, 370, 464; **29:** 292

Proteus
The Two Gentlemen of Verona **6:** 439, 450, 458, 480, 490, 511; **40:** 312, 327, 330, 335, 359; **42:** 18

Puck
A Midsummer Night's Dream **45:** 96, 158

Quickly (Mistress Quickly)
Henry V **5:** 186, 187, 210, 276, 293; **30:** 278

Regan
King Lear **31:** 151; **46:** 231, 242

Richard (King Richard II)
Richard II
artistic temperament **6:** 264, 267, 270, 272,

277, 292, 294, 298, 315, 331, 334, 347, 368, 374, 393, 409; **24:** 298, 301, 304, 315, 322, 390, 405, 408, 411, 414, 419; **39:** 289
Bolingbroke, compared with **24:** 346, 349, 351, 352, 356, 419; **39:** 256
characterization **6:** 250, 252, 253, 254, 255, 258, 262, 263, 267, 270, 272, 282, 283, 304, 343, 347, 364, 368; **24:** 262, 263, 267, 269, 270, 271, 272, 273, 274, 278, 280, 315, 322, 325, 330, 333, 390, 395, 402, 405, 423; **28:** 134; **39:** 279, 289
dangerous aspects **24:** 405
delusion **6:** 267, 298, 334, 368, 409; **24:** 329, 336, 405
homosexuality **24:** 405
kingship **6:** 253, 254, 263, 272, 327, 331, 334, 338, 364, 402, 414; **24:** 278, 295, 336, 337, 339, 356, 419; **28:** 134, 178; **39:** 256, 263
loss of identity **6:** 267, 338, 368, 374, 381, 388, 391, 409; **24:** 298, 414, 428
as martyr-king **6:** 289, 307, 321; **19:** 209; **24:** 289, 291; **28:** 134
nobility **6:** 255, 258, 259, 262, 263, 391; **24:** 260, 263, 274, 280, 289, 291, 402, 408, 411
political acumen **6:** 263, 264, 272, 292, 310, 327, 334, 364, 368, 374, 388, 391, 397, 402, 409; **24:** 405; **39:** 256
private vs. public persona **6:** 317, 327, 364, 368, 391, 409; **24:** 428
role-playing **24:** 419, 423; **28:** 178
seizure of Gaunt's estate **6:** 250, 338, 388
self-dramatization **6:** 264, 267, 307, 310, 315, 317, 331, 334, 368, 393, 409; **24:** 339; **28:** 178
self-hatred **13:** 172; **24:** 383; **39:** 289
self-knowledge **6:** 255, 267, 331, 334, 338, 352, 354, 368, 388, 391; **24:** 273, 289, 411, 414; **39:** 263, 289
spiritual redemption **6:** 255, 267, 331, 334, 338, 352, 354, 368, 388, 391; **24:** 273, 289, 411, 414

Richard (King Richard III, formerly Richard, Duke of Gloucester)
Henry VI, Parts 1, 2, and 3
characterization **3:** 35, 48, 57, 64, 77, 143, 151; **22:** 193; **39:** 160, 177
as revenger **22:** 193
soliloquy (*3 Henry VI*, Act III, scene ii) **3:** 17, 48
Richard III
ambition **8:** 148, 154, 165, 168, 170, 177, 182, 213, 218, 228, 232, 239, 252, 258, 267; **39:** 308, 341, 360, 370, 383
attractive qualities **8:** 145, 148, 152, 154, 159, 161, 162, 165, 168, 170, 181, 182, 184, 185, 197, 201, 206, 213, 228, 243, 252, 258; **16:** 150; **39:** 370, 383
credibility, question of **8:** 145, 147, 154, 159, 165, 193; **13:** 142
death **8:** 145, 148, 154, 159, 165, 168, 170, 177, 182, 197, 210, 223, 228, 232, 243, 248, 252, 258, 267
deformity as symbol **8:** 146, 147, 148, 152, 154, 159, 161, 165, 170, 177, 184, 185, 193, 218, 248, 252, 267; **19:** 164

inversion of moral order **8:** 159, 168, 177, 182, 184, 185, 197, 201, 213, 218, 223, 232, 239, 243, 248, 252, 258, 262, 267; **39:** 360
as Machiavellian villain **8:** 165, 182, 190, 201, 218, 232, 239, 243, 248; **39:** 308, 326, 360, 387
as monster or symbol of diabolic **8:** 145, 147, 159, 162, 168, 170, 177, 182, 193, 197, 201, 228, 239, 248, 258; **13:** 142; **37:** 144; **39:** 326, 349
other literary villains, compared with **8:** 148, 161, 162, 165, 181, 182, 206, 213, 239, 267
role-playing, hypocrisy, and dissimulation **8:** 145, 148, 154, 159, 162, 165, 168, 170, 182, 190, 206, 213, 218, 228, 239, 243, 252, 258, 267; **25:** 141, 164, 245; **39:** 335, 341, 387
as scourge or instrument of God **8:** 163, 177, 193, 201, 218, 228, 248, 267; **39:** 308
as Vice figure **8:** 190, 201, 213, 228, 243, 248, 252; **16:** 150; **39:** 383, 387

Richard Plantagenet, Duke of York
Henry VI, Parts 1, 2, and 3 See **York**

Richmond
Richard III **8:** 154, 158, 163, 168, 177, 182, 193, 210, 218, 223, 228, 243, 248, 252; **13:** 142; **25:** 141; **39:** 349

the Rival Poet
Sonnets **10:** 169, 233, 334, 337, 385; **48:** 352

Roman citizenry
Julius Caesar
portrayal of **7:** 169, 179, 210, 221, 245, 279, 282, 310, 320, 333; **17:** 271, 279, 288, 291, 292, 298, 323, 334, 351, 367, 374, 375, 378; **22:** 280; **30:** 285, 297, 316, 321, 374, 379; **37:** 229

Romeo and Juliet
Romeo and Juliet
death-wish **5:** 431, 489, 505, 528, 530, 538, 542, 550, 566, 571, 575; **32:** 212
immortality **5:** 536
Juliet's epithalamium speech (Act III, scene ii) **5:** 431, 477, 492
Juliet's innocence **5:** 421, 423, 450, 454; **33:** 257
maturation **5:** 437, 454, 467, 493, 498, 509, 520, 565; **33:** 249, 257
rebellion **25:** 257
reckless passion **5:** 419, 427, 431, 438, 443, 444, 448, 467, 479, 485, 505, 533, 538, 542; **33:** 241
Romeo's dream (Act V, scene i) **5:** 513, 536, 556; **45:** 40
Rosaline, Romeo's relationship with **5:** 419, 423, 425, 427, 438, 498, 542, 575

Rosalind
As You Like It **46:** 94, 122
Beatrice, compared with **5:** 26, 36, 50, 75
charm **5:** 55, 75; **23:** 17, 18, 20, 41, 89, 111
disguise, role of **5:** 75, 107, 118, 122, 128,

Cumulative Critic Index

Critic Index

Critic Index

Critic Index

Critic Index

Critic Index

Critic Index

Cumulative Topic Index

The Cumulative Topic Index identifies the principal topics of discussion in the criticism of each play and non-dramatic poem. The topics are arranged alphabetically. Page references indicate the beginning page number of each essay containing substantial commentary on that topic. A parenthetical reference after a topic indicates that the topic is extensively discussed in that volume.

Topic Index

Topic Index

Topic Index

Cumulative Topic Index, by Play

The Cumulative Topic Index, by Play identifies the principal topics of discussion in the criticism of each play and non-dramatic poem. The topics are arranged alphabetically by play. Page references indicate the beginning page number of each essay containing substantial commentary on that topic. A parenthetical reference after a play indicates which volumes discuss the play extensively.

Topic Index, by Play

Topic Index, by Play

Topic Index, by Play

Topic Index, by Play

ISBN 0-7876-3144-2

90000

9 780787 631444